THROUGH THE EYE OF A NEEDLE

THROUGH THE EYE OF A NEEDLE

Wealth, the Fall of Rome, and the Making
of Christianity in the West, 350–550 AD

PETER BROWN

PRINCETON UNIVERSITY PRESS

Princeton and Oxford

Copyright © 2012 by Princeton University Press
Published by Princeton University Press, 41 William Street, Princeton, New Jersey 08540
In the United Kingdom: Princeton University Press, 6 Oxford Street,
Woodstock, Oxfordshire OX20 1TW

press.princeton.edu

Jacket photograph: A hoard of gold and silver coins buried in a wooden chest,
along with precious ornaments and tableware, at Hoxne in East Anglia (Britain).
Copyright © The Trustees of The British Museum; photo credit: Art Resource, NY

Library of Congress Cataloging-in-Publication Data
Brown, Peter, 1935–
Through the eye of a needle : wealth, the fall of Rome, and the making of Christianity
in the West, 350–550 AD / Peter Brown.
p. cm.
Includes bibliographical references and index.
ISBN 978-0-691-15290-5 (hardcover : alk. paper) 1. Church history—Primitive and early
church, ca. 30–600. 2. Wealth—Religious aspects—Christianity—History. 3. Rome—
History—Empire, 284–476. I. Title.
BR162.3.B77 2012
270.2—dc23   2011045697

British Library Cataloging-in-Publication Data is available

This book has been composed in Garamond Premier Pro

Printed on acid-free paper. ∞

Printed in the United States of America

1 3 5 7 9 10 8 6 4 2

For Betsy

Jesus said to him: "If you would be perfect, go, sell what you possess

and give to the poor, and you will have treasure in heaven;

and come, follow me." When the young man heard this

he went away sorrowful; for he had great possessions.

And Jesus said to his disciples, "Truly, I say to you, it will be hard

for a rich man to enter the kingdom of heaven. Again, I tell you,

it is easier for a camel to go through the eye of a needle

than for a rich man to enter the kingdom of God."

When the disciples heard this they were greatly astonished, saying:

"Who then can be saved?" But Jesus looked at them and said to them,

"With men this is impossible, but with God all things are possible."

—Matthew 19:21–26 (Revised Standard Version)

CONTENTS

CONTENTS

CONTENTS

CONTENTS

CONTENTS

xiii

MAPS

ILLUSTRATIONS

PREFACE

In this book I wish to examine the impact of wealth on the Christian churches of the Latin West in the last centuries of the Roman empire and in the first century of the post-imperial age, roughly from the middle of the fourth century AD to the consolidation of the post-Roman, barbarian kingdoms in the period conventionally associated with the "Fall of Rome."

I will begin with four opening chapters that set the scene. The first will describe Roman society in the fourth century AD. The second will examine the social standing of the Christian churches in the transitional period between the conversion of Constantine in 312 and the entry of the rich in ever greater numbers into the churches in the course of the 370s. The next two chapters will juxtapose the traditional ideal of giving to the city with the novel Christian ideal of placing treasure in heaven through gifts to the church and to the poor. The issues raised by the contrast between these two ideals will remain with us for the rest of the book.

The next thirteen chapters will introduce the reader to well-known figures, each one of them in a particular landscape. Each represents a different option for the use of wealth and for the formation of attitudes to it. We will meet the great pagan, Quintus Aurelius Symmachus, in the Rome and southern Italy of his time. Then we will go north, to the Milan and northern Italy of his Christian contemporary, Ambrose of Milan. For three chapters we will follow the young Augustine, a very different person from a more modest background, from Africa to Italy and back again, as he lived and thought his way through a series of religious communities, each of which was characterized by distinctive attitudes toward the use of wealth among its members. We will leave Augustine in 397 as the newly installed bishop of Hippo and as the head of a monastery so as to go far to the north—to the Gaul of Ausonius of Bordeaux. In Gaul, and in the adjoining provinces, we will savor the wealth of the rich landowners and courtiers, the remains of whose villas still amaze us. We will do this in order to appreciate the mystique of wealth and the attitudes toward the natural world that circulated among such people. For this was the wealth Paulinus of Nola formally renounced in 394. We will see how Paulinus came to make this renunciation; how he viewed his own self-chosen poverty; and how he came to devote his wealth to a building project around the shrine of Saint Felix in Nola in southern Italy, which he described in such a way as to make him the poet of wealth renounced and found again as treasure in heaven. Then we will turn back to Rome—but to the Rome of the Christian churches. We will examine the circumstances in which the churches gained wealth and standing in Rome from the time of Constantine onward. The situation created by this slow buildup explains the tensions that accompanied the arrival in Rome in 382 of Jerome, his abrupt departure in 385, and the controversies about wealth, poverty, and patronage that he helped provoke and that we know of largely through his vehement writings in the 390s and early 400s.

After Jerome, the pace of the book changes. We have entered an age of mounting crisis. The spectacular renunciation of their property by a young noble couple (Pinianus and Melania the Younger) coincided with the onset of the Visigothic advance on Rome. The sack of Rome in 410 brought another radical Christian, Pelagius, along with his Roman patrons, as refugees to the shores of Africa. When in Italy, Pelagius's followers had circulated vehement criticisms of wealth. They had insisted on its total renunciation. The consequent battle of ideas between Augustine and Pelagius amounted to a Punic War of the mind between Italy and Africa. But it was not simply a war of ideas. As far as Augustine was concerned, the pious habits of an entire Christian landscape were at stake. Hence we shall go back a century so as to appreciate the fierce sense of agency that had enabled the African churches to build up a position for themselves in African society through drawing on the gifts of the faithful. We will then follow the attitudes toward wealth and religious giving that emerged from the preaching of Augustine in the cities of Africa in the 400s. It was these attitudes that Augustine placed in the path of the radical call to renunciation associated with the views of the supporters of Pelagius. The message from Africa was firm. Wealth was not to be thrown away in headlong renunciation; it was to be used in the churches. Above all, it was to be used to expiate sin. In all subsequent centuries, Augustine's notion of the intimate relation between sin and religious giving infused the giving practices of the Latin churches with a somber dye. Already in Augustine's old age, his views made themselves felt throughout the Latin West. This was in the last days of the united empire. By 430 (as chapter 24 will show), all these concerns came to be engulfed in the general crisis of the western empire. This crisis brought to an abrupt end the affluence of the previous century and placed the wealth of those who had survived the storm on a very different footing.

We are dealing now with an impoverished society in the aftermath of violent dislocation. The regions of the Roman world had drifted apart. Each region fared differently; some did a lot better than others. Hence the surprising vividness of the intellectual life associated with the still-prosperous enclave of Provence, which produced, at this time, the programmatic statements on monastic poverty of John Cassian, a succession of startling charismatic leaders associated with the island of Lérins, and the memorable diagnosis of the ills of the western empire in its last days written by Salvian of Marseilles. In Italy also much of the old world appeared to have continued. But this continuity masked deep changes. By the end of the fifth century, the popes of Rome had ousted the Senate as the patrons of the lower classes of the city. The estates of the Roman church had come to rival, for the very first time, the wealth of the lay nobility.

In the last two chapters we will look at western Europe as a whole. We will follow the manner in which the Christian churches came to administer and deploy their wealth. Last of all, we will see how the discreet pressure of wealth used for religious ends (by bishops and by lay donors) altered the texture of Christianity itself. With this, we have come to stand on the threshold of another world, one very different from the ancient world with which we began our story. By 600 AD, the structures of the church and the expectations of the laity had brought about a slow turning of the age. At last—after three long centuries, and only then—the Christians of Europe began to face toward the Catholicism of the western middle ages.

It might be helpful to readers if I made plain why my book has taken this particular shape.

First: the geographical shape. This is not a book about the Roman world as a whole. It is about the western, Latin world (from the western Balkans to Britain and from Trier to the edge of the Sahara). I have made this choice in large part because of the richness of the material provided by well-known Latin authors and because of the intrinsic interest of the social structures and of the historical developments that were distinctive to the Roman West. But I have also done so because the healthy state of late Roman studies as a whole has left me free to concentrate on that one region with the confidence that there are and will be many other scholars capable of doing justice to the equally fascinating theme of the relation between church, wealth, and society in the eastern provinces of the empire.

Second: the chronological shape. As my title makes plain, I have chosen to concentrate on the period between 350 and 550. This is, in many ways, an arbitrary choice, which I myself have not observed strictly. But I made it as much to remind myself as to remind my readers of a crucial fact: many of the basic dates of the late Roman period are less important than we think. To begin our account with the conversion of Constantine in 312 and to end it with the formal cessation of the western Roman empire in 476 or with the death of Pope Gregory the Great in 603 might seem a straightforward way to bracket a conventional narrative of the period. But to use these dates would be to smuggle in a deceptive teleology. It would encourage us to press the fast forward button—to assume that the conversion of Constantine looked forward, almost as a foregone conclusion, to the passing of the Roman empire and to the triumph of the church in western society summed up in the papacy of Gregory the Great.

The temptation to foreshorten history in this way is to be avoided at all costs. The growth of wealth in the churches did not proceed at the brisk pace implied by conventional narratives. The conversion of Constantine in 312 did not automatically lead to the enrichment of the Christian church. This came later, in the last quarter of the fourth century. The papacy of Gregory I did not mark the apogee of a triumphant church, ready to take over the governance of the post-Roman West. It was a good half century earlier that the churches of Europe began to feel, somewhat to their surprise, the weight of their own wealth. And they felt this weight in a world where bishops had become partners of the great but had by no means become their lords.

Hence the third aspect of the shape of this book. My concern throughout has been to do justice to the pace and to the diversity of developments that do not fit easily into conventional narratives of political and ecclesiastical history. To a large extent, I have attempted to do this by concentrating on a series of distinctive figures, each of whom was placed in a distinctive landscape. In each such landscape history moved at a different pace.

We meet these figures in roughly chronological order as our story unfolds. (Only in Christian Rome and in Christian Africa do we need a flashback across an entire century to set the scene for figures such as Jerome and Augustine.)

I have done this because the more I have studied the theme of wealth in the churches the more I am convinced that the Roman empire was made up of distinctive regions. The Christian churches in each region (despite their frequent interchanges and despite the theoretical claim to forming part of a universal institution—the Church, with a capital "c") were as much the product of local conditions as was any other feature of the Roman world. A true history of Latin Christianity requires an unremitting sense of place. Each Christian region had a landscape of its own. In delineating its distinctive features, one can never be circumstantial enough: the archaeology of sites, the evidence for the circulation of coins and ceramics, styles of inscriptions on dedications and on tombstones, works of local authors—indeed, anything that the historian can find—must be brought to play in building up our picture of a particular landscape. Rather than advancing triumphantly toward a clear goal along a single high road, the regional churches of the West proceeded each at its own pace. They were frequently ignorant of the affairs of their neighbors, and all were equally ignorant of the future that lay in store for them. To view them separately, generation by generation, struck me as the best way to convey the diversity of the Christian churches of the late Roman West and the unforeseen nature of their rise in Roman society.

By contrast, the fact that, in my narrative, each of these landscapes should be related to a single figure or group of figures comes from a choice of my own. The reader should know that, in concentrating on individual authors (Symmachus, Ambrose, Augustine, Paulinus, and so on), I am making a virtue out of a necessity. I am doing the best I can with the bad hand the past has dealt us. So much evidence has not survived, and what has is distributed in ways that reflect the accidents of survival quite as much as the intrinsic importance of the regions to which the evidence refers. The later prominence as Fathers of the Church of authors such as Ambrose, Augustine, and Jerome has ensured that their abundant and circumstantial writings have survived to illuminate the Christian worlds of Milan, Africa, and Rome. We can never be sufficiently grateful for this fact, and not least because, in the case of these authors, their writings illuminate key regions of the late Roman world. But this was a wide world. We must remain aware that there were many other authors—pagan quite as much as Christian—in other regions (or in the same region as our main authors) who have been lost to us, as well as the fact that there are many regions that have remained strangely silent.

It is poignantly easy to imagine an alternative history of the churches in the Roman West. I frequently ask myself what this history would have looked like if, for example, a writer of the ability and manifold activities of Augustine of Hippo had emerged in southern Spain or beside the Danube; if the bishops of Trier had been the subject of a collective biography like the *Liber Pontificialis—Book of the Pontiffs*—of Rome; or if the shrine of Saint Alban (at Verulamium, Saint Albans) in southern Britain had produced a hagiographer whose chronicle of miracles—replete with vivid local data—had survived from post-Roman Britain to act as a companion to the works of Gregory of Tours.

This is neither an idle nor necessarily a gloomy speculation. Even with figures apparently as well-known to us as Augustine, the recent discovery of hitherto unknown sermons and letters—not to mention documents that throw a new light on the Manichaean movement to which he belonged for a time—shows us how much there is left to be discovered. Entire landscapes of the Christian West may yet come to be better known to us through further discoveries of texts and through the mobilization of other forms of evidence.[1]

But the issue remains. How representative were the authors on which I have concentrated? It can be argued that they were not: that their writings reflect the high-strung preoccupations of an intellectual elite far removed from the earthy certainties associated with issues of wealth and poverty. I am unconvinced by this argument. In matters of religion—and especially in the study of major religious movements such as the formation of the Christian churches—the word "elite" can be misleading. It invites us to assume an absence of contact between leading minds and the wider body of opinion and practice that surrounds them. This is a false assumption. I prefer the judgment of Louis Gernet, writing on Greek religion in the classical period: "An elite does not invent. It renders explicit what many others think."[2]

It is because of this that I have chosen to concentrate on the theme of wealth in the Christian churches. Wealth was a theme that lay heavy on everybody's mind. The issue of wealth flowed like a great braided river through the churches and through Roman society as a whole. Wealth was not only about budgets and rent books; the streams of that great and diverse river touched many banks. We do not immediately think of all of these banks when we think of the economy of the Roman empire. To take a few examples: The yearly miracle of the harvest touched on the issue of the relation between man and the physical universe, and between God or the gods and the abundance of nature. The less welcome prodigy of administrative effort that brought the imperial tax collectors and the collectors of rents to shops and villages all over the Roman world raised the issue of the legitimacy of wealth itself and of the empire that extracted it. By the time the year was out, there would have been very few issues—social and personal, secular and religious—on which the great and manifold stream of preoccupation with wealth had not touched.

Hence it was natural to focus on the issue of wealth in the Christian churches. Some of the reasons for this choice were obvious. The New Testament had passed on to the Christian communities of the later empire the challenge of Jesus to the Rich Young Man, along with his equally disturbing comment on the young man's failure to meet this challenge: that it was *easier for a camel to go through the eye of a needle than for a rich man to enter the kingdom of God* (Matt. 19:24). Once the truly rich had entered the churches, at the turn of the fourth and fifth centuries, these words took on a new immediacy. I am tempted to call this period the Age of the Camel. Christians of ascetic temperament watched expectantly to see which—if any—of the very large camels of their age were prepared to pass through the eye of the needle through renouncing their wealth. Those who did so received instant acclaim and have been studied with alacrity ever since. Compared with the heroes and heroines of renunciation, the silent majority of Christians who retained their wealth have been allowed to sink back into obscurity. We have tended to assume that they remained content with their failure to *sell all and give to the poor* (Matt. 19:21). But failures they remain for us. We then go on to describe (in a somewhat ironic tone) how worldly-wise bishops offered the average rich Christian a series of compromises—almsgiving, church building, testamentary bequests—as so many consolation prizes for having failed the primal test of passing through the eye of a needle. We point out that it was from these shamefaced compromises with the "world" (that is, with the norms of Roman society) that the wealth of the churches grew—and grew only too successfully.

I have written this book in part because I am dissatisfied with this way of seeing things. To treat the renouncers of wealth as the heroes and heroines of a "true" Christianity and to view all other forms of religious giving as somehow a betrayal of the essential radicalism of the Christian movement is to merely echo the high-minded language of the ascetic movement. It is remarkable how many sober scholars in our own days write about the growing wealth of the church as if it were no more than a regrettable result of the failure of late Roman Christians to live up to the ideals of their faith. Many write about the growing wealth of the church in a tone worthy of Jerome. For Jerome, the persistent advocate of ascetic renunciation, the history of the Church was a history of decline from the first, heroic days of the Apostles to "the dregs of our own times," where the Church "has grown great in power and riches and has shrunk in spiritual energy."[3]

To adopt this disapproving attitude is to overlook a crucial fact. We are in a society where—for pagans, Jews, and Christians alike—religious giving was thought of as a religious transaction. Renunciation of wealth was not the only act on which the hand of God rested. Gifts to the poor, donations to the church, weekly offerings, offerings for the payment of vows: each and all joined heaven and earth in ways that were all the more deeply installed in the consciousness of believers for not being exhaustively analyzed. The imagined course of wealth from earth to heaven through humdrum acts of pious giving was just as important to Christian believers as was the occasional act of renunciation among the few. Those who shied away from or who toned down the command of Jesus to the Rich Young Man were not mere shirkers. Rather, they had surrounded their use of wealth with a different imaginative charge from that of the advocates of radical renunciation. This charge empowered their daily acts of kindness and generosity. It was from this rich imaginative humus, common both to the wealthy and to distinctly ordinary persons, that the wealth of the church sprang.

Hence the task of reconstructing the imaginative content of religious giving (the flow of wealth from earth to heaven) has proved quite as important to me as has been the business of following that flow on earth—through establishing the relative value of sums raised through great acts of renunciation, through donations, and through daily offerings in the churches. Here I would appeal to my friends in Jewish studies to come to my aid. For they also study, throughout the Roman period, the considerable imaginative shift that accompanied the change from a religion whose giving practices had once been focused on the economy of a vast Hellenistic temple—the Temple of Jerusalem—to the low-profile but tenacious giving habits of synagogues and of Jewish communities scattered throughout the Roman world. It seems as if this imaginative shift in Judaism echoes, in reverse, the history of the growth of Christian wealth. In Christianity, we begin with religious giving on a modest scale (such as we will meet in early fourth-century Aquileia and in the church pavements of northern Italy in subsequent generations) and we end with the great temple-like enterprises of the shrines of sixth-century Gaul and Italy. In both cases—Jewish and Christian—a history of the imaginative background to religious giving remains to be written. This book can offer only a portion of this imaginative history, limited to a particular time and region in the great, extended nebula of Christianities, which reached from Britain to Central Asia and which, at this time, was flanked in almost every region by Jewish communities where religious giving was motivated by cognate and comparable imaginative patterns.[4]

But there is more to it than that. The issue of wealth in general touched on all aspects of the life of the Roman empire and of the societies that succeeded it. For this reason, the issue of wealth can be used as a diagnostic tool. To see wealth in this way enables us to enter into the very heart of Roman society. To study the creation and distribution of wealth in the fourth century; to follow (both in pagan and in Christian sources) the disquiets and the controversies sparked by the accumulation of wealth in the late Roman society of the fourth and fifth centuries; to sense the mystique of wealth that, at that time, drew together a governing class staffed equally by pagans and Christians; to trace, in the course of the fifth and sixth centuries, the evaporation and the restructuring of wealth in times of barbarian invasion, civil war, and regional state building: to do this is not merely to write yet another social and economic history of the later empire. It is to use the theme of wealth itself as a doctor uses a stethoscope. Through paying attention to the issue of wealth, we can listen in to the Roman empire of the West in its last centuries and to western Europe as a whole in its first century without empire. To do so is like overhearing the creaking of a great ship caught in a storm on the high seas.

This has meant that this book has been the most difficult book to write that I have ever undertaken. For it was only by keeping together the abundant discourse on wealth generated in the pagan and Christian literature of the period with a sense of the realities of wealth in Roman and post-Roman society that I could use the issue of wealth as a diagnostic tool in order to listen in to the process I have called "the Making of Christianity in the West." I was determined not to keep separate the history of the religion and culture of the later empire from the history of its society. Brave words, but hard to live up to in modern conditions. For we live in the middle of a dam burst in the study of the society and economy of the period. A dramatic turn in the study of the concrete circumstances of the Roman world has come to alter our image of late Roman society as a whole and, consequently, of the role of Christianity in this society.

Nothing is quite as it used to be. Let me sum up a few of these breakthroughs, as they directly affect the history of Latin Christianity, in the form of a list of *ifs* and *thens*. If the conversion of Constantine did not decisively place the Christian churches on the high ground of Roman society, then we must look elsewhere (to the very end of the fourth century) to see this process happen. Then, and then only, did Christianity dare to think of itself as potentially a majority religion, because sure of the support of the wealthy. If it is shown that we have seriously underestimated the vigor and diversity of the middling classes in the cities of the late Roman West, then we must rewrite large tracts of the history of the Christian communities in these cities, including the history of the recruitment and the social horizons of their bishops and clergy. If Roman society in the West was not characterized by the unchallenged dominance of a few great landowners, then we must revise much of what has been written about the role of Christianity in Latin society both before and after the fall of the empire. To begin with, we must question the reality content of the fiery sermons of Saint Ambrose against the landowners of northern Italy. They may not have been as ruthless and as all-powerful as he implied. Rather than concentrate on the role of a few exorbitantly rich senators, we must seek out the role of lesser figures, such as the minor nobility of Rome and the provinces, who played a crucial role in the endowment and building of churches and in patronizing Christian clergymen and teachers. Furthermore, if the senatorial aristocracy did not colonize the upper ranks of the churches of Italy and Gaul as thoroughly and as rapidly as many scholars have asserted, then the entire issue of the buildup of the wealth of the church and of the rise of the status of the bishop in fifth- and sixth-century society becomes that much more complex, more conflicted, and (thank God!) more interesting.

Having spelled out these few but crucial themes on which I have been led to change my mind in the past decade, I trust that my readers will follow me attentively through my notes. I hope that they will catch, behind the cramped list of titles, something of the excitement these titles inspired in me, as each of them opened a window through which I saw what I never thought I would see—a vista of late Roman society from which many of the accustomed landmarks that had once dominated the landscape of late Roman studies have vanished or have come to seem less prominent than they had once been. Given the explosion of late antique studies, it has been no easy task to keep up-to-date with current literature and with new discoveries. I have attempted to do this up to around the end of 2010. To take a notable example, Brent Shaw's masterly study of fourth- and early fifth-century Africa, the draft of which he kindly shared with me, has only now appeared in print—Brent D. Shaw, *Sacred Violence: African Christians and Sectarian Hatred in the Age of Augustine* (Cambridge: Cambridge University

Press, 2011). I commend it to the reader as a uniquely rich, vivid, and original portrayal of the Africa of Augustine. I should also mention a yet more recent book: Kyle Harper, *Slavery in the Late Roman World, AD 275–425* (Cambridge: Cambridge University Press 2011), which adds nothing less than an entire new dimension to our view of Roman society in the fourth century. I am well aware (indeed, I look forward with relish to the prospect) that new work, some of which I have overlooked—scattered as it now is through so many publications in Europe and in the English-speaking world—will challenge readers to revise yet further our views on the relation between Christianity and society in this hotly debated period.

This scene changing has been a hard-won achievement. Much of it has taken place through the reinterpretation of well-known texts. But there is one direction from which a new wind has arisen: the field of late Roman archaeology. I trust that I have made clear the extent of my debt to this field in the notes. As far as my book is concerned, what is new about the field is less the material that it addresses than the novel way in which this material has come to be interpreted. Rather than remain content to use archaeological material merely to add further documentation of known events, many young archaeologists have set out to discover landscapes no one had known before. The landscapes they have discovered are often as thrillingly different from our conventional ideas of what late Roman society and late Roman Christianity were like as are the first images of the surface of a distant planet beamed back to earth by a space probe. For a historian of the Christian churches, the thrill is precisely that it is well-known landscapes (the Roman catacombs being the most notable among them) that have been rendered disturbingly unfamiliar. The reinterpretation of basic Christian practices through the skilled reinterpretation of archaeological material (such as the Christian care of the dead, the nature of Christian votive piety, Christian memorial inscriptions, and the Christian construction of places of worship) has lifted the veil of clerical words on which so much of our text-based knowledge of the daily life of Christians had depended up until now. In entering a world rendered strange again by the interpretative skill of archaeologists, we have been brought that much closer to the unsung heroes and heroines of this book. We meet the lay men and women on whose habits of giving the Christian churches depended. Their pious practices and their expectations speak to us more clearly from their graves, from the pavements of their churches, and from their graffiti at the tombs of saints than they do from the pages of the Fathers of the Church.

In this book I intend throughout to keep together the study of religion and the study of what is now often called (in tones that invite unquestioning approval) "material culture." To maintain the joining of these disciplines has become more difficult every year. The astonishing expansion of late Roman studies has brought with it a danger of over-specialization. In many ways, specialization is welcome, but over-specialization poses a danger to synthetic ventures and to attempts to see societies in the round—to take their religion and culture quite as seriously as their material bases.

Yet we must struggle to maintain this unitary vision. Rigid distinctions between disciplines are not helpful. They bear little relation to the actual experience of research in the field. We soon learn that all aspects of the history of the later empire are difficult of access. From the most seemingly ethereal theological texts to the most seemingly concrete archaeological surveys, each body of evidence, each in its different way, is a frail bridge to the past. None offers unambiguous results. In all our efforts, we are left peering over the edge of an abyss that drops into an unimaginably distant world. We should be aware of the intellectual vertigo that is inherent in our profession. I am told that, when they reach a certain high altitude, French mountaineers change from formal terms of address—the *vous*—to the more intimate *tu*. It is an admirable practice. It breeds the right spirit of solidarity in a group which, like ourselves, lives by dangling at great heights. For the thrill is always there. No matter by which route we may approach the late Roman period—through Patristic texts, through historical works, through legislative documents, through inscriptions, through excavations, or through mapping patterns of trade revealed by the distribution of ceramics—we are up against the fact that the rise of Christianity in the West is a daunting theme.

> But it is just in this that the fascination of history lies; the student feels himself confronted by forces too mighty to be measured by any instruments at his disposal.[5]

If I have communicated to readers of this book a little of this fascination, I will only be passing on to them the joy of learning that so many of my friends and colleagues in the field have, over my years of writing it, passed on to me.

It is for this reason that I feel particularly indebted to my friends and colleagues. I have been more than fortunate. I can look back on the writing of this book as marked by a succession of acts of rare intellectual generosity on the part of many readers to whom I showed it in its many drafts. An *annus mirabilis* brought as visitors to the Institute of Advanced Studies two of the luminaries in my own heaven—Rita Lizzi and Jairus Banaji. They followed my earliest draft with unstinting care and critical discussion. Soon afterward, Johannes Hahn came to the Princeton campus as a visitor. I could not have wished for a more alert reader. His regular comments, perceptive and precise, gave a new dimension to the notion of academic friendship. Julia Smith and Hamish Scott further strengthened my resolve by readings that were as tenacious as they were frank. Throughout, I have been enlivened and guided by the comments of Kimberly Bowes and Ed Watts. Their warm and searching readings kept me in mind of the sheer joy of scholarship, as we entered together (in constant lively conversation) into landscapes as yet barely opened up for the study of late antiquity. Helmut Reimitz and Jamie Kreiner have shepherded this manuscript (both intellectually and cybernetically, as we now say) as it reached the early medieval period and as it emerged, in innumerable ill-edited files, to its full length. One cannot be grateful enough for such care, offered with such infectious zest. Many others at different times have seen chapters or parts of this manuscript. It has been an encouragement and a discipline for me to have their comments. Let me mention, if only to express a debt that goes far beyond the writing of this book, Glen Bowersock, whose presence and example have been an encouragement to me for many years. Last but not least, I have been more than fortunate in the academic enivronment in which I found myself in the years when I wrote this book. In the Program in Hellenic Studies I found a warm hearth around which so many scholars of the history and of the regions that I have long loved have been brought together, year after year and event after event, by the skill and energy of Dimitri Gondicas.

Last, but by no means least, I would like to acknowledge the work of those connected with Princeton University Press—Jennifer Backer, Julia Livingston, and Debbie Tegarden. With the greatest skill and good nature they have enabled a manuscript which was (I must confess) something of a camel to pass through the needle's eye, and to achieve that standard of craftsmanship and beauty that has been a hallmark of Princeton books.

Throughout all this, my wife, Betsy, stands out. She has supported me unsparingly from beginning to end. She has set aside time at all times to read each draft with an unswerving eye for obscurities and for infelicities of expression and organization. She has constantly contributed her own rich store of historical knowledge and her own distinctive sense (at once humane and wry) of the workings of human nature in the past.

We have traveled together to the many regions in which this history took place. I offer her this book in the old and heavy sense of a vow completed, which I have read on so many Jewish and Christian inscriptions of the later empire: I give to her only a little of what she has given to me.

Princeton
March 24, 2011

PART I

Wealth, Christianity, and Giving at the End
of an Ancient World

CHAPTER I

⟨꙳⟩

Aurea aetas: Wealth in an Age of Gold

From *Rusticulus* (Little Farmer) to *Censor* (Civic Worthy)

WEALTH, PRIVILEGE, AND POWER

In this chapter we will start with general considerations. We will deal first with the distinctive manner in which wealth and social status came together in Roman society. Then we will look at the way in which wealth was taken from the land. After this, we will focus on a single century. We will attempt to sketch, inevitably briefly, the structure of upper-class society in the Latin West in the fourth century A D. We will look at what was, in many ways, a new society, where new forms of status and new ways of showing wealth had emerged as a result of a profound reordering of the Roman empire in the period after 300 A D.

Let us begin by asking the first question: What was "wealth" in late Roman society? Those who observed the wealthy at this time tended to give a simple answer. In the overwhelming majority of cases, wealth was land turned by labor into food, which, in the case of the rich, was turned into sufficient money to be turned into privilege and power.

We can see this process at work on many levels of society. It can be illustrated by a success story from the hinterland of fourth-century Africa. An inscription from Mactar, a city on the edge of the inland plateau of southwestern Tunisia, tells how a truly "poor" man came into both wealth and privilege. His name is missing from the tomb that he set up, but he is known to scholars as the "Harvester of Mactar." He recorded his life in a long inscription. He was never entirely landless. Having barely scraped a living from his own land, he made his way up as a foreman of one of the great gangs of laborers (many of them landless men much poorer than himself) who would spread out over the plateau of eastern Numidia (between modern Tunisia and Algeria) as harvest laborers. Twelve years spent

3

working "under the rabid sun" made him, at last, "the master of a house"—the owner of a comfortable farm. Finally, the income from his property made him eligible to membership of the town council of Mactar.

> I sat in the Temple of the City Council [the "sacred" council hall of Mactar] and from a little farmer [a *rusticulus*] I have become a civic elder—a *censor*.

His life of labor had "reaped the fruit of honors."[1]

By joining the town council, our "Harvester" crossed the most significant social threshold in the Roman world. This was not the modern threshold between poverty and wealth. It was the all-important, Roman threshold between facelessness and "honors." Membership in the governing body of a Roman city such as Mactar linked the "Harvester" to privilege and to power. He ceased to be a mere *rusticulus*—a little farmer. As a town councillor (a *curialis*—a member of the *curia*, the town council—or a *decurio*, which was a similar term) he became an *honestior*, a more honorable person. For instance, he could no longer be flogged or tortured. That, in itself, was no small privilege, which the average subject of a notoriously cruel empire could not claim. His place on the town council and the "honors" associated with his activities on its behalf made him a little aristocrat in his own region.[2]

There were five hundred cities like Mactar in Africa alone. In what is now northeastern Tunisia, they covered the land in a tight grid. The nearest cities to Mactar were only ten miles away on either side. Most had populations of little more than two to five thousand inhabitants. A modern observer would have called them "agro-towns." But this was not how they saw themselves. Technically each was an autonomous republic sheltered beneath the vast umbrella of the Roman empire.[3]

To a modern person, this can appear to be a bizarre situation. It is as if the infrastructure of France and Italy was made up of a network of little princedoms of Monaco and Republics of San Marino. But while, in modern times, these quirky survivals from the world of petty principalities and city-states are tax shelters, notorious for being uncooperative in making money saved within their territories available to the revenue officers of France and Italy, in the Roman empire it was precisely the opposite: cooperation with the imperial authorities in the collection of taxes made the cities important and bound their elites to the empire.

We must always remember that, by modern standards, the Roman empire was a "truly minimal state."[4] It delegated to local groups almost every task of government except the control of high justice and the army. Police, maintenance of roads, fortification, and, most important of all, the collection of taxes were tasks delegated to the town councils of some 2,500 cities scattered like fairy dust over the surface of an immense empire. The empire rested heavily on the members of these town councils. But it did so in return for giving them a free hand to bear down as heavily as they wished on everybody else. A town councillor entered the world of honors so as to become, also, a little tyrant. His principal duty was to act as an agent of extortion in the name of the empire.

Mactar (like so many other Roman cities) spoke of its town council as the *splendidissimus ordo*—"the most resplendent governing body."[5] It governed a territory that extended around the town (in the case of Mactar) within a radius of five miles. But it was the duty of the town councillors—and not (except in states of emergency) of the representatives of the Roman state—to go out each year to extract from the inhabitants of every ecological niche in this small territory the taxes due to the state in money, labor, food, livestock, and other useful materials.

Taxes and demands for labor were presented to each city by the imperial bureaucracy as lump sums. It was for the councillors to divide up these sums among themselves and to collect them from all the inhabitants of their midget state. As a result, in the case of Mactar and of innumerable small cities in every province, the decisions of groups of between thirty and one hundred persons directly affected the fate of thousands through the distribution of the tax load and through its yearly collection.

The Roman system of delegation to the cities ensured that this was an empire where power was never limited to the top. It seeped downward to the smallest city. The *curiales* (the members of the town council) policed the urban *plebs* on behalf of the empire. Outside the city, the *curiales* patrolled a countryside inhabited by *rusticuli*—the "little farmers" whose fate the "Harvester of Mactar" had avoided. From these farmers they drew their own income (in the form of rents and produce) and, at the same time, they flexed the muscle of the Roman state at their expense by collecting from them the taxes due to the emperor.

Thus, in the late Roman empire, the rich remained rich because their persons were sheathed in public authority. Even a modest farmer such as our Harvester expected to wrap the authority of the empire around himself once he joined the town council. It was in this direction that his laboriously accumulated wealth had led him—and in no other. In Rome there were no persons such as there were in ancient China who could be acclaimed (as the great historian Sima Qian had acclaimed the spectacularly rich merchants and monopolists of the Han empire) as members of an "un-titled nobility."[6] Wealth and "honors" were made to converge. The one could not be achieved or maintained without the other. For this reason, when approaching wealth in the later empire (as in most other periods of Roman history) we must make a fundamental transition "from a [modern] mental cosmos in which power depends largely on money to one where money depends ... largely on power."[7]

To a modern person, this situation produces strange tricks of perspective. It is hard to judge social distances in the later empire. Persons and institutions that seem to be separated by unbridgeable chasms of wealth often appear closer to each other than we expect. Our Harvester was probably not notably richer than many of the *rusticuli* among whom he grew up. All that was required to be made a member of a town council was a capital of three hundred *solidi* (gold pieces). This amounted to an income of around twenty-five to thirty *solidi* a year.[8] But the "honors" associated with membership in the town council of Mactar placed him (and would certainly have placed his descendants had he succeeded) within sight of the very top of Roman society. Once our Harvester became a member of the town council, legally and institutionally he and a senator had more in common with each other in terms of the privileges that they shared than he had with any of his former neighbors, whose very bodies remained at the mercy of the Roman state.

We should always bear in mind the effects of this situation. The cities themselves were enormously diverse. Mactar was far from being a Roman town based on a single, cookie-cutter model. It had a gnarled identity all its own that reached back for over half a millennium. In the third century BC it had been the capital of a Numidian kingdom. Its town council maintained Punic titles for their civic offices up to the second century A D. In the fourth century, Punic may well have been spoken in its streets and in the countryside. But these diversities had been folded into the wider structure of the empire by a remarkable system of delegated power.[9]

If there was any such thing as a "political nation" in the later Roman empire (such as Sir Lewis Namier has delineated in his studies of the background of the members of Parliament in eighteenth-century England), it was not to be found only in the Roman Senate, with its venerable past and traditional membership of around six hundred persons. It was also to be found in the vast reservoir of talent provided by some sixty-five thousand *curiales* (what we call the "curial class," made up of members of the town councils) spread throughout the cities of the western empire, not to mention the further tens of thousands of such persons in the yet more heavily urbanized provinces of the Roman East.[10]

The city-based nature of late Roman society determined the geographical range of this "political nation." Let us conjure up for a moment a map of the Roman West that shows the relative density of cities in each region. In the northeastern tip of Africa (stretching inland some 125 miles from Carthage), in Sicily, in central Italy, and, far to the west, in southern Spain, cities lay no more than ten miles (half a day's journey) apart. Abutting this dense area was a larger block, where cities appeared every twenty-five miles. This included northern and parts of southern Italy, the Dalmatian coast, the Mediterranean regions of Gaul, most of modern Spain and Portugal, and much of north Africa to within sixty miles

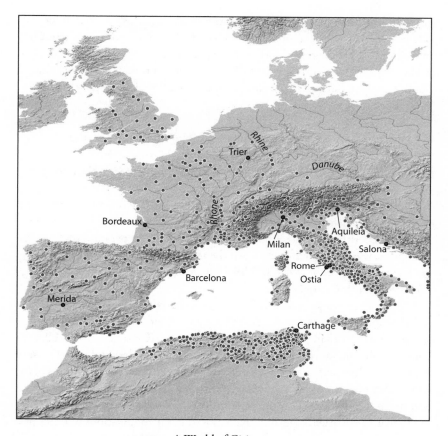

MAP 1. A World of Cities, ca. 400 AD

The reader should know that this map of the overall distribution of cities in the Latin West in 400 AD was derived from a map of Christian bishoprics in ca. 600 AD. Roman cities survived largely because they formed the basis for the early medieval network of bishoprics in most regions of Europe.

inland from the coast. Beyond this vivid core, in much of Gaul, in Britain, along the Danube, and in the hinterlands of Africa, cities lay more distant from each other. The impact of their distinctive structures was muffled by great stretches of a countryside occupied by villages, estates, and rural sanctuaries.[11]

Almost without exception, the principal protagonists of this book, Christian and non-Christian alike, lived in the first two zones. Apart from a few of senatorial origin, almost all the authors that we meet came from curial families. Indeed, until the very end of this period, the alarms and excitements associated with the rise of Christianity in the Roman West took place only on the brightly lit stage of ancient cities, which ranged from the off-scale megalopolis of Rome, through cities such as Milan, Carthage, Bordeaux, Barcelona, and Arles, to innumerable little towns such as Mactar in north Africa and their equivalents elsewhere. Only in Augustine's Africa, in the fourth century, can we catch the voices of Christians in the countryside. Only after the fifth century does a rural Christianity emerge out of tantalizing silence in the countryside of Gaul, Spain, and Italy.

The Wider View: The Rich in a Changing Empire, 100–400 AD

Now let us, for a moment, take a big step backward, so as to view the rich against the landscape of Roman society as whole.

The first thing that we notice is that our Harvester of Mactar was very low on the scale of the rich. Even in his own region, many town councillors would have been far richer than he was. Above him stretched a steep pyramid that became vertiginously high and narrow toward the top. At the very top of this pyramid lay fortunes the likes of which would not be seen again in Europe until the millionaires of the industrial age.

We must remember that this was a very small pyramid compared with the overall population of the empire. From top to bottom, all the rich put together made up no more than what modern modelers of the Roman economy call, with commendable moral restraint, "the fortunate decile" of the total population of the empire. They were the lucky 10 percent. Ninety percent of the subjects of the empire did not partake in the relative prosperity that the Harvester of Mactar and his like had achieved. Most persons lived miserable lives, at a standard of living that never reached beyond that enjoyed by the populations of other preindustrial empires, such as Moghul India. Like Moghul India, the Roman empire was a colorful place. But the color wore off very quickly as one descended the social scale. We should always bear this in mind. The noise generated by a vivid Christian discourse on wealth and poverty (written by members of the curial class and largely addressed to the inhabitants of the cities) affected only a small proportion of the overall population. It has to be set against the vast silence of a wider world "that failed even to begin to share in the moderate amount of economic growth" that had placed our Harvester and many like him in the town halls of cities such as Mactar.[12]

Taking a wider view of Roman history, many scholars have been tempted to think that the fourth century itself was an age dwarfed by the achievements of the empire in previous centuries. Romans of the fourth century have often been presented as the inhabitants of a deeply impoverished empire, busied among the ruins of their former greatness and engaged in desperate and violent attempts to hold back, for a moment, an ineluctable process of decline that had begun around the year 200 AD. It used to be widely believed that the decline and fall of the western empire in the generations after the Gothic sack of Rome in 410 only marked the end of a story of progressive breakdown. The damage had already been done. Socially, economically, and culturally the ancient world had come to an end in the crisis of the third century. The fourth century was already a sinister prelude to the European middle ages.

This melodramatic view dominated the historiography of the first part of the twentieth century. Readers of this book will soon realize that this is not the opinion of this author. From the late 1940s onward, a dam burst of studies on every aspect of the culture, economy, and society of the fourth century has revealed it to be a period in its own right, marked by a strange vigor all its own.[13]

But the issue of proportion cannot be dismissed. The fourth century AD was not the second century AD. The economic explosion that had accompanied the consolidation of Roman rule in the first two centuries had been a prodigious event. It left its imprint in a Mediterranean whose bottom is still littered with the wrecks of Roman ships in numbers that tower above those of the wrecks of any previous or future century until modern times. The lakes of Sweden and the ice-caps of Greenland show deposits of lead that spike in the same period, almost certainly as a result of an unprecedented volume of emissions into the atmosphere associated with the mining and purifying of silver in huge quantities in Roman Spain.[14] The fourth century lies on the far side of this great peak of wealth. But how far down the slope had it fallen? What were the chances that, having slipped that far, it would continue to be a recognizably Roman society? By what devices, and at what human cost, could further slippage be avoided?

Very briefly, the answer may prove to be that it is the second century AD that needs explanation, not the fourth. The second century has rightly been called "this most unusual period of European history."[15] We should not see it as a golden age, against which to measure the achievements and expedients of all later centuries. Rather, it was a costly fluke. Coming after a century of peace, the second century was characterized by extensive overbuilding in many regions, as new local elites competed to become more Roman than the Romans. Traces of ecological strain already appear along the Rhineland frontier in the second century.[16] The impact of plague from the 170s onward may well have led to a long-term demographic downturn whose slow rhythm escapes the conventional periodizations of imperial history.[17] Altogether, this was a society that had pushed hard against the limits of the possible for any preindustrial empire.

From the third century onward, the Roman empire had to face up to the limitations that were usual for any empire. As a result, it passed through what we call the "crisis of the third century." But this crisis is better seen not as a catastrophe but as a return to reality after a period of extraordinary good fortune. After 200 AD, the empire came up against problems all great empires have had to face. It found itself confronted by enemies it could no longer dominate with effortless ease. The relatively peaceful manner by which the imperial office had been passed on from one super-rich Italian family to another gave way to a series of military coups. These, in turn, led to civil wars that drained the provinces of supplies in an unpredictable manner and without the compensation of new conquests. Shaken at the top by usurpations, civil wars, and serious military defeats, the vast mass of the empire settled down to the *grauer Alltag*—to the gray normality of surviving as best it could.

Most great empires face the problem of survival most of the time. In the case of the Roman empire, however, the extraordinary flare of prosperity associated with the second century has tended to make all succeeding centuries of Rome seem to be periods of decline. But it may be better to see the third and fourth centuries less as centuries of irrevocable disaster than as periods marked by a strenuous effort to mobilize the resources of what remained an impressively resilient society in order to survive for the long haul.[18]

Somewhat paradoxically, the empire was saved in the crisis of the third century by the regionalism of Roman provincial society. The sheer size and diversity of the empire cushioned the impact of repeated crises at court and along its frontiers. These crises were localized. In the vast federation of regions that made up the empire, there were always resources to fall back upon in safer and more prosperous provinces. By working through the cities, the Roman system of taxation had co-opted this regionalism rather than undermined it.

And the regions held firm. Many provinces emerged from the crisis of the third century largely unscathed. We tend to forget this because survival lacks glamour. Survival creates silences. These silences do not happen only because things have gone wrong; they often happen because things have kept on keeping on. For example, provinces that had once flaunted the benefits of Roman urban life (such as the cities of Spain) held onto their gains. The cities continued. But the thrill of novelty had worn off. No one felt any longer the need to erect those upbeat inscriptions, recording feats of generosity and public building in the cities, which delight historians of the second century A D.[19]

Africa, in particular, was a world little touched either by civil war or by major barbarian invasion. In and around Mactar and other regions, rural settlement continued to pile building upon building like a coral reef throughout the third and fourth centuries. Pottery kilns producing fine wares covered the countryside.[20] Inscriptions recording public works and acts of generosity continued in the cities of Africa. But even there, by the end of the third century, the pace of building had slackened.[21]

This was partly because, in many provinces of the West, the priorities for public building changed in a significant direction. In many parts of Gaul and Spain (and even eventually in Rome itself, with the Walls of Aurelian, put up in the 270s) walls replaced theaters, baths, and temples as the public building works par excellence. We should not think of these walls as mere fortifications hastily thrown up in panic at the approach of barbarians. Carefully designed and massively built, they radiated the message of a calculated intention to survive, and to survive with Roman grandeur, even in a world that was felt to be less secure than it had been two centuries earlier.[22]

What survived was the empire itself. The emperors and their servants were more than usually vocal on that point. In the third century, the empire passed the crucial test of loyalty. It was widely thought in most regions that the alternative to Rome was chaos. To have survived this test was no small achievement. A century later, after the barbarian raids of 405–6 and the sack of Rome in 410, the western empire would fail to conjure up the same degree of loyalty. It fell apart irrevocably after a generation of barbarian invasion and civil war that was no more severe than that through which the empire had passed in the course of the third century.

For this reason, it is important to note the terms on which the empire survived the crisis of the third century. It did so by harnessing many of the most daring innovations of a time of emergency to ancient Roman institutions whose kinetic energy, gathered over the centuries, had by no means come to a stop. For instance, taxation was sternly rationalized. It was extended to all provinces and exacted with unprecedented determination.[23] But the collusion between cities and empire, which had begun in the first days of Roman rule, still provided the mechanism through which these taxes were collected. It is for this reason that any account of the particular profile of fourth-century society in the West must begin at the roots of wealth—with the harvest, with the taxes, and then with the unusual manner in which, in the fourth century, tax, harvest, and markets were brought together with decisive effect to restructure the life of the Roman rich.

Harvest Shocks

First let us deal with what had barely changed since previous ages. Wealth came mainly from labor on the land. This means that, every year, over 60 percent of the wealth of the Roman empire was gathered at harvesttime by a labor force that amounted to over 80 percent of the overall population. Every year the harvest of basic crops swept across the Roman world, beginning in the Middle East, circling the Mediterranean, and ending in Britain and on the Rhine. The harvest of grain began in spring in the Middle East and was not over until late summer in northern Europe. Throughout the Mediterranean, wine and oil came in the late fall and in early winter. Only Egypt, where the Nile rose and fell in a heavy, mud-red flood between June and September, was miraculously exempt from the march of the seasons.[24]

Before the time of the harvest, rich and poor alike waited. The Mediterranean is notorious for the variability of its harvests, due to unstable climatic conditions. The carefully tended fields were menaced by flattening cloudbursts, by random scything by hailstorms, and by the perpetual menace of prolonged drought (along its eastern and southern shores) and of "dry" winters (winters without snow and thus without moisture) in the plateaus of its hinterlands, notably in Anatolia. "Harvest shocks" caused by unforeseen shortfalls in the crops were the norm. In all areas except Egypt, yields could vary by over 50 percent from year to year.[25]

Not surprisingly, therefore, wealth was widely thought of as lying in the hands of the gods. A good harvest was the smile of God or of the gods spreading across an obedient landscape. In 311, one of the last pagan emperors (the eastern emperor Maximin Daia) informed the citizens of Tyre that his persecution of the Christians had pleased the gods. The weather itself had changed for the better:

> Let them look at the standing crops already flourishing with waving heads
> in the broad fields, and at the meadows, glittering with plants and flowers,
> in response to abundant rains and to the restored mildness and softness of
> the atmosphere.[26]

Christians, also, took no chances. They resorted quite as much as did non-Christians to supernatural measures to protect and nurture their lands. Like everybody else, they called in ritual experts with a reputation for success in such matters. A southern Spanish council of the early fourth century forbade Christian landowners to call in Jews to bless their fields "lest they make invalid and ineffective, our [Christian] blessing on the fruits of the earth which they receive from God."[27] Examples of magical spells have survived. In the Oued Siliane in Tunisia, a stone was placed in the hills looking down over the fields:

> Oreobezagra, Abraxas, Mokhtar ... Adonaï, lords and gods, keep away,
> turn away from this estate and from the fruits which grow in it—from the
> vines, from the olive-trees, from the sown fields—the hail, the mildew,
> the anger of hurricanes, the swarms of locusts, so that none of these
> plagues may attack this estate and the fruits that are all found there.
> Rather, protect them, always intact and healthy, as long as these stones,
> on which these sacred names are inscribed, remain in place in the earth
> and all around.[28]

From January onward, the year was scrutinized for omens of the coming harvest. The Feast of the Kalends of January caught the imagination of pagans, Jews, and Christians alike,[29] for it was a frank feast of wealth present and of wealth to come. The inhabitants of Provence would pile their tables with good things on the day of the Kalends of January. They hoped, through this uncanny display of abundance in bleak midwinter, to bring about the miracle of abundance at the next harvesttime.[30]

The rabbis of Palestine knew what was at stake all over the Mediterranean and beyond. They pointed out that the great prayers of the Jewish New Year were made for dew and rain, "So that, finally, the members of God's people should not come to depend upon each other like slaves."[31] In the eyes of contemporaries, the primary cause of social stratification was the crushing imbalance in exposure to the risk of harvest shocks between the rich (who were cushioned against such shocks) and the poor farmers, whose sole resources lay dangerously open to the weather. It was these harvest shocks that all too often tipped the balance toward misery, debt, and dependence in a rural population that had to produce enough to raise the money needed to pay their rents and taxes.

For everyone, the harvest was a time of finality. The piles of grain gathered on the threshing floor were all that there was. And only a small portion of these piles would remain in the hands of the farmers. For, far away, in January also, the emperor decided the tax budget of the year. Copies of the document, stating the liability of each province, would then be passed down to every city within the province. Members of every town council were held responsible for raising a given sum from within the territory of their city. Vested with imperial authority, the town councillors descended on the villages and farmsteads within the territories of their city.[32]

Then they came again, not as collectors of taxes but as landowners calling in their rents. Altogether, by the time the tax collector and the landowner (who were often one and the same person) had passed by, there was not much left for the farmer. It is usually calculated that, with rent and taxes deducted, the farmers would have to face the coming year with under one-third of the harvest on which they had labored. A peasant family could live on such amounts. But, given the prevalence of harvest shocks throughout the Mediterranean, the farmers had very little buffer against risk, should the sky not "soften" in the coming year.[33]

Furthermore, a complex system of rent collection enabled many urban landowners (especially those resident in great cities) to be like the emperor. They were distant figures, with little or no direct involvement in the life of the peasantry. The *dominus*, the ultimate owner of the land, was represented on the spot by a hierarchy of little *domini*—major tenants and estate administrators on the make.[34] It was they, and not the distant landlords, who were the little tyrants of the locality. In this respect, estate managers were not unlike the *curiales* who bullied the peasantry in the name of the emperor. Managers shielded their masters from direct experience of violence and extortion on the land. Outside Hippo (Bône/Annaba, Algeria), a bailiff once raped a nun who had come to the estate to buy wool. As bishop of Hippo, Augustine could do nothing about this outrage on the spot. We know about the incident only from a letter Augustine wrote to an absentee landowner, for whom such matters must have appeared as distant as the far side of the moon.[35]

The insistence on the payment of rents in-kind should not be seen (as it once was by scholars of the early twentieth century) as a symptom of the reversion of the Roman world to a primitive economy, reduced to the bartering of food.[36] The opposite was the case: a demand for payment in foodstuffs assumed a market for foodstuffs. Farmers could bring their produce into the nearest town. But the rich had privileged access to wider and more lucrative markets. They alone could defeat distance. They could move their goods over large distances so as to supply major cities and hungry armies. The rich alone could also defeat time. They could store the abundance of the harvest and wait to sell when the prices were at their highest. Even in good years, the price of grain edged slowly upward to double its price as it became more scarce in the months before the next harvest. Those who could store the surplus of the harvest by gathering it into their granaries were the ones who could take advantage, every year, of this rise in prices. Further harvest shocks might turn the regular sale of grain into a "killing" in times of shortage.[37]

Not surprisingly, therefore, granaries emerge as the economic villains of the ancient world. Quite as much as does the sight of factories spewing toxic waste into the atmosphere in modern times, great granaries were a sight calculated to trigger disquiet in late Roman minds. Large Roman villas flaunted the wealth of their owner by being built up on solid granaries, endowed with heavy, locked gates.[38] The ruins of the granaries of the great fourth-century villa of São Cucufate, in southern Portugal, still stand ten feet high above the plain of the Alentejo, adjacent to the huge cylindrical weights, which are all that survive of the villa's olive presses.[39] The greatest granary of all, of course, was that of the emperor. Every year, the emperor of Constantinople led a solemn procession to the great Imperial Granary outside the city to watch the first installments of the grain levy from Egypt pile ever higher on its floor.[40] Inhabitants of Constantinople called this warehouse, bluntly, *Lamia*—"Jaws."[41]

A New Age of Gold

Since the time of Hesiod and the great grain silos of the Bronze Age, the storage and sale of foodstuffs was an unchanging feature of the landscape of the Mediterranean. What changed significantly in the fourth century was the manner in which the tax system of the Roman empire created a situation in which the rich were able to change food into gold to their great advantage.

To sum up a complex development: From Constantine onward, the Roman state flooded the economy with gold. The gold *solidus* became the symbol of a new order. As its name suggests, the *solidus* was a solid drop of gold. In the reign of Constantine, a pound of gold yielded seventy-two gold coins. It was with these coins that the emperor consolidated loyalty at the top through spectacular feats of generosity. He paid his army and his high officials in this new, strong currency. Following this example, the imperial bureaucracy as a whole insisted on receiving as many taxes as possible in gold. The result was a situation where those with access to gold coins towered above those whose only wealth still consisted in debased bronze coinage or in the unsold produce of their own fields. Silver coinage survived throughout the fourth century, but it tended to be pushed to one side by the prestigeful, new gold coins.[42]

By the end of the fourth century, a "poverty line" had come to be drawn in the social imagination of contemporaries between the areas of society where the mighty *solidus* circulated and a bleak social hinterland where the *solidus* was absent or difficult to obtain. In the words of the anonymous author of a treatise entitled *De rebus bellicis* (*On Military Problems*), who wrote, perhaps, in the 360s:

> It was in the age of Constantine that extravagant grants assigned gold instead of bronze ... to petty transactions ... [and hence] there ensued an even more extravagant passion for spending gold, which is considered the more precious substance ... which meant that the houses of the rich were crammed full and their splendor increased to the detriment of the poor—for those of little means went under, as the result of [official] violence.[43]

As the writer pointed out, the *Aurea aetas* (golden age) of which the ancients had dreamed, as a moneyless utopia at the dawn of time, had become a new and frightening "age of gold," characterized by violence and a degree of social stratification that was unprecedented even by Roman standards. The humblest servants of the Roman state now found that they could collect their fees and salaries in golden *solidi*. Town councillors extracted as much money as possible from taxpayers or, failing that, stored and sold for gold the food that they had collected from the countryside. At the top of society, emperors and senators came to express their incomes in terms of entire *centenaria*—hundred-pound ingots of pure gold.[44] All categories of the rich and the potential rich were brought together in one stupendous effort. They drove a primitive system of taxation and markets to its limits in order to perform, each year, the magic by which mere natural produce—the resources of a predominantly agrarian society—reached them as revenue, in the form of golden *solidi*.

It is perhaps more than a coincidence that Christian preaching on *treasure in heaven* should have taken on such a strong imaginative resonance in the cities of the Mediterranean and on the estates of Christian landowners at this time. For this was a time when, in the form of the *solidus*, so much treasure had, indeed, become available—charged, as only valuable coin can be, with the hint of infinite possibilities: for (in the words of Jorge Luis Borges, in his chilling story "The Zahir") "any coin ... is ... a repertory of possible futures ... money is future time."[45]

Let us follow for a moment the track of gold at the very top of Roman society in the fourth century.

In late Roman society, as in all other periods of Roman history, wealth had to be seen to be believed. And what was seen at the top—notably, but not exclusively, at Rome—was expected to border on the incredible. A full decade after the Gothic sack of Rome, in 410, Olympiodorus, a Greek diplomat, visited Rome. In his *History* he described a city bathed in memories of recent glory:

> Each of the great houses of Rome contained within itself ... everything which a medium-sized city could hold.... Many of the Roman households received an income of four thousand pounds of gold per year from their properties, not including grain, wine and other produce which, if sold, would have amounted to one-third of the income in gold. The income of the households at Rome of the second class was one thousand or fifteen hundred pounds of gold. When Probus, the son of Olybrius celebrated his praetorship [in 423–25] he spent twelve hundred pounds in gold [on the spectacular public games associated with this occasion]. Before the capture of Rome [in 410] Symmachus the orator [a pagan senator, whom we will have many occasions to meet in upcoming chapters] ... spent two thousand pounds when his son ... celebrated his praetorship. Maximus, one of the wealthy men, spent four thousand pounds on his son's praetorship. The praetors celebrated their festive games for [only!] seven days.[46]

We should be grateful for this set of numbers. They are some of the few statistics that we possess from the late Roman world. But we must be careful. As with all other ancient statistics, the credibility of these huge sums hangs on a slender thread.[47] Assuming that the figures originally given by Olympiodorus were not either grossly exaggerated or garbled by later transmission, we are looking at persons whom Chris Wickham has rightly described as "the richest private landowners of all time."[48]

What mattered to Olympiodorus and his readers were the memorable expenditures on the games incurred by individual senators. For the games placed the wealth of each family on display. Hence the sums spent by a senator such as Quintus Aurelius Symmachus amounted to 144,000 gold *solidi*. This was thirty times more than any senator of the eastern empire was expected to expend on games in Constantinople. The incomes of Roman senators were derived from rents and from the sale of produce. Olympiodorus may have been less precise in recording them than in recording the costs of the games. They formed the looming backdrop to the explosions of wealth made visible in vast palaces and in headlong shows. But, at 288,000 *solidi* a year, the incomes of major senators of Rome amounted to the equivalent of the tax revenue of an entire province or the cost of supplying Rome with grain for an entire year.[49]

What we know best is the blaze of this wealth, not its sources. It was the blaze that contemporaries wished to tell us about. Not surprisingly, the moment that Christian members of the Roman aristocracy began to renounce their family fortunes, their biographers seized on the opportunity to provide statistics that were intended to be quite as stunning as those offered by Olympiodorus. For instance, the young heiress Melania the Younger was remembered as having enjoyed, around the year 405, an annual income of 120,000 gold *solidi* (some 1,660 pounds of gold).[50] Thirty years later, as an old woman, presiding over a convent in the Holy Land, Melania told her biographer an eerie story. The inner chambers of her palace, where a part of her wealth had been stored in the form of gold coins and ingots of pure gold, prior to distribution to the poor, had seemed to shimmer with an unearthly glow. A thought sent from the Devil crossed her mind at that moment. How could *any* kingdom—even the kingdom of heaven—equal such wealth?[51]

Contemporaries had no illusions as to the relationship between wealth and power among such persons. Power was expected to accompany wealth and to draw yet more wealth to itself in mighty gulps. Writing around 390 AD, Ammianus Marcellinus, the last great pagan historian of Rome, fastened on a larger-than-life figure from the immediate past, Sextus Petronius Probus (who died around 388):

> Then [in 368] Probus was summoned from Rome to take up the Praetorian Prefecture—a man known throughout the Roman world for the brilliance of his family background, for the power of his influence and for the sheer extent of his riches, owning estates scattered here and there in every part of the empire. Whether these were justly come by or not, it is not for the likes of me to judge (*non iudicioli est nostri*).[52]

Not surprisingly, descriptions of the wealthy in the late Roman West have been tilted in the direction of the super-rich. Olympiodorus gave his stunning figures for the incomes and outlays of senators out of frank admiration. He was delighted to note that so much old-world splendor had survived in Rome after the Gothic sack of 410.[53] By contrast, the portrait of the rapacity of Probus was offered by Ammianus Marcellinus as a criticism. Ammianus Marcellinus had his own ax to grind: he was a pagan and Probus was a leading Christian senator.[54] But social historians have tended to put the two accounts together. In so doing, they have created a memorable stereotype of a corrupt grandee. In the words of Domenico Vera, Probus (in effect, the Probus of Ammianus Marcellinus, not the Probus we might know from other sources) has become "both a mythical figure and, at one and the same time, the Ideal Type of an entire class."[55] What we must now do is proceed down the social ladder, to meet the rich of the provinces. Here we find persons whose wealth was less spectacular than that of the super-rich of Rome. But they were considerably more vigorous than we had once been led to suppose.

Salvo Vitale felix Turissa: While Vitalis is alive and well,
Turissa prospers

THE RICH IN THE PROVINCES

The tendency to look at only the very top of late Roman society has created a more than usually tenacious stereotype. It stands in the way of our understanding of late Roman society in the West as a whole. We have allowed ourselves to assume that fourth-century society was dominated without exception by a class of great landowners such as we imagine Petronius Probus to have been. This was how the great Russian historian Mikhail Rostovtzeff described them, with characteristic vigor and confidence, in the last chapter of his *Social and Economic History of the Roman Empire* of 1926:

> Purchase, lease, patronage ... were all used to make the senatorial class the class of large landowners *par excellence*, and to form vast estates scattered all over the provinces and resembling small principalities. Few lived in the capital or in the cities. The majority of them built large and beautiful fortified villas in the country and dwelt there, surrounded by their family, their slaves, a real retinue of armed clients, and thousands of rural serfs and dependents. We are well acquainted with their mode of life from the descriptions of Ausonius, Paulinus of Pella [and others,] ... from the numerous ruins of their villas, and from some mosaics which portrayed on their floors the beauty of their châteaux.... Thus, more than ever before, society was divided into two classes: those who became steadily poorer and more destitute, and those who built up their prosperity on the spoils of the ruined Empire—real drones, who lived on the toil and travail of other classes.

To give further weight to his words, Rostovtzeff placed on the adjacent page an illustration of a late Roman mosaic from north Africa. In it, the landowner is shown riding out, already in "barbaric" hunting costume (with flowing cloak and embroidered tunic), from a villa that had apparently taken on the aspect of a walled fortress.[56]

It is important to linger on Rostovtzeff's view of the great landowners of the West. For by correcting it, we can measure the progress of late Roman scholarship since his days.

First: Archaeological surveys in many regions have effectively demolished what has been called "The Black Legend of the *Latifundium*."[57] There is little evidence on the ground for the existence of huge estates "resembling small principalities." Even the greatest villas stood in a landscape dotted with small properties.[58] The work of Domenico Vera has shown that, in many regions, the wealthy drew a large proportion of their wealth from the rents of innumerable small farms. The *microfundium* and not the *latifundium* was the most prominent feature of the late Roman countryside.[59] Furthermore, there is little evidence that the rural population became "steadily poorer and more destitute" in the course of the fourth century.[60]

Second: Rostovtzeff spoke of the labor force of the villas as if they were "rural serfs." He had in mind the serfs of the middle ages or of his own Russia in modern times. But this was not necessarily the case. In the fourth century, tenant farmers were not tied to the land by the Roman government working in collusion with the great landowners, as happened to the peasants of eastern Europe in the seventeenth and eighteenth centuries. The work of Jean-Michel Carrié has cast serious doubt on this particular view of the late Roman peasantry. He has argued that what has come to be called "the late Roman colonate" may not have been as widespread or as coercive a system as we had thought. It did not turn peasants into serfs.[61]

Ever since Carrié's groundbreaking studies on the colonate, disagreement reigns as to whether a system of enforced residence on the estates existed at all and, if it did, whether it was an empire-wide institution. What is at stake in this disagreement is not a purely legal issue. The debate centers on the extent to which agrarian production in the later empire was based on forced labor and, if so, on what kind of forced labor. Were landowners guaranteed a stable labor force through state coercion? Or did they use their own, rough methods to make sure that their tenants remained in place and that enough workers turned out every year to take in the harvest?

It seems that an element of constraint hovered in the background even when the landowners' relations with their farmers took the legal form of free contracts between landlords and tenants. The threat of violence (both physical and through the calling in of debts) was constantly brought to bear upon the peasantry. For this reason, the estates of the later empire were brittle structures. The passing of an army in a civil war or the dislocation caused by a barbarian raid could mean a loss of control in the countryside. It could be the signal for the massive emigration of farmers in search of freedom and of better conditions elsewhere. The peasantry had not been immobilized by law. But the fear of their potential mobility and a wish on the part of the landowners to tie them down was in the air.[62]

Altogether, a tense relationship had developed between landowners and their farmers in many regions. Landowners faced tenants who could not be treated out of hand as "rural serfs." But nor were these tenants contented little farmers who paid rent alone to a distant landlord. The fourth-century scramble for gold ensured that the rural population was driven as hard as, if not harder than, in any other period of ancient history. In the words of Andrea Giardina (in a vigorous defense of the traditional view of the Roman colonate as a coercive institution): "Productivity and suffering may well go hand in hand."[63]

The crisis of the fifth century put this cruel system to the test. The landowners of the West, great and small alike, found that they could no longer take their peasantry for granted. They could no longer rely on a weakened Roman state to enforce their demands. As a result, landowners had to work harder to retain control of their labor force in the face of higher levels of violence and dislocation caused by civil war and barbarian invasions. Many devices—from the provision of fortified refuges to the building of churches on the estates—show a novel concern to strengthen vertical links between peasantry and landowners such as had not existed in the insouciant days of the fourth-century age of gold. Those who strengthened their links to the peasantry on the ground had a better chance of surviving, while the scattered holdings of absentee members of the super-rich (which had depended, to a great extent, on a strong and unified empire) were easily dismantled.

Third: Rostovtzeff (and many scholars after him) placed the landowners of the later empire firmly in the countryside. They believed that the crisis of the third century had left the cities of the Roman West irrevocably depleted. It was assumed that the late Roman aristocracy took to the land en masse. It became a ruralized class, whose power over the land anticipated that of feudal lords of later times. One of the great excitements of the scholarship of the last half century has been the realization that, in the fourth and early fifth centuries, no such thing happened. The landed aristocracy never abandoned the cities. From Britain to Carthage, their villas were usually placed within easy distance of the towns and of the Roman roads that led through the towns. Their town houses were quite as magnificent as their country villas.[64] Even the mosaic Rostovtzeff chose to illustrate the castle-like isolation of a fortified villa of the later empire has been convincingly reinterpreted as conveying a diametrically opposite message. The walls in the background were city walls. The mosaic advertised the landowner's proud relationship to his own city; it did not celebrate withdrawal from the city to a fortified dwelling in the depths of the countryside.[65]

Fourth: The stereotype inherited from Rostovtzeff has caused us to imagine that all late Roman landowners were on the scale of a Petronius Probus or a Melania. They were no such thing. Most were rich town councillors; they were not members of the super-rich. None of them, in any region, could think of himself as the unchallenged lord of the countryside. Each landowner found himself competing with rivals who were usually his equals in provincial society. In most regions, they were not overshadowed by great absentee landowners such as Probus and Melania.

This can be seen through the archaeology of the villas of the late Roman West. Some fourth-century villas—such as Piazza Armerina in Sicily or Carranque in Spain—are enormous. They are, as it were, the Petronius Probuses of villa architecture. Just as Petronius Probus has become notorious for his wealth and corruption, so these villas have become well-known for their overpowering grandeur.[66] But they were not the only villas. Many more have been discovered in Britain, Spain, Gaul, and Italy. They were smaller affairs, often clustered within short distances of each other. They did not stand out as lonely châteaux, dominating the region as if they were the centers of a medieval seigneurie. Rather, they were designed to make a splash. As befitted monuments to success, they were bright and ingeniously built. They radiated a sense of good taste and of luxury enjoyed in a peaceful land. They were not the work of proto-feudal lords but the products of a highly competitive class of local, urban aristocrats. The ambitions of such persons were intense, but they were usually limited to the horizons of their city and their province.[67]

And many such landowners did succeed. On the Mediterranean coast of northeastern Spain, the mosaic of a late Roman villa shows a figure crowned with a walled crown. Normally such a figure was the emblem of the Good Fortune of a city. But, in this case, it represented the Good Fortune of the land, intertwined with the good fortune of its owner. The inscription reads:

Salvo Vitale Felix Turissa.

(While Vitalis is alive and well, Turissa prospers.)

Vitalis was proved right. Boosted in his own time by the landowner's careful attention, Turissa still survives today, as Tossa de Mar (Gerona, Spain).[68]

But what is significant about this buoyant inscription is that Vitalis of Turissa was not a member of the super-rich. Nor, as far as we can see, was he the owner of a vast *latifundium*, such as Rostovtzeff's peremptory words had long encouraged us to imagine him to be. The villa of Turissa was owned by a "little big man"—by a provincial landowner, probably drawn from the urban nobility of a neighboring city on the Mediterranean coast, such as Barcelona.

New Elites in a New "Age of Gold"

The case of Vitalis of Turissa makes us realize that, in the later empire, as in many other periods of ancient history, the great landowners, though spectacular, never stood alone. They were never the sole masters of their world. In a pertinent critique of the views of many social historians, Walter Scheidel has pointed out that we have been misled by a "binary tunnel vision." This presents Roman society as brutally divided between the very rich and the very poor, with no intermediary groups. He has rightly insisted that "It is perfectly possible to reconcile the dominance of a disproportionately affluent elite with the presence of a substantial middle."[69]

Let us look, for a moment, below the great, toward Scheidel's "substantial middle." We will find, throughout the provinces of the West, a social landscape densely populated with vivid and resilient figures. In the society of the fourth-century West, the future lay not with grandees such as Probus but with landowners of the provinces, like Vitalis of Turissa.

This had happened because of a major reshuffle of the upper classes of the West. Here the long reign of Constantine (306–37) proved crucial. As in the days of the "Roman Revolution" of the emperor Augustus that followed the civil wars of the Roman Republic, so, in the reign of Constantine, the emperor turned to a wider social constituency than hitherto to find support for a new style of empire. Constantine and his successors reached out to the widespread "political nation" represented by the elites of the town councils in the provinces. Many of the persons recruited and honored by Constantine were not only leaders in their individual cities. Their wealth and marriage connections made them leaders of provincial society as a whole. They were far from being upstarts; many came from long established families in their region. Their incomes amounted to thousands of gold coins. They towered above little men such as our Harvester of Mactar. But they were not members of the super-rich like Petronius Probus, whose estates spanned southern Italy, north Africa, and other regions of the Mediterranean like the branches of a modern "multinational" company. From Constantine onward, the emperors tipped the balance in favor of these provincials by making membership of the Senate available to them.[70]

Provincial aristocrats were joined by imperial servants—by courtiers, bureaucrats, and military men. As a result, the traditional Senate of Rome was dwarfed by an empire-wide class of newly minted members, all of whom were granted the senatorial title of *vir clarissimus*—"most brilliant man"—and their wives and daughters that of *femina clarissima*. At least two thousand persons at any one time now settled back into local society with the privilege of senatorial rank. As a result, hardy relics of the ancien régime, linked by long traditions to the Roman Senate, fought for honor, power, and riches alongside the *barons d'empire* created by a succession of new Napoleons—by the emperors Constantine, Constantius II, and Valentinian I.[71]

As a result of this new situation, the small group of nobles closely associated with the Senate of Rome found themselves jostled—even in Rome itself—by an influx of provincials and government servants. The resident nobles of Rome showed great tenacity when faced by this situation. Despite the fact that they had lived under Christian emperors since the conversion of Constantine in 312 AD, many nobles remained staunch pagans throughout the fourth century. They were by no means sidelined. Their vast wealth and inherited prestige gave them access to governmental circles. Petronius Probus was not the only Roman senator of the fourth century who remained a vigorous political player.[72]

In the newly reconstituted elite of the empire, the nobles of Rome represented Old Money. Many noble families reached back for centuries. They had also enjoyed centuries of residence in a region of exceptional economic prosperity. We must always remember that southern Italy and north Africa (and not northern Italy, Gaul, or Spain) were the economic center of gravity of the late Roman West.[73] This was where the Roman families connected with Old Money were to be found. Yet, despite the advantages such persons still enjoyed, an influx of new men set the power of the Roman nobility against a backdrop far more diverse than had existed in previous centuries. The huge wealth of men such as Probus no longer enabled them to dominate west Roman society as a whole.

The *Album* of Timgad

STATUS AND PRIVILEGE IN THE FOURTH-CENTURY WEST

Economic and social historians still debate the extent and the causes of the aggressive monetarization of the late Roman economy. In these debates, the role of the late Roman state is central. There are those who think that no preindustrial empire as cramped by distance and by primitive agrarian methods as that of Rome could have produced a state apparatus that was capable of galvanizing an entire economy through its tax demands alone. The fourth-century Roman state may not have been as effective as some recent scholars have come to believe that it had been. Many have argued that, at best, the fourth-century empire witnessed a flexing of state power that was unusual but doomed to be short-lived.[74]

These are valid doubts. Yet we cannot deny that the most remarkable feature of the fourth century was the manner in which the emperors and their court took center stage in determining the hierarchy of Roman society. Gradations of wealth also took on a more blatant quality. Those who received imperial privileges stood out above the rest. This new stratification was connected in the public mind with access to the mighty *solidus*, gained in the first instance through imperial service.

When he described the effects of the post-Constantinian gold rush, the writer of the tract *On Military Problems* went on to add that *adflicta paupertas*—the resentful state of the newly impoverished—was responsible for the crime and political instability of his age. His use of the word *paupertas* should not mislead us. As with so many other Roman authors, the "poverty" he referred to was not that of the peasantry or of the urban poor. What was at stake was not poverty: it was impoverishment—the impoverishment and loss of power of persons who, until then, had not considered themselves to be "poor." The author addressed a segment of Roman society (in which even members of the traditional Senate might be included) who resented the fact that they had missed out on the new age of gold.[75] Let us look at how this restructuring of Roman society happened on the ground, at the level of the cities.

In 367–68, an inscription was set up inside the hall of the imposing *curia*, the City Hall, of the Numidian city of Thamugadi (modern Timgad in southern Algeria). The town councillors of the city were listed in order of precedence. Known to us as the *Album* of Timgad, it amounted to a social diagram of a provincial society in the post-Constantinian empire.[76] Ten *viri clarissimi* (newly created senators) stood out at the very top. At least five of these were local men. A further thirty councillors led the town council of Timgad. They were a true oligarchy. They were usually referred to as the *principales*, the "leading men" of the city. Then came the rank and file. In Timgad, this consisted of around 150 *decuriones* or *curiales*.

These *curiales* were ordinary town councillors (such as the Harvester of Mactar had become). Though sheathed in the honor of public service, and raised by that honor alone above the "little farmers" of the countryside and the *plebs* of their city, they were the group on which "afflicted poverty" threatened to fall most heavily. They were held responsible both for the dreary work of local government, linked to the supervision of the life of the city, and for the financially risky and grim task of collecting the imperial taxes. They were made responsible for any shortfall in the tax yield of the area controlled by their city. If they failed, their precious privilege of freedom from torture and the lash could be withdrawn. Yet, though harassed, this group was far from consisting only of little men. Some *curiales* bore family names that reached back, in Timgad, for at least one and a half centuries.[77]

Most interesting of all, a full seventy former members of the town council of Timgad, though they came from local families, were exempt from service in the town council. For they had become bureaucrats, serving as officials of the government in Timgad and all over Africa. They now served not the city but the empire. In this manner, an original group of sixty to seventy families, who had ruled a city of ten thousand inhabitants and its region for at least two centuries, had come to be splintered by the new age of gold. The gap between the privileged and the less privileged groups in the town council was determined by imperial privileges gained through imperial service. Some were exempted, as a result of this service, from the demands made by their city upon their money and their time. Others, less fortunate, were "grounded." They were tied to the narrow horizons of their hometown. They might be rich, but they had every reason to feel insecure and resentful in the face of their more successful peers who had sought out new opportunities as imperial servants.[78]

Altogether, this vivid and precise glimpse into a provincial society, provided by the *Album* of Timgad and by related inscriptions, places the wealth of the very rich in perspective. Seen from the ground up, Roman senators—let alone men of legendary wealth and influence such as Petronius Probus—were distant figures. The people who usually mattered were the landowners, the government servants, and the holders of imperial privileges in cities such as Timgad, scattered throughout the Roman West.[79]

Amici maiores

PATRONAGE AND POWER

This was a social system that put a premium on upward social mobility. Like a similar, vast, and protocol-ridden organization (the British Navy in the days of Scott of the Antarctic), late Roman society was structured in such a way that "Ambition was not an option ... but a necessity."[80] For lesser members of the town council, the only way out of a life of boredom and occasional humiliation at the hands of the imperial authorities was to escape toward the top, by seeking wealth, power, and privilege in a new system of honors linked to imperial service. Hence the crucial importance, in this period, of a very ancient Roman institution, *patrocinium*. Recent studies have shown that patronage was as strong as ever in the later empire and that patronage still wore its ancient, Roman face.[81] Patronage was a fact of life. As a *Calendar of 354* made plain, a Roman was supposed to note that when the moon was in Taurus, Leo, Scorpio, or Aquarius the time had come yet again "to ask for a favor, to have a conversation with a man of power."[82]

Let us look for a moment at the career of one well-known son of a town councillor—Augustine, the future bishop of Hippo. From the early 370s up to the time of his conversion in 386, Augustine's career depended at every stage on the patronage of others. As a young teacher, he was supported by a patron from his home town of Thagaste, Romanianus. Romanianus gave Augustine financial support and almost certainly intervened to make him exempt from the duties he owed to the city of Thagaste as the son of a town councillor.[83] It was this exemption that set Augustine free to rise to the top. He moved from patron to patron as he made his way up, moving ever further from Thagaste. In Rome, in 384, the patronage of friends from a sectarian group, the Manichees, made him known to none other than Symmachus, who was a well-known pagan and senator in the traditional mold. Chosen to teach at Milan, he may have traveled north with Symmachus's backing.[84] A year later, he was at it again. Now he hoped for a governorship through the intervention of *amici maiores*, "friends in high places," whose *salutatio*—the daily reception held for clients and petitioners—he struggled to attend regularly, despite his heavy workload as a teacher.[85]

Augustine's friend Alypius was no different. Unlike Augustine, who was the son of a town councillor of modest means, Alypius came from the inner circle of the elite of Thagaste. But he also followed the same strategies for advancement as did Augustine. When studying in Carthage, Alypius went out of his way to make himself known through regular attendance at the *salutatio* of a senator who resided in Carthage.[86] Arrived at Rome, Alypius soon came up against the more sinister face of patronage. He was working as the legal adviser to a high official:

> There was at that time an extremely powerful senator. Many people were kept under his power by bribes or subdued by terror. He wanted as usual to use his influence to obtain something which by the laws was unlawful. Alypius resisted. A bribe was promised. He scorned it.... Threats were made. He kicked them away, and everyone was amazed at so exceptional a character who neither wished to have a friend nor feared to have as an enemy a powerful person ... who had innumerable methods of either benefiting or injuring people.[87]

However, when we next meet Alypius, at Milan in 385, he was out of a job. The upright young provincial may have picked the wrong senator to offend.

If there was any traditional Roman mechanism that might have held a fractured elite together, it was the well-tried mechanism of patronage. We need only look at the correspondence of the Roman senator Quintus Aurelius Symmachus to see a major patron at work. One quarter of his letters were ones of recommendation. Through his letters, Symmachus reached out to spin a spider's web that led from his palace in Rome to every level of the upper classes of the western empire. Mauretanian bishops appear alongside Spanish horse breeders; high courtiers and formidable barbarian generals were addressed on behalf of up-and-coming rhetors and doctors. Symmachus's letters are a microcosm of a remarkably diversified elite.[88] But the sheer diversity of the social world that Symmachus attempted to cover through his letters was a cause of weakness. In the fourth century, there were too many patrons, drawn from too many potentially conflicting groups. No single line of patronage could reach from top to bottom to the advantage of a single, established group. For all too many persons on the make, all roads no longer led to Rome.

Splendor

THE ÉCLAT OF THE LOCAL RICH

What was remarkable—and distinctively late Roman—about the members of these differing sections of the wealthy was the extent to which their shared implication in the imperial system imposed on them a rare homogeneity in dress and styles of living. They stood for a new ordering of society. They were expected to look the part.

For instance, the new rich and powerful shared a radically new dress code. Late Roman dress broke significantly with the classical restraint associated with traditional Roman clothing. The new clothes of the elites carried into every locality the values of the court and of the army. Based on military uniforms, they pointedly elided the distinction between military and civilian, Roman and barbarian. A tight, belted tunic, decorated with great panels of woven silk, was worn over subtly embroidered trousers. A heavy cloak (also bright with colored stripes and patches) hung over the body, held on the right shoulder with a golden *fibula* brooch of barbarian workmanship.

With this style of costume went a new way of expressing social distance. The carefully folded Roman toga had to be carried with classical poise. The toga stressed the supremacy of civilian values even in a society committed to war. It demonstrated the role of a classical education in producing persons whose self-control and poise in public were as delicately balanced as were the sentences of the ancient authors whose writings they had internalized. The folds of expensive but simple cloth that hung on their bodies in the form of a toga reflected a similar unruffled poise.[89]

Not so the wearer of the new style of dress. This dress spoke of the energy of persons stepping into new and strenuous roles. It consisted of contrasted layers. The tunic and trousers closed in the body, sheathing it in opulent textures. But the great cloak held in the "bite" of a *fibula* brooch swung from the shoulder with a barbaric sweep. It billowed out behind hunters in the chase. It fluttered around the great as they swept past their clients like ships in full sail, showing to the outside world "great painted walls" of floating, embroidered silk.[90]

Such dress ensured that, in the provinces as in Rome, the rich looked like nobody else. The dress of upper-class women was not affected by the specifically male desire to imitate the barbarian taste of the military. It showed itself, rather, in spectacular jewelry and in the use of precious textiles—pendant earrings, bracelets, necklaces, and heavy golden chains falling over brightly dyed silks and cloth of gold. Given the restrictions on women's ability to dispose of property, the most available form of wealth, for a woman, was the splendor that sheathed her body. In that sense, women represented disposable wealth at its most alarmingly mobile—a fact that was not lost on the critics of clergymen who studiously paid court to Christian matrons. Women carried liquid wealth on their own bodies and kept it stored in great chests in their own bedrooms. Christian women from the aristocracy could load a church with silk veils and altar coverings made from textiles taken from their private wardrobe. A noble woman could finance the foundation of an entire basilica in the middle of Rome through the sale of her jewelry alone.[91]

Altogether, rich men and women alike were expected to stand out like birds of paradise in a flock of starlings. Looking at the inventories of the goods of townsmen in sixth-century Ravenna, one can see immediately who was poor, by late Roman standards, and who was rich. Stephanus had a shirt of silk and cotton in scarlet and bright, leek green, a silk robe of variegated green, linen trousers, two woven tapestries, and a slave called Proiectus. Guderit, by contrast, was a freedman. He had one old dyed shirt, one decorated shirt, and an old short coat of thick material. Guderit was no beggar. He owned a little property and had a roof over his head in a major Roman city. But he was colorless. He lay on the dim side of the sharp, late Roman boundary between rich and poor.[92]

Yet we must remember that dress and other vibrant signs of wealth were not seen only as advertising private gains. Luxury and drama served public needs. From the third century onward, the tendency had been to replace massive public buildings by splendid ceremonial occasions. Public shows continued when civic architecture, with its more lasting impact, slackened. From the emperor downward (in his pearl-studded diadem and purple robes as heavy with religious reverence as church vestments), those who held public power condensed this power on their own persons. The public appearances of emperors, governors, and city leaders were mere nanoseconds of display compared with the silent mass of the classical buildings that former centuries had piled up to show the glory of their cities. But these high ceremonial occasions were seen as explosions of *splendor*, of éclat, that spoke of the majesty of city and empire in a fully public manner that was intended to leave the onlookers stunned.[93]

Last but not least, the signs of wealth in the later empire could be modulated according to the means of their owners. Late Roman dress was flashy. It was clearly marked by striking features—by great embroidered bands and roundels woven into stretches of heavy material, held in place by the costume jewelry of brooches and ornamented belts. But, precisely because such costume was so vivid, it could be reproduced in non-precious materials. Among the lesser gentry of the provinces, carefully dyed wool and linen substituted for the silk and cloth of gold of the truly rich.[94] In the same manner, in the villas and town houses of provincial notables, ingenious stucco work, frescoed walls, and carefully laid floor mosaics imitated the encrusted splendor of gold and marble with which the houses of the truly rich blazed with unimaginable opulence.[95] African ceramics—masterpieces of a thriving fourth-century industry—relayed, in cheap but skillful copies, the exuberant scenes of classical mythology associated with the silverware of the great. Ceramic reproductions of plaques in ivory and precious metal echoed, on the tables of notables in provincial cities, the splendor of high office and the thrill of the great games associated with the nobility of Rome.[96] There was room for many differing levels of the rich, associated with differing uses of precious materials. Far from the centers of power, landowners in what is now southern Portugal might dine in exquisitely constructed halls, decorated by elegant, small pieces of statuary. But they dined without display. They were content to use local pottery, carefully molded to echo the sophisticated wares of Africa.[97]

What is striking about the local elites of the fourth-century West was that they never lost sight of the imperial court. Fragmented and highly factionalized, local families competed fiercely to display their new wealth. And they did so by drawing on a common language which, to a surprising degree, was empire wide. Architectural styles that had been developed in imperial capitals or in vast imperial villas were picked up and circulated throughout the provinces, often skillfully miniaturized to suit the pockets of local clients. Such borrowings brought a touch of "imperial" solemnity and architectural sophistication to town houses and country villas, some of which were no more than expanded farmhouses.[98]

This was true down to the most humble details and in the most distant regions. In Britain, an empress could appear in the form of a pepper pot on the table of a Roman military man (whose buried utentsils and hoard of coins were discovered at Hoxne in East Anglia). She was made of light silver, rendered solemn and opulent by having her diadem and jewelry highlighted by a thin wash of gold.[99]

Indeed, it is in southern Britain that we can best appreciate the reach of empire in the fourth-century world. In a major villa at Woodchester, fifteen miles west of Cirencester, an exquisite piece of mythological sculpture has been found. It stood near a large mosaic of Orpheus, in a palatial hall.[100] Woodchester villa may have been the official residence of the governor of the province of west Britain. The province stretched from the Cotswolds across the Severn valley to the barely Romanized mountains of Wales. Thus, the governor's mansion at Woodchester lay on the farthest edge of the late Roman social order set in place by Constantine. Yet the marble statue in refined classical style that was discovered in the villa came all the way from the eastern Mediterranean. It may even have been produced by a workshop set up by the emperor Theodosius I in Constantinople in the years after 380.[101] If this is the case, then the statue at Woodchester villa provides an extraordinary instant photograph of the speed with which precious objects followed those engaged in governmental service from one end of the empire to the other.

The glory of a villa such as Woodchester is all the more poignant because we know that it had not many years to go. Within half a century, Britain would no longer be part of the Roman empire. After 410 the Roman imperial government withdrew, and the sharp, state-created hierarchies of the fourth century vanished in a swift and brutal flattening out of post-imperial British society.[102] In continental Europe, the crisis of imperial authority associated with the barbarian invasions of the fifth century brought the age of gold to an end, if in a less dramatic and irrevocable manner than in Britain. In the later part of this book, from the 420s onward, we will enter a different, less buoyant age. For what happened in the fifth century was a replay of the crisis of the third century from which, however, no restored empire would emerge.

But this is to anticipate. So drastic a development could not have been foreseen in the mid-fourth century, when our story begins. At that time, the message from on high was plain: in their dress, in the elaborate décor of their homes, even in the tableware and in the precious objets d'art that linked them to persons and ceremonials associated with the very summits of wealth and power, the rich were different from everybody else—and they were different because they were, all of them in differing ways, implicated in the workings of a mighty empire.

And so, as we have seen, the fourth-century age of gold was also an age of empire. It was this combination of large disposable incomes reckoned in gold coins with imperial privileges gained through imperial service or through imperial favor that gave a distinctive flavor to the wealth of the wealthy. It is against this background that we should now turn to examine the position in fourth-century society of the most novel (and, certainly, the most unexpected) group of all to receive the privileges Constantine had offered so lavishly to his supporters. Let us look at the leaders of the Christian churches and their congregations to whom Constantine decided to grant both peace and privilege as a result of his famed conversion to Christianity in 312 AD.

CHAPTER 2

Mediocritas

The Social Profile of the Latin Church, 312–ca. 370

A Transitional Age

This chapter is about the Christianity of the Roman West in the period roughly between the conversion of Constantine in 312 and the election of Ambrose as bishop of Milan in 374. It is not easy to approach this period, as it is a tantalizingly transitional age.

By contrast, we are used to the more brilliant—indeed, more strident—Latin Christianity of the late fourth and early fifth centuries. This was the age of Ambrose, Jerome, Augustine, and Paulinus of Nola. It has been aptly characterized by Sir Ronald Syme as the last (and in many ways the richest) of the "three classical epochs" of Latin literature.[1] In that age, Latin Christianity was caught, for the first time in its history, in the arc light of an abundant literature. For this reason alone, the brilliant period between 370 and 430 will form the heart of this book.

To approach the age that preceded it is like stepping out of bright sunlight into the shade of a catacomb. We have to adjust our eyes to an unaccustomed dimness. Yet, like many apparently dim ages, the sixty years that fell between the conversion of Constantine and the election of Ambrose set the stage for the shimmering epoch that succeeded them. It is important to go back to that earlier time in order to understand the low-profile but tenacious Christianity that gave way to the more assertive religion that emerged after 370 AD.

This chapter, therefore, will lead up to a decisive change in the tone and pace of Latin Christianity. It will show that the distinctive features of the period between 312 and 370 derived, in large part, from a strange paradox. The first Christian emperor thrust the bishops and clergy of the Christian church forward as a privileged body. But, at the same time, he denied them any purchase on the upper reaches of west Roman society. Having looked at the consequences of

31

Constantine's policies, the chapter will then examine the social composition of the churches in the first half of the fourth century. It will conclude with a brief sketch of the social tone of the Christian communities at the moment when, slowly but surely, these communities came to be joined by representatives of the wealthy classes. It was the gathering pace of the entry of the rich into the Christian churches in the period after 370—and not the conversion of Constantine in 312—that marks the true beginning of the triumphant Catholicism of the Middle Ages.

Seu gentilis seu christianus quaecumque: Whether a pagan or a Christian, whoever [he or she] might be

CHRISTIANITY IN A PAGAN WORLD

In order to understand the situation of the Latin churches at the beginning of our period, we must tackle (inevitably briefly in the compass of one chapter) two of the most intractable problems that beset any historian of late antiquity. We must come to some conclusion about the nature and the implications of the conversion of Constantine in 312.[2] Then we must confront the equally daunting prospect of establishing the social niche in which the Christianity in the Latin world of the first half of the fourth century had developed.

The two themes are interrelated. For what we think of the aims of Constantine and of the role he intended the Christian churches to play in Roman society affects what we think of the social texture of the Latin Christian communities and of the pace and the impact of the entry of the rich into the Christian churches at this time and in subsequent generations.

Let us begin with the paradox inherent in the conversion of Constantine in 312. In converting to Christianity, Constantine set himself aims that were considerably narrower than we might at first expect from a decision whose consequences were to prove so momentous for the history of Europe and the Middle East. Though the first Christian emperor has been the subject of intense study, it is still difficult to discover his intentions at the time and, above all, to determine the extent of his ambition on behalf of the Christian faith. A few general remarks (offered with due hesitancy, given the highly complex and contested nature of the field) might help clear the ground.[3]

Constantine did not act out of political calculation. He did not perceive that Christianity was on the way to becoming a majority religion in any part of his empire—not even in the more densely Christianized East and certainly not in the Latin West, where Christianity seems to have made considerably less progress.[4] If Constantine intuited Christianity as the wave of the future, it was not in terms of the observed expansion of the Christian communities.[5] Rather, in the austere words of James Bury, Constantine's conversion had been "the most audacious act ever committed by an autocrat in defiance of the vast majority of his subjects."[6]

If Constantine calculated, he did so in supernatural terms in an age that took the choice of supernatural protectors seriously. His conversion to Christianity was an act of supreme willfulness, such as only a charismatic Roman emperor could have undertaken. He put himself under the protection of the Christian God, and in so doing, he deliberately chose a God as big and as new as himself. He chose an all-powerful and transcendent deity who owed nothing to the past. The Christian God and those who worshiped Him had no need of other, smaller gods. Constantine hoped that this God would protect both himself and his empire as effectively as He seemed to have protected His church and His people, the Christians, in times of persecution.[7]

In return for this protection, Constantine rewarded the Christian clergy with appropriate privileges. For it was they (and not the average Christian) who were the ritual experts. They knew best how to conduct "the worship of the Most High God."[8] Furthermore, in order to enjoy the continued protection of his new God, Constantine was prepared to devote great pains to keeping the worship of that God immune from error and division. From 312 to his death in 337, Constantine, and then his son, Constantius II (337–61), patrolled the Christian episcopate ceaselessly to make sure that the worship they offered to God was correct and pleasing to Him.[9]

But that was almost all that Constantine was prepared to do. The non-Christian subjects of his empire were left largely to themselves; the Roman West remained a predominantly pagan world. The eastern provinces of the empire, reorganized around Constantine's personal foundation—the city of Constantinople—were the laboratory in which he and his successors were encouraged by Christian enthusiasts to carry out the grandiose experiment of a fully Christian empire. But what might have begun to seem possible to Christians in Constantinople and the Levant was still beyond the bounds of the imagination in Rome and the western provinces.

To understand this apparent shortfall in the long-term aims of Constantine, we must be clear about the horizons of the possible that were envisioned by Christians themselves in the early fourth-century West. Constantine certainly thought of himself as a Christian. But he was not a Christian of the middle ages, nor was he even a Christian of the late fourth century. It was enough for him that the Christian God should be recognized, that Christians should no longer be persecuted, and, above all, that the Christian clergy should be privileged and protected.

Christians of the age of Constantine appear to have accepted this narrow estimate of the limits of the possible. If they looked to the future, they did not envision the emergence of Christianity as a majority religion. They had always claimed that Christianity was a "universal" religion, but by universal they meant that anyone anywhere could become a Christian. They were proud of the fact that Christians could be found everywhere. But this did not mean that they expected that everyone everywhere would become a Christian. As Claire Sotinel has put it: Christians of that time could imagine "Christianity as present in all parts of a [social] universe, but not a social universe that was entirely Christian."[10] That awareness only came later. But it did come. Ninety years after the conversion of Constantine, Christian Latin preachers found that they could propose a "majoritarian" rather than a merely universal brand of Christianity. Preaching at Boseth, a small town in Africa, in 404, Augustine of Hippo claimed that

> All are astonished to see the entire human race converging on the Crucified, from emperors down to beggars in their rags ... persons of every rank have already come, of every level of income and of every form of wealth. It is high time for all and sundry to be inside the Church.[11]

But this was the voice of a strident new age. No such voice was to be heard in the age of Constantine.

Altogether, we are dealing with what Paul Veyne has recently called a bipolar society.[12] The Roman empire was not a "Christian empire" but one in which the religion of the new Christian God had unexpectedly become prominent. But it was also an empire where Christians expected (and were expected by others) to remain no more than a privileged minority.

Vivid evidence from Britain shows what it was like to live in such a bipolar society. Some time in fourth-century Britain, Annianus, son of Matutina, had a purse of six silver pieces stolen from him. He placed a leaden curse tablet in the sacred spring of Sulis Minerva at Bath in order to bring the miscreant to the attention of the goddess. On this tablet, the traditional list of antithetical categories that would constitute an exhaustive description of all possible suspects— "whether man or woman, boy or girl, slave or free"—begins with a new antithesis: *seu gentilis seu christianus quaecumque*, "whether a gentile or a Christian, whomsoever." As Roger Tomlin, the alert editor of the tablets, has observed, "it is tempting to think that a novel *gentilis/christianus* pair was added as a tribute to the universal power of Sulis."[13]

At the shrine of Sulis Minerva at Bath in the fourth century, "Christianization" meant little more than knowledge of yet another worldwide category of persons whose deeds were open to the eye of an effective goddess of the post-Constantinian age. It is a glimpse of Christians set in a landscape still crowded with other gods.

"Our State is sustained more by religion than by official duties, physical toil, and sweat"

CHRISTIANITY AND PRIVILEGE

This situation goes some way toward explaining the uncertain public profile of Latin Christianity up to at least the 370s. It was a privileged religion. But its leaders were by no means socially dominant. They lacked the raw muscle of wealth and inherited status that distinguished the traditional leaders of late Roman society.

From 313 onward, Constantine granted to bishops and clergymen the same privileges that had always been accorded by Roman emperors to those who furthered the cultural and religious ends of Roman society. The Christian clergy merely joined a long list of privileged persons, which already included pagan priests (whose exemptions Constantine maintained), professors, doctors, and the leaders of Jewish synagogues.[14] These privileges consisted of exemption from many forms of public service and even (but more grudgingly) from certain forms of personal taxation.[15]

What was at stake in these privileges was not mere monetary advantage; it was the precious commodity of leisure. As we have seen, the Roman empire had always been a "minimal state." It worked through delegating as many tasks of government as possible to local authorities—especially to the town councillors (the *curiales*) and to the trade associations (the *collegia* and the *corpora*) in the cities.[16] These duties varied widely from building roads and city walls to collecting firewood for the public baths and driving herds of horses for delivery to the Roman cavalry, to mention only a few. Imperial demands for labor bit into the time of town councillors—and even, for the average townsman (who was subject to corvée labor), into their own bodies—quite as deeply as the imperial taxes bit into their pockets.

To receive exemption from such duties was to step into an altogether enviable oasis of leisure. This was the precious leisure Constantine went out of his way to ensure that every Christian bishop and Christian priest would enjoy so that they could devote themselves wholeheartedly to the worship of their God. In the words of a law issued by Constantius II, the pious son of Constantine, in 361, the exemptions given to bishops and clergymen had been granted because "our State is sustained more by religion than by official duties, physical toil and sweat."[17]

It was not a popular ruling. Members of the Christian clergy who claimed exemptions were instantly challenged by their fellow townsmen. This is not surprising. *Curiales* and *collegiati* had always looked with hard eyes on shirkers who claimed exemptions of any sort. For taxes and tasks were allotted to groups. The more members each group lost through some of their number receiving personal exemptions, the more "official duties, physical toil and sweat" would be left to be borne by the few who remained. We are dealing with a zero-sum situation of the nastiest sort. We know of Constantine's privileges for the clergy through edicts that show that they were frequently challenged and frequently needed to be defined and reasserted.

Yet despite the alarm and jealousy caused by Constantine's grants of exemptions to bishops and clergymen, a strict ceiling was placed on them. First things came first. Except for a few years at the end of the reign of Constantius II, neither the Christian bishops and clergy nor their churches were ever granted exemption from the land tax, which was the principal tax of the empire.[18]

Hence a paradox. These privileges contributed greatly to the social status of the clergy. But, in themselves, they did not place Christian bishops and clergymen anywhere near the top of Roman society. Put briefly: the clergy became distinguished because they were privileged. By contrast, most leaders of local society in the senatorial or curial class had gained their privileges because they were already distinguished. Many had been substantial landowners before they were folded into the imperial system of honors fostered by Constantine. This was not so with the Christian clergy. Of all the "new men" thrown up by this age of change, the Christian clergy were by far the newest. As a result, around 350, the Christian church stuck out somewhat awkwardly in the Latin world, like a skeleton on which the flesh and sinews of real social power had not yet grown.

This was in no small part due to the fact that the Christian clergy still stood at the head of an invisible class. They were the leaders of religious communities that had grown up in the interstices between rich and poor in the cities of the Roman world. It is to these low-profile persons that we must now turn.

Mediocritas

CHRISTIANITY AND THE *PLEBS*

As long ago as 1958, in a lecture given at the Warburg Institute in London A.H.M. Jones, the great social historian of the later Roman empire, suggested that "the main strength of Christianity lay in the lower and middle classes of the towns, the manual workers and clerks, the shop keepers and merchants."[19] Though delivered in passing and in a somewhat impressionistic manner, all subsequent research (especially that conducted on the social origins of the clergy) has proved Jones's insight to be substantially correct.[20]

What is more difficult to assess is how such persons of the "lower and middle classes of the towns" fit into the society of the fourth century. It is here that significant changes in scholarly opinion have taken place. It used to be widely believed that the principal characteristic of the late Roman cities had been a drastic polarization between the wealthy few and a deeply impoverished majority. The rich life of the trade associations (the *collegia*) of classical Roman times was said to have vanished in the crisis of the third century. Scholars assumed that by the year 300, the "middle" had been well and truly taken out of the Roman city.

But the recent, careful work of Jean-Michel Carrié has made clear that the members of the *collegia* continued to play a significant role in the organization and social life of every late Roman town.[21] Far from having withered away, they continued in much the same way as they had done in classical times. They were organized by the government so as to provide reserves of labor and money, but the *collegiati* never became mere cogs in a fiscal machine. They feasted together, marched together in civic processions, and continued to bury their members in common burial grounds irrespective of religious affiliation.[22]

It was precisely among such persons that the Christian congregations had developed. To appreciate this, we need only go out to the catacombs of Rome. For those who like to imagine Christianity as a religion of the humble and oppressed, these catacombs come as a surprise. Despite their romantic modern associations, only small sections of them go back to the days of the persecuted church. Most of what has survived dates from after the conversion of Constantine. What the Roman catacombs reveal is not a world of the oppressed but the exuberant and socially differentiated urban society in which the Christians of the fourth century participated fully.

In the galleries of the catacombs we find the tomb inscriptions of men and women whose livelihood derived from the needs of the rich in a great city known for its luxuries and for its games.[23] Unlike the great marble sarcophagi of the truly rich, the simple plaques that covered graves carved into the tufa rock were not luxurious. In the words of one such plaque, these tombs were created *de parbula mediocritatem* [*sic*]—"from the humble means" of their owners.[24] The plaques refer to artisans, tradesmen, and minor officials. We meet women as weavers of silk. We meet men as makers of mirrors. We meet barbers with their instruments. We meet grooms leading fine horses.[25] Most surprising of all, in a Christian cemetery, we meet a comic pantomime artist, Vitalis:

> O death, what shall I do with you ...
> You know nothing of merriment.
> You do not appreciate jokes.
> But from these jokes I won out.
> I became known through the whole world.
> From these I gained a handsome house and income.[26]

Medieval pilgrim-monks were puzzled to discover this fourth-century fragment of Cockney cheerfulness close to the church of San Sebastiano on the Appian Way outside Rome. They opined that Vitalis was "the son of Cato, a great Court Jester of his time."

Rome, as a vast metropolis, might be considered an exception. But the Christian sarcophagi of a small provincial city, Salona (modern Solin, a little to the north of Split on the Dalmatian coast of Croatia), show a similar grouping of minor officials and tradesmen. Sarcophagi were not cheap: they were sold for ten to fifteen *solidi*, the equivalent of a quarter to a third of a year's salary for a teacher of Latin grammar.[27] Those who owned such sarcophagi must have stood at the top of the little pyramids formed by the trade associations to which they belonged—engravers, glassmakers, candlestick makers, traders, lawyers, and members of government bureaus.[28] Many must have been employers rather than mere workmen.[29] But they were there. They had not vanished in the crisis of the third century.

People such as these provided the local Christian communities with their clergy. We know of this because of one of the fiercest zero-sum conflicts of all to be fought out in the cities on the issue of "official duties, toil and sweat." Town councillors had never been a closed caste. They constantly reached out to recruit richer members of the *plebs* so as to increase the number of persons who could share the collective burden of taxes and other duties. All over the empire, town councils were on the lookout for wealthy plebeians (farmers or townsmen) who had been caught in an updraft of financial success. Their income exposed such persons to forced co-optation into their local town council. Though this promotion might be a cause for self-congratulation (as we saw in the case of the Harvester of Mactar), it was also a bid on the part of the town council to mobilize every possessor of wealth in the area to perform the gray tasks of taxation and of maintaining law and order.[30]

But the town councils were not the only group interested in rich plebeians. Christian communities also turned to them to act as clergymen. Like their bishops, many clergymen sought ordination so as to avoid civic duties.[31] Yet ordination was never simply a tax dodge. It was a recognition of a person's standing within the Christian community. Rich plebeians were the natural leaders of a congregation that consisted largely of the sections of the *plebs* who were integrated into trade associations. As late as the 420s, Augustine wrote that in the cities of Africa, when the *collegiati* suffered, the clergy also suffered. In more comfortable times, the *collegia* were prepared to let go of a few of their members so as to serve in the local church. This permission was not forthcoming when taxes and civic corvées became heavy.[32]

Altogether, the social niche of the Christian congregations of the earlier part of the fourth century seems to have consisted largely of moderately well-to-do townsfolk. They did not think of themselves as rich. But they were by no means paupers.[33] Indeed, their cheery comfort shocked the bishop of Barcelona; around 380, he tried to preach to his congregation on the need for penance and self-abasement in the Lenten season. As they told their bishop:

> It is good that we are middling persons [*mediocres*]. It is not for us to live in houses sheathed with marble, to be weighed down with gold, in flowing silks and bright scarlet. But all the same we have our little places in gardens and by the sea-side. We have good quality wine, neat little banquets and all that goes with a sprightly old age.[34]

De Dei dono: From the gift of God

CHRISTIAN GIVING AND THE WEALTH OF THE CHURCHES

Mediocris is an open-ended term. The bishop of Barcelona did not necessarily use it only in reference to plebeians. It applied as well to minor landowners and to lesser members of the town councils. But the word pointed toward a contrast. It referred to a world beneath the rich whose complexity and resilience we have tended to underestimate. In order to appreciate the resources of this world, we should go to Aquileia, northeast of Venice, now lying some miles inland from the head of the Adriatic. For a modern visitor to Aquileia, the great mosaic floor unearthed beneath the medieval basilica is an astonishing, silent testimony to a long-lost Christianity. This mosaic covered the floor of a substantial basilica (56 feet wide by 122 feet long) that had been built by bishop Theodorus, probably soon after the conversion of Constantine.[35]

At the top of the main nave, a mosaic inscription on a circular disk summed up Theodorus's achievement as bishop of Aquileia:

> O happy Theodorus, with the help of Almighty God and the help of the flock given to you by heaven you have blessedly accomplished and gloriously dedicated all these things.[36]

The mosaics in the middle of the nave made plain what the inscription meant. Wealth had flowed into the church. Octagonal panels of mosaic showed chubby servants in late Roman dress as they gathered the good things of the earth. Their busy activity evoked the many scenes of bucolic, innocent prosperity that were placed on the mosaics of contemporary villas. At the center, a winged Victory, with a laurel crown on her head and a palm in her hand, stood above two full baskets. These were the "first fruits" offered by the laity to the church.

Further down the nave, eight bust-length mosaic portraits made clear who the members of this flock might be. They show three generations of men and women with dress that indicated (or at least aspired to emulate) senatorial status. There could hardly have been a more clear celebration of the generosity and relatively high social status of "the flock given [to Theodorus] by heaven."[37]

The pavement (and, one suspects, the entire building) had been funded by lay donors working in collaboration with their bishop. The floor mosaic alone would have cost at least four hundred golden *solidi* to lay down. This was a small outlay compared with the vast wealth of a senator, but it was not an inconsiderable sum. It was the equivalent of the annual income of eighty poor families, or of the combined yearly salaries of ten teachers of Latin grammar.

Thus, at the very beginning of the Christian empire, the church of a major port city such as Aquileia (the fourth-century "Queen of the Adriatic") was already surprisingly rich. The economic position of Aquileia may account for the presence of so much wealth, but it does not account for the manner in which this wealth was acquired and used. We are dealing with polyfocal wealth. It was wealth pointedly divided between the bishop and a local lay elite, some of whom were of considerably higher status than the clergy and the average members of the congregation.

For the laity, to give to the church in this manner was a pious act. Another mosaic inscription, which may have been laid down at the same time in an adjoining part of bishop Theodorus's basilica, showed that a single person, Januarius, had given an impressive donation of 880 feet of mosaic (861 square feet, which cost around fifty *solidi*). He did so *de Dei dono*: "from the gift of God."[38] This succinct phrase echoed the solemn prayer of King David, when he endowed the first temple of Jerusalem: *For all things come from Thee, and of Thine own have we given Thee* (1 Chron. 29:14).

This was a votive formula shared by Jews and Christians. It also occurred in Jewish synagogues, such as that at Aphrodisias in Caria (in modern southwestern Turkey)[39] and—if at a later time—at Sardis.[40] As in the synagogue, wealthy Christian donors claimed that by contributing to the church, they were giving back to God a little of the wealth He had showered upon them.

Yet despite the wealth of many of its members, the church of Aquileia remained the center of a surprisingly low-profile Christian community. As Claire Sotinel has pointed out in a decisive recent study of late Roman Aquileia, there is a significant hiatus between the precociously opulent basilica of bishop Theodorus, perched on the riverside within full view of the port, and the "timid Christianity" of the city as a whole. We are dealing with a rich Christian community. But it was not a church prepared to take over the high ground of Aquileian society.[41]

Christians were not alone in maintaining a prosperous but essentially low-profile existence. In the fourth century and later, Jewish synagogues throughout the empire thrived in exactly the same manner.[42] Church and synagogue alike provided a space where the moderately rich could shine through pious dona-tions. In the inscriptions on the pavements of both churches and synagogues we can look below the stunning expenditures still offered by the truly rich to their hometowns as a whole (which we will describe in chapter 3). Instead, we meet a more unassuming form of giving, practiced by a class that usually hovers on the edge of invisibility. In religious buildings, such as churches and synagogues, do-nors gave gifts to their community. But when they gave, they made clear that they gave also—indeed, primarily—to God. In 244–45 the leaders of the Jewish community at Dura Europos (on the Euphrates in modern Syria) placed their names on a row of tiles on the ceiling of their great, newly frescoed synagogue. Over twenty feet above the floor, they could barely be read by the congregation. Rather, these inscriptions were intended for the eyes of God alone. On them, the builders announced that they had brought their work to completion, "with their money ... and in the eager desire of their hearts." In this phrase, they echoed the prophet Isaiah: *The desire of our soul is to Thy Name, and to the remembrance of Thee* (Isa. 26:8).[43]

Altogether, in churches and in synagogues, panels of mosaic and inscriptions dedicated by relatively small men and women were the common coin of a new style of beneficence, proudly displayed within the walls of holy buildings. The church of Theodorus at Aquileia is an early example of what later became wide-spread. When more wealth became available to the churches, around 400, the "polyfocal" habit of giving remained and flowered. From Brescia to Ljubljana, from Aquileia to Florence, mosaic pavements made up of panels contributed by individual donors or by their families became regular features of the churches.[44]

In terms of the overall expense of building the church itself (which might have cost as much as two thousand *solidi*), mosaic panels on the floor were a small item.[45] As pavements are usually all that survive, we do not know whether the rest of the church was also paid for by individual contributions; whether the bishop paid for the rest out of church funds; or whether he relied on a single rich patron or group of rich patrons. What matters is the message these mosaics com-municated. Individual members of the congregation—laity and clergy alike—went on record as fully paid-up contributors to their local church. They did so "with glory and rejoicing."[46]

Compared with the vast sums lavished by Roman aristocrats on their palaces and shows, all this was small change. But the gifts offered by the faithful were frequent, and the habit of pious giving was extraordinarily widespread. In the little city of Durobrivae (Water Newton, on the edge of the Fens), the prosperity of the Christian community may have been related to the neighboring iron mines. The church boasted an impressive silver Eucharistic chalice, given by a pious donor—"Dependent on Thee, I honor Thy holy altar." The church also contained a collection of thin silver leaves, each marked with the XP Christogram. These leaves were similar to those offered, as ex-votos, in pagan temples in Britain. Even in the transitional generations that followed the conversion of Constantine, this steady pattern of pious giving had begun to impart solidity and a touch of splendor to churches even in a little town such as Durobrivae, which lay at the far edge of the Latin West.[47]

It is important to note the connection of many of these acts of Christian giving with the Eucharist. At this time, the Eucharistic liturgy was the most stable condensation of the ideal of offerings made to God that would be blessed by Him and then redistributed to the faithful. The paradigm of the Eucharist ensured that different forms of giving in the churches were treated as equally important. Giving panels of mosaic to the church was a holy action; it was just as much a gift to God as was giving alms to the poor. We moderns might see a difference between Christian charity to the poor and Christian support for the infrastructure of their local churches. Fourth-century Christians seldom made this distinction; all pious gifts were treated as equally significant. All were offerings made to God from the good things that He had given to humankind. All were thought of as springing from a single paradigm of giving—first to God and then to one's fellows—that was summed up in the solemn offering of the Eucharist.[48]

Operatio

GIVING IN THE CHURCHES, FROM CYPRIAN TO CONSTANTINE

Mosaic pavements showed Christian donors in action as supporters of their local churches. They could not show the other side of Christian giving—the poor who gathered to receive alms in the church, at the church door, or at the houses of the faithful. Yet almsgiving also was an integral part of Christian practice. Long before the conversion of Constantine, the Christian care of the poor had been impressive.[49] In the works of bishop Cyprian of Carthage (248–58) *operatio*— giving alms to all categories of persons in distress—was a key word. For Cyprian, *operatio* was the secret of the "vigor" of the church. It showed that the Spirit of God was at work in the community.[50] Pious giving was never a random expression of compassion. The leaders of the churches were careful to steer it toward a clear purpose. Pious giving was mobilized to maintain the resilience of the churches in times of persecution—to support those put in prison by the authorities and to provide shelter for refugees from other cities. Poorer members of the congregation who had stood firm at a time when others had lapsed were rewarded by being singled out to be the recipients of alms raised by collections among the faithful.[51]

A bishop such as Cyprian was also aware that the flow of alms helped bridge social fissures within the Christian community. After Rome, Carthage was the wealthiest city of the western Mediterranean. Ever since the days of Tertullian in the early third century, its Christian community had included some rich and well-placed persons.[52] A bishop of frankly "absolutist" temperament, Cyprian was determined to rule these rich members as effectively as he ruled all other members of his flock.[53] He did so by insisting that the rich should spend their money on the church that he himself headed and on no other. He urged rich virgins to let only the poor "feel the weight" of their wealth. They were not to use their money outside his church. Still less were they to use their money to patronize rivals to Cyprian within the church by funding individual clergymen.[54] He also insisted that those who had lapsed in times of persecution should do penance in his church. This meant, in practice, that they should expiate their sins through generous alms to Cyprian's poor alone.[55]

Cyprian's view of almsgiving had been fiercely inward looking. Christians were to support Christians; there was little or no outreach to the non-Christian poor. Yet precisely because of his fierce emphasis on solidarity, Cyprian had been able to mobilize a remarkable amount of money. On one occasion, he gathered through donations from the faithful one hundred thousand sesterces to ransom fellow Christians captured in a raid by Berber tribesmen.[56] This was the equivalent of a month's salary of three thousand workmen (or half the yearly salary of an imperial secretary). His letters were full of such movements of funds. They provide "practical evidence of the church constituting a society within a society."[57]

Cyprian was not alone in this. Rome was the richest church in the Latin West. By 251, its bishop claimed to be able to support 1,500 widows and distressed persons—a body of persons as large as the largest of the artisan associations of the city.[58]

"For the wealthy must support their duties to the secular world"

PRIVILEGE AND THE CARE OF THE POOR AFTER CONSTANTINE

Thus when Constantine turned to Christianity what he saw were not only the worshipers of an all-powerful God but a community of pious givers to the poor. It was precisely this aspect of the Christian churches that enabled him and his successors to add a significant quid pro quo to the privileges they had granted to the churches. The imperial laws made clear that the bishops and clergy received their privileges not only because they prayed for the empire but also because they looked after the poor.[59]

What was equally obvious, however, was the de haut en bas tone with which these privileges were granted. The bishops and clergy were privileged precisely because they were not expected to be the equals of the rich. They were not to look above themselves, by recruiting members of the curial class. They were not even allowed to receive wealthy plebeians into the clergy. Instead, their business was to look downward to the poor. As Constantine explained in an edict issued in 329: "The wealthy must be there to support the obligations of the secular world, while the poor are maintained by the wealth of the churches." In the words of Rita Lizzi Testa, commenting on this edict, imperial privileges presented the clergy "as poor and as principally occupied with the poor."[60] This was a view with which the overwhelming majority of the populations of the Roman West (Christian as much as non-Christian) were expected to concur.

Yet it was a view that was rapidly becoming out of date. At the end of the century (around 390), the pagan historian Ammianus Marcellinus (to whom we owe the memorable portrait of the sinister wealth of Petronius Probus) looked back with calculated disapproval at the novel splendor of some Christian bishops. He sketched a memorable vignette of the contested election by which Damasus had become bishop of Rome a generation earlier, in 366. Riots had accompanied this election: "In a single day, a hundred and thirty seven corpses of the slain were found." The moral of the tale for Ammianus and his readers (Christian and non-Christian alike) was that clergymen had got above themselves. Even at the end of the fourth century, the ideal clergyman was still one whose role in society had been laid down in the laws of Constantine—an unobtrusive figure. Many clergymen, so Ammianus claimed, still exemplified this ideal. Damasus and his rival should have

> followed the example of some provincial bishops, whose extreme frugality in food and drink, unpretentious attire and downcast eyes commend them to the Eternal Deity and His true worshippers as pure persons who know their place ... *ut puros et verecundos.*[61]

It is worthwhile to pay attention to this passage. We do not often see the Christian clergy described from the outside by a non-Christian. Ammianus chose his words carefully. For a Roman, *verecundus* was a charged word. It summed up the quintessentially Roman virtue of knowing one's place. *Verecundia* was a virtue of the subelites. Experts such as schoolteachers, grammarians, and doctors were expected to show *verecundia* in the presence of their social superiors. For all the indispensable skills they communicated to their patrons, they remained "social paupers" compared with the real leaders of society. They were not to be "pushy." In Ammianus's opinion, Christian bishops should be no different. *Verecundia,* and no virtue of a more thrusting kind, was what suited the clergy best.[62] Clergy-men had their niche in Roman society; they should stay there.

Aula pudoris: A hall of restraint

THE RICH IN THE CHURCHES, CA. 350 AD

Of all the developments in the history of late Roman Christianity, the entry of the rich and powerful into the church was, in many ways, the most predictable. Despite Christian rhetoric of identification with the humble and oppressed, the Christian communities had never been socially monolithic. They were open at both ends, both to those considerably poorer than the well-to-do plebeians who made up the bulk of the Christian congregations and to those who were consid-erably richer and more distinguished. By the year 350, the rich were already there, waiting in the wings, as it were, to make their presence felt in the churches.

In 343 the Latin bishops assembled at Serdica (modern Sofia, Bulgaria) ex-pressed concern that "a rich man or a jurist from the forum or a former adminis-trator" might be chosen by a congregation as their bishop without having served in the clergy. Their ruling against "quickie" ordinations of this kind betrayed the alarm of studiously "mediocre" persons, groomed by long years of service in a low-profile institution, at the prospect of being taken over from on top.[63] Their fears were justified. Only a generation later, Ambrose—a senator and an acting governor—would step directly into the bishopric of Milan with no preparation whatsoever. But what of the rich laity who did not seek clerical office? What sort of rich were they, and what did they hope to find in the churches? Let us con-clude by suggesting a few answers to these questions.

Taking a wide view of the matter, there is nothing surprising about the fact that rich Christians should appear in increasing numbers as the fourth century progressed. The "hands-off" policy of Constantine with regard to paganism it-self was flatly contradicted by the social revolution he himself had furthered. As we saw, this amounted to a restructuring of the traditional elites in such a way as to ensure that more roads than ever led to the court and fewer to the traditional centers of social power. Apart from the brief and chilling reign of the pagan emperor Julian the Apostate (361–63), the rulers of the Roman world remained Christian. One should not underestimate the "gentle violence" brought to bear on upper-class society by the permanent presence of a Christian court, even in times when the policies of the emperors (and their choice of pub-lic servants) tended to remain religion blind. To be close to the court was to be increasingly surrounded by persons for whom the old religion meant little or nothing.

The statistical study conducted by Michele Salzman on the religious choices of the elites of the western empire in the fourth century has provided a sociological chart of the Christianization of the West. Her results agree with common sense. Salzman found many upper-class Christians among those whose careers took them close to the emperor. Many Christians also came from provincial elites where imperial service and imperial privileges had proved decisive in reshaping traditional society. Far fewer conversions to Christianity seem to have occurred in regions such as Rome, its hinterland, and parts of Africa, where (as we have seen) old money still ruled and where the traditional classes and their clients were most solidly entrenched.[64]

What we should think of is a map of western Europe where, in large areas of Britain, Gaul, Spain, and the Balkans, Christianity was confined to the cities and dwarfed by a largely pagan countryside. In Rome and in large parts of Italy, despite a vivid Christian presence, the old religion remained prominent. Elsewhere the local elites were as fragmented in their religious loyalties as they were in everything else. But they were more open to the Christianity of the court because they were even more dependent on the favor of the emperor than were the nobility of Rome.

A commonsense map of this kind has much to commend it. But it offers a somewhat flat picture of the religious texture of the Christian churches of the West to which the upper classes turned. It does not explain what members of the upper classes (whether they were converts or came from Christian families) found to be agreeable—even thrilling—in the churches themselves. Let us try to evoke something of the attraction that becoming members of a Christian congregation held for such persons.

Many Christian writers and thinkers emphasized the fact that it was not easy to be a Christian. The Christian basilica itself was presented as a *sedes iustitiae*, an *aula pudoris*: "a seat of righteousness ... a hall of restraint."[65] All classes met in it to worship a deity who was "implacable on sin"; whose eyes were not "blocked by stomach walls" but penetrated straight to the heart; and whose commands "left no room for the dissident will."[66] Thus wrote Lactantius, the African Christian rhetor and tutor to the son of Constantine. It is an austere and authoritarian picture, such as one might expect from a person entrusted with the education of the son of an absolute monarch.

But the churches were not only presented as places of moral zero tolerance. They were also seen as places of forgiveness, which implied the breaking of boundaries. In the tradition of Cyprian, release from the imprisoning bonds of sin was vividly concretized, on a day-to-day basis, by the breaking of social boundaries through outreach to the poor. The uncannily unmoved deaths of the martyrs proved that death, the ultimate boundary, had been erased. Furthermore, the growing cult of the martyrs was based to a large degree on the previous Christian conviction that the dead remained close to the living.[67] Boundaries between the rich and the poor, between the living and the dead, between heroic figures (the martyrs) and the average believer were not abolished. But they were held in delicious suspense in the imagination of fourth-century Christians. This imaginative erosion of boundaries contradicted the common sense of the abrasive and compartmentalized world around them.

Taken altogether, the combination of moral rigor with a sense of deliverance from many of the burdens associated with the normal world ensured that the Christian churches might be viewed by some as places of relief. In that sense, Christianity can be seen as having provided the last of a series of "escape hatches" such as Roman society had always offered to members of the upper classes. As Seth Schwartz has recently pointed out, countercultural communities of various kinds had long acted as places of consolation and as safety valves for well-to-do persons who found the pace of life too fast and too expensive—driven too relentlessly by considerations of honor and reciprocity.[68]

The best known of these countercultural communities had been the little groups of like-minded souls that had gathered around philosophers in classical Greece and in early imperial Rome. These groups had allowed harassed or disillusioned members of the elite to experiment with forms of alternative living. Ideals of friendship, of a shared, disinterested search for wisdom, of relaxed hierarchy and indifference to money matters were supposed to predominate in such groups. One should not underestimate the attraction of such groups both in classical Rome and in late Roman times.

But philosophical circles had always been small and were limited in their social outreach. Most were devoted to non-supernatural therapies. By contrast, the Christian churches claimed to offer all this on a wider scale in a manner that joined all classes and took account of heaven as well as earth.[69] Indeed, by the year 350, the Christian churches were already the largest escape hatches that had ever been opened in the ancient world. Supposedly led by high-minded, "pure," and unpretentious persons—studiously separated from secular power—they had the air of a dignified, morally bracing, and even exciting experiment in countercultural living.

The Constantinian revolution needed such a counterculture. It had involved an upheaval of society that resulted in the widespread and abrasive fracturing and reconstitution of the upper classes. Whether they came into the churches as winners or losers, the rich Christians of the middle and late fourth century were largely products of that revolution. They would have found through membership in a Christian congregation the equivalent of a social and moral urban lung.

If we look carefully, we can see traces of what the churches offered not only in texts (where these offers might be suspect as being no more than wishful thinking) but on the ground. The overall impression given by well-known Christian artifacts and sites (such as the Roman catacombs and the mosaic pavements of northern Italy) is of patterns in giving and burial that pointed to what may best be called an atmosphere of relaxed hierarchy. This was no utopian equality of the sort that romantic historians of the early church once imagined in the nineteenth century. Nor are we faced with a revolutionary democracy. But what we do see is significant. It is late Roman society with a gentler face.

In a brilliant recent study of the distribution of space and monuments in the Roman catacombs, John Bodel has pointed to the absence of clear social boundaries in the Christian monuments of this time. Social differences were by no means obliterated. By 350, the catacombs included Christian family vaults with brilliant paintings and marble inlays, in which great sarcophagi rested. But neither were these differences insisted on. The Christian vaults were not fenced off as many pagan mausolea and *columbaria* had been. The great rows of graves provided for household dependents in a pagan *columbarium*, which rose from the ground like the slots of a dovecote, had been clearly marked off by border stones and fences, "the traditional boundaries of place in the Roman world."[70] By contrast, Christian family vaults were not hemmed in by marks of privacy. One passed them, like open palaces abutting on a crowded lane, in order to reach the humbler graves that lay all around them. To enter a predominantly Christian catacomb was to enter "an alien, somewhat disorientating world,"[71] characterized by

A heterogeneous mixture of persons of different wealth and status [which appeared to have] no distinctively unifying beliefs about the representation of privilege and rank.[72]

The panels on mosaic pavements give the same impression. These panels varied from city to city; some were more frank about hierarchy than were others. In Vicenza, for instance, there was no mistaking the importance of the votive mosaic panel laid down by Felix, a *vir clarissimus* (honorary senator) and his womenfolk. It was placed in the middle of the church, opposite the door as one entered.[73] But in Verona, by contrast, the three-hundred-foot donation of a similar *vir clarissimus*, Rufinus, was both off-center and matched by two other donors who did not flaunt a title.[74]

It was the same with other Christian artifacts. The sarcophagus of Marcia Romania Celsa (which has been discovered at Arles), the wife of Januarinus, one of Constantine's Christian consuls, was no different from many others that were purchased from Rome by less well-known persons. There is a striking contrast between the somewhat subdued statement of Celsa's status, through a barely finished sarcophagus, and the splendidly assertive masterpieces of marble carving that had been used by pagans of the same class in the third century.[75]

These are small hints in themselves, but they point to a distinctive social tone. In entering the churches, the rich might well have found a countercultural niche, a little to one side of the abrasive realities of the late Roman social system. One should not underestimate the attractions of such a situation. A Christian church, like a burial complex, could act as "a sort of oblique expression of an ideal social order divorced from the compromising realities of life."[76]

A place where hierarchy could be muted without being abandoned had considerable appeal in a competitive and ceremonious age. Nor should we underestimate the dangerous thrill—one that was continuous with former Roman philosophical countercultures—associated with the opportunity for symbolic dissidence provided by the cult of the martyrs. In an age of absolutism, the Christian cult of the martyrs made it possible to establish a small area of inner distance from the powers that be. Though the imperial system was never directly resisted, it could be relativized. It was treated as a mere "power of this world." It was robbed of its overbearing mystique by a comforting sense of the superior power of the God for whom the martyrs had died.

But there were problems in store for such churches, not the least of which was the fact that the Christian churches were by no means the only places where easier social relationships could happen among Christians. If the church presented itself (in a countercultural manner) as one big family, so one big family could just as well present itself as a church. It is an anachronism to think that to be a Christian in the age of Constantine inevitably meant becoming a member of a particular Christian congregation, subject to the rule of priests and bishops who were usually of lower social standing than the richer members of the congregation.

To write a history of the relations between the laity and the clergy in the later empire involves a silent first step. The laity had to become a laity in the strict sense—a *laos*, a people *of* the church *in* the church. They had to relate to their clergy within the walls of a specific building that was associated first and foremost with the clergy. We should not take this step for granted. The work of recent scholars such as Kimberly Bowes (on household religion in town and countryside),[77] Kate Cooper (on the aristocratic houses of Rome),[78] and Claire Sotinel (on the nature of the Christian community in Aquileia)[79] have pointed to alternative histories of the churches.

The seemingly straightforward history of the relationship between bishops, clergy, and laity in the fourth, fifth, and sixth centuries was played out against the shadow of an alternative ordering of the Christian community. This was a household-based Christianity in which bishops and clergymen played a less prominent role than they might have wished. It was a tenacious alternative that did not vanish in the bright new dawn of the Constantinian age. Private Christian cult continued to take various forms long after the official recognition of the Christian church and its leaders and the consequent consolidation of the power of the bishops. It took forms that ranged from pious groups assembled around favored teachers in the palaces and villas of the rich to chapels set up beside family mausolea in the depths of great estates. Throughout this book we shall follow a constant, muffled dialogue between the public church and more private, "unchurched" forms of Christianity that lasted up to the end of the sixth century.

"Interesting Times"

THE END OF THE CONSTANTINIAN SYSTEM IN THE WEST

But this is to anticipate. In many ways the Constantinian system had shielded the Christian communities from their own rich members. The clergy had been encouraged by Constantine to look to the emperor, not to local leaders of society, for protection and for occasional, stunning donations. But it was an expensive system. It assumed the ready availability of imperial funds and an infinite willingness, on the part of the emperor, to micromanage the affairs of the church in all regions of his empire.

This could not last. After the disastrous defeat of the emperor Julian in Persia in 363 there was less money to go around. Imperial grants to the churches were cut back and their tax exemptions were more strictly delimited.

The empire was weakened and divided.[80] The western emperor, Valentinian I (364–75), was a parsimonious military man. His priorities in spending lay along the frontiers of the empire on the Rhine and the Danube. He was sincerely committed to maintaining consensus within the churches. But he was unwilling to go to great pains to enforce it and still less to lavish money on bishops.[81] By so doing, he left the field open to a class of persons who had previously been held in check by the Constantinian system—militant faction fighters who had come to enjoy the support of rich patrons.

The shift in the balance of power between rich patrons and hitherto low-profile Christian communities was a largely silent process we can follow only in stray hints. But the results of this shift became plain in a series of sharp local conflicts within the Christian communities. These conflicts were connected with the victory of a theological faction in what we now call the "Arian Controversy." Put very briefly: the empire-wide consensus of bishops around a single, agreed creed that had been painstakingly negotiated by Constantius II was challenged. The creed supported by Constantius II was deemed, by its enemies, to be tainted with the "Arian" heresy. The accusation was a travesty, but it was a rallying cry that enabled a new guard of bishops to take over crucial sees as upholders of orthodoxy and as vocal opponents of the "Arian" heresy.

These men were ultras. They were known for their uncompromising loyalty to the Nicene Creed—to what they took to be the original statement of Christian belief produced at the Council of Nicaea in 325. They were prepared to dismiss the ecclesiastical establishment set in place by Constantine and his son Constantius II as an antiquated and hubristic tyranny.[82]

The ultra-Nicene party could afford to dismiss the Constantinian system in this high-handed manner. Although they were few in number, they were notable for their connections with persons of wealth and power. Three of them will hold our attention, for varying reasons, in subsequent chapters. Martin had served in the Imperial Guard. In 371 he was elected bishop of Tours against the wishes of the provincial bishops and their distinctly mediocre urban clergy. Rather, Martin enjoyed the support of a network of substantial landowners.[83] In 374 Ambrose stepped straight from a governorship into the see of Milan with the support of none other than Petronius Probus, the Roman magnate of legendary wealth and tentacular influence whom we met in chapter 1.[84] In 383, in distant Spain, Priscillian became bishop of Avila, again through the support of wealthy zealots.[85]

As we shall see, the victory of these ultras was never total. Though they established their own version of doctrinal orthodoxy with great effect, the other radical programs they advanced were less successful. Many regions of the Latin West remained largely unaffected by the emergence of these few vivid figures in major cities. Part of the drama of the generation that followed the installation of Martin, Ambrose, and Priscillian was that, despite the energy they deployed in pushing through programs of reform, the less articulate majority of Latin Christians did not give way. They continued to make their views felt in the churches.

Hence a situation that led to conflict and to vehement polemics. In the case of Priscillian, the opposition to his promotion culminated in a series of denunciations by local bishops that concentrated on Priscillian's relations with his upper-class supporters. These denunciations led to his execution as a sorcerer. Not every new-style bishop suffered so dramatic a fate, but they met with much silent opposition. The monasticism that made Martin a hero to the villa-owning aristocracy of Gaul was long resented and resisted by the more middling clergy of many Gallic cities. The ambitious image of a model clergyman, which Ambrose propounded in his writings, remained a dead letter even in cities that lay in the shadow of the see of Milan. But the emergence of such leaders showed that the times had changed. The conflicts that were brought to the surface by figures such as Martin, Ambrose, and Priscillian marked the beginning of the end of *mediocritas* as the dominant feature of the Latin churches.

There is a Chinese malediction that says: "May you live in interesting times." After the 370s, interesting times began to happen in the West. To persons who had grown up in the bipolar society accepted by Constantine and his successors, this came as a shock. The majority of persons in the Roman West—pagans, Jews, and, indeed, most Christians—were not used to the novel trenchancy of leaders such as Ambrose nor to the degree of social muscle he could summon up in support of his cause.

But before we follow this change, decade by decade and region by region, we must step back to take a wider view of the forms of giving to which the rich had been accustomed in their lives outside the Christian churches. We will then examine the distinctive features of giving within the Christian churches. Last but not least, we must attempt to characterize the challenging blend of novelty and continuity that emerged in the course of the late fourth and early fifth centuries, when rich persons found themselves expected to act as givers not only in their cities but now also within the Christian churches.

CHAPTER 3

Amor civicus: Love of the city
Wealth and Its Uses in an Ancient World

A Debate on Giving

In this chapter and the next, I will attempt to juxtapose non-Christian and Christian attitudes toward wealth and giving. In doing this, I will seek to avoid stark contrasts between the two groups, based on purely abstract considerations. Rather, I shall begin by pointing to the large middle ground of attitudes shared by Christians and non-Christians alike. Both groups, as we will see, placed wealth, as it were, on parole. Both insisted that the possession of wealth should be legitimized (or at least be given a more gentle face) by acts of generosity.

Yet when it came to how this generosity should be expressed, the attitudes of the two groups appeared to diverge sharply. Each form of generosity condensed a very different model of society. The Christian bishops constantly complained that money lavished by the rich on great buildings and on flamboyant games should have been spent on the poor. The one was driven by mere love of display, while Christian generosity (so the bishops claimed) was driven by compassion.

Yet we must remember that a conflict between two models of society implied by two different styles of giving—clear-cut and dramatic though this conflict might appear in retrospect—does not necessarily translate into conflict on the level of day-to-day behavior. Not all rich pagans funneled their money into giving great games. Not all Christians gave only to the poor.

For this reason, our subsequent chapter (chapter 4) will fall into two parts. It will begin by making clear the differences between traditional forms of generosity to one's city and Christian forms of giving to the poor and to the church. This divergence amounted, in the long run, to an imaginative difference of momentous proportions. Not only were the ideal recipients of the Christian gift—the poor—different from the traditional recipients of urban benefactions—the citizens, many of whom were by no means poor—but the imagined effects of giving were also profoundly different. Behind the Christian notion of giving to the poor lay the novel idea that giving to the poor (and to other pious causes) involved a transfer of wealth from this world to the next, summed up in the notion of placing *treasure in heaven*.

But chapter 4 will end firmly on earth. It will describe the manner in which different styles of giving, taken from different traditions and from different social milieux, fueled the "takeoff" of Latin Christianity in the crucial decades after the 370s, when wealth and the wealthy came to enter the churches.

Common Sense on Wealth

First and foremost, however, we must be aware of what Christians and non-Christians saw in a similar fashion when they looked at the society around them. Nothing makes this more clear than the utterances of major Christian preachers of this time. We might expect them always to be saying something new, but this was by no means the case. Those who attended Christian sermons would not have been greatly surprised by much of what they heard. Indeed, their bishops did not expect them to be surprised. On one occasion, Augustine of Hippo made this plain when he began a long sermon on the theme of avarice. As we know, Augustine was not a man short of original ideas. But, on the subject of avarice, he insisted that he had nothing new to say:

> I do not know how it is, but avarice has such an effect on human hearts that all (or, to be more truthful and accurate, almost all) wish, in words, to hold it guilty, even if, in their actions, they show that they have a special soft spot for it. Many have uttered many opinions against avarice— eminent opinions, opinions of great weight, all of them true. Poets, historians, orators, philosophers, every sort of writer and every professional person has had so much to say against avarice.[1]

When they spoke about wealth, Augustine and preachers like him spoke as the heirs of a very ancient world. The certitudes to which they appealed had bobbed up and down for over a millennium in a veritable Saragossa Sea of *idées reçues*. Thus, when Augustine propounded ideas about society that were taken straight from the pagan classics, we should not think that he was doing this in a self-conscious effort to impress pagans with his culture or to woo them into the church by citing their favorite authors. He did it as unthinkingly as we, today, say that the earth is round and that the law of gravity is universal. It was true truth about the social world in which he lived and which he shared with all other thinking persons of his age. He presented much of what he had to say on the topic of avarice (as on many other aspects of wealth) as a matter of common sense.

Let us consider for a moment what this means. Over thirty years ago, the anthropologist Clifford Geertz showed that the common sense of a given society always depended upon "a relatively organized body of considered thought." But this thought was presented in a distinctive manner. As Geertz wrote in his essay "Common Sense as a Cultural System":

> Common-sense wisdom is shamelessly and unapologetically ad hoc. It comes in epigrams, proverbs, *obiter dicta*, jokes, anecdotes ...—a clatter of gnomic utterances—not in formal doctrines, axiomized theories, or architectonic dogmas.[2]

Hence the mute certainty of commonsense judgments. They claim not to represent only the fine-spun and closely argued opinions of an intellectual elite. Rather, they claim to speak with the heavy voice of an imagined majority of right-thinking persons. Commonsense judgments do not have the clear quality of "axiomized theories, or architectonic dogmas." Rather, they are characterized by the inconsistencies and by the multiplicity of meanings we associate with folklore and proverbial wisdom.

If for "common sense" we read "discourse on wealth," we will avoid many false expectations when we sit down to read the pagan and Christian writers of late antiquity. We need not expect from this literature a single, coherent classical or Christian doctrine of wealth. What we get is, perhaps, of greater interest to the historian. Attention to discourse on wealth as a form of common sense—as a heavy sediment of notions and not as a set of doctrines—enables us to explore the horizons of the social imagination of late Roman culture. We can delineate both the resources of that culture and its blind spots—what it was prepared to think about and what it was content to ignore. Let us look first at the blind spots.

In the first place, for late Roman persons (even for late Roman intellectuals such as Augustine), wealth was not a topic to be analyzed in a systematic manner, as we moderns have done since the seventeenth century and as a few outstanding ancient Greeks—such as Aristotle—had done at the very beginning of the classical period. This reluctance to theorize needs to be explained. It did not mean that late Roman persons were ignorant or indifferent to economic phenomena.[3] But their thoughts were not directed toward free and consequential inquiry into the nature of their society.

There is a brutal reason for this lacuna. The Roman empire was not a free world. Wealth and its inseparable shadow, power, were topics that had to be approached circumspectly. For many centuries, educated persons had been the subjects of an authoritarian regime, which claimed to be the protector of the Roman social order. In the wry words of a modern scholar, the emperor Augustus had "made the world safe for oligarchy."[4] In this, the aristocracies of the fourth century AD, both senatorial and local, were little different from their predecessors.

They had no intention of questioning an imperial system that was all of four centuries old. There was only so much that they felt free to say.

Even for the most courageous, many topics were taboo. Reading the stirring sermons of a bishop such as Ambrose of Milan, for instance, one has the impression that denunciations of the rich in general were a substitute for criticisms of the policies of the court in particular. In a court city such as Milan this was a real issue. Ambrose once had to intercede for a man who was being led off to be executed for treason simply because he had said that the present emperor (the young Gratian) was unworthy of his father, Valentinian I.[5] As a result, social criticism tended to be general and studiously non-specific. One suspects that the evil rich—invariably presented in tracts and sermons as generic monsters of avarice and luxury—acted as the whipping boys of public opinion in a world where more precise grievances (such as resentment over high taxation and ill-advised political decisions) could not be expressed.

Yet we should not be in too great a hurry to condemn this retreat from the political as due only to fear or to intellectual inertia. Persons formed by a late antique rhetorical education treated certain issues with deadly seriousness. But these issues did not touch on the overall structure of society. Rather, a rhetorical education brought its full weight to bear on issues of personal behavior. Put bluntly: to the ancients, how individuals acted mattered far more than did the structures within which they acted.[6] In such a view of the world, rich and poor did not meet as classes related to each other within a wider society. Instead, they were seen as two distinct groups of persons from each of which a certain form of behavior was expected. The rich were expected to be generous and good natured; the poor were to be suppliant and grateful.[7]

As a result, social relations were almost always seen, as it were, in close-up—in terms of asymmetrical interactions between individuals. This is not surprising. We are dealing with a steeply hierarchical society, held together by innumerable chains of dependence. It was the behavior of the link in the chain on whose good graces one's own fate hung—whether an emperor, an official, a patron, or a landlord—which mattered most.[8] Hence an intense personalization of social relations. Much talk on the relations of rich and poor assumed situations that seem almost to follow the logic of the folktale. In the folktale, two protagonists alone dominate each incident; neither is seen as part of a group. In the same manner, discourse on wealth and poverty tended to focus on a single encounter and on a single, primal act of giving that linked two persons, one rich and one poor.[9] The poor were those who "looked always to the fingers of the rich."[10] The rich were those whose hands were expected to open in mighty gestures of beneficence or amnesty. From the exquisitely minted coins that showed the emperor Nero reaching out his hand to distribute rations to the people of Rome[11] to the image of the emperor Constantius II scattering gold coins as consul, in the *Calendar of 354*,[12] the cohesion of the entire Roman social order was condensed in the movements of the hands of the great.

In a social situation that was so sharply stylized in this manner (as a series of encounters between givers and suppliants), persuasion was the most important—indeed, the most urgent—tool of action. Speculation could wait. It was not the business of bishops or of rhetors—when they preached, when they framed petitions to the emperors, when they praised and pleaded with governors—to propound "formal doctrines, axiomized theories or architectonic dogmas." Rather, their task was to pick the heavy locks that held the hearts of the mighty. They had to make sure that those locks slid open so as to allow acts of generosity and mercy. In the art of persuasion, it was appeals to common sense (and no fine-spun theories) that did the job.

Sobria vetustas: The sobriety of ancient times

This did not mean that late Roman persons had surrendered the capacity to criticize the society in which they lived—far from it. Pagans and Christians alike looked back on a rich tradition characterized, both in Greek and in Latin, by an unrelenting suspicion of wealth and the wealthy.

In the Latin world, in particular, one feature of Roman collective memory had long stuck out as remarkable. This was the fact that the founders of the Roman Republic were believed to have lived in a state of high-minded, indeed heroic, poverty. For those who looked back at classical accounts of the history of Rome, the coming of wealth was held to have marked the beginning of the end of Roman virtue. It had brought about the fall of the Roman Republic; it could bring about the fall of the empire. Though highly stylized, this representation of the history of Rome gave late Roman Latin writers a language with which to discuss the ills of their own times.[13]

Let us take the opinions of the non-Christian historian Ammianus Marcellinus. Writing around 390 AD in the aftermath of the crushing defeat of the Roman armies by the Visigoths at the battle of Adrianople in 378 AD, Ammianus offered his own remedy for the crisis of his times. It was a call to the rich to return to the *sobria vetustas*, to "the sobriety of ancient times." He assured his readers that Rome had suffered worse disasters and had survived them:

> But this was because the sobriety of ancient times had not been infected by the effeminacy of a laxer way of life, and there was no craving for ostentatious banquets and ill-gotten gains: high and low agreeing with one another and united in a single-hearted enthusiasm hastened to face a glorious death on behalf of the state as if setting out to reach some calm and peaceful harbor.[14]

What gives unusual sharpness to the otherwise unexceptionable opinions of Ammianus was the fact that this was no nostalgia trip on his part. He made plain that he regarded the fateful loss of sobriety among the rich to have been of recent origin. He traced the decline in civic virtue back remorselessly to the court of the Christian emperor Constantine and of his Christian successors. It was the rich of the new age of gold who had begun the rot. Ammianus identified these as the great courtiers and senatorial landowners of his time. Hence his memorable portrait of the most exuberant example of all of the tainted rich—the great Christian aristocrat Petronius Probus, whom we will continue to meet throughout this book.[15]

Ammianus's opinions delineate clearly the sense of discomfort with which Romans had always looked at any extraordinary accumulation of wealth in their midst. But we must remember that this discourse on wealth took place among peers. We are looking at the rich with the eyes of the rich. The issue was never whether or not the rich should be rich; it was how the rich should relate to each other. If the rich had victims, these victims were not thought to be the poor: they were their fellow rich. The rich feared that they might at any time be made to feel "poor"—in the sense of helpless—in the face of overmighty members of their own class. Their eyes fixed on each other, the rich of the late Roman world expected that it would be they who would be the first to suffer from the immoderate wealth of others. They gave little thought to the manner in which threatening accumulations of wealth affected the distant, faceless poor.

Thus, what the common sense of their age purveyed to persons such as Ammianus was not disquietude about riches in themselves. It was a set of stereotypes, vicious as an album of caricatures, of the wrong sort of rich person. Thought on wealth tended to settle down to denunciation of the luxury, pretentiousness, and avarice of the evil rich. To this one should add that, for many writers, the evil rich were usually the new rich (the upstart courtiers and overambitious senators castigated by Ammianus) whose rise to prominence in the fourth century was thought to threaten the more discreet ascendancy of old money.

But it was precisely this stereotypical divide between the bad rich and the good rich that offered the wealthy the opportunity to reestablish themselves in the good graces of their peers. Denunciations of the rich usually ended by offering the one remedy for suspect wealth on which everyone agreed: liberality—opening the heart and the hand in grand gestures of giving.

An Empire of Gifts: From Patronage to *Humanitas*

The Roman empire has been called an "empire of honor."[16] But it can equally well be called an "empire of gifts." In late Roman quite as much as in classical times, the Roman empire was held together by personal ties expressed and cemented through massive giving. The legacies and gifts of one senator alone, the younger Pliny, are an astonishing example of this flow of beneficence.[17] This did not change in the later empire. Constantine's giving had been legendary and, in the opinion of his critics, disastrous.[18] The rich and powerful followed the example of the emperors; they held their followers together by gifts. This is what Petronius Probus had done in the 370s and 380s. As Ammianus Marcellinus wrote, he "enjoyed enormous power ... by bestowing gifts."[19] It was for his generosity that Probus was praised after his death by a court poet:

> He did not hide his wealth in dark cellars nor condemn his riches to the nether gloom, but in showers more abundant than the rain he would ever enrich countless throngs of men. The thick cloud of his generosity was ever big with gifts. Waves of clients washed into his palace, coming in as poor to emerge made rich. His headlong hand outdid the [gold dust–bearing] rivers of Spain in pouring out gifts of gold.[20]

The memory of Probus's open house and open hands was deemed sufficient to launder the great senator's vast and suspect wealth. In the dry words of Elias Bickerman: "In Vergil's Hell there are not robber barons but niggardly millionaires."[21] That was as true in the fourth century as in any other century of the history of Rome.

The issue, of course, was how this generosity would be shown, which groups in society (the poor among them) might be expected to benefit from it, and from what motives this generosity arose. Here we should avoid stark contrasts between charitable attitudes toward the poor encouraged in Christianity and Judaism and the apparent absence of such concern among pagans.

It has become a commonplace for scholars to talk of the "harsh moral climate" of the Greco-Roman world.[22] This is because, as we will see, classical society did not invest acts of generosity to the poor with the same, high ideological charge as did Jews and Christians. But the contrast between pagan and Christian times is somewhat forced. A society without a Christian sense of "charity" found room, on many occasions, for what Greek contemporaries called "philanthropic" actions.[23] Provided that they fit into recognizable categories to which the rich felt that they owed some obligation—as clients, as dependents, as relatives, and as fellow citizens—there was no lack of outreach to the distressed.

As Anneliese Parkin has put it, referring to gifts to the poor in the classical Roman world, "We can fight too hard to argue away every possible reference to almsgiving."[24] Beggars crowded around temples to receive coins and to eat their share of the offerings of food and the meat of sacrifices. They were not totally ignored.[25] But what was lacking was a sense that humanity was most vividly summed up through starkly asymmetrical relations, in the manner of Jewish and

Christian alms to the poor. Alms implied outreach to perceived inferiors. Indeed, the very act of giving alms stressed the helplessness of those who received them.

But almsgiving was never the only form of giving favored among pagans—or, indeed, among Christians. The exchange of gifts and favors between equals was just as important. "Philanthropic" giving offered a safety net to friends and neighbors. To take one example: in a world with few banking institutions, small personal loans to one's peers often played the role of alms.[26] Nor did all acts of mercy take the form of gifts. This was particularly the case in the countryside. Landowners showed generosity by granting rebates of rents and by holding over the payment of debts, even if they usually did this less out of mercy than to maintain control of their tenants by prolonging their indebtedness.[27]

Above all, generosity varied according to one's position in society. The very rich might be rendered impervious to the poor by the "protective bubble" of clients and administrators who surrounded them.[28] But, as we have seen, there was room in late Roman society for a wide spectrum of relatively rich persons, many of whom lived close to the misery around them.[29] Not all hardened their hearts. Doctors were expected to treat poor patients.[30] Associations of tradesmen collected money for beggars (if only to keep them away from their shops).[31] Children were taken in for fostering.[32] A rich widow could be praised for her "piety" in looking after impoverished women who were widows such as herself.[33] Hospitality could be extended to strangers. A poor fisherman once encountered the survivor of a shipwreck:

> Seeing that he was a man of distinguished appearance, he was moved by compassion ... to comply yet more with his compassionate sensibilities, he took off his threadbare little cloak, cut it in half and gave half to the young man.[34]

This is not the famous scene where Saint Martin cut his cloak in half so as to clothe a beggar at the gates of Amiens. It is a scene from a novel of the third century AD. It serves as a reminder that dramas of mercy were by no means limited only to the imagination of Christians.[35]

Even the terrible institution of slavery was expected to soften occasionally.[36] Under the empire, upper-class society found room for countercultural situations in which slaves and masters could be imagined to live happily together in a domestic idyll that resembled the idealized relations between Russian landowners and their serfs in the nineteenth century.[37] Violence to slaves was frowned upon by philosophers.[38] But their advice did little to advance the spread of humane feelings. What little "humanization" occurred in the treatment of slaves did so for a chilling reason: the Roman state made plain that it had no intention of surrendering to the masters and mistresses of slaves its monopoly of cruel and unusual punishments. The emperors ruled that slaves should not be subjected to the fearsome tortures associated with public justice. By this legislation, the emperors declared that they, and only they, intended to suppress with equal savagery both slaves and the "humble" free persons who made up the majority of their subjects.[39] Despite these measures, violence between owners and their slaves continued. Around 300 AD, the Christian bishops at the council of Elvira in southern Spain had to deal with cases of slaves who had died as a result of beatings ordered by their Christian mistress.[40] Altogether, the grim logic of the slave system lay like a vast icecap along the edge of late Roman society. It was calculated to keep humanitarian sentiments (among Christians and pagans alike) in deep freeze.

Slavery apart, however, we are dealing with a morally less frigid society than Christian authors would lead us to believe. We should not dismiss as hypocritical the lists of social virtues which, in many regions, continued without a break from pagan times up to the end of our period. *Clemens, patiens, mancipiis benigna, miranda voluntas, umanetas in eo sates laudanda*—"clement," "patient," "benign to her slaves," "of admirable good will," "endowed with thoroughly praiseworthy humanity": crudely carved on gravestones from the Rhone valley of the early seventh century AD and expressed in distinctly homespun Latin, the laudatory phrases in these inscriptions reach back for centuries.[41] They show a Roman society which, up to the very end, had retained an ideal of humane sociability that was one of the most widespread and most exigent aspects of the civilization of Greece and Rome.[42]

Christian apologists might make much of pagan heartlessness compared with Christian charity. But experienced Christian preachers, such as Augustine, took for granted that Jews and pagans also practiced works of mercy and that many were more zealous in doing so than were Christians.[43] In a newly discovered sermon on Christian gifts, Augustine even made plain that humane acts of generosity were frequently practiced outside the church. These sprang from *humanitas*, from a virtue shared by Christians and non-Christians alike: "They take the form of the humane treatment which one person shows to another because of the common bond of a shared human nature."[44]

Tot tantaque beneficia: So many and such great benefactions

GIVING TO THE CITY

Human decency, alas, finds few historians. This is not only because it is often taken for granted by contemporaries but also because it tends to be a fragmented phenomenon. In the Roman world it followed the contours of a society which, as we have seen, thought of social relations as broken up into innumerable face-to-face encounters between suppliants and givers. Benefactors made their own arrangements to relieve the distress that came their way—whether these distressed persons were friends, relatives, clients, neighbors, or unknown victims of misfortune. Broken up in this manner into innumerable small acts of kindness, the non-Christian practice of *humanitas* lacked a clear focus. A general ideal of humanity was widespread, but the actions that sprang from that ideal were scattered erratically throughout society. They never congealed into a single social action that summed up everyone's ideal of a signal act that combined generosity and humanity in the way that almsgiving to the poor was consistently exalted in Jewish and Christian circles as the pious act par excellence.

For this reason, contemporaries looked elsewhere to find the perfect scenario of generosity. They found it close at hand. For centuries, the most vivid and esteemed form of giving was held to have occurred on the occasion when a rich person gave unstintingly—and in the full blaze of public acclaim—to his or her city by providing new buildings, by repairing old ones, and by laying on splendid games for its citizens.

What we now call "civic euergetism" was the tradition of performing *euergesiai*—"good deeds"—to one's city. Such euergetism was seized upon as a gesture of generosity that summed up an entire urban civilization. Individual benevolence, even when practiced on a wide scale, was like a soft, fine rain. Civic euergetism, by contrast, was a mighty flash of lightning that lit up the principal features of the traditional social landscape, leaving lesser forms of giving (many of which may well have been motivated by compassion) in darkness.

Civic euergetism riveted the attention of contemporaries. It has also riveted the attention of modern historians who rightly consider it to be one of the most striking and idiosyncratic features of the Greco-Roman world.[45] Last but not least, it riveted the attention of Christian bishops throughout the fourth and fifth centuries. Their vocal disapproval of this practice (because it contained no element of compassion for the poor) has served, if anything, to exaggerate the extent of urban euergetism at this time.

The bishops were right to devote so much attention to civic euergetism. They knew a rival for the wealth of the rich when they saw one. For the rich who came in increasing numbers to listen to the bishops had been conditioned since their earliest years to see civic generosity as both a duty and a delight. We meet such rich persons in the Christian catacomb of Santa Cristina at Volsinii (modern Bolsena, about seventy miles north of Rome). Their gravestones date from the last quarter of the fourth century. One (who buried his wife in 376) had been *curator* (financial officer) of the city. The other, Maecius Paternus, had acted as *curator* and had supervised the city's supplies to the army. He had also restored the public baths (called the baths of Tuscianus, in memory of a former benefactor) out of his own pocket. "Proved worthy by the judgment of all," he had been named "patron" of the city. He doubtless had offered games and banquets on these occasions. These offices and honors were proudly listed on Christian grave inscriptions, which ended with the phrase "Peace to you with the saints."[46] Christian or non-Christian, persons of high status belonged to a giving class. They could no more expect to avoid generosity to their city than a medieval knight could avoid the rituals of chivalry without losing his honor.

What was implied by this situation is made plain by an inscription from a generation earlier. In 347 the citizens and town council of Paestum (a city 170 miles south of Rome, now known for the great Greek temples that stand on the lonely seashore) gathered to confer on the young son of a local family the honor of "patron of the city" formerly held by his father:

> for there come from the family of Aquilius Nestorius, that upright young man, such numerous, great and splendid benefactions, with which our city has been adorned, which are visible to the eyes and minds of every one of us citizens, especially when each citizen looks around and sees the public works which this family has erected. They have to such an extent rendered stately the aspect of our city, that the people of the city have resolved to give in return for such great services and other acts of munificence to the city ... the honor of a priesthood of the imperial cult....
>
> And as Aquilius Nestorius, in consideration of this return of honor to himself, always deigns to show to us citizens a unique degree of affection; and as his son, Aquilius Aper, is sure to show us similar affection ... it pleased the citizens to offer him the title of "patron of the city."[47]

A characteristic product of the bipolar world ushered in by Constantine, the XP (Chi Rho: Christogram) monogram of Christ was placed on the head of the plaque presented to Aquilius Nestorius. We do not know if any of the Aquilii were Christians. What is important is that this did not matter. The document (which was discovered in 1990) reveals a little city that still breathed deeply the air of a very ancient world to which Christianity was irrelevant.

Amor civicus: Love of the city

The phenomenon of civic euergetism was so widespread in the Greco-Roman world and its manifestations were so vivid—indeed, so voluble—that it is easy to lose a sense of proportion when approaching its continued manifestations in the fourth century. Let us be clear about what exactly was involved. We are not dealing with an indiscriminate, one-way flow of wealth from the rich to the city but a studied duet between the city and the rich. This took the form of an exchange of honors. The family of Aquilius Nestorius had shown honor to the city of Paestum by rendering splendid its urban profile. The town council and citizens of Paestum returned this honor with the counterhonor of a priesthood and the honorific status of "patron of the city."[48]

This duet laid great emphasis on the wholehearted enthusiasm of both parties. The family of the Aquilii had shown "a unique degree of affection" for Paestum. It was in the hope that this affection would continue in the next generation that the city offered marks of honor with equally spontaneous enthusiasm. Giving was about a very special sort of love—*amor civicus*, love for the city and its citizens. A rich person who showed this love was acclaimed as an *amator patriae*—a lover of his or her hometown. It was the most honorable love that a wealthy person could show.[49]

Amor civicus was written all over the temples, the forums and public buildings, the arches, the colonnades, and the vast places of public entertainment—the theaters, the amphitheaters, and the stadium-like circuses—which still amaze the tourist to any Roman site in almost any region of western Europe and north Africa. In the eyes of the rich, everything that had made a Roman city what it was sprang from this, the most acceptable of all enthusiasms: the love of a leading citizen for his hometown.

The statues in the forums and in front of the temples of so many towns proved this. These statues were lifelike. Many were painted and would be carefully washed on memorial occasions. They amounted to a waxworks of the generous dead. Family by family, generation by generation, their serried ranks turned the forum and other public places into open-air galleries of civic love.[50] They stood on bases that were covered with easily legible inscriptions, from which we scholars now derive the abundant evidence for civic euergetism in classical and late Roman times. At Calama, for instance (modern Guelma in Algeria, which stood at the head of the Seybouse valley on the edge of the plateau of Roman Numidia), Annia Aelia Restituta received no less than five statues and one of her father, "so as to render thanks for her exceptional liberality to her fellow citizens in adding stateliness to her home town."[51]

Much of the evidence for civic benefaction in its heyday comes from the second and early third centuries. But the phenomenon was not limited to that period. One of the major advances in scholarship on the later Roman empire has been our realization of the extent to which the ancient drive of civic love had continued from its flowering in the high empire deep into the fourth and fifth centuries. This has been shown especially for Africa by the monumental and groundbreaking work of Claude Lepelley on the cities of late Roman Africa[52] and by the more recent treatment, by Christophe Hugoniot, of the spectacles still offered in these cities.[53] But the extent of the phenomenon has also been revealed in central and southern Italy through the careful studies of scholars such as Giovanni Cecconi.[54]

These continuities occurred in a world where much else had changed. Things were not as they had been. Scholars find it easy to draw up a gloomy picture of civic euergetism in the fourth-century West. They emphasize the loss of scale and range compared with earlier times. They have pointed out that this loss of momentum was not due solely to economic recession. In Africa, an economic recession did not occur, but even there civic building withered. This was because, as we saw in chapter 1, civic life itself had changed. Members of the inner circle of provincial society now felt that they no longer needed to cut a figure by showing love to their own city. The love of the emperor, gained at a distant court, meant more to them than did the acclaim of their fellow citizens at home.[55] If they decorated cities at all, they did so from the top down. They restored their cities as imperial governors, making use of imperial funds.[56]

Furthermore, the regions where civic love continued to be expressed shrank to a few privileged areas, placed around the heartlands of the Mediterranean.[57] Africa stood out as a homeland of ancient civic values. In the fourth century, there was no more clear sign of the position of Africa as the economic center of gravity of the western empire than the remarkable tenacity with which traditional love of the city maintained its momentum. But, even in Africa, the pace of building was drastically reduced. The high wave of euergetism associated with the second and early third centuries had clearly passed its peak.[58]

Yet it is the tenacity of the tradition of euergetism that is its most striking feature in the later empire. The language of civic love and no other was the language the rich of the most prosperous areas of the western empire continued to use in relation to their cities. The template for euergetism as the model form of generosity may have been reduced in size, but its distinctive shape was unchanged. Civic love, though it was practiced on a smaller scale, was considerably more than a mere ghost of its old self. It had a remarkable capacity to condense the distinguishing features of a given social order. Why was this so?

"That is what it is to have wealth!"

THE PEOPLE AND THE GAMES

We must never underestimate the sheer physical presence of the past in a late Roman city. In a province such as Africa, the boom of public building had happened relatively recently, in the first part of the third century. The monuments among which a city dweller such as Augustine moved as a boy and later as bishop of Hippo were not romantic reminders of a golden past, only distantly connected with the present. Many of these buildings were no older than the great opera houses, the banks, and the flamboyant railway stations of nineteenth-century Europe now seem to us. They were old. But they had not yet been condemned to history. Indeed—like the Milan Opera House, Saint Pancras Station, or the British Museum—they marked the beginning of a "modern age" that was thought by persons of the fourth century to have continued without a break up to the present.[59]

Christian preachers such as Augustine wished that these great piles would sink into the past. Augustine even hinted, with satisfaction, that they were falling down.[60] They were doing no such thing. They had not fallen down, and many were still being repaired—often by the families of those who had first built them over a century earlier. And they continued to be packed.[61]

They were packed because the *populus* also counted for something in the cities. The role of the *populus*—the citizen body—in the late Roman city is difficult for us to appreciate fully. The role of these citizens is less fully documented than is the exuberant self-promotion of their benefactors. But they were there. The *populus* was an integral part of the constitution of each city. As we have seen, the Roman cities of the West were *res publicae*. Each was a Rome in miniature. Each had its *ordo*—its legally defined class of town councillors and notables gathered in the "temple" of the city hall. And each *ordo* faced its eternal doublet, the *populus*.[62]

The *populus* would gather in the theater, in the amphitheater, and in the circus.[63] We tend to imagine that these great buildings were primarily places of entertainment. But for Romans they remained charged with political significance. Games were happy occasions, but they were more than that. Shared joys were the privilege of a citizen body. Those who sat in the theater or around the circus were as much a *populus*—a gathering of fellow citizens—as they had ever been in the forum.

In the theater and in the circus the citizen body made clear that they were entitled to a voice in the affairs of their city. Far from being passive in the later empire, the *populus* used the theater and the circus to perfect techniques with which to put pressure on their superiors. The use of chanted acclamations by theater crowds is documented all over the empire at this time. Acclamations took the form of chanted slogans. The rhythmic chanting of such slogans protected the anonymity of those who shouted them. Furthermore, such chanting conferred a sense of frightening mass upon the wishes of the people. Rhythmic acclamations seemed to carry with them an uncanny charge of inspired unanimity.[64]

It was in this remorselessly well-lit environment that civic notables learned the art of generosity. We can follow their education in giving most clearly in the case of the *spectacula* (the shows) and the *ludi* (the games). These could include anything that gripped the people's attention, from relatively cheap productions, such as dramas, festivals of song, pantomime, striptease, and boxing shows, to stunningly expensive and murderous displays, such as chariot races and the slaughter of wild beasts. What matters is that they were the gift of a wealthy person to the *populus*—to the citizen body—of his or her city.[65]

Putting on shows and games gave a sharp personal profile to civic love. Hence their unusual importance in the fourth and fifth centuries. Even at the height of the prosperity of the empire, the erection of public buildings had been prohibitively expensive. They had usually been built through a collective effort, in which individual donations were supplemented by the use of civic funds administered by the town council as a whole. In Africa and elsewhere, in both the classical and in the late Roman periods, paying out of one's own pocket for public buildings had always been a gesture of exceptional generosity. To leave one's name on an entire public building was "the icing on the cake" for private benefactors. Only the very rich hoped to do this.[66]

By contrast, grand shows were well within the range of individual pockets. They could be given by one person alone and had an immediate and vivid impact. Furthermore, in the fourth century, they fit in very well with the general drift toward stunning personal display which, as we have seen, characterized the rich of the later empire.[67] It was at the games that the hearts of the rich could be seen most clearly to positively whir with "civic love." And they whirred because the *populus* made them whir.

An inscription on a mosaic from the middle of the third century illustrates this. Magerius, a notable of a little town to the southwest of Hadrumentum (modern Sousse in Tunisia) gave a *munus* (a gift of games) to his fellow citizens. It was not a big affair. Only four panthers were killed by members of a professional team of beast fighters—*venatores* who were the Roman equivalents of matadors. But Magerius went out of his way to celebrate the event and, above all, to demonstrate his own generosity on a mosaic that was discovered in the village of Smirat. The mosaic decorated the reception hall of Magerius's town house. The *venatores* are shown in action, braced on tiptoe, with their lances plunging into the lithe beasts. Equally important, however, was the fact that Magerius recorded, on the mosaic, the acclamations of the people. Looking at the mosaic in the museum of Sousse, we can almost hear, in a rare transcript of spoken Latin, the heavy roar of the *populus*. They were engaged in a dialogue with Magerius about generosity. The beast fighters first asked the assembled people for a suitably generous reward. In reporting this request, the herald addressed the people as "My lords." As "lords" of the show, the people then turned to Magerius to give the beast fighters lavish prizes:

Let all who follow you learn from your example! Let all who have preceded you hear of this!... You are the one who gives a game worthy of the quaestors of Rome [members of the senatorial super-rich]. You are giving a game from your own wealth. What a day! Magerius gives! That is what it is to have wealth. That is how to be able to use it! That is it![68]

The *Populus* and the Poor: Citizen Entitlement

This brief summary of the continued importance of civic euergetism in the wealthiest and most secure regions of the late Roman West should make one thing clear. When the bishops preached to the rich in favor of giving to the poor they were not faced by a neutral audience that only needed to be stirred out of their inertia so as to give to a new, deserving cause. Rather, the advocates of Christian charity had been preempted by a long-established and highly esteemed habit of giving that claimed to spring from a deep-seated love. Many of the Christian rich who came to listen to their bishops had been almost genetically wired, by generations of family tradition, to be givers. But they had also been wired to give in one way and in one way only. It was to tame and redirect the urge to give in persons through whom the adrenalin of civic love still pounded that bishops such as Ambrose and Augustine preached urgently. As we shall see, they often did so in vain. Why was this the case?

In order to understand the difficulties experienced by the bishops we have to make a considerable leap of the social imagination. We have to enter a world where the poor themselves lacked the sharp social profile they came to have in later times. The primary division of society was not that between rich and poor but between citizens and non-citizens. The benefactors of cities gave to their "fellow citizens" and never to the poor. Some of these citizens might well be poor, but their poverty in itself entitled them to nothing. They received entertainment, public comforts (such as great bathhouses), and (in many cities) considerable doles of food. But they did not receive them on the basis of need. They received them because they were members of a privileged group. They were the *populus* or *plebs* of the city. This was the imagined, vigorous core of the urban community. To love the city was also to love its citizens with "unique affection"—and to love no one else.

The abiding sense of the entitlement of a privileged core of citizens was a decisive legacy from the classical past to the cities of the later empire. It had lost none of its power. It was not based on a vague sentiment of belonging but on a jealously preserved sense of the rights of resident citizens. Whenever a major benefaction (such as a corn dole) was given to a city, the inhabitants had to come forward to prove that they had been long-term residents and the descendants of citizens in order to benefit from the gift.[69]

In changing times, this core of citizens struggled to maintain the entitlements that went with their civic identity. It was not enough that they were citizens of the Roman empire. They still wanted to be known as citizens of the miniature Rome of their hometown. Bolstered by this privilege, they refused to merge into the anonymous mass of the mere poor. They wished to stand out, if only a little, from the gray poverty of the destitute in the cities and from the huge, faceless world of the countryside around them. To receive food and entertainment not only made them comfortable; it made them feel different from everybody else. A lover of the city cared for them and for them only.

Even in a small town, the citizen group did not coincide with all the inhabitants of the city. Strangers and the non-citizen poor (often immigrants from the countryside) were always present. But they remained marginal. To visit a theater in a city in Africa and elsewhere was to be taught to know one's place in a traditional civic order that had not changed over the centuries. The citizens sat together. In some cities they were divided into professional associations, where each association sat on its own row of marked benches. The right-less poor and strangers were not excluded, but they huddled in the back rows while the *populus* sat down below, close to the show and adjacent to the benches of the town council and the seat of the benefactor for the day.[70]

We can see the working out of the harsh logic of citizen entitlement most clearly in the gigantic city of Rome. In Rome, the *populus Romanus* (or the *plebs Romana*) may have amounted to less than half of the overall population of the city, perhaps two hundred thousand in a city of half a million.[71] Their privileged position would have been glaring. For what was at stake in Rome was the privilege of access to the food provided by the famous *annona civica*—that is, to a dole of grain and of other foodstuffs that was reserved for the citizens of Rome.[72]

In a world characterized by harvest shocks and fear of famine, citizen privileges or their absence were a matter of life and death. Much of the population of Rome was miserably poor. Excavated mass burials show the ravages of disease and malnourishment from which they suffered. But only members of the *populus Romanus* were entitled to free grain and other foodstuffs at reduced prices. The rations made available by the *annona* at Rome could not support an entire family throughout the year, but they could shield them from famine.[73]

Poor though some may have been, even the most needy among the *populus Romanus* did not receive their food as beggars but as citizens. Not surprisingly, the people of Rome were fiercely attached to their privileges. During times of famine, the *plebs* collaborated wholeheartedly with the Senate to drive strangers out of the city. They did so to ensure that there was enough food to go around.

Rome was their city and no one else's.[74] They carried with them to the outlets from which food was distributed a leaden or bronze tessera (the equivalent of an ID card or a passport) to prove that they were members of the *plebs frumentaria*—citizens entitled to grain.[75] To be inscribed on the register of recipients of the *annona* was a title that could be placed with pride on one's tombstone. For in Rome and in many other cities of the later empire (if on a smaller scale), to receive a dole of food did not make one a beggar. It made one a citizen.[76]

In sum, the *populus* was not the poor and did not wish to be treated as the poor. For a civic benefactor to look past the *populus* by showing generosity to the many thousands of beggars and immigrants who lingered on the margins of the city was not an act of charity. It was a snub to the citizen body. Only the most arrogant could threaten to do that. Ammianus Marcellinus noted one such insufferable maverick. The senator Lampadius (who was urban prefect in 365) emerges as very much the Roman aristocrat:

> His vanity was such that he took it very ill if even his manner of spitting was not extolled for its unique adroitness. When he gave a magnificent show as *praetor* [that is, as a young man, some time around 330] and distributed largesse on a most generous scale, he could not bear the demands of the *plebs* that he should make gifts to undeserving favorites [as star performers]. So as to demonstrate both his generosity and his contempt for the crowd, he summoned beggars from the Vatican, and loaded them with rich gifts.[77]

At that time, the Vatican was not yet associated with the great Christian shrine of Saint Peter. It was a no-man's-land, a cemetery area in which beggars lived. But the whimsical gesture of Lampadius showed, without a hint of Christian meaning, that in Rome the *plebs* and the poor were thought of as starkly different groups.

We should remember that this ancient view of the community was still very much alive in many regions throughout the fourth century and beyond. It had continued unchanged alongside the Christian churches. In retrospect, Christian preaching in favor of extensive outreach to the poor might seem to represent a novel surge of humane feeling. But it had its shadow side. It blurred traditional boundaries. To present poverty as the sole requirement for generosity from the rich devalued the status of thousands of persons who thought of themselves as citizens first and only then as poor. It treated them as part of the same miasma of misery as the beggars, the homeless, and the immigrants who crowded into every city. So wide and so indiscriminate a vision undermined the delicate balance of institutionalized groups—benefactors, town councillors, and *populus*—on which the life of the cities of the Roman empire had depended for centuries. The world would have to change considerably (as it did in just these centuries) before a classical view of society as made up of a honeycomb of civic groups was replaced, across Europe, by the gray and universal vision of a world divided only between rich and poor.

For many persons (and not only for the rich) around the year 370 AD, this was a chilling prospect. As we shall see in the course of this book, to move from one model of society to the other was to move from the age of the classical city to what has recently been called a "post-Roman late antiquity," in which the classical model of the city finally relinquished its grip on the social imagination.[78] Let us turn to the next chapter so as to see the beginnings of this great transition, as it was prepared by Christian preaching on the poor, by the new role offered to the poor within the Christian communities, and by the Christian emphasis on the otherworldly efficacy of pious gifts both to the poor and to the church.

CHAPTER 4

"Treasure in Heaven"
Wealth in the Christian Church

Quia non clamat populus ut pauper accipiat: Because the people
do not roar that the poor should receive anything

THE GAMES, THE *POPULUS*, AND THE POOR

In conjuring up Christian attitudes toward wealth and poverty in the Latin West
at the end of the fourth century we will often find ourselves in the world of the
Christian sermon. There is nothing strange about this. In her groundbreaking
study *Christianity and the Rhetoric of Empire*, Averil Cameron speaks of Christian sermons as "the hidden iceberg" in the life of the Christian communities.[1]
Regular preaching—week in and week out, community by community—was the
air the Christian churches breathed. The formal works of Christian authors, which
now fill so many shelves in our libraries, are mere islands that jut out here and
there from the immense and largely hidden oceanic shelf of oral discourse created by the Christian sermon. As bishop of Hippo, Augustine emerged as one of
the most brilliant of these preachers. It has been calculated that in his thirty-five
years as bishop of Hippo, he must have preached at least six thousand sermons.[2]

As we will see later (in chapter 21), Augustine preached extensively on the
relations between the rich and the poor. Among these sermons, the juxtaposition between civic generosity (such as we have described) and Christian giving
to the poor was prominent. A series of sermons only recently discovered in the
cathedral library of Erfurt show that he planned entire campaigns of preaching
on the topic. The campaigns included teach-ins to his own clergy as to how best
to preach against the games and in favor of Christian charity. Rich members of
the congregation who supported the games were to be "condemned, rebuked
and changed for the better."[3] The only use of these wild displays of generosity
was to provide Christians with examples of heroic giving,

by which lazy members of our churches are to be challenged to action, seeing that they barely break a single loaf of bread to feed the starving Christ [in the poor], while those who lavish wealth on the theater [spend so heavily that they] leave hardly a loaf of bread for their own sons.[4]

These sermons were preached at Hippo, at Carthage, and in the little cities of the Medjerda valley. Placed at the very center of the most urbanized region in the Latin West, where the traditions of civic love had remained most vigorous, Augustine challenged the phenomenon of civic euergetism head-on.

Augustine chose his target carefully. In his sermons, his criticisms never touched the great *annona* system that kept the *plebs* of Rome in food, although (as we have seen) this system revealed so brutally the difference between an old-world benefaction made to citizens and the new style of Christian charity to the poor. For the *annona* was an imperial matter. The *annona* had been granted by the emperor Augustus, acting as an urban benefactor on a grand scale, as his gift to the people of Rome.[5] Every year the collection and transport of the *annona* for Rome filled the docks of Hippo and Carthage with ships laden with grain and oil. The *annona* was the secret of much of the wealth of fourth-century Africa.[6] For this reason alone, the *annona* of Rome was untouchable.

But the local games were different. Still performed with gusto in Carthage and elsewhere, they laid bare the mechanisms that caused so much money to flow in what was for Augustine the wrong direction—away from the poor and the churches. The games made clear, every time they were offered, that the rich listened only to the ancient, civic voice of the *populus* and not to the voice of their bishops: "They treat the poor with disgust because the people do not roar [in acclamations] that the poor should receive anything."[7] As Augustine saw it, things had not changed since the days of Magerius at Smirat, almost two centuries before. The people were the "lords" of the games. And the people had no use for the poor.

It is worthwhile to linger a little on what constituted the originality of Augustine's approach. Many of his criticisms of the games would have struck his hearers as thoroughly conventional. The games had been denounced for centuries, and not only by Christians. They had long been the butt of a high-minded counterculture. Philosophers had frequently criticized the games for their sensuality, for their potential for violence, and for the crazy vanity they inspired in those who gave them.[8]

But only Augustine and his Christian contemporaries saw the games in terms of a conflict of giving. This was new. They also saw them in terms of a conflict of loves: "love of the city" was pitted against "love of the poor." In this, Christian preachers deliberately echoed the mystique of civic euergetism. Urban benefactors had taken great care to project an image of themselves as persons driven to dramatic acts of generosity by deep love—love of their city. As a result, the givers of the games could be presented as sinister doubles of the Christian almsgiver. *Amor civicus* and charity were twins. Both were said to be driven by fierce love. As for the theater itself, it was not only a place of cruelty and debauch, as many philosophers had complained; it was also a place of social bonding. In that respect it was a counterchurch. The wild enthusiasms and the glowing sense of solidarity the theater conjured up on high occasions made it, in the words of an eastern writer, nothing less than "the Church of Satan."[9]

Church and Circus: A Tug of War?

In preaching in this way, Augustine deliberately engineered the imaginative collision of two worlds. He juxtaposed the city and the church in terms of two distinctive and seemingly incompatible styles of giving. In doing this, he and his Christian contemporaries (who preached in much the same vein in other parts of the empire) created what can best be called a "representation" of the relation between church and city in late Roman society, in which there was constant competition between the one and the other.

Scholars have often been misled by the vivid contrasts evoked by such preaching. It has become a commonplace to write about the changes in the late Roman city (and indeed, about changes in the empire as a whole) in terms of a straightforward tug of war between church and city for the control of wealth. In the brisk words of Arnaldo Momigliano:

> Money which would have gone to the building of a theatre or an aqueduct now went to the building of churches and monasteries. The social equilibrium changed—to the advantage of the spiritual and physical conditions of monks and priests, but to the disadvantage of the ancient institutions of the empire.[10]

But we must always remember that real life in the later Roman empire did not move as quickly as Christian preachers hoped that it might. The idea that church and city were locked in a relentless zero-sum conflict for limited resources and that the church eventually won because it emptied the pockets of the rich in its favor does not bear close scrutiny for two reasons.

First: So far we have studied only the self-image of the games. But we must be careful not to confuse this self-image with their actual practice. Public representations of civic life expected the games to be expensive. A benefactor was supposed to court financial ruin on behalf of his city. But this rarely happened in reality. Planned for long in advance and often presented with a canny sense of economy, the games were seldom the "status bloodbaths" that they claimed to be.[11] Outlay on the civic games was a relatively small item in the overall budget of the rich. The best comparison may be with the outlays of parliamentary candidates in the conduct of elections in eighteenth-century England. Apart from a few instances, these rarely amounted to crippling sums. What mattered was that in such elections (as in the games of the later empire), the candidate should claim to have made a splash in wooing the voters. For a hotly contested election (with all the rowdy junketing and outright bribery associated with it) was like the Roman games. Both happenings condensed an entire image of society: an England proud to be a land of "free suffrages" that needed to be canvassed; a late Roman city proud to be the gathering place of a free *populus* that needed to be entertained.[12]

Second: The more we study in detail the behavior of the Christian rich throughout the empire (such as those of whom we have a hint from their gravestones in the catacomb of Santa Cristina at Bolsena), the more we realize that few of them maintained the stark opposition between almsgiving in church and civic benefactions in the circus on which their clergy had come to insist. Many rich persons doubtless did both. To take one revealing example: African councils of the time of Augustine condemned the sons of bishops who had laid on games. As members of the class of town councillors, they had plainly inherited from their fathers both the obligations and the tastes of civic benefactors.[13] They saw no inconsistency between their public roles in the city and their Christian piety. They were unimpressed by the either-or choice presented to them by the clergy. It bore little relation to the complexities of their real life as members de rigueur of a class of givers.

"Men may have no use for them, but God has"

THE POOR AND THE BOUNDARIES OF SOCIETY

Altogether, the rise of Christianity in the cities of the late Roman West cannot be explained simply in terms of the collapse of civic euergetism in favor of almsgiving. We are dealing with a change more profound than a straightforward switch in the beneficiaries of public giving, by which giving to citizens was replaced by giving to the poor. The emergence of the poor as highly charged objects of concern involved an imaginative revolution. Let us linger for a moment on what this might involve.

It is easy to forget that Christianity, though we like to study it with alert interest in terms of its impact on late Roman society, was above all a religious movement. Not unlike the Buddhism that entered so dramatically into the somewhat stolid world of imperial China (between the fifth and seventh centuries AD),

Christianity was a religion "avid for the incommensurable."[14] Christians needed to create their own image of society on a scale worthy of the vaulting spiritual ambition of their faith. They tended to do this by placing in society itself a series of unmistakable—even shocking—"markers." These markers served, as it were, as wakeup calls. They would challenge believers and outsiders alike to realize the unimaginably wide horizons opened up to humanity by the Christian message.

Because of this, the most vocal advocates of Christianity in the late fourth and fifth centuries tended to focus attention on extreme states of the human condition. It is no accident that the torrent of Christian preaching on outreach to the poor coincided with a sharp elevation of forms of total sexual renunciation—of virginity, of monastic withdrawal, and even, in certain circles, of clerical celibacy. The same authors often expatiated on both themes: one thinks of Jerome who combined high-strung vignettes of virgin girls sheltered in the depths of noble palaces[15] with praise of Christian senators as they made their way through crowds of beggars, scattering alms as they proceeded to the Senate house, and swabbed the sores of the poor in hospitals they had founded.[16] Outreach to the poor and the adoption of virginity and celibacy were both held to be actions that went against the normal grain of human nature. Both were tinged with a sense of heroic *démesure* that demonstrated the supernatural superiority of the Christian religion, which could inspire its adherents to do such extraordinary things as abandon sex and love the poor.[17]

For this reason, giving to the poor tended to be presented as an act of altruism in its purest and most challenging form. We should not underestimate the imaginative impact of such altruism. Late Roman society (like any other ancient society) was a world held together at every level by intense networks of reciprocal gifts. These ranged from the friendly exchange of services in neighborhood associations to the euphoric dialogue between civic benefactors and their "people," by which the gift of civic pleasures was instantly repaid by the countergift of honor and acclaim. It was a world that appeared to be ruled by iron laws of reciprocity. In such a world, it was considered bad luck to dream that one gave money to a beggar. The dream foretold death: "For Death is like a beggar, who takes and gives nothing in return."[18]

It is only against this background that we can understand the frisson attached by Christian writers and preachers to the ultimate, non-reciprocated gift—the gift to the poor. In the challenging words of Lactantius, writing at the beginning of the reign of Constantine, such giving showed that "The only true and certain obligation is to feed the needy and useless.... Hope of a return must be absolutely missing.... Men may have no use for them, but God has."[19]

Charity to the poor in the fourth century was presented by many Christian writers in much the same way as the "gratuitous act" was once presented by existentialist writers of the 1950s. It was an almost terrifying statement of potential boundlessness. But it was also an act of imaginative conquest. To claim such use-less persons as part of the body of the Christian community was to claim society as a whole, in the name of Christ, up to its furthest, darkest margins.

But this dramatic attitude toward the poor created an imaginative dilemma among Christians. Christel Freu has drawn attention to this dilemma in an out-standing study, *Les figures du pauvre dans les sources italiennes de l'antiquité tar-dive*. As Freu has shown, the image of the poor in Christian preaching swayed with dizzying zest between two poles: the poor were treated either as "others" or as "brothers." Were the poor "others"—to be treated as creatures at the very edge of society to which Christians were expected to reach out in defiance of common sense, as writers such as Lactantius seemed to imply? Or were they "brothers"—to be treated as neighbors and fellow members of the church? Ideas of what a Chris-tian society should be like differed greatly according to the imaginative pole at which the image of the poor rested.[20] Let us follow this tension in the Christian preachers and authors of the fourth and fifth centuries.

First of all, Christian preaching was responsible for a dramatic, if unintended, diminution of the image of the poor in late Roman society. The poor were fre-quently seen to represent an extreme of the human condition, persons teetering on the brink of destruction and condemned to the outer margins of society. Con-gregations all over the Roman world were urged by their preachers to concen-trate their attention on such persons. To use the well-chosen words of Gertrude Himmelfarb (when speaking of representations of the poor in Victorian London), the imaginative logic of such preaching had

> the conceptual effect of pauperizing the poor by first creating the most dis-tinctive, dramatic image of the lowest class, and then imposing that upon the lower classes as a whole.[21]

Christian authors of this time contributed with zest to this tendency to "pau-perize the poor." When, around 404–5, the poet Prudentius wrote about the third-century martyr Saint Lawrence, he used the occasion to paint an image of the poor of Rome that was as violently bizarre as a baroque painting. Lawrence (a deacon of the Roman church and thus responsible for its finances) was be-lieved to have told his persecutor, the Prefect of Rome, that he would hand over to him the fabled wealth of the Christian church. And sure enough he did: he assembled the poor of Rome.

> He runs about the city gathering into one flock the companies of the in-firm and all the beggars who cry out for alms.... There a man showing two eyeless sockets directs his straying, faltering footsteps with a stick; a crip-ple with a broken knee; a one legged man.... Here is one whose limbs are covered with running sores.... Such people he seeks out through all the

public squares, used as they were to being fed by Mother Church.... There stood the company of poor men in their swarms, a ragged sight. They greet the Prefect with a roar for alms.[22]

In this scene, Prudentius made plain what contemporary bishops asserted.[23] The wealth of the church existed only to take care of such miserable persons.

It was a heady image of society. In my book *Poverty and Leadership in the Later Roman Empire*, I drew attention to the working out of this dramatic representation of the poor.[24] Put bluntly: the "pauperizing" rhetoric of Christian authors has contributed heavily to the "binary tunnel vision" that still bedevils the writing of the social history of the later Roman empire.[25] It is largely under the influence of Christian preaching that we tend to think of late Roman society as divided irrevocably between rich and poor and of the poor as living always in a state of abject poverty. As we have already seen, our study of the intermediate classes of the Roman world has suffered seriously from this crude image of the structure of late Roman society.

To this I would now add that the binary vision projected by Christian preaching not only had the effect of pauperizing the poor. It also had the effect of "divitizing" the rich. It tended to present all members of the rich as equally outrageously wealthy. The significant differences in wealth within the senatorial class and within the elites of the cities are ignored.

For the logic of Christian preaching was to encourage the rich to reach out to the poor in such a way as to join the very top of society to the very bottom. In this way, Christianity could be seen as vertically as well as horizontally all inclusive. Not only did the churches reach out to the very edges of society—to the ominous crowds of beggars gathered in public places. Through the charitable activities of the rich, Christianity was supposed to reach downward from mighty palaces to beggars' hovels. Top and bottom—the very rich and the very poor—faced each other in a one-to-one relationship in which all the intermediate gradations of society had been elided.

This emphasis on the unmediated relationship between the imagined very rich and the very poor changed the temper of a long tradition of Roman social criticism; it began to take on a more radical tone. As we have seen, previous traditions of criticism of the rich had tended to be generated by the rich themselves as they patrolled the behavior of their fellow rich. The division that had mattered was that between the "good" and the "bad" rich—effectively, between your rich and the other rich. It was not the division between rich and poor. By contrast, when Ambrose stood up to preach in Milan (between 374 and 397 but especially in the 380s), he did not do so only to castigate the lifestyle of the bad rich. He spoke as an advocate of the oppressed poor. For if the rich were to be urged, for the first time, to be their brothers' keepers, then they could also be held to account for being their brothers' oppressors.[26]

"Not Justice, But a Cry"

THE MODEL OF ANCIENT ISRAEL

The intervention of a preacher such as Ambrose, toward the end of the fourth century, showed that the poor could no longer be spoken of only as "others"—as beggars to whom Christians should reach out across the notional chasm that divided the rich and the poor. They were also "brothers," members of the Christian community who could also claim justice and protection.

Christians had been challenged to think of the poor in this way because they had come to breathe the air of a non-classical society that had slowly but surely become part of their imaginative world. In the Hebrew Scriptures (read in the West in Latin translations that varied from region to region) rich and poor were presented as facing each other directly. They did so in the prayers of the Psalms, in the denunciations of the Prophets, and in vivid incidents in the history of the kingdom of Israel. But in the pages of the Old Testament the poor did not face the rich as beggars asking for alms. Rather, in the manner of an ancient Near Eastern society, the poor came before the powerful in search of justice. They spoke of themselves as "poor" not because they were destitute but because they had deliberately cast off their social advantages and presented themselves as helpless and in need of justice and protection. They challenged the powerful to give judgment in their favor. They came as plaintiffs, not as beggars.[27]

The cry of the poor in the Old Testament was a cry for justice. It was a cry made by free men and women, often of moderate—some even of considerable—means. It was the cry of victims. But these were not the victims of poverty so much as they were the victims of violence and oppression brought upon them by persons more powerful than themselves.[28] It was this relation of petition to justice that gave weight to the Hebrew assonance by which *ze'aqah*—"the cry"—was expected to be met by *zedaqah*—"righteousness." And "righteousness" was achieved through an act of justice granted by the powerful to the weak. The word only later came to mean alms given by the wealthy to the poor. This "elegant juxtaposition of words" did not escape the alert eyes of Jerome, in 408–10, as he commented on the classic phrase of the prophet Isaiah: *He looked for justice, but behold, bloodshed; for righteousness (zedaqah) but, behold, a cry (ze'aqah)* (Isa. 5:7).[29]

The absorption of the language and history of the Hebrew Scriptures in the Christian communities between the fourth and sixth centuries slowly but surely added a rougher and more assertive texture to the Christian discourse on poverty. The poor were not simply others—creatures who trembled on the margins of society, asking to be saved by the wealthy. Like the poor of Israel, they were also brothers. They had the right to "cry out" for justice in the face of oppressors along with all other members of the "people of God."

Auxilium civibus: Help to the citizens

FROM "POOR OF THE CHURCH" TO *PLEBS*

This was a distinctive Christian reading of the Old Testament. Its rise to prominence was slow, but once it had been established, in the course of the fifth and sixth centuries, it represented a decisive change in the role of Christianity in the late Roman world. The preachers of the fourth and early fifth centuries still strove for a victory over the circus. But it was the redefinition of the Christian poor (derived from the Old Testament) that did the most to secure the eventual triumph of Christianity in the cities in the course of the fifth century. The adoption of a view that saw the poor not only as beggars but also as persons in search of justice and protection reflected mounting pressure within the Christian communities themselves to engage in forms of social action that had wider effects than mere charity to the destitute.

As we read the texts of the late fourth and fifth centuries, we must bear in mind the double movement in the image of the poor to which Christel Freu has drawn attention. The image of the poor sank dramatically due to the demands of a Christian pathos that concentrated on the need to reach out to the "needy and useless." However, this downward focus on the destitute was countered by an upward slippage of the notion of the poor, largely associated with the language of the Old Testament. In ancient Israel, the "poor" had never been the "needy and useless." They had been much more like the *plebs* of Rome, as they saw themselves—vulnerable persons compared with the rich but by no means beggars. They belonged to the traditional core of society, not to its margins. They were persons with rights for which they might cry out.

Very soon, the *plebs* of many cities realized that the poor of Israel were more like themselves than were the wretched poor of Christian preaching. A language taken from the Hebrew Scriptures gave to the average inhabitant of late Roman cities a new purchase on the powerful. It also provided them with new advocates in the persons of Christian bishops and clergymen. Christian bishops such as Ambrose could bring the "cry of the poor" for justice to the attention of the great by claiming to be modern avatars of the prophets of ancient Israel.

This upward slippage (which became increasingly plain in the course of the fifth century) had decisive consequences, which we will follow generation by generation and region by region in this book. It reflected the social texture of the Christian communities. As we have already seen, the resilience of Christianity sprang from its firm base in the middling and lower classes of the cities. Throughout the fourth and fifth centuries, this *mediocritas* remained the solid keel of the Christian congregations. Many of the clergy also came from this stratum of urban society. As a result, the success of the churches cannot be explained only by their outreach to the very poor, as this was proposed by Christian preachers. But nor can it be explained only by a switch in giving on the part of the class of rich urban benefactors. It is best understood as a result of the zest with which the lesser townsfolk rallied to the church by taking on themselves the role of the poor of Israel. Like the poor of Israel, they felt entitled to raise a cry in the face of oppression and impoverishment and to turn to their religious leaders for protection.

Ultimately, the Christian bishops rose to prominence neither through fostering the very poor nor through persuading the very rich to switch their generosity from the circus to the churches. It was through winning the middle. This happened when members of the *plebs* came to see themselves as avatars of the "poor of Israel." They did not present themselves as "others"—as beggars—but as "brothers." In the course of the fifth century, they brought with them into the Christian churches a sharp sense of entitlement. They claimed the care of the bishop with the same insistence that they had formerly shown when they had elicited generosity from urban benefactors as the *populus* of the city. This view of the relation between the bishop and the urban community as a whole emerged slowly. Ambrose, in Milan, was perhaps the first to state it clearly, in the 380s. But by the first quarter of the sixth century, the results were plain. Around 530 a bishop of Abellinum in Campania (modern Avellino) was praised on his sarcophagus for having performed a double duty. He was an almsgiver—"a constant source of comforts for the needy"—but he was also an *auxilium civibus*—"help to the citizens."[30] Once bishops began to take on both roles, the cities would soon be theirs.

Christianity and the City: Continuity or Rupture?

Faced with this long-term evolution, which we will follow throughout the entire course of this book, it is tempting to think that for all the sharp antitheses drawn by Christian preachers, little changed in the cities of the West in the course of the fourth and fifth centuries. It is widely believed by historians of the period that Christianity rose to prominence because the church emerged as a viable substitute for civic life. It is said that the bishop and his clergy replaced the town council; that the generosity of benefactors was diverted away from the circus to the church; that the drama of the liturgy and of the festivals of the martyrs replaced the mystique of the forum and the theater; and that the sense of urban privilege associated with membership of a *populus* was given a new lease on life under the capacious label of the bishop's care of the poor. One is tempted to say *plus ça change, plus c'est la même chose.*

It would not be entirely wrong to say this. *Plus ça change, plus c'est la même chose* has proved to be a sound adage. A sober respect for the continuities of Roman institutions and of Roman elite behavior within the Christian churches of the fourth, fifth, and sixth centuries has inspired some of the very best studies of the rise of Latin Christianity in modern times. But there is a danger that the adage can cease to be an interpretive tool and become, instead, a mantra.

This danger is to be resisted. For there is an implicit teleology in an approach that emphasizes only continuity in the emergence of the Christian churches in late Roman society. Behind this approach lies the assumption that traditions and values inherited from the classical past were bound to survive in one form or another and that the Christianization of the Roman world was an event that was somehow external to the deeper continuities in worldview and social structure.

Many skeptical scholars have said that Christianity added only a superficial wash to this basic continuum. Bishops might rise to prominence, but business as usual remained the order of the day. The clergy merely took over the duties and the attitudes of the local magnates whose religion they claimed to have replaced but whose social habits they continued with little break deep into the early middle ages. Posed in this way, the answer to the question "What difference did Christianity make?" should be, bluntly: "Very little."[31]

Other scholars are of more pious disposition. Whether this piety is directed toward the Christian church or ancient Rome, they claim that Christianity did, indeed, transform the Roman world. But they insist that this was a benign transformation that took place without major fractures. Christianity identified itself with the values of Roman civilization in such a way as to ensure that much of the dignity of Rome would survive, if in a new "baptized" form, in the Catholic church of the early middle ages. Christianity, as it were, "took the place" of Rome. We are dealing with a "permanence of traditions and values inherited from the past ... in the midst of a society progressively conquered by the new faith."[32]

In either case, a view that emphasizes continuity alone insists that we are not faced with the brutal end of a society.

Altogether, this is a comfortable narrative. It is a narrative that relies on what Kimberley Bowes, in her recent book, *Private Worship, Public Values and Religious Change in Late Antiquity*, has acutely characterized as a "swap sale" model of change:

Christianization narratives generally tend to formulate ... social changes as a swap sale; they describe how the senator exchanged his consular robe for a bishop's miter; how the civic bureaucracy was charged with building churches and hostels instead of amphitheaters and baths.... This unalloyed confidence that one practice, thing or social role was exchanged for another assumes a tacit teleology.[33]

Such teleology can be misleading. It makes the rise of Christianity in the West seem to result from an almost foreordained convergence of Christian practices with the habits of an earlier, non-Christian world. As we will see, accounts of the Christianization of Roman society that are framed in this manner fail to do justice to the elements of novelty that also accompanied the rise of Christianity in the later empire. It is to them that we must now turn.

Caelum donis terrestribus emit: He bought up Heaven with earthly gifts

"TREASURE IN HEAVEN" AND THE WORKING OF THE GIFT

In the last few sections I summed up the views of those who argue for continuities in outlook and practice between non-Christian institutions (such as civic euergetism) and the development of the Christian church. I do not do this so as to reject them in their entirety; they contain a large measure of truth. But it is important that we supplement them. This is because certain aspects of Christian giving represented a novelty not only in the professed aim of this giving—to give to the poor—but in the motivations ascribed to the giver. What differed most of all was the emphasis on the supernatural efficacy of the Christian gift. We are dealing with a system of religious giving within a religious community that had a profile all its own. It could not be "swapped" unthinkingly for forms of giving that had been dominant in the non-Christian world. Something new had emerged.

In this respect, we must not underestimate the slow but sure development of a Christian common sense of wealth that had already taken root. The bishops, preachers, and donors of the post-370 generation did not step into an imaginative and ritual vacuum that their Roman habits—and their Roman habits alone—sufficed to fill. Far from it. They came to take part in an inherited conglomerate of Christian notions about pious giving, many of whose components were shared with contemporary Judaism and whose outlines reached back for almost a millennium (through the writings of the Old Testament) to the days of the Achaemenid empire and to the Wisdom Literature of the Hellenistic period.

In this respect, the rich who entered the Christian communities came to breathe a largely novel air. The notion of the working of the gift itself was different. In some way or another, to give within the Christian churches was to open a path to heaven. With vertiginous incongruity, any Christian gift, from the smallest to the greatest, was thought to be instantly magnified out of all proportion in an other world. It became "treasure in heaven." This was the conclusion that preachers drew insistently from the story of the Rich Young Man. In this story, Christ had said to the Rich Young Man: *Sell what you possess and give to the poor; and you will have treasure in heaven* (Matt. 19:21 with Mark 10:21 and Luke 18:22). He had repeated this command to his disciples: *Sell your possessions, and give to the poor; provide yourselves with ... a treasure in the heavens which does not fail* (Luke 12:33, cf. Matt. 6:19–20). Late Roman Christians of all classes and levels of culture took these sayings of Jesus seriously. They seemed to imply a joining of heaven and earth that a non-Christian would have perceived as utterly incongruous. A small example shows this. In the mid-fifth century, an inscription was placed above the reused classical sarcophagus in which the famous bishop, Hilary of Arles, was buried. Part of the inscription was utterly traditional. Hilary "had left the husk of his flesh to fly up to the stars." This would have made sense to any pagan. But the inscription went on to state that Hilary had also carried his wealth with him to that high place. For the inscription continued:

Caelum donis terrestribus emit.

(He bought up Heaven with earthly gifts.)[34]

That wealth despised on earth should somehow follow the ethereal soul up to the stars opened up a new horizon.

We should linger on the novelty of this attitude to the joining of heaven with earthly wealth. It is one that is in many ways strange to us. Indeed, it has caused exquisite embarrassment to modern scholars. In no modern dictionary of the Christian church does the word "treasure" appear! Yet, if we wish to understand the economic upsurge of the Christian churches at this time, it is important that we overcome a prudery no late Roman Christian would have shared.

The reason for our modern hesitation lies deep in our own society. In the words of John Parry, in his discussion of the relation between gift giving and monetary exchange:

As other transactions become increasingly differentiated from other types of social relationship, the transactions appropriate to each become ever more polarized in terms of symbolism and ideology.[35]

We have now created two distinct spheres—the world of buying and selling and the world of religious actions. To join the language of one sphere—that of commerce and treasure—with the sphere of religion now strikes us as a joining of incompatibles so inappropriate as to seem almost an off-color joke.

Plainly Roman Christians did not share this modern inhibition. They did not consider themselves to be dealing with two distinct spheres—commerce and religion—in which the ethos of one sphere was considered deeply inappropriate to that of the other. Rather, they thought in terms of two different orbits of exchange.[36] Purely earthly gifts moved, as it were, on a quick circuit. Money exchanged hands. Clients and patrons exchanged favors and support. The grand gift of the urban benefactor was greeted, instantly, by the roar of the countergift of praise. All of these exchanges happened in this world only. The urban benefactors whose statues crowded the forum sought posthumous fame only "in the sweet air" of the living.[37] They hoped that their glory might last on earth, but there was no thought that their gifts might ever follow them to heaven.

Gifts to the other world were different. They were thought of as having set off on an orbit so far distant and so divorced from human time as to leave the imagination haunted by thoughts of incommensurability. What was the relation between the earthly gift and what it might bring in a world beyond the stars? We should not look with modern primness at the fact that, for late Roman Christians, giving took place in the expectation of reward. Gifts to God or the gods had always been made in the expectation of benefits. What interests the historian of the late Roman imagination is the buildup of a new pattern of religious giving that was different from the sacrifices and ex-voto dedications of traditional paganism.

This new pattern was based on an imaginative tension that was generated by the joining of two incommensurables. Earth and heaven were brought together by the Christian gift. And this was done through the daring extension of the earthly language of exchange, commerce, and treasure (the world of the short, quick orbit, as it were) to the unimaginable world of heaven. It has been correctly remarked that seldom in any literature have money and images borrowed from commerce bulked so large as in the literature of late Roman Christianity.[38]

There were many reasons for this. Some lay deep in the past appropriated by Christianity from Judaism through sharing the same Scriptures. Ever since the sixth century BC, the explosion of commerce associated with the invention of money and with the creation of a vast common market in the Achaemenid Persian empire had influenced Jewish notions of religious giving. Commercial metaphors conveyed a sense of infinite possibilities and a capacity for instant change. Sins were seen as debts. And debts could be canceled overnight by the mercy of God. Gifts to the poor could be seen as loans to God. God would repay them with unimaginable interest. Altogether, what seems at first sight to modern persons to be the most crude commercialization of the religious imagination was favored precisely because, at the time, it infused relations with God with a sense of the infinite that echoed the breathtaking expansion of the horizons of the possible that accompanied the rise of a monetarized economy. The volatility, the seemingly limitless opportunities for profit, and the sheer shimmer of such an economy were adopted as apposite ideograms for the incalculable mercy of God.[39]

The language of the Hebrew Scriptures of the Persian period, along with the Wisdom literature, was shared by Jews and Christians. To this a further dimension was added through the sayings and parables of Christ. These also emphasized the vertiginous hiatus between small human actions and their unimaginable repercussion in an other world. Christian preachers and writers derived an entire aesthetic of inverted magnitudes from the words of Christ. They emphasized Christ's praise of the widow who offered her small coin to the treasury of the Temple:

> *Truly I say to you, this poor widow has put in more than all those who are contributing to the treasury. For they [the others] all contributed of their abundance; but she out of her poverty.* (Mark 12:43–44; Luke 21:3–4)

They constantly repeated Christ's promise of heaven to those who gave "even a cup of water" to the poor and to his wandering disciples (Matt. 10:42). A gift of copper coins and of basic food and clothing to a beggar reverberated with a sense of their exact opposite—the off-scale quality of the reward in heaven that awaited these small acts.

These were no fine-spun metaphors. They infused the humdrum practices of Christian giving with a sense of drama. In Augustine's Hippo, the regular poor box was called "the Quadriga." It was seen as a four-horse chariot that swung low to sweep the alms of the faithful (as it had once swept the prophet Elijah himself) far beyond the stars to heaven.[40]

Such a notion of giving was not the only one that circulated in Christian circles. But it soon became widespread. This may be because it was a notion that was peculiarly well fitted to a socially diverse religious community. First and foremost, it flattened the hierarchy of the givers. To place treasure in heaven empowered the average donor. For the reward of the gift was thought to be utterly out of proportion to the gift itself. Heroic giving was no longer seen as the monopoly of the truly rich. Every gift, however small, brought about nothing less than the joining of heaven and earth.

Nor did the right to give become a cause for competition. Fierce interfamily rivalries had goaded urban benefactors to compete in giving to their cities.[41] We can see this happening even more clearly on the higher level of the Roman Senate. In the fourth century, the financing of the major games of Rome had become a sort of financial sumo wrestling. The *nobiles* of Rome—the possessors of old money—brandished the sheer weight of their incomes and the stunning sums they were prepared to pay for the games of their family in order to push upstart senators—usually of bureaucratic background—out of the limelight.[42]

This was not the case with Christian giving. As we saw, members of the rich often came to the church so as to find there a social urban lung. They valued in the churches a certain lowering of the sense of hierarchy and a slowing down of the pace of competition. They found that, in the churches, they did not have to give so much at any one time, provided that they gave frequently. The sense that the glory of heaven stood behind their every gift enabled the Christian rich to contribute regularly and with that much less strain. By giving in the Christian churches, they took part in a communal religious venture tinged with expectations of limitless rewards. For in this common venture the value of individual gifts was amplified. The weight of hundreds of pious offerings gave momentum to one's own generosity.[43]

Hence the double aspect of the Christianity that had emerged in the Latin West in the crucial period between 370 and 400 AD. A new institution had become prominent in a society that knew what it was to give. Its upper classes had always valued the exhilarating "rush" associated with giving to an esteemed public cause, of which civic euergetism was the most spectacular and the most certain of acclaim. Great opportunities for giving now opened up in the relatively new Christian churches. But how would these traditions of highly personalized display impinge on a group that had hitherto been notable for its capacity for collective action?

This was a real dilemma. Ideally, giving was open to all Christians. But this was a myth. It was no more true in the fourth century than was the nineteenth-century myth that the great Catholic Cathedral of Saint Patrick's in Manhattan was built "through the pennies of Irish chambermaids." (In reality, the first building of Saint Patrick's was made possible through a campaign by which the bishop approached a hundred leading figures for $1,000 each.)[44] Furthermore, what sociologists of modern religion call "skewness" appears to be an iron law in religious giving: 20 percent of the congregation usually contribute 80 percent of the funds of the religious community that they support.[45]

Nevertheless, in late Roman conditions, a skewness in giving that mobilized even 20 percent of all believers was a remarkable phenomenon. It would have touched a large and diversified section of the community, drawn from beneath the levels of the elite. We have seen this social diversity in action on the mosaic floors of the fourth-century churches of northern Italy. To hold together such a socially differentiated group of givers was one of the great achievements of the Christian churches of this time. It was based on a creative synergy between new wealth (brought by rich Christians) and a low-profile religious group that had already been schooled to engage in collective ventures. Above all, it was a group whose members were driven by a notion of the gift that dwarfed the size of individual contributions. For each gift opened up a path that led directly from earth to heaven.

Yet we need only look at the church buildings of the fourth century to see that the fingerprints of wealthy donors were already clearly visible all over them. As far apart as Africa and northern Gaul, many Christian basilicas bore the name of their builders, many of whom were rich laypersons.[46] Names were carved everywhere. At the shrine of Saint Alexander on the Via Nomentana close to Rome, the names of lay donors were carved on the rails around the tomb and on the bases of the columns that supported the canopy above it. They jostled the name of the local bishop.[47] Looking at these names, we could be looking at the products of yet another generation of benefactors driven by civic love. But these benefactors had found a home in a different community. Their names lay on the columns of altars and on the pavements of basilicas. They were not to be read on inscriptions placed on the bases of statues in the forum. And these gifts were now thought to have gained acclaim in a distant heaven and not only the cheers of a *populus* on earth.

Pseudomorphosis: Giving in an Age of Transition

The contrast between euergetism in the city and pious giving in the churches seems clear to us now. But we must always remember that in the late fourth century and the early decades of the fifth, it was not all that clear. This was because the gifts themselves carried many meanings. Some could be seen as grand acts of patronage in an ancient tradition. Others could be seen as made to expiate sin, to thank God, or to open up the road to heaven. The notion of "treasure in heaven," though it later proved to be central, was not the only one that directed Christian generosity. This uncertainty is not surprising. As a recent study of gift giving has reminded us, gifts are "not given fixed entities, but contested constructions."[48] They do not always bear unambiguous labels. Much depends on how they are seen by others and on the constructions placed upon them by the givers themselves.

In a transitional age, such as the late fourth century, these "contested constructions" could vary widely. Not every Christian gave for the same reasons. Indeed, not every Christian knew for certain exactly why he or she was giving. For many, almsgiving to the poor was simply a good habit. It merged easily into other, more traditional forms of humane behavior such as had long been practiced by pagans, Jews, and Christians alike. Religious giving was widespread, but we do not know whether it invariably carried the heavy freight of meaning that preachers and Christian apologists wished to place upon it.

In this respect, we must always remember that we do not meet the average Christian in the pages of books or in the texts of the sermons of Christian bish-

ops. We meet such persons, rather, on their tombstones. One such was Karissimus, the Dearest One, who was buried at Tharros on the west coast of Sardinia
some time in the fourth century. We know him from the inscription that was
placed on the little table beside his tomb, at which his friends and the poor
would gather to dine in his honor. The inscription was content to merge many
worlds. It spoke of Karissimus as "a good provider for his friends, he [also] kept
the commandments concerning [care of] the poor." Beneath the inscription is
an image of a circus horse. Flanked by a palm of victory, it trots briskly with the
Chi Rho (XP) monogram branded on its rump. Those who set up Karissimus's
monument evidently chose an image associated with the ancient mystique of the
hippodrome to emphasize their friend's victory over death and the good cheer
that his modest foundation provided both to themselves and to the poor.[49]

None of those gathered around the table of Karissimus could have realized
that, eventually, the ever clearer and more ambitious constructions placed by
leading Christians on the practice of religious giving might usher in the middle
ages. Yet the middle ages did come. A large part of this book will be concerned
with how practices as low profile and as open to multiple constructions as the
good-natured piety of Karissimus and his friends came to be massaged over time.
They came to bear the stamp of ever clearer meanings as we move from the
fourth into the fifth and sixth centuries.

As we shall see, chapter by chapter, these clear meanings did not emerge all at
once and only from the minds of the leaders of the churches. Like pebbles slowly
polished into smoother and more regular shapes in the swirling waters of a great
river, the constructions placed on Christian giving emerged as the result of the
constant (and frequently abrasive) interaction of differing constituencies within
the Christian churches—clerical and lay, ascetic and married, aristocratic, middling, and popular. Behind the apparently unambiguous shape of a Christian
ideal of giving that was passed on to the Catholic middle ages, there lies nothing
less than an entire social history of Latin Christianity in the stormy years between 350 and 550 AD.

For the time being, however, as we study the fourth century, we must resign
ourselves to not yet knowing the outcome of Christian habits of giving that still
seem to waver between many worlds, between the old and the new. In this,
we are in a situation resembling that of Chinese mandarins of strict Confucian
training when faced with the rise of Buddhism in their midst. They discovered to
their annoyance that the rise of Buddhist religious practices meant that things
were no longer quite what they seemed. An official of the Ming empire reported
that the Buddhists in his province had shown great zeal for building bridges.
This was a public venture of which any traditional Chinese gentleman was bound
to approve. But the official learned that the Buddhists were building bridges for
entirely the wrong reasons. They were acting on the belief that they would gain

personal karmic merit in another existence by contributing to the building of such a bridge. A seemingly public-spirited action that was totally intelligible in terms of a long-established Chinese tradition of public benefaction was being driven by a private need for salvation. The mandarin was shocked: "Mixing this up perversely, they care only for karmic reward and do good [public] works only for this.... This is all contrary to the spirit of good works!"[50]

Late Roman history is full of similar surprises. Writing about the quality of late Roman civilization as a whole, the great historian of late antiquity Henri-Irénée Marrou once resorted to an image taken from the field of crystallography. Some crystals undergo what has been called pseudomorphosis: their surface appearance remains the same, but the inner structures that support that surface have changed entirely.[51] In the next chapters we will look at the development of Christianity in a world whose inner structures were rapidly changing despite the appearance of so many features that gave the impression of an unchanged surface continuous with traditions and with ways of acting rooted in a very ancient world.

But in around 370 AD this story still lay in a future that was unknown to everyone. A formerly low-profile Christianity stood on the verge of an influx of the rich. An economy and a social structure, whose boom and bust qualities heightened the pace and drama of the rich in their relationship to the Christian churches, seemed firmly in place—only to be succeeded in the first half of the fifth century by a chilling crash. Forms of urban spending that summed up the aspirations of an ancient civic order still attracted wealthy donors. In order to appreciate the variety of social landscapes and of the options that were still open at this time, we should begin by visiting Rome and its environs as mirrored in the life of a pagan senator who wished to be known above all as an ardent and old-style lover of his city: the nobleman Quintus Aurelius Symmachus.

PART II

An Age of Affluence

CHAPTER 5

⌘

Symmachus

Being Noble in Fourth-Century Rome

Nobilissimi humani generis: The most noble persons
in the human race

It is usual to approach the Roman nobleman Quintus Aurelius Symmachus
(ca. 340–ca. 402) as if he were a "contemporary ancestor" of the Christians of his
time. He is often presented as an isolated figure, cut off from the brave new world
of a triumphant Christianity by his traditional paganism, by his loyalty to the
Senate of Rome, and by his choice of Rome and old-world Campania as his favored places of residence. Yet this is not so. Symmachus was never out of touch
with the world around him. He may well have been on personal terms with Ambrose of Milan; he patronized the young Augustine; he would doubtless have
known of the youthful career of Paulinus of Nola and was a firm friend of Paulinus's teacher, the poet Ausonius of Bordeaux. Rather than standing as a lonely
relic of the past, Symmachus represented an ever-present, living alternative to
Christian versions of what the Roman empire and its cities should be like. In
working through the abundant evidence presented by his letters, his speeches,
and his official memoranda, we can enter into the hopes and fears of a fourth-
century nobleman and "lover of his city." Symmachus provides us with what we
need—a benchmark against which we can measure the changes in attitudes toward wealth and its uses that had become ever more apparent in the lives and
writings of his Christian contemporaries. Let us first place Symmachus in his
world.

Around 350, a traveler from the eastern provinces described Italy:

Italy is a province abundant in everything, especially as it possesses this,
the greatest of all goods: the most great, the most eminent, the imperial
city ... Rome.... It has a great Senate of rich men. If you would wish to

93

look at them closely, you would find that everyone has either been a governor or will soon be one; or there are those who are powerful but are unwilling [to hold offices for long periods], preferring to enjoy their wealth in security.[1]

To take the measure of such persons, it would be best to visit their palaces. These lay in the depths of great gardens on top of the seven hills of Rome. The palace of the greatest of them all—that of the family of the Anicii—lay on the Pincian Hill in the northeast corner of Rome, looking out over the city toward the Capitol. It was famous for the multicolored splendor of the marbles that paved its walkways and sheathed its walls.[2] At this time, it was the Roman residence of Sextus Claudius Petronius Probus. We have already met Probus as a man of outstanding and suspect wealth, gained and protected by frequent spells of high office.[3]

Outside the Anician palace lay a courtyard like a miniature forum. It was filled with statues bearing honorific inscriptions set up by grateful clients from all over the Roman world. A loyal address offered to Probus by the inhabitants of the north Italian provinces he had governed was discovered on this site. It was carved on the base of a statue that had been erected to him. The delegation spoke of themselves as the *peculiares* of Probus, his "very own" people. They praised him in a string of adjectives that brought together (like the quarterings of a great heraldic shield) the elements that exemplified "nobility" in fourth-century Rome. As a man of culture, Probus was "the light of letters and eloquence." As a governor, he was a "master of [wise] provisions and regulations." As a person, he was a "model of good nature." As a servant of the emperors, he was a veritable "high priest of loyalty." It was the combination of these qualities that made Probus "the high peak of nobility."[4] Probus was not alone. Similar inscriptions have been found, scattered all over Rome. They were written on the bases of statues that stood in the halls and forecourts of the palaces of other noblemen.[5]

For Romans of the fourth century (as of all previous ages), *nobilitas* was a highly charged word. It meant, originally, to be well-known, to stand out from the crowd. To be a *nobilis* in this way involved the convergence of a triple claim to excellence: birth, culture, and high office had to come together to make a true nobleman.[6] In the conditions of the fourth century, there was something challengingly indefinable about such claims. The Roman notion of nobility escaped the definition of society associated with the reforms of Constantine. Constantine's extension of the senatorial title of *vir clarissimus*—"most brilliant person"—to the leading members of the provincial elites had seemed to make the aristocracies of the empire into a single legally defined class. But this regulation had little effect in Rome. The "nobility" of the *nobiles* of Rome was not an exclusively legal status. In the words of Christophe Badel, it was a "nobility conferred by nobility."[7] Nobility was not a rank laid down by others; it was a "social frontier." And it was the *nobiles* themselves who patrolled this frontier—not the emperors.[8] They decided who could join them as peers and who could not.

The notion of nobility as a social frontier guided their marriage strategies. Nobles could decide whether to keep non-nobles out of the marriage market or to let them in, to the advantage of their own family. They could marry downward, so as to draw on the new wealth of up-and-coming provincial families. Or they could marry upward, by marrying members of the imperial family of the day.[9] Usually they were careful to marry only among themselves. Unlike the aristocracies of early modern and modern Europe, Romans did not consolidate their wealth through primogeniture or entails. Instead, they maintained their wealth, generation by generation, through carefully planned marriages. Intermarriage was the secret of their vast fortunes. Wealth gained from the spoils of office played a prominent role in contemporary perceptions of men such as Petronius Probus. But these gains were incidental. What really mattered were the massive coagulations of wealth that occurred as cousins married cousins within the charmed circle of the nobility.[10]

As a result, the wealth of the *nobiles* of Rome had a different flavor from the wealth of other families. Their wealth was not that of parvenus, gained only recently from collaboration with the new empire of Constantine. Rather, they were the parvenus of an earlier age. Many of the families of fourth-century Rome had first come into wealth through supporting a leader who had been quite as ruthless as Constantine—the emperor Septimius Severus (193–211). Like Severus himself, many came from Africa. They weathered the crisis of the third century, and by 350 they were solidly established in Africa, Sicily, and southern Italy.[11] They represented old money.

But they could never be talked of only as wealthy. They were *nobiles*. To be recognized as "noble" they had to shine in the proper, Roman style. To do so, they needed public office. But unlike their wealth and their culture, public office could not be summoned up, as it were, from within themselves. Office had to come from the emperor. Ultimately, through the bestowal of governorships, prefectures, and consulships, the court could reach into the very heart of the nobility's own definition of themselves. Put bluntly, a nobleman needed an official post (even if he held it for only a short time) to make his nobility complete. For this reason, the *nobiles* of Rome were less autonomous than they wished to appear. They were as dependent on the imperial system as were the lesser nobility of the provinces.[12]

A nobleman would begin as a young man with a provincial governorship; the most prestigious one was the Proconsulship of Africa. These junior posts would be followed, in middle age, by the Prefecture of the City of Rome. But the ultimate honor of a nobleman was the consulship. It is a commonplace to speak of the consulship of the fourth century as if it were an office stripped of all authority.

It was usually held by the emperors and, at times, even by military men of barbarian origin. But for a Roman nobleman, the prestige of the consulship remained undimmed. It was a numinous office, heavy with archaic grandeur. A momentary avatar of the kings of ancient Rome, swathed in stiff, gold embroidered robes, the consul gave his name to the coming year—with all the magic associations of prosperity the celebration of the Feast of the Kalends conjured up.[13] To take up the consulship was to become part of the deep past of Rome. Consuls nominated in the 370s and 380s could think of themselves as holding an honor that reached back for 870 years to the dawn of the republic.

What is remarkable, when we consider the conditions of the fourth century, is the extent to which the nobility of Rome took their honors for granted—or, at least, they claimed to be able to do so. In this they differed from the new aristocracies that had been created in the provinces by imperial favor. We need only look at the famous *missorium* traditionally associated with the emperor Theodosius I (379–95) to appreciate this difference. The huge silver dish makes plain how the bestowal of high office was regarded outside Rome. Hovering, as it were, against a sky of pure silver, the emperor was shown as larger than life. His head was surrounded by a halo. Framed by the arches of his palace, he sat on a throne, staring into the distance, far above a tiny figure into whose hands (reverently veiled in the folds of an official cloak) he dropped a document of appointment. The *missorium* may not have been produced by the court; it may have been made by the recipient of the honor. Placed among the family's silverware, it went out of its way to remind the aristocracies of the region that nobility came from the court alone.[14] For a provincial, nobility was not a "nobility conferred by nobility." It came from above. When Ausonius of Bordeaux, a mere provincial nobleman from a family of town councillors in Aquitaine, received the consulship in 379, he spoke of it as nothing less than a miracle. Like the grace of God, it was given to him by an act of "unspoken will": "for what merit? I know of none."[15] It could be the words of a later Christian bishop ruminating on predestination and the grace of God. This was not how the nobles of Rome saw themselves. In the words of Quintus Aurelius Symmachus (to whom we will turn for the remainder of this chapter), they saw themselves as the *nobilissimi humani generis*—"the most noble persons in the human race."[16] High office was supposed to come to them as their due.

Landscapes of the Heart: Symmachus between Senate, City, and Countryside

Most nobles of fourth-century Rome remain two-dimensional figures for us. We see them only from the outside, through honorific inscriptions and occasional mentions by contemporaries. But we do know one nobleman in greater detail. This was Quintus Aurelius Symmachus, who was born around 340 and died some time after 402. He preserved for posterity over nine hundred letters, a dossier of *Relationes* (official memoranda from his time as Prefect of Rome), and some speeches. Symmachus's letters notoriously lack intimacy. They were public documents, written to innumerable friends and colleagues so as to get things done—to maintain friendships, to shore up alliances, to obtain favors, to advance the careers of protégés. Each one said next to nothing. Rather, their stilted and ambiguous phrases were like Chinese visiting cards—ornate ideograms that were supposed to ring the right bell in those who received them.[17]

But this is precisely their value to us. They were prepared for publication partly by Symmachus himself and possibly by his son, Memmius.[18] Filled with creaking phrases endlessly repeated, they were, in a sense, Symmachus's own honorific inscription set up to himself. They show him not as an individual (as we might hope of a modern letter writer) but as he would have wished to be seen by his contemporaries. Here was a statue of a nobleman of Rome, made up of letters and not of stone. The letters showed Symmachus doing what every other nobleman was doing, though their letters did not survive. They show him as standing at the center of a web of friendship and influence that stretched from one end of the Roman world to the other. But they also showed him on his home ground. He was an *amator patriae*, a "lover of his home town," writ large. He was the lover of no ordinary *patria*, for his *patria* was Rome itself. It is on this aspect of his life that this and the following chapter will concentrate. For Symmachus's letters give us the opportunity to explore the various levels on which "love of the hometown" could be expressed by a Roman nobleman of the fourth century.

Symmachus, indeed, stayed closer to his *patria* than did many of his more ruthless colleagues. His career never took him away from the regions where the wealth of his own family had lain for generations. In 365—in his mid-twenties—he was governor of Lucania and Bruttium (modern Basilicata and Calabria). In 373 he became Proconsul of Africa. It was a term of service in an area of great senatorial wealth. It ended with a personal visit to shore up his estates in distant Mauretania. This was his only visit to the southern Mediterranean. In 384 he became Prefect of Rome for five months; in 391, he became consul. Altogether, Symmachus did no more than replicate the career of his father.

Symmachus was later known as a senator "of middling wealth."[19] This means "middling" for a nobleman of his status; he was, in fact, extremely rich. But he was a man of middling ambitions. He was known as Symmachus "the orator." His principal successes were those of a diplomat (where he could shine as low key and eminently "representative") rather than those of an administrator and a courtier.

In recent years we have increasingly come to realize that Symmachus was far from being a backwoods peer. Carefully studied by Cristiana Sogno, his letters show him to have been an adroit senatorial politician. The learned and refreshingly disabused study of the "last pagans of Rome" by Alan Cameron has confirmed this impression.[20] But we must remember that we have discovered this by not taking Symmachus at face value. Rather, we have done so through patient, cumulative work which, as it were, takes a peek behind the lapidary self-portrait Symmachus has left us in the edition of his letters.

Let us look at this self-portrait for a moment. What is striking about it is the skill with which Symmachus presented himself as a man set in a shimmering landscape of the heart.

The most prominent landmark in this landscape was the Senate House of Rome. As a young man, in 376, he reported with delight that his speech before the Senate had been well received. The *pars melior generis humani*—"the elite of the human race"—had rallied to him.[21] It was a memorable phrase. We should, however, remember that not many members of the human race were present when the Senate met, in the narrow, high-roofed hall at the head of the Forum, beneath the Capitol. Symmachus would usually have addressed an audience of little more than fifty persons. Yet he was sincere in his words. For him, the *amplissimus ordo*, the "Grand Assembly" gathered in the Senate House of Rome, was the living center of his life as a nobleman. In the well-chosen words of a French scholar, he went to the Senate regularly—"as a practicing Catholic goes regularly to Mass."[22]

Symmachus regarded the Grand Assembly as an intimate college of noblemen. The relation between the Senate of Rome and the senatorial order as a whole was fragile in the extreme. As we have seen, the reforms of Constantine had expanded the senatorial order to include two thousand persons. In the view of Symmachus and his father, only around eighty of these nominal senators counted as true noblemen.[23] The rest were "new" men. They were pale figures compared to the "blazing sun" of a *nobilitas* represented by a small group of families such as his own.[24] He made perfectly plain (at least when speaking to his peers) what he thought of these new colleagues: "The offspring of a family, the more they are distant from being 'new' men, the more they have advanced towards the heights of true nobility."[25] No matter how widely he might cast his net of patronage, Symmachus made clear that he did so from a position of unchallenged superiority. He and a small, self-chosen group of fellow nobles occupied "the heights of true nobility."

In the same way, Symmachus presented himself as living in a narrow world bounded by Rome and its neighboring regions. He settled back among the familiar hills of Rome itself. What may have been his palace has been discovered on Caelian Hill. It was a vast complex with a suitably old-fashioned peristyle courtyard, dating from the last days of Marcus Aurelius.[26] He moved from villa to villa in the immediate neighborhood of the City, along the Tiber and as far south as the Bay of Naples in Campania. He looked on this entire region as his own, beloved *patria*, whose heart was Rome.

Symmachus claimed that he was nowhere happier than when he was in Campania in the early fall. The fertile land positively "glistened" with abundance. Rich fruit did honor to the orchards. At the ancient seaside resort of Baiae, the air was washed clean by the occasional shower. Nature piled its wealth onto the tables to meet the needs of regiments of guests. Earth and sea combined to provide menus worthy of the gods. As an old, sick man, he felt that to return to the bright sunlight of the Bay of Naples lifted his spirits.[27]

He lovingly described his Campanian villas. They were not mere pleasure palaces for him. Each was attached to a carefully managed estate.[28] Above all, each was redolent with a long Roman past. The villa of Symmachus's father-in-law, Memmius Vitrasius Orfitus, had once been owned by the fabulously wealthy Hortensius, with whom Cicero had crossed swords in the trial of Verres, the infamous governor of Sicily. But, unlike the wealth of Verres, Orfitus's wealth (so Symmachus insisted—at a time when we know from other sources that Orfitus had recently been charged with the embezzlement of state funds) was innocent wealth. For it was family wealth—wealth that came from the past. Orfitus's possession of the ancient villa site showed that "Fortune has run from Heaven itself to take up residence with powerful lords, for the fame of the location does not allow drab owners to take over."[29]

Traveling through the cities of Campania and neighboring regions, Symmachus surveyed with pleasure evidence of how the old civic values had survived. Euergetism was alive and well. He once passed Beneventum just as the city was being restored by its local notables after an earthquake. He was pleased to see "lovers of the homeland" at work as they should be:

> While the city itself is great, its individual notables are greater still. They are passionate lovers of literature. Their good behavior is outstanding.... They compete to exhaust their private fortunes for the adornment of their city.... Broken stones are met by undefeated hearts.[30]

But we must always remember that this was Symmachus's Campania. It was a carefully constructed landscape of the heart. As Michele Salzman has observed acutely, Campania provided Symmachus with the "image of a world unchanged in time or space." Symmachus had traveled elsewhere. He had once visited Trier and frequently made his way across the Apennines to Milan. But those journeys did not inspire him and were not expected to inspire his future readers. His letters betray "an unwillingness to celebrate or even to describe at length untraditional locales."[31]

It is even far from certain that all of Campania "glistened" with natural abundance. Archaeological surveys of northern Campania show that to reach the Bay of Naples, Symmachus and his entourage would have had to pass through an emptied landscape, an agrarian slum, with scattered cottages perched in the ruins of what had once been centers of thriving agro-business in the late republic. Symmachus and those like him could not treat Campania as a secure breadbasket. They remained dependent for their wealth on the income of more distant estates across the sea, in Sicily and Africa, with all the anxieties and administrative problems that absentee landownership brought with it.[32]

No example of the Campanian villas that Symmachus describes—sheathed with smoothly fitting marbles, rendered exciting by curved porticoes and by staircases that seemed to float in midair[33]—has yet been discovered. His villas may not have been as spectacular as those set up by provincial noblemen and courtiers in other parts of the empire, such as we will meet in the Gaul and Spain of Ausonius and Paulinus of Nola. In reality, Symmachus did not live an encapsulated existence in a privileged zone. Like any other *amator patriae* of the fourth century, his fate was determined by his involvement in a vast and complex imperial system.

Forma vetustatis: The old model

Symmachus adjusted to this wider world by writing incessantly. Letters poured from him. For up-and-coming young men or for provincials in difficulty, they were the great nobleman's most precious gift.[34] For Symmachus himself, the letters were his lifeline. They kept him in contact with the highest powers and ensured that his name was always present to top bureaucrats, to courtiers, to generals—to anyone who had access to the inner counsels of the emperor. It was through his letters that Symmachus played the master politician. Seemingly as thin as spiders' webs, they wove a safety net around him. They ensured that this proud nobleman of Rome would never fall (as so many did, in the hard-driving world of fourth-century politics) or, if he did, he would soon bounce back.[35] Symmachus was a survivor. For those who read his letters with hindsight, after 402, Symmachus's letters would have served as a pattern book on the art of survival, which other noblemen were well-advised to read and imitate.

This, of course, was not how they were presented. To use the phrase of John Matthews, Symmachus presented his letters as "a museum of late Roman *amicitia*"—they were models of the Roman art of friendship.[36] Friendship, for a Roman, meant maintaining constant contact with others through the exchange of favors. It was through friendship of this kind that Symmachus attempted to bridge the many fissures that divided the upper classes of the later empire. Fellow senators and Praetorian prefects, court eunuchs, barbarian generals, even a leading Christian bishop (Ambrose of Milan)—Symmachus approached them all as if he could take for granted that they all lived in a single, undivided world. They met as friends, bound together by the ancient *religio amicitiae*—the binding protocols of friendship. Nothing, therefore, could be more natural, he would hint to the recipient of his letter, than that they, as friends, should instantly recognize the justice of Symmachus's requests and grant what he demanded. A *religiosus animus*—a "soul attuned to the duties of friendship"—hardly needed to be reminded of what was the right thing to do: he must, of course, oblige Symmachus in this or that matter.[37]

This accounts for the cloying, old-fashioned collegiality with which Symmachus approached his correspondents in high places. But it was precisely this strategy that marked him as a *nobilis*. A nobleman of Rome, he was friend to all but subject to no one but the emperor. He was proud of the fact that in his letters he always maintained the *forma vetustatis*—"the Old Model." He addressed each correspondent by his name only and never mentioned his official rank. "May it help others to be raised high by elevated titles": but this was not for a friend of Symmachus.[38] Seen against the background of fourth-century society, it was a decisive political move. The stark asymmetry of power relations, conferred by imperial office on the persons whom Symmachus approached, was quietly censored. We need only compare Symmachus's deliberately low-key style of address, on the old model, with other letters of the period to realize what this meant. When, as a bishop, Augustine wrote to the powers that be and to noblemen of the same background as Symmachus, the manner in which he framed the greetings in his letters was punctilious in the extreme. We have the impression of a provincial, always looking upward, careful to do justice to every nuance of status and official rank among the great.[39] Not so Symmachus. One was a friend or nothing. Symmachus's nine hundred letters might seem tedious to us. But he had written them in such a way that he would never be seen, by his peers or his descendants, to have groveled.

Religio amicitiae: The religion of friendship

PAGANS AND CHRISTIANS IN THE WORLD OF SYMMACHUS

There was, however, one fissure that had begun to develop across the smooth surface of a world held together by the old-time religion of friendship: the presence of Christianity. Symmachus was what we now call a "pagan." He has even been acclaimed by modern scholars as one of the "last pagans" of Rome. It might be more accurate to call him the "first pagan." He was the first member of the Roman nobility whom we can see adjusting to an unprecedented situation. He was being labeled by others in confessional terms as a "pagan"; this was not a label he would have chosen for himself.

The word "pagan" itself only began to circulate widely in the 370s. It was a word used in a religious sense only by Latin Christians. ("Hellenes," followers of the religion of the ancient Greeks, was the term used by Greek Christians.) Originally the term had nothing to do with religion. *Paganus* originally meant a mere civilian—a person who did not enjoy the honors and prestige attached to service of the emperor. Christians used the term to brand those who did not serve the true emperor, Christ. Such persons were outsiders; they were not fully enrolled members of the empire of God.[40]

"Pagan" was not necessarily a hate word. It was often used in a relatively neutral manner as a convenient, idiomatic term for non-Christians. But the term did a profound injustice to Symmachus. He was not a "pagan." He "worshiped the gods" as he had always done, and that was all there was to it. He simply did not see his fellow Romans (Christians or non-Christians) as divided between insiders and outsiders in this sectarian manner. Whatever their beliefs, he wished to treat members of his class as peers held together by the old-fashioned "religion of friendship."

In thinking this way Symmachus was neither inert nor oblivious to the world in which he lived. He simply had better things to do than to apply religious labels to his friends and colleagues. We modern persons are the heirs of the novel Christian attitudes, which only became fully public in the 370s and 380s, at a time when Symmachus was already in his thirties. We take religious differences seriously. Even in a secular age, we tend to give priority to religious belief—should it occur in a given society—as the most profound and most genuine of all emotions. It takes a real leap of the modern imagination to grasp that, in the world of Symmachus, this was by no means the case.

Christianity itself, though rendered prominent, even troublesome, by Constantine, was still, in the Rome of the 370s as in almost every other region of the West, a church of "mediocre" persons whose opinions barely scratched the granite surface of the high nobility of Rome. Symmachus stood far above the Christian church; his tolerance of Christians was based on great distance. For instance, he could cheerfully extend his patronage to Christian bishops. He wrote to his brother about bishop Clemens from Caesarea in Mauretania (modern Cherchell in Algeria)—a city where Symmachus happened to have property: "You may be astonished to find me recommending a bishop. But it is his case, not his sect, that has persuaded me." Bishop Clemens had not appealed on behalf of his church but on behalf of his city, so as to obtain a tax relief for the community of Caesarea as a whole. Symmachus expected his brother to approve of that: "He has rendered the service of a good man on behalf of Caesarea, which is his *patria*—his home town."[41] In Symmachus's world, a Christian bishop was a "lover of his homeland" first and the leader of a religious "sect" very much second.

Lest we consider this attitude to be out of touch with the times, we should remember the atmospheric weight of reverence that pressed down upon late Romans
of the upper classes (whatever their religious persuasion) as they approached the
institutions and rituals that they had inherited from a past untouched by Christianity. It was not that pagans were lukewarm and Christians were zealous. Between
the two groups lay a massive middle ground that could hold the hearts of pagans
and Christians alike. State and city were still bathed in a majesty all their own.

This situation was by no means limited to Symmachus's Rome. As Christophe
Goddard has shown in a subtle and convincing study of the imperial cult in
fourth-century central Italy, the ceremonies by which loyalty to the emperor was
expressed retained almost every aspect of their former ritual. Only blood sacrifice was avoided, out of respect for the personal prejudices of a Christian emperor. But to agree to avoid sacrifice did not amount to committing religious
suicide. Sacrifice was not central to all pagan rituals. Solemn processions, public
banquets, and great games continued to carry a heavy religious charge. High ceremonies of this kind evoked an awe that rivaled the newfangled tingle associated
with the activities of religious "sects." In a late Roman city—and especially in
Rome—the venerable town hall, the Forum, the circus, and the triumphal ave-
nues that passed beneath ancient arches could be the scene of ceremonial occasions quite as heavy with the thrill of worship as was any Christian basilica.[42]

Nothing shows this more clearly than the fact that, in the 370s, not all senators of Rome were pagans. The great Petronius Probus, to cite only one instance,
came from a Christian family pushed forward by Constantine.[43] Yet the public
life of Rome had continued unchanged. For the Christianity of Probus and his
fellow believers paled in the sunlight of a nobleman's duty to his city. A study of
the bronze tokens (the *contorniati*) issued on the occasion of the Roman games
has shown that representatives of Christian noble families presided at the Circus
Maximus and the Colosseum over spectacles that were as thrilling, as cruel, and
as calculated to cause the raw, pre-Christian adrenalin of worship for the city
and the empire to flow in their veins as were those laid on by any pagan family.[44]
And we know about many of these Christians through Symmachus's letters. He
had corresponded with them all—pagans and Christians alike—as "friends."

Non uno itinere: Not by one avenue alone

———

SYMMACHUS, THE VESTAL VIRGINS, AND
THE ALTAR OF VICTORY, 384

This was the situation Symmachus wished to maintain when, in May 384, he
took over the office of Prefect of the City. One of his first acts was an attempt to

reverse a governmental decision handed down from the court of Trier two years before. In 382 the emperor Gratian (367–83) had decided to cut back on the privileges of the college of the Vestal Virgins in Rome. The college, which consisted of seven virgins drawn from noble families, was not abolished, but its tax exemptions were removed. The virgins were forbidden to receive legacies in land (though not forbidden to receive cash gifts). Furthermore, the virgins were denied a free share of the *annona*—the imperial grain supply of the city. And that was all. Far from signaling a general disestablishment of paganism, it was a mean-minded budgetary cut, framed by bureaucrats in a distant city. It merely applied to a Roman pagan priesthood the same pruning of exemptions that had been imposed on the Christian clergy when Gratian's father, the parsimonious emperor Valentinian I, had cut back on the lavish privileges that had been granted to the church in the glory days of Constantine and Constantius II.[45]

But, of course (like many measures imposed by gray men in the name of fiscal restraint), there was more to it than that. It was seen in Rome as a calculated act of dishonor to an age-old public institution. The removal of the privileges of the virgins (especially their share of the *annona*) called into question the relation between Roman religion and the Roman state. For the virgins received public money and privileges because they prayed for the public good. Like a challenge to the charitable status of a modern institution, such as a university or a church, the measures drafted by Gratian's advisers were explosive. The issues they raised were bound to escalate, especially after the death of Gratian at the hands of usurper in 383 left the matter unresolved.

There were those who wished this particular issue to escalate. By the time Symmachus (in his capacity as Prefect of the City) wrote his official memorandum in support of restoring funding to the Vestal Virgins—his famous *Third Relatio*—Ambrose had already become bishop of Milan. He posed as the keeper of the Christian conscience of Gratian's younger half brother, Valentinian II. He virtually threatened Valentinian II with excommunication if he gave way to Symmachus.

In intervening in this manner, Ambrose blew up the issue out of all proportion. He insisted that the disestablishment of the virgins was only a beginning. He claimed that Gratian had intended to uproot paganism in Rome in its entirety and to go back on Gratian's measures was to bring back paganism as a whole: "to set up an altar and to grant money for impious sacrifices."[46] Seldom have the implications of a bureaucratic half measure been distorted in so melodramatic a manner and with such lasting consequences, as in the confrontation between Symmachus and Ambrose in the year 384.

Ambrose's intervention made his own reputation, both in his own time and in all later centuries, as a militant Christian bishop. But in doing so Ambrose also made Symmachus's reputation. Symmachus was placed at center stage. He was presented by Ambrose as the defender of paganism as a whole. Ambrose wrote as if paganism was about to receive its coup de grâce. The more impressive a figure Symmachus cut as the defender of a doomed religion, the more spectacular would be Ambrose's victory over him. In this scenario of Christian triumph, Symmachus had to be presented as the positively last pagan. For there were to be no pagans after him. Ambrose went out his way to include a copy of Symmachus's *Third Relatio* (so-called because it was the third memorandum he had written to the emperors on the diverse issues he had handled as Prefect of the City) among his letters. It served as an introduction to the bishop's demolition of Symmachus's case. This studied juxtaposition of Symmachus and the bishop of Milan ensured that Symmachus would be remembered, in all later centuries, as the quintessential "last pagan" and his *Third Relatio* as the swan song of the religion of ancient Rome.

But Symmachus, as we have seen, had no intention of being a "last pagan." He saw himself, rather, as the first pagan. He was the first prefect to find himself dealing with an unprecedented and unwelcome situation. The majestic consensus of the Senate had been shaken by a hitherto unheard-of religious issue.

Symmachus's response was "both cautious and acute."[47] He brought to bear the weight of long-established arguments, which many Christians may have shared with their pagan colleagues. Symmachus's *Third Relatio* should not be read as the work of a die-hard pagan. Rather, it was a carefully planned attempt to regain the old consensus between pagan and Christian members of the Senate. He argued with great force that all responsible and public-spirited persons could be expected to agree that, whatever their own beliefs, the cults of Rome should continue as they had always done.[48]

What Symmachus presented as shocking, in Gratian's measure, was the implicit abandonment of an ancient maxim. In Rome, public wealth—revenues provided originally by the state—should be devoted to public worship of the gods for the protection of the city and people of Rome. The safety of the empire as a whole, and of Rome in particular, hung on the prayers of the Vestals. In the words placed on the base of a statue set up to a Vestal Virgin in the third century:

> Through her moral discipline and skillful performance of the rites, the *Respublica* [the commonwealth of Rome] has experienced from day to day a felicity due to her merit.[49]

Symmachus sincerely believed that invisible beings hovered above Rome. They had been entrusted with the "care and protection" of the city. They demanded punctilious worship: "for the benevolence of a superior power, if not maintained by worship, is lost."[50] In cutting off the support of the virgins through denying them a share in the *annona*, Gratian had interrupted the millennial exchange of wealth for blessing that had bound the gods to Rome. Only wealth that came directly from the ancient soil of Italy and its provinces, as a gift from the state, could be offered to the gods. The portion of the *annona* of Rome allotted to the Vestal Virgins did not represent a large sum. But this offering was heavy with symbolic significance. Fruits of the earth, the Vestals' share in the *annona* represented the perpetual sacred exchange between the earth and the gods, which ensured the protection of the empire and of the stupendous human settlement of Rome.

In the manner of a sacred tithe, the grain given to the Vestal Virgins out of the *annona* was believed to keep alive the fertility of the provinces that had provided it. In a world which, as we have seen, always teetered on the brink of shortages due to harvest shocks, to neglect the gods in this way was a serious matter. In 383–84 Symmachus was proved right. The cessation of the exchange of gifts between the earth of the empire and the gods was followed by a widespread drought. He warned the emperor: "Sacrilege has made the year go dry."[51]

But Symmachus did not appeal only to religious fears. The climax of his *Relatio* was a speech he placed in the mouth of Rome herself. It gave cosmic weight to the arguments of an *amator patriae* of the old school. The diversity of cities and their cults was no accident. God had allotted to each city its own guardian spirit, which hovered over its charge. These spirits gave each city its individuality and presided over its collective destiny. For this reason, religious diversity was written into the very fabric of the universe. It was the will of God that each region should be subject to its own, distinctive forms of divine care:

> Everyone has his own customs, his own religious practices. The Divine Intellect has assigned to different cities different religions to be their guardians. Each man was given at birth an individual soul. In the same way each people is given its own special genius [its guardian spirit] to take care of its destiny....
>
> For this reason we [of the Senate] ask for peace for the gods of our fathers, for the gods of our native land.... We look up at the same stars, the same sky covers us all, the same universe compasses us all.... Not by one avenue only can we arrive at so tremendous a secret.[52]

This was no vague plea for tolerance. It was a statement that religious diversity—and not religious uniformity—was part of the fabric of the universe. Christian emperors might adhere to their own sect; they did not trouble Symmachus. Like cities, they could have their own divine guides. For all we know, Symmachus, like many others in his time, may have believed that a faceless High God, unknown to the traditional pantheon, had, indeed, intervened to act as the protector of Constantine and his successors. But this God had no right to push aside his better-established divine peers—the gods of Rome.[53]

Of course, we can list Emperors of either faith and either conviction: the earlier Emperors venerated our ancestral religious rites, the later did not abolish them.[54]

What troubled Symmachus was the thought that a religious establishment as complex, massive, and deeply soaked in time as was the universe itself should be made subject to the personal whim of a single ruler, acting under pressure from a single religious faction.

On this issue, Symmachus misjudged the mood of the emperors. It was not that Gratian and Valentinian II were bigoted Christians. First and foremost, they were autocrats. The "institutionalized egotism" that was part of the late Roman imperial system left little room for delegated cults in distant cities.[55] The issue was who could claim to be closest to the beneficent power of Victory: the Senate in faraway Rome or the emperor in his palace? Hence the shrewdness of Ambrose's decision to present his battle with Symmachus as if the Altar of Victory in the Senate House (and not the privileges of the Vestal Virgins) were the central issue. It was Ambrose and not Symmachus who ensured that the debate between the bishop and the prefect has gone down to history under the misleading name of the "Altar of Victory Controversy."

Up to 382, the Senate House had contained an altar that stood before a beautiful statue of a winged Victory, first taken as loot from the city of Tarentum. This statue had been placed there by the emperor Augustus. Every session of the Senate was supposed to begin with an offering of incense at the altar, on behalf of the emperor.

For Gratian and Valentinian II, the statue of Victory and even its attendant altar were not in themselves repugnant. But they were unnecessary. A fourth-century emperor did not need to be catechized by Christian bishops, such as Ambrose, to come to this conclusion. The emperor had always been encouraged to view himself as the darling of Victory. This view was widely accepted. In 365 Symmachus's own father dedicated a bridge in honor of Gratian's father, the emperor Valentinian I. The bridge spanned the Tiber, joining Trastevere to the Campus Martius. Statues of the emperor were faced by great winged Victories in bronze. The inscription written on the parapets of the bridge hailed Victory as the *Comes*, the peculiar, divine "Companion" of the emperor.[56] In late Roman terms, Victory was the guardian angel of the emperor. She was linked to him by a bond created in heaven itself.[57] Statues of Victory appeared all over the empire at this time. But they referred to the emperor alone; no one mentioned the Senate. For Victory was the emperor's companion, wherever he found himself and in whatever city his statues were erected.[58] The emperor's Victory was placeless. It did not need to be tied down to a single building in a faraway city, where a coterie of proud nobles gathered beneath a classical work of art, as suspect, pagan smoke rose from the altar.

Symmachus's memorandum was turned down, and Ambrose's reputation rose yet further in Christian circles. But the real winner was the emperor. An autocrat in a distant court, Valentinian II made clear, in his rejection of Symmachus's memorandum, that he did not need to depend either on the Senate or on the ancient rituals performed in Rome to be sure of the unique and still numinous protection of Victory.

Yet Symmachus's defeat in 384 did not mean in any way that paganism as a whole was suppressed in Rome. Ambrose had deliberately exaggerated the extent of Gratian's measures. The Vestal Virgins were disendowed, but they continued to meet and to pray. The other pagan cults were not disestablished. The priestly colleges continued to receive donations.[59] Individual pagan worship was maintained by generous givers. As late as the end of the century, Tamesius Olympius Augentius repaired a shrine of Mithra in the area near the modern church of San Silvestro, off the Corso. It was a modest affair. But the inscription, written in small and elegant script on the back of a used block of marble, made plain that the withdrawal of imperial support had not in any way affected his piety:

> Once my ancestor Victor, devout worshipper of Heaven and the Stars, founded a temple of the Sun through royal gifts. Now his grandchild surpasses him in piety. He builds the sacred caves. Nor, Rome, does he require your funds. For the pious, loss is preferable to gain. Who can be richer than he, who, as a provident heir, shares his estate with the heavenly gods?[60]

This was not the language of Christian renunciation. Augentius did not *sell all*. Rather, it was the language of an *amator patriae*, proud to accept financial loss for the sake of his hometown, transferred, with new intensity, to his love of the gods.

Nor did the old gods vanish from Symmachus's own landscape of the heart. There was a good reason for this, built into the structures of late Roman government. Senators were encouraged to act as governors of provinces in central and southern Italy. They added their prestige as noblemen to the routine business of government. They were encouraged, in their locality, to act as viceroys of the emperor himself. They could say *L'État c'est moi*.[61] But the state represented by an old-world grandee such as Symmachus was not the new Christian empire of an Ambrose. For many senatorial governors the empire remained a largely pagan thing, and the cities they visited also remained largely pagan places.[62]

Only three years after Ambrose claimed to have defeated Symmachus, an imperial rescript was solemnly recorded on an inscription erected in the theater of Capua. The rescript declared that, in Campania at least, nothing had changed. The emperors permitted the amphitheater to be filled with roses on May 25 for the pagan festival of the *Rosalia*, held in memory of the dead. Sacred "washings" were to continue to take place in the local rivers. The accustomed procession was expected to make its way up from the city to the temple of Diana on Mons Tifata. At that temple, the pious could still view hunting trophies offered as exvotos to the goddess—antlers recently presented by a sportsman-poet and the awesome skull of an elephant, a triumphal votive gift offered by none other than the great Sulla.[63]

Nonetheless, Symmachus's landscape of the heart proved progressively less comfortable than the studiously unruffled tone of his letters implied. By the time Symmachus entered middle age, Rome had found itself robbed by imperial egotism of parts of an ancient, imaginative system that had upheld among upperclass Romans a sense of the collective majesty of their city. The more religious among the senators (Symmachus among them) felt that they faced a dangerous and fractured world, shorn of the protection of the gods. If the gods withdrew, anything might happen.

But this was not their only anxiety. As outstanding residents of Rome, Symmachus and his fellow *nobiles* found themselves caught between a *populus,* a People of Rome, whom they were supposed to love—to entertain and to feed (if only so as to sleep safely in their beds)—and a distant court, which provided, in the chillingly spasmodic fashion of any overextended bureaucracy, the material means by which this love of the people was to be shown. In our next chapter, we will see how Symmachus faced this dilemma by means of a constant (and far from happy) dialogue between himself and the People of Rome.

CHAPTER 6

❧

Avidus civicae gratiae: Greedy for the good favor of the City

Symmachus and the People of Rome

Securitas Romani populi: The safety from hunger
of the Roman People

In 370 AD the city of Rome was probably the largest human agglomeration on earth. Its population has been variously estimated at half a million to a million.[1] What can be deduced with greater certainty from official documents is that, out of this shadowy mass, 120,000 to 200,000 members of the *populus Romanus* depended (in the manner described in chapter 3) on the arrival of over 175,000 tons of grain, gathered principally from the hinterland of Africa and shipped from its coastal cities to the port of Ostia. This great levy of grain was the heart of the *annona civica*—the food supply provided for the citizens of Rome.[2]

Rome depended on this supply of food. Every year, the Prefect of Rome and the Senate could be thought of as waiting on the quays of Ostia, as the great armada of ships bearing the *annona* edged its way, all too slowly, up the coast of Italy from Africa. Ancient religiosity was real on such occasions, as they looked out anxiously over the heaving sea. This had happened in 359 AD:

> The prefect (Tertullus), who had been harassed by riots, was now faced with the threat of imminent destruction from the increasing fury of the mob . . . had he not had the wit to take his small sons and show them to the populace. . . . "These," he said with tears, "are your fellow-citizens, who will share your fate (which heaven forbid) unless our affairs take a happier turn. . . ." This pathetic speech soothed the mob . . . it fell silent, and calmly awaited its fate. Soon afterwards, through divine providence . . . while Tertullus was sacrificing in the temple of Castor and Pollux . . . . the sea became smooth and the wind changed to a light southerly breeze. The ships entered harbor under full sail and replenished the storehouses with grain.[3]

The historian Ammianus Marcellinus told this story, some forty years later, because it had a happy ending. It was an ending he could believe to have been brought about by the worship of the ancient gods. Such beliefs died slowly. Up to the sixth century, the People of Rome, led by the Prefect of Rome, would gather at the temple of Castor and Pollux at the mouth of the Tiber to celebrate "a merry festival."[4] The yearly gathering was a reminder of the fragility of a gigantic city whose principal supply of food came to it from across the sea.

The Rome of Symmachus remained overshadowed by this stupendous legacy inherited from the classical past. Ever since the time of Augustus, it was the emperor who showed that he was the greatest *amator patriae* of all. As the leading citizen of Rome, he expressed his overwhelming love for the People of Rome by making available to the citizens of Rome an annual supply of grain. The grain had originally been shipped both from Africa and Egypt; but in the fourth century, Constantinople received the grain of Egypt, leaving Rome to make do largely with that from Africa and southern Italy.[5]

Though it might appear headlong in its generosity, we must always remember that the *annona civica* was never given to the population of Rome as a whole. As its name made plain, it was a bluntly "civic" affair; it had nothing to do with poor relief. The only recipients of the emperor's bounty were the registered citizens of Rome. They carried passports—leaden tesserae—to prove their entitlement.[6] Lists of their names and the amounts of their rations were set up at all points of distribution. To the *annona* of grain, later emperors had added substantial rations of pork and wine. These were not distributed free but were sold at reduced prices. No citizen could live off the rations provided by the *annona* alone.[7] But the distributions of bread and other foodstuffs to the registered citizens of Rome through the *annona* conveyed an enviable privilege. In a Mediterranean haunted by the fear of famine and by perpetual shortages of food, they alone enjoyed the time-honored *securitas Romani populi*: guaranteed safety from hunger.[8]

The *annona* had originally been set in place when the emperors resided in Rome. But by the fourth century things had changed. The emperors lived hundreds of miles from Rome in cities such as Trier, Milan, Constantinople, and Antioch. Rome was like a gigantic nuclear power plant inherited from earlier, more heedless generations. It was now entrusted to a skeleton staff and could explode at any moment. The Prefect of the City and the Senate were left alone (as Tertullus had been left in 359) to face the demands and recriminations of the Roman people. And now that the emperor's Praetorian Guard had been abolished, they found themselves confronted by a city of at least half a million inhabitants with a greatly diminished police force.[9] Fourth-century Rome has often been spoken of as no more than a "museum city," a "theme park" of the Roman past. It was no such thing. It was a perilous laboratory of aristocratic rule to which urban elites all over the Roman world looked for both encouragement and warnings of what could go wrong in their own city.

In later chapters we will follow the working out of this dilemma. It is sufficient for the moment to concentrate on Symmachus. For, from his earliest years, the life of Symmachus was deeply implicated in the vicissitudes of the food supply of Rome. The many incidents revealed to us by Symmachus's letters summed up the dilemma of an entire group of nobles. Intensely aware of their privileges, the People of Rome could not be suppressed. They could only be controlled by appearing to be loved. The nobles were encouraged to shine as "lovers of the homeland" if only so as to patrol their city. They used every device of patronage and largesse to hold in check the population of a murmurous mega-city. And yet, no matter how much they were encouraged to cut a fine figure in Rome, they were also all too frequently reminded that their love of their fellow citizens depended, ultimately, on the emperors. For it was the emperors who provided the food for the city and the funds for most of its games.[10]

The yearly collection and transport of the *annona* was both costly and easily mismanaged. It took constant effort to ensure that the gigantic spasm of organization that took place every year to feed the privileged People of Rome worked as it should. Only by putting constant pressure on top politicians and bureaucrats could the senators of Rome be certain that enough food would arrive. In this situation, Symmachus' gifts as a lobbyist came into their own. His friends in high places were constantly mobilized to ensure that the "Sacred Ears" of the emperor always heard about the needs of Rome.[11]

In a letter written in 389, Symmachus reported in euphoric terms on the safe arrival of the *annona* at the wharves of Rome. Looking down "on our dear Tiber" from a villa near Ostia, he wrote that he could watch the grain barges as they made their way up the river, bearing the precious grain on the last stage of its journey from distant regions:

> I see with pleasure what grain arrives day by day, and what supplies from Macedonia [from northern Greece and the Vardar valley of the southern Balkans] have been brought into the warehouses of Rome. For, as you remember, because of delays in Africa, famine was almost at our doorstep, when our most clement emperor, born for the salvation of all, prevented it, through mobilizing levies from this other area.[12]

The arrival of the emergency consignment was presented by Symmachus as a triumph of persistent lobbying on his part. In this way, the spider's web that Symmachus had woven over the years was set to work not for himself and his protégés but on behalf of the city of Rome as a whole. To secure food for Rome Symmachus reached out to persons in very high places. The recipient of this particular letter was the Frankish career general Ricomer. Ricomer belonged to the distant world of the court and of the frontiers. But Symmachus went out of his way to share with the great barbarian news of the pleasant view from the banks of the Tiber. Symmachus invited Ricomer (as a good friend and colleague, of course) to share with him "in the joy of us all." He also reminded Ricomer to be sure to tell "the Lord of the World" of the safe arrival of the grain.[13] What the letters of Symmachus make plain is that the annual arrival of supplies at Rome involved a yearly miracle—a miracle of organization spurred on by a miracle of lobbying. And this lobbying assumed that it was the emperor (and not the gods Castor and Pollux) who was the true "god" who stilled the waves and brought food to Rome.[14]

Vilis plebeius: A low-down creature of the *plebs*

Symmachus was proud to record his interventions on behalf of the People of Rome. Indeed, the record of his relations with the *populus Romanus* (which was also referred to as the *plebs Romana*) was the theme that called for the most strenuous celebration of all in his collected letters. If, however, we look at the situation in which Symmachus found himself, we realize that this was no easy task; it was fraught with real danger. We first meet Symmachus after his family had suffered a major mishap. In one of his earliest letters, written in 376, he reported that his father had withdrawn from Rome to the countryside "so as to simmer down after the loss of his palace."[15] Ammianus Marcellinus tells us what had happened. Sometime in 374–5, the Roman people, with whom Symmachus's father had once been popular, turned on the family:

> They set fire to his beautiful palace across the Tiber [in what is now Traste-vere] enraged by a story invented without a shred of evidence by some low down creature of the *plebs* (a *vilis plebeius*), that Symmachus [the elder] had said that he would rather use all his wine to pour on his lime-kilns than sell it at the reduced prices that the people hoped for.[16]

The incident was a violent reminder of what a nobleman's traditional constituency—the People of Rome—could do. As we have seen, the People of Rome were not a faceless body. They were by no means the poorest of the poor: they had been pulled out from the mass of the inhabitants of Rome so as to receive the privilege of the *annona*. But neither were the People of Rome a body of entirely "free" citizens, obliged to no one. They were linked by overwhelming economic bonds to the upper-class residents of the city. These bonds were strenuously maintained through patronage and through the nobility's control of rental properties in the city. Those who were not clients of the nobility were very often dependent on them as tenants. Extensive patronage exercised by the great families of Rome (which reached right down the social scale through noble patronage of the trade associations of the city) was what kept the city quiet on a day-to-day basis. But it was precisely their "civic" status that ensured that large numbers of the people of Rome were far from being subservient clients. They were members of the ancient *plebs Romana*. Somewhat like the Westminster Mob in eighteenth-century London, this membership gave them a formidable privilege. They enjoyed the "right to riot." When they burned the palace of the Symmachi, they used this right to riot in no uncertain manner on a crucial issue—their entitlement to food.[17]

The *plebs* felt justified in burning noble mansions. The emphasis Symmachus placed on his abiding concern for the successful arrival of the *annona* only told half the story. For he and his peers faced a conflict of interests. The wealth of the great landowners in southern Italy, Sicily, and Africa was due largely to the fact that Rome still provided them with a market of unparalleled size for the sale of the agrarian produce of their own estates. It was sale to the cities (especially to the city of Rome) of huge quantities of grain, wine, and pork that helped men such as Symmachus generate, every year, stunning sums of gold.[18] As landowners, they could make large profits from selling the produce of their estates on the open market. Yet as "lovers of the city" and as administrators of the imperial *annona*, they were forced to flood the city with food at cheap rates that had been fixed by the imperial bureaucracy in the interests of the Roman people.

Hence the rage with which the Roman people had rounded on the elder Symmachus. His proud remark had challenged the ancient mystique on which the relationship between a lover of the city and his people depended. The *plebs* argued that if the old man had truly regarded the Roman people as "his" people, he would have seen them as fellow citizens. He would have helped ensure that they received the benefit of cheap wine (sold, probably, at a discount of around 25 percent). He should have sold the produce of his vineyards at low prices subject to imperial price-fixing. Instead, he treated them as mere customers. He forced them to buy his wine at high prices set by him alone.[19]

Avidus civicae gratiae: Greedy for the good favor of the city

The burning of his father's palace when he was a young man was, perhaps, the most significant tremor known to us in the world of Symmachus. It revealed the tensions that underlay the seemingly placid surface of a nobleman's existence. It put the rest of Symmachus's life in perspective. We know Symmachus best as the author of the defense of the privileges of the Vestal Virgins. But his defense of traditional paganism was only a side issue, connected with his short tenure as urban prefect. By contrast, a tense dialogue with the people of Rome was the very stuff of life for him and his peers.

The dialogue reached its climax in the last years of his life. Twenty years after the burning of his father's palace, Symmachus had a chance to engage in a distinctly more euphoric interchange with the people of Rome. In 393, his son, Memmius, made his debut as a senator by taking on the ancient office of quaestor. The young Memmius solemnly presided at the age of ten over the *quaestura*—the quaestor's games. The organization of the games on behalf of his son gave Symmachus the opportunity to shine before "his" people. Eight years later, in 401, Memmius went on to celebrate the yet more spectacular *praetura*—the praetor's games. These last were deliberately postponed so that Symmachus (who had to attend a court function in Milan) should be seen sitting beside his son, in full view of the Roman people when the games were given.[20]

The sums Symmachus spent on the praetor's games of Memmius in 401 made his reputation. A whole generation later he was remembered as having spent 2,000 pounds of gold on them.[21] This amounted to one-third again of Symmachus's entire revenue for one year—which was 1,500 pounds of gold. It was 400 pounds of gold more than the Senate as a whole had once given as a New Year's gift to the emperor Valentinian I. It was also the equivalent of a year's rations for 130,000 recipients of the *annona*.[22]

The giving of the games involved the sudden release of an avalanche of wealth devoted to nothing other than the joy of the Roman people. Or so Symmachus said. In reality, the games were the tip of an iceberg. They not only displayed the financial muscle of those who gave them. For someone such as Symmachus, this in itself was no great matter. Saved for in advance, with ten years' notice, the praetor's games did not ruin those who paid for them.[23] But the games were the testing point of a nobleman's influence. They were the crowning demonstration of his *potentia*—his ability to get things done.[24] Only the truly great could give truly great games. This was why Symmachus wished to be known as *avidus civicae gratiae*: "greedy for the good favor of the city." He could display his wealth and influence by ensuring that the *plebs* of Rome got nothing but the best.[25]

To this end, he petitioned insistently for the right to exceed the financial limits usually placed on a praetor's games. As Prefect of the City, in 384, he had written a memorandum that condemned the "ugly ostentatiousness" of rich senators, whose costly displays had made lesser senators (often "new" men) unwilling to put on games of their own. On that occasion, he spoke as a bureaucrat.[26] He did not apply this maxim to himself. His edgy relationship with the "new men" of the Senate came out only too clearly in his letters on the games of his son. He wanted to show such people who was a true noble of Rome and who was not. He asked the court for permission to hold a theatrical display in a flooded amphitheater. He also asked for permission to reward the performers with silk robes. He wanted to use the mighty Colosseum itself.[27] Altogether, Symmachus was determined that his lesser colleagues—the newly minted members of the Senate—would feel the weight of his fortune.

Romani animi speciosum calorem: The fine ardor of a Roman soul

Technically, it was the Roman emperors who were the lords of the games at Rome. Of the 177 days a year set aside for games and festivals, 98 were devoted to the history of the emperors and to the triumphs of the reigning dynasty.[28] All these games were paid for by the absent emperors. Each year, however, the emperors yielded a space for men like Symmachus to win glory for their sons. The time allotted to the games of the praetor was short—a little over a week. But while the imperial games tended to lose pace as they dragged on throughout the year, the young praetor could bring in a magic week of games, which coincided with the summer season of the year.[29]

We must remember what these games meant to the "Roman people" who witnessed them. They consolidated the ancient bond between *plebs* and Senate. The nobility turned out in force to attend these games. They sat, family by family, arranged in hierarchical ranks on the benches of the Colosseum and the Circus Maximus. But the games themselves were more than a grand parade of the nobility. They were a time of wonder for all. Huge stocks of gold evaporated in a week so that the amphitheater could be turned into a place of miracles. For a blessed moment, the rules of normal life were held in suspense. Tightrope walkers and ballet dancers defied gravity in vertiginous leaps. Land and sea were joined, as specially constructed amphitheaters filled up with water for naval spectacles. Great organs played as the hot crowd was drenched in fountains of perfumed water.[30]

Above all, the animal world poured into the midst of the city. And what an animal world! Symmachus went out of his way to bring them all to Rome. Crocodiles from the Nile[31] and bears from the Balkans;[32] great Irish wolfhounds brought all the way from Britain in iron cages;[33] lions from the southern mountains of north Africa;[34] antelopes and gazelles trapped along the edges of the Sahara.[35] There was no frontier of the Roman empire not represented by this parade of exotic beasts. Their sheer diversity amounted to a celebration of the immensity of the Roman world.[36] Like the empire itself, their capture and eventual slaughter represented a triumph of human order over a savage world.[37]

Most beasts were lethal. They were destined to be slaughtered by skilled *venatores*—fearless huntsmen, armed with pikes, who were (as we have seen) the matadors of the classical world. And this was done in a solemn mood. What happened in the circus and the amphitheater was more than a blood sport. It was a fortifying lesson in the triumph of civilization. It celebrated the victory of human energy, human skill, and human courage over the wild. For this reason human animals also made their appearance. Like the animals, they were also destined for slaughter. As quaestor, little Memmius received imperial permission to use the Colosseum for a show more ancient and more deadly than was usual for the average quaestor. Saxon prisoners of war were sent to Rome to serve as gladiators, condemned to fight to the death in front of the Roman people. The deaths of vile pirates who had been rounded up along the coasts of the English Channel were intended to make plain, in the middle of Rome, the most magical of all energies— the eternal victory of empire along the frontiers of the North.[38]

We know of all of this from Symmachus's letters concerning the two games of his son, Memmius—those he put on as quaestor, in 393, and the yet more magnificent shows of the praetor in 401. It is one of the few times that we are able to look behind the façade of ancient euergetism. Symmachus's letters on this topic do not always do him credit. His largesse was less exuberant than he claimed. In the same letter in which he declared himself to be "greedy for the good favor of the city," he wrote that he had promised twenty slaves in all to the stables of the rival circus teams of Rome. Could his daughter's father-in-law (in the midst of preparing to fight a civil war) please look out for slaves on the frontier? Slaves were cheaper there. "Choose them for their age and good health, not for their looks."[39]

What we see above all is unceasing anxiety. Nothing seemed to go right. Bears promised from the Balkans were delayed; only a few starved cubs reached Italy. The emperor had to be petitioned for a grant of lions to save the day.[40] Of a consignment of crocodiles, hurried up from Egypt along the coast of Sicily, all but two died of starvation.[41] Worst of all, a disaster took place such as only the teachings of Socrates had allowed him to weather with an unshaken mind: the twenty-nine Saxons committed suicide, strangling each other with their own hands in their prison cells! So much for that rebellious "band of slaves worse than any Spartacus." He would have to petition the emperor, once again, for yet more lions.[42]

At second glance, however, these letters represent (as they must have done to those who read them at a later time) the triumph of the world Symmachus had wrapped around himself with such care over the course of so many decades. There was hardly a single correspondent, high or low, who was not given the opportunity, by Symmachus, to put the seal upon their friendship through granting him some favor—some *industria*, some personal burst of energy in high or distant places on behalf of his preparations—that would make the great event shine.[43] Symmachus's circle of correspondents were offered the chance to put their "handprint," as a class, upon the glory of one of their members. Symmachus implied that he would do the same for them when their turn came. From negotiations that led to the waiving of customs duties on Dalmatian bears[44] to the little silver baskets and exquisite ivory tablets distributed as gestures of thanks and celebration to senatorial friends and to high dignitaries of the court (the emperor, of course, received his tablet framed in gold),[45] these letters document the heady torrent of gifts and mutual favors that bound together the rich and powerful of his age.[46]

Symmachus reached out in all directions. He called in favors, he prodded clients, he browbeat administrators. But it was not simply a matter of power. Throughout the western Mediterranean, the games of Rome had remained exemplary. They were the model on which innumerable civic notables still based their own appearances before the people of their own cities. These men were less wealthy than Symmachus. They might substitute local bears for exotic crocodiles and boxing matches for the deadly clash of gladiators.[47] But the spirit was the same. Everywhere might be a little Rome and every giver of games a little Symmachus.

This happened all over the West. Fourth-century mosaics show the Circus Maximus on the floors of villas as far apart as Piazza Armerina, in the middle of Sicily, and in Gerona, on the northeastern coast of Spain. At Gerona, a figure sits at the head of the circus, in a special box, extending his right hand in a triumphant gesture.[48] The charioteers, the *venatores*, and the spectacular racing horses associated both with local games and with the games at Rome appear both in Carthage and in distant Mérida.[49] In Spain and Africa, one suspects that the games of the great senators of Rome led to an annual flow of gold to inland provinces in order to buy horses and wild beasts.[50] The imaginative range of the games was even wider. Far to the north, in distant northern Britain, on the mosaic of the villa of Rudston in the East Riding of Yorkshire, a panel shows a *toro bravo* of the amphitheater—a clumsily drawn circus bull labeled "Homicide."[51]

Through his son, Symmachus stood at the peak of a pyramid of admiration. For a moment, the entire western world had become part of the glory of his family. And it was an ancient glory, which suited the possessor of ancient wealth. In 399 he wrote to a rancher in distant Spain, from whom he hoped to buy pedigree horses for the chariot races associated with the games:

> I do not think that I need to fear that you will take me for someone interested only in the praise of persons of the *plebs*. You are wise enough to know that tight-fisted attitudes do not suit the magistracies of a great city. You know your Cicero: even he laid down that, in private life, high-spending luxury was to be condemned, but not magnificence in public matters. For this reason, help to the full extent of your resources the fine ardor of a Roman soul.[52]

Within a little over three years, Symmachus was dead. He died after his return from one last embassy from the Senate of Rome to the court at Milan in 402. The embassy had been a rushed affair, undertaken in the middle of winter. For the Gothic troops of Alaric had crossed the Alps and had begun to probe the defenses of Italy. The Senate wanted to make sure, once again, that the emperor would not forget them in a time of crisis.

By 402 much had happened in the world outside Rome. Ambrose of Milan was the same age as Symmachus. He had become bishop of Milan in 374, when Symmachus was in his thirties. Symmachus outlived Ambrose by six years. Younger men had also begun to come to the fore. Augustine had been chosen by Symmachus in 384 (when he was acting as Prefect of the City) to be a teacher of rhetoric in Milan. Augustine returned to Africa a changed man. As bishop of Hippo, he wrote his *Confessions* only a few years before Symmachus died.

The world had begun to change. Wealth, abandoned by high aristocrats, slipped into the church. By 402 a man whose social position was closer to that of Symmachus than was that of any other Christian—the nobleman Paulinus—had begun to rebuild, at Nola, in the heart of Symmachus's beloved Campania, a Christian shrine, whose inlaid marbles (quite as sumptuous as those of the Anician palace) have recently caused amazement to the archaeologist. In Ambrose, Augustine, and Paulinus of Nola, governmental know-how, high culture, and great wealth entered the upper reaches of the Christian churches in such a way as to usher in a new epoch in the history of Latin Christianity.

But it is to Symmachus's letters that we still turn to measure the density of a way of life that only Christians such as Ambrose, Augustine, and Paulinus claimed (somewhat unconvincingly) to be out-of-date. Symmachus was by no means out-of-date. He was not the "last" of anything. Rather, he was a reminder of the resilience of a social order that had only recently found a place for ambitious Christians. It was these newcomers who were strange. Symmachus, by contrast, was as familiar and as solid as the warm stones on which we can still read the ancient phrases of honorific addresses. Symmachus was the way the world worked. In cities and villas all over the West, the majority of the rich still wished to be like Symmachus, a man of his city, still endowed with "the fine ardor of a Roman soul." But not everyone thought that way. Let us now turn to Ambrose, Augustine, and Paulinus to trace the new images of society and the new views on the proper use of wealth with which each one of them grappled—each in a different manner—as a result of their commitment to the Christian church.

CHAPTER 7

꙳

Ambrose and His People

Pro vestro speciali fastu: Typical of your noble airs

FROM GOVERNOR TO BISHOP

With hindsight, it is difficult to realize the extent to which the election of Ambrose as bishop of Milan in 374 and his subsequent activities as a public figure, up to his death in 397, came as a surprise. His election was an unforeseen event whose impact on the Christian churches of the West was both a symptom and a cause of changes in the texture of Christianity that were more decisive, in the long run, than had been the conversion of Constantine in 312 AD. This chapter and the next will concentrate on the nature of Ambrose's impact. They will trace the manner in which Ambrose created a novel power base for himself among the people of Milan. They will also sketch the image of society Ambrose proposed (in intimate dialogue with the works of Cicero) as the basis of this daring alliance between bishop and people. Last but not least, chapter 8 will examine the relation between Ambrose's general stance toward society and his vivid denunciations of the rich of northern Italy.

Little of this could have been foreseen in the late 370s. What was certain was that the empire itself had entered into a new phase of crisis. On August 9, 378, the emperor Valens, along with the major part of the eastern army of the Roman empire, vanished into a heavy cloud of red dust thickened by bush fires and was trampled to death by the Visigoths on the plains outside Adrianople. The effects of a military catastrophe at the farthest end of the Balkans (outside modern Edirne, in European Turkey) were immediately felt in Italy. It seemed for a moment as if only the Alps, their passes hurriedly blocked with felled trees, stood between Milan and the barbarians. Prudent and collegial as ever, Quintus Aurelius Symmachus approached an acquaintance in Rome. He advised Uranius Satyrus (a man roughly his own age and, like himself, a former provincial governor) not to go north. Northern Italy, he said, "was aflame with war." Satyrus, however, did not take Symmachus's advice. He was hurrying to Milan with news of the family estates to report to his younger brother, Aurelius Ambrosius.[1]

Ambrosius (whom we know as Saint Ambrose) had become bishop of Milan in 374. Of all the leading figures of the Latin church, Ambrose is the most difficult to see in true perspective. Hindsight has made him seem, at one and the same time, both larger than life and strangely unremarkable.

He is principally known to us as the bishop who brought to heel a succession of emperors. It was Ambrose who (as we have seen) blocked the petition of Symmachus on behalf of the Vestal Virgins in 384 by a direct appeal to the boy prince Valentinian II. Between 385 and 386 he shamed the court by refusing to yield a church in Milan for the use of the "Arian" members of Valentinian's entourage. In 391 he imposed on the emperor Theodosius a memorable penance for the massacre of civilians at Thessalonica in 390. As a result of these dramatic confrontations, an air of baroque drama has come to surround his person. When visiting the Duomo—the cathedral—of Milan in 1764, Edward Gibbon noticed the wooden bas-reliefs in the choir that portrayed the actions of Saint Ambrose:

> The work is of great beauty, and I imagine that every ecclesiastic must consider with pleasure the scene where the great emperor Theodosius is humbled at the feet of a proud prelate.[2]

Yet we have come to take Ambrose's successes for granted. We expect him to be a "proud prelate" and we expect him to be successful in this role. The language he used in humbling the emperors entered the mainstream of western Catholicism, and his sonorous certainties were echoed by all later Catholic prelates. As a result, they have ceased to be surprising. We forget that this was the very first time that a Latin bishop had raised his voice in such a tone when dealing directly with an emperor and that these certainties were first enunciated in situations where Ambrose was far from certain of success.

The image of Ambrose is further blurred by his association in the popular mind with Saint Augustine. Ambrose is often treated as little more than the bishop who "converted" Augustine to Catholicism in 386–7. He becomes a vague authority figure, overshadowed by the brilliant young Augustine. Yet, as we shall see, the two men barely overlapped. When he was in Milan, Augustine saw Ambrose only from the outside: "Ambrose himself I thought a happy man as the world judges things, for he was held in honor by the great and powerful."[3]

It is the aim of this chapter to trace the manner in which Ambrose built up for himself a position in Milan so that, though a mere Christian bishop, he came to be "held in honor by the great and powerful." It will concentrate on only that aspect of his life as a bishop and leave to one side Ambrose's role in high politics.

It will also deal selectively with the baffling richness of Ambrose's preaching. Instead, it will try to gain a clearer sense of what it meant for a bishop of upper-class background to link up with a Christianity hitherto characterized (especially in northern Italy) by a low social profile. For it was precisely through his acceptance and elaboration of the links that held him to a large and predominantly "middling" congregation that Ambrose was able to create a power base for himself in Milan. In the words of Wolfgang Liebeschuetz:

> It is fashionable to belittle the seemingly astonishing political feats of Ambrose, but there can surely be no doubt that he gained a remarkable hold over a large part of the population of Milan. Without that his defiance of the court [on the occasions we have mentioned] would have been impossible.[4]

The career of Ambrose shows that the entry of members of the upper classes into the affairs of the churches was not a mere "takeover" of Christianity by the rich. It was a novel alliance that joined different layers of late Roman society to form a hitherto unprecedented grouping. We need only compare Ambrose with Symmachus in these crucial decades. While the great Symmachus teetered, as if on high stilts, far above the turbulent People of Rome, Ambrose bonded directly with his "people." He could claim that, as bishop of Milan, he had gathered around himself an entire *populus*—an entire "Christian people." Led by a bishop such as Ambrose, a new force had entered the cities of the Roman world.

In the early 370s, however, this development lay in the future. Ambrose had come to Milan (in around 370) as *consularis*—as governor of "consular" rank of the joint province of Aemilia and Liguria. His ordination as bishop of Milan three years later, in 374, came as a complete surprise. It was a sociological anomaly. It could only have happened at a time when the church system created by the "Arian" policies of Constantius II (and largely continued by the emperor Valentinian I) had begun to break down. Ambrose was not only the first aristocratic bishop in the Latin West. He was the first great faction fighter to find himself at the head of a major see close to the center of power. His ordination represented the victory of an ultra-Nicene group. Alienated and fierce for power, this group presented themselves (as we have seen) as the true upholders of the Trinitarian doctrine declared at the Council of Nicaea in 325. They were prepared to brand all opponents as "Arians." But the ordination of Ambrose did not represent a straightforward victory of Catholicism over Arianism. It opened the way to a more decisive long-term development. It marked the beginning of the end of the low-profile Christianity of the previous generations, to which we were introduced in chapter 2.[5]

Not all of this was apparent at the time. Until challenged by the direct presence of the imperial court, which did not settle in Milan until 383, Ambrose handled the "Arian" legacy in his own city with tact. But what was immediately apparent to contemporaries was that Ambrose was not an ordinary bishop. He was still bathed in the aura of a senatorial governorship.[6] It is even possible that the robes Ambrose wore on festive occasions have been preserved. Known as the "Dalmatics of Saint Ambrose," they are the robes of a nobleman. They are made of precious silk. One of them is a damask cloak woven with scenes from a lion hunt, such as was fashionable at the time among the senators of Rome.[7]

Furthermore, Ambrose was rich. He brought to Milan the wealth of an entire family. Ambrose's elder sister, Marcellina, had been consecrated as a nun in 357. She was content with an annuity from the family estates. Ambrose was celibate. Though a layman, his brother Satyrus also refused to marry. No heir could claim a share of the family lands. With this wealth, Ambrose endowed the church of Milan, though he may well have kept some of it back for his private use. In the tradition of a civic benefactor, he used this private wealth to leave a personal mark on the church through almsgiving and ambitious building projects.[8] The poor of the church were said to have received their alms in gold coins (at a time when the scattering of gold coins to the crowd was a privilege usually reserved for emperors alone).[9] By 385 Ambrose had already built one large basilica on the outskirts of Milan. It was the burial place of Satyrus and was intended to be the burial place of Ambrose himself. It came to be known, simply, as the *Ambrosiana*— Ambrose's church.[10]

Ambrose's ecclesiastical enemies were the first to realize what they were up against. When the "Arian" Palladius was summoned by Ambrose to Aquileia to give an account of his faith, in 381, he claimed that he had expected a debate among equals, conducted in an assembly room open to the general public. Instead, he was ushered into a narrow, closed hall—the *secretarium* (audience hall) of the local bishop. Built with an apse at one end, it resembled a governor's courtroom. Stenographers stood ready to record every word. Ambrose sat on a raised throne in the apse. From this throne, set up *pro vestro speciali fastu*—"typical of your noble airs"—Ambrose proceeded to browbeat Palladius as if he were a Roman governor interrogating a criminal. This was Ambrose in action—a man determined to bring to an end the compromises of an earlier, less demanding age.[11]

But exactly what sort of nobleman was Ambrose? It is important to be precise. As we have already seen, the late Roman nobility was made up of many layers. Symmachus had approached Satyrus as a *parens*. But this does not mean that their families were related. *Parens* was a term of courtesy, used of each other by members of the upper classes, much as *cher cousin* was used in modern times among entirely unrelated European monarchs. The two families did not meet as equals. Unlike Symmachus, Ambrose did not represent old money. He had been born in Trier in 339, the son of an acting Praetorian Prefect. His father was one of those many persons who had sought "nobility" through government service under the sons of Constantine. He vanished with the fall of his emperor—executed as a traitor in a time of civil war. Ambrose grew up in Rome with his widowed mother. He was a member of a Christian family come down in the world in interesting circumstances.[12]

The later empire was filled with recently ennobled families whose offspring trembled on the edge of downward mobility. The fact that the imperial bureaucracy provided careers for persons of non-noble status is well-known and has been much studied. But the governmental machine also drew on young nobles anxious to avoid slipping back into genteel poverty. And government service was not for amateurs. Ambrose went for the "hard" sciences. Unlike Symmachus, "the orator" who was content to shine only in Latin, Ambrose mastered Greek. He also mastered Roman law and probably dabbled in theology and philosophy. Like many laypersons, he may have taken sides in the theological conflicts of his time with greater zeal than did any clergyman. Altogether, drawn from a less secure and hence more strenuous layer of the aristocracy, Ambrose had the makings of a faction fighter. Once he became bishop of Milan, the issue was whether he would carry the city with him in a new mood of intransigence.

Libertatis laetitia: The rejoicing of a free people

AMBROSE AND THE CHURCH OF MILAN

We should not be misled by the confident tone of Ambrose's own letters and preaching. The Christian congregation of Milan was never a creation of Ambrose's will alone; nor was it held together only from the top down, by his own forceful style of leadership. It was a community waiting to happen. In the conditions of a city such as late fourth-century Milan, a Christian church met a real need. As we have seen, a Christian church might have appealed to many as a sort of sociological urban lung. In a society where the elites and the subelites were more than usually fragmented and set in competition one with each other, a church provided a space where groups of different background could come together. The hard outlines of status (which cut so sharply in the outside world) were softened within its walls. Not only were potentially conflicting segments of the privileged classes brought together in a benign environment. The formation of vertical links between the great, the not so great, and the "middling" plebeians—not to mention the poor—was actively encouraged.

These vertical links had always meant much to Romans. The great faction leaders of the republic had known how to be close to the *plebs*. But times had changed. The discomfiture of Symmachus's family at Rome showed that noblemen may have lost their touch. They were less skilled at establishing vertical links with the *plebs Romana*. But the nobles of Rome lived in a real city. Their relation to the *plebs* was soured by conflicts related to the supply of basic foodstuffs. A Christian church was different. What happened in it was not quite real and, for just that reason, doubly precious to those who had to face a tension-ridden world. Vertical links with all classes could be thought to exist (if only for a few hours each week) in the weight-free space of an assembly of the "people of God."

We must remember that Milan offered Ambrose more than usually malleable human material for the creation of such a community. As Neil McLynn has pointed out (in what are some of the most perceptive pages in a brilliant book), Milan was a city more than usually full of well-to-do strangers and of persons without a secure niche in society.[13] Milan was a somewhat faceless town. It did not boast a firmly rooted class of town councillors, drawn from a circle of long-established local landowners, as was the case in many cities in Roman Africa, central and southern Italy, and southwestern Gaul. Nor was there a strong aristocratic presence. Real noblemen, such as Symmachus, came and went; they did not reside in Milan. With the arrival of the court, in 383, Milan became a city of minor bureaucrats and of provision merchants.[14] Ambitious provincials lingered impatiently on the edge of the court. Beneath this fragile crust lay a solid class of "middling" persons—such as the maker of textiles whose clumsy sarcophagus stands at the entrance of the museum of the Castello Sforzesco. On this sarcophagus, wool tunics are shown, hung out for display outside the owner's shop. Beneath these plebeians were the "poor." They were probably present in manageable quantities in Milan—unlike the heartrending masses of great cities, such as Rome, Antioch, and Alexandria. All these were, to use McLynn's phrase, "Ambrose's People."

Between the summer of 385 and Easter Sunday (April 5) of 386, this "people" received its baptism of fire. The issue was whether the emperor had the right to assign a church to be used for public worship by non-Catholic members of his court—in this case, by Gothic soldiers and by the entourage of the empress mother, Justina, who were known "Arians." By the standards of the old Constantinian establishment, Valentinian II and his advisers were entirely within their rights. The church of Milan was a more than usually imperial church. The grand cathedral of Milan had been built by Constantius II. It has been argued that the so-called Basilica Portiana was what is now the splendid circular church of San Lorenzo. No certainty exists on this identification, but, wherever the Basilica Portiana may have been, by refusing to allow any church in Milan to be used by non-Catholics, despite the fact that some of the grandest of these churches had been built by "Arian" emperors, Ambrose showed "nerve" in both senses of the word.[15]

Asked for a church, Ambrose first appealed to a sense of sacrality that was worthy of Symmachus. He replied that churches were "temples." They were holy things and could not be allotted at the whim of an emperor as if they were neutral public spaces.[16] But Ambrose did what Symmachus could not have done: he brought out the crowd. A demonstration in which military force had to be used followed Ambrose's first visit to the palace.[17] Within the crowded basilica, the decisions connected with the bishop's campaign were made by acclamation. In this way, Ambrose's congregation acted as if it was a fully constituted *populus*, assembled in the theater. The proposals of imperial messengers were greeted by the roar of a well-organized crowd.[18] According to Ambrose's enemies, the poor were mobilized, through lavish distributions of gold coin, to act as a militia for the bishop.[19]

For weeks on end, the basilicas were filled with the sounds of war. The traditional readings of the Psalms were replaced by antiphonal chanting, where one group answered the other, as if in the rhythmic slogans used by the people in the theater.[20] Then Ambrose introduced the singing of hymns that he himself had composed. These made complex theological issues widely accessible in the form of memorable verses that could be sung by all. The bishop told his congregation that through chanting such hymns, everyone could be a "teacher"—an instant theologian, like himself.[21] In the course of this confrontation, Ambrose had created "an intellectual community with a wide public to a degree unusual in the ancient world."[22]

The court withdrew its claims, but the sound continued in the Christian basilicas of Milan. Looking back, around 390, Ambrose conjured up the heady sense of community generated by the chanting of the Psalms.

> [A Psalm expresses] the praises of a *plebs*, the applause of all ... the rejoicing of a free people—*libertatis laetitia*—... It is indeed a great bond of unity, by which the *plebs* gathers together with one voice.[23]

Sitting in the Colosseum with little Memmius (at almost this time), Symmachus could not have expected better from the *plebs Romana*, which he had brought together for a passing moment and at such ruinous expense. Ambrose did it every week, through chanting and theology in the miniature but magic theater of a Christian church.

"A Call to Duty"

CICERO, AMBROSE, AND THE *DE OFFICIIS*, 388

In around 388, Ambrose summed up the previous fifteen years of his life as a bishop. He wrote the *De officiis*—"On Duties."[24] The book might better be called "A Call to Duty." In it, Ambrose set himself up to rival and to replace the *De officiis* of the great Cicero. It amounted to a statement of the role of the Christian bishop in Roman society.

In writing his own *De officiis*, Ambrose deliberately echoed Cicero point by point. Cicero had written the *De officiis* for his son, Laelius. Ambrose wrote for his "spiritual sons"—primarily for the clergy of Milan and for the circle of like-minded bishops whom he had gathered around him. Like Cicero's Laelius, they must learn to be public men. Like Laelius, Ambrose's "sons"—the clergy—were expected to usher in "a renaissance of sound leadership."[25] This meant, in effect, that Ambrose went out of his way to ensure that his bishops and clergy would not be like the clergy of an earlier, more relaxed generation. He made clear that they were not to involve themselves in trade or business. He declared that it was best for a priest to gain his living either from the church alone or from "his own little bit of land." It is a coy phrase. When a late Roman writer wrote "little bit" he or she usually meant "quite a lot." Ambrose expected that some bishops and clergymen, at least, would be independently wealthy persons drawn from the upper ranks of the town councils.[26]

He also expected them to be celibate. Married bishops and clergymen were normal. But even they were expected to abstain from sex with their wives once they had been ordained. Ambrose implied (in the face of all the evidence, which points to widespread clerical marriage) that only "backwoods" communities accepted married men as their bishops and priests.[27]

We should not make too much of Ambrose's program for the "gentrification" of the clergy, as he sketched it out in the *De officiis*. The patient work of Claire Sotinel has shown that the bishops and clergy of Italy remained as a whole essentially "middling" men. They did not become little Ambroses overnight.[28] But the social history of the region around Milan in these decades may have worked in favor of Ambrose's ambitious program. The court began to reside frequently in Milan. In a characteristically late Roman manner, the presence of the Roman state, as the most powerful consumer of all, stimulated the economy of the region.[29] Towns that up until then had only harbored low-profile Christian communities found themselves on the *annona* routes that brought supplies to the court and to the army. These routes crossed the Po valley, westward toward Vercelli and Turin and north, over the Alpine passes, through Brescia, Verona, and Trent. The redecoration of villas around these towns show a modest boom in the late fourth century.[30] It was in communities that had been touched with new wealth, brought about by the presence of the court, that Ambrose placed many of his most successful "model" bishops. As a result, the social and imaginative gap between the Forum and the church, which (in a city such as Aquileia) had seemed so considerable a generation before, came to be closed. Led by dignified bishops, known to be close to the great Ambrose, the Christian communities edged closer in the 380s and 390s to the social and cultural high ground in northern Italy.[31]

Magnus itaque iustitiae splendor ... aliis potius nata quam sibi:
What a splendid thing justice is ... [to be] born for others rather than for oneself

AMBROSE IN ACTION

Ambrose's *De officiis* was his own *Apologia pro Vita Sua*. He wrote it at the age of fifty. He had lived a very busy life as a bishop for almost fifteen years. And he was proud of it. It is hard not to recognize in Ambrose's portrait of the man of perfect "justice" a portrait of Ambrose himself in action as bishop of Milan:

> What a splendid thing, then, justice is. Born for others rather than for itself, justice aids the community and strengthens the fellowship that exists between us. It occupies the moral heights.... [The man of justice] brings help to others. He will give them money. He will never refuse to fulfill his duties towards them. He will assume other people's dangers as his own.[32]

The *De officiis* contain autobiographical passages that highlighted the moments when Ambrose had fulfilled his public duties as a "man of justice." Early in his episcopate, he wrote, he had melted down church plate to ransom the victims of Gothic invasion in the Balkans before and after the battle of Adrianople in 378. This was *aurum utile*—"useful gold." It had once been given to the church; Ambrose made it flow again abundantly to help the victims of calamity.[33] Gold must flow from the church. But, once entrusted to the church, it was to remain inviolable. Ambrose recounted how only recently he had steeled the resolve of the bishop of Pavia to resist attempts by the highest fiscal authorities of the empire to confiscate money deposited by a well-to-do widow in the vaults of the church. Without Ambrose's intervention the little man would have crumpled in the face of imperial officials.[34]

So much for spectacular narratives of wealth given away and of wealth preserved. But Ambrose was careful to point out that *misericordia*, mercy to the needy, was the *officium* that made every Christian soul acceptable to God.[35] What forms did this *misericordia* take? It is typical of Ambrose that we do not know. He went out of his way to view the poor, first and foremost, as fellow members of the Christian *populus*. Because of this he avoided emphasizing the chasm between rich and poor, which fueled the anger of preachers in the cities of the Greek East—such as Basil of Caesarea and John Chrysostom.[36] In any case, many of the "poor" with whom Ambrose had dealings were not the long-term, systemic poor who formed the underclass of the great eastern cities. Many were refugees from the war zones of the Danube. They were only recently impoverished and more than usually dependent on the hospitality offered to them by Christian churches in order to make a new start.[37] Whatever the composition of the poor in Milan may have been, Ambrose was not the man to tell us. His main preoccupation was that the poor should be absorbed almost unnoticed into the Christian community. The Christians of Milan were urged to see them as brothers, not as charged "others."

It was typical of Ambrose that he used the church's care of the poor in arguments on public policy in order to disparage his religious rivals. When, in 384, he blocked the appeal of Symmachus on behalf of the ancient cults, he went out of his way to contrast the "worldly" privileges attached to pagan priesthoods with the social mission of the Christian church.

> For her own benefit the Church owns nothing.... These rents and these revenues ... the Church gives away. The possessions of the church are expenditure on the poor. Let them [the pagans] count up how many captives the temples have ransomed, what nourishment they have offered to the poor, to how many exiles they have given resources for a livelihood.[38]

Devincire: To cement yet more closely

Despite his proud answer to Symmachus, outreach to the poor was not a central issue for Ambrose. What weighed more heavily with him was a very Roman issue: cohesion, based on a primal sense of solidarity, was central to his notion both of society and of the church.

In this, Ambrose resembled Cicero on a deep level. He sensed across the centuries a real convergence between his own concerns for the Church and the concerns of the great orator of the Roman Republic in its last days. Cicero wrote his *De officiis* in a time of mounting crisis, between late 46 and December 44 BC. He wrote to mobilize support for a system of aristocratic government that was rapidly falling apart. The book was "a manual of civic virtue, a theoretical treatment of the obligations which a citizen still owed to the Republic."[39]

Cicero's *De officiis* carried an urgent message. It was a book about loyalty to the community. Only through wholehearted acceptance of their obligations to society and to each other could human beings hope to maintain a civilized existence, which could never be taken for granted. Cicero's *res publica* was an oasis of sanity and order in a relentless world, swept by warfare and murderous civil strife. *Devincire*, "to cement"—and to cement ever more tightly—was a word crucial to Cicero in the *De officiis*.

But to whom did this drive to cement the bonds of society apply, and how widely did these bonds extend? Cicero had no doubts on that issue. Bonding was at its most intense among fellow Romans:

> For when with a rational spirit you have surveyed the whole field, there is no social relation among them all more close, none more dear than that which links each one of us to our country—our *res publica*. For this, our native land—our *patria*—weaves together fast around itself all our loves.[40]

But Cicero was also a philosopher. He wished to root the highly particular system of the Roman *res publica* in human nature itself. The Roman citizen who met his obligations to the *res publica* in particular did so because he was guided by all that was best in humanity in general. Nature itself led him

> to contribute to the general good by an interchange of acts of kindness, of giving and receiving; and thus, by our skill, our industry and our talents to cement human society ever more closely together, binding man to man.[41]

Ambrose fastened on this pair of concentric circles in the thought of Cicero. He strove to re-create in his own times the link between the intensely particular loyalty to the *res publica* of Cicero the politician and the studiously universal concern of Cicero the Stoic philosopher. He rewrote Cicero's *De officiis* in such a way as to bring to the fore the two aspects of Christianity. As bishop of Milan, he knew what his *res publica* was. He stressed the peculiarly intense cohesion and militancy of the Catholic Church. But he was also a religious thinker, haunted by the immensity of God. Christianity reached out to the limitless circle of humanity as a whole. Only through a universal benevolence that radiated beyond the tight community of the local congregation could a universal Catholic Church come to embrace and reunite a fractured world.

Everyone knew Cicero in the circles in which Ambrose moved. But they had known Cicero, above all, as a writer on friendship. They turned to him as a pattern book for the ponderously collegial phrases that ornamented their letters to each other. This was what Symmachus had learned from Cicero, as he wove his adhesive web across the governing classes of the Roman world. Ambrose, however, had learned something else. He concentrated on Cicero the politician and the theorist of cohesion. He did so in order to create within the church a new republic for modern times.

"The force of virtue … weakened and warped by primeval greed":

AMBROSE ON PROPERTY AND SOLIDARITY

In canvassing the possibility of a new, more cohesive social order, Ambrose was committed to a view of society that was rooted in a distinctive view of human history. He was the heir of a long tradition of what has been called "ancient primitivism." It was widely believed that there had been a Golden Age somewhere in the past of the human race. It was against the effortless harmony of that age that contemporaries measured the present state of society and found it wanting.[42] All that was bad in society came from the slow decline of humanity from a state of social innocence into its present state of social vice. In this, Ambrose looked back not to Cicero but to the more uncompromising Seneca, the Stoic philosopher:

> There was once a fortune-favored period when the boundaries of nature lay open to all, for men's indiscriminate use, before avarice and luxury had broken the bonds that held mortals together.

[In the words of Vergil's *Georgics* I.125–28:]

> No ploughman tilled the soil, nor was it right
> To portion off the boundaries of property.
> Men shared their gain, and earth more freely gave
> Her riches to her sons who sought them not.[43]

Ambrose took Seneca's words seriously. They were in the back of his mind when, in the *De officiis*, he challenged Cicero's definition of "justice." For Cicero, private property was sacrosanct. Justice consisted in preserving the private rights of individuals provided that the public interest was not weakened.[44] But Ambrose wanted to go beyond Cicero. Christians should embrace a more heroic and expansive definition of justice. To hold onto one's private property was not enough. Property was not there to be owned; it was there to be shared. In order to foster this view, Ambrose followed Seneca. He invoked a time of social innocence, before the balance of nature had been upset by private acts of appropriation.

> For nature generously supplies everything for everyone in common. God ordained everything to be produced to provide food for everyone in common; his plan was that the earth should be, as it were, the common possession of us all. Nature produced common rights, then, it is usurping greed [*usurpatio*, in a negative sense] that has established private rights.[45]

Ivor Davidson, the most recent commentator on the *De officiis,* has written somewhat impatiently that "an enormous amount of scholarly ink has been spilt over these words."[46] But Ambrose's words should not be dismissed as mere

theorizing. To appreciate the power of Ambrose's account of the violent imposition of private property upon an abundant earth we have to recover something
of the meaning of nature itself to Ambrose and his contemporaries.

What Ambrose had in mind was no cold carving up of a dead and abstract
"nature." Behind his views on the common rights of nature lay an ancient person's sense of the numinous fecundity of the earth, a view shared by Christians
and pagans. Mother Earth had barely ceased to be divine; she can still be seen on
a great fourth-century silver dish—the Parabiagio Plate—that was discovered in
a grave outside Milan. It may have been connected with the suburban villa of a
wealthy courtier or landowner. Propped up on one arm beside a full cornucopia,
her naked torso lying wide open, Mother Earth gazes placidly at four cherubs
who gather the fruits of the four seasons. A similar figure also appears at the
bottom of the great silver missorium of Theodosius I, beneath the hieratic scene
in which the emperor conferred high office on a courtier.[47] This was how nature
should be. For human beings to have divided up among themselves so luxuriant
a source of common wealth, so teeming with life, was an act of hubris as absurd
as attempting to measure out properties on the face of the heaving ocean. Human
avarice had done the one and was quite capable of trying to do the other.[48] Ambrose wrote so as to remind his readers that their own cramped rights to the land
were dwarfed by the abundance of nature.

The issue was how much Ambrose was prepared to turn back the clock of society in an attempt to recapture that "natural" first community of goods. Classical
Romans had tended to view mankind's first age of innocence with nostalgia. It
was the world they had lost—and lost forever. The ineluctable sequence of the
ages had condemned it to prehistory. Ambrose did not wish them to be so sure.
He did not advance the idea of an original community of property as the basis
for a specific social program in the here and now. But he did embrace the idea
as one of those "deep humane dreams"[49] that encouraged Christians to resist the
present. They should at least imagine a society that might yet be as open to all as
was the undivided earth.

The notion of humanity's slow decline from an original perfection set Ambrose's efforts as a preacher of benevolence against the background of world history. In the *De officiis* and in his other works, Ambrose was not greatly preoccupied
with the original Fall of Adam and Eve.[50] He did not interpret humanity's fall in
Paradise as Augustine would later do—as a single, abrupt act, which was the only
truly catastrophic event in the history of the human race. Rather, Ambrose
thought along more classical lines. The fall that interested him was less dramatic
but no less tragic in the long run. It was the gradual corruption of society over
the ages. Like Cicero, Ambrose thought that he lived at the end of a long decline.
The world was going to pieces. But, like Cicero again, a sense of decline acted as a
spur to action. As bishop, his *officia*, and the *officia*—the good deeds—he elicited

from others, did something to halt this decline. He strove to roll back a little the creeping injustice that had numbed human society for so many centuries.

> Who would not want to occupy this citadel of virtue [the state of total justice among men] had not the force of virtue in all its glory been left weakened and warped by primeval greed?[51]

In this, Ambrose was an optimist. What had been weakened and warped in society could in some measure be restored. Human "benevolence"—the warm goodwill of human beings for each other—had begun with Adam and Eve. Adam and Eve had been united *in one flesh* and (Ambrose adds significantly) "in one spirit." The human race had issued from a moment of deep harmony. Its members had been created to help each other.

> Having set out from Paradise, good will has filled the whole world.... This good will is now enhanced by the communal nature of the church, by our partnership in faith, by our kinship as recipients of the grace of baptism, and by our sharing in the Mysteries [of the Eucharist].... By these means the congregation of the holy church grows ever upwards [*adsurgit*] into *one body*, joined and bound together in the unity of faith and love.[52]

Hence Ambrose's insistence that giving to the poor should be based upon a strong sense of human solidarity. As Christel Freu has seen so clearly, Ambrose worked hard to reverse the imaginative effects of standard Christian rhetoric on the poor. He did not wish the poor to be seen only as charged outsiders, sent by God to haunt the conscience of the rich. Hence a decisive upward slippage of the image of the poor in Ambrose's sermons and writings. On many occasions, Ambrose spoke of the poor as interchangeable with "the plebeians" and "the people." To call them plebeians in this way made them members of the same Christian community as the prosperous. The poor were part of the "people" who rallied in a solid mass behind their bishop.[53]

For this reason, Ambrose went out of his way to make sure that Christians did not see almsgiving as a de haut en bas gesture. Rather, they were encouraged to see it as the gracious repayment to their fellow humans of an ancient debt.

> It is not anything of yours that you are bestowing on the poor; rather, you are giving back something of theirs. For you alone are usurping what was given in common for the use of all. The earth belongs to everyone, not to the rich.... Hence Scripture says to you: *Incline your soul to the poor, give back what is owed, and answer him with peaceable words in gentleness.* (Sirach/Ecclesiasticus 4:8)[54]

Generosity to the poor was more than a reaching out to the pathetic fringes of society. Rather, it was supposed to awaken memories of human community in a happier world lost in the depths of time. In the words of Mikhail Bakhtin, speaking of the theater and its relation to the early modern carnival, it triggered, if only for a moment, "the mighty aspiration to abundance and to a universal spirit."[55]

The miracle of joys shared by all citizens, which Symmachus had laid on, for one week only in the circus and amphitheaters of Rome, had become, with Ambrose, a permanent aspiration, tinged with classical memories of the Golden Age and with a Christian hope for Paradise Regained. It also gave the bishop of Milan an imaginative platform from which to launch a series of famous attacks upon the avarice of the rich.

CHAPTER 8

"Avarice, the Root of All Evil"

Ambrose and Northern Italy

Avarice or Sacrilege?

THE ILLS OF ITALY

By the time Ambrose came to write the *De officiis*, at the end of the 380s, the mood of terror sparked by the disaster of Adrianople in 378 had passed. Northern Italy settled down to a period of prosperity, linked to the presence of an imperial court. From 383 to 388, under Valentinian II and then on occasions under Theodosius I, Milan was an imperial capital. The court brought to the upper classes of the region the benefits of the late Roman age of gold. Fortunes were to be made in Milan, either through government service or through exploiting the new capital's need for foodstuffs.[1] Two of the great warehouses of Milan have been excavated. Each was twice as large as the *Ambrosiana*, the church Ambrose had built from his own money. These warehouses would be filled with grain provided by the local landowners.[2] It is not altogether surprising that, in a boom or bust economy based on the unremitting turning of agrarian produce into gold, some of Ambrose's most famous sermons should have touched on the theme of wealth. Indeed, in the words of Richard Newhauser, they marked the beginning of a "concentrated and sustained emphasis on *avaritia* [the sin of avarice] in Western Christian literature."[3]

We tend to take Ambrose's preaching against the rich for granted. It is an aspect of his career that has long appealed to modern persons. From the time of the Counter-Reformation onward, Milan has been the center of a long tradition of Catholic engagement with social issues. It was the city of Saint Carlo Borromeo (1538–84), the noble archbishop of Milan who was remembered in the city for his love of the poor. In the nineteenth century, the famous historical novel *I Promessi Sposi* (*The Betrothed*) by the Romantic Catholic Alessandro Manzoni took its readers back to the time of Saint Carlo's cousin, archbishop Federico (1564–1631), who was famous for having fed the poor during the great famine of 1629. Manzoni's novel was a moving story of the vicissitudes of a poor couple, placed at the mercy of the pride and violence of the rich and protected only by representatives of the Catholic Church. In more modern times, Milan witnessed the first Catholic reactions to the labor movements that emerged as a result of the industrialization of northern Italy. Thus a tradition of Catholic social concern was firmly rooted in Milan. It looked back to an Ambrose who was very different from the "proud prelate" of Edward Gibbon—to Ambrose as the preacher of social justice in an age of avarice.[4]

This view of Ambrose has tended to overlook the original context of his preaching. Ambrose is assumed to have breathed the same charged air of Christian engagement with the poor as do humane modern persons. For many scholars, Ambrose seems to be no more than "a simple keen observer of his times." He did not like what he saw.

> His observant eye discerned the details of society's moral degradation.... He visited patrician homes, noted walls inlaid with gold and ivory, saw their thorough-bred horses ... calculated from how far the gourmet food had been brought. He witnessed the concentration of riches in the hands of a few and knew that the race of Achab [the land grabber] never dies.

We are not surprised that the bishop of Milan "lashed out at the spectacle."[5]

Furthermore, we go on to assume that when he described the social ills of his time, Ambrose has provided us with an unvarnished picture of the social and economic state of late fourth-century Italy. His statements have been taken as conclusive evidence that the Roman empire in the West was a doomed society. The greed of the great landowners (as Ambrose described them in his sermons) is assumed by many scholars to have brought Roman society to the verge of collapse.[6]

In fact, Ambrose was a lot less like us than we think. His decision to preach on social issues was not inevitable; it represented a new departure. To many contemporaries it might even have seemed to represent a diversion of attention from more urgent issues. In the late fourth century, not everyone worried about the social ills of Italy. They worried about a more basic issue—the flight of the gods. It is we who link the decline of the Roman empire to the avarice of the rich. Pagans, however, linked it to the loss of supernatural protection caused by Christian blasphemy.

We must remember that paganism was widespread in northern Italy.[7] As we have seen, it still held the high ground in Rome and in much of southern Italy. Many of Ambrose's contemporaries were quietly convinced that the ills of Roman society had a supernatural origin. Many of the sharpest critics of their age were not Christians; they were pagans. For them, bad times had begun with the "national apostasy" of Constantine. The rampant avarice denounced by pagan authors was thought to go hand in hand with the spoliation of the temples and the abandonment of the old religion.[8]

Ambrose had to answer such views. He did so by subtly secularizing the contemporary discourse on decline. He turned what many thinking persons considered a religious crisis into a crisis of social relations. We moderns tend to applaud Ambrose for the perspicacity of his diagnosis of the weaknesses of Roman society. But pagans such as Symmachus would have regarded Ambrose's criticisms of society as mere whistling in the dark. Symmachus knew why things had gone wrong. The moment that the first fruits of the fields of Italy that had fed the Vestal Virgins for 1,200 years were withdrawn (in 382), the link between the land and the gods was broken. The earth lost its abundance. Ambrose would have remembered what Symmachus had written in 384 in his famous *Third Relation* in defense of the Vestal Virgins: "Sacrilege has made the year go dry."[9]

And, indeed, Symmachus's worst fears were confirmed on that occasion. Rome was threatened by famine. As Prefect of the City, Symmachus was forced to initiate a drastic measure. In the late summer of 384 he expelled all foreigners from the city so as to ensure that registered citizens only—the *plebs*, the People of Rome—received the food to which they were entitled. He could only pray: "Oh gods of my country! Forgive us our neglect of the rites! Drive away the misery of this famine."[10] It was a shameful moment for him. In Symmachus's edition of his *Relationes*—of his official reports to the emperor as prefect— the document in which he would have reported the expulsion of foreigners is missing.[11]

Ambrose always had men such as Symmachus in view. Bonds of class and interest kept them together. Symmachus did not drop out of Ambrose's world after his clash with the bishop over the issue of the Vestal Virgins. The two men maintained a somewhat frigid correspondence throughout their lives on matters of business. Symmachus wrote to Ambrose about the protection of shared clients.[12] He also rebuked Ambrose for showing ignorance of the law (and even bad manners) by attempting to claim certain lawsuits for the jurisdiction of the new bishops' court.[13]

Ambrose also continued to seek out opportunities to criticize the great pagan. Barely four years after the famine of 384, he went out of his way to comment on Symmachus's handling of the crisis. When discussing love of one's neighbor in the *De officiis*, Ambrose denounced the heartlessness of an unnamed pagan prefect. He branded the decision to expel immigrants who had long resided in the city of Rome as an inhumane act. Ambrose's criticism of the measure was a transparent attack on Symmachus.[14]

Ambrose's treatment of the Roman famine of 384 in his *De officiis* was highly tendentious.[15] But he ensured that the whole incident would be seen as a purely economic crisis. He presented it as a crisis in which purely human vested interests—those of the Roman Senate, of the people of Rome, and even, perhaps, of grain dealers from Ambrose's northern Italy—clashed in a situation created by a purely natural disaster. In his account of the famine, Ambrose excluded what for Symmachus was the main cause of the crisis: the anger of neglected gods.

Symmachus himself had few illusions as to the avarice of his peers who had failed to contribute to the common stores of grain.[16] But behind his complaints of avarice and lack of public spirit, there lay the deeper fear of a great city laid open to disaster because deprived of its ancestral rites. Ambrose's preaching against the rich, as if they alone were responsible for the miseries of the times, would have struck pagans as a demagogic maneuver. In their opinion, Ambrose's attack on the rich was designed to distract attention from the real issue—which was that Christian sacrilege had exposed Italy to disaster.

Vidi ego miserabile spectaculum: I have seen
with my own eyes a heartrending scene

———

AMBROSE AS SOCIAL CRITIC

It is with this imaginative displacement of anxiety in mind that we should approach a work Ambrose wrote in the late 380s—that is, in the same years as he wrote the *De officiis*. This was *De Nabuthae, On Naboth*. It was based on the story of King Ahab and Naboth's Vineyard. A brutal tale of the greed of a king who brought about the death of a poor farmer in order to take over his estate, the *On Naboth* was preached against the rich landowners of Milan. It began with a ringing challenge: "The story of Naboth is an ancient tale. But today it is an everyday occurrence."[17]

The *On Naboth* is among the most vivid of Ambrose's works. It was composed from sermons he had recently delivered. Even when rewritten for publication, the abuses it denounced seemed grippingly real. In fact, such directness was unusual for Ambrose. Unlike his great contemporary, John Chrysostom, who preached incessantly on the poor, Ambrose did not preach with the "sense of a [single] concrete message needing to be driven home."[18] Rather, he usually preferred to take his hearers on a mystery tour of the Scriptures. To expound the Bible was to peer into a deep, dark well of spiritual truths with one's back turned on material things.[19] As in the nighttime vigils of his cathedral, filled with flickering light and the sound of chanting, Ambrose's sermons were supposed to take his hearers into a world beyond this world. It was not a style from which great rhetoric on social issues might be expected to grow.

Yet this was not the case in the *On Naboth*. Ambrose's sermons on the wealthy were aimed with precise words at a clear target. When he preached, Ambrose wished "to sound like the Bible."[20] And on this occasion he sounded like a prophet of Israel.

Between Ahab, the grasping landowner, and Naboth the small farmer, Ambrose stepped in as the prophet Elijah. It was he, Ambrose, who delivered the prophet's curse:

> *You have slain, and you have taken possession of the inheritance. Therefore, in the place where dogs licked up the blood of Naboth, dogs shall lick up your blood* (1 Kings 21:19).[21]

Speaking that passage, Ambrose did not even mention the name of Elijah. For at that moment everyone in the church would have known that it was Ambrose who was the prophet. Had he raised his voice at this moment in the original sermon, the effect would have been stunning.

Hence the vivid vignettes of social life that are artfully scattered throughout the *On Naboth*. Coming after the gray wisdom of Ecclesiastes and the book of Proverbs—which merely stressed the vanity of riches, not the evils of the rich—these are sudden lightning flashes that seem to reveal an entire social landscape.

> I myself know of a rich man who, in setting out for the country, was in the habit of counting out the rather small loaves that he had brought from the city, so that from the number of loaves one could estimate how many days he was going to be in the country. He did not want to open his granary, which was sealed up, lest his stores be diminished.... I also found out from trustworthy evidence that, if an egg was added to this, he would complain that a chicken had been killed. I write this so that you may know that God's justice, which avenges the tears of the poor, is poised to strike.[22]

He added accounts of tragic accidents at work and of random acts of cruelty.

> One man tumbled from your roof when he was readying large storerooms for your grain. Another fell from the top of a tree while searching for the sort of grapes to bring down for the proper wines to be served at your banqueting.... Another was beaten to death before your eyes if he happened to do something displeasing, and he spattered your banquet with the blood he had shed....
>
> I myself have seen a poor man led away because he was obliged to pay what he could not.[23]

These descriptions were skillful inversions of the pastoral vignettes of servants tending their lord's estate with sprightly innocence, which feature so regularly on the silverware and on the great villa mosaics of the time. As we have seen, happy peasants even appeared on the floor of Theodorus's basilica at Aquileia, gathering the first fruits of rich Christians. Ambrose's countryside, by contrast, was a brutal place.[24]

Last of all, we meet the rich themselves immured in palatial villas in the depths of a countryside drained of human life to make way for vast hunting reserves: "Or are you uplifted by spacious halls? ... They might hold a crowd, but they exclude the voice of the poor."[25]

Yet the scholar has to pause and look again at just these passages. In them, Ambrose strove to create a "reality effect." But it is not the reality known to modern students of late fourth-century Italy. The social ills Ambrose described are palpably out-of-date. There is no evidence for the growth of *latifundia* in fourth-century northern Italy. Nor do modern surveys support the image of a land emptied of its inhabitants. The late Roman villas of Desenzano (on Lake Garda) and of Palazzo Pignano (close to Milan, near the Aemilian Way and close to a river system that would have provided easy transport for its harvests) were splendid buildings.[26] But there is no evidence that they stood in the middle of a man-made wilderness. If anything, the evidence points to the development of tighter human units—of dispersed settlements gathering into villages and of farmhouses being upgraded by the laying of mosaics and the installation of workshops. What the archaeologist has found is not desolation but "a massive increase in rural activity."[27]

This does not mean that the countryside around Milan was a comfortable world. It was a hard-driven land. The landowners depended on the constant, brutal mobilization of labor. This was where the real hardship lay. And Ambrose knew it. When he wrote a practical letter of advice to the bishop of Claterna—a vulnerable area, where grazing land in the foothills of the Apennines met the plain along the Via Aemilia—what concerned him most was that the gangs of seasonal laborers mobilized to bring in the harvest should receive their wages on time.[28]

By contrast, Ambrose's evocation of the spread of *latifundia* at the expense of small farmers was a traditional grievance, well-known to Roman readers since the days of Pliny the Elder. It was irrelevant to the conditions of the fourth century. To denounce the growth of great estates was as anachronistic as to denounce contemporary industrial society by an appeal to the miseries of chimney sweeps in Victorian London, as these were recounted in the *Water Babies* of Charles Kingsley. Why did this hiatus between rhetoric and reality occur?

We must remember that when Ambrose seemed to strive for reality what he actually strove for was drama. And he found his drama already condensed in the works of other writers and preachers. Once he spoke of a particularly heartrending case of oppression, *Vidi ego miserabile spectaculum*, "I have seen with my own eyes a heartrending scene." Yet both the phrase and the vivid scene that followed appear to have been lifted straight from the pages of Basil, bishop of Caesarea in distant Cappadocia![29]

However, we should not be too quick to dismiss Ambrose's picture of upper-class Milanese society as platitudinous rather than perceptive. For to do this would be to overlook the role of platitudes in ancient rhetoric. Appeal to well-tried stereotypes gave the weight of a diffuse but potent common sense of wealth to Ambrose's arguments. In this common sense, greed and misery were thought of as timeless. To repeat the criticisms of an ancient author merely gave added density and drama to similar ills that were present in one's own society. As the great scholar Henri Irénée Marrou once reminded us (when speaking of literary descriptions of ancient dining habits), "a description can be borrowed from a book without ceasing to be historically true."[30] When studying a similar genre— poems on the sufferings of the poor written in medieval China—Mark Elvin has arrived at the same conclusion. He warns us that "a cliché is not necessarily less true for being familiar." Indeed, he goes on to say that "the point is not that the story this poem tells is heartbreaking, but that it is commonplace."[31] And it is precisely the commonplace quality of the greed of the rich and the misery of the poor Ambrose wished to conjure up.

Ultimately, the issue is not what Ambrose said. Still less is it whether what he said can be used in any way by historians who wish to reconstruct the social profile of the northern Italy of his times. It is why he said it. And he said it for a good reason. The *On Naboth* and similar sermons formed part of Ambrose's continued drive to build up a sense of a Christian community in Milan. As we have seen, this community had already stood the test of fire (in 385–86) in the incident of the basilicas. Now their sense of cohesion would be further sharpened by a challenge to the evil rich.

This can be seen from the tone and timing of Ambrose's sermons against avarice. They appear to have coincided with moments of tension between himself and the court. The confrontational quality that marked Ambrose's sermons during the siege of his basilica in 385–86 still lingered dangerously in his sermons on avarice. There was a thinly veiled streak of populism in them. By identifying with the prophets of Israel Ambrose reminded his hearers that they were the heirs of an ancient *populus*—the people of Israel. As we have seen, the cry of the people of Israel was spoken of as the "cry of the poor." The imagined granaries and the vast villas of the rich were locked against this cry. But the cry of the poor was never that of mere beggars. In Milan, as once in Israel, the cry of the poor was the "consensual cry" of the entire *populus* of a Roman city raised against their oppressors. And Ambrose was the prophet who brought this cry to the ears of the great.[32]

"God has not made you rich out of ill will"

THE DUTIES OF THE CHRISTIAN RICH

Even though Ambrose's sermons dealt in commonplaces, we should not automatically assume that preaching against the rich was an altogether anodyne matter. The cities of the later empire could be dangerous places. Milan was doubly dangerous because it was a court city. It harbored rich courtiers who were often strangers to the region. Such persons could never be certain when the tide of public opinion in the city might turn against them. One sermon might be enough to destroy a politician's reputation. This sermon did not have to be an outright attack. For instance: reading the moralizing diatribes on wealth by John Chrysostom, one could never guess that such sermons made him unpopular with the wealthy political establishment at Constantinople. As we now read them, John's sermons seem to amount to no more than a series of platitudes on the subject of the transience of riches. They seem totally safe. Yet rich courtiers claimed that John "had closed the churches to them." For when he preached "the eyes of all would turn upon them."[33]

Even if it was couched in studiously stereotypical terms, a sermon could be decoded by its hearers. It could be perceived as an attack on known individuals, it might undermine their public reputation, or it could make them seem dispensable to the imperial court. Thus, when the court eunuch Calligonus was executed, in 388, Ambrose reminded his hearers of the eunuch's fall:

> from whose end I shy away, at whose death I shudder.... It does not please me to recall that sermon of mine in which I vented my sorrow [in a seemingly jejune statement on eunuchs in government] forced by the outrage he had done to the church.[34]

An apparently banal sermon preached by Ambrose on the story of Joseph and Pharaoh had played a role in the great courtier's ignominious death.

Altogether, in churches increasingly saturated with a heady rhetoric on wealth and poverty it was not always comfortable to be rich. When they entered a Christian basilica, the rich were exposed to the gaze of a crowd of hundreds drawn from all classes, many of whom might have had good reason to resent them.[35] It was a venue more claustrophobic than was the amphitheater in which the notables of the city had long faced their "people." In this situation, a bishop not only spoke out to defend the poor. He also had it in his power either to shame or to shield the rich.

It is difficult to trace this charged relationship in the works of Ambrose himself. But it can be clearly shown in the case of a known "Ambrosian" bishop. Gaudentius of Brescia was one of the new men put in place by Ambrose.[36] He became bishop of Brescia in 396 at the latest. He had close relations with the leading layman of his city, Benivolus. It was the sort of relationship with the local elites that Ambrose had encouraged. Benivolus was a rich man. He had served in the imperial chancery at Milan. Gaudentius could address him both as the "head of the local nobility" and as the "head of the people—the *plebs*—of the Lord." When Benivolus failed to attend church for many weeks because of illness, his absence was noticed. Benivolus himself thought that his prosperity had brought upon him the curse of God. Others may well have thought the same. Benivolus had been a top bureaucrat and had lived close to the prime source of unclean gold. His wealth could be imagined to be suspect wealth derived from bribery and extortion.

Gaudentius responded to Benivolus's anxiety by giving him a copy of the sermons he had missed. In the preface, he went out of his way to comfort Benivolus:

> God has not made you rich out of ill-will but providentially, so that you should find a medicine to heal your sins through works of mercy.[37]

This was a reassuringly banal solution to Benivolus's anxieties. But the incident as a whole showed that black thoughts lay close to the surface when the Brescians considered Benivolus's fortune.

In ancient Rome, a notable who did not spend his money on public beneficence might find that the *plebs* would turn against him with nasty consequences. As we saw, this had happened in the case of the riot in which the palace of Symmachus's father was burned in 373–74. Now "the *plebs* of the Lord" had its own spokesman, in the form of an eloquent bishop of Ambrosian style. The bishop was expected to monitor the behavior of the rich. Indeed, as bishop of Brescia, Gaudentius acted as the parole officer of the wealthy. He put them on their best behavior. He shielded the sick and demoralized Benivolus from his own guilt at the possession of wealth. In so doing, he also shielded him from the criticism of others. But there was a quid pro quo for this protection. Gaudentius told Benivolus in no uncertain terms where he should put his money. In a Christian *populus* the well-tried remedy of generosity, which had disarmed criticism of the rich in ancient times, now took the form of "works of mercy" to the poor and of donations to the church.

"This avarice was what first brought every evil to Italy"

AMBROSE AND THE LIMITS OF THE POSSIBLE

Ambrose's sermons on the wealthy should not be read as a reportage on the actual state of Milanese society. Nor were they intended in themselves to bring about a program of social reform. What they did do was open up for Ambrose and for similar Christian bishops a space for intervention in society. The sermons were no more than the preliminary bombardment that preceded the action of the bishop as intercessor with the great.

Here again, as so often with Ambrose, it is important to see his activities in perspective. He did not act alone. Rather, he took advantage of a major development in the political culture of his time. He exploited what has been called the "advocacy revolution" of the later Roman empire.[38] This advocacy revolution was by no means limited to the Christian church. It had not come about because of a heightened sense of concern for the oppressed but had been fostered by the imperial government for brutally practical reasons. Perched at the top of an immense and slow-moving bureaucracy, the emperor and his court went out of their way to encourage appeals and denunciations from below. As in the Soviet Union, the emperors realized that "the real power of a totalitarian state results from its being at the disposal of every inhabitant."[39] Lethal denunciations could come from anywhere.

As a result, what Jill Harries has aptly called a "culture of criticism" came into being. For it was by allowing the occasional dramatic petition to come through that the central government monitored what was happening in distant provinces.[40] Many of these petitions were sermons in miniature. They were "groans."[41] In denouncing governmental abuses, the petitions used exactly the same discourse of avarice as did Ambrose.

Petitions to the emperor were answered in equally high-pitched tones. Ambrose lived in an age of sermons from the throne. In 301, for instance, the Price Edict of the pagan emperor Diocletian had inveighed against the avarice of merchants and dealers in foodstuffs in language that was quite as strong as any used by the bishop of Milan: among such persons (the emperor declared),

> the unbridled lust to grab is mitigated neither by abundance of supplies nor by the fertile growth of yearly harvests.... They seek to narrow down the abundance that comes from a propitious climate, the benefits bestowed by the gods and the affluence associated with the good fortune of the state. Considerations of common humanity have led me, o my subjects, to place a limit on avarice.[42]

Ambrose could not have said it better. But he had no illusions as to how this new culture of criticism worked. It was not through high-minded consciousness-raising in church (through the sort of sermons that now fill so many volumes of the Fathers of the Church) but through the dogged task of lobbying the powers that be that Christian benevolence was shown to work in late fourth-century Milan.

Ambrose set about this task with memorable verve. On one occasion, he was believed to have gate-crashed the private circus of the imperial palace—entering through the same gateway as the *venatores*, the skilled beast hunters (that is, onto the open arena where the beasts would appear)—in order to gain amnesty for a nobleman condemned for treason.[43] It was the sort of spectacular intervention people liked to associate with Ambrose.

But we should not be misled by the occasional tour de force. Usually, Ambrose got things done in a low-key manner that differed not at all from the constant lobbying of Symmachus. To take one example: A minor clerk in the administration of the harbor works at Ostia faced confiscation on an unspecified charge. He was the protégé of a well-placed north Italian, Eusebius of Bologna. Prompted by his friend Eusebius, Ambrose set to work immediately:

> As soon as I received your letter, I saw the prefect.... The prefect immediately granted forgiveness and ordered the letter of confiscation to be countermanded.[44]

Such incidents reveal the other side of Ambrose. For all the contestational stances through which he built up the cohesion and morale of his congregation, Ambrose remained an insider. He knew how far he could go. As he wrote in the *De officiis*:

> Here is something else which helps you gain a good reputation: rescuing someone in need from the hands of the powerful, or saving a condemned person from death. The way to go about this, as far as possible, is without making a fuss—*sine perturbatione*: we must avoid giving the impression that we are acting more with an eye to boasting about it than to showing people mercy.[45]

Ambrose also knew that there were certain things that a bishop could not touch. One of them was taxation. As we have already seen, taxation was crucial to the formation of late Roman society. And it was the emperor and his servants—not the bishop—who determined the incidence of the taxes. Ambrose could not avoid noticing that Julian the Apostate (361–63), the last pagan emperor, was still remembered warmly in the West: he had lightened the tax load in a way in which no Christian emperor had done.[46] In the crucial area of taxation and the treatment of fiscal debtors, the late Roman state remained impervious to Christianity.

A generation after his death, people close to Ambrose were aware of the constraints this situation had imposed on the great bishop of Milan. Paulinus of Milan wrote a *Life of Ambrose* at the request of none other than Augustine of Hippo. He had no illusions as to what his hero could not do:

> He groaned deeply when he saw that *root of all evil, avarice*, a drive which neither abundant wealth nor shortage could diminish, increasing more and

more among men and particularly in the holders of high office, so that intervening with them was an exceptionally heavy task because everything [at court] was up for sale. This avarice was what first brought every evil to Italy, and from then onwards everything went to the worst.[47]

Paulinus of Milan knew the limits that were placed on Ambrose's ability to intervene in state affairs. Even when Ambrose was at the height of his career, as an old and respected bishop in 396, imperial agents had marched into church to arrest a political suspect. They pushed past Ambrose and his clergy who had crowded around the altar to protect the fugitive and dragged him unceremoniously from the church before the bishop's own eyes.[48]

Paulinus was no naive acolyte. He was legal adviser and manager of the estates of the Milanese church in Africa. He knew the way the world worked. His description of the growth of avarice in Italy may even have consciously echoed the *History of the Caesars* of Aurelius Victor, a supporter of the pagan emperor Julian, writing of the increased load of taxation placed upon Italy for the first time by Diocletian and increased by Constantine.[49] When it came to the central functions of the Roman state, even the vivid Ambrose was a lightweight. He could attack the avarice of private persons, conjuring up their abuses in the old-fashioned language of the Italy of an earlier age. He could not attack the fiscal system from which so much of the wealth around him must have derived. It was only a decade later, in a more crisis-laden situation when the Roman state itself was maimed by barbarian invasions, that Christian writers and preachers turned explicitly against taxation and tax collectors. But in the Italy of the 380s and 390s this development still lay in the future.

Ambrose died in 397—some six years before his exact contemporary, Symmachus. By that time, a younger generation had become prominent in regions far from northern Italy. We are entering the world of Paulinus of Nola, of Augustine, and of Jerome. Each one came from a region very different from the Italy of Symmachus and Ambrose. Augustine, in particular, came from a layer of Roman society that had little in common with the senatorial world in which Ambrose had moved and of which he never lost sight.

Though he left behind him a striking memory of his actions as a public person, many of Ambrose's works became out-of-date with surprising speed. The *De officiis*, from which we have derived so much of Ambrose's view of himself in the late 380s, seems to have had little immediate impact. It was a strange fate to overtake a book that has been described by a modern scholar as "the first manual of Christian ethics."[50]

In a sense, Ambrose had put himself out-of-date. His work in Milan was like the ground course of a high building. It ceased to be noticed, but it had been decisive. In creating in a major western city a Christian community sheathed in an aura of inviolable cohesion, Ambrose had begun a work that would be continued in many other cities of the West. He gave a language to this great enterprise. He conjured up an imagined community in which the distinction between the poor and the *plebs* was deliberately blurred. He brought the poor into the Catholic community. He presented the care of the rich for the poor as a necessary consequence of the unity of all Christians. Last but not least, Ambrose presented the unity of the Catholic community of Milan as the living core of human society as a whole. A fractured human race could regain its long-lost solidarity by entering the Catholic Church. It was by his attention to social issues, judged in the light of that great hope, that Ambrose came to forge a language that proved to be well adapted to the ambitions of a religion that had dared to think of itself—at last and for the very first time—as a true "majority religion," as the church rose "like a moon waxing in brightness" above the Roman world.[51]

CHAPTER 9

Augustine

Spes saeculi

Careerism, Patronage, and Religious Community, 354–384

Tenuis municeps: A townsman of slender means

To turn to Augustine (354–430) is to meet a figure from a different region and from a very different social world from that of Ambrose. The story of Augustine begins in Africa, and after a hiatus of less than five years spent in Italy, it picks up again in Africa. A younger man than Ambrose, Augustine outlived the bishop of Milan by thirty-three years. It was from Africa, as bishop of Hippo, that Augustine witnessed the unfolding of a crisis of empire, from the Gothic sack of Rome in 410 onward, that was more drastic than Ambrose and any members of his generation could ever have imagined.

This chapter and the next two will deal only with the first forty years of Augustine's life. They will follow him from his early years as a provincial on the make in Carthage, Rome, and Milan, from 373 to 387. Then they will describe his return to Africa, in 388, and his activities up to the time of his ordination as bishop of Hippo in 396 (a year before the death of Ambrose). They will present the history of a career and of a conversion seen very much from the inside. Despite the vividness of Augustine's life, which is surprisingly well documented for us, it is important to maintain this inward-looking focus. For an inner history of Augustine does not mean that we will see him in isolation. On the contrary, such a history throws an unexpected light on the stresses and strains of persons of his social background. It gathers together in a single person the tensions of an entire class.

Augustine's continuous search for a community of like-minded friends goes some way toward explaining the remarkable efflorescence of countercultural religious groups in late antiquity. With Augustine, we can follow this widespread process of group formation in detail from small beginnnings to a momentous conclusion. In the years between 373 and 396, Augustine and his close friends passed, decade by decade, from membership in a radical sect, to the formation of a philosophical community, and eventually to the foundation to a monastery of their own making. Little did they know it at the time, but the monastery Augustine founded in Hippo, and about which he wrote after 391, was destined to become the template for an experiment in communal living that condensed some of the highest aspirations of the medieval Catholic Church in its attitudes toward both wealth and society as a whole.

Let us, however, begin the story when Augustine was thirty and had already begun to taste the fruits of success a year after arriving in Rome from Carthage. Not surprisingly, to come to Rome was to come to Symmachus. In 384, in his first months as Prefect of the City, Symmachus was called upon to perform a routine duty:

> A notification had come from Milan to Rome, that a teacher of rhetoric was to be appointed [for the city of Milan], with travel facilities provided by the imperial post.[1]

The man chosen by Symmachus was an African, Aurelius Augustinus. He had come to Rome a little under a year earlier, having taught rhetoric in Carthage for eight years. It was the decision of Symmachus that ensured that the future Augustine of Hippo moved from Rome to Milan in the autumn of 384.

For Symmachus, it was an unremarkable event.[2] He had constantly recommended young men of culture to the great, whether informally or, in this case, as part of his administrative duties as Prefect of the City, who was the official supervisor of the teaching profession (and of their students) in Rome. Many of his nominees went on to high posts in the bureaucracy or at the imperial court. Their successes reassured him. They showed that "the pursuit of classical literature is a sure path to high office."[3]

Most of the young men Symmachus patronized have remained mere names to us; this cannot be said of Aurelius Augustinus. He has become known to us as Saint Augustine of Hippo. The vivid autobiographical passages that enliven his *Confessions* (which he began to write in around 397), when combined with his other works, enable us to follow from the inside the trajectory of Augustine's career from Thagaste (modern Souk Ahras in eastern Algeria) where he was born (in 354) to Milan as a rhetor (in 384) and back to Africa as a would-be monk (in 388). Through further works of his, we can continue to follow him from his ordination (in around 396) as bishop of Hippo (modern Annaba/Bône on the coast of Algeria) until his death in 430.[4]

Because of the abundance of our evidence, it is possible to place Augustine year by year in a living social context as we can do with no other late Roman person. It is important that we should try to do this. Augustine is so well-known for what he wrote that it is easy to forget the manner in which he lived. Augustine's writings would echo through the centuries. But they are not elevating sounds that come from nowhere. They bore the flavor of a real world. In this, and in subsequent chapters, I wish my readers to take up this challenge—to trace the evolution of Augustine's thought on wealth, religion, and society against the various social contexts in which he found himself in various stages of his life. For each context was never a mere background to his life and writings. Each worked its way into the texture of Augustine's thought in a manner that accounts for his unmistakable intellectual profile.

To do this will not always be easy. It has proved difficult to find a place for Augustine on our conventional map of late Roman society. This is partly the fault of the very crude maps of late Roman society that have been available to modern scholars until very recently. But even to contemporaries, Augustine was hard to place. His social position was shot through with ambiguities. Seen through the eyes of Symmachus, it was obvious that the young African lacked the clear markers of status that characterized Symmachus's world and that of his fellow *nobiles*. Ambrose, though a product of the more recent nobility of service, would also have viewed the young African from a great height. Though he welcomed Augustine to Milan *satis episcopaliter*—"very much as a bishop should do"—Ambrose never put himself out to make intimate contact with him.[5]

Altogether, in 384 Augustine's social status was a blur. The most blatant sign of his lack of clear social markings was the fact that, at the age of thirty, his marital status was uncertain. He had been living with a woman for twelve years and already had a son by her. She was not his wife. But neither was she, in any formal sense, his "concubine." For a concubine was a woman debarred from lawful marriage by the laws that prohibited the union of persons of known high status with persons of low status. Augustine lacked the sort of high status that the late Roman laws against *mésalliance* were designed to protect. He was sufficiently unimportant to be free to marry whomever he wished. His companion was not necessarily his social inferior. As Danuta Shanzer has suggested, in a trenchant article, she may simply have been the woman with whom Augustine lived and whom, for reasons we can only guess, he refused to marry.[6] This situation, in itself, would have told Symmachus that Augustine came from a gray zone, unlike his own. In Symmachus's world, marriages were formally contracted because they were linked to the alliance of families and to the joining of vast properties. Augustine, by contrast, was free to live with whomever he chose and however he chose because he was a man unfettered by the obligations of ancestral wealth.

At the same time, it is misleading to speak of Augustine as if an utterly unbridgeable chasm separated him from the worlds of Symmachus and Ambrose. It has proved easy for his modern biographers to acclaim Augustine as a prodigy—as a poor man, the son of a poor man, who rose from rags to riches by his outstanding talents alone. Some scholars have even called him "a nobody."[7] This is far too dramatic a view. Augustine had never been a nobody. Like many Romans from the little cities of the provinces, he had always been somebody somewhere.

To understand this, we must go back to the intense world of Roman north Africa. As we have seen, every city in north Africa was a little *patria* of its own. Each had its own, clearly defined social hierarchy. Because of this, we should see Roman Africa as littered with little pyramids—the social hierarchies of individual cities. Larger pyramids—whose peaks lay in Carthage within Africa and beyond Africa in Rome and Milan—hung over these little pyramids. Despite the attractive power of major centers, which was a blatant feature of the society of the fourth century, the large pyramids did not absorb the little pyramids entirely. Social status came from one's position in the little pyramid of one's hometown first and only then from one's success in the wider world.

Augustine's family belonged close to the top of the little pyramid of Thagaste. Looking back, from the fifth century, Augustine's biographer Possidius described Augustine's parents as *honesti*.[8] *Honestus* was a word as heavy with a sense of ill-defined superiority as the word "gentleman" used to be in traditional English society. Augustine's family were on the top side of the one truly significant shelf in Roman society. They were members of the town council. Their wealth gave them membership in the group that met in the "temple" of the town hall to manage the affairs of "the most resplendent city" of Thagaste. Augustine's father, Patricius, had an estate. The family owned slaves. Augustine never had to work with his hands.[9]

Augustine was unlike the Harvester of Mactar, whom we met in chapter 1. The Harvester had finally entered the "temple" of the town council of his city after years of labor beneath the burning sun. By contrast, Augustine's eventual ascent as a teacher of rhetoric was not one from rags to riches. In 384 he had done no more than move from one little pyramid (where he had always been somewhat privileged) to a position within sight of the top of the biggest pyramid in the Latin West through being appointed to a teaching post in the court city of Milan.

In the conditions of the fourth century, to be on the upper slopes of a little pyramid was not a particularly comfortable position. When he wrote about his father in the *Confessions*, Augustine chose his words with care. He described Patricius as a *tenuis municeps*. *Tenuis* was an ambiguous word; it had a dignified Ciceronian ring to it. For Cicero, it had referred to those who brought their character, not their bankroll, to the service of the state. For Cicero, it marked such persons off from the irresponsible rich. A *tenuis* was by no means a pauper.[10]

We should not be confused by the fact that in later years (in the late 420s) Augustine once described himself to his congregation at Hippo as "a poor man, born from poor parents."[11] In using the word "poor" on this occasion he was doing no more than many Latin authors had done for centuries. He spoke of himself as "poor" "not as a clearly conceptualized condition of deprivation, but negatively, as the opposite of wealth"—the wealth, that is, of others wealthier than oneself.[12] "Poverty as unwealth"[13] was all that Augustine had in mind when he used the words *tenuis* and *pauper* of his father and himself.

Patricius was, indeed, "poor" in this quintessentially Roman sense. He was poor in relation to a considerably richer group of fellow townsmen who formed the inner circle of the city's town council. It was entry into this inner group that Patricius sought, through nurturing the talent of his son. He paid out money for Augustine's education in the nearby university city of Madauros (modern M'Daourouch, in Algeria) with an *animositas*—with a pigheaded determination —that occasionally outstripped his resources. For one year, at the age of sixteen, Augustine had to linger at home, called back from Madauros for lack of funds. But Patricius was determined to succeed.

> At that time, everybody was full of praise for my father because he spent money on his son beyond his means.... Many citizens of far greater wealth did nothing of the kind for their children.[14]

The praise of Patricius's fellow citizens may not have been offered without reserves. They knew what Patricius was up to. In Augustine he had a *filius bonae spei*—a gifted boy with a future ahead of him.[15] He would spend his money so that, from the rewards of a career in teaching or administration, his son might finally break into the inner circle of Thagaste. Had Augustine not, in 386, abruptly abandoned the *spes saeculi*—the hope of advancement in this world on which his father's heart was set[16]—an *Album* of the town council of Thagaste, such as that which has survived from Timgad (to which we referred in chapter 1), might have shown Aurelius Augustinus at last at the top, as Patricius had wished him to be. He might have appeared as a *honoratus*—a man "honored" by the emperor—who had returned from a successful career in the wider world as a teacher or an imperial servant to settle down in middle age among the leaders of his city.

Far from coming from nowhere, Augustine came from the most vivid and creative section of the Roman society of his time. He did not come from the established nobility of Rome or even from the inner circles of local society in Roman Africa. He came from a far less secure and, for that reason, all the more energetic group. In little towns scattered all over the Latin West (and especially in the towns that lay particularly thick on the ground of Africa), men who had grown up within sight of the top of their own, local society saw no reason why, through their talents, they should not rise to the top of the greater, imperial society that reached beyond the little cities of their region.

That is what Augustine had achieved, by the year 384, at the age of thirty, when he moved from Rome to Milan. It was no small achievement for the son of a *tenuis municeps*. But, while only the occasional nobleman of Rome when threatened by downward mobility might find that he had to fight his way back to the top with exemplary energy—as Ambrose had done as a young man—literally hundreds of young men from town councils all over the West set out in search of the same kind of success as did Augustine. They sought wider fields, beyond the little pyramid of their hometowns, in which to shine through skilled professions, through government service, and, as we shall see, through various forms of intellectual and religious experimentation. Far from being a lonely prodigy, Augustine's career was representative of the hopes of an entire class. Like the hum of a swarm of rising hornets, it was largely the noise created by such persons that gave unparalleled energy to the cultural and religious life of the Latin world in the fourth and early fifth centuries.

To move out of Thagaste, in the 370s, Augustine had to have a patron. His great good fortune was that he got one. Romanianus was a truly rich member of the Thagastan elite. In a work written in Milan in 386, Augustine drew on the ancient image of the urban benefactor to describe Romanianus. He was a man such as Symmachus would have recognized as a provincial version of himself. Romanianus was an *amator patriae* in the old style. He was acclaimed

> through the [shouting] mouths of his clients in city and province alike as "the most humane ... the most generous" ... spotlessly neat in appearance, at the very top of his good fortune.

Like Symmachus—though on a provincial scale—Romanianus had held his fellow townsmen entranced by spectacular games:

> Indeed ... , while you presented to the people of our town public shows that included bears and performances never seen before, the applause of the theater deemed you always to be the most prosperous of men.[17]

We even have tantalizing evidence that Romanianus contributed in the traditional manner to the urban fabric of Thagaste. A fragment of beaded stone found at Thagaste bears the name, carved in fourth-century lettering, of a Cornelius Romanianus.[18]

Romanianus took care of Augustine. He did so for over twelve years, from the time that Augustine was a young student of twenty (in 374) to the time of Augustine's final "conversion" from a career, in Milan (in 386). Romanianus had taken "this poor young boy" into "his house, his payroll and his heart." When Augustine returned from Carthage to teach for a few years in Thagaste in 375, Romanianus brought his gifted friend into the charmed circle in which Patricius (only five years dead) had hoped to place him: "By your favor, by your intimate friendship [your *familiaritas*], by sharing your house with me, you made me, along with yourself, a famous leader of local society." For the next ten years,

Romanianus provided the financial "nest" (we would say the "safety net") that supported Augustine's rapid rise as a teacher of rhetoric at Carthage.[19]

Without Romanianus's protection, Augustine might well have remained locked into the small-town life of Thagaste for the rest of his days. Not only did Romanianus give him financial support. It was probably through the intervention of Romanianus that Augustine took what, in the conditions of the fourth century, was the most important step of all for a young man bent on a career. Augustine quietly slipped out of his obligations to serve in the town council of Thagaste, to which he had become liable after the death of his father, which had occurred around 370. Once he had obtained this precious exemption, the way to the top lay open. His teaching career might even be crowned by governmental posts that gave him entry into the new nobility of service.[20]

Familiaritas

PATRONAGE, FRIENDSHIP, AND GROUP FORMATION

As we have seen, patronage of this kind was crucial to the social mobility that characterized so much of fourth-century society. But it is important that we also look at the impact of this system on the attitudes toward society of those who depended on it. We usually meet the patronage systems of this period as they were administered with bland punctilio from the top, by persons such as Symmachus. In the case of Augustine, however, we get a stark, upward view of the same system. It is like looking up into the branches of a giant tree up which Augustine hoped to scramble so as to reach the top of Roman society. For the son of a minor town councillor, who was wealthy enough to be a gentleman at home but not wealthy enough to enter the wider world without support from others, issues of wealth and poverty faded into the background compared with the ever-present and decisive fact of patronage. Augustine had grown up in a social world where what you owned was less important than who you knew.

This situation gave a distinctive flavor to his subsequent views on society. It accounts for what might strike a modern reader of Augustine as one of his blind spots. Apart from preaching conscientiously on almsgiving once he became a bishop, he has little to say about the poor. This was because Augustine had always been surrounded by poverty of a certain kind. The constant, galling awareness that he did not possess as much as did his more fortunate peers was what had driven Patricius to such lengths to foster the talents of his son. For the first half of his life, Augustine was in very much the same position as Patricius. His social world was not divided primarily between rich and poor; it was divided between those who could get ahead and those who could not. The truly rich could afford to think about the poor. As we saw, part of Symmachus's huge wealth was deployed in a ceaseless, anxious dialogue with the *plebs* of Rome. Ambrose lingered with fierce eloquence on the contrast between the avaricious rich and the victimized poor. But Augustine was no Ambrose, and he was certainly no Symmachus. For him, society was veined from top to bottom by the fact of patronage. As a result, Augustine experienced his social world as a cat's cradle of personal relationships. It was not a world of rich and poor; it was a world of patrons and friends.

This goes some way to explain why friendship, trust, and the concord of wills were always more than abstract notions for Augustine. They had been the building blocks of his social world for the first thirty years of his life. Compared with the robust sweep of Ambrose's Ciceronian vision of a human solidarity made ever more dense and enduring through Christian acts of benevolence, there was an element of tunnel vision in Augustine's early views on society. He did not think big, as Ambrose had done. Rather, he thought in terms of small groups, bonded by intense feelings of friendship based on shared belief.

We should give due weight to this feature of the social thought of Augustine. Put very briefly: in the 380s and 390s, Ambrose's Cicero was the Cicero of the *De officiis*. His view of society was rooted in a sense of natural solidarity. Augustine's Cicero, by contrast, was the Cicero of the *Laelius*. It was the Cicero of friendship.[21] But to this widespread classical ideal of friendship (to which men such as Symmachus paid lip service) Augustine added a dose of urgency tinged with anxiety. For him, human society was not held together by some massive, original bond. It depended for its cohesion on the perilous free play of human affections. Each friendship was a gamble. Each human group was the fragile creation of an interplay of wills. Society was a risky business. Whatever solidarity it managed to create depended on the subtle flow of shared affections and loyalties.

Thus in his earlier writings (from the late 380s to the early 400s) Augustine tended to linger by preference on the quality and tenacity of bonds of friendship and on the primacy of shared religious enthusiasms. His ideal remained a countercultural community of like-minded souls. It was the microsociology of a small community that held his attention—whether it was the cell of a religious sect, a philosophical commune, or a monastic establishment. Put briefly: Augustine was a theorist of friendship and of groups based on shared enthusiasms long before he emerged in middle age as the imaginative architect of a grandiose City of God.

How had this development begun? Part of the answer is simple. Friendship—*amicitia*—had always been the gentler face of patronage. Patronage implied a measure of asymmetry between patron and client, but this asymmetry could be canceled. The patron might promote a client to a more intimate relationship.

Familiaritas might replace dependence, if by any chance the fortunate hanger-on was promoted from the position of a client to that of a friend.

The transformation of patronage into friendship was expected to occur most frequently in intellectual circles. In the many countercultures of late antiquity, friendship was the most precious elixir of all. Differences of social status were elided and even the heavy patron-client bond was transformed through the joining of like minds. Persons of potentially competing statuses within a fragmented upper class could hope to sink their differences in a little group committed to the common search for wisdom.

In around 375, when Augustine was twenty-one, Romanianus took this decisive step. He adopted Augustine, his client, as a friend. This was not altogether surprising. They were the same age. They shared the same high culture. In this case, the patron and his client came together with others to form a group of friends. A friendship based on the joining of like minds was even supposed to cause the hard facts of money to melt into the background. In the words of the ancient saying (which had already circulated for eight centuries): "All things are held in common between friends."[22] In such charmed circles, the issue of who depended on whose wealth was deemed to be of no significance. In the *Confessions* Augustine has left a memorable picture of his days in Thagaste, in around 375, when the little group was first formed:

> These were [the things] which occupied my mind in the company of my friends: to make conversation, to share a joke, to perform mutual acts of kindness, to read together well-written books ... to disagree though without animosity—just as a person debates with himself.... These and other signs come from the heart of those who love and are loved and are expressed through the mouth, through the tongue, through the eyes, and a thousand gestures of delight, acting as fuel and out of many to forge a unity.[23]

What Augustine went out of his way not to tell us in this particular passage of the *Confessions* comes as a surprise to modern readers. The group whose shared enthusiasm Augustine described so vividly had been brought together by shared adherence to the most exotic version of Christianity that had ever appeared in late Roman north Africa. Augustine's first experience of the cohesion of a group was not derived solely from his secular friendships. It was forged through joining a radical religious movement. From the age of nineteen (in 373), to his final taking up residence in Milan (in 384), Augustine and his friends adopted a religion known to us as Manichaeism. (The words "Manichaeism" and "Manichee" come from the Syriac term *Mani de hayye*: "the Mani of Life"—pronounced with a distinctive hard *h*, as in the Hebrew *hayyim*.) Mani was the preacher of "life"—of "salvation." He was a prophet who had appeared a little over a century previously (he died in 277). He had been active far to the east, in what is now southern Iraq. For the remainder of this chapter, we must make the leap of the imagination that is required to understand the role of Augustine's ten-year-long experience of Manichaeism in fostering his desire to live in a countercultural religious community among like-minded friends.

"Sons and Daughters of the Light Mind"

AUGUSTINE THE MANICHEE

From 373 to 384, Augustine was a member of the Manichaean sect.[24] These were crucial years for him. Yet Augustine's later works make it more than usually difficult for us to enter into what this experience must have meant. Once converted to Catholicism, he distanced himself entirely from his former religion. He insisted that he had never penetrated the inner circles of the Manichaean cult. He frequently stated that he had remained a mere "fellow traveler"—an "Auditor," a "Hearer," who did no more than listen to the preaching of the Manichaean "Elect" and who ministered to their material needs.

This was a credible claim. The Elect were the virtuosos of the Manichaean religion. Uncannily pale, sexless, and without appetite, the Elect were like wandering monks. The Hearers who supported them were not subject to the same hyperascetic codes as were the Elect.[25] Augustine also implied that he had never been a fully informed Manichee. He stressed the fact that only the Elect knew the secret doctrines of the sect.[26] He even implied that, for most of the time, he had been a half-hearted adherent.[27]

Furthermore, once he became a Catholic, Augustine consistently presented the Manichees as gross outsiders to the Christian tradition. He attacked them as the upholders of a particularly desperate vision of the universe. He stressed the fact that they held that the material world was utterly corrupt. It was a ruined portion of a Kingdom of Light that had been invaded by a principle of active evil, known as the Kingdom of Darkness. To be a Manichee was to realize that one had been trapped in a cosmic catastrophe. Manichees, as it were, dug among the ruins of a fallen world to find frail but precious portions of light trapped beneath a mass evil matter. They prayed, fasted, and ate together so as to send these portions (which were their true selves) back to their former luminous home beyond the Sun.[28]

Once Manichaeism is reduced to a caricature, as Augustine presented it in his later years, it is hard to imagine what he derived from being a Manichee. In his old age, Augustine's enemies even turned his own bleak summary of Manichaean views against him. They claimed that Augustine had remained a crypto-Manichee. They implied that, like the Manichees, Augustine still held to a catastrophic view of the human condition. They claimed that he had continued to believe, with the Manichees, that sexuality was a demonic force. They pointed out that his doctrine of original sin echoed the Manichaean belief that all human beings were the helpless victims of evil forces that had crushed them since the dawn of time.[29]

Faced by this high wall of stereotypes, we have tended to take one of two stances. Either (like Augustine's later critics) we suspect that, if there was anything that Augustine learned from the Manichees, it was bound to be bad. Or we claim that he had learned nothing—that his adherence to the religion of Mani was no more than superficial dabbling in a New Age cult.[30]

It is time to revise both these views. In the first place, to become a Manichee was by no means to cease to be a Christian. Augustine had grown up in a Christian family. He turned to the Manichees after reading the *Hortensius,* which was Cicero's exhortation to pursue the life of wisdom. He turned to them because, unlike the pagan Cicero, their writings "bore the name of Christ."[31] Mani always claimed to be a reformer of Christianity who had brought the message of Jesus to its final perfection.[32]

Nor was it surprising that Augustine should have fallen upon the Manichees when he was in Carthage. Though bound by so many economic ties to Rome, the port of Carthage also looked to the east, as it had done in the days of the Carthaginians. Carthage was the first major landfall in western waters for ships from Antioch and Alexandria. In the fourth century, the presence of extensive Manichaean communities in Africa marked the westernmost foam of a wave of radical ascetic Christianity that had swept through the Christian communities of Mesopotamia, Syria, and Egypt. Those regions were accustomed to radical forms of Christianity preached by wandering ascetics. In Syria and Egypt, the pale Manichaean Elect—monks on the move like many other monks—did not seem at all strange.[33] In the same way, Manichees were welcomed in Carthage as radical, "reformed" Christians. They were not viewed as the representatives of an irremediably exotic cult.[34]

What mattered most was that Manichaeism was a religion made up of small, intense cells.[35] Each cell was a "Holy Church" in miniature in which creatures of the light gathered together in the midst of a darkened universe. Auditors received the pale Elect into their houses. They fed them, and in return, they received preaching and the blessing of long and mysterious prayers.[36] The atmosphere of the stilled study group, made up of chosen souls gathered at the foot of their teacher, was what a Manichaean assembly offered to Hearers in the "Holy Church" of Mani.

Manichaeism gave Augustine and Romanianus just what they needed—an intensely religious version of the *familiaritas* they had sought to achieve, by more secular means, in the years when their relationship of patron and client took on the more intimate form of a relationship between two like-minded friends. Shared Manichaeism had opened the way to friendship. Augustine himself admitted this in one of his anti-Manichaean works: what held him was the *familiaritas* he found among the Manichees: "A sense of intimate friendship, which crept into me under a false image of goodness, and encircled my neck like the coils of a serpent."[37] It was this *familiaritas*—this sense of intimate friendship—that kept Augustine and his friends for so long in the grip of the religion he later came to travesty. Their ten years together as Manichees had by no means been a superficial experience. It had offered them an intense experience of bonding in one of the most starkly countercultural groups in the Latin West.

This impression has been confirmed by the recent discovery of Coptic Manichaean documents at Kellis in the Dakhleh Oasis of western Egypt. They date from around 340. They include personal letters that show that, on a day-to-day basis, members of the local Manichaean community thought of themselves as bound together by strong ties of spiritual friendship.[38] Their members spoke of each other as "Sons and Daughters of the Light Mind." They were inextricably joined one to the other through the common possession of the "Light Mind"—in Coptic, *pnous ñouaïne*.[39]

The "Light Mind" was, in many ways, the equivalent of the Holy Spirit among more mainline Christians. Within the Manichaean community, it acted with peculiar intensity as a bond of union. The "Light Mind" was an emanation of the Spirit of Jesus. It had inspired the Apostles and was now shared by all members in each Manichaean cell. Auditors and Elect alike shared in the same Light Mind. This was a doctrine of spiritual solidarity of unusual force. It was derived from an intensely physical notion of a shared spirit of light, divided up, as it were, into brilliant particles, lodged in every member of the sect. Each possessed fragments of this light; each soul drew closer to the other in order to create the shared incandescence of the "Holy Church" of Mani. To rescue light from matter was not (as Augustine suggested in his anti-Manichaean tracts) an absurdly mechanical process. The dispersed light of the Manichees was nothing less than an image of their own souls. To gather light and to send it on its way to heaven was to gather kindred souls into a glowing unity of mind.[40]

This view of a shared Light Mind was combined with a poignant hope for transparency between members of the same community. Grouped around their Elect, whose utter quiet and unearthly pallor made them seem as if they already stood on the threshold of the Other World of Light, fellow believers felt that they also would soon enter a better world where the tragic opacities of normal society would be removed. In a letter discovered at Kellis, a son wrote to his mother:

To my mother, my lord lady, very precious to me, the beloved of my heart . . . I pray that The Great Day of Joy should happen to us, the day for which we pray indeed every hour, and that God will grant us that we see the image of each other in full, transparent freedom, and with a smiling face.[41]

This new evidence of the inner life of the Manichaean communities makes it easier for us to understand how the Manichaean sense of community could provide such a potent glue of spiritual friendship for Augustine and his friends. Almost everyone touched by Augustine at this time joined the Manichaean church. Romanianus, his son Licentius, Alypius, and many others became "Sons of the Light Mind" along with Augustine. They all stayed with him in the Manichaean faith for ten years. Some went further than Augustine. Alypius was inspired by the continence of the Elect to adopt a life of celibacy.[42] Even Romanianus seems to have had his sex life in order while he was a Manichee. (This was no small achievement for a grandee: at a later time, as a widower, Romanianus shocked Augustine—who was by then bishop of Hippo—by taking a concubine immediately after the death of his wife.)[43]

It has frequently been pointed out that in all his years of supposed "wandering" from the faith, Augustine never once abandoned Christianity. The "name of Christ" had always been present in whatever religion he adopted.[44] There is a further corollary to this view. Throughout his secular career as a teacher, Augustine always thought in terms of living, in some way or other, in the comforting embrace of a religious community. His experience with the Manichees had given him a heightened sense of spiritual friendship.

This was Augustine's greatest debt to the seemingly exotic religion of Mani. It gave him, from a sect from the distant East, an intense experience of community that classical authors, such as Cicero (whose views on friendship Augustine and Romanianus would have shared, as did every educated person), had promised but had not delivered. Religious bonding was one of the fixed components of Augustine's life as a teacher in Carthage and Rome. As far as the patterns of his social life were concerned, he simply brought these components with him to Milan in 384. More than that: as we shall now see, Augustine's hope for an ideal community took on a different form after 386. It guided him in the years before and after his return to Africa in 388. But, *c'est le premier pas qui coûte*—it is the first step that matters. And, for Augustine, this first step toward a life in a religious community was taken in the "Holy Church" of Mani.

CHAPTER 10

From Milan to Hippo

Augustine and the Making of a Religious
Community, 384–396

Inhiabam honoribus: I was agape for honors

When Augustine took the road from Rome to Milan in late 384, it might have seemed as if he had succeeded in making his way to the top of the Roman world. The imperial court was at Milan. But we must remember that this court was only one of three imperial courts set up in different parts of the immense empire. It was the smallest and the least successful. It was flanked by strong and ambitious rulers. The emperor Theodosius was firmly installed at Constantinople. Gaul and Spain were ruled from Trier by Maximus, who had recently ousted and killed Gratian, the older half brother of Valentinian II. Augustine must have been one of many persons who, on making their way to Milan, realized quickly that they had found the right job—but in the wrong place and at the wrong time.[1] It was time to get busy, before the next regime change blocked further chances of promotion:

> I was agape for honors, high fees and a wife.... What a great thing it is to seek advancement to a high [governmental] office—who could wish for anything higher? We have friends in high places. If nothing else, let us put the pressure on and get, at least, a minor governorship.[2]

Augustine meditated for the very first time in his life a true change in his social position. He would move from a dignified but studiously low-profile role as a teacher of rhetoric into the privileged world of government servants.

But in order to do this, Augustine had to make up his mind about his woman. She was sent away "because she was a hindrance to my marriage." She returned to Africa, "vowing never to know a man again." This may refer to a formal vow.

If so, it was possible that she was taken care of by the Catholic Church as a *sanctimonialis*—a nun.[3] This brutal arrangement had been negotiated by Augustine's mother, Monica, who had followed Augustine to Milan. As a widow, she expected to be housed by her son. It is revealing that Monica and Augustine each had a very different view of what this proposed marriage meant. For Monica, it meant that, with a Catholic wife, Augustine would be baptized—and baptized by none other than Ambrose, the bishop of Milan. The stain of Manichaeism would be washed both from his soul and from his reputation.[4]

Unlike Monica, what Augustine singled out (in retrospect) about the prospect of marriage was the role it would play in his plans to continue a search for wisdom in the company of his friends. Their shared enthusiasm for Manichaeism had cooled. This is not surprising, as they approached a court whose emperors regarded Manichaeism as a peculiarly loathsome heresy. But they had not abandoned their shared enthusiasm for wisdom. The new wife could help Augustine's little group of chosen souls. It was not necessary that she should be a rich heiress; the high-minded professor "would not dare" to think of that. But the cachet of an upper-class spouse would give prestige and protection to Augustine and his friends. Her dowry would set Augustine free to lead the philosophical life without having to spend all his time earning money as a teacher. In this way, the future wife (who was probably only twelve at the time) was envisioned by Augustine, quite bluntly, as a replacement for Romanianus.[5]

This projected marriage remained somewhat up in the air. What was of more immediate importance was a scheme to found a philosophical community.

> Many of our friends and I had been deeply mulling over a scheme, the subject of many discussions, for escaping with scorn from life's onerous churnings. We had all but decided to withdraw from the mass of men and to live a life of philosophical detachment. The detachment would be structured thus: we would pool all our belongings, creating a single household fund, so that in open fellowship no one would own this or that, but the contributions of each there would be common property, the whole of it for each, and all of it shared by all of us. It seemed to us that ten or so people could live in such a community. Some of us were quite wealthy, above all Romanianus.... He was especially enthusiastic for this project, swaying others in discussion of it since his financial means far outstripped everyone else's.[6]

But the fact that Romanianus was in Milan at all was a bad sign. A legal battle with an urbane but tenacious enemy (perhaps a kinsman) had taken him far from his base in Africa. To appeal to the imperial court was a perilous maneuver. To have one's principal patron involved in high-risk litigation did not bode well for the scheme.[7]

Yet this was not the only problem the men of the group had to face:

> Later the thought began to occur to us whether this would be acceptable to the ladies—many of us had wives and I myself wanted to acquire one. On this the entire project which we had so well planned collapsed in our hands: it was broken up and abandoned. We returned to sighs and groans and careers following the broad and well-trodden ways of the world.[8]

The opposition of the women deserves to be stressed. It was not that women were excluded from philosophical communes. The great Pythagoras (on whose example this scheme may have been modeled) was well-known for having welcomed women disciples.[9] But the women gathered in Milan were the mothers or the potential mothers of children. They did not wish to see the inheritances of their sons (and with those inheritances, their own hope of support as widows) vanish into a common pool so as to support the project of a high-minded professor.

Candida iura bonorum: The clear-faced company of the good

CASSICIACUM TO THAGASTE, 386–88

It was for these reasons that the project for a philosophical commune failed in 385. When he looked back, over ten years later, to write the *Confessions*, Augustine brushed past this scheme in only one paragraph. This was because it seemed to him with hindsight as he wrote the *Confessions* that the swift unfolding of God's purposes in the next year had rendered it irrelevant. But this was not entirely the case. As anyone who has followed the story of Augustine knows, he experienced a stormy encounter with select writings of Neo-Platonic philosophers (most notably Plotinus) in the summer of 386. This encounter was followed by a decision to become celibate and to seek Catholic baptism. By the autumn of 386, everything had changed in Augustine himself—everything, that is, except for the social setting in which he intended to live his new life.[10]

When Augustine retired in late August 386 to Cassiciacum in the foothills of the Alps (perhaps at Casciago, near Varese, fifty-five kilometers northwest of Milan), the group that followed him was in many ways similar to the commune of like-minded souls that he had planned in 385.[11] The retreat to Cassiciacum was not a totally new departure; it was a return to the hopes of the previous year. It seems unique to us only because it was the first gathering around Augustine of which we know directly through the writings that he produced at this time— the famous Cassiciacum *Dialogues*.[12]

We know how this group looked to one of its members. Ten years later, Licentius, the son of Romanianus (who had been around sixteen at the time), described in a poem the days that he had spent at Cassiciacum. Against the majestic background of the Alps, the group of friends had spent their time "experiencing along with you the freedom of leisured hours, the clear-faced company of the good."[13]

But what would be the bonds that now held together this "clear-faced company of the good"? Seen from the outside, the retreat to Cassiciacum was a staid affair. Augustine later spoke of it as a period of "*otium* devoted to the Christian life."[14] *Otium* was a charged word. It had unmistakable aristocratic overtones. Symmachus and his friends enjoyed long periods of *otium* in the countryside outside Rome or in Campania. "Tired of the affairs of the city," they liked to "tame their great minds in solitude" on their estates. Senators in *otium* were like Catholics "on retreat." "Turning over the learned writings of the men of old" in the well-watered gardens of their villas, they renewed their allegiance to the culture that was supposed to make them truly noble.[15]

Otium was not mere leisure. It implied engagement in intellectual pursuits. Those who emerged from a spell of *otium* had to have something to show for it. This was particularly the case with Augustine, who was still tied to patrons whose teenage children he continued to educate. For these patrons he developed an elevated intellectual program that he put forward in a series of *Dialogues*. The dialogue *Contra academicos, Against the Academics,* refuted the skepticism of the New Academy, which had been upheld by Cicero. In it, Augustine proved that the human intellect could penetrate to ultimate, otherworldly truth. But this required a grooming of the mind. Hence the next dialogue, *De ordine, On Order*, sketched out an intellectual program that would enable the mind to rise to elevated truths. Finally, *De beata vita, On the Blessed Life,* showed that it was possible to enjoy, through contemplation, the supreme happiness of a life lived in the presence of God.

These dialogues were recorded by stenographers, although they were later reworked by Augustine. Stenographers were a luxury item.[16] Their presence hinted at an aristocratic leisure lived in the countryside surrounded by eager scribes. But this was only a tasteful backdrop. Those who participated in the *Dialogues* were by no means aristocrats. They were a distinctly motley group. They included Augustine's mother, Monica, who was fulsomely praised for her untutored wisdom,[17] and two cousins of Augustine's who were entirely uneducated. These cousins give us a rare glimpse of the low level of the culture of average town councillors, if their fathers did not pay out money for their education, as Patricius had done for Augustine. But Augustine stressed that there was also room for unschooled persons such as his cousins in his program of intellectual grooming: "They have hardly been exposed even to a grammarian [in primary school] ... but their very gift of commonsense I judged necessary for the discussion."[18]

Indeed, Augustine went out of his way to communicate that the one thing that brought together the participants of his *otium* was not a shared upper-class culture. The *Dialogues* were meant to be manifestos for a new Christian culture that spoke to persons of all levels of education and to both sexes. Truths the pagan philosophers had hidden from the masses, in esoteric traditions, had been made available to all by Christ's coming to earth, "through an act of clemency to an entire people."[19]

Behind their somewhat faux classical façade, the Cassiciacum *Dialogues* were written to communicate the zeal of a religious group. The dialogue *On the Blessed Life* ended with Monica chanting a hymn composed by Ambrose.[20] It was one of the hymns that had been used in Ambrose's basilica, in the spring of 386, during his confrontation with the court. Altogether, Augustine's *Dialogues* were a daring venture in the democratization of ideas. Truths once accessible only to a few great philosophers were declared to have been made available to all through the preaching of the Christian churches. In this, the *Dialogues* were an echo of Ambrose's attempt, earlier in the year, to make the higher levels of theology available to all, as he rallied excited crowds in the basilicas of Milan by means of hymns and sermons.[21]

So much has been written in recent years on the stages of Augustine's conversion and on the sources that contributed to his intellectual development that it is easy to forget that Augustine's principal conversion at that time had been to a mighty God. This was God conceived of as the Supreme Beauty in a high Platonic tradition that Plotinus (a Greek philosopher of the mid-third century) had expounded to his followers with mystical fervor. Plotinus's writings had set Augustine on fire.

This is well-known. But what is not often stressed is the manner in which Augustine's new view of God deeply affected his attitude toward the religious friendships that bound his group together. A new God meant a new basis for the group. Augustine and his friends ceased to see themselves as "Sons and Daughters of the Light Mind," bound together by an almost physical sharing of particles of light. Instead, they became Platonic lovers. They were united by the vision of a single Beloved, a Supreme Beauty who was both utterly distant from them and yet hauntingly present. In ceasing to be Manichees, they shifted from a form of intense horizontal bonding thought of as a blending of like minds, such as was characteristic of a sect, to a more starkly pyramidal model. Each one of them strained to reach a Beauty whose sheer delight rendered each one of them forgetful of his or her own self. All were drawn together to share in a common, high joy.

Augustine insisted that if the existence of this Supreme Beauty was certain, then the friendships of those who were joined in seeking this Beauty were also certain.[22] They were friendships made in heaven. They were based on the thrill of a shared love of God. This was what Augustine wanted to make clear to Romanianus in his dialogue *Against the Academics*. Augustine opined that their shared love for God as the Supreme Beauty was so intense and so certain to reach its goal that even Romanianus's rival (a grandee as elegant and cultivated as was Romanianus himself) would give up his lawsuit and join with Romanianus to rush, "panting with desire," to taste, along with him, the beauty of God.[23] This was a shared passion, which blotted out the normal sense of "mine" and "yours." For a shared love of Beauty to lead two late Roman gentlemen to abandon a lawsuit was to expect a lot. But Augustine meant what he said. His euphoric phrases show that he was already thinking his way to a new, even more intense form of spiritual bonding than he had ever experienced when he was a Manichee.[24]

Given the mood we can glimpse in the *Dialogues* of Cassiciacum, it is not at all surprising that Augustine closed the ninth book of the *Confessions* with an account of a shared mystical experience. The famous Vision of Ostia showed that it was indeed possible for two people to be engulfed in a common vision of the One God.

In the autumn of 387, Augustine and Monica were waiting at Ostia to take ship for Carthage:

> It came about, as I believe by your providence, ... that she and I were standing by a window overlooking a garden. It was at the house where we were staying at Ostia on the Tiber, where, far from the crowds ... we were recovering our strength for the journey....
>
> Alone with each other we talked very intimately. *Forgetting the past and reaching forward to what lies ahead (Phil. 3:13)* we were searching together in the presence of the Truth, which is yourself. We asked what quality of life the eternal life of the saints will have, a life which *neither eye has seen nor ear heard, nor has it entered into the heart of man (I Cor. 2:9)*. But with the mouth of the heart wide open, we drank in the waters flowing from your spring on high, *The Spring of Life (Psalm 35:10)* which is with you. Sprinkled with this dew to the limit of our capacity, our minds attempted in some degree to contemplate so great a reality.... That was how it was when at that moment we extended our reach and in a flash of mental energy attained to the eternal wisdom which abides beyond all things. If only it could last! Then this alone could ravish and absorb and enfold in inward joys the person granted this vision.... Is this not the meaning of *Enter into the joy of your Lord (Matt. 25:21)*?[25]

For followers of Plotinus, there would have been nothing strange about this mystical ascent—except for one thing: in the ancient world, the mystical ascent had always been a strictly individual affair. But Monica and Augustine had shared the experience. A shared ecstasy of mother and son is calculated to cause eyebrows to be raised among modern scholars of Freudian persuasion.[26] Augustine would not have been so prudish. Decades of shared religious intensity, first as a Manichee and then for a short time as the pioneer of a philosophical commune, had been greatly sharpened by the months spent at Cassiciacum. It seemed quite natural to him that the search for God should be a venture in which an entire community of like-minded souls might be engaged. Augustine had decided that it was possible to have the vision of God and to live the rest of his life in a group made up of those who shared his longing for this vision. But what exactly would be the form of the community where such a thing might happen?

The Road to Poverty

FROM ITALY TO THAGASTE AND HIPPO, 388–91

In 388 Augustine returned to Africa along with an unusual party of retired bureaucrats and failed would-be courtiers. They eventually settled in their hometown, Thagaste. Thagaste was no place of exile. It lay on the inland plateau of Numidia, but it was well situated on roads that led northeastward, back to Carthage, and directly north, to the port of Hippo Regius on the Mediterranean coast.[27] The little group was a somewhat eccentric version of a well-known phenomenon. It marked the return to their hometown of a cluster of successful careerists. Each one of them, in his own way, had gained distinction through imperial service (as had Alypius) or (in Augustine's case) had held a major teacher's chair at a court city. Their careers would have entitled them to the privileges of *honorati*—"honored men"—in retirement. They had succeeded while their run-of-the-mill peers, the average town councillors, had stayed at home to undertake the routine tasks of local government. Though privileged, they were expected to settle down in Thagaste and to use their influence and new wealth to support their hometown.

But something else would also have struck the inhabitants of Thagaste. They were a group of intellectuals. Excitements of the mind were what they offered to their hometown, not the splash of circus games. Furthermore, most of them had been Manichaeans and "Sons of the Light Mind" a little over a decade earlier. They remained a closed religious group. But they now presented themselves in reassuringly old-fashioned terms as living a life *in otio*. They were no longer members of a suspect esoteric sect. They were a group of men of leisure intent on "becoming like God" through prayer and reading.[28]

But there was one crucial difference between what they had been and what they now were. No rich patron towered above them as the ultimate source of their security, as Romanianus had done when Augustine was a young man. They were an independent commune. They had arranged their life according to a "holy agreement." Originally they seem to have pooled their wealth in a tradition taken from philosophical circles. But the pooling of resources changed its meaning over the years and now took on a Christian flavor. It became associated in their minds with the life of the first Christians of Jerusalem as had been described in the *Acts of the Apostles*.

The formation of what scholars have called the Jerusalem Community was regarded as a foundational act by Augustine and by all later advocates of the monastic life in the Latin West. As a result of the descent of the Holy Ghost at Pentecost, the first Christians had become of *one mind and one soul*. Then—and then only—did they decide to concretize their divinely inspired unanimity by a community of property: "*no one said that any of the things which he possessed was his own, but they had everything in common* (Acts 4:32)."[29]

This was how Augustine and his friends read the *Acts of the Apostles*. There were other ways in which the story could have been read. Preaching at Antioch and Constantinople, for instance, John Chrysostom stressed the fact that the pooling of wealth among the Christians at Jerusalem had taken place so as to make money available for the needs of the poor.[30] But this was not Augustine's reading. The poor did not concern him at that time; unity was all. Shared wealth was no more than the material sign of the divinely inspired miracle of shared minds.

Appeal to the *Acts of the Apostles* justified what was a daring move. By emphasizing their unity in *one heart and one mind*, Augustine and his friends deliberately unhooked themselves from the life support machine of patronage. By pooling their wealth they would "go it alone" in an ideally self-supporting community, such as they imagined the first Christians of Jerusalem to have been. Though they might welcome occasional gifts, they would never again accept patrons.

In order to pool their wealth in the manner of the first Christians, they first had to renounce it. But what exactly did renunciation mean in the late fourth century? When he wrote about this period of his life, in a letter written a quarter of a century later (in 414), Augustine assumed that his Christian readers would know what he had done.

> I, who write this, fell deeply in love with that perfection, of which the Lord spoke, when he said to the Rich Young Man: *Go, sell all that you have, and give to the poor* (*Matthew* 19:21).[31]

But a quarter of a century was a long time in the history of the Latin churches. In 388 the mechanics of renunciation were far from clear-cut. For a town councillor such as Augustine, there was little room for drama in the giving up of wealth. Whatever the size of his property, he could not simply throw it away; the claims of other family members had to be met. Augustine's relations with the town council of Thagaste had to be settled definitively, possibly by the cession of some of his lands to the city. The final decision may not have been taken until the death of his son, Adeodatus. This was a bitter tragedy of the years between

388 and 391, whose exact date we do not even know. Only then would Augustine have been free to alienate his estates without compromising the future of his son. Maybe the final arrangements for the transfer of Augustine's property did not happen until his brother Navigius died, as also happened around this time.[32] Only then was Augustine's wealth free from claims both from his family and from the town council of Thagaste. Altogether, the renunciation of wealth was never the headlong matter that advocates of the ascetic life presented it as being. To *sell all* often meant to sell slowly.

Nor was the wealth realized from Augustine's property given directly to the poor. Gifts to the church tended to be spoken of, in a pious formula, as if they were gifts "to the poor of the church."[33] Most probably, Augustine's estates and those of his friends were quietly donated to the church of Thagaste. In return each may have received an annuity or the usufruct of a portion of the revenues of their estates. They would then contribute this income to the common fund of the new community.

It is also far from certain that Augustine and his friends made themselves notably "poor," in the sense of identifying themselves with the real poor in the streets and countryside of Thagaste. This did not mean that they were either half-hearted or pampered. Rather, they defined "poverty" itself in a particular, old-fashioned manner. What still mattered for them was not the new Christian antithesis between "the rich" and "the poor" but the ancient antithesis between "the rich" and "the wise."[34] What the wise rejected was not wealth itself. It was the dire drive for ever more wealth that characterized the unwise rich. The wise opted for "unwealth." They did not opt for destitution but to be content with what they had and to avoid the very real social and political dangers that went with the active pursuit of riches. This did not mean that they did not live in a relatively comfortable manner, surrounded by books and even, perhaps, by servants. Nonetheless, at Thagaste an important step had been taken. No individual member of the community owned anything. It was the community itself that was "poor." Its members lived modestly so as to make do with their pooled wealth. They lived sparingly, as philosophers had always done. But they were by no means a community of paupers.

Even this step took courage. Fourth-century persons lived in a dynamic social world where it was dangerous to stand still. For just as wealth was a state toward which the rich always strove, poverty was a state toward which one might always slide. Relative poverty, linked to the fear of impoverishment and to the bitter shame of *déclassement*, preoccupied all members of the municipal classes. Augustine had grown up among persons who were dogged by the fear of impoverishment. He and his new group had reason to be afraid that they might slide back into the shabby gentility and unimportance of minor city notables once they loosened their grip on their private properties.

For this reason, it is not sufficient to ask whether Augustine and his friends became poor or remained rich at this time. The issue was, rather, what resources could they draw upon to protect themselves once they had brought to a full stop in themselves the momentum of the drive to wealth. Would they slip back into poverty and social impotence?

The answer to this question was "no." Many of Augustine's friends were rich. Quite apart from his landed wealth, a man such as Alypius had drawn a large salary as a government servant. Within a few years of his return to Thagaste, Alypius was able to engage in one of the most expensive enterprises of all in the ancient world. Travel had always been the privilege of the rich, and some time in the early 390s, Alypius traveled all the way to the Holy Land to gather books from Saint Jerome.[35] He was soon chosen as the Catholic bishop of Thagaste. As bishop he would have found himself administering the properties that he, along with Augustine and others, had given to the church. Like any urban benefactor, he had bought himself into a leadership role by such gifts. As bishop of Thagaste, Alypius remained a pillar of the community. He traveled constantly to and from Italy to bring the affairs of Thagaste and of the African churches in general to the attention of the emperor. Indeed, in the 420s Alypius spent more time in Italy, as a sixty-year-old bishop charged with lobbying the court, than he had ever spent there when making his career as a young man.[36]

To those who knew of it, the community established at Thagaste would have looked like any other gathering of leisured, bookish persons. Augustine intended to contribute to the religious life of the region "by spiritual advice to those present and to those who were absent, as well as by books."[37] Books cost money. To write five books against the Manichees "all duly put together and emended" was an expensive undertaking.[38] In a letter he wrote to Romanianus at this time, Augustine spoke of the material costs of such work. He had already loaned Romanianus his ivory writing tablets for perusal. He wrote to Romanianus that he must be content with cheap and durable sheets of parchment (taken, perhaps, from local herds) rather than with the more elegant format of imported papyri.[39]

It is one of Augustine's last letters to the grandee of Thagaste who had played such a crucial role in his early life. He no longer had any desire to depend exclusively on patrons of the size of Romanianus. Rather, he found himself gravitating, almost insensibly, toward a new, more acceptable but no less demanding set of patrons—the Catholic bishops of Africa. At this time, Augustine wrote many books against the Manichees. But he did not do this only out of "indomitable pugnacity."[40] He wrote out of loyalty to an institution—the Catholic Church in Africa—which had begun to show that it could take care of its own.

We are on the edge of a significant generational change. The fourth-century world had been characterized by an exuberant growth of grassroots religious institutions, whether these were the monasteries of Egypt, the widespread cells of the Manichees, or the Catholic communities in major cities, such as that which Ambrose had conjured up in Milan. Among these institutions, the Catholic churches had begun to pull ahead. After 370, all over the Latin West, real wealth and cultural prestige had begun to tilt in their direction. Smaller groups, such as that founded by Augustine and his friends, had originally based themselves on ancient models of spiritual friendship and on the ideal of *otium*—of leisure devoted to the cultivation of spirit and mind. Such groups were the last of a series of countercultural experiments with long roots in the upper-class culture of the ancient world.

Even when created by Christians, these little groups were notably unchurched. Like many Christian intellectuals, Augustine tried hard not to look down on clergymen. But it was difficult not to do so. As we have seen, the clergy were generally persons of middling or low status. They did their job in shepherding the masses. But, in Augustine's opinion in 388, this left them with little time to pursue the philosophical wisdom that truly healed the soul. This was what he and his well-to-do friends hoped to do in a little community of their own founding.[41]

But now the time had come for the leaders of such small groups to make up their minds. Could they continue to "do it their way"? They had to decide to which larger, richer institution they might turn to guarantee their own survival. It is the logic of this situation, working against Augustine's own conscious intentions, that unexpectedly pushed him toward what, in many ways, was a predictable resolution of the dilemma that faced any small, self-supporting group of religious persons in the late fourth century. He became a clergyman and placed his monastery under the wing of a bishop. Let us see how this happened.

In early 391 Augustine went to Hippo Regius, a coastal city, to give spiritual counsel to a devout layman. The bishop of Hippo, Valerius, aided by a zealous congregation, forced him to become a priest. In the eyes of the Christian "people" of Hippo, their very violence showed that they had been moved by a forcer larger and more compelling than themselves—by the Holy Spirit—much as the *populus* of a city were accustomed to imposing their will by shouting "inspired" acclamations in the theater. Acting in the name of the Holy Spirit, the church of Hippo claimed Augustine as its own by imposing on him ordination as a priest.[42]

In a letter Augustine wrote to Valerius immediately after this event, Augustine laid down the terms on which he would serve the church of Hippo.[43] The monastery must come with him. He would bring a chosen number of his fellows from Thagaste. Valerius gave Augustine permission to set up a monastery in the bishop's garden. This may have been a garden close to the main church, near the episcopal residence within what has been called by archaeologists the "Christian quarter" of Hippo.[44]

In the next few years, the situation of the monastery became more clear. By the time Augustine succeeded Valerius as bishop of Hippo, in 396, the crucial document known as the *Praeceptum—The Command*—had been drawn up. It was addressed to those "who live in the monastery." It began with a masterfully concise statement of principle, drawn from the *Acts of the Apostles*:

> The chief motivation for your sharing life together is to live harmoniously in the [one] house and to have one heart and one soul seeking God—*in deum*. Do not call anything your own. Possess everything in common.[45]

The opening phrases of the *Praeceptum* brought lapidary closure to a decade spent in search of a community fused by the shared vision of God. It had begun with plans for a philosophical community in Milan that would replace the sectarian solidarity of the Manichees. It had continued under the ancient guise of a period of *otium* within sight of the Alps at Cassiciacum. Between himself and Monica, the striving for a shared vision had reached a mystical climax "at a window, overlooking a garden" in Ostia. Now, this vision of the shared life had come to rest in a bishop's garden at Hippo, across the sea from Ostia. In this community, the sharing of wealth had become central. In Augustine's view, shared goods both condensed and further enabled a vibrant unity of hearts. Let us now turn to see what Augustine's monasteries in Hippo were like. Then we will linger on the views on society and on the human person (some very ancient and some very new) that had come to weigh upon Augustine in such a way as to infuse the seemingly straightforward words of his *Praeceptum* with a quite distinctive tone.

CHAPTER 11

❦

"The Life in Common of a Kind of Divine and Heavenly Republic"
Augustine on Public and Private in a Monastic Community

The Monasteries at Hippo

From the time of his ordination as a priest at Hippo in 391 to his death in 430, Augustine's life and thought were inextricably linked to the monastery that he had founded. Its importance in his life is obvious. But, unfortunately, the precise course of its development as an institution is shadowy. For most of the time, except when provoked by the occasional scandal, he took the existence of the monastic backdrop to his daily life for granted and seldom discussed it. As a result, it remains for us the dark side of the moon of the life of Augustine.

But we do know something of the early history of the monastery. In 391 Augustine had brought to Hippo from Thagaste a group that still contained many of his friends. They formed the nucleus of the new monastery in the bishop's garden. But this group soon became more diverse. It was joined by persons with whom Augustine had not previously been acquainted. Many came from social backgrounds different from his own and from that of his friends. It may have been this situation that produced the famous *Rule of Augustine*. It has been cogently argued by George Lawless that this *Rule* was drawn up in around 397. It fell into two parts, an *Ordo monasterii*—a set of *Regulations for a Monastery*, which laid down a daily routine of prayer and work—and the *Praeceptum*, *The Command*, which took the form of a series of commands. This last was a lucid summary of the ground rules of life in a monastery. Like most monastic rules produced in late antiquity, the *Rule of Augustine* was not a foundational document. It was not intended to provide a carefully composed blueprint for a future monastery. Instead, it was a response to crisis in an existing monastery. It laid down rules to handle a new situation that had been brought about by growing social and cultural diversity within the monastery in its first five years in Hippo.[1]

At the same time as the *Ordo monasterii* and the *Praeceptum* were being drafted, the monastery itself split into two parts. When Augustine became bishop of Hippo in 396, he wished to continue to live as he had previously. He found that he could not act effectively as a bishop in the monastery that he had founded in the garden. As bishop, he had to keep open house to lay and clerical visitors from the city and from all over Africa. This could not be done without disrupting the life of the monks. So he moved some monks from the monastery into the bishop's palace and left the others in peace in the monastery in the garden.

The monks who moved to the palace had either already been ordained as clergymen or became clergymen. They formed a little monastery in the palace, subject to the same rules as those which had prevailed in the monastery in the garden—no marriage and, above all, no property.[2] It was they who always shared Augustine's table. Visitors to the bishop's table would have noticed that this was not the table of an ordinary local dignitary. There was no display of wealth at meal times. The cutlery was of silver, but the dishes were of terracotta and wood. Augustine had even written verses on the tabletop, warning those present to avoid malicious gossip.[3]

What Augustine had done, in effect, was a very Roman thing. Roman politicians and governors had always surrounded themselves with a group of *iuvenes*— a handpicked staff of up-and-coming young men. The monk-clerics (as we might call them) who gathered around Augustine in the bishop's palace were his *iuvenes*—his intimate staff. Apart from surrounding himself with his own circle of monks, Augustine made no attempt to impose a monastic life style on all other clergymen. Though he wrote passionately on the topic of monasticism in general, he had no grand policy for the churches of Africa. Many ordinary clergymen in Hippo as elsewhere remained married. All retained their property. But they were not members of Augustine's in-group.[4] It was from this in-group that Augustine chose bishops for cities all over Africa—at least ten persons were chosen in this way.[5] This was exactly what Ambrose had done when he placed "his" bishops (most of whom were not monks) in the little towns of northern Italy. It was also what Symmachus had done by constantly forwarding likely young men to posts at court and in the bureaucracy. In all this Augustine followed the typically late Roman tendency to use personal bonds to conduct public business.

For this reason he did not overlook the remnants of his family. His sister appeared from nowhere (she is not mentioned in the *Confessions*) as the head of a convent of nuns organized along exactly the same lines as Augustine's monastery.[6] His nephew (the son of Navigius, named after Augustine's father, Patricius) found a place as a monk-cleric at Augustine's table.[7] It is a reminder that in the real world outside Augustine's writings on the ideal nature of the monastic community, blood was always thicker than ink. For in late Roman Africa, as elsewhere, blood got things done.

Augustine came to use the word "monastery" for his community. At the time this was a novel buzzword of Greek origin. It had only just begun to circulate in Latin. But the members of the monastery were not called monks. They spoke of themselves as "brothers" and "sisters." They were known in the outside world as "servants of God." Their monastery and convent were not large establishments; each may have housed around twenty persons. Augustine's inner circle of clerical "brothers" in the bishop's palace probably numbered no more than ten at one time.

Nor was the monastery in the garden a remarkable building. Neither the monks in the garden nor the nuns at some other place we do not know were isolated from society by high walls.[8] They mingled freely with crowds of both sexes in church and in the streets. They were exposed to temptations such as could only have occurred for those who lived in a monastery without walls.

> When you see a woman, do not fix your eyes on her.... You are not forbidden to see women when you are out of the house. It is wrong, however, to desire women.... Such lust is stimulated on both sides, not only by tender touches, but by the gaze.[9]

Compared with how we tend to imagine monks and monasteries, based on their later history in the West, Augustine's monasteries and those who lived in them were almost indistinguishable from the world around them. Yet Augustine expected these men and women to participate in the most carefully thought-through experiment in creating a community without private property yet to be imagined in the Christian West. As Adalbert de Vogüé makes plain in his great survey of monastic literature, Augustine's *Regulations for the Monastery* (the supplement to the *Praeceptum*) was "one of the most clear and complete expositions which anyone has made of a monastic community in the ancient world."[10]

"The more you come to give care to the common good ... the more
you will know that you have made progress"

RICH AND POOR IN AUGUSTINE'S MONASTERY

Augustine's monastery was a community with a profile all its own. If we compare the *Regulations* and the *Praeceptum* with other rules from Cappadocia and Egypt, we are struck by how little Augustine had to say on issues to which eastern monastic leaders paid great attention. First and foremost, Augustine refused to take on frontally the issue of social differences within the monastery. Unlike Basil of Caesarea, he made no attempt to blot out the previous social *persona* of the members of his community by imposing a uniform dress code upon them.

Nor, unlike monastic founders in Egypt, such as Pachomius, did he impose a uniform workload on all monks. He was prepared to make allowances for the fact that his brethren came from very different walks of life, had worn very different clothes, and had brought with them very different skills. In the words of Adalbert de Vogüé, rich and poor were thrown into "the crucible of charity, which these communities wished to be, to melt and fuse as best they could."[11]

There may be a good reason for this seeming insouciance. Up to 391, the little group at Thagaste had been made up of persons of roughly the same class as Augustine himself. But the social atmosphere among Augustine's friends at Thagaste was rarefied in the extreme compared with that of a large port city such as Hippo. Sooner or later, Augustine's monastery in the garden, and even the monastery of his clergy, were joined by persons from the middling and lower classes such as had always formed the bulk of the Christian congregation. As in Ambrose's Milan so in Hippo—if on a smaller scale—an active group drawn from the higher levels of society found themselves, for the very first time, sharing the same institution with men and women of distinctly mediocre standing. But what for Ambrose could be presented as the euphoric overcoming of social distances in a crowded basilica was a recipe for grumbling, if not outright hatred, in the small face-to-face world of a monastery.

We should not underestimate the shock of this sudden opening of an elite group to take in more average persons. Each group was disturbed by finding itself at close quarters with the other. Poor monks had to be warned:

> They should not consider their present good fortune to consist in the possession of food and clothing which were beyond their means elsewhere [outside the monastery]. Nor should they put their nose in the air because they associate with people they did not dare to approach in the world.

Rich monks had to be told not to

> belittle their brothers who come to this holy society from a condition of poverty. They should endeavor to boast about their fellowship with these poor brothers rather than about the social standing of their rich relatives.[12]

In fact, Augustine's *Praeceptum* was written as a Zen for the handling of social difference.[13] It assumed that each brother (and each sister, for the document applied equally to nuns) would suffer from innumerable little slights that came from the fact that not all their colleagues were of the same class as themselves.

Take the issue of clothing. What we know about the role of clothing as a blazon of social status in a late Roman society explains Augustine's immense sensitivity to this issue. In the monastery and the convent, clothes were distributed from a common store. But what if the brother or sister received, at random, a shabby robe, very different from the high-quality robes he or she had donated to the monastery? As a concession to their frailty, the *Praeceptum* ruled that such persons could keep a personal robe if they so wished. But they could do this only on the condition that their other robes remained in the common wardrobe. Brothers and sisters alike were expected to accustom themselves, slowly but surely, to the thought that their clothes—and all other kinds of belongings— were no longer their own. They belonged to the community.[14]

Augustine was determined to drive this message home. The *Praeceptum* was to be read out every week. The extent to which each brother (or sister) learned to place the good of the community above his or her own needs (even in apparently banal situations, such as the distribution of clothes) was the benchmark of their spiritual growth: "and in this manner, the more you come to give care to the common good rather than to your own, the more you will know that you have made progress."[15]

It is important to grasp the weight and the long-term consequences of this overwhelming concern, on Augustine's part, for the common good. For this reason, let us move to higher ground. Let us linger on the intellectual preoccupations that lay behind the carefully phrased rulings of the *Praeceptum*.

Res publica

AUGUSTINE, CICERO, AND THE COMMON GOOD

For Augustine, the monastic experiment was in many ways an exercise in applied social theory. The monastery was a microcosm. Life within it revealed the immense, as yet unrealized potentiality for unity of the entire People of God. Augustine remained convinced that the latent possibility of a firestorm of love lurked, largely unseen and unrealized, within the immense, unwieldy macrocosm of the Christian churches. A monastery was simply a place where that fire of love was given the chance to burn more vividly than elsewhere. Like the hot point created by a magnifying glass in the sun, life in a monastery concentrated into a single, burning spot the diffuse love that bound together every Christian community. Augustine was confident that the love generated in a monastery pointed the way to an unimaginable future at the end of time. Then the firestorm of love would engulf the entire company of the blessed: "Out of many souls there will arise a City and a People *with a single soul and heart, turned towards God*."[16]

When it came to speaking about the unity of this City at the end of time, it was Cicero who gave Augustine the language that he needed. For Cicero, as we have seen, was deeply concerned with the cohesion of society and with the conditions that strengthened this cohesion in the face of violence and self-will. But Cicero's overriding concern could be interpreted in many ways. In their differing attitudes toward Cicero we can measure the distance between Ambrose and Augustine. Ambrose wrote his *De officiis* only eight years earlier than the framing of Augustine's *Praeceptum*. Yet the two texts seem to belong to two different ages. Ambrose followed Cicero in claiming to rally Roman society after its original cohesion had been sapped by greed. His was a call to return to a lost solidarity. Augustine also followed Cicero, but he followed a different Cicero. He followed the Cicero who had asked how any society (and especially his own society, the Roman Republic) had come into existence in the first place. Above all, how could a society, once formed, maintain that sense of the public, common good that had first brought it together? How did the all too precarious miracle of human unity around a common goal begin? How was it to be maintained? What would it finally achieve—and when?

Augustine had doubtless repeated Cicero's opinions for years on end as a teacher, long before he became a bishop.[17] What Cicero had passed on to him was an acute sense of the tension between the public and the private good—between unity around a common goal and disunity caused by individual self-interest. This tension had been crucial to Cicero's view of society. He had always urged the claims of the community upon the loyalty and the energy of its private citizens. For him, the word *res publica*—the Commonwealth, the Republic, the Common Cause—carried so heavy a freight of meaning that it is almost impossible to translate the term into a modern language. The shifting relations of Romans to their *res publica* summed up for Cicero the state of Roman society and explained the course—alternately splendid and disastrous—of Roman history.[18]

This was a side of Cicero with which Augustine identified wholeheartedly. For it laid bare a tension of the will in pursuit of two potentially opposed aims. It saw the private will as pitted against the public good. But we must remember the extent to which Augustine further sharpened this tension. He read his Cicero with the eyes of a fourth-century subject of a centralized and autocratic empire. The late Roman empire was committed to a high notion of the rule of law. Like the law of God, the law of the emperor was "public" law in the most stark sense. It was a law for all. To act outside this law was to seek a "private" field of action that was invariably associated in the governmental mind either with private violence or with private dabbling in the occult. "Private," for such persons, meant rebellion and sorcery.[19]

And Augustine was also a religious thinker. After the first optimism of his *Dialogues* at Cassiciacum, he returned to wrestling with the problem of evil, if only to find an answer to the Manichees. He began to take the measure of the catastrophe under which the human race had labored as a result of the fall of Adam. But what sort of "fall" had this been? Augustine came to the conclusion that the fall of Adam had taken the form of a free act of rebellion that had been preceded by the equally free rebellion of the angels. He described both of these events in terms that echoed Cicero. Both were rebellions in which private self-will was pitted against the common good. For God was the common good of all. The rebellion of Satan and then of Adam both stemmed from "a love which the Latin language has judiciously called 'private.'"[20] It was not a love of which Augustine expected his readers (well versed as they were in Cicero) to approve.

But Augustine was prepared to go further than Cicero ever went in order to assert the primacy of the public good over the private will. He defended the public good in a way that Cicero would never have done: he deprived his monks and nuns of private property. For Cicero, the tension between public and private was so dramatic precisely because it was left unresolved. For Cicero, private wealth was a fact of life. It came to an aristocrat from birth, almost like a robust character trait. To suggest a leveling of private fortunes through legislation struck him as "utterly condemnable."[21] For to deprive a statesman of his private fortune was like depriving him of the rugged aspects of his character—his sharp expression, his distinctive quirks, his unmistakable, individual tone of voice—he brought to the service of the public good.[22]

Ultimately, what mattered for Cicero was loyalty, not the abolition of private property. The heroes of the early republic were so vivid in the minds of Roman readers, Augustine among them, because they demonstrated the overriding loyalty of men of property to the *Respublica* they served. The *Respublica* in its heyday had been characterized by a magnificent imbalance between the public wealth of the Roman state and the private *egestas* of its leaders—their simple lifestyle and their lack of interest in accumulating private wealth. These were the qualities for which Augustine praised the ancient Romans in his *City of God*: "Those Romans had a republic richly endowed with all resources ... while they themselves lived in poverty in their houses."[23]

This was unwealth at its most heroic. An age of unwealth stood at the very origins of Roman greatness. For this reason, it is not surprising that Augustine conjured up the figure of no less than Scipio Africanus in order to encourage poor monks to practice their handicrafts for the good of the monastery as a whole and to think no longer of their private gain:

> If the former leaders of this earthly state [the Roman Republic] are commonly set forth as subjects of exceptional praise by Roman authors, because they placed a shared commitment to the interests of the entire people of their city above their own private interests—to such an extent that one of them who had just celebrated the conquest of Africa [Scipio Africanus] could not get together enough private funds even to provide a dowry for the marriage of his daughters—then what should be the attitude to *his* Republic of a citizen of that eternal City, the Heavenly Jerusalem?[24]

These words were written in a somewhat formal text. But if Augustine's message trickled down to the monastery itself, it would have been the first time that an artisan of Hippo had found himself (or herself) likened to the greatest general of Rome. Yet the loyalty of a "brother" or a "sister" in the tiny *Respublica* of the monastery was based on something yet more drastic: the total abandonment of all forms of private property. By insisting on this aspect of the monastic life Augustine made plain that he was not content simply to rally the private to a public cause, as Cicero proposed to do. He was bent on the erasure of the private itself. Unwealth must become no wealth at all. To what other traditions did he turn to justify so drastic a step?

"Not cut off ... but part of the whole"

PLOTINUS AND THE "SPIRITUAL COMMUNISM" OF AUGUSTINE

It has proved relatively easy to trace the "Ciceronian" elements in Augustine's views on society. Cicero has long been familiar to us. The imprint of his thought on Augustine, as on Ambrose, has been exhaustively studied.[25] But Cicero could offer Augustine nothing on the issue of monastic poverty. Indeed, Cicero was committed to the view that private property was essential to a properly ordered society. It is important to realize that Augustine agreed entirely with Cicero when it came to normal human society. Like Cicero, Augustine believed in no uncertain manner that the state existed to protect the property rights of private persons. After Adam's fall, private property guaranteed and protected by a strong state was the best that humans could hope for. Only a regime of private property validated by imperial law could fend off the worst effects of the pride, avarice, and violence that had come to be so deeply rooted in the human condition.[26]

But what happened in normal society had nothing to do with the building up of a monastic community A glass wall stood between the two worlds. Normal society arose from the clash of fallen human wills. It belonged to a doomed present. The union of hearts and minds in a monastery, by contrast, was a glimpse of the future. It showed the first, hesitant stages of the creation of an ideal community that would reach fulfillment only in a Heavenly Jerusalem at the end of time. The abandonment of private wealth was a first step toward that future. It pointed the way to a radically new world in which the private itself would fade away. To give philosophical weight to this ambition, Augustine drew on another, more austere and more exotic source—the thought of Plotinus. Plotinus gave Augustine what he needed. He enabled Augustine to go beyond the tense balance between public duty and private interests that had preoccupied Cicero.

Plotinus was a mystic. He lived as if perched on the edge of a vast ocean of the spirit. For him, the greatest puzzle of human existence remained how to explain the fact that, though bathed in the glorious abundance of the One, the human soul had allowed itself to slip into so many cramping, partial loves. A Greek metaphysician, the Roman tension between "public" and "private" meant little to Plotinus. What he had to explain was how the human soul (as we are usually aware of it) had become such a pathetically cramped thing. It had somehow become "partitioned off" from a greater Unity to which it must return.[27]

For Plotinus, the "private" was invariably tinged with the strong negative valence of "privation" of the Good. Hence Plotinus's repeated call to the soul to "return" to that primal Whole to which it rightfully belonged:

But we ... who are we? We were There, we were different from who we are now.

Some of us were even gods, pure souls, intellects united to the fullness of reality ... not [as we now are] marked off or cut off, but part of the Whole.[28]

In reading the works of Plotinus in Latin translation, Augustine had hit upon these passages. But he read them with Roman eyes, and very soon with the eyes of a Roman Christian who had begun to meditate on the rebellion of Adam. One cannot but be struck by the different tone of the two men. Plotinus evoked the silent, almost mesmerized fall of the soul into matter and, thus, into a cramped and privatized existence.[29] Augustine, by contrast, had before his eyes the fall of the Devil and the fall of Adam. Both the Devil and Adam had been fully conscious rebels. In late Roman style, they had pitted their own private wills against the public law of God. They had acted "boasting as if in their own strength, in their private resources, in which all pride takes its delight."[30]

By writing in this way, Augustine put forward an act of "privatization" as lying at the very root of the fallen human condition. The victory of the private over the public good was not something that had happened in the distant past, at the end of a Golden Age (as Ambrose had suggested when he described the origin of private property). It was the template for all sins—from the first sin of Adam up to the present.

For Augustine, a sense of the dire consequences of the fall of Adam reverberated on every level of society. But it was in the little community of his monastery that he was most passionately committed to combating the "private" will. "Brothers" and "sisters" who pitted their desire for private possession of anything against the common good of the monastery were not merely ignoring the overriding claims of a *Respublica*. They were pitting their private wills against a greater whole. In so doing, they reenacted the fateful rebellion of Adam. And, on a yet deeper level, they also played out once again the fall of the soul into cramped particularity whose tragic consequences Plotinus had traced with serene regret.

Augustine was at his most sharp when he wrote on these themes. In around 395 he wrote to a "brother" who still felt pulled by a sense of responsibility for his mother. In Augustine's opinion, this preoccupation held the would-be monk back from the chance to return to a unity as immense as any envisioned by Plotinus:

> Let each man question himself regarding his soul, to learn to hate in it a private feeling … and to love in it that communion and society of which it is said *They had but one soul and one heart outstretched to God* (*Acts* 4:32). So, indeed, is your very soul not your own; it is also that of all your brothers, whose souls are yours, or rather whose souls combined with yours are no longer souls, but a single soul, the One Soul of Christ.[31]

Augustine was so severe because of his sense that private loves were incommensurably less generous than was a love directed toward higher, wider things. He had drawn from Plotinus the lasting certainty that, in touching God, humans touched an abundance that dwarfed their private striving to possess. From Cassiciacum onward, he had been committed to the notion of the ability of all to share, equally and without the competition of a zero-sum game, in the sweet immensity of Wisdom. Augustine's call to a common enjoyment of Wisdom (in his *Soliloquia* of 386) went out of its way to awaken in his readers almost a frisson, such as had long been associated, in philosophical circles, with remissive thoughts of "philosophical" Free Love:

> A woman will only strip for a single-hearted lover; yet, what limit can be placed on the love of that [Divine] Beauty, in relation to which not only do I not envy others, but I even seek out more and more those who will grab hold of her with me, will gasp to have her with me, will hold her with me and, along with me, have full enjoyment of her: and these will be even better friends to me, the more our darling is shared between us.[32]

Modern readers are more easily shocked by such language than were the ancients. We tend to dismiss such a passage as the product of a youthful exuberance, produced by the somewhat overheated atmosphere of Cassiciacum. But this was not the case. Decades later, the theme of shared delight in Wisdom reappeared in a fully public sermon on the *Psalms*:

> But what does the lover of the Wisdom of God say? *Proclaim along with me the greatness of the Lord.* (*Psalm* 33:4) I do not wish to love alone. It is not as if when I have embraced her no one else can find a place to put their hand. There is such ample space in Wisdom, that all souls may caress her and enjoy her to the full.[33]

In all this, we are dealing with a highly idiosyncratic "bleeding" of one discourse into another. A Roman suspicion of the private as a potential obstacle to the common good took on an even sharper tone when joined with a Plotinian call to transcend the "compartmented" state of normal existence. Whenever he came to speak and write about the community of goods within his monastery, issues of actual wealth were never uppermost in Augustine's mind. Rather, what drove him was a passionate sense of the supreme abundance of God and an aversion to the depletion inherent in all private striving to possess. It is this rare mixture of republican Roman virtue (represented by Cicero) and a mystic's yearning for the infinite (represented by Plotinus) that formed the basis of what has been called by Goulven Madec, its most perceptive exponent, "the spiritual communism" of Augustine.[34]

> This is the life in common of a kind of divine and heavenly Republic—a Commonwealth in which *the poor* [the humble worshipers] *are sent away full* (*Luke* 1:53) for *they seek not their own but the things of Jesus Christ* (*Phil.* 2:21).[35]

"It was good for us to be bathed in that common Light"

Whenever he preached on the theme of unity based on the sharing of a common good, Augustine's voice was tinged with great sadness. The victory of the "divine Republic" would only happen in heaven. And heaven was a long way off. Yet it was not beyond yearning for. Preaching in the early 420s (now an old man, approaching seventy), he brought his sermon to an end:

> I sense that your feelings have been drawn upwards with me to heaven. But now I will put away the copy of the Gospel. You will go home, each your own way.... It was good for us to be bathed [for a moment] in that common Light. It was good that we rejoiced. It was good that we have exulted together. But, as we now walk away from each other, as we go each to our own home, may we not walk away from our shared God.[36]

But that was thirty years ahead, and in sadder times for Africa and for the empire as a whole. In 395, nothing of that future was known. What had happened so far in Augustine's life was no small change. An upwardly mobile member of the class of town councillors (and, for that reason, more than usually dependent on a network of patrons and intimate friends) had found his way, through a series of shared enthusiasms—within a religious sect, within a philosophical community, and finally, within his newly founded monastery—to the ideal of a property-less community. When applied to monasteries, this ideal would remain for all of a millennium the most prominent and the most charged model of human institution building in the Latin West.

Though prepared by a long inner evolution, Augustine's monastic experiment did not take place in a sheltered retreat. Hippo was a major port; Augustine and his monks stood on the edge of the wider world. They were well placed to participate in the web of spiritual friendships that well-to-do Christians had begun to weave around the Mediterranean. In 395 Augustine and his monks in Hippo received a letter that amounted to an invitation to enter into one such spiritual friendship. It came from Pontius Meropius Paulinus, a senatorial nobleman with properties in Italy, Gaul, and Spain. Paulinus had come to settle in Nola, in Campania, having formally renounced his vast fortune.[37]

The conversion of a member of the super-rich such as Paulinus was a remarkable event. For a short time in Milan, Augustine had come within sight of wealth. He knew that the wealth of Paulinus was real wealth. It was not the wealth of a mere careerist, nor was it the wealth of a bureaucrat. It was old money. It was the wealth of a senatorial nobleman, based on generations of accumulation and spread over many provinces. This was wealth woven into the very fiber of Paulinus's being. Augustine was impressed:

> For some mysterious reason, [he wrote, in answer to Paulinus's first letter] superfluous and earthly things hold you more tightly if they are already yours, than if they are merely desired. This was why the Rich Young Man *went away saddened ... for he had great wealth* (Luke 18:22–23).... It is one thing not to wish to make one's own what one does not have, and something very different to tear out what is already part, as it were, of one's own flesh. What we do not have can be refused, like food. To renounce what we already own, is like amputating parts of one's own body.[38]

The renunciation of Paulinus had occurred in the same years as Augustine had been settling back in Africa. To understand it, we have to leave the southern Mediterranean far behind. We have to leave Africa and even Italy to get a sense of what great wealth had meant to Paulinus and to those around him, in his days of comfort in the great villas of Gaul and Spain. We then have to follow what it meant to Paulinus to unravel this fortune and to put it to use, in Campania, as a letter writer, builder, and living exemplar of Christian renunciation in the midst of a region which, for the pagan Symmachus, had been the chosen landscape of his heart.

CHAPTER 12

Ista vero saecularia: Those things, indeed, of the world

Ausonius, Villas, and the Language of Wealth

The Parting of Friends: Ausonius and Paulinus, 394–95

Pontius Meropius Paulinus is known to us now as Paulinus of Nola. He was almost exactly the same age as Augustine. When they first made contact with each other (in 395, a year after Paulinus's definitive rejection of his wealth), each had just entered their forties. Both had made drastic changes in their lives in their mid-thirties. Augustine, the son of a modest town councillor, had abandoned a promising career. Along with a group of his friends he had thought himself ever deeper and deeper into the ideal of a life in a small community radically stripped of private wealth. Given the proliferation of similar small groups at the time, among persons of roughly the same unprepossessing background as Augustine, it was an unremarkable solution. The long-term implications of his setting up a monastery linked to the bishop's palace in Hippo were by no means apparent at the time.

Paulinus, by contrast, had passed through a spectacular conversion. He had abandoned an entire senatorial fortune. It was like the crash of an avalanche. For the first time, Christian ascetic teaching had touched a male member of the super-rich. Ambrose (now in his mid-fifties) was delighted. Writing to a fellow bishop in 394, he took particular pleasure in describing how the colleagues of Paulinus in the Roman Senate (Ambrose's own peers—one can imagine the elderly Symmachus among them) would react to the news:

> What will the nobles say? ... That a man from that family, with that lineage, with so much talent ... has abandoned the Senate and broken the continuity of a noble line: this is intolerable.[1]

Not only was Paulinus's act of renunciation made instantly notorious at the time. It has been preserved for all ages by the poignant exchange of poems that took place between Paulinus and his former mentor, the eighty-year-old Ausonius of Bordeaux.[2] Ausonius was appalled by Paulinus's decision. The poems Ausonius wrote to dissuade his friend and the cruel sublimity with which Paulinus answered them have been the delight of readers of late Latin poetry ever since. More than any other documents, they seem to sum up the turning of an age. In the words of Nora Chadwick:

> We feel the beauty and dignity of these two men, so different in outlook, so incompatible in ideals, the eternal gulf which separates each generation from its predecessor, and which no affection or education can bridge.[3]

The two men stand out with an autumnal clarity: "Ausonius is the last of the untroubled age.... And suddenly," writes Helen Waddell in the opening chapter of her exquisite book, *The Wandering Scholars*, "in the midst of this lacquered correspondence ... the great wind blows."[4]

But we must not let this moving exchange of poems absorb the whole of our attention. We are dealing with more than a clash of personalities. Ausonius and Paulinus stood for two options for the rich of the late fourth century and for the two worldviews that were summed up in these options.

For we must never forget that Paulinus's conversion was about wealth. What he turned away from was certainly not paganism; both he and Ausonius came from Christian families. Nor (despite Ausonius's fears) did Paulinus opt for an asceticism of a punishing and antisocial kind that took him out of Roman society (as was known to have happened in the case of many more radical ascetics). But he had, in no uncertain manner, turned away from wealth. He had slipped out from under the widely diffused mystique associated with great riches. This mystique pressed down on all members of his class with the imperceptible but crushing weight of an entire atmosphere.

For this reason, this chapter will not be concerned with Paulinus. It will deal with the world that preceded his renunciation. It will attempt to convey something of the sheer weight and seriousness of the mystique of wealth that Ausonius shared with his peers and that he, Paulinus, rejected. For only after we have measured the intensity of this mystique can we spell out the implications of Paulinus's refusal to take part in it.

Praesedi imperio: I presided over the Empire

DECIMIUS MAGNUS AUSONIUS AND THE EMPIRE OF TRIER

The best way to enter into this mystique is to look more closely at Ausonius himself. Let us begin by placing Ausonius against the wider landscape of fourth-century Gaul. So far, we have concentrated mainly on Italy and Africa. But to cross the Alps from Italy into Gaul was to enter a very different world. It was a world where, for much of the fourth century, many roads led to Trier—and few to Rome. Trier had been the imperial capital par excellence of the Latin-speaking world for almost a century. Constantine had endowed it with one of the largest public baths in the entire empire. It was second only to the baths of Rome. By the 370s, most of the space of these baths had been taken over by government offices. This vast complex was the Pentagon of the West.

The Porta Nigra of Trier has usually been associated with the emperor Valentinian I (364–75). It is still standing; it is the highest surviving Roman building north of the Alps. Its heavy towers seem to conjure up associations of a medieval castle. It has been presented as the sign of an empire under siege, but at the time it was viewed as a supremely confident monument. It was a triumphal arch that faced aggressively northward toward the frontier of the Rhine, which lay a mere sixty miles away. From the coast of Wales overlooking the Irish Sea to the Iron Gates of the Danube, Trier, and not Rome, was the capital of non-Mediterranean Europe.[5]

Trier was the center of an unusually active state. The more we study west Roman society in the fourth century, the more we realize the extent to which the flow of taxes and supplies to Trier and to the armies of the Rhine primed the pump of the economy from which the landowners of Gaul, Spain, and southern Britain derived their wealth. In the time of Ausonius, a persistent fiscal current flowed through what are now southern England, France, Spain, and Portugal. This fiscal current was not uniform and did not always penetrate deeply into the agrarian landscape of many regions. But it did create what students of the Ottoman empire have called "corridors of empire."[6] It is along those corridors of empire that we find the wealthiest landowners and the most splendid villas. In a world where, from the fiscal point of view, all roads ran to Trier, this was wealth derived (in the irreverent words of two recent scholars) from a landscape "tied to an imperial gravy train."[7]

Ausonius trod the "corridors of empire" to good effect. It was in Trier, in 369, that he met none other than Quintus Aurelius Symmachus, then a young man not yet thirty. Symmachus had made his way, for the first and last time in his life, to Trier. He did it ostensibly for fiscal reasons. He brought to the stern emperor Valentinian I a large sum of gold, collected from the Roman Senate, as a "free will offering" to fund the emperor's campaigns in Germany. Symmachus had also come to Trier to find friends in high places. In this he succeeded. In Ausonius he met a man twenty years older than himself who proved to be one of his most firm allies, "a father and a friend."[8] Had Valentinian I's dynasty proved more enduring, Trier and not Milan might have remained the effective capital of the West. It would have been the city to which Symmachus traveled regularly. We might have heard considerably less of Ambrose. Even Augustine the African might have found himself teaching beside the banks of the Moselle.

Ausonius was in many ways the "shadow" of Symmachus. He was a nobleman by culture without the solid advantages of old money such as Symmachus enjoyed. He had been born in Aquitaine into a circle of civic notables. His family nursed a claim to an ancient nobility that had been lost a century before in the civil wars of Gaul in the 260s. Ausonius's grandfather had come to Aquitaine as a refugee from Autun. His claim to nobility was somewhat tenuous. In reality, he and his family were little more than local landowners and town councillors who had risen by their talents. Ausonius's father was a doctor. Ausonius became a poet and a teacher. Up to 365, the schoolrooms of Bordeaux—and no great ancestral villa—had been the center of Ausonius's life.[9]

But if Ausonius was no Symmachus, he was certainly no Augustine. The aura of faded nobility that seems to have clung to his family proved an advantage to Ausonius. It enabled Ausonius and many of his relatives to marry upward into better-established local families in Aquitaine. One cannot imagine Augustine, the son of a mere *tenuis municeps*, doing this. Romanianus had offered him financial support, but not a bride.[10] Furthermore, to be connected with Bordeaux was very different from being a town councillor of Thagaste. Bordeaux was not only a major cultural center; it was the Trier of the Atlantic. It was the seat of the Vicar (the deputy of the prefect) of the southern provinces of Gaul. The recent excavations of its port have shown wide commercial contacts, which included links with Britain, a silent world whose role in the economy of fourth-century Atlantic Europe has only begun to be explored by numismatists and archaeologists.[11] Two relatives known to Ausonius had traded there.[12]

One suspects that Valentinian I looked with favor on Ausonius in part so as to establish a comfortable relationship with Bordeaux and with Ausonius's pupils, the landowners of Aquitaine. He appointed Ausonius as tutor to his son, Gratian. In 375 he became quaestor (framer of the imperial edicts). When Valentinian died, in 375, to be succeeded by Gratian, Ausonius found himself catapulted into prominence. In 377 he was named Prefect of the Gauls. In 378–79 his prefecture was extended to cover Africa and Italy. In 379 he even became consul for the year. The old professor (now in his mid-sixties) was put on display. He was dressed in the same set of heavy, gold-stitched consular robes that had once been worn by none other than the emperor Constantius II, the son of Constantine. As Ausonius later told his grandson in a celebratory poem, for three euphoric years "I presided over the Empire."[13]

Ausonius (of course!) ascribed his success to the young emperor Gratian's gratitude to his old tutor. In reality, he had emerged as a compromise figure in an elegant public relations maneuver by Gratian's court. Gratian's advisers realized that they had to back down a little from the tradition of hard rule upheld by

Gratian's father, the tight-fisted Valentinian I. The nobility of Rome had to be placated. Records of tax arrears were burned in solemn bonfires. A few scapegoats were found and duly executed as exemplary punishment for their mishandling of Roman senators. But that was as far as Gratian and his advisers were prepared to retreat.[14]

Here Ausonius proved useful to the court. His appointment as prefect and then as consul was the perfect way to send a reassuring message to the nobility of Rome and, at the same time, to block further claims by them. No Roman senator could object to Ausonius. He was a teacher of the classics and an upholder of the ideals to which the senatorial nobility of Rome claimed to be devoted. He was the ego ideal of an entire class, which valued *otium* and the cultivation of classical literature. But, at the same time, Ausonius was not a Roman of Rome. He was a mere professor and no more than a municipal notable. His egregiously humble speech of thanks to the emperor for his consulship (which we considered in chapter 5) showed that Ausonius was mercifully without the arrogance and the sense of entitlement of the real article—the *nobiles* of Rome.

De herediolo: On my little family estate

AUSONIUS AND HIS WEALTH

Ausonius's good fortune did not last. In 383 the British armies, headed by Maximus, took over Trier. Gratian was killed. Ausonius withdrew from Trier to Aquitaine. He spent the last decade of his life alternating between Bordeaux and the estates that lay within easy distance of the city.

In this decade, his poetry and letters took him down memory lane.[15] He wrote on his family (the *Parentalia*). He wrote vignettes on the professors of Bordeaux. His letters and poems dwell lovingly on an Aquitanian landscape criss-crossed by gifts and by visitors perpetually on the move from one well-stocked villa to the other. In doing this, he created, in his seventies, a distinctive landscape of the heart that was quite as vivid, as appealing to modern scholars—and quite as much a fruit of wishful thinking—as was the heritage zone of Symmachus's Campania. This is the Ausonius we know so well: Ausonius the landowner and citizen of Bordeaux, whose last and most poignant poems were written so as to lure his friend Paulinus back to Aquitaine.

Ausonius left the court of Trier because of a brutal regime change. But late Roman gentlemen did not dwell on their political reverses. Time out of office was not treated as a defeat; it was presented as time dedicated to *otium*. As we have seen, *otium* meant many things to different sections of the late Roman upper classes. For Ausonius, *otium* represented a moment of blessed equipoise. Freed

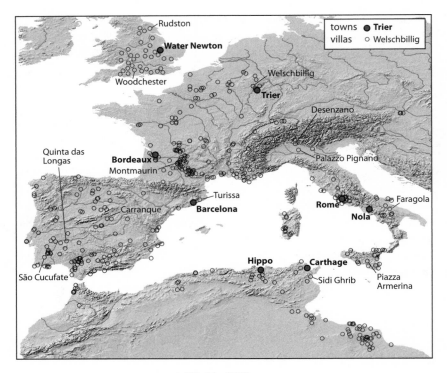

MAP 2. A World of Villas, ca. 400 AD

The reader should know that this map of the distribution of villas is impressionistic. Unlike towns, almost all villas are known to us through modern excavations. Their distribution reflects to a large extent the good fortune or the interest of archaeologists in different regions of Europe.

from the noisy streets of Bordeaux and from the endless personal encounters that were the cost of keeping abreast of the political life of the city, Ausonius could enjoy (if only for a few months in the year) the ultimate reward of a man who had arrived—a nobleman's freedom to do as he pleased:

> You dispose of your times as if you yourself and your affairs were in your own hands, so that there is nothing that you do which you have not yourself willed.[16]

Otium gave Ausonius the chance to turn once again to the Muses. And what better reason to seek their inspiration than to celebrate his own wealth? Hence Ausonius's remarkable poem, entitled *De herediolo*, "On My Little Family Estate." At first sight, the poem is remarkable in its precision. Here we have a late

Roman estate, situated somewhere outside Bazas, that measured (so Ausonius tells us) exactly 1,050 *jugera* (264.411 hectares or 653.33 acres). Of these, 700 *jugera* (436.47 acres) were woodland (woodland was valued not only as a reserve for wild game but as a commercially profitable source of timber and of pitch for ships and wine amphorae); 200 *jugera* (124.70 acres) were plough land; 100 were vineyards; and 50 were meadows. It boasted warehouses (those fateful signs of accumulation) with enough capacity to store food to last for two years. No other literary source in the entire history of the ancient world gives such statistics. It was a substantial estate. On a rough calculation, the arable land alone would have brought in around 1,000 *solidi*. This was the equivalent of one of the large estates given by Constantine to the Roman church.[17]

But Ausonius did not write the poem as a document of social history. Least of all did he write it so as to flaunt his wealth. He wrote it as a sort of economic *Gnôthi seauton*—a "Know Yourself" manual, in which he projected the image of himself as a modest man.[18] The *De herediolo* was not intended to be an account of Ausonius's wealth. Rather, it was an account of the sort of wealth others would allow Ausonius to possess without criticizing him for unseemly greed. It reflected a pose a person of Ausonius's class and culture—a member of the nobility of service—was supposed to adopt.

Furthermore, like Symmachus, Ausonius went out of his way to present his estate as part of his "ancestral" wealth. In reality, it may have come from his deceased wife (the daughter of a local civic notable). But Ausonius wrote of it as if it formed part of the "hereditary realms" handed down from his great-grandfather.[19] Above all, it was an estate appropriate to the measured soul of a "Man of the Muses":

> It is a tiny patrimony, I allow; but never yet did property seem small to those whose souls are balanced.... It is upon the soul—in my measured judgment—that wealth depends, and not a man's soul upon his wealth.[20]

Alas, the unforgiving eyes of modern scholars have discovered, through careful sifting of the correspondence of Ausonius with his friends, what Ausonius never tells us: apart from this "little heritage," the old courtier had managed to accumulate, by the end of his life, at least six other estates.[21] These were scattered around Bordeaux, as far apart as Saintes to the north and Bazas to the south.

Ausonius had come into wealth. Let us linger for a moment on what this wealth looked like, in the form of the villas and the town houses of the fourth century. We will then consider from what sources this wealth was derived, and hence what were the sort of persons who had an interest in displaying it. We will end the chapter on a more general note. We will trace the distinctive imaginative associations of wealth that were shared by villa owners of the age of Ausonius and Paulinus.

Vita bona fruamur felices: Let us, the lucky ones, enjoy the good life

In order to do this, we must abandon a figure for a landscape. Although we know much about the landscape of Gaul from the poetry of Ausonius, we have to look deeper than the shimmering surface these poems present. We must look at the material remains connected with the villas of Britain, Gaul, and the Iberian peninsula (both modern Portugal and modern Spain). What we meet in these remains, even in their present fragmentary state, is nothing less than the stuff of dreams expressed in stone, mosaic, glass, gold, and silverware. We are looking at the splendor of the rich and at what this splendor was meant to convey. We have already seen how much the rich expected to stand out in late Roman society through their brilliant clothes and through the heady moments of their giving of great games. But these were transient flashes of grandeur compared with what we can see in the villas, the town houses, and the baths in which the wealthy lived out their lives both in the countryside and in their cities.

It is a good moment for us to take stock of the mystique of wealth at this time as expressed in material objects. Due to the heartening progress of archaeology all over western Europe and north Africa, a rapidly increasing number of monumental villas of the fourth and early fifth centuries have been revealed by survey and excavation. Their discovery has thrown new light on the horizons and lifestyle of the late Roman rich. In particular, the Spain and Aquitaine known to Paulinus and Ausonius have come to be associated with unusually impressive villas that are now the subject of comprehensive monographs.[22] Visiting late Roman villas as a tourist or an archaeologist, looking at their plans, examining their mosaics, and viewing in museums all over Europe the statuary and silverware associated with them makes us realize that we are not only being presented with economic and social documents that help us measure the power and wealth of those who owned them. We are listening to the heavy voice of wealth in a distant age. These varied artifacts present us with a diffuse but insistent message on the imagined origins and use of riches. They speak to us of

> wealth ... transmitted into ornament, luxury, pleasure ... like an old wine, [it] had let the dregs of greed, even of care and prudence, fall to the bottom of the barrel, leaving only verve and color.[23]

If we want to understand the full implications of Paulinus's rejection of such wealth and of the changing mood in late Roman society that made his renunciation possible, we are well advised to listen to the voice of wealth as it spoke, loud and clear, to the majority of his upper-class contemporaries.

What first strikes us is the *splendor*—the sheer éclat—of late Roman houses. The residences of the late Roman rich—whether their villas or their town houses —were characterized by an explosion of color on their walls and floors, which went hand in hand with the sudden explosion of color in their dress.[24] In the houses of the truly wealthy, the effects of color would have been overpowering. We must remember that we see only the last traces of these splendid mansions. Only the mosaic pavements have survived, laid out like great carpets on ground level. But mosaic was a relatively cheap art form. The real wealth of an upper-class residence lay in the multicolored marbles that covered its walls. The few examples of inlaid marble decoration on the walls of secular buildings that have been discovered are spectacular.[25] Only by going into churches that have survived intact from the late Roman period (such as parts of San Vitale in Ravenna, the apse wall of the basilica at Poreč, or the cascade of colored marbles that pours down the inner sides of the Hagia Sophia in Istanbul) can a modern person glimpse the blaze of opulent color that sheathed the walls of the wealthy from floor to ceiling.

Faced by so much magnificence, there is a tendency among scholars to emphasize that the layout of town houses and villas reflected a stark stratification of late Roman society. Simon Ellis, in particular, has argued that the rich of the fourth century built their villas and town houses in such a way as to dominate their clients and dependents.[26] The open, flowing spaces of the old Roman house were closed in. Reception rooms and rooms for solemn dining came to predominate. These were built as opulent and grandiose stage sets, designed to heighten the status of the master of the house. Oriented toward a domed apse at one end, the great halls were as solemn and as overpowering as courtrooms. These inner halls were approached by long corridors and shielded from public view by exotic tapestries.[27]

Yet we must be careful not to exaggerate this trend. As Kim Bowes has recently pointed out, in an acute revision of the dominant opinion, much of this architecture was built so as to delight quite as much as to overawe. Apses did not always create the effect of a virtual throne room. Often, they simply lightened the spirit. They made each owner's villa seem recondite and surprising.[28] There is a social corollary to this reinterpretation. Villas were not built only by the few, so as to highlight their outright dominance over the remainder of society—far from it. Their pursuit of baroque ingenuity pointed, rather, to the existence of a relatively widespread and competitive class of persons whose incomes might vary considerably region by region and family by family. Like the carefully crafted poems of Ausonius, there was a bijou quality about the architecture of many villas. They could be miniaturized or expanded according to the resources of their owners. As a result, we should not concentrate only on the few truly great villas of the period. Villas came in any number of sizes, from small jewel boxes set in the countryside of Spain and southern Portugal to the overpowering spread of the great villa of Piazza Armerina in Sicily or of Carranque in Spain. Wherever they occurred, villas were not built only by a privileged few. They hint at the strong competitive urges of a widespread class of landowners, each of whom was anxious to stake out a claim on the landscape. In the words of Kim Bowes (adapting a phrase of Le Corbusier), villas were not so much "machines for living" as "machines for competition."[29]

In all this, we are not faced simply with an art *of* the rich. We are dealing with art *by* the rich that was devoted with peculiar zest to the theme of *being* rich. For instance, we are shown the rich dining in great luxury. They had always done this: but now they were shown doing it—and with gusto.[30] The same applies to the other aspects of the activities of the rich. They were shown hunting. They were shown relaxing in front of spacious villas. The architectural features of these villas were often shown on silverware or on mosaics as crowded together so as to indicate in a condensed visual shorthand their opulent and varied appurtenances, right down to the cluster of domes that show active bathhouses from which steam emerges in happy puffs. Villas were shown as if they were little cities. But this was not because they blocked out the city in the imagination of their owners. It was because, like the city, the villa was thought to contain everything necessary to the full life of a nobleman.[31]

Only occasionally did the literary coyness of an Ausonius appear in real life. Even then, this coyness was applied only to the personal behavior of the rich and not to the splendor of the buildings in which they lived. A villa has recently been discovered at the far, eastern end of the Roman empire of the West. It lay very much on a corridor of empire, a few miles off the great imperial road that stretched across the Balkans, in the area between Naissus (modern Niš) and Scupi (Skopje) (in what is now Nerodimlje, near Uroševac in southwest Kosovo). In this villa, a well-appointed apse for dining looked out over a large, regularly patterned mosaic. At the head of the mosaic (where the guests could see them as they passed to their dining couches) were images of the Seven Sages of Greece. Beneath each image was a Latin version of a saying. These sayings were as calculated to dampen the fun as were the sermons of any Christian bishop. Pittacus of Lesbos reminded the diners, "Know Yourself"; Solon of Athens added *Ne quid nimis*—"Do not overdo it"; Creobulus of Myndos chimed in with "Due measure is always useful."[32]

Such moralizing language was usually avoided. The scenes of provincial life (which serve to illustrate so many recent books on the society of the later empire) would not have been there for us to look at if the rich themselves had not wished to show in a peculiarly assertive manner that they were rich, that they intended to remain rich, and that they greatly enjoyed it. An exquisite drinking glass (possibly made in Trier) was found in a fourth-century villa in southern Britain. Around it was written the slogan for a toast: *Vita bona fruamur felices*— "Let us, the lucky ones, enjoy the good life!"[33] This was the motto of the age that produced both Ausonius and the young Paulinus.

Art and Life: Who Were the Villa Owners?

But where did this wealth come from? In answering this question, we must be careful. The interpretation of these glittering artifacts has been affected by deeply rooted historical stereotypes. The splendor of the scenes portrayed on late Roman mosaics and silverware has often been used to illustrate the moralizing discourse of contemporary pagan and Christian texts. As in the sermons of Ambrose, we are invited to see these representations as a direct mirror—as candid camera shots, as it were—of the crass lifestyle of the late Roman rich. We assume that a lifestyle that was patently so luxurious and so supremely self-centered was bound to be bad for late Roman society as a whole. Above all, we are encouraged to believe that this art can be invoked as direct visual evidence for a widespread and sinister social development: the growth of the great estate as an autonomous unit, independent of the city and even of the imperial government.

This impression reflects a deeply rooted trend in the study of late Roman society. The power of the landowners of Gaul and Spain has tended to be viewed as immemorial. For Camille Jullien, the great historian of Gaul of the 1920s, the wealth of the villa owners of the age of Ausonius represented "a return pure and simple to the days of the ancient Gauls."[34] For Jullian and for many others (Mikhail Rostovtzeff among them), landowners like Ausonius were either the last Celtic chieftains or the first medieval barons. They were presented as rural potentates, ensconced at the head of vast pyramids of dependents. Their villas were thought to have looked out like medieval castles over landscapes that they alone controlled. Their leisured lifestyle rested on "the unshakable organism, which a landed aristocracy had formed over ten centuries."[35]

As we saw in chapter 1, the fourth-century reality is significantly different from this view. As we follow it in his letters and poems, the wealth of Ausonius and of his peers in southwest Gaul was considerable. But it was far from stable. It was never independent of the state or of the cities near which these villas lay. The landowners of Aquitaine depended for their wealth on maintaining close relations with the governmental and commercial center of Bordeaux. To live in the countryside alone would have been social and political suicide. Rather, city and estate were the twin foci of an ellipse. Ausonius and the landowners of the region constantly moved between both foci. Aquitaine was a rich agrarian region, which furnished supplies to the Rhine frontier. As a result, the aristocracy of Aquitaine was a court aristocracy in its economic horizons, even if not all of its members had made their way to Trier to become courtiers as Ausonius had done. Their wealth and status did not grow peacefully out of the timeless earth of Gaul. It depended on the vigor of an imperial system that was driven hard from Trier.

It is significant that monumental villas do not turn up in every region of the Roman West. They appear only in regions that served as corridors of empire—

southwestern Gaul, parts of Spain (but not others), the region around Trier, and southern Britain. Villas also appear near the great imperial roads that snaked across the Balkans behind the Danube frontier.[36]

Let us take one corridor of empire that threw up a remarkable number of villas—fourth-century southern Britain. Here we have a profoundly agrarian region whose towns were much smaller than the cities of Aquitaine or Spain. Between twenty and thirty late Roman villas have been discovered, mainly dating from the first half of the fourth century. They stood out in a landscape that was still dotted with round houses of Celtic design that were as distant from the life and values of the owners of the villas as the huddled huts of the villages of nineteenth-century Russia and Poland were distant from the Palladian country houses of the gentry.[37]

But these villas were not lost in the depths of the countryside. They gravitated around the little cities. They were often built within a radius of little more than ten miles from town. These cities in turn were connected, through the fiscal system of the empire, to the principal centers of consumption in the West. They were connected to the imperial court at Trier, to the armies of the Rhineland frontier, and to rich regions such as Aquitaine.

Careful study has shown that the mosaics of the British villas were the products of local schools, each of which radiated from an urban center—such as Dorchester, Cirencester, or Durobrivae (Water Newton, which, at the time, was an important iron town whose church, as we saw, already boasted an impressive collection of silver plate). Through following the spread of the work of each school in its own region we can trace the building activities of a gentry who were intensely aware of each other's buildings.[38] They competed with each other in the common coin of late Roman art. They wished to make their floors radiant with bright mosaics. Their efforts varied. At Thruxton, a long hall that was little more than a Celtic farmhouse was upgraded with a single mosaic added to one end. This showed a wickedly plump and colorful Dionysos beneath the name of the owner along with his clients or kinsmen, who bore the mysterious Celtic name of "the Bodeni."[39] By contrast, at Woodchester, to the west of Cirencester, twenty floors were covered with bright patterns. At least one elegant mythological statue from a contemporary eastern workshop stood in the main hall. The floor of this hall was covered by a large mosaic, made of one and a half million cubes of local stones and brick. It showed Orpheus surrounded by a circle of wild beasts as firmly designed and as forbiddingly muscular as were any of the lions and tigers displayed on the bloodthirsty amphitheater mosaics of north Africa.[40] The conclusions arrived at from the study of these British examples are also valid for Gaul and Spain. They show that a villa was never simply an economic center. Nor was it a proto-feudal castle. It was a monument. It radiated a message to its neighbors that its owner had arrived. And among the fluid and fragmented elites of the fourth century, whether in Britain or in Gaul and Spain, there was no lack of persons anxious to declare that they had arrived.

The end of the villas in the Roman West throws light on the reasons for their unprecedented flowering in the fourth century. The moment that the Roman state and its fiscal energy began to wobble, as a result of civil wars and barbarian invasions, monumental villas of this kind vanished. Many villas survived as economic centers. They served as places for storage and for processing wine and oil. But they became faceless. Their owners left no strong imprint on them. For they no longer served as the blazons of new wealth. By contrast, the lifetime of Ausonius and the early years of Paulinus saw the villas at their height. They stood for a *belle époque*, for a fragile moment of glory associated with the age of gold and a strong empire.[41]

Thus, we should not imagine the owners of villas as a closed group of super-rich landowners solidly ensconced in a position of overwhelming superiority over against all other members of society. Rather, villa owners varied greatly in wealth and in levels of culture. Far from being the unchallenged lords of their region, they were often new men in fierce competition with their peers. They notably lacked the stability that modern scholars have tended to ascribe to them. But what they did have in common was a mystique of wealth, which gave solidity to their own, often fragile fortunes. It bathed their lives in a sense of splendor and excitement. Divided and precarious though they were, they were the *felices*, the lucky ones. It is for this reason that we should listen attentively to the message their art and furnishings conveyed. Let us do this by entering into their villas as if they were palaces of dreams.

Sume!: Take!

AN ICONOGRAPHY OF ABUNDANCE

First and foremost, the late Roman villa was presented as a place of unproblematic abundance. To go out to one's villa in the spring and summer was to claim this abundance as one's own. Even the layout of late Roman dining rooms stressed this fact. The half-circle shape of the late Roman *stibadium* couch derived from the more informal arrangement of cushions in an al fresco picnic.[42] On the *stibadium* couch the guests lay looking outward into the main room rather than facing each other, as on the straight couches of the old Roman triclinium. The most solemn dining occurred in indoor dining halls. In such halls the curved couches lay under the dome of an apse at one end or they were placed around the large hall beneath a series of half domes, arranged in the form of a triconch.[43] But however solemn and enclosed late Roman dining arrangements became, the outdoor picnic remained its model. For it was by eating the diverse products of the land on the land itself that the owner and his friends positively rolled in the agrarian surplus that was the secret of their wealth.

High warehouses for the careful hoarding of the year's grain might be the grim reality. The dream, however, was innocent abundance.[44] Hence the importance of portrayals of the sea and of freshwater products. Fish and *frutti di mare* were pulled from the most abundant and the most innocent source of all—the ocean and lakes and rivers. Such food came from an element free of envy. The liquid immensity of the ocean could never be the object of a zero-sum game. It could never be divided up by estate boundaries, as was the ungenerous earth. Even in the depths of the dry Numidian plateau, at Mactar, a dining room mosaic represented a sea filled with edible fishes.[45]

Ambrose might claim that the abundance of nature was to be shared by all, but the mosaics of those who owned the land spoke in a different voice. They claimed that nature herself would provide the landowner with limitless resources. Significantly, none of these resources was shown as the fruit of human labor. Harvesting is rarely represented. The bitter incidents to which Ambrose referred in his sermons were passed over. Instead, sprightly peasants are shown bearing baskets filled with the good things nature provided with seemingly effortless ease.

At their tables, hosts made sure that their guests would not lack tokens of the unforced generosity of nature. In the great villa of Montmaurin on the river Touch, southwest of Toulouse (a true pleasure palace, it is one of the most grand and frankly delightful villas of Aquitaine), archaeologists discovered six fish tanks, one of which was still filled with unopened oysters from the Atlantic coast.[46] They had been brought 150 miles inland from the beaches near Bordeaux. Such food was offered in the same spirit as Symmachus had gathered crocodiles and Irish wolfhounds to put on display before the people of Rome. They showed that the rich could reach out to the very edges of the known world so as to provide their guests with unexpected delights.

Hence the importance of the little gifts of food and fruit known as *xenia*. Ausonius, for instance, sent to his son, Hesperius, ducks from the marshes with legs of crimson red and rainbow plumage, along with twenty thrushes that had flown into the net as if "wishing to be caught."[47] Signs of the submission of nature itself, such *xenia* were also used as tokens of submission to those who owned the land. Carefully chosen items of food accompanied the rents of tenants to their landlords and the petitions and bribes of inferiors to those above them.[48]

Eating, therefore, was more than a pleasure for the rich. It was an assertion of something bigger: it was a celebration of abundance. It ratified the unfaltering, cosmic energy of the natural world from which all wealth was thought to derive with an ease as ineluctable as was the unfolding of the seasons of the year. As in previous centuries, mosaics of the four seasons remained an essential element in the decoration of the floors of villas and town houses. Representations of the four seasons presented the natural world as charged, through the succession of the seasons, with the promise of perpetual, ever-recurring affluence.[49]

In fourth-century mosaics, nature itself took on a muted divinity all its own. Individual gods and goddesses associated with fertility were no longer shown.[50] Rather, a diffuse cosmic force was thought of as pulsing through the natural world. The world now danced, as it were, with its own divine energy, without help from the old gods. The mosaic of a recently discovered town house in Ravenna shows the four seasons as happy children, dancing in a ring.[51] In a similar grand house at Ravenna (known as the "palace of Theodoric"), an inscription beneath the Seasons urges the reader, *Sume!*—"Take!": "Take what Autumn, what Spring, what Winter and what Summer bring back again and again, and what good things come into being in the whole round world."[52] Derived from ancient themes, the theme of cosmic abundance (summed up in the dance of the seasons) was the new, more faceless but no less potent god of the new rich.

Salvus lotus: Washed and healthy

THE HAPPY BODY

But nowhere did the late Roman rich wish to draw on the life-giving pulse of the universe more than in the care of their own bodies. Late Roman persons held that the human body was in a very intimate manner a microcosm of the great macrocosm of the *mundus*, of the physical universe as a whole. The same energies that pulsed through the stars also pulsed through their bodies.[53]

For this reason, the bodies of the rich were presented as eminently happy ones. For the healthy and energetic body of the individual participated in the same pulse of cosmic exuberance as did the natural world from which his or her own wealth derived. Like food, health also was at the beck and call of the rich. Not for them the fate of the poor, as described by the fourth-century astrologer Firmicus Maternus as dim souls, born under sluggish stars: "miserable, humiliated ... condemned to labor and always occupied in inglorious tasks, whose bodies and mouths are rendered vile by a foul stench."[54]

Moralizing historians have often regarded this pushing forward of the well-bathed body as a symptom of the luxury and self-indulgence of the late Roman rich and as a sure omen of the imminent decline of Roman society. It was no such thing. It was a personalization—one might say a somatization—of the energy and good fortune which, in their own mind, characterized the successful members of the wealthy classes.

To obtain this fighting trim, the rich went frequently to the private baths of their villas and palaces. Throughout the fourth century, they devoted constant effort and expense to making these baths ever more splendid and delightful. But we must be careful how we interpret this phenomenon. The building of private baths has often been represented as a withdrawal into a purely private world at the expense of the great baths of the city. There is little evidence for this view. In Africa, where urban public baths have been much studied (not least, most recently by Anna Leone), public baths did not decline.[55] Rather, the city still lingered in the imagination of those who built private baths in the countryside. They often wrote of the building of their private baths as if they were a form of civic benefaction, offered by the owner to the restricted *populus* of his or her clients and friends. Let us look at one vivid example of such a bath.

Nineteen miles southwest of Carthage, an exquisite late Roman bath complex was found (in 1983) at Sidi Ghrib. It was built quickly, almost as a "folly," by a fortunate pair. Through this bath, husband and wife set their mark for a generation upon a hot and dusty landscape.[56] The builder of the bathhouse advertised his achievement on an inscription placed in the high-domed *frigidarium*—the deliciously cool and spacious hall (roughly twenty-five by twenty-five feet) that formed the sociable center of the complex. It read: "I have built more than my income allowed, but never as much as I would have liked." It was the old boast of a "lover of the city." But the builder of the bath at Sidi Ghrib had not strained his resources to lavish good things on a large citizen body. He had built only for himself and for the circle of his peers:

> If you like it, it is all for you. Whether you like it or not, it is mine. Three
> words: *cato sedes ebria*—for those who appreciate such things, it is a place
> of intoxicating charm.[57]

The bath was "a place of intoxicating charm" precisely because (in the words of Yvon Thébert) it was a "building filled with wonders."[58] The bathhouse was thought of as a miniature universe. With its complicated heating arrangements, the separate spaces of the bathhouse echoed the miraculous blending of the antithetical powers of fire and water and of hot and cold, on which the universe itself depended. And the bath, in turn, worked mysteriously on the balance of the humors within the human body itself. To move between the *caldarium* and the *frigidarium* of such a bath was to recover, from a charmed atmosphere in which steam and coolness mingled, the correct balance of the humors within oneself.[59]

It is not surprising then that a conversational manual in Greek and Latin, associated with Trier (and perhaps even with colleagues of Ausonius himself), should have instructed those who met each other in the baths to greet each other with the phrase, *Salvus lotus:* "Be healthy, Have a Good Wash."[60] Emerging from the baths with firm tread, with exuberant, well-groomed hair, and with the glowing complexion of the well fed and the well washed, the rich emerged at their peak.

Wealth, the Universe, and the Gods

Altogether, the mystique that surrounded the rich as they ate and went to the baths reveals an aspect of the religious climate of the age that we tend to overlook. Traditionally, the fourth century is presented as an age dominated by the conflict between Christianity and paganism. The more we study the period, however, the less this conflict bulks large in it. When we turn to the mystique of wealth in the fourth century, this conflict is almost entirely absent. The late Roman language of abundance and good health was "secular" and "worldly" in the deep, ancient meaning of the two terms. It was in no way irreligious. It carried with it a numinous thrill whose intensity we should not underestimate. This was the thrill evoked by a sense of the beauty and abundance of the *mundus* or the *saeculum*, the physical universe (of which our word "secular" is a pallid echo). The charm of a rich landscape was thought of as an emanation of the glory of the *mundus*—of a material world shot through with invigorating energies. In the fourth century, it was quite possible to neglect the traditional gods of paganism. But landowners still treated with due respect the invisible powers who lurked close to the earth in the lower levels of the universe. For those hidden beings tended the fields, the woods, and the fruits of the harvest.[61]

When Augustine preached to north African congregations, many of whom had been Christian for considerably longer than most of the Christian inhabitants of Gaul had been, he made plain that what really stood between his own, austerely monotheistic definition of Christianity and the attitude toward the natural world of his hearers were not specific pagan rites directed to specific gods. It was, rather, the sense of a hiatus between God and the material universe (the *mundus* or the *saeculum*) that had remained fixed in the back of the minds of the majority of late Roman persons:

> There are those who say: "God is good, he is great, he is supreme, eternal and inviolable. It is he who will give us eternal life and that incorruption which he promised at the resurrection. But those things, indeed, of the [physical] world (*ista vero saecularia*) ... belong to the *daemones* and to the Invisible Powers."
>
> They leave aside God, as if these things did not belong to him; and by sacrifices, by all kinds of healing devices, and by the expert divination of their fellows ... they seek out ways to cope with what concerns the present life.[62]

Among the rich, Christian monotheism had by no means drained the world of its numinous qualities. Christianity had merely placed a new god far above the visible universe. Christ was a high god. He was a god appropriate to an other life, in another world beyond the stars. Since Constantine, Christ had also been the god of the emperors. He was a high god, suitable to the high purposes of a head of state.

Here it is important that we return for a moment to the figure of Ausonius. Careful reading of his writings has enabled us to seize the texture of a confidently "worldly" Christianity very different from the Christianity of the younger generation of ascetics with whom Paulinus chose to ally himself.[63] Here we are dealing with a generational change of great significance. Ausonius was by no means a hypocrite or a crypto-pagan. He was probably born a Christian and may even have represented a Christian faction within the teaching profession of Bordeaux.[64] But, by the 390s, the old man's Christianity was out-of-date (or, rather, it had been declared to be out-of-date by a small but vocal minority in the churches of the Latin West). The Christianity of Ausonius was the Christianity of the Constantinian age. It was a form of Christianity that now seems deeply alien to us. But this is because Christianity itself changed in the last years of Ausonius's life and in the decade after his death. As a result, the Christianity of the old poet seems reticent to the point of seeming insincere when compared with the sharp contrasts between Christians and pagans and between divine and "worldly" affairs that were played up in the public rhetoric of new-style bishops such as Ambrose and by converts to the ascetic life such as Augustine and Paulinus.

Put briefly, Ausonius's religion was by no means wishy-washy or insincere. As befitted a man who grew up in the reign of Constantine and his immediate successors, it was fashionably transcendental. It was in tune with current philosophical notions of an immaterial god, who was to be worshiped in spirit alone.[65] But this was a transcendentalism that left the *mundus*—the physical universe—undisturbed. It revered Christ, but it kept Him out of this world. It limited His power to the ethereal realm to which He properly belonged. Truly high powers on earth, such as the emperor, might be close to Christ. Thanking the emperor Gratian for his consulship, Ausonius could say that to turn his thanks and prayers from Gratian to God "was to make only a small detour"![66] Christ was close to Gratian, as befitted an emperor. But there was no reason why He should be close to Ausonius.

By contrast, what was close to Ausonius was the *mundus* and all that went with it—the shimmer of the landscape, the sparkling variety of an ancient literature filled with delightful stories of the gods, the warm breath of the Muses on the hearts of poets like himself. Christ did not challenge Ausonius's world. From a safe distance beyond the stars, He simply guaranteed it.

Many thought as Ausonius did. For that reason, it is not at all surprising that astrology was so immensely popular among the upper classes of the later empire. For astrology was a system of thought and practice that concentrated whole-heartedly on the workings of the material universe. It focused on the relationship between the stars, the planets, and events on earth. By doing so, it did not deny the existence of God or of the gods. But (like Ausonius) it kept them at a distance. The god of the astrologers lived in lonely majesty above the stars. He made contact with human beings only indirectly, through the influences the planets shed upon the earth. He was as distant from the world as Christ could be thought to be distant by persons such as Ausonius. Thus, there is nothing strange in the fact that the most complete astrological manual of the time—the *Mathesis*—*The Teaching*—of Firmicus Maternus—was written for a Roman nobleman by a man who may well have been a Christian at the time of writing, or who soon became one.[67]

The attitude of Firmicus to the *mundus* was very like that of Ausonius and of others like him. Firmicus believed that a great God ruled the universe, but He had delegated "worldly" things to an intricate interplay of energies, which radiated from the planets and the stars within the universe itself.[68] The farther from heaven and the deeper into the material world one went, the more powerful these influences became. The art of the astrologer was to interpret the interplay of influences by following the courses of the planets as they slid with sinister effect across the Zodiac. Each movement of the planets stirred up eddies of hatred, love, success, or failure in the world below. The destinies of their clients depended on those subtle eddies, whose movements the astrologer claimed to be able to predict.[69]

We meet persons who dabbled with astrology in every section of the upper classes. Ausonius's grandfather had practiced astrology "under cover."[70] A Gallic doctor, Vindicianus, whom Augustine met when Proconsul of Carthage, told Augustine that he had been tempted to become a professional astrologer as well as a doctor. Used to scanning the opaque body for signs of health and illness, as an astrologer Vindicianus would have been doing much the same. He would have scanned the vast body of the sky in an attempt to detect (in the shifts in the relations between the individual planets, traced against the background of the Zodiac) the source of the ripples of fortune and misfortune raised, among human beings, by the conflicting energies associated with the planets.[71] Altogether, astrology was the default religion of the upper classes of the later empire. It was so attractive precisely because it concentrated attention on the alternation of good and evil fortune, played out in a living, material universe. This universe—the *mundus* or the *saeculum*—lay close at hand, far below the somewhat faceless supracelestial realm of the new High God of the Christians. It was from this universe that wealth came, in a mighty, heartening tide, to the fortunate rich.

Living Myths

Securely rooted in the *mundus*, at a safe distance from the High God who reigned above the stars, the rich reached back with gusto to the classical myths that had always given life and drama to their lives on earth. They did this to express their claims to abundance, good health, and success in all their ventures. In so doing, they drew on an imaginative universe in which Christianity was almost totally absent. When dealing with the use of classical mythology in the fourth century, it is important to stress its majestic indifference to the hard-and-fast religious divisions that had developed in certain circles at this time. When we turn to the art of the wealthy classes of the fourth-century Latin West, we have to adjust our ears to the deafening silence on the religious issues that bulk so large in Christian texts. In the mosaics, statues, and silverware of the rich, the conflict between paganism and Christianity might as well be happening on another planet.

There was nothing frivolous or, indeed, irreligious about this absence of clear signs of Christianity and paganism in the use of mythological scenes by the rich. This art spoke to weighty issues that were charged with diffuse religious overtones. What was needed was a language with which to do justice to the aspirations of an entire class, irrespective of their religion. Wealth was a serious matter. It demanded a heavy voice, tinged with religious awe. In the fourth century, this voice could only be found in an imagery taken from a past that owed nothing to Christianity. Let us end this chapter by seeing how this was done.

In certain situations, well-to-do Christians were prepared to signal their special religious adherence. The Christogram—the XP monogram of the name of Christ—is to be seen everywhere in the domestic as well as in the public art of the period. But it is revealing to see exactly where the Christogram appeared. It appeared only in places traditionally associated with good fortune: on the thresholds of houses and at the center of reception rooms, flanked by the Seasons and by similar classical emblems of abundance.[72]

One such Christian was Sevso, probably a military man whose massive plate (recently discovered in mysterious circumstances) signaled rare success. He is portrayed with his wife, presiding over a picnic that marked the successful conclusion of a hunt. His favorite horse—carefully inscribed with its name, Innocentius—is shown beside him. His guests have begun to tuck into a large fish. An inscription ran around this happy scene, placed in the middle of a massive plate, made from over nineteen pounds of solid silver.

> May these, o Sevso, yours for many ages be,
> Small vessels fit to serve your offspring worthily.

Though dwarfed by the inscription and by the sheer shimmer of so vast a plate, the Christogram was present. It hung above the heads of the couple like a beneficent star. It declared that Christ (and no other god) guarded the fortune of Sevso and his wife.[73]

Sevso appears to have owned a further 130 pounds of silverware, which bore no sign of Christ. Heavy silver vessels were emblazoned with scenes from Greek mythology and from Greek drama. They were placed on the plates (along with images of charioteers and of wild beasts from the amphitheater) like so many decals. They advertised Sevso's allegiance to the classical past. To judge from his name, Sevso may have been a cavalry man of Alan background. But Sevso wished to show that he shared with persons as different from himself as Symmachus, Ausonius, and the young Augustine a love of the classics.[74]

Altogether, the art of the fourth century was an art framed for a diverse class of rich persons. All were rich; but some were a lot less rich and less certain of their place in society than were others. Some, indeed (like Sevso), were barely Romans. Such persons needed a shared visual culture (much of which hinted at a shared literary culture) so as to get along with each other.

Hence the enormous appeal of classical myth. The appeal to myth was by no means a sign of unreflecting conservatism. The artists of fourth- and fifth-century mosaics deliberately pulled these myths into the present. They implied that the owners of the mosaics and of the silverware were, themselves, "living myths" in their own time.[75] For only classical mythology could do justice to the glorious démesure, to the epic "larger-than-life" quality of the rich, in all their activities, from the strenuous courage of the hunt to the sexual magnetism that was supposed to radiate from their privileged bodies.

The myths were "modernized." They became, as it were, part of the heraldry of the great—much as, in medieval times, the heads of feudal lineages made their own the courage, the ferocity, and the loyalty of the beasts that decorated their shields. But the myths provided more than emblems of status. In the age of Ausonius, we are still in a deeply polytheistic world. The gods still filled the imagination of most persons. Compared with the deathless energy of the gods, human passions and human delights were thought of as thin and fleeting in themselves. They gained a numinous "fourth dimension" through being associated with the heroes of the past and with the figures of gods and goddesses.[76] The gods might still be worshiped as divinities by some, but their stories were known by all.[77] They lived in an uncanny alternative world at once "intimate and strange" that gave meaning and glory to the lives of mortals.[78]

For this reason, gods and goddesses still hovered around the rich. They added a touch of majesty to the high moments of their lives. Every young bride on her wedding day might still look into her mirror while above her hovered an image of female beauty more solid and vivid than herself—the voluptuous shape of Venus (with her hair done up in the late Roman manner, with great pendant earrings and with a heavy necklace draped across her naked body) as she rode with her retinue across the waves. This was how the young Christian girl, Proiecta, was shown on a great fourth-century silver toilet case—the Esquiline Casket of the British Museum (so-called because it was discovered on the Esquiline Hill, a region of great palaces). An inscription complete with Christogram wished the married couple "long life in Christ." The inscription was attached to the casket in such a way that it ran between the portrait of the young bride and the splendid Venus above her. If anything, the inscription was an invocation of Christ to make the myths come true—for Venus and the bride to merge, so that beauty and delight might flourish in the ancient manner in a family of rich Christians.[79]

In the same way, all over the western provinces (from Britain to the south of Spain) Bellerophon is shown piercing the chimera. Rather than referring to some finespun allegory, the figure of the triumphant Bellerophon was seen as the ego ideal of the owner of the house—a vigorous hunter on a flying horse.[80] Indeed, the myths had become so much a part of the texture of life that gods and goddesses, heroes and heroines, were often no longer shown in proper classical dress. In Malaga, Bellerophon was shown as a huntsman of the later empire complete with the cloak and trousers that distinguished the gentry in every province. The ancient past and the modern present were merged.[81] On a sarcophagus from northern Portugal, the deceased was shown surrounded by the traditional Muses. But he was no longer dressed in the classical toga, as had been normal when a gentleman was shown communing with Muses. Far from it: he was shown in entirely up-to-date dress, with the wide cloak, the fibula brooch, and the trousers of an imperial official.[82]

Not all areas produced mosaics with mythological scenes. The mosaics of Aquitaine, for instance, are surprising for their absence of mythological scenes, compared with the full-blown iconography of Spain, Africa, and Britain. But, wherever they lived, whether they were Christians or pagans, it was the air of the classical tradition the rich chose to breathe, drawing in its oxygen in deep and cheering breaths. For them, there was no other air.

Nothing shows this more clearly than the recent discoveries of sculptures that decorated late Roman villas all over the West. The statuary of the villas of El Ruedo (near Cordoba) and Valtorre de Jarama (south of Madrid), in Spain, echo the stunning collections previously discovered at Chiragan (near Toulouse) and at St. Georges-de-Montagne (near Bordeaux) in Gaul. These villas housed large private collections of classical and imperial statues.[83] Placed in the courtyards of late Roman villas in the West, works of classical sculpture provided their owners with epitomes of Greco-Roman history and culture. The long pool of the villa of Welschbilling (outside Trier) was enclosed with a line of busts placed on the pillars of a balustrade. In this way, the figures of Socrates and Demosthenes, of Caesar and Marcus Aurelius, were brought to a villa that lay only sixty miles away from the northernmost frontier between Rome and the barbarian world. They were a reminder of the heritage a fourth-century villa owner such as Ausonius was expected to cherish and defend.[84]

We, who know about the withering of the great villas in the crisis of the fifth century, find that there is something hauntingly distant about the secular art and literature of the age of Ausonius. It seems to lie on the far side of a divide between the pagan and the Christian world. Yet what we have seen is an art of the Christian rich quite as much as that of pagans. We are looking, in fact, not at a pagan world so much as a world where a distinctive Christianity—the Christianity of the age of Constantine and his successors—had come to coexist, for a moment, with a classical heritage that seemed at the time to be unshakable and unproblematic.

Ausonius was a sincere representative of the Christianity of that generation. The rich, pagan and Christian alike, still felt at ease in the world. But Ausonius and the many like him could not have foreseen the emergence of a new attitude toward wealth among a small but vocal section of their Christian peers. This new attitude cast a cold shadow over the *mundus* as a whole. For those who listened to the message of Christian ascetics, wealth could no longer be seen as the unproblematic overflow of the imagined abundance of the universe. The "world" was a dark place. Its beauties were a source of temptation. Wealth was "slime."[85] It was not an exuberant by-product of the semi-divine world of nature. It was a burden that had to be shed if the soul were to fly away from a world of dull materiality to join Christ "in the air."[86] Wealth could be tolerated only if it passed continuously upward (through pious acts) into a silent, unseen world, which lay beyond the stars. Like the Rich Young Man of the Gospels, the eye of the needle must be faced. *Treasure on earth* had to be renounced so that it could become *treasure in heaven*. Let us turn in our next two chapters to see how Pontius Meropius Paulinus, the friend of Ausonius, became (to Ausonius's great distress) the spokesman of this radical new mood.

CHAPTER 13

༭ఞ

Ex opulentissimo divite: From being rich as rich can be

Paulinus of Nola and the Renunciation
of Wealth, 389–395

Lacerataque centum per dominos veteris Paulini regna: The hereditary
domains of old Paulinus torn apart by a hundred [new] owners

PAULINUS, RENUNCIATION, AND CIVIL WAR

The great villas of Aquitaine have been described by Catherine Balmelle as "dynamic and complex places ... that lay at the heart of a network of sociability."[1] This is certainly how they appeared to Ausonius in the poignant last decade of his life, after he had left the court of Trier in 383. In his letters and poems, he presented the region around Bordeaux as a charmed world, held together by the punctilious exchange of poems and of little gifts of food between like-minded neighbors.

It was important for Ausonius that this world should hold together. For behind the gracious luxury and cultural wealth displayed in these exchanges lay a weightier reality—the need for solidarity within a regional nobility, probably the richest and most enviable in Gaul, caught in a time of intermittent civil war. In 383 Maximus replaced Gratian; in 388 Theodosius replaced Maximus. The roundabout of regime changes would continue until, in the dire years after 406, civil war and barbarian invasion became disastrously intermingled in the politics of Gaul and Spain.

As we saw, the landowners among whom Ausonius moved were not insulated against these events. They were not the great owners of *latifundia* that many scholars have imagined them to have been. They did not live ensconced in the depths of the countryside on virtually autarkic estates while political regimes came and went. They were a class partly created by the late Roman state. For this reason, they were directly vulnerable to the impact of court revolutions and civil war. Hence it was more than usually important for them to maintain their solidarity. They did this by rallying to a distinctive way of life of which their villas and their shared classical culture were the most secure landmarks. For one of them to abandon this style of life was not only to break up a friendship. It was to betray their class and their region at a moment of danger.

This was precisely what Ausonius's friend and former pupil, Pontius Meropius Paulinus, did. Around 389, Paulinus moved out of Aquitaine to the estates of his wife, Therasia, in Spain. The couple settled in Complutum (Alcalá de Henares), on the austere plateau of Castile, twenty miles from modern Madrid. A fourth-century town house at Complutum has been excavated. Its mosaic floors spoke with characteristically late Roman zest of the good life. A line of servants, with well-cut tunics and healthy, bulging calves, were shown on the corridor leading to the dining room. One mosaic panel showed Jupiter in the form of a cheeky swan, leering expectantly upward at Leda as her dress slipped from her shoulders to reveal her naked body.[2]

Such scenes were not for Paulinus and Therasia. Three years of soul-searching, rendered tragic by the death of their only child, ended with a joint decision by Paulinus and Therasia to adopt a life of continence (they would produce no further heir) and to sell up their properties. Paulinus went further. The couple moved to the Mediterranean coast. On Christmas Day 394, Paulinus was ordained a priest at Barcelona, by the acclaim of the Christian people, inspired by the Holy Spirit—just as Augustine had been ordained at Hippo only three years before. With the exception of Ambrose (who immediately became a bishop), no member of the senatorial order had ever become a mere clergyman. Ordination distanced Paulinus yet further from his noble background.[3] But he did not stay in Barcelona. In 395 Paulinus and Therasia crossed the Mediterranean to Campania and settled at Nola, in the shrine of Saint Felix in Cimitile—the "Cemetery"—which lay a short distance outside the town.

Ausonius died around 395, at the age of eighty-five. He only witnessed the opening years of Paulinus's religious odyssey. But what he saw in his last years did not reassure him. The series of poetic letters he sent to his friend show that he feared that Paulinus was bent on committing social suicide. In his first letters, he pleaded with his friend not to lock himself away in melancholy isolation in the middle of the rough landscape of Spain. When Ausonius later heard (in the spring of 394) that Paulinus had also renounced his wealth, this was the last straw. For the only time in his poems to Paulinus, Ausonius turned to the Christian God to pray to Christ that such a thing would not happen:

Lest we have to mourn that the family wealth of the Paulinus of old [probably an ancestor of the third century or even of the second century AD] be grabbed and scattered, and his hereditary domains [his *regna*] be torn apart between a hundred owners.[4]

Ausonius did not use the word *regna* to conjure up estates the size of kingdoms, as many modern scholars assume. He had used the same word for his own "Little Heritage." It was the fact that these were ancestral estates heavy with a sense of heritage that mattered, not their size. He wished to warn Paulinus that if such ancestral lands could go, then anything might go. Why had Paulinus acted in so drastic a manner?

One suspects that Paulinus had moved to Spain in 389 for reasons that were not entirely religious. Hence the alarm Ausonius expressed at his withdrawal. Color-blind as always to confessional issues, Ausonius was far more concerned with the political and social implications of Paulinus's departure from Aquitaine than with his religious preoccupations. After the fall of Maximus, in 388, Gaul had become reconquered territory. It was now ruled by Theodosius I, an emperor based on Constantinople. Until recently Aquitaine had been a privileged province. It was the breadbasket of Trier. Now Aquitaine found itself on the margins of a tenuously united empire ruled, in effect, from distant Constantinople. It is as if in modern times the administration of Bordeaux had switched from Paris to Istanbul. Ausonius the old courtier knew that if the nobility of his region were to have any say in the new regime, they should hang together. This was why he wished to lure Paulinus back from Spain to Bordeaux so as to remain active in the political life of the region. In so doing, Ausonius could present himself to Theodosius as a "patronage broker" who had rallied the Aquitanian landowners, Paulinus among them, to the new regime.[5]

But Paulinus had had enough of politics. There was a good reason for this. He came from a family that was both more wealthy and more vulnerable in times of civil war than was a mere civic notable of Bordeaux such as Ausonius. Though closely associated with Bordeaux, Paulinus's family was not limited to that one region. It had roots in the senatorial aristocracy of Rome and southern Italy. Paulinus's wealth was more like that of Symmachus than that of Ausonius or even of Ambrose. It was old money. His family owned land in Italy. He found it easy to marry into an aristocratic family of Spain which, like Paulinus, had also maintained its links to Rome. He could step with ease across the western Mediterranean. Ausonius knew that, like a multinational company, Paulinus could pull out of Bordeaux with little difficulty. Hence Ausonius's urgent concern to tie Paulinus to his own region and his fear that Paulinus, as a member of the super-rich, could have taken himself and his wealth to reside in any number of other localities.

But, in times of civil war, this scattered wealth spelled danger. With estates in every region, persons like Paulinus were temptingly wealthy. At the same time, they lacked the local support networks (built up over the years by canny marriages and by well-maintained relations with local allies) that protected humbler members of a mere provincial aristocracy. Put bluntly, members of the super-rich were the piggy bank that new regimes, chronically short of cash, were tempted to raid.

Paulinus's family may well have counted as one such piggy bank. At some time in the late 380s, Paulinus's brother had been executed—Paulinus uses the grim word *caesus* of his mysterious death. Paulinus himself was in danger of having his own estates confiscated.[6] He may even have bought himself out. This is what Symmachus may have done, a year earlier, after he had committed the near-fatal error of having rallied to the cause of Maximus of Trier only a few months before Maximus was defeated by Theodosius I.[7] Though the selling off of Paulinus's estates was eventually rendered memorable by being presented as an act of Christian renunciation, his family fortunes may already have been on a downward slide. Certainly, when Paulinus retired to Spain, he was already a man with wealth very much on his mind. Coming to Spain, he found himself in a province where the Christian churches also were greatly preoccupied with the issue of wealth—with how rich Christians might spend their fortunes.

The Shadow of Priscillian

The memorable intensity of Ausonius's reaction to the withdrawal of Paulinus and the high-minded response of Paulinus to his aged mentor have tended to dominate our perceptions of the entire story of Paulinus's withdrawal and renunciation. Scholars of classical inclination have lingered on Paulinus's conversion as if it were a quiet affair—a dignified farewell to the Muses. But this view has excluded any consideration of what was happening in the Christian churches of the time. In reality, as we will now see, Paulinus's public renunciation of his wealth came as the trenchant solution to a little-known but bitter dispute on the role of the wealthy in the Christian churches that had already raged in Gaul and Spain for a decade. It is to this that we must now turn.

To be very brief: behind Paulinus stood Priscillian, and behind Priscillian stood the remarkable decade that saw the end of the age of consensus in the churches imposed by Constantine and his so-called Arian successor, Constantius II. As we have seen, this decade witnessed the unexpected entry into positions of ecclesiastical power of ultra-Nicene dissidents, whose wealth and social standing marked a new departure for the churches of the West. We know that this happened in northern Italy with the emergence of the maverick *nobilis* Ambrose as bishop of Milan in 374.

We often forget that the same thing happened a decade later in the churches of Spain and Aquitaine. In this region, however, the crisis took on a peculiarly acute form. It was associated with controversy over the views and person of a well-educated and charismatic Spaniard—Priscillian. Priscillian was a teacher of extreme ascetic views, based on what struck his enemies as a Gnostic, even Man-ichaean, worldview. The controversy first became public in 380 and gained in vehemence when Priscillian became bishop of Avila in 381. It ended, sometime between 384 and 386, suddenly and in a gruesome manner, with Priscillian's ex-ecution at Trier.

Priscillian was not executed as a heretic. The bishops of Spain who had rallied against him treated his ordination as invalid. He was tried as a layman and con-demned not for his beliefs but for having practiced sorcery and seduced noble ladies. Yet the trial itself had been set in motion in response to clamorous denun-ciations of Priscillian, while still a bishop, by his fellow Spanish bishops.[8]

This was because there was more to Priscillian than his role as a guru. He crystallized the hopes of an entire disaffected party of well-to-do Christians. As Victoria Escribano has recently shown, Priscillian was supported by extreme members of the pro-Nicene faction. It was with their support that he became bishop of Avila in 381. To those who mistrusted him, Priscillian looked much as Ambrose had looked to his "Arian" enemies in 374. He was an intruder who had come from outside the lackluster circles of the Spanish episcopate. He had been pushed into a bishopric by a ginger group of rich lay zealots.[9] But Ambrose sur-vived while Priscillian did not. This was because Ambrose had been a senatorial governor and was independently wealthy. Priscillian was merely the darling of a faction within the Christian aristocracy. He represented a troubling alliance be-tween a religious leader and the wealth of a new class of lay patrons. In Spanish conditions, the sudden pushing forward of Priscillian represented a real threat to the other bishops. If the dubious Priscillian came forward, who else might follow him as protégés of the new Christian rich?

This anxiety was exacerbated by an imbalance between city and villa. Thus, to understand the savagery of the reaction of the bishops to Priscillian, we should go out of the towns to the great villas of the Spanish aristocracy. In a series of recent articles, Kim Bowes has drawn attention to a peculiar disparity in the so-cial landscape of fourth-century Christian Spain. The urban churches of Spain of the fourth and early fifth centuries were strikingly modest. They were the product of a low-profile, urban Christianity, supported by distinctly middling persons, as had been the case in so many other churches of the Latin West (one thinks of the Christian communities of northern Italy before the days of Ambrose).

In Spain, however, the low social profile of the urban churches stood in un-usually sharp contrast to the wealth the Christian landowners of the region had deployed in building mausoleums and churches adjacent to their own villas.[10] As we saw in the last chapter, these villas were by no means cut off from the cities. Country villas were only one focus on the ellipse which, throughout the year, joined local elites to the city when in the countryside and to the countryside when in the city. It was taken for granted that, at certain seasons, an urban notable might retire to the countryside so as to conduct the business of the city in the comfort of his villa. Provincial governors had to be warned not to do this. They were often tempted to accept the invitation of local villa owners to conduct the business of state out of town, in "delightful retreats" away from the heat and noise of the city. Such governors had to be reminded that they were supposed to reside in the city in the governor's official mansion.[11]

Laypersons took this alternation of city and countryside for granted. But the Christian communities within the cities were more recent. Their leaders felt less secure. It mattered to bishops that rich members of the congregation did not attend church in the city's principal basilica. They suspected the worst of those who "lingered in villas" during the Lenten season. Such persons threatened to turn what had been a season of communal penance in the city (in which all classes were joined and in which the *mediocres* predominated) into the religious equivalent of an aristocrat's *otium*—a time of intense devotion, at a distance from the city, in the select company of one's family and friends. Even worse, during such periods of *otium*, men and women might also mingle freely, as they had always done in the high-minded house parties of the great. Favored teachers of uncertain orthodoxy might be brought in to instruct these little gatherings. Thus, absenteeism from the ceremonies of the city and the suspect mingling of the sexes at religious conventicles held around charismatic teachers in country retreats were the twin refrain of the bishops assembled at Saragossa (Zaragoza) in 380:

> The women of the Catholic church should be separated from assemblies of strange men.... They should not join together with them to learn or to teach.
>
> At the time of Lent ... no persons should absent themselves from the churches.... They should not go out to the villas of others to attend meetings.... No one should remain in their house or reside in their villa or seek out mountain retreats, but all should run together to the churches.... Let no one take for themselves the title of Teacher.[12]

Altogether, the Spanish bishops who aired their suspicions at the council of Saragossa felt threatened by the splendor of the villas that ringed their cities. These villas were impressive places. The owners of many of them were newly wealthy. Many had been successful courtiers in capitals as far apart as Trier and Constantinople. Most of the art they patronized was soundproof to Christianity; this was art that did justice to their worldly glory. But, as Christians, they also had to make provision for the afterlife. They continued the tradition of placing impressive mausolea on their properties. Excavations of the villas of Spain and Portugal show that in doing this they deployed a "dizzying array of plans and materials" to provide themselves with impressive buildings linked to private

Christian cult and to private burial on their estates. To take only one example: the great domed building that was erected close to the villa at Carranque contained architectural echoes of the great Church of the Holy Apostles, founded by Constantine at Constantinople as his own burial place. It represented, in the middle of a Castilian plateau dotted with distinctly mediocre cities, a daring combination of saint's shrine and private mausoleum, built by a wealthy person who may have been a leading courtier.[13]

It was among such persons that the followers of Priscillian were thought by the bishops to lurk. This social tension was crucial to the fate of Priscillian. It was not the ascetic nature of the movement itself nor yet the troubling esotericism associated with the teachings of Priscillian that fueled the moral panic that passed through many of the major Spanish churches between 380 and 385. It was Priscillian's access to the wealth and support of persons from outside the proud but socially unprepossessing circles of the Spanish urban clergy.

The problems raised by this imbalance did not apply only to Spain, although they were felt most acutely in that region. It is worthwhile lingering for a moment on this situation. Nowadays, we tend to assume that the ascetic movement shocked contemporaries for much the same reasons as it shocks us. It was world denying. It emphasized self-mortification. It led to the abandonment of social duties. It deprecated marriage and exalted the suppression of sexual drives. This was the view of a pagan, Rutilius Namatianus, who described a colony of monks on the island of Capraria (modern Capraia between Elba and Corsica), which he passed when sailing home to his estates in Gaul a generation later:

> squalid the isle and filled
> With men who shun the light: they call themselves
> "Monks", a name in Greek, because they wish
> To dwell alone [as *monoi*: alone], observed by none....
> What madness of a brain diseased so crazed
> As fearing evil, to refuse all good.[14]

Though the most vocal of the critics of monks were pagans, many were also Christians. We take their judgments as a sufficient explanation for the unpopularity of monks and virgins in this period. We do so because we tend to agree with them. After all, monks were extremists and world haters. Yet the fact remains that, in the later empire, ascetics of all kinds were less often criticized for their world-denying practices than for their relations with wealthy devotees. The relation between holy men and their financial backers was a highly charged issue. In the words of the pagan emperor Julian, referring to monks: "They are ... men who by making small sacrifices gain much ... from all sources ... levying tribute on specious pretenses, which they call 'alms.'"[15] These suspicions were by no means limited to pagans. In 403 Augustine had to write an entire tract against monks who made a practice of begging for alms rather than working for a living—the *De opere monachorum*, "That Monks Should Work." He also rebuked a lady Ecdicia who had given away her husband's fortune to two such charismatic beggars.[16] These practices reminded him of his younger days, when he and others had supported the Elect of the "Holy Church" of Mani. We will see, in a later chapter, how the fund-raising activities of the ascetic Jerome among the pious women of Rome raised a storm of protest. Altogether, whenever the relationship between ascetics and lay donors appeared to be excessive or dubious, late Roman Christians (quite as much as late Roman pagans) were more than usually unforgiving. Suspicion of the wealth of rich supporters was a principal reason for opposition to the ascetic movement in the Latin West. This suspicion was justified. The new wealth of many Christians frequently made itself felt in the churches in an invidious manner through patronizing ascetic stars at the expense of the run-of-the-mill clergy.

Priscillian was one of the first ascetics in the West to fall victim to these suspicions. He had failed to clarify his relations to the wealthy persons who supported him. He was by no means a Manichee in his beliefs, but, in his social profile he was, in many ways, a throwback to an earlier age of Gnostic spiritual guides. As a person, he was "above" money. But he remained surrounded by a disquieting aura of great riches. His followers in Spain and Aquitaine were well-to-do local aristocrats. They ministered to him. They did not renounce their wealth but used it for the cause of their leader. Their considerable funds were deployed at court in order to defend their leader and to secure the condemnation of his enemies.[17]

This was unforgivable. Priscillian, the bishop of Avila—a would-be Ambrose of Castile—was hounded to death by his episcopal colleagues as a sorcerer and a seducer of noble women. When Paulinus moved definitively out of Aquitaine to live on his wife's estates in eastern Spain, we must remember that barely six years (at the longest) had elapsed since the body of Priscillian—headless and bearing the marks of torture—had been taken back to Spain by a group of followers who continued to honor him as a martyr.

We should bear these recent events in mind when we consider the options Paulinus faced when in retreat on his wife's estates between 389 and 394. He faced many options as to what he would do with his wealth. What exactly were they?

It is important to realize that the option he may have known best offered him least guidance when it came to planning his future. This was the life of Saint Martin of Tours. Paulinus had been a sincere admirer of Martin of Tours. Sometime around 387 (when the old monk-bishop of Tours was in his seventies) he had met Martin and had even been cured of an infection of the eye by him. His closest friend and correspondent in the years immediately following his conversion was none other than Sulpicius Severus, the author of the famous *Life of Martin*.[18]

Paulinus once wrote that in Sulpicius "Saint Martin still breathes."[19] But this was a Martin who had surprisingly little to say on the issue of wealth. A member of an earlier generation, the bishop of Tours had not given much attention to the precise manner in which laypersons could dispose of their wealth when they adopted the ascetic life. Most of Martin's monks had been well-to-do. On conversion, they had given property to the monastery at Marmoutier and lived off the income. They did not work. Like aristocrats in *otium* they were engaged in higher pursuits. They devoted their time to contemplation, to reading, and to copying. Ordinary peasants worked the land for them with the heavy oxen of northern Gaul while they themselves occasionally went fishing in the river Loire.[20] Martin and his monks took their relative poverty for granted. Their conversion had not been preceded by a spectacular and widely publicized renunciation of wealth.

But Paulinus could no longer afford to be offhand about his wealth, as Martin and his monks had been. Not only was he more than usually rich. In the years when he retired from Aquitaine, the shadow of Priscillian had fallen across the landscape of Spain and southern Gaul. Paulinus had to make clear quickly and for all to see and hear what was his own stance to his own, vast riches. The Christian communities of his region needed to know exactly how a man as rich as Paulinus intended to use his wealth—how much of it he would retain, and, should he sell up his properties, where exactly all that money would go.

Hence Paulinus's decision to make a public declaration (probably at the Easter festival of 394). He said that he would follow to the letter Christ's command to the Rich Young Man. He would *sell all*. He would *give to the poor*. He would place his *treasure in heaven*. He himself ensured through his own correspondence that his conversion was acclaimed throughout the western Mediterranean in the stark terms provided by the Gospel story.[21] Seen against the background of the churches of Spain, the subtext of the message was clear: Paulinus was "clean." He had freed himself from the aura of undeclared wealth that had made the followers of Priscillian appear to be a sinister and incalculable faction.

Homo quondam ex divite pauper: A man who
from being rich became poor

FROM AQUITAINE TO NOLA

Paulinus, therefore, announced the renunciation of his wealth with an archaic starkness that impressed like-minded Christian contemporaries. The elderly Martin of Tours was predictably delighted with the news:

"There," Martin kept exclaiming, "there is someone to imitate." He held that our generation was blessed in possessing such an example. For Paulinus, a rich man with great possessions, by *selling all and giving to the poor* [as Christ had asked the Rich Young Man to do in Matthew 19:21] has illustrated Our Lord's saying. He has proved that *what is impossible with man is possible with God (Matthew 19:26).*[22]

As we have seen, Ambrose also was thrilled.[23]

For persons such as Martin and Ambrose (as later for Augustine), Paulinus instantly became, in the words of Dennis Trout, his most skilled recent biographer, a "Verbal Icon."[24] He was a living reminder that the story of Jesus and the Rich Young Man could have a happy ending. Paulinus, a very large camel, had indeed been able to *pass through the eye of a needle* by abandoning his fortune. This was how Augustine presented his friend in the first book of the *City of God*: "*Paulinus noster*: Our Paulinus … who, from being rich as rich can be, [*ex opulentissimo divite*] made himself extremely poor."[25]

But the very starkness of this "Verbal Icon" is precisely what has rendered Paulinus's actual financial arrangements in the years after 394 opaque to the historian. In the economic conditions of the later empire, to live up to an ascetic promise to *sell all* was as cumbersome and as slow an operation as was the mobilization of wealth that followed the promise of a senator such as Symmachus to give splendid games. Paulinus had to confront the obstacles that faced any absentee landowner forced to raise money quickly or to secure unaccustomed deliveries of supplies. Whether this was crocodiles from the Nile, as for Symmachus, or wine for the poor of Nola, for Paulinus, these ventures required constant attention and the support of friends. In 396 Paulinus wrote to Sulpicius Severus with a request to give him help on the spot to ensure that old wine he had stored at Narbonne was transported to Nola: "for my freedmen, slaves and brothers have let me down."[26]

But at least on one point the fears of Ausonius were proved to be ill-founded. The ancestral lands of the Paulini did not fall entirely into the hands of foreign carpetbaggers. Paulinus may not have put them up for sale before offering first choice to his kinsfolk and neighbors. We have no account of exactly what Paulinus did in 394, but a text from the sixth-century Christian East gives us some idea of what may have occurred. When Thomas, a great landowner of Armenian royal descent, decided to get rid of his properties, he

> sent a message to the magnates of the district, his neighbors, and stated that, if they were willing they could buy his lands which bordered upon theirs, and, if they were not willing, they were not to be annoyed if strangers came in and bought them.[27]

Paulinus and his agents may well have done the same. In Aquitaine, it appears that another branch of the Paulini (the descendants of Paulinus's brother) survived into the late sixth century. We may meet the last of his line in the 560s, in the person of Leontius, the bishop of Bordeaux. As described by the Italian poet Venantius Fortunatus, Leontius had refurbished the villa at Preignac where Paulinus's brother had lived 150 years before. Lying at ease in old Roman style on his *stibadium* couch, Leontius looked out over flowing pools filled with fish set in a landscape of wheatfields, which waved in the breeze like heavy blond hair.[28] Venantius had read his Ausonius. In the world of poetry, at least, Ausonius's idyllic landscape remained unchanged. It had not been destroyed by Paulinus's isolated act of renunciation. It was still there, in the hands of comfort-loving persons with classical tastes. Even if he was a bishop, Leontius belonged to a class that had continued to appreciate the poetry of Ausonius and of those, such as Venantius, who imitated him. Though ruled by Frankish kings, they wished to be thought of as living like Roman gentlemen.

Yet the unwinding of so much property would have been a noteworthy event, not unlike the massive confiscations that scythed the fortunes of the aristocracy at times of civil war or in the wake of trials for sorcery or treason. A grim edict of the emperor Valentinian I, issued in 369, shows what was at stake:

> If any person … should suffer the sentence of proscription, an investigation of his property shall be very thoroughly made.… A full inventory … shall include the extent and character of the rural property … what is the charm and attractiveness of the various parts; what is the equipment of the buildings and landholdings; how many slaves … are contained on the estate, and in what skills such slaves have been trained … the amount of gold and silver, clothing and jewelry … and what is found in the storerooms.[29]

Such was the wealth Paulinus had abandoned, in 394, in a dramatic act of autoproscription.

Yet, despite the apparent trenchancy of Paulinus's renunciation, things moved slowly. Money seems to have continued to come in to Paulinus from his estates for many years. As we shall see, in the next chapter, he used this money to fund ambitious building projects at the shrine of Saint Felix at Cimitile. These projects lasted until at least 404, if not later. Paulinus became bishop of Nola in around 408. He died only a year after Augustine, in 431. By then, Paulinus of Bordeaux (as Ausonius wished him to be) had become saint Paulinus of Nola.

Nola was not a place of exile for Paulinus. Nor was it a hiding place, as the hinterland of Spain might have been. To move to Nola was to move close to the center of a very ancient world. Nola lay near the Via Appia as it crossed the mountains of Samnium, toward Brindisi and the East. Travelers who made their way along the tax spine of the later empire, which joined Rome to Africa, would also have found it easy to visit Nola. African bishops on their way to the court often stopped by to visit Paulinus at Nola and to pass on to him the letters of Augustine.[30]

Nor was Nola a new city for Paulinus. The shrine of Felix had been known to him since his youth, as it lay close to properties owned by his family. At the age of twenty six (in 380–81), Paulinus had served as senatorial governor of Campania. As governor, he had added a porch to the shrine and had improved the road that led to it.[31] Nor did Paulinus limit his gifts to Nola. Like Symmachus, his family had contacts with many towns. In 404 he gave a brand-new basilica to the Christians of Fundi, on the Appian Way as it approached Rome. He spoke of his gift as if it were the action of a civic benefactor, such as Symmachus would have recognized. He had built a basilica for the local Christians "as a token of my love for the city and in memory of the estate my family used to own there."[32] Altogether, Paulinus had chosen to settle in a region heavy with memories of his own family. His renunciation had not led him to flee his homeland but to return to it on different terms.

Yet Paulinus's settlement at Nola should not be seen only as an example of the untroubled continuity within the Christian church of the lifestyle of a senatorial benefactor and patron. Despite the presence of family lands and the continued pressure of social expectations and of habits of thought inherited from his senatorial background (indeed, one suspects, because of the challenge presented by such continuities), Paulinus went out of his way to ensure that he would not be mistaken for his old self. He did this by emphasizing his new poverty.

But what sort of poverty would this be? It is understandable that modern scholars, when confronted with Paulinus, should stress the continuities of his life. Revenues continued to trickle in from his estates. He continued to assume that his clients in Aquitaine would still obey him and be rewarded for their services. When he set about rebuilding the shrine of Felix at Cimitile, he showed a "proprietary sensibility" worthy of the builder of any great villa. These traits make us doubt that Paulinus had become "poor" in any obvious sense.[33] Modern parallels with movie stars who insist on living the simple life have made us skeptical when dealing with great senators turned monks. The wicked phrase "designer poverty" springs to mind.[34]

But to be too skeptical is to ignore what we saw in the last chapter—the very specific semiotics of wealth in a late Roman society. We have seen that to be rich was not simply to have an income. It was to advertise the fact, all the time, in as assertive and as visible a manner as possible. To possess and to show *splendor*—éclat—was what being rich was all about. To be poor (whether as an unsuccessful professor, an impoverished country gentleman, or a pauper—it was all the same) was to lose this éclat. Once one's "little light of glory" dwindled (to use Ausonius's telling phrase), one sunk into a state of dim anonymity.[35]

Splendor—éclat—was the key term in the definition of wealth. *Splendor* assumed income. But the practice of *splendor* gave little thought to financial matters in themselves. Rather, it had everything to do with how one looked, how one dressed, how one ate, how one traveled, and, last but not least, how often one bathed. Wealth sheathed the bodies of the rich with a set of unmistakable signals of prosperity and good fortune. By contrast, with Paulinus and Therasia, that *splendor* was well and truly dowsed.

It was in terms of a retreat from splendor that Paulinus communicated his new lifestyle to his spiritual friends. In a language of fierce precision, he took apart and inverted, at every point, the social semiotics of the fourth-century rich. In describing himself and his fellow ascetics, Paulinus left a memorable portrait of "poverty" not as "unwealth" but as "anti-wealth." The state of anti-wealth was as dramatically lodged in the body through ascetic practice, as the state of wealth had been lodged in the body, through a privileged lifestyle.

For this reason, Paulinus lingered on the strangeness of the group of men with whom he had chosen to identify himself at Cimitile. His description is like the negative of a photograph. From its dark patches, we can print out the sharp brilliance of wealth as it was usually displayed by persons of Paulinus's background. He and his fellow monks no longer lived in great villas. Instead, they gathered in cramped cells that overlooked the shrine of Felix at Cimitile. They were not shielded from the world by an entourage of dependents. They lived in close contact with the drab masses of the poor gathered in the hostel-portico below.[36] When they traveled, they no longer used great coaches. Many walked all the way. This is what the monk Victor did when he carried letters between Paulinus in southern Italy and Sulpicius Severus in Aquitaine, covering hundreds of miles every year on foot like "a two legged post horse."[37] They wore strikingly simple dress, dark, coarse, and drained of all color—the antithesis to the brilliant polychromy of the dress of the late Roman upper classes. Their hair was roughly cut. It was more like the scalped hair of a Roman convict than the oiled ringlets of a late Roman nobleman.[38] They ate plain food with a minimum of wine from earthenware and wooden vessels: no silver was to be seen. (Paulinus knew all too well what silverware meant as an assertion of wealth on the tables of his peers: he was more resolute in excluding it than was Augustine, who retained silver spoons at the bishop's table in Hippo.) Cooks of peasant stock provided "rustic" food: "beans pounded with millet, in order that I might learn more quickly to lay aside the refined choosiness of a senator."[39]

"All of us have pallid faces."[40] Paulinus and his fellow monks showed their diet in their gait. They adopted the grave, slow movements of those for whom plentiful food was no longer available as a source of energy to fuel the firm tread—the proud *incessus*—of the nobleman. Above all, they were enveloped in the dull smell of the underbathed. This was the sure mark of poverty in the ancient world.

It always carried with it a disquieting reminder of the ultimate victory of the stench of death. This was the exact opposite of the sweet, buoyant smell of life carried by the bodies of the rich as they emerged well washed and well perfumed from the magic, energizing world of their private bathhouses.

For Paulinus, it was utterly appropriate that this dim, unscented company should have come to be assembled around the tomb of Saint Felix. Felix had been a bishop of Nola toward the end of the third century. As Paulinus portrayed him in the annual poems he composed to celebrate the saint's festival, Felix was the mirror image of Paulinus. He had been the son of a rich immigrant to Nola. Felix had not even been a martyr; he had faced torture as a priest, but he died in his bed as a bishop, a poor man. He had surrendered his share of the family property to a greedy brother. He ended up cultivating a rented garden. Felix was what Paulinus wished to be. For Felix had lived "that form of life which was the image of that which the Lord Christ had lived on earth: once a rich man but now poor."[41]

Abjectio

THE IMITATION OF CHRIST

Paulinus's notion of poverty as anti-wealth was so cogent to his like-minded contemporaries because its distinguishing marks were grounded in intimate identification with the person of Christ.[42] He rooted his identity and that of his friends in the drama of a High God come down to earth. As he wrote to Sulpicius Severus in 400:

> Let us remember that we are the limbs of Him Who conquered when condemned, Who prevailed by yielding, Who rose again to glory by falling into death, Who has ensured that we will rise up in resurrection because of the headlong drop of his Crucifixion.... *This is our God and there shall be no other in comparison to Him* (Baruch 3:36).[43]

But what Christ was this? The Christ of Paulinus was very much the Christ of a particular generation. One might even say that He was a Christ whose image in Christian devotion was calculated to resonate with Christians of a particular class faced by a particular theological dilemma. Let us look at this more closely.

The figure of Christ that had emerged in the piety of intransigent Nicene Christians in the Latin West was unusually charged with paradox. The victory of their party had heightened a tension in attitudes toward the person of Christ. The Gospel accounts had shown Christ to have been at times weak and helpless. Yet, for the Nicene party, He was also God. He was not some secondary figure whose weaknesses were what one might expect from a being who was not truly divine, as the Nicene ultras believed (often incorrectly) that the Arians had implied. Thus, Nicene Christians faced an acute tension between the idea of Christ as an unprepossessing human being and the idea of Christ Who was also the "fullness of the Divinity." The answer to this imaginative dilemma was given by Ambrose of Milan and then by Paulinus, who followed Ambrose: God Himself had decided "for us and for our salvation" to expose Himself wholeheartedly, in Christ, to the fullness of human weakness.[44]

It is important to seize the specifically late Roman nuance of this solution. The Christ of Ambrose and of Paulinus was by no means the humanized Christ of later medieval and modern piety. He was very much a late Roman Christ. His humility was all the more stunning because it was based upon a conscious act of self-effacement on the part of the majestic God whom He continued to be. The *splendor* of God had dimmed itself in an awesome gesture of condescension. If, in the late Roman social imagination, power and wealth were things that had to be asserted in order to exist, then no *abjectio*, no "stepping down," could be more stunning than the "stepping down" by which God Himself had abandoned, for a time, His assertion of power. Christ, as God, had been the aristocrat of aristocrats, the wealthiest of the wealthy. Yet out of His immense goodness and of His own free will, He had renounced this wealth. He had veiled the éclat of His divinity in the drab colors of the human condition. But this éclat was still there. In the words of a hymn composed by Ambrose, which made its way into the liturgy of the Latin churches: Christ emerged from His human birth like "a giant of two-fold nature."[45] He confronted the human race as a God and a poor man in one.

The Christ of Paulinus was "poor" because He was a God who had hidden his splendor through an act of mighty self-effacement. "Humility" and "humble" are words to which Paulinus returns incessantly when speaking of Christ. And by "humble" Paulinus meant a posture to the world that was defined in more sharply social terms than can be conveyed by the sentimental modern associations of the word: to be *humilis* in the later Roman empire was to be, quite bluntly, "unimportant."[46]

In this sense, Paulinus's Christ was very much the Christ of the great marble sarcophagi in which the Christian aristocrats of Rome, Spain, and southern Gaul were buried at this time. In them, Christ appeared as a hauntingly muted figure. He was far removed from the destitution and blatant poverty of a later medieval Man of Sorrows. Rather, he stood with dignity before Pilate in a simple, well-folded robe. Yet it was precisely the total reticence of Christ's stance that would have weighed heavily with a late antique viewer. This was not the figure of an ancient philosopher, complete with bristling beard and exposed torso, which advertised the philosopher's active courage and sharp mind.[47] Christ was not like this. He was dressed in a plain robe that made no social assertion whatsoever. His glory rendered nondescript by His simple clothes, he stood before a Pilate whose throne and dress were overburdened with emblems that represented the untamed pride of a ruler of this world.[48] This was the quiet God who had stepped down to earth in Christ.

It was an ominous contrast. It also meant that, like Christ, Paulinus and similar ascetics would not vanish from the earth. Like Christ, he would continue to move among his fellows. Paulinus had no intention of becoming lost to the world on a desert island, as had the monks who shocked Rutilius Namatianus when he sailed past Capraria. Paulinus intended to stay around. Though surrounded by monks who looked pointedly poor, his life at Cimitile was by no means enclosed. It lay open to visitors from all over the West. And he did all this in the very heart of traditional Roman Italy.[49] Writing to Sulpicius Severus, Paulinus cited the current version of Isaiah 42:14: *I have been silent, but surely I will not always be silent.* These were the words of God. As followers of Christ, His poor could now echo these words: for "God is powerful, now, powerful to keep silence in us also."[50] In such a way, a converted aristocrat and his circle, who had carefully dismantled in themselves the strident denotators by which persons of wealth, power, and status had stood out in the late Roman world, faced their society as the bearers of a Christ equally shorn—but only for the time being—of His majesty.

CHAPTER 14

~

Commercium spiritale: The spiritual exchange
Paulinus of Nola and the Poetry of Wealth,
395–408

Marcus votum reddidit domno Felici sancto: Marcus has paid his vow
to the Lord Saint Felix

WEALTH IN A VOTIVE SHRINE

Between 395 and 408, Paulinus wrote a yearly poem for the festival of Saint Felix of Nola. In these poems, he wished his readers to know that he had always been destined to serve Saint Felix at his tomb. As a result, we tend to take very much for granted Paulinus's move to Campania and his taking up residence beside the shrine of Felix at Cimitile—the Cemetery—on the outskirts of Nola. We assume that, in arriving at Nola, in 395, Paulinus had realized his goal in life. This was "to end his days at Nola, serving the altar of a village saint."[1] All that followed were "idyllic years of pastoral."[2]

A series of outstanding recent studies of the life of Paulinus (by Dennis Trout), of the networks created by his correspondence (by Sigrid Mratschek), and of the spiritual content of his letters (by Catherine Conybeare)[3] have shown that this was not at all the case. They have recaptured the skill and the pertinacity with which Paulinus established himself as a leading figure in southern Italy. His correspondence ensured that his voice was heard by select groups of friends both in Gaul and in Africa.

This work has revealed very clearly how much of Paulinus the grandee survived in Paulinus the convert. Paulinus might dim his former status in a drastic act of *abjectio*. He might strip away the marks of high status in order to imitate the awesome condescension of Christ. But, for all this, he continued to enjoy the supreme privilege of a nobleman—the freedom to do what he wished with his life.

Nothing shows this more clearly than his attitude toward his own priesthood. Ordinary persons, when ordained, were expected to remain with the community that had chosen them. For at that time, the priesthood was not an ecclesiastical office that could be practiced anywhere, once conferred. Ordination was ordination to a specific local Christian community and to that community only. Priests ordained in one city were not encouraged to move to another.

Paulinus blithely ignored this restriction. He was ordained at Barcelona, but he left the city within a few months, taking his priesthood and his wealth with him. As a result, Paulinus received a frigid reception from the bishop of Rome, Siricius, when he arrived in Italy. Siricius had a high sense of the esprit de corps of an urban clergy. They were to stay with their bishop, just as officials in the imperial bureaucracy were supposed to stay in their department. Like officials, they were expected to work their way up a clear ladder of promotion. Siricius had no love of freelance clergymen with ascetic pretensions. Ten years before, in 386, he had helped drive Jerome out of Rome. Despite his spectacular renunciation, seen through the eyes of Siricius, Paulinus looked all too like the eccentric Priscillian.[4]

Even Paulinus's monastic establishment in Nola would have struck contemporaries as a classic example of an unchurched, household Christianity. It was largely a family affair. Paulinus may well have inherited a villa in the neighborhood of the shrine of Felix; he turned this into a monastery building.[5] But the boundary between this establishment and the outside world was unclear. Therasia, his wife, had accompanied him to Cimitile. We know nothing of her actions. This may simply have been because her presence at the side of her husband was taken for granted, as would have been the case in aristocratic circles. At a time when clerical pens were busy all over the Mediterranean denouncing the dangers of cohabitation between male and female ascetics among more commonplace Christians, the nobleman Paulinus's continent cohabitation with Therasia was an open secret no one dared challenge.[6]

We also know nothing of the role of the bishop of Nola. There is no evidence that Paulinus served him as a priest. The bonding of an upper-class clergyman with the *populus* of a city, which had meant so much to Ambrose, appears to have meant little to Paulinus. A former landowner to the last, his poems dealt not with townsfolk but with peasants. Even when we make allowances for the limitations of Paulinus's writings as evidence (for each poem and letter was written for a highly specific purpose), the omission of a wife, a bishop, and a city are significant silences.

At some time after 408, Paulinus became bishop of Nola. He steered his community through the Gothic invasion of 410–11. At that time, Saint Felix was said to have appeared on the walls of the city.[7] Paulinus wrote yet another poem of thanks to Felix. It spoke of the inhabitants of Nola set free at last to till the neighboring fields as the Gothic army withdrew. He may have bought them off.[8] In 419 he was brought in as arbitrator during a disputed papal election. When he died, in 431, he died as a good bishop was expected to die, mourned by all the citizens of Nola:

> For not only Christians, but even Jews and pagans, came together for the last rites of Lord Paulinus.... With a single voice, together with us, all bewailed the patron, defender and guardian snatched from them by death.[9]

But this last scene (from a text written in the 430s) merely shows how much the world had changed since 395. By then a bishop was expected to be a local figure and a patron of his city. In 395, however, Paulinus was not a "patron, defender and guardian" to anyone anywhere. What would have struck contemporaries was the exact opposite. It was the freedom to move around enjoyed by Paulinus as an aristocrat. He was not tied down to any city, to any church, or to any conventional public role. He did it his way. And nowhere was this more apparent than in the manner in which he chose to dispose of his wealth. He decided that his wealth should go to building up the shrine of Saint Felix.

Paulinus's decision should not be taken for granted. Many options existed in the minds of fourth-century Christians when they thought of the way in which their wealth could be used for pious purposes. As we have seen, when he announced his conversion Paulinus claimed to follow the outlines of the story of the Rich Young Man. He had followed the command of Christ to *sell all*. But there remained many ways in which to *give to the poor*. Not every rich convert was expected to spend his or her money on the cult of a local saint, as Paulinus would do.

In order to justify his decision, Paulinus fell back on an ancient pattern of pious giving that was already well-known in Christian and Jewish circles. Paulinus insisted on treating his wealth as a gift from God. This wealth had been preserved for him by Saint Felix at the time of his brother's execution when he himself had faced the threat of confiscation: You [Felix] ... removed the sword from my throat and the treasury officials from my estate. You kept me and my possessions in trust for Christ the Lord."[10] Preserved by God through Felix, Paulinus's wealth was given back to God by being spent on Felix. The income derived from the sale of Paulinus and Therasia's estates was not "scattered" among the poor in the regions where these estates lay. It was not sent to distant monasteries in Egypt and the Holy Land (as many Roman aristocrats had begun to do). It was not spent on founding hospitals. Nor was it sent to the distant frontiers, so as to ransom captives (as Ambrose had done). Rather, the wealth of Paulinus flowed, slowly but surely, toward Cimitile. Much of this wealth was frozen in buildings that made visible the splendor of saint Felix.

Paulinus's choice to see his wealth as votive wealth offered back to God was characteristic of him. It was both grand and humble at the same time. In the first place, to give in this way marked Paulinus's actions off from those of the usual urban benefactor. Unlike the urban benefactor, Paulinus did not give his wealth from an unshakable height so as to prove his exalted standing. He gave so as to show deep abasement. He insisted that his wealth was not his own; it lay in the hands of God.

Nor did these gifts spring from a previous relationship to any earthly place or group. The upper-class residents of Beneventum whose "undefeated hearts" had impressed Symmachus when they rallied to repair their city after an earthquake had done so out of a loyalty to their hometown that stretched back over generations. Symmachus himself had shown "the fine ardor of a Roman soul" as part of the longstanding dialogue between his family and the Roman people. By contrast, Paulinus's giving was tilted toward heaven. It was part of a timeless dialogue between himself, God, and Saint Felix. No matter how impressive the shrine at Cimitile may have been, the "people" whose "favor" Paulinus sought were invisible people. They were God and his saints.

And it was a dialogue that was open to all. As we have seen (in the case of the mosaic panels in the basilica of Aquileia and in churches and synagogues elsewhere), both in Judaism and in Christianity votive giving came in all sizes. It was not only for the very wealthy.

This had been particularly true of the shrine of Felix. Nola lay where two zones met, where the fertile Terra di Lavoro behind Naples came close to the hill villages of Samnium. For at least two generations before Paulinus brought his wealth to the shrine, the tomb of Felix had been a center of considerable, low-profile religious activity. Large numbers of graffiti have been discovered at the shrine, most of which take the form of mere scratches. They are the sign of crowds of non-literate pilgrims, anxious to leave their mark beside "the Lord Felix."[11]

An aura of sacred giving reached far into the surrounding countryside. Up in the hills to the east ranged the great herds of pigs that supplied part of the *annona civica* for the Roman people. Felix was believed to protect these herds. Prize pigs were dedicated to him from as far away as Beneventum. Some were so fat that it was a miracle in itself that they could make it to the shrine.[12] On arrival, they were slaughtered in fulfillment of vows made at home to Felix. The poor would gather excitedly at the promise of yet another meal of votive pork.

Paulinus lingered on these incidents in his poems. They added a bucolic touch to his description of the cult of Felix. They also show that Paulinus was not the only donor to the shrine. While his generosity was striking, it was not unique. It followed a pattern of giving laid down by thousands of humbler persons with whose piety he identified wholeheartedly.[13] Though not couched in the language of poetry, the graffiti at the shrine of Felix gave the same message as did Paulinus:

Marcus / votum reddidit / domno Felici s[anc]to.[14]

(Marcus has repaid his vow to the Lord Saint Felix.)

Let us see how Paulinus repaid his vow.

Mea gesta ... Felicisque manu: My deeds ... by the hand of Felix

THE BUILDING OF A SHRINE

Archaeological studies of Cimitile—best represented in the publications of Carlo Ebanista and in the definitive monograph of Tomas Lehmann—have taken us by surprise.[15] They show the speed and the ambition of Paulinus's building plans. Within seven years of Paulinus's arrival, the modest shrine of Felix was transformed. If ever wealth left its footprints on a site outside a city—as it had done in the late Roman villas of Spain and Aquitaine—it was in Paulinus's Basilica Nova (New Basilica) and in the adjacent buildings that came to surround the tomb of Felix. The new basilica measured 115 by 66 feet. It was larger than the reception hall of all but the greatest late Roman villa. Its pavement (made up of sections of multicolored marble) has been judged, by Tomas Lehmann, to be the most exquisite example of *opus sectile* in its time.[16] Marbles of eleven different colors were gathered from all over the Roman world for the columns, for the pavement, and for the casings of the shrine of Saint Felix itself. To gather together so much precious stone implied not only great wealth but *potentia*—the working of patronage networks and the claiming of privileges in a manner similar to that with which Symmachus had assembled the wild animals and horses needed for his son's games. Paulinus seems to have had access to government deposits of columns and unused blocks, as well as the use of government means of transport.[17]

The new basilica ended in a triconch apse (a great apse rendered sinuous by the inclusion, within its curve, of two side apses). It was a unique experiment that echoed the solemn dining halls of contemporary villas. The former apse of the old shrine of Felix was torn down to give a free view from the new basilica into the tomb itself. Joining the two buildings lay a small but exquisite courtyard. Everything that made a villa a place of splendor and delight was to be found there in miniature. A covered portico made up of many-colored columns sheltered a row of bright paintings. The entrance portico of the villa of Paulinus's ancestor at Burgus (Bourg, on the estuary of the Garonne) had contained similar frescoes. These frescoes had shown the ancestors of the Pontii Paulini. In the courtyard at Cimitile, by contrast, scenes from the Old Testament made plain that Paulinus now viewed the saints of old as his true ancestors. Each painting was accompanied by a poetic inscription, much as both Symmachus and Ausonius had placed poems beneath portraits of their own fathers.[18]

In the center of the courtyard were well-kept gardens and fountains filled with splashing water, which showed that Paulinus, like any other owner of a Roman villa, had made himself lord of the region's water. The recently discovered fragment of an exquisite marble basin echoed in miniature the great basin for ablutions that stood in the atrium of the shrine of Saint Peter at Rome.[19]

Altogether, the rebuilt shrine at Cimitile was Paulinus's dream villa. The green lawns and the shaded garden paths that led to the church; the splashing water of fountains in a little jewel of a courtyard; the solemn hall of the basilica, sheathed in marble and lit by great candelabra that cast pools of light surrounded by opulent shadows (as in the dining rooms of the rich)—these were the signs of late Roman villa architecture at its most luxurious.[20]

Paulinus had drawn across the former, assertive brilliance of his aristocratic persona an almost uncanny veil of dimness. But his buildings still spoke of the *splendor*—the éclat—of great wealth. Altogether, we should not underestimate what Kim Bowes has called "the audacity of his Nolan foundation."[21] We can detect in all this splendor a "Spanish symptom." Like the villas of Castille, Estramadura, and southern Portugal with their ambitious mausolea, the rebuilt shrine of Felix was to be Paulinus's monument and eventually his own mausoleum.

The wealthy had always been aware of the adrenalin of social self-assertion that went into the act of building their villas. Only a decade or so earlier—and only thirty miles away from Nola, on the bay of Naples—Symmachus had been tempted by an architect's plan for a new, curving portico that would mark the entrance to one of his villas. He wrote of it to a friend with the coy reticence we have learned (from the example of Ausonius) to expect when the rich spoke in person about their own wealth. His friend must not "bring upon me the itch to build ... you are positively pushing me to act against my sense of restraint—my *verecundia*."[22]

By invoking *verecundia*, Symmachus invoked a precious Roman social virtue. In an aristocrat, *verecundia* involved restraining the urge to make a splash, lest it awaken the envy of peers and the suspicion of emperors who were always on the lookout (in a time of frequent usurpations) for overmighty subjects.[23]

No such reticence held back Paulinus. For he did not build for himself; he built for God. He also encouraged his friend Sulpicius Severus, who had settled in a villa at Primuliacum (somewhere between Narbonne and Aquitaine), to do the same. At Primuliacum, Sulpicius Severus built two basilicas side by side joined together by a baptistery. As at Cimitile, the walls of these buildings were covered with images explained by inscriptions in verse. At Primuliacum, both Sulpicius Severus and Paulinus were represented as founders. Their portraits (in mosaic or fresco) flanked an image of the recently deceased Saint Martin. The essentially private nature of the complex at Primuliacum could not have been more forcibly expressed. This was Sulpicius's own building, placed under the protection of his very own saint. As in Nola, so in Primuliacum: no bishop played a role in the building project.

We know so much about the buildings at Primuliacum and at Cimitile because Paulinus advised his friend Severus on the decoration of the buildings at Primuliacum. He also described to Severus and to other friends every step of his own construction at the shrine of Felix.[24] Yet, although Paulinus shone as a builder, he was careful to present himself as humble in the sight of God. The sensitive studies of Maria Kiely and of Gaëlle Herbert de la Portbarré-Viard have recently shown that Paulinus was like no other Latin Christian author before him in drenching every detail of his new building in a torrent of mystic words. The careful and often high-handed process of building a new shrine was presented as echoing, step by step, what Paulinus wished God to do in rebuilding his own dilapidated soul.[25] In his poems, Paulinus presented himself as passive in the hands of God, the Master Builder. God had worked on him just as he, Paulinus, had worked on every detail of the shrine of Felix—right down to the scruffy vegetable garden once filled with debris and with old huts that he turned (to the understandable annoyance of their occupants, whom he evicted without a qualm) into well-cut lawns to grace the inner courtyard of his shrine.[26] Rebuilt by God, Paulinus built for Felix. Describing the buildings to a visiting bishop, Paulinus spoke of his building activities as: *Mea gesta ... Felicisque manu*: "My deeds ... by the hand of Felix."[27]

We sense in such a remark a total absence of the inhibitions that were imposed on secular noblemen by the centuries-long discipline of an aristocratic peer group. Symmachus had to pretend to be embarrassed by spending so much money on the porticoes of his villa. Not so Paulinus. We are dealing with a phenomenon that accounts in no small part for the vividness of the age: the fierce sense of agency that was released when a convert such as Paulinus stepped clear of the restraint imposed by his peer group and placed himself and his wealth in the hands of God. He could build as extravagantly as he wished for Felix.

Commercium spiritale: The spiritual exchange

Settled in Nola with his wealth dedicated to the Lord Felix, Paulinus was free to linger in his letters and poems on the subsequent, otherworldly destiny of his riches. It needed a poet such as Paulinus to rise to such a theme. In speaking of the transfer of wealth from earth to heaven, he had to break the imaginative barriers imposed by common sense.[28] He had to describe the joining of two incommensurables. Wealth and heaven, instinctively thought of as utter opposites, had to be shown to be continuous.

When speaking the language of poetic paradox, Paulinus deliberately swung between the denigration of wealth in this world and intimations of the incommensurable, unimagined glory associated with the same wealth once it was stored in heaven. By writing in this way, he distilled the sensibility of an age. The ability to contrast and then to connect opposites was deeply embedded in the late antique aesthetic sense. Each dramatic image was expected to conjure up its antithesis. For an early Byzantine Christian, to hear of the dry and empty pit into which Joseph had been lowered by his brothers was to "trigger" in a subliminal manner the image of a baptismal pool, filled to the brim with living waters.[29] For a pious pagan to read of the most obscene, surreal actions of the gods of ancient mythology was to be reminded—by an instinctive reversal of the mind—of the exact antithesis of such disturbing images: it was to catch an echo from the very dome of heaven of the gods in their transcendent glory.[30]

Paulinus did the same. Opposites changed into each other as if by magic. The labile "slime" of wealth on earth became solid treasure in heaven. "Brittle stones" formed a staircase of the mind that reached beyond the stars.[31] In his poems on wealth and heaven, Paulinus emerged as the Wordsworth of his times:

> The song would speak
> Of that interminable building reared
> By observation of affinities
> In objects where no brotherhood exists
> To passive minds.[32]

But in the case of Paulinus, lest anyone think that "that interminable building" was no more than the creation of a poet's fancy, they needed only to enter the new basilica of Cimitile. In its scented depths, where the golden roof waved like a great sea in the flickering light of innumerable oil lamps, they could see with their own eyes that a drop of imagined treasure had, indeed, fallen back from heaven to earth in the unearthly beauty of a Christian shrine.[33]

The message was clear. Wealth—"worldly" wealth, wealth that stood for all that was most brittle in this world, most unspiritual, most stubbornly rebellious to the will of God, and most heavy with death—could be transmuted through the act of pious giving into all that was most glittering and glorious in an eternal world beyond the stars. This was what Paulinus told his friend Severus, in the summer of 404, as they discussed the building of their respective shrines in Italy and Aquitaine: *Videte commercium spiritale*—look and see, we have here an exchange—an exchange taking place in the very world of the spirit."[34]

The notion of *commercium spiritale* (or *spirituale*) was central to the thought world of Paulinus. In order to recapture the imaginative weight of such a notion we must remember that, in Latin usage, the word *commercium*—from which our own word "commerce" is derived—did not carry with it the brash and calculating overtones that "commerce" and "exchange" now evoke. Rather, the word *commercium* evoked any form of profitable bonding. It conjured up the idea of fruitful reciprocity. More generally (to use the well-chosen words of Carole Newlands in her study of Statius's *Silvae*), *commercium* implied "a harmony within duality."[35]

Thus, the word *commercium* came to Paulinus already charged with expectations of "harmony within duality." Such harmony pointed to a world redeemed. Paulinus used the word in relation to pious giving. But the notion of a spiritual exchange through pious giving was only a special case. Behind the *commercium* by which earthly wealth flowed upward to heaven lay the decisive joining of heaven and earth brought about by the coming of Christ. The incarnation of Christ had been the foundational act of "exchange." It had rendered possible and thinkable all other forms of contact between God and humanity. Paulinus wrote this to Ausonius as early as 394: "God has clothed himself in us, entering into eternal links of exchange between mankind and God."[36]

In the words of Catherine Conybeare, through the Incarnation of Christ "each nature—man and God—laid down its essential unlikeness."[37] For late antique persons, the stark contrast between human and divine, between material and spiritual, between body and soul, and between the heavy, turbulent earth and the serenity of the star-filled world beyond the moon had been fixed components in their imaginative universe. No joining could have been more improbable and no paradox more audacious than to bring these antitheses together in such a way that God joined humankind and base, earthly wealth joined the distant purity of the heavens.

Paulinus wrote to make gloriously transparent to the imagination of his readers the invisible exchange by which their own wealth might make its way to heaven:

> For this hope does not abruptly deprive us of our possessions. If it prevails and faith conquers, it changes for the better and transforms our wealth according to God's law, making it no longer brittle but eternal, removing it from earth and setting it in heaven.[38]

Spiritual Exchange and the Care of the Poor: Rome, 396

It is in this paradox-laden language of exchange that Paulinus described the relations between rich and poor. In order to do justice to this theme he seized upon a memorable occasion in Rome. In 396 the Christian senator Pammachius gave a lavish feast to the poor of Rome on the anniversary of the death of his wife, Paulina.[39] The entire courtyard of the basilica of Saint Peter's at Rome was filled with tables. There was nothing new about this practice; Christians had always celebrated the memory of their dead with banqueting. Now Christian aristocrats offered yet bigger and better feasts. Only a few years previously, the great Petronius Probus had died. The great Anician had received an ostentatious Christian burial in a large mausoleum that abutted the apse of the basilica of Saint Peter's. This mausoleum included a *mensa*—a table for the feasting of the poor on the day of the commemoration of Probus's death—that was so grand that it was later believed to have been the *mensa* set up by Saint Peter himself.[40]

One should add that not everyone in Rome was enchanted by that occasion. Symmachus refused to attend Probus's funeral. His frank view of the great Christian senator was that

> it is a law of courtesy that, for those for whom one has had little esteem and from whom one has been distant, one can offer not the testimony of grief, but, at least, the polite gesture of keeping one's opinion to oneself.[41]

But Christians were duly impressed. An aristocrat such as Probus set a new standard of magnificence for the traditional memorial banquet. In celebrating the memory of his wife, Pammachius could not hope to outshine Probus. But the literary brilliance of his friend Paulinus made up for what the occasion lacked in material splendor. Paulinus turned a routine act of Christian piety into a high moment of *commercium*. By feeding the poor on the occasion of his wife's death, Pammachius caused the incommensurable worlds of heaven and earth to come together.

In doing this, Paulinus placed his own, poetic stamp on a well-established Christian practice. Like any other Early Christian memorial occasion, Pammachius's banquet had been given for the *refrigerium*—the refreshing—of the soul of Paulina. On such occasions the living and the dead had always been thought to be joined to each other through a pious feast. Paulinus, however, made clear exactly how this joining happened. The feeding of the poor made the invisible event in heaven visible on earth. By laying on the banquet, Pammachius "formed anew the blood-drained bodies of the needy."[42] But this was not simply an act of charity, carried out on earth. It was an action that mirrored heaven on earth. The pink flush of good cheer that crept over the diners as they ate and drank "doubled" with satisfactory exactness the unimaginable refreshment of Paulina's soul in the other world.

> For Christ's hand poured over her the gifts which you expended on the poor, as *in the blink of an eye* (1 Corinthians 15:51–52) that earthly food was transformed into heavenly nourishment. All the money which you

cheerfully gave, pouring it from your laden hands into the twin palms of the recipients, was deposited in the bosom of a rejoicing Lord by angels who intercepted it in flight, to be restored to you [in Heaven].[43]

It is revealing that Paulinus (by writing "in the blink of an eye") seems to have almost instinctively applied to the process of the transformation of Pammachius's wealth into treasure in heaven the phrase with which Saint Paul described the onset of the greatest transformation of all—the final climax of the *commercium* between God and humanity: the resurrection of the dead. By being turned into alms for the poor, dead wealth had been redeemed and brought to life.

As Paulinus presented it to Pammachius, the *refrigerium* of Paulina was an event shot through with the dizzying paradox of a joining of heaven and earth. But we should also note that the splendid memorial banquet was a very staid occasion. The poor of the church sat in orderly rows, filling the courtyard outside the great, gold-roofed basilica.[44] They held out both hands to receive their gifts of coin, straight from the right hand of Pammachius. Their thankful prayers resounded over the city like the well-organized acclamations that echoed in the Circus Maximus and the Colosseum.

What a good, tumultuous roar to shake the City.... O Rome, you would not need to fear the threats made against you in the Apocalypse, if your senators always gave games such as yours, Pammachius.[45]

In Paulinus's opinion, Pammachius had provided a Christian answer to the spectacles for which Symmachus was already making preparations and which he would eventually lavish on the Roman people in honor of the praetorship of his son, Memmius in 401.

We must keep a sense of proportion when faced by these daring comparisons. There was no chance that Pammachius's feeding of the poor could be regarded as in any way a real replacement for the great games of Rome. What mattered for Pammachius was not the overall size of the ceremony nor the extent of his outlays: compared with 2,000 pounds of gold (which was sufficient to support 130,000 recipients of the *annona* for a year) spent on crocodiles, gladiators, and silk robes for star charioteers, Pammachius's banquet for the poor was a trivial matter. But we should not underestimate the social message of Paulinus's description of the banquet. Pammachius had not scattered alms to a heaving sea of faceless beggars. Rather, he had brought together in miniature the twin components of a stable civic order—a rich giver was brought face-to-face with an orderly and grateful *populus*, even if this *populus* was no more than the Christian poor.

It was for this reason that Paulinus described Pammachius as having offered a *munus*—a show—to the poor that was met by the acclaim of the poor. In so doing, Paulinus sketched out unwittingly the future of Christian Rome. A century later, as we shall see (in chapter 27), the poor of the church protected by the pope came to be promoted to a position resembling that of the old *plebs Romana*. It is an evolution Pammachius could not have dreamed of in practice. But the art of Paulinus—with its daring comparison with the games of Rome—had made it thinkable.[46]

Rich and Poor at the Shrine of Saint Felix

Apart from his letter to Pammachius, Paulinus's vision of the proper relation between rich and poor is best seen in the orderly architecture of the shrine of Felix. At Cimitile, Paulinus was constantly in contact with the poor. He met them, first and foremost, as pilgrims who gathered at Cimitile on the feast day of Felix that occurred in January. This was a period of high unemployment and hunger in the plains of Campania and in the hills of Samnium. He fed those who came to the shrine as pilgrims on that occasion with open-handed generosity. He provided them with warmth and wine.[47]

But Paulinus also met the poor as a permanent mass of destitute persons. It is important to stress this fact. The most poignant Christian discourse on the poor had been generated in the great cities of the eastern Mediterranean. In Antioch and Constantinople, the rich were urged by a preacher such as John Chrysostom to look over the edge of a social precipice into a swirling and anonymous crowd of beggars, buffoons, and homeless immigrants gathered around them in a great city.

But in the Roman world, rural poverty was just as grim and as widespread as was poverty in the cities. This was true of Paulinus's Campania. It was a piebald province. Vivid villas and intensively cultivated estates (such as those owned by Symmachus) alternated with agrarian "rust belts"—ugly swathes of deeply impoverished land. For all its exquisite buildings, the shrine of Felix was far from being an idyllic retreat. It may also have become the human rubbish tip of the region, to which the poor made their way in search of the food and shelter the shrine provided.[48] One of Paulinus's last actions before his death was to pay a quite substantial sum (forty *solidi*) to cloth merchants, which he had owed them for clothes for the poor.[49]

Faced by such misery, what Paulinus advocated was the notion of a mystical symbiosis between rich and poor. The architecture of the shrine itself was interpreted in light of this symbiosis. Paulinus and his monks lived in the upper stories of the courtyard. Their cells looked down directly on to the shrine of Felix. The poor gathered in the porticoes and in the enclosed spaces of the hostel on ground level. For Paulinus, this was not simply a device of social segregation. It was a deeply satisfying concretization of his notion of exchange. He had given the poor material things—sustenance and a roof over their heads. They would offer in return the ethereal essence of their prayers.[50] God Himself had allowed this exchange to happen. For, in a spectacular act of amnesty (like that of a Roman emperor), "He had extorted from His own omnipotent sense of justice" the concession that the rich would not be excluded from the Kingdom. They were not condemned to be forever camels. By pious giving (to the saints and to the poor) they might bypass the terrible, cramped eye of the needle. They were allowed by God to use their earthly treasure so as to purchase heaven through giving to the poor.[51]

Ultimately, the story of the Rich Young Man (which had haunted so many of his ascetic contemporaries) did not obsess Paulinus as much as did the story of Dives and Lazarus. This was Christ's story of the rich man and the beggar who lay at his gate, as told in Luke 16:19–31. Again and again in his works Paulinus returned to the terrible *vicissitudo*—the flip-flop—by which the miserable Lazarus went to heaven and the happy rich man, feasting among his friends in the full éclat of a nobleman, had gone to hell. He feared that this could happen to him: that the scarlet robe that drew all eyes would, in the other world, burst in an instant into a sheet of flame. Yet, Paulinus insists, if Dives had only stopped to look at Lazarus and pressed some alms into his hands he would not have been in hell.[52]

Once again, Paulinus did no more than put his own, distinctive stamp on traditional ideas shared in a more wordless manner by Jews and Christians. A story in the Babylonian Talmud tells how the Roman governor Turnus Rufus once challenged the rabbis:

> "If your God loves the poor, why does He not support them?" The rabbi Meier replied: "So that through them [by giving alms] we [the rich] may be saved from the punishment of Gehinnom."[53]

We may have the inscriptions Paulinus placed on the low marble screen around the tomb of Felix. They take the form of citations from the Bible.[54] The command to *sell all and give to the poor* is not among them. But they did urge almsgiving: *Lock up your alms in the bosom of the poor and it* [the alms themselves, not the poor] *will pray for you* (Eccl. 29:5). Last but not least, the inscriptions copied out Paul's citation from an otherwise unknown saying of Jesus: *It is more blessed to give than to receive* (Acts 20:35).[55] Though known in the world at large and to later ages as the prime example of the total renunciation of wealth, in his letters, poems, and activities at the shrine of Felix Paulinus emerges, rather, as an advocate of the flow of wealth between heaven and earth and between rich and poor.

Divisionem cum Deo facito: Go part shares with God

CHRISTIAN LANDOWNERS AND THE USE OF WEALTH

For wealth to flow in this way, it had to be endowed with a certain imaginative solidity. In the long run, Paulinus's persistent emphasis on the transferability of wealth from earth to heaven laid down a highway in the mind by which real wealth could be set to work by real persons to build a real Christian future. Let us end by seeing how Paulinus opened the door to this process. To do this we should follow the outlines of what Dennis Trout has acutely characterized as Paulinus's "Salvation Economics."[56]

Some time around 400, a ship of Paulinus that carried money to support his building projects—specifically named by him as *argentum illud sacri commercii*—had landed during a storm on the beach of an estate owned by his friend Jovius.[57] Jovius was represented by Paulinus as having thought that the safe landing of the ship had been no more than a matter of chance. By thinking in this manner, Jovius implicitly denied that wealth could play a providential role in the sacred exchange between God and humanity. For he believed that God Himself had had no hand in the creation of this wealth in the first place. Wealth was not a gift of God; it was a gift of fortune. It did not, therefore, need to be given back in gratitude to God.[58]

We only know Jovius through Paulinus's presentation of his attitude. But he is an entirely credible late fourth-century aristocrat. He was a man of the *mundus,* much as Ausonius had been. He had no difficultly in believing in the existence of God. The providence of a One High God might rule supreme in heaven, but this providence did not necessarily extend downward into the sublunary world far below the heavens. For the world below the moon was a messy place touched only indirectly, if at all, by the hand of God. It was ruled either by chance or by the complex interactions of the planets. Or it had been left to the ministrations of lesser powers—to gods and angels, many of whom still bore the accustomed faces of the gods of ancient paganism. As we have seen, these lesser powers still mattered. They stood between humanity and a still distant God who was relegated, even by Christians, to the higher reaches of the heavens.

We must always remember that Paulinus and Jovius still lived in a profoundly polytheist society. Respect for the lower gods clung like a benign ground mist over large tracts of the countryside. The mosaics and statue collections of the great villas of Aquitaine and Spain showed a preference for themes taken from the myth of Dionysos. These themes celebrated the effortless renewal of nature—of the rich plough lands and of the vineyards from which the wealth of the villa owners was drawn. In this mystique of abundance, wealth was thought to nestle, as it were, in the bosom of a natural world endowed with an energy all its own, tended since time immemorial by a multitude of invisible nurturing powers.[59]

Paulinus wrote to Jovius knowing that such beliefs were widespread. He did not in any way encourage Jovius to abandon his wealth. It was sufficient that Jovius should know that this wealth did not come from nature but from God:

> *Divisionem cum Deo facito:* Go part shares with God for your possessions, and render to the Supreme Father thanks for the gift that has been loaned to you by Him.... You and your household can keep all that you possess, provided that you take good care to declare that God is the donor of these things as well.[60]

In 400 AD this was a less banal comment than we might suppose. What Paulinus implied was that Jovius did not owe his wealth to the abundance of nature, miraculously fostered by the little gods of the countryside. Rather, the providence of the One God reached down in a great arc through every level of Roman society to touch the fields and those who owned them.

In proposing this view of wealth, Paulinus followed a wider shift in Christian attitudes toward society in general and the imperial system in particular. What has been aptly called a "ministerial" theory of the imperial power had been developed in the late fourth-century West, largely under the influence of Saint Ambrose. In this ministerial theory, the imperial power was demystified. The emperor was no longer bathed in a quasi-divine aura in such a way that the image of the emperor wavered between that of a god and an ordinary mortal. The emperor was an ordinary human being. He was expected to behave as a pious Christian. But he was no less powerful for that. The brute weight of the imperial system was enthusiastically accepted provided that it was used for a higher aim—the defense and extension of the Christian faith. In this ministerial view, the emperor was thought of as acting as the servant of God, to whom he owed directly the gift of empire.[61]

What Paulinus proposed to Jovius was, in effect, a ministerial theory of landed power, a notion that did not come naturally to landowners at this time. To think that their wealth lay in the hands of a single, all-powerful God, to whom they were accountable for its use, was a novel idea. Far away, on the banks of the Nile, the great Egyptian abbot Shenoute of Atripe was told quite bluntly by Gessios—a largely imagined pagan interlocutor, the equivalent of Paulinus's Jovius—that he should mind his own business. Gessios told Shenoute that he had received his wealth from his own father, not from God. He owed God nothing and the church even less.[62]

Paulinus's answer to persons such as Jovius was both daringly counterfactual and basically safe. Their wealth was not their own; it came from God. But they could keep it as long as they followed the will of God. From the imaginative point of view, nature was stripped of its ancient mystique of abundance. It was the will of God alone—and not the semi-divine energy of nature—that caused the harvests to flourish every year. Nature was desacralized and cut down to size—so that it might remain firmly in the hands of pious human owners.

This message was not unwelcome to the landowners. Indeed, they may have been subliminally prepared for it by aspects of the art of their own mosaics. In an acute analysis of the mosaics of the villas of this period, Lambert Schneider drew attention (in his book *Die Domäne als Weltbild*) to a notable feature of late Roman mosaics. In many of these, nature itself was shown, as it were, pulled into the orbit of the great. No product of the wild or of the cultivated land was shown in its own right. All of nature was presented as if it existed only so as to be "offered up" to the *dominus*, the owner of the estate—preferably by ranks of neatly dressed and deferential peasants. The numinous bounty of the land was undeniable. But it had, as it were, been tilted toward human owners. It existed only to be given to the lords of the land.[63]

We need only to go forward for a century, and to the eastern Mediterranean, to find vivid visual evidence for this change of emphasis. In the votive mosaics of churches of the fifth and sixth centuries, which have survived in large numbers in Israel, Syria, and Jordan, we can see that this sharply "vertical" view of the natural world (as existing for the landowner alone) was transposed to a higher plane. God was now seen as the *dominus*—the great landowner—and it is now the *domini* themselves—the local landowners—who are shown as if they were obedient peasants bearing to Him the produce of their estates. They are shown offering baskets of first fruits, close to the altar to which their offerings would have been brought during the Eucharistic liturgy. They were proud yet deferential figures. They were what Paulinus saw himself to be and what he wished Jovius to be: they were "sharecroppers" of the Lord. They held their lands under God. Their wealth came from God so that part of it might be sent on to heaven by being used for the purposes of God through the support of His poor and through the endowment of His churches.[64]

Such, in general outline and effect, was the message of Paulinus to the wealthy. What is remarkable is that we only know of it for little more than thirteen years—from the first great poems to Ausonius to the last surviving poem for the feast day of Felix, delivered in 408. Yet Paulinus lived until 431. He continued to write works that have not come down to us. The reason for the sudden silence is revealing. Paulinus did not preserve his own letters, as Symmachus had done and as Augustine would do, piling up copies on the shelves of the bishop's library of Hippo. An Aquitanian gentleman to the last, he lived for his friends and he wrote for his friends. It was his friends in Aquitaine who appear to have kept copies of these letters and poems. As Catherine Conybeare has pointed out, these letters were written as "meditative texts" to nourish the souls of small groups of committed Christians, many of whom were landowners as he himself had been.[65] And it must be confessed, a little Paulinus goes a long way. By 408 his friends may have felt that they had received enough of this rich diet. But it was precisely among circles of leisured, landed Christians that the poetry of wealth proposed by Paulinus continued to work, molding the imagination for centuries to come.

Paulinus ensured that the debate on Christian wealth now took place among truly wealthy persons. For some years even before Paulinus had settled in Nola and Augustine had settled in Hippo, this debate had already flared up in Rome itself. In Rome, the debate on wealth increasingly looked eastward across the sea, toward an imagined Outremer—to the ascetic settlements of Egypt and the Holy Land. The acrimony and drama of the debate was sharpened by the intervention of persons who wished to act in Rome as ascetic mentors of the rich. They were not always popular. To see why this was so, we must go back for almost a century to describe Christian Rome from the days of Constantine onward. For the developments of that time formed the backdrop to the differing groups of upper-class Christians, some of whom supported and some of whom rejected the industrious and unforgettable Jerome.

CHAPTER 15

Propter magnificentiam urbis Romae: By reason
of the magnificence of the city of Rome

The Roman Rich and Their Clergy,
from Constantine to Damasus, 312–384

A spectacle as beautiful as a stage painting: Rome in 370

PALACES, *SUBURBIUM,* AND CHURCHES

In the fourth century, Rome was still a stupendous city. A traveler who entered Rome from the south through the Appian Gate would take an hour of brisk walking through a landscape of continuous stone and brick before finally exiting the city at its northern end through the Salarian Gate. The same traveler could have walked through Trier in twenty minutes. The traveler would have passed through monumental areas that were calculated to leave the visitor stunned.[1] On all sides of the monumental center, a population of over half a million was squeezed into high, rickety buildings in the valleys that led up from the Tiber toward the hills. Compared with the chaos below, the hills that ringed the eastern horizon "presented to the eye a spectacle as beautiful as a stage-painting."[2] Crowned by green gardens, in whose depths luxurious palaces might be glimpsed, the hills of Rome were where the residential aristocracy of Rome were to be found. It was the world of the noble *domus*—of palatial building complexes, many of which were centuries old.[3]

The other pole of the life of the rich of Rome was the *suburbium*. Residences in the *suburbium* were the equivalent of the villas that ringed the cities in other provinces. The *suburbium* was a "quasi city."[4] It was an almost unbroken extension of Rome itself, a landscape partly dedicated to the dead and partly more than usually alive. The tombs of generations of Romans stretched along the Appian Way (as along all the other roads into the city). Burial grounds increasingly identified with Christians (such as the funerary area now visited by tourists as the catacombs of San Sebastiano) lay a little to one side of the main basalt road. But in between places given over to the dead, the land bloomed. It was a zone of palatial villas, intensive garden agriculture (largely dependent on slave labor), and artisanal industries that served the city.[5]

It was in the *suburbium* that the rich of Rome found a place where they could breathe in the summer months, while a pall of death (largely due to the falciparum malaria that had held the Tiber valley in its grip for centuries) hung over the city.[6] Symmachus had five villas in the *suburbium*.

It was in the *suburbium* also that villas given over to spiritual *otium* were to be found, like those we have met in the Cassiciacum of Augustine and in the Spanish villas to which Paulinus of Nola had retired before his conversion. These were favored by the Christian rich as much as by their pagan colleagues. From the 350s onward, the pious Christian widow Marcella regularly left her palace on the Aventine for an estate in the *suburbium*. Jerome wrote to her there in 385. He imagined her happy among fresh lettuces as she looked back (in traditional Roman fashion) on the vanities of the city that lay only an hour's walk from her farm: "Let Rome have its riots, let savage carnage rage in the arena, let the citizenry go wild, let the Senate of First Ladies continue to exchange daily visits."[7] Sheltered in the quiet harbor of her suburban residence, Marcella was free to read the Psalms among the twittering birds.

Through the correspondence of Jerome and other documents, we know a lot about individual rich Christians in Rome from the 380s onward. But what was recognizably Christian in this gigantic cityscape around the year 350? The answer is surprising to modern persons: next to nothing. Entering Rome proper, the traveler would have entered a city almost totally empty of Christian monuments. At most, twenty-five churches lay scattered in the midst of an urban fabric made up of fourteen thousand housing blocks. What churches there were merged with the surrounding buildings. At best, they looked like modest town houses, such as were owned by the lesser nobility—a reception hall surrounded by a few subsidiary buildings entered from a courtyard. In a city of half a million, the existing churches of Rome provided room for only twenty thousand worshipers. To eyes accustomed to a traditional city, Christianity was invisible within the walls of Rome.[8]

This could not be said of the *suburbium*. In that area, a Christian donor had already left the footprint of vast wealth upon the land. That donor was Constantine. It was by building spectacular Christian shrines and mausolea connected with Christian sites on the edge of Rome that Constantine made clear his conversion to Christianity in 312.

Constantine founded two major basilicas: Saint Peter's on the Vatican Hill and the basilica in the Lateran gardens that stretched across the hills on the southeast side of Rome (now known as San Giovanni in Laterano). To these two churches alone he gave spectacular liturgical vessels, candelabra, and altars— almost 500 pounds of gold and 12,760 pounds of silver. He endowed the Roman

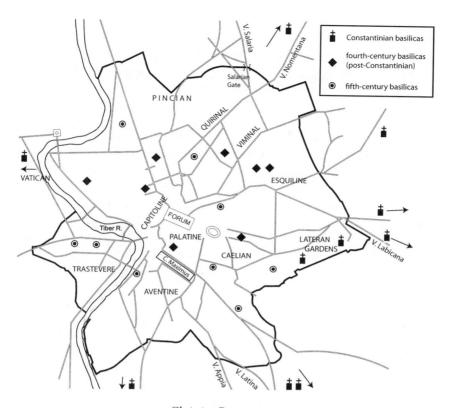

MAP 3. Christian Rome, 300–500 AD

Note the largely peripheral nature of the church buildings erected by Constantine, and the slow growth of churches within the city. The hills marked on the map were the principal places of residence for the aristocracy.

church with a substantial revenue of around 25,000 *solidi* (roughly a quarter of the annual income of Symmachus). But most of this revenue was earmarked for the support of the basilicas that he himself had founded. Over 4,000 *solidi* a year (four times the estimated revenue of Ausonius's "little estate") went to maintaining the lights of the Lateran basilica and of its neighboring baptistery.[9]

These imperial churches were votive monuments. They proclaimed Constantine's victories over his rivals. The splendid basilica he established at the Lateran was built over the barracks of the crack troops of Maxentius, the rival he had defeated in 312. It flanked the palace where Constantine held court when he resided in the city. This palace had a private chapel (now known as Santa Croce in Gerusalemme).[10] Though given to the bishop of Rome to act as his cathedral, the Lateran basilica was a church built for the greater glory of Constantine and not for the greater glory of the local Christians.

The vast shrine over the tomb of Saint Peter in the graveyard area on the Vatican Hill is traditionally associated with Constantine. He may only have begun the building. It was left to his pious sons, and especially to Constantius II, to complete and dedicate what at the time was a frankly imperial monument built to demonstrate the piety of Christian emperors.[11]

The footprint of imperial wealth was even more clear in the *suburbium* proper. Imperial mausolea appeared close to the tomb of Saint Agnes (Sant'Agnese, on the Via Nomentana) and to the tombs of Peter and Marcellinus (SS Pietro e Marcellino, on the Via Labicana). These mausolea were devoted to the memory of female members of Constantine's own family. The mausoleum of Constantine's sister, Constantina, beside the catacomb of S. Agnese is the present-day church of Santa Costanza. But it was not founded as a church. Its vault was decorated with merry cherubs treading the wine harvest. A cheerfully secular mausoleum built for a great princess, it later became known to some as "the Tomb of Bacchus."[12]

Such buildings were both spectacular and highly personalized. The huge tower of the mausoleum of Constantine's mother, Helena (now known as Tor Pignattara), dwarfed the neighboring underground chamber that held the tombs of Saints Peter and Marcellinus. It was a building of uncanny grandeur. An altar made of two hundred pounds of silver stood beneath a dome that hung over seventy feet above the floor. Offerings for the soul of Helena would have been laid on this altar. The Eucharistic furnishings of the altar included a solid gold plate of thirty-five pounds and three heavy gold chalices studded with jewels (each of which weighed ten pounds). Four immense silver candelabra, each weighing two hundred pounds, along with twenty other smaller silver chandeliers, filled the mausoleum with light. Hundreds of pounds of nard, balsam, and spices mixed in the oil of the lamps filled the entire building with an unearthly perfume.[13]

Constantine gave nothing like this to any of the churches attended by the average Christians of Rome. A typical urban benefactor (if on an imperial scale), Constantine gave the Christians large spaces in which "his" people could assemble in hitherto undreamed-of splendor. This was a sufficient gift. The great basilicas were particularly well suited to a Christianity that was a largely "festal" religion. The average believer did not necessarily go to church regularly. But he or she was certain to turn out for the great festivals of the year—Easter and feast days of the martyrs. Constantine's buildings on the edge of Rome were perfectly adapted to such grand occasions. But within Rome itself, apart from a few token gifts, Constantine's generosity did not extend to the local churches.

The disparity between the wealth lavished by Constantine on the edges of Rome and the modest establishment of the Roman church inside the city was typical of the age of Constantine and of his immediate successors. It was the sign of a transitional age marked by the strange alliance between an exuberant emperor and a religious institution still characterized by its *mediocritas*, without real wealth of its own and devoid of traditional social status. The church still had a long way to go before its own resources matched those of rich laypersons. The history of the growth of the wealth of the Christian churches of Rome (and of the conflicts that went with this growth) does not begin with Constantine. It begins, effectively, in the last decades of the fourth century. As we shall see, it was not only a history of the bishop of Rome and his clergy but also of the richer members of the Christian laity.

Constituit titulum: He set up a *titulus*

PRIVATE AND ECCLESIASTICAL ENDOWMENT
IN THE CHURCHES OF ROME

There is a tendency to allow the huge sums lavished by Constantine on his own churches at Rome to cause us to underestimate the wealth that the church of Rome itself may have brought with it into the Constantinian age. This could have been considerable. But it was wealth derived in the old manner. It did not come from single great patrons; it came from the gifts of a large number of basically low-profile persons. When Silvester, the bishop of Rome at the time of Constantine, founded his own church, he endowed it with a revenue of 413 *solidi* (one-tenth of the annual revenue set aside for the lighting of the Lateran basilica alone) along with a mere 55 pounds of silver plate and one small gold dish.[14] What we witness in the course of the fourth century is the slow build-up of the wealth of the churches within Rome itself through the gifts of private persons, clerical and lay alike. In this slow and largely hidden process, the last quarter of the fourth century was far more decisive for the ultimate fate of Christianity in Rome than was the spectacular but limited intervention of Constantine.

Given its long-term importance, the accretion of wealth by the Roman churches was a strangely silent process. The historian can trace it only through fragments that are as tantalizing as they are vivid. The most elusive issue of all concerns the finances of the individual churches of Rome. Many churches in the city bore a distinctive name. They were called *tituli*—"titular churches." To the historian, the term has all the opacity of a technical term whose meaning was taken for granted by contemporaries. They felt that the term required no explanation, leaving us to guess what exactly it meant in the context of a church foundation. In Roman law, the word *titulus* was used of property acquired through a legal transfer that guaranteed full title to the new owner. In reality, it was a word that veiled a complex scenario. We have only one glimpse of the foundation of a titular church. Sometime in the pontificate of Innocent (401/2–417), an aristocratic lady Vestina (an *illustris femina*—the daughter or widow of a high official) built a church to the Milanese martyrs Gervasius and Protasius. (The church is now known as San Vitale on the Quirinal Hill.) The building of the church was organized by three clergymen close to Innocent.

> This woman had directed in the text of her will that the basilica should be constructed from the sale of her ornaments and pearls at an expert estimate. When the basilica was completed, Innocent set up in it a *titulus* in Rome (*titulum Romae constituit*) from the properties assigned by the illustrious woman.

The revenue for the *titulus* came from urban real estate—from a bakery, a bath, and a toll gate—and from a scatter of estates in Etruria and Campania. The total revenue was 1,016 *solidi* (the equivalent of the estimated revenue of Ausonius's family estate). Preserved in the archives of the Roman church, the record of Vestina's *titulus* offers a precious glimpse of a church founded by lay initiative through the sale of spectacular items of personal adornment. Furthermore, the maintenance of the church and the payment of the clergy were financed by the gift of revenues from Vestina's country estates and from a still-buoyant urban economy.[15] A century later, the priests connected with the church built by Vestina still spoke of themselves as priests of the *titulus Vestinae*. In this way, the name of the lay donor who had built the church and provided its revenue remained as important as that of the name of the saints to which it had been dedicated.

Between 366 and 432, ten such *tituli* were founded. In 499 there were priests for at least twenty-nine *tituli*. Though they were by no means the only churches founded at this time, the "titular" churches emerged as the spine of the parochial system of Rome. In some way or other, each one bore the mark of private wealth provided by laypersons. It was through such churches that Christianity moved, in the course of the fourth and early fifth centuries, from a state of virtual invisibility around the year 350 to being a religion whose presence was felt throughout the city. The churches were little specks of splendor that echoed, if on a smaller scale, the proud houses on the hills. It was in such churches that the city of Rome found not its Constantine but its many little Paulinuses.[16]

Indeed, one friend of Paulinus may well have founded a *titulus* of his own. Pammachius, whom we met in the last chapter being praised by Paulinus for placing his treasure in heaven by feasting the poor of Rome in 396, may be the same person who turned a house halfway up the Clivus Scauri, which ascends the Caelian Hill above the Colosseum, into a church that was known as the *titulus Pammachii* (present-day Santi Giovanni e Paolo). Vast marble columns, bearing initials at their base that marked them as having come from imperial storehouses, framed the narthex. Long poems explained the scenes of Old Testament events that were placed on the walls. The inscription at the entrance was frank about what the converted house of Pammachius now offered: the splendor of the entrance alone "shows how great a God dwells within."[17]

Whether the founder of this *titulus* was Paulinus's friend or another Pammachius, the message was as clear in Rome as it was in Nola. By the late fourth and early fifth centuries, the footprint of real wealth could now be seen in Christian churches all over the city. This change is barely documented in any literary source. Yet it is probably the most decisive step of all in the rise of Christianity in Rome. The rich decided to put their money into Christian churches. But what did this mean for the organization of the Christian communities? And who exactly were these rich?

The predominant scholarly opinion about the *tituli* is that proposed by Charles Pietri, the great historian of Christian Rome. He saw the titular churches as deriving their wealth from permanent, lay foundations. Each church had its own finances, based on its original lay endowment. As a result, the titular churches of Rome were not like parish churches in a modern centralized diocese, directly dependent on their bishop. They were more like medieval chantry chapels or their modern equivalents, the comfortably endowed colleges of Oxford and Cambridge.[18] Following Pietri, it was possible to imagine an entire cast of lay patrons standing in the shadows behind each titular church. Loyalty to donors based on ancient notions of patronage and of respect for the rights exercised by civic benefactors over their foundations could be thought to have ensured that these churches enjoyed a rare measure of independence from the bishop of Rome. A "whisper of tensions" can be assumed to have surrounded the relations between the bishop of Rome and the priests and patrons of the new *tituli*.[19] It has been the peculiar delight of modern historians of Christian Rome to unveil these lay patrons. Many scholars claim to be able to see the hand of rival Roman families at work in the ecclesiastical conflicts of the city and in the formation of legends attached to particular churches.[20]

Other scholars differ from Pietri precisely as to the degree of autonomy enjoyed by the *tituli*. Julia Hillner has argued cogently against the notion of a permanent endowment that maintained the interests of the donor and his or her family. She points out that foundations of this kind were rare in Roman practice. It was more trouble than it was worth for a family to retain its interest in a long-term foundation. Urban benefactors preferred to be known for single, one-off donations. These were the sort of gifts that reaped immediate glory. As a result, the family of the donor need not be imagined to have become a permanent presence in the titular church they had founded. What was remembered, in the name attached to the *titulus*, was the outstanding gift that had made the church possible in the first place. In the hectic conditions of late fourth-century Rome, many Christian families competed as equals. The splash of a new church building combined with a gift of revenues reaped quite sufficient glory. There was no need to tie a neighborhood church to any one particular family for generations to come.[21]

The great unknown in these scholarly debates is who exactly were the donors. For the degree to which laypersons could act as independent patrons of the churches they had founded depends on what we think of their resources and their social status. This is something we do not know for certain. Therefore, let us look at the social structure of the residents of fourth-century Rome so as to cast some light on this question.

The Church and the New Aristocracy

It was the singular merit of Charles Pietri to have made plain that the period that began with the pontificate of Damasus (366–84) amounted to nothing less than a "second establishment" of the Church of Rome.[22] Pietri's erudition and sure historical instinct linked the flow of wealth into the ordinary churches of Rome to the activity of pious lay aristocrats, not to the bishop and his clergy. In Pietri's words, the late fourth century and first decade of the fifth were the *belle époque*, "the golden days" of an *aristocratie évergète*—an aristocracy that continued, for the benefit of the Christian churches of Rome, the long-established habits classical euergetism.[23]

Yet Pietri himself warned that "the word 'aristocracy' should not delude us."[24] "Aristocracy" meant many things in fourth-century Rome. Not all aristocrats in Rome were aristocrats as Symmachus would have wished them to be or as modern scholars (following the views of Symmachus) seem to expect them to be. By looking only at the cream of the nobility of Rome, we have tended to turn the exuberant mega-city in which they lived into a singularly rarefied and rigid place. This is not what fourth-century Rome was like.

Rather than being members of the inner circles of the *nobiles*, the Christian rich were, with a few exceptions, "new" men. Socially and culturally, Rome was not the sole preserve of the great noble families who claimed to run the city. It was a microcosm of post-Constantinian society as a whole. A large proportion of its well-to-do residents were not noble in the exclusive sense that Symmachus upheld. They were often dependent for their income on careers as state servants. They derived their status from a frankly imperial system of honors. In this they were no different from their provincial cousins in Bordeaux or Timgad.[25] They did not enjoy the towering prestige or the overwhelming economic advantages in the city that Symmachus and his peers enjoyed. But they were there. They bore the coveted title of *clarissimus*. Already in the reign of Constantine, we find the names of minor senators from the provinces carved on the seats of the Colosseum.[26]

It is notoriously difficult to calibrate the wealth and social presence of these groups who gathered on the middle slopes of a social pyramid that reached its highest pitch in Rome in noblemen such as Symmachus and Petronius Probus. They are a largely invisible class. But recent archaeological discoveries have made it easier to seize their wealth and horizons. Fourth-century Rome has been revealed to be dotted with small town houses. They were not as grand as were the palaces of the nobles. Often forced into a crowded urban fabric without the spacious gardens and forum-like courtyards of the truly noble, they nonetheless flaunted whatever signs of wealth and status that were within the means of their owners. The houses had éclat. They were all sheathed in polychrome marble. But the quality of the marble varied greatly. The lack of spread associated with a true noble *domus* had to be compensated for by the grandeur of a single, apsed reception hall.[27] In at least four cases, the reception hall and courtyard of such houses were eventually converted into Christian churches. For what the rich could offer to the church in Rome was the inestimable gift of real estate in a crowded city.[28]

Placed between the riotous "People of Rome" and a proud core of *nobiles* who considered themselves "the most noble persons in the human race," the new rich of Rome added a further, potentially unpredictable element to the social texture of the city. They remind us of the classes in Rome and Italy who had fastened on the luxuries and cultivated lifestyles of the Greek East in the last centuries of the republic. In the words of Andrew Wallace-Hadrill (in his aptly entitled book, *Rome's Cultural Revolution*): "Luxury ... comes into its own ... in the dynamic situation where there is expansion, new money and new social groups contesting claims to prominence."[29] If, instead of "luxury" we read the founding or embellishment of churches, the patronage of vivid intellectuals, and zealous engagement in theological controversies, then we can understand a little better the dynamism that drove many rich Christians in Rome in the fourth century.

As we have seen, one of the characteristics of Christianity was that it tended to reach down the social scale so as to incorporate "wealthy urban classes below that of the senatorial aristocracy."[30] As Julia Hillner has shown (in an article that is refreshingly free of the sociological stereotypes that tend to focus our attention on only the upper nobility of Rome), these classes could include the priests of the *tituli* themselves and even members of the upper reaches of the trade associations of the city. Such persons had an interest in what Andrew Wallace-Hadrill calls "sub-luxury": "Down-market imitations which nevertheless serve to maintain distinctions at a lower level."[31]

Thus we find a situation in Rome in which members of the upper reaches of the senatorial class, such as the "illustrious" lady Vestina and Pammachius (if the founder of the titular church is, indeed, the same person as the friend of Paulinus), were outnumbered by a larger and more open group of persons. Such persons wished to stand out from their peers and from their fellow Christians who were lower down the social scale. They did this by placing their money and their energy at the disposal of the churches of Rome and by engaging in the excitements associated with Christian controversies.

The epigraphy and archaeology of the catacombs of Rome enable us to follow the silent massing of a distinctive class around the new religion. The age of Constantine had been a time in which well-to-do Christians began to monumentalize themselves with carved sarcophagi in good marble. In doing this, they acted in much the same way as provincial landowners as far away as distant Britain had acted when they monumentalized their villas by providing them with mosaic floors. Sarcophagi belonged to the world of "sub-luxury"; they cost around fifteen *solidi*. Seventy sarcophagi from Rome showed owners who bore the title of *vir clarissimus* and *femina clarissima*. They were all "senators." But they have remained mere names to us. Only two out of that seventy could count as *nobiles* who had held traditional high offices.[32]

The development and grouping of these sarcophagi follows a significant curve in the course of the fourth and early fifth centuries. In the 320s and 330s impressive groups of family tombs were placed in the corridors of the catacombs. By the end of the century, however, family mausolea had come to be constructed around the shrines of the *suburbium*. They were often placed close to the burial sites of martyrs, in a manner that implied special privileges. Put bluntly: they made plain to all that holy ground was, first and foremost, the ground of the rich. Many of these mausolea and large burial chambers within the catacombs were sheathed in the same bright marble as were the town houses in the city.[33] We know that some of those who built these tombs were connected with the imperial administration. The delightful *Cubiculum Leonis* in the catacomb of Domitilla belonged to Leo, an official of the *annona*—a government office whose bureaucrats had plagued Symmachus when he was Prefect of the City.[34]

It is among such people, and not in the great noble palaces that crowned the hills of Rome, that we should look to find the supposed "aristocratic" benefactors who were most responsible for the new wealth of the church of Rome in the age of Damasus and beyond. Let us look, therefore, at Damasus himself.

Ostentatio rerum urbanarum: The swank of city life

THE AGE OF DAMASUS, 366–84

We have long realized that Damasus was a crucial figure in the development of the Roman church. But it remains difficult to place Damasus on the social map of Rome. His relations with the aristocracy are far from clear. It may well be that Damasus did not wish to be exposed to the patronage of the higher levels of the aristocracy. Rather, he turned to the lower levels of the aristocracy. He sought out the new families brought to the fore by the Constantinian system. This was not only because such persons were more likely to be Christian than was the inner core of pagan noble families who claimed to represent the "true" Rome. An alliance with less important aristocrats offered the bishop and his clergy a way to keep open a space for themselves within the city.

It is worthwhile emphasizing this fact. Damasus has usually been presented as an assiduous courtier of the upper nobility. He is treated as a man noted for his aristocratic pretensions. We tend to like him for this. In the fine words of André Piganiol, Damasus was *fastueux et mondain*—"given to display and a lover of fashionable society": "In his struggle against the State, Ambrose has been compared to Gregory VII. It is to a pope of the Renaissance that we must liken the great Damasus."[35]

It has proved agreeable for modern persons to imagine that the Catholicism of fourth-century Rome could be represented by so urbane a prelate as Damasus, so very different from the angular Ambrose. Furthermore, the idea that a natural alliance between pope and aristocracy was initiated by Damasus fits all too well into the conventional, triumphant narrative of the Christianization of Rome. It is often said that the popes absorbed the city of Rome swiftly and without conflict and that they did so by reaching an accommodation with the nobility and with the ancient traditions of the Senate. We like to imagine that high senators and urbane priests were brought together through a gentlemanly process of social osmosis in such a way as to ensure that the best of the classical heritage of Rome was passed on to future ages by the Catholic Church. It has proved comforting to think that the Rome of the Senate morphed effortlessly into the Rome of the popes in this manner.

Yet there is little support for this amiable narrative. Damasus himself was no Borgia. He was the son of a priest, who had worked his way up in the service of the church of Rome. When he founded his own church (San Damaso in Lucina, in the Campus Martius, near the Cancellaria) all that he did was widen his father's house by adding a nave to either side. He offered to it silver vessels that weighed, in all, one hundred pounds and provided it with a revenue of four hundred *solidi*, which came partly from an estate in a town forty miles away and partly from the revenues of an adjacent bath. This was a comfortable but hardly breathtaking endowment.[36]

In any case, Damasus was once bit twice shy in his relations with the higher levels of the Christian nobility. His election had been challenged, in 366, by a rival candidate, Ursinus. On one occasion, 137 deaths resulted from a fierce clash of partisans in a crowded basilica. The divisions caused by this disputed election lasted for the rest of his life. Rita Lizzi Testa has argued ingeniously that his rival Ursinus may have been supported by a particularly intransigent party of aristocrats, some of whom were of higher status than most other Christians. After 366, Damasus was in no mood to forgive the high-minded noblemen and women who had helped prolong the opposition of his rival. Nor did he want to be unduly beholden to those who had supported him at this time.[37]

The interest of Damasus does not lie in his reputed flirtation with the Roman aristocracy. What was decisive was the skill with which he pushed forward the clergy of Rome (with himself at their head) as an effective Third Estate.[38] He stood for a clerical option. This is not surprising. We should always remember that Damasus came to power as an old man. Born in 300 and the son of a priest, the memories of his family reached back before the days of Constantine to the Great Persecution. He was a generation older than Ambrose and a full half century older than either Augustine or Paulinus. He had lived his life in the service of the church. His heroes were the martyrs of Rome and not its nobles.[39]

But he knew how to reach out to accommodate the new rich. We have already met the little girl Proiecta. Her marriage casket (which was part of what is known as the Esquiline Treasure in the British Museum, from the place of its discovery in a palace on the Esquiline Hill) had presented her preparations as a bride under the protection, still, of the numinous beauty of Venus. Proiecta received an epitaph from Damasus when she died—perhaps no more than a few years after her marriage. It was a touching poem that spoke of Proiecta as already in heaven, able to bring comfort to her grieving loved ones through her prayers as if she were a saint.[40] It is a poignant glimpse of an upper-class marriage for which the only surviving evidence is a silver marriage casket and the fragment of a tomb. But the marriage itself is revealing. Proiecta was the daughter of Florus, a successful imperial servant. She married Turcius Secundus, an aging representative of a noble family. For Florus, his daughter's marriage was an upward alliance similar to that which Ausonius had achieved by marrying into the old nobility of Bordeaux. Damasus favored such persons.[41]

It was into this world of family piety focused on the dead and widely shared by all levels of the Christian community that Damasus discreetly introduced himself, his deacons, and his priests. In order to do this, he turned to the cities of the dead that covered the *suburbium*. He filled the catacombs outside Rome with large plaques of marble, which described the stories of the martyrs in Vergilian verse and were elegantly inscribed by a master calligrapher. The verses were written with condensed, almost incantatory power.[42] They were intended to be read as the "signatures" of the bishop of Rome, placed by Damasus on sites that lay outside Rome in the calm of a countryside traditionally dominated by the emperors and the aristocracy. Through these inscriptions, which would have been read by many pilgrims as well as by Romans visiting their dead, Damasus ensured that the bishop of Rome would not be forgotten in the *suburbium* of Rome.[43]

In writing these verses, Damasus did not nurse the illusion (dear to modern scholars of classical inclination) that by writing Vergilian verse he might somehow swing the mighty Senate to the Christian cause. His aims were more clearly focused. He wrote to express the solidarity and the separate identity of the Christian community. They were a "holy people," an "assembly of saints"; and it was the martyrs (not the emperors, and not the aristocracy) who kept them holy, with the help of their bishop and clergy. Roman Christians shared together the glory of being an undivided, elect group. They were the church of Rome—the church of the greatest city in the world. Damasus was their head, and Rome itself was the head of the empire. With or without the Senate and the great profane city that stretched all around their churches, to be a united holy people chosen by God in a world capital was glory enough for Damasus and his flock.[44]

Damasus's basically inward-looking vision struck a chord in a substantial section of the lesser aristocracy and of the newly rich residents of Rome. Here we are dealing with one of the most delicate issues in the study of the fourth century. The Christian churches were sought out as environments that were perceived to be appropriate for persons whose worldview had been formed through their social experience as particpants in an imperial system. Let us look at how this happened.

The mere *clarissimi* and *clarissimae* whom we meet on the Christian sarcophagi of Rome looked to the court and to the imperial *militia* rather than to the Senate as the arbiters of taste. We should not underestimate the cumulative imaginative consequences of this fact. Looking at the sarcophagi of Rome (as elsewhere), we can see how Christian devotion was expressed through images taken directly from the court and the army. These citations from contemporary life gave sharp focus to the ancient sense that Christians were soldiers in the army of the Lord and servants of Christ, their emperor.[45] By the end of the century, the imperial overtones on these sarcophagi had become even more pronounced. While pagan aristocrats of the third century had shown themselves sitting or standing face-to-face with the Muses, the Christian sarcophagi of the late fourth century show the deceased as small figures, bowing before Christ, their emperor. They are shown in the same pose as courtiers when they bowed to "adore" the emperor by kissing the hem of his great purple robe.[46]

Often drawn from the imperial *militia* themselves (as soldiers and bureaucrats), the lesser aristocracy wished to look up to a clergy that had the same hierarchical quality as the imperial service from which they themselves derived their wealth and status. Hence the clergy emerged as a Third Estate in Rome with the tacit consent of members of a minor aristocracy that was the late Roman equivalent of a *noblesse de robe*. Clergy and laity alike wanted a religion in the image of the society in which they lived—hierarchical, strenuous, and loyal, though shorn of the abrasive qualities with which hierarchy was normally displayed in the world outside the churches.

They were prepared to pay for such a church. By the end of the life of Damasus, the financial muscle generated by their giving was visible to the highest circles in Rome. Writing in around 390 (that is, a generation after the events he described), Ammianus Marcellinus left a vivid account of the manner in which the disputed election of Damasus in 366 had disrupted the peace of the city. He ended with a memorable judgment. Such violent behavior was only to be expected:

> Considering the ostentatious luxury of life in the City [*considerans ostentationem rerum urbanarum:* the sheer swank of life in Rome] it is only natural that those who are ambitious should engage in the most strenuous competition to obtain their goal. Once they have reached it [as bishop of Rome] they are assured of rich gifts from ladies of quality; they can ride in carriages, dress splendidly, and outdo kings in the lavishness of their table.[47]

What we forget about this passage is that it does not describe the effortless entry of Damasus into high society. Far from it. It treats the bishop of Rome as an upstart. Such was the view of a writer loyal to the values of an older Rome for whom a man such as Damasus was a troubling anomaly.

Ammianus reflected the reactions of the true nobles of Rome as they looked over the edge of their high world to survey the undignified skirmishes of those who had gathered at their feet. A new Rome was emerging through an alliance between rich new families from the lower nobility and the Christian clergy. The wealth and prestige of the bishop of Rome derived in large part from this alliance. When the great pagan Prefect of the City, Praetextatus (one of Symmachus's closest friends), was approached by Damasus on one occasion, he met the bishop's suggestion that he should become a Christian with the quip: "Make me bishop of Rome, and I will instantly become a Christian."[48]

This was not only the view of pagans. Many Christians also had been pushed to one side by Damasus. They thought much the same of him as did Ammianus. He was accused by his ecclesiastical enemies of being an *auriscalpius matronarum*, usually translated as "ear tickler of ladies of quality." But, for Romans, the sexual innuendo was not nearly as vicious as was the financial slur. Damasus was the ear pick (the Q-tip) of the ladies. He wielded his little scoop with the adroitness of a beautician removing the surplus wax that built up in their ears. This was how the bishop of Rome was thought to skim off the surplus wealth of the Christian rich.[49]

Officia et in se habent gloriam: Offices in themselves have glory

<hr/>

HIERARCHY AND SOCIETY IN THE WORLD OF AMBROSIASTER

Damasus emerges as so forceful and so contested a figure that we often forget that his principal achievement had been to ensure that a low-profile but tenacious body of men rallied behind him. This was the clergy of Rome. We are fortunate to be able to look into the mind of one such clergyman of the time of Damasus. He was a "stubbornly anonymous" writer who is known to us, somewhat contemptuously (since the days of Erasmus), as Ambrosiaster—the Would-Be Ambrose. He wrote commentaries on the *Epistles* of Saint Paul and a set of *Answers to Questions on the Old and New Testaments*. These writings give us a clear sense of the moral and social horizons of a well-educated Roman priest, in constant dialogue with lay questioners.[50]

In the first place, as Sophie Lunn-Rockcliffe has shown in her recent study, Ambrosiaster was an out-and-out monarchist.[51] Firm, unitary rule was the ideal of his society. He explained that Adam had to be created alone, so as to be a unique symbol of the sovereignty of God: "So that, in the person of one man, one God should be seen to have retained the authority of single rule, to the confusion of the Devil."[52] As the inheritor of Adam's function as single ruler of the world, the emperor (and not the Christian bishop) bore "the Image of God" on earth.[53]

Furthermore, Roman law was of crucial importance to Ambrosiaster. And this was not classical law, nor was it the law preserved by the Senate as an aspect of the "liberty" of Rome. It was the authoritarian law of the Roman state. Ambrosiaster believed that the alternative to firm government was *potentia*, the naked graft and violence of the super-rich. Without imperial laws, "the powerful would not be able to be endured, nor would there be any freedom."[54] When Ambrosiaster discussed Paul's doctrine of obedience to the "powers that be," he did not think of criminals. He had in mind those "who sin by their *potentia*." Such persons thought that they could evade the law with impunity in order to oppress the poor. (One thinks of the encounter in Rome between Augustine's friend Alypius and the corrupt and powerful senator whose demands he refused. Alypius was acting as a lawyer at that time. He would have read Ambrosiaster's words on the function of law as a check on the corrupt actions of the great with considerable pleasure.)[55]

For Ambrosiaster, hierarchy was both necessary and glorious. As in the *militia* of the palace, so with the clergy; the office itself conferred dignity on its holder: "Offices in themselves have glory ... and the honor of a position renders its holder glorious."[56]

Altogether, Ambrosiaster thought of the church on the model of the imperial bureaucracy. When he criticized the pretensions of the deacons of Rome he did so because he recognized in them the power of a clique of top bureaucrats ensconced at the head of an extensive clerical *militia*. In his opinion, the power of the deacons of Rome was a result of the sheer size of Rome: it had grown *propter magnificentiam Urbis Romae*, because of the "magnificence of the city of Rome, which is seen to be the head of all cities."[57] His enthusiasm for Rome was transparent. But it was not for the Rome of the Senate.

Clergymen such as Ambrosiaster served Rome well. They were well aware that they lived in an unmanageable and potentially dangerous city. Like Symmachus, they carefully noted whenever food shortages and famines occurred in any part of the world because these shortfalls would directly affect the food supply of Rome.[58] Ultimately, what the clergy of Rome prayed for at every liturgy was what every well-to-do resident of Rome (Symmachus included) desired: "That public joy may prevail, helped by an abundance of supplies and by the removal of all upheaval and sedition."[59]

Gratus nobilibus ... officio sanctus: Popular with the nobles ...
holy by reason of his office

THE ROMAN CLERGY IN THEIR EPITAPHS

In many ways Damasus was like Ambrose. He laid the ground course for the future build-up of Christianity in Rome. That ground course was so solid that it passed unnoticed in subsequent years. But the two men had acted in very different ways. While Ambrose created bonds with the entire *populus* of Milan, Damasus did not reach out to the Roman people as a whole. Already marked out, in the 380s, as a man from an older generation, the prospect of the conversion of Rome as a whole lay beyond the imaginative horizon of Damasus. His principal appeal was to the ideal of a unified Christian congregation. He reached out only to the People of God already gathered within the Christian churches of the city and to their leaders—the Roman clergy. His principal concern was to build up the strength of his own profession. Those who welcomed him most were fellow clergymen such as Ambrosiaster.

We meet clergymen like Ambrosiaster in the inscriptions of the Roman catacombs of the late fourth and early fifth centuries. The epitaphs on the tombs of individual priests and deacons show a group of persons who had begun to make their own a code of living as self-conscious as that of any other of the professional groups who jostled each other in Rome—lawyers, doctors, bureaucrats, and soldiers.

They were a basically stolid group of men. They accepted the social order. The first evidence that we have for the *titulus* of San Clemente is a slave collar marked with the Christogram: "Catch me for I have fled and return me to Victor the acolyte at the Lord's House of Clemens."[60]

It is notable that the clergy's care of the poor of Rome was not charged with any great urgency or pathos. Ambrosiaster spoke of the duty of Christians to support the "needy who appear in public." He simply assumed that these poor were regularly fed and clothed out of church funds. By contrast, real glamour surrounded the "holy poor." These were persons like himself. They were discreet clergymen and pious Christians of modest means. He insisted that the rich had been nominated by God to act as nothing less than the legal "guardians" of such persons. They were responsible for their financial well-being. Altogether, his commentary on Paul's frequent references to the *poor among the saints* amounted to an exhortation to the rich to support their local clergy.[61] Some priests were praised as "friends of the poor." But rather than representing "the emergence of a new humanitarian urge," the title may have been little more than an aspect of their professional persona as clergymen.[62]

This fact should be stressed. Clerical "love of the poor" was a matter of routine. It was not expected to lead to heroic mixing with the destitute; such actions were reserved for individual laypersons of extreme piety. Pammachius the friend of Paulinus of Nola was one such person. In 396 Jerome praised Pammachius and his collaborator, the lady Furia, for their hands-on care of the foul-smelling and diseased poor in the charitable hospital they had established in the Port of Ostia. This heroic condescension to the poor was evoked by Jerome through a verse taken from the sixth book of the *Aeneid*. It was a veritable descent into the Underworld.[63]

We do not know whether the noble patrons whom Jerome addressed actually did this. But we do know that such dramatic behavior was not demanded of the clergy. What was expected from them was a more general benevolence. To take one example: The deacon Dionysius continued to practice as a doctor. As befitted the practitioner of an *ars honesta* (a skill appropriate to a gentleman), Dionysius "scorned sordid gain ... and often, with a generous right hand, fostered the work of saving pity by helping men of slender means."[64] In doing this, Dionysius did little more than what the emperor Valentinian I had insisted that doctors who drew public salaries should do in Rome: "They should prefer to minister to the poor in an honorable manner, rather than shamefully attend only on the rich."[65] Eventually Dionysius's skill and good nature served him well. He survived captivity among the Goths after the sack of the city in 410 by acting as their doctor.

Altogether, the values of the clergy, as we read them on their tombstones of this and later times, were those of prudent but proud men, enrolled in the *militia* of God. They were anxious to appear to be beholden to no one. The deacon Tigridas was spoken of as "popular with the nobles." (He may have been a successful fund-raiser.) But his epitaph also made plain that he met the nobles as an equal. He was "holy by reason of his office."[66] The epitaph of the priest Sissinius was more stern: "Content with his own, he ignored the palaces of the rich."[67]

One can imagine the disquiet of such persons when, in 382, the old Damasus—then in his eighties—was solicited to extend his patronage to a total outsider, to a priest-monk from Dalmatia recently arrived from the East—Eusebius Hieronymus, known to us as Saint Jerome. Strenuously learned, a passionate advocate of the new asceticism, and abrasive as only an expert could be, Jerome soon showed that he was not a man to "ignore the palaces of the rich."

FIGURE 1. *Profusio*

The emperor Constantius II (337–361), dressed in the heavy embroidered robes of a consul, scatters gold coins among the people. Ambrose, bishop of Milan (374–397), was accused of usurping an imperial privilege by scattering gold coins to the poor of his church.

From Andre Grabar, *Early Christian Art: From the Rise of Christianity to the Death of Theodosius*, Odyssey Press, 1968.

FIGURE 2. New Clothing

A married couple on the lid of a great silver casket found on the Esquiline Hill in Rome. The man wears the heavy cloak and Germanic-style fibula brooch of an imperial servant. The woman's neck and hairdo are heavy with jewelry. As we will see (figure 12), the casket was made for the marriage of the daughter of a successful courtier.

Courtesy of Art Resource/The British Museum, © The Trustees of the British Museum/ Art Resource, NY

FIGURE 3. The Touch of Empire

The Empress as a pepper pot.
Part of the treasure found at Hoxne
in East Anglia (Britain).

Courtesy of Art Resource/The British
Museum, © The Trustees of the British
Museum/Art Resource, NY

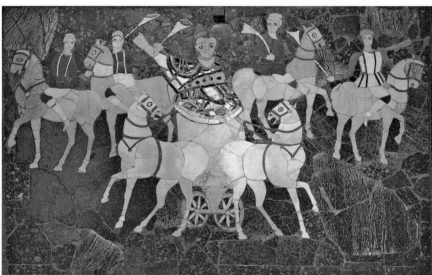

FIGURE 4. The Giver of the Games

Inlaid in marble on the walls of the Roman palace of Junius Bassus, the consul for the year
331, this panel shows him leading a circus procession, accompanied by grooms riding chariot
horses. In around 470, the palace was in the hands of a general of barbarian background,
who donated it to the pope to be made into a church. The church lasted until the end of the
seventeenth century, with this exuberantly secular panel preserved on its walls.

Courtesy of Art Resource/Museo Nazionale Romano (Palazzo Massimo alle Terme), Rome,
Italy. Photo: Vanni/Art Resource, NY

FIGURE 5. *Populus*

This mosaic from Gafsa (Tunisia), a city close to the Sahara, shows circus races witnessed by citizens massed in a hippodrome. Rather than representing a local circus, this may be a folkloristic echo of the circus in Carthage, where the games were challenged in the sermons of Augustine, bishop of Hippo (396–430), who complained that the *populus* acclaimed those who gave money to the games, not those who gave to the poor.

Courtesy of Art Resource/Musee National du Bardo, Tunis, Tunisia. Photo © Gilles Mermet/Art Resource NY

FIGURE 6.
From the Gifts of God

From the mosaic floor of the large basilica of Aquileia (Italy) around 320, this pastoral vignette of a serving girl carrying large grapes communicates the abundance of nature offered up to God.

Courtesy of Art Resource/ Basilica Patriarcale, Aquileia, Italy. Photo: Scala/Art Resource NY

FIGURE 7. A Collective Venture

A detail from a mosaic floor of the original Euphrasian Basilica, Poreč, Croatia (late fourth century). The legend records that Clamosus, a schoolteacher, and his wife donated funds for 100 square feet of the mosaic; the same panel also records that another family donated 400 square feet, and another, 100 square feet. This amounted to 580 square feet of mosaic at a total cost for all three families of 18 gold *solidi*—a quarter of a pound of gold.

FIGURE 8. Honor from on High

Seated in majesty, the emperor Theodosius I (379–395) places a diploma of appointment in the veiled hands of an official. Beneath, the reclining figure of Mother Earth communicates a message of unstinting abundance.

Courtesy of Art Resource/Academia de la Historia, Madrid, Spain. Photo: Scala/Art Resource NY

FIGURE 9. A Moment of Family Glory

Seated in a box at the races in the Circus Maximus in Rome, an entire family (the Lampadii) is grouped around the giver of the games. Symmachus sat with his son Memmius in this manner.

Courtesy of Art Resource/Museo Civico dell'Eta Cristiana, Brescia. Photo: Scala/Art Resource NY

FIGURE 10. *Splendor*

Detail of apse paneling, c.540, Euphrasian Basilica, Poreč, Croatia.
Encrusted marble walls were the glory of late Roman buildings. Unlike their floor mosaics
(which were considerably less expensive), few such walls have survived. The sixth-century
marble work in the apse of the basilica still gives an idea of their sumptuousness.

FIGURE 11. Enjoying the Fruits of the Earth at Table

This reconstruction of the newly-discovered villa at Faragola in southern Italy shows a combination of intimacy and grandeur. The guests recline on the half-circle *stibadium* couch in the apse of a hall, where the floor is cooled by a shallow film of water. Lamps cast pools of light, as they would have done also in a Christian basilica.

Courtesy of Giuliano Volpe. Photo © Giuliano Volpe

FIGURE 12. The Goddess and the Bride

The bride, Projecta, arranges her hair in a mirror directly beneath the figure of Venus,
who echoes her gesture. The daughter of a successful imperial servant, Projecta was marrying
into an old Roman family. She died soon after. Her epitaph was written by
none other than Pope Damasus (366–384).

Courtesy of Art Resource/Musee de l'Arles antique, Arles, France.
Photo: Erich Lessing/Art Resource NY

FIGURE 13. *Abjectio:* Christ before Pilate

Dressed in a simple robe devoid of all grandeur, Christ confronts a Pilate dressed with imperial splendor. The idea of a God who veiled his majesty by "dressing down" in this manner haunted the imagination of such well-to-do Christians as Paulinus.

Courtesy of Art Resource/Musee de l'Arles antique, Arles, France.
Photo: Erich Lessing/Art Resource NY

FIGURE 14. *Mediocres*

(a) The guild of the barrel-makers, a 4th-century fresco from the *cubiculum*
of the Bottai Catacombs of Priscilla, Rome, Italy.

Essential for the hotly contested wine supply of the city, this trade association had a burial
chamber for its own members—Christian and pagan alike. It was from such guilds—
collegia—of well-to-do plebeians that the Christian congregations often drew their clergy.

Courtesy of The Bridgeman Art Library. Copyright status: out of copyright

(b) Marble burial plaque of Constantius the groom or seller of horses

From Bisconti, *Mestieri nelle catacombe romane : appunti sul declino dell'iconografia del
reale nei cimiteri cristiani di Roma* (2000), fig. 5. Reproduced courtesy of the Pontifical
Commission for Sacred Archaeology

FIGURE 15. Christianity in the Home

A small oratory of a martyr placed at the end of a mezzanine landing in a house beneath the
present-day church of Santi Giovanni e Paolo on the Caelian Hill in Rome.
Worshipers prostrate themselves at the feet of a martyr who is framed by drawn curtains. A
man and a woman bearing offerings approach the martyr from each side. The Caelian Hill
was an area of noble residences. The church of Santi Giovanni e Paolo may have originally
been a palace owned by Pammachius, the friend of Paulinus of Nola. Given to the church, it
was known as the *titulus Pammachii*.

From Hugo Brandenburg, *Die frühchristlichen Kirchen Roms vom 4. bis 7. Jahrhundert*,
Schnell und Steiner, 2004. p. 158, left; photo by Arnaldo Vescovo

FIGURE 16. An Argument in Stone: An African Basilica

The mosaic shows the church as a tall building, flanked by twin towers and lit by high clerestory windows. It emphasizes the opulent curtains that veiled the many entrances. Noblewomen such as Melania the Younger could provide these curtains from their personal wardrobes.

Courtesy of CSU Images. Photo © Kathleen Cohen

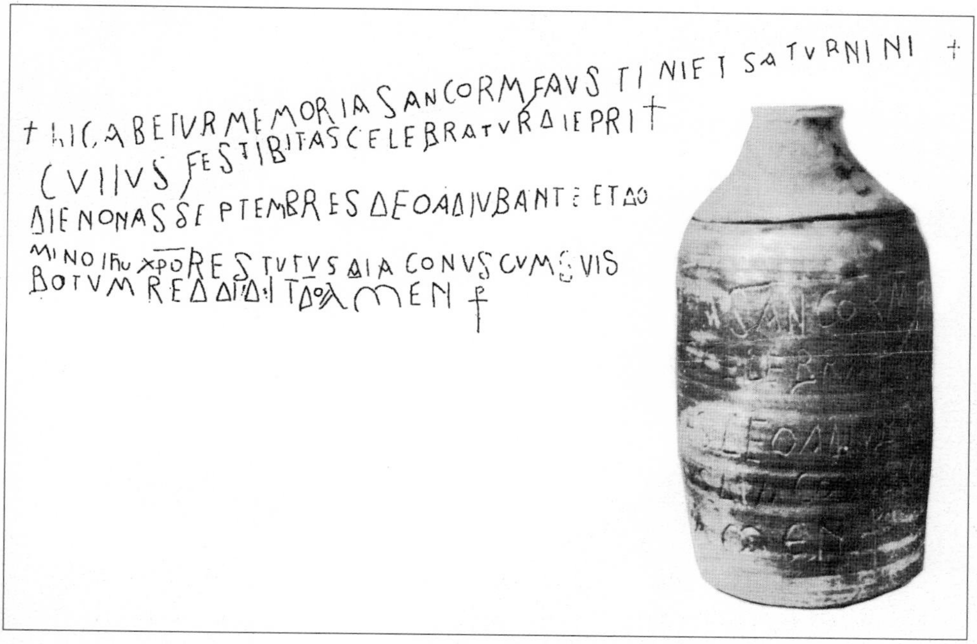

† hIC,ABEIVR MEMORIA SanCORM FAVS TI NIEI SaTVRNINI †
CVIIVS FESTIBITAS CELEBRATVR AIE PRIT
AIE NONAS SEPTEMBRES AEO AAIVBANTE ETAO
MI NO IhꝻ XPO RES TVTVS AIA CONVS CVM SVIS
BOTVM REAAIAIT AOAMEN †

FIGURE 17. *Votum reddidit*: He or she has repaid their vow

Retitutus (a deacon) and his family dedicate relics of the martyrs to a church at Henchir Mdila (Algeria). The relics are contained in a simple jar on which the dedication is scratched in popular Latin: for instance, *votum* is spelt *botum*.

From "Un nouveau reliquaire africain et l'évêché Midilensis" (*Notes d'archéologie chrétienne nord-africaine* XXV), pp. 245–62, fig. 13. Photo © Nöel Duval and Victor Saxer

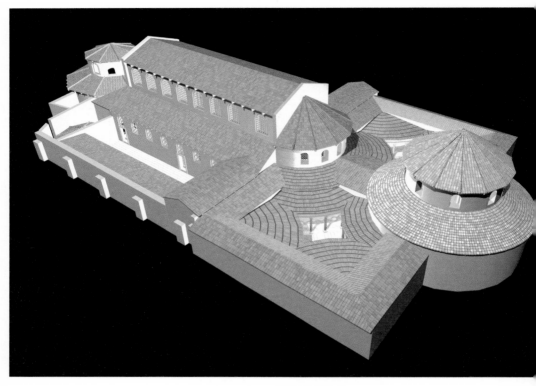

FIGURE 18. Halls of Light

A reconstruction of the spacious sixth-century pilgrimage church recently excavated
at Bir Ftouha in Carthage (Tunisia).

From "Bir Ftouha: A pilgrimage church complex at Carthage," by Susan T. Stevens,
Angela V. Kalinowski, and Hans vanderLeest, *Journal of Roman Archaeology*,
Supplementary Series no. 59, 2005 (graphics by B. Dayhoff), frontispiece and fig. 12.3.
Courtesy of the *Journal of Roman Archaeology*

FIGURE 19. The Managerial Bishop

Bishop Euphrasius rebuilt the cathedral basilica of Poreč (Croatia) in around 540.
He is shown bearing a model of the church as his offering to God. His archdeacon Claudius,
shown bearing the Gospels, may well be his brother. Claudius's son (Euphrasius's nephew)
bears the candles that represent the costly lighting of the basilica. Lamps and candles
often burned perpetually in the basilica so as to represent the eternal light
of paradise in which the soul of their donor hoped to rest.

Courtesy of Art Resource; photo credit: Cameraphoto Arte, Venice/Art Resource, NY

CHAPTER 16

"To Sing The Lord's Song in a Strange Land"

Jerome in Rome, 382–385

Ingentis est otii, laboris et sumptuum: Matters that require profound
leisure, hard work, and much money

JEROME AS AN EXPERT IN ROME

Damasus knew how to act as a patron of the arts. He liked to summon experts
and put them to work. He wanted the best. The exquisite lettering for the verses
he wrote for the tombs of the martyrs in the catacombs had been designed by
one such expert—Furius Dionysius Filocalus.

Filocalus worked for noblemen and women. On one occasion, he composed
and executed an inscription for a bathhouse set up by the elder Melania, a Spaniard and a wealthy relative by marriage of Paulinus of Nola, on one of her estates
in north Africa. He was one of those figures who fit awkwardly into the oversim-
plified image of the society of Rome to which we are accustomed. He was not
a *nobilis*, nor was he a mere artisan. As Alan Cameron describes him, with characteristic good sense: "He was a man of respectable (if not aristocratic) origins
and comfortable means who simply chose to spend his time doing what he did so
well."[1]

Filocalus's most famous work was a spectacular illustrated *Calendar* for the
year 354, made for a certain Valentinus.[2] The *Calendar of 354* was very much a
product of a new Rome, many of whose upper-class residents were poised between their civic duties and the demands of the new religion. It combined without a trace of embarrassment lavish pictures of traditional Roman feasts and of
the gods associated with them with a list of the bishops of Rome and of the dates
of the feasts of the martyrs.[3] The expense and skill that went into such a production ensured that a calligrapher such as Filocalus was valued as the Benvenuto
Cellini of his age.

When he arrived in Rome, in 382, Jerome presented himself to Damasus as yet another Filocalus. He claimed to be a man of formidable expertise, whose service would add luster to the pope. Like Filocalus, he was prepared to work for the bishop of Rome "on matters that require profound leisure, hard work and much money."[4]

Jerome was born in 341 in Stridon, a small city that has entirely vanished. It probably lay near the imperial high road that led from the Danube frontier to Aquileia. Like Augustine, Jerome had grown up in a town of the hinterland. But, unlike Augustine, Jerome had rich parents. He was sent straight to Rome. There he acquired a remarkable literary culture. He had no intention of using this culture to pursue a career as unglamorous as that of a teacher, as Augustine had done. He may have been independently wealthy. We know that he and his brother, Paulinianus, owned estates around Stridon.

By 368 (around age twenty-seven) Jerome was at Trier. He arrived there only a few years after Ausonius had entered the court of Valentinian I and a year before Symmachus arrived on his senatorial mission. On the edge of a formidable bureaucracy, he busied himself copying Christian manuscripts. Wellborn, well educated, with a zest for expertise and a gift for languages, Jerome would have made an excellent imperial agent, traveling on delicate missions throughout the Greek and Latin parts of the empire. But an administrative career was not exciting enough for Jerome. Ecclesiastical politics offered access to an even wider world than service in the bureaucracy would have done.

Within a few years, the excitements of the anti-Arian dissidence swept Jerome from Trier to Antioch. He eventually settled outside Antioch in 375, on the estate of a remarkable patron, Evagrius of Antioch. Evagrius was a restless soul. He had been a failure as a provincial governor, so he switched to the church. He spent time in Italy as a follower of the ultra-Nicene bishop Eusebius of Vercelli. He translated into Latin Athanasius's famous *Life of Anthony*. But in the 370s very few Latin Christians were attracted to the monastic life in its own right. They usually went East to pitch in in favor of the Nicene Creed. This is what Jerome did, by following the eccentric Evagrius back to Antioch.[5]

At almost exactly the same time (in 373), the great Roman widow Melania the Elder made her way to the East.[6] Melania may have been as wealthy as her younger in-law Paulinus of Nola. But she belonged to a generation unaccustomed to spectacular renunciations. She never formally renounced her wealth, nor did she vanish suddenly from Rome. Her later admirers claimed that she had always longed to go to the Holy Places. In fact, she took her time about moving to Palestine. Widowed in 362, she had been content to reside in Rome for over a decade until she saw her son Publicola properly enrolled in the Senate. Furthermore, when she came to the eastern Mediterranean, Melania did not come only as a pilgrim. She came as the supporter of an ecclesiastical faction. She set sail from

Rome bearing funds to support the Nicene cause. She did not go straight to Jerusalem. She arrived in Alexandria with a ship loaded with gold and silver to help the monks of the Nile Delta, whose lay support had been cut off by the repressive measures of the pro-Arian emperor Valens. Going on to Palestine, she helped feed three thousand Egyptian monks in exile. Her funds tipped the balance in favor of the anti-Arian party among the monasteries and hermitages of northern Egypt.[7]

Jerome also came to the East as an activist and not only as a seeker of monks. But, above all, he came so as to make himself an expert. In his later letters Jerome spoke dramatically of his life in a monastic cell, perched in "the vast desert that stretches along the frontier between the Roman and the barbarian world." In fact, he continued to live like a scholar. He was never far from great libraries. He settled on an estate of Evagrius, called Maronia, in the territory of Chalcis only thirty miles east of Antioch. This estate was more like a place of learned *otium* than the hermit's cave in the broiling desert that Jerome later described to Roman readers.[8] As Megan Williams has made abundantly clear in her fine study of Jerome as a scholar, "His attraction seems to have been to the ascetic idea rather than to the ascetic life."[9]

But there was nothing idle about Jerome's *otium*. He read ferociously. He stretched his linguistic capacities beyond that of even the most ambitious Latin clergyman. Not only did he learn Greek, but he went on to make a beginning on Hebrew. It was with these hard skills in hand that Jerome arrived in Rome in 382.

Jerome knew that Damasus needed experts. He was quick to present himself as indispensable as a translator and a critic of texts. He produced for Damasus a more up-to-date Latin version of the Gospels. He went back to the original Greek. It was the beginning of the monumental project from which the Latin "Vulgate" grew.[10] We must remember, however, that the fame of Jerome's Vulgate dates only from the early middle ages. At the time, the venture struck most Latin clergymen as a dangerous and unnecessary tampering with a holy text. Faced with these suspicions, Jerome reacted by setting himself up as the scourge of the half educated. Unlike the amateurs who criticized him, he claimed to offer the hard stuff—study of the Scriptures based on unremitting toil and on the mastery of difficult languages.

Jerome needed to stress his unique expertise. For he was presenting Damasus with an expensive project. He demanded access to costly books and to expensive professional stenographers. To heighten his profile as an expert, he talked down as many as possible of his contemporaries. He pointed out that Ambrose had plagiarized a Greek author (the famous Alexandrian exegete Didymus the Blind) when writing on the Holy Ghost. He claimed that the bishop of Milan had borrowed from Greek authors so as to dress himself up "like a crow in borrowed feathers."[11] Those who criticized his retranslation of the New Testament were dismissed as "two legged asses." We now know that one of these "two legged asses" was none other than the Roman clergyman known to us as Ambrosiaster![12] This was not an attitude calculated to make him popular with the clergy of Rome.

In Rome, Jerome rose with Damasus and fell with Damasus. The moment his patron died, on December 11, 384, Damasus's successor, the new bishop Siricius, sent Jerome back to Antioch where he had originally been ordained as a priest.[13] (As we have seen, Siricius later snubbed Paulinus of Nola in 395 for having deserted Barcelona where he had been made a priest.) Siricius was very much the product of a clergy that had been pushed forward as a Third Estate by Damasus. This clergy had produced careful and basically conservative writers like Ambrosiaster. They had no use for self-promoting outsiders such as Jerome. In the summer of 385, Jerome left Rome never to return. As he wrote bitterly to the nun Asella: "Fool that I was to think that I could *sing the Lord's song in a strange land*."[14]

"The Palace of Holy Paula": Jerome and the Noblewomen of Rome

In the months before he left Rome, Jerome protested that his relations with noble ladies had been the true cause of his downfall:

> Before I came to know the palace of holy Paula, all Rome was enthusiastic for me. In the judgment of almost all, I was worthy of the rank of highest bishop. My stylish pen gave voice to Damasus himself.[15]

This was a preposterous claim. But it puts in perspective Jerome's relations with a circle of remarkable Roman women between the years 382 and 385. It was the male, self-consciously clerical world that had gathered around the aging Damasus that had made and then broken Jerome. Anxious to carve out a niche for himself in the clergy, women had been of secondary interest to him. He certainly did not come to Rome only to act as the mentor of Paula and her circle. Nor did these noblewomen seek him out. He wished himself upon them by his brilliant letters.[16] To begin with, Jerome may have approached Paula and other devout ladies as a fallback to his main career in the service of Damasus.

But the moment Damasus died, the protection offered by his patronage was removed. Jerome was fair game to his enemies. The issues raised by Jerome's relations with noblewomen emerged immediately. He became the object of sexual innuendos. In just these years, the drama of Priscillian was unfolding in distant Spain. As the fate of Priscillian showed, accusations of inappropriate relations with noblewomen could be a matter of life or death. This was especially the case when they were combined with issues of financial support. For his enemies, Jerome's activities fit all too well into the classic stereotype of the charismatic fund-raiser of dubious morals: "The chink of coin in the hand ... the conversation laced with innuendo ... the eye [that] leered lustfully."[17]

Faced by this potentially lethal accusation, Jerome's nerve did not desert him. He decided that assertion was the best form of defense. Far from distancing himself from accusations of relations with women, he decided that if he had to leave Rome he would be known to have done so not because he had been chased out by his male colleagues in the clergy but because he had preached a heroic brand of eastern asceticism in the palaces of noble ladies. He immediately published a series of letters he had written while at Rome to two leading ladies. One was the sixty-year-old widow Marcella, who lived in a palace on the Aventine when she was not living in pious retirement on her estate in the *suburbium* of Rome. The other was the forty-year-old widow Paula, who would soon follow him to the Holy Land. These remarkable letters have ensured that the two women and those around them are "the most recognizable faces of the female monastic movement in the late fourth century."[18] The letters to Marcella and Paula made Jerome famous at the time and in all future ages because they raised what for fourth-century Romans were the ever-interesting and closely related issues of sex and money.

First, let us deal with sex. In the spring of 384, Jerome wrote his *Letter 22* to Paula about the ascetic grooming of her twenty-year-old daughter, Iulia Eustochium. This letter was a brilliantly contrived amalgam of ascetic *idées reçues*. In it, Jerome made a bid to become a presence in the houses of the rich.[19] He achieved this effect through the insistent physicality of his ascetic advice. The letter echoed in reverse the meticulous attention to diet and to the care of the body that Romans had long expected of the skilled house doctors who haunted the palaces of the wealthy. Ancient doctors had written so as to encourage a healthy warmth to blow through the bodies of the young. This would lead the girl to nurture the capacity for sexual delight on which (according to ancient medical theory that linked female orgasm with conception) her chances of fertility depended. With hot and healthy bodies, the young couple could set to with appropriate vigor to found a family. Jerome now stepped in as the house doctor of asceticism. He gave advice as to how to put the energizing process into reverse. He urged Paula to "freeze" the sexual urge in Eustochium. She would do this through long fasts and vigils, through an austere diet, and through total abstinence from wine.[20]

At the same time, Paula was insistently reminded by Jerome that this was an asceticism now practiced by aristocrats. The body of Eustochium was recognizably the body of a noble girl. The sheen of wealth lay on her skin. It penetrated her entire physical being.

Born of noble pedigree, always surrounded by delights, always laid in feather beds, you claim that you can not abstain from wine and from the more succulent of foods.[21]

Furthermore, Eustochium's body was intensely private. It was a *corpusculum*, a "hot little body.[22] It was shielded from the world by the majesty of a late Roman house whose long corridors and doorways, veiled by silken curtains, led to the shrine-like intimacy of the *cubiculum*—the inner room. The inner room did not function exclusively as a bedroom, as in a modern house. It was a guarded place, set aside for intimate conversation, for Christian worship, or (for the unregenerate majority of the rich whose erotic mosaics we have seen in villas all over the empire) for the vigorous joys of love.[23]

Jerome's emphasis on the *cubiculum* deserves our attention for it contained a challenge to contemporary values. Jerome did not aim to create monasteries outside the home. Instead, he wished his correspondents to turn their entire palaces into ascetic fortresses, closed against the outside world. Nothing could have been more contrary to Roman habits. A noble palace had always been a partly public place. Its spacious courtyards and reception halls were supposed to be open to the world at large. It was in these great, open spaces quite as much as in the Forum that the ruling class of Rome conducted the business of the city. To extend to the palace as a whole the sense of intimate seclusion associated with a woman's bedroom was to slam the door in the face of the wider world. It was to create a more than usually charged notion of the "private."

In Jerome's writings, the bedroom absorbed the palace. He presented it as a garden of spiritual delights given over to the reading of the Scriptures. In Christian circles, meditation on the Scriptures was expected to be an experience as erotic and as tantalizing as anything that could be found in the works of Plato and Plotinus when they wrote on the thrilling beauty of the One. It involved a search for ecstasy. At this time, Jerome translated Origen's *Commentary on the Song of Songs*. This great love poem from the days of the ancient kings of Israel was read by Origen and other Christians as a guide to seekers of spiritual sweetness.

For Origen, the "touch" of the Bridegroom on the body of the beloved was a moment of intellectual frisson, which occurred during the reading of the Scriptures.[24] A contemporary of Plotinus, Origen and his Greek readers took such moments of mystical awakening for granted. But Jerome was more colorful than Origen. When he wrote of Eustochium experiencing such thrills, as a noble girl with a hot little body, enclosed within the *cubiculum* of a noble house, no reader (fourth century or modern) could have avoided thinking that the verse—*and may He touch your belly*—referred to something more charged, perhaps, than the chaste excitement of a professor in his library.[25]

We moderns have become strangely prudish in our attitudes toward ecstasy and intellectual frissons. We conclude that such passages reveal in Jerome "his consummate sense of style, and his dirty mind."[26] But, as we have already seen in the case of Augustine, late antique persons were less troubled than we are by the language of spiritual delight. They would have noticed something more disturbing. In Jerome's program, the spiritual exercises of Eustochium cut her off from the public life of the churches. Jerome advised Paula to keep Eustochium at home. She was not to visit the great shrines of Christian Rome. She was to avoid the crowded gatherings associated with the feasts of the martyrs. Rather, the martyrs were to visit her.

This was unusually drastic advice. Nighttime vigils in honor of the martyrs (where the great basilicas of the *suburbium* shone in the dark like giant lanterns) were the high point of the life of the Christian community of Rome. It was not for nothing that the rich needed a list of feasts of the martyrs such as that provided by Filocalus in his famous *Calendar*. By being present at these gatherings, the Christian rich established relations with the poor and with their fellow believers that echoed, in miniature, the ancient dialogue between the nobles and the people of Rome.[27] For rich and pious families to be urged to withdraw from such occasions was a danger sign. Jerome's high-pitched advocacy of total ascetic seclusion in upper-class circles aimed to create a world of elect souls who felt themselves superior to the average Christian. It threatened to undermine the unity of the Christians of Rome as a single "holy people" that Damasus and those around him had worked so hard to maintain.

There is a cloying physicality and an insistence on private space in Jerome's writings that rivet our attention. He expected that this would be the reaction of his readers. A superabundant modern literature on Jerome and women shows that he succeeded.[28] But the purpose of letters such as *Letter* 22 was not simply to close the bodies and the houses of noble virgins and widows against the perils of sex. It was to ensure that these widows and their virgin daughters closed the doors of their palaces against an outside world that was eager less for their bodies than for their money.

Nudos amat eremus: The desert loves those stripped to the bone

---

JEROME ON WEALTH AND POVERTY

On the subject of money, Jerome felt entitled to write with more than usual vehemence. He claimed to have come to Rome from Syria as a self-professed Old Desert Hand. In fact, he knew very little about the Christian Middle East. His experience had been limited to Syria alone. In particular, his notion of poverty showed the clear marks of Syrian piety at its most unflinching. This was a notion of poverty based on identification with the imagined absolute poverty of Christ.

The Syrian ideal of poverty was more radical than that adopted by other ascetics in other regions. It involved a total emptying of the social self. Applied to Christ and to his followers—the monks—the word *msarrqûtâ* (from *srq*—to strip) conjured up to Syrian ears something more awesome than the *abjectio* of Christ on which (as we have seen) the piety of persons such as Paulinus had concentrated.[29] For Paulinus, *abjectio* was associated with the manner in which Christ had "stooped to conquer" by becoming a humble human being. It had involved Paulinus and his monks in a studied dimming down of the current semiotics of wealth in upper-class society. The pale, ill-shorn, and roughly dressed monks who gathered around Paulinus at Cimitile were a sight to make one think. But behind them always lay the shadow of an epic stepping down. Just as Christ, for all the deliberate eclipse of his éclat, had been and, indeed, still *was* God (and all the more God for being silent), so Paulinus's monks remained aristocrats, even when they were pointedly humbled.

In Syria the notion of the self-depletion of the monk went further. To follow Christ's self-emptying meant more than a toning down of the marks of power and wealth. It meant a total whiteout of the social person. On occasions, it even led to the erasure of the boundary between humanity and the animal world. Some Syrian monks were known as "grazers." In full view of an admiring laity, groups of monks moved like herds of animals, eating the wild herbs and grasses of the mountains that overlooked prosperous cities.[30] They sat on the edge of villages, sheltering in the bottom of dry cisterns with no roof above their heads but the sky itself.[31] The monks of Syria had not simply humbled themselves within society. They had stepped outside society itself. Their very presence mocked the world. In this, they were the direct heirs of the Cynics.[32]

With the enthusiasm of a foreigner, Jerome saw these distinctive holy men through the lens of a long classical tradition. He acclaimed them as the Cynics of his time. They seemed to him to live lives as stripped bare of material objects as was the hard rock of the empty cisterns in which they squatted. In his earliest manifesto for the ascetic life, he coined the vivid phrase *Nudos amat eremus*: "The desert loves those stripped to the bone."[33]

Jerome had developed this stark vision early. When still in Syria (in 379), he wrote the vivid *Vita Pauli—Life of Paul the Hermit*. He presented Paul the hermit as a standing reproach to the conscience of the rich.[34]

Those of you, whose estates are so far flung that you do not know where they are, who sheathe your palaces in marble, who string your villas, one after another, estate by estate—what was ever lacking, I ask you, to that old man? You drink from jeweled cups, he from a natural stream. You sew gold thread into your robes, he wore clothes that not even the most exploited of your slaves would wear.... Covered with the meanest dirt, Paul lies at rest, sure to rise again in glory. The stones of carefully constructed tombs rest on you, with all your riches—sure to burn in Hell.[35]

It was a merciless message to bring from northern Syria to the Christian rich of Rome. Over the years, the contrast between gross wealth and stark poverty was advanced by Jerome in a series of dramatic antitheses that gathered cumulative momentum—wealth was to poverty as Dives was to the shivering Lazarus, as the Jewish Patriarchs of the Old Testament, comfortably ensconced in material goods, were to the penniless Apostles, as married sex was to pure virginity, ultimately as Christ was to "the world."[36] The thought of the naked Christ, identified with the shivering poor, was what enabled Jerome to act as the superego of his patrons. Writing to Paula about the great illuminated Bibles that had begun to be produced for rich Christians, Jerome wrote: "The parchment page is dyed deep in purple, the letters are a trickle of gold, the bound volumes are dressed in gems—and the naked Christ lies dying at the gate."[37]

Once he had established himself in Rome, however, Jerome's ominous sense of the contrast between wealth and destitution was applied to a different task than the care of the poor. It enabled him to become a consummate satirist.[38] Addressing the Christian rich of Rome, Jerome stepped with ease into a time-honored literary stance. He, Jerome the monk, was the poor man faced with the foibles of the rich. Like the poet and satirist Martial before him, Jerome invoked the ideal of poverty "almost always to achieve a distance from wealth." As Greg Woolf has written recently of Martial: "the affectation of poverty gives [him] a perspective, a kind of license.... [It] marks out the moral gulf that ... separates [him from the rich]."[39]

Indeed, what Jerome wrote about upper-class Roman society had the delicious triviality of great satire. His unfailing pen picked on the vivid minutiae of the day-to-day life of the fashionable rich. We are told that pagans flocked to make copies of his *Letter* 22 to Eustochium.[40] It was an album of wicked caricatures of persons whom they would have recognized. Jerome showed "The First Lady of Rome" (possibly Faltonia Proba, the wife of none other than Petronius Probus) as she paraded through the courtyard of Saint Peter's, surrounded by her entourage of eunuchs. Once she punched a beggar with her own hands when he came back to ask for more than one coin.[41] He also described a Roman clergyman with well-oiled ringlets and pretty sandals hurrying from one fashionable gathering to another. Once arrived, the clergyman would pass the chamber pot to an elderly donor. He would kiss the old man's head while holding out his hands, not to administer the priest's blessing but to grab the customary "tip" given by the rich to clients at their *salutatio*.[42]

Waspish though it might be, all this was safe stuff. Jerome was untouched by the fierce populism that drove Ambrose in Milan to preach at just this time on the avarice and violence of the rich. If anything, what Jerome wrote was reassuring for Christian Roman readers. Jerome did not treat Rome as a doomed city, irrevocably tainted by centuries of idolatry. These fears were still present in the 370s and 380s. The staid Ambrosiaster had written constantly against the paganism of the *nobiles* who held the cultural high ground in the city.[43] A decade later, when he wrote to Pammachius, Paulinus of Nola would speak of Rome as a city that still lay under the threat of the Apocalypse. The Rome that Paulinus saw was still Babylon—the great, doomed city of the Apocalypse.[44] Jerome's shimmering word pictures banished these dark thoughts. A reader of Jerome was not expected to see a doomed city. All that was wrong with Rome was the piquant misbehavior of Christians in fashionable society.[45]

Discite superbiam sanctam: Learn a holy pride

MARRIAGE STRATEGIES IN THE CIRCLES OF JEROME

But fashionable society, as Jerome and every other Roman knew very well, was not only about dining, sex, and soirées. It was about a relentless round of sociability driven by the marriage market. The dinner parties Jerome urged Eustochium and her mother to shun were like the London Season in eighteenth-century England. They were places where heiresses were put on show and where the "Senate House of Ladies" met to discuss the merits of potential brides. For this reason, we should step back for a moment to look carefully at the women who received Jerome's ascetic admonitions to avoid such occasions.[46]

Jerome's letters to Marcella and Paula give us a precious glimpse of two noblewomen and of the extensive network of relatives, in-laws, and dependents who gathered around them. But we must remember that it is a glimpse through a mere crack in the wall compared with what we could (but may never) know about upper-class society in Rome as a whole. The two groups were interrelated; Pammachius was the link between them. Pammachius was a cousin of Marcella. He married (perhaps at this time) Paulina, the second daughter of Paula (and the elder sister of Eustochium). This was the Paulina whose memorial banquet would be described by Paulinus of Nola in 396. Pammachius had been a fellow student with Jerome in the 360s. He may have provided Jerome with an entry to the houses of both women. We may well be looking at a grouping of families that had already opted to be inward looking. Both Marcella and Paula seem to have been concerned to maintain shared religious traditions through a more than usually careful choice of friends and in-laws. Elective affinities as fellow Christians may always have weighed with them more than did more crudely dynastic considerations in their choice of spouses and in-laws.

There was good reason for this. As we have seen, the resident aristocracy of Rome was far from monolithic. It was as multilayered as that of the provinces. Families securely established in the inner circle of the *nobiles* constantly looked down the social ladder in search of marriage partners that they might absorb so as to make use of the new wealth and the political skills such persons had obtained through making their careers in the fourth-century imperial system. We saw this happening in the series of upward marriages by which Ausonius and his relatives had established themselves among the older noble families of Bordeaux. (As we saw, a similar upward marriage may have linked the family of Proiecta to her husband's family, the noble Roman family of the Turcii.) To older families, a downward marriage represented an infusion of talent and new money.

Paula seems to have belonged to a family that had recently brought provincial wealth into Rome. Her father, Rogatus, was said to be descended from Agamemnon. One might smile at this claim. But Christian provincial families in Greece already claimed Homeric ancestors: a lady buried at Demetrias, near Volos, claimed descent from "the family of Achilles."[47] More to the point, Paula owned the entire city of Actium (near modern Preveza in Greece) on the coast of Epirus.[48] Her mother was supposedly descended from the Scipios and the Gracchi. An air of old nobility, partly evaporated, may have clung to Paula through her mother. But her mother's family had evidently been glad to take aboard the resources of an enterprising Greek.[49]

Marcella found herself in a similar position. She had once been the target of a downward marriage, planned by a member of the high nobility. When widowed after a few months, in the early 360s, her mother offered her to an outstanding figure, Naeratius Cerealis. Cerealis had been a consul. He came from a family that had long dominated Samnium and had even established relations with the emperor through a marriage to "royals" of the dynasty of Constantine. But at the moment when he approached Marcella, Cerealis was down on his luck. He had been tainted with a failed rebellion against Constantius II.[50] He may have sought, at this moment, to bolster his uncertain position by marrying downward into a rich family. Marcella did not accept him. Even if she had not wished to remain a widow so as to be a pious Christian, she might in any case have rejected Cerealis—a failed grandee—as a bad investment.

Altogether, both Paula and Marcella seem to have come from families who were placed in an awkward position. They were above the average *clarissimi* and *clarissimae* whose sarcophagi litter the catacombs of Rome. But they were still marginal to the inner core of the nobility of Rome. The nobles looked on rich provincials such as the family of Rogatus and his daughter Paula in a manner not unlike the English and French nobility of the late nineteenth century when they considered marrying the daughters of American industrialists. It was a situation that gave the families of "new" men considerable leverage, provided that they could offer virgins and widows to potential noble spouses.

Furthermore, widows could be very rich; they had rights in their father's inheritance. The sooner they were remarried the better. Virgins, also, were not encouraged to remain virgins for long. They were to be placed briskly on the marriage market so as to widen the social and political outreach of an up-and-coming family.[51] In a world dependent in this way on the circulation of its women, Jerome made constant propaganda for widowhood and virginity as immobile, consecrated states. By idealizing perpetual virginity and by praising perpetual widowhood, Jerome did nothing less than threaten to freeze two vital moving parts in the structure of the Roman aristocracy. He wrote to Paula about Eustochium in his notorious *Letter* 22: "Learn in these matters a holy pride of birth. Know that you are better than them."[52] This memorable phrase was immediately taken up by other ascetic writers. It has usually been interpreted as a general exaltation of an elitist form of Christianity. In fact (as is so often the case with Jerome), it was bitterly precise. Eustochium was to avoid the salons of married ladies where the business of the marriage market of Rome was conducted. For Eustochium, marriage was to be avoided. More than that: in Jerome's opinion, for an elect soul such as Eustochium, marriage itself was the ultimate *mésalliance*.

"Let the patrician set thunder against me": Ascetic Vocations and the Flow of Wealth

Jerome, of course, expected the aristocracy of Rome to be suitably shocked by his proposal. Writing ten years later, in 396, to the lady Furia (a relative by marriage of Paula—we are in a very small world), he told her that the moment he touched on the themes of virginity and widowhood, he could expect outrage in high places:

> I am fully aware that I am now putting my hand in the fire. Let the nobles rise up against me, let the Patrician Set thunder against me—call me a sorcerer, a seducer, a person to be bundled off to the end of the world.[53]

But we must remember that if Jerome was skilled in manipulating his own persona, he was equally skilled at caricaturing the attitudes of his opponents. He liked to have someone to hate him. But if we look carefully at the families whom Jerome addressed, one is surprised, if anything, by the flexibility and lack of sexual panic with which the male members of the Christian rich handled their daughters and widows. This reflects a certain sense (which is not unusual in upwardly mobile families) that not all strategies for advancement had to pass through the marriage bed. We are not dealing with a city entirely dominated by a closed caste of nobles whose women were valued only as the human clamps that linked together vast blocks of hereditary property. The Anicii might consolidate their legendary wealth through marrying a succession of cousins. Lesser families could afford more diverse strategies, which left room for a fair number of mavericks who were simply content to drop out of the marriage market. Ambrose is an example of this kind. He and his brother remained celibate. His sister, Marcellina, became a "virgin of the church" as early as 355. Nobody seems to have minded.[54]

Furthermore, Romans (pagans and Christians alike) were by no means as shocked by the notion of virginity as Jerome expected them to be. But they valued a different sort of virginity from that propounded by Jerome. They valued a "votive" virginity, safely linked to the home and validated by the local church. Decades before Jerome brought his newfangled ascetic expertise from the East to Rome (indeed, in as early as the 340s), the father of the nun Asella—whom Jerome came to know in Rome—dreamed before her birth that "a virgin had been presented to him in a phial of shining glass, more pure than any mirror."[55]

Asella was marked out from birth as a household virgin. Her virginity and her regular prayers ensured the supernatural protection of a family which, at that time, included both pagans and Christians. In the transitional religious world of the mid-fourth century, the Vestal Virgins were still widely respected. There was nothing strange or particularly shocking about Asella's role as a joining point between heaven and the house in a family where half of the members were still pagan. If virgins such as the Vestals were good for the Roman state, a virgin— even a Christian virgin—in the family could be good for a Roman clan.[56]

What concerned contemporaries was that these individual vocations should not block the movement of property from one generation to the next. This problem was solved in differing ways. By the time Jerome met them, both Marcella and Paula had already arranged with their kin (at some time in the 370s) to divert the principal resources of the family in such a way that the tide of wealth flowed around them to the next generation. This flow of wealth was not blocked by the decision of the two women not to remarry. Marcella retained her inheritance. But she had to buy out her mother by surrendering her jewelry and furniture.[57] As we saw in the case of the church founded by the illustrious lady Vestina through the sale of her jewelry, this would have amounted to no small sum. Jewels were not only valuable; they were seen as heirlooms heavy with a sense of heritage. A later law (issued in Milan in 390) made clear what was at stake. The law declared that such jewels were "the embellishments of a sumptuous home." They were not to be sold off for the benefit of the clergy and the faceless poor.[58]

Unlike Marcella, Paula simply allowed her own inheritance to bypass her. It went to her son, Toxotius, who remained in Rome to carry on the family, while she herself soon joined Jerome in the Holy Land. Yet she was never without money when she started to build a monastery, a hostel, a defensive tower, and a large library for Jerome in Bethlehem.[59] In all these cases, it was the vertical link between the generations that mattered. Older women, as widows, negotiated successfully for their own freedom and for the interests of their own children, either to protect them as virgins or to endow them for a future marriage.

Altogether, it is important for the historian to avoid seeing fourth-century Rome in the melodramatic broken light of Jerome's letters. What was not at stake, at this time, was the fate of entire dynasties or the potential dilapidation of entire fortunes. As John Curran has noted, even among Christian families touched by asceticism, "the careful management of property" was the rule.[60]

Jerome's intervention in Roman affairs was limited in its impact to a few families. But the tensions this intervention raised were real and affected a far wider circle of Christians. In Rome, the arrival and departure of Jerome had coincided with a new development. The 380s saw an increased religious and cultural stratification within the Roman community. As we saw, this development can be traced on the ground in the emergence of ever more prominent family mausolea close to martyr's shrines in the catacombs. Social stratification undermined the Roman Christian ideal of an undivided "holy people." Nowhere was this social stratification shown more blatantly than by increased cultural stratification. Certain families went out of their way to distance themselves from their peers in their zeal and in their scholarly pursuits. It was to these families that Jerome had gravitated.

This was not a matter that involved only the relations of a few reclusive *âmes d'élite* with their chosen gurus. Ascetic piety such as that advocated by Jerome cost money. It involved the transfer of large sums to monastic settlements in Egypt and the Holy Land. It also involved the considerable expense connected with high scholarship—the assembling of libraries and the production of books. There was a danger that, compared with these new enterprises, supporting the local churches of Christian Rome might come to seem to lack glamour. The wealth of rich and pious persons might vanish to distant regions. It might be expended on the theological vendettas of expatriate scholars rather than disbursed in the courtyards of the churches of Rome. Whether this actually happened is a different matter. But in the 390s and 400s, the thought that it could happen was enough to raise alarm. The possibility added a note of tension to the affairs of Rome and (of course) provided the ever-ready pen of Jerome with material for yet more letters and pamphlets. In this case, however, what was at stake for Jerome was not sex and money. It was the cost of cultural endeavors and the rival networks of patronage on which such endeavors depended.

CHAPTER 17

❦

Between Rome and Jerusalem

Women, Patronage, and Learning, 385–412

"I have found what my soul has sought after"
Women and Learning in Rome

We must never underestimate the fierce intellectualism of many upper-class Romans. This intellectual commitment had long roots. In advocating monasticism and intensive meditation on the Scriptures, Jerome claimed to have brought to Rome an exciting novelty from the East. In fact, he had many pagan predecessors. Those to whose palaces he came could look back to at least one and a half centuries of teach-ins conducted by spiritual mentors from the eastern provinces.

When the great Neo-Platonic philosopher Plotinus came from Egypt to Rome around 243 he found himself at the center of a whole circle of zealous Romans. Women were prominent among them.

> Several women were greatly attached to him amongst them Gemina, in whose house he lived, and her daughter, called Gemina, too, after the mother, and Amphiclea, the wife of Ariston ... all three devoted themselves assiduously to philosophy.[1]

Jerome ministered to persons who came from roughly the same social niche as did those who had listened to Plotinus. The study circles around Plotinus were not drawn from the very top level of the *nobiles* but from the new aristocracy that had begun to emerge in the course of the military crisis of the third century. The pagan sarcophagi of the age of Plotinus frequently showed the deceased in the company of philosophers and the Muses. Some of the most impressive of these were commissioned by members of the new service aristocracy of soldiers and administrators. These persons were the sociological equivalents (in the third century) of the newly created *clarissimi* and *clarissimae* of the fourth century. In both the age of Plotinus and in the age of Jerome, we are dealing with men and women for whom the search for nobility included the cultivation of a true nobility of the mind. In this area, at least, they could rival or outshine the better-established families of Rome. Hence the patronage of scholars and of religious guides was of more than usual importance for them.[2]

Despite his suffocating emphasis on physical asceticism, Jerome was the heir of the great spiritual mentors of the third century. But he did not look back to the pagan Plotinus. He looked back to the Christian Origen. Like Plotinus and Origen, Jerome moved in circles that expected women to be as intellectually engaged as men. What he offered them was a study of the Scriptures that was as endlessly thrilling as the mystical quest for the One had been in Neo-Platonic circles.

It is important to do justice to this aspect of the activity of Jerome. At first sight it seems incongruous. The scholarly labor of Jerome emphasized the need to seize the literal meaning of the Scriptures gained by translation from the original languages. This might seem to us to distance the Bible from mystical endeavors. But this is a modern view, based on a modern preference for what we call an "objective" and "historical" study of the Bible. For Jerome and those whom he taught, it was the exact opposite. The entire Bible was thought of as an encoded message from God. To learn Greek and then Hebrew was to advance yet further in cracking this code. It was to learn how to pierce through secondary layers of imprecise or misleading translations. Once these layers had been removed, it was possible to glimpse the hidden Sun of the Wisdom of God that blazed in the very depths of the Scriptures: *I have found what my soul has sought after. I shall hold Him and shall not let Him go* (Song of Songs 3:4).[3] Even the crushing ascetic regimes Jerome propounded for his charges were linked to that endeavor. For only a body whose own sensuality had fallen silent would thrill with a purified and sharpened sensibility to the mystic joys hinted at in the text of the Bible.[4]

Jerome belonged to a generation of great women readers. They were driven by a search for the inner meaning of the Scriptures that was at one and the same time scholarly and mystical. Melania the Elder was believed to have read three million lines of Origen and two and a half million lines of more recent authors. She had read a body of Christian literature (mainly devoted to commentaries on the Scriptures) that was three hundred times larger than Homer's *Iliad*: "And she did not read them once only and in an offhand way, but she worked on them, dredging through each work seven or eight times."[5] Her granddaughter, Melania the Younger, was no different. Once settled on her estate in Africa, in 411, Melania began to read and to copy. She read through the Old and New Testaments four times a year. She made copies of the Scriptures with her own hands.

Often, when she was sitting in silence or writing, her mother would enter the room. Unless she had completed her work or her reading, she would not answer or ask her mother anything. Realizing this, her mother would withdraw, respecting her silence, with wonder and reverence.[6]

Bene nummatus: Well loaded

RUFINUS, JEROME, AND THEIR PATRONS

Such biblical reading (like the philosophical inquiries of an earlier age) seemed to be a peculiarly weight-free and otherworldly exercise. But it assumed a world cluttered with books. In Roman times, the philosopher had always been a man of simple life and heavy bookshelves. A third-century sarcophagus in Cagliari (Sardinia) shows one such philosopher. Dressed in a simple robe, he sits gesturing from an open scroll to a disciple who is also holding a scroll. Behind him is a huge locked cupboard on which a further sixteen scrolls are piled. The first discoverer of the sarcophagus thought that it represented a philosophical discourse on the vanity of wealth. It was no such thing. The locked cupboard and the scrolls *were* the wealth of the philosopher. Though dedicated to elevating thoughts, the cultural world of the philosopher, and of his successor the Christian exegete and spiritual mentor, was far from financially weight free.[7]

Modern persons in a world glutted with cheap books forget that the tradition of learned, contemplative reading propounded by Jerome represented a prodigious investment of money. Each copy of the Gospels alone cost as much as a marble sarcophagus. The setting up of a library stocked with texts of the Holy Scriptures and with their commentaries (not to mention other Christian writings) left a footprint of real wealth. It was an act of monumentalization that was as costly as the building or redecoration of a villa.[8]

The age of Plotinus and Origen (in the mid-third century) and the age of Jerome (in the late fourth and early fifth centuries) were not only ages of mystical endeavor. They were ages of the book. Anthony Grafton and Megan Williams have recently shown that behind the proliferation of Christian libraries lay a revolution in book production. At just this time, the no-nonsense codex (the direct ancestor of the bound book) replaced the scroll. These codices quickened the pace of scholarship and led to ever greater accumulations of books. The libraries owned by some Christian scholars were overwhelming. The library created in the 240s by Origen at Caesarea Maritima in Palestine (and later preserved by the bishops of Caesarea) was "one of the greatest single monuments of Roman scholarship."[9]

Jerome expected his spiritual charges to set up such libraries and to help him do the same. It is, indeed, one of the great paradoxes of the Christian culture of this time (elegantly explored by Megan Williams in her recent study *The Monk and the Book*) that a monk such as Jerome both claimed to be an advocate of total poverty and at the same time spent his life in the shadow of great libraries. He was tied irrevocably to wealthy persons who paid for the libraries on which his literary endeavors depended. In Antioch he had depended on the library of Evagrius. In Rome he had sought out the patronage of Damasus. From 385 (when he left Rome) until his death (around 420) he lived in Bethlehem, drawing on a library in a monastery built, endowed, and even fortified for him by the Roman widow Paula. Altogether, this was a thoroughly incongruous situation. But Jerome would not have been Jerome if he had not been able to mask, through ingenious rhetorical flourishes, the paradox inherent in his combination of a monastic persona committed (as we saw) to a doctrine of extreme poverty with that of a scholar tied to expensive books.[10]

Jerome, however, was merciless when confronted with enemies who did not veil their dependence on wealthy patrons as successfully as he did. We can see this in his relations with Rufinus of Aquileia, a former friend who ended up as Jerome's most deadly enemy. Rufinus was a mirror image of Jerome. Like Jerome, he was both a monastic scholar and a dependent of the rich. He had traveled with Melania the Elder to Alexandria in 373 and went on with her to Jerusalem. He returned to Italy in late 397 and remained in the environment of Rome (almost certainly settled in one of the villas of Melania) except for a short visit to Aquileia. He died in Sicily in 412 as a refugee from the Goths. He had fled to Sicily in the company of Melania's granddaughter, Melania the Younger, and of her husband, Pinianus. He had been able to live a life of learning for almost forty years because of the patronage of one very rich lady and her relatives.[11]

Rufinus did not reach out into Hebrew as Jerome had done. Instead he was content to channel the wisdom of the Greek East into the Latin world. He translated the *Rule* and *Homilies* of Basil of Caesarea, as well as the Bible commentaries of the great Origen. To his eventual misfortune, he also translated Origen's *On First Principles*. This was the great Alexandrian's most challenging work. In it, Origen had defended the freedom of the will and the justice of God in terms of a vast cosmic drama that involved him in risqué speculations on the preexistence of the soul.[12] Rufinus found himself declared guilty by association for having translated such daring views. But he was not deterred by accusations of heresy. Nor were those who patronized him. Rufinus was needed. His role as a link between Rome and the Holy Land was just as important as was that played by Jerome. One of his admirers once dreamed of a ship coming into port bearing a precious cargo from the East: it was yet another translation from the Greek by the indispensable Rufinus![13]

Rufinus could not have engaged in his monumental work of translation without the funding and protection provided by Melania the Elder. Melania's foundation of a monastery on the Mount of Olives and her prolonged residence there

(374–99) marked a new departure. Previously, aristocrats had traveled to the Holy Land and back as pilgrims. To decide to settle permanently in the Holy Land and to found a monastic community just outside Jerusalem involved an entirely new set of financial outlays. Frequent visitors had to be housed. Monastic communities in both Egypt and the Holy Land had to be kept in funds. This was no small burden. For, although the monastic communities of Egypt claimed to be self-supporting, they rarely succeeded in surviving without substantial gifts from rich foreigners such as Melania.[14] Above all, long residence in Jerusalem exposed Melania and her protégé Rufinus to the theological rancors of the eastern clergy.

In 397 a quarrel exploded between Rufinus (with Melania) and Jerome (with Paula) over the proper use of the works of Origen. This controversy need not concern us. What it did do, however, was unleash a stream of innuendoes that began in the Holy Land but soon echoed throughout Italy. These had nothing to do with sex and everything to do with money. Writing to rally support in Rome, Jerome claimed that Rufinus was *bene nummatus,* "well loaded." He was indecently well funded by the rich Melania. Supported by a rich patron, Rufinus plodded comfortably through life with the ridiculous pomposity and slowness of a tortoise. He was not a real scholar or a real monk. His work lacked the wiry vigor of a true ascetic. Unlike Jerome's own incessant labor, there was no *sudor*—no sweat—behind it.[15]

Rufinus answered in kind. He accused Jerome of having broken his vow never to have anything to do with pagan literature. He claimed that Jerome had employed Latin calligraphers in Rufinus's own monastery to make copies of the works of Cicero. He had paid top prices for these heathen classics. Rufinus vouched for it: he had seen the folded sheets before they were cut and bound.[16] These were trivial accusations in themselves, but they take us into the workshops of two great monasteries, in each of which book production played a major role. They also reveal the dilemma of both Jerome and Rufinus. Both were Christian monks and scholars. And both depended on resources only rich patrons could provide.

If anything, part of Jerome's personal bitterness toward Rufinus was due to the fact that Melania the Elder had managed her affairs better than had Paula. Unlike Paula, Melania never sold up her estates or allowed them to slip past her to her children. Instead, she managed them carefully in such a way as to provide a steady flow of funds to the Holy Land for decades on end. When she suddenly returned to Italy, in 399, it was said that she had done so in order to protect Rufinus (who had preceded her by two years). But she may also have returned so as to mobilize the income of her estates and raise further funds by campaigning for the ascetic life among her relatives, many of whom were friends and relatives of Paulinus of Nola.[17] Going up against a formidable network that included persons such as Paulinus of Nola, Jerome and Paula were outclassed.

The imbalance between the resources of Jerome and Rufinus showed in many ways. For instance, Rufinus mocked Jerome's continued involvement with pagan classical literature. He himself had deliberately adopted a style of anodyne simplicity. It was a style consonant with his humble persona as a Christian monk untouched by worldly rhetoric.[18] But Rufinus, with the financial backing of Melania the Elder, could afford to be simple. He was well funded. He did not have to show off so as to raise funds.

Jerome, by contrast, was tied to Paula. She was a less provident and less wealthy patroness than was Melania. For this reason, Jerome always had to look around for other, supplementary donors to his monastery and its library. Held hostage by the perilous state of the finances of his monastery, Jerome was forced to appear to wealthy Christians in Italy, Spain, and Gaul perpetually dressed, as it were, in his Sunday best. He had to shine as a literary genius. If rich donors were to send him funds, he had to send them letters and prefaces written in scintillating Latin, filled with echoes of classical authors.[19]

The solidity of Melania's endowment is shown in the sinister last years of the life of Rufinus.[20] After 403 the peace of Italy ended. Gothic armies marched back and forth across northern Italy and eventually crossed the Apennines to close in on Rome. But Rufinus stayed at it, doggedly translating into Latin in his slow, uncharismatic manner the great commentaries of Origen on the books of the Old Testament:

> What place is there for the pen, when enemy arms are feared; what place for reading, when the eyes are filled with the destruction of town and countryside; where flight must brave the perils of the sea, lest exile itself be still beset by fear?[21]

Rufinus wrote these words in 411 as he and Pinianus (the ascetic husband of Melania the Younger) looked out across the straits of Messina from the safety of a Sicilian villa as flames engulfed Rhegium (Reggio di Calabria, on the Italian side of the straits), torched by the Visigoths. A man who had grown up in the last generation of the Constantinian epoch was looking out on a scene that reminds us, rather, of the war-torn Italy of Cassiodorus and the Northumbria of the Venerable Bede. And, like Cassiodorus and Bede, only one thing was certain—*scripta manent*: in dangerous times books, at least, would survive, housed in libraries supported by massed wealth.

It is worthwhile stepping back to see what was at stake in this remarkable history of two scholars and their Roman patronesses. Megan Williams puts the matter clearly. The Origenist Controversy, which swept through the monasteries of Egypt and Palestine and led to a falling-out between the supporters of Rufinus and of Jerome in Rome, was about one thing: "The right of monks to be intellectuals and of intellectuals to be monks."[22]

Although they look to us like modern scholars (in their enthusiasms, in their expertise, and in their hatreds), we should not forget what an extraordinary phenomenon Jerome and Rufinus represented in their own time. Both were clergymen; but neither belonged to a bishop. Damasus had patronized Jerome; he had not taken him on his clerical staff. Furthermore, when he arrived in Bethlehem, Jerome assembled his library in a gravity-free zone. It was housed in an independent monastery, founded by a noble patroness and intermittently supported by further donations from admiring readers. It may not have been as great as the vast library of Origen at Caesarea, which boasted the eight hundred works of the master and the forty vast tomes that contained Origen's famous *Hexapla*—variant translations of the Old Testament, set beside the Hebrew in six columns. But, by the fourth century, it had become a bishop's library, supported by the wealth of the church and controlled by the ecclesiastical establishment.[23]

By contrast, the library of Jerome owed nothing to the local church and its bishop. It was as well stocked and as autonomous as was the private library of any senator.[24] We need only compare Jerome with Augustine to appreciate the significance of Jerome's freedom. Returning to Africa in 388, Augustine had tried to go it alone without a single, rich patron. He had managed to do this for just three years. Without a Paula or a Melania to support it, Augustine's monastery and the intellectual life that it had fostered was sucked inexorably into the orbit of the Catholic Church. From the moment of his ordination as a priest and then as a bishop in Hippo, Augustine, for all his formidable originality, was a bishop and spokesman of the church of Africa first and an intellectual second. Augustine adapted wholeheartedly to his role as a bishop among bishops. But one wonders what the course of Latin theology might have been like if Augustine had remained a freelance scholar protected by a noble patron in the way that Jerome and Rufinus had been.

In the years between the return of Rufinus in 397 and his death in 412, the Christians of Rome witnessed a flexing of the muscles of aristocratic patronage of a kind they had not experienced before. Despite ecclesiastical condemnations of his alleged "Origenist" tendencies, Rufinus went untouched. He continued to work. The conditions of late Roman book production ensured that his writings were protected. His books circulated along lines laid down by patronage networks and by alliances between friends and relatives. The friends of Melania the Elder and the friends of her friends made themselves responsible for the expensive task of copying and passing on to others the bulky manuscripts of the works of Rufinus. Jerome complained that he could not even get copies of these works so as to challenge them.[25]

Altogether, loyalty to Rufinus and distrust of Jerome became an axis along which sections of the Christian nobility of Rome were divided. Paulinus of Nola rallied instantly to the side of Melania, to whom he was probably related through his wife, Therasia. With Melania the Elder came her granddaughter Melania the Younger and her husband, Pinianus. Paulinus welcomed an entire new generation of would-be ascetics and admirers of Rufinus to the shrine of Saint Felix at Cimitile. In Rome, Jerome found himself frozen out by the rallying against him of an entire network of relatives, friends, and clients of Melania the Elder.[26]

"The Poor among the Saints": Jerome and Vigilantius

In itself, the Origenist Controversy between Jerome and Rufinus was a storm in a teacup. It was deemed to be a *querelle de moines*, a theological debate best left to monks.[27] Nor is it possible to quantify the amount of money that went from Rome and elsewhere in the West to the Holy Land. What matters is that this flow happened in a society that had come to watch with ever-greater suspicion the activities of charismatic fund-raisers in the Christian churches.

The fear of rival fund-raisers had always been present in Rome. A generation previously, the election of Damasus had given rise to divisions in which rich lay Christians had been involved. After this experience, Damasus had determined that if money was given to Christian causes in Rome, it should be given directly to himself alone as the bishop of Rome. He wished to be recognized as the sole representative of the Christian churches in the city. He wished to ensure that wealth would not be given to individual priests and holy men. As early as 370, he obtained from the emperor Valentinian I a ruling that

> Ecclesiastics ... and those men who wish to be called by the name of "Continents" [that is, monks] shall not visit the homes of widows and females under guardianship ... [in order to receive legacies].[28]

The edict was to be read aloud in the churches of Rome. It has usually been interpreted as an imperial rebuke delivered to Damasus for his activities as a fund-raiser and as an "ear tickler of ladies of quality." It was no such thing.[29] It was a preemptive strike, by the bishop, against potential rivals for funds. By obtaining this edict, Damasus attempted to ensure that, in Rome, no clergyman or monk would be given money or legacies for ventures of their own. All donations must go to the bishop, so as to become part of the wealth of the Roman church.

As we have seen, Jerome trod a thin line in his own dealings with ladies such as Paula. He mercilessly caricatured monks and clergymen who fawned on the rich for money. But, to outsiders, it looked very much as if he was doing just what these spongers had been doing. He protested vehemently on his departure: "Whose money did I accept? What gifts, small or great, did I not spurn? Did the money of anyone clink in my hand?"[30]

The suspicions remained. Funds continued to flow out of Rome and the West toward the Holy Places and the monasteries of Egypt. Rome could afford this drain. But in the provinces propaganda for the ascetic movement and the fostering of pilgrimage to the Holy Land threatened to undermine the finances of the less well-endowed local churches. In the years before 406, the issue exploded. The monasteries around Jerusalem came under attack. They were accused of having diverted the wealth of rich Christians away from their local churches through soliciting overseas donations to the Holy Land.

It is revealing that these criticisms arose in southern Gaul, a region that had recently witnessed the rise and fall of Priscillian and the abrupt transfer of the fortune of Paulinus out of Gaul and Spain to Italy. Local clergymen resented the drain of gifts that were made by the rich to support ascetics, especially ascetics settled at the far end of the Mediterranean. They preached that the local rich should use their wealth to give to the local poor and to the local churches. They had been inspired by Vigilantius, a monk from Saint-Martory, in the diocese of Saint Bertrand-de-Comminges, on the slopes of what is now the French side of the Pyrenees.[31]

Vigilantius was a dangerous critic. He had traveled both to the Holy Land and to Nola. He had known both Paulinus of Nola and Jerome. He had been impressed by neither, but for different reasons in each case. His acquaintance with Paulinus and his circle had made him aware of the gentle violence great wealth could bring to bear on traditional Christian piety. This led him to confront directly the issue of the cult of the saints. Could the saints be thought of as both in heaven and still on earth? Was the worship that they received on earth misplaced and reminiscent of paganism? Vigilantius found the cult of saints, such as Paulinus had promoted at the shrine of Saint Felix at Cimitile, disquieting. The splendor of such shrines made the saints seem still "present" on earth. But the saints were not on earth; they were with God, in heaven. They were bathed "in the Light of the Lamb." They did not linger on earth at their shrines. To worship them in the ostentatious manner that Paulinus had promoted amounted to a return to paganism.

> Under the pretext of religion we see a ritual that is practically pagan being introduced into the churches. While the sun is shining, piles of candles are lit.... Great honor do people of this sort offer to the most blessed martyrs, who (so they think) need to be illuminated by cheap little candles, when the Lamb Himself, Who sits on the throne, illumines them. [cf. Revelation 21:23, 22:5][32]

Vigilantius's protest was the only frontal attack on the cult of saints to appear in Latin Christianity. Though he appears to have made no direct mention of it, his arguments were very much directed against the splendor of shrines such as

Paulinus had built in Cimitile and Fundi, with their shimmering mosaics, altars sheathed in imperial purple, and vast candelabra in which oil lamps burned day and night.

It was Jerome, not Paulinus, who answered Vigilantius. His defense of the cult of the saints was brisk. But he rose instantly to the issue of money. He defended the monks of the Holy Places. He pointed out that they were like the Jewish students of Torah, whose study in the Holy Land was supported by contributions from synagogues all over the world.[33] The monks were the "holy poor." They were the direct heirs of the *poor among the saints in Jerusalem* (Romans 15:26) for whose welfare Paul had organized so many collections.[34]

Furthermore, in the parable of the Unjust Steward, Christ had encouraged the rich to use the *mammon of iniquity*, to win *friends* who would welcome them into *eternal tabernacles* (Luke 16:1–9). Such "friends" were not to be found among the ordinary poor:

> Surely these are not the poor, among whom burning lust still rules the ruin of a body wrapped in rags.... Alms are all they need. Rather, the rich should give their money to the "true" poor, who blush to receive and grieve when they do so, [so that the rich] may sow earthly goods and receive, in return, a spiritual reward.[35]

Only by giving to holy monks in the distant Holy Land—and not to the faceless and unsavory poor of their own region—could the rich engage in a "spiritual exchange" that was certain to place their *treasure in heaven*.

"Be not proud. You also are a member of the Church": Jovinian against Jerome, 390–94

In Rome itself, the alarm raised by Jerome had even deeper roots. It was not related only to the drain of funds from the local churches toward the Holy Land. The diversion of funds to ventures outside Rome was seen, rather, as the symptom of a more widespread development which troubled traditional Christians in the city. Jerome's elevation of widowhood and virginity awoke deep suspicion. This was not because denial of the body was, in and of itself, repugnant to Romans. Nor (as we have seen) was it only because it withdrew women from the marriage market and affected the transfer of property from one generation to the next. Rather, it introduced a spiritual stratification within the Roman Christian community that seemed to echo all too faithfully the growing social stratification to which we have already alluded when discussing the appearance of splendid mausolea beside the Christian shrines of the *suburbium*.

Jerome's ascetic propaganda seemed to challenge a central belief of the Roman Christian community. This community did not wish to see its members as sharply divided into separate grades. More than that: they did not wish to see these grades laid down in terms of whether Christians were married or abandoned marriage. Virginity and widowhood were all about sex; they were not about good works and should not be used to claim a status that was automatically superior to that of all other Christians.

To claim a separate rank within a single baptized community solely on the strength of one's distance from sex caused very real disquiet among Roman Christians. It marked the end of an older sense of the Christian community as a place where differing groups—aristocrats and plebeians—could mingle as fellow believers (indeed, as fellow "saints") with a touch of countercultural insouciance. Damasus, in his inscriptions, and Ambrosiaster, in his commentaries, had repeatedly emphasized the fact that Christians were still special as a whole. They formed a single "holy people." Now Jerome and his ascetic supporters claimed that within this single holy people, some were a lot holier than others.

This was bad news for the married. Let us take one example. In 382 (the year Jerome came to Rome) the lady Theodora was buried in the catacomb at the church of Saint Agnes. In the words of her bereaved husband, Theodora had been "an excellent observer of the [Christian] Law, a teacher of the faith.... For this reason she now reigns amid the exquisite odors of Paradise."[36] Now it seemed as if Jerome and his supporters had implied that, as a married woman, the lady Theodora and persons like her had been no more than second-class Christians. Only unmarried women—widows and virgins such as Marcella, Paula, or Eustochium—could claim to be full observers of the Christian Law, to be teachers of the faith, and to be certain of a place in Paradise.

But it was not only bad news for the married. Not all the ascetics of Rome were content with Jerome's views. Rome must have had many Marcellas and not a few Paulas. But Jerome had no use for them. For instance, he ignored the circle around Marcellina, the sister of Ambrose. He treated other groups of virgins and widows than his own as no more than "sham Christians." But this, of course, was by no means the case.

We now know of one such dedicated virgin, of whose existence we could not have guessed had we read only the works of Jerome. Ucceia was the wife of Viventius, a successful career bureaucrat from Pannonia who had been a popular Prefect of the City in 363–367—no mean feat for an outsider from the Balkans. In 389 Ucceia gave a marble sarcophagus for the burial of the consecrated Pannonian virgin Maximilla. Ucceia did this "because of the friendship with which we were joined together." Maximilla was all that a dedicated virgin should be: "Powerful to serve the covenants of Christ and to preserve her own vocation."

Maximilla's admirers could rest assured that they also would go to heaven "if the mind recalls the one faith given equally to all."[37]

Owned by a leading government servant whose wife was linked by a spiritual friendship to a pious virgin, the estate of Viventius in the *suburbium* would have been little different from the retreat of Marcella or one of the *domus* visited by Jerome. But Maximilla is a mere name to us. She had no Jerome to make her famous. The sarcophagus in which she was placed, in 389, was discovered only in the mid-1930s, buried in the family mausoleum of Viventius beside the apse of San Sebastiano on the Appian Way.[38] The message of the inscription placed on the sarcophagus was clear. For the circle around Maximilla, it was shared membership in the baptized community within a shared faith—and not virginity alone—that offered entry into heaven.

Between 390 and 394 (that is, only a few years after Jerome had left Rome in 385) the irritation caused by Jerome's advocacy of the outright superiority of ascetics over all other Christians exploded in the discourses of the monk Jovinian. Jovinian was an ascetic. But he was also a conservative upholder of the Roman ideal of an undivided holy people.[39]

Jovinian argued that those who claimed special merit for virgins and widows were in danger of introducing a novel division into the Christian community of Rome. It was a division that resembled the absolute superiority of the Elect over the Auditors, which had distinguished the "Holy Church" of Mani. As we have seen from the early years of Augustine, the division between Elect and Hearers had been basic to the Manichaean movement. Manichaeism was alive and well in Rome. The Elect were known. The reverence that the rank and file of the Manichaean laity were expected to show to them—on the strength of their uncanny pallor and abstention from meat and wine—was frequently remarked upon.

Jerome expected his widows and virgins to be accused of being like the Manichaean Elect because of their long fasts and pale faces. He dismissed this accusation as an ill-informed slur. But, in fact, he expected such widows and virgins to be surrounded by a reverence similar to that which the Auditors of the "Holy Church" of Mani had bestowed on their Elect. This was precisely what Jovinian feared—the emergence of a binary system within the baptized community of the faithful.

This potential development was not without social consequences. As we have seen, the families addressed by Jerome came from a precarious segment of Roman upper-class society. They needed to distinguish themselves from the rich plebeians below them and from the haughty noble families above them. They had done this in large part by switching the flow of wealth in the direction of religious causes. The new exaltation of virginity would further affect this flow of wealth. The two irrevocably different grades of Christians—the sexless and the married—

might be joined by an ethereal spiritual exchange: as in Manichaeism, wealth would go to the perfect and not to the poor.

To avoid this situation, Jovinian invoked the ancient theme of the Church as a single, undivided community of "saints," rendered equal by baptism. His message to virgins and widows was firm. Jerome quoted him as saying: "Do not be proud. You belong to the same Church."[40]

Jovinian went too far. He was instantly condemned by clergymen who had come to adopt celibacy as the mark of their own superior status within the Christian community. Siricius and Ambrose united against him. Within a holy people, the clergy had every intention of being more holy than anyone else. But, despite his failure to rally clerical opinion, Jovinian had touched a raw nerve. Once an elite based on as elemental a principle as sex and its renunciation was allowed to emerge within the Christian community, money would follow it. Money habitually spent in "good works" for the poor and for the endowment of local churches would go instead to the support of a separate, revered group.

The danger was real. The Manichaean Elect had usually been persons of low social status, elevated by their abstinence alone. They could be supported at very little expense by moderately well-to-do Hearers (as Augustine had done when he was a young teacher). But the would-be Elect of the Christian community of Rome (its widows and virgins) were not like that. They included among their members some of the richest women in the entire empire. They would not receive money; they would give money. Where their money would go, nobody could tell. The cases of Melania and Paula, as well as the careers of Rufinus and Jerome, showed that it might go far beyond the seas—and that it might be used, not to support the local church, but to fund the rancors of freelance polymaths.

The 390s, however, were still a quiet time. We, who know that the barbarian invasions were about to begin, easily forget how peaceful Italy must have seemed in those years. In Rome, the sheer "magnificence" of a vast city allowed potentially conflicting factions to coexist without crisis. But important changes had happened in this time of peace. In many ways, the vivid exchanges between Jerome and his enemies are misleading. They tend to mask the more silent and more decisive developments. Let us end by indicating some of these.

Slowly but surely, following the lead of Damasus, the Roman clergy consolidated its position as a Third Estate in the city. At the same time, the upper nobility and the clergy drew closer. As bishop of Rome, Siricius (who had hounded out Jerome in 385) gained a reputation for having protected nobles who sought sanctuary in the church in times of civil war. Though implicated with usurpers (first with Maximus in 388 and then with Eugenius in 394), they and their families received mercy from Theodosius I, through the intercession of Siricius, on the understanding that they would become Christian.[41] (Even Symmachus once sought sanctuary in a Christian church, after he had been heavily involved with Maximus, having praised the usurper in a panegyric. But, canny as ever, he made sure not to flee to a church of the bishop of Rome. Instead, he sought sanctuary in the separate, schismatic church of the Novatians.)[42]

More decisive yet, leading Christian families began to take a more direct interest in their local Christian communities. We can trace this development in the case of the Anicii. The head of the family, Petronius Probus, had long been known as a Christian. As we saw, he was buried around 390 in a magnificent mausoleum that abutted the apse of the shrine of Saint Peter on the Vatican. He lay as near as possible to the tomb of the saint.[43] Statues erected in his honor by his sons may even have stood close by.[44] But Probus did not have the area to himself. The graves of persons from the lesser nobility of service also clustered around the apse of Saint Peter's. Their presence emphasized the relative openness of Christian burial even in this privileged location.[45]

But this was precisely what Probus and his descendants would have wished. The placing of his mausoleum in a place of shared worship ensured that Probus remained in the public eye. Unlike many nobles, Probus was not buried in the privacy of a suburban villa. His mausoleum and the statues around it stood out among a cluster of graves in a place where the Christian people assembled in large numbers. It remained a prominent monument. In the Renaissance, the tomb was known as the Temple of Probus. When workmen opened the great marble sarcophagus in 1452, they found in it the remains of gold filaments. A grandee to the last, Probus had been buried in a robe of heavy gold cloth.

But Probus himself had been baptized only on his deathbed. He belonged to an earlier generation, still dominated by habits established at the court of Constantine. The great patronized Christianity, but they did not necessarily take part in the life of the local churches. In maintaining this distance they followed the example of their emperor. Though acclaimed as the first Christian emperor, Constantine was never seen in a Christian church outside his palace. Emperors only began to attend church services in public after his death in 337.[46]

In the late fourth century and the beginning of the fifth, the distance between the upper nobility and the local churches began to close. We can see this change in small details. In 408 a member of another branch of the Anicii, Anicius Auchenius Bassus, became consul. His consulship seems to have been celebrated in Africa (where the Anicii owned large estates) with a terra cotta plaque—possibly the lid of a box—in which a consul was shown flanked by the figures of Saints Peter and Paul. This unprecedented merging of the civic mystique of the consulate with the mystique of the twin patron saints venerated by the Christian community of Rome marked a new departure.[47]

These developments showed that Jerome had become a little out-of-date. The groups to whom he had appealed were less prominent than before. They had belonged to the lesser aristocracy. They were now in danger of being overshadowed by families of the super-rich such as the Anicii. How long could such groups maintain a superiority based on an appeal to "true" nobility derived from intellectual activities and from superior spiritual prowess, as both Jerome and Rufinus had urged them to do? They were in danger of being swamped by rich Christians who did not share their concerns.

The silent majority of well-to-do Christians had rallied to the clergy and to the ideal of membership in a well-organized and undivided "holy people" that went back to the days of Damasus. They were glad that their money counted for something in the churches of Rome. With the possible exception of Pammachius, the surge in the foundation of titular churches in the late fourth and early fifth centuries seems to have owed little or nothing to persons connected with the circles addressed by Jerome and Rufinus. Compared with that surge of wealth, accompanied by impressive buildings, the little study groups of persons such as Marcella, Paula, and Melania seemed ever more peripheral to the life of the church.

Nonetheless, not a few Roman Christians remained determined to retain their intellectual ambitions. They continued to seek an extra nobility of the spirit by following mentors such as Jerome or Rufinus much as their ancestors had followed pagan sages. Well educated, tenacious, and not dulled by the punctilious routines of the inner circle of the nobility, they were the storm center from which new controversies could easily blow up.

But here also times had changed. As we have seen (in the case of the Origenist Controversy between Jerome and Rufinus), the rancors of such groups had been safely encapsulated. But after 403, with the increase of Gothic raiding into Italy, the political situation worsened dramatically. The headstrong behavior of even a few ascetic zealots threatened to have serious social and political repercussions, especially if these hotheads came from the higher nobility. This happened after 406 when Melania the Younger and Pinianus—both of them truly members of the super-rich—decided to sell up their vast ancestral properties, as Paulinus had done ten years before. But they did so now at a time of mounting crisis, as the Visigoths of Alaric closed in on Rome.

More dangerous yet, real *nobiles* might at last come to take a personal interest in Christian theology. It was far from certain that they would invariably patronize safe figures. In around 390 the British monk Pelagius came to Rome. He moved in high circles. The circle around Melania and Rufinus seems to have welcomed him and to have provided him with intellectual ammunition.[48] He wrote a long letter defending his ideas to Paulinus of Nola.[49] More significantly still, Pelagius seems to have gained the respect of the Anicii. In 413 he was invited to write a letter of spiritual exhortation for none other than the granddaughter of Petronius Probus—the would-be virgin of the church, Demetrias.

This was not surprising. Pelagius's views on human nature found a ready echo in the high circles in which he had moved in Rome. These views were robustly aristocratic and optimistic. But when they were brought to Carthage in 410, by aristocratic refugees from Rome who had fled to Africa after the Visigothic sack, they came as a shock to the clergy of Carthage and to Augustine of Hippo. Until then, neither region had paid much attention to the other. Two very different Christianities, related to two very different churches and to their distinctive social contexts, had developed in Rome and in Africa. The two intellectual worlds had been kept apart by the waters of the Mediterranean. Awareness of the differences between the Christianity of Rome and that of Africa was slow to develop. Now, as refugees streamed into Carthage from Rome, the two traditions were abruptly brought together with explosive effect. The beginning of the famous Pelagian Controversy dates from this moment. It is to the double crisis associated with the renunciation of Melania the Younger and Pinianus (in around 406) and with the opening phases of the Pelagian Controversy (between 411 and 414) that we must now turn.

PART III

An Age of Crisis

"The Eye of a Needle" and "The Treasure of the Soul"

Renunciation, Nobility, and the Sack of Rome,

405–413

"Through a very narrow crack": Melania and Pinianus, 405–8

What is commonly known to us as the Pelagian Controversy has often been treated as a theological event involving a fundamental clash of ideas between Augustine of Hippo and the followers of Pelagius. In these two chapters, however, we will look at the controversy from a different angle. The Pelagian Controversy was also an incident in the history of the Christian aristocracy of Rome. It coincided with a crisis of wealth within this aristocracy, occurring at a time when the Gothic invasion of Italy and the subsequent sack of Rome in 410 ensured that Christian debates on wealth, renunciation, and nobility took place in an atmosphere tinged with a sense of public peril. This chapter will sketch the development of the crisis. The next will examine one of its products—a strikingly radical critique of wealth written at this time by a follower of Pelagius.

Let us begin with a remarkable incident and its repercussions. In Rome in around 404–5, the possession of a vast family fortune had been sufficient to cause nightmares to a young Christian couple. Valerius Pinianus (then twenty-four) and his twenty-year-old wife, Melania the Younger (named after her grandmother, Melania the Elder, the patroness of Rufinus), had retired to their villa in the *suburbium* of Rome. Following the call of the ascetic life, they had begun to divest themselves of their fortune:

> One night [Melania said] we went to sleep, greatly upset, and we saw ourselves, both of us, passing through a very narrow crack in a wall. We were gripped with panic by the cramped space, so that it seemed as if we were about to die. When we came through the pain of that place, we found huge relief and joy unspeakable.[1]

The dream plainly referred to the words of Christ: *It is easier for a camel to go through the eye of a needle than for a rich man to enter into the Kingdom of Heaven* (Matt. 19:24). But this was a dream with no camel and no needle. Instead, the words of Christ were transformed into an experience of primal horror. The dream relived with terrible intensity the constriction of the rich. The narrow crack was not only the eye of a needle; it was an excruciatingly tight birth canal. Only through the abrupt and total renunciation of their riches could the young couple hope to be "reborn" and get to heaven.

We know of this dream from the exceptionally vivid *Life of Melania the Younger*, which has survived in two, closely related versions, one in Latin and one in Greek. It was originally written in Jerusalem by the priest Gerontius in 452–53—that is, over a decade after Melania's death in 439. It was based on memories of Melania, as she looked back thirty years later to events of the early 400s. The excitement of these events still lingered in her memory. It is a glimpse from a distant land of Rome in the last years of its magnificence.[2]

Wealth was central to the *Life of Melania the Younger*. Reading it, we find ourselves listening in to the truly wealthy as they mused on the nature of their own riches. What Melania remembered most vividly was her villa on the Mediterranean coast, either of Campania or of Sicily:

> She said [to Gerontius]: "We had an extraordinary piece of property, and in it stood a bath that surpassed any in worldly splendor. On one side of it was the sea, and on the other, a forest with diverse vegetation, in which roamed wild boar, male deer and does and other forms of wild life. From the pool, the bathers could see, on one side, ships sailing in the breeze, and, on the other, wild animals in the wood. The Devil ... set before me the multicolored marbles of the villa and its inestimable revenue. For the estate had sixty-two settlements on it [the Latin version adds: with four hundred rural slaves] built around the bath."[3]

In this villa, strange things happened:

> "And then, again," she said, "we had collected an untold mass of gold to send away to the poor and to the saints—45,000 gold coins in all. When I went into the reception hall [the apsed triclinium: the Latin has the more private inner "bedroom"], it seemed, through an illusion brought about by the inspiration of the Devil, that the entire house was made resplendent, as if on fire, through the sheer mass of shimmering coins."[4]

We are introduced to the life of the rich in all its details. For instance, the *Life of Melania* was explicit about the manner in which clothes worn by the young couple had acted as the blazon of their wealth. Renunciation of fine clothing was presented as having meant more to them than did the renunciation of sex. Melania told Gerontius of a conversation she had had with her husband. On his conversion, Pinianus had opted for a simple cloak of good Cilician cloth. Homespun and solid though it was, the Cilician robe was not "beat up" enough to satisfy Melania. She approached him tactfully, in a roundabout manner:

> "Tell me," she asked, "from the time when we began to carry out our promise to God, has your heart ever harbored a thought of lust towards me?"
>
> [To which Pinianus affirmed,] "From the time when we gave our word to God and entered on the chaste life, I have looked on you in the same way as I look on your holy mother Albina."

The trivial matter of sexual desire disposed of, Melania got to the main point—Pinianus's dress: "'Then be persuaded by me, as your spiritual mother and sister, and give up those Cilician clothes.'" From then on, writes Gerontius, Pinianus wore reach-me-downs from Antioch, made of undyed, coarse wool, each of which cost less than a *solidus*.[5] As for Melania herself, an extraordinary anecdote shows how she remembered herself as a young girl. Her memory was of a tender body, sheathed in splendor. The very contact of the embroidered panels on her silken robe, rendered stiff and heavy with gold thread, would raise a bruise on her delicate skin.[6] Over the decades, all this would change. The last glimpse we have of the couple is through the eyes of Peter the Iberian, a Georgian prince turned monk. Peter had heard of Pinianus as a man well-known in Jerusalem in the 420s for wearing nothing but a robe made up of "crushed straw, humble and worthless."[7]

Vivid though it is, the *Life of Melania the Younger* disappoints us on one crucial point. With the benefit of hindsight, it takes for granted the motives of Pinianus and Melania in doing what they did. The *Life* never explains why they made their great renunciation. In considering the motivations of the young couple we should bear in mind that they had come close to Paulinus of Nola through Melania's grandmother, Melania the Elder. Melania the Elder was a Spaniard and may well have been a relative of Therasia. Furthermore, Paulinus was also an enthusiastic supporter of Rufinus. These two figures—Rufinus the intellectual and Paulinus the former aristocrat—may have been the source of the radical ideas on which Pinianus and Melania acted. Each contributed in a different way.

Rufinus accompanied Pinianus when the young couple fled to Sicily in 410. He may have passed on to Pinianus his knowledge of the asceticism of the East, with its emphasis on the ideal of the absolute poverty of monks.[8] But the dramatic act of renunciation itself may have been prompted by Paulinus. Like the renunciation of Paulinus—but with greater drama—the renunciation of Pinianus and Melania was overshadowed by a sense of the coming of the end of the world. There was an apocalyptic strain in the worldview of Paulinus. This may seem paradoxical. His use of wealth at the shrine of Saint Felix seemed to radiate solidity.

But Paulinus built fast because he thought that he built under the shadow of the end of time. He was a man whose Christian piety was driven by an acute sense of the approach of the Last Judgment. As we saw, when he first came to Campania, Paulinus gave a basilica to the Christians of Fundi. It was the first basilica in Italy to show a scene of the Last Judgment in its apse. The mosaic was intended to warn the Christians of Fundi that the end was near.[9] When the senator Pammachius commemorated the death of his wife through lavish almsgiving, Paulinus wrote: "Rome, you would not need to fear those earnest threats of the *Apocalypse* if the entertainments presented by your senators were always such as this!"[10] Paulinus meant it. In the company of persons such as Paulinus, it was not impossible for young Romans such as Pinianus and Melania to think that to throw away their vast wealth might be a sacrifice that saved the great city from destruction. Or, if their conversion and renunciation of wealth did not save Rome, at least they would remove that wealth to heaven before Rome's destruction came.

We can only conjecture *why* Pinianus and Melania did what they did from 405 onward. But we do know *when* they did it. It could not have been at a worse time. The social and political state of Italy ensured that their action had a resonance far beyond what had been normal in more peaceful times. For, as we know, the Apocalypse did not come to Rome. But Alaric, the king of the Visigoths, did.

Rome under Siege: Pinianus, Melania, and the Senate, 408–10

Alaric did not act against Rome out of barbaric bloodlust. He had no wish to destroy Rome as the symbolic center of the Roman empire. He was like any other Roman general in a time of civil war. He headed an army that needed bonuses. He would raise the money that he needed through ransoms and through the systematic pillage of great cities. The spoils of Rome would make him the richest general in the empire.[11]

Having probed northern Italy a few years earlier, Alaric finally arrived outside Rome in November 408. Throughout the next year, he systematically bled Rome. At first, the Senate paid him ransom. They agreed to hand over 5,000 pounds of gold, 30,000 pounds of silver, and 5,000 pounds of precious, oriental pepper (the sign that Rome was still an unparalleled center of luxury).[12] Huge sums, larger than the dreamlike expenditures that great senators had laid out for the games, made their way to the Gothic camp.

Only in the following year did Alaric finally "sack" Rome. This meant, in effect, that he allowed his troops to enter Rome on August 24, 410, in order to clean out the city. Far from being a bloodbath, the Visigothic sack of Rome was a chillingly well-conducted act of spoliation. The gilded statues of the Forum vanished. Huge loads of cash along with gold and silver plate left the city when the

Visigoths marched out again only three days later. Their booty even included (among many other pickings) the great silver dome placed by Constantine over the baptismal basin adjoining the Lateran basilica—a ton of solid silver.[13] In 414, when Ataulph, the brother-in-law of Alaric, celebrated his marriage, he could afford to do it in Roman style:

> Along with other wedding gifts, Ataulph gave his bride fifty handsome youths dressed in silken clothes, each carrying in his hands two huge plat-ters of silver, one of which was full of gold and the other of priceless gems. These had come from Rome, having been taken as booty by the Goths in the sack of the city.[14]

Whether for Alaric, who lusted for it, or for Pinianus and Melania, who craved to be rid of it, great wealth such as only Rome could harbor was being shaken loose in these years. What the young couple did with their fortune was magnified by being set against the backdrop of unparalleled spoliations in north-ern Italy and then in Rome. Whole fortunes vanished at that time. In the atmo-sphere of mounting crisis that led up to the sack of 410, the decision of Pinianus and Melania to dispose of their wealth was bound to have a wide impact. It hap-pened at a moment when the upper-class residents of Rome could no longer tolerate eccentricity.

The young couple's decision was unexpected. But so was the nature of their fortune. Their fellow Romans had not been prepared for the accident of trans-mission by which two stupendous blocks of wealth, held by two well-known families of Rome, ended up in the hands of a young couple who had no heirs. As we saw in our last chapters, this was not a contingency to which ascetics were accustomed. In the 370s and 380s, the patterns of inheritance within rich Chris-tian families had been manipulated in such a way as to ensure that the ascetic renunciation of wealth and marriage by one member of the family did not affect the flow of property to other heirs.

With Pinianus and Melania things were different. Both were heirs to large inheritances. Converted in their teens to the ascetic life, they ended up after a few years of indecision determined not to have children.[15] Pinianus once told Gerontius that he had a yearly revenue of 120,000 *solidi*. Even if we allow for exaggeration and lack of precision in her later, ascetic biographers, this was the wealth of the super-rich. Through her grandmother, Melania the Elder, Melania the Younger was a member of a distinctive group of families whose wealth lay both in Spain and in Italy, as had the wealth of Paulinus and Therasia. The couple also had large estates in Sicily and Africa.[16] Marcella, Paula, and the other families around Jerome had nothing like this wealth.

Of the two, Pinianus's inheritance seems to have been the more beleaguered. The vast palace of the Valerii sprawled in old-fashioned grandeur across the top of the Caelian Hill. A bronze lamp found on the site showed Saint Peter at the tiller of the Ship of the Church, with an inscription that may refer to the baptism of Pinianus's father—"The Lord gives the Law to Valerius Severus."[17] But Valerius Severus had died young, leaving Pinianus and his brother (also called Severus) vulnerable. They were minors who stood in need of protection. It was Symmachus (now in his sixties) who intervened to protect the heirs of a fellow senator. He wrote to the Head of the Treasury that he should shield the sons of Severus: "for unless they enjoy the help of good governors, they will fall victim to spoliation and injustice."[18] Symmachus's concern for the finances of his peers was genuine. What he could not have foreseen (and did not live to see) was that the young Pinianus would despoil himself in an act of self-proscription quite as drastic as that performed by Paulinus of Nola ten years previously.

Altogether, the young couple represented an alliance of vast wealth with eccentricity not usually encountered even in late Roman Rome. As they were not yet of age, they depended on the good will of their peers and on the support of the imperial authorities to carry out their resolve. For that reason their renunciation immediately became a public matter, as would not have been the case with ascetics whose conversion had taken place (as had that of Paulinus) when they were fully grown up.

Their first mistake was to start on the divestment of their properties in the wrong place. In around 408, they began to sell up their estates in the *suburbium* of Rome. As we have seen, the *suburbium* was prime land. It was devoted to intensive agriculture for an urban market. For this reason, it was a land of slaves. Pinianus and Melania instantly manumitted eight thousand slaves. This measure was high-handed and extremely ill-advised. Far from being overjoyed, the remaining slaves refused their freedom. Those who remained tied to properties the couple intended to sell were equally outraged. They did not wish to be handed over to new owners. Pinianus's brother Severus had to intervene. He offered to buy up the remaining slaves at a cut price. The *Life of Melania* said that he had been prompted to do this by the Devil. In fact, Severus may well have been attempting to bring some order to the area by showing that he did not intend to allow long-established dependents of the family to be cut loose in this brutal fashion.[19]

Severus did the right thing to intervene in this way. Loss of control over the agrarian workforce was a serious matter. As we saw in our first chapter, the super-rich had always been absentee landowners on a massive scale; they felt little responsibility toward their dependents. Distance and the complex administrative systems needed to extract and pass on rents attenuated their presence on the land. An entire hierarchy of little lords stood between the super-rich and their slaves and tenants. Christian renunciation of the dramatic sort practiced by Pinianus and Melania simply carried this heartless system to its logical extreme. Through renunciation, absentee lords became something worse than absent. They vanished, leaving an entire region at a loss as to what would happen next. By suddenly manumitting their slaves and selling off their properties, the couple severed what little remained of the vertical bonds between slaves, tenants, and owners that had enabled late Roman landowners to run what had always been a cruel and coercive system.

Late Roman forms of landowning (with their scattered estates and thinly veiled forms of forced labor) had worked as long as the landowners maintained at least some presence on their estates through their agents. When this presence was suddenly withdrawn, through massive manumissions and sales to outsiders, the power of landowners over the land was as seriously weakened as if a barbarian invasion had passed through the countryside. Nobody knew what might happen next.

As for the slaves of Pinianus and Melania, they protested for good reasons. A high-handed act of Christian piety would have thrown them on the labor market at a time when they needed, above all, not freedom but protection. A cruel system of forced labor, slavery at least offered the chance of being fed by one's owners in times of war. To free slaves in such numbers was to make plain that they could no longer count on being protected in any way by their masters. Subsequent events proved the slaves right. Only a little later, in 409, crowds of slaves streamed out of Rome to join the army of Alaric as it approached Rome. These slaves may have been barbarian prisoners of war, many of whom were Goths. They followed a "freedom trail" to the Gothic camp. But they may also have been Roman household slaves who had been brutally cut loose. They were freed and told to leave so that their masters would not have to feed them during the impending siege.[20]

The stability of the intensely cultivated countryside around Rome had always been a major preoccupation of the resident nobility. They had feared runaway slaves and brigands quite as much as they feared barbarians. But brigands and runaway slaves had tended to head for the hills of Samnium and Lucania (the modern Basilicata). Now the actions of Pinianus and Melania in the *suburbium* brought large numbers of resentful slaves and dependent workers cut loose from their former masters up to the very walls of the city.[21]

Faced by the revolt of their slaves and by the opposition of their relatives to the sale of family property, the young couple appealed directly to the imperial court. In early 408 Melania went straight to Serena, the older first cousin of the emperor Honorius and the wife of the generalissimo, Stilicho. At that time Stilicho was the power behind the throne.[22] Serena was residing in Rome. Melania asked Serena to make sure that the sale of her property went through without delay. Serena solved the problem by obtaining an imperial edict that placed the couple's estates under a form of "positive proscription." The edict ruled that the estates of Pinianus and Melania were considered, technically, to have been confiscated by the emperor. They became imperial property that could be sold off in public auctions. The governors, official staffs, and town councils of every province were made responsible for this sale. But the money thus raised would go to Pinianus and Melania, not to the imperial fisc.[23]

By means of this fiction, the wealth of Pinianus and Melania was made to stand out as special, protected wealth. Technically, it belonged to the "divine" properties of the emperor. But it was also viewed as belonging to a yet greater Emperor. It was property given to Christ for His poor. The fact that it had been sold in fulfillment of Christ's command—*Go, sell all that you possess, and give to the poor* (Matt. 19:21)—sheathed it with inviolability. Serena, Pinianus, and Melania claimed that to interfere with the disposal of wealth dedicated in this manner to the poor was "to rob the altars of God."[24]

Whose wealth was holy and whose wealth was not was still a hotly contested matter in Rome. When the generalissimo Stilicho fell, at the end of 408 (blamed for his disastrous mishandling of Alaric), Serena was condemned to death by the Senate.[25] She was strangled. Pagans said that this death was due to the vengeance of the gods. Ten years previously, Serena had reached out and snatched the votive necklace that still hung around the neck of the great statue of the Mother of the Gods. She put the necklace around her own neck.

> And when an old lady, the last of the Vestal Virgins, reproached her to her face for such impiety, she abused her roundly and told her attendants to drive her away.[26]

There were many who believed that it was the fatal desecration of the goddess's necklace that drew the noose around Serena's neck. To pagans, quite as much as to Christians, some wealth was a lot holier than others. God or the gods stood by to avenge those who attempted to divert it to other ends.

Many members of the Senate may still have regretted the spoliation of the temples: this had been true sacred wealth to them. They certainly had little sympathy for the novel fiction that wealth could be made sacred and untouchable through being kept for the poor. They needed the wealth of Pinianus and Melania to save the city. In the winter of 408–9 Alaric blockaded Rome. The Roman people began to starve. In the Circus Maximus they chanted to the prefect: "*Pone pretium carni humanae*: Go, fix the price of human flesh."[27]

In order to survive, the Senate had to tax its own members. Faced with this unprecedented emergency, the factionalism of the upper nobility exploded. Noble families proved notably selfish. The family of the Anicii (represented by the sons of Petronius Probus and by his widow, Faltonia Proba) were said by their enemies to have blocked all schemes for a fair assessment. They did so "because they controlled virtually all the city's wealth."[28]

Because Pinianus and Melania had been tarnished by their association with Serena and Stilicho, their wealth seemed easier game than that of the still-powerful Anicii.[29] In early 409, the Prefect of the City, Pompeianus, summoned an early morning meeting of the Senate. He proposed that the properties of Pinianus and Melania be confiscated. They would contribute "to the resources of the Roman state." Then he went in procession to make this decision public from his official throne (probably close by in the Forum): "Suddenly a riot of the people flared up because of the shortage of bread.... He was dragged from his seat and stoned to death in full sight of the whole city."[30] This was the only time in a century of imagined perils that a Prefect of the City had actually been lynched. This gruesome act of violence (told with relish by Gerontius) freed the young couple. At last, their wealth was their own to throw away.

"What city or country did not have a share of their good deeds?": The Dispersal of a Fortune, 410–17

Once they found themselves free to dispose of their wealth, Pinianus and Melania proved to be less arbitrary and lightheaded in the distribution of their fortune than their ascetic biographers suggest and than many modern scholars assume. Their renunciation of wealth was not an aimless bonfire of the vanities.[31] It marked the entry into the politics of the church of a very wealthy couple determined to fund good causes of their own choosing.

Their gifts were extensive. As Gerontius wrote: "What city or country did not have a share of their good deeds?"[32] The principal beneficiaries of these good deeds were the monks, not the poor. It was the "holy poor"—the *poor among the saints* whose right to financial support Jerome had defended with such vehemence only a few years earlier (in 406)—who received cash gifts of thousands of *solidi*: 35,000 *solidi* went to the monasteries of the East and only 10,000 to those of the West. A further 10,000 went to monks established on offshore islands in the Mediterranean. Innumerable little spurs of karst and lava, pushed up by the tectonic plates of Europe and Africa, these islands had been places of grim exile in classical times. Now, due to the support of the wealthy (who bought up whole islands for the purpose), offshore islands became the potential moon stations of a new, pan-Mediterranean monasticism. Along the coast of Dalmatia alone there are nine hundred little islands. Not all were mere rocks for shivering hermits. Some offshore islands (such as Muline/Ugljan, off the northern coast of Croatia) were the sites of substantial villas, where a monasticism based on aristocratic notions of *otium* could easily develop, much as it had developed off the coast of Italy (as we saw, at Capraria) and as it would soon develop at Lérins, off the coast of southern Gaul.[33]

These subsidies were not indiscriminate. The giving of Pinianus and Melania was as focused as that of Melania the Elder had been. Just as Melania the Elder had intervened (over thirty years previously) to strengthen the resistance of the Nicene party among the monasteries of Egypt, so Melania the Younger lavished money on the supporters of John Chrysostom, the contentious bishop of Constantinople. These embittered dissidents had been scattered as exiles throughout the eastern empire after their charismatic leader had been deposed in 404. By giving to the "Johannites"—the party of the supporters of John Chrysostom—Pinianus and Melania helped keep an ecclesiastical faction alive until its triumphal return to Constantinople in the last years of Melania's life.[34]

Last but not least, their luxury itself was consecrated. It became votive wealth. The silverware and silken robes of Melania were donated to churches. The passing of secular opulence into the opulence of churches through such gifts was a privileged moment in the alchemy of wealth. As with the shimmering buildings of Paulinus at Cimitile, everyone could see, with satisfying precision, exactly how *treasure on earth* became *treasure in heaven*[35] in the form of the opulent veils and silverware donated to the churches.

As we will see, in a subsequent chapter, their flight from Rome was by no means the end of the story for Pinianus and Melania. The couple fled to Sicily and from there to Africa, where the economic impact of their presence proved to be considerable. Only in 417 did they finally arrive in Jerusalem. Obsessed by the imagined poverty of the first Christians, they put themselves on the poor roll of the church of Jerusalem. This was by no means because they had run out of money.[36] Within a few years they were able to distribute large sums to the monks of Egypt.[37] They would later sponsor the construction of a series of buildings on the Mount of Olives.[38] Rather, their enrollment as members of the "poor of the church" was a poignant attempt on their part to relive, in their own times, the imagined life of the Apostolic Community of Jerusalem, where all Christians were thought to have lived in poverty, fed from the common fund. Settled in the Holy Places, the lives of these two former members of the super-rich were absorbed into the great myth of the primal poverty of the Early Christians.

From Rome to Carthage: Anician Ladies in Exile, 410–13

Alaric had created the crisis that had made the renunciation of Pinianus and Melania a matter of public urgency. He was also unwittingly responsible for the Pelagian Controversy. The flight from Rome of so many leading residents of Rome, along with their clients and spiritual mentors, brought about a situation that in more peaceful times would never have occurred. Let us see how this happened.

Part of the Roman aristocracy withdrew to Carthage. It was a natural choice. Protected by the sea and close to the huge estates they owned in the Medjerda valley and on the plateau of Numidia, Carthage could be for them a second Rome in Africa. Nobody knew how long they would have to stay in Africa. It was quite possible, in the alarming months of the winter of 410 and the spring of 411, that Carthage might emerge as the sole remaining bastion of the western empire, as barbarian armies marched unopposed throughout the provinces of the northern Mediterranean. If that happened, the refugees would soon cease to be passing strangers. They would become a heavy presence on the land and in the local churches.

The aristocracy brought their mentors with them. This meant that, after 410, the upholders of forms of Christianity that seemed quite natural in Rome found themselves in a foreign land. At Carthage they were brought face-to-face with the African clergy. From the African point of view, a disquieting sense of "otherness" hovered around the views of many of the most vocal Christian intellectuals who had come from Rome. It was from this growing sense of otherness—as Christian thinkers fostered in one great urban tradition brushed against the accepted wisdom of another—that what we call the Pelagian Controversy exploded.[39]

To understand how this could be so, we must change perspective slightly. So far we have followed two young noble persons in the act of disposing of their fortune, as recorded in the gripping narrative of Gerontius's *Life of Melania the Younger*. But, as we saw in our last chapter, noble Christians had not only been encouraged to throw away their wealth. They had also been urged to use it as patrons of intellectual endeavors. Noble patrons expected their protégés to serve them as mentors—like the house doctors and house philosophers of earlier times. In return, they would support their protégés. They would make them well-known and protect them against the envy of their rivals. In Christian times, this meant that they would stand between their protégés and accusations of heresy. In their role of patrons of Christian scholars and Christian spiritual guides, great lay families considered themselves to be as much the judges of the limits of orthodoxy in their region as were the bishops and clergy. The protection Melania the Elder and her friends and relatives extended to Rufinus showed the extent to which Christian intellectual activity in Rome remained rooted in the *domus*—in the town houses of the wealthy and in the patronage the owners of these houses exercised—quite as much as in the churches.[40]

The position of the Christian nobility as the patrons of spiritual guides explains an event that seems surprising to those who, like ourselves, know about the eventual course of the Pelagian Controversy. In the years immediately after 410, the greatest Christian family of all—the Anician family of Petronius Probus himself—turned to the British monk Pelagius (soon to become notorious as the opponent of Saint Augustine) for spiritual advice.[41] They did this because Pelagius had established himself in Rome as a spiritual mentor with a style all his own.

Pelagius may have come to Rome from southern Britain in around 390. He had made a reputation for himself as a commentator on the *Epistles* of Saint Paul and as an ardent proponent of the perfect life. It was his mission "to set alight and to stir up frozen souls, made sluggish and inert, by means of Christian exhortations."[42]

There was nothing lukewarm or even particularly "liberal"—in a cozy modern sense—about Pelagius. He remained a layperson and shied away from the use of the originally Greek word "monk" (the "m-word," which Jerome had brandished with gusto on every occasion so as to shock and thrill his readers):

> I want you to be called a Christian, not a monk, and to possess the virtue of your own personal claim to praise rather than a foreign name which is bestowed to no purpose by us Latins.[43]

Yet, despite this disclaimer, Pelagius was always regarded by others as a "servant of God." He had a clear ascetic agenda. It was because of this agenda that Pelagius was approached, in around 412–13, by the widow of Petronius Probus—Anicia Faltonia Proba—and by Proba's daughter-in-law—Anicia Juliana, the recent widow of the son of Probus, Olybrius, who had been consul in 395—to write a letter of praise and advice. The letter was written to celebrate the taking of the veil by Probus's granddaughter—Demetrias.[44] The invitation to write such a letter had been a tribute to Pelagius's gift for ascetic exhortation.

Because of the disruption caused by the sack of Alaric, the veiling of Demetrias did not take place in Rome but in Carthage. The *velatio*—the solemn bestowal of the veil on Demetrias by Aurelius, bishop of Carthage—was intended to be a fully public ceremony. The giving of the veil by the paterfamilias had been part of the Roman marriage ceremony. Hence the bestowal of the veil on Demetrias by Aurelius, as a bishop and so as a spiritual father, highlighted the occasion. This was no private vow; it was the spiritual marriage of a top aristocrat to Christ. The marriage took place in the cathedral church of Carthage. The amount of publicity the event received resembled that which surrounded the great games that marked the debut of a senator of Rome. Indeed, the ceremony of the games was echoed even in small details. Gifts were distributed to bishops, much as Symmachus had distributed ivory diptychs and little silver baskets among his peers on the occasion of his son's games as praetor. As bishop of Hippo, Augustine received one such present. He thanked Proba and Juliana with studied delight:

> What words could express, what herald could be worthy of such news, to make plain how incomparably more glorious and fruitful it is that Christ should have virgins of the blood of the Anicii, than that the world should have consuls?[45]

At the time, the Anicii needed a grand ceremony. They had been blamed for refusing to part with their vast wealth to save Rome. Later legend held Proba herself responsible for opening the Salarian Gate (close to the palace of the Anicii on the Pincian Hill) so as to let in the Visigoths of Alaric.[46] She and her retinue appear to have been escorted safely out of Rome. By contrast, Jerome claimed that his friend Marcella had been caught in her palace on the Aventine Hill and that she had eventually died from the beatings she received from Visigoths in search of treasure.[47] The very safety of the Anician ladies suggested that they had struck a deal with the barbarians. As a result, Proba and her family may well have arrived in Carthage under suspicion of treason. Heraclianus, the count of Africa, claimed at that time to be an ardent imperial loyalist. It gave him an excuse to shake down Proba and her retinue in the name of the distant emperor Honorius, who had retreated to Ravenna.[48]

But uncomfortable though their arrival had been, for the moment Carthage—and not Rome—was the only place where the Anicians could hope to shine. They chose to shine as loyal members of the church—through their womenfolk. Demetrias may even have been saved by her vow of virginity from a *mésalliance*. Their reputation shattered by recent events in Rome, the Anician ladies may have been under pressure to recoup their finances and to gain protection in a hostile land through marrying downward into a rich provincial family.[49] It was also a time to keep the family patrimony intact. By becoming a consecrated virgin, Demetrias stepped out of the marriage market and saved her family the expense of providing a dowry.[50]

Characteristically, all these were scenarios alluded to by Jerome, who had also been approached to write a letter to Demetrias. Jerome's letter showed the old satirist's gift for conjuring up the imagined workings of a noble family. We do not have to believe him. But, given the situation of the Anicii at this time, the scenarios to which Jerome referred are credible. Equally credible was Jerome's evocation of the supernatural significance of the ceremony. In dangerous times, the Anicii could hope for the spiritual protection afforded (as in the recent days of the Vestals of Rome) by the presence their midst of a "votive" virgin taken from their own family.[51]

"Spiritual riches no one can give you other than yourself": Pelagius and Demetrias, 413

Pelagius received his invitation to write for Demetrias when he was already far from Rome and Carthage, in Jerusalem. The Anician ladies paired him with Jerome, the other Latin luminary of the Holy Places. For them, Jerome and Pelagius were two great ascetics, placed as it were on the panel of experts summoned to congratulate and to advise Demetrias.

Pelagius's letter was utterly distinctive. It was not the letter of a monastic enfant terrible, such as Jerome wrote. Jerome had included innuendoes of family pressure first placed on Demetrias to accept a husband. He had conjured up the moment when Demetrias had resisted these pressures and when the heavy marriage gifts (the equivalent of the casket of Projecta and the other items of the Esquiline Treasure) were stowed away for good.

Pelagius's letter contained none of these titillating bedroom dramas. Rather, it was the letter of a skilled teacher. He treated Demetrias as a beginning student. He assured her that she possessed the innate gifts necessary to succeed. Then he told her how to succeed.[52] Altogether, the *Letter to Demetrias* was a measured work, which proposed a measured style of life. The great connoisseur of Latin monasticism Adalbert de Vogüé has detected in Pelagius's *Letter to Demetrias* turns of phrase and recommended practices that look straight forward to the *Rule of Saint Benedict*.[53]

But the *Letter to Demetrias* was also a manifesto. In it, Pelagius made plain to an audience of admirers, now gathered in Carthage as they had once been gathered in Rome, the theological principles that underlay his own, distinctive style of spiritual guidance. An unmistakable and challenging view of the human person (the fruit of decades of commentary, writing, and debate in Rome) lay at the heart of his message.

Human nature was sound. It could take the strain of an exacting ascetic education:

> Whenever I have to speak on the subject of moral instruction and the conduct of a holy life, it is my practice first to demonstrate the power and quality of human nature and to show what it is capable of achieving.[54]
>
> First, then, you ought to measure the good of human nature by reference to its Creator.... If it is He who has made all things *exceeding good*, how much more excellent do you suppose He has made humanity itself.[55]

The human mind had always been taught by its own nature—by a "natural law" implanted in the human conscience—to pursue the right. The moral heroism even of pagans made this clear: "even without God, we humans show that we have been made by God."[56] Job, for instance, was one such upright pagan. Taught by nature alone, he had been "a man of the Gospel before the Gospels. He has taught us how great is the treasure of the soul."[57]

The only problem, then, Demetrias had to face was how to ensure that the clear directives of the mind were translated into action. It was here that Pelagius sought to make his message more than clear. His life's work was at stake on this issue.

In Pelagius's opinion, there was no element in the human person and no force within the universe itself that made it impossible for a serious Christian to carry out what his or her conscience demanded. The moral universe, as created by God, was made up of free wills alone. Human beings might use this freedom to do terrible evil. But they acted as totally free agents. There was no heart of darkness in human nature, just as there was no heart of darkness in the universe. No innate force existed that might resist, much less control, the will. To think that such a force existed was to think like a Manichee. Only the ignorant, the inert, or the blasphemous conjured up such imagined forces, so as to give Christians an excuse for not fulfilling the law of God: "Only those who do not want to change their lives, persuade themselves that they are up against 'human nature' itself."[58]

Holiness came from the human will alone. Demetrias did not need to wait to receive the grace of God to realize her spiritual ambitions. Pelagius made clear that he thought it was profoundly wrong to talk of the "grace of God" as if it came as a totally new and unexpected gift from God, given "out of the blue" as it were. To treat grace in this way, as if it were a force that came from outside the self, was to do no more than objectify one's own inertia:

> we languish in ignorance, due to our own sloth and idleness ... struck with amazement, we come to think that sanctity is conferred upon us from some outside source.[59]

By contrast to this affectation of passivity, Demetrias was urged to remember her inner resources. She must learn to draw upon her own true wealth.

> Everyone realizes that your physical nobility and your material wealth belong to your family ... but spiritual riches no one can give you other than yourself.... Spiritual riches can not be there, unless they come from you alone.[60]

This proved to be a fatal sentence for Pelagius. It appeared to imply that God gave nothing to Demetrias. She already had all the spiritual riches she needed to live a perfect life. Over four years later, Augustine and Alypius reminded Anicia Juliana of this passage. In a joint letter written to Juliana in late 417–18, after she had returned to Rome, they warned her:

> To write, "these goods [wealth and nobility] can not be true goods" ... is straightforward, solid food. But what he wrote, [that spiritual riches] "come from you alone": that is poison.[61]

The head of a great *domus*, Juliana was unimpressed by their protests. The two African bishops received a distinctly chilly answer. She assured them that her *domuncula*—her "dear little house"—had never harbored heresy. No breath of suspicion had ever touched a member of the Anicii. In effect, she told Augustine and Alypius to mind their own business. The original of Pelagius's letter remained with the Anician family and was plainly read with approval.[62]

"Let all that dignity ... be transferred": Pelagius and Nobility

Juliana had no reason to be disturbed by Pelagius. For, in the *Letter to Demetrias*, he had implicitly validated the nobility of her family. He derived the prospective sanctity of Demetrias directly from her Anician descent: the one led to the other. As Jean-Marie Salamito has acutely observed, this aspect of the *Letter to Demetrias* involved a maneuver that was more audacious than was usual among late Roman Christian writers. In their relations with the Anicii, as with other nobles, Augustine and Jerome had been prepared to praise the noble origins of their correspondents. But they treated this as mere "worldly" nobility, which the true Christian should strive to forget. Normal nobility stood in sharp opposition to the true nobility of the soul. Thus, Augustine wrote to Juliana in 413 that the Anicii had provided "the world" with consuls; but Christ received virgins "in a manner incomparably more glorious and fruitful." There was no hint, in this flattery, that producing consuls might in any way contribute to producing holy virgins. The one nobility did not lead naturally to the other in such a way that noble birth in and of itself helped guarantee nobility of spirit.[63]

With Pelagius, this was not the case. He urged Demetrias not to forget who she had been. On the contrary:

> Let all that dignity which you derive from your famous family and the illustrious honor of the Anician blood be transferred to the soul; let that person be counted famous, lofty and noble, who guards that nobility, keeps it intact and thinks it demeaning to be a slave to vice.[64]

As Salamito has pointed out, such passages implied a causal link between Christian perfection and noble birth.[65] For Pelagius, earthly nobility was not the antithesis to Christian nobility: the one could lead directly to the other. Demetrias had transferred her excellence; she had not left it behind. Pelagius expected her to draw on a sense of noblesse oblige that was as secure (and as much an inseparable part of herself) as were the inalienable spiritual riches of her mind.

Altogether, readers of Pelagius's *Letter to Demetrias* could not have avoided noticing in it a clear echo, in the spiritual realm, of that high sense of autonomy that had always distinguished the inner circle of the *nobiles* of Rome. As we saw when we discussed the social world of Symmachus, theirs was a nobility conferred by nobility. It was not a nobility that depended on the grace and favor of an emperor. It had not dropped upon them (as it did upon mere provincials, such as Ausonius) as if from heaven itself. It was fully theirs, rooted in their nature, as unshakable and as utterly autonomous as was the "natural nobility" of the soul upheld by Pelagius.

We will have occasion, in a further chapter, to examine in greater detail what this aspect of Pelagius's message meant to Augustine and to the clergy of Africa, and why they decided to oppose it with such vigor. To the Roman refugees in Carthage in 413, however, it meant one thing. Shaken by the sack of Rome, the Anicii had maintained their innate nobility. Demetrias had not abandoned all trace of her noble birth through dispossession and headlong flight to foreign lands—as her peers, Pinianus and Melania the Younger, were intent on doing. Demetrias, indeed, had no intention of vanishing to the East. She returned quickly to Rome with her family as soon as peace was restored. Like Melania the Younger, she died as an old lady, in the 450s. But she had not withdrawn into a cell in the Holy Land. Rather, she continued to live (as Pinianus and Melania had once done) in the *suburbium* of Rome. She was buried in a shrine dedicated to Saint Stephen, which she had built into her large villa on the Via Latina, three miles out of Rome. Nor, as far as we can see, did she turn this villa into a convent. It remained a noble *domus*. Written in large monumental lettering, her epitaph described her as

Demetrias Amnia Virgo.[66]

(Demetrias the virgin of the Anician race.)

Demetrias still represented (in the age of Atilla the Hun) a fragment of a stable world.

In 413 the Anicii had received from Pelagius a heightened sense of their own nobility at a time of crisis. Other followers of Pelagius, however, would treat the rich less kindly. Let us turn to the remarkable anonymous author of the Pelagian *De divitiis*—the vehement treatise *On Riches*, which was written around 410 and became known to Augustine in Africa around 414.

CHAPTER 19

Tolle divitem: Take away the rich

The Pelagian Criticism of Wealth

"The sword of the free will": Pelagius, Habit, and the Social Dimensions of Wealth

Pelagius's *Letter to Demetrias* was a celebratory manifesto, written for a very special aristocratic occasion. Concentrated on the convergence in the young virgin Demetrias of nobility of birth with a "natural" nobility of the mind, it shunned the issue of the huge wealth of her family. Altogether, on the issue of wealth Pelagius tended to be thoroughly conventional. A typical mentor writing for well-to-do disciples, he stressed un-wealth, not poverty. A teacher should be above money. His students, like the "saints" addressed in the *Epistles* of Saint Paul, should avoid snobbery and undue concern with petty social distinctions. It was the morality of an aristocratic philosophical counterculture, of which we have already seen many examples among the study groups of late antiquity.[1]

But there was one theme on which Pelagius's thought had taken on a sharper profile than was usual. That was his notion of habit. Committed to a view of the absolute freedom of the will, Pelagius explained the human sense of difficulty in fulfilling the commands of God by stressing the cumulative resistance to the good created by human custom. No inert or malign force of nature cramped the will. But nevertheless, when confronted by God's challenge to do good, Christians, despite their possession of free will, found themselves cramped by their own past—by the slow piling up of bad habits in the self, derived from previous, free acts of the will.

> Nor is there any reason why it is made difficult for us to do good other than the fact that a long habit of doing wrong has infected us since childhood and corrupted us little by little over many years and ever after holds

us in bondage ... so that it seems, somehow to have acquired the force of
nature.[2]

But not only was the individual held in the grip of his or her own past. Society
itself was also responsible for the bad habits that opposed the will. Society as a
whole was held in the grip of evil customs. These customs were the mute deposit
of past ages of willful sinning by individuals. Nonetheless, when faced by the
weight of social custom, Pelagius remained optimistic. Custom was not insuper-
able. What the free will had created, the free will could undo. Habit remained
external to the will. It was like rust that had come to form around the moving
parts of a machine. Pelagius would teach Demetrias how to file away that rust so
as to recover her natural freedom to do good.[3]

This view of custom had radical implications. Society might seem immobile,
but its immobility was only apparent. It was the result of the free actions of former days. The effects of these actions could be reversed; wealth did not have
to be seen as an irremovable feature of society. Rather, it could be treated as
nothing more than another bad habit inherited from the past. Like any other
bad habit, human beings could shake it off by an act of renunciation. Pelagius
wrote for those who were prepared, in the words of his *Letter to Demetrias*, to
wield "the sword of the free will" in cutting through the bonds that held them to
great wealth.[4]

Pelagius did not pursue this theme in his writings. But his view of habit provided a theoretical justification for the supreme willfulness of persons such as
Pinianus and Melania in forcing through the dispersion of their inheritance.
What the young couple had dared to do, Pelagian writers dared to think. They
wrote so as to exhort others to follow a course of radical ascetic renunciation.
Wealth was a bad habit. It was the result of innumerable free acts of avarice and
violence. A free act of renunciation would reverse that sinister process. Wealth
could drop off the rich like a great cake of rust.

Pelagius was surrounded by a fringe of followers who were often considerably
more radical than he was. Many were attached to noble houses and wrote for
noble patrons. They breathed the heady atmosphere of an ascetic movement in a
time of real crisis, when entire fortunes were being shaken by public calamities.
They had been present at moments of dramatic renunciation and self-imposed
exile. Followers of Pelagius had formed part of the entourage of Pinianus and
Melania as they fled from Italy to Sicily and from thence to Africa. They had been
armed by their teacher with a quite distinctive constellation of ideas, to which
the notions of freedom and habit were central. They looked back in anger at the
passing of an age of affluence that the sack of Rome appeared to have brought to
an end. Wealth was for one thing only—to be renounced.

"Flowers which bloom from crime": The Pelagian *De divitiis* and the Origins of Wealth

The most striking example of this streak of social thinking was the anonymous Pelagian treatise entitled *De divitiis*—*On Riches*. It was written some time between 408 and 414. Its author is a shadowy figure. He was first introduced to English-speaking scholarship in the 1960s by John Morris under the somewhat raffish name of the "Sicilian Briton." Morris presented the author as a refugee to Sicily from a Britain already in the grip of the social upheaval that (in Morris's opinion) had accompanied the withdrawal of the Roman armies from the province. Along with other Pelagian tracts, the *De divitiis* was supposed to have circulated in war-torn Britain as part of an ideology of revolution.[5]

In recent years, however, the exemplary study of Andreas Kessler has removed much of this imagined background. The "Sicilian Briton" has declined into the less colorful "Anonymous Roman."[6] He did not come from a Britain in the throes of revolution. Rather, he grew up in the world of the exuberantly rich in Rome and Sicily. Kessler points out that he was not interested in the redistribution of property. Almsgiving to the poor was notably absent from his concerns. It was the nature of wealth itself and the urgent need for its renunciation that preoccupied him. He did not envisage the reorganization of late Roman society as a whole.

What cannot be denied, however, is the sharp profile of the treatise itself. Scholars have reacted to the *De divitiis* in very different ways, depending on their ideological commitments. John Morris claimed that "the crisp argumentation ... is by any definition socialism."[7] Georges de Plinval (a sober exponent of the thought of Pelagius) was less impressed. For him, it represented "the first, methodical attempt to distort the thought on wealth of the Fathers of the Church."[8] To Jean-Marie Salamito, it was an exercise in "ascetic brinkmanship," startlingly different in tone from the measured convergence of nobility and spiritual excellence canvassed by Pelagius. It was a rant, not a contribution to social thought.[9]

These judgments tend to isolate the *De divitiis*. They ask both too much and too little of it. They look for a revolutionary program and tend to be disappointed when they find in it, on a first reading, no more than the usual array of catchwords employed in contemporary ascetic tracts. But we should look at the *De divitiis* against the background of late Roman denunciations of wealth as a whole. The recent, patient study of Santo Toscano has placed the *De divitiis* against that background. Toscano shows that the tract was characterized by an unusually spirited rearrangement of conventional arguments and by real knowledge of the contemporary world.[10]

It is this rearrangement of conventional arguments for a radical purpose that gives the author of the *De divitiis* a sharp profile. It rescues him from anonymity.

So far we have dealt with known authors (such as Ambrose, Augustine, and Paulinus of Nola) whose life and social context we can attempt to explore. Here we have something different. We do not even know the name of the author of the *De divitiis*. We can only have a rough idea of the date it was written and of the milieu from which he came. But we can see that the *De divitiis* was the treatise of a master disputant. The author's whole-hearted concentration on the issue of renunciation led him to scan the entire range of attitudes toward wealth that had been common to Christians and pagans in the ancient world (whose outlines we have seen in earlier chapters). He found that the common sense of wealth, which had been accepted by even the most daring writers, was inadequate. In the course of his argument, he dismissed an entire inherited conglomerate of notions that had made wealth seem tolerable in the Christian communities. He treated these notions as no more than special pleading in favor of the rich. His readers were to be left with no excuse for not taking the road through the narrow crack of total renunciation, which Paulinus of Nola, Pinianus, and Melania the Younger had taken.

First and foremost, we are dealing with a treatise deeply influenced by Pelagius's sharp sense of the autonomy of the will. For the author of the *De divitiis*, wealth had no existence outside the will. There was no such thing as simply "being" rich in an unproblematic manner. Wealth was the product of avarice, which was the *wish* to be rich. When, in his *First Letter to Timothy* (1 Tim. 6:9), Paul spoke of the rich as those "who wish to be rich," our author claimed that Paul had made clear that wealth was "located squarely in the will." And this was not simply a will to have more than one should have. It was a dire and tenacious will to have, *tout court*.[11]

If the will to have was evil in itself, then traditional restraints on wealth (Christian and non-Christian) were ineffective. Most exegetes of Paul, when faced by the *First Letter to Timothy*, had been content to fall back on the comfortable distinction between "good" wealth and "bad" wealth. This distinction drew attention to the good or bad drives of those who were already rich and to the good or bad uses to which this wealth could be put—whether for luxury or for sober living, for miserliness or for generosity. This attitude, in effect, put the wealth of the wealthy on parole. It urged the rich to be content with what they already had. It was only weakness of character on the part of the bad rich that led them on to avarice. Personal failings—sensuality, pride, and the lust for power—drove them to increase their wealth. Discourse on wealth was, in effect, not a discourse about society. It was a moral discourse about the impact on society of the personal vices to which the rich were most exposed—such as love of luxury, cruelty, and ambition.

For the author of the *De divitiis*, this was not so. Avarice was not luxury, nor was it sensuality, nor even the lust for power. These conventional sins of the bad rich were only secondary manifestations of a deeper and more sinister drive. Avarice was a pure product of the will. It was ensconced (as the will must be) in the very heart of the human person. Indeed, there was a frightening permanence and bodilessness about the drive to wealth. While sex might be satiated, avarice was not.[12]

Because it was a product of the human will, wealth had a history. And it was a grim one. Wealth in the present was based on an apparently endless regress of free acts of greed and power that reached back for thousands of years. The lush "flowers of wealth" pushed their roots deep into "a bed of crime."[13]

Here the author of the *De divitiis* proposed an unexpectedly radical version of the history of human society. We have seen (in the case of Ambrose) that a tradition of primitivism was deeply rooted in the Greek and Roman worlds. It had played an essential role in Ambrose's social thought. Ambrose believed, as did many others, that there had once been a Golden Age when an abundant nature had provided human beings with their needs. Only later was the Golden Age followed by the zero-sum game by which human beings had usurped the common earth through claiming parts of it as private property. This, in turn, had led to the present state of society—a society characterized by estate walls, locked storehouses, land grabbing, violence, and war.[14]

For many Christians, this Golden Age appeared to have lingered for millennia. Sulpicius Severus (whom we have already met as a friend of Paulinus of Nola) wrote in his *Chronicle* that the first human war had been the war between Abraham and the kings, in the valley of the Dead Sea. This war had occurred precisely 3,312 years after the creation of Adam.[15] In writing in this way, Sulpicius assumed that the history of the human race included millennia of social innocence, without property and without war. This was a comforting belief. If social innocence had been the norm among humans for so long, it might yet be recaptured.

The Golden Age might return in modern times, if only in a few outstanding individuals. Describing the ascetic regime of John the Baptist in the desert—where he fed on wild herbs and honey—Paulinus of Nola wrote of John as having lived as life had once been lived "in the first freshness of the human race."[16] John emerged from the desert as a living avatar of the Golden Age. Christians were expected to strive to bring back echoes of those more sober times in their social life. When, in around 406, Paulinus wrote an *Epithalamium* for the marriage of the young deacon Julian of Eclanum (of whom we will hear more in the course of the Pelagian Controversy), Paulinus urged Julian and his wife (the daughter of a bishop) to avoid the excesses of a fashionable marriage. They should opt instead for "the holy simplicity of our first ancestors."[17]

Altogether, the idea that a long stretch of "holy simplicity" had ended only recently (when seen against the full span of human time) was a fixed component in the social imagination of Christians in Rome. Most Christian Romans, however, did not imagine the Golden Age as a radical utopia. It was not an age of undifferentiated innocence, with no property and no social distinctions. Rather, what they usually imagined was a softer version of the present world, not unlike the softer, kinder version of contemporary society they hoped to find in the Christian churches. We can see this in the poetry of a remarkable figure from the highest ranks of the Christian aristocracy.

Faltonia Betitia Proba was the grandmother of Faltonia Proba. In the 350s she wrote a *Cento* on the life of Christ (composed from ingeniously chosen half verses of Vergil). She drew on the memorable description, in book 8 of the *Aeneid*, of the dire onset of the *discolor aetas*, of the "tarnished age" of avarice and war that had succeeded more innocent centuries:

> There came the craze of war, and greed.
> Justice made tracks as she withdrew from earth.[18]

Betitia Proba went on to describe the call of Christ to the Rich Young Man as a call to regain the Golden Age. Her poem did not report Christ's challenge to abandon all, still less the *follow Me* that would haunt the generation of Paulinus, Jerome, and Melania the Younger. Instead, in Proba's rendering of the Gospel incident, the spoiled richling was challenged to step back into the Golden Age. Proba did not present him as having been urged by Christ to become poor. Rather, he was told by Christ (in a series of echoes of Vergil) to behave like an aristocrat of a gentler age, when Good King Saturn had ruled in Italy. He was to be generous to his dependents and to use his power to protect the suffering.[19]

By contrast, the author of the *De divitiis* nurtured no such comfortable dreams. He was uninterested in the notion of a Golden Age and of the consequent emergence of property. He believed that as long as human beings had free wills, they had been capable of avarice and hence of accumulating wealth.[20] This was a remarkably demystified view. It had direct imaginative repercussions. It robbed the rich of an idealized past in which wealth had been innocent. There were no good rich men in the deep past to whom rich Christians could look as models that excused their own possession of wealth. For most rich Christians, the Patriarch Abraham had been the prime example of the good rich man: he had combined holiness with great wealth. The present-day rich assumed that if they used their wealth in the right way, they could be the Abrahams of their own times—generous, hospitable, and protectors of the weak. And, if they imitated Abraham in this respect, they could retain their wealth with an easy conscience.[21]

The author of the *De divitiis* denied this belief categorically. He insisted that Abraham had been an exception—almost a sport of nature. Abraham did not show that other rich men could be holy; he only showed that to be both rich and holy was an exception. The modern rich could not claim to be like him. Abraham had been loved by God because he had been unrepeatable. Abraham had used his will in a manner starkly different from what had already become the grim norm of humanity and what would remain the norm after his death up to modern times.

This view of Abraham implied an unusually disabused view of human history. Abraham had not been preceded by a long age of innocence, still less by other examples of good rich persons. All human time before Abraham had been occupied by tyrants and by men of power in a world whose social order had been created by the clash of human wills alone, acting in a purely human space left vacant by God.[22]

To contemporaries, this was a truly chilling conclusion. In the words of Boniface Ramsay: "This argument effectively removes wealth from the ambit of divine providence."[23] The author of the *De divitiis* did not think that wealth had been granted to some men by God through his providence so as to be used by them as stewards of His bounty. At best, God had reluctantly acceded to the creation of disparities of wealth much as He had condoned the proud gesture with which the people of Israel had set up a king, despite the warnings of the prophet Samuel.[24]

Put bluntly, God's providence played no part whatsoever in the existence of great wealth. Still less had God given great wealth to some so that they could offer it back to him as votive wealth. This was what Paulinus had claimed to do. He did not show a hint of disquiet about his own wealth, provided that he offered it to God by building the shimmering shrine of Saint Felix at Cimitile. The *De divitiis* could have been written as a rebuke to just such a person as Paulinus.

Tolle divitem et pauperem non invenies: Take away the rich and you will find no poor

Who, then, were the rich? In the first place, the author of the *De divitiis* asserted that no one could claim to be an *originarius dives*—rich from birth and, for that reason, innocent of avarice.[25] By this statement, he brushed aside the traditional distinction between family wealth and "new" wealth. Family wealth had tended to be treated as unproblematic wealth, wealth that had always been there. Such wealth was thought to be as stable as the land itself. As we saw in the case of Symmachus and Ausonius, wealth of this kind tended to be validated by a strong sense of heritage. It was guiltless wealth. Only new wealth, wealth that the wrong sort of rich had gained through violence and sharp dealing, was worthy of opprobrium. On the contrary, as the *De divitiis* pointed out, every inheritance had its own, dark history: "I was talking not so much of the possession of riches as of their source, since I think that they can hardly have been acquired without some injustice."[26]

To late Roman readers, this in itself was a platitude. There was a common proverb, cited on one occasion by Jerome, which stated that "a rich man is either a wicked man or the heir of a wicked man."[27] But it was the consequentiality of his answer, not the question itself, that distinguished the author of the *De divitiis*. He turned a much-repeated adage into an inexorable social law.

> "Riches are evil then," you will say. First discover what riches are.... The human race is divided into three classes: the rich, the poor, and those who have enough.... To be rich is to have more than is necessary; to be poor is not to have enough; and to have enough ... is to possess no more than is absolutely necessary.[28]

"To have enough"—to possess *sufficientia*—was the measure of the difference between wealth and poverty. And, for the author of the *De divitiis*, this measure had to be calibrated and maintained with more than usual strictness. In his view, the distribution of wealth and poverty in society was the result of an unforgiving zero-sum game. Those who went beyond the measure of sufficiency could do so only by taking from the poor. Excess in the few automatically led to dispossession in the many:

> Does it seem just to you then that one man should have an abundance of riches, over and above his needs, while another does not have enough even to supply his daily wants? That one man should relax in the enjoyment of his wealth, while another wastes away in poverty?[29]

As we saw in the case of Paulinus of Nola, the juxtaposition of rich and poor, of Dives and Lazarus, was a theme calculated to trouble the conscience of the Christian rich. Paulinus had solved the issue by insisting on the mystical *commercium*, the providential symbiosis, by which God had allowed the poor to cluster round the rich so that the rich could save their own souls by almsgiving. By contrast, the author of the *De divitiis* stripped the juxtaposition of rich and poor of any hint of providential purpose. Rich and poor were not just two groups, made eternally distant one from the other by the hidden will of God. Rather, wealth and poverty were causally interconnected. Whether they were aware of it or not, the rich had actively created the poor. For the rich had won the remorseless tug-of-war for limited resources, which took place to the benefit of the rich. Every time someone overstepped the divinely ordained line of mere sufficiency by becoming rich, others were pulled down into poverty.

Sufficientia was not a classical term.[30] It was taken, originally, from the book of Proverbs (30:8), where the Hebrew *lehem huqi* referred to the daily bread allotted to each person by the hand of God. It conjured up the ideal of contentment and gratitude to God for whatever wealth had already come one's way. It was a term that usually allowed a generous fudge factor in what counted as "sufficient" possessions. In the *De divitiis*, however, *sufficientia* was a polemical slogan. It traced, with unforgiving clarity, an economic poverty line below which the poor had been dragged by the very existence of the rich.

Tolle divitem et pauperem non invenies:
> Get rid of the rich and you will not find the poor. Let no man have more than he really needs, and everyone will have as much as they need, since the few who are rich are the reason for the many who are poor.[31]

We should not underestimate the sharpness of this view. Speaking of critics of the wealthy in the Hellenistic Age, the great Russian historian Mikhail Rostovtzeff (himself an exile from the Bolshevik regime) once observed: "For them, the rich were not, as for some of their modern successors, criminals, but fools."[32] Most Christian writers and preachers of late antiquity (even Ambrose) had been content to treat the rich as fools. They had misused in foolish ways the good wealth bestowed on them by God. The author of the *De divitiis* went one step further: for him, the rich were criminals. They were creatures of free will, and they had made society what it was by their free actions. This was a society starkly divided between rich and poor. The one had caused the other. The extent of the wealth of the rich spelled out with implacable precision the extent to which they had dispossessed the poor.

"Is this really *the wealth of their own hands?*": Wealth and Power

The argument of the *De divitiis* was pushed through with such rhetorical zest that many have doubted its seriousness and, hence, its relevance to contemporary conditions.[33] Yet there is a precision about the description of the rich in the *De divitiis* that rings true for a certain class and region. The rich of the *De divitiis* were not the rich of Ambrose. The rich of Ambrose were presented as archetypal owners of the land. They were monsters of the social imagination, whose profile derived from a long Roman tradition that had viewed with disquiet the growth of *latifundia* and the dispossession of the small farmer.

The *De divitiis* mentions in passing the greed of those who yearned for "boundless estates ... measureless spaces."[34] But the persons who truly angered him were not the great landowners but the *judices*—in the first instance, provincial governors acting as judges. They were the overbearing servants of the emperor. Their oppression of the poor was not linked to the growth of great estates but to the workings of the imperial judicial system. It was the relation between wealth and government power the Pelagian writings chose to denounce with unusual vehemence.

In this, the *De divitiis* was not alone. Other partisans of Pelagius wrote treatises that showed the same obsessive focus on the relation between wealth and administrative violence. The writer of the treatise *De vita christiana*—*On the Christian Life*—pointed out that many such persons had fallen victim, in his own days, to bloody revolts:

> Others again, who had unjustly executed and dispossessed a countless multitude of men were torn apart limb from limb and piece from piece, so that the number of their divided members was no smaller than the number of those they had caused to be killed.[35]

It is not at all surprising, given the vigor of such passages, that John Morris should have imagined that he had caught in them a distant echo of popular vengeance in a world turned upside down by the withdrawal of the Roman government from southern Britain. But similar events had happened in Rome (not least the unprecedented lynching of a Prefect of the City described in the *Life of Melania*). In this respect, we should remember the composite nature of the noble class in Rome. In the 410s (as in the 370s) not all nobles were like Symmachus or the Anicii. A very large number of them would have been new men who had risen to wealth through government service. It was they who produced the *judices* who were denounced, in the Pelagian writings, by authors who came from much the same class as they did.

Hence a division within the Pelagian movement. Nobles such as Demetrias and her mother, Juliana Anicia, might patronize Pelagius. He spoke to them in high terms of their capacity to draw upon an innate nobility of the soul that seemed to echo their own high opinion of themselves. But those who applied the ideas of Pelagius to social issues seem to have come from the lower layer of the nobility, which (as we have often had occasion to see) was a fertile breeding ground of mavericks. The *enfant terrible* of the Pelagian movement, Caelestius, was a "noble by birth" and, at the same time, a student of administrative law. Caelestius was almost the exact social equivalent of what Augustine's friend, the young Alypius, had once been—a notable making his way as a lawyer in Rome. One of the principal opponents of the Pelagians, Constantius, was a retired *vicarius*: he had been an administrative stand-in for the Praetorian Prefect (a high official, such as Alypius had served when he had been a legal adviser in Rome).[36]

Members of this class had no illusions as to the source of their own wealth. It was not immemorial acres; it was access to gold, gained by official power. Nor had the Roman congregations any illusions as to the wealth of the wealthier lay members of their church. Assembled in great basilicas, the People of God watched the wealthy every Sunday as they solemnly processed up the aisle to leave their offerings on special tables placed near the altar. The deacons would bring these offerings to the altar to be offered to God with a solemn prayer of thanks and blessing by the priest.[37] At that moment, in the Roman church and elsewhere, the names of those who brought donations would be read aloud to the acclamations of the congregation. We know of this practice from a remark of Jerome's. It is characteristic of the inveterate satirist that he should have added:

> But is this really *their own wealth* (*Proverbs* 13:5)? We see many who oppress their farmers, the poor and their clients—not to mention the violence of servants of the emperor [*militantes*—bureaucrats as well as soldiers] and governors, who despoil through the use of official power.... The deacon may read out aloud the names of those who bring offerings—"She has brought so much," "He has promised such and such a sum." They bask in the plaudits of the populace, while their conscience should torment them.[38]

By creating ceremonies that echoed in the churches the face-to-face civic encounter of the city's rich with "their" people in the circus, the bishops had unwittingly re-created the tradition of criticism that had always existed as a dark undercurrent to the dialogue between the rich man and his admirers. Wealth given to the people (whether to the shows or to the church) was only too often wealth that needed to be laundered.

The Old Testament notion that "wealth from rapine" must not be offered at the altar of God empowered Christian critics of the rich. In every city, recurrent ceremonies of offering and the creation of pious foundations (such as Paulinus's poorhouse at Cimitile or the hospital of Pammachius and Furia at Rome) provided a moment when local opinion might judge the Christian rich. The rich could always be criticized for offering wealth tainted by rapine. In the words of the Pelagian *De vita christiana*:

> These are not the sort of alms that God asks for.... It is better for you not to give alms at all than to cause a great number to be despoiled of money from which you put a roof over the heads of a few.[39]

The author of the *De divitiis* had no illusions as to the relation between wealth, power, and public cruelty. His portraits of the rich were even more memorable than were the cruelties of the great landowners conjured up by Saint Ambrose:

> Before your eyes human bodies ... battered with a scourge of lead or broken with cudgels or torn apart with claws or branded in the flames ... and you, the upholder of riches and of the sale of offices, recline without a care, resting on thick carpets piled high beneath you ... and entertain your guests with the tale of the man whom you have savagely tortured ... and lest anyone present ... be struck with horror at the story, you go on to claim, in doing this, that you are beholden to the laws.[40]

Christ before Pilate

Last but not least, in the Pelagian writings, the horror of a society dominated by the rich was thrown into high relief by the silent presence of Christ. It was not the poor nor the monk who was the living rebuke to the conscience of the rich—it was Christ Himself. True to Pelagius's emphasis on the power of example to move the will, Pelagian writings focused with unusual power on the humility of Christ.[41] In this, they reflected the sensibility of a post-Jerome generation. The ascetic notion of the utter poverty of Christ, which owed much to Jerome's fierce linking of the absolute poverty of Christ to the poverty of the monks, formed the foundation of the Pelagian critiques of the rich.

Times had changed. For Paulinus of Nola and others of his generation, the *abjectio*, the stepping down of God Himself from heaven to earth, had been abasement enough. As we saw in the case of Pinianus and Melania the Younger, this stepping down was mirrored in a drastic change of dress. But this was not an emptying out that totally destroyed the social person. The Christ of the Pelagians (like the Christ of Jerome) had stepped down even further. He was down and out in Rome. He was imagined, by Jerome, to linger quite literally among the poor who gathered at the steps of the great marbled palaces.[42]

The author of the *De divitiis* was less moved than was Jerome by pathos for the poor. What counted most for him was the stark contrast between poverty and worldly power. In His utter, silent depletion, Christ confronted the rich directly, as the exact opposite of their own existence, much as He had once stood before Pilate.

> So let us see if the rich man's way of life has any similarity with that of Christ. There is none that I can see…. The rich, with vainglorious and proud spirit … are accustomed to solicit earthly power and to take their seat upon the tribunal before which Christ was heard…. He stood humbly before that tribunal; you sit on the tribunal, above those who stand before you, perhaps about to judge a poor man…. He said that His kingdom was not of this world, but to you the glory connected with an earthly empire is so desirable that you procure power in it at vast expense or at the cost of unworthy and wearisome servitude and flattery.[43]

Altogether, the author of the *De divitiis* was categorical. When Christ had said that *It is easier for a camel to go through the eye of a needle than for a rich man to enter into the kingdom of heaven* (Matt. 19:24), he spoke of an outright impossibility. His words could not be palliated by allegory, by special pleading, or by ingenious textual emendation—unless, he added, the rich were to find a very large needle or a very small camel.[44] Only those who, like Pinianus and Melania, had squeezed through that agonizing crack in the wall by totally abandoning their property could hope to come out on the other side to the Kingdom of God.

This was a pamphlet calculated to send shock waves through the community of Christians both in Rome and in exile. As far as we know, Augustine never read the text of the *De divitiis*. But in 414 (that is, only a year after the arrival of Pelagius's *Letter to Demetrias* in Carthage) a certain Hilarius wrote from Syracuse to Augustine at Hippo. Hilarius listed five propositions "on which certain Christians in Syracuse are holding forth." One proposition said:

> A rich man who remains in his riches will not enter the Kingdom of God unless he sells all that he has: nor will those riches be of any use to him [in securing salvation] even if he uses them to fulfill the commandments [that is, for almsgiving].[45]

Augustine instantly associated these propositions with the opinions of Pelagius's more extreme followers. By 414 he and his colleagues had begun to take the measure of the spread of Pelagian ideas. Pelagianism—that is, an -ism made up of heretical ideas—had begun to take shape in their minds. They found themselves confronted with two distinctive statements, which summed up two different wings of the same movement—Pelagius's letter to Demetrias and the *De divitiis*, the Pelagian treatise *On Riches*. Both statements had been generated in Rome. Both had been provoked by the actions of leading members of Roman society—by the vocation and veiling of Demetrias and by the renunciation of Pinianus and Melania. Both had come to Augustine's doorstep as a result of the massive displacement of personnel caused by Alaric's sack of the city in 410. Both caused grave disquiet to Augustine and to the bishops of Africa.

This new challenge came to Augustine when he had already had fifteen years of experience as a bishop in Africa behind him. When we meet him now, in 414, we meet a different man from the priest, the newly ordained bishop and the advocate of monastic poverty of the 390s. Augustine was now an old man. He had entered his sixties. He had breathed the distinctive air of Africa for a long time. This was a province whose Christianity had taken on a particular form, hardened by a century of grassroots growth and by the bitter confrontation of two great local churches.

Africa was a different world from the Rome and Gaul where we have lingered in our most recent chapters. It was with his experience of Africa behind him that Augustine faced the new challenge that had been brought to him, almost by accident, by noble persons from across the sea. The Pelagian Controversy that began with this encounter was never a mere war of minds alone. It quickly became a clash between two Christian landscapes. For this reason, we must go back for at least a decade (to the early 400s) to follow Augustine as a pastor and preacher in Africa. Only by giving due weight to his day-to-day experiences in the churches of Africa can we appreciate the nature of Augustine's reaction both to Pelagius and to the disturbing views on wealth that had only recently been reported to him from Syracuse.

CHAPTER 20

❧

Augustine's Africa

People and Church

Horrendo et perseverantissimo clamoris fremitu: With a frightening
and persistent roar of acclamations

PINIANUS AND MELANIA AT HIPPO, 411 AD

For the next three chapters and for much of the fourth, we will find ourselves in
Africa. This means, of course, that we will return to Augustine. But we will not
return only to Augustine. We will find ourselves in an extensive and strange landscape in which Augustine, for all his prodigious output as a writer, was no more
than one figure among many. He was not necessarily the most important figure.
Indeed, as we shall see, many African Christians (perhaps, indeed, the majority)
regarded him as an unwelcome interloper who attempted to forward the claims
of his own church at the expense of a long-established form of local Christianity.
For Africa was not only a large and diverse province. It harbored the oldest and
most solidly established Christian landscape in the Latin West. No area outside
the great city of Rome could boast of so long a Christian past. And in no other
Latin region had the Christian past been so heavy with disagreements between
two nearly identical versions of the same Christian faith.

For this reason, we must look first at the overall landscape of Christian Africa
in order to understand the zest with which competing Christian communities
had poured their wealth into the creation of churches. As a result of this, the
African Christianity of the fourth century became the first grassroots Christian
movement to appear in the Latin West. In the following chapter we will examine
the manner in which Augustine preached on the themes of wealth and poverty
to boisterous communities. Then we will see the manner in which Augustine
placed the views that had been formed by such preaching in the path of the very
different attitudes toward wealth espoused by radical upholders of the cause of

Pelagius. The last of these chapters will cross the sea again from Africa. It will deal with the manner in which the African church secured the condemnation of Pelagius in Italy. It will then examine the implications of the victory of Augustine and his African colleagues for the relations between church and empire throughout the West in the generation before the imperial system set in place with such confidence by Constantine and his successors collapsed in the face of an unprecedented combination of civil war and barbarian invasion.

Roman Africa was as large as Italy. In the fourth century, much of it was more prosperous than Italy. But it was a world of its own. Africa was different. Romans always spoke of it as "an other sky"—as if it was a different hemisphere.[1] Roman refugees who arrived in Africa after the Gothic sack of Rome in 410 soon realized that they had come to a strange land. At the very end of 410, for instance, the noble Roman couple Pinianus and Melania the Younger together with Albina, the mother of Melania, arrived in Africa. They made straight for inland Numidia, where estates belonging to their families may well have existed for centuries. Outside Thagaste (Souk Ahras, Algeria), they owned one such enormous property.

> [The villa settlement] had a bath and employed many artisans who worked in gold, silver and bronze, along with two bishops, one of our [Catholic] faith and one of the [Donatist] heretics.[2]

This estate was given to the church of Thagaste, where (as we have seen) Augustine's friend Alypius had been bishop since 395. Viewed through the eyes of these great Romans, Thagaste seemed "small and exceedingly poor." Pinianus and Melania's estates in the area were believed to be larger than the entire territory controlled by the city. The pious couple set about to remedy the poverty of Alypius's church:

> She [Melania] adorned the church of this holy man [Alypius] with revenue as well as with offerings of both gold and silver treasure and valuable silk veils, so that this church which formerly had been so very poor now stirred up envy of Alypius on the part of the other bishops in that province.[3]

It looked as if Pinianus and Melania might turn the church of Thagaste into the Cimitile of Numidia.

Other Christian congregations in other cities were quick to react to this new influx of wealth. Intercity rivalry had always been the stuff of civic life in Africa. The constant striving to do better than one's neighbors had thrown up the spectacular buildings of an earlier age. The Christian communities wanted to do the same. They wanted larger basilicas, a better-paid clergy, more funds for poor relief. The best way to do this was to attract rich benefactors.

Thus, when Pinianus and Melania, led by Alypius, made their way down to the coast to visit Augustine at Hippo in the spring of 411, the Christian *populus*— Augustine's congregation at Hippo — was waiting for them. At a church service, Augustine and Alypius found themselves cornered by a determined crowd. The bishops stood on the slightly raised floor beneath the apse at the end of the church. The *populus* occupied the main body of the church. "With a frightening and persistent roar of acclamations" they demanded that Pinianus be made a priest at Hippo.[4] Augustine and his Roman visitors had no illusions as to why they did this. The congregation had acted "so as to retain among them a man of wealth who was known to despise money and to give it away freely."[5]

As we have seen, urban benefactors had long been subjected to similar pressures to show generosity to the *populus* of their cities. But this pressure had been brought to bear in vast open-air circuses and amphitheaters. By contrast, the basilica of Hippo may have measured 120 by 60 feet, with standing room for only a few hundred persons. In such an enclosed space, the zeal of the *populus* as it pressed forward toward the apse was terrifying. Alypius did not dare step down from the slightly raised floor for fear that he would be set upon by the crowd, who viewed him as the rival for Pinianus's money because he was bishop of Thagaste.[6]

In expressing themselves in this vehement manner, the Christian *populus* thought of itself as inspired by God. Their unanimous *clamor* was not a mere roar. It probably took the form of the rhythmic acclamations that accompanied the bringing of gifts up to the altar. This was the high point of the involvement of the laity with the solemn drama of the Mass. Hence the pressure put on Pinianus at this moment to accept the priesthood and to swear an oath not to leave the city. Pinianus's acceptance of these demands would have been seen as his Sunday offering. By giving in to the chants of the people, Pinianus would in effect have surrendered his vast wealth to the church of Hippo.

Twenty years previously, Augustine himself had been made priest at Hippo in the same high-handed manner. Paulinus of Nola also had been ordained a priest at Barcelona (on Christmas Day 394) "by the force of a [Christian] *plebs* suddenly inflamed [by God]." Pinianus was to be for the Christian people of Hippo what the Christian people of Barcelona had wished Paulinus to be—a rich benefactor permanently tied to their city as a member of the clergy.

But the "Christian people" of Hippo underestimated the sheer idiosyncrasy of a noble family. At the very moment Augustine was holding the pen to append his signature to the oath extracted from Pinianus, Melania simply said: No.[7] That was the end of the matter. Melania's was the voice of the super-rich, whose members felt entitled (as did Paulinus of Nola) to live where they wished and to take their money with them. The congregation dispersed. Augustine was left to explain the incident to his injured colleague Alypius and to the great Albina, the mother of Melania, who regarded the whole matter as a shabby attempt by a provincial church to grab the money of the great. The noble refugees returned, thoroughly alienated, to their country estate outside Thagaste. Gerontius, the writer of the *Life of Melania the Younger*, passed over the incident at Hippo in complete silence.

We only know of the incident from two embarrassed letters Augustine later wrote to Alypius and to Albina. What they reveal is the extent to which the congregation of a provincial church in Africa had been swept up in a moment of collective greed. Pinianus's arrival in Hippo had given them a now-or-never opportunity to gain real wealth.

The incident is a reminder that wealth such as that of Pinianus had not come near the churches of Africa. It was not that the church of Hippo was not wealthy. Augustine told Albina that, as bishop of Hippo, he himself managed estates that were twenty times larger than his family property had been at Thagaste. (One would love to be able to quantify this remark. If the revenue of a modest town councillor was 50 *solidi* a year, then the revenue of the estates of the church of Hippo would have amounted to 1,000 *solidi* a year. This was no small sum. It was roughly the same as the estimated revenue of Ausonius's "little" hereditary estate.) But as Augustine pointed out, an income of this size was nothing compared with the income of Pinianus, which may have been as much as 120,000 *solidi* a year:

> For in whatever church, especially in this our Africa, our friend Pinianus might be ordained (I do not say as a priest, but even as a bishop), he would still be in deep poverty compared with his former affluence.[8]

Compared with the wealth of Albina and her family, the churches of Africa bore the indelible mark of *mediocritas*. In the early fourth century, the largesse of Constantine had largely passed them by. Throughout the fourth century no African church had received windfalls from eccentric senators. No African city—not even Carthage—had attracted a bishop such as Ambrose. Nor had any city gained a Paulinus of Nola. For over a century, from the age of Constantine onward, the wealth of the churches of Africa was thought of as having grown from the ground up as a result of determined, low-profile giving by its local congregations—its *populi* and *plebes*.[9]

Altogether, the noble families of Rome who landed in Africa in 410 found themselves in an unaccustomed Christian landscape. It was the landscape in which Augustine, now almost sixty, had worked for twenty years, first as a priest and then as a bishop. For this reason we must first take a large step backward so as to place Augustine against the wider world of Africa.

Augustine's Africa: Many Landscapes, Two Churches

By "Africa," of course, we mean Roman Africa—what we would now call North Africa or, in Arabic, the Maghreb (effectively the territories of western Libya, Tunisia, Algeria, and Morocco). For Romans, this region was "Africa" and its inhabitants were the "Africans." Roman Africa was not the same as our Africa. Apart from the ancient land of Egypt, the remainder of the vast continent was virtually unknown to the Romans. Sub-Saharan, equatorial Africa and what is now South Africa were cut off from the Mediterranean fringe of north Africa by the Sahara Desert, as if by an impassable ocean of sand.

For Augustine, the first and most important landmark in his life as a bishop in Africa was the city of Hippo itself. It was not for nothing that Hippo (modern Bône/Annaba in Algeria) derived its name from the Punic *ûbôn*—harbor. It was the "Harbor of the Kings." In ancient times, it had been the window onto the Mediterranean of the great inland kingdom of Numidia. Though only a quarter of the size of Carthage, Hippo was the second largest port on the Mediterranean coast of Africa. For centuries, grain levied for the *annona* of Rome had passed directly from the plateau of Numidia to Hippo and thence to Ostia.[10] As bishop of Hippo, Augustine found himself in one of the hubs of the Mediterranean world. Hippo was a place where news from the outside world arrived quickly and from which Augustine's voice (in the form of his writings and letters) could be heard in places as far apart as Gaul, Italy, and the Holy Land.

To the east of Hippo, all roads led to Carthage. As a bishop, Augustine spent a third of his life outside Hippo. He traveled regularly to and from Carthage to attend the councils of the African church.[11] It is important to do justice to this part of Augustine's life. Despite his huge personal output, Augustine was very much a team player. He was always careful to present himself as no more than one bishop among many. He loaned his pen as a writer and his voice as a preacher to decisions that were taken in large councils of bishops gathered at Carthage from all over Africa. These decisions had been masterminded by Aurelius, the bishop of Carthage and honorary head of the African churches, and by Augustine's episcopal colleagues, his forceful friend Alypius among others. When we speak of "Augustine" (especially in connection with the churches of Africa) we must remember that we are not dealing with a lonely genius but the spokesman of what contemporaries called "the churches (or the church) of Africa." Behind Augustine stood a body of men whose capacity for collective action made them the most formidable pressure group in Latin Christianity.

Augustine traveled to Carthage by land. Each journey would take around ten days on horseback or by carriage. Sometimes he took the coast road, but more usually he struck inland to join the well-used road system that led from the plateau of Numidia down the Medjerda valley (the ancient Bagradas) to Carthage.

Traveling along that road, Augustine would have passed through a densely settled landscape dotted with little Roman cities that were as confidently embedded in a classical Roman past as were the cities of the heritage zone of Symmachus's Campania.[12]

Thus, when we talk of "Augustine's Africa" we must always remember that we are talking of a distinctive, clearly delimited landscape—the northeastern quadrant of Roman Africa, between Hippo and Carthage. As we have seen, this region had become the economic center of gravity of the late Roman West. In it, the traditional life of the cities had been maintained with peculiar intensity.

But Augustine's Africa was only a small part of all of Roman Africa. Augustine was well aware that at his back lay a world as large as all of Italy, and many times more diverse. Stretching south for 200 miles to the Sahara and for over 1,100 miles from the Gulf of Syrtes (modern Libya) to the Atlantic coast of modern Morocco, Roman Africa was a confederation of sharply contrasting landscapes. Even Augustine's own diocese was full of contrasts. It stretched thirty miles inland from the alluvial plain of the Seybouse into the foothills of the Numidian Alps. Already along the inland fringes of the territory of Hippo one entered a different world. Punic, not Latin, was spoken in the mountain villages.[13]

Yet farther south lay a world very different from that of Mediterranean Africa. On the huge plateau of Numidia, the grid of cities (which was so tight along the Medjerda valley) only covered parts of a vast, dry landscape. The agrarian settlements on the wide plains of Numidia were a world apart. Their inhabitants were deliberately kept underdeveloped by Roman standards. Their villages were denied any form of corporate existence and were frequently named after the estates on which the villagers worked, held to the land by various forms of bonded labor.[14]

The economic and social needs of this extensive subcivic world were met by intermittent rural markets—by *nundinae*.[15] These markets were, at one and the same time, essential to the owners of the great grain fields and feared by them as perpetual flash points of violence. Grain harvesting took place in the early summer; harvesting of the olives came later—in the autumn and early winter. Both harvests required the mobilization of large gangs of workers. A significant number of these gangs were wage laborers from distant regions. Such were the gangs that had been led out, "under the rabid sun" of eastern Numidia, by the Harvester of Mactar, whom we met in chapter 1.[16] These gangs were made up of strong and desperate men who were tied to their employers by debt. Their hope of reward depended on the random oscillation of crop yields in a dry region. Numidia was not the effortless breadbasket of Rome that Romans liked to imagine. It was a land of dangerous shortages. In the fourth century, grain production was driven by taxation and by the lure of profits across the sea. It pushed against the ecological limits of the possible. Landless men or sharecroppers waited, year by year, to see if they would return home with money in their pockets and the landowner's wine in their bellies, or if they would sink yet further into debt due to bad harvests.

A wave of violence had rocked southern Numidia in the late 340s. Significantly, the principal aim of this violence had been the cancellation of debts. What is equally significant was that the violent bands of which we happen to know were led by Christians. Two otherwise unknown figures, Axido and Fasir, were acclaimed as "leaders of the saints." The bands that were mobilized at this time were called by their supporters Agonistici: "Fighters [for the Lord]." Their enemies called them *circumcelliones*—Circumcellions. In all probability, "Circumcellion" was originally a religiously neutral term. It was used of the laborers who attempted to scrounge a living by gathering around the warehouses, the *cellae*, on the great estates in the hope of employment or of handouts of food.[17]

We know of the Circumcellions largely through Augustine's account of them. He presented them as a religious phenomenon. He spoke of them as dangerous "crazies"—as a species of terrorist monks given to murder, mayhem, and suicide. The outside world was encouraged to believe that the Circumcellions were a constant threat to law and order throughout the countryside of Africa and that they were the strong-arm men of the rival church to Augustine's own Catholic community. In this way, a phenomenon born of the gray misery of rural Numidia has come to be known to us almost exclusively from the works of Augustine writing hundreds of miles away, in the distant coastal city of Hippo. He consistently presented them as a melodramatic, religious phenomenon.[18]

We should always be aware of Augustine's distortion of the evidence. When we talk of Augustine's Africa we must bear in mind that what Augustine presents is a landscape deliberately viewed through religiously tinted glasses through which we can see only so much of a vast and complex world. We must strive to free ourselves from Augustine's vivid but narrow vision so as to take in fourth-century Roman Africa as a whole.

First and foremost, we must remember that Augustine had good reason to present a lopsided view of his home province. Quite as much as Ambrose, he found himself in the position of a faction fighter. He was determined to bring an age of compromise to an end and to install a new Catholic order in what he considered to be a backward region. From the moment he became a priest and then a bishop in Hippo he was committed to a bitter confrontation with a near-identical Christian church that was quite as strong and popular as his own. He had to confront what he called "the Donatist schism." In this confrontation, he weighed in with all his energy on the side of a group of forceful bishops (his friend Alypius among them) who were determined that their church, and their church only, should be recognized as the "true" Catholic church of Africa.

We usually speak of the history of Christianity in fourth-century Africa as if it was dominated by the Donatist schism. But this impression is largely due to the polemical skill of Augustine. He claimed that his church was the "true," Catholic church of Africa because his community had been recognized by all churches spread throughout the Roman empire. By contrast, he claimed that the church of his rivals had turned their backs on the wider Catholic world and had chosen to remain a local splinter group confined to Africa. They had followed Donatus—in Augustine's opinion, a figure of dubious charisma—who had formed a separate church, which he had headed as bishop of Carthage between 311 and 355. It was for this reason that Augustine and his colleagues named their rivals "Donatists." He and his colleagues were determined that others should see the Donatist church as no more than an obstinate minority—alien, tainted by violence and altogether unworthy of respect.[19]

In his brilliant new book *Sacred Violence* and in other publications, Brent Shaw has effectively dismantled this powerful and enduring stereotype.[20] Shaw makes clear that Augustine's insistence on the otherness of his rivals and on their resolutely local vision of themselves as the only surviving church in Christendom obscured the fact that, for a century, the two groups that he called "Donatists" and "Catholics" had competed as equals all over Africa. Their rivalry had been part of the general spread of Christianity in Africa.

Indeed, the rivalry of the two churches was far from being a spiritual catastrophe, as Augustine would have us believe. In reality, it greatly accelerated the process of Christianization. What Augustine presented in doctrinal terms as a fruitless conflict between Donatists and Catholics was experienced on the ground as the vigorous replication (region by region, city by city, and village by village) of two barely distinguishable forms of the same Christianity, each claiming to be more zealous than the other.

Until the imperial authorities weighed in massively in support of Augustine's party (which only occurred in a persistent manner after 411), neither church had enjoyed an overwhelming social or financial advantage over the other. Both churches appealed to much the same constituency as had the other churches of the Latin West in the post-Constantinian generation. There was nothing very exciting about the personnel of either church. Members of the lower echelons of the town councils, schoolteachers, and lawyers provided the leaders. The average inhabitants of the cities and the inhabitants of the villages provided the followers. Although Augustine frequently denounced the social disruption caused by the existence of two churches, African society as a whole was not greatly affected by their rivalry.

This was because Christianity in Africa, though vocal, was strangely encapsulated. Paganism was still widespread. Even many laypersons who were Christians felt that they had better things to do than involve themselves in disputes raised by their bishops and clergy. As in Rome, so in the cities of Africa, the higher levels of the civic elites remained closed to the affairs of the church. Many leading civic notables were pagans. Even when they were Christian, the "temple" of the town council with its solemn rituals and its unceasing, yearlong involvement with concrete, non-religious problems—entertaining the people, maintaining law and order, and collecting taxes—made religious conflicts between Christians seem of secondary importance.[21]

When Augustine became bishop of Hippo (in 396), he found that his own party was in a minority in the city. For all his talent, he did not hold the social high ground. He was faced by local elites who appeared not to take the division between the two churches very seriously. At the top of society, Donatists and Catholics married each other with little thought to the views of their respective bishops. For such persons, blood and class were a lot thicker than baptismal water. Notables who looked favorably upon Augustine's rivals blocked his efforts to force the pace of religious controversy.[22]

To persuade such persons to support the Catholic cause was not simply a matter of persuading them to take sides as Christians for one church or another. It involved a more drastic change of attitude. They had to be persuaded to look at the world in terms to which they were not yet accustomed. They had to be taught to see Africa through the same, religion-tinted glasses as did Augustine and his colleagues. In the generation before Augustine became bishop and for many decades afterward, they had not yet put on those glasses. The "civil religion" of the cities, whose continued strength we evoked in chapter 3, was what still held their attention, not the divisions between two Christian churches, each of which was staffed by busy but largely insignificant persons.

Yet, despite the nonchalance toward Christian affairs of the elites of Africa, the division between Catholics and Donatists had created facts on the ground on a massive scale. No other Christian region in the West could boast so many bishops. When the two parties were summoned to a conference, which met at Carthage on June 1, 411, over 560 bishops trooped into the city from territories as far apart as western Libya, Tunisia, and Algeria. Each church had around 280 bishops.[23] (As late as 600, Italy had only 240 bishops—under half the number of those who competed so fiercely in the towns and villages of fourth-century Africa.) The aristocratic refugees from Rome who arrived in Carthage at roughly the same time as the conference between the two churches would have witnessed a parade of massed bishops through the streets of the city that was inconceivable in any other province of the West.

The conference of Carthage of 411 marked the climax of a dramatic change of pace in the rivalry between Catholics and Donatists in Africa. Constantly lobbied by the representatives of the Catholic church to which Augustine belonged, the emperors finally decided to take in hand the religious affairs of the province. They outlawed the Donatist church. Its buildings were confiscated, and its bishops were exiled from the cities. Upper-class lay supporters were penalized, and their legacies to the Donatist church were declared invalid. No one was executed (as Priscillian had been executed) or forced directly to change their belief—unless they were peasants on the estates of a particularly zealous landlord. They were simply deprived of their church and faced with a painful choice. Leading local figures had to decide between loyalty to the emperor and loyalty to the Donatist church in their city, which the emperor had declared to be a non-church.[24]

Not surprisingly, given the role of the imperial system in the establishment of status and honors at all levels in provincial society, a large number of lay-persons joined the Catholic church. They waited to see if the imperial policy would change back to tolerance. Only the Donatist clergy remained intransigent. Theirs was the "church of truth." Through using the power of the state to establish itself, the so-called Catholic church simply showed that it was a fake church, as the Donatist clergy had always claimed it to be. It was a church "of the persecutors"—a church based on force.

This situation only developed after 411. A decade earlier, however, in 400, it was far from certain that the emperor would intervene so massively. The two churches of Africa faced each other as equals. Both had expanded largely untroubled in the easier days of the post-Constantinian empire. Without ever becoming a dominant religion, Christianity had come to occupy a distinctive niche in Roman Africa. Throughout the fourth century, the elites of Africa and the provincial governors who came to Africa from overseas (men from senatorial families in Rome, like Symmachus) took for granted the bipolar world set in place by Constantine. In this bipolar world, a vigorous but socially unprepossessing Christianity was given free rein provided that the internal differences between Christians did not impinge unduly on the affairs of the upper classes of the cities.

Thus, neither church was allowed to occupy the social high ground in the cities of Africa. But what the elites of the cities did not realize was the vigor with which the two churches had set about creating worlds of their own. They did this by competing with each other. This rivalry mirrored the spirit of competition that had once been the lifeblood of the cities of Africa. The two churches competed—as the cities had always competed—by spending their money. The war of words (of which we know so much from the copious works of Augustine) was accompanied by a silent and determined war of wealth that is hardly ever mentioned in our otherwise voluble sources. It is to this war of wealth that we must now turn.

Quid imperatori cum ecclesia: What has the Church
to do with an Emperor?

THE AUTONOMY OF CHURCH WEALTH

Here we must pause to do justice to the very real religious passions that fueled
the rivalry between two, nearly identical churches. The cause of the schism itself
lay in the past. The Donatists accused the Catholics of having tolerated bishops
who had lapsed by offering sacrifice and by surrendering copies of the Holy
Scriptures to be burned at the time of the last great persecution in 303. Catholics replied that these accusations were false; that Donatist bishops also had
lapsed; and that, in any case, the failure of a few of its members did not drive the
Holy Spirit from the church as a whole. But that was a hundred years ago. No
reconciliation between the two parties had occurred. Why had this stalemate
happened?

A principal reason was the fact that both parties were fiercely attached to a
belief in the absolute spiritual autonomy of their own church. This was not a
vague doctrine. Every local church was presented as the only place in its locality
where the Holy Ghost was to be found. We cannot understand the sharpness of
the rivalry between the two churches unless we enter into the conviction of the
bishops and clergy of each of them that it was their church—and their church
alone—in which God dwelt. The church of their rivals was an empty shell, devoid of the presence of God. Its bishops lacked the Holy Spirit. Spiritually, they
were dead men walking. They could not offer salvation to those who followed
them. Their churches were fake churches, even more sinister than pagan temples
had been. Pagan temples reeked with the smoke of incense and sacrifice. They
were plainly alien. But dead churches, though they still pretended to be Christian, were as toxic as any temple. This was the ultimate trick of the Devil. It had
brought to Africa a foretaste of the days of Antichrist, when ultimate evil could
masquerade, in an uncanny fashion, in the form of a persecuting Christian
church supported by emperors who claimed to be Christian.[25]

In churches who held such a view of themselves, the wealth of each local
church could not be treated as a purely worldly matter. This wealth was regarded
as the concretization, in financial terms, of each church's unique possession of
the Holy Spirit. In matters of church finance, as in so much else, the bishops of
both churches looked back directly to the example of Cyprian of Carthage in the
mid-third century. As we saw in chapter 2, Cyprian had propounded an intensely
sacralized and inward-looking notion of religious giving. Only money given to
the bishop by members of the true church could count as holy offerings. Only
the bishop could redistribute these offerings as holy alms. The flow of wealth in the
churches was thought of as a watertight system. The Christian *plebs* gave to the

bishop, who stood at their core as the guarantor of the presence of the Holy Spirit in each congregation. Vigor in giving not only provided financial muscle. It was a clear sign of the energy of the Holy Spirit at work in the congregation.[26] By contrast, wealth that came from outside the church and wealth that was redistributed without the bishop was dead wealth. It was empty of the Holy Spirit. Both Catholics and Donatists believed this intensely. Outside their church there was no salvation. Nor could there be any spiritually efficacious pious giving. Only by giving in the right church could sins be expiated and treasure on earth be placed in heaven.

In a famous incident in 346, Donatus, bishop of Carthage, made plain this attitude toward the wealth of the church. He was faced by an unprecedented situation. The emperor Constans had attempted to intervene in the affairs of the churches of Africa. Constans had hoped to introduce a Constantinian style of church government into the province. In other provinces, the Constantinian system had worked well. As we have seen, conformity to the imperial definition of Christianity was bought by the judicious distribution of privileges and, above all, by the infusion of imperial funds into the local churches. In 346 imperial commissioners arrived in Carthage bearing funds to distribute to the poor. This would not have been a random almsgiving. Individual local churches who accepted the imperial preference for the "Catholic" rivals of Donatus would have found their wealth increased through imperial funding offered in the name of the poor.

But the emperor had miscalculated the religious mood of Africa. Donatus reacted instantly. He refused imperial subsidies with a phrase that made him famous: *Quid imperatori cum Ecclesia?*—"What has the Church to do with an Emperor?"[27] This phrase did not refer to any abstract issue of the relations between Church and State. It was made in the spirit of Cyprian. Only the bishop could distribute wealth within the churches, in a closed circuit of holy giving that began with the offerings of the faithful within the church to their bishop and that continued through the outward flow of wealth in the churches from the holy hands of the bishop. By contrast, wealth that came directly from an emperor came from outside the church. It was wealth untouched by the Holy Spirit. It was wealth without blessing. With all the confidence of an Ambrose (but a whole generation earlier), Donatus played the upright Daniel to the emperor Constans's Belshazzar: *May your gifts remain with you, O King.*[28] It was a resounding snub to the Constantinian system.

Nor was Donatus alone. A little later, the imperial commissioners, still carrying money boxes full of coins for the poor, reached southern Numidia. In the 340s that part of Numidia had been a zone of agrarian distress, recently shaken by the activities of Axido and Fasir. Faced by the arrival of the commissioners, the Donatist bishop of Bagai (also called Donatus) turned his church into a public warehouse. He was accused of laying in stores because he intended to stand siege in his basilica. But the warehouse set up in the bishop's church was not only a sign of readiness for war. It was the symbol of the role of the bishop as the only true distributor of food to the poor of the region.[29] Many churches have been discovered in Africa ringed by storehouses.[30] Complaints by the rival bishops at the conference of Carthage reveal that to put a country church out of action involved two acts—desacralizing it by breaking its altar and denying its role as a center of holy alms by carrying away its store of grain.[31]

Non opus est procerum ... sed rectoris: This is no work of [worldly] magnates, but of a bishop, ruler of the flock

WEALTH AND BUILDING BETWEEN TWO CHURCHES

We know about these vivid incidents through the lively war of words that took place between the polemists of both churches, Augustine being the most prolific among them. But we can also trace this war on the ground. A long tradition of archaeology first pursued by the French in their north African territories and then continued in the modern states of Tunisia, Algeria, and Morocco has revealed an entirely new dimension to the struggle of the churches. Of all the provinces of the Latin West, it is only in the Roman Africa of the age of Augustine that we can see the emergence of a Christian landscape in towns and countryside alike.

These excavations have revealed a fact almost too big to be seen. Like central France in around the year 1000, the landscape of Africa began to be "covered with a white robe of churches." Each church was an argument in stone in favor of one church or the other. Each was a place where the Holy Spirit was to be found. In the High Plains north of Timgad (in southern Algeria), the ground is covered with the ruins of churches: seventy-three were charted in one survey alone of central Numidia. Many settlements eventually came to have three, four, or even seven churches.[32] The ruins of these churches represent a hidden Africa, of which we have little or no hint in the copious works of Augustine. It is impossible to decide which of these churches were Donatist and which were Catholic. Nor are they easy to date; fourth, fifth, and sixth centuries blur together. But what is evident is the unflagging enthusiasm with which these churches were set up.

Let us look at a few examples. Perhaps the most spectacular was the great basilica associated with the shrine of Saint Crispina at Theveste (modern Tebessa in eastern Algeria). It appears to have been built in a single campaign that must have involved a huge mobilization of wealth and labor. Rising on a high podium outside the city, it dominated the road that led up from Carthage into Numidia. Flanked by a hostel and entirely surrounded by a row of strong storerooms, each closed with an ingenious lock, the basilica stood above a wide courtyard framed on either side with triumphal arches that deliberately echoed the Roman monuments of the city. The basilica was reached by mounting a broad flight of steps, in the manner of a Roman temple. Once inside, the visitor would find a door in the right wall that opened into a small three-conched shrine of the martyrs. The shrine was sheathed in marble and domed with golden mosaic.

The basilica of Theveste had an unusually high roof, lit by clerestory windows. But—unlike the martyr's shrine—its walls were covered only with painted plaster. This was no opulent jewel-box, like Paulinus's Cimitile. Rather, the building complex as a whole had a gruff Roman monumentality. It was a "City of God" in stone.[33] This "City of God" lay just outside an "earthly city" whose ancient customs had by no means disappeared. At just the same time as the great shrine was being erected, the families of civic notables of Theveste were busy repairing the amphitheater of the city, as their ancestors had done, over a century before.[34] These two enterprises—the building of a great Christian shrine and the repair of an ancient amphitheater—are a reminder of the fact that the rivalry of the two churches of Africa with each other took place against the wider background of a rivalry between Christianity as a whole and robust traditions of civic life to which Christianity had remained peripheral.

The great basilica at Theveste may have been a Catholic building. Far to the south, at Timgad, it was the Donatists who had flexed the muscle of church wealth to best effect. As late as 368, the ancient capitol of Timgad was restored by a leading town councillor who was praised for "having repaired the city." By the 380s, however, the city's capitol looked out over a huge new basilica set in a church complex that measured 541 by 380 feet. The inscription on the floor of the basilica made clear that this was a house of God built by the wealth of God: "This was done and perfectly completed by the command of Optatus, High Priest of God." Optatus was the Donatist bishop of Timgad. He was by no means a little man. Between 388 and 398 he was a leading figure in the province. He was so close to the generals who were charged with the defense of Africa that he is one of the very few bishops in the history of the Early Church who enjoyed the considerable (if dubious) distinction of having been executed for his role in a civil war.[35]

It was figures such as Optatus who brought the Constantinian system to an end in Africa. Optatus no longer fitted into a model of society that assumed bishops would rule a lively but essentially low-profile church under the disengaged eyes of the true elites. Optatus stood for a new option. It was an African option. For, unlike Ambrose, who had come into the church from on top, Optatus had risen from the ground up, like his basilica. He may well have come from a humble background. But his office as Christian bishop had raised him into prominence. His great basilica showed to the world at large that he was the guardian of sacred wealth provided by the offerings of innumerable pious givers.

The tide of holy giving did not show itself only in the basilicas that appeared on the edges of the major cities. The smaller cities also were studded with churches built by their congregations. Constant rivalries sharpened the collective urge to build. When the Donatist bishop of Membressa (a small town at the head of the Medjerda valley) was ousted from his church by a rival faction, his congregation instantly built him yet another basilica![36]

But to understand the strength of this surge of building, we have to go to Numidia. The villages of Numidia have provided the most vivid evidence for the enthusiasm of humble congregations. Occasionally we meet groups of donors. Such were Publius, Petronius, and Tunnius, from Henchir Guesseria, a little church fifteen miles northeast of Timgad. On the mosaic in front of the apse they declared that they had "promised and completed their vow to God and to His Christ," *favente Deo*, "through the good favor of God." They then added, on a note of communal pride, *Gadiniana floret*: "Hurrah for the *plebs* of the Gadinii."[37] Other churches were built through the collaboration of neighboring villages:

> The Venusianenses began it, the Mucrionenses donated five columns, the Cuzabatenses donated six columns, all paved the apse: the Cuzabatenses decorated it the most. Rogatus the priest and Emilius the deacon planned the building.[38]

This combination of local pride and clerical guidance characterized the African churches.

The sense of autonomy was by no means limited to Donatists alone. Some time in the late fourth century, the Catholic bishop Alexander built a church of the martyrs on the western promontory of the bay of Tipasa, 320 miles west of Hippo. It looked across the bay to the prominent shrine of Saint Salsa. Alexander's inscription made plain that, as a builder, he owed nothing to the lay world:

> Here, where the walls are rendered praiseworthy by a light-filled roof, where the vaults shimmer and you see the holy altar: this is not the work of any magnates. No: the glory of such a deed redounds through all ages to Alexander, Ruler [of the flock].[39]

Populus: A Grassroots Christianity

The spread of Christianity reconfigured the countryside of Africa. It brought a new sense of identity to the many faceless settlements that had lain in the shadow of the Roman cities. In a remarkable new book entitled *Peasant and Empire in Christian North Africa*, Leslie Dossey has shown that the emergence of a country-based episcopate represented a revolution in the history of rural Africa. Formerly the villages had been held at arm's length by the cities. They were not allowed to function as autonomous units. The appearance in them of bishops gave them a new pride, an identity, and a capacity for collective bargaining they had not enjoyed previously. As Dossey points out, this development did not take place only because of initiatives taken at the top. In many cases, the pressure came from below. Villagers made skillful use of the division between the two churches so as to obtain a bishop for their own village. All over the countryside of Africa, but especially on the great plains of Numidia, a sense of privilege once associated with the grant of municipal status came to be expressed, in the fourth century, in religious terms through the installation of a bishop with his church and clergy.[40]

The arrival of a bishop brought many things. It turned a hitherto faceless settlement into a holy *plebs*—a people of God, in whose midst the Holy Spirit dwelt. The bishop could also represent the community in secular matters. As a bishop, he could challenge the great. He could carry petitions to the authorities all the way to Italy. His curse might be feared by the powerful.[41] If he was a Catholic bishop (and in most areas, even if he was a Donatist bishop), he was treated as a *vir venerabilis*—a man to be revered. Even when he was of low social status, his body was untouchable. He could not be flogged in the way that any other peasant could be flogged.[42]

Thus, over the course of the fourth century, a new world came into being in the countryside. A new style of Christian bishop emerged as a village leader. Concentrating as he did on the highly urbanized world between Hippo and Carthage, Augustine may not have been fully aware of the extent of the revolution this represented. But, in his old age, Augustine experienced one such country bishop. It was not a happy experience for him. Let us conclude by looking for a moment at this vivid incident.

In late 411 Augustine had chosen Antoninus, a monk from his own monastery, to be bishop of the *castellum*—the hill village—of Fussala, in the Numidian Alps on the southeastern edge of the territory of Hippo. He did so, ostensibly, so as to counter Donatist influence in the region. By 422, however, Augustine had come to regret his choice. In his opinion, Antoninus had turned out to be a petty tyrant. But this was not everyone's view of Antoninus. On the spot, the young bishop was far from unpopular. As a bishop, Antoninus put a new face on Fussala. He built an impressive bishop's palace in the village. He united around him the local strongmen—the guardians of the city walls, headed by a retired soldier. He also brought new legal skills—a stenographer from Augustine's monastery and a legal agent, a *defensor*, paid for by the church. He received from the primate of Numidia letters that enabled him to travel as far as Italy so as to secure the release of prisoners arrested by the Count of Africa, the commander in chief of the Roman forces in the province.[43]

In 422 Augustine and his colleagues attempted to depose Antoninus for violence and extortion. Antoninus did not give in easily; he appealed directly to the bishop of Rome. We know about his career because Augustine was forced to write an embarrassed letter on the subject to bishop Celestine of Rome. This letter (*Letter* 209) has long been known. It can now be supplemented by another letter on the case of Antoninus (*New Letter* 20*) that was discovered by Johannes Divjak in 1975 in a collection of hitherto unknown letters from Augustine's old age.[44]

The new letter shows that Antoninus had created a solid position for himself at Fussala. It was Augustine who was insecure. In the late summer of 422 Augustine found himself forty miles from Hippo in the hill country of Numidia. It was not his world. Everyone in the villages claimed to speak only Punic. They were far from passive. After one group had been berated in Punic by a Numidian colleague of Augustine's, they all walked out of the church—even (Augustine adds) the local nuns, women whose chastity symbolized the holiness of the local church. Augustine and the other Latin-speaking bishops were left stranded.[45]

Augustine wrote the *New Letter* 20* to Fabiola, an upper-class Roman lady. She had offered hospitality to Antoninus in Rome. The energetic young bishop from the backlands had evidently brought her a heroic tale of persecution at the hands of the powerful.[46] Fabiola was as high as you could get; she may well have been the daughter of Fabiola, the correspondent of Jerome who had collaborated with none other than Pammachius, the senatorial friend of Paulinus of Nola, to found a hostel in the Port of Rome.[47]

Dubious character though he may have been, Antoninus of Fussala was a sign of the times. Half a century previously, in the days of Symmachus, a steady trickle of deferential clients had come to Rome as the "special people" of one or another great Roman aristocrat. They had placed statues and laudatory addresses in the courtyards of their palaces. This practice continued. But, by the 420s, figures like Antoninus had also begun to make an appearance. Bishops from lower-class backgrounds felt free to approach the palaces of the great in Rome. Antoninus joined many worlds. He was bilingual in Latin and Punic, and his official position as the spiritual head of a mountain village gave him and his congregation access to a wider world. Even if his stories were self-serving, they were the sort to which Christian aristocrats were now expected to pay attention. He brought directly to the highest circles of Roman Christian society vivid tales of misery, injustice, and hard dealing from the very ground of Africa. It is against this background of increasing pressure from below that we must place the preaching of Augustine before the *populus*—the far-from-passive Catholic congregations of Hippo and Carthage.

CHAPTER 21

"Dialogues with the Crowd"
The Rich, the People, and the City in the Sermons of Augustine

"Dialogues with the crowd": Augustine and the *Populus*

In late antiquity, a bishop was supposed to be a *seminator Verbi*—a "Sower of the Word."[1] He did not have to write books, but he was expected to preach. Augustine preached ceaselessly. In the thirty-five years in which he was bishop of Hippo (between 396 and 430) he preached over six thousand sermons. He was a magical speaker. In reading sermons of Augustine, we can usually be certain that we are not reading carefully reedited texts (as was the case with Ambrose). We are reading his own words as they were first heard. This is because rich members of the congregation would pay skilled experts in shorthand to take down every word as it came from his lips.[2]

Of this torrent of words, only around one-tenth has survived. Of these, many of the original sermons were cut down by medieval copyists, who were only interested in certain parts of them. They wanted to know about the theology of Augustine and not about the Africa of Augustine. They often found that many of these sermons were too full of local color to be of interest (or even to be intelligible) to persons who now read them many centuries later in a Gothic Europe where north Africa—by then a Muslim region—seemed infinitely remote. Hence the importance of the recent discovery by the great French scholar François Dolbeau of a series of sermons by Augustine that had been copied in their entirety in a late medieval monastery in Mainz. These sermons had not been cosmeticized. They were complete and full of vivid local details. Some had been star performances. One such sermon took over two hours to preach. In the Mainz sermons (now called the Dolbeau sermons in honor of their discoverer) we can hear again the voice of Augustine, almost as if on a tape recording.[3] But we can also catch an echo of the voice of the congregations to which Augustine preached. What we hear is not quite what we expected. Brilliant as a preacher, Augustine faced a *populus*—a surprisingly vigorous Christian people—in front of whom he was not always at his ease.

The late antique sermon was an open-ended occasion. In the course of the Christian church service, the sermon preceded the high drama of the Mass. It came just before the solemn procession in which the laity brought their gifts to the altar. For the unbaptized in the audience (and we know that there were many such persons) the sermon was the last thing they heard of the Christian faith before they were invited to leave the church so that the baptized alone could continue with mysterious rites in which others (unbaptized Christians quite as much as non-Christians) had no part.[4]

During the sermon, the preacher interacted with his audience in the most face-to-face manner possible. There was no raised pulpit. There were no confining pews. The congregation stood on the spacious floor of the basilica. They were free to move around. They would surge up to the edge of the slightly raised area in front of the apse in order to listen to the preacher. The preacher would come forward toward them from his seat in the middle of the semicircular bench on which he and his clergy sat with their backs to the circular wall of the apse. Or he would step down from the apse into the center of the church so as to preach beside the altar that stood near the middle of the basilica, set apart by low railings of wood or carved marble. A mobile lectern of light wood was all that the preacher needed, to hold the copy of the Bible from which he sowed his words. Delivered extempore in front of, or in the midst of, a standing audience that could move as it wished, Augustine's sermons have rightly been called "dialogues with the crowd."[5]

They were not always successful dialogues. A long and vivid sermon from among those recently discovered by Dolbeau has enabled us to glimpse a notable moment of failure. It happened on January 22, 404, when Augustine was preaching at Carthage. The basilica in which he preached was considerably larger than his own church in Hippo. It may have had room for two thousand persons. On this occasion, it was crowded. In order to be heard better and to create a mood of intimacy, Augustine first stepped down from the apse so as to deliver his sermon at the altar. But he then saw that a large section of the crowd had already pushed up to the edge of the apse to hear him from that position. He hesitated for a moment and then turned away from the altar to make his way back to toward the apse. The moment he turned, a rhythmic cry went up from the crowd gathered around the altar. They ordered him to hurry back down and to speak to them there. Instantly, Augustine turned his back on the hecklers, mounted the raised floor of the apse, and sat down on the high bench beside his colleague, Aurelius of Carthage. This indicated that he refused to preach until order had been restored.[6]

It was a brittle and seemingly arrogant gesture on Augustine's part. He had pointedly placed the distance of the apse between himself and the *populus*. His gesture was met by instant protest from those who remained at the altar, in the middle of the church. They used the same techniques as were used in the circus and the amphitheater. An acclamation went up: "Get on with the Mass!"—which meant, in effect, "Cut the sermon!"[7] The Christian *populus* of Carthage made plain what they thought of Augustine's seemingly dismissive attitude.

The next day Augustine preached again. He had to explain his behavior to a congregation who plainly expected him to apologize. He was considerably less contrite than his listeners thought that he should have been. The sermon was entitled *On Obedience*. He made clear that he did not approve of their spirited heckling:

> I beseech you.... Make a distinction between the Church of God and the theater.... Here, jumping to one's feet [in a massive surge, as if from the benches of the theater: in church, of course, the congregation would already have been standing, though they may have swayed ominously as they shouted], setting up a rhythmic chant, calling the shots—may God shield your hearts from all that.[8]

He preached in vain. The Christian basilicas of Africa were not immune to the makeshift democracy of a late Roman *populus*. It was not only the countryside that had found a new voice within the Christian churches. Urban congregations used their church to experiment in new, abrasive forms of civic life. The moment that Augustine entered his own basilica at Hippo or stood up to speak in one of the spacious basilicas of Carthage, he realized that the crowd gathered beneath its high, wooden roof was not the united "people of God" that it was supposed to be. The old divisions of the city had survived. In every church, a *populus* was pitted against its *ordo*. But now the *ordo* they challenged was not the town council. It was the bishop and his clergy. The possibility of conflict was in the air. In church, a majority of poor citizens could jostle and barrack their clergy. They could also turn their voices against the rich whom they had reason to resent, in much the same manner as they had been accustomed to doing in the bright light of day from the benches of the theaters.[9] It is against this distinctive background that we should place the manner in which Augustine approached the rich in his preaching and offered them an active role in the Christian community.

Isti soli vivunt: They alone have a life

THE RICH, THE POOR, AND THE *POPULUS*

But when we turn to Augustine's sermons we must remember that he was no Ambrose. His sermons were not rewritten as polished treatises. What we get, rather, is the ad hoc, seemingly inconsequential quality of an extempore speaker, constantly adjusting his tone of voice to the mood of an audience whose presence we can sense behind his words. Vivid images, snatches of anecdotes from real life, and condensed phrases are scattered almost randomly in the flow of words. It is like listening in to only one side of a lively conversation. In this conversation, whom was Augustine addressing and what did he tell them?

This section will deal with three groups—with the rich and with two categories of the "poor," which we must keep apart in our minds though they tend to be blurred in modern usage. Let us first look at what we moderns would call the poor—the destitute. Augustine preached regularly on almsgiving to the poor. His sermons on this topic have been studied with admirable skill by Richard Finn in his book *Almsgiving in the Later Roman Empire*.[10] Augustine took this part of his routine duties as a bishop seriously. But the care of the poor was seldom uppermost in his mind. When he wrote to Albina about the incident of Pinianus in 411, he claimed that in Hippo only "a small number of the indigent" needed support from the church.[11]

When it came to charity to the poor, Augustine did not preach in a notably heartless society. He recognized that Jews and pagans also gave alms to beggars and showed sympathy for the weak and destitute quite as much as did many Christians.[12] Nor did he live in a region desperately challenged by the presence of the poor. Throughout the fourth century, cities such as Hippo and Carthage were spared the worst effects of famine, unemployment, and disease. It was in the hill country south of Hippo that real, grinding poverty was to be found. The members of a village occupied by a sect known as the Abelonii (the Sons of Abel the Just) were able to reject marriage—in the manner of the Shakers—and still maintain themselves for generations through adopting the children of the neighboring peasantry. Poor families were only too glad to part with their children so as to have fewer mouths to feed. In the 420s families of poor peasants outside Hippo were quite prepared to sell their children as slaves in order to raise money.[13]

As far as we can see, nothing as terrible as this happened in the cities. In Carthage and Hippo, the number and needs of the destitute varied with the seasons. In the cold months of winter work at the docks and on building projects ceased and the unemployed filled the streets. In the winter of 410, Augustine wrote to his congregation in Hippo to urge them that the alarm of the sack of Rome (which had led to instant hoarding) should not make them less generous than before in their annual collection and distribution of clothes for the poor. In Carthage, late spring was the worst time. Supplies diminished and food prices rose before the next harvest. Preaching in Carthage, Augustine urged the hands of charitable Christians to "work" with more than usual zeal by giving alms in that low season.[14]

When Augustine preached about the poor in this manner, his hearers would have known what category of poor persons he referred to. The poor of the church and the poor who lived from alms alone were an easily recognizable underclass. Above these poor stood the majority of the population of the cities. They were far from a monochrome group. There were many layers of them, ranging from prosperous artisans and shopkeepers to day laborers. The recent archaeological survey of Anna Leone has shown that the people of Carthage, as in Rome, benefited from the presence of rich residents and from the regular performance of great games. The organization of the games led to a proliferation of little associations, each with their club room and semi-private baths. Members of the trade associations played a crucial role in the public life of the city.[15] They turned out on festival days so as to march in processions. Catering to the rich, the bazaar of the silversmiths was world famous.[16] Further down the social scale, the work of the docks, the preparation and dying of textiles, and the processing of fish for export (in Carthage and in other African cities) supported a substantial population in industrial neighborhoods.[17]

These people spoke of themselves as *pauperes*, as poor. They did so much as average Americans tend to say that they are "middle class." For them, the word *pauper* did not automatically conjure up the image of a "pauper"—of a beggar and a homeless person in need of food, clothes, and shelter. Rather, it conjured up a contrast. One was poor over against others who were not poor. *Pauper* was a relational term; it assumed the presence of its opposite, the rich. In the Roman cities of Africa, as elsewhere, the poor stood toward the rich in an attitude that was at one and the same time assertive and fearful.[18]

It is important to keep in mind this distinction between the outright poor and the *pauperes* to whom Augustine preached in Hippo and Carthage. If we do not do so we are left with a profoundly polarized image of the late Roman city. As we have seen, the tendency to treat all *pauperes* as if they were paupers has contributed to a warped vision of urban life in this period.[19] In reality, the self-styled *pauperes* of the cities were an energetic and far from homogeneous group. They had their own hierarchy. They were often organized in trade associations. Those who stood at the head of the associations formed a group of their own. They were the true *plebs media*—the rich plebeians of the city. As we have seen, in Africa as elsewhere, the Christian churches had drawn on this group for their financial support. It was also from this group that the churches recruited their clergy. As a result, the bulk of the clergy of Africa remained close to the social world of the *pauperes* who made up the bulk of the *populus* of every city. They shared their fears and resentments.

Bishops were somewhat different. As Claudia Rapp has shown, "a glass ceiling in promotion" stood between clergymen recruited from humble backgrounds and the ranks of the episcopate. Bishops were more likely to come from the class of town councillors, as did Augustine.[20] But Africa was a land of small towns and thriving country bishoprics. The glass ceiling in promotion did not block the ascent of humbler persons into the episcopate as much as it did in other provinces. In Africa, membership in the clergy still offered a *carrière ouverte aux talents* to members of the self-respecting poor. The career of Antoninus of Fussala is a prime example of this fluidity. His mother and stepfather had been so poor when they first came to Hippo that they were placed on the poor rolls of the church. Antoninus himself was, in effect, given to Augustine's monastery so as to be housed and fed, much as the peasants in the hills around Hippo gave their children to the community of the eccentric Abelonians or sold them to slave dealers. But Antoninus's activities at Fussala showed that his humble origins did not stand in the way of his becoming a forceful bishop, capable of establishing contacts with the great.

Ultimately, social differences within the Christian clergy were less significant than was the primary, secular division between the rich and the *populus* within the cities of Africa. In cities the size of Hippo and Carthage the *populus* could be dangerous. In around 412 the *populus* of Hippo dragged an imperial official out of sanctuary in Augustine's own basilica and lynched him. Merchants and artisans were involved in the incident.[21] In 419 the chief commander of the armed forces in Africa was killed in a riot at Carthage. The ringleaders found sanctuary in the city's basilicas. They finally received an imperial amnesty—but not before a delegation of African bishops had traveled some 1,800 miles, from Carthage to Ravenna and then to the foothills of the Pyrenees and back, to plead for mercy.[22]

The *populus* was not only feared, it was consulted. Approval by the *populus* was required for the appointment of special tax collectors. Outgoing Proconsuls of Africa (usually, as we have seen, representatives of the highest nobility of Rome) found that their tenure of office was subject to the judgment of the people, in the form of acclamations or hisses, which were carefully recorded and publicized.[23] Furthermore, Christian congregations began at this time to intervene directly as pressure groups in the politics of the city. In June 401 the Christian congregation of Carthage protested the appointment to a high office in the town council of a pagan banker who had only recently been baptized as a Christian so as to qualify for the office. The Christian *populus* had chanted that they would not be ruled by pagans.[24] Altogether, the *pauperes* of major cities were by no means a group of aimless indigents. They had remained a *populus* in the old Roman sense—a citizen body with a right to shout and riot.

Augustine faced this *populus* in his basilica. He may not have faced all of them; it is difficult to know the exact social composition of a preacher's audience at this time. A large number of the working poor may never have found time to come to church except at high festivals. Beggars would have stayed outside the basilica, for this was where the money was. Pious Christians gave alms at the church door or in the courtyard outside the church. As a result, Augustine would have found himself preaching to the rich (who enjoyed the leisure to take religion seriously) and to the upper layers of the *populus*—to artisans, to members of the guilds, to small landowners, and to minor town councillors. It was precisely such persons who felt most acutely the stresses and strains inherent in the social structure of a late Roman city.

In this mixed congregation, the rich stood out. They were very much in the public eye:

> when the poor catch sight of them, they murmur, they groan, they praise and they envy, wanting to be their equals, grieving that they can not make it. In between the praises of the rich, they say: "These are the only ones who matter; these are the only ones who know how to live—*Isti soli vivunt.*"[25]

If anything, it was the presence of such rich persons that made the average towns-man feel poor. One did not have to be a beggar to come up short against the high wall of power and status that surrounded the rich. For most of the time, Augustine appears to have preached to relatively prosperous members of the *populus* who, nonetheless, still saw themselves as permanently at a disadvantage in comparison with the rich.

Here we are dealing with a characteristically Roman division of society where power, and the security that came from power, counted for more than mere income. What even the most prosperous members of the *populus* lacked was not money—it was security. They were not poor, but they always lived in fear of impoverishment. Impoverishment, not poverty, was the condition that haunted their social imagination. Like the inhabitants of eighteenth-century Lyons, the *pauperes* of Hippo and Carthage were *paupérisables*—"impoverishable."[26] They felt themselves on a slope that always tilted perilously toward the bottom of society.

Where fourth-century Africa may have been different from eighteenth-century France was the stark clarity with which members of the *populus* were able to trace their misfortunes directly back to the rich and to place a human face upon their oppressors. We are dealing with relations of power that were more than usually blatant. Oppressing the poor was a face-to-face matter. Indeed, it was an "in the face" matter. Describing the rich of Rome, Ammianus Marcellinus wrote of how great senators when approached even by well-to-do clients would reject the old-fashioned client's kiss. They would turn their face away "like an ill-tempered bull about to charge." Instead, they offered their knee for adoration, as if their clients had come to them as suppliants for mercy and not as friends.[27] What happened in the palaces of Rome happened just as openly in the towns of Africa. When the rich and powerful strode across the forum, surrounded by their brightly dressed entourage, it was wise to scramble to one's feet and to bow deeply as they passed.[28]

These persons were indeed formidable. Their presence was felt in every town. In the course of the fourth century, an oligarchy of leading town councillors and holders of imperial privileges had tended to take over the government of their region at the expense of their poorer and less privileged colleagues on the town council. They did so by controlling the allocation of taxation. It was they who determined the impact of potentially crippling levies, privileging themselves and penalizing others. This was power at its most naked. It was power derived from implication in the imperial system at its most formidable and most exacting.

But this power could not be challenged. The imperial tax system was identified with the emperor—it was out of bounds to criticism. Ambrose had realized this in Milan. Augustine observed the same prudent attitude in Hippo and Carthage. His image of the rich was deliberately vague. We only learn by inference how they gained their power and wealth. We will have to wait until the early 440s—until the height of the crisis of empire caused by the barbarian invasions—for a Christian writer, Salvian of Marseilles, to describe and denounce the actual mechanisms of taxation, which made the inner circle of the town councils the "tyrants" of their region.[29] But he did this in a fiery tract, *On the Government of God*, which may not have circulated widely. We may doubt whether he did so in a sermon, as he stood eye to eye with the rich in his own church.

What Augustine did refer to were the side effects of the imperial system. He expected his audience to have no illusions as to the manner in which the life of the average person depended on two closely related powers—on patronage and on *potentia* (a crushing power to harm others wielded by the rich as a result of their control of public office). Augustine's sermons are shot through with references to these two forces. It is not surprising that the most convincing study of the workings of patronage in the late Roman West (by Jens-Uwe Krause) should draw so heavily on the sermons of Augustine.[30] For the average person, it was patronage that tipped the balance between prosperity and spoliation.

> Brethren, you know how people boast of their patrons. To those who threaten him, the client of a greater patron answers: "By the head of so-and-so, my patron, you can do nothing against me."[31]

These were the "poor," as Augustine knew many of them. They were not beggars. Rather, they were, at different times in their life, both vulnerable to impoverishment and zestful in bringing impoverishment on others:

> But perhaps you have been made utterly poor and destitute. You had some little family property that had supported you, which was taken away from you by the tricky dealing of a rival. You groan, you grumble against the times you live in.... Yesterday, this person was groaning that he had lost his property. Today, backed by a greater patron, he is grabbing the property of others.[32]

In late Roman conditions, no person could be certain that he would keep clear of the powerful. For instance, someone might be proud that he would never value his property so much that he would commit perjury for it. Only the great did this: "I am a poor man, a *plebeius*—a member of the *plebs*—one of the crowd, when could I ever expect to be a provincial governor?" Yet, as Augustine pointed out, when the occasion came, such a person, though unable to commit the gross sins of the great, would still be tempted to commit perjury when pressured by a *potens* to lie on his behalf in a lawsuit:

> He is a man of power. He can drag up a suit against you, so that you lose your land. He has great power at the moment.... Indeed, you say: "He need only lodge a complaint against me, and I will have my property confiscated."[33]

Altogether, the *pauper* of Augustine's sermons was not usually a beggar. He was a typical Roman *plebeius*. He could also be a minor town councillor and a modest landowner threatened by abrasive forms of power both old and new. Such persons enjoyed a modest independence, provided that they kept a low profile. But they had few ways of resisting pressure that came to them from on top, from great landowners, and from imperial officials. In that sense, plebeians and minor members of the town councils (such as Augustine's family had been) shared a common fate. All of them stood on the razor's edge of vulnerability to those above them. It was to the fears and resentments of this group—not the poor in the modern sense but those who faced impoverishment—that Augustine spoke most convincingly.

Tolle superbiam: Get rid of pride

AUGUSTINE ON RICH AND POOR

Augustine preached not only to the *pauperes*. The rich were also present in the basilica. These were the leading town councillors and major landowners in the region, the local representatives of the imperial bureaucracy and their staffs, privileged honorary senators, and, occasionally, military men with their retinues. They stood out in their bright robes.[34] They may have stood at the head of the congregation, nearest to the bishop and his clergy in the apse. These were the "more honored and respected persons" who stepped up to the apse to negotiate with Augustine in 411 when the crowd was clamoring for the ordination of Pinianus.[35]

Bishops took seriously the sensibilities of the rich. In around 400 Aurelius, bishop of Carthage, rearranged the entrances to major churches so as to enable the wives of the great to enter through a separate women's door. They no longer had to make their way to the women's section by pushing through the crowd, where they had been exposed to "the comments of cheeky, boisterous slaves."[36] Often the rich put in no more than a token appearance. Augustine was aggrieved when one local landowner, Romulus, appeared in church at Hippo on Sunday but left immediately after the service. He did not stay behind to discuss with Augustine the case of peasants on his estates, who claimed that he had charged them double rent.[37]

The way in which Augustine faced this group throws a vivid light on his priorities as a pastor and as a social thinker. The ideal of the unity of the Catholic congregation was of paramount importance to him. There were good reasons for this emphasis on unity. The rivalry between the two churches of Africa offered Christians a choice of bishops in their city. If one bishop did not please them, they would go to the other. Members of each church—faced with the perpetual opportunity to cross over to the church of its rivals—needed to be persuaded to stay together.

But we have already seen that concern for unity had deep roots in Augustine's own thought and worldview. In his sermons of the 400s and 410s we meet very much the same man whom we met, twenty years younger, in the early 390s, when he drew up the precepts for his monastery. He had remained a passionate preacher of unity and concord. But now his concern for unity had widened. The monastery Augustine had set up and for which he wrote his *Precept* and his *Rule* in 395 was a tiny, cohesive group of possibly no more than twenty persons. Now, as a bishop, Augustine had to face an entire community. As we have seen, he did not always do it very well. But he still strove to communicate to his hearers what he believed most deeply: in heaven they would reach a unity of loving souls in a City of God of which the tight world of the monastery was supposed to offer a foretaste on earth. Heaven was a long way away. But a hint of a future glorious unity could be sensed in the euphoric moments when the entire congregation (many hundreds of them) chanted the Psalms along with their bishop:

> Now let us hear, brothers, let us hear and sing. Let us pine for the City where we are citizens.... By pining we are already there; we have already cast our hope, like an anchor, on that far shore.[38]

The grand theme of the unity of the City of God grew out of Augustine's ceaseless "dialogues with the crowds" in the 400s and 410s. It was only later spelled out with monumental certainty in the pages of his *City of God*.[39]

But the concern for unity came with a price. Augustine's passion for unity imposed a reticence on him in his dealings with the rich that other more frankly populist preachers had not observed. Augustine was no Ambrose. Unlike Ambrose, he never set himself up in church to denounce the rich as the Ahabs of his time. The vivid vignettes of oppression, fear, and corruption we extract from his

works were never brought together to form part of a single, targeted denunciation of the rich, as Ambrose had done in Milan in the 380s.

Altogether, Augustine kept close to the contours of the possible when facing
a real audience of rich and powerful persons in a late Roman city. There was a
large element of prudence in this attitude. If alienated, the rich could easily go
over to the Donatist church of his rivals. In any case, Augustine was a law and
order man. He did not relish the freedom of the *populus*. In Carthage, where
the *populus* was a large and vocal body, he was usually brought forward by his
colleague Aurelius to dampen the enthusiasm of the Christian crowd, not to stir
it up.[40]

So what exactly did he offer to the rich? He had no doubt that, as a group,
they had their own besetting sins.

> Certainly, many sins are seen to be particular to the rich. The more actively
> engaged they are, the more they have to administer their properties, the
> more they have to take care of extensive properties, the more difficult it is
> for them not to bring on themselves ever more sins.[41]

But there was a remedy for such behavior. Preaching at some time after 411
(at a time when Pelagian views already circulated in Carthage and Hippo), Augustine coined a phrase that may have been an echo in reverse of the brilliant
slogan of the Pelagian *De divitiis—tolle divitem et pauperem non invenies*: "Get
rid of the rich and you will find no poor."[42] Augustine's phrase, by contrast, stressed
not wealth but pride:

Tolle superbiam: divitiae non nocebunt.

(Get rid of pride, and riches will do no harm.)[43]

In Augustine's preaching, pride, not wealth, was the true Last Enemy of the
Christian. The real division of the world was not between the rich and the poor.
It was between the proud and those who were enabled by God's grace to be humble before God and before their fellows.[44] In practice this meant a view of society
where the inequalities created by wealth could be accepted as long as they were
softened by the abandonment of the toxic by-products of wealth—arrogance,
violence, and the abuse of power.

In many ways, Augustine's message was reassuringly traditional. It drew a firm
line between the traditional "good" rich and the "bad" rich. It also reinforced the
Roman tendency to regard a *Concordia ordinum*—a balance between rulers and
ruled in every city—as the formula for social peace. In the ancient world, it was
agreed that the rich could lead the city provided that they treated those below
them with good nature and that they showed "civic love" by spending money on
games and buildings. To this well-worn maxim Augustine merely added that the

rich should show good nature by abandoning pride and that their generosity should take the form of giving alms.

Yet, at the time, Augustine's emphasis on the renunciation of pride (rather than the renunciation of wealth) represented a significant shift. We should linger for a moment on this shift. In the generation that had preceded Alaric's sack of Rome in 410, a more starkly economic view of wealth had come to circulate among radical Christians. This view fostered a horror of wealth in and of itself. It found memorable expression in the radical writings of the partisans of Pelagius. Altogether, the traditional common sense on wealth had taken on a more dramatic and confrontational tone. All rich threatened to become the "bad" rich. Augustine reacted against this current. He found a place again in the church for the "good" rich. He did it through giving the good rich a new role. They were to act as the pillars of a hierarchical society that functioned for the greater glory of God. Frank superiorities of wealth and power might exist, but they existed only on the condition that they were wielded without disruptive arrogance. For once the rigid stance of pride was removed, wealth and power could be used without inhibition to promote the concord of a Christian society.

What this meant, in fact, was shifting the definition of the good rich by seeing them, first and foremost, as those who wielded power. The good rich were not only persons who knew how to give but also persons who knew how to rule. For Augustine, power meant order. In his thought world, order was maintained at every level of society by firm rule. Heads of families ruled their children and dependents. City worthies ruled the people of their cities. Imperial administrators and generals ruled their subjects and their soldiers. At the top stood a Christian emperor, commissioned by God to rule a potentially anarchic society.

In this hierarchical view of society, the good rich were expected to be also the good governors. It was a shift with a long future before it. From the time of Charlemagne onward, medieval clerics who mined the works of Augustine realized they were reading the ideological charter of a high-pitched but cohesive society not unlike the feudal world in which they themselves lived. Power, not money, was what mattered. And even power could be taught to be humble before God and to bend down (from time to time) to hear and to protect the powerless.[45]

Given the long-term impact of this vortex of ideas and the clarity with which Augustine expressed it, it is easy to delineate what Augustine said. But it is considerably harder for the historian to step back and estimate how what he said was heard by those who first listened to him in the basilicas of Hippo and Carthage.

What would have been immediately apparent to any hearer was Augustine's determination to avoid an outright confrontation between rich and poor. He made clear that, as their bishop, he viewed his congregation as an absolute democracy of hearts, leveled beneath the gaze of God. As a bishop, sin was his business. And Augustine was relentlessly even-handed in his treatment of the sins of both the rich and the poor. The members of each group sinned, even if each sinned differently:

> Look here, brothers and sisters; in this whole congregation listening to this, how many rich people are there? ... If only there could be as few [who go to hellfire] as there are rich people in the human race![46]

He insisted that, alas, Hell had room for more than one class. A poor man might have heard with pleasure the words of the Gospel, that *It is easier for a camel to enter through the eye of a needle than for a rich man to enter into the kingdom of heaven* (Matt. 19:24).

> He hugged himself and laughed out loud when it was said that the rich will not enter into the kingdom of heaven. "I will," he said. "These shabby clothes will ensure that I do. Those people who do violence to us and who oppress us will not get in."

But even the beggar should be careful:

> Certainly, such people [the evil rich] will not get in. But you too, just see whether you will enter. What if, as well as being poor, you are greedy; what if you are both weighed down with want and on fire [inside] with avarice?[47]

Augustine's emphasis on the primacy of inner states of mind was central to his ethical thought. But, in church, this insistence was used also as a blocking move. Augustine wished to discourage the members of his congregation from judging the rich solely by the external signs of their social status.

> A rich man finds it all too easy to say: *Male serve!* "You lousy slave!" That sounds arrogant. But if he does not say it, he may fail to control his household. Frequently, he controls it better by a harsh word than by a savage beating. He says this under the pressure of a need to keep his household in order. But let him never say it inwardly. Let him never say it deep down in his heart. Let him not say it before the eyes and ears of God.[48]

Seldom in Christian preaching had the semiotics of power—which included the high-handed habit of command Augustine described—been judged so lightly. It was the same with the heavy eating of the rich. Christian moralists—such as Ambrose—had swooped in on this well-known attribute of wealth and power. In doing so, they followed a long philosophical and medical tradition of distaste for the vulgar sensuality of the "bad" rich.[49] Augustine, by contrast, accepted heavy eating as part of the custom of a class. When drawing up his monastic *Praeceptum* in the 390s, he had dealt surprisingly lightly with the weaknesses of the rich—their need for special food, special clothing, and special forms of work. He was equally tolerant of these weaknesses in his sermons. Heavy eating was regrettable; but, compared with worse sins, it was tolerable—if only for the time being. Time alone would tell whether God's grace would cause that particular bad habit to drop away.[50]

"Let him be rich in good works ... let him share"

Yet seldom had the quid pro quo of this tolerance of the externals of wealth been spelled out so clearly as Augustine did in his sermons. It was not enough for the rich to say that they had their heart in the right place:

> God knows, I do not have haughty ideas about myself. And if I shout and use harsh words, God knows my conscience, that I say such things from my need to exercise control, not because I consider myself a cut above all others.

Augustine would not accept this excuse. He pointed out that Paul had not only said: *Command the rich of this world not to be proud* (1 Tim. 6:17). They should also be generous.

> So, what next? *Let them be rich in good works....* This is not something you do behind closed doors. Either it is done, and is visible to all, or it is not done.... *Let them be rich in good works, let them give readily, let them share* (1 *Timothy* 6:18).... If rich people are like that, they need have no worries; when the Last Day comes, they also will be found in the Ark ... they will not form part of the destruction brought by the Flood.[51]

Once again, those who listened to Augustine would have picked up an old-fashioned message, communicated in the homely wisdom of the *Letter to Timothy* ascribed to Saint Paul. The *Letter to Timothy* was not a very exacting text. It did not demand the renunciation of wealth; it simply cautioned the rich against the transience of earthly goods and advised them to be generous—*to give readily, to share.* As in the Roman city, so now in the church, the rich were put on parole. They could be rich—but they had to be generous. And Augustine went on to tell them in no uncertain terms not only that they should be generous. He showed clearly to what causes they should give. Let us end this chapter by turning to these good causes and to the styles of giving which, in Augustine's opinion, stood in their way.

Gloriosa … effusionis insania: Crazy expenditure … as a source of glory

CARTHAGE AND THE GAMES OF 403

Augustine's sermons were never abstract lucubrations on his part. The discoveries of François Dolbeau have shown that the sermon on the relations of rich and poor that we have just cited formed part of an entire campaign of preaching that had been conducted by Augustine at Carthage in the last months of 403.[52] The sermons coincided with a major event in the life of the city. Every year, between October 26 and November 1, the priests of the imperial cult met in Carthage to celebrate the games that expressed the exuberant loyalty to the emperor of the provinces of Africa. Not all of these priests were pagans. The office was a title of honor that had also come to be held by Christians. But the assembly of the priests at Carthage was an annual reminder of the fact that African upper-class society had remained predominantly urban and resolutely secular.[53] It basked in notions of glory and status that owed everything to the past and nothing to Christianity.

The games of Carthage were second only to those of Rome. They followed a pattern of display of which the games laid on by Symmachus for his son (which had been held in Rome only a few years earlier, in 393 and 401) were a more lavish version. Of all the ceremonials of worldly power that had survived largely unchanged throughout the fourth century, these games were the most stunning and unashamedly non-Christian events that were to be seen in Africa. They began with *venationes*, with matador-like combats with wild beasts. They went on to elaborate mime dances. They culminated with chariot races. Last but not least came the solemn bestowal of expensive robes on star performers.[54]

These games involved deeply serious matters. As they presided in the amphitheater, the priests of the imperial cult wore golden crowns bearing icons of the emperors. They made vows for the safety of the empire, for the abundance of Africa, and for the continuing "Good Fortune" of the city. The Genius of Carthage had retained a numinous power. She needed no blood sacrifice to keep her memory alive. She was a majestic presence in the theater, in the amphitheater, and in the circus of Carthage as she presided over the annual explosion of the games.[55]

The games were supposed to be ostentatiously expensive. To appear to court bankruptcy by lavish giving was a matter of pride.[56] This was a moment of *gloriosa effusionis insania*—"crazed expenditure as a source of glory"—to which the urban elites of Carthage and the provinces were supposed to look forward with zest. It was because of this that Augustine preached against the games for hours on end, over a period of many weeks.

We know of these games only from Augustine's sermons. Their luxury and expense may well have gained in the telling. Like Symmachus, Augustine knew what great games should be like even if, like Symmachus, the games themselves were not always as great a success as their image suggested. Nor (as we saw in chapter 4) were they necessarily as heavy a burden on the rich as the rich themselves claimed they were. What mattered was that, for Augustine, the games were utterly appropriate to his own rhetoric of almsgiving. They were the exact inverse of the pattern of giving he had proposed to the rich when they came to church. It was not only the amount of money that flowed on these occasions that he denounced: it was the way it flowed and the direction in which it flowed.

With a sure sense of the psychology of civic display, Augustine seized on the *démesure* of the games—on the heroic scattering of resources that was supposed to indicate the measureless reserves of love and loyalty the rich harbored for their city. The games were supposed to be a time of collective madness. They were characterized by the fierce loyalties of circus factions for their respective charioteers.[57] They carried the thrill of death, as the *venatores* pitted themselves against wild and agile beasts and the chariots hurtled around the circus. They were a time for heedless spending by the rich, which was summed up in the distribution of disproportionately expensive silk robes and money prizes to star performers. And all of this was thought to have resulted from a dialogue with the *populus*. The rich did not simply display their wealth before the people. The people of Carthage encouraged this spending by the heavy roar of acclamations. This for Augustine was what was truly intolerable about the games.

> Driven crazy by this and puffed up with pride ... they even wish to lose their fortunes by giving—giving to actresses, giving to cabaret artists, giving to wild-beast hunters, giving to charioteers. They pour forth not only their inherited resources, but their very souls. They draw back with disgust from the poor, because the People do not shout for the poor to receive largesse. But the People roar for the *venator*—the matador—to have his prize.[58]

The games summed up the attitude of an entire urban society: "crazy expenditure is treated as a source of glory and works of [Christian] mercy—*opera misericordiae*—are held in derision."[59]

Non vides in arcam inanem praepositi tui. Vides certe vel surgentem fabricam: You can not see into the empty coffers of your leader; but you certainly can see the empty shell of his building as it goes up

———

GIVING TO THE CHURCH

What was at stake, in Augustine's preaching, was a war of giving. And this involved not only giving to the poor but also giving to the church for other causes. In these years, Aurelius of Carthage had begun a campaign of building that eventually led to the construction of a large cathedral basilica within the city and another outside it.[60] Augustine preached at a time when large churches, still without their roofs, were rising above the city:

> Your bishop may not lack for clothes or need a roof above his head [like the poor]. But perhaps he is building a church. You cannot see into the empty coffers of your leader; but you certainly can see the empty shell of his building as it goes up.... May God grant that I do not say this in vain.[61]

The campaign of fund-raising to build churches also included a collection of money for the support of the clergy. A series of sermons that have recently been discovered in a manuscript at Erfurt show that Augustine may have been challenged to justify his appeals in favor of this form of giving. His hearers expected him to preach about giving to the poor. They felt cheated when a sermon did not end with the rousing challenge of the prophet Isaiah: *"Share your bread with the hungry, and bring the homeless poor into your houses; when you see the naked, clothe them* (Isa. 58:17). Why then did the bishop take them on a detour by talking about collections for the clergy?

Augustine justified his preaching by appealing to the fund-raising activities of Saint Paul. It was a primal duty of Christian congregations to support with material goods the clergy who bestowed on them the spiritual goods of prayer and preaching. Those who gave to the clergy would receive the same incommensurately great rewards in heaven as did those who gave to the poor.[62]

But unlike the Manichees whose Elect were supported by the Auditors, and unlike the "holy poor" among the monks whose right to alms was defended so fiercely by Jerome, the African clergy who received collections did so in part so as to serve the community by building churches. Of all the activities funded by collective giving, building churches involved the greatest sums and had the most spectacular results. This was an activity that brought together rich and poor alike. As we saw in our last chapter, churches built in this way were enduring arguments in stone for the divinely inspired zeal of the congregations who had built them.

They had sprung up all over Africa. Augustine once preached in one such church:

> The fact that you build a church means, with God's help, that you build it for yourselves. What you give to the poor is different. They come and go. This church you build for your own selves. It is the house of your own prayers, the house where you all come together.[63]

Like the *Dolbeau Sermons*, the sermon that referred to this enterprise did not find a place in the standard medieval collection of Augustine's sermons. It is a relatively recent discovery. Writing in 1937, the discoverer of this sermon referred to the fact that the church had been built by the contributions of its congregation as "a touching detail."[64] At the time, however, the show of energy behind such building was considerably more than that. It revealed a slow but sure determination on the part of the African churches to flex their financial muscle. Any church that wished to be dominant in Africa had to establish generous and regular giving by all classes, but most especially by their richer members.

That was why Augustine preached with such gusto against the games. The rich had to be headed off from the glamour of such occasions. They had to break with their background as civic benefactors and learn to give to the church instead. Augustine's sermons aimed at the creation of new habits of generosity among a traditional class of heavy givers.

But (as we saw in chapter 4) we must be careful in interpreting this preaching. Augustine presented the issue as a zero-sum game between the upholders of profane, civic spectacles and a new, Christian ideal of giving to the poor and to pious causes. As a result of Augustine's use of oppositional rhetoric of this kind, scholars have tended to assume that the zero-sum competition between alms and circuses that Augustine conjured up with such gusto actually happened. They have suggested that giving to the churches undermined and finally replaced civic benefaction. In fact, in Africa and elsewhere, the two patterns of giving continued side by side for a long time, without the one necessarily draining funds and energy from the other. In many cities of the Latin West, the end of the games came more slowly than we might expect. There was no easy transition by which wealth that had previously flowed into the cities quietly changed course and flowed, instead, into the Christian churches.

Something else was at stake. By contrasting civic with Christian giving Augustine was attempting to draw a clear line in the sand. For by 403, the line was already in danger of being rubbed out. The boundaries between the world of the civic elites and that of the bishops had become blurred. Augustine stressed the absolute incompatibility of games and almsgiving. For those who listened to him the reality had already become more complex. Over the years, the social and cultural gap between the civic upper classes of the cities and the personnel of the

Christian church had shrunk. A generational change had taken place. In major cities, bishops came to be drawn from the same class as the civic givers.

We are no longer in the world of the 380s, when Optatus, the Donatist bishop of Timgad, had erected his great basilica within sight of a capitol repaired by a group of persons very different from himself. Notables and bishops had begun to seem interchangeable. In 417 the Catholic Council of Carthage summed up previous rulings that forbade the sons of bishops from offering public games. Their fathers had evidently come from elite families before they had entered the clergy. Their sons had inherited the obligations—and the extravagant tastes—of civic benefactors.[65] Augustine could even say that he expected that many who sat in the amphitheater would eventually sit beside him on the bench of bishops.[66]

Surprising details show the extent to which the two groups—the civic notables and the bishops—had drawn close to each other. At the very end of Augustine's life, in 428, one of his most touching letters among those discovered by Johannes Divjak (*New Letter* 2*) was a courteous exchange between Firmus, a nobleman of Carthage, and the old bishop. Firmus was a figure poised between two worlds. He had received from Augustine copies of the *City of God* and advice on how best to circulate it. He himself had read the *City of God* as far as book ten. He had been present for three afternoon sessions, when book eighteen had been read aloud. In return, Augustine had asked Firmus to send him the school exercises of his son, a boy whom Augustine called affectionately "our little Greek." The old bishop wished to be told the boy's age and the progress of his studies. Firmus was married to a Christian wife, though he himself still delayed his baptism.[67] Recently, Firmus's name has been identified, carved in bold letters on a seat of the amphitheater of Carthage. He bore the title of *vir clarissimus*—he was an honorary senator. A reader of the *City of God* and good friend of Augustine, Firmus had sat with his peers presiding over the games of their city up to the very last days of Roman Africa.[68]

Faced by persons such as Firmus, it was important for Augustine and his colleagues to carry the war of giving to the highest levels of African urban society. By the beginning of the fifth century, the churches in Africa were well equipped to engage in this war. Based on traditions that reached back over 150 years to the days of Cyprian of Carthage, the bishops of Africa had created and maintained an impressive ideology of collective giving, both for the poor and for the needs of the clergy. They had generated a prevailing wind of generosity in the churches. This generosity reflected the energy that we can sense in the headstrong actions of the Christian *populus* all over Africa—from the creation of country bishoprics to the lynching of unpopular officials. These had been impressive gains, unparalleled in other provinces. But in the last analysis, in Africa as elsewhere, only the intervention of the traditional rich could raise the local church above the level of tenacious mediocrity to the glory that such a church felt it deserved.

History had come full circle in Augustine's Africa. Two centuries before, the forums, temples, theaters, and circuses that amaze us in the ruins of the Roman cities of Africa had been created through a surge of giving by the municipal upper classes. In the words of Ramsay MacMullen: "The physical magnificence of imperial civilization rested ultimately on sheer willingness."[69]

Now was the time for the "sheer willingness" of the churches of Africa to make itself felt. But there was a difference. In the Christian churches both rich and poor were expected to contribute. There was no fixed class of givers. It is against this background that we should see the consequences in Africa of the unforeseen arrival on its shores, after 410, of the super-rich of Italy, accompanied by spiritual guides such as Pelagius and his disciples. The views on wealth and on the human condition held by the mentors of the Roman aristocracy were very different from those Augustine had preached for over a decade in the churches of Hippo, Carthage, and the Medjerda valley. They were views that seemed to privilege a group of special givers—great renouncers or open-handed families of the super-rich, now proud to produce noble virgins. Seen with African eyes, this was a moment of danger. The spectacular behavior of Pinianus and Melania, Pelagius's praise of the "natural" nobility of soul of the Anician Demetrias, combined with the extreme statements of the Pelagian *De divitiis* betrayed different, more melodramatic views of wealth that had been nurtured in a specifically Roman environment at a moment of acute crisis. Now the two views collided for a few years on the soil of Africa. Let us move forward, therefore, from the time of Augustine's sermons on the duties of the rich—such as he had preached in Carthage at the time of the games of 403—to the sermons he preached after 413 against the ideas of Pelagius and of his radical followers.

CHAPTER 22

Dimitte nobis debita nostra: Forgive us our sins

Augustine, Wealth, and Pelagianism, 411–417

"Place your hopes in your own self": Augustine and Pelagianism in Africa

In the last chapter we followed Augustine in action as a preacher. In his sermons of the 400s, he had come to frame a distinctive attitude toward wealth and its uses in the African churches. The arrival from Rome of patrons and supporters of Pelagius constituted an unwelcome intrusion. For a moment, Augustine's intense but somewhat isolated world—the world of African Christianity—was thrown open to views that challenged those to which he had become wedded as a result of decades of preaching and activity at Hippo and in Carthage. Let us see how Augustine and his African colleagues reacted to this challenge.

In 411 the shores of Africa were "awash with displaced senators."[1] Some noble refugees, such as Albina, Pinianus, and Melania, went straight to their ancestral estates in the hinterland, thereby putting a safe distance between themselves and a coastline still exposed to the threat of barbarian invasion from Italy. Others remained in Carthage. Not all of these refugees were Christian. Many were embittered pagans who had their own views on the disaster that had struck them. The uncle of Melania, Rufius Agrypnius Volusianus, was the son of a Roman priestly family.[2] In many ways Volusianus lived in what was already a post-pagan world. He would have exercised no priesthood. His mother was a Christian. But he continued to harbor grave doubts as to the truth of Christianity. He also doubted the political advisability of a Christian empire. His criticisms were first aired in a salon of cultivated gentlemen in Carthage.[3] Volusianus voiced the resentment of pagans, in both Rome and Africa, who believed the fall of Rome had happened because of neglect of the worship of the gods. The need to answer pagan criticisms led Augustine to embark on the masterpiece of his old age—the "great and arduous work" of the *City of God*. He wrote the *City of God* because the views of persons like Volusianus counted for much in African provincial society.[4]

At that time, nobody knew how long the refugees from Rome would remain in Africa. As a result of the Visigothic invasions in Italy and the related collapse of the Rhine frontier in Gaul, the political geography of the Latin West had changed. The western empire imploded dramatically toward the south. All roads no longer led to Trier, as they had done in the days of Ausonius. Nor was Milan any longer a safe staging post between Gaul and the Balkans. In a world where Gaul and even Italy north of the Apennines were zones of danger, Rome and Carthage were brought face-to-face in a manner that had not happened since the days of the Punic Wars. Africa was now the only rich and loyal province in the western empire. The future was unknown. In a worst-case scenario, Carthage might well have become a "Rome in exile"—a bulwark of high Romanity that faced across the Mediterranean to a ruined world. It was crucial for Augustine to influence the opinions of the noble refugees around whom an alternative to Rome might emerge. Expatriate Christian nobles from Rome could have settled down to become the lay leaders of the church in Carthage and elsewhere in Africa. If they protected the ideas of Pelagius, his ideas and those of his followers would spread throughout the province with alarming speed.

Nor was Augustine concerned only with the Romans of Rome. He was well aware that a large and influential floating vote of local figures existed in Hippo, in the proud little cities of the Medjerda valley, and in Carthage. Many were small-town intellectuals, nurtured on Neo-Platonic and Stoic ideas. In one of the largest houses of Bulla Regia (a town through which Augustine passed regularly on his way to Carthage) a mosaic panel lay in the middle of the floor of the dining room. It spelled out in golden letters on a blue background a motto in Greek: *en seautô tas elpidas ékhé*: "Place your own hopes in your own self." The Greek was not perfect, but the message was plain. It advocated exactly the same degree of self-reliance Augustine considered to be a central and heretical element in the views of Pelagius.[5] In Augustine's eyes, the shadow of Pelagius not only fell over the Christians of Africa. It also fell over a large middle ground of undecided pagans for whose minds Augustine had battled inconclusively for decades. A Christianity patronized by nobles from Rome and supported by converted intellectuals of Stoic background from among the urban elites would have had a very different flavor from the sort of Christianity Augustine had propounded in Africa for the previous twenty years. Hence the tenacity with which Augustine pursued the ideas associated with Pelagius and his followers in the course of what has come to be known as the Pelagian Controversy.

Dimitte nobis debita nostra: Forgive us our sins

AUGUSTINE AND DAILY PENANCE

The Pelagian Controversy finally erupted after Pelagius's *Letter to Demetrias* (in 413) and the arrival from Sicily of news of the doctrines canvassed in the Pelagian treatise *De divitiis* (in around 414). It could never be a war of ideas alone. It was a battle that was fought from the ground up. The piety of an entire Christian region was involved. Augustine decided early on to fight it as a battle to uphold the pious customs of the African churches. Its opening phases included a campaign of preaching by Augustine in Hippo and in the great basilicas of Carthage. In these sermons Augustine aimed to persuade his listeners that the ideas of Pelagius and of his more extreme followers were not only misplaced but denied the most cherished religious practices of the African churches.[6] Thus, the denial of original sin appeared to undercut the practice of infant baptism "for the remission of sins."[7] Pelagius's emphasis on free will independent of the grace of God appeared to deny the solemn prayers of the bishop at the end of every church service: "May He grant us to persevere in His commandments and to walk in the right way."[8] The notion that a human being might use his or her free will to live without sin flouted the daily recitation of the Lord's Prayer: *Forgive us our sins.*[9]

Nowhere was the appeal to common practices more plain than in the manner in which Augustine approached the subject of wealth and of religious giving within the Church. He spoke to his hearers on the assumption that he shared with them the certainty that almsgiving was an obligatory pious practice. He also insisted that almsgiving had always had an expiatory function. Alms atoned for sins. The command of the prophet Daniel to king Nebuchadnezzar was a command to every Christian: *Redeem your sins with alms and your injustices by compassion on the poor* (Dan. 4:24). It was this certainty Augustine invoked incessantly against the ideas of Pelagius and his followers. Let us see why he did this.

Augustine may never have read the text of the *De divitiis* itself. But his informants in Syracuse made sure that he understood its message in terms of traditional religious practice. The message of the treatise was not so much that the rich should not exist. It was that they could not be saved. Unless they gave away everything, their almsgiving would be to no avail.

> A rich man who remains in his riches will not enter the Kingdom of God unless he sells all that he has: nor will those be of any use to him [in securing salvation] even if he uses them to fulfill the commandments [that is, by giving alms].[10]

Faced by such views, Augustine expected his audience to agree that to have denied the rich the chance to save themselves through almsgiving was a serious matter. It touched directly on two central issues: on Augustine's particular notion of sin and penance, and on more general notions, current in the African churches as elsewhere, on the expiatory nature of religious gifts.

There is little need to linger on the first of these issues. By the age of sixty, Augustine had believed for some time that the life of a Christian was a life of continual penance.[11] He had already made this plain in a vivid image in one of his sermons of 403. The pious Christian was a human hedgehog. He or she was covered from head to foot with the tiny, sharp spines of daily, barely conscious *peccata minutissima*—tiny little sins.[12] It was to expunge these tiny sins that the Christian should pray every day *Dimitte nobis debita nostra*: *Forgive us our sins* (Matt. 6:12).

As Anne-Marie de la Bonnardière showed in a masterly article written over half a century ago, this passage in the Lord's Prayer was crucial to Augustine. He seized upon it from the opening years of the Pelagian Controversy. It became for him the touchstone of orthodoxy.[13] Recited by the baptized before receiving the Eucharist, the phrase *Dimitte nobis debita nostra—Forgive us our sins*—left no room for the Pelagian claim that baptized Christians could live without sin. To Augustine, the prayer was a daily reminder of a daily state of sinfulness, which cried out for daily forgiveness. To deny this was to strike at the very heart of his religion. By the year 415, Augustine's notion of what the Christian society of the future might look like was simple in the extreme: it consisted of being able to hear the thunder of thousands of persons beating their chests, every day, as they recited the Lord's Prayer and remembered their sins.[14]

"Let the hands go round and round to work the pump": Daily Sins and Daily Alms

Overwhelmingly interested as we are in the history of the Augustinian notion of sin and its effects on Christian subjectivity in all future ages, we have tended to overlook the concrete, financial corollary of his insistence on daily penance for sin. Like all other Christian preachers of his generation, Augustine never doubted that prayer for forgiveness should be accompanied by almsgiving.[15] Of all the practices he expected his hearers to take for granted, the link between almsgiving and expiation was the one most solidly installed in the back of their minds. It was a source of hope for the average Christian. Writing against popular errors concerning the Last Judgment, in the second to last book of the *City of God*, Augustine reported that perhaps the most tenacious popular error of all was the belief that Christians who gave alms would never, no matter what their sins, end up in the perpetual fire of Hell. They might pass through this fire for a time; or they might be released from it at given times. But, unlike those who did not give alms, they would never end in the fire of Hell forever without hope of remission.[16] Like many of the popular misconceptions disapproved of by Augustine, this was by no means a view limited to the uneducated. Paulinus of Nola, for instance, seems to have taken such a view for granted. Like little drops of water, alms accompanied by prayer on behalf of the dead somehow dampened the fires that raged around sinners in the other world.[17] For most believers, a good Christian was an almsgiving Christian.

Augustine had serious reservations about many aspects of this popular belief. He did not believe that the power of alms alone would save hardened sinners in the other world. But, as far as this life was concerned, he wholeheartedly accepted the view that linked almsgiving to the forgiveness of sins. He made clear in his sermons that almsgiving provided the "wings" that brought the *Dimitte nobis* of the Lord's Prayer up to heaven.[18] Without such wings no prayer could fly.

Faced by Pelagius, Augustine pulled the traditional notion of almsgiving as a remedy for sin into the powerful gravitational field of a notion of the need for the daily expiation of sins that was implied in the daily recitation of the Lord's Prayer. "Daily"—*cottidiana*—was the ever-recurrent word Augustine used, whether he spoke of sin, of prayer, or of almsgiving. The human condition demanded this. The soul was a leaking vessel on the high seas. Little trickles of daily sins constantly seeped through the timbers, silently filling the bilge with water that might yet sink the ship if it were not pumped out. And to man the bilge pump was both to pray *and* to give alms:

> And we should not only pray, but also give alms.... Those who work the bilge-pump lest the boat go down do so [chanting sea shanties] with their voices and working with their hands.... Let the hands go round and round.... Let them give, let them do good works.[19]

Altogether, when he came to preach against the Pelagians, Augustine placed behind the largely unreflecting practice of expiatory giving the heavy weight of a view of human nature that made daily expiation a necessity. Religious giving was part of daily life because daily life itself was defined by sin. It took place against the noise of the steady creak of the bilge pump of prayer, fasting, and almsgiving.[20]

"May he have salvation from his sins": Expiatory Giving in Africa

The rich of Africa heard this message with a certain relief. Indeed, their expected reaction to Augustine's preaching fits in very well with the realities of their social condition. Even if they were good Christians, none of them suffered from the vertigo of wealth that had swept through Christian Roman families of the super-rich. Pinianus and Melania were rare birds. But their actions had provoked and corroborated a widespread critique of wealth in Roman circles, addressed to some of the richest persons in the empire. The local landowners of Africa were different. They had no wish to be told to renounce their wealth in its entirety, as the author of the *De divitiis* urged that they should do. The Christian message they had continuously received from their bishops (Catholic and Donatist alike) was not that they should renounce their wealth but sacralize it by giving it on a regular basis to the church.

A century of confrontation between the two churches of Africa had created something of a lifeboat mentality among the rich supporters of either church. Each local church had needed constant collective support. A fierce sense of the autonomy of the wealth of the church in Africa had built up over the years. It had created a mood that did not expect ostentatious, one-off personal acts of generosity to the church, such as had led Paulinus to rebuild the tomb of Saint Felix at Cimitile or Pammachius to found the splendid church that bore his own name at Rome. Rather, if the rich were to use their wealth, they were to do it on a regular basis and with a low profile. For this reason, it was best that giving should be associated with regular penitential habits the rich shared as fellow sinners with all other members of the congregation. Giving to the Christian community "for the remission of sins"—and not for one's own glory—was the surest remedy for pride. It also reassured the ever-vigilant Christian *populus* that those who led the community in wealth did not lead it with the habitual arrogance of the rich and powerful. To give in expiation of sin marked out the gift as a humble religious transaction, not as a gesture of self-promotion. It muted the profile of the benefactor.

We should, of course, always remember that Africa was a large place. Not everyone from every region accepted the studiously subdued image of the good Christian giver to which Augustine appealed in his sermons. Further to the west from Hippo, leading figures in provincial society (such as the great Moorish generals of the time) had no qualms whatsoever about erecting votive shrines that bore their names and those of their family. Such a person was Flavius Nuvel, who built a basilica at Rusguniae, in Caesarean—that is, eastern—Mauretania (on the coast, twenty miles east of modern Algiers), along with his wife and family: "He has [now] dedicated the basilica which he promised with a vow and offered it to God." A semi-independent prince, Flavius Nuvel was the Paulinus of his region. He had even been able to obtain and install in his basilica a fragment of the True Cross that had been brought all the way from the Holy Land. The building made clear that Nuvel and his family enjoyed the protection of God. It did not declare that they were sinners.[21]

By contrast, Augustine had preached a somber democracy of sin. This meant, in practice, that he left room among the possible lay donors to the church for persons with lesser fortunes than grandees such as Nuvel. All could give because all were equally sinners. And the gifts of all would be equally acceptable to God. Each gift, of whatever size, worked equally to expiate the sins of the donor. This attitude encouraged relatively humble persons to come forward as donors to the church. Such was Umbrius Felix, a schoolteacher in the little town of Mina (modern Ighil Izane, Algeria), far to the west of Hippo, on the inland road that crossed Caesarean Mauretania. In an inscription carved between two rosettes, he wrote in 408 AD:

> from the Gifts of God and Christ, Umbrius Felix, the *magister*, made this. He has repaid his vow to God. Let prayer be made for him and may he have salvation from his sins.[22]

Augustine was not alone in thinking in this way. The notion of constant expiation provided background noise to the building activities of many bishops. At Tipasa, bishop Alexander placed at the entrance of his basilica an unusually elegant and explicit inscription:

> *Clausula iustitiae est martyrium votis optare.*
> *Habes et aliam similem, aelemosinam viribus facere.*

(The highest pitch of righteousness is to wish for martyrdom. You have another like it: to give alms to the best of your ability.)[23]

And all this could be cheap. As we saw in chapter 4, the Christian notion of the incommensurability between the gift and its heavenly reward fostered an attitude that favored regular, small donations. Each gift, however small, was charged with a magic all of its own. In the words of a later inscription from a church at Tigzirt (on the coast of Mauretania, in modern Algeria): "Seek heaven with a pious heart, through [donating] a few cubes only of mosaic."[24]

"If you wish to have a memorial forever": Renunciation, Endowment, and Provincial Society

As always with Augustine, there was a practical side to his deep musings on sin, grace, and free will. His doctrine of the need for daily expiation, summed up in the phrase *Forgive us our trespasses* in the Lord's Prayer, served to empower the pious practices of the average rich member of his congregations.

This was a doctrine that spoke to the habits of a class that had come, over the years, to rally to Augustine's church in Africa. It was not a doctrine that had meant much to the pious aristocrats Melania and Pinianus when they first arrived in Africa. Up to 411, their notion of renunciation had involved the dizzy scattering of gold. Wealth was there to be "vaporized." Nothing did this more effectively than turning it, as quickly as possible, into the most liquid (and portable) of all substances—golden coins—and sending it as far from home as it could go to the imagined ends of the earth.[25]

The bishops of Africa would have none of this. Augustine makes only one appearance in Gerontius's *Life of Melania* (the ugly incident in Hippo having been excluded). In the passage in question, we see how, in coming to Africa, Melania and Pinianus entered a very different zone of Christian piety. Regular endowment meant more to the local bishops than did the spectacular but spasmodic acts of giving to which they had been used in Italy:

> When the blessed ones decided to sell all their property [in Africa], the most saintly and important bishops (I mean blessed Augustine, his brother-bishop Alypius, and Aurelius of Carthage) advised them saying, "The money that you now furnish to monasteries will be used up in a short time. If you wish to have a memorial forever in heaven and earth, give an estate and its income to each monastery."[26]

We do not know to what extent the young couple put this advice into practice. In any case, they left Africa for Jerusalem within a few years, in 417. They spent the remainder of their wealth in the Holy Land and in Egypt. The great noble ladies of the Anician house also left Africa. They returned to Rome the moment that peace returned to Italy. After 417 the Catholic churches in Africa buckled down to make the best they could of what they had. They drew on the "sheer willingness" (to use Ramsay Mac Mullen's phrase) that had already been built up over the previous generations among the local laity. These reserves of willingness had become considerable. A new class of persons began to bring wealth to the churches. Their emergence in African society at this time was a relatively recent development that was connected with a change in the structures of landholding in the province. Let us see how this happened.

Africa had always been associated, in the Roman mind, with the massive landholdings of the emperor and of the nobility of Rome. These estates were imagined at the time (and continue to be imagined by modern scholars) to have been *latifundia*. We tend to think of them as vast, autonomous tracts of land that were as seemingly endless as the somber chaparral of southern Texas, with its huge ranches and stunted towns. Given such widespread ideas about Africa, it was easy for the biographer of Melania, writing in distant Jerusalem in the 450s, to imagine that his heroine had been ensconced in one such grandiose estate outside Thagaste.

But in many parts of Africa (and especially in the Medjerda valley, which Augustine knew well) the reality on the ground was significantly different from the stereotype.[27] In the course of the fourth century, a vigorous provincial society had grown up under the shadow of these immense blocks of land—and, ultimately, at the expense of their absentee owners. As in Ireland or Hungary in the nineteenth century, land owned by a few great, absentee landowners had fostered the growth of an entire class of lesser figures, drawn from local society. This class was made up of tenants on long leases, of administrators on behalf of absentee landlords, and of entrepreneurs involved in the mobilization of labor and the sale of agrarian products. These men, of course, still towered above the *pauperes*—the small farmers and townsmen of their region. Most had family property of their own. Many came from the elites of the cities. But they were not the great *latifondistas* that modern historians frequently imagine them to have been. In fact, they preyed on the *latifondistas*. They fell on the land of the emperor and of the Roman *nobiles* and turned much of its profit to their own advantage.[28]

New forms of leasing had made this possible. In the course of the late third and fourth centuries, the great landowners (led by the emperor) came to prefer the stability offered by long-term tenancies over the rapid, revolving door practice of five-year leases. Such tenancies were known as tenancies for *emphyteusis*—for "the planting up of the land." They seem to have encouraged the growth of new cash crops. In many areas, they were associated with the spectacular extension of olive cultivation.[29] They attracted improving landowners drawn from local society.

We know of one such landowner. This was the Donatist bishop of Calama (modern Guelma, in Algeria), Crispinus. Crispinus's notion of improvement was not everybody's notion. The moment he obtained the emphyteutic lease of an imperial estate, he rebaptized eighty of its previously Catholic peasants. By doing this he put the Holy Spirit back into them, by baptizing them properly. It was all part of the reorganization of his new property.[30] Augustine, of course, was duly shocked. But Crispinus's action was a sign of the times. Town councillors, bishops, and local landowners were enabled to become leading figures in their region through enterprising use of a new system of leases that gave them access to the land of great absentee landowners. It was a situation that tended to pit local figures against the distant grandees whose lands they had virtually made their own in return for rent.

These people needed to commemorate themselves; they now did so in the churches. Whatever they may have thought about the Catholic church associated with the party of Augustine and his colleagues (for many local notables were former Donatists), the imperial laws issued after 411 had ensured that it was now the only church in town. Wealth that had been divided between two churches now flowed into only one. The result was yet another surge of building. On the floor of one such new basilica—the basilica that may have been built around this time at Cuicul (modern Djemila, in Algeria)—we meet the provincial rich of Africa who had contributed to it. Mosaic panels celebrated individual donors' gifts that had enabled the laying of an extensive pavement. As we have seen, such panels were common in the churches of northern Italy. They were rare in Africa. (African inscriptions had tended to give prominence to the bishop as the administrator of sacralized wealth collected from many donations.) The names of the donors on the panels in the basilica of Cuicul were a concise gazetteer of the gentry. The titles they used echoed faithfully the local hierarchies that had been created by the imperial system. They were a commentary on the structuring of local African society first revealed to us, sixty years previously, by the stone inscription of the *Album* placed in the town hall of Timgad in the 360s. But they are now placed on the floor of a Christian basilica. Flavius Paulus was an honorary senator and former tribune; Flavius Felix was an honorary senator and former head of a provincial government office; Iulius Adeodatus was a priest of the imperial cult. This proud civic title, associated with pagan cult, was taken for granted by its holder. He plainly saw nothing wrong in flaunting it on the floor of a Christian basilica! Two others were simply *viri honesti*, respectable town councillors such as Augustine and his father had once been.[31] The mosaic gives us a glimpse of the face of the rich within the churches of Africa in the last decades of Augustine's life.

Augustine and his colleagues had given such persons a doctrine for the long haul. Suffused by a sense of the daily need to expiate sins, the "sheer willingness" that had always been expected of the rich in Africa had lost much of its vividness. It could not be associated either with the startling *démesure* of civic prodigality or with the new and equally startling scenarios of Christian ascetic renunciation. But what it had lost in vividness, pious giving had gained in a sense of an indefinite future, driven by the perpetual motion of the need to expiate sin. Giving to the church and to the poor could never be a spasmodic, one-off business. Sin was permanent. Its momentum was almost subliminal. For (as Augustine presented it) personal sin was linked to a shared, unplumbed complicity in the sin of Adam—a vast sin from the very dawn of time that had infected the whole human race. For this reason, religious giving also had to be permanent, regular, and devoted to the advancement of a collective venture in salvation. The unimaginable scale of this venture (as Augustine conjured it up in the pages of the *City of God*) did justice to the majesty of the rise, in Africa and throughout western Europe, of a new institution in the form of the Catholic Church. It is to the place of the church in society both in Africa and elsewhere that we must now turn by following the years of mounting crisis throughout the Latin West (associated with the sack of Rome and the collapse of the Rhine frontier), which coincided with the dénouement of the Pelagian Controversy, from around 415 to the death of Augustine in 430.

CHAPTER 23

❧

"Out of Africa"

Wealth, Power, and the Churches: 415–430

"A new heresy ... secretly spreading its tentacles": Pelagius between
Africa, Palestine, and Rome, 415–17

There was a saying among the ancient Greeks and Romans: *Ex Africa semper
aliquid novi*: "Out of Africa there is always something new."[1] In the 410s and
420s, the churches of Africa, with Augustine as their spokesman, brought yet
another startling set of novelties from their strange land. The rallying of the
church of Africa behind Augustine against the views of Pelagius involved ma-
neuvers that were unprecedented in the history of Latin Christianity. An entire
provincial church gathered in councils attended by up to two hundred bishops
so as to condemn the views of a single lay teacher. No less surprising was the manner in which the bishops asserted that they could derive an entire set of theological doctrines from the day-to-day practices of their own church. Matters that
had previously been regarded as impenetrable and as open to disagreement among
experts—such as the relation between grace and free will, the exact nature of
original sin, and the exact meaning of the baptism of children—were handled
with peremptory certitude by Augustine and his colleagues. Theological conclusions of unusual rigor were derived from simple rituals, such as infant baptism
and the recitation of the Lord's Prayer.

Most striking of all was the confidence with which the bishops of Africa
claimed that others should share their certainty on these issues. Having met in
solemn council in 416 to condemn the ideas associated with Pelagius, they
passed on their judgment to the bishop of Rome and to the emperor as if they
expected their views to be ratified without further question.[2] Africa had spoken
with unprecedented, massed conviction. The issue was whether anyone else would
listen to the novel dogmatic statements that came—very much as new things—
out of Africa.

Between 415 and 418, it seemed as if nobody would listen. Up to 418, Augustine heard nothing but bad news. The fate of Pelagius lay beyond his control and that of his colleagues. Pelagius had gone straight from Africa to Palestine, where he received a mixed reception. He was met by the hostility of Jerome. Jerome's enmity may have been related to Pelagius's close relations to Pinianus and Melania the Younger, who was the granddaughter of Melania the Elder, the famous patroness of Jerome's enemy Rufinus. Pelagius was also followed by accusations from the West, but they did not impress the local Palestinian bishops. Pelagius was cleared of heresy and accepted as orthodox at a council held at Diospolis (Lydda/Lod, in Israel) on December 20, 415.[3]

In early spring of 416, one of the first boats to sail into the harbor of Hippo at the end of the winter closure of the Mediterranean carried a pamphlet written by Pelagius. In this pamphlet, Pelagius announced to the world that he had been cleared of heresy by the bishops of Palestine. A fragment of the sermon with which Augustine greeted this unwelcome news has recently been discovered. It shows him reacting instantly to the challenge from Pelagius. From then on, the gloves were off. As he told his congregation on that occasion, "There is a new heresy lurking about, and secretly spreading its tentacles far and wide."[4]

Augustine could no longer ignore the views of Pelagius. His heresy had to be quashed. Immediately, two councils were summoned—one of the bishops of Numidia at Milevis and one at Carthage. They sent to Innocent, bishop of Rome, a list of the views of Pelagius and Caelestius. As we have seen, the Africans presented their list of errors in the expectation that such errors would be instantly condemned.

But Innocent did not wish to be hurried. He was reluctant to condemn a man known for his Christian zeal and for his relations with leading Christian families of Rome, such as the Anicii. Faced by a united and indignant church in Africa, he agreed that if such thoughts were being entertained by anyone, it was, indeed, a serious matter. But he hinted that it was up to him (and not to the Africans) to judge whether Pelagius actually held them. He would decide for himself. He elicited a statement of the faith from Pelagius. Caelestius, Pelagius's leading disciple and a more radical figure than Pelagius, reappeared in Rome.

Then, in March 417, Innocent died. He was succeeded by Zosimus. Like Innocent, Zosimus wanted to be the judge of this case. But while Innocent had been an old, experienced man, capable of biding his time, Zosimus was a new bishop in a hurry to get things done. In the late summer of 417, a gathering to investigate the ideas of Pelagius took place in the courtyard of what is now the modern church of San Clemente. This was a titular church, named after an unknown Clemens. But it was already associated in the popular mind with Saint Clement, the disciple of Saint Peter. It was an eminently suitable place for the successor of Saint Peter to give judgment. Zosimus exonerated both Caelestius and Pelagius of the charges leveled against them. In September 417 Zosimus's letter arrived in Carthage. The African bishops received a lecture on the evils of false testimony and on the dangers of over-rigid theological speculation. It was a calculated snub. Zosimus treated the African bishops as a group of doctrinaire heresy hunters in a strange land.

Characteristically, Augustine and his colleagues replied by calling a yet larger council. A "universal" council of over two hundred bishops was abruptly summoned to Carthage by Aurelius. The council sent bishops to Italy. But they did this so as to seek judgment from another, more reliable source. The bishops avoided Rome and went directly to the imperial court at Ravenna. They secured from the emperor an outright condemnation of both Pelagius and Caelestius.[5]

"Who judge it to be a sign of plebeian baseness to think the same as everybody else": Roman Society and the Condemnation of Pelagius, 418

Looking back a few years later, the followers of Pelagius were convinced that Alypius of Thagaste had brought a gift of eighty Numidian stallions to bribe leading courtiers in order to secure the condemnation of their hero. If this was true, it was a well-timed gift. The ravages of the Visigoths and Vandals in Spain had cut off the supply of fine horses that had been provided by the ranches of Lusitania on which Symmachus had drawn for his games twenty years previously. Eighty stallions was a lavish gift. A horse cost a minimum of twelve *solidi*. Even if there was no truth in this accusation, the rumor itself showed that, in the eyes of the world, the church of Africa was not only a church very certain of its opinions but a church experienced in the ways of the court. It was now also a very rich church. The recent absorption of the estates of the Donatist church had left it uniquely wealthy. To outsiders it seemed as if the longstanding economic dominance of Africa in the economy of the western Mediterranean had been transmuted into a theological dominance also, due to the lobbying power of rich African bishops.[6]

It has proved easy to agree with the supporters of Pelagius that the appeal of Augustine and his colleagues to the imperial court at Ravenna was a high-handed and corrupt maneuver. It is often assumed that their intervention alone secured the condemnation of Pelagius. Making vivid use of a metaphor from a soccer game, Brinley Rees, the translator of the letters of Pelagius, has said that

> the match [between Pelagius and Augustine] may well have ended in a draw; instead, it went into "extra" time and at the end of that Augustine and his team won with the help of questionable decisions made by the referees and the touch-judges.[7]

Basically, in appealing to the emperor Augustine and his African colleagues had not played fair.

Though this view is common among modern scholars, it does not do justice to the complexity of Italian local politics and to the involvement of the emperors themselves in the affairs of Rome. It is, therefore, to Rome and not to Ravenna that we must turn in order to understand the sudden swing of opinion that led to the final condemnation of Pelagius and his followers.

The Rome to which the Roman refugees returned and in which Caelestius made his appearance before bishop Zosimus in 417 was not the Rome of pre-410. It was not an entirely ruined city. But it was a city whose nerve had been shattered by the famine days of the Gothic siege of 409 and by the methodical depredation of the Gothic sack of 410. The different groups within it—the upper nobility, the lesser nobles (many of whom were government servants), the well-to-do plebeians, and the clergy—had seldom shared the same interests. This had not mattered greatly in more prosperous days. Now each of them was concerned to get back on its own feet, on its own terms.

The nobles faced a formidable governmental task. To keep Rome quiet had been difficult enough in the days of Symmachus. Now this task was rendered more intractable by the dislocation of the imperial *annona* and by the drop in income from the estates of the nobles in southern Italy as a result of the Gothic invasions. At the time, neither recession seemed irreversible. The great estates would regain their yield (provided that they regained their manpower that had been dispersed by war and through capture by the barbarians). The *annona* was reorganized. But the strain of the effort was plain in these years.[8]

Furthermore, the Christian members of the nobility had come to be divided. In previous decades they had become accustomed to in-fighting among fellow Christians. Leading families acted as the patrons of increasingly radical teachers. The division of Roman families between the supporters of Jerome and of Rufinus in the 390s was exacerbated as these families inherited other, yet more assertive spiritual guides. As we have seen, Pelagius stepped into the slot once occupied by Rufinus. Furthermore, it seemed as if the leading Christian family of Rome—that of the Anicii—had also supported Pelagius. Religious factionalism linked to the Christian aristocracy and its clients had become a major feature of upper-class life in Rome.

Factionalism of this kind was a matter of immediate concern to emperors who resided in Ravenna. We tend to think of Ravenna as a distant court city, occupied by the emperor and his servants, while Rome lay deserted.[9] But in the generation after 410, the exact opposite was the case. Ravenna was not a true alternative to Rome. It was not a governmental capital, totally removed by distance and by ethos from Rome, as Trier and Milan had been. Rather, Ravenna was a co-capital with Rome. Ravenna was the northern focus of an ellipse of imperial power that straddled central Italy and the Apennines. The other focus was Rome.[10] We should bear this in mind when we judge the actions of the African bishops. To go to Ravenna was not to bypass the bishop of Rome in seeking a purely "secular" judgment on a religious matter. That is a modern assumption. For the emperor and for many upper-class residents of Rome, theology and due order in their city were not separate issues. The one had to be solved so as to ensure the other. If the bishop of Rome failed to bring about consensus, the emperor and his advisors would do it for him.

It is, therefore, not surprising that, on April 30, 418, the Praetorian Prefect, Flavius Junius Quartus Palladius, received an imperial edict that brushed aside bishop Zosimus's acquittal of Pelagius and Caelestius. The imperial edict condemned them both by name as "the nefarious originators of a new heresy." They must leave the city. Their followers—clergy and laity alike—could be denounced by any person. Their teachings had damaged the peace "of our most holy City."[11]

Palladius was not a distant courtier, attached to the emperor in the faraway marshes of Ravenna. We know from an inscription made public in 1928 (that seems not to have been considered in the context of the Pelagian Controversy) that Palladius had been a link between Rome and the court. His palace stood at the foot of the Aventine Hill. The inscription was set up outside this palace. It stated that he had represented the Senate to the emperor on four occasions.[12] More important, Palladius may well have been the same Palladius who, in the terrible years of 409–10, had presided over attempts to make all senators contribute equally to collections of money with which to buy the safety of the city from the Goths.[13]

If that is the case, then Palladius would have seen the Christian aristocracy at its worst. The Anicii had protected their vast wealth by refusing to make any contribution to the common fund. Faltonia Proba was even believed by her enemies to have opened the gates of Rome to the Goths. The young Pinianus and his wife, Melania the Younger, had decided to sell up their fortune at just the time when a part of it was needed by the *Respublica* for the common good of Rome. Palladius (if he was the same person) was in no mood to forgive yet further factionalism among the nobles.

Thus, Pelagius and Caelestius were not condemned only so as to please the Africans but also for having led a disruptive faction in Rome. They were presented in the imperial edict as a group that claimed, on the basis of their perfectionist theology, to be superior to everybody else:

> Judging it to be a sign of plebeian baseness to think the same as everybody else, and a signal mark of expertise to destroy what has been approved of by all in common.[14]

The draconian edict fits all too well into the tense mood of the time. After 410 a lifeboat mentality had developed in Rome. Divisions of religious opinion were a luxury inherited from a more affluent age. They had no place in a city that had been shaken by barbarian invasion.

"In almost the entire West a dogma has been pushed forward that is no less idiotic than it is impious": Julian of Eclanum, 418–ca. 450

Faced by an imperial edict that claimed to bring order back to an anxious city, the varying groups in Rome capitulated. Zosimus did an about-face. The clergy of Rome also rallied against Pelagius. Many leading priests and deacons had previously supported him. They included future bishops of Rome—Celestine (422–32) and Sixtus (432–40).[15] Even the bearer of letters from Rome to Carthage, the young acolyte Leo, may well have been the future Leo the Great (440–61).[16] The switch of allegiances among these well-placed clergymen made plain that they wished the clergy to maintain their position as the true Third Estate of Rome. As clergymen, they were prepared to accept the hardline doctrines laid down by fellow ecclesiastics—by the African bishops—rather than to follow the views of Pelagius, a layman whose principal protectors had been laypersons from the upper aristocracy.

The only consequential opposition to the ideas of Augustine came from outside Rome. Julian, the young bishop of Eclanum, in southern Italy, refused to sign the document condemning Pelagius. It is worthwhile lingering for a moment on this remarkable person. His career shows the impressive cultural resources on which a Latin clergyman of good family could draw.[17]

Eclanum was a small city in the hills behind Campania, about ten miles from Beneventum. Now known as Mirabella Eclano, it looked out to the dry, rolling hills of Apulia (modern Puglia) and to the road that led from Rome to Brindisi and the East. Julian belonged to a relatively new social group—an aristocracy of clergymen. His father had been a bishop, and his two sisters were nuns. He was born into a circle of clergymen that had recently established itself on the edge of Campania. This was the region Symmachus had regarded as his favored landscape of the heart in the 370s and in which Paulinus of Nola had settled in 395. We first meet young Julian in 407, when Paulinus wrote an *Epithalamium* for him. This poem was written to celebrate Julian's marriage to the daughter of Aemilius, the bishop of Beneventum.[18] At that time, the young man was already destined for the priesthood. Bishop Aemilius, Julian's father-in-law, was a good friend and the social equal of Paulinus. Socially, Julian's marriage to the daughter of Aemilius may well have represented a step upward for the young man. It had been made possible through the tight bonds established between members of a regional clergy, despite their original differences in wealth and status.[19]

At some time, perhaps in the mid-410s, Julian was ordained bishop of Eclanum. Either before or after his consecration, he impressed the Christian nobility of his region by giving alms to relieve the needy during a food shortage—caused, perhaps, by the passing of the Visigothic armies in 411–12.[20] Seen from the outside, by an admiring gentry, Julian would have resembled the town councillors, whose public spirited rallying to the repair of their native Beneventum after an earthquake in 375 had been celebrated forty years previously by the young Symmachus.

These details of Julian's life and background have helped give the young bishop of Eclanum an agreeably old-fashioned air.[21] But Julian was not an aristocrat of the old school. He was a clergyman from a generation in which the clergy had begun to create for themselves a high culture of their own. He was part of the world that drew on the scholarship of Jerome and Rufinus and exploited the new opening to the Greek East associated with the growth of Latin pilgrimages to the Holy Land.

Julian was shocked by the victory of Augustine's ideas. He thought that the clergy of Rome and the bishops of Italy should have supported Pelagius. Instead, they had succumbed to a putsch masterminded in Carthage. In his opinion, they had been forced by fear of the imperial laws to subscribe to a declaration of faith that amounted to a denial of free will, to a demonization of marriage, and to the victory within the church of a neo-Manichaeism propounded by Augustine, who was known to have once been a Manichee. In the words of one of Julian's many appeals to his episcopal colleagues, the bishops of the Christian West had allowed themselves to be bullied and bamboozled: "In almost the entire West a dogma has been pushed forward that is no less idiotic than it is impious."[22]

Julian was exiled in late 418. Like Cicero before him (in 51 BC), Julian took the road to Brindisi and hence to Cilicia. But he did this as an exiled bishop and not, like Cicero, as a Roman governor. He settled down in relative comfort as an expatriate. He became a follower of the great Greek exegete Theodore of Mopsuestia. He adapted rapidly to a new and congenial intellectual environment. His polemic against Augustine was the fruit of an unexpected and felicitous joining of East and West.[23]

Julian was a rare bird. He was a Latin writer who learned remarkably quickly to think like a Greek. This enabled him to offer to his readers in the Latin West a glimpse of the rich intellectual world of the eastern Mediterranean of which Augustine and his colleagues in Africa had remained stubbornly ignorant. Antioch and Cilicia were regions that had long nurtured sunnier views of the human condition. These had been elaborated in reaction to the spread of Manichaeism from further east. Julian applied the anti-Manichaean arguments developed in Antioch in such a way as to demolish the views of Augustine on original sin.[24]

For the next ten years, Julian wrote unceasingly. He succeeded in piling tome after tome on Augustine's desk—four volumes of Julian to answer one of Augustine's (in mid-419) and a further eight, which arrived in Africa in 427–28, finally causing the old, sick man to abandon all other tasks so as to respond to Julian's withering attack. In this continuous flood of ridicule, the description of Augustine as *Patronus asinorum*—"Lord of the Donkeys"—was only the least offensive.[25] Having haunted the old age of Augustine by his voluminous attacks, Julian later returned to Italy. He died in Sicily around 450.[26]

Quite apart from the relentless intelligence he demonstrated in his attack on Augustine as a neo-Manichee, Julian showed acute political sense. He began his campaign by approaching a powerful layman. In 419 Valerius was a count at the imperial court and on his way to become Master of the Cavalry.[27] He was the man to whom Alypius of Thagaste was said to have brought the gift of eighty Numidian horses. Still a young man, Valerius wished to found a family. Julian went out of his way to ensure that Valerius knew that, when it came to sex and marriage, Augustine had remained an out-and-out Manichee. Sex, to Augustine (so Julian claimed), was no natural instinct. It was a demonic urge, planted irrevocably in the human body. Even when begotten in lawful wedlock, children were a result of "the Devil's gift."[28] Married laypersons such as Valerius should think twice before supporting so outrageous a view of married intercourse as that proposed by Augustine and his crypto-Manichaean followers in Africa.

It is easy to dismiss Julian's portrayal of Augustine's thoughts on sex and marriage as a malicious caricature.[29] But what mattered at the time was that it was a caricature directed to a non-clerical audience. It was the presence of married lay readers, such as count Valerius, that gave a distinctive tone to the final decades of the Pelagian Controversy. This was the last great debate in the Latin West, between the fifth century and the Reformation, to be conducted before an audience that included influential and cultivated married persons on issues (such as sex and marriage) that directly touched their own lives.

Cogita unitatem: Think unity

AUGUSTINE, WEALTH, AND THE CHURCH

In the 420s, both Julian and Augustine knew that large books mattered. In the increasingly dislocated conditions of the Latin West, imperial laws and ecclesiastical pronouncements had little power in themselves. Modern scholars (projecting back into the later empire the image of a modern totalitarian state) sometimes think that major controversies in early Christianity could be closed by an imperial ukase. They claim that state power alone tipped the balance between Augustine and Pelagius, with sad results for all future ages. Both Augustine and Julian knew better than that. They knew that imperial laws were only the opening shots. A bitter war of words to sway public opinion was bound to follow.

This was particularly the case when it came to the application of laws on religious matters. Despite the high-flown intolerance of their language, imperial edicts against heresy took second place to overriding, frankly secular concerns. What had always mattered most for the imperial government was the gigantic annual spasm connected with bringing in the taxes. Laws on religion were never imposed as resolutely as were laws on taxation.

If laws against heretics were unpopular or seemed irrelevant, they lacked bite. They were often ignored for decades on end. They had to have public opinion behind them if they were to be enforced. Public opinion meant, in effect, the opinion of the educated class who applied the laws as governors or as heads of their cities. Hence Julian's choice of the recipients of some of his most vehement works. As courtiers and administrators, laypersons—and not the clergy—still held the keys of power. And laypersons worried about marriage.

They also worried about wealth. Augustine saw this clearly. His letters to powerful officials in the 420s placed great emphasis on his notion of the Catholic Church as an all-embracing institution and on the possibilities for the pious use of wealth within it. Images of the good Christian rich, which Augustine had already framed in his sermons of the 400s, were now passed on to high-up politicians and generals on active service. Through being summed up in carefully composed letters from around 417 onward (and not simply scattered as so many "seeds of the Word" in sermons), Augustine's view of wealth came to be part of the common sense of wealth throughout the late Roman and early medieval West.

Put very briefly: Augustine rendered wealth unproblematic because its origins were held to be opaque. Like grace itself, wealth was a phenomenon Augustine had removed from human scrutiny. Wealth was among the gifts of which Saint Paul had written: *But each one of you has his own gift from God* (1 Cor. 7:7). Augustine wrote this (in 418) to Boniface, the future Count of Africa (the head of the armed forces in the region). He treated Boniface's official rank, physical courage, and wealth as, all of them, equally gifts of God. They were gifts to be used in the service of the Catholic Church.[30] To treat a political office and the wealth attached to it in the same way as a personal charisma (which is what Paul had meant by "gift") might strike a modern reader as illicit. It was not so for Augustine. For him, wealth, like everything else, derived from the hidden providence of God. The only issue, then, was how, like any other gift of God, wealth might be used for the collective good of the church. It was a bracing message for an officer stationed on the Saharan frontier of the empire.

Such a view of wealth depended on a strong sense of the majesty of the Catholic Church. Wealth gained meaning and solemnity through being used to serve a worldwide institution with a grandiose future. In 417 Augustine wrote a similar letter to another politician, Dardanus, a former Prefect of Gaul. Dardanus was now living in retirement. He did so prudently, behind the walls of a fortified village named Theopolis—"City of God" (or "City protected by God"). Theopolis lay in a seemingly remote and dreamlike valley of the Alpes Maritimes (at Saint-Geniez, east of Sisteron). But it was close to an escape route into Italy through a network of minor mountain passes.[31] Dardanus needed security. In 413 he had suppressed a usurpation through a bloodbath of the Gallic nobility. He was even supposed to have killed the usurper with his own hands. Dardanus was later known to his admirers as a *vir strenuus*. He was a hard man for hard times. Dardanus had stood firm for the emperor of Ravenna.[32] Augustine reminded him of a yet more splendid institution to which he should be loyal: *cogita unitatem*— "When you think of where God dwells, think of the unity of the gathered saints [massed in heaven]."[33] Dardanus could best serve God by placing his wealth and power behind the unity of the Catholic Church on earth.

Augustine's justification of wealth came at the right time. In a world that had been unexpectedly shaken by renewed civil war and by barbarian invasion, there was no point in denouncing the rich for the manner in which they had gained their wealth. Those whose wealth had survived the shocks of this new crisis were unlikely to feel guilty about what little of it was left to them. The radical critiques of wealth and the wealthy associated with the preaching of Ambrose and with the Pelagian *De divitiis* were out-of-date. Such radicalism had been the product of an age of affluence. It had played on the disquiet of the comfortable rich of the fourth-century age of gold. It had less effect on persons who now faced the prospect of losing everything.

As we will see in our next chapter, by 420 the age of gold was well and truly over. As the empire unraveled and lost its power in the western provinces, an emphasis on the need for firm local hierarchies came to the fore. This took the form of attempts to establish stronger vertical links with one's own dependents, such as had not been considered necessary in an earlier age. The fourth-century age of gold had been characterized by extensive and impersonal forms of absentee landownership that depended on the support of a strong, unified empire. Now was a time for retrenchment and for the strengthening of local roots. Dardanus's fortification of Theopolis was a sign of the times. Solidarity was at a premium. In a society that strove to hang together, the worst sin was pride, not avarice. If the nobility was to survive, they had to mobilize the loyalty of those beneath them. They had to learn to stoop to conquer—and they did so in a manner now taught them by the bishops and clergy of the Catholic Church. As Kate Cooper has pointed out, letters and treatises of advice to leading laypersons—to men and women alike—became a regular feature of the literature of the Latin West. These treatises were no longer written in favor of the renunciation of wealth. They were about the correct use of wealth as an instrument of power.[34]

Augustine's writings at this time formed part of this change of viewpoint. He made clear that the best way to stoop to conquer was to join the throng of fellow believers of all classes in the Catholic Church and to do so as a sinner along with other sinners. Writing against Julian, Augustine presented his victory over the ideals of Pelagius as a victory of the common man over an icy and elitist perfectionism. There was room in Augustine's image of the church for distinctly average sinners:

> Who indulge their sexual appetites, although within the decorous bonds of marriage.... Who hold on to what they possess. Who give alms, if not very lavishly.... But who, through all this, see themselves as small and God as glorious.[35]

Such persons were encouraged to put their money where their heart was. A community of sinners was to be a community of givers. Not everyone did this in the spirit that Augustine intended in his famous sermons on almsgiving and expiation. The epigraphy of Italy, Gaul, and Spain in the fifth and sixth centuries shows that many continued to give and to build for thoroughly un-Augustinian reasons. They offered their wealth as part of a vow. They wished to bring glory to their local church as they had once brought glory to their city. They wished to ensure that they and their family would not be forgotten. But, in the writings and sermons of his old age, Augustine had caused the wind of Christian piety to set in a distinctive direction. In later centuries, the joining of generosity to the expiation of sin would become the prevailing breeze throughout the churches of the West.

Small details show this turning of the wind. Already in the late 430s, when the fiery Salvian of Marseille looked back to the days of Paulinus of Nola, he chose a verse that came from the poem Paulinus had asked Sulpicius Severus to place under his own portrait, which Sulpicius had placed beside that of Saint Martin in the church at Primuliacum. Martin was the saint and Paulinus was the sinner. For Salvian, Paulinus was the right sort of sinner. He knew how to expiate his sins by giving. He showed that it was possible "to redeem sins through scattered coins."[36]

Altogether, what Augustine offered was an attitude by which wealth came to be accepted on a "no questions asked" basis provided that much of it was spent within the church to redeem sins. Many writers and preachers all over the Latin world could have thought what Augustine thought. This is not surprising. Augustine did not strive for novelty on the issue of wealth and expiation. In his writings and sermons he had always been careful to stick close to the inherited conglomerate of notions he shared with readers and hearers in both Africa and elsewhere. But he had put all of this into memorable words. In certain circles, these words remained. We may first meet Leo, the future bishop of Rome, as a young acolyte who brought letters to Carthage in the summer of 418. A loyal reader of the works of Augustine, Leo had no doubts on the issue of wealth. When Leo became bishop of Rome in 440 and began to preach on wealth and almsgiving, it was to Augustine that he turned:

> For even earthly and material riches come from His generosity.... For riches are good. They greatly add to the bonds of human society when owned by the benevolent and the generous.... Many use wealth, whether come by justly through inheritance, or gained in any other way, as an instrument of piety.[37]

By this time, Augustine's ideas had crossed the Mediterranean. No longer confined to Africa, they were becoming part of the common sense of Latin Christianity. How had this come about?

"We groan in vain for those poor persons": Bishops and Society between Africa and Italy, 419–28

For those of us who are used to conventional biographies of Augustine, which stress the significance of his irrevocable return from Milan to Africa, it comes as a surprise to learn that this was by no means what happened to his friends. Between 419 and 428, Alypius, now a bishop in his seventies, along with other colleagues, hovered for years on end around the imperial court. He did not do this only to extort legislation against the Pelagians. He was charged with bringing to the ears of an all-too-distant emperor repeated news of the social woes of Africa.

This fact had not been known until recently. In 1975 the Austrian scholar Johannes Divjak discovered a hitherto unknown collection of letters from the last decades of Augustine's life. We have already seen what a rich store of information these letters contained. They include both the full story of Antoninus, bishop of Fussala, and the delightful letter Augustine wrote, in his very last years, to Firmus of Carthage. But, most important of all, the *Divjak Letters* (as they are usually called) have allowed us to witness a silent but decisive change in the pace of the relations between a major provincial church (the church of Africa) and the empire to which it was subject. Many of these letters were cast in the form of *commonitoria*. They were drafted as memoranda that would serve as the basis for pleading at the imperial court. They were drafts for the petitions Alypius and his colleagues brought to the emperor and his advisors at Ravenna.[38]

They were written so as to attract the attention of the emperor. For this reason, they make alarming reading. They carried the voices of distant Christian communities to governmental circles in Rome and Ravenna. They not only illustrate the distance between Italy and Africa but reveal a more profound inner distance. Though favored at Ravenna, the African bishops still faced an administration that was only nominally Christian. The Roman state had changed very little. Its profane energy had in no way diminished, or become any gentler, since the days of Ambrose.

The *Divjak Letters* are full of complaints about the high-handed manner in which clerical privileges were brushed aside. Sanctuary in Christian churches did little to protect fiscal debtors. A letter of Augustine to Alypius, in mid-March 420, made plain that those who owed money for unpaid taxes were unceremoniously dragged out of the churches where they had sought refuge. Bishops and their staff who resisted the tax officials were sued for obstructing "necessities of state." Those who could not seek sanctuary were pillaged: "We groan in vain for those poor persons, to whom we can offer no help."[39]

In the same letter, Augustine also reminded Alypius to point out to the court that fiscal oppression had sapped the clergy of Africa. Town councils and trade associations found themselves too poor to allow any of their members to serve in the church. The little groups that had been the pride of the cities were being ground down by "the hard dealing of high up officials."[40] Augustine suggested that *defensores*—legal advocates authorized to challenge tax abuses—should be set up in Africa, as they had been set up in other provinces. Augustine recommended that bishops suggest reliable laymen as candidates for this office.[41]

In 428 Augustine forwarded yet more alarming news from Africa. Slave dealers had invaded the province, raiding isolated villages in the hills behind Hippo. They captured free Romans and sold them overseas. (They probably sold them directly across the sea to the Italian owners of great estates, whose labor force had been dislocated by the Gothic invasion and the sack of Rome.) Augustine added that only a few of these captives had been legally sold to the dealers by their parents. To sell one's children in this way was a grim expedient usually connected with times of famine. It was barely legal. As a bishop, Augustine was always anxious to work within the limits of Roman law. He consulted a local lawyer on the validity of such sales.[42] Most of the victims, however, had been free Roman citizens, snatched without even the formality of a legal sale. Alypius was urged to search the archives of Rome for laws that could be applied to the slave dealers in such cases. But most important of all, the emperor in Italy—six hundred miles away from Africa across a heaving sea—must be made aware of "this evil of Africa, the news of which, I cannot believe, is silent even where you are now."[43]

Ground down by illness and by the dogged defense of his own reputation against Julian of Eclanum, the old rhetor took the time to sketch for Alypius the former lawyer the phrases that might yet stir the court:

> Barbarians are resisted when the Roman army is in good condition for fear that Romans will be held in barbarian captivity. But who resists these traders who are found everywhere, who traffic, not in animals but in human beings, not in barbarians but in Roman provincials? ... Who will resist, in the name of Roman freedom—I do not say the common freedom of the Roman state but of their very own selves?[44]

Altogether, the *Divjak Letters* document a significant change in the "tone" of Latin Christianity both inside and outside Africa. They reveal only too clearly the limits of the possible for Christian bishops. They had to work in a society where public life still bore a resolutely profane face. Even if the balance of privilege might seem to have tilted toward the Catholic Church in the previous decades, the balance of raw power had not done so. Taken with other evidence, the *Divjak Letters* give no support to standard narratives of the triumphant rise of Christianity in the Latin West. The Catholic Church did not come to replace the failing empire in a smooth and uncontested transition. As we shall see in subsequent chapters, the *Respublica*—the Roman state—remained a profane institution whose sense of its own majesty and traditions of hard rule owed nothing to Christianity. In the course of the fifth century, the Roman state handed over very little to the bishops. Eventually the empire went down fighting beneath the unloving eyes of many Christians, who considered it an empire that had failed to give effect to their own aspirations for a Christian society.

Given their studiously alarmist tone, the *Divjak Letters* tend to be read as texts that document a mounting and ineluctable crisis in African society. This was not the case. There was hardly a single abuse mentioned in them that had not already made its appearance at an earlier time. But one change had happened. In the 420s the bishops had become more ambitious. They moved with greater urgency (though not necessarily with greater success) into areas of taxation, slavery, and sanctuary, which they had not entered previously.[45] Over the decades, they had come to sense their power as a pressure group. The imperial condemnation of Pelagianism had been obtained through their skill in lobbying the court—a skill they had previously shown in the defeat of their Donatist rivals in Africa after 411. But the laws against the Pelagians and the Donatists were only one side of the coin. The other side was a growing confidence that bishops who arrived at Ravenna faced an empire ruled by "Christian princes" where they could expect that their views would be heard.

This was the great mirage of the late 420s. The rhetoric of an empire ruled by "Christian princes" grew in strength at this time. Signals from the court encouraged such a view. In 426 the great votive church of John the Evangelist was built by the empress Galla Placidia in Ravenna. She did this so as to celebrate her return to power after a short-lived civil war. The splendid new church (whose original decoration, alas, no longer survives) was as much an extravagant display of gratitude to God for His protection in a time of danger as was the shrine of Cimitile that had been erected by Paulinus of Nola thirty years earlier. But this was no longer a personal ex-voto. It was intended to be a statement of the union of church and empire. It stood beside the palace. Its apse was ringed by portraits of the imperial family since the days of Valentinian I, crowned by an image of Constantine. Such a sight was calculated to cheer a bishop arriving with petitions from the provinces.[46]

But, as the *Divjak Letters* have shown, not all of these petitions were answered. For the bishops were not the only pressure group at work at this time. They had to compete with lay rivals—with bureaucrats, landowners, and town councillors. As a result, the administrative structure of the empire remained opaque to Christianity. Bishops had no more direct control of the crucial business of tax collection than they had enjoyed forty years previously, in the days of Ambrose. They were still marginal to the workings of the Roman administrative machine.

This is demonstrated in small but revealing details. In a brilliant recent article, Avshalom Laniado has shown that a law ascribed to the year 409, which appeared to scholars to have given Italian bishops a place in the committee charged to elect a *defensor* for their city, had been misdated. It had usually been dated to 409 and placed in Italy. But Laniado shows that it was, in fact, a law of the early sixth century that had been wrongly dated in the *Code* of Justinian. This means that scholars have projected backward, onto the western empire of the time of Augustine, a role for the bishop that only emerged a century later and in the eastern (not the western) parts of the empire.[47]

Laniado's study is devoted to this one detail alone. But it brings a significant adjustment to our perspective on the role of the church in society in the Latin world. Though now ruled by ever more demonstratively Christian emperors, the business of the *Respublica* remained largely closed to Christian bishops. In the west there was as yet no regular machinery by which a bishop could take part in the affairs of his city as a peer and colleague of the traditional civic elites. In the very last days of Augustine's life, we are still looking at a compartmentalized society. The Christian church remained pinned into a niche of its own in late Roman society. It was kept there by the sheer weight of a profane Roman state and by the robustly secular attitudes of those who ran it.

This was a situation that most persons who had grown up in the second half of the fourth century took for granted (Augustine and Alypius among them). The Christian bishops still had less impact than they might have wished on the public life of the empire. But, at the time, this shortfall of Christian influence in crucial matters such as taxation and sanctuary was accepted as the price the churches were prepared to pay for enjoying the overall protection and privileges provided by a seemingly solid empire.

However, this situation would not last forever. The fifth century would prove to be a time of unpleasant surprises, the most unpleasant of which was the realization that the empire itself was far from solid. Starting around 405–6, the weakness of the empire was revealed ever more clearly, decade by decade. Within a few decades, even Africa was involved in the common disaster. In the very last year of Augustine's life, in 429, a Vandal army suddenly appeared before the walls of Hippo, having crossed the straits of Gibraltar and swept unopposed and largely unobserved for nine hundred miles through western north Africa. A decade later, in 439 (nine years after the death of Augustine in 430), the unthinkable happened. Carthage fell to the Vandals. In the words of Quodvultdeus, the successor of Aurelius as bishop of Carthage, it was the end of an age: "Where is Africa, which was for the whole world a garden of delights?"[48]

It is time to turn away from Africa to consider the crisis of empire that had already engulfed the provinces of the northern Mediterranean. In order to do this, we must return to Gaul around the year 400.

CHAPTER 24

"Still at That Time a More Affluent Empire"
The Crisis of the West in the Fifth Century

The Iron and the Clay: Civil War and the "Barbarian Invasions," 405–39

This chapter will deal with the general crisis of the western empire throughout the fifth century A.D. It will describe the onset of the crisis that reduced the empire, within a generation, to a shell of its former self. It will then linger on the adjustments the wealthy of the provinces most affected by this crisis were forced to make (and the opportunities many of them seized) in an increasingly regionalized world. It will end by pointing to the survival of the empire in some of these regions and to the loyalty it could still inspire in many figures before the empire itself vanished from the West, leaving some of its most vocal supporters in a fragmented world deprived, for the first time in half a millennium, of an imperial core.

The chapters that follow this one will be devoted less to the end of an empire than to the end of an age of Latin Christianity. They will introduce the reader to landscapes that remained in imperial hands throughout most of the fifth century. They will describe the brilliant and controversial circles associated with Marseilles and with the island of Lérins in Provence; the fiery tracts of Salvian of Marseilles; the Rome of the Senate and the popes; and the countryside of southern Italy. The last two chapters (chapter 28) of this book will view the West as a whole in an age without empire. They will sketch the emergence of a new Christianity. The first of these two chapters will describe the manner in which the Christian churches became aware of their own, great wealth and the steps they took to protect and display it. The last chapter (chapter 29) will survey the Latin Christian world of the sixth century. It will trace the manner in which the weight of wealth, in the hands of new donors of a post-imperial age, caused Christianity itself to take on a new and sharper profile, very different from the religion we first met two centuries before in the hesitant days around 350.

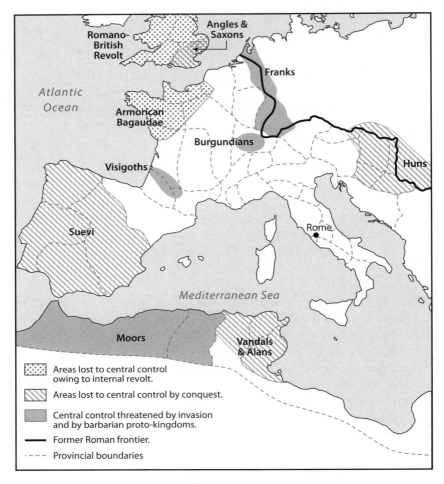

MAP 4. The Crisis of Empire, ca. 450 AD

But now let us turn to the beginning of the crisis from which all this derived. We must do so by returning to Gaul. In the middle of the fourth century, a traveler from the East (who was probably a Syrian) wrote of Gaul: "It is a very great province, and for that reason always needs to have an emperor present. It produces an emperor of its own."[1]

This seemingly naïve description was doubly accurate. A strong emperor was needed in Gaul in order to keep watch over the Rhine from Trier. When such an emperor was lacking, the local armies instantly proclaimed a usurper, so as to fill the threatening vacuum of power. The absence of an emperor was a signal for usurpation and civil war. This had already happened twice in the first part of the fourth century. By contrast, the reign of Valentinian I at Trier, from 364 to 375, had been a moment of peace and prosperity. The steady flow of goods and taxes to Trier fostered the affluence of the villa owners of southern Britain, Gaul, and Spain known to us through archaeology and through the works of Ausonius, whom we met in chapter 12.

After the death of Valentinian I, Gaul began to feel again the chill of imperial absence. The center of gravity of the Roman world swung south and east— toward northern Italy, the Balkans, and Constantinople. Once again, emperors were proclaimed in Gaul. Each was committed to defending his title by engaging in an empire-wide civil war. Twice in six years (with Maximus, in 388, and again with Eugenius, in 394) emperors from Gaul found themselves forced to strip the garrisons of Britain and the Rhine in order to wage war in Italy. These troops were fed into the meat grinder of major battles with fellow Romans—the eastern armies of the emperor Theodosius I (379–95). Only a skeleton force of professional troops remained along the northwestern frontiers of the empire. The provincials held their breath.[2]

One such provincial was Sulpicius Severus (whom we have met as the friend of Paulinus of Nola and the author of the *Life of Saint Martin*). In around 400– 404 he finished a world chronicle in the quiet of his villa at Primuliacum, between Toulouse and Narbonne. He viewed his times with alarm. He wrote that the Roman empire was "once the strongest of all empires." But now it was the weakest. Like the great statue in the *Book of Daniel*, it was an empire with feet of clay. It was doomed to disintegration.

> For it is not ruled by any one, single emperor, but by many emperors, who are always divided by military confrontations and by conflicts of basic interests ... while the soil of the Roman empire has been occupied by foreign or rebellious nations.... in such a way that barbarian tribes have come to be mixed up with us [like fissile clay inserted into the iron of a Roman order] in our armies, in our cities and throughout our provinces.[3]

In 405 Sulpicius was proved right. Civil war mixed with the "clay" of ill-absorbed barbarians (who were used in lieu of regular troops by contending Roman emperors) created the perfect storm. It raged for a generation throughout Britain, Gaul, Spain, and Africa. Sulpicius himself survived. But he and those like him emerged to find themselves in a world from which their leisured way of life (the product of strong rule and of an aggressive fiscal system) had vanished for good.

The story of this perfect storm can be told briefly.

On December 31, 405, a large confederacy of barbarian groups—Vandals, Sueves, and Alans, drawn originally from the middle Danube (and with little previous contact with Roman populations)—crossed the Rhine near Mainz. They came to plunder and (for all we know) to seek employment.[4] The armies of Britain created an emperor to deal with them—Constantine III. Constantine pinned the barbarians down in northern Gaul. His main concern, however, was to establish himself as the rightful emperor of the West. In 407 he moved quickly south (as the emperor Maximus had done, for the same reason, twenty years earlier) so as to invade Italy. In the next year, the murderous confederacy from across the Rhine reappeared in Aquitaine, the richest region of Gaul, already known to us as the homeland of Ausonius, Paulinus of Nola, and Sulpicius Severus. A tsunami of violence swept over southern Gaul. The barbarians had found their way into "the very bowels of the Roman empire."[5]

But the barbarians had not fought their way to the south. They were there because Constantine III needed them. He had discreetly relocated them from the north to southern Gaul so as to use their violence in his civil war. Like any other desperate army at a time of civil war (Roman troops included), they were paid for their services by license to plunder.[6]

In October 409, the same groups crossed the passes of the Pyrenees into Spain. Again, they had not moved of their own accord. They had been invited by yet another usurper, now set up in Saragossa. Vandals, Alans, and Sueves fanned out across the wide spaces of the Iberian peninsula. They looted the countryside and shook down cities. These depredations are usually referred to, somewhat dramatically, as the "barbarian invasions." They were no such thing. They were "collateral damage" brought upon the provinces by contending emperors. The vagaries of civil war, and not any headlong momentum of "invasion" on their part, accounted for the movements of barbarian groups at this time.[7]

Many "barbarians" were little more than freelance pillagers and highwaymen, such as had always appeared in the Roman provinces in times of disorder. They were like the gangs of slave traders who had raided the mountain districts around Hippo in these same years. Outside Tarragona, for instance, one band of "barbarians" robbed a priest of the case of books that he was carrying and then took them to the nearest town (Lérida) to see if they could find a purchaser![8] These random gangs were troublesome, but they were hardly the bloodthirsty cavalcades that we imagine when we speak of "barbarian invasion." Archaeological surveys of the area around Tarragona show that throughout this period of upheaval, the countryside remained populous and productive.[9]

But the more usurpers there were, the more conglomerations of barbarian military manpower converged to offer their services. The confederacy of the Vandals, Alans, and Sueves that had come down from the north was soon met by another barbarian group, which had come up from the south. Having sacked Rome in 410, the Goths moved out of Italy into southern Gaul. They also claimed to come as the servants of emperors. They supported a usurper of their own for a few years. Then they allied themselves with the "legitimate" emperors of Ravenna. Moving into Spain, their superior numbers enabled them to wipe out most of the Alans and an entire subtribe of the Vandals. In 418 they were rewarded by being settled in Aquitaine. This was, in many ways, a state-sponsored land grab. Direct access to landed estates (and, perhaps, some scholars speculate, to tax revenues) was the most acceptable form of all of the license to pillage that had been extended by rival emperors to other barbarian militias in lieu of pay.[10] The settlement of the Visigoths in Aquitaine was their bonus for having participated on the right side in a decade of civil war.

A state of imminent civil war also provided the background to the most extraordinary exploit of all of this time. In 429 the Vandals of King Genseric crossed from southern Spain into north Africa. (This was in the last year of Augustine's life.) Boniface, the Count of Africa (the commander of the only Roman forces in the province), had been a correspondent of Augustine. In 429 he was engaged in a confrontation with rivals across the sea in Italy. With his back turned on the hinterland of Africa, he was taken totally by surprise when the Vandals suddenly emerged from the west. Again, in September 439, Genseric took Carthage at a time when the relief of the city had been held back because of divisions at the court of Ravenna.[11] Altogether, it was civil war—and no bloodthirsty drive of their own—that had moved barbarian militias from one end of the Roman West to the other in under a generation.

The loss of Africa marked the end of an era. Civil war waged by novel means— that is, through the use of barbarian militias—had destabilized the provinces of Britain, Spain, and Gaul. But the Vandal conquest of Carthage did more than this. It broke the "tax spine" of the western empire.[12] In the words of Jill Harries: "The battle for Gaul [and, one might add, for Britain and Spain] had been lost in Africa."[13]

Already in the 430s, articulate contemporaries knew that they lived in a generation that had seen the end of a *belle époque*. When, in 431, the emperor Valentinian III chose to please the Senate of Rome by honoring a Roman worthy of the age of Symmachus—the great pagan, Nicomachus Flavianus, who had died in 394—there was an element of a nostalgia trip about the gesture. The long inscription that was placed on the base of the statue of Flavianus in the Forum of Trajan emphasized the manner in which he had used his high offices to preserve and increase "the wealth of what was still at that time [*adhuc*] a more affluent Empire [*Respublica*]."[14]

By 431 the tax revenues of the empire had probably dropped by 50 percent. After the loss of Carthage, they dropped further. The *Respublica* was left with a quarter of the resources it had enjoyed under the emperor Valentinian I. The empire had suffered a dramatic loss of revenue. More serious still, what had been crippled was the motor force of hard government from on top, which had enabled wealth accumulated through taxes to be turned into seemingly unchallengeable social hierarchies by the wealthy in the glory days of the fourth-century age of gold. The great machine that had made the rich so very rich had stalled.

Indigne invidioseque: Improperly and spitefully

FACTIONALISM AND IMPOVERISHMENT: THE CASE OF PAULINUS OF PELLA, 376–459

It is easier to describe the stages of this debacle than to say what exactly had happened to west Roman society in these crucial thirty years. Here the sources do not help us. When they looked back from mid-century, vocal Roman writers tended to blame everything on the barbarians. In 452 a chronicler wrote in the Mediterranean city of Marseille that, after 405–6, "the madness of hostile peoples tore all Gaul to pieces."[15] Given the inherited prejudices of all educated Romans against barbarians, and given the behavior of the armed bands who had been granted license to pillage the civilian population by warring Roman emperors, this melodramatic view is not surprising. It has always proved easy to string together a series of blood-curdling quotations from contemporary authors who described the hardships suffered by the Roman population at this time.[16]

But this catalogue of woes is essentially superficial. It does not, in itself, explain the profound changes in Roman provincial society itself that set in around the 410s and had become irreversible over much of the West by 450. What we call the "barbarian invasions" are better seen as the jets of water that suddenly announce the breaking of a dam. The real collapse of the dam came from within. The "clay" of barbarian military groups established on Roman territory acted as the catalyst for an abrupt reshuffling of social hierarchies among the Romans themselves. We are dealing with a social edifice which, even in its glory days, had been capable of changing at a touch. It is the edifice, and not the barbarians who touched it, that deserves our attention.

First of all, we should never underestimate the factionalism of the Roman provincial elites when faced with a situation of civil war. When civil war was mixed with the dangerous "clay" of barbarian bands, the local elites were far from being content to remain the passive victims of barbarian violence. They pitched in with gusto to despoil each other. We can see this in the case of the author of an autobiographical poem, Paulinus of Pella.[17] Paulinus was the grandson (through his mother) of none other than Ausonius of Bordeaux. He had been born at Pella in northern Greece in 376, where his father had held a governmental post that had been secured for him by Ausonius in the heyday of his influence at the court of Trier in the 370s. Paulinus was an "empire brat." As a baby, he had been in Carthage, where his father was proconsul. He had passed through Rome. On his return to Bordeaux, he inherited a palace and set to work improving his wife's properties in Aquitaine.

This all happened before 405. Paulinus looked back to those "days of old-world peace" with calculated nostalgia.[18] Seldom do we see so clearly an author creating for himself the gilded image of an ancien régime. In those happy days, he had hunted with his father. He had begotten children with his slaves. (Never, he assures us, had he raped a woman nor had he accepted the favors of a freeborn girl.)[19] In describing his lifestyle at that time, Paulinus made his own the cramping coyness of his grandfather Ausonius.

> This was what suited my status as one who looked for moderate satisfactions, delightful but far removed from self-display: A house equipped with spacious rooms, each suited to a different season of the year. A rich and attractive table, many servants, and young men at that ... silver plate distinguished for its refinement, not for its mere mass. Workmen skilled in various crafts to meet my commissions. Stables filled with well-conditioned beasts and coaches to carry me around safely and in style. But I was less concerned to expand these things than to preserve them. I was not excessively anxious to increase my revenue nor to seek out high office.[20]

But, for Paulinus as for so many other Roman provincials, the villa owner's ideal of a restrained life on the land, uninvolved in politics, was somewhat of a pose. The moment the chance of imperial office came his way, Paulinus (like the old Ausonius at the court of Trier) jumped at it. He found an emperor on his doorstep. The emperor Attalus had been set up in 414 by the Visigoths in southern France. Paulinus rallied to Attalus, who made him Count of the Sacred Largesses. This post involved Paulinus in the ugly business of handling the properties of proscribed persons. In times of civil war, business was more than usually brisk in that department.[21]

Unfortunately, Attalus was no Valentinian I. He was bankrupt. Short of pay, angry Visigoths burned Paulinus's palace in Bordeaux. Paulinus wrote so vividly of this burning that a reader might be expected to believe that all of Bordeaux had been set on fire by the barbarians. This was not the case. We are not dealing with widespread destruction. Rather, what Paulinus of Pella described was a thoroughly Roman event—the torching of the house of an unpopular official. (The house of Symmachus's father had suffered the same fate in Rome forty years previously.)[22]

In the long run, Paulinus's luck ran out. He ended his life as a poor man, partly dependent on the charity of the church of Marseilles. His plot of only four *iugera*, perched on the rocks outside Marseilles (even when it went with a town house and was supplemented by ingenious rental arrangements), compared badly with the 1,050 *iugera* of his grandfather Ausonius's "little inheritance" outside

Bazas.[23] But, if Paulinus was impoverished, it was not because of the passing of the barbarians through Aquitaine. It was because of the factional violence among Romans themselves in a time of civil strife. In 388 his namesake, Paulinus of Nola (who had been a friend of Ausonius), had almost lost his own life and property in a similar situation when he was caught in the backlash of the civil war that followed the usurpation of Maximus. A civil war had always been a time of massive confiscations and for the settling of scores between local notables. In the studiously bland language of an imperial law issued in 416, Paulinus of Pella's progressive expropriation had been just one of those things that happened *indigne invidioseque*—"improperly and spitefully"—in times of civil strife.[24]

Local Romanness against Central Romanness

Paulinus's account of his career is so vivid that we forget when it was written and for what purpose. It took the form of a poem titled *Thanksgiving to God* the old man wrote at the formidable age of eighty-four in 459. It was written to thank God for having enabled him, Paulinus, to establish good relations with the court of the Gothic king now established in his former home city of Bordeaux. Paulinus's sons had previously returned to Bordeaux: "Both were fired with the desire for freedom which they thought they could find in greater measure at Bordeaux, albeit in collaboration with the settled Goths."[25]

One of Paulinus's sons was no more successful as a politician than his father had been. The Gothic court was not an easy place. "Tossed between the good friendship and the anger of the king," he had been as thoroughly despoiled as his father had been. But this was not done by the Goths. It was done by his fellow Romans.[26] Yet it had not been for lack of trying. Romans quickly learned that they could make their fortunes at barbarian courts in the fifth century (if on a smaller scale) much as they had done at the court of emperors in the fourth century: "For we know of many who have flourished through the favor of the Goths."[27] Ultimately, it was the development of barbarian courts (such as the Gothic court first at Bordeaux and then at Toulouse) to which enterprising young Romans might turn—and not the colorful rampages of the first decade of the barbarian invasions—that sealed the fate of an imperial order in the West.

What needs to be explained, therefore, is the relative ease with which, already by the late 450s, local barbarian strongmen (such as the Goths at Bordeaux) had come to use their armies to create alternative power structures to those of the empire. It is the digging in of the barbarians—and not their first (imagined) headlong progress through "the very bowels" of the empire—that poses the real problem to historians of the Roman West in its last century. With remarkable speed, local power blocs appeared. In each, a royal court emerged as a center of patronage and government. Not all of these power blocs were set up by barbarians. Some were ruled by self-consciously "Roman" figures—such as emerged in northern Gaul and, perhaps, among the competing tribal regions in Britain.[28] But they were all disturbingly isomorphic, on a smaller scale, to the *Respublica*—the legitimate Roman empire. It was the creation of these alternatives to empire that changed the rules of the game by which the wealthy became wealthy in a new age.

How did this happen? The answer lies, perhaps, in the strong regionalism of the provinces of Gaul and Spain—and even more so of Britain, where pre-Roman tribal identities may have reemerged. Local nobilities had always drawn their wealth from relatively small catchment areas. Their ambitions had tended to center on their province alone. This regionalism reached back to the very beginning of the empire. The Roman empire in the West had always been a federation of regions. The appearance of the barbarians dislocated the mechanisms by which this federation had been held together for so many centuries. In the words of Guy Halsall, "The key factor in the break-up of the Empire was the exposure of a critical fault line between the imperial government and the interests of the regional elites."[29]

In many ways, the fourth-century age of gold had been unusual. An active imperial court had created a service aristocracy that was more fluid and more tied to the imperial center than had ever been the case previously. As we saw, the world of Ausonius was not a world of self-contained owners of *latifundia* who were able to "sit out" periods of civil disorder. It was a world of courtiers and of courtiers manqués. Even on the wide plateau of Spain, the basis of the wealth of those who owned the great villas of the fourth century came from their implication in a network of imperial tax collection. An aristocracy created, to a greater extent than ever previously in Roman history, by close involvement with state power was bound to change when this state power changed—when it weakened, when it withdrew, and, above all, when it was replaced by other, more local power blocs.

What the relatively small armies of the Goths, Sueves, and Vandals (and later the Franks and the Burgundians) offered to the regional elites was what the sons of Paulinus of Pella sought at the Gothic court in Bordeaux—a return to wealth through service at a center of state power. But this time it was a local center. In effect, barbarian kings and their armed retinues offered the regional elites a Rome at home. These little Romes were largely run by local Romans. They drew to themselves courtiers and litigants from the region. They proved more accessible as a source of justice and wealth than was the increasingly impoverished *Respublica*—the legitimate empire that now ruled Gaul from a distance, across the Alps in Ravenna and Rome.

We are dealing with a powerful reversal of the mechanisms set in place in the West under Constantine and his successors. In the fourth century, the presence of an imperial court in the West had enabled the wealthy to partake in ever wider pyramids of influence. They held office throughout the empire. They owned land in many provinces. In the fifth century, the emergence of local courts worked in the opposite direction. In many parts of Gaul, Spain, and Africa, late Roman society was miniaturized. Regional elites dug themselves in around local centers of military power. They did so in a world whose horizons had shrunk and where the opportunities for widespread enrichment (even in the service of an active barbarian king) had, with very few exceptions, closed down to the level of a single region.

Reviewing the history of the fifth-century West, Peter Heather has described the process of the fall of the Roman empire in terms similar to those of Halsall. The end of the empire was the story of the "destruction of central Romanness." But what replaced this "central Romanness" was not barbarism but forms of "local Romanness"—a social order that had grown from the ground up as the Roman regional elites opted for local leaders, local armies, and local systems of patronage, all of which were offered by barbarian kings and their followers.[30]

Tuitio ... communis: A common refuge to all

VIOLENCE AND SOCIETY IN THE FIFTH CENTURY

What was it like to be a "local Roman" at this time? It is important to redress the anti-barbarian bias of our texts by emphasizing the Roman side of the equation— the violence of Romans to each other and the zest with which the Roman regional elites of the former imperial West collaborated with barbarian warlords to create for themselves new centers of government. But this process did not bring peace. The creation of rival courts around rival leaders led to a state of unresolved political instability in Gaul and Spain. A climate of violence spread across Gaul and Spain in the course of the fifth century.

This climate of violence, rather than any notable slaughter or the sack of any large cities, was what slowly but surely changed the face of Roman society. The last true "barbarian invasion" happened in 451, when the armies of Attila the Hun entered Gaul only to be defeated in a major battle at the Catalaunian Fields (near Chalons) by Count Aetius, who led an alliance of the Roman and the Visigothic armies against the Huns. After that last great war, Gallic society was left to grind itself into a new shape in what the French historian Fernand Braudel (speaking of a similar phenomenon—the rise of piracy in the early modern Mediterranean) has called "an age of undeclared wars."[31] How had this situation come about and what were its effects?

In negotiating with barbarians in the early decades of the fifth century, Romans flattered themselves that the barbarians could be treated as farmers manqués—they could be quieted by gifts of land. This calculation ignored many factors. Young warriors liked to fight. Kings needed to fight so as to maintain their prestige against competing brothers and aristocrats. All needed the wealth that came from war. And this wealth was best obtained through little wars. The goal of most of these wars was not extensive conquest. The Visigoths of Aquitaine (about whom we know most) regularly went on campaign for strictly limited aims—to assert control of a neighboring region here, to shake down or to occupy a single city there. For this reason, the Visigothic campaigns (like those of the Sueves who had established themselves in northwestern Spain) were largely wars of nerves. A campaign up to the walls of a city would end with the systematic pillage of the rich countryside around it. This was how the Visigoths set to work outside Bazas (the former hometown of Ausonius) in 414:

> The enemies ravaged the villages [or villas] all around. They set fire to farm buildings. They ruined vineyards and grain fields by driving livestock into them.[32]

This carefully administered violence to the land was calculated to cause the inhabitants of a region or a city to reconsider their loyalties. They would open their gates or would offer to buy off the invaders. There was usually a faction within the city that favored such a course. In 453 a church council in Angers laid down that a cleric who had played a role in betraying his city to the enemy was to be not only excommunicated but barred from public banquets. This was the ultimate ostracism, imposed by a little community in a time of little wars.[33] But it also showed that there were always people ready to collaborate with barbarians for the sake of peace and quiet.

Wealth came from plunder and, above all, from a lively slave trade.[34] The terrible scenes Augustine had portrayed in Africa, in the late 420s, became normal in the Gaul and Spain of the later fifth century. Not all captives ended up as slaves in distant lands. Rather, the culmination of a successful little war consisted in selling back to a pillaged region its own inhabitants. As a result, the Christian pious act of ransoming captives came, in Gaul, to be more than a gesture of sending contributions to a distant frontier, as had been the case in the fourth century. It became an intensely local matter. It involved the healing of the social fabric of an entire war-torn region through the return of its workforce. Christian charity ensured that farmers and slaves were brought back to their former masters.[35]

Looking down from northern Britain, Patricius (our Saint Patrick, who had already served his time as a slave in Ireland) saw Gaul as a land of ransoms:

It is the custom of the Roman Gallic Christians to send suitable holy persons to the Franks and to other tribes with so many thousands of *solidi* so as to ransom baptized captives.[36]

It was through ransoms, rather than through any other pious actions, that the wealth of the wealthy was deployed in the churches in this time of brutal little wars. For ransoms implied liquidity. Large sums of cash or bullion had to be made immediately available in a way that was beyond the means of the more modest members of the local congregations. Hence the praise of the lady Eugenia on her sarcophagus in Marseille: "With her wealth she freed captives from the chains imposed by violence and brought those driven away back to their lands."[37]

One suspects that it was the spoils of little wars and money raised from ransoms that account for the fact that the Visigothic territories along the Garonne valley, from Toulouse to Bordeaux, remained an oasis of prosperity. It is only in this region that villas appear to have survived. They were paved no longer with haunting scenes of pagan mythology but with exuberant designs of flowers and vegetation. These patterns were well within the powers of local craftsmen, who reproduced them with unusual zest. The "Aquitainian sarcophagi," though notoriously difficult to date, may well have come from this period. Carved in stone from local quarries, they signaled the emergence of a distinctive local form of prestige goods. They were adapted to family mausolea and to displays of upper-class burial around the tombs of saints. They no longer looked to the great marble sarcophagi of Rome for inspiration. It was an art of local Romans for local Romans. They may serve as a reminder that a province such as Aquitaine could be both prosperous and already "post-Roman" (by fourth-century standards) under barbarian management.[38]

At the same time, the Christianity of Gaul changed its texture as a response to the new levels of instability. It is not as surprising as it seems that the age of the barbarian invasions of Gaul coincided with a golden age of church building. As we will see in a subsequent chapter, these new cathedrals were directly linked to the need to maintain the morale of the inhabitants of the cities in a world where they were often called upon to withstand sieges.[39] Within these cathedrals Christian preaching came to emphasize, above all, the value of cohesion.

It was pride and envy, not wealth, that were most abhorrent to Gallic preachers in this period. There was good reason for their emphasis on those two vices. In the unstable conditions of Gaul, pride and envy translated only too readily into factionalism. And factionalism, as we have seen, was what exposed Romans to each other quite as much as it exposed them to the barbarians. Let us take the example of a set of anonymous sermons known as the sermon collection of "Eusebius Gallicanus," which have recently been studied in detail by Lisa Bailey. They were preached in the Rhone valley at the end of the fifth century. It is no coincidence that they should have emphasized a need for solidarity among ordinary Christians that was as exacting as any imposed on monks. The inhabitants of little cities facing the prospect of siege were as cramped and as dependent upon each other as were the monks in any monastery.[40]

One preacher of the mid-fifth century, Valerianus of Cimiez (a hill town perched above the Roman road that passed Nice), went out of his way to control even sarcasm and witticisms among his flock. It was unwise to make jokes about the physical traits of one's fellow citizens—to call a man of swarthy complexion "Mr. Silver Shine" or an elder compatriot "baba."[41] Revenge for such a slight might take the form of treason. Looking back from a later time, the inhabitants of Trier believed that their city had once been betrayed to the barbarians and sacked because of the anger of a leading citizen who had been provoked by a coarse joke at the expense of his wife.[42]

Christian sources provide vivid and uniformly self-congratulatory evidence for the role of the church in maintaining the morale of the cities of Gaul in this time. Christian hagiography presents us with images of heroic bishops standing on the walls of their cities and of great Christian basilicas filled with refugees in search of sanctuary. But these incidents were exaggerated in retrospect. There was only so much that the Christian churches could do. Laypersons (and especially the wealthy, who owned properties outside the cities) had to fend for themselves. Many did this none too badly. But it is harder to follow what they did in the face of crisis. Only by using archaeology as well as written sources can we reconstruct something of what was happening.

In the first place, the landowners had to act quickly if they were to preserve their properties. They had to become more resolutely local than they had been in the fourth century. What was needed now were not large incomes, gathered from many regions, but power on the spot. The great age of absentee landownership ended. Paulinus of Pella simply gave up all hope of gaining revenues from his mother's estates in distant Greece:

> For there were extensive farms, well-stocked with numerous peasants, scattered but not too widely separated, which even for a prodigal or careless lord might have provided an abundant income.[43]

Paulinus's failure to draw on these distant lands marked the beginning of his decline into poverty. As a contemporary writer in Provence observed:

> Men rendered conspicuous by official honors, placed at the top of the empire by occupying high posts, with revenues drawn from everywhere and properties that stretched throughout the Roman world ... now appear to us figures in a fairytale.[44]

The world of the super-rich, associated with persons such as Petronius Probus, had well and truly passed.

But we must remember that in Gaul and Spain there had been few such persons, even at the height of the age of gold.[45] As we saw, the rural landscape of these provinces had not been dominated by the vast estates of absentee landowners or even by *latifundia* owned by local figures. It was largely owned by competing petty noblemen, whose villas clustered around the towns. They were comfortable but not outstandingly wealthy. Modern archaeological surveys have enabled us to measure the horizons of the possible for such persons. To take one example: careful excavations of the rubbish tip of Quinta das Longas (in Lusitania; now in Elvas, in southeastern Portugal) have shown that it was possible to have an elegant, even a recherché villa and yet to eat on dishes produced by regional potteries.[46]

In the fourth century, the owners of a villa such as Quinta das Longas were representatives of the local elites. They were the little big men whom we met in chapter 1. We have attempted to glimpse their features (alas, not always successfully, given the state of our evidence) beneath the glare of publicity generated by the Christian members of the super-rich, such as Paulinus of Nola and the two Melanias. For such petty noblemen, the fifth century was not necessarily an age of catastrophe. It opened up new opportunities for them. In many regions, they found themselves no longer overshadowed by grandees connected with an empire-wide system. Service at a barbarian court gave them a degree of local power they had not enjoyed previously to such an extent. The fifth century was the age of the little big man.

But this process happened at a cost to both their standard of living and, to a certain degree, their Romanness. It is remarkable how quickly the villas built or rebuilt in the fourth century disappear from the archaeological record in the course of the fifth century. As we have seen, in many regions villas had shown most clearly the footprint of wealth in the countryside. With the "end of the villas" it is as if the wealth of an entire class has vanished from our radar screen.[47] Although it may have been accumulated with more difficulty and on a less massive scale, wealth had not vanished. But it had lost its clearly recognizable Roman face. No one attempted to shine in fifth-century Gaul and Spain through building a villa. Service at the barbarian court, the maintenance of a townhouse in cities such as Mérida, Toulouse, and Bordeaux, and a reliable retinue were what was needed. With this went a slow but sure change in lifestyle. In a less secure age, skills developed in hunting changed easily into skills of cavalry warfare. Armed retinues, both for self-protection and to assert equality with barbarian kings and their army, cost local Romans as much as mosaics and private bathhouses had once done.[48]

In many regions distant from the centers of power a prestige-full burial seems to have replaced the villa as the way in which wealth was put on show. Both in northern Gaul and in the Duero valley, burials with grave goods, which scholars had once associated only with Germanic barbarians, have been shown to be the work of Romans. On such occasions, the members of the local elite were put on display throughout their funeral. They lay on their biers adorned with status symbols that still carried echoes of an earlier, more affluent age—military brooches and buckles in northern Gaul, hunting equipment and horse harnesses in Spain. The *dominus* might still wish to be seen as a great hunter. But this dominance was no longer expressed through great mosaics and sarcophagi, which had shown him as the mythological lord of the hunt in fourth-century Spain, in southern Gaul, and in southern Britain. A graveside ceremony was enough. The rest of the income of a local big man may have been spent on warfare and on building up supporters through gifts and feasting.[49] Altogether, we now face a world where it is harder to distinguish rich from poor in the archaeological record. For in many regions of the West the rich had lost the strident attributes of wealth that had rendered them so gloriously visible in the fourth century.[50]

Those who wished to remain rich knew that their first priority had not changed since imperial times. They had to control their labor force. This had always been difficult in times of violence. We can only guess at the scenarios of retrenchment and control that were adopted. Recent archaeological surveys have offered scattered hints of what may have happened on the ground. The region outside Béziers, for instance, shows a marked falloff of dispersed settlements and the emergence of a few, large conglomerations in the course of the fifth century.[51]

Some landowners went so far as to offer fortifications to their peasantry. Dardanus, the former Prefect of Gaul, opened up the road to the upland valleys east of Sisteron in the Alpes Maritimes. He and his brother left a public inscription beside the road to proclaim their feat. The model village (as we saw in the last chapter) was even called Theopolis (City of God)—Dardanus had placed it under the protection of God: "They furnished walls and gates, which, established on their own estate, they wished to serve as a common refuge to all."[52] A ruthless and unpopular servant of the Roman state, Dardanus had every reason to wish to feel safe. But the language of the inscription makes plain that this was no private castle in the making. Dardanus's fortification of Theopolis was presented as an act of loyalty to the empire. The walls had been put up for the public good. In doing this, Dardanus used a language of public building which, up till then, had been more common in the forum of a city. Now Dardanus was prepared to set up a grand inscription that advertised his care for mere villagers.[53]

Dardanus knew that if he had not provided this fortification, the inhabitants of a rich upland valley might have scattered farther into the hills. Their labor would have become lost to him and his heirs within a generation. A recent survey in Spain enables us to trace this danger as it emerged on the ground. The survey studied the plain of the Jarama and the plateau land between Toledo and

Madrid. There is no evidence of depopulation or of destruction in this area. Rather, what we see is what in the long term would have spelled the ruin of a landowner of late Roman style: a population that had once been held in place through a network of villas, which in turn had linked them to the city and its tax collectors, slowly but surely scattered into informal groupings of low-profile farms and villages. The villages remained stratified. These were no happy communes of equals freed from the burden of rents and taxes. But the old mechanisms of extracting these rents and taxes had unraveled. Once the farms and villages had broken loose from the tight net spread by the villa, it was next to impossible to extract from them the high level of wealth that had supported the affluent residences of the fourth-century age of gold.[54]

New Romans for Old: From the Bacaudae to Sidonius Apollinaris, 430–ca. 480–90

Altogether, by the mid-fifth century we are looking out on a new West. Beyond the Alps, Gaul and Spain had broken up into a mosaic of differing regions. The *Respublica* still survived; impoverished though it was, it remained the largest single political unit in Europe. It was unshaken in Italy and was still a vivid presence in southern Gaul. Geographically, we are in a world that had returned to the days of the Punic Wars in the third century BC. At that time, Italy and the rim of the western Mediterranean had faced Africa, while at their back a vast, uncontrolled hinterland stretched behind the coastline to the north and west. Now, in the fifth century AD, central Romanness—in the form of the legitimate Roman empire, the *Respublica*—reached up from Italy to hold the Mediterranean shores of southern Gaul and eastern Spain. But this enclave of central Romanness based on the Mediterranean was ringed to the north and west by gray zones of local Romanness that had emerged in much of Gaul and Spain, while to the south lay a formidable rival—the Vandal kingdom of Carthage.

Vandal Carthage showed exactly what ruthless state power could still do. As far as we can see, the Vandal state was not based on any tacit arrangement between local Romans and a barbarian court, as happened with the Goths of Bordeaux and Toulouse. Major Roman landowners in Proconsular Africa and Byzacena were abruptly dispossessed so as to leave a glacis around the hinterland of Carthage that was occupied by Vandal warriors alone.[55]

Worse than that: the Vandals did not hide the fact that they were Arian and not Catholic Christians. Within a decade, Catholic bishops were exiled as "heretics." The Vandals even used the former anti-Donatist laws that had imposed exile on Donatist bishops after 411. Vandal rulers applied these laws unchanged to the Catholic clergy. By a strange (and not wholly undeserved) irony of fate, many of the friends of Augustine (notably Possidius of Calama, his biographer) ended their lives as exiles in Italy. They had been driven from their cities by the same laws against heresy that they had petitioned for, thirty years before, in order to drive out their Donatist rivals.

What is revealing is that the African cities did nothing to protect their bishops. In the 430s and 440s, as in the 420s, the cities of Africa had remained robustly secular. Despite decades of preaching by Augustine and his colleagues, they had not become massively Catholic cities. Their town councillors now found themselves in a dilemma. They were forced by a strong Vandal state of Arian views to choose between loyalty to their Catholic bishops and clergy (as Catholic believers) and the loss of their lay privileges, or conformity to the new regime and the retention of their status in their hometowns. Conformity to Arian rule, in effect, enabled them to continue to be loyal to the little *respublica* of their own city. This was what had always mattered most for them. Not surprisingly, they chose the city over the altar. They did not rally to support the Catholic Church. Nor did they become zealous Arians. Accustomed to politic conformity by the suppression of Donatism only a generation earlier, the lay elites of Africa kept a low profile. They left the two groups of clergy—Catholic and Arian—to fight it out between themselves while they governed their little cities as they had always done.[56]

The failure of the African elites to stand up for the Catholic Church deserves to be stressed. It showed how precarious the position of the church still was in many regions. Despite a vocal Christian literature that celebrated the merging of church and city in Gaul and Spain, this alliance may have come more slowly than we think and certainly more slowly than the bishops and clergy wished.

Yet the paradox of the Vandal kingdom is precisely that, after these draconian measures, what remained of the Roman society of Carthage and eastern Africa (the old provinces of Proconsularis and Byzacena) settled down to thrive with indecent vigor. Large palaces appeared in the city. Roman officials staffed the Vandal administration. Roman shipowners helped man the Vandal war fleets. This was probably more profitable to them than had been the annual effort to stir into action the great dinosaur of the *annona* fleet that had once sailed from Carthage to Rome.

Not all subjects of the Vandals sailed the seas as pirates. Freed from the levies connected with the *annona* for Rome, African ceramics and African wines flooded into the market throughout the eastern Mediterranean. The ancient link across the southern Mediterranean between Africa and the Levant, which had characterized Punic Carthage, was revived in the fifth century. Our word "vandalism" was derived from the Vandals, who came to enjoy an odious reputation in later ages. Yet they had not brought destruction to Africa. Rather, through their commercial outreach the Vandals of Carthage "presided over something of an Indian summer for the ancient economy."[57]

Latin poets came to frequent the Vandal court. They praised the Vandal ruler as a "Sun King." They inscribed elegant verses on still-functioning suburban bathhouses. If the old world lived on anywhere, in the West, in a manner that would have been recognizable to fourth-century villa owners, it was in the pirate city of Carthage and its surrounding countryside.[58]

This extreme option—as well as the gray zones in Britain, Gaul, and Spain where the emperor's writ no longer ran—would have been known in southern Gaul. They form a backdrop to one of the most remarkable phenomena of this period: that is, the rallying of loyalty to the legitimate empire—usually spoken of as the *Respublica*—in those areas where imperial rule had continued. An influential segment of Gallic upper-class society rejected forms of local Romanness. They opted instead for the "central Romanness" represented by the surviving empire, depleted though this empire had become.

It is important to note this phenomenon. We have spent much of this chapter examining the way in which whole regions of Gaul and Spain opted slowly but surely for forms of regional government that tacitly excluded the empire. But this was an almost covert process—a somewhat shameful open secret. It can only be reconstructed with difficulty, as it left little trace in Roman sources. Only very few writers (the remarkable Salvian among them) referred to the awkward fact that there were now "Romans out there"—*illic Romani*—who prayed never again to become subjects of the Roman state.[59] What we more usually hear in the sources of this time is the voice of a vocal faction committed to the *Respublica*—to the structures and attitudes of the Roman empire as it had been inherited from the fourth century and as it would survive (if only, outside Italy, in a series of increasingly embattled enclaves) until the late 470s.

We are dealing, in effect, with the emergence of a new style of Roman patriotism. In the fourth century, the Roman empire had been seen as a universal empire. It had no challengers other than barbarians outside its frontiers. It was a true *orbis terrarum*, a "civilized world" as vast and as seemingly immovable as the universe itself. By the mid-fifth century in the West, this universal empire survived in Gaul and Spain only as a constellation of enclaves. Central Romanness was no longer a given; it had become an option. But it was an option for which many writers voted with their pens. Confronted by widening pockets of local Romanness, these enclaves were breeding grounds for a distinctive kind of hyper-Romanity. If anything, this hyper-Romanity increased in intensity as the imperial enclaves themselves shrunk over the decades.

Nothing shows more clearly the fierce intransigence with which upholders of the surviving imperial order viewed their world than their reaction to one of the most mysterious phenomena of the age—the Bacaudae. On the subject of the Bacaudae, learned fantasies (largely but by no means exclusively of the Marxist persuasion) have flourished. We still do not know who the Bacaudae were. Some have treated them as a peasant *jacquerie*; others have seen them as local landowners who resorted to violent means to defend their region in a world bereft of imperial protection.[60] The word itself is Celtic: it may come from *baga*, "warrior." We do not even know whether a Bacauda was a person or a happening— like the Fronde in seventeenth-century France. Nor do we know whether it was an urban event (perhaps the equivalent of a tax riot) or an exclusively rural movement, as most scholars have tended to assume.[61]

But we do know one thing. We know how the Bacaudae were perceived by others. Two chroniclers (Hydatius, bishop of Chaves in northern Portugal, and the anonymous Marseilles author of the *Chronicle of 452*) are the only sources who make frequent mention of their activities at this time. These activities are recorded for Gaul in 435, 437, and 448 (in the *Chronicle of 452*) and in Spain for 441, 443, 449, and, once again, in 454 (by Hydatius). Both authors referred to their suppression with undisguised satisfaction. In Spain, in 443, a general "broke" their "insolence."[62] In Outer Gaul (the northern provinces bordering Britanny and the English Channel) a leader called Tibatto led the region to "secede from membership of the Roman order"—*a Romana societate*—in 435. He caused "the slaves of almost all Gaul to conspire in *a* Bacauda." Two years later, in 437, the "commotion" was suppressed, "with much slaughter." This event was recorded with evident satisfaction by the *Chronicle of 452*.[63]

Nowhere did either author pretend that the Bacaudae were barbarians. They had been Romans. For almost the first time in the history of the Roman empire, Roman armies took the field not against barbarians or the armies of a rival emperor but against Roman subjects. These disaffected Romans were declared to be "public enemies"—"suicidal rebels" against whom a war of reconquest was to be waged. It was a war (often waged by barbarian troops in Roman pay) of which most writers in the territories of the *Respublica* approved wholeheartedly.[64]

Altogether, forced on to the defensive by so many unwelcome and alternative ways of being Roman, which now ranged from an abandoned Britain, through ill-defined zones of unrest in Gaul and Spain, to the pirate capital of Carthage, the *Respublica* in its last decades was by no means dead. But it was not a pretty thing.

Indeed, the *Respublica* had become, in many ways, an ancien régime. Derived from the ambitious state of the fourth century, the fifth-century empire, as it impinged on Gaul, lacked the cohesion between its top and bottom levels that had made the empire of Valentinian I formidable but flexible. What had happened in the crisis of the third century recurred in fifth-century Gaul. A split developed between what Jean-Michel Carrié (talking of the end of the third century) has called the *milieux dirigeants*, the inner circles of government, and the "governing classes" at large.[65] Ruthless generals sent from Italy allied with Gallic families who had already clambered onto the imperial bandwagon in the days of Valentinian and Theodosius. These families expected to retain a monopoly of high offices in Gaul. They were considerably less open than before to the "governing classes" as a whole—that is, to persons recruited from the lesser nobility of the cities. They did not promote them. They did not listen to their views. The control exercised by these privileged families over the higher levels of the administration created "a situation in which politics had become the preserve of the already powerful."[66]

As a result, the social mobility that had energized the imperial administration in the fourth century dried up. To opt for the *Respublica* in the latter half of the fifth century was not to opt for the Roman empire as it had been in the days of Constantine, Valentinian, and Theodosius. It was to support a more than usually proud and top-heavy system, deeply wedded to a sense of its own excellence.

It is against this background that we can best appreciate the career and writings of Sidonius Apollinaris (430–ca. 480–90). Born in Lyon, Sidonius spent most of his life in the imperial enclaves of the Auvergne and the Rhone valley; he also went to Italy twice. Yet it was part of the literary genius of Sidonius that he ensured that his "Rome"—the Rome of a hyper-Roman, who viewed the world through narrow slits—has become to a large extent our Rome. For Sidonius presented what remained of the empire as a model society that was worthy of unquestioning loyalty. To be loyal to Rome was to be loyal to civilization itself. As a result, it is Sidonius's Rome that we see pass, majestically and tragically, into the imagined twilight of a barbarian age. Yet, as we read his letters and poems, we can glimpse the many alternative forms of being Roman that already pressed in around him. It was this alternative, more provincial form of Romanness that would win out at the end of his life.[67]

We first meet Sidonius at Arles in 449. As a nineteen-year-old boy, he had stood in a solemn row of figures swathed in glittering robes behind the throne of the consul of the year (the general Asterius, who had crushed the Bacaudae in Spain eight years before). Sidonius was careful to record that, though a young man, he stood close to the consul's throne. For

> my father, father-in-law, grandfather and great-grandfather had glittering careers, holding urban and praetorian prefectures and masterships at court and in the army.[68]

Sidonius's background made him very much a representative of the inner "governing circles" who stood at the top of the fifth-century *Respublica* in Gaul. For him, high office in the service of the empire was the one sure criterion of status. The other clear landmark was high culture. Ideally, the two converged. On the occasion of Asterius's consulship, the stunning visual display of high officers of state gathered around the consul was echoed by the speech of a famous orator:

> The consular robe, soaked in Tyrian purple, with embroidered palm-leaves crackling on its fringes, was enhanced by a speech yet more richly colored and more suffused with gold.[69]

The heir of Pliny and Symmachus, Sidonius also knew how to depict a landscape of the heart. He conjured up his beloved Clermont more vividly than Symmachus ever did for his Campania:

> The cultivated plain where waves of wind undulate across the grain ... gentle to travelers, fruitful to the tiller, delightful to the hunter, where the ridges of the mountains encircle the plain with pasture, the lower slopes with vineyards, lowlands with villas and the rocky peaks with forts.[70]

As a writer, Sidonius had a gift for making time stand still. We walk around his own villa and those of his friends as if they were just as they had been in the fourth (or, indeed, in the first) century AD.[71] It is only occasionally that we notice small details that show that the times had changed. Sidonius's bathhouse was no longer painted to create a magic world like that of Sidi Ghrib in fourth-century Africa. Its walls were covered only with plain plaster on which he had written short verses.[72]

Sidonius ended his life as bishop of Clermont. He did so because he was a victim of the factionalism of Roman politics. In 469 his career in the *Respublica* came to an abrupt end under suspicion of association with a traitor. As Jill Harries has shown, Sidonius's consecration as a bishop was no happy promotion to a spiritual honor that was considered interchangeable with his worldly dignity. It was not a triumphant shift from the toga to the miter, as many have imagined. It was a comedown.[73]

It is to Sidonius's credit that, despite this setback, he rose to the occasion with a vigor which (of course!) he took care to render memorable through many vivid letters. When he became bishop, Clermont was still within the territories of the empire. Yet even when he attempted to defend Clermont from absorption into the expanding Gothic kingdom of King Euric, he met with opposition within Clermont itself.[74]

We know why. Many local Romans saw no great advantage in being subjects of the emperors. Their relatives and peers were already making good careers at the Gothic court. In 478 Sidonius wrote to one such Roman—Namatius. Namatius was not a servant of the *Respublica*. He was serving Euric as admiral of the Gothic Atlantic fleet stationed at Bordeaux. A local figure with a tinge of nobility (such as Ausonius had once been), Namatius did not treasure family memories of high office in the *Respublica* that dated from the age of gold, as Sidonius did.

Indeed, Namatius did not need the *Respublica* to make him feel great or even to make him feel Roman. It was enough for a man of energy and intelligence such as himself to follow "the standards of a victorious people"—the Goths, who now represented the only viable state in southern Gaul.[75]

Such persons were devout Christians. They exemplify the piety of the new class of rich that had formed around barbarian courts. They were not interested in building villas. They were not rich enough to build the shimmering new basilicas that had begun to decorate the cities of Gaul. But they did know how to put their money into relatively cheap demonstrations of Catholic piety. Above all, as good Catholics, they knew a saint when they saw one. Such a person was Count Victorius. He was Euric's first military commander in Clermont after the city had been handed over to the Goths. Like Namatius, he had risen as a military leader in Gothic service. When a holy hermit (who had come all the way from Mesopotamia to Gaul) was on his deathbed, Victorius bent over the dying man: "He bent his office low, as low as his own knees." He was careful to weep. He paid for the cost of a reverential funeral. Writing in 477, after the *Respublica* had vanished in the West, Sidonius was pleased to observe such piety in the new governor of Clermont.[76] Victorius was also careful to leave his mark on the surrounding countryside. He set up a row of columns at the popular rural shrine of Saint Julian in Brioude (to the south of Clermont). He brought relics of Saint Lawrence to a church he built on an estate.[77]

It is more than likely that Victorius considered that these acts of devotion were done for the atonement of his sins. There were many who thought that such atonement was needed. Writing a century later, Gregory of Tours remembered Victorius's pious donations with approval. But he added a further anecdote. Victorius arrested the "senator" Eucherius, a former "illustrious" man from the days of the old empire.

> One night he ordered him to be dragged from the prison in which he had been placed, and, having tied him next to an ancient wall, he ordered this very wall to be pulled down on top of him.[78]

It was a lesson in post-imperial politics, Romano-Gothic style.

Sidonius died between 480 and 490, after the empire had vanished from the West. On his sarcophagus, he made no mention of his bishopric. His offices in the *Respublica* and his literary activities were what mattered for him. Nor did he date his death by the reign of any local king. Instead, he dated his death by the reign of the eastern emperor, Zeno. Sidonius considered Zeno, as emperor at Constantinople, to be the sole surviving head of the legitimate Roman empire.[79]

Sidonius's descendants, by contrast, took to the new politics of local Romanness like ducks to water. His son, Apollinaris, led out the militia of Clermont to fight for the Goths against the Franks at the famous battle of Vouillé in 507.[80]

His grandson, Arcadius, played an important and sinister role at the Frankish court. He helped the sons of Clovis get rid of their young nephews, who might claim the throne. It was Arcadius who appeared before the boys' grandmother carrying a sword and a pair of scissors. He gave her the choice of having them tonsured as clergymen or killed. Only one opted to be tonsured.[81] This happened in the 520s; a lot can happen in one hundred years. Only a century before, in the 420s, Augustine was still alive, petitioning the imperial court about the slave trade in Africa. Genseric was still in Spain. Galla Placidia's great votive shrine was being built beside the palace at Ravenna. The *Respublica* had only just begun to feel the first tremors that preceded its collapse in Gaul, Spain, and Africa.

It is important for us to understand the texture of the fifth-century West as a whole before we deal in detail with the manner in which wealth was thought about and used in the new age ushered in by the developments we have described. But it is important for us to have this panorama in mind for another reason. Not only did a general crisis overcome the western empire in the fifth century, but the crisis itself was viewed and judged by a remarkable succession of Christian authors who wrote in the imperial enclave of Provence and in the southern valley of the Rhone. These writers are a listening station for us. It is through them that we can still hear the voices of a world in crisis. Their writings touched, in vivid and pertinent ways, on every aspect of the relation between Christianity and society. So let us now turn, first, to the "saints"—to the Christian intellectuals of Marseilles and to the monk-bishops from the monastery of Lérins—and then to the most remarkable personality of all to emerge from this circle—Salvian, the priest of Marseilles.

PART IV

Aftermaths

CHAPTER 25

Among the Saints

Marseilles, Arles, and Lérins, 400–440

The *Sancti* of Provence

Up to the end of the empire in the West—until the 470s—Provence and the southern valley of the Rhone (from Lyons to Arles and Marseilles) remained an imperial enclave. The region also stood out as a distinctive cultural and religious landscape. In this chapter, we will follow the debates among Christian intellectuals in Provence—mainly of monastic background—on topics that ranged from the nature of wealth in the monastery, through the qualifications for leadership in the churches, to the fate of the foundering empire. In the next chapter, we will consider the Roman empire in the West in the early 440s as viewed from Provence by a vivid and idiosyncratic author—Salvian of Marseilles.

The cities of Provence welcomed newcomers from less secure parts of Gaul. Some time in the 420s or 430s, Paulinus of Pella finally decided to make the best he could of his new poverty by settling in Marseilles. He added that he had been drawn there by his love for "the many saintly persons"—the *sancti*—who lived there.[1] This was very much the right thing to say about Marseilles and the Christian intellectuals who lived there. Fifth-century Provence as a whole was marked by vibrant overlapping circles of "saints." Marseilles itself stood between an "island of the saints"—the monastery of Lérins (modern Ile Saint Honorat, three miles off the coast of Cannes)—and the city of Arles, at the mouth of the Rhone. For over half a century, from the 420s to the 470s, the constant competition between these three centers made southern Gaul the most vibrant region of Christian writing in the western Mediterranean.

Each center was different from the other. Arles was not intended to be a city of saints. It was the "little Rome of Gaul." Throughout the fifth century, Arles was the secular heart of what remained of the *Respublica* in Gaul and eastern Spain. The city was crowded with governmental buildings. It was a center of frankly worldly pageantry. The secular nobility of Gaul were encouraged to gather regularly at Arles, in their full finery of silk and cloth of gold, to lend their massed presence to the sort of ceremonies of state the young Sidonius Apollinaris still witnessed in 449.[2]

By contrast, Christian intellectuals—priests, monks, and laymen alike—gathered at Marseilles. Marseilles had emerged unscathed from the disorders that followed the invasion of 405–6 and the subsequent collapse of imperial rule in much of Gaul and Spain. It reverted to the role it had played when first settled by Greeks in classical times. It became an emporium for foreign goods. Marseilles also regained some of the reputation the old Greek colony of Massilia had once enjoyed. It became a place for leisured eccentricity, an Athens of the West.[3]

Lérins was a different matter. It was the most successful of a series of island monasteries that had been deliberately chosen for their sheer "horror." Spiritual Counts of Monte Cristo, the upper-class converts to the monastic life who lived at Lérins and on similar bare islands claimed to have brought a touch of the awesome desert of Egypt to within sight of the Côte d'Azur.

The persons connected with these three very different centers were held together by an unusually tenacious upper-class culture. The sense of a shared culture made it easy for upper-class monks to move from a monastery to the episcopate or to the priesthood—from Lérins to Arles, to Marseille or to the little cities of the Alpes Maritimes and the valley of the Rhone. To name only the most prominent of these lateral promotions from desert island to the bishopric of a major city: in 426–7 Honoratus, who had been abbot of Lérins since 410, became bishop of Arles until his death in 428. In 430 his relative Hilarius (best known to English speakers as Hilary of Arles) moved from Lérins to Arles to become bishop until his death in 449. Some abbots boasted connections with the higher nobility of Gaul. But connections in high places may have been exceptional, if not invented. What mattered more than such claims to nobility was the literary culture that all protagonists had in common. This culture held together the differing layers of the provincial elites of Provence much as it had held together the variegated elites of Aquitaine in the time of Ausonius.[4]

The reputation of Lérins was as much the creation of a literary movement as of an ascetic experiment. Even when they were thought of as cut off from the world by the vast silence of the sea, the abbots of Lérins kept in touch with a circle of friends and admirers that embraced all of Provence and much of the Rhone valley. Honoratus was said to have "poured the honey back into the bees' wax of his tablets" by the charm of his letters.[5] Hilary, Honoratus's successor as bishop of Arles, went out of his way to be seen plaiting baskets in the manner of the great monks of Egypt.[6] But this did not deter him from being the center of a literary circle, made up of cultivated and politically active laymen. He even received formal panegyrics from local poets—one of whom, called Livy (!), was quite prepared to say that "if Augustine had come after you, he would have been thought a lesser figure than you."[7]

In such circles we do not feel, as we do when reading the sermons of Augustine, a Christian culture resting on an oceanic shelf of weekly preaching to socially mixed congregations. Rather, we are looking at the culture of a leisured class, close to that of Paulinus of Nola, of Sulpicius Severus, or of the patrons of Jerome and Pelagius. Letters of exhortation; panegyrics of recently deceased monastic heroes; pamphlets carefully dedicated to like-minded patrons—often written under an assumed name (the sure sign of an "in group" who could be trusted to recognize the pen names of their friends):[8] these were the principal products of the circles of Lérins, Marseilles, and Arles. Created in this way by competing literary cliques, the evidence for the Christianity of Provence has rightly been characterized as at one and the same time "extraordinarily dense and extraordinarily one sided."[9]

Altogether, we are faced with a phenomenon we did not find in Africa but we did find in Rome. A remarkable group of persons were committed to drastic changes in their own lives. Yet they were not recluses. They remained surrounded by a wide penumbra of lay supporters. Some of the *sancti* may have been bound by blood to high-placed persons. They certainly shared their culture. But it was not simply a matter of a common background. An intense religious relationship was involved. Upper-class laypersons treated the monks of Lérins as *sancti*—living saints, holy men. They were bound to them by a strong psychological bond. They entered into a spiritual exchange through which the *sancti* received reverence and material support from laypersons, who received their blessing in return. This bond was always more vibrant—and less predictable—than were the normal bonds of shared class and culture because it was based on a sharp sense of the unresolved opposition between the sacred and the profane.

For this reason, the relations between the "saints" and laypersons of similar class and culture were not without their problems. The writings that came from Marseilles, Lérins, and Arles concentrated to an unusual degree on defining the uneasy boundary between the new demands of the ascetic movement and the average Christianity of well-to-do secular persons.

The unspoken presence of a cultivated Christian laity as patrons and admirers put constant pressure on the monks and monk-bishops of Provence to emphasize the drastic tenor of their own, ascetic life. It provoked constant debate as to which Christianity was authentic and which was a half-hearted compromise. Equally vigorous was the debate among monks themselves as to who were true monks and who were tepid amateurs. This situation generated arguments on almost every aspect of Christian behavior and of Christian society—from the nature of grace and free will to the fate of the Roman empire. Furthermore, the need for consequentiality among the "saints," in their pursuit of the highest standards of ascetic Christianity, accounts for the radicalism that runs like a live current throughout the Christian literature of Provence, from the works of John Cassian in the 420s to the denunciations of the *Respublica* itself by Salvian in the 440s. It is to these challenges that we must now turn. They took many different forms.

Ne … inhaeserit ei vel unius nummi contagio: Lest there remain in him the infection of a single coin

WEALTH AND THE MONASTERY

The first and, in retrospect, the best-known challenge to come from the *sancti* of Provence came from a mystery man who had only recently settled in Marseilles. John Cassian may originally have come from the farthest end of the Latin world— from Scythia, the Dobrudja region of modern Romania, where the Danube flows into the Black Sea. He had traveled in Egypt and the Middle East at the end of the fourth century and came to Gaul at some time in the 410s. He claimed to be the bearer of the authentic spiritual goods of Egypt. Cassian tells us next to nothing about himself. He made his own the total anonymity he expected of a true monk.[10] His first treatise, *De Institutis Coenobiorum*, was written in 420–24. Usually called Cassian's *Institutes*, it is best translated as "Basic Rules for the Foundation of a Monastery." It was addressed to a Provençal bishop (Castor of Apt) who wished to found a monastery.[11] A little later, between 426 and 428, Cassian wrote his *Collationes* (*Conferences*).[12] These were a collection of spiritual sermons ostensibly elicited by Cassian and by his companion Germanus from various wise monks of Egypt, whom they had visited a generation earlier in the 380s and 390s. With these *Conferences*, Cassian reached out to the islands along the coast. One set of *Conferences* were dedicated to Honoratus, the abbot of Lérins. A further set went to the monks on the Iles d'Hyères.

In all his writings, Cassian claimed to offer the real thing. He invariably compared the haphazard and fissile monastic experiments of Gaul unfavorably with the uncanny solidity of the monasteries of Egypt. In Egypt alone, so Cassian claimed, something of the original fervor of the Primitive Church was still alive. Relics of the brotherly love, based on the abandonment of wealth and on the sharing of goods that had characterized the Jerusalem Community of the first Christians, were still to be found among some monks in the depths of the monasteries and hermitages of Egypt.

As we saw, the Jerusalem Community, as described in chapters 2 and 4 of Acts, had haunted Augustine in his early experiments in the monastic life. For Augustine, that moment of total sharing had been linked to the shared ecstasy of the coming of the Holy Ghost at Pentecost. It was an ecstasy of brotherly love toward which Augustine's monks labored painfully in this life. But it remained a dream for the future, one that would come to fruition only in a Heavenly Republic beyond this world. For Cassian it was no such thing. Deep community linked to prayer and contemplation was a living experience among some monks of Egypt. He wrote his treatises to ensure that the living experience of community (similar to that of the earliest Christians) he had found in Egypt could be transferred to the monasteries of Gaul.[13]

But how would this be done? Like the writings of other *sancti* in Marseilles, Cassian's works were polemical tracts for their time. They were not a dispassionate travelogue of the monasteries of Egypt but a mirror held up to the monks of Gaul. Especially in his *Institutes*, but also in his *Conferences*, Cassian used the example of the monks of Egypt to mount a consequential criticism of the half-hearted monastic experiments he had observed in Gaul. This criticism concentrated on the issue of wealth and poverty in the monastery.

As Richard Goodrich has pointed out in a perceptive study of Cassian, the principal target of his criticism was the gentlemanly attitude toward wealth that had characterized the monks of Gaul.[14] From the days of Saint Martin onward, monasticism in Gaul had been modeled to a large extent on the leisured life of the villa owners who had protected and admired Martin. Cultivated advocates of asceticism had continued to live from the revenues of their estates or (if they had renounced these estates by giving them to the church, as Sulpicius Severus appears to have done) from annuities paid by the church. Monasteries were also kept afloat by the pooled donations of well-to-do members. Basically, the monks did not have to think about money because money would always be there. In effect, they practiced "unwealth"—a life of restricted needs in a stripped-down villa. They continued the same sublime indifference toward wealth that had long been associated with the ideal of *otium* in aristocratic and philosophical circles. But indifference toward wealth was not the same as having no wealth whatsoever. In Cassian's view, such persons could never be real monks. For they had spared themselves the sharp taste of real poverty.

In Cassian's opinion, monasteries could survive and thrive only if the issue of wealth was resolved in the very first steps taken by the monk who wished to enter a monastery. The postulant must come to the door of the monastery already stripped of his worldly goods. No portion of his former wealth was allowed to enter the monastery, not even in the form of a pious donation.[15] Augustine had admitted such donations. Similarly, from time to time the altar at Lérins would be piled with goods, money, or documents brought to the monastery by well-to-do recruits.[16]

This was not what Cassian wished to happen. He insisted that the monk should enter the monastery sterilized of wealth. Not even "the infection of a single coin" was allowed to adhere to him.[17] He was admitted to the monastic community by a ceremony that stressed the fact that he did not own even the clothes that he stood up in. He received directly from the hands of the abbot a uniform, neutral robe.[18] It was a foundational ceremony, as awesomely irrevocable as the vesting and rewarding of an officer in the late Roman army. But here the largesse of the abbot was the gift of total poverty. Henceforth, the monk depended for his clothes and rations on the monastery, in which the abbot was a little emperor.

Cassian offered his readers an inside tour of a monastery stripped bare of riches. And he did this so as to present a community stripped bare of the dire willfulness of the rich. To surrender wealth was a sine qua non. But this dispossession was always seen as a synecdoche of a surrender of the self that was intended to be even more drastic than the surrender of personal wealth. Self and wealth were fused; true renunciation involved both. The monastic life

> consisted in the despoiling of the self from all property and in a total stripping down, so that, apart from the will of the abbot, hardly any will should be alive in us.[19]

Dispossession meant "de-dominization." The monk ceased to be a *dominus* of any thing and of any person. Most of all, he ceased to be the *dominus* even of himself.[20] In this Cassian was "the great equalizer."[21] All monks were equal, because equally dependent on the will of their abbot.

We must remember that Cassian was writing for well-to-do readers and for recruits to the monastic life drawn from the provincial elites. For such aspirants to the monastic life Cassian insisted on a leveling down that admitted no half measures. By contrast, Augustine had been quite prepared to offer concessions to upper-class recruits in matters of dress, food, and work schedule. Cassian offered no such thing. From the very beginning, the monk should learn "not to be ashamed to be leveled to the poor, that is, to the body of the brotherhood."[22]

Accustomed as we now are to the notion of monastic poverty, as practiced for centuries under the *Rule of Saint Benedict*, it is easy to forget how very drastic this view of the ideal monastery must have appeared to fifth-century readers. Read with Roman eyes, Cassian's ideal monastery resembled a slave barracks. Under the eye of the abbot, every monk was expected to jump to his task with alacrity "in a way that no slaves ever showed in the service of even the most harsh and over-bearing lord."[23]

Cassian's ideal monastery was, indeed, a very strange place. In it, free men became slaves and the wealthy became paupers. Everything that a Gallic farmer had good reason to dread in times of war and famine; everything that a nobleman made destitute by barbarian violence and by civil war might experience: all the social ruin of Gaul was turned, as if by a kind of magical inversion, into the basis of a perfect society. One wonders, indeed, whether voluntary impoverishment of so drastic a kind did not hold a special, almost unconscious appeal to members of a class that had recently experienced so much involuntary impoverishment. Compared with the great fear of total financial ruin brought about by civil war and barbarian plundering, monastic poverty that brought former aristocrats down to the level of the poor was, at least, a state that was freely chosen.[24]

In Cassian's view of the monastery, the monk had not only stepped downward (as Paulinus of Nola had done, with his dark robes, unwashed body, and ill-cut hair) to follow the *abjectio*, the stepping down of Christ. Cassian's monk did more than cancel out in himself all previous denotators of wealth and status while still carrying with him tantalizing hints of former grandeur. He had entered a monastery so as to realize what he really was before God—the equivalent of a total social shipwreck:

> He was a refugee immigrant in this world, a landless man. He should think of himself as an estate-born slave and odd-jobs-man of the monastery rather than presume that he was the owner of anything at all.[25]

Stripped of wealth, the monks of Cassian's monastery were expected to work to support themselves by the labor of their hands. There was an element of bravado in this claim. The monasteries of Egypt never became economically self-sufficient. Nor did the monasteries of Cassian's Provence. Monks might follow Cassian by becoming totally poor. Regular, hard work might become increasingly prominent as the sign of a true monastery. But total economic independence from the outside world always remained no more than a dream.[26]

Cassian insisted on the myth of monastic autarky largely so as to drive home his challenge to the tepid monks of Gaul. In Cassian's opinion, the monk was the exact opposite of the leisured rentier. He was the only productive member of society. He depended on himself to feed himself. Everyone else was like a beggar, living on the *agape*—the handouts—of others. Landowners collecting rents; emperors collecting taxes: compared with monks, they were all parasites, expecting to be fed by others.[27]

For Cassian, monks were the one exception to the dire rule of human society. For millennia, society had been characterized by the exploitation of the weak by those who did not wish to work. Ever since the Days of the Giants before the Flood (the biblical equivalent of the Age of Bronze, which brought to an end the original social innocence of the Golden Age in pagan thought), the powerful had "preferred to base their lives on plunder rather than live from the sweat of craftsmanship and labor."[28]

It is important to note the harsh tone with which Cassian spoke of society outside the monastery. He viewed the social structures of the lay world with notably disabused eyes. Like the Pelagian writer of *On Riches*, he gave little credence to the widespread idea that personal wealth was a providential gift to its owner. When Cassian described the manner in which the great Egyptian hermit,

Abba Moses, gave alms, he did not present him as the administrator of wealth sent to him by God. Abba Moses gave alms, frankly, in order to remedy a little the inequities of an unjust society:

> inequality will continue to rage [until the end of time] due to those who occupy those things which have been granted [by God] for the use of all in common for their own use alone—and do not even use them.[29]

But what mattered for Cassian was not that social inequality (shocking though it might be) should vanish from the world. What concerned him was that no trace of such inequality should linger in the sterile environment of his monastery. For this reason, the very radicalism of Cassian's views on monastic poverty brought an old-fashioned debate on wealth to a halt. This debate was, quite literally, left at the monastery's door. The old distinction between good wealth and bad wealth did not apply in a monastery: it was a place where no wealth existed.

If avarice was denounced, it was done so only as a function of the total dispossession of the monk. Cassian followed the ravages of avarice with microscopic precision. But the avarice he observed had nothing to do with gold and wide acres. It was a chill ghost within the self. It could lead monks to shameful acts—petty thefts; manic fits of overwork; the pathetic hoarding of food or small coins; a miser's terror of old age, illness, and the onset of penury. These personal temptations of the monks were so bizarre and so humiliating that Cassian—who wrote without a hint of embarrassment about sexual temptations and wet dreams—thought that it was better that laypersons not read his chapters on avarice in the monastery.[30] But these disquisitions on the vice of avarice bore no relation to the bad rich outside the monastery, as these had been excoriated by Ambrose and by Pelagian writers.

This marks a change. Only two decades earlier, the Pelagian movement had shown what storms could arise when ascetic demands for total renunciation were allied with a consequential body of social criticism. Pelagian tracts were known in Marseilles. Some were still admired as models of ascetic exhortation. But Cassian's single-minded concentration on monastic poverty put the issues that those tracts had raised out-of-date. The storm clouds parted. The two issues—wealth and renunciation—ceased to be so vehemently intertwined. In order to foster renunciation, one did not have to launch an attack on Roman society as a whole, as the Pelagian authors of *On Riches* and *On the Christian Life* had done.

For Cassian, renunciation, true renunciation, was for experts only. He wrote for them. For those who read Cassian on monastic poverty, his critique of wealth could not be seen as directed at society in general. It was a call for utter consequentiality to would-be monks in their own ascetic vocation. Later writers from Marseilles, such as Salvian, were merciless in attacking half-hearted converts to the religious life who thought that they could be good monks and good clergy-men while keeping control of their own money. Such persons were dismissed by Salvian as *monstra*—as freaks. They were *demi vierge* ascetics.[31] Alas, our friend Paulinus of Pella (who cheerfully combined professions of dedication to God with descriptions of his most recent real estate ventures) would have appeared to Salvian as one such freak.

But this was a radicalism voiced by professionals judging other professionals. Cassian's call to poverty barely affected persons in the world; they were not called upon to make such all-or-nothing choices. The Christian common sense of wealth was sufficient for them. It was possible to be a member of the good rich provided that one did not claim to be a monk. Generosity, a sense of solidarity, and the giving of alms for the forgiveness of sins were virtues that were expected of the laity. They were virtues that continued to be praised in secular persons in fifth-century Gaul as, indeed, in all later centuries. Only in the narrow confines of a monastery was it now considered necessary to face *the eye of a needle*—to contemplate the total renunciation of wealth. Wealth no longer needed to be a source of widespread, ill-defined anxiety. The wealthy were now offered a clear-cut choice of roles. Either one remained rich and became a pillar of the church as a donor and almsgiver, or one betook oneself to a monastery.

But now let us turn to the island of Lérins to see how real monks related to real laypersons in the Provence to which Cassian had brought the News from Nowhere of the wealthless monastery.

Circe's Island: Lérins, 400–449

When, in around 428, Cassian dedicated books eleven through eighteen of his *Conferences* to the abbot Honoratus, the monastery on Lérins had already ex-isted for over twenty years. In the opinion of its admirers (an opinion the exigent Cassian may not have entirely shared), this monastery had already brought Egypt to the edge of Gaul. Chosen in around 400–410 by Honoratus as the site for his monastery, Lérins was a low-lying, offshore island, rendered difficult of access by reefs and a strong current. Its sweltering, snake-infested flatland had attracted him. The *squalor* of the island—the bleak absence of human cultivation—was held to resemble the deserts of Egypt.[32]

The reality, however, was somewhat different. Not all offshore islands of the Mediterranean were deserts or needed to remain deserts. The close neighbor of Lérins—Lero, the present-day Ile Sainte Marguerite, separated from Lérins by a narrow strait—had boasted villas, makers of rafts, and even a cult center duti-fully frequented by Ligurian pirates.[33] Lérins quickly ceased to be a desert. It became a miniature, monastic version of Lero.

This happened for a variety of reasons. Manual labor was obligatory for all monks. What may well be the first rule of Lérins—the *Rule of the Four Fathers*—insisted on six hours of labor each day, despite the "murmuring" of monks who may have found this pointedly "Egyptian" regulation surprising.[34] But a successful monastic settlement on Lérins was only possible because well-to-do recruits brought their own slaves with them. These slaves were expected to settle down as "brothers" to their former masters.[35] Their labor was brought to bear to turn the squalor of Lérins into the equivalent of an intensively cultivated villa. The imagined desert island became one of a chain of island villa sites that stretched across the entire northern shore of the Mediterranean, from the Balearic Islands to the Adriatic coast of modern Croatia.[36] Furthermore, monks entering Lérins were encouraged to make oblations to the monastery—a practice of which Cassian certainly disapproved.[37] In his own small and intensely cultivated estate, cut off from the mainland by the sea, the abbot of a monastery such as Lérins did not have to face the problem of the evaporation of his labor force, which drove a lay landowner, such as Dardanus, to lavish walls upon his peasants in the upper valleys of the nearby Alpes Maritimes as much to keep them in place on his estates as to defend them. A labor force made up of obedient monks was quite as effective as any gang of slaves.

For these reasons, Lérins emerged at a time when older ascetic lifestyles, frequently tied to villas in the open countryside, were endangered by a rising tide of violence. Sulpicius Severus, the friend of Paulinus of Nola, may well have been a victim of this change. His villa at Primuliacum seems to have lain close to the main road between Toulouse and Narbonne. In the peaceful last years of the fourth century, Primuliacum had been a "spiritual caravansary," a perfect joining place for like-minded ascetics within easy distance of major cities. But, after 406, as war bands roamed the roads, to be close to a major highway was the wrong place to be. The monastery-like settlement at Primuliacum, with its baptistery and twin churches covered with pictures and inscriptions, was lost without a trace. Sulpicius himself may have found himself forced to join the clergy in order to gain a living.[38]

This change affected more than one individual. The cult of Saint Martin in Gaul had been largely fostered by a network of leisured villa owners such as Severus. This cult fell almost completely silent for over half a century until it was revived in the 460s at Martin's grave at Tours.[39] By contrast, the intensely organized "island of the saints" at Lérins, hemmed in by the sea and careful to maintain an "Egyptian" image of industry, stood out ever more prominently as the security and affluence of an earlier age vanished from large parts of Gaul.

Within a decade, the monks of Lérins came to colonize the churches of Provence. Honoratus moved to Arles in 428. His relative Hilary, also from Lérins, became bishop of Arles in 430. Others soon followed to other sees. One such

was Eucherius. Eucherius had been a lay admirer of monks. He had first settled
with his wife on neighboring Lero, much as Paulinus of Nola had settled with his
wife, Therasia, at Nola. He later crossed the water to Lérins. He became bishop
of Lyon in 435. Maximus, another former abbot of Lérins, became bishop of
Riez in 433, as did his successor as abbot, the brilliant Faustus, who went to Riez
as bishop in 468. Their careers proved that Lérins was a Circe's island. It was a
place of "astonishing transmutations." Circe had turned men into pigs. Lérins, by
contrast, turned sinners into saints and then, in a manner equally magical, sent
them out into the world as bishops.[40]

This fact is well-known, but it is not easy to explain. Modern scholars have
advanced the notion that because the monks of Lérins came from aristocratic
backgrounds, it seemed natural to them not to treat the monastic life as a lifelong commitment but rather as analogous to the traditional spell of withdrawal
from public life associated with the aristocratic ideal of *otium*. Loyalty to their
hometown and to the traditions of government associated with their class led
them back to the cities of Gaul as bishops. In their capacity as bishops, the products of Lérins are supposed to have set about maintaining an austere Christian
version of the Roman way of life in precisely the regions where this way of life
was being threatened by barbarians.[41]

Modern scholars have a soft spot for the monks of Lérins. Their writings on
each other and on the spiritual life appear to "breathe the spirit of the educated
Roman upper class."[42] They strike modern readers as unusually measured, at times
even bucolic. Their descriptions of the saints of Lérins are often praised because
they are mercifully free of the miracle stories that usually thrived in an ascetic
environment—whether in distant Egypt or around the person of Saint Martin.[43]
Altogether, the monks of Lérins tend to be seen as among the last—and, perhaps, the nicest—of the "last Romans." Last but not least, it is widely believed
that the remarkable constellation of monk-bishops associated with Lérins was a
sign of the future—an encouraging one. It showed that aristocratic and ascetic
values could merge, thereby opening the way for the triumphant colonization of
the Gallic church by members of the Roman senatorial aristocracy in the course
of the fifth and early sixth centuries.[44]

This view has much to commend it. But it misses something of the sharpness
of the age. It suggests altogether too simple an image of southern Gaul as it passed
through the crises of the 420s and 430s. In the first place, we must remember the
complexity of the Gallic aristocracy at this time. We should not be lured into
following too literally the aristocratic discourse contained in the writings of the
circle of Lérins. These writings emphasized the high position in society that abbots, monks, and bishops were supposed to have enjoyed before they abandoned
the world to become monks. Hints of high status heightened the value of their
renunciation. Furthermore, monastic leaders were presented as having passed

effortlessly from worldly nobility to a yet higher, spiritual nobility as abbots and bishops. In a later generation, writers would emphasize the smooth—indeed the providential—transition of their heroes from high status in the world to high status in the church.[45]

But we should be careful not to take such rhetoric too literally. The notion of nobility it put forward was studiously vague. As in the days of Ausonius, "nobility" in Gaul was a fluid concept. It was claimed by many and (as the case of Ausonius himself makes plain) it tended to be inflated in retrospect. We need to be more careful as to what exactly had been the social status of the main protagonists of the monastic movement associated with Lérins. Honoratus and Hilary may have come from well-placed local families, attached to the little "senates"—the town councils—of their cities. In the Rhone valley, such town councils came to speak of themselves in the fifth century as "councils of the noble."[46] The horizon of these self-styled nobles seldom reached beyond their province. At most, they might hold land in other provinces in Gaul and be linked to other Gallic cities. But they had never been members of the empire-wide class of the super-rich, which had been so prominent in the fourth century.[47] For them, the world of multiprovincial aristocrats, such as Paulinus of Nola, already belonged to a *belle époque* that had passed forever in the first quarter of the fifth century.

Furthermore, as we have seen, the links between the provincial nobility and the grandees who controlled the upper echelons of the *Respublica* had become weaker than they had been in the fourth century. An adversarial relationship had developed between the real power brokers of the empire (those who came from privileged Gallic families, such as the families of Sidonius Apollinaris and his friends) and a lesser nobility. It was they—and not the great families close to the court—who had borne the brunt of barbarian violence and ruthless civil wars. It has been rightly suggested that many of the founding members of the Lérins circle had come to Provence as refugees. But they had not all fled from the barbarians. In many cases, their families may have been thrown loose (as Paulinus of Pella had been) by the vehement infighting of Romans themselves in the decades of civil war that followed the great raid of 405–6.[48] A streak of resentment runs through the writings of the *sancti*. It was directed against the upper echelons of the nobility and their allies, the high-ups in the imperial administration, who were the effective rulers of fifth-century Gaul. The anger of the lesser nobility emerges most clearly in Salvian's denunciations of the high officers of the empire.

In a society whose upper classes were fractured in this way there was a certain a jaggedness in the relations between the first generation of Lerinians and the lay world around them. Their own rhetoric of nobility renounced and found again attempted to patch over an all-too-real hiatus between their monastic persona and the profane world with which they found themselves confronted. The monks of Lérins may have been aristocrats in their own small way. But they entered the social world of southern Gaul as isotopes of Egypt. On their "Circe's island" they had made themselves starkly different from the normal aristocrat. Indeed, their value to those who wielded real power in the governmental center at Arles was precisely that they were not like the other lesser nobles from whose ranks they came.

A hairy man, girded up with a belt of leather (2 Kings 1:8): Monks as Bishops

In the later 420s, governmental circles in Gaul needed the right sort of bishops. They could no longer afford to be indifferent as to who headed the Christian congregations in the cities. Bishops had been involved in the civil wars of the 410s. When Constantius, the head of the armed forces for the court of Ravenna, crushed Constantine III in 411 and settled the Visigoths in 418, he included the bishopric of Arles as part of his settlement of southern Gaul. He may even have lavished a new Christian basilica on the city, called the Basilica Constantia.[49] He set up "his" bishop in Arles—Patroclus (412–26). But Patroclus was too close to government circles for his own safety. In 426 he was murdered by an officer from a rival faction in the military. In an age used to violent controversies in the church, Patroclus was one of the very few bishops ever to be assassinated. It was time to look for a safer sort of bishop.[50]

The safer sort proved, in the short run, to be the odder sort. The high-ups went for the monks of Lérins. This is not altogether surprising. The careers of Martin and Priscillian already showed that when wealth spoke in the churches of the West, it often spoke in favor of ascetics and mavericks. The wealthy and powerful supported such figures precisely because they were both like themselves and yet utterly different. As ascetics, they had made themselves the antithesis to the average member of their own class. They represented a notion of the holy that was starkly opposed to the profane world.

This cliff face of difference was crucial. It ensured that holy men were holy and that they could bring blessing and empowerment to laypersons who desperately needed it in dangerous times. In the case of the rapid transfer of two outstanding monks from Lérins—first Honoratus and then Hilary—the common links of family and class (though present) may not have weighed so heavily with their lay patrons as did religious considerations. In a monk from Lérins they found an Elijah for their own, troubled age: *A hairy man, girded up with a belt of leather* (2 Kings 1:8). Such persons were not perceived as being anymore members of the "upper" class. In the well-chosen words of Pascal-Grégoire Delage, they stood for an "out class" heavily endowed with spiritual power.[51]

But there was more to the presence of a former monk as bishop than the expectation of the occasional blessing. With Honoratus as bishop, the laity could be sure that their souls and those of their kin and loved ones would truly benefit from the gifts they had offered to the church. Honoratus's prayers on behalf of the dead made these endowments effective in the other world. This was not only because of the efficacy of his prayers. Honoratus's parsimony as a former monk made sure that wealth given to the church for the benefit of the souls of the dead would not be dispersed or wasted on mere display.[52] The administration of church property by monk-bishops was guided by a horror of excess. This horror did not derive directly from Cassian, who wrote only about monasteries and not about the goods of the church. But it was based on a starkly minimalist attitude toward the handling of wealth that had been honed to a new sharpness by Cassian's writings on monastic poverty.

Somewhat paradoxically, monk-bishops proved to be enormously successful fund-raisers. They were successful because they were reputed to have had no contact with wealth. Their hands were clean. Hilary of Arles (430–49) continued to work in the fields when he was a bishop, "though not physically suited for it, as he came from a distinguished family and had not been brought up for such things."[53] He constructed machines with which to drain the salt-pans along the coast.[54] The fact that he had "taken on rustic labors for the sake of Christ" was even mentioned on his tombstone.[55] This studied display of self-sufficiency on the Egyptian model only served to heighten the flow of gifts to the church. A later writer remembered Hilary with pride: "He did not only hold on to the wealth which the church then had, but he expanded this wealth through many inheritances given by the faithful."[56]

Yet, despite his reputation in lay circles as a man to be trusted with wealth, there was a *terribilità* about Hilary the monk that fits ill with the notion of a nobleman morphing effortlessly into a bishop. He came to Arles from Lérins as a prophet to awaken Provence.[57] He used his lay connections to the full so as to turn the see of Arles into a mega-metropolitan see. But he did this so as to impose his own high notions of ecclesiastical order. He brought a whole new network of bishoprics into existence along the fringes of the Rhone. Not surprisingly, these bishops were often drawn from circles connected with Lérins.[58] He rushed from city to city. He summoned councils. He deposed bishops at will.[59] Challenged in 444 by Pope Leo, he crossed the Alps in winter, striding on foot all the way to Rome.[60] When the two men met, there was an explosion of words between them. Hilary, said Leo, uttered "things such as no layman should speak and no bishop ever have to hear."[61]

Viewed from Rome, Hilary's charismatic dominance in southern Gaul represented all that governmental circles in Italy had come to distrust in Gallic versions of local Romanness. It was a Bacauda within the church—a balkanization of ecclesiastical politics within the very territories of the *Respublica*. As the emperor Valentinian III declared (at Leo's behest) in 445: Hilary "had violated the majesty of imperial government ... with the lone recklessness of a usurper."[62] The hero of the saints of Lérins, Hilary was not necessarily the hero of everybody else.

"A new brotherhood of ... outsiders": Monks and the Churches of Southern Gaul

Hilary died in 449. His memorable clash with Leo, in the last years of his life, should not be treated in isolation. It was the climax of long-term resentments that had grown up in Gaul itself. The style of ecclesiastical government represented by monk-bishops of Lérins such as Hilary threatened notions of church order that were well established in Italy and Africa and that had been taken for granted in much of Gaul and Spain as well. What was at stake was nothing less than the sociology of the local Christian communities. Would the churches continue to be churches of the *mediocres*? Or would a new model of ecclesiastical leadership, imposed from on top by vivid leaders of monastic background such as Hilary, establish itself as the norm? This development threatened to brush aside the combination of *plebs* and clergy that had accounted for the low-profile tenacity of the Christian churches in most provinces of the West.

A sense of alarm at the appearance of the high-handed style of leadership represented by Hilary and the monastic clique of Lérins had ensured that the bishop of Rome was fed with anti-monastic petitions from the clergy of many Gallic cities. Letters from Rome responded to these petitions. They accepted the grievances of a local clergy who felt pushed to one side by the forceful "saints" of Lérins.

The bishops of Rome based their case on a strong sense of the clergy as a Third Estate. As we have seen, this sense had developed in Rome since the days of Damasus. But the Roman model was not linked to Rome alone. It was a model that could also be applied to provincial churches. It suited the social profile of the urban communities from which the clergy were still recruited, both in Italy and in many other provinces.

In most Gallic cities, the clergy and their bishops had remained relatively little men, drawn from the town councillors and the rich plebeians. Aware of their precarious position in the social pyramid, the clergy were held together by a fierce sense of privilege. They modeled themselves on their social equals—on members of the lower ranks of the imperial bureaucracy. A clerical career was supposed to resemble that of a civil servant working his way to the top in a governmental office. Promotion within the clergy was to be by seniority. Ideally, a bishop should rise from the ranks of the clergy of his hometown.[63] It was expected that the bishop would be chosen by a broad constituency of the "people" of that city, acting in collaboration with their clergy. These were relatively free elections. They were by no means always dominated by other bishops or by local magnates.[64]

Hence the vigor with which the clergy of many cities in southern Gaul reacted to the rising prestige of monks. In 428 Pope Celestine echoed their grievances in a long letter to the bishops of Provence. Celestine condemned this "new brotherhood of wanderers and outsiders ... who did not grow up in the church, but came from another religious setting."[65] The resentment of the small-town clergy did not focus on the average monk. It was the super-monk who appeared to have come out of a privileged background such as Lérins that concerned them. Celestine insisted that such monks should not be chosen as bishops over the heads of the clergy. The orderly ranks of clergymen, dressed in ceremonious, Roman style, were not to be pushed aside by men who positively wished to look like Elijah the Tishbite—hairy men, dressed in strange monastic robes.

"Diversity and separation in one church": Prosper of Aquitaine at Marseilles, 428–33

The rise of the monk-bishops also met with a theological challenge raised in the name of Augustine by a lay intellectual: Prosper of Aquitaine.[66] Prosper was a married man with strong theological opinions. He was like Sulpicius Severus in his sharp pen and like Paulinus of Nola in his poetic verve. A product of the leisured culture of previous decades, Prosper was an example of the easy symbiosis of lay and clerical circles that characterized the Christianity of Provence. He had little sense that, as a layman, he was debarred from issues debated by the clergy and by experts in the monastic life. He needed heroes, and he found one in Augustine. He also needed enemies. He moved from Aquitaine to Marseilles in the 420s. Once there, he went out of his way to pick a quarrel with the local *sancti*. In 428, when Augustine was still alive, Prosper attempted to get the bishop of Hippo involved in discussions on grace and free will which, so he said, were taking place at Marseilles. He told Augustine that he represented a circle of "intrepid lovers of the full doctrine of grace."[67]

In 432 Prosper went further. He picked on Cassian. He wrote a tract called *Contra Collatorem* (*Against the Sermonizer*) to answer what he claimed to be a veiled attack by Cassian in the thirteenth book of his *Conferences* on Augustine's notions of grace and free will. He even went so far as to accuse Cassian of harboring "remnants" of Pelagian ideas. By choosing a pseudonym for Cassian, he avoided singling him out as the object of a personal attack. But, in so doing, he also relieved himself from any obligation to understand Cassian's highly nuanced views on grace and the human will on their own terms. As "the Sermonizer," Cassian was no more than a straw man for Prosper. He was made to stand for currents of opinion Prosper considered dangerous because different from the views of Augustine.[68]

Not surprisingly, the "saints" of Marseilles remembered Prosper somewhat coolly. He was feisty—*nervosus*, a man of "muscular assertiveness." His attack on Cassian was ill conceived.[69] Modern scholars tend to agree. They speak of the attack on Cassian as "Prosper's red herring." It was "a singularly ill-considered and regrettably influential interpretation of Cassian's writings."[70]

Yet on one issue Prosper touched a raw nerve. He wrote when monks of Lérins had begun to take over the governmental capital of Arles as bishops. Prosper sensed that it was time to look at the qualifications of these persons from a strictly theological point of view. They plainly brought to the cities advantages of culture, class, and ascetic training, both from Lérins and from their secular background. But did they think that their activity had sprung from the grace of God alone? Or had part of their success sprung from their background—from "merits" accumulated by their own unaided will, independent of the grace of God?[71]

In this, Prosper did not claim to write only as a theologian of grace and free will. He claimed to be concerned with the structure of the Christian community. He caricatured Cassian's guarded language. To Prosper (if not to Cassian's more sympathetic modern exponents), Cassian seemed to hold back a residue of free will in the human person. Devout persons brought this precious residue of free will to the service of God. They placed it entirely in the hands of God, to use as He wished. Yet even this humble attitude rang alarm bells for Prosper. In his opinion, to speak of such a residue of free will was the thin end of a wedge.

This was because Prosper perceived that free will was not a purely abstract, sociologically neutral notion. It could act as a shorthand for the possession of social and cultural advantages. Once believers claimed that part of their actions had derived from their free will alone, independent of the grace of God, this will itself—the good will, that is, which led to good religious actions—could be invested with sociological overtones. Those who came to God of their own free will might be tempted to think of themselves (and, more important, to be thought of by others) as having brought with them an entire spectrum of social and cultural advantages that had been achieved by their own free will. Culture, class, and ascetic know-how might be among them. The church might come to be ruled by an elite of self-made saints, who could be thought to have owed as much to their social background and ascetic grooming as to the grace of God.

For this reason, Prosper claimed that Cassian's views would bring about a fateful "diversity and separation in one church."[72] The very wrongheadedness of the accusation, when applied to Cassian, showed how much weight Prosper attached to the issue.[73] He accused Cassian of having implied that some persons could be thought to have brought considerably more of their own free will to the service of God than had others. God would be disposed to "protect and embrace" them precisely because of these qualities. They had "anticipated God's call with fervor and alacrity."[74] They already showed, in effect, that they deserved to lead the Christian community: "[They] abound in glory ... who devoutly and in their own strength have offered to God what they had not received [from Him, but from their own past]."[75]

The leaders of the Lerinian movement were not immune to this criticism. Faced by the raw secular world of Arles, they strove to establish for themselves "visible moral status in the here and now."[76] Humble though they might be in themselves, their admirers were quite prepared to acclaim them as men of spiritual power, won through ascetic labors on the isle of Lérins and discreetly bolstered by their noble background.

Against this view, Prosper upheld the utter leveling of all wills before God. To be "called" by God was to be entirely remade by Him. It was to enter a space of magical transformation, invisible to human eyes and incapable of being measured by human criteria.[77] Social status and culture were irrelevant to this transformation. If that was so, they might also be irrelevant to the church's choice of its leaders. The strong institutional sense of the clergy, preserved in the Roman model, fostered a social and cultural leveling where only the grace of God (and no visible social advantages) counted. Only the invisible grace of God could confer distinction on persons rendered equally faceless by their offices in the church. As far as Prosper was concerned, lower-class bishops could emerge in due order from the drab ranks of the clergy. Such a bishop was as certain of the blessing of God (provided that he was among the elect) as was any vivid holy man of aristocratic background who might be brought in from Lérins.

Servitutis officum: "The due return of service"

FREEDOM, SERVICE, AND THE GALLIC CONSENSUS

Prosper's attack on Cassian was his last contribution to the argumentative world of the *sancti* of Marseilles. We should be careful not to give it undue prominence in the overall religious landscape of the Provence of his time.[78] What Susan Wessel has called "the ongoing conversation" about Augustine and the Pelagian Controversy continued in Gaul.[79] But it did not continue on Prosper's terms. What has been called a "Gallic consensus" emerged.[80] This consensus did not reject Augustine. Rather, when writing of grace and freedom, authors from Lérins and Marseille chose their words carefully. They agreed with much of what Augustine had said, but they did so on their own terms. Above all, they placed a screen of language between themselves and the bishop of Hippo. When they spoke of grace and free will, they avoided speaking in the way that Augustine and his enthusiastic admirers, such as Prosper, were prepared to speak. We should linger on this phenomenon, if only for a moment, as it reveals something of the social world these authors took for granted.

What the Gallic writers had in common with Augustine was the need to express the extent of human dependence on God. They shared with him a "spirituality of dependence."[81] Prosper's caricature of Cassian tends to make us forget that, for both parties, Pelagius was the odd man out. He was "a crazy."[82] His talk of the natural nobility of the soul and of the total autonomy of the will came from another world than their own. We see this clearly when, at the very end of the fifth century (in 473–74), bishop Faustus of Riez summed up the issues that had been discussed for generations in Provence. He wrote a treatise titled *On Grace.* In it, Pelagius's view of the human person was presented as that of a free laborer who expected—indeed demanded—to gain his reward "by work alone, without the patronage extended by grace." Faustus rejected Pelagius's views out of hand. Human beings needed a lord to serve heart and soul. Pelagius offered them not a lord but only a distant paymaster from whom they could claim fair wages.[83]

But how was this acute sense of dependence on God to be expressed? Here the two sides diverged significantly. Augustine had tended to speak of the relation between God and human beings in terms of a swamping of the person by the grace of God. He and his followers used a language of dependence that always went deeper than the human will. Dependence on God was expressed in terms of inspiration, of illumination, of a mystical union between God and the soul. It is perhaps no coincidence that many vocal Augustinians (such as Prosper) were also poets. Used to the idea of the poet "possessed" by the Muses, they saw nothing theologically dangerous in a notion of grace that flooded the entire person, to create from scratch something totally new because totally inspired. In the words of a minor poet who celebrated his conversion at this time:

> O Father, if it seems good to grant, put Your whole self within me,
> Into my deepest depths, into the marrow of my soul.
> All that I can do is yours; even to will is barely left to me.[84]

In clear contrast to this language of mystical absorption, authors such as Faustus and his predecessors in Provence chose to speak of grace and free will in terms of a root metaphor derived from the world of social relations. It was a metaphor taken from the high-pitched world of the relations between patrons and clients. Impoverished by Adam's fall, the human being approached God as a down-and-out client might approach a patron. Human freedom had been "stripped of resources" by sin.[85] But, nonetheless, the approach of a sinner was that of a client, not a slave. It was the choice of a free person. Though they might be utterly dependent on their patron, such clients still brought to his service an *officium,* the return of a free man anxious to add what little he could to further the cause of his lord: "So that God may retain the full rights of a lord and the believer may give in return the freely offered service of subjection."[86] It is a metaphor that bore the stamp of the age. The landowners of Gaul had struggled at this time to establish ever tighter vertical relations with their peasants. What they wished from their dependents was not servitude (which had become harder to enforce in a world dislocated by intermittent violence) but, rather, the dependable service of clients. This was exactly what the authors of Provence proposed when speaking of the services rendered by human beings to God.

Your lightnings have gone forth over the whole earth (Psalm 76:19): Prosper and the Roman Empire

It was in this way that Provençal authors spoke of the same issues as did Augustine and his admirers. They often did it to the same purpose—to stress the absolute dependence of human beings on God. But they did it their way. They also held distinctive views on the fate of their own society and of the Roman empire. These differed significantly from those proposed by an Augustinian such as Prosper.

It is worthwhile looking at Prosper's view of the prospects of the Roman empire. It merits greater attention than does his squib against Cassian. In Prosper's opinion, the Roman empire already appears as a mere sideshow. Put bluntly: his Augustinianism convinced him that nothing in the past contributed to what happened in the present, just as nothing—no social advantage, no cultural gift, no ascetic labor—could precede the workings of grace in the individual heart. Everything was a new creation. Every event was touched by a sense of vertigo—it marked a new departure where the hidden hand of God alone had moved. *Ecce faciam nova* (Isa. 43:19): "Behold, I shall do new things"—the words of God to the prophet Isaiah summed up Prosper's challenge.[87] The Roman empire in itself contributed nothing to the daily miracle of the newborn will. Impressive, infinitely ingenious, and strictly necessary if a human race guided by their evil hearts was not to destroy itself entirely, the old Roman order stood to one side of the world of grace.[88] The two worlds touched in no way.

At a stroke, Prosper rendered the history of the church majestically independent of the history of the beleaguered *Respublica.* It did not greatly matter to Prosper if the Roman empire declined. For, to use a modern phrase, Rome was no longer "where the action was." The world of God's grace was a world without a clear human center. Grace could happen at any time and in any region. The future held any number of surprises. Not all of these were necessarily nasty surprises; many, indeed, might be glorious. But they had nothing to do with the march of human history, not even with the march of Rome—far from it. These novel glories happened and would continue to happen because of the mighty pulse of God's all-powerful grace within the Catholic Church alone: "*Your lightnings have gone forth over the whole earth (Psalm 76:19).*"[89]

Prosper left Marseille for Rome in 433 to put his pen at the service of the pope. It is significant that, once in Rome, he chose to sum up his own worldview in a *Chronicle* and not in a theological tract.[90] In Prosper's *Chronicle* the *Respublica* was ousted from center stage. For Prosper, the history of the fifth century was not the history of barbarian invasions at the expense of the empire. His history was a *Gesta Dei per ecclesiam*—the history of the great acts of God that continued to happen through his church. These acts of God provided plenty of good news. Thus, the entry for 431 assured the reader that even the terrible Irish had come to believe in Christ. They had done so through bishops alone. At one stroke, because of the God-given energy of bishops, Britain had ceased to be Pelagian and utter pagans on the edge of the world had become Christian.[91] The *Respublica* had nothing to do with that triumph along the former frontiers of Rome. The message was clear. Even if the empire vanished, such events would continue to occur: "for the glory of the saints is this, that the whole world should come to be subjected to God and to His laws."[92]

Altogether, in his *Chronicle*, Prosper viewed the world around him with "an almost surprising serenity."[93] This was because he had rendered the workings of God's grace in the church in the West as independent of the Roman empire as he had rendered active service of God, in those touched by God's grace, independent of any claims to previous qualifications derived from lay status or from ascetic prowess.

Such serenity was by no means to be found among the *sancti* of Marseilles. We have already met the unknown author of the *Chronicle of 452* in the previous chapter. He was no lover of Augustine or of those who loved Augustine. In an early entry, he spoke of the spread, in Gaul, of the "heresy" of "those who believe that they are among the predestinate, which is said to have originated with Augustine."[94] In the *Chronicle of 452*, the *Respublica*—the Roman empire—remained the center of attention. The chronicler recorded, with glum brevity, the years in which whole provinces, or groups of provinces, fell off the edge of his world—made subject to barbarians or separated from Rome by Bacaudic revolts.[95] In 451 he concluded that "in this time, the state of the empire—of the *Respublica*—appeared to be pitiable in the extreme."[96] Rather than the high Augustinian optimism of Prosper, which looked past the *Respublica* to the continuous, grace-filled triumphs of the Catholic Church, these were chill views. In southern Gaul, serious persons had begun to allow themselves, for the first time, to think the unthinkable: "Why is it that the condition of the barbarians is so much better than our own?"[97] In the early 440s, a memorable and far from reassuring answer to this question came from another *sanctus* of Marseilles—an admirer and, perhaps, a former monk of Lérins, now working as a priest in the city: Salvian of Marseilles.

CHAPTER 26

Romana respublica vel iam mortua: With the empire

now dead and gone

Salvian and His Gaul, 420–450

A Report on the State of the Nation: Salvian's *De gubernatione Dei* in Modern Scholarship

The most vivid and by far the best known commentary on the state of the Roman empire in the 430s and 440s was provided by yet another refugee to Provence—Salvian. It is to one work of Salvian in particular, his *De gubernatione Dei*—*On the Government* (that is: [*On the providential rule*] *of God*)—that all historians of the social history of the later empire turn so as to learn about the social ills of the Roman empire in the fifth century.[1] Writing in 1899, Samuel Dill could say of Salvian:

> He feels a burning indignation against the selfishness of the wealthy and official class, and an equally passionate pity for the poor and oppressed, which, had he lived in the nineteenth century, would certainly have made him a Socialist of the extremest type.[2]

In the words of his English translator, Salvian's *De gubernatione Dei* "might well be entitled *A Report on the State of the Nation*."[3] It was a damning report. Throughout the last century, the *De gubernatione Dei* has been quarried for evidence for the abuses that are held to have caused the fall of the Roman empire in the West. Salvian has been treated as our principal source for the imperial tax system, which sapped the resources of the cities and which drove even well-to-do Romans to seek freedom among the barbarians and the Bacaudae.[4] He is regarded as a prime witness for the oppression of the peasantry by the great landowners, which has seemed to many scholars to announce the coming of the Middle Ages: "Salvian described a primitive feudal system, an obvious precursor to the political structure of medieval France."[5] Last but not least, Salvian's insistence on making invidious comparisons between the vices of the Romans of his day and the virtues of their barbarian conquerors has led him to be alternately denounced as a defeatist, even as a "collaborator," by Frenchmen and to be acclaimed by Germans for having foreseen the future of early medieval Europe. To use the words of Salvian's translator: "Salvian looks to the future and realizes that the destiny of Europe belongs to the Teutonic tribes."[6]

Yet we do Salvian a disservice by quarrying his work in this way for pieces of raw evidence for causes of the decline of the empire. We treat him as no more than the writer of "A Report on the State of the Nation." We look less at Salvian himself than at what he tells us about the symptoms of the terminal illness of west Roman society. We argue about whether Salvian's diagnosis was correct. We do not ask why he wrote as he did or why he emphasized certain symptoms rather than others. Salvian has become for us a source. He is not often considered as a person.

In fact, Salvian was a vivid person with his own, idiosyncratic take on the problems of his day. In his writings we catch the hopes and fears associated with a particular juncture in the crisis of the empire—of the *Respublica*—in a particular region. He wrote in the late 430s and early 440s, probably in Marseilles and certainly for the *sancti* of southern Gaul.[7]

Let us look for a moment at the world that Salvian and his readers looked out on from the relative security of Provence. In the 430s and 440s it had become plain that what had once been a universal empire had begun to unravel. The territories around Marseilles and Arles had become a self-conscious imperial enclave. They were lands of the *Respublica*. But Salvian now looked out at a world where the *Respublica* was only one state among others. The "central Romanness" associated with the *Respublica* (to use the well-chosen term of Peter Heather) had come to be challenged by powerful alternatives in both Gaul and Spain. Provence and the southern valley of the Rhine were ringed by barbarian kingdoms in the making and by ominous, stateless zones associated with the Bacaudae. Far to the south across the Mediterranean, Africa had recently fallen to the Vandals. Salvian wrote no longer for the citizens of a world empire but for the inhabitants of an enclave in which the grandeur of an ancien régime still lingered. He wrote to warn them that the Roman order of which they remained so proud hung on by a thread. The *Respublica* was almost dead and gone: "Now dead or at least drawing its last breath in that part of the world where it appears to be still alive."[8]

We have to understand why Salvian was prepared to say this. It was not simply because of the social abuses he described so vividly—these were mere signs for him of the progress of a more deep-seated malady. This was the implacable working out of the judgment of God against an entire society that claimed to be Christian. The Christians of the empire had abandoned God. In the last analysis, for Salvian the church and not the empire was the Sick Man of Europe. The empire might fall because the church had already fallen. How had Salvian come to this startling conclusion?

"A teacher of bishops": Salvian at Marseilles, ca. 420–ca. 480

We know very little about Salvian, but what we do know is revealing. In the first place, Salvian was no Paulinus of Pella. He had not declined quietly into genteel poverty. Nor was he a man of the south, like Prosper of Aquitaine. He had come from the far north. He had been present as the Roman order that had seemed so secure in the days of Ausonius collapsed along the frontier of the Rhine. Trier, the former northern capital of the Roman world, was sacked four times within a decade. Salvian claimed that he had seen rows of decomposing corpses outside its walls.[9] We learn from one of his letters that a female relative had been left stranded in Cologne. Utterly impoverished, she was too poor to flee. She had become dependent on the good graces of barbarian ladies from the new Frankish governing class that had taken over the city. Salvian had sent this letter so as to raise funds from fellow saints to support her son, a boy "of not insignificant family."[10]

Salvian came to the deep south as a refugee from a region where the imperial order appeared to have fallen to settle in territories where this imperial order had survived. He did so as a *conversus*—a convert to an ascetic form of Christianity. His wife had joined him in this *conversiuncula*—this "little conversion of ours." We know this from an awkward letter he wrote to his parents-in-law, who had been pagans. But even when they became Christians, they remained deeply hostile to the asceticism of their daughter and son-in-law. The letter shows that, for Salvian, to be a *sanctus* was always to be on the outs with ordinary Christians.[11]

In the mid-420s, Salvian appeared at Lérins. He joined persons who were as resolutely alienated from the world as he was. He may have lost his wife at that time. He wrote in heady terms about the abbot of Lérins, Honoratus. He called him "our very own sun in Christ." The slightest absence of the abbot caused a chill to fall upon his monks, as if a cloud had covered the sun.[12] But it was not as an admirer of Lérins but as a preacher in the church of Marseilles that Salvian established himself. He became a priest. He lived to a ripe old age; he was still alive in 480. He had outlived the *Respublica* whose imminent demise he had declared around 440.

Unlike the abrasive Prosper, Salvian was remembered fondly in the *Catalogue of Illustrious Authors* written by Gennadius of Marseilles. Gennadius wrote of him with evident admiration as a "teacher of bishops." He was well-known for his many works, "written in a rhetorical and forthright style."[13] Despite the challenging idiosyncracy of the writings of his middle age, Salvian was not necessarily an isolated figure. He expressed and may have molded the views of an entire body of opinion—of monks, clergymen, and impoverished members of the local aristocracies. The anger of this group at the rulers of their own society lingers in Salvian's pages.

Salvian always wrote for saints about the preoccupations of their fellow saints. His works circulated among the monk-bishops drawn from the monastic circle of Lérins. In the 420s he had been the tutor of Salonius, the son of Eucherius. Eucherius was one of the best known of the admirers of Lérins. When Eucherius became bishop of Lyons in 435, Salonius was placed by his father as bishop of Geneva at some time before 440. Geneva was a crucial city. It was a watching point into the valleys of Switzerland; it stood on the edge of a region wide open to the barbarian world. In 443 Burgundian militias were settled there, in order to offer much needed defense. It is, perhaps, significant that Salvian chose to write for a bishop whose city lay on the frontier of the receding empire.

Illa egregia ... dudum primitivae plebis beatitudo: That outstanding blessedness which the first community [of Christians] once enjoyed

SALVIAN AND THE WEALTH OF THE CHURCH

Bishops such as Salonius worried not only about the barbarians but about the solvency of their own churches. They needed donations from the laity. But their attention was not directed only to the laity. As members of the circle of Lérins, they had more intensely inward-looking preoccupations. Like John Cassian, they had to face the issue of the renunciation of wealth. Was renunciation obligatory for all monks and clergymen? Could they expect those "devoted to religion"—as lay penitents, as ascetics, and as members of the clergy—to surrender all their wealth to Christ? More important yet, would they renounce their wealth by giving it to the church?

The first known work of Salvian, written sometime between 435 and 439, addressed this theme. It was called *Ad Ecclesiam*—an *Open Letter to the Church*—and came to be known as *On Avarice*. Characteristically, for a member of a Provençal in-group, Salvian adopted a pen name. He was Timothy—the Timothy to whom Saint Paul had written so much advice on the management of the church. He went out of his way to justify both the pen-name and the book itself in a long letter to Salonius.[14]

The *Ad Ecclesiam* was typical of the mood that was current among the *sancti* of Provence. A streak of radicalism ran through all their writings. They wrote so as to challenge a chosen few to adopt ever more consequential and more drastic attitudes toward the world around them. What Salvian attacked with particular ferocity in the *Ad Ecclesiam* were not the weaknesses of the average lay Christians. Those who claimed to be true Christians—as monks and clergymen—and who nonetheless refused to give their wealth to the church were the principal target of his contempt.

The tension between real ascetics and sham ascetics gave vigor to Salvian's pen as he wrote the *Ad Ecclesiam*. We see this most clearly in his idealization of the life of the first Christians. In this idealization of the Jerusalem Community (as this had been described in chapters 2 and 4 of the *Acts of the Apsotles*), his view of the church had been influenced by debates in Marseilles, stirred up by the monasticism of Lérins and by the writings of John Cassian. He proposed a fundamentally monastic vision of the original purity of the Primitive Church. For Salvian, the early Christians had lived in a "time of exceptional blessedness." Judged against this vibrant utopia, the contemporary church seemed deeply fallen.[15]

Salvian's ideas converged with those of John Cassian. Both men were strangers to Provence. Cassian was a Latin-speaking east Roman from the Danubian frontier; Salvian was a refugee from the Rhineland. Both thought of the Christian church in their own days as overshadowed by the imagined perfection of the *ecclesia primitiva*, the church in its first days. But Cassian was the more optimistic of the two. For Cassian, a precious remnant of the first solidarity of Christians appeared to have survived, despite a massive cooling off of zeal among the majority of believers. It could still be found in the monasteries of Egypt and might be renewed in properly founded monasteries in Gaul.[16] Salvian, by contrast, made plain in the opening pages of his *Ad Ecclesiam* that this perfection had all but totally vanished:

> That exceptional and outstanding blessedness which once the first community—the *primitiva plebs*—had enjoyed has passed away.... How different the Christian people are now from what they had been! ... In a new and hitherto unheard of manner ... the Church wanes as it reaches its fullness, slipping back as it advances.[17]

For Salvian, the vibrant image of the Primitive Church hovered above his age as a permanent rebuke—a historical superego.

The Primitive Church of Salvian was very much an image of his own making. It was more like fifth-century Lérins than first-century Jerusalem. He thought of it as a community of the wealthy who had renounced their properties in favor of the church. In a mighty upsurge of zeal, the rich Christians of Jerusalem had followed the words of Christ: *If you would be perfect, go, sell what you possess and give to the poor, and you will have treasure in Heaven* (Matt. 19:16). Salvian placed far less emphasis than had Augustine—or even Cassian—on the sharing of goods and hearts associated with the Jerusalem Community. Rather, he presented the Jerusalem Community as a gathering where the rich had made a massive purchase of paradise by surrendering their wealth to the church in return for *treasure in heaven*.[18] When speaking of the early Christians, Salvian used the same language as that with which the monk-bishop Hilary of Arles was praised, a decade later, on the inscription placed on his sarcophagus. Here was a man who had "purchased heaven by earthly gifts rendered, now, perpetual."[19]

Aimed at heaven, this was a sharply upward-tilted use of wealth. The poor are all but absent from Salvian's view of the Primitive Church. Those "in need" who benefited from the pooled goods of the first community were not the real poor. They were the "holy poor," the "poor among the saints" of Salvian's times. They were poor monks and clergymen who expected to be supported by rich members of the laity, much as Jerome had expected them to be supported thirty years previously when he wrote against Vigilantius.[20]

On Avarice: Family Strategies and Donations to the Church

Not surprisingly, the *Ad Ecclesiam* was described somewhat unkindly by a German scholar of the nineteenth century as "a manual of the clerical art of extortion, a guide to legacy hunters."[21] The tract was known to contemporaries as *On Avarice*. But the avarice attacked in it had nothing to do with the denunciations of the rich that we have seen in the preaching of Ambrose and in the Pelagian treatise *On Riches*. The themes of luxury and self-aggrandizement are absent. What mattered for Salvian was not how the rich had gained their wealth nor even how they used it. It was where they would eventually place it. The avarice Salvian attacked was the retentiveness of potential wealthy donors to the church. These were persons who would rather bequeath their property to anyone but clergymen.

The *Ad Ecclesiam* reminds us that in fifth-century Gaul, we have silently entered a new age. This is not the fund-raising of Augustine's sermons, addressed still to socially diverse congregations. With Salvian we are dealing with heavier matters—with transfers of wealth from rich families through testamentary bequests to the church. Because of this, the *Ad Ecclesiam* takes us back to a very ancient, very Roman world. *Captatio*—legacy hunting—had been one of the principal "social pressure points" of Roman upper-class society.[22] This was because an element of sheer willfulness, even whim, had always been associated with the distribution of legacies. The testator was encouraged to include his friends among the beneficiaries of his will. As a result, members of the dying man's family lived in perpetual fear that overgenerous legacies to friends might rob them of a large share of the inheritance. In the words of Edward Champlin: "Captation ignites the tensions at a major social frontier between family and friendship."[23]

In the straitened conditions of fifth-century southern Gaul, the ancient tension between family and friendship flared up with unusual intensity around the issue of gifts to the church.[24] This was because, in many cases, the laity had become as dependent on the church as the church was on the laity. Well-to-do families had come to use the church so as to husband their own threatened resources. It struck them that Christian renunciation was not such a bad idea if it reduced the number of competitors for the family inheritance. Girls were forced to become nuns so as to save on dowries. The emperor Majorian was called upon to rule on this issue in 458. He ruled that young girls should not be forced to take the veil. He plainly did so in answer to petitions by rich senators, some of whose colleagues had taken advantage of this new form of estate planning.[25] These strategies affected boys as well as girls. Young men of good family were placed in the clergy or they were allowed to become monks—but only on the condition that they lost their share of the inheritance to their married brothers and sisters. In this way, would-be monks and clergymen found themselves disinherited by their own families. They were denied the financial means to express devotion to the church—through donations, through the foundation of monasteries, and through almsgiving to the poor.[26]

Salvian's sharpness on this issue is a reminder that many local churches may not have looked only to the wealthy laity for financial support. When it came to substantial endowments, they expected to receive more from persons who were already members of the church's hierarchy. As we saw in the case of Pinianus at Hippo in Africa, real wealth was expected to come to the church from rich persons who had joined the priesthood. Priests, bishops, wealthy monks, and laypersons who lived the religious life as penitents (of which there were a number in Gaul) formed a small but dependable constituency of potential donors. What appalled Salvian more than did the selfishness of the normal rich was the fact that many religious persons, even clergymen, preferred to pass on their wealth to their kinsfolk or to rich patrons rather than give it to the church.[27]

"One tiny flicker of hope": Deathbed Gifts and the Other World

In much of the *Ad Ecclesiam*, Salvian repeated the preaching of former bishops. Bishops had long encouraged their parishioners to remember the church in their legacies. Augustine in Africa and Valerianus of Cimiez in Provence both urged their hearers to think of Christ as if He were an extra son—thereby ensuring that the church received a share of each family's inheritance.[28]

But Salvian did it his way. He only mentioned that particular option in passing. Instead, he went out of his way to make clear to the laity that he was not making the same absolute demands on them that he made on his fellow saints. He stressed the fact that he did not expect all Christians equally and without exception to give all their wealth to the church, as the first Christians had done at the time of the Jerusalem Community.[29]

Salvian conceded with ponderous condescension that the majority of his readers were far too weak to follow such advice. They would never be persuaded to renounce their wealth in their own lifetime. Rather, he insisted that, for such weaklings, God had offered an "extremely soft" option. Gifts could be made on their deathbed, for the world to come. Deathbed donations to the church gave average believers "one tiny flicker of hope" as their souls left the body at the hour of death.[30] Such gifts enabled the soul to cross the awesome threshold of death. One gave to the church so as to avoid a Hell that loomed just beyond the moment of death.

We have become so used to the medieval practice of gifts for the soul that it is easy to forget that Salvian's vivid focus on death and the other world struck a new, sharp note. Previously, donors had given for less clearly focused reasons. They had given so as to increase the glory of their local church. They had spoken vaguely of donations for "the salvation of their souls." But they had not given much thought to the exact mechanisms by which this salvation might be achieved in the other world through gifts and memorial services. Indeed, they had not been encouraged by their clergy to give much thought to such obscure matters.[31] Even Augustine's notion of alms for the expiation of sins was mainly concerned with regular almsgiving in this world. His preaching and writing is notably free of other-world scenarios.

But if there was anything the monks of Lérins brought to the Christianity of their time, it was a novel, overwhelming sense of judgment in the other world. Hilary of Arles came to be known for his preaching of hellfire.

> Who could have shown more vividly the terrible ordeal of the Last Judgement? Who could inspire such terror by conjuring up the dark fire of Hell? Who could express the agonies of the searing river of fire, as it swept the sinners away?[32]

Hilary had used these images to inspire penance. Salvian did so to inspire gifts. Faced on their deathbed by the serried ranks of their own family—"a yoke made heavy by the solid flesh of kinship"—donors should think of the serried ranks of angels and of demons who awaited them in the next life: "Behold, the staff of the Sacred Tribunal awaits you as you leave this life. The torturing angels and the ministers of undying punishments stand at the ready."[33] It is as if we were suddenly transported, across half a millennium, to the scenes of bliss and terror that decorate the portals of the Romanesque churches of France. Altogether, with Salvian a new, chill wind blew through the churches of southern Gaul. In this world, as well as in the next, the judgment of God had come dramatically close: *In every place, the eyes of the Lord look out upon the good and the wicked* (*Prov.* 15:3).[34]

De praesenti iudicio: Judgment in the Here and Now

Salvian's next work was dedicated directly to Salonius. It was his famous tract *De gubernatione Dei*. Written at some time after 439 and not completed, it was all too aptly known to contemporaries as *De praesenti iudicio*: "Judgment in the Here and Now."[35] It is important to realize the extent to which an overpowering awareness of the imminent presence of God as the judge of human sins—and not a modern historian's sense of the abuses of Roman society—drove Salvian to produce his tract for the times.

Salvian's insistence on the judgment of God made him a writer who was as powerful as he was idiosyncratic. There were many options he did not take when wrestling with the fate of his society. These other options had been canvassed in Provence. For Eucherius of Lyons, for instance, the ills of the present merely proved that Christians lived in the "old age" of the world. It was better for them to think of their own old age and approaching death than to focus in too concrete a manner on the ills of contemporary society. Like everything else, it would soon pass away.[36] Indeed, seen from a monastery, the world seemed a somewhat diaphanous place. It was as pallid as a moon in the morning sky.[37] Not so for Salvian. He held his focus with fierce determination on the real ills of a real empire. He did so to persuade his readers that they were in the presence of a God who judged human sins in the here and now with terrifying particularity.

In writing in this way, Salvian showed that he was part of the general "Gallic consensus" in theology. This consensus included a strong sense of the unrelenting rigor of the Law of God. Salvian's emphasis on the Law of God resembled the insistence on total obedience to the commandments of God that had been put forward in Pelagian writings that were still read in Marseilles. Human beings were free—but they were free only to serve God. They did this by observing His Law to the full. The Law of God had been given to every Christian. To fail to observe it was not an excusable sign of human weakness but amounted to a direct act of rebellion against God. What God wished from the Christian people was total transparency to His Law: "The life of a Christian should be as pure—as crystal clear—as the clear, bright fluid in the pupil of the eye."[38] God's Law was clear for all to obey. God's judgment for breaches of this Law was also clear for all to see. A terrible sense of the transparency of the justice of God in punishing the empire for Christian breaches of His Law made the *De gubernatione Dei* quite unlike any other contemporary writing.[39]

Why was this remorseless logic of crime and punishment so important to Salvian? It was because, at the back of Salvian's mind, there lay a lingering conviction that, in some way or other, the Roman empire was the Israel of modern times. Like the ancient Israel, it was a state subject to the peculiar care of God. This fact conferred a sense of privilege on the inhabitants of the surviving territories of the empire. But it also laid a heavy responsibility upon them.[40]

As David Lambert has made plain in a thoughtful study, Salvian wrote about the Christian Roman empire of the fifth century as if it was an avatar of the kingdom of Israel: "It had become a politico-religious entity of the same kind as Israel under Moses."[41] The empire was an Israel writ large. The former intimacy of the link between Israel and the Law of God haunted Salvian when he thought about the present. There had once been a time on Sinai when "men and angels had joined in a single school" to learn the Law of God.[42] Israel was a privileged society because it had once been brought near to the Law of God. The Christian Roman empire could have done the same. Instead (again like Israel), it neglected God and His Law.

Thus, Salvian fastened on the widespread tendency of his contemporaries to identify the Christian empire with ancient Israel. But he drew a different conclusion from this identification. His message was so terrible because he claimed that the Christian Roman empire was, indeed, an Israel but a failed one. Its inhabitants had rejected the opportunity to be an Israel obedient to the Law. For this reason, Roman Christians lived in an Israel in its last days, an Israel deserted by God. And this was the fault of the Christians. For they had rebelled against the Law of God. The moral backsliding of the Christian congregations had drained the churches of the supernatural virtue that had once been attached to the very name of Christian.[43] A church whose prayers should have acted to "placate" God had come to "exacerbate" Him.[44]

Vos non estis populus meus: "You are not my people" (Hosea 1:9). These words of Hosea to an abandoned Israel summed up, for Salvian, the extent of the peril the surviving *Respublica* now faced.[45] It had been betrayed from within by its own Christians as certainly as Israel had been betrayed by its own inhabitants when they had rebelled against the Law of God. Like the ancient kingdom of Israel in its last days, the Romans of the late 430s and early 440s were paying the price for their abandonment of God. For this reason, God's judgment upon them could not have been more just or more chillingly clear:

> The Romans were once the strongest of all, now they are powerless.... Barbarian peoples used to pay tribute to them. Now we are tributary to the barbarians. They rent to us the very sunshine. Our entire safety is up for sale.[46]

Deus noster propitius esto Reipublicae Romanae: Our God, may You
be propitious to the Roman state

SALVIAN AND CONTEMPORARY OPINION

In order to write as he did, Salvian deliberately brushed aside alternative, more
comforting ways of seeing his world. He notably passed over the high Augustinian optimism of Prosper of Aquitaine. For Prosper, as we have seen, the workings
of God's mighty grace in the church effectively cut the history of Christianity
loose from the history of the empire. Prosper's world of pure grace was a world
with no center. The hand of God was as likely to show itself on the shores of
Ireland as in Arles. And the workings of God's providence were beyond human
scrutiny. A velvet opacity screened the relation between sin and judgment.

Nothing could be more different from Prosper's serene mystification of the
workings of grace and of God's providence than the remorseless clarity of Salvian's sense of a direct relation between God's Law and God's judgment in the here
and now. Nor did the centerless world proposed by Prosper mean anything to
Salvian. His view of the *Respublica* as an avatar of the kingdom of Israel kept his
attention focused on the existing territories of the empire. For it was there that
the Law of God should have been observed in its fullness; and so it was there
that the blows of God's judgment had fallen with inexorable force and in a manner that was clear for all to see.

In adopting this view, Salvian pointedly dissociated himself from the incipi-
ent Christian patriotism of his contemporaries in the territories of the *Respublica*.
We who read Salvian's *On the Government of God* with the advantage of hindsight tend to treat the Roman empire of the late 430s as a doomed institution.
But this was not how it appeared to many contemporaries. The 430s and early
440s were seen by many as a time of consolidation after the terrible events of the
early decades of the fifth century. Having experienced widespread violence, the
Christian communities of southern Gaul began to dig in. As we have seen, a siege
mentality bought townsfolk together around their local churches. For the first
time in their history, the cities of Gaul gained major cathedrals. In Clermont, a
new Christian basilica (built by the bishop, a rich senator) occupied a large proportion of the newly fortified citadel.[47] In Geneva itself, Salonius (the recipient
of the *De gubernatione Dei*) found himself in a complex of new Christian buildings that occupied a sixth of the area of the newly walled city.[48]

This defiant mood was most prevalent in cities that stood on the frontiers of
the *Respublica*. Narbonne lay within striking distance of the Visigoths of Toulouse and had been besieged by them. It needed divine protection. In 445 bishop
Rusticus of Narbonne rebuilt the city's basilica. He did this not only as a bishop
but as a public figure. An inscription placed on the lintel in clear monumental

script made plain that the Praetorian Prefect of Gaul himself had urged Rusticus to undertake the building. The prefect also contributed part of the state's income, along with building materials and workmen, to the amount of 2,100 *solidi*. Set up "through the mercy of Christ," the cathedral of Narbonne was a sign that Christianity had become the state cult of the Roman Empire.[49] The prayers of the Church were believed to have maintained the protection of God for the *Respublica*. It was the same elsewhere. Now buried in the long grass beside the Christian basilica of Salona (Solin, on the Dalmatian coast of Croatia, a little north of Split), a similar lintel declared in large capitals: *Deus noster propitius esto Reipublicae Romanae*—"Our God, may You be propitious to the Roman State."[50]

Salvian's answer was a firm "no." God would not be propitious to the *Respublica*. For all its rhetorical style, the *On the Government of God* was not a purely literary confection. It was an icy blast directed against the mood of recovery and consolidation that had comforted Salvian's compatriots. What did Salvian offer them instead?

The Footsteps of God: Salvian and the Barbarians

Salvian proposed, for the very first time, a novel map of Gaul. This was a strictly moral map. What he traced upon it were the differing shades of knowledge of the Law of God in differing regions and among differing groups. Some groups could claim diminished responsibility—they had not known that Law. Others, such as the Romans, could make no such claim—they had known the Law. They were entirely responsible for their sins. They must face the full rigor of God's judgment.

In an unusually illuminating article, Michael Maas has pointed out the "imaginative leap" involved in propounding such a view of the world. For Salvian's map was not like the usual Roman map. It did not divide the world in cultural terms. No chasm stood between the uncivilized barbarian and the civilized Roman. Compared with knowledge of the Law of God, such distinctions were trivial.[51] Let us see what this shift of perspective involved.

Salvian's insistence on knowledge of the Law of God as the only criterion according to which God judged any human society had the effect of rearranging the barbarian groups of Gaul as if they lay around the *Respublica* in a series of concentric circles. Gaul was ringed by an outer fringe of unconverted, pagan barbarians—Saxons, Huns, Franks, Gepids, and Alamans. They were a supremely nasty lot. Salvian (who had seen them at work along the Rhine) had little use for non-Christian barbarians. But, unlike the Romans, they could at least claim ignorance of God's Law. For that reason, they would suffer less harsh punishment than would the Romans.[52]

Next came an anomalous gray zone. Goths and Vandals were not pagans. They were Christians. But they were misinformed Christians. They were Arian heretics. Proud to be old-fashioned (and proud of their links to the eastern empire), the Goths had remained loyal to what had been the imperial religion in the days when the mighty pro-Arian emperors Constantius II and Valens had been their patrons along the frontier of the Danube.[53] In Salvian's opinion, the Goths could not have known the Law in its entirety because they were Arians. They had received only a partial version of this Law from their Roman Arian teachers. For that reason, they could not be judged as harshly for their errors as Roman Christians would be judged. They erred in good faith. Only the Catholic, Roman Christians of Salvian's own time had no excuse. They could expect no mercy.[54]

For this reason, Salvian singled out the Christian Visigoths and Vandals as the privileged agents of the judgment of God. This was not difficult. These two groups had been the barbarians whose successes needed most to be explained. They had done most to humiliate the *Respublica*. Salvian ended his work with a description of the Vandal conquest of Carthage in 439. More than any other barbarian victory, this had inflicted a body blow that left the empire stunned. If this catastrophe was not "judgment in the here and now" then nothing was.

Altogether, Salvian saw the barbarians (and especially the Visigoths and Vandals) as the traveling assizes of God. They seemed to him to move from province to province in a manner that was grimly intelligible. Each province in turn had deserved its fate. As a result, Salvian made the tentative advance of barbarian war bands from region to region, as they followed the fortunes of Roman civil war like flitting wolf packs, seem inevitable and overwhelming. The confident lines and arrows that show the "barbarian invasions" in conventional modern textbooks owe more than we think to Salvian's merciless vision. For Salvian, this series of unexpected conquests seemed to hang together in a single, dramatic pattern. They were the footsteps of God as He strode in judgment across the West in the here and now.[55]

Dicam quomodo: Let me tell you how

SALVIAN AND ROMAN SOCIETY

In Salvian's view of the world, barbarians appear largely as executors of the judgment of God against the Romans who had known and abandoned His Law. As we have seen, this view has stimulated vehement debate among European scholars. But we must remember that Salvian's daring shift of perspective toward the barbarian world was not as important to him (or, one suspects, to his readers) as was his treatment of the sins of the Romans themselves. Here Salvian was quite unusual. Far from indulging in ill-focused jeremiads, he was prepared to spell out in detail what sins in particular had earned the wrath of God. He wrote not only to tell "why" but to tell both "what" and "how"—what had gone wrong in Roman society and by what mechanisms this wrong had come to happen. *Dicam quomodo*: "Let me tell you how" was Salvian's refrain.[56] Though he is often dismissed as a purveyor of rhetorical exaggerations, the very tenacity with which Salvian held his focus on the ills of his time make him quite unusual.

In the first place, Salvian confronted his contemporaries with a shocking anomaly. Romans had begun to flee *to* the barbarians where formerly they had fled *from* the barbarians in horror, as Salvian himself had done when fleeing from the Rhineland.[57] Now they fled toward the territories of their former enemies. They had been forced to do this because of Roman oppression: the authorities of the *Respublica* had come to treat Roman citizens as little better than barbarians. For Salvian, the Bacaudae were a glaring example of this dire process. Branded with the opprobrious name of "Bacaudae," freeborn Romans found themselves the target of vicious campaigns of repression by Roman armies. They were treated as if they were public enemies of the Roman state.[58]

> They are forced to be barbarians.... It is the unjust rule of Romans (*Romana iniquitas*) which makes them cease to be Romans.[59]

Salvian did nothing to soften the impact on his readers of this ultimate anomaly. He did not share the interest of modern historians in the emergence of new styles of local Romanness around barbarian courts or in the no-man's-land of the territories controlled by the Bacaudae. He had no sense whatsoever that a new, barbarian-Roman world was emerging. Rather, he still looked at Gaul and Spain with the hard eyes of a man who wrote from within the territories of the *Respublica*. He was well aware of the ideology of those who governed his region. Any province under barbarian rule was, technically, a province taken "captive" by the enemies of Rome. In such a captive province, there simply should not have been Romans who were happy to be *illic*—"over there"—in barbarian territory. Yet such Romans now prayed that they would never again become subjects of the empire.[60]

For Salvian himself there was little that was romantic about barbarians. God might judge them and excuse them according to his Law. But that was a God's-eye view. For Salvian and his readers, barbarians—even Christian barbarians— were different. They even smelled different. Stench clung to their bodies and to their clothes.[61] Yet well-born Romans of high culture preferred to live among them: "they prefer to live as free men in a captive land than to live as captives under the name of Roman freedom."[62]

Other authors had written about Romans who found it easier to live with barbarians than to pay taxes to the empire.[63] That, in itself, was not new. What was new was the manner in which Salvian drew attention to this flight as a shocking inversion of the normal order of things. The *Respublica* should be the place of liberty. Augustine had said so, in no uncertain terms, only a decade previously, when he drafted his petition to halt the slave trade in Africa. Roman armies were there to fight for "Roman liberty" lest Roman citizens become the captives of barbarians.[64] Now the most sinister transformation of all had taken place. It was within the *Respublica* itself that Salvian perceived the ultimate anomaly—a new birth of captivity.

"Strangled, as if by thugs, with the bonds of taxes": Salvian and Taxation

We must be clear as to what Salvian regarded as the root cause of this sinister development. He focused on an all-too-well-known object—the fiscal apparatus of the Roman state. Inherited in all its abrasive vigor from the fourth century, the imperial tax machine still struggled in the face of massive dislocation and losses of territory to pay the armies and to maintain a governmental class whose wealth still derived in large part from their control of taxes.

Thus, in his emphasis on taxation, Salvian did not simply repeat the perpetual and general grievances of all subjects of the later empire against the weight of taxes. His comments reflected a precise moment in the crisis of the Roman state. From the military point of view, what remained of the *Respublica* had rallied with unexpected vigor in the 430s and early 440s. Covering with mobile forces a vast area between the Rhineland and the Danube, Count Aetius had rendered the empire a power still to be reckoned with. In the words of Guy Halsall, Aetius's campaigns amounted to a form of "government through punitive expedition."[65] Quite apart from the brutality of such campaigns, they had been extremely costly. The cavalry units used by Aetius were crushingly expensive to maintain. A policy based as much on diplomacy as on the use of force drained money in the form of subsidies.[66]

In both Gaul and Italy, taxes had to be collected even more stringently than before. Traditional exemptions were curtailed or overridden. The reaction of the rich—especially the high-ups in government circles—had been to protect themselves against high taxes by shifting the burden onto lesser taxpayers. This abuse now became more than usually flagrant and unpopular. A rhetoric of the public good had long been deployed by subjects of the empire in their petitions for tax relief. The same rhetoric was echoed back to taxpayers in imperial edicts. In 441 the chancery of Valentinian III in Italy denounced tax evaders in the same language as did Salvian:

> Since they serve only their domestic profits and deprive the common good, in which is contained their true and substantial welfare.... The burden which the rich man refuses ... only the weaker man bears.[67]

The language used in the imperial edicts shows that Salvian was no innovator. He partook in the widespread culture of criticism to which we referred when speaking of Ambrose. But what was different was the implacable finality of his judgment: "the *Romana respublica* is now dead ... strangled, as if by thugs, with the bonds of taxes."[68]

Salvian's relentless precision on matters of taxation betrays the clear but narrow focus of his own field of vision and of those who read him. An impoverished local notable himself, he spoke with rare anger on behalf of the minor nobility of the provinces. Such persons felt increasingly alienated from the narrow government circles who controlled imperial policy. It was this class of minor notables that felt particularly threatened by ruthless taxation. When Salvian spoke of the *pauperculi*—the "poor little guys"—who were devastated by high officials, he did not mean the lower classes in the modern sense.[69] His "poor" were rarely peasants. They were never the down-and-out poor of the cities. They were people like himself. In the 430s it was they who risked sliding down the steep slope into impoverishment as refugees and as fiscal debtors.[70] And they did so because they were victimized by their own more fortunate and more ruthless peers. The immediate villains of Salvian's tract were local ones. They were the leading town councillors—the *principales*—of the cities. As in the fourth century so in the 430s and 440s: the duty of the leading councillors was to extract all that they could from their weaker colleagues as well as from the peasantry. Ever since the fourth century, they had grown rich through manipulating the tax machine of the Roman state at the expense of their peers.

> What place is there where the *principales* do not devour the very guts of the widows and orphans, and even of the *sancti* [the clergy, whose duty it was to protect them]?[71]

Salvian seldom lifted his eyes from the brightly lit scene of local, city-based extortion. Yet he singled out the high-ups of government as the real culprits. For it was they who had set the imperial tax machine in motion: "*Praefectura ... praeda*: a Prefecture confers a license to pillage.... The whole world is destroyed so that a few should bear the title of *Vir Illustris*."[72] These were bitter words. Salvian knew that the title of *vir illustris* conferred by high office gave access to the upper ranks of the nobility. Former holders of high offices entered the charmed circle of ex-prefects and sons of prefects to which Sidonius Apollinaris belonged and to which he clung so tenaciously in the generation after Salvian. In Salvian's account we can hear distinctly the angry voice of men less privileged than Sidonius and his friends. This was the voice of members of the lesser aristocracies linked to their region and to its provincial cities. In writing as he did, Salvian expressed the anger of an entire group, directed against what was fast becoming an isolated ancien régime—an upper aristocracy closed against newcomers and tarnished by association with the systematic violence of the Roman state. If this was "central Romanness," then, Salvian implied, it got what it deserved.

Labores manuum nostrarum manducamus: We are eating the bread of our own making

OUTER CAPTIVITY, INNER OPPRESSION

High taxation meant impoverishment. And impoverishment meant a quickening of the most sinister process of all—the enslavement of Romans by Romans within the territories of the *Respublica* itself. Salvian went out of his way to explain exactly how this happened. Faced by the weight of taxes, poor farmers found that they did not have the means to emigrate to the barbarians. Instead, they did what little they could do: they handed themselves over to the rich as clients in return for protection. The rich took over title to their lands under the pretext of saving the farmers from the land tax. The patron registered the farmer's land on the tax rolls under his (the patron's) own name. Within a few years, the poor farmers found themselves without land, although they were still hounded for personal taxes. Such patronage by the great, so Salvian claimed, turned free men into slaves as surely as the magic of Circe had turned humans into pigs.[73]

This was an unpardonable transformation. Salvian had no objection to patronage in itself. He wrote that it showed "greatness of soul" in a powerful man to offer to help the weak.[74] But to turn a free client into a slave in this way went against the whole grain of his view of society. As we have seen, the Gallic consensus on theology had assumed a view of society that accepted sharp asymmetries as long as the partners remained free agents. The relation of patron and client provided the root metaphor for the relations between God and human beings. Salvian shared this view. Dependence on God—or on the great—was not the same thing as slavery. Free men in distress might approach the great as abject clients. But they should not be made into slaves. As far as Salvian was concerned, Gallic society could remain steeply hierarchical. But (in the words of Cam Grey) this hierarchy was to be based on "reciprocal vertical relationships" between patrons and clients, not on the unilateral enslavement of the clients.[75]

It is important that we should not be misled by Salvian's dramatic picture of the oppression of clients by their patrons in the Gaul of the 430s. It is far from certain that enslavement through patronage happened on an unprecedented scale at this time. Still less is it certain that such patronage represented a new development—a harbinger of feudal links of dependence that bound the peasantry as serfs to their lords. There is much to be said for the less dramatic view proposed by Jens Uwe Krause: such patronage did not mark a new departure. Salvian was not describing the sudden emergence of a new, "proto-feudal" order throughout the countryside of Gaul. He was only describing the normal ups and downs of farmers forced to sell part or all of their land to richer neighbors so as to cover their tax debts.[76]

But what this deflation of the phenomenon of rural patronage in Gaul does not explain is the intensity with which Salvian himself fastened on it as a privileged symptom of the miseries of the Romans. He did so for a reason that was deeply rooted in his thought on the justice of God. The justice of God was always apposite. By a relentless *lex talionis*, the Romans suffered at the hands of the barbarians precisely what they were inflicting on their fellows: nothing more, nothing less: "Are we surprised that the barbarians capture us, when we make captives of our own brothers?"[77]

If Salvian has misled social historians of the fifth-century West by exaggerating the power exercised by rural patrons over their dependents, it was because he wished his readers to know that any captivity Romans inflicted on each other was bound to be as brutal as that which any barbarian had inflicted on Romans. For the justice of God to stand, the one captivity—that imposed by patrons on their clients—had to be presented as just as oppressive, as widespread, and as inexorable as was the other—the captivity inflicted on Romans by barbarians. For the one to be a punishment for the other, both had to be presented as equally disastrous and equally irrevocable.

Here Salvian's rhetoric struck a contemporary note. "Captivity," "subjugation," and "unconditional surrender" were the ugly words with which contemporary chroniclers spoke of the rise of the barbarians at the expense of the Roman empire. The *Chronicle of 452*, for instance, recorded the dates when province after province fell under the "captivity," the *ditio*—the "power"—of barbarian groups.[78] Faced by this rhetoric of subjugation used by contemporary upholders of the Roman order when talking of the world outside the territories of the *Respublica*, Salvian invited his readers to look inward. Everything that they, as Romans, complained about in the outside world was happening within Roman society itself. It was because of the sinister growth of "captivity" in their own society that they suffered "captivity" at the hands of barbarians. *Labores manuum nostrarum manducamus* (Psalm 127:2): "We are eating the bread of our own making."[79]

Sonus populi: The sound of the people

As a convert to the ascetic life and a clergyman, Salvian expected to be a lonely figure. In the words of Robert Markus:

> Salvian has sharply divided the world: the utterly corrupt Roman world on the one side, the few who have renounced it on the other. The division of the world into the few—or the very few, as he likes to add—reverberates like a scarcely muffled drumbeat through Salvian's pages.[80]

But his sense of belonging to a beleaguered group did not mean that Salvian was isolated from reality. He saw the world through narrow slits. But these slits were no more narrow than those through which Sidonius Apollinaris viewed (with calculated euphoria) the traditional *Respublica* in its last days. What Salvian saw he saw clearly. This was a robustly profane society. The upper reaches of this society might revere the "saints"—as they had revered the striking monk-bishops of Arles, Honoratus, and Hilary. But this honor had been based on an ancient compact. The world of the holy (represented by ascetic bishops) was not supposed to mingle with the world of the profane and still less to modify it. The "saints" could do nothing to remove the stain of deep profanity from the empire itself.

The unredeemed profanity of the public life of the later empire was essential to Salvian's view of the world. He piled up a unique denunciation of the social sins of the Romans—the merciless collection of taxes and the imposition of new slavery on dependent farmers. But, as far as he was concerned, even if the Roman empire of his time had been strong and just, it had remained a proud institution deaf to God's Law.[81] As Hervé Inglebert has seen clearly, the surviving *Respublica* represented for Salvian the "absolute triumph of the earthly city." It had remained an empire oblivious to God.[82]

For Salvian, the Christian façade of the empire amounted to no more than a set of "emperor's clothes." In reality, the Roman state was stark naked. The empire had not opened itself to the values of the Christian church it claimed to patronize. The church itself had lost its power to pray for the safety of the empire.[83] The clergy were snubbed by tax collectors and by high officials.[84] Those who adopted the monastic life were mocked by their fellow nobles and were deprived of their inheritances by their families.[85] Salvian himself remembered how he had once been sent packing by a *praepotens*, a high official to whom he had appealed on behalf of a man whose livelihood was threatened. With "blazing eyes," the high-up told Salvian that he had sworn to Jesus Christ to ruin the poor fellow. He would not go back on his oath.[86]

This was not simply a personal failure on Salvian's part. In his works, we can catch the same sense of frustration that the correspondence of Augustine and Alypius had conveyed a decade previously in Africa. When taxation and the necessities of state were involved, the empire, though ruled by Christian princes, presented to the bishops a cliff face of secular power largely untouched by the appeals of churchmen. This was not a state that was in any mood to surrender its prerogatives to bishops and clergymen.

One aspect of the empire showed this clearly. The high ceremonies of state remained heavy with profane elements. There was little or no sign of Christianity in the ivory diptychs with which the consuls of the fifth century continued to celebrate their elevation, as Symmachus had done in the fourth.[87] The splendid scenes in Arles, which Sidonius Apollinaris remembered as a youth from the late 440s, would also have been soundproof to Christianity. Salvian even claims that the auspices were still taken on these occasions.[88] Roman generals on campaign at the head of still largely pagan armies made up of barbarian mercenaries were happy to use non-Christian forms of divination on the eve of battles.[89] Many bishops viewed the ideology of empire itself as still bathed in sinister grandiloquence. Bishop Quodvultdeus, who had been driven from Carthage by the Vandals in 439, was by no means impressed by the empire to which he had fled. He was convinced that one of the signs of the approach of Antichrist and the end of the world was the ease with which petitions to the emperor still spoke of "your Godhead, your Altars, your Perennial Being."[90]

This robust profanity was also to be seen in all aspects of the life of secular persons. The numinous link between abundance and the turning of the seasons (on which we touched when discussing the world of Ausonius) continued to haunt the imagination of the rich. In the court city of Ravenna, the Feast of the Kalends was still celebrated with ancient gusto. Dressed as the mighty gods who ruled the planets, actors danced from house to house through the streets of the city.[91] An exquisite mosaic has recently been discovered beneath the Via d'Azeglio in Ravenna. It shows children dressed as the seasons participating in a round dance. It may date from this time.[92]

But what shocked Salvian most of all was the fact that in the cities of Africa and Gaul, the sense of solidarity on which the morale of the citizens depended owed little to the Christian churches and still less to the preaching of bishops. It continued to be generated by the roar of the circus. This was what still drew townsmen together in times of crisis. For the games had never been occasions for mere amusement. They had linked the cities to the destiny of the empire. Salvian had seen this happen in his native Rhineland. In 421 the notables of Trier sought from the newly created emperor Constantius III funds to celebrate his accession through circus games. They would have solemnly gathered in the amphitheater on the Petrisberg above a city already blackened by the fires of war. The wild explosion of worldly joy associated with such games (and by no means the prayers of the saints) were held to be the most effective remedy for the upheavals of the past decades.[93]

Altogether, to go to the circus in a time of crisis was not to succumb to luxury but to show a robust, civic patriotism. To love one's city was to love the games. Salvian reports that as the Vandal armies closed in around the governmental capitals of Africa—first Cirta (Constantine, Algeria) in Numidia and then Carthage—they were met by "the sound of the people as it roared acclamations in the circus."[94]

Salvian wished to treat these heavy symbols of collective loyalty as if they were dispensable. They were frivolous luxuries. To support the games in times of "calamity for the imperial treasury" was to throw good money down the drain. He claimed that financial restraints had already led to the widespread abandonment of games in most of the cities of Gaul.[95] Historians have tended to take Salvian at his word. They readily link the end of circus celebrations in the West to the economic recession of the fifth century.[96]

Yet there is only limited truth in this assertion. As we have seen, games had already come to be less numerous in the fourth century. Even in a prosperous province such as Africa, they tended to be concentrated in certain "flagship" cities. But in such cities they survived; their ideological weight had not been diminished. Major government centers in the West maintained their circuses throughout the fifth century and even longer. In Saragossa, for instance, at the extreme western edge of the surviving territories of the *Respublica* in Spain, a spectacle was laid on in the circus in honor of the new consul in the 490s.[97] As late as 577, the first reaction of a Frankish king to a challenge to his rule was to build circuses in Soissons and Paris, "for he was keen to offer spectacles to the citizens."[98]

Salvian would have taken little comfort from this sign of continuity. His view was that, like a patient high on drugs (Sardinian herbs that were used to bring on uncontrolled laughter), the Roman people "laughed as it died."[99] He wrote to declare that the time for laughing was over. The profane world associated with empire was all but dead. Yet it had refused to die. It is possible to read Salvian's "Report on the State of the Nation" against the grain of its author's intentions. Careful reading of *On the Government of God* and of a wide array of contemporary sources shows that in the 430s and 440s, Salvian still faced an imperial society that had remained deeply profane. The exercise of power in the *Respublica* had retained an ancient, pre-Christian tone. Only when that ancient core finally gave way, in the course of the sixth century, could it be said that the West had definitively entered a "post-Roman" age. Only then—but not before, and certainly not in the time of Salvian—did the Christian church finally come into its own. For it was only then—in the later fifth century—that the church emerged as the owner of great wealth that made it for the first time the equal of the landed aristocracy. This was a decisive change. Let us end, then, in these last three chapters, by turning first to Italy and then back to Gaul, Spain, and Africa to see how this—the last stage of our story—came about.

CHAPTER 27

❦

Ob Italiae securitatem: For the security of Italy

Rome and Italy, ca. 430–ca. 530

Fifth-Century Italy

In 439 Count Aetius returned to Rome after a series of wide-ranging campaigns in Gaul. The Roman Senate celebrated his return by erecting a golden statue to him in the Atrium Libertatis—a building near the Senate house at the top of the Forum. The base of the statue has survived. It is a modest block covered with elegant, small letters that now stands beside the entrance of the Senate house unnoticed by passing tourists. In this inscription, the Senate praised Aetius for victories that had "returned Gaul to the Roman empire." But they thanked him above all "for the security of Italy" obtained by his distant wars.[1]

It was a resolutely local view. It reminds us that after the first fateful spasm of violence that began in 406 and culminated in 439 with the Vandal conquest of Carthage, the unity of the western empire had shattered. Many regions had abandoned (or would soon abandon) the sense of belonging to the *Respublica*, to the empire. As in the days of Symmachus (now half a century in the past), the Roman Senate that erected the statue to Aetius still saw itself as the symbolic core of the Roman world. But this world had changed. The members of the Senate (most of them from families based in Rome) now looked out across the Alps to a Gaul and a Spain that had become war zones. It seemed as if Italy alone, as it stretched in a succession of rich and diverse landscapes from the Alps to the Ionian sea, was a land of rare security.[2] In Italy the *Respublica* that Salvian, writing about Gaul, had declared in just these years to be "almost dead and gone" appeared still to be very much alive.

A strong sense of the unbroken survival of the Roman ancien régime prevailed in Rome and in central and southern Italy. By contrast, northern Italy, between the Alps and the Apennines, was a different world. A corridor between

Gaul and the Balkans, it was frequently dislocated by warfare. Furthermore, northern Italy was used to the presence of barbarians. For centuries the Roman civilian population had been flanked by a large military establishment of preponderantly barbarian origin. Ever since the days of Ambrose, the Romans of the north had derived much of their wealth from supplying the armies gathered around the court in government centers such as Milan and Ravenna. It was not surprising, therefore, that the establishment of barbarian rule in Italy finally came from the inside and not as a result of invasion. It was a result of the final winning out of a non-Roman military faction in northern Italy. After 476 the emperor simply withdrew, leaving power in the hands of a series of strongmen who emerged from barbarian contingents that had long been stationed in northern Italy and the Balkans—first Odoacer (476–93) and then Theodoric (493–526).[3]

Compared with the "political hothouse" of northern Italy,[4] Rome, central Italy, and the Mezzogiorno moved to a slower rhythm. For the upper classes of the region, the "security of Italy" meant two things: the preservation of the stupendous stage set of Rome itself and, alongside this, the development of an agrarian economy capable of supporting them in new, less affluent times. How did the Christian church, especially in Rome, fit into this situation?

Complexity: A New Narrative for Rome

In order to answer this question, it is important that we should abandon two narrative modules that are deeply embedded in modern scholarship on the history of fifth-century Rome. The one asserts that after the Gothic sack of 410, the emperors abandoned Rome forever, leaving a vacuum of responsibility that was rapidly filled by the popes. It is believed that in the course of the fifth century, a Rome without the emperors rapidly became "the Rome of the popes." The other belief is a corollary of this narrative. It is said that the Senate of Rome rallied briskly around the bishop of Rome. It is often assumed that the wealth of Christian senators fueled the rise of an opulent church from the early fifth century onward and that the result of this alliance was the emergence of a Christianity deeply tinged with aristocratic Roman values. This has been presented as an altogether happy evolution. It is said to have preserved the continuity of the traditions of classical Rome in Christian form. In a darkening age, marked by so much violence and destruction in other regions of the West, what values—we tend to think—could have been more worthwhile preserving than Roman values? It has always proved heartening, both to scholars and to general readers, to imagine a fifth-century Rome where little had changed. For the leaders of the Christian church itself had become more Roman than the Romans. Rome, it is said, became the preserve of

> a papacy sure of itself and penetrated by the old educated classes, Christian by now yet conscious of the obligation to carry on the traditions of the classical past.[5]
>
> [For] the pope and his clergy, allied to the great Roman families, embodied the Church in Rome.[6]

These are the warm words of Richard Krautheimer, the master exponent of the Christian architecture of fifth-century Rome. Yet we have come to learn (if only in the last decade) that the story is not so simple. In the words of Federico Marazzi, who has summed up the new view in a luminous essay: "The key to understanding the city of Rome ... is complexity."[7]

Marazzi rightly insists that the fifth century was not characterized by an effortless mutation of pagan Rome into the Rome of the popes. Rather, we are dealing with a more tension-laden situation that continued the abrasive dynamics of the Rome of the fourth century. As we have seen, in fourth-century Rome many groups had been content to go their own way. No one group achieved outright dominance over all the others in the city. This situation continued throughout much of the fifth century. In a world characterized by compartmentalized endeavors, the final emergence of the bishops and clergy of Rome as dominant players in the urban scene came late. It happened only in the late fifth and early sixth centuries—in the pontificates of Simplicius (468–83), Gelasius (492–96), and Symmachus (498–514).

These bishops did not emerge as leading figures in Rome as a result of an alliance with the Senate. They emerged, in many ways, in defiance of the Senate. They did so as the upholders of a high view of ecclesiastical autonomy. By the year 500 AD, this sense of autonomy was given weight by the possession of solid landed wealth, carefully administered by the bishop and his agents all over southern Italy. In asserting their autonomy, the bishops and clergy looked past the Senate. They were the heirs of the development we have traced since the days of Pope Damasus. Damasus and his successors had pushed the clergy to the fore with the support of the minor nobility. The conditions of the fifth century favored the further emergence of the clergy as a Third Estate in Rome. We must look now at how the eventual victory of the clerical element in the city came about.

In order to do this, we must abandon the notion that the emperors were absent from fifth-century Rome. In fact, the emperors resided in Rome far more frequently than they had ever done in the previous two centuries. Rome quite as much as Ravenna was their capital. It provided the ruler of a diminished empire with what was still a spectacular backdrop for himself and his court. When they resided in Rome, the court and its resident officials could be kept in supplies by an ingeniously revamped *annona* system.

The court made its presence felt in the churches. For the entire first half of the fifth century, the great basilicas of Rome owed as much to the emperors and to their courtiers as they did to local donors. In the succinct words of Andrew Gillett:

> Sixtus [432–40] and Leo [440–61] transformed the urban landscape of Rome ... but their works, often seen as an expression of the pope's new-found local authority within the city ... occurred in the presence, not the absence of the western emperors.[8]

For instance, Sixtus III completed the great basilica of Santa Maria Maggiore at the top of the Esquiline Hill. It dwarfed the titular churches around it. It made the pope present in an area previously dotted with senatorial houses.[9] The great mosaic that can still be seen on the arch before the apse spelled out, in the visual language of Roman triumphal art, the claims of the bishop of Rome to be the head of a Christian religion that was as worldwide as the empire itself. The church was dedicated by Sixtus to the *plebs Dei*, to the Roman congregation as a privileged and holy People of God.[10]

But the building of Santa Maria Maggiore owed less to the unaided initiative of Sixtus than we once thought. Probably built on imperial property, it had been aided at every step by the emperor.[11] It is notable that Sixtus donated to Santa Maria Maggiore "a twelve pound wine jug of the finest gold." Gold was the fingerprint of empire; its use betrayed the active participation of the imperial court. At Santa Maria Maggiore and elsewhere, golden liturgical plate made its first appearance in Rome since the days of Constantine.[12] The age of Sixtus III has often been described as the first great age of papal Rome. For the emperor and for the governing circles resident in Rome, the foundation and endowment of basilicas such as Santa Maria Maggiore represented, rather, a momentary return, fostered by the court, to the golden age of Constantine.[13]

It is also far from certain that, in the fifth century, the great Roman families were any more committed to the economic support of the church of Rome than they had been in the fourth century. Some families did contribute; many others did not. Compared with the resident aristocracy of Constantinople, who poured money into new shrines and monasteries, the great families of Rome were a minor presence. Courtiers, officials, and, later, military men were the figures who left their marks on the churches of Rome. It was they, and not the nobles, who made repairs, provided mosaics, and offered ex-votos. Indeed, when it came to giving land to the church, the upper nobility was more than usually ungenerous. They kept the best land to themselves. In the *suburbium*—the intensely cultivated area outside the city that was a zone of prime real estate dominated by the nobility—the church held only 5 percent of the land in around 500 AD. In the fifth century there had been no avalanche of noble wealth in the direction of the church.[14]

For many leading nobles in the fifth century—as in the fourth—Rome was first and foremost a stupendous ancient city. It was notable for traditions that were thought to reach back a thousand years. It had by no means become a city dominated by Christian shrines. Resident Roman senators blended easily into the ancient, pre-Christian backdrop of the city. Many remained crypto-pagans for longer than we might expect. We have already met Volusianus, the uncle of Melania the Younger, whose criticisms of Christianity immediately after the sack of Rome provoked Augustine to write his *City of God*. As late as 437 Volusianus was still a pagan, though nominally enrolled as a catechumen of the Christian church. He was only baptized on his deathbed.[15] There were many like Volusianus both in Rome and in Constantinople. Their existence in high society was screened by an "ideology of silence." They were there; one simply did not talk about them. For their very existence mocked the public ideology, which claimed that Christianity had become the sole religion of the Roman world and that paganism no longer existed.[16] As Arnobius, an African writer in mid-fifth-century Rome, put it, there were still many members of the rich for whom the Christian Psalms and the teaching of Christ on almsgiving were *frigidae naeniae*, "uninspiring ditties."[17]

These attitudes were surprisingly long-lasting. As late as 494, Pope Gelasius claimed to be outraged that members of the Senate still supported the festival of the Lupercalia, which dated from the days of Romulus. Every February 14 naked youths dashed through the city whipping ladies suspected of immorality and singing obscene ditties—which, on this occasion (so as to keep up with the times) may have included songs about the adulteries of a member of Gelasius's clergy.[18]

Even good Christians of the noble class spent more time and money maintaining the joy of their city and the glory of their families in the Colosseum and the Circus Maximus than they did in the churches. In 494 Flavius Turcius Rufius Apronianus Asterius was consul. His very name represented a confluence of great families, like the quarterings of a late medieval heraldic shield. We know from the subscription of two surviving manuscripts that Asterius had edited both the *Eclogues* of Vergil and the works of Sedulius, a recent Christian poet. But he had spent his money on Rome. As consul, he had "thrown away his revenue as a matter of pride" for his beloved city.[19] But what was this city like?

Apparet quantus in Romana civitate fuerit populus: It is evident
how great the population of the city of Rome has been

POPULATION AND SUPPLY IN FIFTH-CENTURY ROME

Those who study Rome in the fifth and early sixth centuries have to resign themselves as best they can to a peculiar lacuna in their evidence. The one factor that is crucial to any convincing narrative of the social and economic history of Rome in this period remains unknown: the population of the city. Legislation on the organization of the Roman *annona* in the fourth and early fifth centuries provides us with a series of spectacular figures. There may have been as many as 300,000 recipients of cheap pork in 367. There were still 120,000 after the Gothic sack. As late as 452, 3.5 million pounds of pork were provided for some 141,120 citizens. Despite the sharp drop after 410, Rome seemed (on paper at least) to have remained one of the largest and best provisioned cities of the Mediterranean.[20]

Yet, for many scholars, these figures seem too good to be true. They argue that this level of population could not have been maintained throughout the fifth century. They assume that the loss of massive levies of grain and oil from Africa due to the Vandal conquest of Carthage must have had drastic consequences.[21] Furthermore, field archaeology in the *suburbium* of Rome and in southern Etruria appears to point to a "sudden and unforeseen" emptying of land that had once been given over to intensive agriculture for the Roman market.[22] The sudden death, after 450, of entire tracts of countryside around Rome may be a warning sign that we are looking at the traces at one remove of an otherwise silent and gigantic catastrophe—the emptying out of a city which, in 400, had been the largest human settlement on the face of the planet.

Yet, even if we subscribe to a dramatic view of the recession of Rome during this period, we still know little about the pace of this collapse. Somehow, Rome does not seem to have collapsed as rapidly or as drastically as the model to which historians appeal to explain this collapse would lead us to expect.[23] Thus, when, in 533–35, the bureaucrat Cassiodorus wrote of the Rome of his times, he toyed with the contrast between the present and the glorious past of the city:

It is evident how great was the population of the city of Rome, seeing that it was fed by supplies even from far off regions.... For the vast extent of the walls bears witness to the throngs of citizens, as do the swollen capacity of the places of entertainment and the wonderful size of the baths.[24]

But Cassiodorus's edict showed that he did not think that he was living among ruins. He was still busily organizing pigs for Rome. In the form of livestock, at least, the *annona* for Rome had continued to be gathered throughout southern

Italy, if not in such prodigious amounts. When King Theodoric visited Rome in 500, he confronted a *populus Romanus* that could be thought to be as large as 120,000. Theodoric also provided 8,500 *modii* of grain for the poor gathered around the shrine of Saint Peter. This was the equivalent of a year's supply for 300 persons.[25] In the words of Sam Barnish, Rome in the early sixth century still gave "the impression of a great city."[26]

Behind this impression there lies a largely hidden history of the redeployment of Italian agriculture in the south to make good the losses of supplies from Africa.[27] This redeployment did not reach the same levels as in the age of the *annona* at its height in the fourth century. But it did ensure the one thing that mattered. The People of Rome continued to be honored by receiving civic rations in one form or another. On occasions, these may have been no more than token distributions of honey and rare wine. Pork continued to be provided from the ever-available herds of pigs in the toe of Italy.[28] Through these somewhat makeshift devices, Rome retained an outstanding ancient tradition. It remained a city of the *annona*, which meant that it also remained a city of the *populus Romanus*.

Ad maiorem gratiam voluptatemque populi Romani: To the greater charm and delight of the Roman people

Rather than lock ourselves into false certainties, either way, as to the size of Rome at this time, it is better to attempt to envision the changes in the texture of its urban life and the relations between different groups at this time. Fifth-century Rome was not a ghost city. But it had become somewhat of a parody of its former self. The houses of the senatorial aristocracy came to dominate the city more than ever. In the hills of Rome, houses with splendid marble pavements held the high ground up to the end of the sixth century.[29] But they now stood in the midst of deserted gardens and the emptied, charred ruins of former, even greater palaces.

It was a world in which the urban framework had fallen apart. Vivid islands of continued habitation stood out more clearly in the midst of a degraded urban landscape.[30] This applied also to the Christian churches and shrines of Rome. Some were gentrified. They were made into oases of civilized living, like the noble palaces of the same period. In 461–68, for instance, Pope Hilarus set up a fountain and a porch in brightly colored marbles in front of Santa Croce in Gerusalemme (near the Lateran). He also endowed the great suburban shrine of Saint Lawrence (San Lorenzo fuori le mura) with a little palace hall (a *praetorium*), an indoor and an outdoor bath, and two libraries.[31]

The great families who still lived in these palaces treated the city as their own. The dislocation of the old *annona* system and its replacement by less massive supplies made the inhabitants of Rome if anything more dependent on food supplies drawn from the estates of the nobility. We do not know, but we can reasonably imagine, that a large proportion of the *plebs* of Rome depended on the great families as clients, for employment, and even for food. The *nobiles* were tempted to behave as if they owned the *populus Romanus*. When, in 509, the supporters of a pantomime began to heckle their own patrons (the family of the Decii) in the Circus Maximus, the Decii simply sent armed slaves into the amphitheater to beat up their rebellious clients.[32] A century earlier, such high-handed treatment of the People of Rome would have cost Symmachus his palace, if not his life.

But, though perhaps more dominant, the nobles were poorer than they had been before. Traditional forms of self-advertisement came to a virtual end as the century progressed. Except on rare occasions, the upper nobility no longer received statues from their peers and admirers.[33] In the same manner, lesser figures did without the marble sarcophagi that had been the glory of the Christian catacombs of the fourth century.[34]

Yet Rome remained a splendid stage set for its resident nobility. Throughout the fifth century, members of the Senate worked hard to create within the city a series of "museum islands" devoted to their own version of the past of Rome. The buildings around the Senate House (where Aetius's statue was placed) were carefully restored. Deserted buildings full of rubble were hidden behind repaired façades. The paving of the Forum was maintained.[35] This was not merely an exercise in museum-like conservation. It was about the collective memory of an entire class. The continuity of the Senate with its own past was stressed. Leading pagans of the late fourth century (such as Nicomachus Flavianus) were brought back into public view by statues to which long inscriptions were attached. Christian senators placed their inscriptions beside those of their pagan ancestors, as if to emphasize an unbroken continuity of civic pride to which religion was irrelevant.[36]

This determination to continue the civic past of Rome was particularly visible in the mighty Colosseum. The seats around the arena of the Colosseum were regularly repaired up to the 530s.[37] Even today, we can sit where the last senators of Rome once sat in massed family groups. They presided over games that had the same ingredients (if not lavished on the same scale) as those once celebrated by Symmachus and his son. Only the gladiators who had given a savage thrill to the praetorian games of little Memmius were absent.[38] Occasionally a cross, now carved so as to mark the divisions between the seats of different families, gave a hint of Christian times.[39] But what happened in that great building was soundproof to Christianity. The only noise in it was that of the People of Rome. In 438 the Prefect of the City (Flavius Paulus) restored the Colosseum after an earthquake. He did so *ad maiorem gratiam voluptatemque [populi romani]*, "for the greater charm and delight of the Roman People."[40] At the same time, however, Paulus and his family were careful to make their vows to Saint Paul by contributing to the marble sheathing of the great basilica of Saint Paul Outside the Walls.[41]

Great Works and Little Works: *Annona*, Almsgiving, and the People of Rome

What we find, in the Rome of the mid-fifth century and in subsequent decades, is an uneasy balance between two very different efforts. The lay elites of the city strove to maintain the civic life of Rome as they had had inherited it from their grandparents of the fourth century. At the same time, the bishop of Rome and his clergy attempted to reach out to the population of the city as a whole in the name of the care of the poor. What was at stake was a redefinition of who exactly were the "People of Rome." It was only when this redefinition occurred (at the very end of our period—indeed, at the very end of the sixth century) that the "People of Rome" came to overlap, in the social imagination of contemporaries, with the "poor of the Church" who had always been subject to the care of the bishop of Rome. The Roman church, and not the emperor and the nobility, became the protector and the nourisher of the People of Rome. This was the crucial change. Then, and only then, could Rome be truly called "the Rome of the popes."

This was not an evolution we can take for granted. At first sight, the two forms of care were utterly disproportionate. The amounts spent on maintaining the *annona* and the games dwarfed the sums spent on poor relief.[42] For example, in the early sixth century, the bishop of Ravenna was the head of one of the richest churches in Italy. He was expected to spend 3,000 *solidi* a year on the poor.[43] But, in 452, the cost of pigs alone for the *annona* of Rome amounted to 14,700 *solidi* a year.[44] A century before, the sons of senatorial aristocrats had spent 86,400 *solidi* in a few weeks on their praetorian games at a time when the yearly revenue of the church of Rome may have been a mere 26,000 *solidi*.[45] Between the two forms of giving, and the wealth mobilized to meet the demands of each, there was no contest.

In this respect, one is reminded of the debates of Chinese mandarins at the court of the T'ang emperor in the eighth century. As Buddhism spread in western China, conservative Confucian scholars (the nearest equivalent that we might find in all of Eurasia to men such as Symmachus and Cassiodorus) contrasted scornfully the "little works" carried out by Buddhist monasteries in times of hardship—in the form of almsgiving, orphanages, and soup kitchens for the poor—with the "great works" undertaken by the emperor and his bureaucracy. Only supplies of food from the great imperial warehouses (and not the "little works" of the Buddhist monks) could relieve the famine of whole provinces.[46] In the fourth, fifth, and early sixth centuries, many conscientious administrators of the *annona* of Rome (such as Cassiodorus) would have thought the same way. Christians might give alms to feed the poor at a time of famine. Some did this in a memorable fashion. For instance, in the 470s, Gallo-Roman aristocrats in Clermont and the Rhone valley united to transport food to the cities and to take care of famine victims at their villas.[47] But ultimately, as in China, it was the state that controlled the greatest warehouses and so could do the greatest good. As Cassiodorus told King Theodoric, for a ruler in Roman style, "The best troops... are his well-stored granaries."[48] The cargoes of grain released from state granaries in times of crisis or diverted to feed the people of Rome (as Theodoric had done when he visited the city in 500 AD) were still considered to be stunning proofs of the generosity of the emperor. The "small works" associated with the Christian care of the poor took second place.

But things were not as simple as they seemed to a bureaucrat such as Cassiodorus. "Conspicuous overprovision" had always been part of the ideology of the *annona*.[49] Even in the fourth century, one wonders whether all those pigs, all that grain, and all that oil solemnly earmarked for the Roman people ever arrived at Rome each year in the quantities laid down in the laws. In scale alone, the hiatus between the *annona* and Christian almsgiving to the poor may have narrowed in the course of the fifth century. The amounts provided by the *annona* diminished while the church emerged, slowly but surely, as the safety net of the Roman people as a whole. But this, of course, depended on the ability of the clergy to elicit donations. In order to do this, they had to provide the rich families of Rome with a rationale for the pious use of wealth. Let us see how they set about doing this.

Sub quadam procuratione: Under contract as an estate manager

DEMETRIAS, PROSPER, AND THE USE OF WEALTH

The process of gathering wealth for the church was well under way by the time that Leo the Great became pope (440–61). Already, a decade earlier, in around 433, an intellectual very different from the disabused Salvian arrived in Rome from Marseilles. Prosper, the pugnacious defender of Augustine (whom we met in chapter 25), came to Rome to act as secretary and advisor to the popes. He also held strong opinions on how the Christian rich should view their wealth. One of his first works may have been a letter on this subject to Anicia Demetrias, entitled *De vera humilitate—On True Humility*.[50] If Prosper is the author of this tract, it would have constituted his visiting card to a remarkable lady.

In the 430s, Demetrias was a living reminder of the *belle époque* of fourth-century Rome. She was the granddaughter of none other than Petronius Probus. We last met her receiving letters of spiritual advice both from Jerome and from Pelagius on the occasion of her consecration as a nun at Carthage in 413. Now she lived three miles out of Rome on an estate near the Via Latina. Some time before her death, she built a large shrine to Saint Stephen within the center courtyard of her villa. Though completed at the urging of Pope Leo and with the help of a Roman priest, the shrine was, nonetheless, very much *her* shrine. It was possibly built to be her mausoleum, placed at the heart of her villa.[51]

Whether it was Prosper or someone else who wrote the *De vera humilitate,* the author did so very much as Demetrias's client. He was made to show his paces. He was to demonstrate to Demetrias and to those around her how a holder of high Augustinian views such as Prosper made sense of the legendary wealth associated with her family. The treatise on humility turned out to be, in fact, a treatise on wealth.

The treatise advanced an unusually trenchant justification of wealth provided that it was used on behalf of the church. The author was austerely Augustinian. Unlike Pelagius, twenty years previously, he denied to Demetrias any sense of "natural" nobility. Like everyone else, she was a fallen creature. Her virtues were given to her by God alone. They did not grow upward naturally from her pedigree, as Pelagius had seemed to imply.[52] But the same mighty hand of God that had placed His grace in her heart had also placed Demetrias in the midst of huge wealth. This wealth need not taint her. It did not have to be thrown away (as Melania and Pinianus had done in the hectic days of Demetrias's youth). Once her heart was detached from wealth through the grace of God, she was able to approach her fortune with a dispassionate and firmly focused sense of purpose, as if from an Archimedean leverage point outside it. She was not its owner; she was its manager.[53]

On this point, the author was unusually explicit. He did not simply exhort Demetrias to restrain herself or to learn to be more generous, as the ancient platitudes on wealth had long insisted. Rather, he presented the use of wealth as a form of relationship to God. Wealth was a gift of God that asked to be managed. Demetrias was to think of herself not as the owner of vast lands but as an estate manager, a *procurator* placed in charge of the properties of God. Carefully administered by the wealthy, the revenues of their estates were to be paid into the church on a regular basis in the name of the poor:

> They should treat their properties in no other way than if they were in charge of goods for the poor and for the useful purposes of the church. It is as if they were serving under contract as an estate-manager—*sub quadam procuratione.*[54]

Furthermore, Demetrias was not only urged to give to the poor. She was also encouraged to use her wealth to support an entire hierarchical society, held together on every level by deference.

> The first application of humility is to the good relations associated with our life in common, by which divine mercy is elicited and human society is woven together. For it does much to strengthen love when *in honor preferring one another* (*Rom.* 12:10) ... those beneath love to serve and those above them are not swollen with pride; where the poor do not hesitate to acknowledge the precedence of the rich and the rich take pleasure in treating the poor as equals. So that those at the top take no pride in the brilliance of their pedigrees, but nor do the poor rise up in the name of a shared human nature.[55]

Voluntaria et sancta collectio: A voluntary and holy collection

THE SERMONS OF POPE LEO (440–61) AND THE REDEFINITION OF THE POOR IN ROME

The same language was adopted by Pope Leo (440–61). Indeed, Leo's language overlapped so completely with that of the writer of *De vera humilitate* that many have thought that he, and not Prosper, was its author. Leo opted heavily for the Augustinian view of wealth. In his sermons, he always treated wealth as a providential fact of life. It had to be accepted on a "No questions asked" basis. How wealth had been obtained was no longer an issue for him. What mattered was how it would be used: "For although we can do nothing to create the world of nature, we can, however, put to full use the material goods that we have received through the grace of God."[56] What is revealing is the extent to which Leo used this view of wealth to foster forms of Christian practice that reached out, discreetly but unmistakably, beyond the immediate needs of the poor so as to steady the city of Rome as a whole.

In the mid-440s Leo instituted a special collection—a *collecta*—for the poor. It occurred in the summer months, which, for the average inhabitant of Rome, were hard months. They were months of heat, fever, and scarce food before the arrival of the harvest. But the church collections were also timed to coincide with the Ludi Apollinares in the Circus Maximus, which took place in early July. These were weeks of heavy giving. The page in the *Calendar of 354* that illustrates the month of July showed a great sack full of gold coins that symbolized the huge sums spent on the games at this season.[57] As we saw in the case of Symmachus, part of these *ludi* were provided by senatorial families on behalf of their sons, as praetors. On that occasion, Symmachus had spent on little Memmius in one week a sum that was equivalent to over three times the yearly revenue of the church of Rome. Leo made explicit that one purpose of the collection was to counter the dazzle of such shows. He even claimed that the practice of the *collecta* dated back to the "days of idolatry," when the charity to each other of a small and heroic band of Christians stood out in a pagan city.[58]

The collection was a feast of unity. Leo expected that all Christians would converge on their neighborhood churches to bring their free-will offerings as alms for the poor.[59] Given the fragile relations between the bishop of Rome and the clergy established in the various *tituli*—the neighborhood churches, whose near independence of the bishop had been shown on many occasions—Leo's collection represented an unparalleled flexing of papal muscle. With this collection, he intended to draw all Christian Rome together around a single holy venture. More than that, it was a feast of solidarity. The gifts were offered by an undivided people of God. The poor were urged to think of their contributions as being just as important as those of the rich.[60] Charity was not a matter of ostentatious giving, by which the rich distinguished themselves from everybody else. Leo was careful to leave room for the *mediocres*, even for the poor. It was the "resources of the multitude" that enabled this *voluntaria et sancta collectio*.[61]

But who felt the weight of this giving? Here we may be dealing with two different definitions of the poor. Alms doubtless continued to be distributed on the spot to the destitute in the different *regiones* of Rome. Indeed, in a dramatic and still mysterious incident, a Roman deacon, Titus, had been assassinated in 426 by men of the commander in chief, Felix, when distributing alms to the poor in the city. Felix was also said to have engineered the assassination of Patroclus, the bishop of Arles in the same year.[62] (A few years later, Felix and his wife, Padusia—plainly undisturbed by these events—added new mosaics to the papal cathedral at the Lateran!)[63] In the tense conditions of the 420s, bishops in key cities and almsgiving in key neighborhoods in Rome had both come to carry a political charge that they had not carried previously.

But Leo and his successors went further than their predecessors in taking control of the care of the destitute. They ensured that almsgiving was sacralized and centralized by being linked to the cult of the saints. As we saw from Paulinus of Nola's description of the memorial feast of Pammachius for his wife, the *atrium* of Saint Peter's had already become a place where alms were distributed and the poor were fed. Leo told the rich that by distributing alms in the courtyard of Saint Peter's, their granaries (those dark symbols of wealth retained) might be redeemed—and, indeed, filled with yet more grain in the coming year.[64] Major churches became points on which the poor converged. In 472 Anthemius, one of the very last emperors of Rome, hoped to escape with his life after having been deposed. In order to escape detection, he "mingled with the beggars and joined the supplicants" who had gathered around the church of Saint Chrysogonus in Trastevere.[65]

Yet Leo's "poor" were strangely faceless. His sermons gave no sense of a city filled with large crowds of the destitute. It is a significant silence. Preaching at Ravenna, Leo's contemporary Peter Chrysologus (Peter of the Golden Words) lingered with pathos on the destitute. He wished to shock. He spoke of Lazarus lying at the door of Dives, with every sore on his body an open mouth crying out to touch the heart of the rich.[66] Peter may well have had to face a higher incidence of conjunctural poverty than did Leo. He preached in a region that had been exposed to frequent dislocations, such as Attila's terrible raid into northern Italy in 452.

There are no such brutal juxtapositions in the sermons of Leo. Rather, a new form of poverty had begun to preoccupy him. This was the poverty of what later ages called the "shame-faced" poor. Such persons were impoverished noblemen and citizens, not beggars. Leo insisted that the "shame-faced" poor also should be covered by the church's care of the poor.[67] With this, Leo spread a wider net in Rome, both financially and imaginatively, than ever previously. His concern for the shame-faced poor was the thin end of the wedge. It meant that Christian discourse on the poor had changed from obsessive concentration on the afflicted "poor" as standing for the nadir of the human condition to a less dramatic but more general concern for the impoverished members of an entire city. The imaginative pendulum that had swung dramatically throughout the fourth century between seeing the poor as "others" and seeing them as "brothers" (which we sketched out in chapter 4) now came to rest in favor of the poor as "brothers"—as fellow citizens entitled to care in times of stress.

In preaching in this way, Leo followed Ambrose. His language when speaking of the poor stressed the cohesion of the urban community as a whole. It was language consonant with the lifeboat mentality we also observed in the cities of Gaul. But, with Leo, the sense of an afflicted community achieved a yet deeper resonance. Like Ambrose, he spoke of the Christian congregation in terms borrowed from the history of ancient Israel. Leo implied that the Christian congregation was a new Israel. It was notionally coextensive with the entire urban community. He also spoke of the poor no longer as creatures confined to the margins of society.[68] Rather, he spoke of them as like the poor of Israel—as self-respecting citizens down on their luck who needed justice and protection quite as much as they needed food.[69] His strong notion of compassion was not only directed toward generating pathos for the poor. It was attuned to embrace all Rome, great and small alike, in the wider community of a suffering human race.[70]

Thus, a double development took place in the last half of the fifth century. The church of Rome grew richer. The senatorial aristocracy grew poorer, mainly as a result of the loss of their overseas estates in Africa and the Balkans. These losses could not be compensated for by the development of Italian agriculture alone. As the nobility got poorer and the church grew richer, the incomes of the two groups (which had previously admitted no comparison) began to level up. At the same time, an imaginative leveling up occurred. Through the preaching of Leo, the Christian congregations were actively encouraged to view the poor as fellow members of the same urban community. Entitlement to protection and to supplies of food that had once been associated exclusively with the civic rights of the Roman People to their share in the *annona* came to be offered to all distressed Romans by the pope and his clergy.

By the time of Gregory the Great (590–604) the "great works" of the *annona* and the "small works" of Christian charity had merged. There are no grounds for the view that the popes of Rome consciously took over what remained of the *annona* system.[71] Instead, they offered their own support on their own terms. But what they offered converged on what the People of Rome had been accustomed to expect. The difference was that it was now the poor who were said to be privileged and not the *plebs*. But the level of care remained the same. In the time of Gregory I, three thousand refugee nuns in Rome received, as an annual payment, almost exactly the same amount as Roman citizens had once received, each year, from the *annona*.[72] Gregory also ensured that the true heirs to the citizens of Rome were not only the beggars of Rome but also the "shame-faced" poor— impoverished members of the nobility and other inhabitants of the city. The names of these poor were duly registered in account books kept in the Lateran palace. Their standard of living was guaranteed as honorary members of the "poor of the church."[73]

Even in the care of the poor, Rome remained distinctive: its citizens were privileged. One of the most valued privileges of the People of Rome had been to be supported by the products and labor of others. Gregory continued this tradition. He went out of his way to obtain barbarian prisoners of war as slaves. He explained to local governors and to generals who were responsible for this slave trade that he did so because the labor of barbarian slaves on the estates of the church enabled him to care for "the poor of the church" in Rome.[74] That slaves should serve the poor in a gulag situated in the *suburbium* of Rome (where slaves had always been prominent) strikes a modern reader as a wry paradox. But Gregory was too much a Roman to see anything strange about this arrangement. In Gregory's Rome, the poor of the church were recognizable avatars, if somewhat the worse for wear, of the once triumphant *populus Romanus*—a privileged citizen body destined still to be served by the nations of the barbarian world.

Massae ... iuris nostri ... a me ipso Dei favore et iuvamine fundatae:
[The church] of an estate ... owned by me ... founded by myself
with the favor and help of God

THE WEALTHY AND THEIR CHURCHES

But this is to anticipate a time when the church of Rome had finally become the greatest landowner of Italy. The terrible wars brought upon Italy by the invasion of the emperor Justinian, after 535, well and truly leveled the playing field between the wealth of the church and that of the Roman aristocracy. After those wars the church became the only great landowner left standing in Italy. At the end of the sixth century, Gregory I inherited a very different Italy from that of a century before.

Around the year 500, however, such a drastic evolution could not have been predicted. Instead we find a situation of "vibrant complexity" (to hark back to the well-chosen words of Federico Marazzi).[75] Lay landowners were still very much a presence in the city and in Italy as a whole. But they found themselves caught up in a series of conflicting relationships with the wealth of the church. Let us see how this situation had come about.

The rich of Rome and Italy had not contributed as much to the wealth of the church as conventional narratives have suggested. This wealth had grown up beside them, not because of them. Emperors, courtiers, and relatively modest persons had been the principal donors in fifth-century Rome. But once the wealth of the church was there, senatorial landowners became involved with it. They did so very much for their own reasons—as founders of churches on their own estates in the provinces and as the guardians of public order in Rome itself.

We can see this clearly in the case of one major donor from the end of the fifth century. *Flavius Valila qui et* [also known as] *Theodobius* could hardly claim to have been a scion of the Roman aristocracy. He was a military man of Gothic origin closely attached to the court. He represented the military muscle of the *Respublica* and of its successor, the barbarian kingdom of Italy under Odoacer. Yet this man of war had his seat among the senators at the Colosseum.[76] Flavius Valila/Theodobius is the best-known lay donor to the Christian church in the entire course of the fifth century.

In Rome itself, Valila left to Pope Simplicius (468–83) the splendid palace on the Esquiline of Junius Bassus, the consul of 331. This was a magnificently profane building, whose inlaid panels of multicolored marble showed Bassus in his chariot presiding over the consular games with a triumphant sweep of the arm.[77] Simplicius consecrated the palace as a church. The pope's inscription made plain that by the act of consecration, Valila's donation of the palace to the church—made "with devout mind"—now worked for the good of his soul. "Adapted to celestial matters" by becoming a church, the donation was Valila's very own treasure in heaven. The worshipers were to learn from the donation of the pious Goth how "through this series of exchanges [*commercia*] kingdoms on high can be sought out through earthly wealth."[78]

It was the language of Paulinus of Nola. But Valila may have had other, more earthly reasons to make the donation. He may have received the palace and its adjacent properties as confiscated land, passed on to him as a reward by the emperor or by Odoacer. To place a church in the middle of these properties was a way to secure them for his family and to gain the protection of the Roman church for himself in a time of violent regime change.[79]

In any case, Valila had already been a Paulinus of Nola in his own way. In 471 he placed a church on his estate, the *massa Cornutiana* (now Santa Maria in Cornuta), within sight of Hadrian's villa at Tivoli. In the words of his foundation document (copied in a medieval collection of charters), this church was built on an estate that was "ours by right," *a me ipso Dei favore et iuvamine fundatae*—"built and founded by myself, with the favor and help of God." The church was placed beside the farmhouse of the estate, with a carefully fenced row of buildings and allotment gardens for its priests. The sheer splendor of its accoutrements made it a little Cimitile. Silver plate, chalices, and incense burners for the Eucharist lay on the altar. Silver crowns and great candelabra hung over the altar and along the nave—"fifty four pounds and seven ounces of silver by the measure of the City." Worth around 650 golden *solidi*, it was as much silver as Pope Damasus had given to his own family church in Rome. But Valila also included seventy-seven different textiles, with careful instructions as to where each precious curtain should hang.

Last but not least: Valila made clear that the moment that any future bishop or priest attempted to detract in any way from this little oasis of splendor, through alienation of its precious objects or through transferring them to another church, the donation would be null and void. The entire foundation would revert to Valila or to his heirs.[80] This was the sort of rich man who, all over Italy, in the course of the fifth century had come to think of churches as part of the footprint of their own wealth and power on the land.

Pro sua devotione ... in possessionibus suis: For his [or her] loyal devotion ... on his [or her] estates

CHRISTIANITY AND AGRICULTURE IN ITALY

In order to understand the complex relation between the rich and the Christian churches we must look far beyond Rome, and most especially we must look south, to the Mezzogiorno. Here we meet churchmen and landowners alike adjusting to changes in the agrarian economy of Italy that had begun to take effect after the loss of Africa to the Vandals. It has long been possible to follow this development through papal correspondence concerning the estates of the church, that becomes increasingly abundant at the end of the fifth century and in the sixth century. But this evidence has now been placed in a concrete and vivid context by a series of archaeological discoveries that (in the words of Domenico Vera) amount to "a rediscovery of Late Antiquity in southern Italy."[81]

Apart from raids from Vandals (in the 440s and 450s), one punitive expedition by the east Roman fleet (in 508), and a violent eruption of Vesuvius (which, among other disasters, almost buried Paulinus's shrine at Cimitile sometime during 507–10), the Mezzogiorno did not experience the sinister climate of violence that had ground down the structures of the old order in Gaul and Spain. Furthermore, in Italy, unlike Gaul, two large court cities remained to be fed—Rome on the west coast and Ravenna on the Adriatic. Sicily and Apulia adjusted to provide for both cities. The grain fields of both regions expanded at this time to make good (if on a smaller scale) the loss of the African *annona*. Above all, the "burning" fields of Apulia, which stretched in a monotonous plain from the mountains of Samnium to the Adriatic, became the new Numidia of Italy—a breadbasket set in place by unrelenting toil and supervision.[82]

In the last decade, the remarkable work of Giuliano Volpe and his colleagues has shown what this new southern Italy looked like to those who owned the land. Great villas linked in varying ways to estate production and to export have been discovered in Apulia, Bruttium, and Lucania in the heel and the toe of Italy. The villas themselves varied greatly. The recently discovered villa at Faragola (Ascoli Satriano, south of Foggia) was close to the main road system. It rested against the hillside of the valley of the Carapelle, beside a road that joined the Appian Way to the Via Traiana. A dining hall laid with panels of *opus sectile* in glass and marble was dominated by a perfect *stibadium* (a half-moon dining couch) made of inlaid marbles and decorated with bas-relief panels that show a scene from a mystery cult. On hot days, the entire mosaic floor in front of the dining area could be covered with a delicious film of shimmering water ingeniously led from the neighboring river. A harbor stood beside the river to transport the products of the estate. All this was built in the later fifth century, at a time when traditional villas lay deserted all over Gaul and Spain.[83]

It was the owners of such villas who decided to plant churches on their estates. In this, Apulia did not resemble fourth-century Numidia. In Apulia the owners of the land acted first. Unlike Augustine's Africa, there seems to have been less upward pressure from the villagers themselves to have their own churches and clergy. The churches were founded by local landowners. But few if any of these founders were senatorial landowners. Rather, they were men on the spot. Many were thriving *conductores*—managers who had become rich by renting the estates of the emperor and of other absentee landlords. As with the parvenu courtiers of the Visigoths in Aquitaine (such as count Victorius), to found a church in the fifth century was a relatively inexpensive way of leaving one's mark on the countryside.

The letters of Pope Gelasius (492–96) cast a vivid light on this situation. Faced by newly established churches, Gelasius had clear views as to what the donors should do. The lay donor who wished to found a church *pro sua devotione … in possessionibus suis*—"out of loyal devotion … on his [or her] estates"—must first approach the local bishop with a petition that included a deed of donation (such as that which Flavius Valila had provided for his church outside Tivoli). It was for the bishop to consecrate the church and to provide the priest (though the bishop usually chose a candidate suggested by the owner). The free-will offerings of the faithful were to go to the priest. The founder himself or herself was left with only the right of *processio* "such as any Christian can have." This meant little more than the right to take the Eucharist in the building that he or she had provided.[84]

Yet the word *processio* itself had always implied more than that. It derived from the solemn procession of the faithful to bring gifts to the altar. It was a ceremony associated with an act of public giving by a benefactor. Such gifts were expected to receive some return in forms of recognition and of rights granted to the benefactor by a grateful people. Yet Gelasius insisted that, in church, giving made the giver in no way different from any other member of the congregation.

We can guess why Gelasius took such an austere stance toward the lay founders of churches. He was attempting to curb a vigorous conglomerate of assumptions as to the use and status of privately founded churches. Lay founders did not share the pope's views. For centuries, owners had been in the habit of maintaining a greater stake in their foundations than Gelasius allowed. Some pocketed the offerings made at the newly founded church.[85] Others expected a family foundation to serve the region as a whole. Magetia, a *spectabilis femina*—a "high-ranking" woman—near Sora (Frosinone), had wished to have a burial church in which to lay the dead of her family. Plainly she expected that this family mausoleum would function as a church for the estate as a whole. It was to be open to the entire population as a center for public Mass. Gelasius cut Magetia down to size. Only private masses for the souls of the departed could be celebrated at the tombs of her kin. In effect, as a laywoman, Magetia was denied any religious role other than the care of her own dead.[86]

Other founders had assumed, like Magetia, that their family mausoleum could also serve as a church for the neighborhood, even if this mausoleum contained the graves of non-Christian ancestors. Prayers might even be offered in the names of the departed. For these were ancient and venerable names, associated with the family who owned the land. Gelasius professed to be shocked. This could not happen "if any sense of Christianity is clear or deeply-rooted in these regions."[87]

Plainly Gelasius's "sense of Christianity" was not that of every landowner. His letters represent, on paper at least, a ringing defeat for ancient, Roman notions of religion as a matter for "friends and family." This notion of religion had been normal on the estates of the great. From time immemorial, countrymen and owners alike had been joined together by sharing an ancient cultic landscape that the owners helped orchestrate by founding shrines.[88] By contrast, Gelasius's letters were characterized by so fierce a determination to limit the rights of lay founders that we already seem to hear in them the voice of Hildebrand (Pope Gregory VII) and his fellow reformers at the time of the eleventh-century Investiture Contest.

In fact, it is the other way around. We hear Gelasius because the partisans of Hildebrand listened to him. They read him and made extracts of his letters. Most of Gelasius's letters on the state of the churches in Italy take the form of fragments. They consist of passages copied from his letters to be used as proof-texts by late eleventh-century canon lawyers whose principal concern was to defend the rights of the church against encroachment by laypersons.[89] Yet if we look more closely at those extracts, we will see that, on the ground, the interests of laypersons and the pope converged as often as they were in conflict. Let us see how this was so.

Publica disciplina: Public order

CLERICAL PRIVILEGE AND UNFREEDOM ON THE ESTATES

The foundation of churches on estates posed, immediately, the problem of who would act as priests in them. To be a clergyman—whether a priest or a deacon—was to "put on the belt of the clerical order."[90] The term echoed the old words *cingulum militiae*, the military belt that had distinguished members of the imperial bureaucracy. In using this term of the clergy, the popes' letters showed that the spread of Christianity had imported yet another layer of privileged persons into the countryside. Enterprising locals were only too happy to become members of this new privileged class through joining the clergy. By doing so, they threatened to undermine the grip of the landowners over their lives. Gelasius was told that many who became priests and deacons had been slaves. Many more had been *obnoxii*—farmers permanently tied to the estate on which they were registered as taxpayers. Clerical status freed them from these bonds. This happened at a time when the landowners of southern Italy depended on their ability to control a large pool of tied labor in order to bring in the yearly harvest on which their wealth depended.[91]

Harsh though he might be in limiting the rights of lay founders, Gelasius supported the landowners wholeheartedly when it came to controlling their own peasants. Ordination to the clergy was not to become an escape hatch for slaves and tied peasants. In 494 he told the bishops of the Mezzogiorno that

> almost everybody is complaining about the way in which here and there slaves and hereditary tied farmers are fleeing from legal dependence and from estates under the cover of taking up a religious life.

This must stop,

> lest a practice associated with the name of Christianity should seem to cause a breach in the rights of others and to subvert the *publica disciplina*—the order of society as laid down by law.... Nor should the dignity of the clerical ministry be tarnished by persons subject to such obligations.[92]

On this matter, the pope saw eye to eye with the wealthy laity. Disrupting the social order by allowing tied persons to join the clergy amounted to a pollution—a blot on the scutcheon of the Christian church. Gelasius meant what he said. The antithesis between bound and free and between those subject to hereditary obligation and those who were unencumbered free farmers had deep roots in his thought on the human condition. Like Leo, Gelasius was an Augustinian. When he learned that a bishop was propagating Pelagian ideas in Picenum, Gelasius was duly shocked. The bishop (appropriately named Seneca) had claimed that babies were free of sin. Seneca had argued that they did not need to be baptized at an early age. God had formed every human being in the womb. Seneca went on to claim that, because of this, no human being carried the taint of an original sin, inherited from Adam. All human beings had been born free. They were innocent of an inherited taint such as could only be expiated by baptism.

How wrong could bishop Seneca be! For Gelasius, obligation from the dawn of time, not freedom, was the stuff of the human condition. With rock-like certainty, the social metaphor of the great estate slid into place in Gelasius's condemnation of the views of bishop Seneca. Gelasius asserted that no human being could claim to be born free. All were born into an unfreedom inherited from Adam. All were subject to sin, as if they they were peasants bound to the land: "tied to their registered place of origin, because born into a state of servile dependence."[93]

As we saw, the Gallic writers of Provence at this time went out of their way to avoid such language. They admitted a steep degree of dependence of human beings on God. But, for writers such as Salvian and Faustus of Riez, the metaphor that made sense of this dependence had always been that of a patron approached by a destitute client. For all his misery, the client remained a free man. By contrast, Gelasius's instinctive resort to the language of slavery and hereditary obligation as the master metaphor of the human condition may give us a glimpse of the strain of social effort on which the "security of Italy" rested on the great estates of the fifth-century Mezzogiorno.

Ut quae vel pro salute vel requie animarum suarum unusquisque venerabili ecclesiae pauperum causa contulerit: Whatever somebody for the sake of his salvation and the repose of his soul will have donated ... to the venerable church on behalf of the poor

————

LAY BEQUESTS AND CLERICAL CONTROL

Though they were reassured by Gelasius and other popes on a central issue of the social order, lay landowners continued to view the clergy with unrelenting suspicion. They had no wish to surrender their wealth to an institution that failed to respect their wishes. The donation of Flavius Valila made plain the fears of every founder. They worried once their church fell into the hands of the bishop's administration, they would lose all say in what happened to it. A treasure house of family piety, as solid and as splendidly appointed as any villa, would be neglected. Its holy vessels might be appropriated by the bishop, passed on to other churches, or sold outright to raise funds.

The greatest worry concerned the misuse of land donated to the church. Nowhere was this anxiety more acute than in Rome itself. Upper-class Romans feared that land that had been given by their predecessors might be sold off by ambitious popes to finance ecclesiastical schemes for charities and for building operations. Candidates for the papacy might do worse: they might bribe supporters with promises of church lands. As a result, individual clergymen might emerge greatly enriched at the expense of their lay superiors—the senatorial donors. This was a serious matter. For the first time, it raised the issue of the balance of wealth in the city between the clergy and the *nobiles*. Until then, the pope and clergy had not counted as competitors. But this had ceased to be the case in the last decades of the fifth century.

These anxieties coincided with a regime change in northern Italy. In 476 the last Roman emperor, Romulus Augustulus, resigned. He was replaced by a barbarian strongman, Odoacer (476–93), who ruled as king of Italy. Odoacer stayed in Ravenna; Rome ceased to be an imperial residence. For this reason alone, Odoacer needed the approval of the Senate even more than had previous emperors. For the Senate was the shop window of his regime. It was only through the Senate that Odoacer could make his power felt in the ancient center of the empire. Recognition by the Senate gave his ad hoc regime a reassuringly old-fashioned look.

Furthermore, both Odoacer and his successor, Theodoric (493–526), were not Catholics. They were Arians. Religious issues among Catholics could not be resolved in their palace. As a result, the kings turned to the Senate. Here was a lay organism. Even though most of them were staunchly Catholic, senators were still dependent on the patronage of the court of Ravenna as members of the clergy were not. In effect, Odoacer and Theodoric placed the Senate between themselves and the popes. They treated the Senate as if it was the traditional caretaker of Rome. As caretaker, the Senate, and not the pope and his clergy, was given a mandate to patrol the clergy's use of wealth.[94]

The Senate soon had the opportunity to show its powers. In 483 Pope Simplicius had died without naming a successor. A contested election seemed imminent. Acting as Praetorian Prefect and as the representative of the absent king, Flavius Caecina Decius Maximus Basilius—as his name implied, a grandee of the grandees—summoned the clergy to a meeting in the mausoleum of the emperors beside Saint Peter's.[95] He and his family knew about wealth and how it should be spent at Rome. In 484 his brother Decius Marius Venantius Basilius would complete a reconstruction of the arena of the Colosseum *proprio sumptu*—out of his own pocket—as a gift to the city of Rome.[96] As a representative of the Senate, Maximus Basilius intended to teach the clergy how to use their wealth properly for the good of the city. He presented them with an ultimatum in the form of a document—a *scriptura*. No future election of a pope was to happen without prior consultation with the king and the Senate. Above all, no church lands or ornaments were to be alienated under any pretext:

> For it is unjust and equal to a sacrilege that, whatever somebody for the sake of his salvation and the peace of his soul will have donated or securely bequeathed to the venerable church on behalf of the poor should be transferred to somebody else.[97]

The language invoked in this ultimatum was old. Gifts to the church had long been defined as gifts to the poor made for the sake of the souls of the donors. But the situation in 483 was new. This was the first time that a major public debate took place on the wealth of the church. Basilius's document betrayed a new urgency. The church had become rich, but nobody, least of all the clergy, knew exactly how this wealth should be administered. No one could say for certain who actually owned the properties of the church. When we speak, often somewhat glibly, of the "wealth of the church" in the fifth century, we must realize that we are referring to what had remained a conceptual and managerial morass.[98]

Nobody had yet defined to what extent a bishop could dispose of the wealth of the church on his own initiative. Nobody agreed on how much he had to attend to the views of his colleagues and his own clergy when handling church property. Last but not least, individual donors had been given no guarantee that their wishes would continue to be respected or that family properties would not be broken up or alienated to serve the general purposes of the church.

Hence the Senate's support for the document prepared by Basilius. Not surprisingly, Basilius's proposal rankled in clerical circles. Almost twenty years later, in 502, Pope Symmachus presided over a large synod at Rome. Symmachus and his episcopal colleagues haughtily rejected the document that had been drawn up by Basilius. But they did this by taking the wind out of his sails. They incorporated Basilius's principal complaint, agreeing that the wealth of the church should be inalienable. But it was the pope—not the Senate—who would ensure that its integrity was preserved in perpetuity. The decree of their synod was to last "for as long as the doctrine of salvation of the Catholic Church, under the plan of God, will remain in place."[99]

It is the language of eternity applied to a mighty institution. Four hundred years previously, in 95 AD, a Roman citizen in distant Phrygia (west-central Turkey) had declared that his will (which provided, among other things, for an annual gift of roses to his tomb) should stand "for as long an age as the rule of the Romans shall be maintained." Four hundred years later, in 871–99, a Saxon nobleman made his gift to the church of Canterbury in Britain. The gift was to stand "as long as baptism should last and money can be raised from the land."[100]

Pope Symmachus's proud words mark the beginning of a new age. In the course of the fifth century, the wealth of the church had piled up more slowly than we might think and in the course of many contests between clergy and donors in Rome and all over Italy. But it had come to stay. In our next-to-last chapter, let us look a little more closely at how the wealth of the churches had been accumulated and mobilized throughout the Latin West. This will help us understand by what devices, both theological and practical, the wealth of the church came, by the middle to the end of the sixth century, to stand out sharply as different from the wealth of laypersons because it was wrapped in the magic of eternity.

PART V

Toward Another World

CHAPTER 28

Patrimonia pauperum: Patrimonies of the poor

Wealth and Conflict in the Churches
of the Sixth Century

Istam omnem rerum ecclesiasticarum procurationem: The whole
management of the properties of the church

FROM HIPPO TO ARLES

In the course of the fifth century, the face of western Europe changed irrevocably. This time, the revival of an imperial order, such as had followed the dislocations of the third century, did not take place. The Latin West became a post-imperial world. Regional power blocs replaced the former western empire. The wealthy suffered as the ambitious engine of enrichment driven by the needs of an imperial state was brutally dismembered. Parts of this engine survived, but it worked now on a more local level and at a lower scale of intensity. On all levels of society (and not only among the rich) a general impoverishment set in. The fourth-century age of gold became a memory. Furthermore, if we are to believe some scholars, western Europe began to feel the long-term effects of a "climatic anomaly"—the edging southward as far as the Mediterranean of a colder and more rainy climate. Meteorological changes that had taken place over Greenland (two thousand miles to the north of the territories of Rome) may have added their silent weight to the slow unraveling of the Roman agrarian landscape in the very heartlands of post-imperial Europe.[1]

Yet, despite rapid changes on many levels, strong links with the past remained. The grandchildren of persons who had been alive in the old age of Augustine, Jerome, Pelagius, and John Cassian would have lived through the final establishment of Frankish rule throughout Gaul, in around 500–520, and might even have lived to witness the ominous arrival of the east Roman war fleets of the emperor Justinian along the coasts of Africa, Sicily, and southern Italy in 533–35.

In the Christian churches of the West, some problems remained. Indeed, one of the most remarkable features of the period we will now consider (essentially the sixth century) was the dogged continuation within the Latin churches of debates inherited from a more prosperous age.

We are dealing with a phenomenon that is peculiar to the period Hervé Inglebert has aptly named *une antiquité tardive post-romaine*—"a post-Roman late antiquity."[2] Despite the disappearance of the Roman state, the cultural resources piled up in the Christian churches of the fourth and early fifth centuries continued to be deployed. The crisis of the age did not lead to discontinuity in this field. Rather, the thoughts of the golden age of the Fathers of the Latin Church (the age of Ambrose, Jerome, and Augustine with which we began this book) were brought to bear to meet new circumstances. Hence the paradoxical mingling of high thoughts and down-to-earth reality that characterizes much of the sixth century. This is not merely an accident of the sources. It is part of the character of an age. In a world where so much had changed, Christian writings devoted to major problems of faith and organization maintained an unbroken arc that spanned the seemingly vertiginous gap between the late 300s and the late 500s—joining the world of Augustine and Jerome to that of Gregory of Tours.

Not the least of these problems was a continuing uncertainty as to the exact nature of the wealth of the church. How would bishops, monks, and clergymen relate to the wealth that had come to pile up around them in the course of the fourth and fifth centuries?

To understand the nature of this situation we must return for a moment to the Hippo of the old age of Augustine. A few incidents that seemed to be of minor, quotidian importance at the time reveal the dilemmas a Christian bishop had to face.

In the spring of 411, as we have seen, the congregation of Hippo made an attempt to grab the wealth of the pious senator Pinianus by ordaining him a priest at Hippo, thereby tying him and his fortune to their city. Augustine was accused of colluding with this attempt. It was said that he wanted to increase the wealth of his church.

Augustine reacted with transparent embarrassment to this insinuation. He complained that bishops such as himself were treated as if they were like any other landowner. It was assumed that they had total control of the wealth of their church, *tamquam possessores et domini*—"as if they were landowners and lords."[3] To counter this accusation, Augustine went out of his way to explain that he merely acted as a manager of the wealth of the church of Hippo. As bishop, he was in charge of "the whole management (the *procuratio*) of the properties of the church."[4] But he did not own these properties.

Furthermore, Augustine insisted in a later letter that he undertook this "management" only on behalf of the poor: "For if we possess anything, it is not ours, but goods of the poor over which we exercise, in some way or other—*quodammodo*—a kind of manager's control."[5] This statement, too, had been prompted by an embarrassing situation. Augustine had to explain (to none other than Boniface, the ill-fated Count of Africa, whom we met in chapter 23) why the Catholic Church had grown appreciably richer through taking over the confiscated estates of its Donatist rival.

In both cases, laypersons were presented with a paradoxical notion of wealth. Their local Christian church could be wealthy. But the wealth of the bishop was not supposed to be like the wealth of any other landowner. It was wealth that was not owned but "managed." And it was managed in the name of those who could never own anything—the poor. Put bluntly: a non-owner presided over the wealth of non-persons. Ideally, the bishop was a managerial figure. He was not a landowner but a Good Steward. His position was like that of the managers of the great imperial estates (many of whom had been slaves). He did not own any of the wealth that had been entrusted to him. Altogether, the wealth of the church was a strange form of wealth. It was wealth held at a distance, by an inner hiatus that distinguished sharply between ownership and administration.[6]

Augustine had placed the weight of a lifetime behind this option. As we saw, his monastery had been founded so as to realize the ideal of a community shorn of the divisive particularity associated with private property. He had also gathered around himself an inner group of clergymen who had vowed to live as monks. These monk-clergymen were supposed to have renounced all personal ties to property.

At the very end of his life, in late 425, it became clear that this renunciation had not been understood by everyone in the radical manner that Augustine had understood it. One of Augustine's monk-clergymen, the priest Januarius, had recently died. It was revealed that he had stashed away a sum of money. He bequeathed all this money to the church of Hippo, having pointedly cut both his daughter and his son out of his will.[7]

This incident has usually been seen as a tragic moment for the old Augustine. It was "tinged with the twilight tones of the end of a long reign."[8] But this may not be the case. The incident sprang from an elementary misunderstanding as to what the wealth of the church was supposed to be. Januarius was no secretive curmudgeon. Nor did he necessarily think that he had broken Augustine's rule of poverty. What mattered for Januarius was not that he owned wealth but that he did not own "lay" wealth. He had kept his wealth strictly within the church. He had not given any of it to laypersons. Both of his children were already supported by the church: his daughter was a nun, his son was a monk. The precious sum of silver went to the church of Hippo. The money of a man of the church had passed to the church. Many of Augustine's congregation thought that nothing particularly untoward had happened and that Augustine should accept Januarius's legacy.[9]

Augustine acted to rebut this claim with remarkable fierceness. His great sermons on the affair of Januarius (*Sermons* 355 and 356) became classics. Monks referred to them, treating them as a charter for the total autonomy of monasteries. They drew the conclusion that a monastery was a self-supporting body. Its monks lived from the revenues of the properties they had handed over to the common fund and from those properties alone. For this reason, they claimed that they did not depend on the wealth of the local church. In 525 a group of monks in Byzacena, south of Carthage, used Augustine's sermons in this way to show that their monastery was independent of the bishop because it was financially independent of the local church.[10]

But Augustine was not concerned with monks pure and simple. What he had insisted on was monastic renunciation for the clergymen in his service. Compared with the ideal monks imagined by John Cassian, these clerical monks lived in a more ambiguous situation. They were not cut off from the world. They had not entered a community protected by the glacis of a real or imagined desert. Instead, they were surrounded by a dense penumbra of wealth. What would be the relation of such persons, deprived of personal wealth, to the corporate wealth of the church they served?

In his final sermon on the affair (*Sermon* 356), Augustine made plain what this situation could mean. He publicized the arrangements made by one priest in particular—Leporius. For Augustine, Leporius was the model monk-priest. He was a living example of a man who had never strayed far from wealth but who had never owned a penny of what he had handled.

Leporius had come to Hippo from war-torn northern Gaul.[11] He was a Salvian —a refugee who had ended up not at Marseilles but in Africa on the far, southern shore of the Mediterranean. He had renounced his own private wealth before Augustine came to know him. He came to Hippo technically "poor"—that is, without anything that he could call his own. There he settled down as an enterprising dealer in real estate. Untainted by private wealth, he proved to be a gifted fund-raiser. With funds raised in this way, he built a monastery, a poorhouse, and a chapel of the martyrs at Augustine's command. He had even bought a house that was rented out to provide yet further income for the church. But none of this was his.

Having itemized the many ways in which Leporius had spent the money that he had raised, Augustine then turned to the congregation to make clear that they should not even entertain the thought that anything apparently owned by Leporius was other than property owned by the church as a whole:

> Let nobody any longer say, "At the priest's house," "In front of the priest's house." ... Here's where the priest's house is. It is here [in the monastery of

the clergy], where my house is. He has no other house, except for God, who dwells everywhere.[12]

Seldom in late antiquity had the fingerprints of personal wealth been wiped off more thoroughly from the properties of the church than in this final settling of accounts between Augustine and the monk-clergy of Hippo.

Later generations continued to ponder Augustine's words. In around 500–510, Julianus Pomerius, himself a refugee from Africa and a loyal disciple of Augustine, wrote his book *On the Contemplative Life* at Arles. Under its bishop, Caesarius (502–42), Arles was one of the richest and most active sees in Gaul. Pomerius wrote to persuade admirers of the monks that it was still possible to be both a monk and an active bishop such as Caesarius.[13]

In the Gaul of the early sixth century, to reassure monks that they could be bishops meant persuading them that the wealth of the church had come to stay. It was there. The only issue was how to deal with it. Pomerius went out of his way to prove that involvement with the wealth of the church need not pollute them or detract from their spiritual life. It was possible to be both a contemplative and an administrator. The tantalizing disjuncture between the wealth of the church and the studied wealthlessness of its nominal owner, the bishop, was central to Pomerius's argument. Pomerius insisted that the wealth of the church could be administered—indeed, even increased—by persons inspired by the austere distinction between wealth and its mere "managers" delineated by the old Augustine.

Pomerius looked back on the bishops of the previous century. He praised Hilary of Arles for having greatly increased the wealth of his see.[14] He also praised Paulinus of Nola. Indeed, in the pages of Pomerius, we do not meet Paulinus the great renouncer and the flamboyant builder of the shrine of Saint Felix. We meet a very different Paulinus—a Paulinus for the sixth century: Paulinus, the canny bishop of Nola, who "did not despise the wealth of his church, but administered it with the utmost conscientiousness."[15]

Central to the argument of Pomerius was the notion that the wealth of the church was not like any other wealth. It was not personal wealth, which caused the coarse adrenalin of lordship to surge within those who owned it. It was wealth directed as if from a higher sphere by aloof "managers." Above all, it was wealth bathed in a mystical aura all its own. It was wealth piled up through innumerable transactions with the supernatural, to which all sexes and to all classes had contributed. Above all, it was wealth that was collected and administered on behalf of the poor:

For they [the bishops and clergy] should know that the goods of the church are nothing other than the fruit of vows made by the faithful, the various prices which they offer for their sins, they are the *patrimonia pauperum*—the patrimonies of the poor.[16]

"Ill defined according to the ancient laws"

GIFTS TO THE CHURCH: CHRISTIAN PIETY AND ROMAN LAW

We modern persons, who have come to take for granted the notion of the impersonal administration of wealth in corporate bodies—in churches, universities, and large companies—need to make a leap of the imagination to recapture the extent to which Pomerius's high doctrine of wealth without a *dominus* flouted the common sense of centuries. Roman law had recognized the existence of corporate bodies—of town councils, trade associations, and similar *collegia*. But Roman lawyers did little to define exactly how these bodies should act in relation to their wealth. The lawyers offered no guidelines as to who were entitled to take decisions and who could represent the corporation.[17]

The Christian churches of the fourth and fifth centuries inherited this lacuna in Roman legal thought. In 321 Constantine ruled that "every person shall have liberty to leave at his death any property that he wishes to the most holy and venerable council of the Catholic Church."[18] It was a characteristically expansive edict. It appeared, at first sight, to open the sluice gates for wealth to pour into the churches. But this did not happen. The law was plainly issued because legacies to the church had been challenged and continued to be challenged. Made close to death, legacies to the church threatened to exclude rightful heirs. As we saw in chapter 26, when we discussed the writings of Salvian of Marseille on giving to the church, the conflict between a prospective donor to the church and his own family was an ancient Roman issue that had flared up with peculiar intensity in the course of the fifth century.

But there was more to it than this. Such wills were not only unpopular. They were vulnerable by the standards of strict Roman law. In naming a "holy and venerable council" as the recipient of gifts, Christian donors named a vague entity whose legal status had not been fully established. The bishops had not done their homework. In the laws of Constantine and his successors, "the idea of a church's civil personality [was] taken for granted rather than worked out."[19]

In the centuries that followed, Roman lawyers continued to look with a cold eye on the lack of definition inherent in Constantine's ruling. They moved slowly. There was a significant time lag between the language of Christian piety and the norms of Roman law. Christians had long been encouraged to give "to the poor" and "to Christ." As we have seen, for a writer such as Pomerius, the properties of the church were all (in some way or other) gifts to the poor. But in Roman law "Christ" and the "poor" were vague terms. They were *personae incertae*— "individuals of whom a testator could form no specific concept."[20] They were to be avoided as a potential cause of litigation.

In the 430s Salvian had urged Christians to name Christ in their will.[21] But as late as 530, the east Roman lawyers of the emperor Justinian were still at work, attempting to make sense of Christian bequests "of which we have found many that seem ill-defined according to the ancient laws." A law of Justinian referred to an unnamed donor, "a person of illustrious background, well-educated in law and rhetoric," who had brought on complicated litigation through having named only "Our Lord Christ" as the beneficiary of his will. Justinian's lawyers attempted to steer such dangerously open-ended bequests toward a clear recipient— preferably the bishop of the city in which the testator had lived.[22]

Faced by the problems raised by ambiguously worded legacies, Roman lawyers instinctively chose this solution. They favored the bishop. He was singled out as the one clear representative of an otherwise ill-defined association. It was expected that gifts to the church (in whichever form they came—shares of an inheritance, an entire inheritance, legacies, or simple offerings) would be made "to So-and-So, bishop of the church of such and such a place" or "to the church of such-and-such a place, whose bishop is so-and-so."[23] As a result, bishops were not what Augustine said that they should be—mere "managers" of the wealth of others. The common sense of an entire society still bathed in Roman law made them *domini* whether they liked it or not.[24] And, as we will see, many liked it greatly.

"Nowadays … avarice has grown in the Church as it has done in the Roman empire": Bishops and Their Critics

Needless to say, not every bishop was an Augustine. But this was not simply because other bishops were less conscientious or less other-worldly. They were caught in an unresolved dilemma. Roman law made them lords while Christian sentiment wished to think of them as mere managers. Left to himself, a bishop was a lord of the wealth of the church in his own city. The only restraints placed on his initiative in using this wealth were a sense of decorum, spasmodically reinforced by the pressure of colleagues, by provincial councils, and by the invocation of previous rulings of the ancient church (in the form of the "canons" of councils, whether real or invented). These often proved to be flimsy mechanisms of control. Usually we hear of a bishop's actions when these restraints had failed. And in the late fifth and sixth centuries, we come to hear a lot. There is a good reason why this should be so.

It has been said of the constitution of the Roman empire that it was an autocracy tempered by assassination. The position of the Christian bishop in his own church was much the same. It was an autocracy frankly tempered by character assassination. The only way to check a bishop's autocratic rule over the wealth of his church was to denounce him for his misuse of that wealth.

Historians of the social and economic role of the church in late Roman society have every reason to be grateful for this situation. There is hardly any evidence for the nature of the wealth of the church and for the mechanisms of its distribution that does not come to us from denunciations of individual bishops for some abuse or other in the administration of the goods of the church.

Such denunciations occurred frequently. We'll look at just a few examples from the Latin West in this period. In 475 Pope Simplicius issued a famous ruling on the fourfold "Roman" division of the revenues of the church. He ruled that such revenues were to be divided in equal shares among the bishop, the clergy, an allotment for the upkeep of the churches, and the poor. It is a central piece of evidence for the finances of the churches of Italy at this time. Yet it is known to us only because the bishop of Aufinum (Ofena: L'Aquila) had been denounced by his clergy for keeping the last three years of revenue all for himself.[25]

We also know that the revenues of the see of Ravenna in the early sixth century amounted to 12,000 *solidi* a year. It is one of the very few figures that we have for the income of any church in the late antique period. But how do we know this? The precious statistic has only come down to us as a result of conflicts within the church of Ravenna that led to the descent of a delegation of sixty angry clergymen on Pope Felix III (526–30) in Rome. They came to claim their rights to a full "Roman" fourth of the revenues their bishop had refused to disburse. The clergy settled for that: 3,000 *solidi* (which, multiplied by four, has given historians the sum of 12,000 *solidi* per annum as the revenue of a major Italian see).[26]

These and innumerable other incidents make plain that the most vociferous and most unforgiving watchdogs of the bishops were not the laity but their own clergy. And what they watched most intently was the bishops' use of the wealth of the church. In the words of an anonymous treatise probably written in the fifth century by a fierce supporter of the rights of the clergy over against their bishop:

> Nowadays because avarice has grown in the Church as it has done in the Roman empire, individuals who take advantage of the power and influence associated with the name of bishop … reduce the entire order of deacons to their own use … while the unhappy clergyman goes begging in the streets.

The wicked bishop, apparently, had imposed a pay freeze on his priests![27]

Recognoscite dominum vestrum: Recognize your master

BISHOPS, CLERGY, AND THE WEALTH OF THE CHURCH

Though the forms it took varied from region to region, the conflict between the bishop and his clergy was a Europe-wide phenomenon. It had roots in the deep past. Ever since the third century, the role of the bishop as the undisputed leader of the Christian community in every city had never been entirely secure. What historians of the Early Church call "mono-episcopacy" was established considerably more slowly than we might think. Many urban churches of the fourth and fifth centuries remained "polyfocal" in practice. Priests and deacons were often more present to their congregations than was the distant bishop (especially if that bishop, as a public figure, was constantly absent attending councils or lobbying at the imperial court). A strong whiff of proprietary rights still lingered in many churches. In Rome congregations attended churches that were known to have been endowed by lay donors from families that may have continued to be dominant in the neighborhood. Priests and deacons might enjoy the patronage of rich and cultivated persons in a way that rendered them virtually independent of their bishop.[28] We are looking at a formula for factionalism. As far as the three-cornered conflict between the bishop, his own clergy, and their lay supporters was concerned, little had changed between the fourth and the sixth centuries.

This was particularly the case in Rome. In the time of Pope Symmachus (498–514)—whom we met at the end of the last chapter—the schism caused by the simultaneous election of Symmachus and the priest Laurentius revealed how powerful these centrifugal forces had remained. It was a memorable schism. In the words of Henry Chadwick, the conflict between Symmachus and Laurentius led to "a dreadful four years of gang warfare."[29] Leading clergymen were killed as rival factions clashed in the streets of the city.

The backdrop to this schism was a Rome that had broken up into a loose confederation of neighborhoods. It was dotted with islands where groups of fine buildings (both ecclesiastical and aristocratic) stood out in the midst of a sprawling and degraded urban landscape. These dispersed islands of well-maintained residences were the power bases of rival clergymen and their lay allies. The tenacity of the opposition to Pope Symmachus mounted by the clergy who supported Laurentius shows that a bishop's control of his own clergy could never be taken for granted.

In these situations, wealth was the key to episcopal power. Symmachus rode out the storm because he could flex the financial muscle of the wealth of the church. Loyal clergymen were said to have received threefold pay raises. The poor were looked after as seldom before. As lord of his church's wealth, Symmachus reestablished himself as lord of the churches of Rome.[30]

Rome was exceptional both for its size and for its traditions of clerical independence linked to lay patronage. Elsewhere in Italy, as in Gaul and Spain, the conflict between the bishop and his own clergy took place on a more narrow stage. It is best seen as the last playing out of a very ancient Roman style of urban politics.

As we have seen, the secret of the Roman social order in the West had been the ability of small groups to hang together at the top of local society. The *curiae*—the town councils—had played that role for centuries. But they only did so for as long as they held together. The town councils declined in the fourth and fifth centuries, not because their members sank into undifferentiated poverty but because they had fractured. An inner group of *principales* (such as those denounced by Salvian) became separate from the run-of-the-mill town councillors. The town councillors who had gathered for centuries in the "temple" of the town hall lost their sense of cohesion. Excluded and victimized by a new oligarchy of *principales* and imperial servants, town councillors had sought their fortunes elsewhere (often by entering government service), or they had turned to the protection of powerful patrons outside the city.[31]

This story is well-known and has been told often. But by the sixth century, the conflict between the town council and its leaders had come to be replicated within the Christian church. All over the West, the clergy lost out to their bishop. The bishop and his personal staff emerged as the new *principales*. The clergy took on the role of lesser town councillors. They saw themselves as the disgruntled losers in a battle with a high-handed oligarchy now centered on the bishop's palace. Bishops refused to treat their clergy as equals in much the same way as the oligarchic inner core of *principales* had browbeaten their weaker colleagues in the town councils.

The battle between the bishop and his clergy was fought in very much the same manner as the battle between different sections of the town council had been fought in previous centuries. In the late fourth century, average town councillors were accused of "hiding in the shadow of the powerful" so as to avoid their duties in the city.[32] Now, in many church councils of sixth-century Gaul, priests were denounced by their bishops for doing much the same. They lingered by preference in the "oratories and villas of the powerful" so as to keep the bishop's officials at bay and to avoid turning up to attend the bishop's ceremonies in the city.[33]

The conflict between the bishop and his own clergy did not simply replicate the infighting of the town councillors. It was exacerbated by the mechanisms of episcopal elections. Ideally, bishops were supposed to be drawn from the local clergy. But the result of this practice was that a bishop would have to live for the rest of his life with resentful colleagues whom he had defeated. Outsiders were frequently chosen so as to avoid this situation. In the fifth century, this solution goes some way toward explaining the demand in the cities of Provence for monk-bishops trained in Lérins. In sixth-century Gaul, it was more usual to choose outside candidates from distinguished "senatorial" families or from among the growing cadre of royal servants. Only prestige-full outsiders could bridle the ri-valries within the local clergy that had been unleashed by the election of their bishop.[34]

To make matters worse, disputed elections were a financial bloodbath for the local church. They were often as expensive to the rival parties (in terms of the wealth that they had to mobilize in proportion to their other outlays) as the dis-plays of "civic love" had been for those who had competed for eminence by lav-ishing shows on their city in earlier centuries.[35] Much of the money spent on these occasions went into bribes. It has been calculated that the Frankish kings gained 10,000 *solidi* a year in gifts from rival parties in contested elections.[36] This is some indication of the intensity with which the clergy of the cities pursued their feuds. In such a situation—whether he was a winner from inside or had been introduced from outside as a tiebreaker—no bishop could feel secure.

Bishops could only feel secure if they had the wealth of their church behind them. Bishops who did not act quickly to establish control of the wealth of their church frequently found themselves helpless. They had to face senior clergymen who were already firmly ensconced at the head of the administration of the properties of the church. Nothing shows this more clearly than the way in which Gregory, bishop of Tours (573–94), wrote about Sidonius Apollinaris in his *Book of Histories*. As we saw, Sidonius had become bishop of Clermont in 468 in unusual circumstances. He was ill prepared for the job. Remembered a century later, he appeared to Gregory to be a poignant figure. Gregory wrote that Sido-nius had been a former prefect, "from the very first ranks of the senators of Gaul." He was the relative by marriage of a Roman emperor. For Gregory, Sidonius was the "real thing."[37] Yet as a bishop Gregory remembered him as a pathetic figure. Two priests "took away from him all power over the estates of the church and reduced him to a pittance, with great ignominy."[38] That was how a former gran-dee appeared to an observer of the conflict-ridden churches of late sixth-century Gaul.

Only a bishop who made full use of his power as the *dominus* of the wealth of his church could hope to control his clergy. In 580 Riculf, a priest of Tours, made a bid to replace Gregory as bishop of Tours at a time when Gregory was absent and out of favor at the Frankish court. Riculf knew exactly how to conduct a cleri-cal putsch. He immediately took over the bishop's palace and made an inventory of the money he found there. Then he took over the estates of the church. He repaid his supporters with gifts and with advantageous tenancies of choice fields and vineyards. The minor clergy—usually young boys already enrolled at an early age in the service of the church—he simply flogged. *Recognoscite dominum vestrum:* "Recognize your master" was Riculf's boast.[39] Gregory portrayed Riculf as an upstart and a barbarian. But he was no such thing. He was a well-established priest and administrator of church property. He had contacts at court. He was simply doing, if high-handedly and in a hurry, what any other bishop (Gregory included) would have done to secure himself as head of his own church.

"Made rich by the devout or stripped by the faithless": Wealth and the Churches in the Sixth Century

These vivid anecdotes of small-town politics Latin Christian style do not only litter the vivid works of Gregory of Tours. They can be found in almost every other source for the sixth century. They point to a more decisive but more silent development. At some time during the late fifth and early sixth centuries, the Christian churches of the West realized that many among them had become, indeed, very rich. The weight of this development can be sensed in the nature of the sources. It is not entirely an accident that we know considerably more about the finances of the churches after the late fifth century than we know from any earlier period.

Let us take the example of the *Liber Pontificalis* (*Book of the Pontiffs*) of Rome. It was written in around 510 by a priest possibly connected with the papal administration in the Lateran at the time of Pope Symmachus. A series of biographies of the popes from Saint Peter to the early sixth century, the *Book of the Pontiffs* could have taken many forms. For this reason, the form that it did take is all the more surprising. It turned out to be a book about wealth. It is a treasure trove for historians of the late Roman economy. It contains twenty of the thirty inventories of church plate available for the entire Roman world in the period between 300 and 600.[40] It preserves some of the only evidence that we have for the revenues and distribution of church estates and for the financing of church foundations. Yet we seldom stop to think why we are treated to such unique evidence. It is because this was the work of a man who wrote at a time when issues of church wealth had played a crucial role in the conflict between the supporters of Pope Symmachus and those of the priest Laurentius.[41]

It is the same with Gregory, who became bishop of Tours in 573. Gregory finished his *Histories* in 591. The relation of Gallic society as a whole to the wealth of the church was a central theme of his narrative. He made it clear that he intended to write about the ways in which "the churches have either been made rich by the devout or stripped by the faithless."[42] Altogether, in the Latin churches of the sixth century wealth was in the air.

The awakening of the churches to great wealth was a new development. It could not have been foreseen in the fourth and early fifth centuries. Yet we often fail to realize the novelty of this situation. Certain deeply entrenched historical stereotypes stand in our way. At the risk of being brusque, it is important to remove these.

First, we must begin by making clear what we mean by speaking of "the wealth of the Church." As far as wealth was concerned, there was no such thing as "the Church" with a capital C. There was only the wealth of individual churches. Each bishop was the little lord of the wealth of his own church and of his own church only. Hence the distribution of wealth among the churches was highly stratified. It followed the contours of a steeply pitched hierarchy of cities that had been set in place in the later empire. Imperial capitals, metropolitan cities, and government centers had come to draw wealth and talent to themselves, leaving the minor cities to their fate. Most small cities shrunk; some collapsed entirely.

The wealth of the churches was distributed in the same uneven manner as was the wealth of individual cities. We find glaring contrasts between the wealth of individual churches in the Latin West.[43] Rich cities had rich churches. In Italy the churches of Rome and Ravenna had revenues of 26,000 and 12,000 *solidi*, respectively. They towered above their neighbors. By contrast, in central Italy in the shadow of Rome, the churches of the little towns were dirt poor. In Ferentis (Ferento, Viterbo) the bishop had only one vineyard with which to support himself and pay the expenses of his church. In Aquinum (Aquino, Frosinone) the dying bishop foretold the future of his see in around 540. It was not a rosy future. The next bishop would be a former provider of donkeys at the local roadhouse. His successor would be a fuller. After that, there would be no more bishops. The see would vanish, ground down (as so many of the little cities of Italy were ground down in the 540s and 550s) by plague and war.[44]

The second stereotype that must be avoided is the assumption that the rise to wealth of the Christian churches was fore-ordained. Many accounts of this period assume that the wealth of the Church (very much with a capital C) was an inevitable consequence of the conversion of Constantine. In reality, as we have seen, Constantine did little to place the leaders of the Christian churches on the high ground of Roman society. He assumed that this high ground would remain occupied by others. For many churches the road to wealth was hesitant and surprisingly spasmodic. In the fourth and fifth centuries, different regions drew on very different constituencies of donors. As a whole, bishops tended to rely less on wide acres and more on the legal and fiscal privileges granted to them by Christian emperors. They did not feel that they could compete on their own turf with great landowners and successful courtiers. Up to the end of the empire, even the most prosperous churches of the West still lay in the shadow of massive complexes of lay wealth. It was only the unexpected collapse of the great lay fortunes in the course of the fifth century that left the Christian bishops standing, for the first time, as major landowners in every locality.[45]

The third stereotype has led us to suppose that the wealth of many churches grew because they inherited the wealth of the secular aristocracy.[46] It is asserted that large numbers of senators became bishops and clergymen. They brought their wealth with them. The "aristocratization" of the church is held to be the one truly major development of Latin Christianity as a whole from the fifth century onward. This view rests on a misunderstanding. It extends to all regions of the West conditions that were peculiar to certain enclaves of senatorial power in Gaul. Patient work on the personnel of the Christian churches in other regions has shown that an aristocratization of the church did not happen in Italy and in many other parts of Gaul, Spain, and Africa.[47]

Even in Gaul, aristocratic dominance in the churches was less widespread and less deeply rooted than many scholars assert. Martin Heinzelmann has claimed that aristocratic dominance had "distant roots in the state of Constantine and had been firmly established in Gaul since the second half of the fifth century."[48] But this may not be the case. The work of Heinzelmann has been of inestimable value in pointing to the elements of continuity between the ruling elites of Gaul in Roman and post-Roman times. But it is less certain that the continuity of Roman aristocratic values and of aristocratic styles of dominance to which Heinzelmann drew our attention led the bishops inexorably to a position of unchallenged wealth and power in Gallic society. Still less did it lead to the formation of what Heinzelmann has called a *Bischofsherrschaft*—a "bishop's lordship" over the cities of southern Gaul and elsewhere.[49] The tendency to exaggerate the density of the senatorial presence in the churches has caused us to imagine a situation where bishops of Roman noble background came to rule virtually autonomous city-states. We even assume that Gregory of Tours wrote his *Histories* and his *Books of Miracles* in order to provide an ideology for this supposed bishop's lordship.[50]

But this is not the case. In reality, the bishop's position in the cities of Gaul was considerably more fragile than the image of a solid bishop's lordship suggests. By the last decades of the sixth century (that is, when Gregory was writing), what dominance the senatorial families had once enjoyed in the churches of Gaul was fast becoming out-of-date. A new aristocracy (partly Roman and partly barbarian) had formed around the courts of the Frankish kings. Its representatives were quite prepared to push aside honored relics of an earlier age.[51] Senatorial families lost their influence. They became poorer. This meant that there was little or no old money left for the churches of Gaul to fall back on as a source of endowments.

Last but not least, we cannot assume that the Christian clergy possessed failsafe mechanisms for the accumulation of wealth. We must reject the romantic stereotype that has presented the Catholic Church as rising ever higher on a flood of pious donations.[52] Nor can we adopt the mirror image of this devout imagining—the image of a church that cynically set out in quest of legacies. There is, for instance, no support for the view that Christianity altered patterns of marriage (by increasing prohibitions on marriage between cousins) in such a way as to produce a surplus of unmarried or unmarriageable persons whose inheritances would go to the church.[53]

In fact, as the sermons of Augustine and the tracts of Salvian make plain, late Roman Christians were not necessarily great givers to the church. And even when they gave, their gifts were frequently challenged—by kinsfolk, by fiscal agents, and by other interested parties. This situation did not change in the sixth century. There were plenty of Roman lawyers in Frankish Gaul and elsewhere who were expert in "breaking" testaments by finding reasons to have bequests to the church declared invalid.[54] We must never forget the sheer secularity of the post-imperial barbarian kingdoms. They were the heirs of an empire that (to the great horror of Salvian, as we have seen) had remained resolutely untouched by Christian values in its day-to-day handling of property matters and taxation.

To take one well-known example: King Chilperic of Neustria (561–84) still upheld this unabashed secular tradition. He was Gregory's bête noir. Gregory called him "the Herod of our times."[55] He recorded with evident disapproval the fact that, as late as 577, Chilperic had built amphitheaters at Soissons and Paris.[56] Above all, Chilperic was "assiduously devoted to the breaking of wills in favor of the churches."[57] He also resented the fiscal privileges of bishops. He would frequently complain: "Behold, our fisc has remained poor and our riches are passed over to the churches."[58] This remark has been cited constantly by historians of the Frankish kingdoms. But there was nothing new about Chilperic. Far from registering the king's reaction to a novel crisis brought about by the imbalance between a grossly wealthy church and an impoverished Merovingian state, Chilperic's remark merely showed that he was a vigilant ruler who took the interests of the fisc—the revenue office—seriously. His like had been around in Gaul since the days of the tight-fisted and effective emperor Valentinian I.[59] Such persons acted as a constant brake on the expansion of church property.

Altogether, gifts to the church were not always productive of wealth. Many were legally vulnerable. Many donations consisted of widely scattered properties that were not always of high quality. They included tracts of underpopulated land, which appear to have become more common in an agrarian world overshadowed by recurrent violence and, perhaps, by climatic anomaly. Or they were awkwardly placed plots that were not worth fighting over with one's kinsfolk or neighbors. They could be handed over without regret to the church. In this situation, the frequent addition of properties did not automatically add up to growth.[60]

We must remember that corporate wealth, in itself, had never been a formula for economic success in the ancient world. The fate of the town councils in the fourth and fifth centuries showed this clearly. The towns owned extensive properties. But, as Gilles Bransbourg has shown in a brilliant recent article, these properties were notoriously mismanaged. They seriously underperformed in producing revenue and were regularly pillaged by those who were supposed to administer them.[61] There was no reason why the lands of the church should not have gone the same way.

The lesson of the later empire had been that corporate bodies and their lands were only safe when protected by imperial privileges. Dependence on exemptions granted by the state lasted into post-imperial times. The clergy knew, for instance, that those who worked on imperial estates had claimed personal immunities from corvée labor and similar burdens. This was a privilege many churches went out of their way to obtain for their own lands. By the sixth century, the lands associated with major shrines—such as the lands of Saint Martin around Tours—were supposed to enjoy such exemptions. Passing armies could not requisition goods and labor from the peasants who worked on them. In this manner, the exemptions formerly associated with the "divine household" of the emperor were now claimed by the "household of God"—the church. They were now granted by kings.[62] Long after the empire had vanished, fiscal privileges inherited from imperial times and renewed by local kings remained crucial to the social position of the churches. Landed wealth, in and of itself, was not enough.

Erat strenuus in labore, ecclesias erigere, domos componere: He was
strenuously active, setting up churches, organizing estates

———

THE RISE OF THE MANAGERIAL BISHOP

Yet none of these advantages could be taken for granted. They had to be fought for. What the situation demanded was a bishop who was prepared to take the offensive. First of all, he had to have skilled lawyers at his disposal in order to hold onto what he received. We can see this happening all over Europe. From the mid-fifth century onward, ecclesiastical *defensores*—lawyers skilled in defending the interests of the church—make their appearance in ever greater numbers. They emerged as the right-hand men of the bishops. By the time of Pope Gelasius (492–96), the *defensores* of the church of Rome had come to be treated as members of the clergy.[63] Having secured his lands by means of such lawyers against the lawyers employed by angry family members, against fiscal agents, and against rapacious neighbors, the bishop then let loose upon his lands a team of administrators who were devoted to making the best out of what properties the local church had been able to retain. Hence the importance of the emergence of a new figure in the landscape of wealth—the rise of what may best be called "the managerial bishop."

To be a managerial bishop was not for everyone. In 558–59, Pope Pelagius I (556–61) wrote that the bishop of Narni should resign. He was far too nice for the job:

> For the gentleness which goes with such inborn simplicity as his cannot govern the patrimony of the church. He cannot stand up to the city councilors in matters of taxation, nor can he get himself involved in the troublesome business of hounding those who retain ecclesiastical properties.[64]

Pelagius himself knew only too well what qualities were needed; he displayed them himself. Writing in around 560 to Julianus, bishop of Cingulum (Cingoli: Macerata), about the workforce on the estates of the Roman church, he added (possibly with his own hand):

> As for those peasants who could take out leases or become tenants, if you let go of a single hair of their heads, there will be no way in which you will be able to regain my good favor.[65]

Such bishops are better documented in Italy from the lively correspondence of the popes. But they were also important in Gaul and Spain. Gregory of Tours admired just such qualities in his maternal uncle, Nicetius, who was bishop of Lyons from 552 to 573: "He was a great almsgiver and strenuously active. He was most diligently engaged in setting up churches, organizing estates, sowing fields and digging and trenching vineyards."[66]

There were many bishops and clergymen like him in Gaul. A sixth-century letter adressed an archdeacon of Metz: "I salute Mactaric the archdeacon—a man who pants with enthusiasm for the re-establishment of the church and is always on the watch out for its material advantages."[67] Even the great north Frankish politician duke Chrodinus funded his gifts to the church by model farming: "For he was often at work, setting up estates from scratch, planting vines, building farm houses, reclaiming land."[68]

The success of managerial bishops showed that one did not have to be a former aristocrat to be an effective guardian of the church's wealth. It was not that aristocrats were innocent of estate management. But when it came to increasing the wealth of the church, the skills of a government clerk proved just as effective as was an aristocrat's command of the classics and long pedigree. The need for efficient administrators ensured that the clergy remained a *carrière ouverte aux talents*. Epiphanius, bishop of Pavia (466–96), had been a mere *ingenuus*, a freeborn citizen of Pavia. Enrolled in the church, he started learning shorthand at an early age. By the 460s he was a subdeacon, conducting litigation on behalf of the church among the farmers of the Po valley. Epiphanius's biographer, Ennodius, came from a noble family of southern Gaul. He presented his hero as the darling of the nobility. But Epiphanius himself was not a nobleman. He had not come in from the top as an aristocrat might have done. He had risen from relatively humble origins as a bureaucrat in the service of his church.[69]

For all his nostalgia for the senatorial families of earlier days, Gregory of Tours was very much the child of the new age of the managerial bishop. He was the first boy in his family to grow up from childhood as a member of the clergy. He may even have learned shorthand as a boy, as a preparation for administrative duties.[70] As Martin Heinzelmann has made clear, he took his senatorial background very much for granted. What he wished to be was not a senator but a man of the church.[71] He was a tenacious upholder of canon law procedures.[72] We would not have been able to read in the works of Gregory so many vivid tales of rancor, treachery, and egotism among the clergy of Gaul if it were not for the fact that Gregory regarded such actions as breaches of a church law to which he was deeply committed. He liked a bishop to be *strenuus in labore*, an active and no-nonsense administrator, loyal to the laws of the church. He even noted with a certain approval that the last act of bishop Praetextatus of Rouen, when mortally wounded in 585 from a dagger thrust delivered by an assassin in the pay of Queen Fredegund, was "to put in order his *domus*." Propped up in bed, he continued to organize the administrative staff gathered in his palace.[73]

Patrocinium immortalis ecclesiae: The patronage of the undying church

INSTITUTIONAL CONTINUITY AND CONTROL OF THE PEASANTRY

To emphasize the relative novelty of the figure of the managerial bishop is not to claim that ecclesiastical landownership was in any way qualitatively different from that of the lay world, either in the gentleness and honesty of its day-to-day management or in its economic success.[74] Both types of property—lay and ecclesiastical—attempted in their high-handed manner to make the best they could of difficult times. Both faced recurrent warfare that threatened to scatter their labor force. Many peasants were taken captive. Many more, one may suspect, took advantage of the momentary breakdown of law and order to run away from their lords.[75] Both groups—lay and clerical alike—staggered through a possible downturn in the weather. The letters of the popes show the same administrative practices and the same determination to control the land and those who worked on it as was shown by great secular landowners. The correspondence of

Gregory I reveals forms of estate management that are richly documented from the papyri of similar great landowners in sixth-century Egypt.[76]

But the estates of the church did have time on their side. Given to God and the poor, the wealth of the church was deemed to be eternal. And so was the supervision exercised by the administrators of the church. This is shown very clearly in the language of church councils when they touched on the charged issue of the fate of freed slaves. For former slaves the bishops offered both good news and bad news. The bishops gathered at the council of Mâcon in 585 declared that slaves who had been manumitted on the estates of the church (or who had been given as freedmen to the church) could not be reenslaved. They were protected by the "patronage of the undying church."[77] But this did not mean that they were freed from all obligations. Patronage came with a cost. Freedmen merely changed from slaves into servants. The old Roman law had insisted that freed slaves should continue to render *obsequiuum*—personal service—to their masters. This law was maintained with particular vigor in the church.[78] In the words of the fourth council of Toledo (in 633 AD), the descendants of all slaves freed by the church were expected to continue to owe "service and obedience" to the church. They did this "because the church never dies."[79]

In a society where wealth depended on the annual mobilization of labor to bring in the fruits of the land, the ability to control persons was decisive. It was quite as important as the ownership of extensive lands. By offering protection to freedmen from reenslavement in return for insisting on their continued obligations as servants of the church, the bishops of Gaul and Spain gave their weight to a more widespread development. This was the emergence of estates worked by a closely supervised labor force made up of slaves and semi-servile peasants.[80] In the late sixth and seventh centuries, work based on tight control over manpower, and not the collection of rent from widely scattered holdings (as had been the case in the fourth century), was what the powerful needed in order to generate their wealth. By insisting on their perpetual rights over freedmen and over other forms of tied labor, the administrators of the estates of the church pointed the way toward a general movement to reassert and tighten control over those who worked the land.

The strenuous bishops admired by Gregory of Tours had the future before them. In collaboration with the Frankish kings, the newly formed nobility of northern Gaul reversed the effects of the dislocation of the fifth century. Far from continuing indefinitely into an ever deeper spiral of disorder (as we sometimes imagine when talking of "Dark Age" Gaul), the nobles and bishops of the age of Gregory of Tours brought to a close the "Time of Troubles" associated with the breakdown of the Roman empire in the course of the fifth century. Having regained control of their peasants, the great landowners of the Frankish kingdoms (ecclesiastical and lay alike) came into greater wealth than did the aristocracy of any other region in the West. They emerged in the seventh century as "the first truly medieval nobilities of Europe."[81] They did this partly by sharing in the managerial skills deployed by the bishops as guardians of the wealth of the "undying church."

An Age of Light: Building in Gaul and Italy

This development only got under way at the end of the sixth century. It did not happen everywhere. We can see this if we look at ecclesiastical building in different regions. Here, signs of regression were evident all over the West, with the possible exception of Africa.[82] It is usually stated that in the sixth century southern Gaul came to be covered with a white robe of churches due to the wealth "of that Gallo-Roman aristocracy, regenerated by Christianity."[83] But, in reality, the building record of the cities of southern Gaul shows a notable slowing of pace. Bishop Rusticus's basilica at Narbonne had taken four years to complete in 445. Bishop Namatius's impressive basilica at Clermont, built in the 460s, took twelve years. It took Gregory seventeen years to complete the repair of his own cathedral in Tours; and its walls were covered with frescoes, not precious mosaics.[84] The greatest churches in Gaul were not those built by the bishops. They were built by members of the Frankish royal family.[85]

When Venantius Fortunatus, the poet from northern Italy, came to Gaul in 566–67, he was surrounded by bishops who expected their churches to be praised. He presented each such church as a towering shrine, with golden ceilings and inner domes in which "wandering light is caught and blazes with radiance without a sun."[86] But the judgment of the archaeologist is somewhat more harsh. Speaking of the excavation of the church dedicated to Saint Mary in Bordeaux, for which Venantius praised bishop Leontius, the authors of the *Topographie chrétienne ... de la Gaule* remark that "the modest proportions of the construction that has been revealed barely agrees with the emphatic tones of Venantius' poem."[87]

It is to sixth-century Italy that we should turn to find real wealth and skill deployed in the building of churches. The classic monuments of sixth-century Italy are the well-known churches of Ravenna. But the splendid churches of Ravenna were the product of unique conditions created by a major government center. A changer of gold—Julianus Argentarius—spent 36,000 *solidi* on the now famous church of San Vitale. Along with his son, Julianus spent at least 60,000 *solidi* in all on San Vitale and on other churches in Ravenna. He was not a great landowner. Rather, he offered crucial financial services to the aristocracy and the state.[88]

For this reason, the foundations at Ravenna are somewhat unrepresentative. If we want to appreciate what the new style of managerial bishop could do in an

Italian city that was not a government capital, we should look to the south, to Canusium (Canosa di Puglia), on the Appian Way that led to Bari and to Brindisi. At Canusium, bishop Sabinus (531–542/552) remodeled the entire city so as to place the bishop's stamp upon it.[89] Above the former pagan shrine of Minerva he placed a daring building, made up of four great conch-like apses arranged in a square.[90] He expanded the episcopal center at San Pietro, drawing water from an ancient aqueduct in order to feed a fountain near a large baptistery.[91] Another center at another corner of the city (Piano di San Giovanni) was also expanded.[92]

Sabinus even had his own brick factory. Brick stamps that bear his name show that Sabinus left his mark on the church of the neighboring coastal port of Barletta.[93] Nothing like this was happening in distant Gaul. And yet Sabinus was not an aristocrat but a bishop who knew how to get the most out of the wealth of his church. On one occasion, he narrowly avoided being poisoned by his own archdeacon. This, in itself, was a tribute to an active man. Sabinus knew how to set his administrators to work so as to create a see that a fellow administrator, his archdeacon, was (quite literally) prepared to kill for.[94]

Not all of this building can be ascribed solely to economic success. The churches were also triumphs of skill. Looking at the sixth-century churches of Italy, one is struck by the ingenuity with which bishops adjusted to harsher times. The churches they built or repaired show that, in the West, the days of vast basilicas had passed. Instead, churches were small but magical places, such as Venantius Fortunatus had praised in Gaul. Light seemed to be trapped in them. The aim was to secure a play of light on mosaic. The light itself was made to fall from unexpected angles. The ever-changing shimmer of reflecting surfaces infused cramped spaces with a sense of immensity. In around 510 the sanctuary that contained the grave of Saint Felix at Cimitile was rebuilt. It still stands adjacent to the ruins of the great basilica Paulinus of Nola had built a century before. The new sanctuary was smaller than its predecessor, but it was built with such skill and elegance that it appears as a world in itself, filled with a mysterious radiance: "A light now opens on to wide spaces."[95] Within one century, at Cimitile as elsewhere, we have passed from a massive age of gold to a more economical but no less magical age of light.

Nothing illustrates this change more effectively than the remarkable study by Ann Terry and Henry Maguire on the mosaics of the basilica rebuilt in 543 by bishop Euphrasius of Poreč (former Parenzo in Istria, Croatia). Their patient work has revealed the extraordinary skill shown by the mosaic artists who worked on the building. This was a large building by sixth-century standards. But this fact makes the economy of means employed by bishop Euphrasius all the more impressive. The artists set about their task with "both skill and frugality."[96] They were sparing in their use of the most precious types of mosaic pieces. They used these to produce an enormous variation of hues around central figures. They used gold "as a wild card … [to] achieve a rippling, iridescent shimmer." Yet this gold was prudently mingled with plain, cheap stones so as to achieve maximum effect for the least outlay.[97] Patiently observing every tilt of the mosaic chips and the mixture of precious and ordinary materials in the overall decoration of the building, Terry and Maguire have taken us as far as we moderns can go to enter the imaginative world conjured up in the poems of Venantius Fortunatus. We are in smaller buildings than before, but they have been endowed, through the unsurpassed skills of craftsmen, with what the great basilicas of earlier, more prosperous times could not achieve: "the apparent power to generate sacred light."[98]

Furthermore, it is in such buildings that we still can look into the eyes of the bishops who commissioned them. Euphrasius at Poreč, Ecclesius and Maximianus in San Vitale at Ravenna stand out for the robust realism with which they were represented. With half-shaven chins, furrowed brows, and great, gray eyes, they stand out from the ethereal, idealized figures of saints and angels with whom they mingle.[99] These were manager-bishops who knew how to bring glory to the churches of the sixth-century West.

CHAPTER 29

Servator fidei, patriaeque semper amator: Guardian of the faith, and always lover of [his] homeland

Wealth and Piety in the Sixth Century

The Bishop and His City: Pastoral Power

It is a thrill for a historian of the west Roman empire in its last days to arrive (through rooms devoted to a clutter of Victorian chinaware) at the small exhibit of early medieval tombstones in the Museum of the Carmarthenshire Antiquarian Society in southwest Wales. The crude inscriptions carved in local sandstone speak of a region in western Britain that was fast losing its Roman face. One local figure, named Voteporix, still bore the Roman military title of *protector*. But his name was also carved in Irish ogham script on one side of his tall memorial stone. He was a leader in a post-Roman society that looked across the Irish sea rather than to continental Europe. In the midst of such monuments to early Welsh and Irish warriors, it is a surprise to find broken portions of a smaller square stone, whose clumsy lettering and erratic spelling reveal on closer inspection a carefully composed Latin inscription: "Here lies Paulinus *servatur fidaei patrieq[ue] semper amator* guardian of the faith and always a lover of his home land."[1]

Paulinus may well have been a mid-sixth-century bishop in an area (near Caio, Carmarthen) that still bears his name—Pant-y-Polion: "Vale of Paulinus." Paulinus was praised as "always a lover of his *patria*"—his homeland. It was a phrase that was also used across the sea in Gaul. Venantius Fortunatus, the Italian poet and friend of Gregory of Tours, used it frequently in poems in praise of the bishops of the cities of Gaul. Paulinus of Pant-y-Polion and the bishops addressed by Venantius Fortunatus were almost exact contemporaries. Fortunatus honored his patrons with phrases such as *Decus Patriae*, "Ornament of his Homeland," *Tutor Patriae*, "Guardian of his Homeland," and *Urbis Amator*, "Lover of the City."[2] The message was plain. If a leading Roman was to love anything, it was above all his *patria*—his hometown—which was supposed to claim his love. The inscrip-

503

tion of Paulinus in distant Wales shows that as late as the mid-sixth century the Christian bishop was expected to continue this deep-rooted Roman love for a specific community.

Those who praised bishop Paulinus were the heirs of a long tradition. Two centuries before, the title *amator patriae* had been used in faraway Lepcis Magna (Libya) on the southern shore of the Mediterranean. It was a common phrase, with long roots in the ancient world.[3] For instance, it had been used in around 300 to praise Porphyrius, a rich citizen of Lepcis Magna. Porphyrius had shown himself to be a "lover of the city and of his fellow-citizens." He had provided four live elephants for the circus games. "The most splendid town council" of Lepcis Magna had repaid his gesture by literally putting him on a pedestal. A statue that showed him driving a two-horse chariot was set up in the city's market upon a massive base marked twice over with his name—Porphyrius.[4]

Paulinus of Pant-y-Polion and the Gallic bishops praised by Venantius Fortunatus no longer provided elephants in order to prove their love for the community. The change in what they were expected to provide sums up the turning of an age. But what, exactly, had changed? One aspect of the change is obvious: Paulinus was also praised as a *servator fidei*, a "guardian of the faith." He was a religious leader. What is less obvious is the specific nature of the power that came from such leadership. As a Christian bishop, he wielded a "pastoral" power. It is worthwhile to linger a little on the peculiarity of that kind of power, which had come to the fore in Roman society with the spread of Christianity in the fourth, fifth, and sixth centuries.

In a series of lectures to the Collège de France in 1977–78 (which have only recently been published), the French philosopher Michel Foucault drew attention to the oddity and to the long destiny in European thought of the notion of "pastoral" power. It had deep roots in the ancient Near East and in Early Christian discourse. It was "absolutely specific and different from political power" as it had usually been conceived in the Greco-Roman world.[5] It was a power that was thought of as more than usually insistent, wide-ranging, and absorptive. It was "directed to all and each" member of a flock of believers.[6] The bishop was supposed to love the members of his flock. He loved each one of them equally. And he loved them all—up to the very edge of the human community, where (as we have often had occasion to see) the poor gathered like a black band on the far horizon, marking the extreme edges of society.

Indeed, the bishop's pastoral love for his flock was no more than a specific, localized manifestation of the inexhaustible love of God Himself for all humankind.[7] Even in his own *patria*, the bishop's love was not cramped by civic boundaries: it extended to all classes and it spilled over in such a way as to erase (or, at least, in practice, to erode) the primary distinction between townsfolk and the people of the countryside. Porphyrius, by contrast, like any other ancient civic benefactor, did not have to stretch his love so far. It was enough for him to love only the city of Lepcis Magna and, within Lepcis Magna itself, only the clearly defined core of the city, which consisted of his fellow citizens.

More important still, pastoral power was unique in one other respect. To use Foucault's words, it was a form of power shorn of "all those disturbing features that make men tremble before the power of kings."[8] The ideal relation of a bishop to his flock was that of a father to his children and of a shepherd coaxing his sheep. He was supposed to be bound by innumerable strands of fellow-feeling to all members of his congregation, like a head to a vast body.

Sixth-century persons did not need to be reminded by an alert French philosopher of these peculiar aspects of the power ascribed to their bishops. One need only turn to the poems of Venantius Fortunatus to be made aware of this. Venantius described bishop Leontius of Bordeaux (a hardy relic of the ancien regime, complete with a senatorial pedigree that may have reached back to the family of Paulinus of Nola) as "second to none in nobility." But he then went on to describe Leontius's relations to his congregation in Bordeaux in purely Christian, pastoral terms. He was their father, not their lord:

> One would say that he had begotten this people as their father. For he admonished them in so gentle a voice that you would think that he was speaking to parts of his own body.[9]

In reality, we know that the Christian churches in east and west alike had produced their fair share of bishops who were thugs, would-be warriors, and lordly rulers, just as the administrators of the wealth of the church included its fair share of misers, land grabbers, and petty tyrants. But these were treated as exceptions. For a bishop to flaunt any power other than "soft" pastoral power of the sort Venantius praised in bishop Leontius of Bordeaux was to destroy the basis of his legitimacy. By the middle of the sixth century, the bishop and his clergy had found a niche for themselves by exercising just such soft power— power that was pointedly not normal power—in the heart of every Christian city of the Roman and post-Roman world.

The division between church and state had been unknown in the classical world. It emerged only slowly in late antiquity and in very different ways in different regions. It was a division that grew from a remarkable polarization of the social imagination, by which nonviolent pastoral power was pitted against mere "worldly" power. It was a development which, in the year 300, had been unimaginable to persons such as Porphyrius as it was to the overwhelming majority of the population of the Roman world who were not yet Christian. How was this strange polarity between pastoral and worldly power expressed throughout the sixth-century West, and what was the relation (both real and imagined) between this power and the new wealth of the church?

Necatores pauperum: Murderers of the Poor

POVERTY AND THE SACRED

In the first place, we should not take for granted that the nonviolent pastoral power of the bishops went unchallenged in the cities of the sixth century. Still less can we claim that this power had morphed effortlessly into another, hybrid form of power in which spiritual and worldly power were joined in the person of bishops who acted as the heads of what have been called *Bischofsherrschaften*—bishops' lordships.

In fact, lay power had by no means withered away in the sixth-century West. If we think that this happened, it is because of the peculiar quality of our sources for the period. The literature of the age was overwhelmingly clerical and mainly hagiographic. Like a photographic plate, which privileges blue tones over red, a literature devoted to the deeds of saints and bishops did not register certain colors as clearly as others. The vivid blues of a bishop's activities stand out sharply, while the great red mass of lay life against which these deeds were set remains subdued— much as, in astronomers' photographs of the constellation of Orion, the vivid blue of a dwarf star tends to swamp the prodigious red globe of Betelgeuse.[10]

But if we look carefully at a city such as Tours, we find that a bishop such as Gregory of Tours had to deal constantly with forceful representatives of worldly power over whose activities he had far less control than he wished. The fiscal agents of the Frankish kings remained as aggressive and as conscious of their rights as had been the agents of any Roman emperor in the fourth century. As in earlier times, the local lay elites fought each other over the distribution of taxes. This involved recourse to tax registers over which Gregory, as a mere bishop, had no control.[11] Above all, it was the count (the representative of the king) and not the bishop who led the militias of the cities out to war. War was a serious matter in a city such as Tours whose geographical position (as a place of transit between northern and southern Gaul, and between the Rhone valley and the Atlantic) placed it at the center of disputes between rival Frankish rulers. In the crisp words of Simon Loseby, a *Bischofsherrschaft* without a *Heer*—a bishop's lordship without command of an army—amounted to little.[12] In a world where worldly power had by no means backed off to leave the bishop in undisputed control of the city, soft, pastoral power was what the bishop had and soft power only.

The peculiar nature of the wealth of the church played a crucial role in the exercise of this distinctive form of power. Obviously, the wealth of the church provided the bishop with financial muscle. In many cities, the bishop's landed wealth had finally made him the equal of any other landowner. The bishop's role in local decision making derived from his position as one of the richest figures in the region. It did not derive from any formal grant to the bishop of powers that had once been wielded by lay officials. The bishop did not succeed the lay *defensor* of the cities (the small-claims judge and legal representative set in place in many cities in the fourth century).[13] Nor was the bishop made an official head of the town council. Rather, he was co-opted into the town council on the strength of his wealth and persuasive abilities.[14] It was a powerful position, but it was not a position that was institutionally formalized. It was his to lose. And the bishop would lose it if he did not make skillful use of the prestige that came from what was unique about him—his pastoral power.

Given this situation, the bishop's standing in the community depended on his ability to draw on a form of wealth that was carefully constructed as being quite as distinctive as was his own unique power as a pastor. For just as the bishop's power took the strange form of power without power, so the wealth of the church took the equally strange form of wealth without wealth. It was nominally "the wealth of the poor." It was wealth held in trust for non-persons. It was through basing themselves on counterfactual power joined to counterfactual wealth that the bishops and clergy of the sixth century rose to prominence in a society where worldly, lay power had remained as solid and abrasive as ever before.

Let us, therefore, linger a little on the implications of the cluster of expectations that gathered around the wealth of the church and its relation to the care of the poor. What exactly did contemporaries mean when they spoke of the estates of the church as the "patrimonies of the poor"? In this, we are dealing with the construction of a model of society that carried a considerable imaginative charge, derived from very real preoccupations in society at large. These preoccupations were shared by both those who administered the wealth of the church and those who contributed to that wealth as donors. In the long run, it had palpable effects, on the ground, for the deployment of wealth by the bishops. For it soaked the routine administration of the wealth of the church with a pathos and a sense of the untouchable that was lacking in any form of lay landownership.

In the first place, the notion that the wealth of the church was the wealth of the poor was mobilized to ensure that the administration of church lands was kept clean. To disperse, embezzle, or misuse these properties was to rob the innumerable, helpless persons for whom this wealth was said to be held in trust. Appeals to the rights of the poor brought to bear a heavy language of disapprobation on erring bishops and clergymen. The very last *Senatus consultum* of which we know was issued by the Senate of Rome in 532. It was inscribed on marble plaques that were set up in the great courtyard of Saint Peter's. It concerned church property. It warned competing candidates in an upcoming papal election that they should not mortgage the lands of the church for funds to support their election campaigns: "In such a way the properties of the poor are burdened with debt so as to pay for election promises."[15] In the opinion of the Senate of Rome, to rob the poor in this manner was unpardonable.

But the appeal to the notion of the poor as the victims par excellence of the misuse and appropriation of church wealth derived its power from yet wider concerns. In the canons of the councils of fifth- and sixth-century Gaul we can see the emergence of a distinctive discourse that linked the integrity of church property to the perpetual rights of the poor. Those who robbed the church of its lands—both those who directly appropriated church property and those who held back bequests made to the church by members of their family—were deemed to be nothing less than *necatores pauperum*, "murderers of the poor."[16] They were solemnly cursed. At the council of Tours in 567 bishops and their clergy were urged to gather together so as to chant the solemn malediction of Psalm 108 in unison against such defaulters:

> *Because he did not remember to show mercy but persecuted the poor and needy and sought to kill the broken hearted* (Psalm 108 [109]:15).[17]

Everyone knew who the *broken hearted* were. They were not the poor gathered in the courtyard of the church but the bishop and his clergy whose rights (exercised on behalf of the poor) had been flouted.

We are witnessing the mutation of an old Christian theme. In the fourth century, to give to the poor had been presented as a supremely counterfactual gesture. Christians who gave to the poor—rather than lavish comforts on the narrow core of their fellow citizens—were thought to have reached out to claim the furthest edges of society for the church. By the sixth century, this notion had hardened into a means to protect the fragile edges of the lands of the church. The notion that the poor were the "endangered species" of sixth-century society, for whose preservation the bishop was responsible, placed a cordon around the properties of the church. The notion had the effect of setting up a system of alarms that were calculated to go off at the slightest touch. Any attempt to appropriate the wealth of the church or to misuse church funds was immediately presented as an attack on the helpless poor.

The bishops and clergy might use high words in defense of the poor, but their curses were not always heeded. However, the notion of the poor as victims was not without weight. It derived its explosive force from merging with more widespread anxieties specific to the sixth-century West. Let us look for a moment at what these were.

In the fluid world of the post-imperial kingdoms, the honeycomb of carefully graded social statuses that had protected free Romans—as senators, as town councillors, as *honestiores*—had collapsed. What had survived best was the brutal binary model in which the rich faced the poor with no intermediary classes in between. This stark model of society had been conjured up for at least two centuries by Christian preaching. Over the years, as we have seen, it had subtly changed. It had become fused with a model of society derived from the Old Testament. On this Old Testament model, the "poor" were not invariably thought of as beggars. They were average persons who cried out for justice. What they lacked was not money but power. In the same way, the rich were not simply the wealthy. They were the powerful—the *potentes*. What they were expected to give to the poor were not alms but justice.[18]

It was to this Old Testament image of the poor that bishops and lay statesmen alike turned, so as to think about the nature of rule in the new, post-Roman kingdoms. It was easier to advise a king, a queen, or a count to show mercy on the poor (in the manner of an Old Testament monarch) than to deliver a lecture on the complicated rights of Roman citizens.[19] As a result, talk about the poor became a way to talk about the charged issue of what it was to be the subjects of new, non-Roman rulers. The decisions of the second council of Mâcon, in 585, made this plain:

> Those to whom the cares of great affairs have been entrusted [as royal governors] should not pass over as of little esteem the affairs of the very smallest persons. For it so happens that, when the smallest of the land are despised, matters slowly grow to a great evil.[20]

Put bluntly, to tread on the poor was to threaten to tread on everybody else. In Gaul and elsewhere, the bishops were able to crystallize intense feelings of victimization around the figures of the poor "who lived beneath the veil" of their protection. In so doing, they were able to bring to the surface the grievances and fears of entire regions and of groups of persons who were far from being beggars. The language mobilized for the protection of the poor had become the language of all potential victims of the power of kings and their representatives.[21]

Hic fuit amator pauperum et clerum ampliavit: He was a lover of the poor and expanded the clergy

When talking of the imaginative logic that lay behind sixth-century images of the poor and their relevance to the anxieties of society at large, we should not be too detached. Human feeling played a significant role in relations to the poor. Many bishops did, indeed, love the real poor with real warmth. The pathos of the identification of the poor with the humbled incarnate Christ (which had once stirred great aristocrats such as Paulinus and had sharpened the pen of Jerome against the rich of Rome) was still very much alive in the sixth century. Gregory of Tours wrote with particular warmth of bishop Quintianus of Rodez:

> This holy bishop was magnificent in his giving of alms. Indeed, when he heard poor men cry out he used to say: "Run, I beg you, run to that poor

man.... Why are you so indifferent? How do you know that this poor person is not the very One [Christ Himself] Who ordained in his Gospel that one should feed Him in the person of the poor."[22]

As this quote shows, the notion that Christ was present in the poor in general (upheld by so many preachers of the fourth and fifth centuries) had become focused on the idea that, among the anonymous crowd of normal beggars, one might light on at least one beggar who was Christ in disguise. The notion of a hidden savior living among the poor was a theme of folklore common to Jews, to Christians, and eventually to Muslims. Its spread in eastern and western Christianity alike summed up an entire view of society. This was a society tested by God not only from above—from the vault of heaven—but from below: from the silent ranks of the poor among whom Christ lingered.[23]

Quintianus, however, was something of a maverick. He was a refugee from Vandal Africa and the bishop of a small see. Gregory relished the flamboyant style with which he cared for the poor and rebuked the rich. The average bishop of a major see found that he faced a more delicate task. He had to show love not for one group alone but for two. He had to love the poor, but he was also well advised to try to love his clergy. It is revealing that the two groups now appear together for the first time in many texts. For both groups depended on the bishop's generosity: the poor for their sustenance and the clergy for their salaries.

The result of this situation was that clergy and poor tended to become amalgamated. In many great shrines (such as that of Saint Martin at Tours) select members of the poor were promoted to a para-clerical role. The long-established practice of enrolling the poor on the *matricula* of the church took on a new meaning. Persons chosen from the poor roll formed the equivalent of a guild of licensed beggars. They were called *matricularii*. These groups were not large: they ranged from twelve to forty at most shrines. They stood out from the gray mass of beggars as visible and well organized.[24] They divided up the alms they had been given at the church door. Heaven help the member of the worshipful company of beggars who tried to keep for himself the alms he had received without sharing them with his fellow members of the "blessed poor"![25] The *matricularii* felt that they owned the shrine quite as much as did the clergy. At times of crisis, the *matricularii* joined in, pelting the retinues of Frankish noblemen with roof tiles in order to avenge the honor of Saint Martin when these retinues attempted to drag fugitives from sanctuary at the saint's tomb.[26]

But it was the clergy—and not the poor—who were most vociferous in bringing to bear on their bishop the ancient Roman pressure to show generosity to his dependants. We can see this very clearly in the case of Rome. For the first time, popes were praised as lovers both of the poor and of their own clergy. The author of the *Liber Pontificalis* (*The Book of Pontiffs*) wrote of Pope Gelasius (492–96) that he took good care of both groups: *hic fuit amator pauperum et clerum ampliavit*—"he was a lover of the poor and expanded the clergy."[27] Gelasius was a stern manager of the estates of the church. As we have seen, he could be adamant in asserting the rights of the church and in upholding the social order by excluding slaves and tied farmers from the clergy. Compassion was not a notable trait in his letters. But Gelasius knew to whom he should be generous—and that included not only the poor but also the proud clergy of Rome.

Pope Symmachus (498–514) followed Gelasius's example. Symmachus needed to be more than usually generous. A Sardinian from a pagan family, he was an outsider to the clerical oligarchy of the city. He had made his way to the top as an administrator. As we have seen, his authority was challenged for years on end by a rival pope, Laurentius, who may have enjoyed more support from noble families than did Symmachus. A high-handed and obstinate man, Symmachus had a reputation that was further tarnished by rumors of a liaison with a mistress called Conditaria (Spice Girl).[28] But he knew how to use the wealth of the church. Symmachus was a model of generosity. He ransomed captives. He provided money and clothing for bishops exiled from Vandal Africa. He paid his clergy well.

Above all, Symmachus loved the poor. To love the poor was to love all Rome. As we have seen, Rome had fallen apart into separate islands of settlement, many of which were dominated by the supporters of Laurentius, his rival. But the fine dust of the poor that lay at the bottom of society was what all neighborhoods had in common. Drawn from all over the city to receive alms at the shrine of Saint Peter, the poor were the nearest thing to a united *populus Romanus* that remained in the divided city of Rome. Symmachus made sure that the poor of Rome knew who was their true pope and their true benefactor. He built hostels for the poor near major shrines. He fitted out baths. He even installed a public lavatory beside the courtyard of Saint Peter's.[29]

The tradition continued. In the 580s, in distant Mérida in southwestern Spain, bishop Masona—a former courtier of the Visigothic kings—knew the rules of the game. His generosity extended equally to the poor and to the clergy. On becoming bishop, he immediately used what may have been his private fortune to set up an ambitious scheme of hospitals, food centers, and a bank for cheap loans to the poor.[30] But he also went out of his way to look after his clergy. Thanks to his free spending, his clergy "and even the servants in his palace" were able to appear in the great Easter procession dressed in silk robes "as if they were marching in the procession of a king."[31]

If we look at panegyrics of sixth-century bishops in action all over Europe, the payment of the clergy and the care of the poor tended to merge into a single golden blur. Together they created the hum associated with a well-run bishopric.

In the case of the poor, the seemingly limitless nature of their demands was used by hagiographers to heighten the impression of the bishop's limitless wealth. Hagiographic narratives of this period stressed the miraculous abundance of wealth used for the poor. They contained stories that presented holy bishops (such as Caesarius of Arles) as having been approached by tight-fisted church administrators who told them that they no longer had funds with which to feed the poor. Undeterred by the parsimony of his officials, the bishop proceeded to the storehouse only to find it filled with miraculous piles of grain. The imaginative logic of these miracles was plain. If the poor were endless and ever-present, then the wealth that passed to them from the bishop's palace could also be imagined to be inexhaustible.[32] In this way, the care of the poor was wrapped in an aura of boundless wealth that contrasted strangely with the prudent setting up of small and privileged begging associations, hostels, and food centers for groups of "blessed poor" that rarely appear to have risen above forty.[33] In reality, love of the poor was never headlong. When, in 616, the great courtier-bishop Bertram of Le Mans drew up his will we find that he gave only one-tenth of his vast wealth to the poor.[34]

This shortfall needs to be explained. No great poorhouses emerged in western Europe as they did in the contemporary eastern empire.[35] This was not due entirely to economic recession or to lack of generosity on the part of the bishops. What mattered was that the poor should be localized and, wherever possible, organized into small, manageable groups. The localization of the care of the poor in the vicinity of holy places represented the culmination of a process that was already under way in 400 AD in the porticoes and dining hall adjacent to the shrine of Saint Felix at Cimitile and in the great open square in front of Saint Peter's in Rome. Treasure on earth could be imagined with greatest ease to be transferred to heaven through giving to the poor at such shrines. For heaven and earth were already joined at the tomb of a saint and through the constant prayers of the monks and clergymen gathered in the shrine. Alms given to the poor in these places were all the more certain to reach heaven.

But we should also remember that poverty had its own, sixth-century face. Society had changed. The poor of Gaul, Spain, and even Italy were not the great urban masses imagined by the preachers of earlier times—the "systemic" poor who formed a permanent underclass in the crowded cities of the fourth century. The poor of the sixth-century West were very largely what social scientists have called the "conjunctural poor." They were families ruined by crop failure (sad indicators, perhaps, of the climatic anomaly posited by some modern scholars) and by warfare. They had been forced to take to the roads. When the council of Tours met in 567, among other items of business it had to deal with the needs of a society tensed against the imminence of civil war. The "fury of the kings" threatened to send a new wave of poor persons into the towns and villages in search of food and alms. In order to cope with the emergency, local parishes were urged to feed their own poor rather than driving them to seek alms elsewhere.[36]

But (in the eyes of a bishop such as Gregory of Tours) it was precisely the terrible rootlessness of the conjunctural poor that caused an aura of the sacred to flicker around the great shrines of Latin Europe. For, in the atrium of the shrine of Saint Martin at Tours (as elsewhere), it was as if the "hidden hand" of providence itself had brought pilgrims with some money together with the broken victims of war, crop failure, and physical disability.

A fresco at the west entrance to the shrine of Saint Martin at Tours showed the story of the Widow's Mite. Beneath it was an inscription on almsgiving. It reminded every pilgrim that "rich and poor alike are liable to this law."[37] One was ill-advised to enter into the presence of Martin without having given alms to the poor gathered in the great courtyard outside the shrine (and especially to the licensed *matricularii* who surrounded the sanctuary).

Modest pilgrims would bring food and wine to feed the poor. One woman was cured of a paralyzed arm simply through the act of endlessly mixing punch at the banquet tables around which the poor would gather.[38] There were terrible sights in that courtyard. A horribly deformed girl had first been paraded around the countryside as a freak show before she was finally dumped at the shrine of Saint Martin to be supported by gifts from pious pilgrims.[39] There were also sights of worldly glory brought low. Queen Ultrogotha (the wife of Childebert I) "presented many gifts" before she even dared to pass from the great courtyard into the shrine, so as to stand before the sarcophagus in the presence of Saint Martin himself.[40]

We know so much about these shrines from the vivid writings of Gregory of Tours. But we know very little about what happened outside them. One suspects that there was considerably more religious mobility allied to the rootlessness of poverty than Gregory's accounts betray. The surprising evidence of graffiti at the caves of hermits in both Gaul and Spain points to an ominously mobile population consisting of the poor and of religious wanderers. They were like the *Bozhii ljudi*, "God's folk" in old Russia—notorious spreaders of rumors and extravagant pious tales. Their Christianity was not necessarily the well-groomed Catholic "reverence" advocated by Gregory of Tours.[41]

At times of plague and war, dangerous figures emerged. What is striking is the speed with which they gathered money through donations from their followers (some of whom, Gregory noted with horror, were clergymen). In 591 a prophet began his preaching outside Bourges: "A crowd of the common people flocked to him.... They brought him gold and silver and robes."[42] In 585 a diviner appeared outside Verdun: "Every day she gathered gold and silver, processing around the countryside loaded with jewelry, as if she was some divine being."[43]

Te itaque, sanctam ecclesiam catholicam ... in qua omnis populus christianus exorat remedia peccatorum: [I give to] You, holy Catholic Church ... in Whom all Christian people pray for the healing of their sins

For a bishop such as Gregory these were disturbing incidents. But for the historian of religious sentiment in the sixth-century West, they reveal a situation that is otherwise almost too big to be seen. Clergy and laity alike wished to give to religious causes. As we have seen, they were not always generous in their gifts, nor were they inevitably moved by deep piety. But they knew what they wanted both from religious figures (even from the most bizarre figures of diviners, prophetesses, and wandering holy men) and from a religious institution. They wanted remission of their sins and safety for their souls.

The profile and the aims of lay donors are strangely muted. They are underexposed, as it were, compared with the vivid snapshots of bishops, monks, and clergymen that dominate the literature of the period. We have easier entry into the minds of the clergy. But just because the world of the laity is difficult of access does not mean that it is entirely closed to us. What we can follow, throughout western Europe, is the process by which the pressure of giving imposed a distinctive shape upon the churches. Generation after generation, pious givers molded the Latin Christianity of their time into their own image, as a church that deserved to receive their gifts.

It was this pressure of giving that did most to create a hiatus between the Christianity of the sixth century and the Christianity of previous generations. That earlier Christianity had grown from the soil of an ancient world that now seemed glorious but strange. As Robert Markus has made plain in his luminous short book, *The End of Ancient Christianity*, a profound change happened between the age of Augustine and the age of Gregory the Great (between 400 and 600 AD).[44] But it has proved easier to describe this change than to account for it. It did not come about only because of changes in the culture of the clerical elite. Those particular changes have been brilliantly described by Markus. He points to the process of cultural depletion, simplification, and "cognitive erasure" that took place among the leading thinkers of the church. This process led to a "retreat of the secular" and to an extension of Christian religious values to aspects of society and culture that had hitherto been considered neutral.

But there is more to the story than this. We tend to assume that the cultural depletion to which Markus refers is easily explicable in terms of the narrowing of cultural resources in the Latin churches, brought about by prolonged warfare and economic recession. But the "end of ancient Christianity" did not happen only because of a loss of cultural riches and a clamping down of intellectual horizons. This is too narrow and too intellectual a view of what happened between

400 and 600 A D. We also have to reckon with a significant change of goals within Christianity itself. In order to sense the turn of the tide that brought about this change of goals we must look away from the clergy to the wide and dimly visible ocean of religious giving from which this tide arose.

For this we have precious evidence. A few original wills and charters written on papyrus have miraculously survived in the church treasuries of Ravenna and Gaul. What they show is the force of a piety focused on the need to obtain the forgiveness of one's sins through the intercession of others. All over the West, churches and similar pious institutions received legacies because (in the words of a papyrus preserved in Ravenna) they were the places *in qua omnis populus christianus exorat remedia peccatorum"*—"in which all Christian people pray for the relief of their sins."[45]

In these formulae, Augustine's somber sense of daily giving for the expiation of sins and Salvian's dramatic close-up of judgment beyond the grave were brought together. Religious giving was placed against the grand setting of the Last Judgment (as it was imagined in the sixth century), the final, grand theater of amnesty.[46] This is not exactly what it had been in the Gospels. In the great scene of the Last Days in chapter 25 of the *Gospel of Matthew* (Matt. 25:31–46), Christ ("the Son of Man") separated the sheep from the goats. The sheep who had shown mercy on others were placed on His right hand and were welcomed into His kingdom. But Christ showed no mercy to the goats. They were told to "go away into eternal punishment." In the sixth century, by contrast, it was precisely the potential goats who expected Christ's mercy. They expected to gain that mercy through the intercessions of the saints. Sinners could hope to receive *venia*—"amnesty," "forgiveness"—from God at the very last moment of the Last Judgment.[47] Gregory of Tours had no doubts as to the working out of that scenario:

> And when, at the Last Judgment, I am to be placed on the left hand [among the goats destined for Hell], Martin will deign to pick me out from the middle of the goats with his sacred right hand. He will shelter me behind his back, as the angels tell the King: "This is the man for whom Saint Martin pleads."[48]

This is what the great bishop Bertram of Le Mans also had in mind when he drew up his will: *vel venia*—"forgiveness at the very least"—was what he wanted: "May God, through the wide-handed grace of His pity grant some kind of amnesty."[49] It was wrong to ask for more than mere forgiveness. "Glory" belonged only to the saints, whose intercessions at the Last Judgment Bertram went on to elicit by drawing up a list of bequests and pious foundations that originally filled a papyrus roll seven meters long.

We are looking at a rare focusing of the religious gift around a single purpose. In Christian circles, the religious gift had become the central transaction of a "vibrant piety of intercession" whose rise in the West has recently been evoked by Tom Head.[50] It is worthwhile to linger a little on what this means. Intercession demanded intercessors. And, in the sixth-century West, the most effective intercessors were deemed to be those figures who in this life and the next were most starkly different from the donor. It was the difference that mattered. Put in a nutshell: the way to the great Other beyond the grave lay through human beings who, themselves, had (in one way or another) become "other" to the average Christian. The poor, the monks, the saints, and the priests who offered the Eucharist on behalf of the faithful were each—if each in a different way—seen as intercessors whose effectiveness derived from their otherness.

Hence the manner in which the churches of Latin Christianity came to be surrounded by a coral reef of institutions devoted to intercession. Many of these had not enjoyed such prominence or so clear a function in earlier centuries. Often they now became prominent because they were compact. The associations of *matricularii*, the hospitals, and the hostels for the poor that were founded at that time were never enough to absorb the gray poverty that surrounded them. But their appeal was precisely that "small is beautiful." These carefully organized groups made the otherness of the poor visible, orderly, and, for that reason, efficacious.

This was not an entirely recent development of the sixth century. As we have seen, the rhetorical logic of the preaching of fourth-century Christians had always teetered as if on an imaginative tightrope between reaching out to the poor as "brothers" and treating them as "others"—as total outsiders, whom only the paradox of Christian mercy could embrace. The sixth-century logic of intercession came down firmly on the side of the latter view, at least for a selected segment of the poor. As humane modern persons, we may regret a situation in which "weaker members of society are seen as others rather than brothers."[51] But it was only through being seen as the ultimate others in society that the poor in the courtyard of Saint Martin and of similar shrines could be believed to lead the average believer who gave them alms into the unthinkable otherness of heaven.

It was also as a function of the imaginative logic of a search for a way to the Other through others that monasteries and convents suddenly leaped into focus in the sixth century. As Albrecht Diem has made plain in his groundbreaking study, *Das monastische Experiment* (The Monastic Experiment), the principal goal of the monastic reformers of Gaul and elsewhere in the sixth century was to create powerhouses of prayer. Although the monks were expected to work, on the Egyptian model propounded by Cassian, these powerhouses of prayer were not self-supporting. They were almost entirely supported by lay giving.[52]

This was a significant change. Previously, monasteries had been founded by individual spiritual guides. It was the abbot who was imagined to have "built" the monastery by gathering his disciples around him. Now, all over the West, it became possible for a pious clergyman or a layperson to state that he or she had built a monastery *for* the abbot and his monks. They set up and endowed carefully constructed monasteries in which they placed either monks or nuns as masters of intercessory prayer. For instance, the monastery attached to the shrine of the Theban martyrs at Saint Maurice d'Agaune (Valais, Switzerland) was built for its monks by King Sigismund of Burgundy "with great care and attention to detail."[53] In so doing, donors showed that they had found an other who could be relied upon to bring them to God. As the monastic foundations of the Frankish nobility and of their kings made clear toward the end of the sixth and throughout the seventh century, lay patrons were prepared to put a lot of money into these magnetically attractive others, established in well-organized convents and monasteries.[54]

In this way, monks gradually came to eclipse the poor as the privileged others of the Christian imagination. The monks alone had become the "holy poor." In a contemporary monastic rule, lay gifts were instantly sanctified and made effective by being brought into the chapel to be prayed over by the nuns or monks.[55] It is a solution whose high-pitched emphasis on the "holy poor"—on monks and nuns to the exclusion of the real poor—as the only truly reliable, because truly other, recipients of alms for the safety of the soul would have struck a fourth-century Christian as vaguely Manichaean.[56] With this shift from the poor to the monks as the primary intercessors for the sins of all Christians, an ancient Christianity died.

Toward the Great Simplification: The "Othering" of the Clergy

In the sixth and early seventh centuries, the pressure of religious giving accounted for the most striking feature of the age. As givers, the laity came to insist that the clergy should be clearly other to themselves. If they were not, gifts to the churches would not work for the relief of the sins of the givers.

Hence we witness a progressive "othering" of the clergy. They became a sacral class. Their dress, hairstyle, and sexual behavior were increasingly expected to be sharply different from that of the laity. Religious dress became sharply distinguished from lay dress.[57] The tonsure was taken on as a sine qua non of both the clerical and the monastic state. It is notable that the origins of the tonsure did not lie in any clerical regulations. It came from the ground up. The cutting of hair (both of beards and of the top of the head) had long been treated by Romans as a sign of special dedication. The tonsure emerged as a response to lay demand for such a sign. Those who interceded for the laity, as a sacral class, were to be clearly designated by means of a ritual of shaving the crown of the head that had deep roots in the ancient folklore of hair.[58]

Above all, continence was imposed on all grades of the clergy. Slowly but surely, roughly between 400 and 500 AD and at different paces in different regions, every member of the clergy of the Latin churches—bishops, priests, deacons, and even sub-deacons—came to be expected to refrain on a permanent basis from intercourse. For, at one moment or another during the celebration of the Eucharist, their hands had touched holy things—the body and blood of Christ and the sacred dishes and vessels (the patens and the chalices) in which these divine substances were carried.[59]

We must be careful, at this point, not to allow modern debates on the celibacy of the clergy in the Roman Catholic Church to lure us into anachronism. What was at stake at this time was not the commitment of the clergy from childhood onward to a permanent renunciation of sex. Many clergymen did adopt this practice (one thinks of Ambrose, whose lifelong celibacy puzzled the unconverted Augustine).[60] But such celibacy was never mandatory. What mattered was what one might call "post-marital" celibacy. It was taken for granted that a priest or a bishop might have had a wife and children. But ordination meant that they had to cease sexual relations with their wives.[61] It was deemed prudent that spouses should no longer live together. The bishop's or the priest's wife moved out, often to the safety—and the relative comfort—of a convent. This last was a precautionary measure that was not invariably acted on by aristocrats. As we saw in chapter 14, Paulinus of Nola had continued to live with his wife, Therasia, when already a priest. The wife of Sidonius Apollinaris was remembered (by Gregory of Tours) as creeping out of the bishop's palace—where she still lived—to buy back the family silverware that her husband had lavished improvidently on the poor.[62]

Not all contemporaries saw this development with the same sense of inevitability as do modern scholars. Post-marital celibacy was not taken for granted by every wife of every bishop. Gregory of Tours tells how (as late as the 550s) the wife of bishop Felix of Nantes was convinced that her spouse had ceased to have sexual relations with her for the obvious reason—the bishop had a mistress. Bursting into his room at the time of the siesta, she saw Felix sleeping alone with a radiant lamb curled up on his chest. Christ had claimed Felix from her, as His bishop and as the dispenser of His holy things.[63]

In the fifth and sixth centuries, the issue of the continence of the clergy loomed so large precisely because the boundary between the celibate and the lay world was still so precarious. Formerly married persons, who had been accustomed to having sexual relations with each other, were expected to refrain from intercourse simply because of the husband's involvement with the Eucharist. It was a prohibition that was notoriously difficult to maintain.

In this situation, the price of purity was eternal vigilance. As early as the 400s, the clergy of Bruttium (modern Basilicata in southern Italy) were denounced by a layman (appropriately enough, a retired *agens in rebus*—a former member of a cadre of imperial agents who were notorious for their spying activities) for "polluting" the church by continuing to beget children.[64] The insistence on the continence of the clergy at this time is striking. One-third of the rulings of the sixth-century councils of Gaul were concerned, in one way or another, with this issue. Modern scholars speak with ill-disguised discomfort of "the obsessive drive to regulate" that provoked a veritable *luxe de précautions*—an overkill of precautions.[65] Why did this attempt to patrol so fragile a boundary become so marked a feature of the sixth-century church?

The usual tendency of modern scholarship has been to blame the clergy. Historians of the early medieval church all too readily assume that any rulings that offend the sensibilities of our own age (such as the imposition of celibacy on the clergy and the segregation of women from contact with male priests) must have derived from the decisions of an austere elite of clergymen. They are the villains of the story. They are assumed to have imposed their own ascetic codes upon their weaker colleagues and upon an otherwise fun-loving but passive laity. Altogether, there is a tendency to view the history of Christianity in the early Middle Ages in terms of a top-down model. On this top-down model, clerical power is seen as always triumphing over the laity—and usually with results of which we disapprove. Such a view is to be strongly resisted. The demand for a continent clergy came as much from the bottom up as from the top down. It is significant that in Africa, among churches where (as we have seen) the views of the *populus* counted for much, the imposition of continence did not result from any conciliar ruling. The bishops of Africa merely adopted the lay custom of demanding celibacy of their clergy.[66]

The imposition of celibacy on the clergy was what we would call "consumer driven." In 567 the bishops gathered at the council of Tours set in place an entire set of rulings to preserve the chastity of their clergy. Priests who traveled in the countryside on church business were to be chaperoned. Any form of cohabitation between clergymen and women was to be avoided.[67] But these minute regulations were drawn up so as to satisfy the laity. They were intended to counter "the suspicion of the populace" that their priests were not true others to themselves.[68] The effectiveness of the Eucharist as a privileged vehicle of intercession was at stake. In the words of a bishop summing up similar regulations taken at the council of Mâcon in 585, a priest had to be continent "because he did not come forward as intercessor for his own sins only, but for those of others."[69]

In the inland regions of Gaul, the laity were wealthy and, for that reason, doubly exacting. We need only move 150 miles to the west—to the Atlantic coast of Brittany—to find holy priests who traveled from house to house in order to celebrate the Eucharist with the help of *conhospitae*—women companions. To the bishops of Gaul, this was a practice "which can not be spoken of without a shudder of the soul."[70] But the Bretons were a society of recent settlers. They were governed by chieftains of low social profile. Their soul did not shudder at the behavior of their clergy. This was, perhaps, because the Breton laity had less wealth to give to the church; and so they had less money riding on the utter otherness of their clergy. In any case, the Breton bishop Lovocatus, who was denounced by the bishops of western Gaul, was not seen by his Breton flock as a wayward clergyman. A monk-bishop in the ascetic tradition of the Celtic churches, Lovocatus's austerity placed him beyond suspicion even when he consorted with women. His "otherness" was unchallenged. He was later revered in Brittany as a saint and a founder of churches.[71] The average clergyman of Gaul, however, was no ascetic hero. He had to be watched more carefully.

In order to understand the weight of the pressure toward a sacral, celibate clergy, we must remember that the circle of those who depended on monks and the clergy for intercession had widened considerably. For this was the time when Christianity ceased to be confined to the cities and spread throughout the countryside. The creation of a rural Christianity in Spain, Gaul, and Italy remains the dark side of the moon in the study of the churches in this period. Yet it is one of the great changes of the age.[72] In Gaul alone two hundred country parishes are known to have been founded in the fifth and sixth centuries.[73] In southwestern Spain and southern Portugal, small churches appear beside many villas for the very first time.[74]

In Gaul and Spain these churches were staffed by priests. But many of these priests became the equivalent of bishops. They gained control of the wealth of their church and refused to surrender more than a portion of it to their nominal superior, the bishop of the neighboring city.[75] In parts of Italy, one might even say that country Christianity created towns rather than that the towns created country Christianity. Bishops (and not mere priests) appear in a significant number of non-urban sites in Italy, giving them a quasi-urban status.[76] Nothing like this had happened in western Europe since the spread of country bishoprics in fourth-century Africa.

As we saw in the case of southern Italy, in many areas the spread of churches in the countryside owed as much to lay initiatives as to the urban clergy. Lay patrons often did more than did the urban bishops to build shrines and to provide churches. In Spain, for instance, the evidence is painfully fragmentary but vivid. Often no more than fragments of inscriptions survive to mark the activities of lay founders. For instance, at Nativola, near modern Granada in southern Spain, count Gundileva provided three churches for the region between 594 and 610 AD. He did so "with the help of the saints, with the labor of the workers of his estates, at his own expense."[77]

Gundileva's churches were big enough to be marked by the proud inscription that outlasted them all. Others were more modest. In Gaul many little chapels were made of wood.[78] What is striking is that the founders of such churches were by no means great landowners. In Spain some churches were even built by associations of slaves on the royal estates, who contributed "from their poverty" to putting up a shrine.[79] We need only think back to the majestic mausoleum-churches connected to the villas of fourth-century Castile or to the villa-monastery of Sulpicius Severus at Primuliacum (with its twin basilicas, baptistery, and carefully executed mosaic portraits of its founders and their favorite saints, accompanied by inscriptions written in high-quality verse) to realize that we are witnessing a true democratization of religious building in the countryside.[80]

The priests who were hired to serve these modest churches had little to offer by way of culture or preaching. But they did offer the Mass, and to offer the Mass effectively on behalf of their patrons and on behalf of a congregation that may have consisted largely of workers on the lands of their patrons, they had to be continent. Celibacy was the only thing that made members of this "clerical proletariat" different from the peasants among whom they lived.[81] As peasant-priests, celibacy was their only distinguishing mark of otherness. Patrons watched that celibacy closely lest it be lost, with the hard eyes of persons who had paid for intercession.

These were the humble roots from which the principal feature of post-Roman society in the West emerged. This was the division of society into two castes—a caste of priests and a caste of warriors, the one notionally separated from the other by a distinction of archaic sharpness. In a well-chosen phrase, Walter Goffart has described the change from a late antique to an early medieval society as a "process of simplification."[82] This great simplification was well under way in the sixth century.

It was not a development that was confined to "barbarian" northern Europe. One need only visit an urban site in north Africa, such as Sufetula (Sbeitla, in southwestern Tunisia), to see the process of simplification frozen, as it were, on the ground. The last, sixth-century phase of the city (and not the city of Roman times) is what the modern visitor sees first when he or she comes to the site. At one end of the town, the classical amphitheater had become a fortress that housed a garrison. Around the city, fortified towers scanned the horizon. At the other end of Sbeitla, substantial basilicas built in the sixth century stand side by side to form a massive bishop's quarter. In between, the forum, the marketplace, and all the busy life we associate with the center of a classical Roman city had become (and still remains) a faceless open space, crossed by random paths.

It is easy to see, in the stark features of sixth-century Sbeitla, the outlines of the Islamic city of the future, where the mosque and the casbah—the place of religion and the place of armed power, respectively—faced each other across a maze of winding lanes. Already by the sixth century, in what had once been one of the most heavily urbanized regions of the late Roman world, a Roman city with a clear civic center had been replaced by a city divided between the two poles of pastoral and worldly power.[83] This distancing of the two poles and the disappearance of the once vigorous neutral ground that had stood between them (in the form of an ancient city, with its pre-Christian joys and values) is the measure of the change that occurred when the Christianity of the Latin West slipped from its late antique to its early medieval form.

In a perceptive review of Chris Wickham's magnificent analysis of the social and economic developments of the later Roman empire and the early middle ages—*Framing the Early Middle Ages*—Ian Wood has observed: "The extent to which the church came to dominate in the society and economy of western Europe ought to be recognized as truly astonishing."[84] But how had this situation come about? Massive and inevitable though it might seem in retrospect, the emergence of the clergy as a separate and superior caste of sacred persons did not happen automatically. The militarization of society alone does not explain it, nor (as we have just seen) can we blame it on a monasticization of the clergy imposed from on top by an elite of forceful bishops. It was the laity that wanted its clergy to be different. *C'est le premier pas qui coûte*: it is the first step that counts. Once the tacit decision was taken to make the clergy different, the passing of time made them dominant.

Magnum et mirabile Dei donum est: It is a great and amazing gift of God

WEALTH AND THE OTHER WORLD

So what does this change involve for the meaning of wealth itself? Put briefly, we are no longer in a world where wealth could be mythologized, as it had been in the days of the great villa owners connected with Ausonius of Bordeaux. It could no longer be imagined as a shimmering overflow of the abundance of the *saeculum*—a quasi-divine material cosmos on whose riches the wealthy drew with unreflecting zest. Wealth had been problematized. But it had not been demonized. Few Christian thinkers of the later fifth and sixth centuries thought that wealth should be rejected out of hand. The heady days of Pinianus, Melania the Younger, and the Pelagian author of the *De divitiis* were over. What won out was a combination of Paulinus of Nola's poetic sense of the romance of treasure placed in heaven by a spiritual exchange with Augustine's sad emphasis on daily giving as the remedy for daily sin. To this was added the dry view upheld by later Augustinians that wealth itself was a gift of God that demanded forms of management as strict and as careful as that exercised by any procurator on an imperial estate.

But this still leaves us with a psychological riddle. It is an observed fact that other-worldly religions—whether this be late antique Christianity or its exact contemporary at the other end of Eurasia, the Buddhism of central Asia and western China—often manage to become very rich very soon. As Chinese observers noted, with characteristic economy of words, there was a lot of wealth to be gotten from *fo-shih*—from "Buddha business."[85]

We can treat this fact (as many late antique Christians did) as sad evidence of the decline of the church from a first moment of imagined virtue. Or we might be tempted to view it with a certain worldly-wise complacency. After all, we say, idealism never lasts. Traditional social mores tend to prevail. If these are the mores of a Roman aristocracy, we are somewhat relieved. It is comforting to think that the views of upholders of the good old Roman ways did not give way entirely to the extremist views on wealth proposed by doctrinaire Christians. If we are historians of Christian theology, we can even be content to say that the wealth of the church—like the British Empire as described by Benjamin Disraeli —simply happened "in a fit of absence of mind." We do not feel obliged to study it and still less to meditate on the paradox of its existence.

Yet it may be possible to go further than these somewhat banal answers. We need to find some way to integrate the sincere otherworldliness of the Christian movement with its considerable worldly success in the late antique period. I would suggest that, faced with this problem, Buddhists and Christians may have found their way to a common solution. They knew that those who supped with the Devil of wealth needed a long spoon. But it was, perhaps, precisely the length of the spoon that gave them an advantage. An ideal of detachment from worldly things took the glamour out of wealth. But it did not make wealth go away. Indeed, the ideal of detachment subtly reinforced the notion that if wealth was there it was there for a reason. It was there to be used—to be administered in a no-nonsense and effective manner for the good of the church. Bluntly, wealth was given a higher purpose. It was swept into the pastoral image of the church, to which Michel Foucault referred in his lectures to the Collège de France on the nature of pastoral power: it was made subject "to a power that guides towards an end and functions as an intermediary towards that end."[86]

As we have seen, we should not exaggerate the effect of this high view on the actual administration of the wealth of the churches in the sixth century. But it did affect the way in which this wealth was seen by those who approached the church as donors. Because its use was directed toward supernatural and eternal ends, the wealth of the church came to be viewed as wealth that radiated a future even on earth. It was wealth subtly touched by expectations of eternity.

The idea of the wealth of the church rested on a mighty paradox that had long haunted the late antique imagination. Even the smallest gift to the poor or to the church brought about a miraculous joining of heaven and earth. In such gifts, time and eternity were joined. In the words of the donation of Palladius of Auxerre to the convent of St. Julian in 635:

> It is a great and amazing gift of God—*magnum et mirabile donum Dei*—that with things bound by time and destined to bankruptcy prizes can be acquired in heaven that will last without end.[87]

And, as another charter put it:

> *The world perishes and those things that are in the world* (1 John 2:17). That, however, which has been transferred to the churches, to the shrines of saints or to the poor never perishes.[88]

For such donors, wealth did not stand in the way of heaven. Rather, when given to the church, wealth opened a high road to the future and a prospect of properties and institutions that might enjoy an indefinite future on earth because they were bathed in the soft glow of perpetual treasure in heaven. They were little oases of eternity in a changing world. The hopes expressed in the charters were almost proved right. The poorhouse founded in Le Mans by bishop Bertram in 616 lasted until 1789; that founded in Trier by the rich deacon Adalgisel Grimo, in 634, lasted up to the time of Napoleon.[89]

Ut numquam sit neque hora noctis absque luminaria ipsa basilica sancta: That this holy basilica should not be without lighting for a single hour of the night

It is now time to conclude by pointing out how shifts in the style and aims of religious giving may account for some differences between the Christianity of the year 400 and that of the year 600. A Christian of the age of Augustine, had he or she been able to visit a basilica of the year 600, might have noticed certain significant changes.

Looking toward the altar, our visitor would have noticed that certain noisy and bustling ceremonies no longer happened. In many regions, the faithful no longer proceeded in person to the altar bearing gifts. Nor did donors any longer receive the acclamation of the congregation as their names were read aloud. The Mass had ceased to be a ceremony that reached one of its high points in a solemn moment of lay giving. Instead, it had become a high sacrifice, offered by the clergy alone. The holy vessels in gold and silver filled with the body and blood of Christ that stood upon the altar were the true offerings. They were carried by the priests alone who brought them to God on behalf of the laity.[90]

In the body of the church itself, the quality of the light might also have seemed different. In 400, in the great basilicas of Rome, Carthage, and elsewhere, light was thought to stream into the columned hall from the spacious courtyard outside. Perfumed chandeliers blazed throughout the basilica. But this light spoke stridently of the general magnificence and joy of the Christian community. In 600 the newly built churches would have been much smaller. But now they carried within themselves the magic of perpetual light. As we saw in our last chapter, the supreme achievement of the sixth-century mosaic artist had been to create a world where "the day remains through art."[91] To this, donors added lighting in the form of innumerable oil lamps or great candles. They may not have given more of these than had their predecessors. But they now gave them with greater insistence and for a clearer purpose. Bertram of Le Mans insisted in his will that "this holy basilica should not ever be without lighting for a single hour of the night … so that it might blaze without pause all the time."[92] Now that the transport of olive oil from Mediterranean countries had become an increasingly difficult operation, oil to fuel the lamps of churches (once a common commodity) took on associations of almost supernatural luxury similar to that of the bales of Chinese silk that wrapped the great Buddhas of Central Asia.[93]

This was because light now stood for Paradise. More than that, it stood for the individual soul in Paradise. The lights Bertram maintained at great expense at his tomb in the church showed that the great bishop now rested in a world of unflickering, perpetual light. This also was a change. Those who listened to Augustine and to similar preachers in 400 were in no doubt that they belonged to a group on its way to heaven. But, by 600, the church itself had become a little heaven. In a small church, filled with the light of so many lamps and candles, the average believers felt less that they were members of a happy group bound eventually for the Heavenly Jerusalem. Rather, they stared directly, with a longing tinged with fear, into a world beyond this world.

The pavement of the church itself would have told our visitor a similar story. In the fourth and early fifth centuries, a scatter of small mosaic panels had enlivened the pavements of the basilicas of fourth-century Aquileia, northern Italy, and Istria. In the sixth century, these panels no longer spoke of a community supported by small donors. The hierarchy of donors was more clearly defined, leaving less room for minor figures. Only the leaders of local society appeared. When the mosaics of the pavement of the cathedral church of Grado were laid down, in around 550, the names of the local elite, clerical and lay, were carefully distributed in due order around the bishop's dedicatory inscription.[94] In Poreč, in Istria, the basilica of the great managerial bishop Euphrasius rose above a church once paved by little people. The earlier pavement was buried. It had contained a patchwork of donors, such as Clamosus, "the teacher of children," his wife, Secundina, and with other parishioners, each of whom contributed panels worth around three *solidi* each. This was not the case in Euphrasius's magnificent new church. It was a church of the elite, headed by their bishop. It was no longer a church that depended on the support of little men and their families.[95]

Furthermore, the tone of the dedications themselves had subtly changed. In the well-chosen words of Ville Vuolanto: "Donations were no longer seen as made for the community and for the honor of the family, but became a personal matter between God and individuals."[96] The donors of the mosaic dedications were no longer, as it were, looking around them in the basilica to see and to be seen by the community to which they had contributed. Rather, they looked upward, to place their souls in the hands of God.

Nothing shows this shift more clearly than what happened to the splendid inlaid marble benches of the priests that lined the back wall of the apse in the basilica of Euphrasius at Poreč.[97] From the sixth century to the eleventh, the spaces near the benches came to be covered with carved graffiti. These graffiti bore the names and the days of the death of the elite of Poreč—lay and clerical. They were not made at random. Scratched into the priceless panels of marble and mother of pearl, they clustered around the altar where Mass was celebrated. In two centuries we have passed from the Cockney confidence of Clamosus, who added a cheap new mosaic panel to the pavement of his church so as to add to the honor of the Christian community, to a silent array of elite names, pushing close to the altar, where the Eucharistic prayer was recited on behalf of their own souls.

This shift in donors and in what they paid for is the measure of the changing of an age. A Christian community that had bloomed in the last, strident days of the ancient world seems to have turned its back on the warm and sociable light of the Forum and of the cheap but spacious church building of the late fourth century. Its members now sought a future in the light beyond the grave. Whether they turned away in this manner from the world of the living in real life can be doubted. But this was how Christians now wished to spend their money in church, in preparation for the long journey of the soul.

CONCLUSION

The changes that took place between the years 500 and 650 proved decisive. A new conglomerate of notions about the use of wealth, about the nature of the Christian community, and about the destiny of the Christian soul slid into place. In all later centuries, this particular conglomerate of notions—which linked together the wealth of the church, the care of the poor, and the fate of the soul—became fixed in the minds of the populations of western, Catholic Europe.

By the year 1000, western Europeans were supposed to take this inherited conglomerate with them wherever they went, even to the edges of the known world. Some went very far. In 1020 the first European settler in Greenland to become a Christian, Thorstein the son of Eric the Red, lay dying at Lysefjord (Ameralik in Greenland). Just before he died, Thorstein summoned his wife, Gudrid. In a manner associated with Norse tales of prophecy, he sat up suddenly (as if returned from the dead) and gave her this advice: "He bade her beware of marrying a Greenlander and then he urged her to bestow their money upon the church or to give it to the poor; and then he sank back for the last time."[1]

Recounted some centuries later, in the *Saga of the Greenlanders*, the story carried with it the heavy weight of common sense concerning the proper use of wealth shared by all Catholic Christians. It was what any believer, such as Thorstein Eiriksson, was expected to do when he or she faced death, even when settled on the fringes of the Arctic.

In 350 AD, however, little of this was clear. This book has traced a long process. We began with a hesitant age. As a result of the conversion of Constantine in 312 AD, the Christian churches of the West had become privileged. But they had not become wealthy. The majority of the upper-class inhabitants of the Roman West were still encouraged by long tradition to show generosity to their cities and to their fellow citizens—not to the churches and still less to the poor. Only in the last quarter of the fourth century did the wealthy enter the church in growing numbers, often stepping into leadership roles as bishops and as Christian writers. It was the entry of new wealth and talent into the churches from around the year 370 onward, rather than the conversion of Constantine in 312, which marks the turning point in the Christianization of Europe. From then onward, as members of a religion that had been joined by the rich and powerful, Christians could begin to think the unthinkable—to envision the possibility of a totally Christian society.

But this new wealth brought its own problems. The structures of fourth-century society ensured that there would be a lot of new wealth, held in the hands of competing groups. Many of these groups were anxious to make their mark by fostering the new religion. Yet the churches to which the new rich turned in the last quarter of the fourth century were already, in many ways, old-fashioned institutions. They were set in their ways. Christian habits of religious giving reached back for centuries to traditions and to texts shared by Christianity and Judaism. In both Christianity and Judaism these habits had been formed to one side of the dominant models of public benefaction provided for the rich by the cities of the Greco-Roman world.

The imaginative effect of Christian giving was to break down traditional boundaries that had been maintained by the ancient city. Gifts to the city gained fame in this world and in this world only. By contrast, gifts within the churches were thought to join this world to a boundless world beyond the stars. Furthermore, giving was not only for the rich. All believers of all classes were encouraged to contribute to the care of the poor and to the upkeep of the church and clergy. Furthermore, to give to the poor was very different from giving to a clearly defined core of fellow citizens. It was to reach out to a group that was imagined to be as immense and as silent as heaven itself.

Even before the conversion of Constantine, these notions had created a distinctive style of giving for religious causes in Christian circles. In the 250s the letters of a bishop such as Cyprian showed how much financial muscle could be developed—through regular almsgiving and through occasional collections—by communities whose social composition was, for the most part, limited to the moderately wealthy inhabitants of the cities.

The rich encountered such Christian communities toward the end of the fourth century. This encounter did not lead to the smooth absorption of the churches into the orbit of the wealthy. Instead, we enter troubled waters. Between around 370 and 430, we are faced with an explosion of writing on the subject of wealth, associated with writers and preachers such as Ambrose, Jerome, Augustine, Paulinus of Nola, and the supporters of Pelagius. There was good reason for this explosion. In the Christian churches of the time, distinctive traditions of giving and attitudes toward wealth reached back to before the age of Constantine. They were often associated with low-profile styles of leadership that drew their support from distinctly average congregations. These low-profile styles of giving and leadership frequently clashed with the expectations for a bright new age brought into the churches by the wealthy and the vocal few.

Because of this, the famous controversies about the use of wealth in the Christian churches that occurred at this time—such as those connected with Priscillian in the 380s, with Jerome in the 380s and 390s, and with the teachings of Pelagius in the 400s—were no mere rhetorical fireworks. They were impressive eddies raised by the force of currents that flowed deep within the Christian communities themselves, as new wealth and new radical attitudes toward wealth clashed with the tenacious if less articulate habits of the average Christian laity and of the average members of the clergy.

Hence the irony of the situation that emerged when much of the wealth created in the fourth century evaporated or changed its structures in the brutal crisis of the fifth century. Having recently passed from an age of relative mediocrity to an age of affluence, the Christian churches now found themselves in a generally impoverished world.

For this reason we can trace a double movement in the Christian communities of that time. As the fifth century progressed, the central institutions of the Roman world lost much of their mystique. Tensions between the sacred and the profane that had been veiled in a more confident generation were revealed ever more clearly. Faced with massive losses of income and by a widespread weakening of its authority in large areas of the West, the imperial structure inherited from the fourth century showed no intention of surrendering. Instead, the empire—the *Respublica*—went down fighting. And it went down fighting as a frankly secular institution. Government circles made plain that they would not yield any of the prerogatives of the Roman state to the Christian bishops. The disillusionment of the African bishops in their dealings with the court of Ravenna in the late 420s and the memorable anger of Salvian of Marseilles against the abuses of the Roman state in Gaul and Spain in the late 430s document a new, sharp mood.

In this time of crisis, the choice of personnel in the churches also came to be challenged. The lively controversies among the writers of Provence were not driven only by theological issues such as grace, free will, and predestination. They also included a vigorous debate on the nature of Christian leadership in a changed age. This problem had been brought to the fore in the 430s by a clash between new aristocratic ideals of leadership (allied to a vigorous monastic movement) and more old-fashioned, more plebeian models of the Christian community that had been upheld in the cities of southern Gaul and Italy.

At the same time, the crisis of the fifth century had brought about consolidation on the local level. Radical critiques of wealth were abandoned. Rather than denouncing the evil origins of wealth and insisting on its total renunciation, writers of the fifth century came to emphasize how wealth could be used to consolidate the Christian community. In major cities, such as Rome, the outreach to the poor, which had once taken the form of care only for the destitute, slowly but surely changed its function so as to embrace the care of average citizens in times of stress.

Last, but not least, the greatest surprise of all occurred in the late fifth century. The leaders of the churches realized that they—and not the great lay landowners whose fortunes had previously dwarfed the wealth of the churches—were, at last, truly wealthy. The collapse of the traditional aristocracies left the church in a unique position. The administrative and ideological effort deployed by so many bishops and clergymen of the late fifth and sixth centuries in making the best of this new situation—from the popes of Rome and well-known figures such as Gregory of Tours to up-and-coming clergymen as far apart as Mérida, Pavia, and Metz—was truly remarkable. It was an age of managerial bishops and their clerical staffs. We can still admire their skill as administrators and builders in the luminous shrines of Italy and elsewhere. Yet the secret of their success was not a total novelty. The notion of the sacral character of the corporate wealth of the church that flourished at this time went back many centuries to the sense of the collective nature of the wealth of the faithful that had been fiercely maintained, in the name of the care of the poor, among the more low-profile churches of the third and fourth centuries.

It was the weight of this new collective wealth, combined with the support of a new constituency of lay donors—drawn from many levels of society but most prominently from the new aristocracies of the post-imperial West—that exerted a discreet and continuous pressure on the churches of Latin Europe around 600 AD. This pressure hastened the great turn toward the other world that has been held to mark the end of the ancient world and the beginning of the middle ages. Led by a clergy made ever more starkly different from themselves in culture and lifestyle, the laity sought out new ways to place their wealth beyond the grave for the salvation of their souls. As Thorstein Eiriksson made plain in his last moments, wealth for the church and for the poor had become wealth for the dead.

This book has sought to bring readers back to those centuries, roughly between the years 350 and 550 AD. To do this has meant entering a very ancient world in order to encounter a very ancient Christianity. It was in this world that the conglomerate of ideas that medieval persons took for granted was first formed. As we have seen, these ideas emerged slowly, in a hesitant and conflict-laden manner very different from the way that they would later come to circulate in the triumphant Catholicism of the Latin West and in the various Christianities of more modern times. If this book has helped readers make the journey back to a world before our world—a world from which so many of our own views on wealth and poverty have derived—I will be content.

ABBREVIATIONS

CCSL   Corpus Christianorum, Series Latina

CSEL   Corpus Scriptorum Ecclesiasticorum Latinorum

MGH   Monumenta Germaniae Historica

PL   Patrologia cursus completus, series Latina

SC   Sources Chrétiennes

NOTES

PREFACE

1. I think, in particular, of the Latin-speaking Balkans: see esp. S Ćurčić, *Architecture in the Balkans from Diocletian to Süleyman the Magnificent* (New Haven, CT: Yale University Press, 2010). It was a joy and an honor to explore this neglected world through repeated conversations with Danny Ćurčić as he brought to completion his masterpiece of unflinching, all-embracing scholarship. See also the challenging body of neglected evidence assembled by M. Handley, "Two Hundred and Sixty-Four Addenda and Corrigenda to *PLRE* from the Latin-Speaking Balkans," *Journal of Late Antiquity* 3 (2010): 113–57; and the fine fourth-century mausolea at Sopiane (Pécs) in Hungary: K. Hudák and L. Nagy, *A Fine and Private Place: Discovering the Early Christian Cemetery of Sopiane/Pécs*, Heritage Booklets 6 (Pécs: Örökség Ház, 2009).

2. L. Gernet, *Le génie grec dans la religion* (Paris: Renaissance du Livre, 1932), 370.

3. Jerome, *Vita Malchi: Patrologia Latina* 23: 53C.

4. On the nature of the Jewish communities and the meaning of pious gifts within them I have learned much from S. Schwartz, *Imperialism and Jewish Society, 200 B.C.E. to 640 C.E.* (Princeton: Princeton University Press, 2001); and idem, *Were the Jews a Mediterranean Society? Reciprocity and Solidarity in Ancient Judaism* (Princeton: Princeton University Press, 2010); and from J. Niehoff-Panagiotidis, "Byzantinische Lebenswelt und rabbinische Hermeneutik: Die griechischen Juden in der Kairoer Genizah," *Byzantion* 74 (2004): 51–109 at pp. 88–100, on the distinctive meaning of almsgiving.

5. W. K. Lowther Clarke, *Saint Basil the Great: A Study in Monasticism* (Cambridge: Cambridge University Press, 1913), 14.

CHAPTER I
Aurea aetas

1. H. Dessau, *Inscriptiones Latinae Selectae*, no. 7457 (Berlin: Weidmann, 1916), 3:781–82. My colleague Brent Shaw has demonstrated that this inscription dates from

the fourth century: see Shaw, *Bringing in the Sheaves: Economy and Metaphor in the Roman World* (Toronto: forthcoming).

2. P. Brown, *Power and Persuasion in Late Antiquity: Towards a Christian Empire* (Madison: University of Wisconsin Press, 1992), 52–54; see P. Garnsey, *Social Status and Legal Privilege in the Roman Empire* (Oxford: Clarendon Press, 1970); and R. Rilinger, *Humiliores-Honestiores: Zu einer sozialen Dichotomie im Strafrecht der römischen Kaiserzeit* (Munich: Oldbourg, 1988).

3. F. Jacques, *Le privilège de liberté: Politique impériale et autonomie municipale dans les cités de l'Occident romain (161–244)*, Collection de l'école française de Rome 76 (Rome: Palais Farnèse, 1984); H. Inglebert, *Histoire de la civilisation romaine* (Paris: Presses Universitaires de France, 2005), 73–75; and P. Gros, "La ville comme symbole: Le modèle central et ses limites," in Inglebert, *Histoire de la civilisation romaine*, 155–232. A.H.M. Jones, *The Later Roman Empire: A Social, Economic and Administrative Survey, 284–602* (Oxford: Blackwell, 1964), 2:722–57 remains the best short synthesis in English.

4. P. F. Bang, "Trade and Empire—In Search of Organizing Concepts for the Roman Empire," *Past and Present* 195 (2007): 3–54 at p. 13.

5. G. Charles-Picard, "*Civitas mactaritana*," *Karthago* 8 (1957): 1–156; C. Lepelley, *Les cités de l'Afrique romaine au Bas-Empire*, vol. 2, *Notices d'histoire municipale* (Paris: Études Augustiniennes, 1981), 289–95.

6. *Records of the Grand Historian of China, translated from the* Shih Chi *of Ssu-ma Ch'ien*, trans. B. Watson, Columbia Records of Civilization 65 (New York: Columbia University Press, 1961), 499; see Ying-shih Yü, *Trade and Expansion in Han China: A Study in the Structure of Sino-Barbarian Economic Relations* (Berkeley: University of California Press, 1967).

7. J. Lendon, *Empire of Honour: The Art of Government in the Roman World* (Oxford: Oxford University Press, 1997), 30.

8. *Novella of Valentinian III* 3.4 (AD 439). This fixed a minimum below which persons would not be co-opted into the town council: see Jones, *The Later Roman Empire*, 2:738–39.

9. Charles-Picard, "*Civitas mactaritana*," 40.

10. I take this figure from W. C. Scheidel and S. J. Friesen, "The Size of the Economy and the Distribution of Income in the Roman Empire," *Journal of Roman Studies* 99 (2009): 61–91, at p. 77.

11. See the map in Inglebert, *Histoire de la civilisation romaine*, 72–73, and map 1, p. 7.

12. Scheidel and Friesen, "The Size of the Economy," 91.

13. The classic statements are F. Lot, *The End of the Ancient World and the Beginnings of the Middle Ages* (New York: Knopf, 1931); and M. Rostovtzeff, *The Social and Economic History of the Roman Empire* (Oxford: Clarendon Press, 1926). From an abundant bibliography, see the titles that have influenced the present author in P. Brown, "The World of Late Antiquity Revisited," *Symbolae Osloenses* 72 (1997): 5–90. It goes without saying that the debate on this issue remains as vigorous as ever: for views different from my own, see J.W.H.G. Liebeschuetz, *The Decline and Fall of the Roman City* (Oxford:

Oxford University Press, 2001); and A. Giardina, "Esplosione di tardoantico," *Studi Storici* 40 (1999): 157–80.

14. F. de Callataÿ, "The Graeco-Roman Economy in the Super Long-Run: Lead, Copper and Shipwrecks," *Journal of Roman Archaeology* 18 (2005): 361–72; B. Ward-Perkins, *The Fall of Rome and the End of Civilization* (Oxford: Oxford University Press, 2005), 87–104.

15. G. Halsall, *Barbarian Migrations and the Roman West, 376–568* (Cambridge: Cambridge University Press, 2007), 69.

16. Ibid., 72; J. Haas, *Die Umweltkrise des 3. Jahrhunderts n. Chr. im Nordwesten des Imperium Romanum*, Geographica Historica 22 (Stuttgart: Steiner, 2006).

17. R. P. Duncan-Jones, "The Impact of the Antonine Plague," *Journal of Roman Archaeology* 9 (1996): 108–36; M. McCormick, *Origins of the European Economy: Communications and Commerce, A.D. 300–900* (Cambridge: Cambridge University Press, 2001), 30–41.

18. I have found that the best modern accounts are by J.-M. Carrié and A. Rousselle, *L'empire romain en mutation: Des Sévères à Constantin, 192–337* (Paris: Du Seuil, 1999), 49–126, 651–718. D. S. Potter, *The Roman Empire at Bay, AD 180–395* (London: Routledge, 2004), 85–298. See also K. Strobel, *Das Imperium Romanum im "3. Jahrhundert": Modell einer historischen Krise?* Historia Einzelschrift 75 (Stuttgart: F. Steiner, 1993); C. Witschel, "Re-Evaluating the Roman West in the 3rd Century A.D.," *Journal of Roman Archaeology* 17 (2004): 251–81; *Deleto paene imperio Romano: Transformazionsprozesse des römischen Reiches im 3. Jahrhundert und ihre Rezeption in der Neuzeit*, ed. K.-P. Johne, T. Gerdhardt, and U. Hartmann (Stuttgart: F. Steiner, 2006).

19. See C. Witschel, *Krise-Rezession-Stagnation? Der Westen des römischen Reiches im 3. Jahrhundert n. Chr.* (Frankfurt: M. Clauss, 1999), 239–74 on Spain and Britain. See now P. Reynolds, *Hispania and the Roman Mediterranean, A.D. 100–700: Ceramics and Trade* (London: Duckworth, 2010), 24–32, 69–74.

20. R. B. Hitchner, "The Kasserine Archaeological Survey, 1982–1985," *Africa* 11–12 (1992–93): 158–259; idem, "The Kasserine Archaeological Survey, 1982–1986" and "The Kasserine Archaeological Survey, 1987," *Antiquités africaines* 24 (1988): 7–41 and 26 (1990): 231–59; D.P.S. Peacock, F. Bejaoui, and N. Ben Lazreg, "Roman Pottery Production in Central Tunisia," *Journal of Roman Archaeology* 3 (1990): 59–84.

21. C. Lepelley, *Les cités de l'Afrique romaine*, vol. 1, *La permanence d'une civilisation municipale* (Paris: Études Augustiniennes, 1979), 59–120. For Italy, see B. Ward-Perkins, *From Classical Antiquity to the Middle Ages: Urban Public Building in Northern and Central Italy, 300–850* (Oxford: Oxford University Press, 1984), 1–48.

22. Halsall, *Barbarian Migrations and the Roman West*, 83–85; J. Crow, "Fortifications and Urbanism in Late Antiquity," in *Recent Research in Late Antique Urbanism*, ed. L. Lavan, Journal of Roman Archaeology: Supplement 42 (Portsmouth, RI: Journal of Roman Archaeology, 1996), 89–105; P. Garmy and L. Maurin, eds., *Enceintes romaines d'Aquitaine: Bordeaux, Dax, Périgueux, Bazas* (Paris: Editions de la Maison des Sciences de l'Homme, 1996); H. Dey, "Art, Ceremony and City Walls: The Aesthetics of Imperial Resurgence in the Late Roman West," and B. S. Bachrach, "The Fortification of Gaul and

the Economy of the Third and Fourth Centuries," *Journal of Late Antiquity* 3 (2010): 3–37, 38–64; C. Fernández Ochoa and A. Morillo Cerdán, "Walls in the Urban Landscape of Late Roman Spain: Defense and Imperial Strategy," in *Hispania in Late Antiquity: Current Perspectives*, ed. K. Bowes and M. Kulikowski (Leiden: Brill, 2005): 299–340; R. Rebuffat, "Enceintes urbaines et insécurité en Maurétanie tingitaine," *Mélanges de l'École française de Rome: Antiquité* 86 (1974): 501–22.

23. J.-M. Carrié, "Dioclétien et la fiscalité," *Antiquité tardive* 2 (1994): 33–64. G. Bransbourg, "Fiscalité impériale et finances municipales au IVe siècle," *Antiquité tardive* 16 (2008): 255–96 is a significant new contribution.

24. D. Bonneau, *La crue du Nil, divinité égyptienne, à travers milles ans d'histoire (322 av.–641 ap. J.-C.)* (Paris: Klincksieck, 1964). In the sixth century the Nile was still called "Most Sacred": C. Kreuzsaler, "*Ho hierôtatos Nilos* auf einer christlichen Nilstandsmarkierung," *Journal of Juristic Papyrology* 34 (2004): 81–86.

25. P. Erdkamp, *The Grain Market in the Roman Empire: A Social, Political and Economic Study* (Cambridge: Cambridge University Press, 2005), 322–25; P. Horden and N. Purcell, *The Corrupting Sea: A Study of Mediterranean History* (Oxford: Blackwell, 2000), 152; P. Garnsey, *Famine and Food Supply in the Graeco-Roman World: Responses to Risk and Crisis* (Cambridge: Cambridge University Press, 1988), 8–16.

26. Eusebius, *Ecclesiastical History* 9.7.10.

27. *Council of Elvira*, canon 49, ed. E. J. Jonkers, in *Acta et symbola conciliorum quae saeculo quarto habita sunt* (Leiden: Brill, 1954), 16.

28. P. A. Février, *Approches du Maghreb romain: Pouvoirs, différences et conflits*, vol. 2 (La Calade: Édisud, 1990), 17; A. Mastrocinque, "Magia agraria nell'impero cristiano," *Mediterraneo antico* 7 (2004): 795–836.

29. M. Meslin, *La fête des kalendes de janvier dans l'empire romain: Étude d'un rituel de Nouvel An* (Brussels: Latomus, 1970).

30. Caesarius of Arles, *Sermon* 192.3.

31. *Jerusalem Talmud: Yoma* 5.2, trans. M. Schwab, *Le Talmud de Jérusalem* (Paris: Maisonneuve, 1932–33), 3:218.

32. Jones, *The Later Roman Empire*, 1:451–60.

33. Ibid., 1:462–69.

34. D. Vera, "Forme e funzioni della rendita fondiaria nella tarda antichità," in *Società romana e impero tardoantico*, vol. 1, *Istituzioni, ceti, economie*, ed. A. Giardina (Bari: Laterza, 1986), 367–447 at pp. 441–43; and idem, "L'altra faccia della luna: La società contadina nella Sicilia di Gregorio Magno," *Studi Storici* 47 (2006): 437–61. See also C. Wickham, *Framing the Early Middle Ages: Europe and the Mediterranean, 400–800* (Oxford: Oxford University Press, 2005), 68.

35. Augustine, *New [Divjak] Letter* 14* and 15*.3, in Bibliothèque Augustinienne 46B, *Lettres 1*–29** (Paris: Desclée de Brouwer, 1987), 262–69, trans. R. B. Eno, in *St. Augustine: Letters: Volume VI (1*–29*)*, Fathers of the Church 81 (Washington, DC: Catholic University of America Press, 1989), 112–16.

36. J. Banaji, *Agrarian Change in Late Antiquity: Gold, Labour, and Aristocratic Dominance* (Oxford: Oxford University Press, 2001), 16.

37. Erdkamp, *The Grain Market*, 324.

38. Horden and Purcell, *The Corrupting Sea*, 205, 214.

39. J. Alarcão, R. Étienne, and F. Mayet, *Les villas romaines de São Cucufate (Portugal)* (Paris: Boccard, 1990), 149–55.

40. M. McCormick, "Bateaux de vie, bateaux de mort: Maladie, commerce et le passage économique du bas-empire au moyen-âge," in *Morfologie sociali e culturali in Europa fra Tarda Antichità e Alto Medioevo*, Settimane di Studi del Centro Italiano di Studi sull'Alto Medioevo 45 (Spoleto: Centro di Studi sull'Alto Medio Evo, 1998), 35–118 at pp. 35–37.

41. J. Haldon, "*Comes horreorum—Komès tès Lamias*," *Byzantine and Modern Greek Studies* 10 (1986): 203–9.

42. Banaji, *Agrarian Change in Late Antiquity*, 39–88 develops with great force a view inspired by S. Mazzarino, *Aspetti sociali del quarto secolo* (Rome: Bretschneider, 1951), 47–216. See now F. Carlà, *L'oro nella tarda anrichità: Aspetti economici e sociali* (Turin: Silvio Zamorani, 2009), 117–57.

43. *Anonymus de rebus bellicis* 2.1–2, ed. and trans. E. A. Thompson, *A Roman Reformer and Inventor* (Oxford: Clarendon Press, 1952), 94; see Banaji, *Agrarian Change in Late Antiquity*, 46–49; and A. Giardina, ed., *Anonimo: Le cose della guerra* ([Milan]: Mondadori, 1989), with commentary and full discussion of the possible dates and context of the treatise. See now Carlà, *L'oro nella tarda anrichità*, 125–31.

44. J.-P. Callu, "Le 'centenarium' et l'enrichissement monétaire au Bas-Empire," *Ktèma* 3 (1978): 301–16. On the flow of gold in the empire as revealed by hoards of *solidi* beyond the frontier, see esp. P. Guest, "Roman Gold and Hun Kings: The Use and Hoarding of Solidi in the Late Fourth and Fifth Centuries," in *Roman Coins outside the Empire: Ways and Phases, Contexts and Functions*, ed. A. Bursche, R. Ciołek, and R. Wolters, Collection Moneta 82 (Wetteren: Moneta, 2008), 295–307. For a spectacular hoard of *solidi* discovered close to the capital at Trier, see now *Moselgold: Der römische Schatz von Machtum*, ed. F. Reinert (Luxembourg: Musée national d'histoire et d'art, 2008). I owe knowledge of this to the kindness of Johannes Hahn.

45. Jorge Luis Borges, *A Personal Anthology*, ed. A. Kerrigan (New York: Grove Press, 1967), 131.

46. Olympiodorus, *History: Fragment* 41.1–2, ed. R. C. Blockley, *The Fragmentary Classicising Historians of the Later Roman Empire: Eunapius, Olympiodorus, Priscus and Malchus*, vol. 2 (Liverpool: Francis Cairns, 1983), 204–6.

47. W. C. Scheidel, "Finances, Figures and Fiction," *Classical Quarterly* 46 (1996): 222–38.

48. C. Wickham, *The Inheritance of Rome: A History of Europe from 400 to 1000* (London: Allen Lane, 2009), 29.

49. Jones, *The Later Roman Empire*, 2:537–39.

50. *The Life of Melania* 15, ed. D. Gorce, *Vie de sainte Mélanie*, SC 90 (Paris: Le Cerf, 1962), 156, trans. E. A. Clark, *The Life of Melania the Younger* (New York: Edwin Mellen, 1984), 38.

51. *Life of Melania* 17, Gorce, p. 160, Clark, p. 40.

52. Ammianus Marcellinus, *Res gestae* 27.11.1, ed. and trans. J. C. Rolfe, *Ammianus Marcellinus,* Loeb Classical Library (Cambridge, MA: Harvard University Press, 1952),

3:72–74; also trans. W. Hamilton, *The Later Roman Empire, A.D. 354–378* (Harmondsworth, UK: Penguin, 1986), 345–46.

53. A. Gillett, "The Date and Circumstances of Olympiodorus of Thebes," *Traditio* 48 (1993): 1–29.

54. T. D. Barnes, *Ammianus Marcellinus and the Representation of Historical Reality* (Ithaca, NY: Cornell University Press, 1998), 117–19.

55. Vera, "Forme e funzioni della rendita fondiaria," 412.

56. Rostovtzeff, *Social and Economic History of the Roman Empire*, 475–77 with plate IX.2.

57. Summary: *Du latifundium au latifondo: Un héritage de Rome, une création médiévale ou moderne?* Publications du Centre Pierre Paris 25 (Paris: Boccard, 1995), 460. For a similar dismantling of certitudes in Italian archaeology (related to the "slave villa" and the implied rise of the *latifundium*), see A. Marzano, *Roman Villas in Central Italy: A Social and Economic History*, Columbia Studies in the Classical Tradition 30 (Leiden: Brill, 2007), 125–53.

58. P. Sillières, "Approche d'un espace rural antique: L'exemple de Vila de Frades en Lusitanie méridionale," in *Du latifundium au latifondo*, 21–29.

59. D. Vera, *"Massa fundorum,"* *Mélanges de l'École française de Rome: Antiquité* 111 (1999): 991–1025.

60. See esp. P. Van Ossel, "Rural Impoverishment in Northern Gaul at the End of Antiquity: The Contribution of Archaeology," in *Social and Political Life in Late Antiquity*, Late Antique Archaeology 3:1, ed. W. Bowden, A. Gutteridge, and C. Machado (Leiden: Brill, 2006), 533–65.

61. J.-M. Carrié, "Le 'colonat du Bas-Empire': Un mythe historiographique?" *Opus* 1 (1982): 351–70; C. Grey, "Contextualizing *Colonatus*: The *Origo* of the Late Roman Empire," *Journal of Roman Studies* 97 (2007): 155–75.

62. See esp. the vigorous arguments of J. Banaji, "Lavoratori liberi e residenza coatta: Il colonato romano in prospettiva storica," in *Terre, proprietari e contadini dell'impero romano: Dall'affitto agrario al colonato tardoantico*, ed. E. Lo Cascio (Rome: Nuova Italia Scientifica, 1997), 253–80; and idem, "Aristocracies, Peasantries and the Framing of the Early Middle Ages," *Journal of Agrarian Change* 9 (2009): 59–91 at p. 67. For the relation between demands for a tied peasantry and emergencies caused by barbarian raids, see S. Schmidt-Hofner, *Reagieren und Gestalten: Die Regierungsstil des spätrömischen Kaisers am Beispiel der Gesetzgebung Valentinians I*, Vestigia 58 (Munich: C. H. Beck, 2008), 269–87, esp. 276–80. Though based on evidence from the eastern provinces, K. Harper, "The Greek Census Inscriptions of Late Antiquity," *Journal of Roman Studies* 98 (2008): 83–119 at pp. 105–6 is most revealing for the role of slaves and dependent tenants in the labor force of the rich.

63. A. Giardina, "The Transition to Late Antiquity," in *The Cambridge Economic History of the Greco-Roman World*, ed. W. Scheidel, I. Morris, and R. Saller (Cambridge: Cambridge University Press, 2007), 743–68 at p. 752.

64. J. Wacher, *Roman Britain*, 2nd ed. (Stroud, UK: Sutton, 1998), 131–36; Marzano, *Roman Villas in Central Italy*, 141. The landmark works that led to this revision are Mazzarino, *Aspetti sociali del quarto secolo*; L. Cracco Ruggini, *Economia e società nell'*

"Italia annonaria": Rapporti fra agricoltura e commercio dal IV al VI secolo d.C. (Milan: Giuffrè, 1961; 2nd ed., Bari: Edipuglia, 1995); and Lepelley, *Les cités de l'Afrique romaine.*

65. N. Duval, "Deux mythes iconographiques de l'antiquité tardive: La villa fortifiée et le 'chasseur vandale,'" in *Humana sapit: Études d'Antiquité Tardive offertes à Lellia Cracco Ruggini*, ed. J.-M. Carrié and R. Lizzi Testa, Bibliothèque d'Antiquité Tardive 3 (Turnhout: Brepols, 2002), 333–40.

66. The grandeur of Piazza Armerina, in particular, has led to excessively dramatic interpretations of the role of late Roman villas as places for the show of power: see esp. S. Ellis, "Power, Architecture and Décor: How the Late Roman Aristocrat Appeared to His Guests," in *Roman Art in the Private Sphere: New Perspectives on the Architecture and Decor of the Domus, Villa, and Insula*, ed. E. K. Gazda (Ann Arbor: University of Michigan Press, 1991), 117–34.

67. See now esp. K. Bowes, *Houses and Society in the Later Roman Empire* (London: Duckworth, 2010), 77–82, 95–98. One should note the wide range of the sizes and wealth of villas in all regional surveys: see esp. C. Balmelle, *Les demeures aristocratiques d'Aquitaine: Société et culture de l'Antiquité tardive dans le Sud-Ouest de la Gaule* (Bordeaux and Paris: Ausonius and Aquitania, 2001); A. Chavarría Arnau, *El final de las "villae" en "Hispania" (siglos IV–VIII)* (Turnhout: Brepols, 2007); S. Scott, *Art and Society in Fourth Century Britain: Villa Mosaics in Context*, Oxford School of Archaeology Monographs 53 (Oxford: Oxbow, 2000).

68. I. Rodá, "Iconografía y epigrafía en dos mosaicos hispanas: Las villas de Tossa y de Dueñas," in *VI Coloquio internacional sobre mosaico antiguo* (Palencia/Mérida: Associación Español del Mosaico, 1994), 35–42 at p. 35.

69. W. Scheidel, "Stratification, Deprivation and Quality of Life," in *Poverty in the Roman World*, ed. M. Atkins and R. Osborne (Cambridge: Cambridge University Press, 2006), 40–59 at p. 54.

70. For Africa, see esp. P. Leveau, *Caesarea de Maurétanie: Une ville romaine et ses campagnes*, Collection de l'École française de Rome 70 (Rome: Palais Farnèse, 1984), 477–85; for Gaul, see Wickham, *Framing the Early Middle Ages*, 167–74.

71. P. Heather, "New Men for New Constantines? Creating an Imperial Elite in the Eastern Mediterranean," in *New Constantines: The Rhythm of Imperial Renewal in Byzantium, 4th–13th Centuries*, ed. P. Magdalino (Aldershot: Variorum, 1994), 11–34; and idem, "Senators and Senates," in *The Cambridge Ancient History*, vol. 13, *The Late Empire, A.D. 337–425*, ed. A. Cameron and P. Garnsey (Cambridge: Cambridge University Press, 1998), 184–210; Schmidt-Hofner, *Reagieren und Gestalten*, 103–15.

72. R. Lizzi Testa, *Senatori, popolo, papi: Il governo di Roma al tempo dei Valentiniani* (Bari: Edipuglia, 2004), 209–305; idem, "Alle origini della tradizione pagana su Costantino e il senato romano," in *Transformations of Late Antiquity: Essays for Peter Brown*, ed. P. Rousseau and M. Papoutsakis (Farnham, UK: Ashgate, 2009), 85–127 at pp. 120–23.

73. Alan Cameron, "The Antiquity of the Symmachi," *Historia* 48 (1999): 477–505; and F. Jacques, "L'ordine senatorio attraverso la crisi del III secolo," in *Società romana e impero tardoantico*, 1:81–225, with the map on p. 110. This decisive shift to the south of the Roman economy has been revealed through a remarkable tradition of Italian scholar-

ship that is well summed up by C. Wickham, "Marx, Sherlock Holmes and Late Roman Commerce," *Journal of Roman Studies* 78 (1988): 183–93; and now idem, *Framing the Early Middle Ages*, 708–12.

74. B. Shaw, "After Rome: Transformations of the Early Mediterranean World," *New Left Review* 51 (2008): 89–114, an admirably independent-minded review of Wickham, *Framing the Early Middle Ages*.

75. *Anonymus de rebus bellicis* 2.3, p. 94.

76. C. Kelly, *Ruling the Later Roman Empire* (Cambridge, MA: Harvard University Press, 2004), 107–13, 148–58.

77. Ibid., 145–48; Lepelley, *Les cités de l'Afrique romaine*, 2:468–70.

78. Kelly, *Ruling the Later Roman Empire*, 138–45. The two best accounts of the frustrations of the *curiales* in the later empire as a whole remain Jones, *The Later Roman Empire*, 2:737–57; and Lepelley, *Les cités de l'Afrique romaine*, 1:243–92.

79. Halsall, *Barbarian Migrations and the Roman West*, 79–96 provides a fine survey of the regional divergences among the local elites of the late Roman West.

80. D. Crane, *Scott of the Antarctic: A Life of Courage and Tragedy in the Extreme South* (New York: Harper Percival, 2006), 45.

81. J.-U. Krause, *Spätantike Patronatsformen im Westen des römischen Reiches*, Vestigia 38 (Munich: C. H. Beck, 1987), 20–67; P. Garnsey, "Roman Patronage," in *From the Tetrarchs to the Theodosians: Later Roman History and Culture, 284–450 CE. For John Matthews on the Occasion of His 70th Birthday*, Yale Classical Studies 34, ed. S. McGill, C. Sogno, and E. Watts (Cambridge: Cambridge University Press, 2010), 33–54 at pp. 47–53.

82. *Calendar of 354*, ed. T. Mommsen, *Chronica Minora*, MGH: Auctores Antiquissimi 9 (Berlin: Weidmann, 1892), 1:47.

83. Augustine, *Contra academicos* 2.2.2; see Lepelley, *Les cités de l'Afrique romaine*, 2:176–82.

84. Augustine, *Confessions* 5.13.23; see now J. V. Ebbeler and C. Sogno, "Religious Identity and the Politics of Patronage: Symmachus and Augustine," *Historia* 56 (2007): 230–42.

85. Augustine, *Confessions* 6.11.19.

86. Augustine, *Confessions* 6.9.15.

87. Augustine, *Confessions* 6.10.16.

88. J. F. Matthews, "The Letters of Symmachus," in *Latin Literature of the Fourth Century*, ed. J. W. Binns (London: Routledge, 1974), 58–99; R.B.E. Smith, "'Restored Utility, Eternal City': Patronal Imagery at Rome in the Fourth Century AD," in *"Bread and Circuses": Euergetism and Municipal Patronage in Roman Italy*, ed. K. Lomas and T. Cornell (London: Routledge, 2003), 142–66; C. Sogno, "Roman Matchmaking," in *From the Tetrarchs to the Theodosians*, 51–71 at pp. 63–66.

89. M. Harlow, "Clothes Maketh the Man: Power Dressing and Elite Masculinity in the Later Roman World," in *Gender in the Early Medieval World: East and West, 300–900*, ed. L. Brubaker and J.M.H. Smith (Cambridge: Cambridge University Press, 2004), 44–69 at pp. 44–54; for a slightly later period, see P. von Rummel, "*Habitus Vandalorum?* Zur Frage nach einer gruppen-spezifischen Kleidung der Vandalen in Afrika," *An-

tiquité tardive 10 (2002): 131–141. "Barbarian" dress is the dress of courtiers and hunters, not specifically of Vandals. See now P. von Rummel, *Habitus barbarus: Kleidung und Repräsentation spätantiker Eliten im 4. und 5. Jahrhundert*, Reallexikon der germanischen Altertumskunde, Ergänzungsband 55 (Berlin: de Gruyter, 2007), 401–7.

90. R. MacMullen, "Some Pictures in Ammianus Marcellinus," *Art Bulletin* 46 (1964), now in *Changes in the Roman Empire: Essays in the Ordinary* (Princeton: Princeton University Press, 1990), 78–106; F. Morelli, "Tessuti e indumenti nel contesto economico tardoantico: I prezzi," *Antiquité tardive* 12 (2004): 55–78.

91. *Life of Melania* 19 and 21, Gorce, pp. 164, 172, Clark, pp. 41, 44; *Liber Pontificalis 42: Innocent I*, trans. R. Davis, *The Book of Pontiffs (Liber Pontificalis): The Ancient Biographies of the First Ninety Roman Bishops to AD 715* (Liverpool: Liverpool University Press, 1989), 31.

92. *Pap. Ital.* 8.III.7–13, ed. and trans. J.-O. Tjäder, *Die nichtliterarischen Papyri Italiens aus der Zeit 445–700*, Skrifter utgivna av Svenska Institutet i Rom 4.19 (Lund: Gleerup, 1955), 242.

93. C. Witschel and B. Borg, "Veränderungen im Repräsentationsverhalten der römischen Eliten während des 3. Jhrdts. n. Chr.," *Inschriftliche Denkmäler als Medien der Selbstdarstellung in der römischen Welt*, ed. G. Alföldy and S. Panciera (Stuttgart: F. Steiner, 2001), 47–120 at pp. 97–99.

94. H. Maguire, "The Good Life," in *Late Antiquity: A Guide to the Postclassical World*, ed. G. W. Bowersock, P. Brown, and O. Grabar (Cambridge, MA: Harvard University Press, 1999), 238–57 at pp. 242–43.

95. See M. Kulikowski, *Late Roman Spain and Its Cities* (Baltimore: Johns Hopkins University Press, 2004), 137–47, on the contrast between El Ruedo (Cordova), with its local sandstone and stucco work, and the truly imperial use of eastern marbles in Carranque (Toledo).

96. J. W. Salomonson, "Late Roman Earthenware with Relief Decoration Found in Northern-Africa and Egypt," *Oudheidkundige Mededelingen* 43 (1962): 53–95; J. Spier, "A Lost Consular Diptych of Anicius Auchenius Bassus (A.D. 408) in the Mould for an ARS Plaque," *Journal of Roman Archaeology* 16 (2003): 251–54. See now the hoard of nineteen items of copper and lead alloy tableware found by Chris Jarrett at Draper's Gardens, London: G. Cleland, "Unearthed after 1,600 Years, Dinner Set Hidden by Fleeing Romans," *Daily Telegraph*, December 7, 2007.

97. M. J. de Almeida and A. Carvalho, "*Villa* romana da Quinta das Longas (Elvas, Portugal): A lixeira baixo-imperial," *Revista Portuguesa de Arqueologia* 8 (2005): 299–368. I owe this reference to my student Damian Fernández.

98. I. Baldini Lippolis, *La domus tardoantica: Forme e rappresentazioni dello spazio domestico nelle città del Mediterraneo* (Imola: University Press of Bologna, 2001), 73.

99. R. Bland and C. Johns, *The Hoxne Treasure: An Illustrated Introduction* (London: British Museum Press, 1993), frontispiece.

100. J. T. Smith, *Roman Villas: A Study in Social Structure* (London: Routledge, 1997), 182–83.

101. L. M. Stirling, *The Learned Collector: Mythological Statuettes and Classical Taste in Late Antique Gaul* (Ann Arbor: University of Michigan Press, 2003), 128–33, 190.

102. S. E. Cleary, *The Ending of Roman Britain* (London: Batsford, 1989); Wickham, *Framing the Early Middle Ages*, 306–10.

CHAPTER 2
Mediocritas

1. R. Syme, *Ammianus and the Historia Augusta* (Oxford: Clarendon Press, 1968), 210.

2. From a superabundant literature, I have found the most reliable account of the reign and possible intentions of Constantine to be T. D. Barnes, *Constantine and Eusebius* (Cambridge, MA: Harvard University Press, 1981) and now *Constantine: Dynasty, Religion, and Power in the Later Roman Empire* (Oxford: Wiley-Blackwell, 2011). R. Van Dam, *The Roman Revolution of Constantine* (New York: Cambridge University Press, 2007) does justice to the extent and complexity of Constantine's non-religious commitments. See also *The Cambridge Companion to the Age of Constantine*, ed. N. Lenski (Cambridge: Cambridge University Press, 2006); and T. D. Barnes, "Was There a Constantinian Revolution?" *Journal of Late Antiquity* 2 (2009): 374–84. See now K. W. Wilkinson, "Palladas and the Age of Constantine," *Journal of Roman Studies* 99 (2009): 36–60, and idem, "Palladas and the Foundation of Constantinople," *Journal of Roman Studies* 100 (2010): 179–94, important articles which, if accepted, give a more drastic impression of the impact of Constantine on the paganism of the eastern provinces.

3. Readers acquainted with this literature will see that I favor a "minimalist" rather than a "maximalist" view of the intentions—and hence the impact—of Constantine in his support of the Christian faith. The debate is summed up by E. D. Digeser, *The Making of a Christian Empire: Lactantius and Rome* (Ithaca, NY: Cornell University Press, 2000), 167–71. There is much to be learned from the views expressed, with vigor and a characteristic sense of paradox, by P. Veyne, *Quand notre monde est devenu chrétien (312–394)* (Paris: Albin Michel, 2007), now translated as *When Our World Became Christian, 312–394* (Cambridge: Polity Press, 2010).

4. Compare Barnes, *Constantine and Eusebius*, 191, with R. Lane Fox, *Pagans and Christians* (New York: A. Knopf, 1987), 265–335.

5. K. M. Hopkins, "Christian Number and Its Implications," *Journal of Early Christian Studies* 6 (1998): 185–226. On the expansion of Christianity before Constantine, see now M.-F. Baslez, *Comment notre monde est devenu chrétien* (Tours: Éditions CLD, 2008), 127–200, in response to Veyne, *Quand notre monde est devenu chrétien*, 35–91, *When Our World Became Christian*, 17–45.

6. J. B. Bury, *History of the Later Roman Empire from the Death of Theodosius I to the Death of Justinian (A.D. 395–A.D. 565)* (London: MacMillan, 1923), 1:366.

7. N. H. Baynes, *Constantine the Great and the Christian Church*, 2nd ed. with preface by Henry Chadwick (London: Oxford University Press for the British Academy, 1972), 9–10, 29–30; Veyne, *Quand notre monde est devenu chrétien*, 33, *When Our World Became Christian*, 16.

8. Letter of Constantine (of 313) to the bishop of Syracuse: Eusebius, *Ecclesiastical History* 10.5.21.

9. Barnes, *Constantine and Eusebius*, 208–44; idem, *Athanasius and Constantius: Theology and Politics in the Constantinian Empire* (Cambridge, MA: Harvard University Press, 1993), 165–75. See now P. Just, *Imperator et Episcopus: Zum Verhältnis vom Staatsgewalt und christlicher Kirche zwischen dem 1. Konzil von Nicaea (325) und dem 1. Konzil von Konstantinopel*, Potsdamer Altertumswissenschaftliche Beiträge 8 (Stuttgart: F. Steiner, 2003); P. Barceló, *Constantius II. und seine Zeit: Die Anfänge des Staatskirchentums* (Stuttgart: Klett-Cotta, 2004); and Veyne, *Quand notre monde est devenu chrétien*, 141–58, *When Our World Became Christian*, 73–84.

10. C. Sotinel, "La sphère profane dans l'espace urbain," in *Les frontières du profane dans l'antiquité tardive*, ed. É. Rebillard and C. Sotinel, Collection de l'École française de Rome 428 (Rome: École française de Rome, 2010), 319–49 at p. 344; Veyne, *Quand notre monde est devenu chrétien*, 78–91, *When Our World Became Christian*, 39–45.

11. Augustine, *Dolbeau Sermon* 25.25.510, ed. F. Dolbeau, *Vingt-six sermons au peuple d'Afrique* (Paris: Institut d'Études Augustiniennes, 1996), 266, trans. E. Hill, in *Sermons (Newly Discovered) III/11*, The Works of Saint Augustine: A Translation for the 21st Century (Hyde Park, NY: New City Press, 1997), 382; see P. Brown, *Augustine of Hippo: New Edition with an Epilogue* (Berkeley: University of California Press, 2000), 459–61.

12. Veyne, *Quand notre monde est devenu chrétien*, 159, *When Our World Became Christian*, 84.

13. R.S.O. Tomlin, "The Curse Tablets," in *The Temple of Sulis Minerva at Bath*, vol. 2, *The Finds from the Sacred Spring*, ed. B. Cunliffe (Oxford: Oxford University Press, 1988), 323–24.

14. For the general notion of exemptions to cultic practitioners, see R. M. Grant, *Early Christianity and Society: Seven Studies* (New York: Harper and Row, 1977), 44–65; and M. Weinfeld, *Social Justice in Ancient Israel and in the Ancient Near East* (Minneapolis: Fortress; Jerusalem: Magnes, 1995), 16–17, 79–80. Individual performers of rituals could also qualify for exemptions: see J. Alvar, *Romanising Oriental Gods: Myth, Salvation and Ethics in the Cults of Cybele, Isis and Mithras*, trans. and ed. R. Gordon, Religions of the Greco-Roman World 165 (Leiden: Brill, 2008), 266, for exemption for a person who had performed a *taruobolium* "for the safety of the emperor." For exemptions issued by Constantine for the leaders of Jewish synagogues, see *Codex Theodosianus* 16.8.2, 16.8.4; A. Linder, ed. and trans., *The Jews in Roman Imperial Legislation* (Detroit: Wayne State University Press; Jerusalem: Israel Academy of Sciences and Humanities, 1987), 131–38; and M. Jacobs, *Die Institution des jüdischen Patriarchen*, Texte und Studien zum Antiken Judentum 52 (Tübingen: Mohr Siebeck, 1995), 274–84. For teachers as "doctors of the soul," see *Syro-Roman Law Book* 116, ed. and trans. J. Furlani, *Fontes Iuris Romani Anteiustiniani*, ed. S. Riccobono (Florence: G. Barberà, 1968), vol. 2, part 1, p. 794.

15. See esp. *Codex Theodosianus* 16.2.1–16, from 313 to 361 AD, with the edition with notes by R. Delmaire, *Le code Théodosien: Livre XVI*, SC 497 (Paris: Le Cerf, 2005), 122–55. K. L. Noethlichs, "Zur Einflussnahme des Staates auf die Entwicklung eines christlichen Klerikerstandes," *Jahrbuch für Antike und Christentum* 15 (1972): 136–54; R. Lizzi Testa, "Privilegi economici e definizione di *status*: Il caso del vescovo cristiano,"

Rendiconti dell'Accademia Nazionale dei Lincei: Classe di scienze morali, storiche e filologiche, ser. 9, no. 11 (2000): 55–103; C. Rapp, *Holy Bishops in Late Antiquity: The Nature of Christian Leadership in an Age of Transition* (Berkeley: University of California Press, 2005), 234–60; R. Van Dam, "Bishops and Society," in *The Cambridge History of Christianity,* vol. 2, *Constantine to c. 600,* ed. A. Casiday and F. W. Norris (Cambridge: Cambridge University Press, 2007), 343–66 at pp. 345–47. The reader should be aware that the respective dates of many of these laws remain uncertain.

16. See esp. Jones, *The Later Roman Empire,* 2:734–37, 858–59 for a description of the extent and variety of these duties.

17. *Codex Theodosianus* 16.2.16 (361).

18. Lizzi Testa, "Privilegi economici e definizione di *status*," 91–96; Jones, *The Later Roman Empire,* 1:118.

19. A.H.M. Jones, "The Social Background of the Struggle between Paganism and Christianity," in *The Conflict between Paganism and Christianity in the Fourth Century,* ed. A. Momigliano (Oxford: Clarendon Press, 1963), 17–37 at p. 21.

20. For Italy, see esp. C. Sotinel, "Le personnel épiscopal: Enquête sur la puissance de l'évêque dans la cité," in *L'évêque dans la cité du IVe au Ve siècle: Image et autorité,* ed. É. Rebillard and C. Sotinel, Collection de l'École française de Rome 248 (Rome: École française de Rome, 1998), 105–26, esp. at pp. 125–26, reprinted as "The Bishop's Men: Episcopal Power in the City," in *Church and Society in Late Antique Italy and beyond* (Farnham, UK: Ashgate/Variorum, 2010), article VII; idem, "Le recrutement des évêques en Italie aux *IVe* et *Ve* siècles," in *Vescovi e pastori in epoca Teodosiana,* Studia Ephemeridis Augustinianum 58 (Rome: Institutum Pontificium Augustinianum, 1997), 193–204, reprinted in *Church and Society,* article VI; idem, "Les évêques italiens dans la société de l'Antiquité tardive: L'émergence d'une nouvelle élite?" in *Le trasformazioni delle "élites" in età tardoantica,* ed. R. Lizzi Testa (Rome: Bretschneider, 2006), reprinted as "The Bishops of Italy in Late Antique Society: A New Elite?" in *Church and Society,* article VIII; G. A. Cecconi, "Vescovi e maggiorenti cristiani nell'Italia centrale fra IV e V secolo," *Vescovi e pastori in epoca Teodosiana,* 205–24. For the eastern provinces, see now Rapp, *Holy Bishops,* 172–88, 205–44; S. Hübner, *Der Klerus in der Gesellschaft des spätantiken Kleinasiens* (Stuttgart: F. Steiner, 2006). The recent appearance of the *Prosopographie chrétienne du Bas Empire,* vol. 3, *Diocèse d'Asie (325–641),* ed. S. Destephen (Paris: CNRS, 2008) will greatly enrich our knowledge of the social status of the clergy of the eastern provinces.

21. J.-M. Carrié, "Les associations professionnelles à l'époque tardive: Entre *munus* et convivialité," in *Humana sapit,* 309–32.

22. É. Rebillard, *Religion et sépulture: L'Église, les vivants et les morts dans l'Antiquité tardive* (Paris: Éditions de l'École des Hautes Études en Sciences Sociales, 2003), 51–71, now translated as *The Care of the Dead in Late Antiquity* (Ithaca, NY: Cornell University Press, 2009), 37–56.

23. C. R. Galvão-Sobrinho, "Funerary Epigraphy and the Spread of Christianity in the West," *Athenaeum,* n.s., 83 (1995): 421–66.

24. *Inscriptiones Latinae Christianae Veteres,* ed. E. Diehl (Zurich: Weidmann, 1970), no. 666.

25. *Inscriptiones Latinae Christianae Veteres*, vol. 1, nos. 602, 604A, 668. D. Mazzoleni, "Il lavoro nell'epigrafia Cristiana," in *Epigrafi del mondo cristiano antico* (Rome: Lateran University Press, 2002), 39–48 collects the evidence with plates, along with an elevating but insubstantial disquisition on the dignity of labor in Christian circles.

26. *Inscriptiones Christianae Urbis Romae Septimo Saeculo Antiquiores*, ed. Giovanni Battista de Rossi and Angelo Silvagni, n.s., vol. 5, *Coemeteria reliqua viae Appiae*, ed. A. Ferrua (Vatican: Pontificio Istituto di Archeologia Cristiana, 1971), no. 13655, p. 133.

27. J. Dresken-Weiland, *Sarkophagbestattungen des 4.–6. Jahrhunderts im Westen des römischen Reiches*, Römische Quartalschrift Supplementband 55 (Rome: Herder, 2003), 78.

28. Ibid., 73–75.

29. P. Veyne, *L'empire gréco-romain* (Paris: Seuil, 2005), ch. 3, "Existait-il une classe moyenne en ces temps lointains?" 117–62 at pp. 126–29.

30. *Codex Thedosianus* 12.1.53 (362) in general. The most notable laws against the ordination of rich plebeians are *Codex Theodosianus* 16.2.3 (320) and 16.2.17 (364).

31. Athanasius, *Historia Arianorum* 78.1.

32. Augustine, *New [Divjak] Letter* 22*.2, p. 348, trans. Eno, *St. Augustine: Letters VI*, 156.

33. Veyne, *L'empire gréco-romain*, 119.

34. Pacianus of Barcelona, *Sermo de Paenitentibus* 10.3, ed. and trans. C. Granado, *Pacien de Barcélone: Écrits*, SC 410 (Paris: Le Cerf, 1995), 138.

35. *I mosaici della basilica di Aquileia*, ed. G. Marini (Aquileia: CISCRA Edizioni, 2003), 24–27 combines magnificent photos and foldouts of the mosaics with a commentary devoid of scholarly value. See esp. C. Sotinel, *Identité civique et christianisme: Aquilée du IIIe au VIe siècle*, Bibliothèque des Écoles françaises d'Athènes et de Rome 324 (Rome: École française de Rome, 2006), 72–89; and J.-P. Caillet, *L'évergétisme monumental chrétien en Italie et à ses marges d'après les pavements de mosaïque (IVe–VIIe s.)*, Collection de l'École française de Rome 175 (Rome: Palais Farnèse, 1993), 123–41. See now A. Zettler, *Offerenteninschriften auf den frühchristlichen Mosaikfußböden Venetiens und Istriens* (Berlin: de Gruyter, 2001), 138–43; and esp. V. Vuolanto, "Male and Female Euergetism in Late Antiquity: A Study on Italian and Adriatic Church Floor Mosaics," in *Women, Wealth and Power in the Roman Empire*, ed. P. Setälä et al., Acta Instituti Romani Finlandiae 25 (Rome: Finnish Institute, 2002), 245–302.

36. Caillet, *L'évergétisme monumental chrétien*, 139 discusses the possible meanings of this inscription, which is rendered opaque by bad grammar.

37. Caillet, *L'évergétisme monumental chrétien*, 141.

38. Ibid., 410–11; and Zettler, *Offerenteninschriften*, 73–75, 155–56. I have adopted Caillet's view that the inscription is contemporary with Theodorus's basilica.

39. W. Ameling, ed., *Inscriptiones Judaicae Orientis*, vol. 2, *Kleinasien*, Texts and Studies in Ancient Judaism 99 (Tübingen: Siebeck Mohr, 2004), no. 19, pp. 119–22.

40. Ibid., no. 90, pp. 261–62; T. Rajak, "The Gifts of God at Sardis," in *Jews in a Graeco-Roman World*, ed. M. Goodman (New York: Oxford University Press, 1998), 229–39. The date of the Sardis synagogue is disputed: the inscriptions with the distinctive formulae could be considerably later than those in the basilica of Aquileia: see J. Mag-

ness, "The Date of the Sardis Synagogue in the Light of the Numismatic Evidence," *American Journal of Archaeology* 109 (2005): 443–75 at p. 443.

41. Sotinel, *Identité civique et christianisme*, 89–99.

42. Schwartz, *Imperialism and Jewish Society*, 284–88. The subject is now superbly documented and fully discussed with reference to all known synagogues in *Inscriptiones Judaicae Orientis*, vol. 1, *Eastern Europe*, ed. D. Noy, A. Panayatov, and H. Bloedhorn, Texts and Studies in Ancient Judaism 101 (Tübingen: Siebeck Mohr, 2002); vol. 2, *Kleinasien;* and vol. 3, *Syria and Cyprus*, ed. D. Noy and H. Bloedhorn, Texts and Studies in Ancient Judaism 102 (Tübingen: Siebeck Mohr, 2004). For similar mosaic panels in Christian churches in the East, see R. Haensch, "Le financement de la construction des églises pendant l'Antiquité tardive et l'évergétisme antique," *Antiquité tardive* 14 (2006): 47–58.

43. *Inscriptiones Judaicae Orientis*, 3:139–46.

44. Sotinel, *Identité civique et christianisme*, 270–74.

45. Caillet, *L'évergétisme monumental chrétien*, 416, 432–33, 451–59.

46. Caillet, *L'évergétisme monumental chrétien*, 372: an inscription on the mosaic of a baptistery in Emona (Ljubljana).

47. I. Schrüfer-Kolb, *Roman Iron Production in Britain: Technological and Socioeconomic Landscape Development along the Jurassic Ridge*, British Archaeological Reports 380 (Oxford: Archaeopress, 2004); R. E. Leader-Newby, *Silver and Society in Late Antiquity: Functions and Meanings of Silver Plate in the Fourth to Seventh Centuries* (Aldershot: Ashgate, 2003), 82–88.

48. E. Magnani, "Almsgiving, *donatio pro anima* and Eucharistic Offering in the Early Middle Ages of Western Europe (4th–9th Century)," in *Charity and Giving in Monotheistic Religions*, ed. M. Frenkel and Y. Lev, Studien zur Geschichte und Kultur des islamischen Orients, n. F. 22 (Berlin: de Gruyter, 2009), 111–21; and idem, "Du don aux églises au don pour le salut de l'âme en Occident (IVe–XIe siècle): Le paradigme eucharistique," in *Pratiques de l'eucharistie dans les Églises d'Orient et Occident (Antiquité et Moyen Âge)*, ed. N. Bériou, B. Caseau, and D. Rigaux (Paris: Institut d'Études Augustiniennes, 2009), 1021–42.

49. P. Brown, *Poverty and Leadership in the Later Roman Empire*, Menahem Stern Jerusalem Lectures (Hanover, NH: University Press of New England, 2002), 16–26.

50. Cyprian, *De ecclesiae catholicae unitate* 25; *De lapsis* 6 and 35; *De opere et eleemosynis* 2.9 and 26.

51. Cyprian, *Letters* 22.2, 5.1, 7, 10.5, 14.2. These letters are brilliantly translated and commented upon by G. W. Clarke, *The Letters of St. Cyprian of Carthage*, vol. 1, Ancient Christian Writers 43 (New York: Newman Press, 1984).

52. G. Schöllgen, *Ecclesia Sordida? Zur Frage der sozialen Schichtung frühchristlicher Gemeinden am Beispiel Karthagos zur Zeit Tertullians*, Jahrbuch für Antike und Christentum: Ergänzungsband 12 (Münster: Aschendorff, 1984).

53. M. M. Sage, *Cyprian*, Patristic Monographs Series 1 (Cambridge, MA: Philadelphia Patristic Foundation, 1975), 329; H. Chadwick, *The Church in Ancient Society: From Galilee to Gregory the Great* (Oxford: Oxford University Press, 2001), 106. See now J. P. Burns, *Cyprian the Bishop* (London: Routledge, 2002), 16–20; C. García Mac Gaw, *Le*

problème du baptême dans le schisme donatiste, Scripta Antiqua 21 (Bordeaux: Ausonius, 2008): 46–49; and P. Bernardini, *Un solo battesimo, una sola chiesa: Il concilio di Cartagine del settembre 256* (Bologna: Mulino, 2009), 65–125.

54. Cyprian, *De habitu virginum* 11.

55. Cyprian, *De dominica oratione* 32; *Letter* 24.1.

56. Cyprian, *Letter* 62.

57. Clarke, *The Letters of St. Cyprian* 1:165.

58. Eusebius, *Ecclesiastical History* 6.43.11.

59. E.g., *Codex Theodosianus* 16.2.14, justifying clerical exemption from trade taxes. See esp. Brown, *Poverty and Leadership*, 29–32; C. Corbo, *Paupertas: La legislazione tardoantica* (Naples: Satura, 2006), 114–38; and C. Freu, *Les figures du pauvre dans les sources italiennes de l'antiquité tardive* (Paris: Boccard, 2007), 174–77.

60. *Codex Theodosianus* 16.2.6; Lizzi Testa, "Privilegi economici e definizione di *status*," 71.

61. Ammianus Marcellinus, *Res gestae* 27.2.15, Rolfe, 3:20, Hamilton, 336.

62. R. A. Kaster, *Guardians of Language: The Grammarian and Society in Late Antiquity* (Berkeley: University of California Press, 1988), 133.

63. *Council of Serdica*, canon 13 [Latin] = 10 [Greek], trans. H. Hess, *The Early Development of Canon Law and the Council of Serdica* (Oxford: Oxford University Press, 2002), 220, 232. See now P.-G. Delage, "Le canon 13 de Sardique ou Les inquietudes d'évêques d'origine modeste," in *Les Pères de l'Église et la voix des pauvres*, ed. P.-G. Delage (La Rochelle: Histoire et Culture, 2006), 55–74.

64. M. R. Salzman, *The Making of a Christian Aristocracy: Social and Religious Change in the Western Roman Empire* (Cambridge, MA: Harvard University Press, 2002), 69–137, 178–99. For disagreement on the statistical basis of these conclusions, especially as they affect the role of women in the conversion of the aristocracy, see R. W. Mathisen, "The Christianization of the Late Roman Senatorial Order: Circumstances and Scholarship," *International Journal of the Classical Tradition* 9 (2002): 257–78 at pp. 265–67, with the rejoinder of Salzman in 12 (2005): 123–37 and the response of Mathisen in 14 (2007): 123–47. See also T. D. Barnes, "Statistics and the Conversion of the Roman Aristocracy," *Journal of Roman Studies* 85 (1995): 135–47; and Veyne, *Quand notre monde est devenu chrétien*, 185–97, *When Our World Became Christian*, 98–106.

65. *Inscriptiones Latinae Christianae Veteres*, no. 1753.1.

66. Lactantius, *Divine Institutes* 5.19.32, 6.24.14, trans. A. Bowen and P. Garnsey (Liverpool: Liverpool University Press, 2003), 323, 385.

67. S. Diefenbach, *Römische Erinnerungsräume: Heiligenmemoria und kollektive Identitäten im Rom des 3. bis 5. Jahrhunderts n. Chr.*, Millennium-Studien 11 (Berlin: de Gruyter, 2007), 38–80.

68. Schwartz, *Were the Jews a Mediterranean Society?* 18, 31n19.

69. E.g., M. T. Griffin, *Seneca: A Philosopher in Politics* (Oxford: Clarendon Press, 1976), 315–66; J. A. Francis, *Subversive Virtue: Asceticism and Authority in the Second-Century Pagan World* (University Park: Pennsylvania University Press, 1995), 1–19; Veyne, *L'empire gréco romaine*, ch. 11, "Passions, perfection et âme matérielle dans l'utopie stoïcienne," 683–712 at pp. 693–95.

70. J. Bodel, "From *Columbaria* to Catacombs: Collective Burial in Pagan and Christian Rome," in *Commemorating the Dead: Texts and Artifacts in Context. Studies of Roman, Jewish, and Christian Burials*, ed. L. Brink and D. Green (Berlin: de Gruyter, 2008), 177–242 at p. 219.

71. Ibid., 220.

72. Ibid., 224.

73. Caillet, *L'évergétisme monumental chrétien*, 91, 95; see also M. Humphries, *Communities of the Blessed: Social Environment and Religious Change in Northern Italy, AD 200–400* (Oxford: Oxford University Press, 1999), 84–85.

74. Caillet, *L'évergétisme monumental chrétien*, 80.

75. Dresken-Weiland, *Sarkophagbestattungen*, 94; *Repertorium der christlich-antiken Sarkophage*, vol. 3, *Frankreich, Algerien, Tunesien*, ed. B. Christern-Briesenick (Mainz: P. Zabern, 2003), no. 21, p. 21, and plate 11.

76. Bodel, "From *Columbaria* to Catacombs," 222.

77. K. Bowes, *Private Worship, Public Values, and Religious Change in Late Antiquity* (Cambridge: Cambridge University Press, 2008).

78. K. Cooper, *The Fall of the Roman Household* (Cambridge: Cambridge University Press, 2007).

79. Sotinel, *Identité civique et christianisme*, 67–71.

80. See esp. Potter, *The Roman Empire at Bay*, 441–581.

81. Ammianus Marcellinus, *Res gestae* 30.9.1, Rolfe, 3:368, Hamilton, p. 407. For a careful study of the administration of Valentinian in action, see Schmidt-Hofner, *Reagieren und Gestalten*.

82. See esp. H. C. Brennecke, *Hilarius von Poitiers und die Bischofsopposition gegen Konstantius II: Untersuchungen zur dritten Phase des Arianischen Streites (337–361)*, Patristische Texte und Studien 26 (Berlin: de Gruyter, 1984); D. H. Williams, *Ambrose of Milan and the End of the Arian-Nicene Conflicts* (Oxford: Oxford University Press, 1995).

83. J. F. Matthews, *Western Aristocracies and Imperial Court, A.D. 364–425* (Oxford: Clarendon Press, 1975), 145–59.

84. N. B. McLynn, *Ambrose of Milan: Church and Court in a Christian Capital* (Berkeley: University of California Press, 1994), 1–52.

85. V. Escribano, "Heresy and Orthodoxy in Fourth Century Hispania: Arianism and Priscillianism," in *Hispania in Late Antiquity*, 121–49.

CHAPTER 3

Amor civicus

1. Augustine, *Sermon* 177.1.

2. C. Geertz, "Common Sense as a Cultural System," in *Local Knowledge: Further Essays in Interpretive Anthropology* (New York: Basic Books, 1983), 73–93 at p. 90.

3. J.-M. Carrié, "Pratique et idéologie chrétiennes de l'économique (IVe–VIe siècle)," *Antiquité tardive* 14 (2006): 17–26 at p. 18.

4. J. C. Mann, review of *Roman Government's Response to Crisis, A.D. 235–337*, by R. MacMullen, *Journal of Roman Studies* 69 (1979): 191.

5. Sozomen, *Ecclesiastical History* 7.25.

6. Brown, *Power and Persuasion*, 41–61; Lendon, *Empire of Honour*, 15.

7. Freu, *Les figures du pauvre*, 19. It is the same with medieval descriptions of the "orders" of society: O. Brunner, *Land and Lordship: Structures of Governance in Medieval Austria*, trans. H. Kaminsky and J. van Horn Melton (Philadelphia: University of Pennsylvania Press, 1992), 329–33.

8. Rilinger, *Humiliores-Honestiores*, 278 rightly insists that these vertical links were stronger than were more general horizontal categorizations, such as that between *honestiores* and *humiliores*.

9. M. Lüthi, *The European Folktale: Form and Nature*, trans. J. D. Niles (Bloomington: University of Indiana Press, 1982), 56–58.

10. Libanius, *Oratio* 7.12.

11. C. Ando, *Imperial Ideology and Provincial Loyalty in the Roman Empire* (Berkeley: University of California Press, 2000), 26.

12. M. Salzman, *On Roman Time: The Codex-Calendar of 354 and the Rhythms of Urban Life in Late Antiquity* (Berkeley: University of California Press, 1990), figure 13.

13. R. Osborne, "Introduction: Roman Poverty in Context," in *Poverty in the Roman World*, 1–20 at p. 13; E. Gabba, *Del buon uso della ricchezza: Saggi di storia economica e sociale del mondo antico* (Milan: Guerini, 1988), 19–26.

14. Ammianus Marcellinus, *Res gestae* 31.5.14, Rolfe, 3:416, Hamilton, p. 420.

15. Barnes, *Ammianus Marcellinus*, 175–80.

16. Lendon, *Empire of Honour*. For an illuminating comparative treatment, see M. E. Lewis, "Gift Circulation and Charity in the Han and Roman Empires," in *Rome and China: Comparative Perspectives on Ancient World Empires*, ed. Walter Scheidel (Oxford: Oxford University Press, 2009), 121–36.

17. R. Duncan-Jones, "The Finances of the Younger Pliny," *Papers of the British School at Rome* 33 (1965): 177–88; S. Mratschek, *Divites et praepotentes: Reichtum und soziale Stellung in der Literatur der Prinzipatszeit*, Historia Einzelschriften 70 (Stuttgart: F. Steiner, 1993).

18. Zosimus, *Historia nova* 2.38.1, ed. L. Mendelssohn, *Zosimi comitis et exadvocati fisci Historia nova* (Leipzig: Teubner, 1887), 96, trans. R. T. Ridley, *Zosimus: New History* (Canberra: American Association of Byzantine Studies, 1982), 40; *Anonymus de rebus bellicis* 2.1.

19. Ammianus Marcellinus, *Res gestae* 27.11.2, Rolfe, 3:74, Hamilton, p. 345.

20. Claudian, *On the Consuls Probinus and Olybrius* 42–47, ed. and trans. M. Platnauer, in *Claudian*, Loeb Classical Library (Cambridge, MA: Harvard University Press, 1956), 1:4–6.

21. E. Bickerman, *Four Strange Books of the Bible* (New York: Schocken, 1967), 163.

22. P. Veyne, *Le pain et le cirque: Sociologie historique d'un pluralisme politique* (Paris: Le Seuil, 1976), 45, trans. B. Pierce, *Bread and Circuses: Historical Sociology and Political Pluralism* (London: Allen Lane Penguin, 1990), 20.

23. G. Arena, "Il 'potere di guarire': L'attività medica fra politica e cultura nella tarda antichità," in *Poveri ammalati e ammalati poveri: Dinamiche socio-economiche, trasformazioni culturali e misure assistenziali nell'Occidente romano in età tardoantica*, ed. R. Marino, C. Molè, and A. Pinzone (Catania: Edizioni del Prisma, 2006), 387–424 at p. 422; J. Kabiersch, *Untersuchungen zum Begriff der Philanthropia bei dem Kaiser Julian*, Klassisch-Philosophische Studien 21 (Wiesbaden: Harassowitz, 1960).

24. A. Parkin, "'You do him no service': An Exploration of Pagan Almsgiving," in *Poverty in the Roman World*, 60–82 at p. 65.

25. Ibid., 68; Libanius, *Oration* 2.30, 30.20.

26. Veyne, "Existait-il une classe moyenne en ces temps lointains?" in *L'empire gréco-romaine*, 117–62 at pp. 142–48.

27. Veyne, *Le pain et le cirque*, 16, 164n2, English trans., p. 6.

28. G. Woolf, "Writing Poverty in Rome," in *Poverty in the Roman World*, 83–99 at pp. 84–85.

29. Parkin, "'You do him no service,'" 69–70.

30. M. Albana, "Archiatri ... honeste obsequi tenuioribus malint quam turpiter servire divitibus (CTH 13,3,8)," in *Poveri ammalati e ammalati poveri*, 253–79 at pp. 264–66.

31. Libanius, *Oration* 46.21.

32. L. Robert and J. Robert, "Bulletin épigraphique," *Revue des études grecques* 97 (1984): 419–522, no. 468 at p. 500.

33. G.H.R. Horsley, *New Documents Illustrating Early Christianity* (Sydney, NSW: Ancient History Documentary Research Centre, 1982), 2:55–56.

34. *The Story of Apollonius King of Tyre* 12.9, trans. G. N. Sandy, in *Collected Ancient Greek Novels*, ed. B. P. Reardon (Berkeley: University of California Press, 1989), 744.

35. W. Robins, "Romance and Renunciation at the Turn of the Fifth Century," *Journal of Early Christian Studies* 8 (2000): 531–57 at pp. 548–54.

36. B. Shaw, "'A Wolf by the Ears': M. I. Finley's *Ancient Slavery and Modern Ideology* in Historical Context," introduction to M. I. Finley, *Ancient Slavery and Modern Ideology* (Princeton: M. Wiener, 1998), 3–74 at pp. 43–49.

37. E. M. Shtaerman and M. K. Trofimova, *La schiavitú nell'Italia imperiale: I–III secolo* (Rome: Riuniti, 1975), 199.

38. Porphyry, *Letter to Marcella* 35, ed. A. Nauck, *Porphyrii philosophi Platonici opuscula selecta* (Leipzig: Teubner, 1886), 296.

39. S. Knoch, *Sklavenfürsorge im Römischen Reich: Formen und Motive*, Sklaverei—Knechtschaft—Zwangsarbeit 2 (Hildesheim: G. Olms, 2005), 240–50. See now Y. Rivière, "Une cruauté digne des féroces barbares? À propos du *De emendatione servorum* (c.Th. IX.12)," in *Le Code Théodosien: Diversité des approches et nouvelles perspectives*, edited by Sylvie Crogiel-Pétrequin and Pierre Jaillette, Collection de l'École française de Rome 412 (Rome: École française de Rome, 2009), 171–208.

40. Council of Elvira, canon 5, in *Acta et symbola conciliorum quae quarto saecula habita sunt*, 6.

41. *Recueil des inscriptions chrétiennes de la Gaule*, vol. 15, *Viennoise du Nord*, ed. F. Descombes (Paris: CNRS, 1985), 197–98, see esp. the early seventh-century group from Briord, nos. 263–69, pp. 676–99.

42. A. J. Festugière, *La révélation d'Hermès Trismégiste,* vol. 2, *Le Dieu cosmique* (Paris: Belles Lettres, 1981), 301–9, on *philanthropia* in the Hellenistic age.

43. Augustine, *Enarrationes in Psalmos* 83.7.

44. Augustine, *Erfurt Sermon* 4.5, ed. I. Schiller, D. Weber, and C. Weidmann, "Sechs neue Augustinuspredigten: Teil 2 mit Edition dreier Sermones zum Thema Almosen," *Wiener Studien* 122 (2009): 1–34 at p. 104.

45. The classic statement is that of Veyne, *Le pain et le cirque;* see esp. O. Murray, introduction to the English translation, *Bread and Circuses,* vii–xxii at pp. xx. Linked to the Greco-Roman city, euergetism played a prominent role in what was "the most successful and long-lasting form of social organization that man has yet invented."

46. *Inscriptiones Christianae Italiae,* vol. 1, *Volsinii: Regio VII,* ed. C. Carletti (Bari: Edipuglia, 1985), nos. 2 and 18 at pp. 3 and 20.

47. *L'Année épigraphique 1990,* no. 211, at pp. 65–67, admirably commented by J. Harries, "*Favor populi*: Pagans, Christians and Public Entertainment in Late Antique Italy," in "*Bread and Circuses,*" 125–41 at pp. 126–27.

48. Harries, "*Favor populi,*" 128.

49. A. Giardina, "*Amor civicus*: Formule e immagini dell'evergetismo romano nella tradizione epigrafica," in *La terza età dell'epigrafia,* ed. A. Donati (Faenza: Fratelli Lega, 1988), 67–87; P. Le Roux, "L'*amor patriae* dans les cités sous l'empire romain," in *Idéologies et valeurs civiques dans le monde romain: Hommage à Claude Lepelley,* ed. H. Inglebert (Nanterre: Picard, 2002), 143–61.

50. C. Witschel, "Statuen auf spätantike Platzanlagen in Italien und Afrika," in *Statuen in der Spätantike,* ed. F. A. Bauer and Witschel (Wiesbaden: Reichert, 2007), 113–69, esp. p. 124.

51. *Corpus Inscriptionum Latinarum,* vol. 8, ed. G. Wilmanns and T. Mommsen (Berlin: G. Reimer, 1881), no. 5366.

52. Lepelley, *Les cités de l'Afrique romaine.*

53. C. Hugoniot, *Les spectacles de l'Afrique romaine: Une culture officielle municipale sous l'empire romain* (Lille: Atelier National de Réproduction de Thèses, 2003).

54. G. A. Cecconi, *Governo imperiale e élites dirigenti nell'Italia tardoantica: Problemi di storia politico-amministrativa (270–476 d.C.)* Biblioteca di Athenaeum 24 (Como: New Press, 1994); E. Savino, *Campania Tardoantica (284–604 d.C.)* (Bari: Edipuglia, 2005).

55. Liebeschuetz, *The Decline and Fall of the Roman City,* 29–103.

56. Cecconi, *Governo imperiale e élites dirigenti,* 141–56. On a parallel development in the eastern empire, see D. Slootjes, *The Governor and His Subjects in the Later Roman Empire,* Mnemosyne Supplements 275 (Leiden: Brill, 2006), 77–97.

57. See V. Malineau, "Le théâtre dans les cités de l'Italie tardo-antique," in *Les cités de l'Italie tardo-antique (IVe–VIe siècle): Institutions, économie, société, culture et religion,* ed. M. Ghilardi, C. J. Goddard, and P. Porena, Collection de l'École française de Rome 369 (Rome: École française de Rome, 2006), 187–203 on the drastic recession of theaters in Italy.

58. Lepelley, *Les cités de l'Afrique romaine,* 295 (a slender list of buildings and repairs).

59. Hugoniot, *Les spectacles*, 590–92.

60. Augustine, *Sermo Denis* 24.13; *Dolbeau Sermon* 6.13.222–26, in *Vingt-six sermons au peuple d'Afrique*, 466–67.

61. Hugoniot, *Les spectacles*, 113–18.

62. Inglebert, *Histoire de la civilisation romaine*, 63–67 is the most trenchant short summary of this issue.

63. Gros, "La ville comme symbole," 187–209; Jacques, *Le privilège de liberté*, 379–434.

64. C. Roueché, "Acclamations in the Late Roman Empire: New Evidence from Aphrodisias," *Journal of Roman Studies* 74 (1984): 181–99; C. Hugoniot, "Les acclamations dans la vie municipale tardive et la critique augustinienne des violences lors des spectacles africains," in *Idéologies et valeurs civiques*, 179–87.

65. Hugoniot, *Les spectacles*, 97.

66. A. Zuiderhoek, "The Icing on the Cake: Benefactors, Economics and Public Building in Roman Asia Minor," in *Patterns in the Economy of Roman Asia Minor*, ed. S. Mitchell and C. Kaksari (Swansea: Classical Press of Wales, 2005), 167–86; Hugoniot, *Les spectacles*, 825.

67. Borg and Witschel, "Veränderungen im Repräsentationsverhalten," 97–99.

68. Hugoniot, *Les spectacles*, 393–95; K.M.D. Dunbabin, *The Mosaics of Roman North Africa: Studies in Iconography and Patronage* (Oxford: Clarendon Press, 1978), 67–68, with plate xxii, figure 53.

69. R. J. Rowland, "The 'Very Poor' and the Grain Dole at Rome and Oxyrhynchus," *Zeitschrift für Papyrologie und Epigraphik* 21 (1976): 69–73; J.-M. Carrié, "Les distributions alimentaires dans les cités de l'empire romain tardif," *Mélanges de l'École française de Rome: Antiquité* 87 (1975): 995–1101.

70. Hugoniot, *Les spectacles*, 196–200.

71. The groundbreaking study remains Mazzarino, *Aspetti sociali del quarto secolo*, 217–47.

72. On the development of the Roman *annona*, see in general Garnsey, *Famine and Food Supply in the Graeco-Roman World*, 218–68.

73. P. Garnsey, "Mass Diet and Nutrition in the City of Rome," in *Cities, Peasants and Food in Classical Antiquity: Essays in Social and Economic History* (Cambridge: Cambridge University Press, 1998), 226–52; L. V. Rutgers et al., "Stable Isotope Data from the Early Christian Catacombs of Ancient Rome: New Insights into the Dietary Habits of Rome's Early Christians," *Journal of Archaeological Science* 36 (2009): 1127–34.

74. Ammianus Marcellinus, *Res gestae* 28.4.32, Rolfe, 3:158, Hamilton, p. 63; Ambrose, *De Officiis* 3.45–51.

75. C. Virlouvet, *Tessera frumentaria: Les procédés de la distribution du blé public à Rome à la fin de la République et au début de l'Empire*, Bibliothèque des Écoles françaises d'Athènes et de Rome 296 (Rome: Palais Farnèse, 1995), 243–62; D. Vera, "Giustiniano, Procopio e l'approvvigionamento di Costantantinopoli," in *Politica, retorica e simbolismo del primato: Roma e Costantinopoli (secoli IV–VII)*, ed. F. Elia (Catania: Spazio Libri, 2004), 9–44.

76. G. Woolf, "Food, Poverty and Patronage: The Significance of the Epigraphy of the Roman Alimentary Schemes in Early Imperial Italy," *Papers of the British School at Rome* 58 (1990): 197–228 at p. 215; C. Virlouvet, *La plèbe frumentaire dans les témoignages épigraphiques: Essai d'histoire sociale et administrative du peuple de Rome antique*, Collection de l'École française de Rome 414 (Rome: École française de Rome, 2009), 187–270.

77. Ammianus Marcellinus, *Res gestae* 27.3.5, Rolfe, 3:14–16, Hamilton, p. 335; see now Lizzi Testa, *Senatori, popolo, papi*, 77–85.

78. Inglebert, *Histoire de la civilisation romaine*, 483.

CHAPTER 4
"Treasure in Heaven"

1. A. Cameron, *Christianity and the Rhetoric of Empire: The Development of Christian Discourse* (Berkeley: University of California Press, 1991), 79.

2. Based on the calculations of A. Mandouze, *Saint Augustin: L'aventure de la raison et de la grâce* (Paris: Études Augustiniennes, 1968), 624–25.

3. Augustine, *Erfurt Sermon* 4.6, p. 32.

4. Ibid.

5. Veyne, *Le pain et le cirque*, 383–98.

6. J. T. Peña, "The Mobilization of State Olive Oil in Roman Africa: The Evidence of the Late Fourth-Century *Ostraca* from Carthage," in *Carthage Papers*, ed. Peña et al., Journal of Roman Archaeology Supplement 28 (Portsmouth, RI: Journal of Roman Archaeology, 1998), 117–238.

7. Augustine, *Enarrationes in Psalmos* 149.9.

8. See now L. Lugaresi, "*Regio aliena*: L'atteggiamento della chiesa verso i luoghi di spettacolo nelle città tardoantiche," and N. Belayche, "Des lieux pour le 'profane' dans l'empire tardo-antique? Les fêtes entre *koinônia* sociale et espaces de rivalités religieuses," *Antiquité tardive* 15 (2007) [= *Jeux et spectacles dans l'Antiquité tardive*]: 21–34 and 35–46. Veyne, "Païens et charité chrétienne devant les gladiateurs," in *L'empire gréco-romaine*, 545–631.

9. John of Ephesus, *Ecclesiastical History* 5.17, trans. R. Payne Smith (Oxford: Oxford University Press, 1860), 226; see P. Brown, *The Rise of Western Christendom: Triumph and Diversity, A.D. 200–1000*, 2nd ed. (Oxford: Blackwell, 2003), 170–72.

10. A. D. Momigliano, "Introduction: Christianity and the Decline of the Roman Empire," in *The Conflict between Paganism and Christianity*, 9.

11. K. M. Hopkins, *Death and Renewal* (Cambridge: Cambridge University Press, 1983), 9.

12. L. B. Namier, *The Structure of Politics at the Accession of George III*, 2nd ed. (London: Macmillan, 1957), 162–72.

13. *Concilium in Causa Apiarii*, canon 15, *Concilia Africae, a. 345–a. 525*, ed. C. Munier, CCSL 149 (Turnhout: Brepols, 1974), 105.

14. J. Gernet, *Buddhism in Chinese Society: An Economic History from the Fifth to the Tenth Centuries* (New York: Columbia University Press, 1995), 241.

15. Jerome, *Letter* 22.11–25 (to Paula on Eustochium).

16. Jerome, *Letter* 66.5–11 (to Pammachius).

17. P. Brown, *The Body and Society: Men, Women and Sexual Renunciation in Early Christianity*, reprint with new introduction (New York: Columbia University Press, 2008), 341–86.

18. Artemidorus, *Oneirocriticon* 3.53, trans. R. J. White, *The Interpretation of Dreams* (Park Ridge, NJ: Noyes Press, 1975), 171.

19. Lactantius, *Divine Institutes* 6.11.18 and 28 with 6.12.2, Bowen and Garnsey, pp. 353 and 355.

20. Freu, *Les figures du pauvre*, 390–418.

21. G. Himmelfarb, "The Culture of Poverty," in *The Victorian City: Images and Realities*, ed. H. J. Dyos and M. Wolff (London: Routledge; Boston: Kegan Paul, 1973), 2:726.

22. Prudentius, *Peristephanon* 2.141–81, ed. and trans. H. J. Thomson, Loeb Classical Library (Cambridge, MA: Harvard University Press, 1961), 2:116–18.

23. Ambrose, *Letter* 73 (18).16.

24. Brown, *Poverty and Leadership*, 45–48.

25. Scheidel, "Stratification, Deprivation and Quality of Life," 44.

26. Freu, *Les figures du pauvre*, 264–68.

27. S.v. "ʾebyôn," *Theologisches Wörterbuch zum Alten Testament*, ed. G. J. Botterweck and H. Ringgren (Stuttgart: Kohlhammer, 1973), 1:27–43; trans. J. T. Willis, *Theological Dictionary of the Old Testament* (Grand Rapids, MI: Eerdmans, 1974), 1:27–41.

28. See in general Weinfeld, *Social Justice in Israel and in the Ancient Near East*.

29. Jerome, *Commentary on Isaiah* 2.5, PL 24:79C.

30. *Corpus Inscriptionum Latinarum*, vol. 10, *Inscriptiones, Bruttiorum, Lucaniae, Campaniae, Siciliae, Sardiniae Latinae*, ed. T. Mommsen (Berlin: G. Reimer, 1883), no. 1194; Brown, *Poverty and Leadership*, 70–73.

31. R. MacMullen, "What Difference Did Christianity Make?" *Historia* 35 (1986): 322–43, now in *Changes in the Roman Empire*, 142–53.

32. Y. Duval and L. Pietri, "Évergétisme et épigraphie dans l'Occident chrétien (IVe–VIe s.)," in *Actes du Xe Congrès international d'épigraphie grecque et chrétienne*, ed. M. Christol and O. Masson (Paris: Publications de la Sorbonne, 1997), 371–96 at p. 371.

33. Bowes, *Private Worship, Public Values, and Religious Change*, 10.

34. *Inscriptiones Latinae Christianae Veteres*, no. 1062b.5–8.

35. J. Parry, "The Gift, the Indian Gift and the 'Indian Gift,'" *Man*, n.s., 21 (1986): 453–73 at p. 466.

36. M. Bloch and J. Parry, introduction to *Money and the Morality of Exchange*, ed. Parry and Bloch (Cambridge: Cambridge University Press, 1989), 1–32 at p. 2.

37. Dante, *Inferno* 7.122, derived from Virgil, *Aeneid* 6.436.

38. S. Mrozek, "Les phénomènes économiques dans les métaphores de l'Antiquité tardive," *Eos* 72 (1984): 393–407.

39. G. A. Anderson, "Redeem Your Soul by the Giving of Alms: Sin, Debt and the 'Treasury of Merit' in Early Jewish and Christian Tradition," *Letter and Spirit* 3 (2007): 36–69; idem, *Sin: A History* (New Haven, CT: Yale University Press, 2009), 135–51, 164–88.

40. Augustine, *Sermon* 66.5; see R. Finn, *Almsgiving in the Later Roman Empire: Christian Promotion and Practice, 313–450* (Oxford: Oxford University Press, 2006), 47.

41. Lepelley, *Les cités de l'Afrique romaine*, 2:347–352 (competing families at Lepcis Magna).

42. See now S. Giglio, "Il 'munus' della pretura a Roma e a Costantinopoli nel tardo impero romano," *Antiquité tardive* 15 (2007): 65–88.

43. C. Sotinel, "Le don chrétien et ses retombées sur l'économie dans l'Antiquité tardive," *Antiquité tardive* 14 (2006): 105–16 at p. 115, translated as "The Christian Gift and Its Economic Impact in Late Antiquity," in *Church and Society*, article IX.

44. J. P. Dolan, *The Immigrant Church: New York's Irish and German Catholics, 1815–1865* (Baltimore: Johns Hopkins University Press, 1975), 165–67.

45. L. R. Iannacone, "Skewness Explained: A Rational Choice Model of Religious Giving," *Journal for the Scientific Study of Religion* 36 (1997): 141–57.

46. On the *tituli* of Rome, see now Diefenbach, *Römische Erinnerungsräume*, 379–400. On the *basilica Constantia* in Arles (possibly built in the early 420s by the military commander and later emperor Constantius), see M. J. Heijmans, *Arles durant l'Antiquité tardive: De la duplex Arelas à l'urbs Genesii*, Collection de l'École française de Rome 324 (Rome: École française de Rome, 2004), 193–94. For a list of lay patrons who subscribed to the rebuilding of the main basilica at Narbonne in 445, see esp. H.-I. Marrou, "Le dossier épigraphique de l'évêque Rusticus de Narbonne," *Rivista di archeologia cristiana* 3–4 (1970): 331–49. The list was carved on the lintel of the main entrance. For Rheims, see *Inscriptiones Latinae Christianae Veteres*, no. 61 (the church built by Jovinus, a Master of the Cavalry and consul, in 367, which in this period bore his name). On Ambrose's private foundation of a church in Milan that was immediately known as the *basilica Ambrosiana*, see McLynn, *Ambrose of Milan*, 209–11.

47. V. Fiocchi Nicolai, "Evergetismo ecclesiastico e laico nelle iscrizioni paleocristiane del Lazio," in *Historiam pictura refert: Miscellanea in onore di Padre Alejandro Recio Veganzones O.F.M.*, Studi di Antichità Cristiana 51 (Vatican: Pontificio Istituto di Archeologia Cristiana, 1994), 237–52 at pp. 240–41.

48. G. Algazi, "Introduction: Doing Things with Gifts," in *Negotiating the Gift: Pre-Modern Figurations of Exchange*, ed. Algazi, V. Groebner, and B. Jussen (Göttingen: Vandenhoeck and Ruprecht, 2003), 9–27 at p. 10.

49. *Inscriptiones Latinae Christianae Veteres*, no. 997; Finn, *Almsgiving*, 198–201.

50. J. Kieschnick, *The Impact of Buddhism on Chinese Material Culture* (Princeton: Princeton University Press, 2003), 211.

51. H.-I. Marrou, *Saint Augustin et la fin de la culture antique: Retractatio*, Bibliothèque de l'École française d'Athènes et de Rome 145 (Paris: Boccard, 1949), 690. See now the pertinent remarks of J.-M. Carrié, "*Nihil habens praeter quod ipso die vestiebatur*: Comment définir le seuil de la pauvreté à Rome?" in *Consuetudinis amor: Fragments*

d'histoire romaine (IIe–VIe siècles) offerts à Jean-Pierre Callu, ed. F. Chausson and É. Wolff (Rome: Bretschneider, 2003), 71–102 at pp. 77–84.

CHAPTER 5
Symmachus

1. *Expositio totius mundi et gentium*, ed. and trans. J. Rougé, SC 124 (Paris: Le Cerf, 1966), 192.

2. Augustine, *Contra Secundinum* 3. The Anician palace has recently been unearthed: see H. Broise, M. Dewailly, and V. Jolivet, "Scoperta di un palazzo tardoantico nella piazzale di Villa Medici," *Rendiconti: Pontificia Accademia Romana di Archeologia* 72 (1999–2000): 1–17.

3. On Probus in general, see esp. Lizzi Testa, *Senatori, popolo, papi*, 306–19.

4. *Inscriptiones Latinae Selectae*, no. 1265, 1:281.

5. H. Niquet, *Monumenta virtutum tituliique: Senatorische Selbstdarstellung im spätantiken Rom im Spiegel der epigraphischen Denkmäler* (Stuttgart: F. Steiner, 2000), 25–35 and tables of inscriptions on pp. 270–81.

6. C. Badel, *La noblesse de l'empire romain: Les masques et la vertu* (Seyssel: Champ Vallon, 2005); B. Näf, *Senatorisches Standesbewusstsein in spätrömischer Zeit*, Paradosis 40 (Freiburg, Switzerland: Universitätsverlag, 1995).

7. Badel, *La noblesse de l'empire romain*, 188.

8. Ibid., 12, 65–105.

9. Jacques, "L'ordine senatorio attraverso la crisi del III secolo," 135.

10. Jones, *The Later Roman Empire*, 2:555. For the marriages of the Anicii, see most recently A. van den Hoek, "Peter, Paul and a Consul: Recent Discoveries in African Red Slip Ware," *Zeitschrift für Antikes Christentum* 9 (2005): 197–246 at pp. 210–12 and the family tree on p. 230.

11. Cameron, "The Antiquity of the Symmachi"; Jacques, "L'ordine senatorio attraverso la crisi del III secolo," 108–20.

12. Lizza Testa, *Senatori, popolo, papi*, 381–99. See now the trenchant conclusions of John Weisweiler, *State Aristocracy: Resident Senators and Absent Emperors in Late Antique Rome, c. 320–400* (D. Phil, Cambridge, 2011).

13. Meslin, *La fête des kalendes de janvier*, 21–22.

14. *El disco de Teodosio*, ed. M. Almagro-Gorbea, Estudios del Gabinete de Antigüedades 5 (Madrid: Real Academia de la Historia, 2000). Leader-Newby, *Silver and Society in Late Antiquity*, 48–49 provides a convincing reinterpretation of the making and function of this disc.

15. Ausonius, *Gratiarum actio* 5.21–22. See chap. 12, n. 12.

16. Symmachus, *Oratio* 6.1.

17. The letters of Symmachus are now edited with a French translation by J. P. Callu, *Symmaque: Lettres*, 4 vols. (Paris: Belles Lettres, 1972–2002). Exhaustive commentary is provided in a *Commento storico al libro ... dell'epistolario di Q. Aurelio Simmaco* (Pisa: Giardini, 1981–2002)—so far we have vol. 2, G. A. Cecconi (2002); vol. 3, A. Pellizzari

(1998); vol. 4, A. Marcone (1987); vol. 5, P. Rivolta Tiberga (1992); vol. 6, Marcone (1983); and vol. 9, S. Roda (1981); and, for the *Relationes* of Symmachus, D. Vera, *Commento storico alle "Relationes" di Quinto Aurelio Simmaco* (Pisa: Giardini, 1981). See now M. R. Salzman and M. Roberts, *The Letters of Symmachus: Book 1* (Atlanta, Ga.: Society of Biblical Literature, 2011), with an excellent introduction as a commentary.

18. C. Sogno, *Q. Aurelius Symmachus: A Political Biography* (Ann Arbor: University of Michigan Press, 2006), 60–63.

19. Olympiodorus, *History: Fragment* 41.1–2, pp. 204–6; well commented by Cameron, "The Antiquity of the Symmachi," 493–98. See also Matthews, *Western Aristocracies and Imperial Court*, 12–31.

20. Sogno, *Symmachus*, 1–30; A. Cameron, *The Last Pagans of Rome* (Oxford: Oxford University Press, 2011).

21. Symmachus, *Letter* 1.52 (AD 376), Callu, 1:114; see Lizzi Testa, *Senatori, popolo, papi*, 297.

22. A. Chastagnol, "Le Sénat dans l'oeuvre de Symmaque," in *Colloque genèvois sur Symmaque*, ed. F. Paschoud (Paris: Belles Lettres, 1986), 73–92 at p. 75. Lizzi Testa, *Senatori, popolo, papi*, 355–72 offers a substantially new analysis of the wider political aims and ideals of Symmachus.

23. Lizzi Testa, *Senatori, popolo, papi*, 361–64.

24. Symmachus, *Oratio* 6.1.

25. Symmachus, *Oratio* 7.4.

26. Baldini Lippolis, *La domus tardoantica*, 267–68; N. Christie, *From Constantine to Charlemagne: An Archaeology of Italy, AD 300–800* (Aldershot: Ashgate, 2006), 240.

27. Symmachus, *Letter* 1.7.1, Callu, 1:71.

28. D. Vera, "Simmaco e le sue proprietà: Struttura e funzionamento di un patrimonio aristocratico del IV secolo d.C.," in *Colloque genèvois sur Symmaque*, 231–76 at pp. 237–42.

29. Symmachus, *Letter* 1.1.5, Callu, 1:62; A. Chastagnol, "Un scandale du vin à Rome sous le Bas-Empire: L'affaire du Préfet Orfitus," *Annales* 5 (1950): 166–83.

30. Symmachus, *Letter* 1.3.4, Callu, 1:67.

31. M. R. Salzman, "Travel and Communication in *The Letters of Symmachus*," in *Travel, Communication and Geography in Late Antiquity: Sacred and Profane*, ed. L. Ellis and F. L. Kidner (Aldershot: Variorum, 2004), 81–94 at pp. 87, 92; idem, "Symmachus and His Father: Patriarchy and Patrimony in the Late Roman Senatorial Elite," in *Le trasformazioni delle "élites" in età tardoantica*, 357–75 at pp. 368–72.

32. P. Arthur, *Romans in Northern Campania: Settlement and Land-Use around the Massico and the Garigliano Basin*, Archaeological Monographs of the British School at Rome 1 (London: British School at Rome, 1991), 89–94.

33. Symmachus, *Letters* 1.11.3, Callu, 1:77 and 2.60.2, Callu, 1:195.

34. The best introduction in English to this much-studied topic remains Matthews, "The Letters of Symmachus." See also S. Roda, "Polifunzionalità della lettera commendaticia: Teoria e prassi nell'epistolario simmachiano," in *Colloque genèvois sur Symmaque*, 177–207; Smith, "'Restored Utility, Eternal City'"; M. R. Salzman, "Symmachus and the 'Barbarian' Generals," *Historia* 55 (2006): 352–67. See now Cameron, *Last Pagans*, 366–82.

35. Sogno, *Symmachus*, 71–85.

36. Matthews, "The Letters of Symmachus," 62.

37. Symmachus, *Letter* 9.141, Callu, 4:82.

38. Symmachus, *Letter* 2.35, Callu, 1:177.

39. É. Rebillard, "Augustin et le rituel épistolaire de l'élite sociale et culturelle de son temps: Éléments pour une analyse processuelle des relations de l'évêque et de la cité dans l'Antiquité tardive," in *L'évêque dans la cité du IVe au Ve siècle*, 127–52.

40. s.v. "pagan," *Late Antiquity: A Guide to the Postclassical World*, 625. Cameron, *Last Pagans*, 14–25 is a useful discussion.

41. Symmachus, *Letter* 1.64.1, Callu, 1:121–22. See esp. Ebbeler and Sogno, "Religious Identity and the Politics of Patronage," 236; M. R. Salzman, "Symmachus' Ideal of Secular Friendship," in *Les frontières du profane*, 247–72.

42. C. J. Goddard, "Les formes festives de l'allégeance au Prince en Italie centrale, sous le règne de Constantin: Un suicide religieux?" *Mélanges de l'École française de Rome: Antiquité* 114 (2002): 1025–88.

43. Barnes, "Statistics and the Conversion of the Roman Aristocracy."

44. S. Mazzarino, "La propaganda senatoriale nel tardo imperio," *Doxa* 4 (1951): 121–48; P. Brown, "Dalla 'plebs romana' alla 'plebs Dei': Aspetti della cristianizzazione di Roma," in *Governanti e intellettuali: Popolo di Roma e popolo di Dio, I–VI secolo*, Passatopresente 2 (Turin: Giapichelli, 1982), 123–45 at pp. 126–28. See now esp. P. F. Mittag, *Alte Köpfe in neuen Händen: Urheber und Funktion der Kontorniaten*, Antiquitas 3:38 (Bonn: Habelt, 1999), 180–226; and Cameron, *Last Pagans*, 691–94.

45. R. Lizzi Testa, "Christian Emperor, Vestal Virgins and Priestly Colleges: Reconsidering the End of Roman Paganism," *Antiquité tardive* 15 (2007): 251–62 at pp. 254–56; Cameron, *Last Pagans*, 33–51.

46. Ambrose, *Letter 17.9*, trans. J.W.H.G. Liebeschuetz (with C. Hill), *Ambrose of Milan: Political Letters and Speeches* (Liverpool: Liverpool University Press, 2006), 66. See esp. Lizzi Testa, "Christian Emperor, Vestal Virgins," 258; and R. M. Errington, *Roman Imperial Policy from Julian to Theodosius* (Chapel Hill: University of North Carolina Press, 2006), 200–204.

47. Sogno, *Symmachus*, 49.

48. Symmachus, *Relatio 3*, translated by R. H. Barrow, *Prefect and Emperor: The Relationes of Symmachus, A.D. 384* (Oxford: Clarendon Press, 1973), 34–47; and now by Liebeschuetz, *Ambrose of Milan*, 71–78. Outstandingly the best commentary is provided by Vera, *Commento storico alle "Relationes" di Quinto Aurelio Simmaco*, 12–53.

49. *Inscriptiones Latinae Selectae*, no. 4934; A. D. Nock, "*A diis electa*: A Chapter in the Religious History of the Third Century," *Harvard Theological Review* 23 (1930): 251–74 at p. 273, now in *Essays on Religion and the Ancient World*, ed. Z. Stewart (Cambridge, MA: Harvard University Press, 1972), 1:252–70.

50. Symmachus, *Letter* 1.46.2, Callu, 1:109.

51. Symmachus, *Relatio* 3.16, Barrow, p. 45.

52. Symmachus, *Relatio* 3.8 and 3.9, Barrow, pp. 39 and 41.

53. M. Edwards, "The Beginnings of Christianization," in *The Cambridge Companion to the Age of Constantine*, 137–56 at pp. 141–42.

54. Symmachus, *Relatio* 3.3, Barrow, p. 37.

55. P. J. Coveney, introduction to *France in Crisis, 1620–1675*, ed. Coveney (Totowa, NJ: Rowman and Littlefield, 1977), 43.

56. Lizzi Testa, *Senatori, popolo, papi*, 447–54; see *Aurea Roma: Dalla città pagana alla città cristiana*, ed. S. Ensoli and E. La Rocca (Rome: Bretschneider, 2000), 462–63.

57. A. D. Nock, "The Emperor's Divine *Comes*," *Journal of Roman Studies* 37 (1947): 102–16, now in *Essays on Religion and the Ancient World*, 653–75.

58. C. Roueché, "The Image of Victory: New Evidence from Ephesus," *Travaux et mémoires* 14: *Mélanges Gilbert Dagron*, ed. V. Déroche (Paris: Boccard, 2002), 527–46, esp. pp. 541–44.

59. Lizzi Testa, "Christian Emperor, Vestal Virgins," 260.

60. *Inscriptiones Latinae Selectae*, no. 4269. See Cameron, *Last Pagans*, 143.

61. Cecconi, *Governo imperiale e élites dirigenti*, 141–56.

62. C. J. Goddard, "The Evolution of Pagan Sanctuaries in Late Antique Italy (Fourth–Sixth Centuries A.D.): A New Administrative and Legal Framework: A Paradox," in *Les cités de l'Italie tardo-antique (IVe–VIe siècle)*, 281–308; and idem, "Au coeur du dialogue entre païens et chrétiens: L'adventus' des sénateurs dans les cités de l'Antiquité tardive," in *Pagans and Christians in the Roman Empire (IVth–VIth Century A.D.): The Breaking of a Dialogue*, Proceedings of the International Conference at the Monastery of Bosé, October 2008, ed. P. Brown and R. Lizzi Testa (Münster: Lit, 2011), 371–400.

63. D. E. Trout, "*Lex* and *iussio*: The *Feriale Campanum* and Christianity in the Theodosian Age," in *Law, Society, and Authority in Late Antiquity*, ed. R. W. Mathisen (Oxford: Oxford University Press, 2001), 162–78. See now Cameron, *Last Pagans*, 59.

CHAPTER 6
Avidus civicae gratiae

1. On the overall population of fourth-century Rome as this can be discovered from official documents on the *annona*, the groundbreaking study remains Mazzarino, *Aspetti sociali del quarto secolo*, 217–47. No consensus has been reached: see W. V. Harris, introduction to *The Transformations of Vrbs Roma in Late Antiquity*, ed. Harris, Journal of Roman Archaeology: Supplementary Series 33 (Portsmouth, RI: Journal of Roman Archaeology, 1999), 13.

2. On the development of the Roman *annona*, see in general Garnsey, *Famine and Food Supply in the Greco-Roman World*, 218–68. The sheer scale and complexity of this undertaking is studied in all its aspects in *Nourrir la plèbe: Actes du colloque tenu à Genève les 28. et 29. IX. 1989 en hommage à Denis Van Berchem*, ed. A. Giovannini, Schweizerische Beiträge zur Altertumswissenschaft 22 (Basel: F. Reinhardt, 1991); on pork, see S.J.B. Barnish, "Pigs, Plebeians and *Potentes*: Rome's Economic Hinterland, c. 350–600 A.D.," *Papers of the British School at Rome* 55 (1987): 157–85; on oil from Carthage, see Peña, "The Mobilization of State Olive Oil in Roman Africa."

3. Ammianus Marcellinus, *Res gestae* 19.10.1–4, Rolfe, 1:522–24, Hamilton, pp. 177–78.

4. *Cosmographia* 1.25, ed. A. Riese, *Geographi Latini Minores* (Heilbronn: Heinninger, 1878), 83. See now R. Lizzi Testa, "*Insula ipsa Libanus Almae Veneris nuncupatur*: Culti, celebrazioni, sacerdoti pagani a Roma, tra IV e VI secolo," in *Istituzioni, carismi ed esercizio del potere (IV–VI secolo d.C.)*, ed. G. Bonamente and R. Lizzi Testa (Bari: Edipuglia 2010), at pp. 273–76.

5. Vera, "Giustiniano, Procopio e l'approvvigionamento di Costantantinopoli," 9–44.

6. Virlouvet, *Tessera frumentaria*, 243–62.

7. Garnsey, "Mass Diet and Nutrition in the City of Rome."

8. Symmachus, *Relatio* 18.3, Barrow, p. 98; see Vera, *Commento storico alle "Relationes" di Quinto Aurelio Simmaco*, 135–42; E. Lo Cascio, "*Canon frumentarius, suarius, vinarius*: Stato e privati nell'approvvigionamento dell'*Vrbs*," in *Transformations of Vrbs Roma*, 163–82.

9. Jones, *The Later Roman Empire*, 693.

10. On the Rome of Symmachus, see esp. N. Purcell, "The Populace of Rome in Late Antiquity: Problems of Classification and Historical Description," in *The Transformations of Vrbs Roma*, 135–61. See also J. R. Curran, *Pagan City and Christian Capital: Rome in the Fourth Century* (Oxford: Oxford University Press, 2000); and *Aurea Roma: Dalla città pagana alla città cristiana*, the catalogue of a superb exhibition with articles.

11. Symmachus, *Letter* 4.54.2 (AD 397), Callu, 2:133.

12. Symmachus, *Letter* 3.55 (AD 389), Callu, 2:58.

13. Symmachus, *Letter* 3.55.2; Salzman, "Symmachus and the 'Barbarian' Generals."

14. Symmachus, *Letter* 2.6 (AD 385), Callu, 1:155.

15. Symmachus, *Letter* 1.44 (AD 376), Callu, 1:107.

16. Ammianus Marcellinus, *Res gestae* 27.3.3–4, Rolfe 3:14, Hamilton, p. 336.

17. Purcell, "The Populace of Rome," 150–56.

18. Though open to challenge in detail, the groundbreaking study remains Cracco Ruggini, *Economia e società nell' "Italia annonaria,"* 19–152.

19. For the full background of the incident (which suggests the role of noble factions in leading popular opinion), see Lizzi Testa, *Senatori, popolo, papi*, 327–43.

20. Symmachus, *Letter* 7.1 (AD 399), Callu, 3:47.

21. The sums are provided in Olympiodorus, *History: Fragment* 41.1–2, Blockley, pp. 204–6.

22. For these calculations, see F. A. Poglio, *Gruppi di potere nella Roma tardoantica (350–395 d.C.)* (Turin: Celid, 2007), 283.

23. A. Chastagnol, "Observations sur le consulat suffect et la préture au Bas-Empire," *Revue historique* 219 (1958): 221–53.

24. Pelagius, *Letter to Demetrias* 14.2, PL 30.

25. Symmachus, *Letter* 2.78.1 (AD 394), Callu, 1:204.

26. Symmachus, *Relatio* 8.1, Barrow, p. 60; see Vera, *Commento storico alle "Relationes" di Quinto Aurelio Simmaco*, 74–82.

27. Symmachus, *Letter* 4.8 (AD 401), Callu, 2:90–92; A. Marcone, "L'allestimento dei giochi annuali a Roma nel IV secolo d.C.: Aspetti economici e ideologici," *Annali*

della Scuola Normale Superiore di Pisa, Classe di lettere e filosofia, ser. 3, no. 11 (1981): 105–22, now in *La parte migliore del genere umano: Aristocrazie, potere e ideologia nell'Occidente tardoantico*, ed. S. Roda (Turin: Scriptorium, 1994), 293–311.

28. Salzman, *On Roman Time*, 131–46.

29. Hugoniot, *Les spectacles*, 1:628–32; C. Machado, "The City as Stage: Aristocratic Commemoration in Late Antique Rome," in *Les frontières du profane*, 287–317 at pp. 296–304.

30. Hugoniot, *Les spectacles*, 1:658–60.

31. Symmachus, *Letters* 6.43 (AD 401), Callu, 3:26 and 9.141 and 9.151 (AD 398), Callu, 4:81–82 and 88.

32. Symmachus, *Letter* 2.76.2 (AD 393), Callu, 1:203.

33. Symmachus, *Letter* 2.77 (AD 393), Callu, 1:204.

34. Symmachus, *Letter* 2.76.2, Callu, 1:203.

35. Symmachus, *Letter* 9.144 (AD 399–400), Callu, 4:83.

36. S. Settis, "Per l'interpretazione di Piazza Armerina," *Mélanges de l'école française de Rome: Antiquité* 87 (1975): 873–994 at pp. 952–55; see the spectacular foldout illustration facing p. 946.

37. S. Muth, "Bildkomposition und Raumstruktur der 'Grossen Jagd' von Piazza Armerina in seinem raumfunktionalen Kontext," *Mitteilungen des deutschen archäologischen Instituts: Römische Abteilung* 106 (1999): 189–212.

38. Symmachus, *Letter* 2.46.1 (AD 393), Callu, 1:185.

39. Symmachus, *Letter* 2.78.3 (AD 394), Callu, 1:204.

40. Symmachus, *Letter* 2.76.2 (AD 393), Callu, 1:203.

41. Symmachus, *Letter* 6.43 (AD 401), Callu, 3:26.

42. Symmachus, *Letter* 2.46.2–3 (AD 393), Callu, 1:185.

43. Symmachus, *Letter* 5.15 (AD 390), Callu, 2:164.

44. Symmachus, *Letter* 5.62 (AD 391–98), Callu, 3:198.

45. Symmachus, *Letter* 2.81.2 (AD 393–94), Callu, 2:206. See now D. Vera, "Presentazione," in *Eburnea Diptycha: I dittici d'avorio tra Antichità e Medioevo*, ed. M. David (Bari: Edipuglia, 2007), 7–9; D. Kinney, "First-Generation Diptychs in the Discourse of Visual Culture," in *Spätantike und byzantinische Elfenbeinbildwerke im Diskurs*, ed. G. Bühl, A. Cutler, and A. Effenberger (Wiesbaden: Reichert, 2008), 149–66 at pp. 149–50; and Cameron, *Last Pagans*, 712–42.

46. I. N. Wood, "The Exchange of Gifts among the Late Antique Aristocracy," in *El disco de Teodosio*, 301–14.

47. Hugoniot, *Les spectacles*, 428–30, 682–87.

48. J. H. Humphreys, *Roman Circuses: Arenas for Chariot Racing* (Berkeley: University of California Press, 1986), 223–32 (Piazza Armerina) and 239–41, with figure 121 (Gerona).

49. J. W. Salomonson, *La mosaïque aux chevaux dans l'antiquarium de Carthage* (The Hague: Imprimerie Nationale, 1965); Humphreys, *Roman Circuses*, 362–76 (Mérida).

50. Harries, "*Favor populi*," 130–34.

51. S. Johnson, *Later Roman Britain* (London: Paladin, 1982), 26.

52. Symmachus, *Letter* 4.60.3 (AD 399), Callu, 1:141.

CHAPTER 7

Ambrose and His People

1. Ambrose, *De excessu fratris Satyri* 1.32. For the life of Ambrose, I have depended largely on McLynn, *Ambrose of Milan*. See now J.H.W.G. Liebeschuetz, *Ambrose and John Chrysostom: Clerics between Desert and Empire* (Oxford: Oxford University Press, 2011), 57–94. The reader should know that, out of a superabundant bibliography on every aspect of the life and thought of Ambrose, in all the languages of Europe, I have chosen only titles that offer convenient and up-to-date introductions to the topics touched on in this chapter. The numbering of the letters of Ambrose is that of the new edition of O. Faller and M. Zelzer, *Sancti Ambrosii Opera*, CSEL 82:1, 2, and 3 (Vienna: Tempsky, 1968, 1990, and 1982), followed in parentheses by the traditional number, taken from the Maurist edition, printed in PL 16.

2. *Gibbon's Journey from Geneva to Rome: His Journal from 20 April to 2 October 1764*, ed. G. A. Bonnard (London: Nelson, 1961), 47.

3. Augustine, *Confessions* 6.3.3.

4. Liebeschuetz, *Ambrose of Milan*, 132n.5.

5. McLynn, *Ambrose of Milan*, 1–52.

6. S. Mazzarino, *Storia sociale del Vescovo Ambrogio* (Rome: Bretschneider, 1989), 51. Published posthumously, this work by a great historian of late antiquity remains a most suggestive essay.

7. H. Granger Taylor, "The Two Dalmatics of Saint Ambrose," *Bulletin de Liaison, Centre International d'Études des Textiles Anciens* 57–58 (1983): 127–73.

8. McLynn, *Ambrose of Milan*, 69–71.

9. Ambrose, *Letter* 75 A (21A), *Contra Auxentium* 33, Liebeschuetz, p. 158.

10. McLynn, *Ambrose of Milan*, 226–29.

11. Palladius of Ratiaria, *Apologia* 89, ed. and trans. R. Gryson, *Scholies ariennes sur le concile d'Aquilée*, SC 267 (Paris: Le Cerf, 1980), 274.

12. McLynn, *Ambrose of Milan*, 31–37, 263–75. P. Porena, "Trasformazioni istituzionali e assetti sociali: I prefetti del Pretorio tra III e IV secolo," in *Le trasformazioni delle "élites" in età tardoantica*, 325–56 at pp. 334–46 shows that ex-prefects were not readily accepted into Roman noble society.

13. McLynn, *Ambrose of Milan*, 220–25.

14. Ambrose, *Letter* 76 (20).6 and (20).7, Liebeschuetz, p. 163.

15. McLynn, *Ambrose of Milan*, 158–219, esp. at pp. 176–79. Liebeschuetz, *Ambrose of Milan*, 124–36 argues for a different order of events (with a chronological table on p. 135). Recently, the present church of San Lorenzo has been dated to around 400. It cannot have been the scene of the conflict of 385–6: M. Löx, "Die Kirche San Lorenzo in Mailand: Eine Stiftung des Stilicho?" *Mitteilungen des deutschen archäologischen Instituts: Römische Abteilung* 114 (2008): 407–38.

16. Ambrose, *Letter* 75A (21A), *Contra Auxentium* 35, Liebeschuetz, p. 159; *Letter* 76 (20).2 and (20).19, Liebeschuetz, pp. 162 and 169. On the implications of this stance, see B. Caseau, "A Case Study for the Transformation of Law in Late Antiquity: The Legal Protection of Churches," in *Confrontation in Late Antiquity: Imperial Presentation and*

Regional Adaptation, ed. L. Jones Hall (Cambridge: Orchard Academic, 2003), 61–77 at pp. 64–66.

17. Ambrose, *Letter* 75A (21A), *Contra Auxentum* 29, Liebeschuetz, p. 156.

18. Ambrose, *Letter* 76 (20).3, Liebeschuetz, p. 162.

19. Ambrose, *Letter* 75A (21A), *Contra Auxentium* 33, Liebeschuetz, p. 158.

20. Augustine, *Confessions* 9.7.15, 10.33.50.

21. Ambrose, *Letter* 75A (21A), *Contra Auxentium* 34, Liebeschuetz, p. 159.

22. J. Moorhead, *Ambrose: Church and Society in the Late Roman World* (London: Longman, 1999), 142.

23. Ambrose, *Explanatio Psalm.* 1.9, ed. M. Petschenig, CSEL 64 (Vienna: Tempsky, 1919), 7.

24. I will refer throughout to the outstanding introduction, edition, translation, and commentary of I. J. Davidson, *Ambrose: De officiis*, 2 vols. (Oxford: Oxford University Press, 2001).

25. Ambrose, *De off.* 1.7.24, p. 130, with Davidson, *Ambrose: De officiis*, pp. 15–16.

26. Ambrose, *De off.* 1.36.185, p. 224.

27. Ambrose, *De off.* 1.50.249, p. 260.

28. Sotinel, "Les évêques italiens dans la société de l'Antiquité tardive," 388–95.

29. See the groundbreaking study of Cracco Ruggini, *Economia e società nell' "Italia annonaria,"* 84–111. The second edition of this book has an invaluable preface and a fully updated bibliography.

30. Bowes, *Private Worship, Public Values and Religious Change*, 170–74.

31. See esp. R. Lizzi, *Vescovi e strutture ecclesiastiche nella città tardoantica (L'Italia annonaria nel IV–V secolo d.C.)*, Biblioteca di Athenaeum 9 (Como: New Press, 1989), 15–57; and idem, "Ambrose's Contemporaries and the Christianization of Northern Italy," *Journal of Roman Studies* 80 (1990): 156–73 at pp. 164–68.

32. Ambrose, *De off.* 1.28.136, p. 196.

33. Ambrose, *De off.* 2.15.70 and 28.136–43, pp. 306 and 342–48.

34. Ambrose, *De off.* 2.29.150, p. 350.

35. Ambrose, *De off.* 1.11.38, p. 138.

36. Brown, *Poverty and Leadership*, 36–44; C. Tiersch, *Johannes Chrysostomus in Konstantinopel (398–404): Weltsicht und Wirken eines Bischofs in der Hauptstadt des Oströmischen Reiches*, Studien und Texte zu Antike und Christentum 6 (Tübingen: Mohr Siebeck, 2000), 229–50.

37. Ambrose, *De off.* 2.15–16.70–77, pp. 306–10, with Davidson, *Ambrose: De officiis*, 2:744–52.

38. Ambrose, *Letter* 73 (18).16, Liebeschuetz, p. 86.

39. R. Syme, *The Roman Revolution* (Oxford: Clarendon Press, 1939), 145.

40. Cicero, *De officiis* 1.17.57, ed. and trans. W. Miller, Loeb Classical Library (Cambridge, MA: Harvard University Press, 1913), 58–60.

41. Cicero, *De officiis* 1.7.22, pp. 22–24.

42. A. O. Lovejoy and G. Boas, *A Documentary History of Primitivism and Related Ideas*, vol. 1, *Primitivism and Related Ideas in Antiquity* (Baltimore: Johns Hopkins University Press, 1935); B. Gatz, *Weltalter, goldene Zeit und sinnverwandte Vorstellungen*,

Spudasmata 16 (Hildesheim: G. Olms, 1967). Ambrose was preceded in Christian circles by a considerably more radical evocation of the Golden Age and its violent end in frank class dominance by Lactantius, writing at the time of the Great Persecution: Lactantius, *Divine Institutes* 5.5–6, pp. 290–94, with comments on pp. 36–40. We cannot assume that Ambrose had read Lactantius.

43. Seneca, *Epistula* 90.34: Lovejoy and Boas, *Documentary History of Primitivism*, 272–73. See esp. P. Garnsey, *Thinking about Property: From Antiquity to the Age of Revolution* (Cambridge: Cambridge University Press, 2007), 121–30.

44. Cicero, *De officiis* 1.7.20, p. 22.

45. Ambrose, *De off.* 1.28.132, p. 194.

46. Davidson, *Ambrose: De officiis*, 571–76 at p. 571.

47. *Age of Spirituality: Late Antique and Early Christian Art, Third to Seventh Century*, ed. K. Weitzmann (New York: Metropolitian Museum of Art, 1988), cat. no. 164 at pp. 185–86.

48. Ambrose, *Exaemeron* 5.26.

49. A. Dworkin, *Intercourse* (New York: The Free Press, 1987), 128.

50. Brown, *Body and Society*, 351–54.

51. Ambrose, *De off.* 1.28.137, p. 196.

52. Ambrose, *De off.* 1.32.169–33.170 and 3.3.19, pp. 216 and 364.

53. Freu, *Les figures du pauvre*, 245.

54. Ambrose, *De Nabuthae* 12.53, trans. B. Ramsey, *Ambrose* (New York: Routledge, 1997), 135.

55. M. M. Bakhtin, *Rabelais and His World*, trans. H. Iswolsky (Cambridge, MA: MIT Press, 1968), 278.

CHAPTER 8
"Avarice, the Root of All Evil"

1. See esp. Cracco Ruggini, *Economia e società nell' "Italia annonaria,"* 84–111.

2. McLynn, *Ambrose of Milan*, 222n9.

3. R. Newhauser, *The Early History of Greed: The Sin of Avarice in Early Medieval Thought and Literature* (Cambridge: Cambridge University Press, 2000), 72.

4. O. Chadwick, *A History of the Popes, 1830–1914* (Oxford: Clarendon Press, 1998), 307–20.

5. V. R. Vasey, *The Social Ideas in the Works of St. Ambrose: A Study on De Nabuthe*, Studia Ephemeridis Augustinianum 17 (Rome: Institutum Patristicum Augustinianum, 1982), 227.

6. E.g., G. Alföldy, *The Social History of Rome* (London: Croom Helm, 1985), 210, who is unduly dependent on Ambrose for his dark picture of the fourth-century West.

7. Humphries, *Communities of the Blessed*, 207–15.

8. Zosimus, *New History* 2.38.1–5; Ammianus Marcellinus, *Res gestae* 22.4.3; *Anonymus de rebus bellicis* 2.1–2, Giardina, p. 12, with commentary on pp. 51–55.

9. Symmachus, *Relatio* 3.16, Barrow, p. 45.

10. Symmachus, *Letter* 2.7.3 (AD 384), Callu, 1:156–57.

11. Sogno, *Symmachus*, 33.

12. McLynn, *Ambrose of Milan*, 263–71.

13. Symmachus, *Letter* 3.36 (around AD 397), Callu, 2:44–45; Salzman, "Symmachus and the 'Barbarian' Generals," 360–63 provides a good analysis of a distinctly frosty interchange.

14. Ambrose, *De off.* 3.7.45–51, Davidson, 1:380–86.

15. See Davidson, *Ambrose: De officiis*, 2:840–46 for a commentary and review of the diverse opinions of social historians on this passage.

16. Symmachus, *Letter* 2.55.2 (AD 385–86), Callu, 1:191.

17. Ambrose, *De Nabuthae* 1.1. B. Ramsey, *Ambrose*, provides a vigorous translation of the *De Nabuthae*.

18. McLynn, *Ambrose of Milan*, 239.

19. Moorhead, *Ambrose*, 83.

20. McLynn, *Ambrose of Milan*, 240, citing G. Nauroy, "L'écriture dans la pastorale d'Ambroise de Milan," in *Le monde latin antique et la Bible*, ed. J. Fontaine and C. Pietri, vol. 2, *Bible de tous les temps* (Paris: Beauchesne, 1985), 371–408 at p. 404.

21. Ambrose, *De Nabuthae* 11.48, Ramsey, p. 133.

22. Ambrose, *De Nabuthae* 4.18, Ramsey, p. 122.

23. Ambrose, *De Nabuthae* 5.20, Ramsey, pp. 122–23.

24. For example, the idyllic picnic after the hunt in the Cesena Dish: see *Milano: Capitale dell'impero romano, 286–402 d.C.* (Milan: Silvana Editoriale, 1991), 313, 348. See esp. Carrié, "Pratique et idéologie chrétiennes de l'économique," p. 21 on Ambrose's subversion of the *topoi* of the idyllic rural life.

25. Ambrose, *De Nabuthae* 13.56, Ramsey, p. 136.

26. Bowes, *Private Worship, Public Values, and Religious Change*, 147–49; N. Mancassola and F. Saggioro, "La fine delle ville romane: Il territorio tra Adda e Adige," *Archeologia medievale* 27 (2000): 315–31.

27. Christie, *From Constantine to Charlemagne*, 418; P. Arthur, "From *Vicus* to Village: Italian Landscapes, AD 400–1000," in *Landscapes of Change: Rural Evolutions in Late Antiquity and the Early Middle Ages*, ed. N. Christie (Aldershot: Ashgate, 2004), 103–33.

28. Ambrose, *Letter* 36 (2).12: see Lizzi, *Vescovi e strutture ecclesiastiche*, 43–45; and Freu, *Les figures du pauvre*, 297–329. The identification of the bishopric of Constantius with Claterna is not accepted by all: s.v. "*Constantius 5*," *Prosopographie chrétienne du Bas-Empire*, vol. 2, *Italie*, ed. C. Pietri and L. Pietri (Paris: École française de Rome 2000), 473–74.

29. Ambrose, *De Tobia* 8.29 copies Basil, *Homilia in Psalmum XIV*, Patrologia Graeca 29: 277B. See the careful comparison of this and similar texts in Cracco Ruggini, *Economia e società nell' "Italia annonaria,"* 14–16. For Cappadocia as presented in the sermons of Basil of Caesarea, see now R. Van Dam, *Kingdom of Snow: Roman Rule and Greek Culture in Cappadocia* (Philadelphia: University of Pennsylvania Press, 2002), 20–52.

30. H.-I. Marrou, introduction to *Clément d'Alexandrie: Le pédagogue*, vol. 1, SC 70 (Paris: Le Cerf, 1960), 89.

31. M. Elvin, *The Retreat of the Elephants: An Environmental History of China* (New Haven, CT: Yale University Press, 2004), 204, 205.

32. Freu, *Les figures du pauvre*, 264–68.

33. M. Wallraff and C. Ricci, *Oratio funebris in laudem sancti Iohannis Chrysostomi: Epitaffio attribuito a Martirio di Antiochia* 40 (Spoleto: Centro Italiano di Studi sull'Alto Medioevo, 2007), 92. See J.H.W.G. Liebeschuetz, *Barbarians and Bishops: Army, Church, and State in the Age of Arcadius and Chrysostom* (Oxford: Clarendon Press, 1990), 217–23; and Tiersch, *Johannes Chrysostomus in Konstantinopel*, 229–50.

34. Ambrose, *De Joseph* 6.30, 6.33; see McLynn, *Ambrose of Milan*, 196, 217; and G. Nauroy, *Exégèse et création littéraire chez Ambroise de Milan: L'exemple du De Ioseph Patriarcha* (Paris: Institut d'Études Augustiniennes, 2007), 241–350.

35. R. MacMullen, "The Preacher's Audience (AD 350–400)," *Journal of Theological Studies* 40 (1989): 503–11 argues for an audience effectively restricted to the elite. He is countered by P. Rousseau, "The Preacher's Audience: A More Optimistic View," in *Ancient History in a Modern University*, ed. T. W. Hillard et al. (Grand Rapids, MI: Eerdmans, 1998), 2:371–408, with which I find myself in agreement.

36. Lizzi, *Vescovi e strutture ecclesiastiche*, 109–24; and idem, "Ambrose's Contemporaries," 167.

37. Gaudentius, *Tractatus* Praefatio 22, ed. A. Glück, CSEL 68 (Leipzig: Teubner, 1936), 7, and PL 20:835.

38. Brown, *Poverty and Leadership*, 80–84.

39. J. T. Gross, *Revolution from Abroad: The Soviet Conquest of Poland's Western Ukraine and Western Belorussia* (Princeton: Princeton University Press, 2002), 120.

40. J. Harries, *Law and Empire in Late Antiquity* (Cambridge: Cambridge University Press, 1999), 97; Kelly, *Ruling the Later Roman Empire*, 186–231.

41. Gildas, *De excidio Britanniae* 20.1, ed. M. Winterbottom, in *The Ruin of Britain, and Other Works* (London: Phillimore, 1978), 23, 95. See esp. J.-L. Fournet, "Entre document et littérature: La pétition dans l'antiquité tardive," in *La Pétition à Byzance*, ed. D. Feissel and J. Gascou, Centre de Recherche d'Histoire et Civilisation Byzantine: Monographies 14 (Paris: Amis du Centre, 2004), 61–74. For the West, see A. Gillett, *Envoys and Political Communication in the Late Antique West, 411–533* (Cambridge: Cambridge University Press, 2003), 26–35.

42. *Edictum Diocletiani et collegarum de pretiis rerum venalium*, ed. M. Giacchero (Genoa: Università di Genova, 1974), 1:135. S. Corcoran, *The Empire of the Tetrarchs: Imperial Pronouncements and Government, AD 284–324* (Oxford: Clarendon Press, 1996), 207–213, see p. 208: "Greed is a motive everyone can understand." *Avaritia* is mentioned eight times in the preamble of the edict.

43. Sozomen, *Ecclesiastical History* 7.25.

44. Ambrose, *Letter* 26 (54).1.

45. Ambrose, *De off.* 2.21.102, p. 324.

46. Ambrose, *De obitu Valentiniani* 21.

47. Paulinus of Milan, *Vita Ambrosii* 41, ed. M. Pellegrino, Verba Seniorum, n.s., 1 (Rome: Studium, 1961), 110.

48. Paulinus, *Vita Ambrosii* 34, p. 100.

49. Aurelius Victor, *Caesares* 39.3: see Mazzarino, *Storia sociale del Vescovo Ambrogio*, 86.

50. Davidson, *Ambrose: De officiis*, 1:96.

51. Ambrose, *Letter* 73 (18).24.

CHAPTER 9
Augustine

1. *Confessions* 5.13.23. We are fortunate to have two excellent translations of the *Confessions*: H. Chadwick, *Saint Augustine: Confessions* (Oxford: Oxford University Press, 1991); and G. Wills, *Saint Augustine: Confessions* (London: Penguin, 2006). I have based my translations largely on an adaptation of both. In these chapters, I will quote the works of Augustine without author's name, with the conventional Latin titles and their abbreviations. From the superabundant bibliography on the life and thought of Augustine, I will cite only works that have helped me directly in the study of the themes that concern me. For this chapter, which depends largely on the evidence of the *Confessions*, I would especially recommend J. J. O'Donnell, *Augustine: Confessions*, 3 vols. (Oxford: Clarendon Press, 1992).

2. Ebbeler and Sogno, "Religious Identity and the Politics of Patronage," are right to insist that we should not read too much into Symmachus's choice of Augustine.

3. Symmachus, *Letter* 1.20 (AD 378), Callu, 1:84–85.

4. Brown, *Augustine of Hippo* (2000) brings the reader up-to-date, in an extensive epilogue, with newly discovered letters and sermons of Augustine and with other advances in the field. S. Lancel, *Saint Augustin* (Paris: Fayard, 1999), trans. A. Nevill, *Saint Augustine* (London: SCM Press, 2002) is the work of a master of the concrete background of Augustine in Africa.

5. *Confessions* 5.13.23.

6. D. Shanzer, "*Avulsa a latere meo*: Augustine's Spare Rib—*Confessions* 6.15.25," *Journal of Roman Studies* 92 (2002): 157–76 at pp. 172–75.

7. J. J. O'Donnell, *Augustine: A New Biography* (New York: Harper Collins, 2005), 10.

8. Possidius, *Vita Augustini* 1.1.

9. Lancel, *Saint Augustin*, 5–7; B. D. Shaw, "The Family in Late Antiquity: The Experience of Augustine," *Past and Present* 115 (1987): 3–51, esp. pp. 8–9.

10. *Confessions* 2.3.5; see esp. J. Doignon, "L'enseignement de l'*Hortensius* de Cicéron sur les richesses devant la conscience d'Augustin jusqu'aux *Confessions*," *Antiquité classique* 51 (1982): 193–206 at p. 198nn30, 31.

11. *Sermon* 356.13.

12. Woolf, "Writing Poverty in Rome," 93.

13. Ibid., 94.

14. *Confessions* 2.3.5.

15. *Confessions* 1.16.26.

16. *Confessions* 8.12.30.

17. *Contra academicos* 1.1.2.

18. A. Gabillon, "Romanianus alias Cornelius: Du nouveau sur le bienfaiteur et l'ami de saint Augustin," *Revue des études augustiniennes* 24 (1978): 58–70.

19. *C. acad.* 2.2.3.

20. C. Lepelley, "*Spes saeculi*: Le milieu social d'Augustin et ses ambitions séculières avant sa conversion," in *Congresso internazionale su S. Agostino nel XVI centenario della conversione*, Studia Ephemeridis Augustinianum 24 (Rome: Institutum Pontificium Augustinianum, 1987), 1:99–117, now in *Aspects de l'Afrique romaine: Les cités, la vie rurale, le christianisme* (Bari: Edipuglia, 2001), 329–44.

21. s.v. "Friendship," *Augustine through the Ages: An Encyclopedia*, ed. A. D. Fitzgerald (Grand Rapids, MI: Eerdmans, 1999), 372–73.

22. Cicero, *De officiis* 1.16.51.

23. *Confessions* 4.8.13.

24. On Manichaeism in general, see P. Brown, "The Diffusion of Manichaeism in the Roman Empire," *Journal of Roman Studies* 59 (1969): 92–103, now in *Religion and Society in the Age of Saint Augustine* (London: Faber, 1972; Eugene, OR: Wipf and Stock, 2007), 94–118; S.N.C. Lieu, *Manichaeism in the Later Roman Empire and Medieval China*, 2nd ed. (Tübingen: Mohr, 1992); I.M.F. Gardner and S.N.C. Lieu, "From Narmouthis (Medinat Madi) to Kellis (Ismant el-Kharab): Manichaean Documents from Roman Egypt," *Journal of Roman Studies* 86 (1996): 146–69. The literature on Manichaeism is deservedly extensive. I have limited myself to the treatments most relevant to the career and outlook of Augustine.

25. Brown, *Body and Society*, 197–202; J. D. BeDuhn, *Augustine's Manichaean Dilemma*, vol. 1, *Conversion and Apostasy, 373–388 C.E.* (Philadelphia: University of Pennsylvania Press, 2010), 42–69 is a remarkable in-depth study of Augustine the Manichee.

26. *Contra Fortunatum* 3: see BeDuhn, *Augustine's Manichaean Dilemma*, 1:70–105. See also J. K. Coyle, "What Did Augustine Know about Manichaeism When He Wrote His Two Treatises *De moribus*?" in *Augustine and Manichaeism in the Latin West*, ed. J. van Oort, O. Wermelinger, and G. Wurst, Nag Hammadi and Manichaean Studies 49 (Leiden: Brill, 2001), 43–56; J. van Oort, "The Young Augustine's Knowledge of Manichaeism: An Analysis of the *Confessiones* and Some Other Related Texts," *Vigiliae Christianae* 62 (2008): 441–66; and J. BeDuhn, "Augustine Accused: Megalius, Manichaeism and the Inception of the *Confessions*," *Journal of Early Christian Studies* 17 (2009): 85–124.

27. *Confessions* 5.7.13.

28. On the different aspects of Augustine's anti-Manichaean debates and writings, see F. Decret, *L'Afrique manichéenne, IVe–Ve siècles: Étude historique et doctrinale* (Paris: Études Augustiniennes, 1978); R. Lim, *Public Disputation, Power, and Social Order in Late Antiquity*, The Transformation of the Classical Heritage 23 (Berkeley: University of California Press, 1995), 70–108; P. Frederiksen, *Augustine and the Jews: A Christian Defense of Jews and Judaism* (New York: Doubleday, 2008), 211–32.

29. N. Cipriani, "La polemica antiafricana di Giuliano di Eclano: Artificio letterario o scontro di tradizioni teologiche?" in *Cristianesimo e specificità regionali nel Mediterraneo latino (sec. IV–VI)*, Studia Ephemeridis Augustinianum 46 (Rome: Institutum Pontificium Augustinianum, 1994), 147–60 provides the best introduction to a contentious

matter. See E. A. Clark, "Vitiated Seeds and Holy Vessels: Augustine's Manichaean Past," in *Ascetic Piety and Women's Faith: Essays on Late Ancient Christianity* (Lewiston, NY: Edwin Mellen Press, 1986), 291–349. I remain unconvinced by those who wish to trace Augustine's doctrine of original sin directly back to his Manichaean past: P. Brown, review of *Emotion and Peace of Mind: From Stoic Agitation to Christian Temptation*, by Richard Sorabji, *Philosophical Books* 43 (2002): 185–208 at pp. 199–202.

30. O'Donnell, *Augustine: A New Biography*, 4.

31. *Confessions* 3.4.8.

32. M. Franzmann, *Jesus in the Manichaean Writings* (London: T. and T. Clark, 2003).

33. D. Caner, *Wandering, Begging Monks: Spiritual Authority and the Promotion of Monasticism in Late Antiquity* (Berkeley: University of California Press, 2002), 83–157.

34. W.H.C. Frend, "The Gnostic-Manichaean Tradition in Roman North Africa," *Journal of Ecclesiastical History* 4 (1953): 13–36.

35. R. Lim, "Unity and Diversity among the Western Manichaeans: A Reconsideration of Mani's *sancta ecclesia*," *Revue des études augustiniennes* 35 (1989): 231–50.

36. *Confessions* 3.10.18, 4.1.1.

37. *De duabus animabus* 11.

38. *Coptic Documentary Texts from Kellis I*, ed. I. Gardner, A. Alcock, and W.-P. Funk (Oxford: Oxbow, 1999). Many of these have been translated in I. Gardner and S.N.C. Lieu, *Manichaean Texts from the Roman Empire* (Cambridge: Cambridge University Press, 2004).

39. Gardner and Lieu, "From Narmouthis (Medinat Madi) to Kellis (Ismant el-Kharab)," 166.

40. J. D. BeDuhn, *The Manichaean Body: In Discipline and Ritual* (Baltimore: Johns Hopkins University Press, 2000); P. Brown, "Alms and the Afterlife: A Manichaean View of an Early Christian Practice," in *East and West: Papers in Ancient History Presented to Glen W. Bowersock*, ed. T. C. Brennan and H. I. Flower (Cambridge, MA: Department of Classics, Harvard University, 2008), 145–58.

41. *Papyri Kellis Coptici* 25, *Coptic Documentary Texts*, p. 275, Gardner and Lieu, p. 275.

42. *Confessions* 6.7.12.

43. *Letter* 259.2: see Brown, *Augustine of Hippo*, 493.

44. *Confessions* 3.4.8, 5.14.25.

CHAPTER 10
From Milan to Hippo

1. See esp. McLynn, *Ambrose of Milan*, 157–70.

2. *Confessions* 6.6.9.

3. *Confessions* 6.15.25.

4. *Confessions* 6.13.23; BeDuhn, *Augustine's Manichaean Dilemma*, 1:165–92.

5. *Confessions* 6.11.19; *Soliloquia* 11.18. See n. 12 below.

6. *Confessions* 6.14.24; see esp. O'Donnell, *Augustine: Confessions*, 2:379–81.

7. *Confessions* 6.14.24; *C. acad.* 2.2.4.

8. *Confessions* 6.12.24.

9. Iamblichus, *On the Pythagorean Life* 27.132, trans. G. Clark (Liverpool: Liverpool University Press, 1989), 59 with pp. xvi–xviii.

10. *Confessions* 7.9.13–21.27; see O'Donnell, *Augustine: Confessions*, 2:413–18. The most perceptive recent study of this moment and of Augustine's circle at the time is R. Lane Fox, "Movers and Shakers," in *The Philosopher and Society in Late Antiquity: Essays in Honor of Peter Brown*, ed. A. Smith (Swansea: Classical Press of Wales, 2005), 19–50 at pp. 25–31. From a superabundant bibliography on Augustine's stay at Cassiciacum, I have learned most, on the issues that concern me, from D. Trout, "Augustine at Cassiciacum: *Otium Honestum* and the Social Dimensions of Conversion," *Vigiliae Christianae* 42 (1988): 132–46; and C. Conybeare, *The Irrational Augustine* (Oxford: Oxford University Press, 2006).

11. O'Donnell, *Augustine: Confessions*, 2:379–81, 3:80–104 rightly emphasizes the continuity between the two schemes of withdrawal.

12. The *Dialogues* are available in English translation. All three and the *Soliloquia* are translated in *The Writings of Saint Augustine*, vol. 1 (New York: CIMA Publishing, 1948); *Contra academicos*: J. J. O'Meara, *St. Augustine: Against the Academics*, Ancient Christian Writers 12 (Westminster, MD: Newman Press, 1951); *De ordine*: S. Borruso, *On Order* (South Bend, IN: St. Augustine's Press, 2007) with a fine commentary by J. Trelenberg, *Augustins Schrift de Ordine*, Beiträge zur historischen Theologie 144 (Tübingen: Mohr Siebeck, 2009); *De beata vita*, trans. R. A. Brown, *S. Aureli Augustini de beata vita* (Washington, DC: Catholic University of America Press, 1944); *Soliloquia*: K. Paffenroth, *Saint Augustine: Soliloquies* (Hyde Park, NY: New City Press, 2000).

13. *Letter* 26.4, which cites the poem of Licentius: see D. Shanzer, "Arcanum Varronis iter: Licentius' Verse Epistle to Augustine," *Revue des études augustiniennes* 37 (1991): 110–43.

14. *Retractationes* 1.1.1; Brown, *Augustine of Hippo*, 108–9.

15. Symmachus, *Letter* 1.47.2 (before AD 385), Callu, 1:110; Naucellius, *Poem* 5, *Epigrammata Bobiensia*, ed. F. Munari (Rome: Edizioni di storia e letteratura, 1955). See esp. S. Roda, "Fuga nel privato e nostalgia del potere nel IV secolo d.C.: Nuovi accenti di un'antica ideologia," in *Le trasformazioni della cultura nella tarda antichità* (Rome: Bretschneider, 1985), 1:95–108.

16. *C. acad.* 1.1.4.

17. *De ordine* 1.11.31, 2.17.45; *De beata vita* 2.10.

18. *De beata vita* 1.6.

19. *C. acad.* 3.19.

20. *De beata vita* 4.35; see esp. N. Cipriani, "Le fonti cristiane della dottrina trinitaria nei primi Dialoghi di S. Agostino," *Augustinianum* 34 (1994): 253–313.

21. Conybeare, *The Irrational Augustine*, 63–92.

22. *C. acad.* 3.6.13.

23. *C. acad.* 2.2.6.

24. *C. acad.* 2.3.9.

25. *Confessions* 9.10.23–26: on the Vision of Ostia, see O'Donnell, *Augustine: Confessions*, 3:122–37.

26. The peculiarity of this "duet" is clearly seen by F. Troncarelli, *Il ricordo della sofferenza: Le Confessioni di sant'Agostino e la psicoanalisi* (Naples: Edizioni scientifiche italiane, 1993), 181.

27. Lancel, *Saint Augustin,* 121–44 provides the best account of these years.

28. *Letter* 10.2; see G. Folliet, "*Deificari in otio*: Augustin, Epistula X,2," *Recherches augustiniennes* 2 (1962): 225–36.

29. From a vast bibliography on this issue, I have found the most reliable guides to be Mandouze, *Saint Augustin,* 165–242; G. Lawless, *Augustine of Hippo and His Monastic Rule* (Oxford: Clarendon Press, 1987); and L. Verheijen, *Nouvelle approche de la Règle de Saint Augustin*, Vie Monastique 8 (Bégrolle-en-Mauge: Abbaye de la Bellefontaine, 1980), 1:75–84. See in general, A. de Vogüé, *Histoire littéraire du mouvement monastique. Première partie: Le monachisme latin* (Paris: Le Cerf, 1993), 2:109–61. E. Plumer, *Augustine's Commentary on Galatians* (Oxford: Oxford University Press, 2003) offers a view from an unexpected angle on the growth of Augustine's sense of community in these years and on his own role as a spiritual guide.

30. John Chrysostom, *Homilies on Acts* 11.3, Patrologia Graeca 60:96–97. See esp. P. C. Bori, *Chiesa primitiva: L'imaggine della comunità delle origini—Atti 2, 42–47; 4, 32–37—nella storia della chiesa antica* (Brescia: Paideia, 1974), 234–41; for Augustine, see pp. 260–77.

31. *Letter* 157.4.39.

32. O'Donnell, *Augustine: A New Biography,* 24, 349n51.

33. See the case of Gregory Nazianzen: R. Van Dam, "Self-Representation in the Will of Gregory Nazianzus," *Journal of Theological Studies* 46 (1995): 118–48; and J. Beaucamp, "Le testament de Grégoire de Nazianze," in *Fontes Minores* 10, ed. L. Burgmann, Forschungen zur byzantinischen Rechtsgeschichte (Frankfurt: Löwenklau, 1998).

34. *De beata vita* 3.22 (citing Cicero, *Hortensius*); *De diversis quaestionibus* 40.

35. *Letter* 28.1.

36. O. Wermelinger, s.v. "Alypius," *Augustinus-Lexikon*, ed. C. Mayer (Basel: Schwabe, 1986), 1:246–67.

37. Possidius, *Vita Augustini* 3.2.

38. *Letter* 18.1.

39. *Letter* 15.1.

40. Lancel, *Saint Augustin,* 194.

41. *De moribus ecclesiae catholicae* 1.1, 32.69.

42. Possidius, *Vita Augustini* 3.3–4.3; *Sermo* 355.2.

43. *Letter* 21.2: see esp. O'Donnell, *Augustine: A New Biography,* 24–25.

44. See Lancel, *Saint Augustin,* 221–34 for Augustine's monasteries at Hippo.

45. *Praeceptum* 2, ed. and trans. Lawless, *Augustine of Hippo*, p. 80. See esp. T. J. van Bavel, "'Ante omnia' et 'in Deum' dans la 'Regula Sancti Augustini,'" *Vigiliae Christianae* 12 (1958): 157–65.

CHAPTER 11
"The Life in Common of a Kind of Divine and Heavenly Republic"

1. Lawless, *Augustine of Hippo*, 148–52.

2. *Sermon* 355.2.

3. Possidius, *Life of Augustine* 2.5, 2.7.

4. *Sermon* 356.14.

5. Possidius, *Life of Augustine* 11.3.

6. *Letter* 211; Lawless, *Augustine of Hippo*, 152–54.

7. *Sermon* 356.3.

8. Lawless, *Augustine of Hippo*, 48–56 on the fluidity of monastic terminology; H. Dey, "Building Worlds Apart: Walls and the Construction of Communal Monasticism from Augustine through Benedict," *Antiquité tardive* 12 (2004): 357–71, at pp. 360–61.

9. *Praeceptum* 4.4, Lawless, p. 89.

10. Vogüé, *Histoire littéraire du mouvement monastique*, 3:152.

11. Ibid., 2:150.

12. *Praeceptum* 1.6, Lawless, p. 83.

13. See esp. Vogüé, *Histoire littéraire du mouvement monastique*, 3:172–204; and Lawless, *Augustine of Hippo*, 121–61.

14. *Praeceptum* 5.1.230, Lawless, p. 94: see Vogüé, *Histoire littéraire du mouvement monastique*, 3:192.

15. *Praeceptum* 5.2.247, Lawless, p. 94.

16. *De bono coniugali* 18.21.

17. M. Testard, *Saint Augustin et Cicéron* (Paris: Études Augustiniennes, 1958), 1:2–176.

18. M. Schofield, "Cicero's Definition of *res publica*," in *Cicero the Philosopher*, ed. J.G.F. Powell (Oxford: Clarendon Press, 1995), 63–83.

19. *De diversis quaestionibus* 79.1 on magic as a "private" power.

20. *De Genesi ad litteram* 11.15.19. See esp. R. A. Markus, "*De civitate Dei*: Pride and the Common Good," in *Augustine: "Second Founder of the Faith,"* ed. J. C. Schnaubelt and F. Van Fleteren, Collectanea Augustiniana (New York: Peter Lang, 1990), 245–59, now in Markus, *Sacred and Secular* (Aldershot: Variorum, 1994), no. III.

21. Cicero, *De officiis* 2.21.73.

22. Cicero, *De officiis* 1.31.110.

23. *De civitate Dei* 5.18, trans. H. Bettenson, *Augustine: Concerning the City of God against the Pagans* (Harmondsworth: Penguin, 1972), 210–11.

24. *De opere monachorum* 25.32.

25. H. Hagendahl, *Augustine and the Latin Classics*, Studia Graeca et Latina Gothoburgensia 20 (Stockholm: Almqvist and Wiksell, 1967), 1:35–169.

26. *Tractatus in evangelium Iohannis* 6.25–26; see now R. W. Dyson, *The Pilgrim City: Social and Political Ideas in the Writings of St. Augustine of Hippo* (Woodbridge: Boydell, 2001), 105–30.

27. A. H. Armstrong in *Plotinus*, Loeb Classical Library (Cambridge, MA: Harvard University Press, 1988), 6:271, 274.

28. Plotinus, *Ennead* 6.4.14, Armstrong, *Plotinus*, 6:317.

29. See esp. E. R. Dodds, *Pagan and Christian in an Age of Anxiety: Some Aspects of Religious Experience from Marcus Aurelius to Constantine* (Cambridge: Cambridge University Press, 1965), 24–26.

30. *Letter* 140.24.61.

31. *Letter* 243.2: see A. Gabillon, "Pour une datation de la lettre 243 d'Augustin à Laetus," *Revue des études augustiniennes* 40 (1994): 127–42.

32. *Soliloquia* 1.22.33.

33. *Enarratio in Psalmos* 33.2.6.

34. G. Madec, "Le communisme spirituel," in *Homo Spiritalis: Festgabe für Luc Verheijen*, ed. C. Mayer (Würzburg: Augustinus, 1987), 225–39, now in *Petites Études Augustiniennes* (Paris: Institut d'Études Augustiniennes, 1994), 215–31.

35. *Letter* 140.26.63.

36. *Tractatus in ev. Iohannis* 35.9.

37. *Letter* 32: see D. Trout, *Paulinus of Nola: Life, Letters, and Poems* (Berkeley: University of California Press, 1999), 202–5.

38. *Letter* 31.5.

CHAPTER 12

Ista vero saecularia

1. Ambrose, *Letter* 27 (58).3.

2. *Ausone et Paulin de Nole: Correspondance*, ed. D. Amherdt, Sapheneia 9 (Bern: Peter Lang, 2004).

3. N. Chadwick, *Poetry and Letters in Early Christian Gaul* (London: Bowes and Bowes, 1955), 66.

4. H. Waddell, *The Wandering Scholars* (London: Constable, 1929), 2, 3.

5. H. Heinen, *Trier und das Trevererland in römischer Zeit* (Trier: Spee, 1985), 211–365; E. M. Wightman, *Roman Trier and the Treveri* (London: Hart-Davis, 1970), 58–123.

6. D. R. Khoury, *State and Provincial Society in the Ottoman Empire: Mosul, 1540–1834* (Cambridge: Cambridge University Press, 1997), 49.

7. Bowes and Kulikowski, introduction to *Hispania in Late Antiquity*, 25.

8. See esp. Matthews, *Western Aristocracies and Imperial Court*, 32–33; G. W. Bowersock, "Symmachus and Ausonius," in *Colloque genèvois sur Symmaque*, 1–15, now in *Selected Papers on Late Antiquity* (Bari: Edipuglia, 2000), 69–80; and Sogno, *Symmachus*, 5–21.

9. A. Coşkun, *Die gens Ausoniana an der Macht: Untersuchungen zu Decimius Magnus Ausonius und seiner Familie*, Prosopographica et Genealogica 8 (Oxford: Linacre College, 2002), 6–11, 52–62.

10. H. Sivan, *Ausonius of Bordeaux: Genesis of a Gallic Aristocracy* (London: Routledge, 1993), 49–73.

11. See esp. M. G. Fulford, "Economic Hotspots and Provincial Backwaters: Modelling the Late Roman Economy," in *Coin Finds and Coin Use in the Roman World*, ed. C. E. King and D. G. Wigg, Studien zu Fundmünzen der Antike 10 (Berlin: Mann, 1996), 153–77.

12. Ausonius, *Parentalia* 7.2 and 18.8, Green, pp. 30 and 36, *Ausonius* 1:68 and 82. In providing page numbers, I cite first from R.P.H. Green, *The Works of Ausonius* (Oxford: Clarendon Press, 1991) and second from the translation of H. G. Evelyn-White, *Ausonius*, 2 vols., Loeb Classical Library (Cambridge, MA: Harvard University Press, 1951). As this edition has a different numbering of the works of Ausonius from that of Green, I have avoided inextricable complexity by citing the Evelyn-White text and translation by the volume and page numbers only, as *Ausonius*.

13. Ausonius, *Gratiarum actio* 4 and 11, Green, pp. 148–49 and 154, *Ausonius* 2:228 and 249; and *Proptrepticus ad nepotem* 86, Green, p. 24, *Ausonius* 2:80.

14. Ausonius, *Gratiarum actio* 16, Green, pp. 157–58, *Ausonius* 2:206.

15. Poignantly evoked by Bowersock, "Symmachus and Ausonius," 12.

16. Ausonius, *Letter* 4.32, Green, p. 196, *Ausonius* 2:18. See the outstanding study of J. Fontaine, "Valeurs antiques et valeurs chrétiennes dans la spiritualité des grands propriétaires terriens à la fin du IVe siècle Occidental," in *Epektasis: Mélanges patristiques offerts au cardinal Jean Daniélou*, ed. J. Fontaine and C. Kannengiesser (Paris: Beauchesne, 1972), 571–95 at p. 576, now in *Études sur la poésie latine tardive d'Ausone à Prudence* (Paris: Belles Lettres, 1980), 241–65 at p. 246.

17. Ausonius, *De herediolo* 21–28, Green, p. 19, *Ausonius* 1:34. See esp. R. Étienne, "Ausone, propriétaire terrien et le problème du latifundium au IVe siècle ap. J. C.," in *Institutions, société et vie politique de l'empire romain au IVe siècle ap. J. C.*, ed. M. Christol et al., Collection de l'École française de Rome 159 (Rome: Palais Farnèse, 1992), 305–11. This estimate is based on the calculations first made by Cracco Ruggini, *Economia e società nell' "Italia Annonaria,"* 416–17. The reader should be warned that this provides only the most approximate order of magnitude.

18. Ausonius, *De herediolo* 19, Green, p. 19, *Ausonius* 1:34.

19. Ausonius, *De herediolo* 1, Green, p. 19, *Ausonius* 1:32.

20. Ausonius, *De herediolo* 1–10, Green, p. 19, *Ausonius* 1:32.

21. Sivan, *Ausonius of Bordeaux*, 66–69.

22. Balmelle, *Les demeures aristocratiques d'Aquitaine*; Chavarría Arnau, *El final de las villae en Hispania*.

23. Giuseppe Tomasi di Lampedusa, *The Leopard*, trans. A. Colquhoun (New York: Pantheon, 1960), 43.

24. K.M.D. Dunbabin, *Mosaics of the Greek and Roman World* (Cambridge: Cambridge University Press, 1999), 69 (on the late Roman villa at Desenzano, Lake Garda, Italy) and 88 (on the mosaics of Aquitaine). Compare Christie, *From Constantine to Charlemagne*, 432: the villa at Piazza Armerina "oozes with … polychrome mosaics."

25. See the spectacular marble wall discovered at Porta Marina, Ostia: *Aurea Roma*, frontispiece, 251–62.

26. Ellis, "Power, Architecture and Décor"; Smith, *Roman Villas*, 178.

27. For similar outlay in urban palaces, see Y. Thébert, "Private Life and Domestic Architecture in Roman Africa," in *A History of Private Life*, ed. P. Ariès and G. Duby, vol. 1, *From Pagan Rome to Byzantium*, ed. P. Veyne, trans. A. Goldhammer (Cambridge, MA: Harvard University Press, 1987), 313–409 at p. 405. The best recent survey of urban domestic architecture is Baldini Lippolis, *La domus tardoantica*. See now F. Ghedini and S. Bullo, "Late Antique Domus of Africa Proconsularis: Structural and Decorative Aspects," in *Housing in Late Antiquity: From Palaces to Shops*, ed. L. Lavan, L. Özgenel, and A. Sarantis, Late Antique Archaeology 3.2 (Leiden: Brill, 2007), 337–66; and J. Arce, A. Chavarría, and G. Ripoll, "The Urban Domus in Late Antique Hispania: Examples from Emerita, Barcino and Complutum," in *Housing in Late Antiquity*, 305–36.

28. Bowes, *Houses and Society*, 54–60.

29. Ibid., 95. For a set of same-scale plans of Spanish villas, see Chavarría Arnau, *El final de las* villae *en* Hispania, 96–99. Similar plans are available in Balmelle, *Les demeures aristocratiques de l'Aquitaine*; and Baldini Lippolis, *La domus tardoantica*.

30. K.M.D. Dunbabin, *The Roman Banquet: Images of Conviviality* (Cambridge: Cambridge University Press, 2003), 141–74.

31. L. Schneider, *Die Domäne als Weltbild: Wirkungsstrukturen der spätantiken Bildersprache* (Wiesbaden: F. Steiner, 1983), 68–87. This is an exceptionally acute analysis, despite dogmatic Marxist adhesion to the view of the late Roman estate as an autonomous *latifundium*. For a correction, see W. Raeck, "*Publica non despiciens*: Ergänzungen zur Interpretation des Dominus-Julius-Mosaiks aus Karthago," *Mitteilungen des deutschen Archäologischen Instituts: Römische Abteilung* 94 (1987): 295–308.

32. S. Djurić, "Mosaic of Philosophers in an Early Byzantine Villa at Nerodimlje," in *VI Coloquio internacional sobre mosaico antiguo*, 123–34.

33. *The Age of Spirituality*, no. 73, pp. 84–85.

34. C. Jullian, *Histoire de la Gaule* (Paris: Hachette, 1993), 2:832n73.

35. Ibid., 2:464, 832n73, 468.

36. Bowes, *Houses and Society*, 90–95, esp. the map, figure 21 on p. 92. For villas in the Balkans, see now Ćurčić, *Architecture in the Balkans*, 32–40, 63–66.

37. D. Mattingly, "Being Roman: Expressing Identity in a Provincial Setting," *Journal of Roman Archaeology* 17 (2004): 5–25.

38. Scott, *Art and Society in Fourth-Century Britain*, 78–81.

39. Ibid., 118–19; M. Henig and G. Soffe, "The Thruxton Roman Villa and Its Mosaic Pavement," *Journal of the British Archaeological Association* 146 (1993): 1–28.

40. Dunbabin, *Mosaics of the Greek and Roman World*, 99–100.

41. K. Bowes and A. Gutteridge, "Rethinking the Later Roman Landscape," *Journal of Roman Archaeology* 18 (2005): 405–13 is the most recent contribution to a lively debate. See also Wickham, *Framing the Early Middle Ages*, 473–81; and Chavarría Arnau, *El final de las* villae *en* Hispania, 125–41.

42. Dunbabin, *The Roman Banquet*, 169–74.

43. K.M.D. Dunbabin, "Convivial Spaces: Dining and Entertainment in the Roman Villa," *Journal of Roman Archaeology* 9 (1996): 66–80. A spectacular new *stibadium* has

been discovered at Faragola in Apulia. It was designed for an intimate gathering of seven guests: see G. Volpe, G. De Felice, and M. Turchiano, "La villa tardoantica di Faragola (Ascoli Satriano) in Apulia," in *Villas Tardoantiguas en el Mediterráneo Occidental*, ed. A. Chavarría, J. Arce, and G. P. Brogiolo, Anejos de Archivo Español de Arqueología 39 (Madrid: Consejo Superior de Investigaciones Científicas, 2006), 221–51 at pp. 229–30 and figure 30, p. 240. See also L. Bek, "*Quaestiones conviviales*: The Idea of the Triclinium and the Staging of Convivial Ceremony from Rome to Byzantium," *Analecta Romana Instituti Danici* 12 (1983): 81–107; and B. Polci, "Some Aspects of the Transformation of the Roman *Domus* between Late Antiquity and the Early Middle Ages," in *Theory and Practice in Late Antique Archaeology*, ed. L. Lavan and W. Bowden, Late Antique Archaeology 1 (Leiden: Brill, 2003), 79–109 at pp. 80–88.

44. Schneider, *Die Domäne als Weltbild*, 61.

45. Thébert, "Private Life and Domestic Architecture," 365.

46. Balmelle, *Les demeures aristocratiques d'Aquitaine*, 60.

47. Ausonius, *Letter* 1, Green, p. 193, *Ausonius* 2:62.

48. P. Veyne, "Les cadeaux des colons à leur propriétaire: La neuvième *Bucolique* et le mausolée d'Igel," *Revue archéologique* (1981): 245–52.

49. G.M.A. Hanfmann, *The Season Sarcophagus in Dumbarton Oaks* (Cambridge, MA: Harvard University Press, 1951), 1:142–209.

50. P. Kranz, *Jahreszeiten-Sarkophage: Entwicklung und Ikonographie des Motivs der vier Jahreszeiten auf kaiserzeitlichen Sarkophagen und Sarkophagdeckeln*, Deutsches Archäologisches Institut: Die antiken Sarkophagreliefs, vol. 5, part 4 (Berlin: Mann, 1984), 169–77.

51. M. G. Maioli, "Il complesso archeologico di Via d'Azeglio a Ravenna: Gli edifici di epoca tardoimperiale e bizantina," *Corso di cultura sull'arte ravennate e bizantina* 41 (1994): 45–61, figure 4 on p. 52; *Archeologia urbana a Ravenna: La Domus dei tapeti di pietro, il complesso archeologico di via d'Azeglio*, ed. G. Montevecchi (Ravenna: Longo, 2004), 104–9.

52. Hanfmann, *The Season Sarcophagus*, 2:154, no. 192a.

53. Brown, *Body and Society*, 26–28.

54. Firmicus Maternus, *Mathesis* 3.13.13, ed. W. Kroll and F. Skutsch (Stuttgart: Teubner, 1968), 1:191.

55. A. Leone, *Changing Townscapes in North Africa from Late Antiquity to the Arab Conquest*, Munera 28 (Bari: Edipuglia, 2007), 59, 86–87.

56. A. Ennabli, "Les thermes du Thiase Marin de Sidi Ghrib (Tunisie)," *Monuments et mémoires publiés par l'Académie des Inscriptions et Belles Lettres* 68 (1986): 1–59 at p. 49; see now J. J. Rossiter, "Domus and Villa: Late Antique Housing in Carthage and Its Territory," in *Housing in Late Antiquity*, 367–92 at pp. 386–87.

57. Ennabli, "Les thermes du Thiase Marin," 56–57.

58. Y. Thébert, *Thermes romains d'Afrique du Nord et leur contexte méditerranéen: Études d'histoire et d'archéologie*, Bibliothèque de l'École française d'Athènes et de Rome 315 (Rome: École française de Rome, 2003), 477–78.

59. Vindicianus, *Letter to the Emperor Valentinian* 1.7, ed. M. Niedermann, *De medicamentis/Über Heilmittel*, Corpus Medicorum Latinorum 5 (Berlin: Akademie, 1968),

1:50. Exposure to the balance of heat, cold, and moisture in the bath is treated as an integral part of healing for acute indigestion.

60. A. C. Dionisotti, "From Ausonius' Schooldays? A Schoolbook and Its Relatives," *Journal of Roman Studies* 72 (1982): 83–125 at p. 103.

61. P. Brown, *Authority and the Sacred: Aspects of the Christianisation of the Roman World* (Cambridge: Cambridge University Press, 1995), 8–10.

62. Augustine, *Enarratio 1 in Psalm* 34.7.

63. Coşkun, *Die gens Ausoniana an der Macht*, 216–37 is a clear review of opinions.

64. R.P.H. Green, "Still Waters Run Deep: A New Study of the *Professores* of Bordeaux," *Classical Quarterly*, n.s., 35 (1985): 491–506.

65. See esp. Ausonius, *Ephemeris* 1 and 2, Green, pp. 7–10, *Ausonius* 1:14–22: Ausonius's morning prayer. M. Skeb, *Christo vivere: Studien zum literarischen Christusbild des Paulinus von Nola*, Hereditas 11 (Bonn: Borengässer, 1997), 23–60 is a fair and perceptive interpretation of the religion of Ausonius.

66. Ausonius, *Gratiarum actio* 18, Green, p. 159, *Ausonius* 2:266. Close to God, the emperor was above fate: P. Monat, "Astrologie et pouvoir: Les subtilités de Firmicus Maternus," in *Pouvoir, divination, et prédestination dans le monde antique*, ed. E. Smajda and E. Geny (Besançon: Presses Universitaires Franc-Comtoises, 1999), 133–39.

67. As suggested by Edwards, "The Beginnings of Christianization," 141–42. For a different view, see now Cameron, *Last Pagans*, 174.

68. Firmicus Maternus, *Mathesis* 1.2.1, Kroll and Skutsch, 1:6. The *Mathesis* has been translated into English by J. R. Bram, *Ancient Astrology: Theory and Practice* (Park Ridge, NJ: Noyes Press, 1975). There is also a French edition and translation by P. Monat, *Firmicus Maternus: Mathesis*, 3 vols. (Paris: Belles Lettres, 1992, 1994, 1997).

69. E.g., Firmicus Maternus, *Mathesis* 1.7.5 and 3.15.19, Kroll and Skutsch, 1:20 and 133.

70. Ausonius, *Parentalia* 4.16, Green, p. 28, *Ausonius* 1:64.

71. Augustine, *Confessions* 4.3.5; see also Augustine, *Letter* 138.1.3, where Vindicianus's ability to diagnose and to prescribe treatments for his patients is viewed as stemming from an almost occult divinatory power.

72. H. Brandenburg, "Christussymbole in frühchristlichen Bodenmosaiken," *Römische Quartalschrift* 64 (1969): 74–138.

73. *The Sevso Treasure*, Bonham's Private Exhibition (London: Bonham, 2006), 1–12; Dunbabin, *The Roman Banquet*, 141–44.

74. Leader-Newby, *Silver and Society in Late Antiquity*, 139–53.

75. W. Raeck, *Modernisierte Mythen: Zum Umgang der Spätantike mit klassischen Bildthemen* (Stuttgart: F. Steiner, 1992), 98–121. See also the careful and perceptive study of S. Muth, *Erleben von Raum—Leben im Raum: Zur Funktion mythologischer Mosaikbilder in der römisch-kaiserzeitlichen Wohnarchitektur*, Archäologie und Geschichte 10 (Heidelberg: Archäologie und Geschichte, 1998).

76. P. Zanker and B. C. Ewald, *Mit Mythen leben: Die Bildwerk der römischen Sarkophage* (Munich: Hirmer, 2004), 266.

77. A. Cameron, *Greek Mythography in the Roman World* (Oxford: Oxford University Press, 2004).

78. Muth, *Erleben von Raum—Leben im Raum*, 328.

79. K. J. Shelton, *The Esquiline Treasure* (London: British Museum, 1981), esp. pp. 30–33 and plate 11.

80. H. Brandenburg, "Bellerophon christianus? Zur Deutung des Mosaiks von Hinton St. Mary und zum Problem der Mythendarstellungen in der kaiserzeitlichen dekorativen Kunst," *Römische Quartalschrift* 63 (1968): 49–86.

81. J. M. Blázquez, *Mosaicos romanos de Córdoba, Jaén y Málaga*, Corpus de mosaicos de España 3 (Madrid: CSIC, 1981), plate 61A and pp. 77–78.

82. J. M. Arnaud and C. V. Fernandes, *Construindo a memória: As colecções do Museu Arqueológico do Carmo* (Lisbon: Museu Arqueológico do Carmo, 2005), 239.

83. Stirling, *The Learned Collector*; N. Hannestad, *Tradition in Late Antique Sculpture: Conservation, Modernization, Production*, Acta Jutlandica 69:2 (Aarhus, Denmark: Aarhus University Press, 1994), 127–44; M. Bergmann, *Chiragan, Aphrodisias, Konstantinopel: Zur mythologischen Skulptur der Spätantike*, Deutsches Archäologisches Institut, Rom: Palilia 7 (Wiesbaden: Reichert, 1999).

84. H. Wrede, *Die spätantike Hermengalerie von Welschbillig*, Römische-germanische Forschungen 32 (Berlin: de Gruyter, 1972), 46–89.

85. Paulinus, *Letter* 32.23.

86. Paulinus, *Poem* 10.307–14, in Green, p. 716, *Ausonius* 2:146.

CHAPTER 13

Ex opulentissimo divite

1. Balmelle, *Les demeures aristocratiques d'Aquitaine*, 146.

2. Muth, *Erleben von Raum—Leben im Raum*, 420–21 and plate 33.4.

3. Trout, *Paulinus of Nola*, 53–103; S. Mratschek, *Der Briefwechsel des Paulinus von Nola: Kommunikation und soziale Kontakte zwischen christlichen Intellektuellen*, Hypomnemata 134 (Göttingen: Vandenhoek and Ruprecht, 2002), 78–103, 190–243; Coşkun, *Die gens Ausoniana an der Macht*, 99–111. It is important to note that the chronology of these years (and hence the pace of Paulinus's evolution) is not certain. Coşkun prefers a tighter schedule and a faster pace, clearly determined by a rapid succession of "existential threats"—execution of his brother in 390, baptism at Easter 391, subsequent retreat to Spain. By making him retire to Spain in 389, the other authors give Paulinus more time to make up his mind and remain more uncertain than is Coşkun as to the exact sequence of events that may have contributed to Paulinus's renunciation.

4. Ausonius, *Letter* 23.35–38, Green, p. 226, *Ausonius*, 2:108.

5. For an analogy to the position of Ausonius, see S. Kettering, *Patrons, Brokers, and Clients in Seventeenth-Century France* (Oxford: Oxford University Press, 1986). H. Sivan, "The Last Gallic Prose Panegyric: Paulinus of Nola on Theodosius I," in *Studies in Latin Literature and Roman History*, ed. C. Deroux, Collection Latomus 227 (Brussels: Latomus, 1994), 7:577–94 posits active alienation from Theodosius I on the part of Paulinus. This may well be the case.

6. Paulinus, *Poem* 21.416–20, ed. W. von Hartel, *Sancti Pontii Meropii Paulini Nolani Carmina*, CSEL 30 (Vienna: Tempsky, 1894), 171–72; trans. P. G. Walsh, *The Poems of St. Paulinus of Nola*, Ancient Christian Writers 40 (New York: Newman Press, 1975), 186. See esp. H. Sivan, "The Death of Paulinus' Brother," *Rheinisches Museum für Philologie* 139 (1996): 170–79; and Coşkun, *Die gens Ausoniana an der Macht*, 102–4.

7. Symmachus, *Letter* 2.30.4, Callu, 1:174; Sogno, *Symmachus*, 67–76.

8. H. E. Chadwick, *Priscillian of Avila: The Occult and the Charismatic in the Early Church* (Oxford: Clarendon Press, 1976) remains the most learned and reliable guide; see now M. Conti, *Priscillian of Avila: The Complete Works* (Oxford: Oxford University Press, 2010); with V. Burrus, *The Making of a Heretic: Gender, Authority and the Priscillianist Controversy* (Berkeley: University of California Press, 1995); and M. B. Simões, *Prisciliano e as tensões religiosas do século IV* (Lisbon: Universidade Lusíada, 2002).

9. Escribano, "Heresy and Orthodoxy in Fourth-Century Hispania."

10. K. Bowes, "'Une coterie espagnole pieuse': Christian Archaeology and Christian Communities in Theodosian Hispania," in *Hispania in Late Antiquity*, 189–258; see also Bowes, "Building Sacred Landscapes: Villas and Cult," in *Villas Tardoantiguas en el Mediterráneo Occidental*, 73–95.

11. *Codex Theodosianus* 1.16.12 (AD 369).

12. *Council of Saragossa* (AD 380), canons 2, 4, and 7, *Concilios visigóticos e hispano-romanos*, ed. J. Vives (Madrid: Consejo Superior de Investigaciones Científicas, 1963), 16–18.

13. Bowes, *Private Worship, Public Values and Religious Change*, 142–46.

14. Rutilius Namatianus, *De reditu suo* 1:440–46, ed. C. H. Keene, trans. G. F. Savage-Armstrong, *Rutilii Claudii Namatiani De reditu suo libri duo/ The Home-Coming of Rutilius Claudius Namatianus from Rome to Gaul in the Year 416 A.D.* (London: George Bell and Sons, 1907), 144–45.

15. Julian, *Oratio 7*, 224B, trans. W. C. Wright, Loeb Classical Library (Cambridge, MA: Harvard University Press, 1949), 2:122.

16. Augustine, *Letter* 262.5.

17. Sulpicius Severus, *Chronica* 2.46.2, ed. G. de Senneville-Grave, *Sulpice Sévère: Chroniques*, SC 441 (Paris: Le Cerf, 1999), 334–36.

18. The best introductions to Sulpicius Severus and his worldview remain J. Fontaine, *Sulpice Sévère: Vie de Saint Martin*, SC 133 (Paris: Le Cerf, 1967), 1:56, 99; and C. Stancliffe, *St. Martin and His Hagiographer: History and Miracle in Sulpicius Severus* (Oxford: Clarendon Press, 1983); Vogüé, *Histoire littéraire du mouvement monastique*, 2:93–156.

19. Paulinus, *Letter* 27.3, ed. W. Hartel, in *Sancti Pontii Meropii Paulini Nolani Epistulae*, CSEL 29 (Vienna: Tempsky, 1894), 239–40; trans. P. G. Walsh, *Letters of St. Paulinus of Nola*, Ancient Christian Writers 36 (New York: Newman Press, 1967), 2:91.

20. Sulpicius Severus, *Life of Martin* 10.6 and 10.21; *Dialogues* 2[3].10; Vogüé, *Histoire littéraire du mouvement monastique*, 2:48.

21. The reactions of contemporaries to the renunciation of Paulinus are discussed by Trout, *Paulinus of Nola*, 1–15. Mratschek, *Der Briefwechsel*, 80–81, esp. p. 16, shows the

active role Paulinus played in circulating this image of himself. At pp. 608–13, Mratschek collects all contemporary and later references to Paulinus's renunciation. Paulinus's own statements about himself are collected at pp. 605–8.

22. Sulpicius Severus, *Life of Saint Martin* 24.4–5.

23. Ambrose, *Letter* 27 (58).3.

24. Trout, *Paulinus of Nola*, 2.

25. Augustine, *City of God* 1.10.

26. Paulinus, *Letter* 5.22, Hartel, p. 39, Walsh, 1:69. For readers of German, I would particularly commend the edition with introduction and translation of M. Skeb, *Paulinus von Nola: Briefe/Epistulae*, Fontes Christianae 25/1–3 (Freiburg: Herder, 1998).

27. John of Ephesus, *Lives of the Eastern Saints* 21, ed. and trans. E. W. Brooks, Patrologia Orientalis 17 (Paris: Firmin-Didot, 1923), 1:228.

28. See now M. Roberts, *The Humblest Sparrow: The Poetry of Venantius Fortunatus* (Ann Arbor: University of Michigan Press, 2009), 71–82; s.v. "Leontius 4," *Prosopography of the Later Roman Empire 3B*, ed. J. R. Martindale (Cambridge: Cambridge University Press, 1992), 774; see K. Stroheker, *Der senatorische Adel im spätantiken Gallien* (Tübingen: Alma Mater, 1948), 188; M. Heinzelmann, "Gallische Prosopographie, 260–527," *Francia* 10 (1982): 531–718; and C. Settipani, "Ruricius Ier évêque de Limoges et ses relations familiales," Prosopographica X, *Francia* 18 (1991): 195–222. The reader should know that such links remain conjectural.

29. *Codex Theodosianus* 9.42–47 (AD 369).

30. S. Mratschek, "*Multis enim notissima est sanctitas loci*: Paulinus and the Gradual Rise of Nola as a Center of Christian Hospitality," *Journal of Early Christian Studies* 9 (2001): 511–53; J. A. Gutilla, "Dalla Capua di Ausonio (Roma altera quondam) alla Nola di Paolino (post urbem titulos sortitus secundos)," *Journal of Early Christian Studies* 12 (2004): 523–36; Savino, *Campania tardoantica*, 282.

31. Trout, *Paulinus of Nola*, 47–49.

32. Paulinus, *Letter* 32.17, Hartel, p. 291, Walsh, 2:149. See Trout, *Paulinus of Nola*, 46–148.

33. Trout, *Paulinus of Nola*, 145–59.

34. C. Kelly, review of *God and Gold in Late Antiquity* by D. Janes, *Journal of Roman Studies* 89 (1999): 253.

35. Ausonius, *Professors* 10.51, Green, p. 50, *Ausonius*, 1:116.

36. See esp. Trout, *Paulinus of Nola*, 121–32; and Mratschek, *Der Briefwechsel*, 550–52.

37. Paulinus, *Letter* 28.1, Hartel, p. 241; see esp. M.-Y. Perrin, "*Ad implendum caritatis officium*: La place des courriers dans la correspondance de Paulin de Nole," *Mélanges de l'École française de Rome: Antiquité* 104 (1992): 1025–68.

38. Paulinus, *Letter* 22.2, Hartel, p. 55, Walsh, 1:198; cf. Cyprian, *Letter* 76.2.4 on Christians in prison during the Decian persecution: see Vogüé, *Histoire littéraire du mouvement monastique*, 1:9.

39. Paulinus, *Letter* 5.21, Hartel, p. 39, Walsh, 1:69; and *Letter* 23.6, Hartel, p. 163, Walsh, 2:7.

40. Paulinus, *Letter* 22.2, Hartel, p. 155, Walsh, 1:197.

41. Paulinus, *Poem* 21.529–30, Hartel, p. 175, Walsh, p. 190. See G. Luongo, *Lo specchio dell'agiografo: San Felice nei carmi XV e XVI di Paolino di Nola* (Naples: Tempi Moderni, 1992).

42. The best treatment of this theme is in Skeb, *Christo vivere*, 215–60; see also L. Padovese, "Considerazioni sulla dottrina cristologica e soteriologica di Paolino di Nola," in *Anchora vitae: Atti del II Convegno Paoliniano nel XVI Centenario del Ritiro di Paolino a Nola*, ed. G. Luongo (Naples: Redenzione, 1998), 209–24.

43. Paulinus, *Letter* 24.17, Hartel, p. 217, Walsh, 2:67.

44. E. Dassmann, *Die Frömmigkeit des Kirchenvaters Ambrosius von Mailand* (Münster-in-Westfalen: Aschendorff, 1965), 116–22; K. Baus, *Das Gebet zu Christus beim hl. Ambrosius*, ed. E. Dassmann (Berlin: Philo, 2000).

45. Ambrose, *Hymn* 4, cited by Faustus of Riez, *Letter* 7, ed. A. Engelbrecht, in *Fausti Reiensis praeter sermones pseudo-eusebianos opera*, CSEL 21 (Vienna: Tempsky, 1891), 203; Dassmann, *Die Frömmigkeit des Kirchenvaters Ambrosius*, 118.

46. Matthias Skeb, the excellent German translator of the letters of Paulinus, frequently translates "humble" and "humility" as *bedeutungslos* and *Bedeutungslosigkeit*.

47. B. C. Ewald, *Der Philosoph als Leitbild: Ikonographische Untersuchungen in römischen Sarkophagreliefs* (Mainz: Zabern, 1999).

48. To take one example: in the scene of the judgment of Christ on the Traditio Legis sarcophagus in the Musée de l'Arles antique, Pilate is shown wearing quasi-imperial dress faced by a Christ in an utterly simple robe: see *D'un monde à l'autre: Naissance d'une Chrétienté en Provence, IVe–VIe siècle*, ed. J. Guyon and M. Heijmans (Arles: Musée de l'Arles antique, 2002), 66, now in *Picturing the Bible: The Earliest Christian Art*, ed. J. Spier (New Haven, CT: Yale University Press with Kimbell Art Museum, 2007), no. 64, on pp. 242–43.

49. See esp. S. Pricoco, "Paolino di Nola e il monachesimo del suo tempo," in *Anchora vitae*, 59–92.

50. Paulinus, *Letter* 5.7, Hartel, p. 28, Walsh, 1:59.

CHAPTER 14
Commercium spiritale

1. Waddell, *The Wandering Scholars*, 2.

2. Ibid., 12.

3. Trout, *Paulinus of Nola*; Mratschek, *Der Briefwechsel*; C. Conybeare, *Paulinus Noster: Self and Symbol in the Letters of Paulinus of Nola* (New York: Oxford University Press, 2000).

4. Siricius, *Letter* 1.10, PL 13:1143; Trout, *Paulinus of Nola*, 94–95.

5. Bowes, *Private Worship, Public Values, and Religious Change*, 154.

6. Brown, *Body and Society*, 370–73.

7. Augustine, *De cura gerenda pro mortuis* 19.

8. T. Lehmann, "Zu Alarichs Beutezug in Campanien: Ein neu entdecktes Gedicht des Paulinus Nolanus," *Römische Quartalschrift* 93 (1998): 181–99.

9. Uranius, *De obitu Paulini* 9, trans. Trout, *Paulinus of Nola*, 296.

10. *Poem* 21.419, Hartel, p. 172, Walsh, p. 186.

11. G. Otranto, "Paolino di Nola e il Cristianesimo dell'Italia Meridionale," in *Anchora vitae*, 35–58 at p. 48.

12. Paulinus, *Poem* 20.312–87, Hartel, pp. 153–56, Walsh, pp. 167–70.

13. Paulinus, *Poem* 20.67–209, Hartel, pp. 145–50, Walsh, pp. 159–64; D. Trout, "Christianizing the Nolan Countryside: Animal Sacrifice at the Tomb of St. Felix," *Journal of Early Christian Studies* 3 (1995): 281–98.

14. A. Ferrua, "Graffiti di pellegrini alla tomba di San Felice," *Palladio*, n.s., 13 (1963): 17–19.

15. C. Ebanista, *Et manet in mediis quasi gemma intersita tectis: La basilica di S. Felice a Cimitile. Storia degli scavi, fasi edilizie, reperti*, Memorie dell'Accademia di archeologia, lettere e belle arti in Napoli 15 (Naples: Arte Tipografica, 2003); T. Lehmann, *Paulinus Nolanus und die Basilica Nova in Cimitile/Nola: Studien zu einem zentralen Denkmal der spätantik-frühchristlichen Architektur* (Wiesbaden: P. Reichert, 2004).

16. Lehmann, *Paulinus Nolanus und die Basilica Nova*, 62, 104.

17. P. Pensabene, "Marmi e reimpiego nel santuario di S. Felice a Cimitile," in *Cimitile e Paolino di Nola. La tomba di S. Felice e il centro di pellegrinaggio: Trent'anni di ricerche*, ed. H. Brandenburg and L. Ermini Pani (Città del Vaticano: Pontificio Istituto di Archeologia Cristiana, 2003), 129–207.

18. Sidonius Apollinaris, *Poem* 22.158–203; see esp. M. M. Kiely, "The Interior Courtyard: The Heart of Cimitile/Nola," *Journal of Early Christian Studies* 12 (2004): 443–97 at p. 452n35; and J. Elsner, *Imperial Rome and Christian Triumph: The Art of the Roman Empire, AD 100–450* (Oxford: Oxford University Press, 1998), 255–59.

19. A. van den Hoek and J. J. Herrmann, "Paulinus of Nola, Courtyards, and Canthari," *Harvard Theological Review* 93 (2000): 173–219.

20. S. Ellis, "Shedding Light on Late Roman Housing," in *Housing in Late Antiquity*, 283–302 at pp. 292–99.

21. Bowes, "'Une coterie espagnole pieuse,'" 255.

22. Symmachus, *Letter* 2.60.2, Callu, 1:195.

23. R. Kaster, *Emotion, Restraint, and Community in Ancient Rome* (London: Oxford University Press, 2005), 13–27. See Ammianus Marcellinus, *Res gestae* 16.8.8–9, where it is precisely the splendor and the near-imperial ceremony associated with the life of a great villa owner that "destroyed noble houses" in Spain by arousing the suspicion of the emperor.

24. Bowes, *Private Worship, Public Values, and Religious Change*, 155–56. For the novelty of such images in a Christian context, see T. Lehmann, "Martinus und Paulinus in Primuliacum (Gallien): Zu den frühesten nachweisbaren Mönchsbildnissen (um 400) in einem Kirchenkomplex," in *Vom Kloster zum Klosterverband: Das Werkzeug der Schriftlichkeit*, ed. H. Keller and F. Neiske (Munich: W. Fink, 1997), 56–67. For a translation and commentary of Paulinus's letters to Sulpicius Severus on these matters, see R. C. Goldschmidt, *Paulinus' Churches at Nola: Translation and Commentary* (Amsterdam: North Holland, 1940). This study precedes the recent archaeological investigations, which have

largely confirmed Paulinus's descriptions of his own buildings at Cimitile. Alas, Primulia-cum has not survived.

25. Kiely, "The Interior Courtyard"; G. Herbert de la Portbarré-Viard, *Descriptions monumentales et discours sur l'édification chez Paulin de Nole: Le regard et la lumière (epist. 32 et carm. 27 et 28)*, Supplements to Vigiliae Christianae 79 (Leiden: Brill, 2006).

26. Trout, *Paulinus of Nola*, 170–72.

27. Paulinus, *Poem* 27.351–52, Hartel, p. 277, Walsh, p. 283.

28. The best appreciation of Paulinus's use of paradox as a way of dissolving apparent antitheses is Conybeare, *Paulinus Noster*, 40, 120–21.

29. Romanos Melodos, *Kontakion on Joseph I*, Strophe 1, trans. M. Carpenter, *Kontakia of Romanos, Byzantine Melodist II* (Columbia: University of Missouri Press, 1973), 83.

30. Proclus, *Commentary on the Republic of Plato*, Diss. 6, 77.24, trans. A. J. Festugière, *Proclus: Commentaire sur la République* (Paris: Vrin, 1970), 1:95.

31. Paulinus, *Letter* 32.22, Hartel, p. 296, Walsh, 2:154.

32. W. Wordsworth, *The Prelude* 2.383–87.

33. D. Janes, *God and Gold in Late Antiquity* (Cambridge: Cambridge University Press, 1998), 84–93.

34. Paulinus, *Letter* 32.21, Hartel, p. 296, Walsh, 2:153–54.

35. C. E. Newlands, *Statius' Silvae and the Poetics of Empire* (New York: Cambridge University Press, 2002), 145n44. For a more "cosmic" use of *commercium/commercia*, as the joining of heaven and earth, in the work of the astrologer Manilius, see K. Volk, "Heavenly Steps: Manilius 4.119–121 and Its Background," in *Heavenly Realms and Earthly Realities in Late Antique Religions*, ed. R. S. Boustan and A. Y. Reed (Cambridge: Cambridge University Press, 2004), 34–46 at p. 45.

36. Paulinus, *Poem* 10.53–56, Hartel, p. 26, Walsh, p. 59.

37. Conybeare, *Paulinus Noster*, 127.

38. Paulinus, *Poem* 21.431–35, Hartel, p. 172, Walsh, p. 187.

39. On Pammachius, see Mratschek, *Der Briefwechsel*, 347–48; and *Prosopographie chrétienne du Bas-Empire*, 2:1576–81.

40. See M. Schmidt, "Ambrosii carmen de obitu Probi: Ein Gedicht des Mailänder Bischofs in epigraphischer Überlieferung," *Hermes* 127 (1999): 99–116 at pp. 101–3 (I do not accept the author's ascription of the poem to Ambrose); J. F. Matthews, "Four Funerals and a Wedding: This World and the Next in Fourth-Century Rome," in *Transformations of Late Antiquity: Essays for Peter Brown*, ed. P. Rousseau and M. Papoutsakis (Farnham, UK: Ashgate, 2009), 129–46 at pp. 134–38.

41. Symmachus, *Letter* 3.88.1, Callu, 2:79.

42. Paulinus, *Letter* 13.14, Hartel, pp. 95–96, Walsh, 1:130. The implications of Christian *refrigerium* practice have been exceptionally well studied by Diefenbach, *Römische Erinnerungsräume*, 38–80. On a significant detail, see now D. Shanzer, "Jerome, Tobit, Alms, and the *Vita Aeterna*," in *Jerome of Stridon: His Life, Writings and Legacy*, ed. A. Cain and J. Lössl (Farnham, UK: Ashgate, 2009), 87–103 at pp. 98–102.

43. Paulinus, *Letter* 13.14, Hartel, p. 96, Walsh, 1:130. The role of the angels in carrying Pammachius's alms to Christ echoes the offertory prayer of the Eucharist as described

in Ambrose, *De sacramentis* 4.27: see esp. Magnani, "Du don aux églises au don pour le salut de l'âme," 1029n24.

44. Paulinus, *Letter* 13.11, Hartel, p. 93, Walsh, 1:127.

45. Paulinus, *Letter* 13.15, Hartel, p. 96, Walsh, 1:131.

46. See most recently L. Grig, "Throwing Parties for the Poor: Poverty and Splendour in the Late Antique Church," in *Poverty in the Roman World*, 145–61. The terms *munus* and *munerarius* had been used by other Christian writers—Cyprian, *De opere et elemosynis* 21 and Jerome, *Letter* 66.5—but Paulinus's is the most consequential exploitation of the comparison.

47. Horden and Purcell, *The Corrupting Sea*, 447; Brown, *Poverty and Leadership*, 50–51.

48. See esp. Arthur, *Romans in Northern Campania*, 89–94. The Ager Campanus may have been more prosperous than northern Campania: Savino, *Campania Tardoantica*, 207–18, but it has not been surveyed in the same way.

49. Uranius, *De obitu Paulini* 3, Trout, p. 294.

50. Paulinus, *Poem* 21.386–94, Hartel, p. 171, Walsh, p. 185.

51. Paulinus, *Letter* 13.19, Hartel, p. 100, Walsh, 1:135.

52. Paulinus, *Letter* 13.17, Hartel, p. 98, Walsh, 1:132; *Poem* 31.466, Hartel, p. 323, Walsh, p. 323. See, in general, J. Desmulliez, "Paulin de Nole et la *paupertas*," in *Les Pères de l'Église et la voix des pauvres*, 245–63.

53. *Babylonian Talmud: Baba Bathra* 10a, trans. M. Simon (London: Soncino, 1935), 45.

54. A. Ferrua, "Cancelli di Cimitile con scritte bibliche," *Römische Quartalschrift* 68 (1973): 50–68.

55. *Inscriptiones Latinae Christianae Veteres*, no. 2472.

56. Trout, *Paulinus of Nola*, 133–59; see also Mratschek, *Der Briefwechsel*, 120–35.

57. Paulinus, *Letter* 16.1, Hartel, p. 115, Walsh, 1:151; see Mratschek, *Der Briefwechsel*, 139–40, 628. Paulinus also wrote *Poem* 22 to Jovius, effectively summarizing the contents of his letter.

58. Paulinus, *Letter* 16.2, Hartel, p. 115, Walsh, 1:152–53.

59. E.g., D. Vaquerizo Gil and J. R. Carillo Díaz-Pinés, "The Roman Villa of El Ruedo (Almedinilla, Córdoba)," *Journal of Roman Archaeology* 8 (1995): 121–54 at p. 144.

60. Paulinus, *Letter* 16.9, Hartel, p. 122, Walsh, 1:160.

61. G. Bonamente, "Chiesa e impero nel IV secolo: Constanzo II fra il 357 e il 361," in *La comunità cristiana di Roma: La sua vita e la sua cultura dalle origini all'alto medioevo*, ed. L. Pani Ermini and P. Siniscalco (Vatican City: Pontificio Istituto di Archeologia Cristiana, 2000), 113–38; Brown, *Authority and the Sacred*, 16–22; G. W. Bowersock, "From Emperor to Bishop: The Self-Conscious Transformation of Political Power in the Fourth Century A.D.," *Classical Philology* 81 (1986): 298–307 at pp. 303–6, now in *Selected Papers on Late Antiquity*.

62. H. Behlmer, *Schenute von Atripe: De Iudicio (Torino, Museo Egizio: Catalogo 63000 Cod. IV)* (Turin: Museo Egizio, 1996), 267.

63. Schneider, *Die Domäne als Weltbild*, 100–123.

64. P. Baumann, *Spätantike Stifter im Heiligen Land: Darstellungen und Inschriften auf Bodenmosaik in Kirchen, Synagogen und Privathäusern* (Wiesbaden: Reichert, 1999), 195–267.

65. Conybeare, *Paulinus Noster*, 16, 161–65.

CHAPTER 15
Propter magnificentiam urbis Romae

1. Ammianus Marcellinus, *Res gestae* 16.10.13–17 on Constantius II first entering Rome. I wish that the reader had available an imagined walk through Rome in the fourth century, such as Diane Favro has provided for the Rome of Augustus: D. Favro, *The Urban Image of Augustan Rome* (Cambridge: Cambridge University Press, 1996), 255–79. The best introduction remains R. Krautheimer, *Rome: Profile of a City, 312–1408* (Princeton: Princeton University Press, 1980).

2. Strabo, *Geography* 3.5.8.

3. J. Hillner, "*Domus*, Family, and Inheritance: The Senatorial Family House in Late Antique Rome," *Journal of Roman Studies* 93 (2003): 129–45.

4. L. Spera, *Il paesaggio suburbano di Roma dall'antichità al medioevo: Il comprensorio tra le vie Latina e Ardeatina dalle Mura Aureliane al III miglio* (Rome: Bretschneider, 1999), 439–42.

5. See esp. E. Champlin, "The *Suburbium* of Rome," *American Journal of Ancient History* 7 (1982): 97–117; N. Purcell, "Tomb and Suburb," in *Römische Gräberstrasse: Selbstdarstellung, Status, Standard*, ed. H. von Hesberg and P. Zanker, Bayerische Akademie der Wissenschaften: Philologisch-historische Klasse/Abhandlungen, NF 96 (Munich: Bayerische Akademie der Wissenschaften, 1987), 25–41; *Suburbium: Il suburbio di Roma dalla crisi del sistema delle ville a Gregorio Magno*, ed. P. Pergola, R. Santangeli Valenzani, and R. Volpe, Collection de l'École française de Rome 311 (Rome: École française de Rome, 2003).

6. W. Scheidel, "Germs for Rome," in *Rome the Cosmopolis*, ed. C. Edwards and G. Woolf (Cambridge: Cambridge University Press, 2003), 159–76 at p. 159.

7. Jerome, *Letter* 43.3, ed. I. Hilberg, CSEL 54.1 (Vienna: Österreichische Akademie der Wissenschaften, 1996), 320. All citations from the letters of Jerome in this and the next two chapters will refer to the respective volumes and pages of this edition.

8. Curran, *Pagan City and Christian Capital*, 116–36; Lizzi Testa, *Senatori, popolo, papi*, 105–25.

9. C. Pietri, *Roma Christiana: Recherches sur l'Église de Rome, son organisation, sa politique, son idéologie de Miltiade à Sixte III (311–440)*, Bibliothèque des Écoles françaises de d'Athènes et de Rome 224 (Rome: Palais Farnèse, 1976), 3–17, 77–82; R. Krautheimer, *Rome*, 3–31; and idem, *Three Christian Capitals: Topography and Politics* (Berkeley: University of California Press, 1983), 7–40.

10. Curran, *Pagan City and Christian Capital*, 90–114; E. D. Hunt, "Imperial Building at Rome: The Role of Constantine," in *Bread and Circuses*, 57–76. See now R. R.

Holloway, *Constantine and Rome* (New Haven, CT: Yale University Press, 2004), 105–24; and Bowes, *Private Worship, Public Values and Religious Change*, 85–87.

11. See now the critical study of G. W. Bowersock, "Peter and Constantine," in *St. Peter's in the Vatican*, ed. W. Tronzo (Cambridge: Cambridge University Press, 2005), 5–15. But see P. Liverani, "Saint Peter's, Leo the Great and the Leprosy of Constantine," *Papers of the British School at Rome* 76 (2008): 155–72 at p. 161.

12. Holloway, *Constantine and Rome*, 100–101; M. J. Johnson, *The Roman Imperial Mausoleum in Late Antiquity* (Cambridge: Cambridge University Press, 2009), 139–56. D. J. Stanley, "Santa Costanza: History, Archaeology, Function, Patronage and Dating," *Arte medievale*, n.s., 3 (2004): 119–40 argues for a later dating.

13. J. Guyon, *Le cimetière aux deux lauriers: Recherches sur les catacombes romaines*, Bibliothèque des Écoles françaises d'Athènes et de Rome 264 (Rome: École française de Rome, 1987); Holloway, *Constantine and Rome*, 86–104; Diefenbach, *Römische Erinnerungsräume*, 153–212; Johnson, *The Roman Imperial Mausoleum*, 110–18.

14. *Liber Pontificalis* 34: Silvester, now ed. H. Geertman, in *Atti del colloquio internazionale* Il Liber Pontificalis e la storia materiale, Medelingen van het Nederlands Instituut te Rome: Antiquity 60–61 (Assen: Van Gorcum, 2003), 289, 319–20, trans. Davis, *The Book of the Pontiffs*, 14.

15. *Liber Pontificalis* 42: Innocentius, Geertman, pp. 319–20, Davis, pp. 31–32.

16. A clear map of the *tituli* and of the basilicas of Rome is provided in Bowes, *Private Worship, Public Values, and Religious Change*, figure 10, p. 67 and figure 11, p. 73.

17. *Inscriptiones Christianae Urbis Romae*, vol. 2, part 1, ed. G. B. de Rossi (Rome: P. Cuggiani, 1888), 150. I accept this person as the Pammachius of Paulinus's letter: see Pietri, *Roma Christiana*, 488.

18. Pietri, *Roma Christiana*, 571–73; idem, "Recherches sur les *domus ecclesiae*," *Revue des études augustiniennes* 24 (1978): 3–21; and idem, "Donateurs et pieux établissements d'après le légendier romain (Ve–VIIe s.)," in *Hagiographie, cultures et sociétés, IVe–XIIe siècles* (Paris: Études Augustiniennes, 1981), 434–53, now in *Christiana respublica: Éléments d'une enquête sur le christianisme antique*, Collection de l'École française de Rome 234 (Rome: École française de Rome, 1997), 1:127–45, 2:1187–1205.

19. Bowes, *Private Worship, Public Values, and Religious Change*, 71.

20. See, for example, P.A.B. Llewellyn, "The Roman Church during the Laurentian Schism: Priests and Senators," *Church History* 45 (1976): 417–27; and the many suggestive perspectives in *Religion, Dynasty and Patronage in Early Christian Rome, 300–900*, ed. K. Cooper and J. Hillner (Cambridge: Cambridge University Press, 2007).

21. J. Hillner, "Families, Patronage and the Titular Churches of Rome, c. 300–c. 600," in *Religion, Dynasty and Patronage*, 225–61.

22. Pietri, *Roma Christiana*, 461–573.

23. Ibid., 573; with Pietri, "Évergétisme et richesses ecclésiastiques dans l'Italie du IVe à la fin du Ve siècle: L'exemple romain," *Ktèma* 3 (1978): 317–37, now in *Christiana respublica*, 2:813–33.

24. Pietri, *Roma Christiana*, 723.

25. For an overview, see Salzman, *The Making of a Christian Aristocracy*, 69–137.

26. S. Orlandi, *Epigrafia anfiteatrale dell'occidente romano*, vol 6, *Roma*, Vetera 15 (Rome: Quasar, 2004), 554; F. Guidobaldi, "Le *domus* tardoantiche di Roma come 'sensori' delle trasformazioni culturali e sociali," in *The Transformations of Vrbs Roma*, 53–68 at pp. 62–63.

27. See esp. Guidobaldi, "Le *domus* tardoantiche di Roma"; Christie, *From Constantine to Charlemagne*, 240.

28. Guidobaldi, "Le *domus* tardoantiche di Roma," 62, 66; Guidobaldi, "La fondazione delle basiliche titolari di Roma nel IV e V secolo: Assenze e presenze nel *Liber Pontificalis*," in *Atti del colloquio internazionale* Il Liber Pontificalis, 5–12.

29. A. Wallace-Hadrill, *Rome's Cultural Revolution* (Cambridge: Cambridge University Press, 2008), 354.

30. J. Hillner, "Clerics, Property and Patronage: The Case of the Roman Titular Churches," *Antiquité tardive* 14 (2006): 59–68 at p. 60.

31. Wallace-Hadrill, *Rome's Cultural Revolution*, 370.

32. Dresken-Weiland, *Sarkophagbestattungen*, 31–33.

33. L. Spera, "Un cubicolo monumentale nella catacomba di Pretestato," *Rivista di archeologia cristiana* 68 (1992): 279–307.

34. *Die Katakombe "Commodilla": Repertorium der Malereien*, ed. J. G. Deckers, G. Mietke, and A. Weiland, Roma Sotteranea Cristiana 10 (Vatican: Pontificio Istituto di Archeologia Cristiana, 1994), 1:89–104 and color plates nos. 19–31. See also P. Pergola, "*Mensores frumentarii Christiani* et annone à la fin de l'Antiquité (Relecture d'un cycle de peintures)," *Rivista di archeologia cristiana* 66 (1990): 167–84.

35. A. Piganiol, *L'empire chrétien (325–395)*, Histoire romaine 4:2 (Paris: Presses Universitaires de France, 1947), 226–27.

36. See *Liber Pontificalis* 39, Davis, p. 30. See esp. Pietri, *Roma Christiana*, 461–64; and Curran, *Pagan City and Christian Capital*, 144–45.

37. Lizzi Testa, *Senatori, popolo, papi*, 129–70, 195; but see Diefenbach, *Römische Erinnerungsräume*, 224–42, esp. 237; M. Raimondi, "Elezione *iudicio Dei* e *turpe convicium*: Damaso e Ursino tra storia ecclesiastica e amministrazione romana," *Aevum* 83 (2009): 169–208. An unknown *clarissima femina* Anastasia did contribute to the baptistery built by Damasus in Saint Peter's: H. Brandenburg, "Das Baptisterium und der Brunnen des Atriums von Alt-St.Peter in Rom," *Boreas* 26 (2003): 55–71 at pp. 64–65.

38. This is seen clearly by C. Pietri, "Damase, évêque de Rome," in *Saecularia Damasiana*, Studi di Antichità Cristiana 39 (Vatican: Pontificio Istituto di Archeologia Cristiana, 1986), 31–58, now in *Christiana respublica*, 1:49–76. Diefenbach, *Römische Erinnerungsräume*, 289–329 is an outstanding characterization of the inscriptions of Damasus. See now U. Reutter, *Damasus, Bischof von Rom (366–384)*, Studien und Texte zu Antike und Christentum 55 (Tübingen: Mohr Siebeck, 2009), 57–153.

39. Diefenbach, *Römische Erinnerungsräume*, 302, 316n355.

40. J. Guyon, "Damase et l'illustration des martyrs: Les accents de la dévotion et l'enjeu d'une pastorale," in *Martyrium in Multidisciplinary Perspective: Memorial Louis Reekmans*, ed. M. Lamberigts and P. van Deun (Louvain: Peeters, 1995), 157–77 at p. 176.

41. s.v. "Florus 1," *Prosopography of the Later Roman Empire*, 1:367–68.

42. J. Fontaine, "Damase, poète théodosien: L'imaginaire poétique des *Epigrammata*," in *Saecularia Damasiana*, 115–45.

43. J. Guyon, "L'oeuvre de Damase dans le cimetière 'Aux deux lauriers' sur la Via Labicana," in *Saecularia Damasiana*, 227–58 at pp. 253–55. Given their siting we should not exaggerate the contemporary impact of these inscriptions: see N. McLynn, "Seeing and Believing: Aspects of Conversion from Antoninus Pius to Louis the Pious," in *Conversion in Late Antiquity and the Early Middle Ages: Seeing and Believing*, ed. K. Mills and A. Grafton (Rochester, NY: University of Rochester Press, 2003), 224–70 at pp. 229–31.

44. Pietri, "Damase, évêque de Rome," 55–57.

45. C. Pietri, "Le serment du soldat chrétien: Les épisodes de la *militia Christi* sur les sarcophages," *Mélanges d'Archéologie et d'Histoire* 74 (1962): 649–64, now in *Christiana respublica*, 2: 1134–64; M. Dulaey, "La scène dite de l'arrestation de Pierre: Nouvelle proposition de lecture," *Rivista di Archeologia Cristiana* 84 (2008): 299–346.

46. J. G. Deckers, "Vom Denker zum Diener: Bemerkungen zu den Folgen der konstantinischen Wende im Spiegel der Sarkophagplastik," in *Innovation in der Spätantike*, ed. B. Brenk (Wiesbaden: Reichert, 1996), 137–72.

47. Ammianus Marcellinus, *Res gestae* 27.3.14, Rolfe, 3:20, Hamilton, p. 336.

48. Jerome, *Contra Iohannem Hierosolymitanum* 8, PL 23:361C; see M. Kahlos, "Vettius Agorius Praetextatus and the Rivalry between the Bishops in Rome in 366–367," *Arctos* 31 (1997): 41–54.

49. *Gesta inter Liberium et Felicem* 10, *Collectio Avellana*, ed. O. Günther, CSEL 35 (Vienna: Tempsky, 1895), 1:4; see esp. J. Fontaine, "Un sobriquet perfide de Damase: *Matronarum auriscalpius*," in *Hommages à Henri le Bonnec: Res sacrae*, ed. D. Porte and J.-P. Néraudau, Collection Latomus 201 (Brussels: Latomus, 1988), 177–92 at pp. 180–81.

50. S. Lunn-Rockliffe, *Ambrosiaster's Political Theology* (Oxford: Oxford University Press, 2007), 33–86. See also D. G. Hunter, "The Significance of Ambrosiaster," *Journal of Early Christian Studies* 17 (2009): 1–26. Parts of Ambrosiaster's commentaries have been translated: G. L. Bray, *Ambrosiaster: Commentaries on Romans and 1–2 Corinthians* (Downers Grove, IL: InterVarsity Press, 2009).

51. Lunn-Rockliffe, *Ambrosiaster's Political Theology*, 130–45.

52. Ambrosiaster, *Comm. in 1 Cor. 11.7*, ed. H. J. Vogels, CSEL 81:2 (Vienna: Tempsky, 1968), 102.

53. Ambrosiaster, *Quaestio* 35, ed. A. Souter, CSEL 50 (Vienna: Tempsky, 1908), 63.

54. Ambrosiaster, *Quaestio* 115.59, p. 338.

55. Ambrosiaster, *Quaestio* 4.2, p. 25.

56. Ambrosiaster, *Comm. in 1 Cor. 12.3*, p. 131.56; Augustine, *Confessions* 6.10.6.

57. Ambrosiaster, *Quaestio* 101.4, p. 195.

58. Ibid.

59. Ambrosiaster, *Comm. in 1 Tim. 2.4*, 1, CSEL 81:3, p. 260.

60. *Inscriptiones Latinae Christianae Veteres*, no. 94A.

61. S. Lunn-Rockliffe, "A Pragmatic Approach to Poverty and Riches: Ambrosiaster's *Quaestio* 124," in *Poverty in the Roman World*, 115–29.

62. Pietri, *Roma Christiana*, 648 on *Inscriptiones Christianae Urbis Romae*, n.s., 2, ed. A. Silvagni (Rome: Pontificio Istituto di Archeologia Cristiana, 1935), no. 4815; compare *Inscriptiones Latinae Christianae Veteres*, nos. 609, 698.

63. Jerome, *Letter* 66.5, CSEL 54:1, pp. 652–53; *Letter* 77.6.3, CSEL 55:43.

64. *Inscriptiones Latinae Christianae Veteres*, no. 1233.

65. *Codex Theodosianus* 13.3.8 (370). See Albana, "Archiatri ... honeste obsequi tenuiores malint"; Schmidt-Hofner, *Reagieren und Gestalten*, 327–30; and Corbo, *Paupertas*, 138–56.

66. *Inscriptiones Christianae Urbis Romae*, n.s., 4, ed. A. Ferrua (Vatican: Pontificio Istituto di Archeologia Cristiana, 1964), no. 10228.

67. *Inscriptiones Christianae Urbis Romae*, n.s., 6, ed. A. Ferrua (Vatican: Pontificio Istituto di Archaeologia Cristiana, 1975), no. 15839.

CHAPTER 16
"To Sing the Lord's Song in a Strange Land"

1. A. Cameron, "Filocalus and Melania," *Classical Quarterly* 87 (1992): 140–44 at p. 142.

2. Salzman, *On Roman Time*, 201–2.

3. Ibid., 196–204.

4. Jerome, prologue, *Origen on the Song of Songs*, PL 23:1118A.

5. See S. Rebenich, *Hieronymus und sein Kreis: Prosopographische und sozialgeschichtliche Untersuchungen*, Historia Einzelschriften 72 (Stuttgart: F. Steiner, 1992), 21–51; and M. H. Williams, *The Monk and the Book: Jerome and the Making of Christian Scholarship* (Chicago: University of Chicago Press, 2006), 268–76. I would urge the reader to consult these two books for this and all subsequent periods of Jerome's life.

6. The chronology of the life of Melania the Elder is ambiguous, and a correct solution is important for an understanding of the pace of her conversion and the aims of her eventual departure for Alexandria and the Holy Land: see *Prosopographie chrétienne du Bas-Empire*, 2:1480–83.

7. Palladius, *Lausiac History* 46.1–4; see N. Lenski, "Valens and the Monks: Cudgeling and Conscription as a Means of Social Control," *Dumbarton Oaks Papers* 58 (2004): 93–117. On the relations between Melania the Elder and Palladius that can be deduced from the Syriac version of the original edition of Palladius's *Lausiac History*, see S. P. Brock, "Saints in Syriac: A Little-Tapped Resource," *Journal of Early Christian Studies* 16 (2008): 181–96 at pp. 192–94.

8. Rebenich, *Hieronymus und sein Kreis*, 88–89.

9. Williams, *The Monk and the Book*, 31.

10. Ibid., 50–52; A. Cain, *The Letters of Jerome: Asceticism, Biblical Exegesis, and the Construction of Christian Authority in Late Antiquity* (Oxford: Oxford University Press, 2009), 43–67. Despite much justified skepticism, Jerome did not entirely invent his intimacy with Damasus: see Y.-M. Duval, "Sur trois lettres méconnues de Jérôme concernant son séjour à Rome," in *Jerome of Stridon*, 29–40, esp. pp. 31–33.

11. Prologue to *The Translation of Didymus the Blind*, PL 23:103.

12. Jerome, *Letter* 27.2, 54.1, p. 225; Cain, *The Letters of Jerome*, 51–61.

13. P. Nautin, "L'excommunication de saint Jérôme," *Annuaire de l'École Pratique des Hautes Études, Ve section: Sciences religieuses* 80–81 (1972–73): 7–37.

14. Jerome, *Letter* 45.6.2, 54.1:327.

15. Jerome, *Letter* 45.2.2, 54.1:324.

16. Cain, *The Letters of Jerome*, 86.

17. Jerome, *Letter* 45.2.2, 54.1:324.

18. Cain, *The Letters of Jerome*, 90.

19. N. Adkin, *Jerome on Virginity: A Commentary on the* Libellus de virginitate servanda *(Letter 22)*, ARCA 42 (Liverpool: Francis Cairns, 2003) provides a comprehensive commentary on *Letter* 22, which reveals with withering precision the extent to which Jerome placed himself on show in this letter by pillaging the works of others.

20. Brown, *Body and Society*, 376. On the medical background to this advice, see A. Rousselle, *Porneia: De la maîtrise du corps à la privation sensorielle, IIe–IVe siècles de l'ère chrétienne* (Paris: Presses Universitaires de France, 1983); and T. M. Shaw, *The Burden of the Flesh: Fasting and Sexuality in Early Christianity* (Minneapolis: Fortress Press, 1998).

21. Jerome, *Letter* 22.11.1, 54.1:158: Adkin, *Jerome on Virginity*, 90–91.

22. Jerome, *Letter* 22.8.2, 54.1:154: Adkin, *Jerome on Virginity*, 72.

23. Muth, *Erlebnis von Raum—Leben in Raum*, 266–70.

24. Brown, *Body and Society*, 172–73, 367.

25. Jerome, *Letter* 22.25.1, 54.1:178.

26. Adkin, *Jerome on Virginity*, 230.

27. P. Brown, *The Cult of the Saints: Its Rise and Function in Latin Christianity* (Chicago: University of Chicago Press, 1981), 41–46; Bowes, *Private Worship, Public Values and Religious Change*, 84–96; B. Brenk, *Die Christianisierung der spätrömischen Welt: Stadt, Land, Haus, Kirche und Kloster in frühchristlicher Zeit* (Wiesbaden: Reichert, 2003), 98–105.

28. These range in time over the last decades from E. A. Clark, *Jerome, Chrysostom and Friends: Essays and Translations* (Lewiston, NY: Edwin Mellen Press, 1979) to P. Laurence, *Jérôme et le nouveau modèle feminine: La conversion à la "vie parfaite"* (Paris: Institut d'Études Augustiniennes, 1997); K. Cooper, *The Virgin and the Bride: Idealized Womanhood in Late Antiquity* (Cambridge, MA: Harvard University Press, 1996) seeks a new way around this scholarly obsession.

29. S. Brock, *The Syriac Fathers on Prayer and the Spiritual Life*, Cistercian Studies 101 (Kalamazoo, MI: Cistercian Studies, 1987), xxxi–xxxii. See also A. Persic, "La Chiesa di Siria e i 'gradi' della vita cristiana," in *Per foramen acus: Il cristianesimo antico di fronte alla pericope evangelica del "giovane ricco"* (Milan: Vita e Pensiero, 1986), 208–63.

30. Sozomen, *Ecclesiastical History* 6.33.

31. Jerome, *Vita Pauli* 6, PL 23:21B.

32. D. Krueger, *Symeon the Holy Fool: Leontius' Life and the Late Antique City* (Berkeley: University of California Press, 1996), 72–107. The influence goes deep: J. Clackson, "A Greek Papyrus in Armenian Script," *Zeitschrift für Papyrologie und Epigraphik* 129

(2000): 223–58 at lines 20–24 on pp. 240–41 contains sayings of Diogenes in a sixth-century textbook of Greek conversation for Armenians.

33. Jerome, *Letter* 14.1.3, 54:45.

34. Vogüé, *Histoire littéraire du mouvement monastique*, 1:179.

35. Jerome, *Vita Pauli* 17, 28C.

36. Jerome, *Letter* 22.21.1, 54:171, with Adkin, *Jerome on Virginity*, 179–81; *Letter* 49.21.4, 54:387.

37. Jerome, *Letter* 22.32.1, 54.1:193, with Adkin, *Jerome on Virginity*, 307–9. On this patronage, which seems to have produced highly individual manuscripts, see esp. J. Lowden, "The Beginnings of Biblical Illustration," in *Imaging the Early Medieval Bible*, ed. J. Williams (University Park: Pennsylvania State University Press, 1999), 9–55 at pp. 40–43. (I owe this reference to Professor E. Moodey.)

38. D. Wiesen, *St. Jerome as a Satirist: A Study in Christian Latin Thought and Letters* (Ithaca, NY: Cornell University Press, 1964).

39. Woolf, "Writing Poverty in Rome," 98.

40. Rufinus, *Apologia contra Hieronymum* 2.5, ed. M. Simonetti, CCSL 20 (Turnhout: Brepols, 1961).

41. Jerome, *Letter* 22.32.2, 54:193–94.

42. Jerome, *Letter* 22.28.4–6, 54:186.

43. Ambrosiaster, *Comm. in Rom.* 8.20.40, p. 285.

44. Paulinus, *Letter* 13.15.

45. Jerome, *Letter* 46.11.2, 54:341—written by Paula and Eustochium.

46. On this extensive theme the most reliable studies are G. Jenal, *Italia ascetica atque monastica: Das Asketen-und Mönchtum in Italien von den Anfängen bis zur Zeit der Langobarden (ca. 150/250–604)*, 2 vols. (Stuttgart: A. Hiersemann, 1995), 1:36–65; G. Disselkamp, *"Christiani Senatus Lumina": Zum Anteil römischer Frauen der Oberschicht im 4. und 5. Jahrhundert an der Christianisierung der römischen Senatsaristokratie*, Theophaneia 34 (Bodenheim: Philo, 1997); and the eminently sensible treatment of F. E. Consolino, "Tradizionalismo e trasgressione nell'*élite* senatoria romana: Ritratti di signore fra la fine del IV e l'inizio del V secolo," in *Le trasformazioni delle "élites,"* 65–139. For reliable biographical sketches of these women, see *Prosopographie chrétienne du Bas-Empire*, s.v. "Melania 1," 2:1480–83; s.v. "Marcella," 2:1357–62; and s.v. "Paula 1," 2: 1617–26.

47. Jerome, *Letter* 108.3.1 and 33, 55:308 and 350; see C. Habicht, "Spätantikes Epigram aus Demetrias," in *Demetrias*, ed. V. Milojčič and D. Theocharis (Bonn: R. Habelt, 1976), 199–203; C. P. Jones, *New Heroes in Antiquity: From Achilles to Antinoos* (Cambridge, MA: Harvard University Press, 2010), 80.

48. Jerome, prologue to *Comm. in ep. ad Titum*, PL 26:556A.

49. Jerome, *Letter* 108.3.1 and 33, 55:308 and 350.

50. Jerome, *Letter* 127.2.1, 56:146. See esp. H. Sivan, "On Hymens and Holiness in Late Antiquity: Opposition to Aristocratic Female Asceticism in Rome," *Jahrbuch für Antike und Christentum* 36 (1993): 81–93 at p. 86—an article of salutary precision. See now B. Enjuto Sánchez, "I 'Neratii': Legami tra Roma e le città di Sannio nel IV secolo d.C.," in *Les cités de l'Italie tardo-antique*, 113–21.

51. A. Aarjava, *Women and Law in Late Antiquity* (Oxford: Clarendon Press, 1996), 43–75.

52. Jerome, *Letter* 22.16.1, 54.1:163; see Adkin, *Jerome on Virginity*, 130.

53. Jerome, *Letter* 54.2.2, 54:467.

54. Aarjava, *Women and Law in Late Antiquity*, 108–9.

55. Jerome, *Letter* 24.2, 54:215.

56. Sivan, "On Hymens and Holiness," 82–83; see R. Lizzi Testa, "Vergini di Dio —Vergini di Vesta: Il sesso negato e la sacralità," in *L'Eros difficile: Amore e sessualità nell'antico cristianesimo*, ed. S. Pricoco (Catanzaro: Rubettino, 1998), 89–132.

57. Jerome, *Letter* 127.4.3, 56.1:149.

58. *Codex Theodosianus* 16.2.27 (390).

59. Jenal, *Italia ascetica*, 2:474–507. R. Lizzi, "Una società esortata all'ascetismo: Misure legislative e motivazioni economiche nel IV–V secolo d.C.," *Studi Storici* 30 (1989): 129–53 at p. 149n89 collects all the passages from the letters of Jerome that indicate, in equal proportions, *either* that Paula had renounced all her wealth *or* that she had retained much of it for substantial building in her monastery.

60. J. Curran, "Jerome and the Sham Christians of Rome," *Journal of Ecclesiastical History* 48 (1997): 213–29 at p. 227. See esp. J. Harries, "'Treasure in Heaven': Property and Inheritance among Senators of Late Rome," in *Marriage and Property*, ed. E. M. Craik (Aberdeen: University of Aberdeen Press, 1984), 54–70.

CHAPTER 17
Between Rome and Jerusalem

1. Porphyry, *Life of Plotinus* 9.

2. H. Wrede, *Senatorische Sarkophage Roms: Der Beitrag des Senatorenstandes zur römischen Kunst der höhen und späten Kaiserzeit*, Monumenta Artis Romanae 29 (Mainz: P. Zabern, 2001), 101; N. Denzey, *The Bone Gatherers: The Lost Worlds of Early Christian Women* (Boston: Beacon Press, 2007), 85–88.

3. Jerome, *Letter* 36.11.1, 54:277.

4. Brown, *Body and Society*, 172–73, 178–79.

5. Palladius, *Lausiac History* 55.3.

6. Gerontius, *Vita Melaniae Latina* 33.1, ed. P. Laurence, *Gérontius: La vie latine de sainte Mélanie* (Jerusalem: Franciscan Printing Press, 2002), 212.

7. Ewald, *Der Philosoph als Leitbild*, 102, 213–14.

8. Williams, *The Monk and the Book*, 133–66.

9. A. Grafton and M. Williams, *Christianity and the Transformation of the Book: Origen, Eusebius, and the Library of Caesarea* (Cambridge, MA: Harvard University Press, 2006), 131. See now Cameron, *Last Pagans*, 469–75 on the high standards of textual emendation in Christian circles.

10. Willams, *The Monk and the Book*, 187.

11. s.v. "Tyrannius Rufinus," *Prosopographie chrétienne du Bas-Empire*, 2:1925–40.

12. Jenal, *Italia ascetica*, 2:387–417.

13. Rufinus, *Apologia contra Hieronymum* 1.11, p. 44.

14. E. Wipszycka, "Les aspects économiques de la vie de la communauté des Kellia," in *Études sur le christianisme dans l'Égypte de l'antiquité tardive*, Studia Ephemeridis Augustinianum 52 (Rome: Institutum Patristicum Augustinianum, 1996), 337–62.

15. Jerome, *Letter* 125.18.2, 56:137.

16. Rufinus, *Apologia contra Hieronymum* 2.11, p. 89.

17. Palladius, *Lausiac History* 54.4–6.

18. Jenal, *Italia ascetica*, 2:603–8; see now Williams, *The Monk and the Book*, 102 on the sharp differences between Rufinus and Jerome.

19. Jenal, *Italia ascetica*, 2:536–57.

20. C. P. Hammond, "The Last Ten Years of Rufinus's Life and the Date of His Move South from Aquileia," *Journal of Theological Studies*, n.s., 28 (1977): 372–429.

21. Rufinus, *Prologus in Omelias Origenis in Numeros*, ed. M. Simonetti, *Opera*, CCSL 20 (Turnhout: Brepols, 1961), 285.

22. Williams, *The Monk and the Book*, 101.

23. Ibid., 155–66.

24. Ibid., 181–200.

25. Jerome, *Contra Rufinum* 1.1, PL 23:397A.

26. P. Brown, "The Patrons of Pelagius: The Roman Aristocracy between East and West," *Journal of Theological Studies*, n.s., 21 (1970): 56–72, also in *Religion and Society in the Age of Saint Augustine*, 208–26; E. A. Clark, *The Origenist Controversy: The Cultural Construction of an Early Christian Debate* (Princeton: Princeton University Press, 1992), 11–42.

27. Pietri, *Roma Christiana*, 435.

28. *Codex Theodosianus* 16.2.20 (370).

29. Lizzi Testa, *Senatori, popolo, papi*, 109 is to be preferred to Pietri, *Roma Christiana*, 570n3.

30. Jerome, *Letter* 45.2.2, 54:324.

31. The best treatment of the issues involved is D. G. Hunter, "Vigilantius of Calagurris and Victricius of Rouen: Ascetics, Relics, and Clerics in Late Roman Gaul," *Journal of Early Christian Studies* 7 (1999): 401–30.

32. Jerome, *Contra Vigilantium* 4, PL 23:342C, ed. J.-L. Feiertag, *S. Hieronymi presbyteri opera*, CCSL 79C (Turnhout: Brepols, 2005).

33. Jerome, *Contra Vigilantium* 13, Feiertag, p. 26.

34. Jerome, *Contra Vigilantium* 13, Feiertag, p. 25.

35. Jerome, *Contra Vigilantium* 14, Feiertag, pp. 26–27.

36. *Inscriptiones Latinae Christianae Veteres*, no. 316.

37. *Inscriptiones Christianae Urbis Romae*, n.s., 5:13355.

38. A. Bertolino, "'In area Callisti': Contributo alla topografia di Roma tardoantica," *Rivista di archeoloigia cristiana* 70 (1994): 181–90.

39. Notably the best treatment is D. G. Hunter, "Resistance to the Virginal Ideal in Late-Fourth-Century Rome: The Case of Jovinian," *Theological Studies* 48 (1987): 45–64; and idem, "Rereading the Jovinianist Controversy: Asceticism and Clerical Authority in Late Ancient Christianity," in *The Cultural Turn in Late Ancient Studies: Gender,*

Asceticism, and Historiography, ed. D. B. Martin and P. C. Miller (Durham, NC: Duke University Press, 2005), 119–35, now in Hunter, *Marriage, Celibacy, and Heresy in Ancient Christianity: The Jovinianist Controversy* (Oxford: Oxford University Press, 2007).

40. Jerome, *Adversus Jovinianum* 1.5, PL 23:217C.

41. *Inscriptiones Latinae Christianae Veteres*, no. 972.6–7; see Augustine, *City of God* 5.26.

42. Socrates, *Ecclesiastical History* 5.14.

43. Matthews, "Four Funerals and a Wedding," 134–37. See now Cameron, *Last Pagans*, 179–81 on earlier Anicii as Christians.

44. C. Machado, "Roman Aristocrats and the Christianization of Rome," in *Pagans and Christians in the Roman Empire (IVth–VIth Century A.D.): The Breaking of a Dialogue*, ed. P. Brown and R. Lizzi Testa (Münster: Lit, 2011), 493–513.

45. Ibid., 513, referring to Eventius 1, *Prosopography of the Later Roman Empire*, 2:413—a typical career from lawyer to provincial governor.

46. N. B. McLynn, "The Transformation of Imperial Churchgoing in the Fourth Century," in *Approaching Late Antiquity: The Transformation from Early to Late Empire*, ed. S. Swain and M. Edwards (Oxford: Oxford University Press, 2004), 235–70, esp. pp. 236–42 on Constantine.

47. Hoek, "Peter, Paul and a Consul," figure 1a on p. 231.

48. The relationship between Rufinus and Pelagius is even closer if we accept the view that the mysterious "Rufinus the Syrian" was, in fact, Rufinus of Aquileia himself: W. Dunphy, "Rufinus the Syrian: Myth and Reality," *Augustiniana* 59 (2009): 79–157.

49. Augustine, *Letter* 186.1.

CHAPTER 18
"The Eye of a Needle" and "The Treasure of the Soul"

1. Gerontius, *Life of Melania*, Latin version (henceforth *VL* = *Vita Latina*), 16.2–3, ed. and trans. Laurence, *Gérontius: La vie latine de sainte Mélanie*, 186; Greek version (henceforth *VG* = *Vita Graeca*), 16, ed. and trans. Gorce, *Vie de sainte Mélanie*, 160, with translation and appended essays as commentary by Clark, *The Life of Melania the Younger*, 39.

2. Laurence, *Gérontius*, 109–41; Gorce, *Vie de sainte Mélanie*, 54–77; Clark, *Life of Melania the Younger*, 115–52.

3. *VL* 18.2–4, pp. 188–90; *VG* 18, p. 162; Clark, p. 40.

4. *VL* 17.2, p. 186; *VG* 17, p. 170; Clark, p. 39.

5. *VL* 8.5–9, pp. 168–70; *VG* 8, p. 142; Clark, pp. 31–32.

6. *VL* 31.3, p. 210; *VG* 31, p. 186; Clark, p. 48.

7. John Rufus, *Life of Peter the Iberian*, 39, ed. and trans. C. B. Horn and R. R. Phenix, *John Rufus: The Lives of Peter the Iberian, Theodosius of Jerusalem and the Monk Romanus* (Atlanta, GA: Society for Biblical Literature, 2008), 54–55. It is not entirely certain that Peter actually saw Pinianus: he may have heard of him and his dress. See P. Devos, "Quand Pierre l'Ibère vint-il à Jérusalem?" *Analaecta Bollandiana* 86 (1968):

337–50. See now C. B. Horn, *Asceticism and Christological Controversy in Fifth-Century Palestine: The Career of Peter the Iberian* (Oxford: Oxford University Press, 2006), 138–41.

8. See esp. Jenal, *Italia ascetica*, 1:96–97, 2:492.

9. Paulinus, *Letter* 32.17.

10. Paulinus, *Letter* 13.15.

11. P. Heather, *The Fall of the Roman Empire: A New History of Rome and the Barbarians* (Oxford: Oxford University Press, 2006), 145–232 provides a vivid account of these years.

12. Zosimus, *Historia nova* 5.41.4, Mendelssohn, p. 270, Ridley, p. 121.

13. P. Veyne, "La prise de Rome en 410 et les Grandes Invasions," *L'empire gréco-romain*, 713–47 at pp. 726–29. P. Courcelle, *Histoire littéraire des grandes invasions germaniques*, 3rd ed. (Paris: Études Augustiniennes, 1964), 31–77 remains the best evaluation of the literary evidence of destruction; see also B. Brenk, "L'anno 410 e il suo effetto sull'arte chiesastica a Roma," in *Ecclesiae urbis*, ed. F. Guidobaldi and A. G. Guidobaldi, Studi di Antichità Cristiana 59 (Rome: Pontificio Istituto di Antichità Cristiana, 2002), 2:1001–18.

14. Olympiodorus, *Fragment* 24, p. 187.

15. *VL* 3.1 and 5.1–6.3, pp. 160, 162–64; *VG* 3 and 5–6, pp. 132–36; Clark, pp. 29–30. On Pinianus and Melania as "Modell- und Sonderfall"—both model and exception—see Jenal, *Italia ascetica*, 1:81–86, 2:484–87. See now R. Alciati and M. Giorda, "Possessions and Asceticism: Melania the Younger and Her Slow Way to Jerusalem," *Zeitschrift für Antikes Christentum* 14 (2010): 425–44.

16. *VL* 15.1, p. 184, ascribes this fortune to Melania; *VG* 15, p. 156, 157n4 to Pinianus; Clark, p. 38. We must resign ourselves to orders of magnitude that may be conventional exaggerations.

17. B. Brenk, "La cristianizzazione della *Domus* dei Valerii sul Celio," in *The Transformations of Vrbs Roma*, 69–84.

18. Symmachus, *Letter* 7.116, Callu, 3:105.

19. *VL* 10.1, p. 172; *VG* 10, pp. 144–46, 145n6; Clark, p. 33; Palladius, *Lausiac History* 61.5 gives the overall number of slaves that had been manumitted. Palladius had visited the couple in the *suburbium* in 404–5. See esp. K. Cooper, "Poverty, Obligation, and Inheritance: Roman Heiresses and the Varieties of Senatorial Christianity in Fifth-Century Rome," in *Religion, Dynasty, and Patronage*, 165–89 at pp. 165–66.

20. Zosimus, *Historia nova* 5.42.3, Mendelssohn, p. 272, Ridley, p. 122.

21. A. Giardina, "Carità eversiva: Le donazioni di Melania la Giovane e gli equilibri della società tardoromana," *Studi storici* 29 (1988): 127–42 at pp. 139–40. See now B. Pottier, "Entre les villes et les campagnes: Le banditisme en Italie du IVe au VIe siècle," in *Les cités de l'Italie tardo-antique*, 251–66.

22. *VL* 11.1–7, p. 174; *VG* 11, pp. 146–48; Clark, pp. 34–35; Curran, *Pagan City and Christian Capital*, 299–300; G. D. Dunn, "The Care of the Poor in Rome and Alaric's Sieges," in *Prayer and Spirituality in the Early Church*, vol. 5, *Poverty and Riches*, ed. Dunn, D. Luckensmeyer, and L. Cross (Sydney: St. Paul's, 2009), 319–33.

23. *VL* 12.9, p. 180; *VG* 12, p. 152; Clark, p. 37.

24. *VL* 13.2, p. 182; *VG* 13, p. 154; Clark, p. 37.

25. Heather, *The Fall of the Roman Empire*, 216–27.

26. Zosimus, *Historia nova* 5.38.3–4, Mendelssohn, p. 266, Ridley, p. 119.

27. Zosimus, *Historia nova* 6.11.2, Mendelssohn, p. 292, Ridley, p. 130.

28. Zosimus, *Historia nova* 6.7.4, Mendelssohn, p. 288, Ridley, p. 129.

29. It has been suggested that Pinianus and Melania were punished as actual partisans of Stilicho: A. Demandt and G. Brummer, "Der Prozess gegen Serena im Jahre 408 n. Chr.," *Historia* 26 (1977): 479–502. I am less certain, but I do not doubt the importance of political factors in the last stages of the couple's residence in Rome.

30. *VL* 34.1–3, p. 214; *VG* 19, p. 166; Clark, p. 42.

31. Palladius, *Lausiac History* 54.1 on Melania the Elder.

32. *VL* 34.1, p. 214; *VG* 19, p. 166; Clark, p. 42.

33. *VL* 15.6 and 19.2, pp. 186 and 190; *VG* 15 and 19, pp. 158 and 164; Clark, pp. 38 and 41. See Bowes, *Private Worship, Public Values, and Religious Change*, 138–40.

34. *VL* 19.2, p. 190; *VG* 19, p. 168; Clark, pp. 42–43 and 137–38.

35. *VL* 19.4, p. 190 and 21.3, p. 194 (in Africa); *VG* 19 and 21, pp. 164 and 172; Clark, pp. 41 and 44.

36. This is how I would interpret *VL* 35.3, p. 222; *VG* 35, p. 194; Clark, p. 51.

37. *VL* 38, p. 228; *VG* 37–38, pp. 196–98; Clark, pp. 52–53.

38. Melania continued to build constantly at the Mount of Olives. Most notable was a shrine of the Apostles in which both Pinianus and Melania's mother, Albina, were buried: *VL* 49.2, p. 250; *VG* 49, p. 220; Clark, p. 61: see the plan in Laurence, *Gérontius*, p. 340.

39. The development of the African reaction to the ideas of Pelagius and his followers has been studied with great finesse by É. Rebillard, "Sociologie de la déviance et orthodoxie: Le cas de la controverse pélagienne sur la grâce," in *Orthodoxie, christianisme, histoire*, ed. S. Elm, Rebillard, and A. Romano, Collection de l'École française de Rome 270 (Rome: École française de Rome, 2000), 221–40. Among abundant recent studies of high quality on Pelagius, I owe most to O. Wermelinger, *Rom und Pelagius: Die theologische Position der römischen Bischöfe im pelagianischen Streit in den Jahren 411–432*, Päpste und Papsttum 7 (Stuttgart: A. Hiersemann, 1975); and to S. Thier, *Kirche bei Pelagius*, Patristische Texte und Studien 50 (Berlin: de Gruyter, 1999). English readers have reason to be particularly grateful to the translations of B. R. Rees, *The Letters of Pelagius and His Followers* (Woodbridge, UK: Boydell, 1991); see also his summary, *Pelagius: A Reluctant Heretic* (Woodbridge, UK: Boydell, 1998).

40. Brown, "The Patrons of Pelagius," in *Religion and Society*, 210–11; Hammond, "The Last Ten Years of Rufinus' Life," 400n3.

41. P. Laurence, "Proba, Juliana et Démétrias: Le christianisme des femmes de la *gens Anicia* dans la première moitié du Ve siècle," *Revue des études augustiniennes* 48 (2002): 131–63. See now A. Kurdock, "*Demetrias ancilla Dei*: Anicia Demetrias and the Problem of the Missing Patron," in *Religion, Dynasty and Patronage*, 190–224; G. D. Dunn, "The Christian Networks of the *Aniciae*: The Example of the Letter of Innocent I to Anicia Iuliana," *Revue des études augustiniennes et patristiques* 55 (2009): 53–72.

42. Pelagius, cited in Augustine, *De natura et gratia* 82.

43. Pelagius, *De divina lege* 9.3, PL 30:119 (Paris: J.-P. Migne, 1846), Rees, p. 102. See P. Brown, "Pelagius and His Supporters: Aims and Environment," *Journal of Theological Studies*, n.s., 19 (1968): 93–114, now in *Religion and Society*, 183–207. My view

has been modified by Thier, *Kirche bei Pelagius*, esp. p. 9. Thier rightly distinguishes more clearly than I did in 1968 between Pelagius himself and the more sectarian groups that followed him. Recent literature has redrawn the portrait of Pelagius largely through advances in understanding his *Commentaries on the Epistles of Saint Paul*: see H. J. Frede, *Ein neuer Paulustext und Kommentar*, 2 vols. (Freiburg: Herder, 1973–74); T. De Bruyn, *Pelagius' Commentary on St. Paul's Epistle to the Romans* (Oxford: Clarendon Press, 1993); and J. Tauer, "Neue Orientierungen zur Paulusexegese des Pelagius," *Augustinianum* 34 (1994): 313–58.

44. The most nuanced treatment of this occasion is Vogüé, *Histoire littéraire du mouvement monastique*, 5:291–340.

45. Augustine, *Letter* 150.

46. Procopius, *History of the Wars* 3.2.27, ed. and trans. H. B. Dewing, *Procopius*, Loeb Classical Library (Cambridge, MA: Harvard University Press, 1916), 2:18.

47. Jerome, *Letter* 127.13.1.

48. Jerome, *Letter* 130.7.7. See T. Kotula, "Le fond africain de la révolte d'Héraclien en 413," *Antiquités africaines* 11 (1977): 257–66.

49. Jerome, *Letter* 130.5.4.

50. Jerome, *Letter* 130 6.6–7.

51. Jerome, *Letter* 130.6.1.

52. This is clearly seen by N. Cipriani, "La morale pelagiana e la retorica," *Augustinianum* 31 (1991): 309–27.

53. Vogüé, *Histoire littéraire du mouvement monastique*, 5:298–313.

54. Pelagius, *Letter to Demetrias* 2.1, PL 30:16D, Rees, p. 36.

55. Pelagius, *Letter to Demetrias* 2.2, 17A, Rees, p. 37.

56. Pelagius, *Letter to Demetrias* 4.2, 19B, Rees, p. 40.

57. Pelagius, *Letter to Demetrias* 6.3, 22A, Rees, p. 43.

58. Pelagius, *Letter to Demetrias* 3.3, 18B, Rees, p. 39.

59. Pelagius, *Letter to Demetrias* 8.3, 23C, Rees, p. 44.

60. Pelagius, *Letter to Demetrias* 11.1, 26D, Rees, p. 48.

61. Augustine, *Letter* 188.2.5.

62. Augustine, *Letter* 188.1.3.

63. J.-M. Salamito, *Les virtuoses et la multitude: Aspects sociaux de la controverse entre Augustin et les pélagiens* (Grenoble: Éditions Jérôme Millon, 2005), 29–35.

64. Pelagius, *Letter to Demetrias* 22.2, 38B, Rees, p. 60.

65. Salamito, *Les virtuoses et la multitude*, p. 30.

66. *Inscriptiones Christianae Urbis Romae*, n.s., 6, no. 15764. See now Bowes, *Private Worship, Public Values, and Religious Change*, 94–96.

CHAPTER 19
Tolle divitem

1. The best survey of this theme is A. Kessler, *Reichtumskritik und Pelagianismus: Die pelagianische Diatribe De divitiis. Situierung, Lesetext, Übersetzung, Kommentar*, Paradosis 43 (Freiburg, Switzerland: Universitätsverlag, 1999), 36–55.

2. Pelagius, *Letter to Demetrias* 8.3, 23BC, Rees, p. 44. See Brown, "Pelagius and His Supporters," in *Religion and Society*, 195–200; and Thier, *Kirche bei Pelagius*, 75.

3. Pelagius, *Letter to Demetrias* 8.2, 23B, Rees, p. 44.

4. Pelagius, *Letter to Demetrias* 1.1, 15D, Rees, p. 36.

5. J. Morris, "Pelagian Literature," *Journal of Theological Studies*, n.s., 16 (1965): 26–60. This perspective continues to be accepted by historians of post-Roman Britain: see K. R. Dark, *Civitas to Kingdom: British Political Continuity, 300–800* (Leicester: Leicester University Press, 1994); and idem, "The Late Antique Landscape of Britain, AD 300–700," in *Landscapes of Change*, 279–99 at pp. 286–91. Dark explains the observed flattening out of post-Roman British material culture by a violent revolution and a widespread abandonment of luxury, inspired by a Christian ideology of Pelagian inspiration.

6. Kessler, *Reichtumskritik und Pelagianismus*, 104–35.

7. Morris, "Pelagian Literature," 50–51.

8. G. de Plinval, *Pélage: Ses écrits, sa vie et sa réforme: Étude d'histoire littéraire et religieuse* (Lausanne: Payot, 1943), 208.

9. Salamito, *Les virtuoses et la multitude*, 128.

10. S. Toscano, *Tolle divitem: Etica, società e potere nel* De divitiis, Testi e Studi di Storia Antica 19 (Catania: Edizioni del Prisma, 2006). See now P. Garnsey, "The Originality and Origins of Anonymous, *De divitiis*," in *From Rome to Constantinople: Studies in Honour of Averil Cameron*, ed. H. Amirav and B. ter Haar Romeny (Louvain: Peeters, 2007), 29–45.

11. *De divitiis* [henceforth *De div.*] 4.1, ed. and trans. Kessler, *Reichtumskritik und Pelagianismus*, p. 246, Rees, p. 176. The original edition is C. P. Caspari, *Briefe, Abhandlungen und Predigten aus der zwei letzten Jahrhunderten des kirchlichen Altertums und dem Anfang des Mittelalters* (Christiania/Oslo: Malling, 1890; reprint, Brussels: Culture et Civilisation, 1964).

12. *De div.* 1.3, Kessler, p. 244, Rees, p. 175.

13. *De div.* 3, Kessler, p. 246, Rees, p. 176.

14. See esp. Garnsey, *Thinking about Property*, 121–28.

15. Sulpicius Severus, *Chronica* 1.4.3, p. 98.

16. Paulinus, *Poem* 6.263.

17. Paulinus, *Poem* 25.102: see J. Lössl, *Julian von Aeclanum: Studien zu seinem Leben, seinem Werk, seiner Lehre und ihrer Überlieferung*, Supplements to Vigiliae Christianae 60 (Leiden: Brill, 2001), 56–73.

18. Proba, *Cento* 301–2, ed. and trans. E. A. Clark and D. F. Hatch, *The Golden Bough, the Oaken Cross: The Vergilian Cento of Faltonia Betitia Proba*, American Academy of Religion: Texts and Translations 5 (Chico, CA: Scholars Press, 1981), 48.

19. Proba, *Cento* 524, Clark and Hatch, p. 72.

20. *De div.* 7.4, Kessler, p. 260, Rees, p. 182.

21. M. Colish, *Ambrose's Patriarchs: Ethics for the Common Man* (Notre Dame, IN: University of Notre Dame Press, 2005) is excellent on Ambrose's image of Abraham as the model for the good rich.

22. *De div.* 9.1, Kessler, p. 266, Rees, p. 184.

23. B. Ramsey, s.v. "Wealth," in *Augustine through the Ages*, 876–81 at p. 880. The only parallel known to me is the Syrian ascetic treatise (possibly Messalian) that declares

that war does not happen according to the will of God (whether to punish or to give victory) but is only the result of human actions: *Liber Graduum* 9.6, trans. R. A. Kitchen and M.F.G. Parmentier, *The Book of Steps: The Syriac Liber Graduum*, Cistercian Studies 196 (Kalamazoo, MI: Cistercian Studies, 2004), 92–93.

24. *De div.* 9.2, Kessler, p. 266, Rees, p. 184.

25. *De div.* 7.3, Kessler, p. 260, Rees, p. 182.

26. Ibid.

27. Jerome, *Letter* 120.1.7. The topic was also debated in Neo-Platonic circles: Eunapius, *Lives of the Sophists*, ed. W. C. Wright, in *Philostratus and Enapius: The Lives of the Sophists*, Loeb Classical Library (Cambridge, MA: Harvard University Press, 1952), 372–74.

28. *De div.* 5.1, Kessler, p. 250, Rees, p. 177.

29. *De div.* 8.1, Kessler, p. 262, Rees, p. 182.

30. Kessler, *Reichtumskritik und Pelagianismus*, 351.

31. *De div.* 12.2, Kessler, p. 292, Rees, p. 194. See Newhauser, *The Early History of Greed*, 90.

32. M. Rostovtzeff, *The Social and Economic History of the Hellenistic World* (Oxford: Clarendon Press, 1941), 2:1130.

33. Kessler, *Reichtumskritik und Pelagianismus*, 220–37 provides an admirable analysis of the rhetorical strategies of the author.

34. *De div.* 8.1, Kessler, p. 262, Rees, p. 182.

35. *De vita christiana* 3.3, PL 50:387A, Rees, p. 110.

36. *Prosopographie chrétienne du Bas-Empire* 2, s.v. "Caelestius," 1:357–75 (*auditorialis scholasticus*) and "Constantius 11," 1:475.

37. Pietri, *Roma Christiana*, 579.

38. Jerome, *Commentaria in Ezechielem prophetam* 6.8, PL 25:175.

39. *De vita christiana* 11.1 and 12, 396A and 397A, Rees, pp. 119 and 120.

40. *De div.* 6.3 and 6.4, Kessler, p. 256, Rees, p. 180.

41. Kessler, *Reichtumskritik und Pelagianismus*, 166. The dust cover of Toscano, *Tolle divitem* most appositely shows Christ before Pilate as illustrated in the sixth-century Rossano Gospel Book.

42. Jerome, *Letter* 125.5.1.

43. *De div.* 6.2, Kessler, p. 254, Rees, p. 179.

44. *De div.* 18.1, Kessler, p. 306, Rees, pp. 200–201.

45. Augustine, *Letter* 156; see Kessler, *Reichtumskritik und Pelagianismus*, 85–100.

CHAPTER 20
Augustine's Africa

1. Claudian, *De bello Gildonico* 1.2, ed. and trans. Platnauer, 1:98.

2. Gerontius, *VL* 21.4, Laurence, p. 194. For a Roman view of such estates, see Frontinus, *De controversiis agrorum* 2. On the family estates of the Valerii and others, see S. Panciera, "Ancora sulla famiglia senatoria 'africana' degli Aradii," *Africa Romana* 2 (1986): 547–72.

3. Gerontius *VG* 21, Gorce, p. 172, Clark, p. 44; *VL* 20.3, p. 194.

4. *Letter* 126.1. (For the sake of economy, all citations without the name of an author in this and the subsequent three chapters are from the works of Augustine.)

5. *Letter* 125.2.

6. *Letter* 126.1. On the size of the excavated basilica at Hippo that is thought to be that of Augustine, see Lancel, *Saint Augustine* (2002), 240–44.

7. *Letter* 126.5.

8. *Letter* 126.7.

9. H. Jaïdi, "Remarques sur la constitution des biens des églises africaines à l'époque romaine tardive," in *Splendidissima civitas: Études d'histoire romaine en hommage à François Jacques*, ed. A. Chastagnol, S. Demougin, and C. Lepelley (Paris: Publications de la Sorbonne, 1996), 169–91; C. Buenacasa Pérez, "La creación del patrimonio ecclesiastico de las iglesias norteafricanas en época romana (siglos II–V): Renovación de la visión tradicional," in *Sacralidad y Arqueología: Homenaje al Prof. Thilo Ulbert*, Antigüedad y Cristianismo 21 (Murcia: Universidad de Murcia, 2004), 493–509.

10. *Hippone*, ed. X. Delestre (Aix-en-Provence: Édisud, 2005), 19–36, 183–215. See also Brown, *Augustine of Hippo*, 183–97; Lancel, *Saint Augustin*, 211–16.

11. O. Perler, *Les voyages de Saint Augustin* (Paris: Études Augustiniennes, 1969), 25–56, 423.

12. Lepelley, *Les cités de l'Afrique romaine*, 1:46–49.

13. Ibid.

14. L. Dossey, *Peasant and Empire in Christian North Africa* (Berkeley: University of California Press, 2010), 101–24.

15. B. Shaw, "Rural Markets in North Africa and the Political Economy of the Roman Empire," *Antiquités africaines* 17 (1981): 37–83, now in *Rulers, Nomads and Christians in Roman North Africa* (Aldershot: Variorum, 1995).

16. A. Berthier, *La Numidie: Rome et le Maghreb* (Paris: Picard, 1981), 150–52.

17. Optatus of Milevis, *De schismate donatistarum* 3.4, trans. M. Edwards, *Optatus: Against the Donatists* (Liverpool: Liverpool University Press, 1997), 68–69; Augustine, *Letter* 185.4.15—but without mention of Fasir and Axido.

18. B. Shaw, "Who Were the Circumcellions?" in *Vandals, Romans and Berbers: New Perspectives on Late Antique North Africa*, ed. A. H. Merrills (Aldershot: Ashgate, 2004), 227–58; idem, "Bad Boys: Circumcellions and Fictive Violence," in *Violence in Late Antiquity: Perceptions and Practices*, ed. H. A. Drake (Aldershot: Ashgate, 2006), 179–96; Dossey, *Peasant and Empire in Christian North Africa*, 173–89.

19. W.H.C. Frend, *The Donatist Church: A Movement of Protest in Roman North Africa* (Oxford: Clarendon Press, 1952). Though this book is open to criticism, it remains the starting point for the study of Augustine's activity in Africa. See Brown, *Augustine of Hippo*, 207–39, with updates on pp. 460–62, 482–84, and 486.

20. B. Shaw, *Sacred Violence: African Christians and Sectarian Hatred in the Age of Augustine* (Cambridge: Cambridge University Press, 2011). I deeply appreciate the kindness of the author in letting me see the manuscript of this important work. Idem, "African Christianity: Disputes, Definitions and 'Donatists,'" in *Orthodoxy and Heresy in Religious Movements: Discipline and Dissent*, ed. M. R. Greenshields and T. Robinson

(Lampeter: Edwin Mellen Press, 1992), 5–34, now in *Rulers, Nomads and Christians*. O'Donnell, *Augustine*, 209–19 sees clearly the temerity of Augustine's claim to represent the only "Catholic" Christianity in Africa.

21. C. Lepelley, "Le lieu des valeurs communes: La cité terrain neutre entre païens et chrétiens dans l'Afrique de l'Antiquité tardive," in *Idéologies et valeurs civiques*, 271–85; and idem, "De la réaction païenne à la sécularisation," *Cristianesimo e storia* 30 (2009): 423–39.

22. *Letters* 34 and 35.

23. S. Lancel, *Actes de la Conférence de Carthage en 411*, SC 373 (Paris: Le Cerf, 1991), 4:1293–1536.

24. P. Brown, "Religious Coercion in the Later Roman Empire: The Case of North Africa," *History* 48 (1963): 283–305, now in *Religion and Society*, 301–30.

25. B. Kriegbaum, *Kirche der Traditoren oder Kirche der Märtyrer? Die Vorgeschichte des Donatismus* (Innsbruck: Tyrolia, 1986) is the best survey of the ecclesiological assumptions of African Christianity. Now see the trenchant study of C. García Mac Gaw, *Le problème du baptême dans le schisme donatiste*, Ausonius: Scripta Antiqua 21 (Bordeaux: Ausonius, 2008), 175–238. Dossey, *Peasant and Empire in Christian North Africa*, 147–94 is outstanding.

26. Cyprian, *De unitate ecclesiae* 25; Y. Duval, *Les chrétientés d'Occident et leur évêque au IIIe siècle: Plebs in ecclesia constituta* (Paris: Institut d'Études Augustiniennes, 2005), 29.

27. Optatus of Milevis, *Against the Donatists* 3.3, Edwards, p. 62: see G. A. Cecconi, "Elemosina e propaganda: Un'analisi della 'Macariana persecutio,'" *Revue des études augustiniennes* 31 (1990): 42–66.

28. Daniel 5:17 in Optatus of Milevis, *Against the Donatists*, Edwards, p. 67.

29. Optatus of Milevis, *Against the Donatists* 3.4, Edwards, p. 70.

30. See esp. A. Leone, "Clero, proprietà, cristianizzazione delle campagne nel Nord Africa tardoantica: *Status quaestionis*," *Antiquité tardive* 14 (2006): 95–104 at pp. 103–4.

31. *Collatio Carthaginensis* 1.189, ed. and trans. S. Lancel, *Actes de la Conférence de Carthage*, SC 195 (Paris: Le Cerf, 1972), 2:840.

32. A. Berthier, *Les vestiges du christianisme antique dans la Numidie centrale* (Algiers: Maison-Carrée, 1942).

33. J. Christern, *Das frühchristliche Pilgerheiligtum von Tebessa: Architektur und Ornamentik einer spätantiken Bauhütte in Nordafrika* (Wiesbaden: F. Steiner, 1976), 292. This remarkable building complex is well illustrated in C. Briand-Ponsart and C. Hugoniot, *L'Afrique romaine de l'Atlantique à la Tripolitaine, 146 av. J.-C.–533 ap. J.-C.* (Paris: Armand Colin, 2005), 528–29.

34. Lepelley, *Les cités de l'Afrique romaine*, 2:186–88.

35. Ibid., 2:452–55, 471–74.

36. *Contra epistulam Parmeniani* 3.6.29.

37. I. Gui, N. Duval, and J.-P. Caillet, *Basiliques chrétiennes d'Afrique du Nord: Inventaire d'Algérie* (Paris: Institut d'Études Augustiniennes, 1992), vol. 1: text, pp. 224–25 and vol. 2: illustrations, CIX, no. 84, p. 109. See now A. Michel, "Aspects du culte dans les églises de Numidie au temps d'Augustin: Un état de question," in *Saint Augustin, la*

Numidie et la société de son temps, ed. S. Lancel (Bordeaux: Ausonia; Paris: Boccard, 2005), 67–108 at pp. 88–91, with a map of sites dated to the time of Augustine on p. 70.

38. S. Gsell, *Atlas archéologique de l'Algérie* (Algiers: A. Jourdain, 1911), fasc. 27, no. 278, also in *Inscriptiones Latinae Christianae Veteres,* no. 1859.

39. *Inscriptiones Latinae Christianae Veteres,* no. 1825; Février, *Approches du Maghreb romain,* 2:39–41; J. Christern, "Basilika und Memorie der heiligen Salsa in Tipasa: Ein Beitrag zum Verhältnis von Märtyrergrab und Zömeterialbasilika," *Bulletin d'archéologie algérienne* 3 (1968): 193–250; Gui, Duval, and Caillet, *Basiliques chrétiennes d'Afrique du Nord,* vol. 2: illustrations XXVII–XXVII, pp. 26–27; Y. Duval, *Loca sanctorum Africae: Le culte des martyrs en Afrique du IVe au VIIe siècle,* Collection de l'École française de Rome 58 (Rome: Palais Farnèse, 1982), 1:258–366.

40. Dossey, *Peasant and Empire in Christian North Africa,* 125–44.

41. *Letter* 247 with *New Letter* 1*.2–3, pp. 46–48, 421–22, Eno, *Letters,* p. 12, on a minor bishop who excommunicated the entire household of an official who had dragged a man out of sanctuary in his church.

42. *Passio Marculi* 4, ed. and trans. J.-L. Maier, *Le dossier du donatisme,* vol. 1, *Des origines à la mort de Constance II (303–361),* Texte und Untersuchungen 79 (Berlin: Akademie Verlag, 1987), 280, trans. M. A. Tilley, *Donatist Martyr Stories: The Church in Conflict in Roman North Africa* (Liverpool: Liverpool University Press, 1996), 80. It was considered shocking that a delegation of Donatist bishops should be flogged by an imperial commissioner.

43. *New Letter* 20*.11 and 29–31, pp. 311 and 336–40, Eno, *Letters,* pp. 139–40, 147–49.

44. *New Letter* 20*, pp. 292–342 with commentary, pp. 516–20, Eno, *Letters,* pp. 133–49: see Brown, *Augustine of Hippo,* 468–69. See now A. Gutsfeld, "Kirche und *civitas* in der Spätantike: Augustin und die Einheit von Stadt und Land in Hippo Regius," in *Die spätantike Stadt und ihre Christianisierung,* ed. G. Brands and H.-G. Severin (Wiesbaden: Reichert, 2003), 135–44 at pp. 139–42; and N. B. McLynn, "Augustine's Black Sheep: The Case of Antoninus of Fussala," in *Istituzioni, carismi ed esercizio del potere,* 305–21.

45. *New Letter* 20*.20, p. 324, Eno, *Letters,* p. 143.

46. *New Letter* 20*.27, pp. 332–34, Eno, *Letters,* pp. 146–47 with *Letter* 209.5.

47. s.v. "Fabiola 1" and "2," *Prosopographie du Bas-Empire,* 2:734–36.

CHAPTER 21
"Dialogues with the Crowd"

1. F. Dolbeau, "'Seminator verborum': Réfléxions d'un éditeur des sermons d'Augustin," in *Augustin prédicateur (395–411),* ed. G. Madec (Paris: Institut d'Études Augustiniennes, 1998), 95–111.

2. Mandouze, *Saint Augustin,* 595–615.

3. F. Dolbeau, "Nouveaux sermons de Saint Augustin pour la conversion des païens et des donatistes (IV)," *Revue des études augustiniennes* 38 (1992): 69–141 at p. 51. On

these discoveries, see Brown, *Augustine of Hippo* (2000), 443–45. A small group of sermons similar to those discovered by Dolbeau have been found at Erfurt: Schiller, Weber, and Weidmann, "Sechs neue Augustinuspredigten: Teil 2." I am grateful to the kindness of the authors for having allowed me to see this article before its publication.

4. Mandouze, *Saint Augustin*, 615–27.

5. Ibid., chapter 11 (pp. 591–663) was entitled "Dialogues avec la Foule."

6. *Dolbeau Sermon* 2 [359B], Dolbeau, 316–44, Hill, 343–53. Each of the *Dolbeau Sermons* has been placed within the conventional order of Augustine's sermons, to which Hill adheres. I give this number in square brackets.

7. *Dolbeau Sermon* 2.3 and 20, pp. 329 and 342, Hill, pp. 332–33 and 349.

8. *Dolbeau Sermon* 2.23, p. 344, Hill, p. 351.

9. See esp. J. C. Magalhães de Oliveira, "*Vt maiores pagani non sint!* Pouvoir, iconoclasme et action populaire à Carthage au début du Ve siècle," *Antiquité tardive* 14 (2006): 245–62.

10. Finn, *Almsgiving*, 147–50; idem, "Portraying the Poor: Descriptions of Poverty in Christian Texts from the Late Roman Empire," in *Poverty in the Roman World*, 130–44.

11. *Letter* 126.8. See Brown, *Poverty and Leadership*, 63–65.

12. *Enarrationes in Psalmos* 83.7.

13. *De haeresibus* 87 (on the Abelonii); *Letter* 10*.2.34, p. 168, Eno, p. 77 (on the sale of children).

14. *Letter* 122 (at Hippo); *Dolbeau Sermon* 16 [72A].9, p. 126, Hill, p. 70 (at Carthage).

15. Leone, *Changing Townscapes in North Africa*, 59, 66–82.

16. *Registri Ecclesiae Carthaginensis Excerpta* 61, in *Concilia Africae a. 345–a. 525*, p. 197—on Christian members of the associations obliged to be present at civic festivals; *Confessions* 6.9.14 and *Expositio totius mundi et gentium* 61, p. 202—on the street of the silversmiths.

17. A. Wilson, "Urban Production in the Roman World: The View from North Africa," *Papers of the British School at Rome* 70 (2002): 231–73 at pp. 237–50—for Timgad and Sabratha. One can assume similar industry at Carthage and Hippo.

18. Veyne, *L'empire gréco-romain*, 117–62 vividly characterizes this essential feature of Roman society. The best analysis of the social composition of the congregations addressed by Augustine is in Dossey, *Peasant and Empire in Christian North Africa*, 149–59.

19. See Brown, *Poverty and Leadership*, 46–48.

20. Rapp, *Holy Bishops*, 173.

21. *Sermon* 302.13 and 302.16, with J. C. Magalhães de Oliveira, "Le 'pouvoir du peuple': Une émeute à Hippone au début du Ve siècle connue par le sermon 302 de Saint Augustin pour la fête de Saint Laurent," *Antiquité tardive* 12 (2004): 309–24 at pp. 313–14.

22. *New Letter* 15*.2, pp. 264–66, Eno, p. 115; R. Delmaire and C. Lepelley, "Du nouveau sur Carthage: Le témoignage des Lettres de Saint Augustin découvertes par Johannes Divjak," *Opus* 2 (1983): 473–87 at pp. 477–82.

23. *Codex Theodosianus* 11.7.20 (412); Quodvultdeus, *De gloria sanctorum* 15, ed. R. Braun, CCSL 60 (Turnhout: Brepols, 1976), 220.

24. See esp. Magalhães de Oliveira, *"Vt maiores pagani non sint!"* 255–60.

25. *Sermon* 345.1.

26. J. P. Gutton, *La société et les pauvres: L'exemple de la généralité de Lyon, 1534–1789* (Paris: Belles Lettres, 1971), 8–11.

27. Ammianus Marcellinus, *Res gestae* 28.4.10.

28. *Enarrationes in Psalmos* 39.28.

29. Jones, *The Later Roman Empire*, 2:737–63; Lepelley, *Les cités de l'Afrique romaine*, 1:243–92.

30. Krause, *Spätantike Patronatsformen.*

31. *Sermon* 130.5.

32. *Sermon* 14.8.

33. *Sermon* 107. 8–9.

34. *Sermon* 6.2.2.

35. *Letter* 126.1.

36. *Dolbeau Sermon* 2.5, p. 330, Hill, p. 334.

37. *Letter* 247.1.

38. *Enarrationes in Psalmos* 64.3.

39. Brown, *Augustine of Hippo*, 312–29; see now M. Ruokanen, *Theology of Social Life in Augustine's De civitate Dei*, Forschungen zur Kirchen-und Dogmengeschichte 53 (Göttingen: Vandenhoeck and Ruprecht, 1993).

40. Magalhães de Oliveira, *"Vt maiores pagani non sint!"* 247.

41. *Enarrationes in Psalmos* 132.4.

42. *De div.* 12.2.

43. *Sermon* 37.4.

44. Newhauser, *The Early History of Greed*, 93–99.

45. T. F. X. Noble, "Secular Sanctity: Forging an Ethos for the Carolingian Nobility," in *Lay Intellectuals in the Carolingian World*, ed. P. Wormald and J. L. Nelson (Cambridge: Cambridge University Press, 2007), 8–36, esp. pp. 16–18. See also M. M. Gorman, "The Oldest Annotations on Augustine's *De civitate Dei*," *Augustinianum* 46 (2006): 457–79 at p. 461.

46. *Dolbeau Sermon* 5 [114B].9, pp. 441–42, Hill, p. 108.

47. *Dolbeau Sermon* 5.11, p. 443, Hill, p. 109.

48. *Dolbeau Sermon* 5.12, p. 444, Hill, p. 110.

49. H. Savon, *Saint Ambroise devant l'exégèse de Philon le Juif* (Paris: Études Augustiniennes, 1977), 1:249–62.

50. *Sermon* 61.11.12.

51. *Dolbeau Sermon* 5.12–13, p. 445, Hill, p. 111.

52. The series of sermons was identified by A.-M. La Bonnardière, "Les 'Enarrationes in Psalmos' prêchées par Saint Augustin à Carthage en décembre 409," *Recherches augustiniennes* 11 (1976): 52–90. The discovery of *Dolbeau Sermons* that are connected to this series and datable to 403–4 has led to a redating of the series as a whole from 409 to 403: see Dolbeau, *Vingt-six sermons*, p. 374, confirmed by P.-M. Hombert, *Nouvelles recherches de chronologie augustinienne* (Paris: Institut d'Études Augustiniennes, 2000), 563–88.

53. This is the occasion proposed by Hugoniot, *Les spectacles*, 772–73.

54. *Enarrationes in Psalmos* 147.3 and 147.12; 103, sermon 1.13; 81.1 and 81.23; 102.12–13 now with *Dolbeau Sermon* 5.14, p. 446, Hill, p. 112; and 26.1–2, pp. 366–68, Hill, pp. 180–81.

55. Lepelley, *Les cités de l'Afrique romaine*, 1:110–11, 310–14, 2:44–47.

56. *Enarrationes in Psalmos* 147.7.

57. *Dolbeau Sermon* 11 [90A].11, p. 65, Hill, pp. 82–83.

58. *Enarrationes in Psalmos* 149.10.

59. *Letter* 138.2.14.

60. L. Ennabli, *Carthage: Une métropole chrétienne du IVe à la fin du VIIe siècle* (Paris: Centre National de Recherche Scientifique, 1997), 29–31.

61. *Enarrationes in Psalmos*, sermon 3.9–10.

62. *Erfurt Sermon* 2.1 and 3.3.1, ed. Schiller, Weber, and Weidmann, pp. 9–10 and 18.

63. *Sermon* 107A, PL Supplementum 2:777.

64. C. Lambot, "Nouveaux sermons de saint Augustin," *Revue bénédictine* 49 (1937): 233–78 at p. 270.

65. *Concilium in Causa Apiarii* can. 15, in *Concilia Africae*, p. 105.

66. *Enarrationes in Psalmos* 147.7.

67. *New Letters* 1A and 2*.2 and 12–13, pp. 54–58, 62, and 88–92, Eno, pp. 14–16, 19–20, and 28–30; see Brown, *Augustine of Hippo*, 471–73. *New Letter* 1A had already been discovered: see C. Lambot, "Lettre inédite de S. Augustin relative au 'De civitate Dei,'" *Revue bénédictine* 51 (1939): 109–21.

68. Hugoniot, *Les spectacles*, pp. 316–17.

69. R. MacMullen, *Roman Social Relations, 50 B.C. to A.D. 284* (New Haven, CT: Yale University Press, 1974), 61.

CHAPTER 22
Dimitte nobis debita nostra

1. N. B. McLynn, "Augustine's Roman Empire," *Augustinian Studies* 30 (1999): 29–44 at p. 34.

2. P. Brown, "Aspects of the Christianization of the Roman Aristocracy," *Journal of Roman Studies* 51 (1961): 1–11, now in *Religion and Society*, 161–82.

3. *Letter* 135.2.

4. Brown, *Augustine of Hippo*, 297–302.

5. R. Hanoune, "Le paganisme philosophique de l'aristocratie municipale," in *L'Afrique dans l'Occident romain (Ier siècle av. J.-C.–IVe siècle ap. J.-C.)*, Collection de l'École française de Rome 134 (Rome: Palais Farnèse, 1990), 63–75 at p. 71.

6. Rebillard, "Sociologie de la déviance et orthodoxie," 225–32.

7. Wermelinger, *Rom und Pelagius*, 172–76.

8. Augustine, *Sermon* 348 = *Dolbeau Sermon* 30.13.200, ed. F. Dolbeau, "Le sermon 384A de saint Augustin contre Pélage: Édition du texte intégral," *Recherches augustiniennes* 28 (1995): 37–63 at p. 61, Hill, p. 316.

9. A.-M. La Bonnardière, "Les commentaires simultanés de Mat. 6,12 et de 1 Jo. 1,18 dans l'oeuvre de saint Augustin," *Revue des études augustiniennes* 1 (1955): 129–47.

10. *Letter* 156. See Kessler, *Reichtumskritik und Pelagianismus*, 85–100.

11. É. Rebillard, *In hora mortis: Évolution de la pastorale chrétienne de la mort aux IVe et Ve siècles dans l'Occident latin*, Bibliothèque des Écoles françaises d'Athènes et de Rome 283 (Rome: Palais Farnèse, 1994), 148–67.

12. *Enarrationes in Psalmos* 103, sermon 3.18.

13. La Bonnardière, "Les commentaires simultanés," 129–31; idem, "Pénitence et réconciliation de pénitents d'après saint Augustin," *Revue des études augustiniennes* 13 (1967): 31–53 at pp. 47–53.

14. *Enarrationes in Psalmos* 140.18.

15. See, for example, O. Plassmann, *Die Almosen bei Johannes Chrysostomus* (Münster: Aschendorff, 1961); and Brown, *Poverty and Leadership*, 95.

16. *De civitate Dei* 21.27.

17. Paulinus, *Letter* 35. Augustine's view of the eternity and absence of remission in the final fires of Hell after the Last Judgment was by no means as widespread as it later became: see P. Brown, "The Decline of the Empire of God: Amnesty, Penance and the Afterlife from Late Antiquity to the Middle Ages," in *Last Things: Death and the Apocalypse in the Middle Ages*, ed. C. W. Bynum and P. Freedman (Philadephia: University of Pennsylvania Press, 2000), 41–59 at pp. 42–50; Skeb, *Christo vivere*, 88–106—Paulinus showed "astonishing optimism" on this issue.

18. *Sermon* 58.9.10.

19. *Sermon* 56.7.11 and 58.9.10.

20. *Sermon* 9.19.

21. Duval, *Loca sanctorum Africae*, vol. 1, no. 167, pp. 351–53; *Inscriptiones Latinae Christianae Veteres*, no. 1822. See now A. Blackhurst, "The House of Nubel: Rebels or Players?" in *Vandals, Romans and Berbers*, 59–76, at pp. 65–66.

22. *Inscriptiones Latinae Christianae Veteres*, no. 1915.

23. Duval, *Loca sanctorum Africae*, vol. 1, no. 173, p. 366.

24. *Carmina Latina Epigraphica* 119, ed. E. Engström (Leipzig: Teubner, 1912), 35.

25. Compare the tendency of Hindu and Buddhist givers to expiate their sins by gifts to distant shrines: Parry, "*The Gift*, the Indian Gift and the 'Indian Gift,'" 463.

26. Gerontius, *VG*, Gorce, p. 170, Clark, p. 43. See now C. Lepelley, "Facing Wealth and Poverty: Defining Augustine's Social Doctrine," *Augustinian Studies* 38 (2007): 1–18.

27. P. Leveau, P. Sillières, and J.-P. Valat, *Campagnes de la Méditerranée romaine: Occident* (Paris: Hachette, 1993), 181–88 brings welcome precision on the exact size and placing of estates in the widely differing regions of Africa.

28. D. Vera, "Enfiteusi, colonato e trasformazioni agrarie nell'Africa romana proconsulare del tardo impero," *Africa Romana* 4 (1987): 267–93, esp. 284–89; and idem, "Terra e lavoro nell'Africa romana," *Studi Storici* 4 (1988): 967–92, esp. at pp. 979–82.

29. J. Peyras, "Le fundus Aufidianus: Étude d'un grand domaine romain de la région de Mateur (Tunisie du Nord)," *Antiquités Africaines* 9 (1975): 181–222; A. Leone and D. Mattingly, "Vandal, Byzantine and Arab Rural Landscapes in North Africa," in *Landscapes of Change*, 135–62 at p. 154.

30. *Letter* 66.1.

31. Gui, Duval, and Caillet, *Basiliques chrétiennes d'Afrique du Nord*, vol. 2, no. LX-VIII, p. 68. The reader should know that the date of this basilica remains contested; I think that an early fifth-century date is more likely than a later one, by reason of the titles of the donors. This is also the view of J.-P. Caillet, "La réalité de l'implantation monumentale chrétienne au temps d'Augustin: L'exemple de quelques cités de Numidie," in Lancel, *Saint Augustin*, 55–66 at p. 60.

CHAPTER 23
"Out of Africa"

1. Pliny the Elder, *Natural History* 8.17.42.

2. Wermelinger, *Rom und Pelagius*, 46–87.

3. Brown, *Augustine of Hippo* (2000), 354–66. The reader should know that, given the superabundant literature on Augustine and the Pelagian Controversy, I have cited only the books and articles I have found to be reliable and relevant to the themes raised in this chapter.

4. *Sermon* 348 = *Dolbeau Sermon* 30.5.81, Dolbeau, p. 51, Hill, p. 312.

5. Wermelinger, *Rom und Pelagius*, 88–218.

6. *Opus imperfectum contra Iulianum* 1.42.

7. Rees, *The Letters of Pelagius and His Followers*, 11–12.

8. Olympiodorus, *Fragment* 25, Blockley, 2:189; Brown, "Pelagius and His Supporters," in *Religion and Society*, esp. at pp. 186–92.

9. A. Gillett, "Rome, Ravenna and the Last Western Emperors," *Papers of the British School at Rome* 69 (2001): 131–67 effectively demolishes this persistent misconception.

10. Well seen by V. Zangara, "Una predicazione alla presenza dei principi: La chiesa di Ravenna nella prima metà del sec. V," *Antiquité tardive* 8 (2000): 265–304 at p. 267.

11. *Edict of Honorius*, in *Collectio Quesnelliana* XIV, PL 56:490–92 (Paris: J.-P. Migne, 1846).

12. *L'Année épigraphique 1928*, no. 80, p. 22.

13. Zosimus, *Historia nova* 5.41.5: see *Prosopography of the Later Roman Empire*, 2:822–24.

14. *Edict of Honorius*, in *Collectio Quesnelliana*, 491B.

15. *Letter* 192 (to Celestine) and 191.2 (to Sixtus).

16. *Letter* 191.1.

17. The best recent study is Lössl, *Julian von Aeclanum*.

18. Paulinus, *Poem* 25; see Lössl, *Julian von Aeclanum*, 73.

19. Sotinel, "Les évêques italiens," 385–86 is to be preferred to the speculations on Julian's high birth collected in Lössl, *Julian von Aeclanum*, 72n200.

20. Gennadius, *De viris illustribus* 46: see Lössl, *Julian von Aeclanum*, 42.

21. I plead guilty to having succumbed to the temptation to see Julian in terms of this old-world background in *Augustine of Hippo*, 382–84. Lössl, *Julian von Aeclanum* has provided an ample corrective to this view.

22. Julian in Augustine, *Contra II epistulas pelagianorum* 4.33, now in *Iuliani Aeclanenensis fragmenta* 27, ed. L. de Coninck, CCSL 88 (Turnhout: Brepols, 1977), 340.

23. Cipriani, "La polemica antiafricana di Giuliano di Eclano."

24. J. Lössl, "Julian of Aeclanum on Pain," *Journal of Early Christian Studies* 10 (2002): 203–43; and idem, *Julian von Aeclanum*, 127–35; P. Brown, "Sexuality and Society in the Fifth Century A.D.: Augustine and Julian of Eclanum," in *Tria corda: Scritti in onore di Arnaldo Momigliano*, ed. E. Gabba, Biblioteca di Athenaeum 1 (Como: New Press, 1983), 49–70.

25. *Opus imperfectum* 4.46; Brown, *Augustine of Hippo*, 383–99.

26. Lössl, *Julian von Aeclanum*, 320–29.

27. R. Mathisen, "A New Fragment of Augustine's *De nuptiis et concupiscentia* from the *Codex Sangallensis* 190," *Zeitschrift für Antikes Christentum* 3 (1999): 165–83.

28. Julian in Augustine, *Opus imperfectum* 2.88.

29. For corrections of the caricatures of Augustine's views on sex and marriage by Julian and by modern scholars, see Brown, *Body and Society*, 396–427; and idem, review of Sorabji, *Emotion and Peace of Mind*, 192–208; J. Cavadini, "Feeling Right: Augustine on the Passions and Sexual Desire," *Augustinian Studies* 36 (2005): 195–217.

30. *Letter* 189.5–6.

31. H.-I. Marrou, "Un lieu dit 'Cité de Dieu,'" in *Augustinus magister* (Paris: Études Augustiniennes, 1955), 1:101–10; S. Connolly, "Fortifying the City of God: Dardanus' Inscription Revisited," *Classical Journal* 102 (2007): 145–54.

32. *Prosopography of the Later Roman Empire*, 2:346–47.

33. *Letter* 187.12.37.

34. The reflection of this situation in fifth-century treatises of spiritual advice is clearly perceived by Cooper, *The Fall of the Roman Household*, 93–107.

35. *Contra II epistulas pelagianorum* 3.5.14.

36. Salvian, *De gubernatione Dei* 7.3.14, ed. and trans. G. Lagarrigue, *Salvien de Marseille: Oeuvres*, vol. 2, *Du gouvernement de Dieu*, SC 220 (Paris: Le Cerf, 1975), citing Paulinus, *Letter* 32.3.

37. Leo, *Sermon* 24 (*De collectis* 5).1, ed. and trans. R. Dolle, *Léon le Grand: Sermons*, SC 22 (Paris: Le Cerf, 1947), 1:56; and *Sermon* 79 (*De ieiuniis* 7).3, *Sermons*, SC 200 (Paris: Le Cerf, 1973), 4:134.

38. First published by Johannes Divjak, CSEL 88 (Vienna: Tempsky, 1981) and then with a translation and commentaries in *Oeuvres de saint Augustin 46B: Lettres 1*–29**, translated by Eno, *St. Augustine: Letters 1*–29**. I will cite from *Oeuvres de saint Augustin 46B*. M.-F. Berrouard, "Un tournant dans la vie de l'église d'Afrique: Les deux missions d'Alypius en Italie à la lumière des *Lettres* 10*, 15*, 16*, 22* et 23A," *Revue des études augustiniennes* 31 (1985): 46–70 remains the fundamental treatment of this new evidence for the relation of the bishops of Africa to the imperial court.

39. *Letter* 22*.2.40, p. 348.

40. *Letter* 22*.2.32, p. 348.

41. *Letter* 22*.4.58, pp. 350–52; see F. Jacques, "Le défenseur de cité d'après la Lettre 22* de saint Augustin," *Revue des études augustiniennes* 32 (1986): 56–73.

42. *Letter* 24*, pp. 382–86.

43. *Letter* 10*.3.64, pp. 170–72.

44. *Letter* 10*.5.112, p. 176.

45. This was clearly seen in the first discussion of the *Divjak Letters* by P.-A. Février, "Discours d'Église et réalité historique dans les nouvelles Lettres d'Augustin," in *Les Lettres de Saint Augustin découvertes par Johannes Divjak* (Paris: Études Augustiniennes, 1983), 101–15 at p. 109.

46. Zangara, "Una predicazione alla presenza dei principi," 275–98. See now D. M. Deliyannis, *Ravenna in Late Antiquity* (Cambridge: Cambridge University Press, 2010), 63–70.

47. A. Laniado, "Le christianisme et l'évolution des institutions municipales du Bas-Empire: L'exemple du *defensor civitatis*," in *Die Stadt in der Spätantike—Niedergang oder Wandel?* ed. J.-U. Krause and C. Witschel, Historia Einzelschriften 190 (Stuttgart: F. Steiner, 2006), 319–34. This corrects Liebeschuetz, *The Decline and Fall of the Roman City*, 149.

48. Quodvultdeus, De tempore barbarico 2.5, cited by Heather, *The Fall of the Roman Empire*, 288; see pp. 262–91 on the course of the Vandal invasion of Africa.

CHAPTER 24
"Still at That Time a More Affluent Empire"

1. *Expositio totius mundi et gentium* 58, p. 196.

2. For battles in the civil wars as the true "killing fields" of Roman professional armies and the consequent increase in the use of barbarian troops, see esp. B. Shaw, "War and Violence," in *Late Antiquity: A Guide to the Post-Classical World*, 130–69 at pp. 148–52; and A. D. Lee, *War in Late Antiquity: A Social History* (Oxford: Blackwell, 2007), 51–73.

3. Sulpicius Severus, *Chronica* 2.3.2, p. 228. On Sulpicius Severus, see esp. H. Inglebert, *Les romains chrétiens face à l'histoire de Rome: Histoire, christianisme et romanités en Occident dans l'Antiquité tardive (IIIe–Ve siècles)* (Paris: Institut d'Études Augustiniennes, 1996), 365–85.

4. The best recent analysis of this confederation is by W. Goffart, *Barbarian Tides: The Migration Age and the Later Roman Empire* (Philadelphia: University of Pennsylvania Press, 2006), 73–107. Heather, *The Fall of the Roman Empire*, 205–50 tells the story with vigor. See now P. Heather, "Why Did the Barbarians Cross the Rhine?" *Journal of Late Antiquity* 2 (2009): 3–29.

5. Paulinus of Pella, *Eucharisticos* 235, ed. and trans. H. G. Evelyn White, *Ausonius*, Loeb Classical Library (Cambridge, MA: Harvard University Press, 1949), 2:322.

6. See esp. M. Kulikowski, "Barbarians in Gaul, Usurpers in Britain," *Britannia* 31 (2000): 325–45.

7. Kulikowski, *Late Roman Spain and Its Cities*, 151–75; and J. Arce, *Bárbaros y romanos en Hispania (400–507 A.D.)* (Madrid: Marcial Pons, 2005), 31–149.

8. Augustine, *Letter* 11*.2.49, Divjak, p. 188.

9. Halsall, *Barbarian Migrations and the Roman West*, 339.

10. M. Kulikowski, "The Visigothic Settlement in Aquitania: The Imperial Perspective," in *Society and Culture in Late Antique Gaul: Revisiting the Sources*, ed. R. Mathisen and D. Shanzer (Aldershot: Ashgate, 2001), 26–38. The grant of shares of tax revenue (and not of land) as the basis of such settlements was suggested by W. Goffart, *Barbarians and Romans, A.D. 418–584: The Techniques of Accommodation* (Princeton: Princeton University Press, 1980) and is now defended with spirit in *Barbarian Tides*, 119–86. It is a solution of inspired simplicity. It awakens doubt for just that reason. The debate continues: W. Goffart, "The Technique of Barbarian Settlement in the Fifth Century: A Personal, Streamlined Account with Ten Additional Comments," and G. Halsall, "The Technique of Barbarian Settlement in the Fifth Century: A Reply to Walter Goffart," *Journal of Late Antiquity* 3 (2010): 65–98, 99–112.

11. Heather, *The Fall of the Roman Empire*, 266–99.

12. Wickham, *Framing the Early Middle Ages*, 711.

13. J. Harries, *Sidonius Apollinaris and the Fall of Rome, AD 407–485* (Oxford: Clarendon Press, 1994), 246.

14. *Corpus Inscriptionum Latinarum* 6:1783, ed. and trans. in C. W. Hedrick, *History and Silence: Purge and Rehabilitation of Memory in Late Antiquity* (Austin: University of Texas Press, 2000), 1–5.

15. *Chronicle of 452* 55 (406), ed. T. Mommsen, *Chronica Minora*, MGH: Auctores Antiquissimi 9: 1 (Berlin: Weidmann, 1892), 652. See S. Muhlberger, *The Fifth-Century Chroniclers: Prosper, Hydatius, and the Gallic Chronicler of 452* (Liverpool: F. Cairns, 1990), 136–92; and idem, "Looking Back from Mid-Century: The Gallic Chronicler of 452 and the Crisis of Honorius' Reign," in *Fifth-Century Gaul: A Crisis of Identity?* ed. J. Drinkwater and H. Elton (Cambridge: Cambridge University Press, 1992), 28–37. Extracts from the Gallic chronicles and much other material have been translated by A. C. Murray, *From Roman to Merovingian Gaul: A Reader* (Peterborough, Ontario: Broadview Press, 2000). On the literature of barbarian "invasion," see Courcelle, *Histoire littéraire des grandes invasions germaniques*; and M. Roberts, "Barbarians in Gaul: The Response of the Poets," in *Fifth-Century Gaul*, 97–106.

16. As has been done most recently by Ward-Perkins, *The Fall of Rome*, 28–31. But now see the reserves on this use of the evidence by N. B. McLynn, "Poetic Creativity and Political Crisis in Early Fifth-Century Gaul," *Journal of Late Antiquity* 2 (2009): 60–74. Ward-Perkins has accepted these criticisms: "407 and All That: Retrospective," *Journal of Late Antiquity* 2 (2009): 75–78 at p. 78. See in general W. Pohl, "Rome and the Barbarians in the Fifth Century," *Antiquité tardive* 16 (2008): 93–101.

17. Translated by Evelyn White in the Loeb Classical Library as an appendix to the works of Ausonius (see note 5). See also C. Moussy, *Paulin de Pella: Poème d'action de grâces et Prière*, SC 209 (Paris: Le Cerf, 1974). The best commentary is provided by N. B. McLynn, "Paulinus the Impenitent: A Study of the *Eucharisticos*," *Journal of Early Christian Studies* 2 (1995): 461–86; see most recently A. Coşkun, "The *Eucharisticos* of Paulinus Pellaeus: Towards a Reappraisal of the Worldly Convert's Life and Autobiography," *Vigiliae Christianae* 60 (2006): 283–315; and A. Marcone, "Il mondo di Paolino di Pella," in *Di tarda antichità: Scritti scelti* (Milan: Mondadori, 2008), 87–96.

18. Paulinus of Pella, *Eucharisticos* 228, Evelyn White, p. 322.

19. Paulinus of Pella, *Eucharisticos* 159–66, Evelyn White, p. 318.

20. Paulinus of Pella, *Eucharisticos* 204–15, Evelyn White, pp. 320–22.

21. Paulinus of Pella, *Eucharisticos* 291–310, Evelyn White, pp. 326–28; McLynn, "Paulinus the Impenitent," 471.

22. McLynn, "Paulinus the Impenitent," 469.

23. Paulinus of Pella, *Eucharisticos* 520–38, Evelyn White, p. 344.

24. *Codex Theodosianus* 15.14.14 (416).

25. Paulinus of Pella, *Eucharisticos* 500–502, Evelyn White, p. 342.

26. Paulinus of Pella, *Eucharisticos* 514, Evelyn White, p. 342.

27. Paulinus of Pella, *Eucharisticos* 307, Evelyn White, p. 328.

28. On the "kingdom" of Aegidius and Syagrius in northern Gaul, see P. MacGeorge, *Late Roman Warlords* (Oxford: Oxford University Press, 2002), 69–164; on Britain, see C. A. Snyder, *An Age of Tyrants: Britain and the Britons, A.D. 400–600* (University Park: Pennsylvania State University Press, 1998); and S. Laycock, *Britannia the Failed State: Tribal Conflicts and the End of Roman Britain* (Stroud: The History Press, 2008), 109–68.

29. Halsall, *Barbarian Migrations and the Roman West*, 19.

30. Heather, *The Fall of Rome*, 432–43.

31. F. Braudel, *The Mediterranean and the Mediterranean World in the Age of Philip II*, trans. Siân Reynolds (London: Collins, 1973), 2:865–91.

32. Gregory of Tours, *The Glory of the Martyrs* 12, ed. Bruno Krusch, in MGH: Scriptores rerum Merovingicarum 1 (Hannover: Hahn, 1885), 46.

33. *Council of Angers* 453, ed. C. Munier, *Concilia Galliae, a. 314–a. 506*, CCSL 148 (Turnhout: Brepols, 1963), 138; see R. W. Mathisen, *Roman Aristocrats in Barbarian Gaul: Strategies for Survival in an Age of Transition* (Austin: University of Texas Press, 1993), 77–85 at p. 79.

34. R. Samson, "Slavery, the Roman Legacy," in *Fifth-Century Gaul*, 218–27; N. Lenski, "Captivity, Slavery, and Cultural Exchange between Rome and the Germans from the First to the Seventh Century C.E.," in *Invisible Citizens: Captives and Their Consequences*, ed. C. M. Cameron (Salt Lake City: University of Utah Press, 2008), 80–109 at pp. 95–103.

35. W. Klingshirn, "Charity and Power: Caesarius of Arles and the Ransoming of Captives in Sub-Roman Gaul," *Journal of Roman Studies* 75 (1985): 183–203.

36. Patricius, *Letter to Coroticus* 14, ed. and trans. A.B.E. Hood, *St. Patrick: His Writings and Muirchu's Life* (Chichester: Phillimore, 1978), 37, 57.

37. *Inscriptiones Latinae Christianae Veteres*, no. 179.

38. On this hotly debated issue, see esp. N. Duval, "La notion de 'sarcophage' et son rôle dans l'antiquité tardive," and C. Balmelle, "Le répertoire végétal des mosaïstes du Sud-Ouest de la Gaule et des sculpteurs des sarcophages dits d'Aquitaine," *Antiquité tardive* 1 (1993): 29–35, 101–7, along with the other contributions in that volume. Despite the majority opinion of the contributors, I find myself in agreement with Yves Christe (at pp. 21 and 79), who sees a rupture with fourth-century styles rather than a smooth continuity. See now J.-L. Boudartchouk, "Production et diffusion des sarcophages romains tardifs et mérovingiens dans la région de Lourdes (Hautes Pyrénées)," *Gallia* 59 (2002): 53–60.

39. Halsall, *Barbarian Migrations and the Roman West*, 347.

40. L. K. Bailey, "Building Urban Christian Communities: Sermons on Local Saints in the Eusebius Gallicanus Collection," *Early Medieval Europe* 12 (2003): 1–24; and idem, *Christianity's Quiet Success: The Eusebius Gallicanus Sermon Collection and the Power of the Church in Late Antique Gaul* (Notre Dame, IN: University of Notre Dame Press, 2010), 1–38.

41. Valerianus of Cimiez, *Homily* 6.3, PL 52:710D.

42. Fredegar, *Chronicae* 3.7, ed. B. Krusch, in MGH: Scriptores rerum Merovingicarum 2 (Hannover: Hahn, 1888), 94.

43. Paulinus of Pella, *Eucharisticos* 416–19, Evelyn White, p. 336.

44. Eucherius of Lyon, *De contemptu mundi* 273–88, ed. and trans. S. Pricoco, *Eucherio di Lione: Il rifiuto del mondo* (Florence: Nardini, 1990), 74.

45. Wickham, *Framing the Early Middle Ages*, 169–173.

46. Almeida and Carvalho, "*Villa* romana da Quinta das Longas." I owe knowledge of this article and that in note 54 to my student Damian Fernández. See now Reynolds, *Hispania and the Roman Mediterranean*, 60–63 and map 8 on p. 166.

47. For a lively debate on this issue, see T. Lewit, "'Vanishing Villas': What Happened to Élite Rural Habitation in the West in the 5th–6th C.?" *Journal of Roman Archaeology* 16 (2003): 260–74; and Bowes and Gutteridge, "Rethinking the Later Roman Landscape," 412–13. In general, see P. Heather, "Elite Militarisation and the Post-Roman West," in *Istituzioni, carismi ed esercizio del potere*, 245–65.

48. Wickham, *Framing the Early Middle Ages*, 473–81.

49. Halsall, *Barbarian Migrations and the Roman West*, 342–44, 350–51, 364.

50. The abrupt disappearance of Roman denotators of wealth is most clear in post-imperial Britain (see Cleary, *The Ending of Roman Britain*), but it is a Europe-wide phenomenon.

51. S. Mauné, *Les campagnes de la cité de Béziers dans l'Antiquité: Partie nord-orientale (IIe s. av. J.-C.–VIe s. ap. J.-C.)* (Montagnac: Mergoil, 1998), 119–22.

52. *Inscriptiones Latinae Selectae*, no. 1279.

53. Connolly, "Fortifying the City of God." Dardanus may have placed his mausoleum chapel in this valley. See F. Benoit, "La crypte en triconque de Théopolis," *Rivista di archeologia cristiana* 27 (1951): 69–89. For fortification in southern Gaul, see now L. Bourgeois, "Les résidences des élites et les fortifications du Haut Moyen Âge en France et en Belgique dans leur cadre européen: Aperçu historiographique (1955–2005)," *Cahiers de civilisation médiévale* 49(2006): 113–142 at p. 118.

54. A. Vigil-Escalero Guirado, "Granjas y aldeas altomedievales al Norte de Toledo (450–800 D.C.)," *Archivo Español de Arqueología* 80 (2007): 239–84.

55. Y. Modéran, "L'établissment térritorial des Vandales en Afrique," *Antiquité tardive* 10 (2002): 87–122.

56. Y. Modéran, "Une guerre de religion: Les deux Églises d'Afrique à l'époque vandale," *Antiquité tardive* 11 (2003): 21–44 at p. 44.

57. A. Merrills and R. Miles, *The Vandals* (Chichester, UK: Wiley-Blackwell, 2010), 141–76 at p. 176.

58. Y. Hen, *Roman Barbarians: The Royal Court and Culture in the Early Medieval West* (Basingstoke, UK: Palgrave MacMillan, 2007), 59–93; R. Miles, "The *Anthologia*

Latina and the Creation of Secular Space in Vandal Carthage," *Antiquité tardive* 13 (2005): 305–20; C. Balmelle et al., "Vitalité de l'architecture domestique à Carthage au Ve siècle: L'exemple de la maison dite de la Rotonde, sur la colline de l'Odeon," *Antiquité tardive* 11 (2003): 151–66. See also G. Chalon et al., "*Memorabile factum*: Une célébration de l'évergétisme des rois vandales dans l'Anthologie Latine," *Antiquités africaines* 21 (1985): 207–62; and G. Hays, "*Romuleis Libicisque litteris*: Fulgentius and the 'Vandal Renaissance,'" in *Vandals, Romans and Berbers*, 101–32.

59. Salvian, *De gubernatione Dei* 5.8.37.

60. Compare E. A. Thompson, "Peasant Revolts in Late Roman Gaul and Spain," *Past and Present* 2 (1952): 11–23—a brilliant Marxist synthesis—with R. Van Dam, *Leadership and Community in Late Antique Gaul* (Berkeley: University of California Press, 1985), 41–48—a daring reversal of this perspective, in terms of self-defense by local elites. The reader should know that I lean toward the views of J. F. Drinkwater, "The Bacaudae of Fifth-Century Gaul," in *Fifth-Century Gaul*, 208–17. I accept his rejection of the tendency to identify with the "Bacaudic" movement every mention of conflict, of social unrest, and of regional power vacuums in fifth-century Gaul and Spain, unless they are explicitly connected with Bacaudae. A passage in the comedy known as the *Querolus* (scene II.30) has attracted particularly exuberant learned fantasies: see C. Jacquemard-Le Saos, *Querolus (Aulularia). Comédie latine anonyme: Le Grincheux* (Paris: Belles Lettres, 2003), xii–xlii. It may have nothing whatsoever to do with the Bacaudae.

61. See J. C. Sánchez León, *Les sources de l'histoire des Bagaudes* (Paris: Belles Lettres, 1996). Outside Hydatius and the *Chronicle of 452* we are left with only Zosimus, *Historia Nova* 6.2.5; and Salvian, *De gubernatione dei* 5.5.22 and 5.6.24–26. For the use of the term referring to events of the late third century, see Sánchez León, *Les sources*, 119–46. The *Chronicle of 452* uses the singular, "in a Bacauda," on two occasions (117 and 133, for 443 and 448). The fact that a doctor, Eudoxus, was implicated in one Bacauda (*Chronicle of 452* 113—for 448) and that Bacaudae killed a bishop and a garrison in a north Spanish mining town, Tarazona (Turiasso) (Hydatius, *Chronicle* 133—for 449), may indicate an urban setting for some "Bacaudic" events.

62. Hydatius, *Chronicle* 120 (443), ed. and trans. R. W. Burgess, *The Chronicle of Hydatius and the Consularia Constantinopolitana* (Oxford: Clarendon Press, 1993), 96. The work and worldview of Hydatius is brilliantly characterized by Muhlberger, *The Fifth-Century Chroniclers*, 193–266, esp. at pp. 260–64.

63. *Chronicle of 452* 117 (435) and 119 (437), Mommsen, p. 660.

64. This is the view of Salvian, *De gubernatione Dei* 5.6.24; see Drinkwater, "The Bacaudae," 217.

65. Carrié and Rousselle, *L'empire romain en mutation*, 732.

66. Matthews, *Western Aristocracies and Imperial Court*, 347.

67. The study of Sidonius Apollinaris I have found the most perceptive is that of Harries, *Sidonius Apollinaris and the Fall of Rome*.

68. Sidonius Apollinaris, *Letter* 1.3.1, ed. and trans. W. B. Anderson, *Sidonius: Poems and Letters*, Loeb Classical Library (Cambridge, MA: Harvard University Press, 1965), 1:346.

69. Sidonius Apollinaris, *Letter* 8.6.6, Anderson, 2:424.

70. Sidonius Apollinaris, *Letter* 4.2.5, Anderson, 2:142.

71. The mixture of realistic description and timeless stereotypes has not endeared Sidonius to archaeologists engaged in reconstructing what fifth-century villas were really like: see J. Bodel, "Monumental Villas and Villa Monuments," *Journal of Roman Archaeology* 10 (1997): 3–35 at p. 16: "a confused agglomeration of conceits that frustrate rather than aid the reader." See also J. Percival, "Desperately Seeking Sidonius: The Realities of Life in Fifth-Century Gaul," *Latomus* 56 (1997): 279–92. But see the largely successful attempt to reconstruct one such villa (that of the *Burgus Leontii* in Sidonius, *Poem* 22) by Balmelle, *Les demeures aristocratiques d'Aquitaine*, 144.

72. Harries, *Sidonius Apollinaris*, 132; on *Letter* 2.2.5–6, Anderson, 1:420–22.

73. Harries, *Sidonius Apollinaris*, 15.

74. Sidonius Apollinaris, *Letter* 3.2.2, Anderson, 2:8.

75. Sidonius Apollinaris, *Letter* 8.6.16, Anderson, 2:432. See *Prosopography of the Later Roman Empire*, 2:771.

76. Sidonius Apollinaris, *Letter* 7.7.1–2, Anderson, 2:388–90. See *Prosopography of the Later Roman Empire*, 2:1162–63.

77. Gregory of Tours, *Histories* 2.20; ed. Bruno Krusch and Wilhelm Levison, in *Libri historiarum X*, MGH: Scriptores rerum Merovingicarum, vol. 1, 2nd ed. (Hannover: Hahn, 1951), trans. Lewis Thorpe, *Gregory of Tours: The History of the Franks* (Harmondsworth, UK: Penguin, 1974). See Harries, *Sidonius Apollinaris*, 195.

78. Gregory of Tours, *Histories* 2.20. See *Prosopography of the Later Roman Empire*, 2:406.

79. *Recueil des inscriptions chrétiennes de la Gaule*, vol. 8, *Aquitanie première*, ed. F. Prévot (Paris: CNRS, 1991), no. 21 at p. 126.

80. Gregory of Tours, *Histories* 2.37; *Prosopography of the Later Roman Empire*, 2:114.

81. Gregory of Tours, *Histories* 3.18. *Prosopography of the Later Roman Empire*, 2: 131–32.

CHAPTER 25
Among the Saints

1. Paulinus of Pella, *Eucharisticos*, 520–21. On the background of this widely used term, see É. Griffe, "La pratique religieuse en Gaule au Ve siècle: *Saeculares* et *sancti*," *Bulletin de littérature ecclésiastique* 63 (1962): 241–67.

2. S. T. Loseby, "Arles in Late Antiquity: *Gallula Roma Arelas* and *Urbs Genesii*," in *Towns in Transition: Urban Evolution in Late Antiquity and the Early Middle Ages*, ed. N. Christie and S. T. Loseby (Aldershot: Scolar, 1996), 45–70; Heijmans, *Arles durant l'Antiquité tardive*. For continued relations between Arles, Narbonne, and Mediterranean Spain, see Reynolds, *Hispania and the Roman Mediterranean*, 84–85.

3. S. T. Loseby, "Marseille: A Late Antique Success Story?" *Journal of Roman Studies* 82 (1992): 165–85.

4. R. W. Mathisen, *Ecclesiastical Factionalism and Religious Controversy in Fifth-Century Gaul* (Washington, DC: Catholic University of America Press, 1989), 76–78.

5. Hilary of Arles, *Vita Honorati* 22, ed. S. Cavallin, *Vitae Sanctorum Honorati et Hilarii episcoporum Arelatensium* (Lund: Gleerup, 1952), 65. See Mathisen, *Ecclesiastical Factionalism*, 93–96.

6. Honoratus of Marseille, *Vita Hilariti* 15, ed. S. Cavallin, trans. P.-A. Jacob, *La vie d'Hilaire d'Arles* SC 404 (Paris: Le Cerf, 1995), 124. The poet deliberately plays on the way in which Hilary wove his time and duties as skillfully as he wove his baskets.

7. Honoratus, *Vita Hilarii* 14, p. 122.

8. M. Vessey, "Peregrinus against the Heretics: Classicism, Provinciality and the Place of the Alien Writer in Late Roman Gaul," *Studia Ephemeridis Augustinianum* 46 (1994): 529–65 at p. 550, now in *Latin Christian Writers in Late Antiquity and Their Texts* (Ashgate: Variorum, 2005). On the wider implications of these networks as vehicles of master-disciple relationships, see R. Alciati, *Monaci, vescovi e scuola nella Gallia tardo-antica*, Temi e Testi 72 (Rome: Edizioni di Storia e Letteratura, 2009), 119–21, 228. See also M. Dulaey, "La bibliothèque du monastère de Lérins dans les premières décennies du Ve siècle," *Augustinianum* 46 (2006): 187–230. A further aspect of the ecclesiastical culture of Provence, which is less often considered, is now well treated by Bailey, *Christianity's Quiet Success*.

9. S. Baumgart, *Die Bischofsherrschaft im Gallien des 5. Jahrhunderts: Eine Untersuchung zu den Gründen und Anfängen weltlicher Herrschaft der Kirche*, Münchener Arbeiten zur Alten Geschichte 8 (Munich: Editio Maris, 1995), 14–15.

10. See most recently, R. Goodrich, *Contextualizing Cassian: Aristocrats, Asceticism, and Reformation in Fifth-Century Gaul* (Oxford: Oxford University Press, 2007). There is an abundant literature on Cassian: see P. Rousseau, *Ascetics, Authority, and the Church in the Age of Jerome and Cassian* (Oxford: Oxford University Press, 1978), 169–234; idem, "Cassian: Monastery and World," in *The Certainty of Doubt: Tributes to Peter Munz*, ed. M. Fairburn and W. H. Oliver (Wellington, New Zealand: Victoria University Press, 1995), 68–89; C. Stewart, *Cassian the Monk* (Oxford: Oxford University Press, 1998); and O. Chadwick, *John Cassian* (Cambridge: Cambridge University Press, 1968).

11. J.-C. Guy, ed., *Jean Cassien: Institutions Cénobitiques*, SC 109 (Paris: Le Cerf, 1965), from which I cite. Translated by B. Ramsey, *The Institutes*, Ancient Christian Writers (New York: Newman Press, 2000).

12. E. Pichéry, ed., *Jean Cassien: Conférences*, vol. 1, *I–VII*, SC 42 (Paris: Le Cerf, 1955); *Conférences*, vol. 2, *VIII–XVII*, SC 54 (1958); *Conférences*, vol. 3, *XVIII–XXIV*, SC 64 (1959). I will cite from the volume and page number of the SC edition. Translated selections by C. Luibheid, *Conferences* (New York: Paulist Press, 1985); and in full by B. Ramsey, *The Conferences* (New York: Paulist Press, 1997). Vogüé, *Histoire littéraire du mouvement monastique*, 6:173–439 provides a commentary of characteristic erudition and judiciousness.

13. Cassian, *Inst.* Preface 3, p. 29 and 2.2, p. 60. See now Goodrich, *Contextualizing Cassian*, 117–50.

14. Goodrich, *Contextualizing Cassian*, 32–116.

15. *Institutes* 4.4 (126): Goodrich, *Contextualizing Cassian*, 151–207, esp. at pp. 173–74.

16. *Regula Macarii* 24, ed. A. de Vogüé, *Les Règles des saints Pères*, SC 297 (Paris: Cerf, 1982), 1:382, and ed. and trans. S. Pricoco, *La Regola di San Benedetto e le Regole dei Padri* (Verona: Mondadori, 1995), 52.

17. *Inst.* 4.3.1 (124).

18. *Inst.* 4.4 (127).

19. *Inst.* 12.32.1 (498).

20. *Inst.* 1.2.3 (60).

21. Goodrich, *Contextualizing Cassian*, 190.

22. *Inst.* 4.5 (129).

23. *Inst.* 4.19.1 (146).

24. This aspect of Cassianic and post-Cassianic monasticism is well understood by G. Hartmann, *Selbststigmatisierung und Charisma christlicher Heiliger der Spätantike*, Studien und Texte zu Antike und Christentum 38 (Tübingen: Mohr Siebeck, 2006), 51–94 on the Fathers of the Jura.

25. *Inst.* 4.14 (138).

26. Wipszycka, "Les aspects économiques de la vie de la communauté de Kellia"; idem, "Le monachisme égyptien et les villes," *Travaux et mémoires* 12 (1994): 1–44; idem, "Les formes institutionnelles et les formes d'activité économique du monachisme égyptien," in *Foundations of Power and Conflicts of Authority in Late Antique Monasticism*, ed. A. Camplani and S. Filoramo, Orientalia Lovaniensia Analecta 157 (Louvain: Peeters, 2007), 109–54 at pp. 149–50. A. Laniado, "The Early Byzantine State and the Christian Ideal of Voluntary Poverty," in *Charity and Giving in Monotheistic Religions*, 15–43 shows that total individual poverty, such as Cassian proposed, was not considered obligatory for monks until the sixth century. For Gaul, see A. Diem, "Monastic Poverty and Institution Forming: Evidence from Early Medieval Historiography and from Monastic Rules," (paper presented at the Cornell Conference on Medieval Poverty, March 2008).

27. *Coll.* 24.12 (64:183).

28. *Coll.* 8.21 (54:31).

29. *Coll.* 1.10 (32:89).

30. *Inst.* 7.13 (309).

31. Salvian, *Letter* 9.10; *Ad Ecclesiam* 2.3.12 and 2.9.43. Both edited by G. Lagarrigue, in *Salvien de Marseille: Oeuvres*, vol. 1, *Les lettres, les livres de Timothée à l'Église*, SC 176 (Paris: Le Cerf, 1971).

32. Hilary of Arles, *Vita Honorati* 15, Cavallin, p. 54; Eucherius, *De laude eremi* 3 and 6, ed. C. Wotke, CSEL 31 (Vienna: Tempsky, 1894), 178–79. See esp. S. Pricoco, *L'isola dei santi: Il cenobio di Lerino e le origini del monachesimo gallico* (Rome: Edizioni dell'Ateneo e Bizzarri, 1978), 129–64; Vogüé, *Histoire littéraire du mouvement monastique*, 7:58–180, with M.-E. Brunert, *Das Ideal der Wüstenaskese und seine Rezeption in Gallien bis zum Ende des 6. Jahrhunderts*, Beiträge zur Geschichte des alten Mönchtums und des Benediktinerordens 42 (Münster: Aschendorff, 1994).

33. Brunert, *Das Ideal der Wüstenaskese*, 181–83.

34. *Regula quattuor patrum* 3.11, ed. A. de Vogüé, *Régles des saints pères*, SC 297 (Paris: Le Cerf, 1982), 1:194, and ed. and trans. S. Pricoco, *La Regola di San Benedetto e le Regole dei Padri* (Verona: Mondadori, 1995), 16.

35. *Regula quattuor patrum* 2.35, Vogüé, p. 192, Pricoco, p. 14.

36. I. Schrunk and V. Begović, "Roman Estates on the Island of Brioni, Istria," *Journal of Roman Archaeology* 13 (2000): 252–76; Bowes, *Private Worship, Public Values, and Religious Change*, 138–40.

37. *Regula Macarii* 24, Vogüé, p. 382, Pricoco, p. 52.

38. Fontaine, *Sulpice Sévère: Vie de Saint Martin*, 45, with 152 and 170.

39. A. S. McKinley, "The First Two Centuries of Saint Martin of Tours," *Early Medieval Europe* 14 (2006): 173–200 at pp. 178–83.

40. Hilary, *Vita Honorati* 17, Cavallin, p. 61.

41. This dominant interpretation was first suggested by F. Prinz, *Frühes Mönchtum im Frankenreich: Kultur und Gesellschaft in Gallien, den Rheinlanden und Bayern am Beispiel der monastischen Entwicklung (4. bis 8. Jahrhundert)* (Vienna: Oldenbourg, 1965). R. Nouhailhat, *Saints et patrons: Les premiers moines de Lérins*, Université de Besançon: Centre de Recherches d'Histoire Ancienne 84 (Paris: Belles Lettres, 1988) is a thought-provoking but extreme statement of this view.

42. C. M. Kasper, *Theologie und Askese: Die Spiritualität des Inselmönchtums von Lérins im 5. Jahrhundert*, Beiträge zur Geschichte des Alten Mönchtums und des Benediktinertums 40 (Münster: Aschendorff, 1991), 62.

43. See esp. Pricoco, *L'isola dei santi*, 59–74, 177–85. See the reserves of Vogüé, *Histoire littéraire du mouvement monastique* 7:432–34. C. Leyser, *Authority and Asceticism from Augustine to Gregory the Great* (Oxford: Clarendon Press, 2000), 33–34 presents a more complex picture.

44. Mathisen, *Roman Aristocrats in Barbarian Gaul*, 89–104.

45. The most clear statement of this view is in Constantius, *Life of Germanus of Auxerre* 1. We should note that Germanus was a bishop from 407 to 437, but the *Life* was written around 475–80 by a friend of Sidonius Apollinaris. It may not reflect early fifth-century perceptions of Germanus. See Näf, *Senatorisches Standesbewusstsein*, 117–92.

46. The curial background of many "noble" bishops is cogently argued by F. D. Gilliard, "Senatorial Bishops in the Fourth Century," *Harvard Theological Review* 77 (1984): 153–75 at pp. 163–65. The Testament of Ansemundus speaks of the *senatus nobilis* of Vienne: P. Amory, "The Textual Transmission of the Donatio Ansemundi," *Francia* 20 (1993): 163–83 at pp. 180–83; for Lyon, see *Recueil des Inscriptions chrétiennes de la Gaule*, vol. 15, part 11, pp. 220–26—the *nobile consilium* of Lyon.

47. Harries, *Sidonius Apollinaris*, 34, 170–71.

48. Mathisen, *Ecclesiastical Factionalism*, 82–83.

49. On the Basilica Constantia, see now Heijmans, *Arles*, 193–94.

50. Mathisen, *Ecclesiastical Factionalism*, 27–43.

51. *Inst.* 1.1 (36); cf. Celestine, *Letter* 4, PL 50:431B (Paris: J.-P. Migne, 1846): Delage, "Le canon 13 de Sardique," 73.

52. Hilary, *Vita Honorati* 28, Cavallin, p. 69.

53. Gennadius, *De viris illustribus* 70.

54. Honoratus, *Vita Hilarii* 15, Cavallin, p. 126.

55. Epitaph of Hilary, line 9 in Cavallin, *Vitae*, p. 110.

56. Julianus Pomerius, *De vita contemplativa* 2.9, PL 59:453C (Paris: J. P. Migne, 1847).

57. Jacob, *Vie d'Hilaire*, 48.

58. R. W. Mathisen, "Episcopal Hierarchy and Tenure of Office in Late Roman Gaul: A Method for Establishing Dates of Ordination," *Francia* 17 (1990):125–39 at pp. 130–134.

59. M. Heinzelmann, "The 'Affair' of Hilary of Arles (445) and Gallo-Roman Identity in the Fifth Century," in *Fifth Century Gaul*, 239–51.

60. Honoratus, *Vita Hilarii* 22, Cavallin, p. 138.

61. Leo, *Letter* 10.3. The best characterization of the relations between the two men is now S. Wessel, *Leo the Great and the Spiritual Rebuilding of a Universal Rome*, Supplements to Vigiliae Christianae 93 (Leiden: Brill, 2008), 76.

62. *Novella of Valentinian III* 17 (445).

63. Zosimus, *Letter* 9.1.2 (418), PL 20:671AB.

64. This important point is maintained by P. Norton, *Episcopal Elections, 250–600: Hierarchy and Popular Will in Late Antiquity* (Oxford: Oxford University Press, 2007).

65. Celestine, *Letter* 4, 430A–431A, 434B.

66. See in general R. H. Weaver, *Divine Grace and Human Agency: A Study of the Semi-Pelagian Controversy*, Patristic Monographs Series 15 (Macon, GA: Mercer University Press, 1996); and R. Lorenz, "Der Augustinismus Prospers von Aquitanien," *Zeitschrift für Kirchengeschichte* 73 (1962): 217–52. The best study is now A. Y. Hwang, *Intrepid Lover of Perfect Grace: The Life and Thought of Prosper of Aquitaine* (Washington, DC: Catholic University of America Press, 2009).

67. Brown, *Augustine of Hippo*, 400–410; Hwang, *Intrepid Lover of Perfect Grace*, 91–94.

68. Prosper, *Contra Collatorem*, PL 51: 213–76, trans. J. R. O'Donnell, *Prosper of Aquitaine: Grace and Free Will*, Fathers of the Church 7 (New York: Fathers of the Church, 1949).

69. Gennadius, *De viris illustribus* 85.

70. A.M.C. Casiday, *Tradition and Theology in St. John Cassian* (Oxford: Oxford University Press, 2007), 6.

71. Prosper, *Contra Collatorem* 12.4:246B, O'Donnell, p. 380.

72. Prosper, *Contra Collatorem* 18.2:263B, O'Donnell, p. 402.

73. A. Casiday, "Rehabilitating John Cassian: An Evaluation of Prosper of Aquitaine's Polemic against the 'Semipelagians,'" *Scottish Journal of Theology* 58 (2005): 270–84 at p. 280.

74. Prosper, *Contra Collatorem* 18.2:263C, O'Donnell, p. 402.

75. Ibid.

76. C. Leyser, "'This Sainted Isle': Panegyric, Nostalgia and the Invention of Lerinian Monasticism," in *The Limits of Ancient Christianity: Essays on Late Antique Thought and Culture in Honor of R. A. Markus*, ed. W. E. Klingshirn and M. Vessey (Ann Arbor: University of Michigan Press, 1999), 188–206 at p. 190; and Leyser, s.v. "Semi-Pelagianism," *Augustine through the Ages*, 761–66.

77. Prosper, *Pro Augustino responsiones ad excerpta Genuensium* 4, PL51:193A (Paris: J.-P. Migne, 1846).

78. R. A. Markus, "The Legacy of Pelagius: Orthodoxy, Heresy and Conciliation," in *The Making of Orthodoxy: Essays in Honour of Henry Chadwick*, ed. R. Williams (Cambridge: Cambridge University Press, 1989), 214–34; idem, *The End of Ancient Christianity* (Cambridge: Cambridge University Press, 1990), 178–79; with É. Rebillard, "*Quasi funambuli*: Cassien et la controverse pélagienne sur la perfection," *Revue des Études Augustiniennes* 40 (1994): 197–210.

79. Wessel, *Leo the Great*, 82.

80. Leyser, "Semi-Pelagianism," 764.

81. J.-M. Salamito, "Aspects aristocratiques et aspects populaires de l'être chrétien aux IIIe et IVe siècles," *Antiquité tardive* 9 (2001): 165–78 at p. 174.

82. *Chronicle of 452* 44, ad ann. 400.

83. Faustus of Riez, *De gratia* 1.3, ed. A. Engelbrecht, *Fausti Reiensis praeter sermones pseudo-eusebianos opera*, CSEL 21 (Vienna: Tempsky, 1891), 15. See now R. Barcellona, *Fausto di Riez, interprete del suo tempo: Un vescovo tardoantico dentro la crisi dell'impero* (Soveria Manelli: Rubettino, 2006), 39–83.

84. *Ad Deum post conversionem*, ed. A. Hamman PL Supplementum 3:1130 (Paris: Garnier, 1963).

85. Faustus, *Letter* 2, Engelbrecht, p. 166.

86. Faustus, *De gratia*, Prologue, Engelbrecht, p. 3.

87. Isaiah 43:19, cited in Prosper, *De vocatione omnium gentium* 1.9, PL 51:658B (Paris: J.-P. Migne, 1846).

88. Prosper, *De vocatione omnium gentium* 1.4:651A; and *Pro Augustino responsiones ad capitula Gallorum* 13, PL 51:168A (Paris: J.-P. Migne, 1846).

89. Prosper, *De vocatione omnium gentium* 2.4:689D.

90. Muhlberger, *The Fifth-Century Chroniclers*, 48–135.

91. Prosper, *Chronicle of 452* 1307, ad ann. 431, ed. Mommsen, in *Chronica Minora*.

92. Prosper, *Psalmorum C ad CL Expositio*, ad Ps. 149.9, PL 51:424C (Paris: J.-P. Migne, 1846).

93. Muhlberger, *The Fifth-Century Chroniclers*, 130.

94. *Chronicle of 452* 81, ad ann. 418.

95. *Chronicle of 452* 73 (Aquitaine "handed over"); 108 (Vandals "lacerate" Africa); 117 (Gallia Ulterior "separates from the Roman order").

96. *Chronicle of 452* 138.

97. Salvian, *De gubernatione Dei* 3.1.2, Lagarrigue, p. 186.

CHAPTER 26
Romana respublica vel iam mortua

1. I cite from the Sources Chrétiennes edition of the works of Salvian: *De gubernatione Dei*, ed. G. Lagarrigue, *Salvien de Marseille: Oeuvres*, vol. 2, SC 220 (Paris: Le Cerf,

1975), translated as *The Governance of God* by J. F. O'Sullivan, *The Writings of Salvian, the Presbyter*, Fathers of the Church 3 (New York: CIMA, 1947), 23–232; and by E. M. Sanford, *On the Government of God*, Columbia Records of Civilization (New York: Columbia University Press, 1930); *Letters* and *Ad Ecclesiam*, ed. Lagarrigue, *Salvien de Marseille: Oeuvres*, vol. 1, SC 176 (Paris: Le Cerf, 1971), trans. Sullivan, *The Writings of Salvian*, 237–63, 267–371. The best studies of Salvian known to me are J. Badewien, *Geschichtstheologie und Sozialkritik im Werk Salvians von Marseille*, Forschungen zur Kirchen- und Dogmengeschichte 32 (Göttingen: Vandenhouck and Ruprecht, 1980); and, more recently, D. Lambert, "The Uses of Decay: History in Salvian's *De gubernatione dei*," *Augustinian Studies* 30 (1999): 115–30; and L. Pietri, "Riches et pauvres dans l'*Ad Ecclesiam* de Salvien de Marseille," in *Les Pères de l'Église et la voix des pauvres*, 149–61.

2. S. Dill, *Roman Society in the Last Century of the Western Empire*, 2nd ed. (1919; reprint, New York: Meridian, 1958), 137.

3. O'Sullivan, *The Writings of Salvian*, 6.

4. Wickham, *Framing the Early Middle Ages*, 62–64.

5. Goodrich, *Contextualizing Cassian*, 19.

6. O'Sullivan, *The Writings of Salvian*, 15n45. For a sample of the literature from both sides of the Rhine, see esp. Courcelle, *Histoire littéraire des grandes invasions germaniques*, 146–55; and J. Fischer, *Die Völkerwanderung im Urteil der zeitgenössischen kirchlichen Schriftsteller Galliens unter Einbeziehung des heiligen Augustinus* (Heidelberg: Kemper, 1948).

7. Halsall, *Barbarian Migrations and the Roman West*, 354 indicates that Salvian's description of social conditions in Gaul is "usually assumed to refer to northern Gaul." This assumption is based on Salvian's knowledge of the Rhineland and his remarks on the Bacaudae. Northern Gaul is assumed to be a center of Bacaudic activity, but Bacaudae were also known in Spain.

8. Salvian, *De gub. Dei* 4.6.30, Lagarrigue, p. 254.

9. Salvian, *De gub. Dei* 6.15.94, Lagarrigue, p. 416.

10. Salvian, *Letter* 1.5–6, Lagarrigue, p. 78.

11. Salvian, *Letter* 4.6, Lagarrigue, p. 90.

12. Hilary, *Vita Honorati* 19.11, Cavallin, p. 63.

13. Gennadius, *De viris illustribus* 68. See esp. Alciati, *Monaci, vescovi e scuola*, 83–100.

14. Salvian, *Letter* 9, Lagarrigue, pp. 120–32.

15. Salvian, *Ad Ecclesiam* 1.1.2, Lagarrigue, p. 140.

16. Goodrich, *Contextualizing Cassian*, 157–77.

17. Salvian, *Ad Ecclesiam* 1.1.2, p. 140, and 1.1.4, Lagarrigue, p. 142; cf. *De gub. Dei* 6.1.4, Lagarrigue, p. 362.

18. Salvian, *Ad Ecclesiam* 1.1.2, Lagarrigue, p. 140.

19. Epitaph of Hilary, line 7, Cavallin, p. 110.

20. Salvian, *Ad Ecclesiam* 2.9.39, Lagarrigue, p. 214.

21. E. Loening, *Geschichte des deutschen Kirchenrechts*, vol. 1, *Das Kirchenrecht in Gallien von Constantin bis Chlodovech* (Strassburg: Trübner, 1878), 235.

22. E. Champlin, *Final Judgments: Duty and Emotion in Roman Wills, 200 B.C.–A.D. 250* (Berkeley: University of California Press, 1991), 101.

23. Ibid., 102.

24. See now Cooper, *The Fall of the Roman Household*, 93–142.

25. *Novella Maioriani* 6; Jerome, *Letter* 130.6 (written in 413) refers only to a wealthy priest who had placed his daughter in a convent, not to an aristocrat. See esp. S.J.B. Barnish, "Transformation and Survival in the Western Senatorial Aristocracy, c. A.D. 400–700," *Papers of the British School at Rome* 66 (1988): 120–55 at pp. 143–49.

26. Salvian, *Ad Ecclesiam* 3.4.21, Lagarrigue, p. 254.

27. Salvian, *Ad Ecclesiam* 3.13.57–58, Lagarrigue, pp. 282–84.

28. Salvian, *Ad Ecclesiam* 4.7.36, Lagarrigue, p. 334; Augustine, *Sermon* 86.10.13; Valerianus of Cimiez, *Homily* 4.6, 705AB (Paris: J.-P. Migne, 1845). See E. F. Bruck, *Kirchenväter und soziales Erbrecht: Wanderungen religiöser Ideen durch die Rechte der östlichen und westlichen Welt* (Berlin: Springer, 1956).

29. Salvian, *Ad Ecclesiam* 1.3.10, Lagarrigue, p. 146.

30. Salvian, *Letter* 9.8, Lagarrigue, p. 124; and *Ad Ecclesiam* 3.18.31, Lagarrigue, p. 298.

31. Rebillard, *The Care of the Dead* [*Religion et sépulture*], 140–75; Brown, "Alms and the Afterlife," 153–58.

32. Honoratus of Marseille, *Vie d'Hilaire* 16.5, Cavallin, pp. 94–95.

33. Salvian, *Ad Ecclesiam* 3.2.7, Lagarrigue, p. 244 and 3.3.15, Lagarrigue, p. 250.

34. Salvian, *De gub. Dei* 4.14.66, Lagarrigue, p. 286.

35. Gennadius, *De viris illustribus* 68.

36. Eucherius, *De contemptu mundi* 614–25, Pricoco, p. 98.

37. Valerianus of Cimiez, *Homily* 15.2:739A.

38. Salvian, *De gub. Dei* 3.8.38, Lagarrigue, p. 214.

39. Badewien, *Geschichtstheologie und Sozialkritik im Werk Salvians*, 176–99, at p. 189.

40. Salvian, *De gub. Dei* 4.14.58 and 4.14.65, Lagarrigue, pp. 280 and 284.

41. Lambert, "The Uses of Decay," 128.

42. Salvian, *De gub. Dei* 1.9.43, Lagarrigue, p. 142.

43. Salvian, *De gub. Dei* 3.11.59, Lagarrigue, p. 320.

44. Salvian, *De gub. Dei* 3.9.44, Lagarrigue, p. 220.

45. Salvian, *De gub. Dei* 4.1.4, Lagarrigue, p. 234.

46. Salvian, *De gub. Dei* 6.18.93, Lagarrigue, p. 424.

47. S. T. Loseby, "Decline and Change in the Cities of Late Antique Gaul," in *Die Stadt in der Spätantike*, 67–104 at pp. 68–69. See in general Loseby, "Bishops and Cathedrals: Order and Diversity in the Fifth-Century Urban Landscape in Gaul," in *Fifth-Century Gaul*, 144–55; J. Harries, "Christianity and the City in Late Roman Gaul," in *The City in Late Antiquity*, ed. J. Rich (London: Routledge, 1992), 77–98.

48. Loseby, "Decline and Change," 69; J. Guyon, "La topographie chrétienne des villes de la Gaule," in *Die Stadt in der Spätantike*, 105–28, figure 1 at p. 110.

49. Marrou, "Le dossier épigraphique de l'évêque Rusticus de Narbonne," 332–33 and figures 2–3 on pp. 335–37.

50. *Inscriptiones Latinae Christianae Veteres*, no. 773; see now *Salona: Recherches archéologiques franco-croates à Salone*, vol. 3, *Manastirine: Établissement préromain, nécropole, et basilique paléochrétienne*, ed. N. Duval, E. Marin, and C. Metzger, Collection de l'École française de Rome 194:3 (Rome: École française de Rome; Split: Musée archéologique de Split, 2000), 306–9.

51. M. Maas, "Ethnicity, Orthodoxy and Community in Salvian of Marseilles," in *Fifth-Century Gaul*, 275–84 at p. 276.

52. Salvian, *De gub. Dei* 4.14.67–70, Lagarrigue, pp. 284–88.

53. E. A. Thompson, *The Visigoths in the Time of Ulfila* (Oxford: Clarendon Press, 1966), 78–156. See now esp. S. Esders, "Grenzen und Grenzüberschreitungen: Religion, Ethnizität und politische Integration am Rande des oströmischen Imperiums (4.–7. Jh.)," in *Gestiftete Zukunft im mittelalterlichen Europa: Festschrift für Michael Borgolte*, ed. W. Huschner and F. Rexroth (Berlin: Akademie Verlag, 2008), 3–28 at pp. 5–13.

54. Salvian, *De gub. Dei* 5.2.6, Lagarrigue, p. 314 and 5.3.10, Lagarrigue, p. 318.

55. Salvian, *De gub. Dei* 7.2.8, Lagarrigue, pp. 434–36 (Aquitaine); 7.13.54, Lagarrigue, p. 468; 7.16.67–68, Lagarrigue, pp. 478–80 (Carthage).

56. Salvian, *De gub. Dei* 5.7.30, Lagarrigue, p. 334.

57. Salvian, *De gub. Dei* 4.3.15, Lagarrigue, p. 344.

58. Salvian, *De gub. Dei* 5.6.24, Lagarrigue, p. 330.

59. Salvian, *De gub. Dei* 5.5.22–23, Lagarrigue, pp. 328–30.

60. Salvian, *De gub. Dei* 5.8.37, Lagarrigue, p. 340.

61. Salvian, *De gub. Dei* 5.5.21, Lagarrigue, p. 328.

62. Salvian, *De gub. Dei* 5.5.22, Lagarrigue, p. 328.

63. Mamertinus, *Panegyric to Julian*, *Panegyrici Latini* 11.3–4 (AD 362); Orosius, *History against the Pagans* 7.41.1 (AD 417).

64. Augustine, *New [Divjak] Letter* 10*.5.

65. Halsall, *Barbarian Migrations and the Roman West*, 250.

66. H. Elton, "Defence in Fifth-Century Gaul," in *Fifth-Century Gaul*, 167–76; T. Stickler, *Aëtius: Gestaltungsspielräume eines Heermeisters im ausgehenden Weströmischen Reich*, Vestigia 54 (Munich: C. H. Beck, 2002), 155–253.

67. *Novella of Valentinian III*, 10, Preface (441): see Cecconi, *Governo imperiale e élites dirigenti*, 162–67. Compare Salvian, *De gub. Dei* 5.7.31, p. 336.

68. Salvian, *De gub. Dei* 4.6.30, Lagarrigue, p. 254.

69. Salvian, *De gub. Dei* 4.4.21 and 4.15.74, Lagarrigue, pp. 248 and 290.

70. See esp. C. Grey, "Salvian, the Ideal Christian Community and the Fate of the Poor in Fifth-Century Gaul," in *Poverty in the Roman World*, 168–82 at p. 173; with Brown, *Poverty and Leadership*, 67–73.

71. Salvian, *De gub. Dei* 5.4.18, Lagarrigue, p. 324.

72. Salvian, *De gub. Dei* 4.3.21, Lagarrigue, p. 248.

73. Salvian, *De gub. Dei* 5.9.45, Lagarrigue, p. 346. Much false certainty reigns on the issue of rural patronage in Gaul: the best treatments are C. R. Whittaker, "Circe's Pigs: From Slavery to Serfdom in the Later Roman World," *Slavery and Abolition* 8 (1987): 88–122; Grey, "Salvian, the Ideal Christian Community and the Fate of the Poor," 176–80; and idem, "Contextualizing *Colonatus*." On the language of "poverty" and "destitu-

tion" in the establishment of vertical links in Gaul, see now A. Rio, "High and Low: Ties of Dependence in the Frankish Kingdoms," *Transactions of the Royal Historical Society*, 6th ser., 12 (2008): 43–68, esp. pp. 51–52. This language does not necessarily indicate either real impoverishment or total dependence. For a comprehensive and original treatment, see now W. Goffart, "Salvian of Marseille, *De gubernatione Dei* 3.38–45 and the 'Colonate' Problem," *Antiquité tardive* 17 (2009): 269–88, esp. p. 286.

74. Salvian, *De gub. Dei* 5.8.30, Lagarrigue, p. 340.

75. See Grey, "Salvian, the Ideal Christian Community and the Fate of the Poor," 168.

76. Krause, *Spätantike Patronatsformen*, 233–83.

77. Salvian, *De gub. Dei* 5.9.46, Lagarrigue, p. 346.

78. Salvian, *De gub. Dei* 4.2.10, Lagarrigue, p. 238, and 5.6.26, Lagarrigue, p. 332; cf. Hydatius, *Chronicle* 49 (ad ann. 411) provinces of Spain *se subiciunt servituti*; *Chronicle of 452* 126 (ad ann. 442) provinces of Britain *in dicionem Saxonum rediguntur*.

79. Salvian, *De gub. Dei* 5.9.46, Lagarrigue, p. 346.

80. Markus, *The End of Ancient Christianity*, 169.

81. Salvian, *De gub. Dei* 4.11.53, Lagarrigue, p. 276.

82. Inglebert, *Les romains chrétiens*, 663.

83. Salvian, *De gub. Dei* 3.9.46, Lagarrigue, p. 220.

84. Salvian, *De gub. Dei* 5.5.19, Lagarrigue, p. 326.

85. Salvian, *De gub. Dei* 4.7.32, Lagarrigue, p. 256.

86. Salvian, *De gub. Dei* 4.15.74, Lagarrigue, pp. 290–92.

87. *Eburnea Diptycha*, ed. David. By contrast, the emperor was shown bearing the Christian Labarum: A. Cameron, "The Probus Diptych and Christian Apologetic," in *From Rome to Constantinople*, 191–202.

88. Salvian, *De gub. Dei* 6.12.37, Lagarrigue, p. 368.

89. Prosper, *Chronicle* 1335 (ad ann. 439).

90. Quodvultdeus, *Dimidium temporis* 7.14, ed. R. Braun, CCSL 60 (Turnhout: Brepols, 1976), 199.

91. Petrus Chrysologus, *Sermon* 155 and 155 bis, ed. A. Olivar, CCSL 24B (Turnhout: Brepols, 1982), 961–69.

92. Maioli, "Il complesso archeologico di Via d'Azeglio a Ravenna," figure 4 on p. 52; and *La musica ritrovata: Iconografia e cultura musicale a Ravenna e in Romagna dal I al VI secolo*, ed. D. Castaldo, M. G. Maioli, and D. Restani (Ravenna: Longo, 1997), illustration 23, p. 96. See now *Archeologia urbana a Ravenna*, ed. Montevecchi.

93. Salvian, *De gub. Dei* 6.15.85, Lagarrigue, p. 416: see H. Heinen, "Reichstreue *nobiles* im zerstörten Trier," *Zeitschrift für Papyrologie und Epigraphik* 131 (2000): 271–78.

94. Salvian, *De gub. Dei* 7.12.71, Lagarrigue, p. 408.

95. Salvian, *De gub. Dei* 6.8.43, Lagarrigue, p. 390.

96. Markus, *The End of Ancient Christianity*, 172–73.

97. *Consularia Caesaraugustana* 85a: see Kulikowski, *Late Roman Spain and Its Cities*, 207.

98. Gregory of Tours, *Histories* 5.17.

99. Salvian, *De gub. Dei* 7.1.6, Lagarrigue, p. 434, with n. 1.

CHAPTER 27
Ob italiae securitatem

1. *L'Année épigraphique 1950*, no. 50 = *Corpus Inscriptionum Latinarum* VI, part 8:3, ed. G. Alföldy (Berlin: de Gruyter, 2000), 5093–94, no. 41389. See esp. Stickler, *Aëtius*, 255–73.

2. C. Wickham, *Early Medieval Italy: Central Power and Local Society, 400–1000* (London: MacMillan, 1981), 1–14 gives a splendid overview of the regional diversity of Italy.

3. Cracco Ruggini, *Economia e società nell' "Italia annonaria,"* 205–406 remains essential. See especially Barnish, "Transformation and Survival in the Western Senatorial Aristocracy," 138–51. J. J. O'Donnell, *The Ruin of the Roman Empire: A New History* (New York: Harper Collins, 2008), 97–170 is a vivid evocation of the society of Italy on the eve of Justinian's fateful invasion. See now Deliyannis, *Ravenna*, 106–187.

4. Halsall, *Barbarian Migrations and the Roman West*, 331.

5. Krautheimer, *Three Christian Capitals*, 107.

6. Krautheimer, *Rome: Profile of a City*, 52–53.

7. F. Marazzi, "Rome in Transition: Economic and Political Change in the Fourth and Fifth Centuries," in *Early Medieval Rome and the Christian West: Essays in Honour of Donald A. Bullough*, ed. J.M.H. Smith (Leiden: Brill, 2000), 21–41 at p. 22.

8. Gillett, "Rome, Ravenna and the Last Western Emperors," 145.

9. Bowes, *Private Worship, Public Values, and Religious Change*, 72; Gillett, "Rome, Ravenna and the Last Western Emperors," 145n53.

10. R. Krautheimer, "The Architecture of Sixtus III: A Fifth-Century Renaissance?" in *De artibus opuscula XL: Essays in Honor of Erwin Panofsky*, ed. M. Meiss (New York: University of Columbia Press, 1961), 291–302 remains a classic statement of this view. See now J. Martin, *Der Weg zur Ewigkeit führt über Rom: Die Frühgeschichte des Papsttums und die Darstellung der neutestamentlichen Heilsgeschichte im Triumphbogenmosaik von Santa Maria Maggiore in Rom* (Stuttgart: Steiner, 2010), 109–71.

11. Gillett, "Rome, Ravenna and the Last Western Emperors," 145n53.

12. *Liber Pontificalis* 46, Davis, p. 35.

13. Leader-Newby, *Silver and Society in Late Antiquity*, 64–66.

14. D. De Francesco, *La proprietà fondiaria nel Lazio, secoli IV-VIII: Storia e topografia* (Rome: Quasar, 2004), 289. A strong case for a wider range of donors (in which members of the clergy were a significant element) is made by Hillner, "Clerics, Property and Patronage." The list of aristocratic patrons on 59n1 is slim—twelve names only, most of them courtiers, officials, and military men, not nobles.

15. Gerontius, *VG* 53, Gorce, p. 232.

16. Brown, *Power and Persuasion*, 128–29. The phrase comes from C. J. Halperin, *Russia and the Golden Horde: The Mongol Impact on Medieval Russian History* (London: Tauris, 1985), 5. See recently, C. Ando, *The Matter of the Gods: Religion and the Roman Empire* (Berkeley: University of California Press, 2008), 149–86. The reader should know that Cameron, *Last Pagans*, 231–72, 567–626 argues strongly against the idea of a residual paganism among such persons. The issue remains open.

17. Arnobius Iunior, *Commentaria in Psalmos* 95, PL 53:464C (Paris: J.-P. Migne, 1847).

18. N. B. McLynn, "Crying Wolf: The Pope and the Lupercalia," *Journal of Roman Studies* 98 (2008): 161–75.

19. s.v. "Asterius 11," *Prosopography of the Later Roman Empire*, 2:173–74. Writing in 502, Ennodius, *Libellus pro synodo* 133–34, ed. F. Vogel, *MGH: Auctores Antiquissimi* 7 (Berlin: Weidmann, 1885), 66–67 claimed that almsgiving accompanied consular processions. But this assertion is part of a rhetorical juxtaposition between pagan and Christian Rome. It does not describe a Christian practice integrated into a secular ceremony.

20. The significance of these figures was first demonstrated by Mazzarino, *Aspetti sociali del quarto secolo*, 239. The drop after 410 may be exaggerated, as the high figure for 367 remains uncertain. For a clear survey, see R. Hodges and D. Whitehouse, *Mohammed, Charlemagne and the Origins of Europe: Archaeology and the Pirenne Thesis* (Ithaca, NY: Cornell University Press, 1983), 48–51; Christie, *From Constantine to Charlemagne*, 58–61.

21. Wickham, *Framing the Early Middle Ages*, 651–53, 709–13.

22. F. di Gennaro and F. Dell'Era, "Dati archeologici di età tardoantica del territorio dell' *insula inter duo flumina*," in *Suburbium*, 97–121 at p. 120. It is the refrain of the entire volume (but see the cautions of P. Pergola and J. Guyon, on pp. 170–71). For southern Etruria, see Hodges and Whitehouse, *Mohammed, Charlemagne, and the Origins of Europe*, 36–46. For a summary of recent work, see H. Patterson, "The Tiber Valley Project: Archaeology, Comparative Survey and History," in *General Issues in the Study of Medieval Logistics: Sources, Problems and Methodologies*, ed. J. F. Haldon (Leiden: Brill, 2006), 93–117.

23. Liebeschuetz, *The Decline and Fall of the Roman City*, 386: "the delay between the effect and its suggested cause presents an intriguing puzzle."

24. Cassiodorus, *Variae* 11.39.1, trans. S.J.B. Barnish, *Cassiodorus: Variae*, Translated Texts for Historians 12 (Liverpool: Liverpool University Press, 1992), 161. The reader should know that Cracco Ruggini, *Economia e società, nell' "Italia annonaria,"* 315–16, and J. Durliat, *De la ville antique à la ville byzantine: Le problème des subsistences*, Collection de l'École française de Rome 136 (Rome: Palais Farnèse, 1990), 104–7 reach widely different conclusions from this one edict. Durliat uses it to posit a drop of up to 60 percent in the population of Rome since 410; in 1961, Cracco Ruggini already dismissed such a conclusion as "inadmissable." The reader should know that our view of Rome after 410 hangs on such slender threads.

25. *Anonymus Valesianus* 12.64; Procopius, *Anecdota* 26.29.

26. Barnish, "Pigs, Plebeians and *Potentes*," 161.

27. Cracco Ruggini, *Economia e società, nell' "Italia annonaria,"* 205–321, 349–59.

28. Sidonius Apollinaris, *Letter* 1.10; Barnish, "Pigs, Plebeians and *Potentes*," 159–66.

29. See now esp. R. Meneghini and R. Santangeli Valenzani, *Roma nell'altomedioevo: Topografia e urbanistica della città dal V al X secolo* (Rome: Libreria dello Stato, 2004), 33.

30. Diefenbach, *Römische Erinnerungsräume*, 404–13 uses the term "nuclearization" and speaks of "islands" of settlement.

31. *Liber Pontificalis* 48, Davis, pp. 39–40.

32. R. Lim, "The Roman Pantomime Riot of A.D. 509," in *Humana sapit*, 35–42.

33. See now *Statuen in der Spätantike*, ed. Bauer and Witschel. This volume makes plain that financial recession alone does not account for the end of the "Statue Habit." Changing structures of public life and changing tastes also played an important role.

34. H. Brandenburg, "Osservazioni sulla fine della produzione e dell'uso dei sarcophagi a rilievo nella tarda antichità nonché sulla loro decorazione," in *Sarcofagi tardoantichi, paleocristiani ed altomedievali*, ed. F. Bisconti and H. Brandenburg (Vatican: Pontificio Istituto di Archeologia Cristiana, 2004), 1–14.

35. Marazzi, "Rome in Transition," 34.

36. *Corpus Inscriptionum Latinarum* 6:1783 set up to Nicomachus Flavianus, now edited and commented in Hedrick, *History and Silence*; C. Machado, "Building the Past: Monuments and Memory in the Forum Romanum," in *Social and Political Life in Late Antiquity*, 157–92.

37. See the masterly study of Orlandi, *Epigrafia anfiteatrale*, 545–63.

38. Ibid., 114–15.

39. Ibid., 296.

40. Ibid., 102–18.

41. s.v. "Paulus 15," *Prosopographie chrétienne du Bas Empire*, 2:1674.

42. Brown, "Dalla 'plebs romana' alla 'plebs Dei,'" 131.

43. Agnellus of Ravenna, *Liber pontificalis ecclesiae Ravennatensis* 60, ed. and trans. C. Nauerth (Freiburg: Herder, 1996), 272–74, trans. D. M. Deliyannis, *The Book of Pontiffs of the Church of Ravenna* (Washington, DC: Catholic University of America Press, 2004), 172–77.

44. *Novella Valentiniani III* 36.1.

45. Olympiodorus, *Fragment* 41, Blockley, p. 205.

46. H. Scogin, "Poor Relief in Northern Sung China," *Oriens Extremus* 25 (1978): 30–45 at pp. 30–31, citing the memorandum of Sung Ching, AD 717.

47. Gregory of Tours, *Histories* 2.24 and Sidonius Apollinaris, *Letter* 6.12, well commented by R. Mathisen, "Nature or Nurture? Some Perspectives on the Gallic Famine of circa A.D. 470," *The Ancient World* 24 (1993): 91–105.

48. Cassiodorus, *Variae* 12.28. See C. Rapp, "Charity and Piety as Episcopal and Imperial Virtues in Late Antiquity," in *Charity and Giving in Monotheistic Religions*, 75–88.

49. Purcell, "The Populace of Rome in Late Antiquity," 138.

50. *De vera humilitate*, ed. and trans. M.K.C. Krabbe, *Epistula ad Demetriadem de vera humilitate*, Catholic University of America Publications 97 (Washington, DC: Catholic University of America Press, 1956), with extensive arguments for authorship by Prosper. On Prosper in Rome, see N. W. James, "Leo the Great and Prosper of Aquitaine: A Fifth-Century Pope and His Adviser," *Journal of Theological Studies* 44 (1993): 554–84; and Hwang, *Intrepid Lover of Perfect Grace*, 187–234.

51. Bowes, *Private Worship, Public Values, and Religious Change*, 94–96.

52. *De vera humilitate* 1, Krabbe, p. 142.

53. *De vera humilitate* 22, Krabbe, p. 206.

54. *De vera humilitate* 5, Krabbe, p. 158.

55. *De vera humilitate* 3, Krabbe, p. 146.

56. Leo, *Sermon* 90.2, Dolle, 4:220.

57. Leo, *Sermon* 22.1, Dolle, 2:34 with n. 4; Salzman, *On Roman Time*, figure 38 and pp. 102–3.

58. Leo, *Sermon* 72.3, Dolle, 4:74.

59. Leo, *Sermon* 22.1, Dolle, 2:34.

60. Leo, *Sermon* 24.2, Dolle, 2:56.

61. Leo, *Sermon* 75.2, Dolle, 4:92.

62. Prosper, *Chronicle* ad ann. 426.

63. s.v. "Felix 22," *Prosopographie chrétienne du Bas Empire 2*, 1:776.

64. Leo, *Sermon* 86.1, Dolle, 4:176.

65. Priscus, *Fragment* 64, in *The Fragmentary Classicising Historians of the Later Roman Empire*, vol. 2, ed. Blockley, p. 372.

66. Petrus Chrysologus, *Sermon* 121.7, Olivar, 2:730.

67. Leo, *Sermon* 23.3, Dolle, 2:44. See Brown, *Poverty and Leadership*, 58–60; and Freu, *Les figures du pauvre*, 418–28.

68. See esp. Freu, *Les figures du pauvre*, 241–96.

69. Brown, *Poverty and Leadership*, 45–73.

70. See Wessel, *Leo the Great*, 179–257 for a fine evocation of this aspect of Leo. See also M. J. Armitage, *A Twofold Solidarity: Leo the Great's Theology of Redemption* (Strathfield, NSW: St. Paul's Publications, 2005), 169–83.

71. As suggested by Durliat, *De la ville antique à la ville byzantine*, 134–37.

72. Gregory I, *Letter* 7.23.

73. Gregory I, *Letter* 1.39 and 1.44; John the Deacon, *Life of Gregory* 2.28 and 2.30, PL 75:97C and 98A (Paris: J.-P. Migne, 1849). See now E. Caliri, "Povertà e assistenza nella Sicilia protobizantina," in *Poveri ammalati e ammalati poveri*, 145–66 at pp. 157–60.

74. Gregory I, *Letter* 1.73 and 9.124; Brown, *Poverty and Leadership*, 63; A. Serfass, "Slavery and Pope Gregory the Great," *Journal of Early Christian Studies* 14 (2006): 77–103 at p. 87.

75. Marazzi, "Rome in Transition," 41.

76. Orlandi, *Epigrafia anfiteatrale*, 513–16.

77. *Aurea Roma*, 536, catalogue no. 178.

78. *Inscriptiones Latinae Christianae Veteres*, no. 1785.

79. Orlandi, *Epigrafia anfiteatrale*, 515; D. De Francesco, "Aspetti della presenza germanica in Italia: Le donazioni di Valila nel Tiburtino," *Rivista di Archeologia Cristiana* 74 (1998): 415–53.

80. L. Duchesne, *Le Liber Pontificalis: Texte, Introduction et Commentaire*, Bibliothèque de l'École française de Rome (Paris: de Boccard, 1955): cxlvi–cxlvii. See esp. De Francesco, *La proprietà fondiaria nel Lazio*, 95–115. This study also dispels doubt as to the authenticity of the document, which survives only in a medieval copy.

81. D. Vera, "I paesaggi rurali del Meridione tardoantico: Bilancio consuntivo e preventivo," in *Paesaggi e insediamenti rurali in Italia meridionale fra tardoantico e altomedioevo*, ed. G. Volpe and M. Turchiano (Bari: Edipuglia, 2005), 23–38 at p. 25.

82. Cracco Ruggini, *Economia e società nell' "Italia annonaria,"* 205–321; G. Volpe, *Contadini, pastori e mercanti nell'Apulia tardoantica* (Bari: Edipuglia, 1996), 257–392. Some would also add the impact of a meteor that fell in the Abruzzi at this time: R. Santilli et al., "A Catastrophe Remembered: A Meteorite Impact of the Fifth Century AD in the Abruzzo, Central Italy," *Antiquity* 77 (2003): 313–20.

83. G. Volpe, G. De Felice, and M. Turchiano, "Faragola (Ascoli Satriano): Una residenza aristocratica tardoantica e un 'villaggio' altomedievale nella Valle del Carapelle: I primi dati," in *Paesaggi e insediamenti,* 265–97.

84. Gelasius, *Epistulae,* 35–36, ed. A. Thiel, *Epistolae Romanorum pontificum genuinae* (Braunsberg: E. Peter, 1867; Hildesheim: G. Olms, 1974), 1:447: see L. Pietri, "Évergétisme chrétien et fondations privées dans l'Italie de l'Antiquité tardive," in *Humana sapit,* 253–63; and M. De Fino, "Proprietà imperiali e diocesi rurali paleocristiane dell'Italia tardoantica," in *Paesaggi e insediamenti,* 691–702 at pp. 694–97.

85. Gelasius, *Fragment* 21, Thiel, pp. 495–96.

86. Gelasius, *Ep.* 33, Thiel, p. 448.

87. Gelasius, *Ep.* 14.xxxv.25, Thiel, p. 376.

88. Bowes, *Private Worship, Public Values, and Religious Change,* 221–26.

89. F. Marazzi, *I "Patrimonia Sanctae Romanae Ecclesiae" nel Lazio (secoli IV–X): Struttura amministrativa e prassi gestionali,* Istituto storico italiano per il Medioevo: Nuovi Studi Storici 31 (Rome: Palazzo Borromini, 1998), 57. See the cautions of a seasoned medievalist on the limitations of such fragments: W. Ullmann, *Gelasius I (492–496): Das Papsttum an der Wende der Spätantike zum Mittelalter,* Päpste und Papsttum 18 (Stuttgart: Hiersemann, 1981), 227n36; and D. Jasper and H. Fuhrmann, *Papal Letters in the Early Middle Ages* (Washington, DC: Catholic University of America Press, 2001), 61–70.

90. Gelasius, *Ep.* 21, Thiel, p. 388.

91. On the various forms of "servility" through which a labor force was maintained at this period, see now esp. Banaji, "Aristocracies, Peasantries," 72–74.

92. Gelasius, *Ep.* 14.xiv.14, Thiel, p. 370.

93. Gelasius, *Ep.* 6.4, Thiel, p. 328.

94. See esp. G. B. Picotti, "Sulle relazioni fra re Odoacre e il Senato e la chiesa di Roma," *Rivista Storica Italiana* ser. 5, no. 4 (1939): 363–86; T. Sardella, *Società, chiesa e stato nell'età di Teodorico: Papa Simmaco e lo scismo laurenziano* (Soveria Manelli: Rubettino, 1996).

95. See the acts of the Synod of 502, held by Pope Symmachus: Symmachus, *Ep.* 6.II.4–6, Thiel, pp. 685–87. The classic studies of the ultimatum of Basilius of 483 and its relation to the later schism between Laurence and Symmachus are by C. Pietri, "Le Sénat, le peuple chrétien et les partis du cirque sous le pape Symmaque," *Mélanges d'archéologie et d'histoire* 78 (1966): 123–39 at pp. 131–38, now in *Christiana respublica,* 2:771–87; and idem, "Évergétisme et richesses ecclésiastiques," in *Christiana respublica,* 2:813–33. As far as they affect the status of the *tituli,* Pietri's views have been challenged. That form of aristocratic endowment may not have been in question or have functioned as Pietri supposed; see Hillner, "Families, Patronage and the Titular Churches of Rome." See also Diefenbach, *Römische Erinnerungsräume,* 404–87.

96. Orlandi, *Epigrafia anfiteatrale,* 51–56.

97. Cited in Symmachus, *Ep.* 6.III.7, Thiel, p. 687; trans. Hillner, "Families, Patronage and the Titular Churches of Rome," 249.

98. Marazzi, *"Patrimonia Sanctae Romanae Ecclesiae,"* 63, 76.

99. Symmachus, *Ep.* 6.IV.14, Thiel, p. 690; trans. Hillner, "Families, Patronage and the Titular Churches of Rome," 260.

100. Brown, *The Rise of Western Christendom*, 487.

CHAPTER 28
Patrimonia pauperum

1. McCormick, *Origins of the European Economy*, 27–41; F. L. Cheyette, "The Disappearance of the Ancient Landscape and the Climatic Anomaly of the Early Middle Ages: A Question to Be Pursued," *Early Medieval Europe* 16 (2008): 127–65. P. Squatriti, "The Floods of 589 and Climate Change at the Beginning of the Middle Ages: An Italian Microhistory," *Speculum* 85 (2010): 799–826 at pp. 812–19 is more cautious. Many scholars feel no need to invoke "climatic anomaly" to explain the changes of this period: see T. Lewit, "Pigs, Presses and Pastoralism: Farming in the Fifth to Sixth Centuries," *Early Medieval Europe* 17 (2009): 77–91.

2. Inglebert, *Histoire de la civilisation romaine*, 483.

3. Augustine, *Letter* 125.2.

4. Augustine, *Letter* 126.9.

5. Augustine, *Letter* 185.9.36.

6. U. Meyer, *Soziales Handeln im Zeichen des "Hauses": Zur Ökonomik in der Spätantike und im frühen Mittelalter* (Göttingen: Vandenhouck and Ruprecht, 1998), 102–88; V. Toneatto, "I linguaggi della ricchezza nella testualità omiletica e monastica dal II al IV secolo," in *Economica monastica: Dalla disciplina del desiderio all'amministrazione razionale*, ed. V. Toneatto, P. Černic, and S. Paulitti (Spoleto: Centro di Studi sull'Alto Medioevo, 2004), 1–88.

7. Augustine, *Sermon* 355.3.

8. Lancel, *Saint Augustin*, 232. See now O'Donnell, *Augustine*, 166–69. The best summary of the incident is by N. B. McLynn, "Administrator: Augustine in His Diocese," in *Companion to Augustine*, ed. M. Vessey (Oxford: Wiley-Blackwell, forthcoming).

9. Augustine, *Sermon* 355.4.

10. Council of Carthage of AD 525, lines 252–344, *Concilia Africae*, pp. 278–81; D. Ganz, "The Ideology of Sharing: Apostolic Community and Ecclesiastical Property in the Early Middle Ages," in *Property and Power in the Early Middle Ages*, ed. W. Davies and P. Fouracre (Cambridge: Cambridge University Press, 1995), 17–30.

11. s.v. "Leporius 1," *Prosopographie chrétienne du Bas-Empire*, vol. 1, *L'Afrique chrétienne (305–533)*, ed. A. Mandouze (Paris: CNRS, 1982), 634–35.

12. Augustine, *Sermon* 356.10.

13. See esp. W. Klingshirn, *Caesarius of Arles: The Making of a Christian Community in Late Antique Gaul* (Cambridge: Cambridge University Press, 1994), 72–82; Alciati, *Monaci, vescovi e scuola*, 147–76.

14. Julianus Pomerius, *De vita contemplativa* 2.9, PL 59:453C.

15. Julianus Pomerius, *De vita contemplativa* 2.9, PL 59:453B.

16. Julianus Pomerius, *De vita contemplativa* 2.9, PL 59:454A.

17. Y. Thomas, "La construction de l'unité civique: Choses publiques, choses communes et choses n'appartenant à personne et représentation," *Mélanges de l'école française de Rome: Moyen Âge* 114 (2002): 7–39; H. R. Hagemann, *Die Stellung der Piae Causae nach justinianischem Rechte*, Basler Studien zur Rechtsgeschichte 37 (Basel: Helbing and Lichtenhahn, 1953), 24, 36; Marazzi, *"Patrimonia Sanctae Romanae Ecclesiae,"* 34; Hillner, "Families, Patronage and the Titular Churches of Rome," 237–42.

18. *Codex Theodosianus* 16.2.4 (AD 321). See esp. Barnes, *Constantine and Eusebius*, 50.

19. S. Wood, *The Proprietary Church in the Medieval West* (Oxford: Oxford University Press, 2006), 730.

20. S. MacCormack, "Sin, Citizenship and the Salvation of Souls: The Impact of Christian Priorities on Late Roman and Post-Roman Society," *Comparative Studies in Society and History* 39 (1997): 644–73 at pp. 662–63.

21. Salvian, *Ad Ecclesiam* 4.4.21 and 7.3.5, Lagarrigue, pp. 324 and 332.

22. *Cod. Iustinianianus* 1.2.25.1 (530); cf. *Novella* 131.9 (545). See Bruck, *Kirchenväter und soziales Erbrecht*, 120–22.

23. E.g., Augustine, *Tractatus in ev. Iohannis* 6.24.

24. See the trenchant remarks of Carrié, "Pratique et idéologie chrétiennes de l'économique," esp. at p. 25.

25. Simplicius, *Letter* 1.1, ed. A. Thiel, *Epistolae Romanorum pontificum genuinae* (Braunsberg: E. Peter, 1867; Hildesheim: G. Olms, 1974), 1:176. B. Bellomo, "Abusi nell'economia di carità," in *Poveri ammalati e ammalati poveri*, 449–63 offers many more examples.

26. Agnellus, *Liber pontificalis ecclesiae Ravennatensis* 60, Nauerth, 268–80, Deliyannis, 173–77. See O. R. Borodin, "Ekonomicheskie protivorechiia v srede ravennskovo dukhenstva v VI–VIII vv.," *Vizantiiskii vremennik* 56 (81) (1995): 32–44 at pp. 33–36.

27. Pseudo-Jerome, *De septem ordinibus ecclesiae*, PL 30:154B (Paris: J.-P. Migne, 1846).

28. Bowes, *Private Worship, Public Values, and Religious Change*, 71 speaks of a perpetual "whisper of tension" on this issue. *Religion, Dynasty and Patronage*, ed. Cooper and Hillner, examines many of the scenarios of tension this situation can be supposed to have generated.

29. H. Chadwick, *Boethius: The Consolations of Music, Logic, Theology and Philosophy* (Oxford: Clarendon Press, 1981), 37.

30. On the complex situation in Rome, see now esp. Sardella, *Società, chiesa e stato*, 43–66, esp. 46n7 (on the threefold pay raise, which is mentioned in only one version of Symmachus's life in the *Liber pontificalis*); and Diefenbach, *Römische Erinnerungsräume*, 404–32.

31. For two masterly surveys, though largely based on eastern evidence: see Jones, *The Later Roman Empire*, 2:731–63; and Liebeschuetz, *The Decline and Fall of the Roman*

City, 29–136. For Africa and, by implication, for much of the West, Lepelley, *Les cités de l'Afrique romaine*, 1:243–92 remains the best treatment.

32. E.g., *Codex Theodosianus* 12.1.146 (395); *Novella of Majorian* 7.1 (458).

33. *Clermont* (535) c. 4, *Concilia Galliae*, vol. 2, *a. 511–a. 645*, ed. C. de Clercq, CCSL 148A (Turnhout: Brepols, 1963), 106; *Orleans* (541) c. 26, p. 139; *Mâcon* I (581–83) c. 10, p. 225; and *Châlon* (647/53) c. 14, p. 306.

34. For the appointment of noble candidates in order to avoid conflict among the local clergy, see Sidonius Apollinaris, *Letter* 7.9.3, with the characteristic comment— "some priests twittered in holes and corners" (Bourges in 472); Gregory of Tours, *Histories* 4.15 (Tours in 556).

35. In 530 the revenues of the church of Rome had sunk due to bad harvests to such an extent that Felix IV insisted on nominating a successor rather than exposing the church to the costs of a disputed election: L. Duchesne, "La succession du pape Félix IV," *Mélanges d'archéologie et d'histoire* 3 (1883): 239–66 at pp. 245–47. An election without costs was considered to have been a miracle: Gregory of Tours, *De vita patrum* 6.3, trans. E. James, *Gregory of Tours: Life of the Fathers* (Liverpool: Liverpool University Press, 1985).

36. D. Claude, "Die Bestellung der Bischöfe im merowingischen Reiche," *Zeitschrift der Savigny Stiftung für Rechtsgeschichte: Kanonistische Abteilung* 49 (1963): 1–77 at p. 59n290.

37. Gregory, *Histories* 2.21.

38. Gregory, *Histories* 2.23.

39. Gregory, *Histories* 5.49.

40. B. Caseau, "Objects in Churches: The Testimony of Inventories," in *Objects in Context, Objects in Use: Material Spatiality in Late Antiquity*, ed. L. Lavan, E. Swift, and T. Putzeys, Late Antique Archaeology 5 (Leiden: Brill, 2007), 551–79.

41. See esp. Duchesne, *Le Liber Pontificalis*, 1:cxli–cliv; P. Carmassi, "La prima redazione del *Liber Pontificalis* nel quadro delle fonti contemporanee: Osservazioni in margine alla *vita* di Simmaco," in *Atti del colloquio internazionale* Il Liber Pontificalis e la storia materiale, 235–66; K. Blair-Dixon, "Memory and Authority in Sixth-Century Rome: The *Liber Pontificalis* and the *Collectio Avellana*," in *Religion, Dynasty and Patronage*, 59–76.

42. Gregory, *Histories* I, preface 1.

43. Jones, *The Later Roman Empire*, 2:904–7; Hübner, *Der Klerus in der Gesellschaft des spätantiken Kleinasiens*, 217–28.

44. Gregory, *Dialogues* 1.9.2 and 3.8.1, ed. A. de Vogüé, *Grégoire le Grand: Dialogues*, SC 260 (Paris: Le Cerf, 1979), 76, 286.

45. Pietri, "Évergétisme et richesses ecclésiastiques," in *Christiana respublica*, 2:813–33.

46. P. Simonnot, *Les papes, l'église et l'argent: Histoire économique du christianisme des origines à nos jours* (Paris: Bayard, 2005), 12—because of celibacy and aristocratic investment, the wealth of the church "did not cease to grow with clockwork regularity"; see also pp. 161–66. It is a pity to see an intelligent and thought-provoking survey marred by

incorrect information passed on to the author in the form of stereotypes widely accepted in learned circles.

47. Sotinel, "Les évêques italiens" for Italy is decisive. On the limited extent of the "senatorial" enclaves in southern Gaul, see S. Esders, *Römische Rechtstradition und merowingisches Königtum: Zum Rechtscharakter politischer Herrschaft in Burgund im 6. und 7. Jahrhundert* (Göttingen: Vandenhoeck and Ruprecht, 1997), 185. For a differentiated general survey, see Rapp, *Holy Bishops*, 172–207.

48. M. Heinzelmann, *Gregory of Tours: History and Society in the Sixth Century*, trans. C. Carroll (Cambridge: Cambridge University Press, 2001), 190.

49. See esp. M. Heinzelmann, *Bischofsherrschaften in Gallien: Zur Kontinuität römischer Führungsschichten vom 4. bis 7. Jahrhundert*, Beihefte der Francia 5 (Munich: Artemis Verlag, 1976); and *Herrschaft und Kirche: Beiträge zur Entstehung und Wirkungskreise episkopaler und monastischer Organisationsformen*, ed. F. Prinz (Stuttgart: Hiersemann, 1988).

50. A.H.B. Breukelaar, *Historiography and Episcopal Authority: The Histories of Gregory of Tours Interpreted in Their Historical Context*, Forschungen zur Kirchen und Dogmengeschichte 57 (Göttingen: Vandenhoek and Ruprecht, 1994), 266–67.

51. For criticisms of this position, see now especially S. Patzold, "Zur Sozialstruktur des Episkopats und zur Ausbildung bischöflicher Herrschaft in Gallien zwischen Spätantike und Frühmittelalter," in *Völker, Reiche und Namen im frühen Mittelalter*, ed. M. Becker and S. Dick (Munich: W. Fink, 2010), 121–40; P. Brown, introduction to *The World of Gregory of Tours*, ed. K. Mitchell and I. Wood (Leiden: Brill, 2002), 1–28 at pp. 12–13; Esders, *Römische Rechtstradition und merowingisches Königtum*, 184–86; Loseby, "Decline and Change," 90–92; and J.-U. Krause, "Überlegungen zur Sozialgeschichte des Klerus im 5./6. Jh. n. Chr.," in *Die Stadt in der Spätantike*, 413–39 at p. 432. On the strength of the new nobility connected with the royal courts, see Halsall, *Barbarian Migrations and the Roman West*, 356–57.

52. É. Lesne, *Histoire de la propriété ecclésiastique en France*, vol. 1, *Époques romaine et mérovingienne* (Lille: Giard, 1910), 74: "dû à la même rosée que la piété des premiers âges chrétiens, semblables à la fraîcheur d'un matin, verse sur la riche végétation des églises"; see also pp. 143, 146. Despite these effusions, Lesne's study has not been surpassed.

53. J. Goody, *The Development of the Family and Marriage in Europe* (Cambridge: Cambridge University Press, 1983). This is effectively demolished by B. Shaw and R. P. Saller, "Close-Kin Marriage in Roman Society?" *Man*, n.s., 19 (1984): 432–44.

54. E.g., Gregory, *Histories* 4.24 on the lawyer Celsus of Vienne: see D. Liebs, *Römische Jurisprudenz in Gallien (2. bis 8. Jahrhundert)* (Berlin: Duncker and Humblot, 2002), 63.

55. Gregory, *Histories* 6.46.

56. Gregory, *Histories* 5.17.

57. Gregory, *Histories* 6.46.

58. Ibid.

59. The centuries-long background to Chilperic's attitude is well understood by Esders, *Römische Rechtstradition und merowingisches Königtum*, 137–41.

60. Marazzi, *"Patrimonia Sanctae Romanae Ecclesiae,"* 63. The best survey remains Jones, *The Later Roman Empire*, 2:894–910.

61. Bransbourg, "Fiscalité impériale et finances municipales," 261–67.

62. *Codex Justinianus* 11.75.1 (AD 343)—exemptions from corvées for tenants and farmers on imperial estates. See Esders, *Römische Rechtstradition und merowingisches Königtum*, 250.

63. Sotinel, "Le personnel épiscopal," 110–12.

64. Pelagius I, *Letter* 16, ed. P. M. Gassó and C. M. Batlle, *Pelagii I papae: Epistulae quae supersunt (556–61)* (Montserrat: Abbey of Montserrat, 1956), 49–50.

65. Pelagius, *Letter* 84, Gassó and Batlle, p. 206.

66. Gregory, *Histories* 4.36.

67. *Letter of Gogo the referendarius to Peter, bishop of Metz*, ed. W. Gundlach, in *Epistulae Austrasiacae* 22.1, CCSL 117 (Turnhout: Brepols, 1957), 441.

68. Gregory, *Histories* 6.20: s.v. "Chrodinus," *Prosopography of the Later Roman Empire* 3A:312–13.

69. Ennodius, *Life of Epiphanius* 9–10, 21–25; C. Sotinel, "Les ambitions d'historien d'Ennode de Pavie: La *Vita Epiphanii*," in *La narrativa cristiana antica: Codici narrative, strutture formali, schemi retorici*, Studia Ephemeridis Augustinianum 50 (Rome: Istituto Patristicum Augustinianum, 1995), 585–605 at p. 596.

70. Gregory, *Glory of the Confessors* 39, trans. R. Van Dam (Liverpool: Liverpool University Press, 1988), 51 (Van Dam translates *notae litterarum* as "letters of the alphabet": see p. 51n44 for his reasons). For a precise and sympathetic account of the family background of Gregory and his affective ties to particular saints and their churches, see R. Van Dam, *Saints and Their Miracles in Late Antique Gaul* (Princeton: Princeton University Press, 1993), 50–81.

71. Heinzelmann, *Gregory of Tours*, 11. On Gregory's general vision of the church, see pp. 153–201.

72. Esp. Gregory, *Histories* 5.18, but also *Histories* 6.15 and 8.19. This element is well seen by Heinzelmann, *Gregory of Tours*, 45, 75, 97.

73. Gregory, *Histories* 8.31.

74. This is clearly shown by H. G. Ziche, "Administrer la propriété de l'église: L'évêque comme clerc et comme entrepreneur," *Antiquité tardive* 14 (2006): 69–78.

75. The will of Ranilo in AD 553 mentions the need to recall slaves and dependent farmers who had escaped "in this time of war with the barbarians" (the wars of Justinian): *Pap. Ital.* 13.21, Tjäder, 1:304.

76. R. Mazza, "Tra Oriente e Occidente: La gestione del *patrimonium Petri* in Italia meridionale," in *Paesaggi e insediamenti rurali*, 703–715. The strenuous measures of landowners in Egypt are now discussed by P. Sarris, *Economy and Society in the Age of Justinian* (Cambridge: Cambridge University Press, 2006), 227.

77. Council of Mâcon II (AD 585), canon 7, *Concilia Galliae*, 2:242.

78. See esp. D. Claude, "Freedmen in the Visigothic Kingdom," in *Visigothic Spain: New Approaches*, ed. E. James (Oxford: Oxford University Press, 1980), 139–88 and the important recent study of S. Esders, *Die Formierung der Zensualität: Zur kirchlichen*

Transformation des spätrömischen Patronatswesens im früheren Mittelalter (Ostfildern: Jan Thorbecke, 2010).

79. Council of Toledo IV (AD 633), canon 70, ed. Vives, *Concilios visigóticos e hispano-romanos*, 215.

80. Banaji, "Aristocracies, Peasantries," 65–71.

81. Ibid., 64.

82. Ward-Perkins, *The Fall of Rome*, 148–50.

83. M. Vieillard-Troïekouroff, *Les monuments religieux de la Gaule d'après les oeuvres de Grégoire de Tours* (Paris: Champion, 1976), 366, 368.

84. *Topographie chrétienne des cités de la Gaule,* vol. 7, *Narbonne,* ed. P.-A. Février (Paris: Boccard, 1989), 21 (on Rusticus of Narbonne); vol. 6, *Bourges,* ed. F. Prévot (1989), 32 (on Namatius of Clermont); vol. 5, *Tours,* ed. L. Pietri (1987), 28 (on Gregory of Tours). See now B. Beaujard, "La topographie chrétienne des cités de la Gaule: Bilan et perspectives," in *Le problème de la christianisation du monde antique,* ed. H. Inglebert, S. Destephen, and B. Dumézil (Paris: Picard, 2010), 203–18.

85. On Paris, see *Topographie chrétienne des cités de la Gaule,* vol. 8, *Sens,* ed. J.-C. Picard (Paris: Boccard, 1992), 116–21; on Chalon-sur-Saone and King Guntram, see *Topographie chrétienne,* vol. 4, *Lyon,* ed. B. Beaujard (Paris: Boccard, 1989), 76.

86. Venantius Fortunatus, *Carmina* 2.10.17, ed. and trans. M. Reydellet, *Venance Fortunat: Poèmes I–IV* (Paris: Belles Lettres, 1994), 67; see also *Carmina* 1.1.12 (p. 20); 1.2.13 (p. 22); 1.9.19 (p. 29); 1.12.11 (p. 31); 3.7.50 (p. 96); 4.23.30 (p. 121). See now Roberts, *The Humblest Sparrow,* 65–69. Fortunatus brought these images with him from Italy, where they had already been used: e.g., the inscription in the chapel of bishop Petrus Junior in the episcopal palace at Ravenna (which Venantius would have seen): Agnellus, *Liber pontificalis* 50, Nauerth, p. 242, Deliyannis, p. 162. In general, see G. Bührer-Thierry, "Lumière et pouvoir dans le haut moyen-âge occidental: Célébration de pouvoir et métaphores lumineuses," *Mélanges de l'École française de Rome: Moyen-âge* 116 (2004): 521–58.

87. *Topographie chrétienne des cités de la Gaule,* vol. 10, *Bordeaux,* ed. L. Maurin (Paris: Boccard, 1998), 30.

88. S.J.B. Barnish, "The Wealth of Julianus Argentarius: Late Antique Banking and the Mediterranean Economy," *Byzantion* 55 (1985): 5–38. See also F. W. Deichmann, *Ravenna: Hauptstadt des spätantiken Abendlandes,* bd. 2, *Kommentar* 2 (Stuttgart: F. Steiner, 1989), 21–27. See now Deliyannis, *Ravenna,* 223–54.

89. s.v. "Sabinus 7," *Prosopographie chrétienne du Bas-Empire,* 2:1975–77. See esp. G. Volpe et al., "Il complesso sabiniano di San Pietro a Canosa," in *La cristianizzazione in Italia tra Tardoantico e Altomedioevo,* ed. R. M. Bonacasa Carra and E. Vitale (Palermo: Carlo Saladino, 2007), 2:1113–65 at pp. 1129 and 1142. See now also G. Volpe, "Architecture and Church Power in Late Antiquity: Canosa and San Giusto (*Apulia*)," in *Housing in Late Antiquity,* 131–68 at pp. 134–52.

90. Volpe, *Contadini, pastori e mercanti,* 102–5, esp. figure 21 on p. 102.

91. Volpe et al., "Il complesso sabiniano di San Pietro a Canosa," 1114–21.

92. M. Corrente, R. Giuliano, and D. Leone, "Il complesso religioso di Piano di San Giovanni e il problema del primo polo episcopale canosino," in *La cristianizzazione in Italia,* 2:1167–1200.

93. Volpe, *Contadini, pastori e mercanti*, 151.

94. Gregory, *Dialogues* 3.5, Vogüé 274.

95. Ebanista, *Et manet in mediis quasi gemma intersita tectis*, 146.

96. A. Terry and H. Maguire, *Dynamic Splendor: The Wall Mosaics in the Cathedral of Eufrasius at Poreč* (University Park: Pennsylvania State University Press, 2007), 82.

97. Ibid., 90.

98. Ibid., 98.

99. P. Niewöhner, "Vom Sinnbild zum Abbild: Der justinianische Realismus und die Genese der byzantinischen Heiligentypologie," *Millennium* 5 (2008): 163–89 at pp. 176–79.

CHAPTER 29
Servator fidei, patriaeque semper amator

1. C. Tedeschi, *Congeries lapidum: Iscrizioni Britanniche dei secoli V–VII*, Scuola Normale Superiore di Pisa: Centro di Cultura Medievale (Pisa: Scuola Normale Superiore, 2005), Gso-7 at 117–19 with plate XXVI.

2. Venantius Fortunatus, *Carmina* 3.5.9 and 3.8.17, Reydellet, 1:91, 98; 5.3.5, Reydellet, 1:17; Roberts, *The Humblest Sparrow*, 17–27, 38–53.

3. Giardina, "*Amor civicus.*"

4. *The Inscriptions of Roman Tripolitania*, ed. J. M. Reynolds and J. B. Ward Perkins (London: British School at Rome, 1952), no. 603 at p. 159; See also Lepelley, *Les cités de l'Afrique romaine*, 2:353 with 348n63. The term had Punic roots.

5. M. Foucault, *Security, Territory, Population: Lectures at the Collège de France, 1977–1978*, ed. M. Senellart, trans. G. Burchell (Basingstoke: Palgrave MacMillan, 2007), 155.

6. Ibid., 129.

7. Ibid., 168.

8. Ibid., 128.

9. Venantius Fortunatus, *Carmina* 4.9.10 and 4.9.24, Reydellet, 1:140, 141.

10. Gillett, *Envoys and Political Communication in the Late Antique West*, 178–83 is a valuable corrective to this bishop-centered view. Out of forty-one embassies recorded by Hydatius of Chaves, only two were headed by bishops.

11. Gregory of Tours, *Histories* 9.30, cf. *Histories* 4.2, 4.16, 5.23, and 6.45. See esp. J. Strothmann, "Königsherrschaft oder nachantike Staatlichkeit? Merowingische Monetarmünzen als Quelle für die politische Ordnung des Frankenreichs," *Millennium* 5 (2008): 353–81; and M. Hardt, *Gold und Herrschaft: Die Schätze europäischer Könige und Fürsten im ersten Jahrtausend* (Berlin: Akademie Verlag, 2004), 146–48.

12. Loseby, "Decline and Change," esp. at p. 92 is an effective criticism of current overvaluations of episcopal power in the cities.

13. Cracco Ruggini, *Economia e società nell' "Italia annonaria,"* 333–35 on the activities of bishop Datius of Milan during the famine of 535–36. It was the bishop's wealth (as administrator of the wealth of the church of Milan) and not any institutional role that accounted for his importance.

14. G. A. Cecconi, "Crisi e trasformazioni del governo municipale in Occidente fra IV e VI secolo," in *Die Stadt in der Spätantike*, 285–318 rightly insists on the complexity of the evolution of municipal government. There is no straightforward narrative of the decline of town councils and their replacement by the church.

15. Cassiodorus, *Variae* 9.15.1, Barnish, p. 112.

16. Orléans II (549) canons 13 and 16, *Concilia Galliae*, pp. 152 and 154; Mâcon I (581–85), canon 4, p. 224; Valence (583–85), p. 235; Paris (614), canon 9, p. 277; and Clichy (626–27), canon 24, p. 296.

17. Tours II (567), canon 25, *Concilia Galliae*, p. 192.

18. Brown, *Poverty and Leadership*, 68–70; Freu, *Les figures du pauvre*, 264–68—on Ambrose.

19. This is well seen by A. Firey, "'For I was hungry and you fed me': Social Justice and Economic Thought in the Late Patristic and Medieval Christian Traditions," in *Ancient and Medieval Economic Ideas and Concepts of Social Justice*, ed. S. T. Lowry and B. Gordon (Leiden: Brill, 1998), 333–370 at pp. 344–45.

20. Mâcon II (585), canon 12, *Concilia Galliae*, pp. 244–45.

21. Esders, *Römische Rechtstradition und merowingisches Königtum*, 319–38.

22. Gregory of Tours, *De vita Patrum* 4.4, James, p. 46.

23. Gregory of Tours, *De gloria confessorum* 109; see V. Neri, *I marginali nell'Occidente tardoantico: Poveri, "infames" e criminali nella nascente società cristiana* (Bari: Edipuglia, 1998), 61–62. For Elijah and Khidhr as the "living ones" who (like Jesus in Christian and Muslim legend) walk the world unrecognized after their death, see L. Ginzberg, *The Legends of the Jews*, trans. H. Szold (Philadelphia: Jewish Publication Society of America, 1925), 5:202–35; and I. Omar, "Khidhr in the Islamic Traditions," *The Muslim World* 83 (1993): 279–94.

24. The best study is T. Sternberg, *Orientalium more secutus: Räume und Institutionen der Caritas des 5. bis 7. Jahrhunderts in Gallien*, Jahrbuch für Antike und Christentum, Ergänzungsband 16 (Münster in Wesfalen: Aschendorff, 1991), 136–38.

25. Gregory of Tours, *De virtutibus sancti Martini*, ed. B. Krusch, MGH: Scriptores rerum Merovingcarum (Hannover: Hahn, 1885), 1.31.

26. Gregory of Tours, *Histories* 7.29. See now A. E. Jones, *Social Mobility in Late Antique Gaul: Strategies and Opportunities for the Non-Elite* (Cambridge: Cambridge University Press, 2009), 226–49.

27. *Liber Pontificalis* 51, Duchesne, 1:255n5 at p. 256.

28. For a memorable characterization of Pope Symmachus, see Chadwick, *Boethius*, 31–39; see now Sardella, *Società, chiesa e stato*, 41–111, 183–95.

29. *Liber Pontificalis* 53, Davis, pp. 45–46.

30. *Vitae patrum Emeritensium* 5.3.1–8, ed. J. N. Garvin *The Vitas sanctorum patrum Emeritensium* (Washington, DC: Catholic University of America Press, 1946), 192–95.

31. *Vitae patrum Emeritensium* 5.3.11, Garvin, p. 196.

32. E.g., Venantius Fortunatus, *Vita Germani*, PL:12 (Paris: J.-P. Migne, 1846); and Cyprianus of Toulon, *Vita Caesarii* 2.8. On church warehouses and miracles of abundance, see Sternberg, *Orientalium more secutus*, 73–79. For a similar mystification of the wealth of the church of Alexandria, see V. Déroche, *Études sur Léontios de Néapolis*, Stu-

dia Byzantina Upsalensia 3 (Uppsala: Alqmvist and Wiksell, 1995), 238–49—speaking of the "économie miraculeuse" constructed by hagiographers. See now D. Caner, "Towards a Miraculous Economy: Christian Gifts and Material 'Blessings' in Late Antiquity," *Journal of Early Christian Studies* 14 (2006): 329–77.

33. Sternberg, *Orientalium more secutus*, 126–35.

34. M. Borgolte, "*Felix est homo ille qui amicos bonos relinquit*: Zur sozialen Gestaltungskraft letzwilliger Verfügungen am Beispiel Bischofs Bertrams von le Mans (616)," in *Festschrift für Berent Schwineköper*, ed. H. Maurer and H. Patze (Sigmaringen: J. Thorbecke, 1982), 5–18 at p. 13.

35. Sternberg, *Orientalium more secutus*, 150 points to the contrast with the eastern empire.

36. Tours II (567), canon 5, *Concilia Galliae*, p. 178. See Gregory of Tours, *Histories* 4.47–48, 6.41, 7.2, 7.28—on the impact of such warfare.

37. *Inscriptions chrétiennes de la Gaule antérieures au VIIIe siècle*, ed. E. Le Blant (Paris: Imprimerie impériale, 1856), no. 173, 1:234; well translated along with the *De virtutibus sancti Martini*, trans. Van Dam, *Saints and Their Miracles*, 313.

38. Gregory of Tours, *De virtutibus sancti Martini* 2.22, cf. 2.23.

39. Gregory of Tours, *De virtutibus sancti Martini* 2.24.

40. Gregory of Tours, *De virtutibus sancti Martini* 2.12.

41. M. A. Handley, *Death, Society and Culture: Inscriptions and Epitaphs in Gaul and Spain, AD 300–750*, BAR International Series 1135 (Oxford: British Archaeological Reports, 2003), 161–63. See L. Tolstoy, *War and Peace*, book 6, chapter 17, trans. L. and A. Maude (London: Macmillan, 1954), 527–28. On Catholic "reverence," see P. Brown, "Relics and Social Status in the Age of Gregory of Tours," in *Society and the Holy in Late Antiquity* (Berkeley: University of California Press, 1982), 222–50 at pp. 230–35.

42. Gregory of Tours, *Histories* 10.25.

43. Gregory of Tours, *Histories* 7.44.

44. Markus, *The End of Ancient Christianity*, 213–28, esp. p. 225.

45. *Pap. Ital.* 4–5. B VII. 10–11, Tjäder, 1:216. See esp. J. Barbier, "Testaments et pratique testamentaire dans le royaume franc (VIe–VIIIe siècles)," in *Sauver son âme et se perpétuer: Transmission du patrimoine et mémoire au haut Moyen Âge*, ed. F. Bougard, C. La Rocca, and R. Le Jan, Collection de l'École française de Rome 351 (Rome: École française de Rome, 2005), 7–79. See now A. Angenendt, "*Donationes pro anima*: Gift and Countergift in the Early Medieval Liturgy," in *The Long Morning of Medieval Europe: New Directions in Early Medieval Studies*, ed. J. R. Davis and M. McCormick (Aldershot: Ashgate, 2008), 131–54. See also Magnani, "Almsgiving, *donatio pro anima* and Eucharistic Offering."

46. Brown, "The Decline of the Empire of God."

47. W. Levison, "Das Testament des Diakons Adalgisel Grimo vom Jahre 634," *Trierer Zeitschrift* 7 (1932): 69–85, now in *Aus rheinischer und fränkischer Frühzeit* (Dusseldorf: L. Schwann, 1948), 118–38 at p. 125.

48. Gregory of Tours, *De virtutibus sancti Martini* 2.60.

49. M. Weidemann, *Das Testament des Bischofs Bertram von Le Mans vom 27. März 616: Untersuchungen zu Besitz und Geschichte einer fränkischen Familie im 6. und 7. Jahr-*

hundert, Römisch-germanisches Zentralmuseum, Monographien 9 (Mainz: R. Habelt, 1986), 11.

50. T. Head, "The Early Medieval Transformation of Piety," in *The Long Morning of Medieval Europe*, 155–60 at p. 160.

51. M. Rubin, *Charity and Community in Medieval Cambridge* (Cambridge: Cambridge University Press, 1987), 299.

52. A. Diem, *Das monastische Experiment: Die Rolle der Keuschheit bei der Entstehung des westlichen Klosterwesens*, Vita Regularis: Abhandlungen 24 (Münster: Lit, 2005), 178.

53. Gregory of Tours, *Histories* 3.5. For a possible surviving example of one such monastery outside Rome, see E. Fentress et al., *Walls and Memory: The Abbey of San Sebastiano at Alatri (Lazio) from Late Roman Monastery to Renaissance Villa and Beyond*, Disciplina Monastica 2 (Turnhout: Brepols, 2005), 34–70.

54. Brown, *The Rise of Western Christendom*, 252–55.

55. *Regula cuiusdam ad virgines* III, PL 88:1056B (Paris: J.-P. Migne, 1850).

56. Brown, "Alms and the Afterlife."

57. See esp. B. Jussen, *Name der Witwe: Erkundungen zur Semantik der mittelalterlichen Busskultur* (Göttingen: Vandenhoeck and Ruprecht, 2000), 47–53, 176–98. See, e.g., Narbonne (589), canon 1, *Concilios visigóticos e hispano-romanos*, 146, which forbids priests to wear purple, for it was a dress "of worldly dignity."

58. H. Lutterbach, *Monachus factus est: Die Mönchwerdung im frühen Mittelalter*, Beiträge zur Geschichte des alten Mönchtums und des Benediktinertums (Münster: Aschendorff, 1995), 120–22. On the subsequent ramifications of the meaning of the monastic tonsure, see E. James, "Bede and the Tonsure Question," *Peritia* 3 (1984): 85–98.

59. *Canones in Causa Apiarii*, canon 25, *Concilia Africae*, 108–9. See J.-A. Sabw Kanyang, *Episcopus et plebs: L'évêque et la communauté ecclésiale dans les conciles africains (345–525)*, European University Studies 701 (Bern: Peter Lang, 2000), 144–45.

60. Augustine, *Confessions* 6.3.3.

61. See in general Brown, *Body and Society*, 356–59.

62. Gregory of Tours, *Histories* 2.22.

63. Gregory of Tours, *De gloria confessorum* 75.

64. Innocent I, *Letter* 38, PL 20:605B (Paris: J.-P. Migne, 1845).

65. R. Godding, *Prêtres en Gaule mérovingienne*, Subsidia Hagiographica 82 (Brussels: Société des Bollandistes, 2001), 125, 143.

66. T. Sardella, "Continenza e uxorato del clero nell'Africa di Agostino," in *L'adorabile vescovo d'Ippona*, ed. F. E. Consolino (Soveria Manelli: Rubettino, 2001), 183–226.

67. Tours II (567), canon 20, *Concilia Galliae*, p. 183 and canons 13–17, pp. 180–82.

68. Tours II (567), canon 20, *Concilia Galliae*, p. 183.

69. Veranus, *Sententia de castitate sacerdotum*, PL 72:701–2 (Paris: J.-P. Migne, 1849); see Godding, *Prêtres en Gaule*, 130.

70. L. Duchesne, "Lovocat et Catihern, prêtres bretons du temps de saint Mélaine," *Revue de Bretagne et de Vendée* 57 (1885): 5–21; Godding, *Prêtres en Gaule*, 147–49.

71. B. Tanguy, "De l'origine des évêchés bretons," in *Les débuts de l'organisation religieuse en la Bretagne Armoricaine*, Brittania Monastica 3 (Landevennec: Brittania Mo-

nastica, 1994), 6–33 at pp. 13–14. See in general W. Davies, *Small Worlds: The Village Community in Early Medieval Brittany* (London: Duckworth, 1988).

72. Bowes, *Private Worship, Public Values, and Religious Change*, 125–88; S.J.B. Barnish, "*Religio in stagno*: Nature, Divinity and the Christianization of the Countryside in Late Antique Italy," *Journal of Early Christian Studies* 9 (2001): 387–402.

73. C. Pietri, "Chiesa e comunità locali nell'Occidente cristiano (iv–vi d.C.): L'esempio della Gallia," in *Società romana e impero tardoantico*, vol. 3, *Le merci, gli insediamenti*, ed. A. Giardina (Bari: Laterza, 1986), 761–97, in *Christiana respublica*, 1: 475–521. R. Lizzi Testa, "L'Église, les *domini*, les païens *rustici*: Quelques strategies pour la christianisation de l'Occident (IVe–VIe s.)," in *Le problème de la christianisation*, 77–113.

74. Chavarría Arnau, *El final de las* villae *en* Hispania, 43–62. J. Sanchez Velasco, A. M. Rosa, and G. G. Muñoz, "Aproximación al estudio de la ciudad de Cabra y su obispado al final de la Antigüedad," *Antiquitas* 21 (Priego de Corboba: Museo Histórico Municipal, 2009), 135–80 shows what can be done from what are, alas, exiguous remains.

75. Godding, *Prêtres en Gaule*, 331–58; Wood, *The Proprietary Church*, 10–11.

76. G. Cantino Wataghin, V. Fiocchi Nicolai, and G. Volpe, "Aspetti della cristianizzazione degli agglomerati secondari," in *La cristianizzazione in Italia*, 1:83–134.

77. *Inscripciones latinas de la España romana y visigóda*, ed. J. Vives (Barcelona: Consejo Superior de Investigaciones Científicas, 1969), no. 303, p. 101.

78. Vieillard-Troïekouroff, *Les monuments religieux de la Gaule*, 397–98.

79. *Council of Toledo III* (589), c. 15, *Concilios visigóticos e hispano-romanos*, p. 129.

80. Bowes, *Private Worship, Public Values, and Religious Change*, 130–57.

81. Krause, "Überlegungen zur Sozialgeschichte des Klerus," 426.

82. Goffart, *Barbarian Tides*, 136.

83. Y. Thébert, "L'évolution urbaine dans les provinces orientales de l'Afrique romaine tardive," *Opus* 2 (1982): 99–131 at p. 120.

84. I. N. Wood, "Review Article: Landscapes Compared," *Early Medieval Europe* 15 (2007): 223–37 at p. 236.

85. Gernet, *Buddhism in Chinese Society*, 166.

86. Foucault, *Security, Territory, Population*, 129.

87. J. M. Pardessus, ed., *Diplomata, cartae, epistolae, leges aliaque instrumenta ad res Gallo-Francicas spectantia* (Aalen: Scientia Verlag, 1969), no. 273, 2:37.

88. Ibid., no. 241, 1:227.

89. Sternberg, *Orientalium more secutus*, 128, 137.

90. Mâcon II (585), canon 4, *Concilia Galliae*, pp. 240–41.

91. Venantius Fortunatus, *Carmina* 4.23.15, Reydellet, 1:121.

92. Weidemann, *Das Testament des Bischofs Bertram*, 11.

93. P. Fouracre, "Eternal Light and Earthly Needs: Practical Aspects of the Development of Frankish Immunities," in *Property and Power*, 53–81; see Xinru Liu, *Silk and Religion: An Exploration of Material Life and the Thought of People, AD 600–1200* (Delhi: Oxford University Press, 1996).

94. This is well studied by Vuolanto, "Male and Female Euergetism."

95. On Clamosus and his peers, see Kaster, *Guardians of Language*, 254–55.

96. Vuolanto, "Male and Female Euergetism," 262.

97. P. Chevalier, "Les graffitis de l'abside de l'Eufrasiana de Poreč: Un obituaire monumental du haut Moyen Âge," *Mélanges Jean Pierre Sodini: Travaux et mémoires* 15 (2005): 359–70.

CONCLUSION

1. *Eric the Red's Saga* 4, in *The Norse Atlantic Saga*, trans. G. Jones, 2nd ed. (Oxford: Oxford University Press, 1986), 220.

WORKS CITED

⎯⎯⎯⎯⎯⎯ ❧ ⎯⎯⎯⎯⎯⎯

PRIMARY SOURCES

The reader should know that this is not a comprehensive bibliography of all the sources cited in this book. I have chosen only to indicate editions and translations: first, for authors and sources on which I have concentrated in individual chapters; second, for those on which I have depended repeatedly in all chapters; and last, in some cases, for sources that are taken from less well-known authors and where the reader might require an indication of the editions and translations in which they can be found. For many well-known classical and Christian authors, I have been content to cite the traditional titles and abbreviations, with the knowledge that, in modern conditions of reference, readers will be able to find their way to appropriate editions and translations when needed.

Acta et symbola conciliorum quae saeculo quarto habita sunt. Edited by E. J. Jonkers. Leiden: Brill, 1954.

Ad Deum post conversionem. Edited by Adalbert Hamman, in PL Supplementum 3. Paris: Garnier, 1963.

Agnellus of Ravenna. *Liber pontificalis ecclesiae Ravennatensis.*
Edited and translated by Claudia Nauerth, *Agnellus von Ravenna: Liber pontificalis/Bischofsbuch.* Freiburg: Herder, 1996.
Translated by Deborah Mauskopf Deliyannis, in *The Book of Pontiffs of the Church of Ravenna.* Washington, DC: Catholic University of America Press, 2004.

Ambrose of Milan. *De Nabuthae.*
Edited by Karl Schenkl, in *Sancti Ambrosii Opera*, part 2. CSEL 62. Vienna: Tempsky, 1897.
Translated by Boniface Ramsey, in *Ambrose.* New York: Routledge, 1997.
———. *De officiis.* Edited and translated by Ivor J. Davidson, in *Ambrose: De officiis.* 2 vols. Oxford: Oxford University Press, 2001.

Ambrose of Milan. *Letters.*
>   Edited by Otto Faller and Michaela Zelzer, in *Sancti Ambrosii Opera*, part 10.
>   CSEL 82. Vols. 1–3. Vienna: Tempsky, 1968–90.
>   Selected letters translated by J.W.H.G. Liebeschuetz with the assistance of Carole
>   Hill, in *Ambrose of Milan: Political Letters and Speeches*. Liverpool: Liverpool
>   University Press, 2006.

Ambrosiaster. *Commentarius in Epistulas Paulinas.*
>   Edited by Henry Joseph Vogels, in *Ambrosiastri qui dicitur Commentarius in
>   Epistulas Paulinas*. 3 vols. CSEL 81. Vienna: Tempsky, 1966–69.
>   Translated by Gerald L. Bray, in *Ambrosiaster: Commentaries on Romans and
>   1–2 Corinthians*. Downers Grove, IL: InterVarsity Press, 2009.

———. *Quaestiones Veteris et Novi Testamenti.*
>   Edited by Alexander Souter, in *Pseudo-Augustini Quaestiones Veteris et Novi
>   Testamenti CXXVII*. CSEL 50. Vienna: Tempsky, 1908.

Ammianus Marcellinus. *Res gestae.*
>   Edited and translated by John C. Rolfe, in *Ammianus Marcellinus*. Loeb Classical
>   Library. 3 vols. Cambridge, MA: Harvard University Press, 1952.
>   Translated by Walter Hamilton, in *The Later Roman Empire, A.D. 354–378*.
>   Harmondsworth: Penguin, 1986.

Anonymus de rebus bellicis.
>   Edited and translated by Andrea Giardina, in *Anonimo: Le cose della guerra*.
>   [Milan]: Mondadori, 1989.
>   Edited and translated by E. A. Thompson, in *A Roman Reformer and Inventor*.
>   Oxford: Clarendon Press, 1952.

Arnobius Iunior. *Commentaria in Psalmos*. PL 53. Paris: J.-P. Migne, 1847.

Artemidorus. *Oneirocritica*. Translated by Robert J. White, in *The Interpretation of
>   Dreams*. Park Ridge, NJ: Noyes Press, 1975.

Augustine of Hippo. *Confessions.*
>   Edited with commentary by James J. O'Donnell, in *Augustine: Confessions*. 3 vols.
>   Oxford: Clarendon Press, 1992.
>   Translated by Henry Chadwick, in *Saint Augustine: Confessions*. Oxford: Oxford
>   University Press, 1991.
>   Translated by Gary Wills, in *Saint Augustine: Confessions*. London: Penguin,
>   2006.

———. *Contra academicos libri tres.*
>   Edited by Pius Knöll, in *Sancti Aureli Augustini Opera* 1:3. CSEL 63. Vienna:
>   Tempsky, 1922.
>   Translated by John J. O'Meara, in *St. Augustine: Against the Academics*. Ancient
>   Christian Writers 12. Westminster, MD: Newman Press, 1951.
>   Translated in *The Writings of Saint Augustine*. Vol. 1. New York: CIMA Publish-
>   ing, 1948.

———. *De beata vita.*
>   Edited by Pius Knöll, in *Sancti Aureli Augustini Opera* 1:3. CSEL 63. Vienna:
>   Tempsky, 1922.

Translated by Ruth Allison Brown, in *S. Aureli Augustini de beata vita*. Washington, DC: Catholic University of America Press, 1944.

Translated in *The Writings of Saint Augustine*. Vol. 1. New York: CIMA Publishing, 1948.

———. *De civitate Dei.*

Edited by Bernard Dombart and Alfons Kalb. CCSL 47–48. Turnhout: Brepols, 1954–55.

Translated by Henry Bettenson, in *Augustine: Concerning the City of God against the Pagans*. Harmondsworth: Penguin, 1972.

———. *De ordine.*

Edited by Pius Knöll, in *Sancti Aureli Augustini Opera* 1:3. CSEL 63. Vienna: Tempsky, 1922.

Translated by Silvano Borruso, in *On Order*. South Bend, IN: St. Augustine's Press, 2007.

Translated in *The Writings of Saint Augustine*. Vol. 1. New York: CIMA Publishing, 1948.

———. *Dolbeau Sermons.*

Nos. 2–27, edited by François Dolbeau, in *Vingt-six sermons au peuple d'Afrique*. Paris: Institut d'Études Augustiniennes, 1996.

No. 30, edited by François Dolbeau, in "Le sermon 384A de saint Augustin contre Pélage: Édition du texte integral." *Recherches augustiniennes* 28 (1995): 37–63.

Translated by Edmund Hill, in *Sermons (Newly Discovered) III/11*. The Works of Saint Augustine: A Translation for the 21st Century. Hyde Park, NY: New City Press, 1997.

———. *Enarrationes in Psalmos*. Edited by Clemens Weidmann (1–50), Hildegund Müller (51–100), and Franco Gori (101–150). CSEL 93, 94, 95. Vienna: Österreichische Akademie der Wissenschaften, 2001–04.

———. *Erfurt Sermons.*

Nos. 1, 5, and 6, edited by Isabella Schiller, Dorothea Weber, and Clemens Weidmann, in "Sechs neue Augustinuspredigten: Teil 1 mit Edition dreier Sermones." *Wiener Studien* 121 (2008): 227–84.

Nos. 2–4, edited by Isabella Schiller, Dorothea Weber, and Clemens Weidmann, in "Sechs neue Augustinuspredigten: Teil 2 mit Edition dreier Sermones zum Thema Almosen." *Wiener Studien* 122 (2009): 171–214.

———. *Letters 1*–29* [New Letters].*

Edited by Johannes Divjak, in *Sancti Aurelii Augustini Opera* 2:6. CSEL 88. Vienna: Tempsky, 1981.

Edited and translated, in *Lettres 1*–29**. Bibliothèque Augustinienne 46B. Paris: Desclée de Brouwer, 1987.

Translated by Robert B. Eno, in *St. Augustine: Letters: Volume VI (1*–29*)*. Fathers of the Church 81. Washington, DC: Catholic University of America Press, 1989.

———. *Praeceptum*. Edited and translated by George Lawless, in *Augustine of Hippo and His Monastic Rule*. Oxford: Clarendon Press, 1987.

Augustine of Hippo. *Sermons.*
 Reprint of 1683 Maurist edition, in PL 38–39. Paris: J.-P. Migne, 1845–46.
 Additional sermons collected by Adalbert Hamman, in PL Supplementum 2.
  Paris: Garnier, 1960. Includes *Sermones Lambot* 1–29, discovered and edited
  by Cyrille Lambot and published in *Revue bénédictine* between 1933 and
  1958. (See "Secondary Sources" below for specific references.)
 Nos. 1–50, edited by Cyrille Lambot, in *Sancti Aurelii Augustini Sermones de
  Vetere Testamento.* CCSL 41. Turnhout: Brepols, 1961.
 Translated by Edmund Hill, in *The Works of Saint Augustine: Sermons.* 11 vols.
  Hyde Park, NY: New City Press, 1997.
——. *Soliloquia.*
 Translated by Kim Paffenroth, in *Saint Augustine: Soliloquies.* Hyde Park, NY:
  New City Press, 2000.
 Translated in *The Writings of Saint Augustine.* Vol. 1. New York: CIMA Publish-
  ing, 1948.
Ausonius of Bordeaux. Works: *Ephemeris*; *Gratiarum actio*; *De herediolo*; *Letters*;
 Parentalia; *Professors*; *Proptrepticus ad nepotem.*
 Edited by R.P.H. Green, in *The Works of Ausonius.* Oxford: Clarendon Press, 1991.
 Edited and translated by H. G. Evelyn-White, in *Ausonius.* 2 vols. Loeb Classical
  Library. Cambridge, MA: Harvard University Press, 1951.
The Babylonian Talmud. Edited by Isidore Epstein. Translated by Maurice Simon.
 London: Soncino, 1935.
Calendar of 354. Edited by Theodor Mommsen, in vol. 1 of *Chronica Minora, saec. IV. V.
 VI. VII.* MGH: Auctores Antiquissimi, vol. 9. Berlin: Weidmann, 1892.
Cassian, John. *Collationes.*
 Edited and translated by E. Pichéry, in *Jean Cassien: Conférences.* 3 vols. SC 42, 54,
  64. Paris: Le Cerf, 1955–59.
 Selections translated by Colm Luibheid, in *Conferences.* New York: Paulist Press,
  1985.
 Translated by Boniface Ramsey, in *The Conferences.* New York: Paulist Press, 1997.
——. *De institutis coenobiorum.*
 Edited and translated by Jean-Claude Guy, in *Jean Cassien: Institutions Cénobi-
  tiques.* SC 109. Paris: Le Cerf, 1965.
 Translated by Boniface Ramsey, in *The Institutes.* Ancient Christian Writers. New
  York: Newman Press, 2000.
Cassiodorus. *Variae.*
 Edited by Theodor Mommsen. MGH: Auctores Antiquissimi 12. Berlin:
  Weidmann, 1894.
 Translated by S.J.B. Barnish, in *Cassiodorus: Variae.* Translated Texts for Historians
  12. Liverpool: Liverpool University Press, 1992.
Celestine I of Rome. *Letters.* PL 50. Paris: J.-P. Migne, 1846.
Chronicle of 452.
 Edited by Theodor Mommsen, in vol. 1 of *Chronica Minora, saec. IV. V. VI. VII.*
  MGH: Auctores Antiquissimi 9. Berlin: Weidmann, 1892.

Translated by Alexander Callander Murray, in *From Roman to Merovingian Gaul: A Reader*. Peterborough, Ontario: Broadview Press, 2000.

Cicero. *De officiis*. Edited and translated by Walter Miller. Loeb Classical Library. Cambridge, MA: Harvard University Press, 1913.

Codex Iustinianus. Edited by Paul Krueger, in *Corpus Iuris Civilis: Institutiones*. Vol. 2. 11th ed. Berlin: Weidmann, 1954.

Codex Theodosianus.

> Edited by Theodor Mommsen and Paul M. Meyer, in *Theodosiani libri XVI cum Constitutionibus Sirmondianis et Leges novellae ad Theodosianum pertinentes*. Berlin: Weidmann, 1905.

> Translated by Clyde Pharr, in collaboration with Theresa Sherrer Davidson and Mary Brown Pharr, in *The Theodosian Code and Novels, and the Sirmondian Constitutions*. Princeton: Princeton University Press, 1952.

> Introduced with notes by Roland Delmaire and translated by Jean Rougé, in *Les lois religieuses des empereurs romains de Constantin à Théodose II (312–438)*. Vol. 1, *Le code Théodosien: Livre XVI*. SC 497. Paris: Le Cerf, 2005.

Collatio Carthaginensis. Edited and translated by Serge Lancel, in *Actes de la Conférence de Carthage en 411*. 4 vols. SC 194–95, 224, 373. Paris: Le Cerf, 1972–91.

Collectio Avellana. Edited by Otto Günther, in *Epistulae imperatorum pontificum aliorum inde ab a. CCCLXVII usque ad a. DLIII datae: Avellana quae dicitur collectio*. 2 vols. CSEL 35. Vienna: Tempsky, 1895–98.

Collectio Quesnelliana. PL 56. Paris: J.-P. Migne, 1846.

Concilia Africae, a. 345–a. 525. Edited by Charles Munier. CCSL 149. Turnhout: Brepols, 1974.

Concilia Galliae.

> Vol. 1, *a. 314–a. 506*. Edited by Charles Munier. CCSL 148. Turnhout: Brepols, 1963.

> Vol. 2, *a. 511–a. 695*. Edited by Charles de Clerq. CCSL 148A. Turnhout: Brepols, 1963.

Concilios visigóticos e hispano-romanos. Edited by José Vives, with the collaboration of Tomás Marín Martínez and Gonzalo Martínez Díez. Madrid: Consejo Superior de Investigaciones Científicas, 1963.

Coptic Documentary Texts from Kellis. Vol. 1, edited by Iain Gardner, Anthony Alcock, and Wolf-Peter Funk. Oxford: Oxbow, 1999. Selectively translated by Iain Gardner and Samuel N. C. Lieu, in *Manichaean Texts from the Roman Empire*. Cambridge: Cambridge University Press, 2004.

Corpus Inscriptionum Latinarum.

> Vol. 6, *Inscriptiones Urbis Romae Latinae*. Part 8:3, *Titulos et imagines: Titulos magistratuum populi romani ordinum senatorii equestrisque thesauro schedarum imaginumque ampliato*. Edited by Géza Alföldy. Berlin: De Gruyter, 2000.

> Vol. 8, *Inscriptiones Africae Latinae*. Edited by Gustav Wilmanns and Theodor Mommsen. Berlin: G. Reimer, 1881.

> Vol. 10. *Inscriptiones Bruttiorum, Lucaniae, Campaniae, Siciliae, Sardiniae Latinae*. Edited by Theodor Mommsen. Berlin: G. Reimer, 1883.

Cyprian of Carthage. *Letters*.
    Edited by G. F. Diercks, in *Sancti Cypriani episcopi opera* 3. CCSL 3B, 3C.
        Turnhout: Brepols, 1994–96.
    Translated by G. W. Clarke, in *The Letters of St. Cyprian of Carthage*. 4 vols. Ancient
        Christian Writers 43–44, 46–47. New York: Newman Press, 1984–88.
De divina lege.
    PL 30. Paris: J.-P. Migne, 1846.
    Translated by B. R. Rees, in *The Letters of Pelagius and His Followers*. Woodbridge,
        UK: Boydell, 1998.
De divitiis.
    Edited by C. P. Caspari, in *Briefe, Abhandlungen und Predigten aus der zwei letzten
        Jahrhunderten des kirchlichen Altertums und dem Anfang des Mittelalters*.
        Christiania/Oslo: Malling, 1890; reprint, Brussels: Culture et Civilisation,
        1964.
    Edited and translated by Andreas Kessler, in *Reichtumskritik und Pelagianismus:
        Die pelagianische Diatribe De divitiis. Situierung, Lesetext, Übertsetzung,
        Kommentar*. Paradosis 43. Freiburg, Switzerland: Universitätsverlag, 1999.
    Translated by B. R. Rees, in *The Letters of Pelagius and His Followers*. Woodbridge,
        UK: Boydell, 1998.
Edictum Diocletiani et collegarum de pretiis rerum venalium. Edited by Marta Gi-
    acchero. 2 vols. Genoa: Università di Genova, 1974.
Epigrafia anfiteatrale dell'occidente romano. Vol. 6, *Roma*. Edited by Silvia Orlandi.
    Vetera 15. Rome: Quasar, 2004.
Epistulae Austrasiacae. Edited by Wilhelm Gundlach, in *Liber scintillarum, quem
    recensuit Henricus M. Rochais*. CCSL 117. Turnhout: Brepols, 1957.
Eric the Red's Saga. Translated by Gwyn Jones, in *The Norse Atlantic Saga*. 2nd ed.
    Oxford: Oxford University Press, 1986.
Eucherius of Lyon. *De contemptu mundi*. Edited and translated by Salvatore Pricoco, in
    Eucherio di Lione: Il rifiuto del mondo. Florence: Nardini, 1990.
———. *De laude eremi*. Edited by Karl Wotke, in *Sancti Eucherii Lugdunensis Formulae
    spiritalis intelligentiae, Instructionum libri duo, Passio agaunensium martyrum,
    Epistula de laude heremi*. CSEL 31. Vienna: Tempsky, 1894.
Eusebius of Caesarea. *Ecclesiastical History*.
    Edited and translated by Kirsopp Lake. 2 vols. Loeb Classical Library 153, 265.
        London: Heinemann, 1926–32.
    Translated by Hugh Jackson Lawlor and John Ernest Leonard Oulton, in *Eusebius:
        The Ecclesiastical History and the Martyrs of Palestine*. London: SPCK,
        1927–28.
Expositio totius mundi et gentium. Edited and translated by Jean Rougé. SC 124. Paris:
    Le Cerf, 1966.
Faustus of Riez. *De gratia*. Edited by August Engelbrecht, in *Fausti Reiensis praeter
    sermones pseudo-eusebianos opera*. CSEL 21. Vienna: Tempsky, 1891.
———. *Letters*. Edited by August Engelbrecht, in *Fausti Reiensis praeter sermones
    pseudo-eusebianos opera*. CSEL 21. Vienna: Tempsky, 1891.

Firmicus Maternus, Julius. *Mathesis.*
>Edited by W. Kroll and F. Skutsch, in *Matheseos libri VII.* 2 vols. Stuttgart: Teubner, 1968. Reprint of 1897–1913 edition.
>Edited and translated by Pierre Monat, in *Firmicus Maternus: Mathesis.* 3 vols. Paris: Belles Lettres, 1992, 1994, 1997.
>Translated by Jean Rhys Bram, in *Ancient Astrology: Theory and Practice.* Park Ridge, NJ: Noyes Press, 1975.

Fortunatus, Venantius. *Carmina.* Edited and translated by Marc Reydellet, in *Venance Fortunat: Poèmes.* 3 vols. Paris: Belles Lettres, 1994–2004.
———. *Vita Germani.* PL 88. Paris: J.-P. Migne, 1846.

Fredegar. *Chronicae.* Edited by Bruno Krusch, in MGH: Scriptores rerum Merovingicarum. Vol. 2. Hannover: Hahn, 1888.

Gaudentius of Brescia. *Tractatus.* Edited by Ambrosius Glück, in *S. Gaudentii episcopi brixiensis tractatus.* CSEL 68. Leipzig: Teubner, 1936.

Gelasius I of Rome. *Epistulae.* Edited by Andreas Thiel, in *Epistolae Romanorum pontificum genuinae.* Vol. 1. Braunsberg: E. Peter, 1867; Hildesheim: G. Olms, 1974.

Gennadius. *De viris illustribus.* Edited by Ernest Cushing Richardson, in *Hieronymus, Liber de viris inlustribus; Gennadius, Liber de viris inlustribus.* Leipzig: Hinrichs, 1896.

Gerontius. *The Life of Melania.*
>*Vita Graeca* [*VG*], edited and translated by Denys Gorce, in *Vie de sainte Mélanie.* SC 90. Paris: Le Cerf, 1962.
>*VG*, translated by Elizabeth A. Clark, in *The Life of Melania the Younger.* New York: Edwin Mellen, 1984.
>*Vita Latina* [*VL*] edited and translated by Patrick Laurence, in *Gérontius: La vie latine de sainte Mélanie.* Jerusalem: Franciscan Printing Press, 2002.

Gregory I of Rome. *Dialogues.*
>Edited and translated by Adalbert de Vogüé, in *Grégoire le Grand: Dialogues.* 3 vols. SC 251, 260, 265. Paris: Le Cerf, 1978–80.
>Translated by Odo John Zimmerman, in *St. Gregory the Great: Dialogues.* New York: Fathers of the Church, 1959.
———. *Letters.*
>Edited by Dag Norberg, in *S. Gregorii Magni Registrum epistularum.* 2 vols. CCSL 140, 140A. Turnhout: Brepols, 1982.
>Translated by John R. C. Martyn, in *The Letters of Gregory the Great.* 3 vols. Toronto: Pontifical Institute of Medieval Studies, 2004.

Gregory of Tours. *De gloria confessorum.*
>Edited by Bruno Krusch, in MGH: Scriptores rerum Merovingicarum. Vol. 1. Hannover: Hahn, 1885.
>Translated by Raymond Van Dam, in *Gregory of Tours: Glory of the Confessors.* Liverpool: Liverpool University Press, 1988.
———. *De gloria martyrum.*
>Edited by Bruno Krusch, in MGH: Scriptores rerum Merovingicarum. Vol. 1. Hannover: Hahn, 1885.

Gregory of Tours. *De gloria martyrum*.
> Translated by Raymond Van Dam, in *Gregory of Tours: Glory of the Martyrs*.
> Liverpool: Liverpool University Press, 1988.
———. *Histories*.
> Edited by Bruno Krusch and Wilhelm Levison, in *Libri historiarum X*. MGH:
> Scriptores rerum Merovingicarum. Vol. 1. 2nd ed. Hannover: Hahn,
> 1951.
> Translated by Lewis Thorpe, in *Gregory of Tours: The History of the Franks*.
> Harmondsworth: Penguin, 1974.
———. *De virtutibus sancti Martini*.
> Edited by Bruno Krusch, in MGH: Scriptores rerum Merovingicarum. Vol. 1.
> Hannover: Hahn, 1885.
> Translated by Raymond Van Dam, in *Saints and Their Miracles in Late Antique
> Gaul*. Princeton: Princeton University Press, 1993.
———. *De vita patrum*.
> Edited by Bruno Krusch, in MGH: Scriptores rerum Merovingicarum. Vol. 1.
> Hannover: Hahn, 1885.
> Translated by Edward James, in *Gregory of Tours: Life of the Fathers*. Liverpool:
> Liverpool University Press, 1985.
Hilary of Arles. *Vita Honorati*. Edited by Samuel Cavallin, in *Vitae Sanctorum Honorati
et Hilarii episcoporum Arelatensium*. Lund: Gleerup, 1952.
Honoratus of Marseille. *Vita Hilarii*. Edited by Samuel Cavallin. Translated by
Paul-André Jacob, in *La vie d'Hilaire d'Arles*. SC 404. Paris: Le Cerf, 1995.
Hydatius of Chaves. *Chronicle*. Edited and translated by R. W. Burgess, in *The Chronicle
of Hydatius and the Consularia Constantinopolitana*. Oxford: Clarendon Press,
1993.
Innocent I of Rome. *Letters*. PL 20. Paris: J.-P. Migne, 1845.
Inscripciones latinas de la España romana y visigóda. Edited by José Vives. 2 vols.
Barcelona: Consejo Superior de Investigaciones Científicas, 1969.
Inscriptiones Christianae Italiae. Vol. 1, *Volsinii: Regio VII*. Edited by Carlo Carletti.
Bari: Edipuglia, 1985.
Inscriptiones Latinae Christianae Veteres. Edited by Ernst Diehl. 3 vols. Zurich:
Weidmann, 1970.
Inscriptiones Christianae Urbis Romae Septimo Saeculo Antiquiores.
> Vol. 2, part 1. Edited by Giovanni Battista de Rossi. Rome: P. Cuggiani, 1888.
> New series, vol. 2, *Coemeteria in viis Cornelia Aurelia, Portuensi et Ostiensi*.
> Edited by Angelo Silvagni. Rome: Pontificio Istituto di Archeologia
> Cristiana, 1935.
> New series, vol. 4, *Coemeteria inter vias Appiam et Ardeatinam*. Edited by Antonio
> Ferrua. Vatican: Pontificio Istituto di Archeologia Cristiana, 1964.
> New series, vol. 5, *Coemeteria reliqua viae Appiae*. Edited by Antonio Ferrua.
> Vatican: Pontificio Istituto di Archeologia Cristiana, 1971.
> New series, vol. 6, *Coemeteria in viis Latina, Labicana et Praenestina*. Edited by
> Antonio Ferrua. Vatican: Pontificio Istituto di Archeologia Cristiana, 1975.

Inscriptiones Judaicae Orientis. Edited by Walter Ameling. 3 vols.

    Vol. 1, *Eastern Europe.* Edited by David Noy, Alexander Panayotov, and Hanswulf Bloedhorn. Texts and Studies in Ancient Judaism 101. Tübingen: Siebeck Mohr, 2002.

    Vol. 2, *Kleinasien.* Edited by Walter Ameling. Texts and Studies in Ancient Judaism 99. Tübingen: Siebeck Mohr, 2004.

    Vol. 3, *Syria and Cyprus.* Edited by David Noy and Hanswulf Bloedhorn. Texts and Studies in Ancient Judaism 102. Tübingen: Siebeck Mohr, 2004.

Inscriptiones Latinae Selectae. Edited by Hermann Dessau. 3 vols. Berlin: Weidmann, 1892–1916.

Inscriptions chrétiennes de la Gaule antérieures au VIIIe siècle. Edited by Edmond Le Blant. 2 vols. Paris: Imprimerie impériale, 1856–65.

The Inscriptions of Roman Tripolitania. Edited by J. M. Reynolds and J. B. Ward Perkins. London: British School at Rome, 1952.

Jerome. *Contra Vigilantium.* Edited by Jean-Louis Feiertag, in *S. Hieronymi presbyteri opera.* CCSL 79C. Turnhout: Brepols, 2005.

———. *Letters.* Edited by Isidore Hilberg, in *Sancti Eusebii Hieronymi Epistulae.* 4 vols. CSEL 54–56. Vienna: Österreichische Akademie der Wissenschaften, 1996.

———. *Opera.* PL 23–26. Paris: J.-P. Migne, 1844–45.

Pseudo-Jerome. *De septem ordinibus ecclesiae.* PL 30. Paris: J.-P. Migne, 1846.

John the Deacon. *Life of Gregory.* PL 75. Paris: J.-P. Migne, 1849.

John of Ephesus. *Ecclesiastical History.* Translated by R. Payne Smith, in *The Third Part of the Ecclesiastical History of John, Bishop of Ephesus.* Oxford: Oxford University Press, 1860.

———. *Lives of the Eastern Saints.* Edited and translated by E. W. Brooks. 3 vols. Patrologia Orientalis 17–19. Paris: Firmin-Didot, 1923–25.

John Rufus. *The Life of Peter the Iberian.* Edited and translated by Cornelia B. Horn and Robert R. Phenix, in *John Rufus: The Lives of Peter the Iberian, Theodosius of Jerusalem and the Monk Romanus.* Atlanta, GA: Society for Biblical Literature, 2008.

Julian of Eclanum. *Expositio libri Iob; Tractatus prophetarum Osee, Iohel et Amos; operum deperditorum fragmenta.* Edited by Lucas de Coninck. CCSL 88. Turnhout: Brepols, 1977.

Julianus Pomerius. *De vita contemplativa.* PL 59. Paris: J.-P. Migne, 1847.

Lactantius. *Divine Institutes.* Translated by Anthony Bowen and Peter Garnsey. Liverpool: Liverpool University Press, 2003.

Leo I of Rome. *Sermons.* Edited and translated by René Dolle, in *Léon le Grand: Sermons.* 4 vols. SC 22, 49, 74, 200. Paris: Le Cerf, 1947–73.

Liber Pontificalis.

    Biographies from A.D. 311 to 535, edited by Herman Geertman, in *Atti del colloquio internazionale* Il Liber Pontificalis e la storia materiale. Medelingen van het Nederlands Instituut te Rome: Antiquity 60–61. Assen: Van Gorcum, 2003.

Liber Pontificalis.
> Edited by Louis Duchesne, in *Le Liber Pontificalis: Texte, Introduction et Commentaire.* Bibliothèque de l'École française de Rome. 3 vols. Paris: Boccard, 1955–57.
> Translated by Raymond Davis, in *The Book of Pontiffs (Liber Pontificalis): The Ancient Biographies of the First Ninety Roman Bishops to AD 715.* Liverpool: Liverpool University Press, 1989.

Pseudo-Martyrius of Antioch. *Vita Iohannis Chrysostomi.* Edited by Martin Wallraff and Cristina Ricci, in *Oratio funebris in laudem sancti Iohannis Chrysostomi: Epitaffio attribuito a Martirio di Antiochia.* Spoleto: Centro Italiano di Studi sull'Alto Medioevo, 2007.

Naucellius. *Poems.* Edited by Franco Munari, in *Epigrammata Bobiensia.* Rome: Edizioni di storia e letteratura, 1955.

New Documents Illustrating Early Christianity. Edited by G.H.R. Horsley. Vol. 2. Sydney, NSW: Ancient History Documentary Research Centre, 1982.

Novellae. [See *Codex Theodosianus.*]

Olympiodorus. *History.* In *The Fragmentary Classicising Historians of the Later Roman Empire: Eunapius, Olympiodorus, Priscus and Malchus.* Vol. 2. Edited and translated by Roger C. Blockley. Liverpool: Francis Cairns, 1983.

Optatus of Milevis. *De schismate donatistarum.*
> Edited by Karl Ziwsa, in *S. Optati Milevitani libri VII.* CSEL 26. Vienna: Tempsky, 1893.
> Translated by Mark Edwards, in *Optatus: Against the Donatists.* Liverpool: Liverpool University Press, 1997.

Pacianus of Barcelona. *Sermo de Paenitentibus.* In *Pacien de Barcélone: Écrits.* Edited and translated by Carmelo Grandao. SC 410. Paris: Le Cerf, 1995.

Palladius of Ratiaria. *Apologia.* Edited and translated by Roger Gryson, in *Scholies ariennes sur le concile d'Aquilée.* SC 267. Paris: Le Cerf, 1980.

Pap. Ital. Die nichtliterarischen Papyri Italiens aus der Zeit 445–700. Edited and translated by Jan Olof Tjäder. 3 vols. Skrifter utgivna av Svenska Institutet i Rom 4.19. Lund: Gleerup, 1954–82.

Pardessus, Jean Marie, ed. *Diplomata, cartae, epistolae, leges aliaque instrumenta ad res Gallo-Francicas spectantia.* 2 vols. Reprint, Aalen: Scientia Verlag, 1969.

Passio Marculi. Edited and translated by Jean-Louis Maier, in *Le dossier du donatisme.* Vol. 1, *Des origines à la mort de Constance II (303–361).* Texte und Untersuchungen 79. Berlin: Akademie Verlag, 1987.
> Translated by Maureen A. Tilley, in *Donatist Martyr Stories: The Church in Conflict in Roman North Africa.* Liverpool: Liverpool University Press, 1996.

Patricius. *Letter to Coroticus.* Edited and translated by A.B.E. Hood, in *St. Patrick: His Writings and Muirchu's Life.* Chichester: Phillimore, 1978.

Paulinus of Milan. *Vita Ambrosii.*
> Edited and translated by Michele Pellegrino, in *Vita di S. Ambrogio.* Verba Seniorum n.s. 1. Rome: Studium, 1961.
> Translated by F. R. Hoare, in *The Western Fathers.* New York: Harper and Row, 1954.

Paulinus of Nola. *Letters.*
> Edited by Wilhelm von Hartel, in *Sancti Pontii Meropii Paulini Nolani Epistulae.* CSEL 29. Vienna: Tempsky, 1894.
> Edited and translated by Mattias Skeb, in *Paulinus von Nola: Briefe/Epistulae.* 3 vols. Fontes Christianae 25/1–3. Freiburg: Herder, 1998.
> Translated by P. G. Walsh, in *Letters of St. Paulinus of Nola.* 2 vols. Ancient Christian Writers 35–36. New York: Newman Press, 1966–67.
———. *Poems.*
> Edited by Wilhelm von Hartel, in *Sancti Pontii Meropii Paulini Nolani Carmina.* CSEL 30. Vienna: Tempsky, 1894.
> Translated by P. G. Walsh, in *The Poems of St. Paulinus of Nola.* Ancient Christian Writers 40. New York: Newman Press, 1975.
Paulinus of Pella. *Eucharisticos.*
> Edited and translated by Hugh G. Evelyn White, in *Ausonius.* Vol. 2. Loeb Classical Library. Cambridge, MA: Harvard University Press, 1949.
> Edited and translated by Claude Moussy, in *Paulin de Pella: Poème d'action de grâces et Prière.* SC 209. Paris: Le Cerf, 1974.
Pelagius. *Commentaries on the Epistles of Saint Paul.*
> Edited by Hermann Josef Frede, in *Ein neuer Paulustext und Kommentar.* 2 vols. Freiburg: Herder, 1973–74.
> *Commentary on Romans,* translated by Theodore de Bruyn, in *Pelagius' Commentary on St. Paul's Epistle to the Romans.* Oxford: Clarendon, 1993.
———. *Letter to Demetrias.*
> PL 30. Paris: J.-P. Migne, 1846.
> Translated by B. R. Rees, in *The Letters of Pelagius and His Followers.* Woodbridge, UK: Boydell, 1991.
Pelagius I of Rome. *Letters.* Edited by P. M. Gassó and C. M. Batlle, in *Pelagii I papae: Epistulae quae supersunt (556–561).* Montserrat: Abbey of Montserrat, 1956.
Petrus Chrysologus. *Sermons.* Edited by Alexandre Oliver, in *Sancti Petri Chrysologi Collectio sermonum.* 2 vols. CCSL 24, 24B. Turnhout: Brepols, 1975–82.
Plotinus. *Enneads.* Edited and translated by A. H. Armstrong, in *Plotinus.* 7 vols. Loeb Classical Library. Cambridge, MA: Harvard University Press, 1966–88.
> Translated by Stephen MacKenna, in *Plotinus: The Enneads.* Burdett, NY: Larson, 1992.
Porphyry. *Life of Plotinus.*
> Edited and translated by A. H. Armstrong, in *Plotinus.* 7 vols. Loeb Classical Library. Cambridge, MA: Cambridge University Press, 1966–68.
> Translated by Stephen McKenna, in *Plotinus: The Enneads.* Burdett, NY: Larson, 1992.
Possidius. *Vita Augustini.*
> PL 32. Paris: J.-P. Migne, 1845.
> Translated by F. R. Hoare, in *The Western Fathers.* New York: Harper and Row, 1954.

Proba, Faltonia Betitia. *Cento*. Edited and translated by Elizabeth A. Clark and Diane F. Hatch, in *The Golden Bough, the Oaken Cross: The Vergilian Cento of Faltonia Betitia Proba*. American Academy of Religion: Texts and Translations 5. Chico, CA: Scholars Press, 1981.

Prosper of Aquitaine. *Chronicle*.
    Edited by Theodor Mommsen, in vol. 1 of *Chronica Minora, saec. IV. V. VI. VII*. MGH: Auctores Antiquissimi, vol. 9. Berlin: Weidmann, 1892.
    Excerpts translated by Alexander Callander Murray, in *From Roman to Merovingian Gaul: A Reader*. Peterborough, Ontario: Broadview Press, 2000.
———. *Contra Collatorem*.
    Printed in PL 51. Paris: J.-P. Migne, 1846.
    Translated by J. Reginald O'Donnell, in *Prosper of Aquitaine: Grace and Free Will*. Fathers of the Church 7. New York: Fathers of the Church, 1949.
———. *Pro Augustino responsiones ad capitula Gallorum*. PL 51. Paris: J.-P. Migne, 1846.
———. *Pro Augustino responsiones ad excerpta Genuensium*. PL 51. Paris: J.-P. Migne, 1846.
———. *Psalmorum C ad CL Expositio*. PL 51. Paris: J.-P. Migne, 1846.
———. *De vera humilitate*. Edited and translated by M. Kathryn Clare Krabbe, in *Epistula ad Demetriadem de vera humilitate*. Catholic University of America Publications 97. Washington DC: Catholic University of America Press, 1956.
———. *De vocatione omnium gentium*. PL 51. Paris: J.-P. Migne, 1846.

Querolus (Aulularia). Comédie latine anonyme: Le Grincheux.
    Edited and translated by Catherine Jacquemard-Le Saos. Paris: Belles Lettres, 2003.

Recueil des inscriptions chrétiennes de la Gaule. Published under the direction of Henri Irénée Marrou.
    Vol. 8, *Aquitanie première*. Edited by Françoise Prévot. Paris: CNRS, 1991.
    Vol. 15, *Viennoise du Nord*. Edited by Françoise Descombes. Paris: CNRS, 1975.

Regula cuiusdam ad virgines. PL 88. Paris: J.-P. Migne, 1850.

Regula Macarii.
    Edited and translated by Salvatore Pricoco, in *La Regola di San Benedetto e le Regole dei Padri*. Verona: Mondadori, 1995.
    Edited and translated by Adalbert de Vogüé, in *Les règles des saints pères*. Vol. 1. SC 297. Paris: Le Cerf, 1982.

Regula quattuor patrum.
    Edited and translated by Salvatore Pricoco, in *La Regola di San Benedetto e le Regole dei Padri*. Verona: Mondadori, 1995.
    Edited and translated by Adalbert de Vogüé, in *Les règles des saints pères*. Vol. 1. SC 297. Paris: Le Cerf, 1982.

Repertorium der christlich-antiken Sarkophage. Edited by Friedrich Wilhelm Deichmann. Vol. 3, *Frankreich, Algerien, Tunesien*. Edited by Brigitte Christern-Briesenick. Mainz: P. Zabern, 2003.

Rufinus of Aquileia. *Apologia contra Hieronymum*. Edited by Manlio Simonetti, in *Opera*. CCSL 20. Turnhout: Brepols, 1961.

————. *Prologus in Omelias Origenis in Numeros*. Edited by Manlio Simonetti, in *Opera*. CCSL 20. Turnhout: Brepols, 1961.

Rutilius Namatianus, Claudius. *De reditu suo*. Edited by Charles Haines Keene and translated by George F. Savage-Armstrong, in *Rutilii Claudii Namatiani De reditu suo libri duo / The Home-Coming of Rutilius Claudius Namatianus from Rome to Gaul in the Year 416 A.D.* London: George Bell and Sons, 1907.

Salvian of Marseilles. *Ad Ecclesiam*.
    Edited and translated by Georges Lagarrigue, in *Salvien de Marseille: Oeuvres*.
        Vol. 1, *Les lettres, les livres de Timothée à l'Église*. SC 176. Paris: Le Cerf, 1971.
    Translated by Jeremiah F. O'Sullivan, in *The Writings of Salvian, the Presbyter*.
        Fathers of the Church 3. New York: CIMA, 1947.

————. *De gubernatione Dei*.
    Edited and translated by Georges Lagarrigue, in *Salvien de Marseille: Oeuvres*.
        Vol. 2, *Du gouvernement de Dieu*. SC 220. Paris: Le Cerf, 1975.
    Translated by Eva M. Sanford, in *On the Government of God*. Columbia Records
        of Civilization. New York: Columbia University Press, 1930.
    Translated by Jeremiah F. O'Sullivan, in *The Writings of Salvian, the Presbyter*.
        Fathers of the Church 3. New York: CIMA, 1947.

————. *Letters*.
    Edited and translated by Georges Lagarrigue, in *Salvien de Marseille: Oeuvres*.
        Vol. 1, *Les lettres, les livres de Timothée à l'Église*. SC 176. Paris: Le Cerf, 1971.
    Translated by Jeremiah F. O'Sullivan, in *The Writings of Salvian, the Presbyter*.
        Fathers of the Church 3. New York: CIMA, 1947.

Severus, Sulpicius. *Chronica*. Edited and translated by Ghislaine de Senneville-Grave, in *Sulpice Sévère: Chroniques*. SC 441. Paris: Le Cerf, 1999.

————. *Dialogues*. Edited and translated by Jacques Fontaine, in *Gallus: Dialogues sur les "vertus" de saint Martin*. SC 510. Paris: Le Cerf, 2006.

————. *Life of Martin*.
    Edited and translated by Jacques Fontaine, in *Sulpice Sévère: Vie de Saint Martin. Introduction, texte et traduction*. 3 vols. SC 133–35. Paris: Le Cerf, 1967–69.
    Translated by F. R. Hoare, in *The Western Fathers*. New York: Harper and Row, 1954.

Sidonius Apollinaris. *Letters*. Edited and translated by W. B. Anderson, in *Sidonius: Poems and Letters*. 2 vols. Loeb Classical Library. Cambridge, MA: Harvard University Press, 1965.

————. *Poems*. Edited and translated by W. B. Anderson, in *Sidonius: Poems and Letters*. 2 vols. Loeb Classical Library. Cambridge, MA: Harvard University Press, 1965.

Simplicius of Rome. *Epistulae*. Edited by Andreas Thiel, in *Epistolae Romanorum pontificum genuinae*. Vol. 1. Braunsberg: E. Peter, 1867; Hildesheim: G. Olms, 1974.

Siricius of Rome. *Letters*. PL 13. Paris: J.-P. Migne, 1845.

The Story of Apollonius King of Tyre. Translated by Gerald N. Sandy. In *Collected Ancient Greek Novels*. Edited by B. P. Reardon. Berkeley: University of California Press, 1989.

Symmachus. *Letters*. Edited and translated by Jean Pierre Callu, in *Symmaque: Lettres*. 4 vols. Paris: Belles Lettres, 1972–2002.

———. *The Letters of Symmachus*. Book 1. Edited and translated by Michale Renee Salzmann and Michael Roberts. *Writings from the Greco-Roman World* 30. Atlanta, Ga.: Society of Biblical Literature, 2011.

———. *Orationes*. Edited and translated by Jean-Pierre Callu, in *Symmaque: Discours, rapports*. Paris: Belles Lettres, 2009.

———. *Relationes*.

 Edited and translated by Jean-Pierre Callu, in *Symmaque: Discours, rapports*. Paris: Belles Lettres, 2009.

 Edited and translated by R. H. Barrow, in *Prefect and Emperor: The Relationes of Symmachus, A.D. 384*. Oxford: Clarendon Press, 1973.

Symmachus, Pope. *Epistulae*. Edited by Andreas Thiel, in *Epistolae Romanorum pontificum genuinae*. Vol. 1. Braunsberg: E. Peter, 1867; Hildesheim: G. Olms, 1974.

Le Talmud de Jérusalem. Translated by Moïse Schwab. Paris: Maisonneuve, 1932–33.

Uranius. *De obitu Paulini*.

 PL 53. Paris: J.-P. Migne, 1847.

 Translated by Dennis Trout, in *Paulinus of Nola: Life, Letters, and Poems*. Berkeley: University of California Press, 1999.

Valerianus of Cimiez. *Homilies*. PL 52. Paris: J.-P. Migne, 1845.

Veranus. *Sententia de castitate sacerdotum*. PL 72. Paris: J.-P. Migne, 1849.

Vindicianus. *Letter to the Emperor Valentinian*. Edited by Max Niedermann, in *De medicamentis/Über Heilmittel*. Vol. 1. Corpus Medicorum Latinorum 5. Berlin: Akademie, 1968.

De vita christiana.

 PL 50. Paris: J.-P. Migne, 1846.

 Translated by B. R. Rees, in *The Letters of Pelagius and His Followers*. Woodbridge, UK: Boydell, 1998.

Vitae patrum Emeritensium. Edited by Joseph N. Garvin, in *The Vitas sanctorum patrum Emeritensium*. Washington, DC: Catholic University of America Press, 1946.

Zosimus. *Historia nova*.

 Edited by Ludwig Mendelssohn, in *Zosimi comitis et exadvocati fisci Historia nova*. Leipzig: Teubner, 1887.

 Translated by Ronald T. Ridley, in *Zosimus: New History*. Canberra: American Association of Byzantine Studies, 1982.

SECONDARY SOURCES

Aarjava, Antti. *Women and Law in Late Antiquity*. Oxford: Clarendon, 1996.

Adkin, Neil. *Jerome on Virginity: A Commentary on the* Libellus de virginitate servanda *(Letter 22)*. ARCA 42. Liverpool: Francis Cairns, 2003.

Age of Spirituality: Late Antique and Early Christian Art, Third to Seventh Century. Catalogue of the exhibition at the Metropolitan Museum of Art, November 19,

1977, through February 12, 1978. Edited by Kurt Weitzmann. New York: Metropolitian Museum of Art, New York 1988.

Albana, Mela. "Archiatri ... honeste obsequi tenuioribus malint quam turpiter servire divitibus (CTH 13,3,8)." In *Poveri ammalati e ammalati poveri: Dinamiche socio-economiche, trasformazioni culturali e misure assistenziali nell'Occidente romano in età tardoantica*, 253–79. Edited by Rosalia Marino, Concetta Molè, and Antonino Pinzone, with the collaboration of Margherita Cassia. Catania: Edizioni del Prisma, 2006.

Alciati, Roberto. *Monaci, vescovi e scuola nella Gallia tardoantica*. Temi e Testi 72. Rome: Edizioni di Storia e Letteratura, 2009.

Alciati, Roberto, and Maria Chiara Giorda. "Possessions and Asceticism: Melania the Younger and Her Slow Way to Jerusalem." *Zeitschrift für Antikes Christentum* 14 (2010): 425–44.

Alföldy, Géza. *The Social History of Rome*. London: Croom Helm, 1985.

Algazi, Gadi. "Introduction: Doing Things with Gifts." In *Negotiating the Gift: Pre-Modern Figurations of Exchange*, 9–27. Edited by Gadi Algazi, Valentin Groebner, and Bernhard Jussen. Göttingen: Vandenhoeck and Ruprecht, 2003.

Almeida, Maria José de, and António Carvalho. "Villa romana da Quinta das Longas (Elvas, Portugal): A lixeira baixo-imperial." *Revista Portuguesa de Arqueologia* 8 (2005): 299–368.

Alvar, Jaime. *Romanising Oriental Gods: Myth, Salvation and Ethics in the Cults of Cybele, Isis and Mithras*. Translated and edited by Richard Gordon. Religions of the Greco-Roman World 165. Leiden: Brill, 2008.

Amory, Patrick. "The Textual Transmission of the Donatio Ansemundi." *Francia* 20 (1993): 163–83.

Anchora vitae: Atti del II Convegno Paoliniano nel XVI Centenario del Ritiro di Paolino a Nola. Edited by Gennaro Luongo. Naples: Redenzione, 1998.

Anderson, Gary A. "Redeem Your Soul by the Giving of Alms: Sin, Debt and the 'Treasury of Merit' in Early Jewish and Christian Tradition." *Letter and Spirit* 3 (2007): 36–69.

———. Sin: A History. New Haven, CT: Yale University Press, 2009.

Ando, Clifford. *Imperial Ideology and Provincial Loyalty in the Roman Empire*. Berkeley: University of California Press, 2000.

———. *The Matter of the Gods: Religion and the Roman Empire*. Berkeley: University of California Press, 2008.

Angenendt, Arnold. "*Donationes pro anima*: Gift and Countergift in the Early Medieval Liturgy." In *The Long Morning of Medieval Europe: New Directions in Early Medieval Studies*, 131–54. Edited by Jennifer R. Davis and Michael McCormick. Aldershot: Ashgate, 2008.

L'Année épigraphique.

1928. Edited by René Cagnat and Maurice Besnier. Paris: CNRS.

1990. Edited by André Chastagnol, André Laronde, Marcel Le Glay, and Patrick Le Roux. Paris: CNRS.

Arce, Javier. *Bárbaros y romanos en Hispania (400–507 A.D.)*. Madrid: Marcial Pons, 2005.

Arce, Javier, Alexandra Chavarría, and Gisela Ripoll. "The Urban Domus in Late Antique Hispania: Examples from Emerita, Barcino and Complutum." In *Housing in Late Antiquity: From Palaces to Shops*, 305–36. Edited by Luke Lavan, Lale Özgenel, and Alexander Sarantis. Late Antique Archaeology 3.2. Leiden: Brill, 2007.

Archeologia urbana a Ravenna: La Domus dei tapetti di pietro, il complesso archeologico di via D'Azeglio. Edited by Giovanna Montevecchi. Ravenna: Longo, 2004.

Arena, Gaetano. "Il 'potere di guarire': L'attività medica fra politica e cultura nella tarda antichità." In *Poveri ammalati e ammalati poveri: Dinamiche socio-economiche, trasformazioni culturali e misure assistenziali nell'Occidente romano in età tardoantica*, 387–424. Edited by Rosalia Marino, Concetta Molè, and Antonino Pinzone, with the collaboration of Margherita Cassia. Catania: Edizioni del Prisma, 2006.

Armitage, Mark J. *A Twofold Solidarity: Leo the Great's Theology of Redemption.* Strathfield, NSW: St. Paul's Publications, 2005.

Arnaud, José Marais, and Carla Verela Fernandes. *Construindo a memória: As colecções do Museu Arqueológico do Carmo.* Lisbon: Museu Arqueológico do Carmo, 2005.

Arthur, Paul. "From Vicus to Village: Italian Landscapes, AD 400–1000." In *Landscapes of Change: Rural Evolutions in Late Antiquity and the Early Middle Ages*, 103–33. Edited by Neil Christie. Aldershot: Ashgate, 2004.

———. *Romans in Northern Campania: Settlement and Land-Use around the Massico and the Garigliano Basin.* Archaeological Monographs of the British School at Rome 1. London: British School at Rome, 1991.

Atti del colloquio internazionale. Il Liber Pontificalis e la storia materiale. Edited by Herman Geertman. Medelingen van het Nederlands Instituut te Rome: Antiquity 60–61. Assen: Van Gorcum, 2003.

Augustine through the Ages: An Encyclopedia. Edited by Allan D. Fitzgerald. Grand Rapids, MI: Eerdmans, 1999.

Augustinus-Lexikon. Edited by Cornelius Mayer. Basel: Schwabe, 1986.

Aurea Roma: Dalla città pagana alla città cristiana. Edited by Serena Ensoli and Eugenio La Rocca. Rome: Bretschneider, 2000.

Ausone et Paulin de Nole: Correspondance. Edited by David Amherdt. Sapheneia 9. Bern: Peter Lang, 2004.

Bachrach, Bernard S. "The Fortification of Gaul and the Economy of the Third and Fourth Centuries." *Journal of Late Antiquity* 3 (2010): 38–64.

Badel, Christophe. *La noblesse de l'empire romain: Les masques et la vertu.* Seyssel: Champ Vallon, 2005.

Badewien, Jan. *Geschichtstheologie und Sozialkritik im Werk Salvians von Marseille.* Forschungen zur Kirchen- und Dogmengeschichte 32. Göttingen: Vandenhouck and Ruprecht, 1980.

Bailey, Lisa Kaaren. "Building Urban Christian Communities: Sermons on Local Saints in the Eusebius Gallicanus Collection." *Early Medieval Europe* 12 (2003): 1–24.

———. *Christianity's Quiet Success: The Eusebius Gallicanus Sermon Collection and the Power of the Church in Late Antique Gaul.* Notre Dame, IN: University of Notre Dame Press, 2010.

Bakhtin, Mikhail M. *Rabelais and His World*. Translated by Helene Iswolsky. Cambridge, MA: MIT Press, 1968.

Baldini Lippolis, Isabella. *La domus tardoantica: Forme e rappresentazioni dello spazio domestico nelle città del Mediterraneo*. Imola: University Press of Bologna, 2001.

Balmelle, Catherine. *Les demeures aristocratiques d'Aquitaine: Société et culture de l'Antiquité tardive dans le Sud-Ouest de la Gaule*. Bordeaux and Paris: Ausonius and Aquitania, 2001.

———. "Le répertoire végétal des mosaïstes du Sud-Ouest de la Gaule et des sculpteurs des sarcophages dits d'Aquitaine." *Antiquité tardive* 1 (1993): 101–7.

Balmelle, Catherine, A. Ben Abed-Ben Khader, A. Bourgeois, Cl. Brenot, H. Broise, J.-P. Darmon, M. Ennaïfer, and M.-P. Raynaud. "Vitalité de l'architecture domestique à Carthage au Ve siècle: L'exemple de la maison dite de la Rotonde, sur la colline de l'Odéon." *Antiquité tardive* 11 (2003): 151–66.

Banaji, Jairus. *Agrarian Change in Late Antiquity: Gold, Labour, and Aristocratic Dominance*. 2001. Reprint, Oxford: Oxford University Press, 2007.

———. "Aristocracies, Peasantries and the Framing of the Early Middle Ages." *Journal of Agrarian Change* 9 (2009): 59–91.

———. "Lavoratori liberi e residenza coatta: Il colonato romano in prospettiva storica." In *Terre, proprietari e contadini dell'impero romano: Dall'affitto agrario al colonato tardoantico*, 253–80. Edited by Elio Lo Cascio. Rome: Nuova Italia Scientifica, 1997.

Barbier, Josianne. "Testaments et pratique testamentaire dans le royaume franc (VIe–VIIIe siècles)." In *Sauver son âme et se perpétuer: Transmission du patrimoine et mémoire au haut Moyen Âge*, 7–79. Edited by François Bougard, Cristina La Rocca, and Régine Le Jan. Collection de l'École française de Rome 351. Rome: École française de Rome, 2005.

Barcellona, Rossana. *Fausto di Riez, interprete del suo tempo: Un vescovo tardoantico dentro la crisi dell'impero*. Soveria Manelli: Rubettino, 2006.

Barceló, Pedro. *Constantius II. und seine Zeit: Die Anfänge des Staatskirchentums*. Stuttgart: Klett-Cotta, 2004.

Barnes, Timothy D. *Ammianus Marcellinus and the Representation of Historical Reality*. Ithaca, NY: Cornell University Press, 1998.

———. *Athanasius and Constantius: Theology and Politics in the Constantinian Empire*. Cambridge, MA: Harvard University Press, 1993.

———. *Constantine: Dynasty, Religion and Power in the Later Roman Empire*. Oxford: Wiley-Blackwell, 2011.

———. *Constantine and Eusebius*. Cambridge, MA: Harvard University Press, 1981.

———. "Statistics and the Conversion of the Roman Aristocracy." *Journal of Roman Studies* 85 (1995): 135–47.

———. "Was There a Constantinian Revolution?" *Journal of Late Antiquity* 2 (2009): 374–84.

Barnish, S.J.B. "Pigs, Plebeians and *Potentes*: Rome's Economic Hinterland, c. 350–600 A.D." *Papers of the British School at Rome* 55 (1987): 157–85.

———. "*Religio in stagno*: Nature, Divinity and the Christianization of the Countryside in Late Antique Italy." *Journal of Early Christian Studies* 9 (2001): 387–402.

Barnish, S.J.B. "Transformation and Survival in the Western Senatorial Aristocracy, c. A.D. 400–700." *Papers of the British School at Rome* 66 (1988): 120–55.

———. "The Wealth of Julianus Argentarius: Late Antique Banking and the Mediterranean Economy." *Byzantion* 55 (1985): 5–38.

Baslez, Marie-Françoise. *Comment notre monde est devenu chrétien.* Tours: Éditions CLD, 2008.

Baumann, Peter. *Spätantike Stifter im Heiligen Land: Darstellungen und Inschriften auf Bodenmosaik in Kirchen, Synagogen und Privathäusern.* Wiesbaden: Reichert, 1999.

Baumgart, Susanne. *Die Bischofsherrschaft im Gallien des 5. Jahrhunderts: Eine Untersuchung zu den Gründen und Anfängen weltlicher Herrschaft der Kirche.* Münchener Arbeiten zur Alten Geschichte 8. Munich: Editio Maris, 1995.

Baus, Karl. *Das Gebet zu Christus beim hl. Ambrosius.* Edited by Ernst Dassmann. Berlin: Philo, 2000.

Bavel, Tarsicius J. van. "'Ante omnia' et 'in Deum' dans la 'Regula Sancti Augustini.'" *Vigiliae Christianae* 12 (1958): 157–65.

Baynes, Norman Hepburn. *Constantine the Great and the Christian Church.* 2nd ed. Preface by Henry Chadwick. London: Oxford University Press for the British Academy, 1972.

Beaucamp, Joëlle. "Le testament de Grégoire de Nazianze." In *Fontes Minores* 10. Edited by Ludwig Burgmann. Forschungen zur byzantinischen Rechtsgeschichte. Frankfurt: Löwenklau, 1998.

Beaujard, Brigitte. "La topographie chrétienne des cités de la Gaule: Bilan et perspectives." In *Le problème de la christianisation du monde antique,* 203–18. Edited by Hervé Inglebert, Sylvain Destephen, and Bruno Dumézil. Paris: Picard, 2010.

BeDuhn, Jason David. "Augustine Accused: Megalius, Manichaeism and the Inception of the *Confessions.*" *Journal of Early Christian Studies* 17 (2009): 85–124.

———. *Augustine's Manichaean Dilemma.* Vol. 1, *Conversion and Apostasy, 373–388 C.E.* Philadelphia: University of Pennsylvania Press, 2010.

———. *The Manichaean Body: In Discipline and Ritual.* Baltimore: Johns Hopkins University Press, 2000.

Behlmer, Heike. *Schenute von Atripe: De Iudicio (Torino, Museo Egizio: Catalogo 63000 Cod. IV).* Turin: Museo Egizio, 1996.

Bek, Lise. "*Quaestiones conviviales*: The Idea of the Triclinium and the Staging of Convivial Ceremony from Rome to Byzantium." *Analecta Romana Instituti Danici* 12 (1983): 81–107.

Belayche, Nicole. "Des lieux pour le 'profane' dans l'empire tardo-antique? Les fêtes entre *koinônia* sociale et espaces de rivalités religieuses." *Antiquité tardive* 15 (2007): 35–46.

Bellomo, Barbara. "Abusi nell'economia di carità." In *Poveri ammalati e ammalati poveri: Dinamiche socio-economiche, trasformazioni culturali e misure assistenziali nell'Occidente romano in età tardoantica,* 449–63. Edited by Rosalia Marino, Concetta Molè, and Antonino Pinzone, with the collaboration of Margherita Cassia. Catania: Edizioni del Prisma, 2006.

Benoit, Fernand. "La crypte en triconque de Théopolis." *Rivista di archeologia cristiana* 27 (1951): 69–89.

Bergmann, Marianne. *Chiragan, Aphrodisias, Konstantinopel: Zur mythologischen Skulptur der Spätantike.* Deutsches Archäologisches Institut, Rom: Palilia 7. Wiesbaden: Reichert, 1999.

Bernardini, Paolo. *Un solo battesimo, una sola chiesa: Il concilio di Cartagine del settembre 256.* Bologna: Mulino, 2009.

Berrouard, Marie-François. "Un tournant dans la vie de l'église d'Afrique: Les deux missions d'Alypius en Italie à la lumière des *Lettres* 10*, 15*, 16*, 22* et 23A." *Revue des études augustiniennes* 31 (1985): 46–70.

Berthier, André. *La Numidie: Rome et le Maghreb.* Paris: Picard, 1981.

——. *Les vestiges du christianisme antique dans la Numidie centrale.* Algiers: Maison-Carrée, 1942.

Bertolino, Alessandro. "'In area Callisti': Contributo alla topografia di Roma tardoantica." *Rivista di archeoloigia cristiana* 70 (1994): 181–90.

Bickerman, Elias. *Four Strange Books of the Bible.* New York: Schocken, 1967.

Blackhurst, Andy. "The House of Nubel: Rebels or Players?" In *Vandals, Romans and Berbers: New Perspectives on Late Antique Africa,* 59–76. Edited by Andrew H. Merrills. Aldershot: Ashgate, 2004.

Blair-Dixon, Kate. "Memory and Authority in Sixth-Century Rome: *The Liber Pontificalis* and the *Collectio Avellana.*" In *Religion, Dynasty and Patronage in Early Christian Rome, 300–900,* 59–76. Edited by Kate Cooper and Julia Hillner. Cambridge: Cambridge University Press, 2007.

Bland, Roger, and Catherine Johns. *The Hoxne Treasure: An Illustrated Introduction.* London: British Museum Press, 1993.

Blázquez, José María. *Mosaicos romanos de Córdoba, Jaén y Málaga.* Corpus de mosaicos de España 3. Madrid: CSIC, 1981.

Bloch, Maurice, and Jonathan Parry. Introduction to *Money and the Morality of Exchange,* 1–32. Edited by Jonathan Parry and Maurice Bloch. Cambridge: Cambridge University Press, 1989.

Bodel, John. "From *Columbaria* to Catacombs: Collective Burial in Pagan and Christian Rome." In *Commemorating the Dead: Texts and Artifacts in Context. Studies of Roman, Jewish, and Christian Burials,* 177–242. Edited by Laurie Brink and Deborah Green. Berlin: de Gruyter, 2008.

——. "Monumental Villas and Villa Monuments." *Journal of Roman Archaeology* 10 (1997): 3–35.

Bonamente, Giorgio. "Chiesa e impero nel IV secolo: Constanzo II fra il 357 e il 361." In *La comunità cristiana di Roma: La sua vita e la sua cultura dalle origini all'alto medioevo,* 113–38. Edited by Letizia Pani Ermini and Paolo Siniscalco. Vatican City: Pontificio Istituto di Archeologia Cristiana, 2000.

Bonneau, Danielle. *La crue du Nil, divinité égyptienne, à travers mille ans d'histoire (322 av.–641 ap. J.-C.).* Paris: Klincksieck, 1964.

Borg, Barbara, and Christian Witschel. "Veränderungen im Repräsentationsverhalten der römischen Eliten während des 3. Jhrdts n. Chr." In *Inschriftliche Denkmäler als*

Medien der Selbstdarstellung in der römischen Welt, 47–120. Edited by Geza Alföldy and Silvio Panciera. Stuttgart: F. Steiner, 2001.

Borgolte, Michael. "*Felix est homo ille qui amicos bonos relinquit*: Zur sozialen Gestaltungskraft letzwilliger Verfügungen am Beispiel Bischofs Bertrams von le Mans (616)." In *Festschrift für Berent Schwineköper*, 5–18. Edited by Helmut Maurer and Hans Patze. Sigmaringen: J. Thorbecke, 1982.

Bori, Pier Cesare. *Chiesa primitiva: L'imaggine della communità delle origini—Atti 2, 42–47; 4, 32–37—nella storia della chiesa antica*. Brescia: Paideia, 1974.

Borodin, O. R. "Ekonomicheskie protivorechiia v srede ravennskovo dukhenstva v VI–VIII vv." *Vizantiskĭ vremennik* 56 (81) (1995): 32–44.

Boudartchouk, Jean-Luc. "Production et diffusion des sarcophages romains tardifs et mérovingiens dans la région de Lourdes (Hautes Pyrénées)." *Gallia* 59 (2002): 53–60.

Bourgeois, Luc. "Les résidences des élites et les fortifications du Haut Moyen-Âge en France et en Belgique dans leur cadre européen: Aperçu historiographique (1955–2005)." *Cahiers de civilisation médiévale* 49 (2006): 113–42.

Bowersock, Glen W. "From Emperor to Bishop: The Self-Conscious Transformation of Political Power in the Fourth Century A.D." *Classical Philology* 81 (1986): 298–307. Reprinted in *Selected Papers on Late Antiquity*.

———. "Peter and Constantine." In *St. Peter's in the Vatican*, 5–15. Edited by William Tronzo. Cambridge: Cambridge University Press, 2005.

———. *Selected Papers on Late Antiquity*. Bari: Edipuglia, 2000.

———. "Symmachus and Ausonius." In *Colloque genèvois sur Symmaque*, 1–15. Edited by François Paschoud. Paris: Belles Lettres, 1986. Reprinted in *Selected Papers on Late Antiquity*.

Bowes, Kimberly. "Building Sacred Landscapes: Villas and Cult." In *Villas Tardoantiguas en el Mediterráneo Occidental*, 73–95. Edited by Alexandra Chavarria, Javier Arce, and Gian Pietro Brogiolo. Anejos de Archivo Español de Arqueología 39. Madrid: Consejo Superior de Investigaciones Científicas, 2006.

———. "'Une coterie espagnole pieuse': Christian Archaeology and Christian Communities in Theodosian Hispania." In *Hispania in Late Antiquity: Current Perspectives*, 189–258. Edited by Kim Bowes and Michael Kulikowski. Leiden: Brill, 2005.

———. *Houses and Society in the Later Roman Empire*. London: Duckworth, 2010.

———. *Private Worship, Public Values, and Religious Change in Late Antiquity*. Cambridge: Cambridge University Press, 2008.

Bowes, Kimberly, and Adam Gutteridge. "Rethinking the Later Roman Landscape." *Journal of Roman Archaeology* 18 (2005): 405–13.

Brandenburg, Hugo. "Das Baptisterium und der Brunnen des Atriums von Alt-St.Peter in Rom." *Boreas* 26 (2003): 55–71.

———. "Bellerophon christianus? Zur Deutung des Mosaiks von Hinton St. Mary und zum Problem der Mythendarstellungen in der kaiserzeitlichen dekorativen Kunst." *Römische Quartalschrift* 63 (1968): 49–86.

———. "Christussymbole in frühchristlichen Bodenmosaiken." *Römische Quartalschrift* 64 (1969): 74–138.

———. "Osservazioni sulla fine della produzione e dell'uso dei sarcophagi a rilievo nella tarda antichità nonché sulla loro decorazione." In *Sarcofagi tardoantichi, paleocristiani ed altomedievali*, 1–14. Edited by Fabrizio Bisconti and Hugo Brandenburg. Vatican: Pontificio Istituto di Archeologia Cristiana, 2004.

Bransbourg, Gilles. "Fiscalité impériale et finances municipales au IVe siècle." *Antiquité tardive* 16 (2008): 255–96.

Braudel, Fernand. *The Mediterranean and the Mediterranean World in the Age of Philip II*. Translated by Siân Reynolds. 2 vols. London: Collins, 1972–73.

"Bread and Circuses": Euergetism and Municipal Patronage in Roman Italy. Edited by Kathryn Lomas and Tim Cornell. London: Routledge, 2003.

Brenk, Beat. "L'anno 410 e il suo effetto sull'arte chiesastica a Roma." In vol. 2 of *Ecclesiae urbis*, 1001–18. Edited by Federico Guidobaldi and Alessandra Guiglia Guidobaldi. Studi di Antichità Cristiana 59. 3 vols. Rome: Pontificio Istituto di Antichità Cristiana, 2002.

———. *Die Christianisierung der spätrömischen Welt: Stadt, Land, Haus, Kirche und Kloster in frühchristlicher Zeit*. Wiesbaden: Reichert, 2003.

———. "La cristianizzazione della *Domus* dei Valerii sul Celio." In *The Transformations of Vrbs Roma in Late Antiquity*, 69–84. Edited by W. V. Harris. Journal of Roman Archaeology: Supplementary Series 33. Portsmouth, RI: Journal of Roman Archaeology, 1999.

Brennecke, Hans Christof. *Hilarius von Poitiers und die Bischofsopposition gegen Konstantius II: Untersuchungen zur dritten Phase des Arianischen Streites (337–361)*. Patristische Texte und Studien 26. Berlin: de Gruyter, 1984.

Breukelaar, Adriaan H. B. *Historiography and Episcopal Authority: The Histories of Gregory of Tours Interpreted in Their Historical Context*. Forschungen zur Kirchen und Dogmengeschichte 57. Göttingen: Vandenhoek and Ruprecht, 1994.

Briand-Ponsart, Claude, and Christophe Hugoniot. *L'Afrique romaine de l'Atlantique à la Tripolitaine, 146 av. J.-C.–533 ap. J.-C.* Paris: Armand Colin, 2005.

Brock, Sebastian P. "Saints in Syriac: A Little-Tapped Resource." *Journal of Early Christian Studies* 16 (2008): 181–96.

———. The Syriac Fathers on Prayer and the Spiritual Life. Cistercian Studies 101. Kalamazoo, MI: Cistercian Studies, 1987.

Broise, Henri, Martine Dewailly, and Vincent Jolivet. "Scoperta di un palazzo tardoantico nella piazzale di Villa Medici." *Rendiconti: Pontificia Accademia Romana di Archeologia* 72 (1999–2000): 1–17.

Brown, Peter. "Alms and the Afterlife: A Manichaean View of an Early Christian Practice." In *East and West: Papers in Ancient History Presented to Glen W. Bowersock*, 145–58. Edited by T. Corey Brennan and Harriet I. Flower. Cambridge, MA: Department of Classics, Harvard University, 2008.

———. "Aspects of the Christianization of the Roman Aristocracy." *Journal of Roman Studies* 51 (1961): 1–11. Reprinted in *Religion and Society*.

———. *Augustine of Hippo: New Edition with an Epilogue*. Berkeley: University of California Press, 2000.

Brown, Peter. *Authority and the Sacred: Aspects of the Christianisation of the Roman World*. Cambridge: Cambridge University Press, 1995.

———. *The Body and Society: Men, Women and Sexual Renunciation in Early Christianity*. Reprint with new introduction. New York: Columbia University Press, 2008.

———. *The Cult of the Saints: Its Rise and Function in Latin Christianity*. Chicago: University of Chicago Press, 1981.

———. "Dalla 'plebs romana' alla 'plebs Dei': Aspetti della cristianizzazione di Roma." In *Governanti e intellettuali: Popolo di Roma e popolo di Dio, I–VI secolo*, 123–45. Passatopresente 2. Turin: Giapichelli, 1982.

———. "The Decline of the Empire of God: Amnesty, Penance and the Afterlife from Late Antiquity to the Middle Ages." In *Last Things: Death and the Apocalypse in the Middle Ages*, 41–59. Edited by Caroline Walker Bynum and Paul Freedman. Philadephia: University of Pennsylvania Press, 2000.

———. "The Diffusion of Manichaeism in the Roman Empire." *Journal of Roman Studies* 59 (1969): 92–103. Reprinted in *Religion and Society*.

———. Introduction to *The World of Gregory of Tours*, 1–28. Edited by Kathleen Mitchell and Ian Wood. Leiden: Brill, 2002.

———. "The Patrons of Pelagius: The Roman Aristocracy between East and West." *Journal of Theological Studies*, n.s., 21 (1970): 56–72. Reprinted in *Religion and Society*.

———. "Pelagius and His Supporters: Aims and Environment." *Journal of Theological Studies*, n.s., 19 (1968): 93–114. Reprinted in *Religion and Society*.

———. *Poverty and Leadership in the Later Roman Empire*. Menahem Stern Jerusalem Lectures. Hanover, NH: University Press of New England, 2002.

———. *Power and Persuasion in Late Antiquity: Towards a Christian Empire*. Madison: University of Wisconsin Press, 1992.

———. "Relics and Social Status in the Age of Gregory of Tours." In *Society and the Holy in Late Antiquity*, 222–50. Berkeley: University of California Press, 1982.

———. *Religion and Society in the Age of Saint Augustine*. London: Faber, 1972; Eugene, OR: Wipf and Stock, 2007.

———. "Religious Coercion in the Later Roman Empire: The Case of North Africa." *History* 48 (1963): 283–305. Reprinted in *Religion and Society*.

———. Review article on Richard Sorabji, *Emotion and Peace of Mind: From Stoic Agitation to Christian Temptation*. *Philosophical Books* 43 (2002): 185–208.

———. *The Rise of Western Christendom: Triumph and Diversity, A.D. 200–1000*. 2nd ed. Oxford: Blackwell, 2003.

———. "Sexuality and Society in the Fifth Century A.D.: Augustine and Julian of Eclanum." In *Tria corda: Scritti in onore di Arnaldo Momigliano*, 49–70. Edited by Emilio Gabba. Biblioteca di Athenaeum 1. Como: New Press, 1983.

———. "The World of Late Antiquity Revisited." *Symbolae Osloenses* 72 (1997): 5–90.

Bruck, Eberhard Friedrich. *Kirchenväter und soziales Erbrecht: Wanderungen religiöser Ideen durch die Rechte der östlichen und westlichen Welt*. Berlin: Springer, 1956.

Brunert, Maria-Elisabeth. *Das Ideal der Wüstenaskese und seine Rezeption in Gallien bis zum Ende des 6. Jahrhunderts.* Beiträge zur Geschichte des alten Mönchtums und des Benediktinerordens 42. Münster: Aschendorff, 1994.

Brunner, Otto. *Land and Lordship: Structures of Governance in Medieval Austria.* Translated by Howard Kaminsky and James van Horn Melton. Philadelphia: University of Pennsylvania Press, 1992.

Buenacasa Pérez, Carles. "La creación del patrimonio ecclesiastico de las iglesias norteafricanas en época romana (siglos II–V): Renovación de la visión tradicional." In *Sacralidad y Arqueología: Homenaje al Prof. Thilo Ulbert,* 493–509. Antigüedad y Cristianismo 21. Murcia: Universidad de Murcia, 2004.

Bührer-Thierry, Geneviève. "Lumière et pouvoir dans le haut moyen-âge occidental: Célébration de pouvoir et métaphores lumineuses." *Mélanges de l'École française de Rome: Moyen-âge* 116 (2004): 521–58.

Burns, J. Patout. *Cyprian the Bishop.* London: Routledge, 2002.

Burrus, Virginia. *The Making of a Heretic: Gender, Authority and the Priscillianist Controversy.* Berkeley: University of California Press, 1995.

Bury, J. B. *History of the Later Roman Empire from the Death of Theodosius I to the Death of Justinian (A.D. 395–A.D. 565).* 2 vols. London: MacMillan, 1923.

Caillet, Jean-Pierre. *L'évergétisme monumental chrétien en Italie et à ses marges d'après les pavements de mosaïque (IVe–VIIe s.).* Collection de l'École française de Rome 175. Rome: Palais Farnèse, 1993.

———. "La réalité de l'implantation monumentale chrétienne au temps d'Augustin: L'exemple de quelques cités de Numidie." In *Saint Augustin, la Numidie et la société de son temps,* 55–66. Edited by Serge Lancel. Bordeaux: Ausonia; Paris: Boccard, 2005.

Cain, Andrew. *The Letters of Jerome: Asceticism, Biblical Exegesis, and the Construction of Christian Authority in Late Antiquity.* Oxford: Oxford University Press, 2009.

Caliri, Elena. "Povertà e assistenza nella Sicilia protobizantina." In *Poveri ammalati e ammalati poveri: Dinamiche socio-economiche, trasformazioni culturali e misure assistenziali nell'Occidente romano in età tardoantica,* 145–66. Edited by Rosalia Marino, Concetta Molè, and Antonino Pinzone, with the collaboration of Margherita Cassia. Catania: Edizioni del Prisma, 2006.

Callataÿ, François de. "The Graeco-Roman Economy in the Super Long-Run: Lead, Copper and Shipwrecks." *Journal of Roman Archaeology* 18 (2005): 361–72.

Callu, Jean-Pierre. "Le 'centenarium' et l'enrichissement monétaire au Bas-Empire." *Ktèma* 3 (1978): 301–16.

The Cambridge Ancient History. Vol. 13, *The Late Empire, A.D. 337–425.* Edited by Averil Cameron and Peter Garnsey. Cambridge: Cambridge University Press, 1998.

The Cambridge Companion to the Age of Constantine. Edited by Noel Lenski. Cambridge: Cambridge University Press, 2006.

The Cambridge Economic History of the Greco-Roman World. Edited by Walter Scheidel, Ian Morris, and Richard Saller. Cambridge: Cambridge University Press, 2007.

The Cambridge History of Christianity. Vol. 2, *Constantine to c. 600.* Edited by Augustine Casiday and Frederick W. Norris. Cambridge: Cambridge University Press, 2007.

Cameron, Alan. "The Antiquity of the Symmachi." *Historia* 48 (1999): 477–505.

———. "Filocalus and Melania." *Classical Quarterly* 87 (1992): 140–44.

———. *Greek Mythography in the Roman World.* Oxford: Oxford University Press, 2004.

———. *The Last Pagans of Rome.* Oxford: Oxford University Press, 2011.

———. "The Probus Diptych and Christian Apologetic." In *From Rome to Constantinople: Studies in Honour of Averil Cameron,* 191–202. Edited by Hagit Amirav and Bas ter Haar Romeny. Louvain: Peeters, 2007.

Cameron, Averil. *Christianity and the Rhetoric of Empire: The Development of Christian Discourse.* Berkeley: University of California Press, 1991.

Caner, Daniel. "Towards a Miraculous Economy: Christian Gifts and Material 'Blessings' in Late Antiquity." *Journal of Early Christian Studies* 14 (2006): 329–77.

———. *Wandering, Begging Monks: Spiritual Authority and the Promotion of Monasticism in Late Antiquity.* Berkeley: University of California Press, 2002.

Cantino Wataghin, Gisella, Vincenzo Fiocchi Nicolai, and Giuliano Volpe. "Aspetti della cristianizzazione degli agglomerati secondari." In vol. 1 of *La cristianizzazione in Italia tra Tardoantico e Altomedioevo,* 83–134. Edited by Rosa Maria Bonacasa Carra and Emma Vitale. Palermo: Carlo Saladino, 2007.

Carlà, Filippo. *L'oro nella tarda antichità: Aspetti economici e sociali.* Turin: Silvio Zamorani, 2009.

Carmassi, Patrizia. "La prima redazione del *Liber Pontificalis* nel quadro delle fonti contemporanee: Osservazioni in margine alla vita di Simmaco." In *Atti del colloquio internazionale, Il Liber Pontificalis e la storia materiale,* 235–66. Edited by Herman Geertman. Medelingen van het Nederlands Instituut te Rome: Antiquity 60–61. Assen: Van Gorcum, 2003.

Carrié, Jean-Michel. "Les associations professionnelles à l'époque tardive: Entre munus et convivialité." In *Humana sapit: Études d'Antiquité Tardive offeres à Lellia Cracco Ruggini,* 309–32. Edited by Carrié and Rita Lizzi Testa. Bibliothèque d'Antiquité Tardive 3. Turnhout: Brepols, 2002.

———. "Le 'colonat du Bas-Empire': Un mythe historiographique?" *Opus* 1 (1982): 351–70.

———. "Dioclétien et la fiscalité." *Antiquité tardive* 2 (1994): 33–64.

———. "Les distributions alimentaires dans les cités de l'empire romain tardif." *Mélanges de l'École française de Rome: Antiquité* 87 (1975): 995–1101.

———. "*Nihil habens praeter quod ipso die vestiebatur*: Comment définir le seuil de la pauvreté à Rome?" In *Consuetudinis amor: Fragments d'histoire romaine (IIe–VIe siècles) offerts à Jean-Pierre Callu,* 71–102. Edited by François Chausson and Étienne Wolff. Rome: Bretschneider, 2003.

———. "Pratique et idéologie chrétiennes de l'économique (IVe–VIe siècle)." *Antiquité tardive* 14 (2006): 17–26.

Carrié, Jean-Michel, and Aline Rousselle. *L'empire romain en mutation: Des Sévères à Constantin, 192–337*. Paris: Du Seuil, 1999.

Caseau, Béatrice. "A Case Study for the Transformation of Law in Late Antiquity: The Legal Protection of Churches." In *Confrontation in Late Antiquity: Imperial Presentation and Regional Adaptation*, 61–77. Edited by Linda Jones Hall. Cambridge: Orchard Academic, 2003.

———. "Objects in Churches: The Testimony of Inventories." In *Objects in Context, Objects in Use: Material Spatiality in Late Antiquity*, 551–79. Edited by Luke Lavan, Ellen Swift, and Toon Putzeys. Late Antique Archaeology 5. Leiden: Brill, 2007.

Casiday, Augustine M. C. "Rehabilitating John Cassian: An Evaluation of Prosper of Aquitaine's Polemic against the 'Semipelagians.'" *Scottish Journal of Theology* 58 (2005): 270–84.

———. *Tradition and Theology in St. John Cassian*. Oxford: Oxford University Press, 2007.

Cavadini, John. "Feeling Right: Augustine on the Passions and Sexual Desire." *Augustinian Studies* 36 (2005): 195–217.

Cecconi, Giovanni Alberto. "Crisi e trasformazioni del governo municipale in Occidente fra IV e VI secolo." In *Die Stadt in der Spätantike—Niedergang oder Wandel?* 285–318. Edited by Jens-Uwe Krause and Christian Witschel. Historia Einzelschriften 190. Stuttgart: F. Steiner, 2006.

———. "Elemosina e propaganda: Un'analisi della 'Macariana persecutio.'" *Revue des études augustiniennes* 31 (1990): 42–66.

———. *Governo imperiale e élites dirigenti nell'Italia tardoantica: Problemi di storia politico-amministrativa (270–476 d.C.)*. Biblioteca di Athenaeum 24. Como: New Press, 1994.

———. "Vescovi e maggiorenti cristiani nell'Italia centrale fra IV e V secolo." In *Vescovi e pastori in epoca Teodosiana*, 205–24. Studia Ephemeridis Augustinianum 58. Rome: Institutum Pontificium Augustinianum, 1997.

Chadwick, Henry. *Boethius: The Consolations of Music, Logic, Theology and Philosophy*. Oxford: Clarendon, 1981.

———. *The Church in Ancient Society: From Galilee to Gregory the Great*. Oxford: Oxford University Press, 2001.

———. *Priscillian of Avila: The Occult and the Charismatic in the Early Church*. Oxford: Clarendon, 1976.

Chadwick, Nora K. *Poetry and Letters in Early Christian Gaul*. London: Bowes and Bowes, 1955.

Chadwick, Owen. *A History of the Popes, 1830–1914*. Oxford: Clarendon, 1998.

———. *John Cassian*. Cambridge: Cambridge University Press, 1968.

Chalon, Michel, Georges Devallet, Paul Force, Michel Griffe, Jean-Marie Lassere, and Jean-Noël Michaud. "*Memorabile factum*: Une célébration de l'évergétisme des rois vandales dans l'Anthologie Latine." *Antiquités africaines* 21 (1985): 207–62.

Champlin, Edward. *Final Judgments: Duty and Emotion in Roman Wills, 200 B.C.–A.D. 250*. Berkeley: University of California Press, 1991.

Champlin, Edward. "The *Suburbium* of Rome." *American Journal of Ancient History* 7 (1982): 97–117.

Charity and Giving in Monotheistic Religions. Edited by Miriam Frenkel and Yaacov Lev. Studien zur Geschichte und Kultur des islamischen Orients, n. F. 22. Berlin: de Gruyter, 2009.

Charles-Picard, Gilbert. "*Civitas mactaritana.*" *Karthago* 8 (1957): 1–156.

Chastagnol, André. "Observations sur le consulat suffect et la préture au Bas-Empire." *Revue historique* 219 (1958): 221–53.

———. "Un scandale du vin à Rome sous le Bas-Empire: L'affaire du Préfet Orfitus." *Annales* 5 (1950): 166–83.

———. "Le Sénat dans l'oeuvre de Symmaque." In *Colloque genèvois sur Symmaque*, 73–92. Edited by François Paschoud. Paris: Belles Lettres, 1986.

Chavarría Arnau, Alexandra. *El final de las "villae" en "Hispania" (siglos IV–VIII)*. Turnhout: Brepols, 2007.

Chevalier, Pascale. "Les graffitis de l'abside de l'Eufrasiana de Poreč: Un obituaire monumental du haut Moyen Âge." *Mélanges Jean Pierre Sodini: Travaux et mémoires* 15 (2005): 359–70.

Cheyette, Fredric L. "The Disappearance of the Ancient Landscape and the Climatic Anomaly of the Early Middle Ages: A Question to Be Pursued." *Early Medieval Europe* 16 (2008): 127–65.

Christe, Yves. "À propos du décor figuré des sarcophages d'Aquitaine." *Antiquité tardive* 1 (1993): 75–80.

Christern, Jürgen. "Basilika und Memorie der heiligen Salsa in Tipasa: Ein Beitrag zum Verhältnis von Märtyrergrab und Zömeterialbasilika." *Bulletin d'archéologie algérienne* 3 (1968): 193–250.

———. *Das frühchristliche Pilgerheiligtum von Tebessa: Architektur und Ornamentik einer spätantiken Bauhütte in Nordafrika*. Wiesbaden: F. Steiner, 1976.

Christie, Neil. *From Constantine to Charlemagne: An Archaeology of Italy, AD 300–800*. Aldershot: Ashgate, 2006.

Cipriani, Nello. "Le fonti cristiane della dottrina trinitaria nei primi Dialoghi di S. Agostino." *Augustinianum* 34 (1994): 253–313.

———. "La morale pelagiana e la retorica." *Augustinianum* 31 (1991): 309–27.

———. "La polemica antiafricana di Giuliano di Eclano: Artificio letterario o scontro di tradizioni teologiche?" In *Cristianesimo e specificità regionali nel Mediterraneo latino (sec. IV–VI)*, 147–60. Studia Ephemeridis Augustinianum 46. Rome: Institutum Pontificium Augustinianum, 1994.

Les cités de l'Italie tardo-antique (IVe–VIe siècle): Institutions, économie, société, culture et religion. Edited by Massimiliano Ghilardi, Christophe J. Goddard, and Pierfrancesco Porena. Collection de l'École française de Rome 369. Rome: École française de Rome, 2006.

Clackson, James. "A Greek Papyrus in Armenian Script." *Zeitschrift für Papyrologie und Epigraphik* 129 (2000): 223–58.

Clark, Elizabeth A. *Jerome, Chrysostom and Friends: Essays and Translations*. Lewiston, NY: Edwin Mellen Press, 1979.

———. *The Origenist Controversy: The Cultural Construction of an Early Christian Debate*. Princeton: Princeton University Press, 1992.

———. "Vitiated Seeds and Holy Vessels: Augustine's Manichaean Past." In *Ascetic Piety and Women's Faith: Essays on Late Ancient Christianity*, 291–349. Lewiston, NY: Edwin Mellen Press, 1986.

Clarke, W. K. Lowther. *Saint Basil the Great: A Study in Monasticism*. Cambridge: Cambridge University Press, 1913.

Claude, Dietrich. "Die Bestellung der Bischöfe im merowingischen Reiche." *Zeitschrift der Savigny Stiftung für Rechtsgeschichte: Kanonistische Abteilung* 49 (1963): 1–77.

———. "Freedmen in the Visigothic Kingdom." In *Visigothic Spain: New Approaches*, 139–88. Edited by Edward James. Oxford: Oxford University Press, 1980.

Cleary, Simon Esmonde. *The Ending of Roman Britain*. London: Batsford, 1989.

Cleland, Gary. "Unearthed after 1,600 Years, Dinner Set Hidden by Fleeing Romans." *Daily Telegraph*, December 7, 2007.

Le Code Théodosien: Diversité des approches et nouvelles perspectives. Edited by Sylvie Crogiel-Pétrequin and Pierre Jaillette. Collection de l'École française de Rome 412. Rome: École française de Rome, 2009.

Colish, Marcia L. *Ambrose's Patriarchs: Ethics for the Common Man*. Notre Dame, IN: University of Notre Dame Press, 2005.

Colloque genèvois sur Symmaque. Edited by François Paschoud. Paris: Belles Lettres, 1986.

Commento storico al libro ... dell'epistolario di Q. Aurelio Simmaco. Pisa: Giardini, 1981–2002.

Vol. 2, *Commento storico al libro II*. By Giovanni Alberto Cecconi. 2002.

Vol. 3, *Commento storico al libro III*. By Andrea Pellizzari. 1998.

Vol. 4, *Commento storico al libro IV*. By Arnaldo Marcone. 1987.

Vol. 5, *Commento storico al libro V*. By Paola Rivolta Tiberga. 1992.

Vol. 6, *Commento storico al libro VI*. By Arnaldo Marcone. 1983.

Vol. 9, *Commento storico al libro IX*. By Sergio Roda. 1981.

The Conflict between Paganism and Christianity in the Fourth Century. Edited by Arnaldo Momigliano. Oxford: Clarendon Press, 1963.

Connolly, Serena. "Fortifying the City of God: Dardanus' Inscription Revisited." *Classical Journal* 102 (2007): 145–54.

Consolino, Franca Ela. "Tradizionalismo e trasgressione nell'élite senatoria romana: Ritratti di signore fra la fine del IV e l'inizio del V secolo." In *Le trasformazioni delle "élites" in età tardoantica*, 65–139. Edited by Rita Lizzi Testa. Rome: Bretschneider, 2006.

Conti, Marco. *Priscillian of Avila: The Complete Works*. Oxford: Oxford University Press, 2010.

Conybeare, Catherine. *The Irrational Augustine*. Oxford: Oxford University Press, 2006.

———. *Paulinus Noster: Self and Symbol in the Letters of Paulinus of Nola*. New York: Oxford University Press, 2000.

Cooper, Kate. *The Fall of the Roman Household*. Cambridge: Cambridge University Press, 2007.

Cooper, Kate. "Poverty, Obligation, and Inheritance: Roman Heiresses and the Varieties of Senatorial Christianity in Fifth-Century Rome." In *Religion, Dynasty and Patronage in Early Christian Rome, 300–900*, 165–89. Edited by Kate Cooper and Julia Hillner. Cambridge: Cambridge University Press, 2007.

———. *The Virgin and the Bride: Idealized Womanhood in Late Antiquity*. Cambridge, MA: Harvard University Press, 1996.

Corbo, Chiara. *Paupertas: La legislazione tardoantica*. Naples: Satura, 2006.

Corcoran, Simon. *The Empire of the Tetrarchs: Imperial Pronouncements and Government, AD 284–324*. Oxford: Clarendon Press, 1996.

Corrente, Marisa, Roberto Giuliano, and Danilo Leone. "Il complesso religioso di Piano di San Giovanni e il problema del primo polo episcopale canosino." In vol. 2 of *La cristianizzazione in Italia tra Tardoantico e Altomedioevo*, 1167–1200. Edited by Rosa Maria Bonacasa Carra and Emma Vitale. Palermo: Carlo Saladino, 2007.

Coşkun, Altay. "The *Eucharisticos* of Paulinus Pellaeus: Towards a Reappraisal of the Worldly Convert's Life and Autobiography." *Vigiliae Christianae* 60 (2006): 283–315.

———. *Die gens Ausoniana an der Macht: Untersuchungen zu Decimius Magnus Ausonius und seiner Familie*. Prosopographica et Genealogica 8. Oxford: Linacre College, 2002.

Courcelle, Pierre. *Histoire littéraire des grandes invasions germaniques*. 3rd ed. Paris: Études Augustiniennes, 1964.

Coveney, P. J. *Introduction to France in Crisis, 1620–1675*. Edited by P. J. Coveney. Totowa, NJ: Rowman and Littlefield, 1977.

Coyle, J. Kevin. "What Did Augustine Know about Manichaeism When He Wrote His Two Treatises *De moribus?*" In *Augustine and Manichaeism in the Latin West*, 43–56. Edited by Johannes van Oort, Otto Wermelinger, and Gregor Wurst. Nag Hammadi and Manichaean Studies 49. Leiden: Brill, 2001.

Cracco Ruggini, Lellia. *Economia e società nell' "Italia annonaria": Rapporti fra agricoltura e commercio dal IV al VI secolo d.C.* Milan: Giuffrè, 1961. 2nd ed. Bari: Edipuglia, 1995.

Crane, David. *Scott of the Antarctic: A Life of Courage and Tragedy in the Extreme South*. New York: Harper Percival, 2006.

La cristianizzazione in Italia tra Tardoantico e Altomedioevo. Edited by Rosa Maria Bonacasa Carra and Emma Vitale. 2 vols. Palermo: Carlo Saladino, 2007.

Crow, James. "Fortifications and Urbanism in Late Antiquity." In *Recent Research in Late Antique Urbanism*, 89–105. Edited by Luke Lavan. Journal of Roman Archaeology, Supplement 42. Portsmouth, RI: Journal of Roman Archaeology, 1996.

Ćurčić, Slobodan. *Architecture in the Balkans from Diocletian to Süleyman the Magnificent*. New Haven, CT: Yale University Press, 2010.

Curran, John R. "Jerome and the Sham Christians of Rome." *Journal of Ecclesiastical History* 48 (1997): 213–29.

———. *Pagan City and Christian Capital: Rome in the Fourth Century*. Oxford: Oxford University Press, 2000.

D'un monde à l'autre: Naissance d'une Chrétienté en Provence, IVe–VIe siècle. Edited by Jean Guyon and Marc Heijmans. Arles: Musée de l'Arles antique, 2002.

Dark, K. R. *Civitas to Kingdom: British Political Continuity, 300–800.* Leicester: Leicester University Press, 1994.

———. "The Late Antique Landscape of Britain, AD 300–700." In *Landscapes of Change: Rural Evolutions in Late Antiquity and the Early Middle Ages,* 279–99. Edited by Neil Christie. Aldershot: Ashgate, 2004.

Dassmann, Ernst. *Die Frömmigkeit des Kirchenvaters Ambrosius von Mailand.* Münster-in-Westfalen: Aschendorff, 1965.

Davies, Wendy. *Small Worlds: The Village Community in Early Medieval Brittany.* London: Duckworth, 1988.

De Bruyn, Theodore. *Pelagius' Commentary on St. Paul's Epistle to the Romans.* Oxford: Clarendon, 1993.

Deckers, Johannes G. "Vom Denker zum Diener: Bemerkungen zu den Folgen der konstantinischen Wende im Spiegel der Sarkophagplastik." In *Innovation in der Spätantike,* 137–72. Edited by Beat Brenk. Wiesbaden: Reichert, 1996.

Decret, François. *L'Afrique manichéenne, IVe–Ve siècles: Étude historique et doctrinale.* Paris: Études Augustiniennes, 1978.

De Fino, Mariagrazia. "Proprietà imperiali e diocesi rurali paleocristiane dell'Italia tardoantica." In *Paesaggi e insediamenti rurali in Italia meridionale fra tardoantico e altomedioevo,* 691–702. Edited by Guiliano Volpe and Maria Turchiano. Bari: Edipuglia, 2005.

De Francesco, Daniela. "Aspetti della presenza germanica in Italia: Le donazioni di Valila nel Tiburtino." *Rivista di Archeologia Cristiana* 74 (1998): 415–53.

———. *La proprietà fondiaria nel Lazio, secoli IV–VIII: Storia e topografia.* Rome: Quasar, 2004.

Deichmann, Friedrich Wilhelm. *Ravenna: Hauptstadt des spätantiken Abendlandes.* 3 vols. Stuttgart: F. Steiner, 1969–89.

Delage, Pascal-Grégoire. "Le canon 13 de Sardique ou Les inquietudes d'évêques d'origine modeste." In *Les Pères de l'Église et la voix des pauvres,* 55–74. Edited by Pascal-Grégoire Delage. La Rochelle: Histoire et Culture, 2006.

Deleto paene imperio Romano: Transformazionsprozesse des römischen Reiches im 3. Jahrhundert und ihre Rezeption in der Neuzeit. Edited by Klaus-Peter Johne, Thomas Gerdhardt, and Udo Hartmann. Stuttgart: F. Steiner, 2006.

Deliyannis, Deborah Mauskopf. *Ravenna in Late Antiquity.* Cambridge: Cambridge University Press, 2010.

Delmaire, Roland, and Claude Lepelley. "Du nouveau sur Carthage: Le témoignage des Lettres de Saint Augustin découvertes par Johannes Divjak." *Opus* 2 (1983): 473–87.

Demandt, Alexander, and Guntram Brummer. "Der Prozess gegen Serena im Jahre 408 n. Chr." *Historia* 26 (1977): 479–502.

Denzey, Nicola. *The Bone Gatherers: The Lost Worlds of Early Christian Women.* Boston: Beacon Press, 2007.

Déroche, Vincent. *Études sur Léontios de Néapolis.* Studia Byzantina Upsalensia 3. Uppsala: Alqmvist and Wiksell, 1995.

Desmulliez, Janine. "Paulin de Nole et la *paupertas*." In *Les Pères de l'Église et la voix des pauvres*, 245–63. Edited by Pascal-Grégoire Delage. La Rochelle: Histoire et Culture, 2006.

Devos, Paul. "Quand Pierre l'Ibère vint-il à Jérusalem?" *Analaecta Bollandiana* 86 (1968): 337–50.

Dey, Hendrik. "Art, Ceremony and City Walls: The Aesthetics of Imperial Resurgence in the Late Roman West." *Journal of Late Antiquity* 3 (2010): 3–37.

———. "Building Worlds Apart: Walls and the Construction of Communal Monasticism from Augustine through Benedict." *Antiquité tardive* 12 (2004): 357–71.

Diefenbach, Steffen. *Römische Erinnerungsräume: Heiligenmemoria und kollektive Identitäten im Rom des 3. bis 5. Jahrhunderts n. Chr.* Millennium-Studien 11. Berlin: de Gruyter, 2007.

Diem, Albrecht. "Monastic Poverty and Institution Forming: Evidence from Early Medieval Historiography and from Monastic Rules." Paper presented at the Cornell Conference on Medieval Poverty, March 2008.

———. *Das monastische Experiment: Die Rolle der Keuschheit bei der Entstehung des westlichen Klosterwesens.* Vita Regularis: Abhandlungen 24. Münster: Lit, 2005.

Digeser, Elizabeth DePalma. *The Making of a Christian Empire: Lactantius and Rome.* Ithaca, NY: Cornell University Press, 2000.

Dill, Samuel. *Roman Society in the Last Century of the Western Empire.* 1919. Reprint, New York: Meridian, 1958.

Dionisotti, A. C. "From Ausonius' Schooldays? A Schoolbook and Its Relatives." *Journal of Roman Studies* 72 (1982): 83–125.

El disco de Teodosio. Edited by Martín Almagro-Gorbea. Estudios del Gabinete de Antigüedades 5. Madrid: Real Academia de la Historia, 2000.

Disselkamp, Gabriele. *"Christiani Senatus Lumina": Zum Anteil römischer Frauen der Oberschicht im 4. und 5. Jahrhundert an der Christianisierung der römischen Senatsaristokratie.* Theophaneia 34. Bodenheim: Philo, 1997.

Djurić, Srdjan. "Mosaic of Philosophers in an Early Byzantine Villa at Nerodimlje." In *VI Coloquio internacional sobre mosaico antiguo*, 123–34. Palencia/Mérida: Associación Español del Mosaico, 1994.

Dodds, E. R. *Pagan and Christian in an Age of Anxiety: Some Aspects of Religious Experience from Marcus Aurelius to Constantine.* Cambridge: Cambridge University Press, 1965.

Doignon, Jean. "L'enseignement de l'*Hortensius* de Cicéron sur les richesses devant la conscience d'Augustin jusqu'aux *Confessions*." *Antiquité classique* 51 (1982): 193–206.

Dolan, Jay P. *The Immigrant Church: New York's Irish and German Catholics, 1815–1865.* Baltimore: Johns Hopkins University Press, 1975.

Dolbeau, François. "Nouveaux sermons de Saint Augustin pour la conversion des païens et des donatistes (IV)." *Revue des études augustiniennes* 38 (1992): 69–141.

———. "'Seminator verborum': Réfléxions d'un éditeur des sermons d'Augustin." In *Augustin prédicateur (395–411)*, 95–111. Edited by Goulven Madec. Paris: Institut d'Études Augustiniennes, 1998.

Dossey, Leslie. *Peasant and Empire in Christian North Africa*. Berkeley: University of California Press, 2010.

Dresken-Weiland, Jutta. *Sarkophagbestattungen des 4.–6. Jahrhunderts im Westen des römischen Reiches*. Römische Quartalschrift Supplementband 55. Rome: Herder, 2003.

Drinkwater, John F. "The Bacaudae of Fifth-Century Gaul." In *Fifth-Century Gaul: A Crisis of Identity?* 208–17. Edited by John Drinkwater and Hugh Elton. Cambridge: Cambridge University Press, 1992.

Du latifundium au latifondo: Un héritage de Rome, une création médiévale ou moderne? Publications du Centre Pierre Paris 25. Paris: Boccard, 1995.

Duchesne, L. *Le Liber Pontificalis: Texte, Introduction et Commentaire*. Bibliothèque de l'École française de Rome. 3 vols. Paris: Boccard, 1955–57.

———. "Lovocat et Catihern, prêtres bretons du temps de saint Mélaine." *Revue de Bretagne et de Vendée* 57 (1885): 5–21.

———. "La succession du pape Félix IV." *Mélanges d'archéologie et d'histoire* 3 (1883): 239–66.

Dulaey, Martine. "La bibliothèque du monastère de Lérins dans les premières décennies du Ve siècle." *Augustinianum* 46 (2006): 187–230.

———. "La scène dite de l'arrestation de Pierre: Nouvelle proposition de lecture." *Rivista di Archeologia Cristiana* 84 (2008): 299–346.

Dunbabin, Katherine M. D. "Convivial Spaces: Dining and Entertainment in the Roman Villa." *Journal of Roman Archaeology* 9 (1996): 66–80.

———. *Mosaics of the Greek and Roman World*. Cambridge: Cambridge University Press, 1999.

———. *The Mosaics of Roman North Africa: Studies in Iconography and Patronage*. Oxford: Clarendon, 1978.

———. *The Roman Banquet: Images of Conviviality*. Cambridge: Cambridge University Press, 2003.

Duncan-Jones, Richard P. "The Finances of the Younger Pliny." *Papers of the British School at Rome* 33 (1965): 177–88.

———. "The Impact of the Antonine Plague." *Journal of Roman Archaeology* 9 (1996): 108–36.

Dunn, Geoffrey G. "The Care of the Poor in Rome and Alaric's Sieges." In *Prayer and Spirituality in the Early Church*. Vol. 5, *Poverty and Riches*, 319–33. Edited by Geoffrey Dunn, David Luckensmeyer, and Lawrence Cross. Sydney: St. Paul's, 2009.

———. "The Christian Networks of the *Aniciae*: The Example of the Letter of Innocent I to Anicia Iuliana." *Revue des études augustiniennes et patristiques* 55 (2009): 53–72.

Dunphy, Walter. "Rufinus the Syrian: Myth and Reality." *Augustiniana* 59 (2009): 79–157.

Durliat, Jean. *De la ville antique à la ville byzantine: Le problème des subsistences*. Collection de l'École française de Rome 136. Rome: Palais Farnèse, 1990.

Duval, Noël. "Deux mythes iconographiques de l'antiquité tardive: La villa fortifiée et le 'chasseur vandale.'" In *Humana sapit: Études d'Antiquité Tardive offeres à Lellia*

Cracco Ruggini, 333–40. Edited by Jean-Michel Carrié and Rita Lizzi Testa. Bibliothèque d'Antiquité Tardive 3. Turnhout: Brepols, 2002.

———. "La notion de 'sarcophage' et son rôle dans l'antiquité tardive." *Antiquité tardive* 1 (1993): 29–35.

Duval, Yves-Marie. "Sur trois lettres méconnues de Jérôme concernant son séjour à Rome." In *Jerome of Stridon: His Life, Writings and Legacy*. Edited by Andrew Cain and Josef Lössl. Farnham, UK: Ashgate, 2009.

Duval, Yvette. *Les chrétientés d'Occident et leur évêque au IIIe siècle: Plebs in ecclesia constituta*. Paris: Institut d'Études Augustiniennes, 2005.

———. *Loca sanctorum Africae: Le culte des martyrs en Afrique du IVe au VIIe siècle*. 2 vols. Collection de l'École française de Rome 58. Rome: Palais Farnèse, 1982.

Duval, Yvette, and Luce Pietri. "Évergétisme et épigraphie dans l'Occident chrétien (IVe–VIe s.)." In *Actes du Xe Congrès international d'épigraphie grecque et chrétienne*, 371–96. Edited by Michel Christol and Olivier Masson. Paris: Publications de la Sorbonne, 1997.

Dworkin, Andrea. *Intercourse*. New York: The Free Press, 1987.

Dyson, R. W. *The Pilgrim City: Social and Political Ideas in the Writings of St. Augustine of Hippo*. Woodbridge: Boydell, 2001.

Ebanista, Carlo. *Et manet in mediis quasi gemma intersita tectis: La basilica di S. Felice a Cimitile. Storia degli scavi, fasi edilizie, reperti*. Memorie dell'Accademia di archeologia, lettere e belle arti in Napoli 15. Naples: Arte Tipografica, 2003.

Ebbeler, Jennifer V., and Cristiana Sogno. "Religious Identity and the Politics of Patronage: Symmachus and Augustine." *Historia* 56 (2007): 230–42.

Eburnea Diptycha: I dittici d'avorio tra Antichità e Medioevo. Edited by Massimiliano David. Bari: Edipuglia, 2007.

Edwards, Mark. "The Beginnings of Christianization." In *The Cambridge Companion to the Age of Constantine*, 137–56. Edited by Noel Lenski. Cambridge: Cambridge University Press, 2006.

Ellis, Simon. "Power, Architecture and Décor: How the Late Roman Aristocrat Appeared to His Guests." In *Roman Art in the Private Sphere: New Perspectives on the Architecture and Decor of the Domus, Villa, and Insula*, 117–34. Edited by Elaine K. Gazda, assisted by Anne E. Haeckl. Ann Arbor: University of Michigan Press, 1991.

———. "Shedding Light on Late Roman Housing." In *Housing in Late Antiquity: From Palaces to Shops*, 283–302. Edited by Luke Lavan, Lale Özgenel, and Alexander Sarantis. Late Antique Archaeology 3.2. Leiden: Brill, 2007.

Elsner, Jás. *Imperial Rome and Christian Triumph: The Art of the Roman Empire, AD 100–450*. Oxford: Oxford University Press, 1998.

Elton, Hugh. "Defence in Fifth-Century Gaul." In *Fifth-Century Gaul: A Crisis of Identity?* 167–76. Edited by John Drinkwater and Hugh Elton. Cambridge: Cambridge University Press, 1992.

Elvin, Mark. *The Retreat of the Elephants: An Environmental History of China*. New Haven, CT: Yale University Press, 2004.

Enceintes romaines d'Aquitaine: Bordeaux, Dax, Périgueux, Bazas. Edited by Pierre Garmy and Louis Maurin. Paris: Editions de la Maison des Sciences de l'Homme, 1996.

Enjuto Sánchez, Begoña. "I 'Neratii': Legami tra Roma e le città di Sannio nel IV secolo d.C." In *Les cités de l'Italie tardo-antique (IVe–VIe siècle): Institutions, économie, société, culture et religion*, 113–21. Edited by Massimiliano Ghilardi, Christophe J. Goddard, and Pierfrancesco Porena. Collection de l'École française de Rome 369. Rome: École française de Rome, 2006.

Ennabli, Abdelmagid. "Les thermes du Thiase Marin de Sidi Ghrib (Tunisie)." *Monuments et mémoires publiés par l'Académie des Inscriptions et Belles Lettres* 68 (1986): 1–59.

Ennabli, Liliane. *Carthage: Une métropole chrétienne du IVe à la fin du VIIe siècle*. Paris: Centre National de Recherche Scientifique, 1997.

Erdkamp, Paul. *The Grain Market in the Roman Empire: A Social, Political and Economic Study*. Cambridge: Cambridge University Press, 2005.

Errington, R. Malcom. *Roman Imperial Policy from Julian to Theodosius*. Chapel Hill: University of North Carolina Press, 2006.

Escribano, Victoria. "Heresy and Orthodoxy in Fourth Century Hispania: Arianism and Priscillianism." In *Hispania in Late Antiquity: Current Perspectives*, 121–49. Edited by Kim Bowes and Michael Kulikowski. Leiden: Brill, 2005.

Esders, Stefan. *Die Formierung der Zensualität: Zur kirchlichen Transformation des spätrömischen Patronatswesens im früheren Mittelalter*. Ostfildern: Jan Thorbecke, 2010.

———. "Grenzen und Grenzüberschreitungen: Religion, Ethnizität und politische Integration am Rande des oströmischen Imperiums (4.–7. Jh.)." In *Gestiftete Zukunft im mittelalterlichen Europa: Festschrift für Michael Borgolte*, 3–28. Edited by Wolfgang Huschner and Frank Rexroth. Berlin: Akademie Verlag, 2008.

———. *Römische Rechtstradition und merowingisches Königtum: Zum Rechtscharakter politischer Herrschaft in Burgund im 6. und 7. Jahrhundert*. Göttingen: Vandenhoeck and Ruprecht, 1997.

Étienne, Robert. "Ausone, propriétaire terrien et le problème du latifundium au IVe siècle ap. J. C." In *Institutions, société et vie politique de l'empire romain au IVe siècle ap. J. C.*, 305–11. Edited by Michel Christol et al. Collection de l'École française de Rome 159. Rome: Palais Farnèse, 1992.

L'évêque dans la cité du IVe au Ve siècle: Image et autorité. Edited by Éric Rebillard and Claire Sotinel. Collection de l'École française de Rome 248. Rome: École française de Rome, 1998.

Ewald, Björn Christian. *Der Philosoph als Leitbild: Ikonographische Untersuchungen in römischen Sarkophagreliefs*. Mainz: Zabern, 1999.

F. Bang, Peter. "Trade and Empire—In Search of Organizing Concepts for the Roman Empire." *Past and Present* 195 (2007): 3–54.

Favro, Diane. *The Urban Image of Augustan Rome*. Cambridge: Cambridge University Press, 1996.

Fentress, Elizabeth, Caroline J. Goodson, Margaret L. Laird, and Stephanie C. Leone. *Walls and Memory: The Abbey of San Sebastiano at Alatri (Lazio) from Late Roman Monastery to Renaissance Villa and Beyond.* Disciplina Monastica 2. Turnhout: Brepols, 2005.

Fernández Ochoa, Carmen, and Angel Morillo Cerdán. "Walls in the Urban Landscape of Late Roman Spain: Defense and Imperial Strategy." In *Hispania in Late Antiquity: Current Perspectives,* 299–340. Edited by Kim Bowes and Michael Kulikowski. Leiden: Brill, 2005.

Ferrua, Antonio. "Cancelli di Cimitile con scritte bibliche." *Römische Quartalschrift* 68 (1973): 50–68.

———. "Graffiti di pellegrini alla tomba di San Felice." *Palladio,* n.s., 13 (1963): 17–19.

Festugière, A. J. *La révélation d'Hermès Trismégiste.* Vol. 2, *Le Dieu cosmique.* Paris: Belles Lettres, 1981.

Février, Paul-Albert. *Approches du Maghreb romain: Pouvoirs, différences et conflits.* 2 vols. Aix-en-Provence and La Calade: Édisud, 1989–90.

———. "Discours d'Église et réalité historique dans les nouvelles Lettres d'Augustin." In *Les Lettres de Saint Augustin découvertes par Johannes Divjak,* 101–15. Paris: Études Augustiniennes, 1983.

Fifth-Century Gaul: A Crisis of Identity? Edited by John Drinkwater and Hugh Elton. Cambridge: Cambridge University Press, 1992.

Finn, Richard. *Almsgiving in the Later Roman Empire: Christian Promotion and Practice, 313–450.* Oxford: Oxford University Press, 2006.

———. "Portraying the Poor: Descriptions of Poverty in Christian Texts from the Late Roman Empire." In *Poverty in the Roman World,* 130–44. Edited by Margaret Atkins and Robin Osborne. Cambridge: Cambridge University Press, 2007.

Fiocchi Nicolai, Vincenzo. "Evergetismo ecclesiastico e laico nelle iscrizioni paleocristiane del Lazio." In *Historiam pictura refert: Miscellanea in onore di Padre Alejandro Recio Veganzones O.F.M.,* 237–52. Studi di Antichità Cristiana 51. Vatican: Pontificio Istituto di Archeologia Cristiana, 1994.

Firey, Abigail. "'For I was hungry and you fed me': Social Justice and Economic Thought in the Late Patristic and Medieval Christian Traditions." In *Ancient and Medieval Economic Ideas and Concepts of Social Justice,* 333–70. Edited by S. Todd Lowry and Barry Gordon. Leiden: Brill, 1998.

Fischer, Josef. *Die Völkerwanderung im Urteil der zeitgenössischen kirchlichen Schriftsteller Galliens unter Einbeziehung des heiligen Augustinus.* Heidelberg: Kemper, 1948.

Folliet, Georges. "*Deificari in otio*: Augustin, Epistula X,2." *Recherches augustiniennes* 2 (1962): 225–36.

Fontaine, Jacques. "Damase, poète théodosien: L'imaginaire poétique des *Epigrammata.*" In *Saecularia Damasiana,* 115–45. Studi di Antichità Cristiana 39. Vatican: Pontificio Istituto di Archeologia Cristiana, 1986.

———. "Un sobriquet perfide de Damase: *Matronarum auriscalpius.*" In *Hommages à Henri le Bonnec: Res sacrae,* 177–92. Edited by D. Porte and J.-P. Néraudau. Collection Latomus 201. Brussels: Latomus, 1988.

———. *Sulpice Sévère: Vie de Saint Martin. Introduction, texte et traduction.* 3 vols. SC 133–35. Paris: Le Cerf, 1967–69.

———. "Valeurs antiques et valeurs chrétiennes dans la spiritualité des grands propriétaires terriens à la fin du IVe siècle Occidental." In *Epektasis: Mélanges patristiques offerts au cardinal Jean Daniélou,* 571–95. Edited by Jacques Fontaine and Charles Kannengiesser. Paris: Beauchesne, 1972. Reprinted in Fontaine, *Études sur la poésie latine tardive d'Ausone à Prudence.* Paris: Belles Lettres, 1980.

Foucault, Michel. *Security, Territory, Population: Lectures at the Collège de France, 1977–78.* Edited by Michel Senellart. Translated by Graham Burchell. Basingstoke: Palgrave MacMillan, 2007.

Fouracre, Paul. "Eternal Light and Earthly Needs: Practical Aspects of the Development of Frankish Immunities." In *Property and Power in the Early Middle Ages,* 53–81. Edited by Wendy Davies and Paul Fouracre. Cambridge: Cambridge University Press, 1995.

Fournet, Jean-Luc. "Entre document et littérature: La pétition dans l'antiquité tardive." In *La Pétition à Byzance,* 61–74. Edited by Denis Feissel and Jean Gascou. Centre de Recherche d'Histoire et Civilisation Byzantine: Monographies 14. Paris: Amis du Centre, 2004.

Francis, James A. *Subversive Virtue: Asceticism and Authority in the Second-Century Pagan World.* University Park: Pennsylvania University Press, 1995.

Franzmann, Majella. *Jesus in the Manichaean Writings.* London: T. and T. Clark, 2003.

Frede, Hermann Josef. *Ein neuer Paulustext und Kommentar.* 2 vols. Freiburg: Herder, 1973–74.

Frederiksen, Paula. *Augustine and the Jews: A Christian Defense of Jews and Judaism.* New York: Doubleday, 2008.

Frend, W.H.C. *The Donatist Church: A Movement of Protest in Roman North Africa.* Oxford: Clarendon Press, 1952.

———. "The Gnostic-Manichaean Tradition in Roman North Africa." *Journal of Ecclesiastical History* 4 (1953): 13–36.

Freu, Christel. *Les figures du pauvre dans les sources italiennes de l'antiquité tardive.* Paris: Boccard, 2007.

From Rome to Constantinople: Studies in Honour of Averil Cameron. Edited by Hagit Amirav and Bas ter Haar Romeny. Louvain: Peeters, 2007.

From the Tetrarchs to the Theodosians: Later Roman History and Culture, 284–450 CE. For John Matthews on the Occasion of His 70th Birthday. Edited by Scott McGill, Cristiana Sogno, and Edward Watts. Yale Classical Studies 34. Cambridge: Cambridge University Press, 2010.

Les frontières du profane dans l'antiquité tardive. Edited by Éric Rebillard and Claire Sotinel. Collection de l'École française de Rome 428. Rome: École française de Rome, 2010.

Fulford, M. G. "Economic Hotspots and Provincial Backwaters: Modelling the Late Roman Economy." In *Coin Finds and Coin Use in the Roman World,* 153–77. Edited by Cathy E. King and David G. Wigg. Studien zu Fundmünzen der Antike 10. Berlin: Mann, 1996.

Gabba, Emilio. *Del buon uso della ricchezza: Saggi di storia economica e sociale del mondo antico.* Milan: Guerini, 1988.

Gabillon, Aimé. "Pour une datation de la lettre 243 d'Augustin à Laetus." *Revue des études augustiniennes* 40 (1994): 127–42.

———. "Romanianus alias Cornelius: Du nouveau sur le bienfaiteur et l'ami de saint Augustin." *Revue des études augustiniennes* 24 (1978): 58–70.

Galvão-Sobrinho, Carlos R. "Funerary Epigraphy and the Spread of Christianity in the West." *Athenaeum,* n.s., 83 (1995): 421–66.

Ganz, David. "The Ideology of Sharing: Apostolic Community and Ecclesiastical Property in the Early Middle Ages." In *Property and Power in the Early Middle Ages,* 17–30. Edited by Wendy Davies and Paul Fouracre. Cambridge: Cambridge University Press, 1995.

García Mac Gaw, Carlos. *Le problème du baptême dans le schisme donatiste.* Scripta Antiqua 21. Bordeaux: Ausonius, 2008.

Gardner, Iain M. F., and Samuel N. C. Lieu. "From Narmouthis (Medinat Madi) to Kellis (Ismant el-Kharab): Manichaean Documents from Roman Egypt." *Journal of Roman Studies* 86 (1996): 146–69.

Garnsey, Peter. *Cities, Peasants and Food in Classical Antiquity: Essays in Social and Economic History.* Cambridge: Cambridge University Press, 1998.

———. *Famine and Food Supply in the Graeco-Roman World: Responses to Risk and Crisis.* Cambridge: Cambridge University Press, 1988.

———. "The Originality and Origins of Anonymous, *De divitiis.*" In *From Rome to Constantinople: Studies in Honour of Averil Cameron,* 29–45. Edited by Hagit Amirav and Bas ter Haar Romeny. Louvain: Peeters, 2007.

———. "Roman Patronage." In *From the Tetrarchs to the Theodosians: Later Roman History and Culture, 284–450 CE. For John Matthews on the Occasion of His 70th Birthday,* 33–54. Edited by Scott McGill, Cristiana Sogno, and Edward Watts. Yale Classical Studies 34. Cambridge: Cambridge University Press, 2010.

———. *Social Status and Legal Privilege in the Roman Empire.* Oxford: Clarendon, 1970.

———. *Thinking about Property: From Antiquity to the Age of Revolution.* Cambridge: Cambridge University Press, 2007.

Gatz, Bodo. *Weltalter, goldene Zeit und sinnverwandte Vorstellungen.* Spudasmata 16. Hildesheim: G. Olms, 1967.

Geertz, Clifford. "Common Sense as a Cultural System." In *Local Knowledge: Further Essays in Interpretive Anthropology,* 73–93. New York: Basic Books, 1983.

Gennaro, Francesco di, and Francesca Dell'Era. "Dati archeologici di età tardoantica del territorio dell' *insula inter duo flumina.*" In *Suburbium: Il suburbio di Roma dalla crisi del sistema delle ville a Gregorio Magno,* 97–121. Edited by Phillippe Pergola, Riccardo Santangeli Valenzani, and Rita Volpe. Collection de l'École française de Rome 311. Rome: École française de Rome, 2003.

Gernet, Jacques. *Buddhism in Chinese Society: An Economic History from the Fifth to the Tenth Centuries.* New York: Columbia University Press, 1995.

Gernet, Louis. *Le génie grec dans la religion.* Paris: Renaissance du Livre, 1932.

Ghedini, Francesca, and Silvia Bullo. "Late Antique Domus of Africa Proconsularis: Structural and Decorative Aspects." In *Housing in Late Antiquity: From Palaces to Shops*, 337–66. Edited by Luke Lavan, Lale Özgenel, and Alexander Sarantis. Late Antique Archaeology 3.2. Leiden: Brill, 2007.

Giardina, Andrea. "*Amor civicus*: Formule e immagini dell'evergetismo romano nella tradizione epigrafica." In *La terza età dell'epigrafia*, 67–87. Edited by Angela Donati. Faenza: Fratelli Lega, 1988.

———. "Carità eversiva: Le donazioni di Melania la Giovane e gli equilbrii della società tardoromana." *Studi storici* 29 (1988): 127–42.

———. "Esplosione di tardoantico." *Studi Storici* 40 (1999): 157–80.

———. "The Transition to Late Antiquity." In *The Cambridge Economic History of the Greco-Roman World*, 743–68. Edited by Walter Scheidel, Ian Morris, and Richard Saller. Cambridge: Cambridge University Press, 2007.

Gibbon's Journey from Geneva to Rome: His Journal from 20 April to 2 October 1764. Edited by George A. Bonnad. London: Nelson, 1961.

Giglio, Stefano. "Il 'munus' della pretura a Roma e a Costantinopoli nel tardo impero romano." *Antiquité tardive* 15 (2007): 65–88.

Gillett, Andrew. "The Date and Circumstances of Olympiodorus of Thebes." *Traditio* 48 (1993): 1–29.

———. *Envoys and Political Communication in the Late Antique West, 411–533.* Cambridge: Cambridge University Press, 2003.

———. "Rome, Ravenna and the Last Western Emperors." *Papers of the British School at Rome* 69 (2001): 131–67.

Gilliard, Frank D. "Senatorial Bishops in the Fourth Century." *Harvard Theological Review* 77 (1984): 153–75.

Ginzberg, Louis. *The Legends of the Jews.* Translated by Henrietta Szold. 7 vols. Philadelphia: Jewish Publication Society of America, 1909–38.

Goddard, Christophe J. "Au coeur du dialogue entre païens et chrétiens: L'adventus' des sénateurs dans les cités de l'Antiquité tardive." In *Pagans and Christians in the Roman Empire (IVth–VIth Century A.D.): The Breaking of a Dialogue*, 371–400. Proceedings of the International Conference at the Monastery of Bosé, October 2008. Edited by Peter Brown and Rita Lizzi Testa. Münster: Lit, 2011.

———. "The Evolution of Pagan Sanctuaries in Late Antique Italy (Fourth–Sixth Centuries A.D.): A New Administrative and Legal Framework: A Paradox." In *Les cités de l'Italie tardo-antique (IVe–VIe siècle): Institutions, économie, société, culture et religion*, 281–308. Edited by Massimiliano Ghilardi, Christophe J. Goddard, and Pierfrancesco Porena. Collection de l'École française de Rome 369. Rome: École française de Rome, 2006.

———. "Les formes festives de l'allégeance au Prince en Italie centrale, sous le règne de Constantin: Un suicide religieux?" *Mélanges de l'École française de Rome: Antiquité* 114 (2002): 1025–88.

Godding, Robert. *Prêtres en Gaule mérovingienne.* Subsidia Hagiographica 82. Brussels: Société des Bollandistes, 2001.

Goffart, Walter. *Barbarian Tides: The Migration Age and the Later Roman Empire.*
Philadelphia: University of Pennsylvania Press, 2006.

———. *Barbarians and Romans, A.D. 418–584: The Techniques of Accommodation.*
Princeton: Princeton University Press, 1980.

———. "Salvian of Marseille, *De gubernatione Dei* 3.38–45 and the 'Colonate'
Problem." *Antiquité tardive* 17 (2009): 269–88.

———. "The Technique of Barbarian Settlement in the Fifth Century: A Personal,
Streamlined Account with Ten Additional Comments." *Journal of Late Antiquity*
3 (2010): 65–98.

Goldschmidt, R. C. *Paulinus' Churches at Nola: Translation and Commentary.*
Amsterdam: North Holland, 1940.

Goodrich, Richard. *Contextualizing Cassian: Aristocrats, Asceticism, and Reformation
in Fifth-Century Gaul.* Oxford: Oxford University Press, 2007.

Goody, Jack. *The Development of the Family and Marriage in Europe.* Cambridge:
Cambridge University Press, 1983.

Gorman, Michael M. "The Oldest Annotations on Augustine's *De civitate Dei.*"
Augustinianum 46 (2006): 457–79.

Grafton, Anthony, and Megan Williams. *Christianity and the Transformation of the
Book: Origen, Eusebius, and the Library of Caesarea.* Cambridge, MA: Harvard
University Press, 2006.

Granger Taylor, Hero. "The Two Dalmatics of Saint Ambrose." *Bulletin de Liaison,
Centre International d'Études des Textiles Anciens* 57–58 (1983): 127–73.

Grant, Robert M. *Early Christianity and Society: Seven Studies.* New York: Harper and
Row, 1977.

Green, R.P.H. "Still Waters Run Deep: A New Study of the *Professores* of Bordeaux."
Classical Quarterly, n.s., 35 (1985): 491–506.

Grey, Cam. "Contextualizing *Colonatus*: The *Origo* of the Late Roman Empire." *Journal
of Roman Studies* 97 (2007): 155–75.

———. "Salvian, the Ideal Christian Community and the Fate of the Poor in Fifth-
Century Gaul." In *Poverty in the Roman World,* 168–82. Edited by Margaret
Atkins and Robin Osborne. Cambridge: Cambridge University Press, 2007.

Griffe, Élie. "La pratique religieuse en Gaule au Ve siècle: *Saeculares* et *sancti.*" *Bulletin
de littérature ecclésiastique* 63 (1962): 241–67.

Griffin, Miriam T. *Seneca: A Philosopher in Politics.* Oxford: Clarendon, 1976.

Grig, Lucy. "Throwing Parties for the Poor: Poverty and Splendour in the Late
Antique Church." In *Poverty in the Roman World,* 145–61. Edited by Margaret Atkins and Robin Osborne. Cambridge: Cambridge University Press,
2007.

Gros, Pierre. "La ville comme symbole: Le modèle central et ses limites." In Hervé
Inglebert, *Histoire de la civilisation romaine,* 155–232. Paris: Presses Universitaires
de France, 2005.

Gross, Jan T. *Revolution from Abroad: The Soviet Conquest of Poland's Western Ukraine
and Western Belorussia.* Expanded edition with a new preface. Princeton:
Princeton University Press, 2002.

Gsell, Stéphane. *Atlas archéologique de l'Algérie*. Algiers: A. Jourdain, 1911.

Guest, Peter. "Roman Gold and Hun Kings: The Use and Hoarding of Solidi in the Late Fourth and Fifth Centuries." In *Roman Coins outside the Empire: Ways and Phases, Contexts and Functions*, 295–307. Edited by Aleksander Bursche, Renata Ciołek, and Reinhard Wolters. Collection Moneta 82. Wetteren: Moneta, 2008.

Gui, Isabelle, Noël Duval, and Jean-Pierre Caillet. *Basiliques chrétiennes d'Afrique du Nord: Inventaire d'Algérie*. 2 vols. Paris: Institut d'Études Augustiniennes, 1992.

Guidobaldi, Federico. "Le *domus* tardoantiche di Roma come 'sensori' delle trasformazioni culturali e sociali." In *The Transformations of Vrbs Roma in Late Antiquity*, 53–68. Edited by W. V. Harris. Journal of Roman Archaeology: Supplementary Series 33. Portsmouth, RI: Journal of Roman Archaeology, 1999.

———. "La fondazione delle basiliche titolari di Roma nel IV e V secolo: Assenze e presenze nel *Liber Pontificalis*." In *Atti del colloquio internazionale* Il Liber Pontificalis e la storia materiale, 5–12. Edited by Herman Geertman. Medelingen van het Nederlands Instituut te Rome: Antiquity 60–61. Assen: Van Gorcum, 2003.

Gutilla, Joseph A. "Dalla Capua di Ausonio (Roma altera quondam) alla Nola di Paolino (post urbem titulos sortitus secundos)." *Journal of Early Christian Studies* 12 (2004): 523–36.

Gutsfeld, Andreas. "Kirche und *civitas* in der Spätantike: Augustin und die Einheit von Stadt und Land in Hippo Regius." In *Die spätantike Stadt und ihre Christianisierung*, 135–44. Edited by Gunnar Brands and Hans-Georg Severin. Wiesbaden: Reichert, 2003.

Gutton, Jean Pierre. *La société et les pauvres: L'exemple de la généralité de Lyon, 1534–1789*. Paris: Belles Lettres, 1971.

Guyon, Jean. *Le cimetière "Aux deux lauriers": Recherches sur les catacombes romaines*. Bibliothèque des Écoles françaises d'Athènes et de Rome 264. Rome: École française de Rome, 1987.

———. "Damase et l'illustration des martyrs: Les accents de la dévotion et l'enjeu d'une pastorale." In *Martyrium in Multidisciplinary Perspective: Memorial Louis Reekmans*, 157–77. Edited by Mathijs Lamberigts and Peter van Deun. Louvain: Peeters, 1995.

———. "L'oeuvre de Damase dans le cimetière 'Aux deux lauriers' sur la Via Labicana." In *Saecularia Damasiana*, 227–58. Studi di Antichità Cristiana 39. Vatican: Pontificio Istituto di Archeologia Cristiana, 1986.

———. "La topographie chrétienne des villes de la Gaule." In *Die Stadt in der Spätantike—Niedergang oder Wandel?* 105–28. Edited by Jens-Uwe Krause and Christian Witschel. Historia Einzelschriften 190. Stuttgart: F. Steiner, 2006.

Haas, Jochen. *Die Umweltkrise des 3. Jahrhunderts n. Chr. im Nordwesten des Imperium Romanum*. Geographica Historica 22. Stuttgart: Steiner, 2006.

Habicht, Christian. "Spätantikes Epigram aus Demetrias." In *Demetrias*, 199–203. Edited by V. Milojčić and D. Theocharis. Bonn: R. Habelt, 1976.

Haensch, Rudolf. "Le financement de la construction des églises pendant l'Antiquité tardive et l'évergétisme antique." *Antiquité tardive* 14 (2006): 47–58.

Hagemann, Hans Rudolf. *Die Stellung der Piae Causae nach justinianischem Rechte.* Basler Studien zur Rechtsgeschichte 37. Basel: Helbing and Lichtenhahn, 1953.

Hagendahl, Harald. *Augustine and the Latin Classics.* 2 vols. Studia Graeca et Latina Gothoburgensia 20. Stockholm: Almqvist and Wiksell, 1967.

Haldon, John. "*Comes horreorum—Komès tès Lamias.*" *Byzantine and Modern Greek Studies* 10 (1986): 203–9.

Halperin, Charles J. *Russia and the Golden Horde: The Mongol Impact on Medieval Russian History.* London: Tauris, 1985.

Halsall, Guy. *Barbarian Migrations and the Roman West, 376–568.* Cambridge: Cambridge University Press, 2007.

———. "The Technique of Barbarian Settlement in the Fifth Century: A Reply to Walter Goffart." *Journal of Late Antiquity* 3 (2010): 99–112.

Hammond, Caroline P. "The Last Ten Years of Rufinus's Life and the Date of His Move South from Aquileia." *Journal of Theological Studies,* n.s., 28 (1977): 372–429.

Handley, Mark A. *Death, Society and Culture: Inscriptions and Epitaphs in Gaul and Spain, AD 300–750.* BAR International Series 1135. Oxford: British Archaeological Reports, 2003.

———. "Two Hundred and Sixty-Four Addenda and Corrigenda to *PLRE* from the Latin-Speaking Balkans." *Journal of Late Antiquity* 3 (2010): 113–57.

Hanfmann, George M. A. *The Season Sarcophagus in Dumbarton Oaks.* 2 vols. Cambridge, MA: Harvard University Press, 1951.

Hannestad, Niels. *Tradition in Late Antique Sculpture: Conservation, Modernization, Production.* Acta Jutlandica 69:2. Aarhus, Denmark: Aarhus University Press, 1994.

Hanoune, Roger. "Le paganisme philosophique de l'aristocratie municipale." In *L'Afrique dans l'Occident romain (Ier siècle av. J.-C.–IVe siècle ap. J.-C.),* 63–75. Collection de l'École française de Rome 134. Rome: Palais Farnèse, 1990.

Hardt, Matthias. *Gold und Herrschaft: Die Schätze europäischer Könige und Fürsten im ersten Jahrtausend.* Berlin: Akademie Verlag, 2004.

Harlow, Mary. "Clothes Maketh the Man: Power Dressing and Elite Masculinity in the Later Roman World." In *Gender in the Early Medieval World: East and West, 300–900,* 44–69. Edited by Leslie Brubaker and Julia M. H. Smith. Cambridge: Cambridge University Press, 2004.

Harper, Kyle. "The Greek Census Inscriptions of Late Antiquity." *Journal of Roman Studies* 98 (2008): 83–119.

Harries, Jill. "Christianity and the City in Late Roman Gaul." In *The City in Late Antiquity,* 77–98. Edited by John Rich. London: Routledge, 1992.

———. "*Favor populi:* Pagans, Christians and Public Entertainment in Late Antique Italy." In *"Bread and Circuses": Euergetism and Municipal Patronage in Roman Italy,* 125–41. Edited by Kathryn Lomas and Tim Cornell. London: Routledge, 2003.

———. *Law and Empire in Late Antiquity.* Cambridge: Cambridge University Press, 1999.

———. *Sidonius Apollinaris and the Fall of Rome, AD 407–485.* Oxford: Clarendon, 1994.

———. "'Treasure in Heaven': Property and Inheritance among Senators of Late Rome." In *Marriage and Property*, 54–70. Edited by Elizabeth M. Craik. Aberdeen: University of Aberdeen Press, 1984.

Harris, W. V. Introduction to *The Transformations of Vrbs Roma in Late Antiquity*, 9–14. Edited by W. V. Harris. Journal of Roman Archaeology: Supplementary Series 33. Portsmouth, RI: Journal of Roman Archaeology, 1999.

Hartmann, Götz. *Selbststigmatisierung und Charisma christlicher Heiliger der Spätantike*. Studien und Texte zu Antike und Christentum 38. Tübingen: Mohr Siebeck, 2006.

Hays, Gregory. "*Romuleis Libicisque litteris*: Fulgentius and the 'Vandal Renaissance.'" In *Vandals, Romans and Berbers: New Perspectives on Late Antique North Africa*, 101–32. Edited by A. H. Merrills. Aldershot: Ashgate, 2004.

Head, Thomas. "The Early Medieval Transformation of Piety." In *The Long Morning of Medieval Europe: New Directions in Early Medieval Studies*, 155–60. Edited by Jennifer R. Davis and Michael McCormick. Aldershot: Ashgate, 2008.

Heather, Peter. "Elite Militarisation and the Post-Roman West." In *Istituzioni, carismi ed esercizio del potere (IV–VI secolo d.C.)*, 145–65. Edited by Giorgio Bonamente and Rita Lizzi Testa. Bari: Edipuglia 2010.

———. *The Fall of the Roman Empire: A New History of Rome and the Barbarians*. Oxford: Oxford University Press, 2006.

———. "New Men for New Constantines? Creating an Imperial Elite in the Eastern Mediterranean." In *New Constantines: The Rhythm of Imperial Renewal in Byzantium, 4th–13th Centuries*, 11–34. Edited by Paul Magdalino. Aldershot: Variorum, 1994.

———. "Senators and Senates." In *The Cambridge Ancient History*. Vol. 13, *The Late Empire, A.D. 337–425*, 184–210. Edited by Averil Cameron and Peter Garnsey. Cambridge: Cambridge University Press, 1998.

———. "Why Did the Barbarians Cross the Rhine?" *Journal of Late Antiquity* 2 (2009): 3–29.

Hedrick, Charles. *History and Silence: Purge and Rehabilitation of Memory in Late Antiquity*. Austin: University of Texas Press, 2000.

Heijmans, Marc. *Arles durant l'Antiquité tardive: De la duplex Arelas à l'urbs Genesii*. Collection de l'École française de Rome 324. Rome: École française de Rome, 2004.

Heinen, Heinz. "Reichstreue *nobiles* im zerstörten Trier." *Zeitschrift für Papyrologie und Epigraphik* 131 (2000): 271–78.

———. *Trier und das Trevererland in römischer Zeit*. Trier: Spee, 1985.

Heinzelmann, Martin. "The 'Affair' of Hilary of Arles (445) and Gallo-Roman Identity in the Fifth Century." In *Fifth-Century Gaul: A Crisis of Identity?* 239–51. Edited by John Drinkwater and Hugh Elton. Cambridge: Cambridge University Press, 1992.

———. *Bischofsherrschaften in Gallien: Zur Kontinuität römischer Führungsschichten vom 4. bis 7. Jahrhundert*. Beihefte der Francia 5. Munich: Artemis Verlag, 1976.

Heinzelmann, Martin. "Gallische Prosopographie, 260–527." *Francia* 10 (1982): 531–718.

———. *Gregory of Tours: History and Society in the Sixth Century.* Translated by Christopher Carroll. Cambridge: Cambridge University Press, 2001. Originally published as *Gregor von Tours (538–594): "Zehn Bücher Geschichte." Historiographie und Gesellschaftskonzept im 6. Jahrhundert.* Darmstadt: Wissenschaftliche Buchgesellschaft, 1994.

Hen, Yitzhak. *Roman Barbarians: The Royal Court and Culture in the Early Medieval West.* Basingstoke, UK: Palgrave MacMillan, 2007.

Henig, Martin, and Grahame Soffe. "The Thruxton Roman Villa and Its Mosaic Pavement." *Journal of the British Archaeological Association* 146 (1993): 1–28.

Herbert de la Portbarré-Viard, Gaëlle. *Descriptions monumentales et discours sur l'édification chez Paulin de Nole: Le regard et la lumière (epist. 32 et carm. 27 et 28).* Supplements to Vigiliae Christianae 79. Leiden: Brill, 2006.

Herrschaft und Kirche: Beiträge zur Entstehung und Wirkungskreise episkopaler und monastischer Organisationsformen. Edited by Friedrich Prinz. Stuttgart: Hiersemann, 1988.

Hess, Hamilton. *The Early Development of Canon Law and the Council of Serdica.* Oxford: Oxford University Press, 2002.

Hillner, Julia. "Clerics, Property and Patronage: The Case of the Roman Titular Churches." *Antiquité tardive* 14 (2006): 59–68.

———. "*Domus,* Family, and Inheritance: The Senatorial Family House in Late Antique Rome." *Journal of Roman Studies* 93 (2003): 129–145.

———. "Families, Patronage and the Titular Churches of Rome, c. 300–c. 600." In *Religion, Dynasty and Patronage in Early Christian Rome, 300–900,* 225–261. Edited by Kate Cooper and Julia Hillner. Cambridge: Cambridge University Press, 2007.

Himmelfarb, Gertrude. "The Culture of Poverty." In vol. 2 of *The Victorian City: Images and Realities,* 707–36. Edited by H. J. Dyos and Michael Wolff. London: Routledge; Boston: Kegan Paul, 1973.

Hippone. Edited by Xavier Delestre. Aix-en-Provence: Édisud, 2005.

Hispania in Late Antiquity: Current Perspectives. Edited by Kim Bowes and Michael Kulikowski. Leiden: Brill, 2005.

Hitchner, Robert Bruce. "The Kasserine Archaeological Survey, 1982–1985." *Africa* 11–12 (1992–93): 158–259.

———. "The Kasserine Archaeological Survey, 1982–1986." *Antiquités africaines* 24 (1988): 7–41.

———. "The Kasserine Archaeological Survey, 1987." *Antiquités africaines* 26 (1990): 231–59.

Hodges, Richard, and David Whitehouse. *Mohammed, Charlemagne and the Origins of Europe: Archaeology and the Pirenne Thesis.* Ithaca, NY: Cornell University Press, 1983.

Hoek, Annewies van den. "Peter, Paul and a Consul: Recent Discoveries in African Red Slip Ware." *Zeitschrift für Antikes Christentum* 9 (2005): 197–246.

Hoek, Annewies van den, and John J. Herrmann. "Paulinus of Nola, Courtyards, and Canthari." *Harvard Theological Review* 93 (2000): 173–219.

Holloway, R. Ross. *Constantine and Rome*. New Haven, CT: Yale University Press, 2004.

Hombert, Pierre-Marie. *Nouvelles recherches de chronologie augustinienne*. Paris: Institut d'Études Augustiniennes, 2000.

Hopkins, Keith M. "Christian Number and Its Implications." *Journal of Early Christian Studies* 6 (1998): 185–226.

———. *Death and Renewal*. Cambridge: Cambridge University Press, 1983.

Horden, Peregrine, and Nicholas Purcell. *The Corrupting Sea: A Study of Mediterranean History*. Oxford: Blackwell, 2000.

Horn, Cornelia B. *Asceticism and Christological Controversy in Fifth-Century Palestine: The Career of Peter the Iberian*. Oxford: Oxford University Press, 2006.

Housing in Late Antiquity: From Palaces to Shops. Edited by Luke Lavan, Lale Özgenel, and Alexander Sarantis. Late Antique Archaeology 3.2. Leiden: Brill, 2007.

Hübner, Sabine. *Der Klerus in der Gesellschaft des spätantiken Kleinasiens*. Stuttgart: F. Steiner, 2006.

Hudák, Krisztina, and Levente Nagy. *A Fine and Private Place: Discovering the Early Christian Cemetery of Sopiane/Pécs*. Heritage Booklets 6. Pécs: Örökség Ház, 2009.

Hugoniot, Christophe. "Les acclamations dans la vie municipale tardive et la critique augustinienne des violences lors des spectacles africains." In *Idéologies et valeurs civiques dans le monde romain: Hommage à Claude Lepelley*, 179–87. Edited by Hervé Inglebert. Nanterre: Picard, 2002.

———. *Les spectacles de l'Afrique romaine: Une culture officielle municipale sous l'empire romain*. 3 vols. Lille: Atelier National de Réproduction de Thèses, 2003.

Humana sapit: Études d'Antiquité Tardive offeres à Lellia Cracco Ruggini. Edited by Jean-Michel Carrié and Rita Lizzi Testa. Bibliothèque d'Antiquité Tardive 3. Turnhout: Brepols, 2002.

Humphreys, John H. *Roman Circuses: Arenas for Chariot Racing*. Berkeley: University of California Press, 1986.

Humphries, Mark. *Communities of the Blessed: Social Environment and Religious Change in Northern Italy, AD 200–400*. Oxford: Oxford University Press, 1999.

Hunt, E. D. "Imperial Building at Rome: The Role of Constantine." In *"Bread and Circuses": Euergetism and Municipal Patronage in Roman Italy*, 57–76. Edited by Kathryn Lomas and Tim Cornell. London: Routledge, 2003.

Hunter, David G. *Marriage, Celibacy, and Heresy in Ancient Christianity: The Jovianist Controversy*. Oxford: Oxford University Press, 2007.

———. "Rereading the Jovinianist Controversy: Asceticism and Clerical Authority in Late Ancient Christianity." In *The Cultural Turn in Late Ancient Studies: Gender, Asceticism, and Historiography*, 119–35. Edited by Dale B. Martin and Patricia C. Miller. Durham, NC: Duke University Press, 2005.

———. "Resistance to the Virginal Ideal in Late-Fourth-Century Rome: The Case of Jovinian." *Theological Studies* 48 (1987): 45–64.

———. "The Significance of Ambrosiaster." *Journal of Early Christian Studies* 17 (2009): 1–26.

Hunter, David G. "Vigilantius of Calagurris and Victricius of Rouen: Ascetics, Relics, and Clerics in Late Roman Gaul." *Journal of Early Christian Studies* 7 (1999): 401–30.

Hwang, Alexander Y. *Intrepid Lover of Perfect Grace: The Life and Thought of Prosper of Aquitaine*. Washington, DC: Catholic University of America Press, 2009.

Iannacone, Laurence R. "Skewness Explained: A Rational Choice Model of Religious Giving." *Journal for the Scientific Study of Religion* 36 (1997): 141–57.

Idéologies et valeurs civiques dans le monde romain: Hommage à Claude Lepelley. Edited by Hervé Inglebert. Nanterre: Picard, 2002.

Inglebert, Hervé. *Histoire de la civilisation romaine*. In collaboration with Pierre Gros and Gilles Sauron. Paris: Presses Universitaires de France, 2005.

———. *Les romains chrétiens face à l'histoire de Rome: Histoire, christianisme et romanités en Occident dans l'Antiquité tardive (IIIe–Ve siècles)*. Paris: Institut d'Études Augustiniennes, 1996.

Istituzioni, carismi ed esercizio del potere (IV–VI secolo d.C.). Edited by Giorgio Bonamente and Rita Lizzi Testa. Bari: Edipuglia, 2010.

Jacob, Paul-André. *La vie d'Hilaire d'Arles*. SC 404. Paris: Le Cerf, 1995.

Jacobs, Martin. *Die Institution des jüdischen Patriarchen*. Texte und Studien zum Antiken Judentum 52. Tübingen: Mohr Siebeck, 1995.

Jacques, François. "Le défenseur de cité d'après la Lettre 22* de saint Augustin." *Revue des études augustiniennes* 32 (1986): 5–73.

———. "L'ordine senatorio attraverso la crisi del III secolo." In *Società romana e impero tardoantico*. Edited by Andrea Giardina. Vol. 1, *Istituzioni, ceti, economie*, 81–225. Bari: Laterza, 1986.

———. *Le privilège de liberté: Politique impériale et autonomie municipale dans les cités de l'Occident romain (161–244)*. Collection de l'école française de Rome 76. Rome: Palais Farnèse, 1984.

Jaïdi, Houcine. "Remarques sur la constitution des biens des églises africaines à l'époque romaine tardive." In *Splendidissima civitas: Études d'histoire romaine en hommage à François Jacques*, 169–91. Edited by André Chastagnol, Ségolène Demougin, and Claude Lepelley. Paris: Publications de la Sorbonne, 1996.

James, Edward. "Bede and the Tonsure Question." *Peritia* 3 (1984): 85–98.

James, N. W. "Leo the Great and Prosper of Aquitaine: A Fifth-Century Pope and His Adviser." *Journal of Theological Studies* 44 (1993): 554–84.

Janes, Dominic. *God and Gold in Late Antiquity*. Cambridge: Cambridge University Press, 1998.

Jasper, Detlev, and Horst Fuhrmann. *Papal Letters in the Early Middle Ages*. Washington, DC: Catholic University of America Press, 2001.

Jenal, Georg. *Italia ascetica atque monastica: Das Asketen-und Mönchtum in Italien von den Anfängen bis zur Zeit der Langobarden (ca. 150/250–604)*. 2 vols. Stuttgart: A. Hiersemann, 1995.

Jerome of Stridon: His Life, Writings and Legacy. Edited by Andrew Cain and Josef Lössl. Farnham, UK: Ashgate, 2009.

Johnson, Mark J. *The Roman Imperial Mausoleum in Late Antiquity*. Cambridge: Cambridge University Press, 2009.

Johnson, Stephen. *Later Roman Britain*. London: Paladin, 1982.

Jones, A.H.M. *The Later Roman Empire: A Social, Economic and Administrative Survey, 284–602*. 2 vols. Oxford: Blackwell, 1964.

———. "The Social Background of the Struggle between Paganism and Christianity." In *The Conflict between Paganism and Christianity in the Fourth Century*, 17–37. Edited by Arnaldo Momigliano. Oxford: Clarendon, 1963.

Jones, Allen E. *Social mobility in Late Antique Gaul: Strategies and Opportunities for the Non-Elite*. Cambridge: Cambridge University Press, 2009.

Jones, Christopher P. *New Heroes in Antiquity: From Achilles to Antinoos*. Cambridge, MA: Harvard University Press, 2010.

Jullian, Camille. *Histoire de la Gaule*. 2 vols. Paris: Hachette, 1993.

Jussen, Bernhard. *Name der Witwe: Erkundungen zur Semantik der mittelalterlichen Busskultur*. Göttingen: Vandenhoeck and Ruprecht, 2000.

Just, Patricia. *Imperator et Episcopus: Zum Verhältnis vom Staatsgewalt und christlicher Kirche zwischen dem 1. Konzil von Nicaea (325) und dem 1. Konzil von Konstantinopel*. Potsdamer Altertumswissenschaftliche Beiträge 8. Stuttgart: F. Steiner, 2003.

Kabiersch, Jürgen. *Untersuchungen zum Begriff der Philanthropia bei dem Kaiser Julian*. Klassisch-Philosophische Studien 21. Wiesbaden: Harassowitz, 1960.

Kahlos, Maijastina. "Vettius Agorius Praetextatus and the Rivalry between the Bishops in Rome in 366–367." *Arctos* 31 (1997): 41–54.

Kasper, Clemens M. *Theologie und Askese: Die Spiritualität des Inselmönchtums von Lérins im 5. Jahrhundert*. Beiträge zur Geschichte des Alten Mönchtums und des Benediktinertums 40. Münster: Aschendorff, 1991.

Kaster, Robert A. *Emotion, Restraint, and Community in Ancient Rome*. London: Oxford University Press, 2005.

———. *Guardians of Language: The Grammarian and Society in Late Antiquity*. Berkeley: University of California Press, 1988.

Die Katakombe "Commodilla": Repertorium der Malereien. Edited by Johannes Georg Deckers, Gabriele Mietke, and Albrecht Weiland. 3 vols. Roma Sotterana Cristiana 10. Vatican: Pontificio Istituto di Archeologia Cristiana, 1994.

Kelly, Christopher. Review of *God and Gold in Late Antiquity* by Dominic Janes. *Journal of Roman Studies* 89 (1999): 253–54.

———. *Ruling the Later Roman Empire*. Cambridge, MA: Harvard University Press, 2004.

Kessler, Andreas. *Reichtumskritik und Pelagianismus: Die pelagianische Diatribe De divitiis. Situierung, Lesetext, Übertsetzung, Kommentar*. Paradosis 43. Freiburg, Switzerland: Universitätsverlag, 1999.

Kettering, Sharon. *Patrons, Brokers, and Clients in Seventeenth-Century France*. Oxford: Oxford University Press, 1986.

Khoury, Dina Rizk. *State and Provincial Society in the Ottoman Empire: Mosul, 1540–1834*. Cambridge: Cambridge University Press, 1997.

Kiely, Maria M. "The Interior Courtyard: The Heart of Cimitile/Nola." *Journal of Early Christian Studies* 12 (2004): 443–97.

Kieschnick, John. *The Impact of Buddhism on Chinese Material Culture.* Princeton: Princeton University Press, 2003.

Kinney, Dale. "First-Generation Diptychs in the Discourse of Visual Culture." In *Spätantike und byzantinische Elfenbeinbildwerke im Diskurs,* 149–66. Edited by Gudrun Bühl, Anthony Cutler, and Arbe Effenberger. Wiesbaden: Reichert, 2008.

Klingshirn, William. *Caesarius of Arles: The Making of a Christian Community in Late Antique Gaul.* Cambridge: Cambridge University Press, 1994.

———. "Charity and Power: Caesarius of Arles and the Ransoming of Captives in Sub-Roman Gaul." *Journal of Roman Studies* 75 (1985): 183–203.

Knoch, Stefan. *Sklavenfürsorge im Römischen Reich: Formen und Motive.* Sklaverei—Knechtschaft—Zwangsarbeit 2. Hildesheim: G. Olms, 2005.

Kotula, Tadeusz. "Le fond africain de la révolte d'Héraclien en 413." *Antiquités africaines* 11 (1977): 257–66.

Kranz, Peter. *Jahreszeiten-Sarkophage: Entwicklung und Ikonographie des Motivs der vier Jahreszeiten auf kaiserzeitlichen Sarkophagen und Sarkophagdeckeln.* Deutsches Archäologisches Institut: Die antiken Sarkophagreliefs. Vol. 5. Part 4. Berlin: Mann, 1984.

Krause, Jens-Uwe. *Spätantike Patronatsformen im Westen des römischen Reiches.* Vestigia 38. Munich: C. H. Beck, 1987.

———. "Überlegungen zur Sozialgeschichte des Klerus im 5./6. Jh. n. Chr." In *Die Stadt in der Spätantike—Niedergang oder Wandel?* 413–39. Edited by Jens-Uwe Krause and Christian Witschel. Historia Einzelschriften 190. Stuttgart: F. Steiner, 2006.

Krautheimer, Richard. "The Architecture of Sixtus III: A Fifth-Century Renaissance?" In *De artibus opuscula XL: Essays in Honor of Erwin Panofsky,* 291–302. Edited by Millard Meiss. New York: Columbia University Press, 1961.

———. *Rome: Profile of a City, 312–1408.* Princeton: Princeton University Press, 1980.

———. *Three Christian Capitals: Topography and Politics.* Berkeley: University of California Press, 1983.

Kreuzsaler, Claudia. "*Ho hierôtatos Nilos* auf einer christlichen Nilstandsmarkierung." *Journal of Juristic Papyrology* 34 (2004): 81–86.

Kriegbaum, Bernhard. *Kirche der Traditoren oder Kirche der Märtyrer? Die Vorgeschichte des Donatismus.* Innsbruck: Tyrolia, 1986.

Krueger, Derek. *Symeon the Holy Fool: Leontius' Life and the Late Antique City.* Berkeley: University of California Press, 1996.

Kulikowski, Michael. "Barbarians in Gaul, Usurpers in Britain." *Britannia* 31 (2000): 325–45.

———. *Late Roman Spain and Its Cities.* Baltimore: Johns Hopkins University Press, 2004.

———. "The Visigothic Settlement in Aquitania: The Imperial Perspective." In *Society and Culture in Late Antique Gaul: Revisiting the Sources,* 26–38. Edited by Ralph Mathisen and Danuta Shanzer. Aldershot: Ashgate, 2001.

Kurdock, Anne. "*Demetrias ancilla Dei*: Anicia Demetrias and the Problem of the Missing Patron." In *Religion, Dynasty and Patronage in Early Christian Rome, 300–900*, 190–224. Edited by Kate Cooper and Julia Hillner. Cambridge: Cambridge University Press, 2007.

La Bonnardière, Anne-Marie. "Les commentaires simultanés de Mat. 6,12 et de 1 Jo. 1,18 dans l'oeuvre de saint Augustin." *Revue des études augustiniennes* 1 (1955): 129–47.

———. "Les 'Enarrationes in Psalmos' prêchées par Saint Augustin à Carthage en décembre 409." *Recherches augustiniennes* 11 (1976): 52–90.

———. "Pénitence et réconciliation de pénitents d'après saint Augustin." *Revue des études augustiniennes* 13 (1967): 31–53.

Lambert, David. "The Uses of Decay: History in Salvian's *De gubernatione dei*." *Augustinian Studies* 30 (1999): 115–30.

Lambot, Cyrille. "Lettre inédite de S. Augustin relative au 'De civitate Dei.'" *Revue bénédictine* 51 (1939): 109–21.

———. "Nouveaux sermons de saint Augustin." *Revue bénédictine* 49 (1937): 233–78.

Lancel, Serge. *Actes de la Conférence de Carthage en 411*. 4 vols. SC 194–95, 224, 373. Paris: Le Cerf, 1972–91.

———. *Saint Augustin*. Paris: Fayard, 1999. Translated by Antonia Nevill, as *Saint Augustine*. London: SCM Press, 2002.

Landscapes of Change: Rural Evolutions in Late Antiquity and the Early Middle Ages. Edited by Neil Christie. Aldershot: Ashgate, 2004.

Lane Fox, Robin. "Movers and Shakers." In *The Philosopher and Society in Late Antiquity: Essays in Honor of Peter Brown*, 19–50. Edited by Andrew Smith. Swansea: Classical Press of Wales, 2005.

———. *Pagans and Christians*. New York: A. Knopf, 1987.

Laniado, Avshalom. "Le christianisme et l'évolution des institutions municipales du Bas-Empire: L'exemple du *defensor civitatis*." In *Die Stadt in der Spätantike— Niedergang oder Wandel?* 319–34. Edited by Jens-Uwe Krause and Christian Witschel. Historia Einzelschriften 190. Stuttgart: F. Steiner, 2006.

———. "The Early Byzantine State and the Christian Ideal of Voluntary Poverty." In *Charity and Giving in Monotheistic Religions*, 15–43. Edited by Miriam Frenkel and Yaacov Lev. Studien zur Geschichte und Kultur des islamischen Orients, n. F. 22. Berlin: de Gruyter, 2009.

Late Antiquity: A Guide to the Postclassical World. Edited by G. W. Bowersock, Peter Brown, and Oleg Grabar. Cambridge, MA: Harvard University Press, 1999.

Laurence, Patrick. *Jérôme et le nouveau modèle feminine: La conversion à la "vie parfaite."* Paris: Institut d'Études Augustiniennes, 1997.

———. "Proba, Juliana et Démétrias: Le christianisme des femmes de la *gens Anicia* dans la première moitié du Ve siècle." *Revue des études augustiniennes* 48 (2002): 131–63.

Lawless, George. *Augustine of Hippo and His Monastic Rule*. Oxford: Clarendon, 1987.

Laycock, Stuart. *Britannia the Failed State: Tribal Conflicts and the End of Roman Britain*. Stroud: The History Press, 2008.

Le Roux, Patrick. "*L'amor patriae* dans les cités sous l'empire romain." In *Idéologies et valeurs civiques dans le monde romain: Hommage à Claude Lepelley*, 143–61. Edited by Hervé Inglebert. Nanterre: Picard, 2002.

Leader-Newby, Ruth E. *Silver and Society in Late Antiquity: Functions and Meanings of Silver Plate in the Fourth to Seventh Centuries*. Aldershot: Ashgate, 2003.

Lee, A. D. *War in Late Antiquity: A Social History*. Oxford: Blackwell, 2007.

Lehmann, Tomas. "Martinus und Paulinus in Primuliacum (Gallien): Zu den frühesten nachweisbaren Mönchsbildnissen (um 400) in einem Kirchenkomplex." In *Vom Kloster zum Klosterverband: Das Werkzeug der Schriftlichkeit*, 56–67. Edited by Hagen Keller and Franz Neiske. Munich: W. Fink, 1997.

———. *Paulinus Nolanus und die Basilica Nova in Cimitile/Nola: Studien zu einem zentralen Denkmal der spätantik-frühchristlichen Architektur*. Wiesbaden: P. Reichert, 2004.

———. "Zu Alarichs Beutezug in Campanien: Ein neu entdecktes Gedicht des Paulinus Nolanus." *Römische Quartalschrift* 93 (1998): 181–99.

Lendon, John. *Empire of Honour: The Art of Government in the Roman World*. Oxford: Oxford University Press, 1997.

Lenski, Noel. "Captivity, Slavery, and Cultural Exchange between Rome and the Germans from the First to the Seventh Century C.E." In *Invisible Citizens: Captives and Their Consequences*, 80–109. Edited by Catherine M. Cameron. Salt Lake City: University of Utah Press, 2008.

———. "Valens and the Monks: Cudgeling and Conscription as a Means of Social Control." *Dumbarton Oaks Papers* 58 (2004): 93–117.

Leone, Anna. *Changing Townscapes in North Africa from Late Antiquity to the Arab Conquest*. Munera 28. Bari: Edipuglia, 2007.

———. "Clero, proprietà, cristianizzazione delle campagne nel Nord Africa tardoantica: *Status quaestionis*." *Antiquité tardive* 14 (2006): 95–104.

Leone, Anna, and David Mattingly. "Vandal, Byzantine and Arab Rural Landscapes in North Africa." In *Landscapes of Change: Rural Evolutions in Late Antiquity and the Early Middle Ages*, 135–62. Edited by Neil Christie. Aldershot: Ashgate, 2004.

Lepelley, Claude. *Les cités de l'Afrique romaine au Bas-Empire*. 2 vols. Paris: Études Augustiniennes, 1979–81.

———. "De la réaction païenne à la sécularization." *Cristianesimo e storia* 30 (2009): 423–39.

———. "Facing Wealth and Poverty: Defining Augustine's Social Doctrine." *Augustinian Studies* 38 (2007): 1–18.

———. "Le lieu des valeurs communes: La cité terrain neutre entre païens et chrétiens dans l'Afrique de l'Antiquité tardive." In *Idéologies et valeurs civiques dans le monde romain: Hommage à Claude Lepelley*, 271–85. Edited by Hervé Inglebert. Nanterre: Picard, 2002.

———. "*Spes saeculi*: Le milieu social d'Augustin et ses ambitions séculières avant sa conversion." In vol. 1 of *Congresso internazionale su S. Agostino nel XVI centenario della conversione*, 99–117. Studia Ephemeridis Augustinianum 24. Rome: Institutum Pontificium Augustinianum, 1987. Reprinted in Lepelley,

Aspects de l'Afrique romaine: Les cités, la vie rurale, le christianisme, 329–344. Bari: Edipuglia, 2001.

Lesne, Émile. *Histoire de la propriété ecclésiastique en France*. Vol. 1, *Époques romaine et mérovingienne*. Lille: Giard, 1910.

Leveau, Philippe. *Caesarea de Maurétanie: Une ville romaine et ses campagnes*. Collection de l'École française de Rome 70. Rome: Palais Farnèse, 1984.

Leveau, Phillippe, Pierre Sillières, and Jean-Pierre Valat. *Campagnes de la Méditerranée romaine: Occident*. Paris: Hachette, 1993.

Levison, Wilhelm. "Das Testament des Diakons Adalgisel Grimo vom Jahre 634." *Trierer Zeitschrift* 7 (1932): 69–85. Reprinted in Levison, *Aus rheinischer und fränkischer Frühzeit*. Dusseldorf: L. Schwann, 1948.

Lewis, Mark Edward. "Gift Circulation and Charity in the Han and Roman Empires." In *Rome and China: Comparative Perspectives on Ancient World Empires*, 121–36. Edited by Walter Scheidel. Oxford: Oxford University Press, 2009.

Lewit, Tamara. "Pigs, Presses and Pastoralism: Farming in the Fifth to Sixth Centuries." *Early Medieval Europe* 17 (2009): 77–91.

———. "'Vanishing Villas': What Happened to Élite Rural Habitation in the West in the 5th–6th C.?" *Journal of Roman Archaeology* 16 (2003): 260–74.

Leyser, Conrad. *Authority and Asceticism from Augustine to Gregory the Great*. Oxford: Clarendon, 2000.

———. "Semi-Pelagianism." In *Augustine through the Ages: An Encyclopedia*, 761–66. Edited by Allan D. Fitzgerald. Grand Rapids, MI: Eerdmans, 1999.

———. "'This Sainted Isle': Panegyric, Nostalgia and the Invention of Lerinian Monasticism." In *The Limits of Ancient Christianity: Essays on Late Antique Thought and Culture in Honor of R. A. Markus*, 188–206. Edited by William E. Klingshirn and Mark Vessey. Ann Arbor: University of Michigan Press, 1999.

Liebeschuetz, J.W.H.G. *Barbarians and Bishops: Army, Church, and State in the Age of Arcadius and Chrysostom*. Oxford: Clarendon, 1990.

———. *The Decline and Fall of the Roman City*. Oxford: Oxford University Press, 2001.

———. *Ambrose and John Chrysostom: Clerics between Desert and Empire*. Oxford: Oxford University Press, 2011.

———, with the assistance of Carole Hill. *Ambrose of Milan: Political Letters and Speeches*. Liverpool: Liverpool University Press, 2006.

Liebs, Detlef. *Römische Jurisprudenz in Gallien (2. bis 8. Jahrhundert)*. Berlin: Duncker and Humblot, 2002.

Lieu, Samuel N. C. *Manichaeism in the Later Roman Empire and Medieval China*. 2nd ed. Tübingen: Mohr, 1992.

Lim, Richard. *Public Disputation, Power, and Social Order in Late Antiquity*. The Transformation of the Classical Heritage 23. Berkeley: University of California Press, 1995.

———. "The Roman Pantomime Riot of A.D. 509." In *Humana sapit: Études d'Antiquité Tardive offeres à Lellia Cracco Ruggini*, 35–42. Edited by Jean-Michel Carrié and Rita Lizzi Testa. Bibliothèque d'Antiquité Tardive 3. Turnhout: Brepols, 2002.

Lim, Richard. "Unity and Diversity among the Western Manichaeans: A Reconsideration of Mani's *sancta ecclesia*." *Revue des études augustiniennes* 35 (1989): 231–50.

Linder, Amnon, ed. and trans. *The Jews in Roman Imperial Legislation*. Detroit: Wayne State University Press; Jerusalem: Israel Academy of Sciences and Humanities, 1987.

Liu, Xinru. *Silk and Religion: An Exploration of Material Life and the Thought of People, AD 600–1200*. Delhi: Oxford University Press, 1996.

Liverani, Paolo. "Saint Peter's, Leo the Great and the Leprosy of Constantine." *Papers of the British School at Rome* 76 (2008): 155–72.

Lizzi, Rita. "Ambrose's Contemporaries and the Christianization of Northern Italy." *Journal of Roman Studies* 80 (1990): 156–73.

———. "Una società esortata all'ascetismo: Misure legislative e motivazioni economiche nel IV–V secolo d.C." *Studi Storici* 30 (1989): 129–53.

———. *Vescovi e strutture ecclesiastiche nella città tardoantica (L'Italia annonaria nel IV–V secolo d.C)*. Biblioteca di Athenaeum 9. Como: New Press, 1989.

Lizzi Testa, Rita. "Alle origini della tradizione pagana su Costantino e il senato romano." In *Transformations of Late Antiquity: Essays for Peter Brown*, 85–127. Edited by Philip Rousseau and Manolis Papoutsakis. Farnham, UK: Ashgate, 2009.

———. "Christian Emperor, Vestal Virgins and Priestly Colleges: Reconsidering the End of Roman Paganism." *Antiquité tardive* 15 (2007): 251–62.

———. "L'Église, les *domini*, les païens *rustici*: Quelques stratégies pour la christianisation del'Occident (IVe–VIe s.)." In *Le problème de la christianisation du monde antique*, 77–113. Edited by Hervé Inglebert, Sylvain Destephen, and Bruno Dumézil. Paris: Picard, 2010.

———. "*Insula ipsa Libanus Almae Veneris nuncupatur*: Culti, celebrazioni, sacerdoti pagani a Roma, tra IV e VI secolo." In *Istituzioni, carismi ed esercizio del potere (IV–VI secolo d.C.)*, 273–303. Edited by Giorgio Bonamente and Rita Lizzi Testa. Bari: Edipuglia 2010.

———. "Privilegi economici e definizione di *status*: Il caso del vescovo cristiano." *Rendiconti dell'Accademia Nazionale dei Lincei: Classe di scienze morali, storiche e filologiche*, ser. 9, no. 11 (2000): 55–103.

———. *Senatori, popolo, papi: Il governo di Roma al tempo dei Valentiniani*. Bari: Edipuglia, 2004.

———. "Vergini di Dio—Vergini di Vesta: Il sesso negato e la sacralità." In *L'Eros difficile: Amore e sessualità nell'antico cristianesimo*, 89–132. Edited by Salvatore Pricoco. Catanzaro: Rubettino, 1998.

Llewellyn, P.A.B. "The Roman Church during the Laurentian Schism: Priests and Senators." *Church History* 45 (1976): 417–27.

Lo Cascio, Elio. "*Canon frumentarius, suarius, vinarius*: Stato e privati nell'approvvigionamento dell'*Vrbs*." In *The Transformations of Vrbs Roma in Late Antiquity*, 163–82. Edited by W. V. Harris. Journal of Roman Archaeology: Supplementary Series 33. Portsmouth, RI: Journal of Roman Archaeology, 1999.

Loening, Edgar. *Geschichte des deutschen Kirchenrechts.* Vol. 1, *Das Kirchenrecht in Gallien von Constantin bis Chlodovech.* Strassburg: Trübner, 1878.

The Long Morning of Medieval Europe: New Directions in Early Medieval Studies. Edited by Jennifer R. Davis and Michael McCormick. Aldershot: Ashgate, 2008.

Lorenz, Rudolf. "Der Augustinismus Prospers von Aquitanien." *Zeitschrift für Kirchengeschichte* 73 (1962): 217–52.

Loseby, Simon T. "Arles in Late Antiquity: *Gallula Roma Arelas* and *Urbs Genesii.*" In *Towns in Transition: Urban Evolution in Late Antiquity and the Early Middle Ages,* 45–70. Edited by Neil Christie and Simon T. Loseby. Aldershot: Scolar, 1996.

———. "Bishops and Cathedrals: Order and Diversity in the Fifth-Century Urban Landscape in Gaul." In *Fifth-Century Gaul: A Crisis of Identity?* 144–55. Edited by John Drinkwater and Hugh Elton. Cambridge: Cambridge University Press, 1992.

———. "Decline and Change in the Cities of Late Antique Gaul." In *Die Stadt in der Spätantike—Niedergang oder Wandel?* 67–104. Edited by Jens-Uwe Krause and Christian Witschel. Historia Einzelschriften 190. Stuttgart: F. Steiner, 2006.

———. "Marseille: A Late Antique Success Story?" *Journal of Roman Studies* 82 (1992): 165–85.

Lössl, Josef. "Julian of Aeclanum on Pain." *Journal of Early Christian Studies* 10 (2002): 203–43.

———. *Julian von Aeclanum: Studien zu seinem Leben, seinem Werk, seiner Lehre und ihrer Überlieferung.* Supplements to Vigiliae Christianae 60. Leiden: Brill, 2001.

Lot, Ferdinand. *The End of the Ancient World and the Beginnings of the Middle Ages.* New York: Knopf, 1931.

Lovejoy, Arthur O., and George Boas. *Primitivism and Related Ideas in Antiquity.* Vol. 1 of *A Documentary History of Primitivism and Related Ideas.* Edited by Arthur Lovejoy and George Boas. Baltimore: Johns Hopkins University Press, 1935.

Lowden, John. "The Beginnings of Biblical Illustration." In *Imaging the Early Medieval Bible,* 9–55. Edited by John Williams. University Park: Pennsylvania State University Press, 1999.

Löx, Markus. "Die Kirche San Lorenzo in Mailand: Eine Stiftung des Stilicho?" *Mitteilungen des deutschen archäologischen Instituts: Römische Abteilung* 114 (2008): 407–38.

Lugaresi, Leonardo. "*Regio aliena*: L'atteggiamento della chiesa verso i luoghi di spettacolo nelle città tardoantiche." *Antiquité tardive* 15 (2007): 21–34.

Lunn-Rockliffe, Sophie. *Ambrosiaster's Political Theology.* Oxford: Oxford University Press, 2007.

———. "A Pragmatic Approach to Poverty and Riches: Ambrosiaster's *Quaestio* 124." In *Poverty in the Roman World,* 115–29. Edited by Margaret Atkins and Robin Osborne. Cambridge: Cambridge University Press, 2007.

Luongo, Gennaro. *Lo specchio dell'agiografo: San Felice nei carmi XV e XVI di Paolino di Nola.* Naples: Tempi Moderni, 1992.

Lüthi, Max. *The European Folktale: Form and Nature.* Translated by John D. Niles. Bloomington: University of Indiana Press, 1982.

Lutterbach, Hubertus. *Monachus factus est: Die Mönchwerdung im frühen Mittelalter.* Beiträge zur Geschichte des alten Mönchtums und des Benediktinertums. Münster: Aschendorff, 1995.

Maas, Michael. "Ethnicity, Orthodoxy and Community in Salvian of Marseilles." In *Fifth-Century Gaul: A Crisis of Identity?* 275–84. Edited by John Drinkwater and Hugh Elton. Cambridge: Cambridge University Press, 1992.

MacCormack, Sabine. "Sin, Citizenship and the Salvation of Souls: The Impact of Christian Priorities on Late Roman and Post-Roman Society." *Comparative Studies in Society and History* 39 (1997): 644–73.

MacGeorge, Penny. *Late Roman Warlords.* Oxford: Oxford University Press, 2002.

Machado, Carlos. "Building the Past: Monuments and Memory in the Forum Romanum." In *Social and Political Life in Late Antiquity*, 157–92. Late Antique Archaeology 3:1. Edited by Will Bowden, Adam Gutteridge, and Carlos Machado. Leiden: Brill, 2006.

———. "The City as Stage: Aristocratic Commemoration in Late Antique Rome." In *Les frontières du profane dans l'antiquité tardive*, 287–317. Edited by Éric Rebillard and Claire Sotinel. Collection de l'École française de Rome 428. Rome: École française de Rome, 2010.

———. "Roman Aristocrats and the Christianization of Rome." In *Pagans and Christians in the Roman Empire (IVth–VIth Century A.D.): The Breaking of a Dialogue*, 493–513. Proceedings of the International Conference at the Monastery of Bosé, October 2008. Edited by Peter Brown and Rita Lizzi Testa. Münster: Lit, 2011.

MacMullen, Ramsay. *Changes in the Roman Empire: Essays in the Ordinary.* Princeton: Princeton University Press, 1990.

———. "The Preacher's Audience (AD 350–400)." *Journal of Theological Studies* 40 (1989): 503–11.

———. *Roman Social Relations, 50 B.C. to A.D. 284.* New Haven, CT: Yale University Press, 1974.

———. "Some Pictures in Ammianus Marcellinus." *Art Bulletin* 46 (1964): 435–55. Reprinted in *Changes in the Roman Empire: Essays in the Ordinary.*

———. "What Difference Did Christianity Make?" *Historia* 35 (1986): 322–43. Reprinted in *Changes in the Roman Empire: Essays in the Ordinary.*

Madec, Goulven. "Le communisme spirituel." In *Homo Spiritalis: Festgabe für Luc Verheijen*, 225–39. Edited by Cornelius Mayer. Würzburg: Augustinus, 1987. Reprinted in Madec, *Petites Études Augustiniennes*, 215–31. Paris: Institut d'Études Augustiniennes, 1994.

Magalhães de Oliveira, Júlio César. "Le 'pouvoir du peuple': Une émeute à Hippone au début du Ve siècle connue par le sermon 302 de Saint Augustin pour la fête de Saint Laurent." *Antiquité tardive* 12 (2004): 309–24.

———. "*Vt maiores pagani non sint*! Pouvoir, iconoclasme et action populaire à Carthage au début du Ve siècle." *Antiquité tardive* 14 (2006): 245–62.

Magnani, Eliana. "Almsgiving, *donatio pro anima* and Eucharistic Offering in the Early Middle Ages of Western Europe (4th–9th Century)." In *Charity and Giving in Monotheistic Religions*, 111–21. Edited by Miriam Frenkel and Yaacov Lev. Studien zur Geschichte und Kultur des islamischen Orients, n. F. 22. Berlin: de Gruyter, 2009.

———. "Du don aux églises au don pour le salut de l'âme en Occident (IVe–XIe siècle): Le paradigme eucharistique." In *Pratiques de l'eucharistie dans les Églises d'Orient et Occident (Antiquité et Moyen Âge)*, 1021–42. Edited by Nicole Bériou, Béatrice Caseau, and Dominique Rigaux. Paris: Institut d'Études Augustiniennes, 2009.

Magness, Jodi. "The Date of the Sardis Synagogue in the Light of the Numismatic Evidence." *American Journal of Archaeology* 109 (2005): 443–75.

Maguire, Henry. "The Good Life." In *Late Antiquity: A Guide to the Postclassical World*, 238–57. Edited by G. W. Bowersock, Peter Brown, and Oleg Grabar. Cambridge, MA: Harvard University Press, 1999.

Maioli, Maria Grazia. "Il complesso archeologico di Via d'Azeglio a Ravenna: Gli edifici di epoca tardoimperiale e bizantina." *Corso di cultura sull'arte ravennate e bizantina* 41 (1994): 45–61.

Malineau, Violaine. "Le théâtre dans les cités de l'Italie tardo-antique." In *Les cités de l'Italie tardo-antique (IVe–VIe siècle): Institutions, économie, société, culture et religion*, 187–203. Edited by Massimiliano Ghilardi, Christophe J. Goddard, and Pierfrancesco Porena. Collection de l'École française de Rome 369. Rome: École française de Rome, 2006.

Mancassola, Nicola, and Fabio Saggioro. "La fine delle ville romane: Il territorio tra Adda e Adige." *Archeologia medievale* 27 (2000): 315–31.

Mandouze, André. *Saint Augustin: L'aventure de la raison et de la grâce*. Paris: Études Augustiniennes, 1968.

Mann, J. C. Review of *Roman Government's Response to Crisis, A.D. 235–337*, by Ramsay MacMullen. *Journal of Roman Studies* 69 (1979): 191.

Marazzi, Federico. *I "Patrimonia Sanctae Romanae Ecclesiae" nel Lazio (secoli IV–X): Struttura amministrativa e prassi gestionali*. Istituto storico italiano per il Medioevo: Nuovi Studi Storici 31. Rome: Palazzo Borromini, 1998.

———. "Rome in Transition: Economic and Political Change in the Fourth and Fifth Centuries." In *Early Medieval Rome and the Christian West: Essays in Honour of Donald A. Bullough*, 21–41. Edited by Julia M. H. Smith. Leiden: Brill, 2000.

Marcone, Arnaldo. "L'allestimento dei giochi annuali a Roma nel IV secolo d.C.: Aspetti economici e ideologici." *Annali della Scuola Normale Superiore di Pisa, Classe di lettere e filosofia*, ser. 3, no. 11 (1981): 105–22. Reprinted in *La parte migliore del genere umano: Aristocrazie, potere e ideologia nell'Occidente tardoantico*, 293–311. Edited by Sergio Roda. Turin: Scriptorium, 1994.

———. "Il mondo di Paolino di Pella." In *Di tarda antichità: Scritti scelti*, 87–96. Milan: Mondadori, 2008.

Markus, Robert A. "*De civitate Dei*: Pride and the Common Good." In *Augustine: "Second Founder of the Faith,"* 245–59. Edited by Joseph C. Schnaubelt and

Frederick Van Fleteren. Collectanea Augustiniana. New York: Peter Lang, 1990. Reprinted in Markus, *Sacred and Secular*. Aldershot: Variorum, 1994.

———. *The End of Ancient Christianity*. Cambridge: Cambridge University Press, 1990.

———. "The Legacy of Pelagius: Orthodoxy, Heresy and Conciliation." In *The Making of Orthodoxy: Essays in Honour of Henry Chadwick*, 214–34. Edited by Rowan Williams. Cambridge: Cambridge University Press, 1989.

Marrou, Henri-Irénée. "Le dossier épigraphique de l'évêque Rusticus de Narbonne." *Rivista di archeologia cristiana* 3–4 (1970): 331–49.

———. Introduction to *Clément d'Alexandrie: Le pedagogue*. Vol. 1. SC 70. Paris: Le Cerf, 1960.

———. "Un lieu dit 'Cité de Dieu.'" In vol. 1 of *Augustinus magister*, 101–10. Paris: Études Augustiniennes, 1955.

———. *Saint Augustin et la fin de la culture antique: Retractatio*. Bibliothèque de l'École française d'Athènes et de Rome 145. Paris: Boccard, 1949.

Martin, Jochen. *Der Weg zur Ewigkeit führt über Rom: Die Frühgeschichte des Papsttums und die Darstellung der neutestamentlichen Heilsgeschichte im Triumphbogenmosaik von Santa Maria Maggiore in Rom*. Stuttgart: Steiner, 2010.

Marzano, Annalisa. *Roman Villas in Central Italy: A Social and Economic History*. Columbia Studies in the Classical Tradition 30. Leiden: Brill, 2007.

Mastrocinque, Attilio. "Magia agraria nell'impero cristiano." *Mediterraneo antico* 7 (2004): 795–836.

Mathisen, Ralph W. "The Christianization of the Late Roman Senatorial Order: Circumstances and Scholarship." *International Journal of the Classical Tradition* 9 (2002): 257–78.

———. "The Christianization of the Late Roman Senatorial Order *bis*: A Response to Michele Salzman's 'Rejoinder' to Ralph Mathisen's Review Article." *International Journal of the Classical Tradition* 14 (2007): 233–47.

———. *Ecclesiastical Factionalism and Religious Controversy in Fifth-Century Gaul*. Washington, DC: Catholic University of America Press, 1989.

———. "Episcopal Hierarchy and Tenure of Office in Late Roman Gaul: A Method for Establishing Dates of Ordination." *Francia* 17 (1990): 125–39.

———. "Nature or Nurture? Some Perspectives on the Gallic Famine of circa A.D. 470." *Ancient World* 24 (1993): 91–105.

———. "A New Fragment of Augustine's *De nuptiis et concupiscentia* from the *Codex Sangallensis* 190." *Zeitschrift für Antikes Christentum* 3 (1999): 165–83.

———. *Roman Aristocrats in Barbarian Gaul: Strategies for Survival in an Age of Transition*. Austin: University of Texas Press, 1993.

Matthews, John F. "Four Funerals and a Wedding: This World and the Next in Fourth-Century Rome." In *Transformations of Late Antiquity: Essays for Peter Brown*, 129–46. Edited by Philip Rousseau and Manolis Papoutsakis. Farnham, UK: Ashgate, 2009.

———. "The Letters of Symmachus." In *Latin Literature of the Fourth Century*, 58–99. Edited by J. W. Binns. London: Routledge, 1974.

———. *Western Aristocracies and Imperial Court, A.D. 364–425*. Oxford: Clarendon, 1975.

Mattingly, David. "Being Roman: Expressing Identity in a Provincial Setting." *Journal of Roman Archaeology* 17 (2004): 5–25.

Mauné, Stéphane. *Les campagnes de la cité de Béziers dans l'Antiquité: Partie nord-orientale (IIe s. av. J.-C.–VIe s. ap. J.-C.)*. Montagnac: Mergoil, 1998.

Mazza, Roberta. "Tra Oriente e Occidente: La gestione del *patrimonium Petri* in Italia meridionale." In *Paesaggi e insediamenti rurali in Italia meridionale fra tardoantico e altomedioevo*, 703–15. Edited by Guiliano Volpe and Maria Turchiano. Bari: Edipuglia, 2005.

Mazzarino, Santo. *Aspetti sociali del quarto secolo*. Rome: Bretschneider, 1951.

———. "La propaganda senatoriale nel tardo imperio." Review of Andreas Alföldi, *Die Kontorniaten: Ein verkanntes Propagandamittel der Stadt-römischen heidnischen Aristokratie in ihrem Kampfe gegen das christliche Kaisertum. Doxa* 4 (1951): 121–48.

———. *Storia sociale del Vescovo Ambrogio*. Rome: Bretschneider, 1989.

Mazzoleni, Danilo. "Il lavoro nell'epigrafia Cristiana." In *Epigrafi del mondo cristiano antico*, 38–49. Rome: Lateran University Press, 2002.

McCormick, Michael. "Bateaux de vie, bateaux de mort: Maladie, commerce et le passage économique du bas-empire au moyen-âge." In *Morfologie sociali e culturali in Europa fra Tarda Antichità e Alto Medioevo*, 35–118. Settimane i Studi del Centro Italiano di Studi sull'Alto Medioevo 45. Spoleto: Centro di Studi sull'Alto Medioevo, 1998.

———. *Origins of the European Economy: Communications and Commerce, A.D. 300–900*. Cambridge: Cambridge University Press, 2001.

McKinley, Allan Scott. "The First Two Centuries of Saint Martin of Tours." *Early Medieval Europe* 14 (2006): 173–200.

McLynn, Neil B. "Administrator: Augustine in His Diocese." In *Companion to Augustine*. Edited by Mark Vessey. Oxford: Wiley-Blackwell, forthcoming.

———. *Ambrose of Milan: Church and Court in a Christian Capital*. Berkeley: University of California Press, 1994.

———. "Augustine's Black Sheep: The Case of Antoninus of Fussala." In *Istituzioni, carismi ed esercizio del potere (IV–VI secolo d.C.)*, 305–21. Edited by Giorgio Bonamente and Rita Lizzi Testa. Bari: Edipuglia 2010.

———. "Augustine's Roman Empire." *Augustinian Studies* 30 (1999): 29–44.

———. "Crying Wolf: The Pope and the Lupercalia." *Journal of Roman Studies* 98 (2008): 161–75.

———. "Paulinus the Impenitent: A Study of the *Eucharisticos*." *Journal of Early Christian Studies* 2 (1995): 461–86.

———. "Poetic Creativity and Political Crisis in Early Fifth-Century Gaul." *Journal of Late Antiquity* 2 (2009): 60–74.

———. "Seeing and Believing: Aspects of Conversion from Antoninus Pius to Louis the Pious." In *Conversion in Late Antiquity and the Early Middle Ages: Seeing and Believing*, 224–70. Edited by Kenneth Mills and Anthony Grafton. Rochester, NY: University of Rochester Press, 2003.

McLynn, Neil B. "The Transformation of Imperial Churchgoing in the Fourth Century." In *Approaching Late Antiquity: The Transformation from Early to Late Empire*, 235–70. Edited by Simon Swain and Mark Edwards. Oxford: Oxford University Press, 2004.

Meneghini, Roberto, and Riccardo Santangeli Valenzani. *Roma nell'altomedioevo: Topografia e urbanistica della città dal V al X secolo.* Rome: Libreria dello Stato, 2004.

Merrills, Andy, and Richard Miles. *The Vandals.* Chichester, UK: Wiley-Blackwell, 2010.

Meslin, Michel. *La fête des kalendes de janvier dans l'empire romain: Étude d'un rituel de Nouvel An.* Brussels: Latomus, 1970.

Meyer, Ulrich. *Soziales Handeln im Zeichen des "Hauses": Zur Ökonomik in der Spätantike und im frühen Mittelalter.* Göttingen: Vandenhouck and Ruprecht, 1998.

Michel, Anne. "Aspects du culte dans les églises de Numidie au temps d'Augustin: Un état de question." In *Saint Augustin, la Numidie et la société de son temps*, 67–108. Edited by Serge Lancel. Bordeaux: Ausonia; Paris: Boccard, 2005.

Milano: Capitale dell'impero romano, 286–402 d.C. Milan: Silvana Editoriale, 1991.

Miles, Richard. "The *Anthologia Latina* and the Creation of Secular Space in Vandal Carthage." *Antiquité tardive* 13 (2005): 305–20.

Mittag, Peter Franz. *Alte Köpfe in neuen Händen: Urheber und Funktion der Kontorniaten.* Antiquitas 3:38. Bonn: Habelt, 1999.

Modéran, Yves. "L'établissment térritorial des Vandales en Afrique." *Antiquité tardive* 10 (2002): 87–122.

———. "Une guerre de religion: Les deux Églises d'Afrique à l'époque vandale." *Antiquité tardive* 11 (2003): 21–44.

Momigliano, Arnaldo D. "Introduction: Christianity and the Decline of the Roman Empire." In *The Conflict between Paganism and Christianity in the Fourth Century*, 1–16. Edited by Arnaldo Momigliano. Oxford: Clarendon, 1963.

Monat, Pierre. "Astrologie et pouvoir: Les subtilités de Firmicus Maternus." In *Pouvoir, divination, et prédestination dans le monde antique*, 133–39. Edited by Élisabeth Smajda and Evelyne Geny. Besançon: Presses Universitaires Franc-Comtoises, 1999.

Moorhead, John. *Ambrose: Church and Society in the Late Roman World.* London: Longman, 1999.

Morelli, Federico. "Tessuti e indumenti nel contesto economico tardoantico: I prezzi." *Antiquité tardive* 12 (2004): 55–78.

Morris, John. "Pelagian Literature." *Journal of Theological Studies*, n.s., 16 (1965): 26–60.

I mosaici della basilica di Aquileia. Edited by Graziano Marini. Aquileia: CISCRA Edizioni, 2003.

Mratschek, Sigrid. *Der Briefwechsel des Paulinus von Nola: Kommunikation und soziale Kontakte zwischen christlichen Intellektuellen.* Hypomnemata 134. Göttingen: Vandenhoek and Ruprecht, 2002.

————. *Divites et praepotentes: Reichtum und soziale Stellung in der Literatur der Prinzipatszeit.* Historia Einzelschriften 70. Stuttgart: F. Steiner, 1993.

————. "*Multis enim notissima est sanctitas loci*: Paulinus and the Gradual Rise of Nola as a Center of Christian Hospitality." *Journal of Early Christian Studies* 9 (2001): 511–53.

Mrozek, Slawomir. "Les phénomènes économiques dans les métaphores de l'Antiquité tardive." *Eos* 72 (1984): 393–407.

Muhlberger, Steven. *The Fifth-Century Chroniclers: Prosper, Hydatius, and the Gallic Chronicler of 452.* Liverpool: F. Cairns, 1990.

————. "Looking Back from Mid-Century: The Gallic Chronicler of 452 and the Crisis of Honorius' Reign." In *Fifth-Century Gaul: A Crisis of Identity?* 28–37. Edited by John Drinkwater and Hugh Elton. Cambridge: Cambridge University Press, 1992.

La musica ritrovata: Iconografia e cultura musicale a Ravenna e in Romagna dal I al VI secolo. Edited by Daniela Castaldo, Maria Grazia Maioli, and Donatella Restani. Ravenna: Longo, 1997.

Muth, Susanne. "Bildkomposition und Raumstruktur der 'Grossen Jagd' von Piazza Armerina in seinem raumfunktionalen Kontext." *Mitteilungen des deutschen archäologischen Instituts: Römische Abteilung* 106 (1999): 189–212.

————. *Erleben von Raum—Leben im Raum: Zur Funktion mythologischer Mosaik-bilder in der römisch-kaiserzeitlichen Wohnarchitektur.* Archäologie und Geschichte 10. Heidelberg: Archäologie und Geschichte, 1998.

Näf, Beat. *Senatorisches Standesbewusstsein in spätrömischer Zeit.* Paradosis 40. Freiburg, Switzerland: Universitätsverlag, 1995.

Namier, L. B. *The Structure of Politics at the Accession of George III.* 2nd ed. London: Macmillan, 1957.

Nauroy, Gérard. "L'écriture dans la pastorale d'Ambroise de Milan." In *Le monde latin antique et la Bible.* Edited by Jacques Fontaine and Charles Pietri. Vol. 2, *Bible de tous les temps*, 371–408. Paris: Beauchesne, 1985.

————. *Exégèse et création littéraire chez Ambroise de Milan: L'exemple du* De Ioseph Patriarcha. Paris: Institut d'Études Augustiniennes, 2007.

Nautin, Pierre. "L'excommunication de saint Jérôme." *Annuaire de l'École Pratique des Hautes Études, Ve section: Sciences religieuses* 80–81 (1972–73): 7–37.

Neri, Valerio. *I marginali nell'Occidente tardoantico: Poveri, "infames" e criminali nella nascente società cristiana.* Bari: Edipuglia, 1998.

Newhauser, Richard. *The Early History of Greed: The Sin of Avarice in Early Medieval Thought and Literature.* Cambridge: Cambridge University Press, 2000.

Newlands, Carole E. *Statius' Silvae and the Poetics of Empire.* New York: Cambridge University Press, 2002.

Niehoff-Panagiotidis, Johannes. "Byzantinische Lebenswelt und rabbinische Herme-neutik: Die griechischen Juden in der Kairoer Genizah." *Byzantion* 74 (2004): 51–109.

Niewöhner, Philipp. "Vom Sinnbild zum Abbild: Der justinianische Realismus und die Genese der byzantinischen Heiligentypologie." *Millennium* 5 (2008): 163–89.

Niquet, Heike. *Monumenta virtutum titulique: Senatorische Selbstdarstellung im spätantiken Rom im Spiegel der epigraphischen Denkmäler.* Stuttgart: F. Steiner, 2000.

Noble, Thomas F. X. "Secular Sanctity: Forging an Ethos for the Carolingian Nobility." In *Lay Intellectuals in the Carolingian World,* 8–36. Edited by Patrick Wormald and Janet L. Nelson. Cambridge: Cambridge University Press, 2007.

Nock, Arthur Darby. "*A diis electa*: A Chapter in the Religious History of the Third Century." *Harvard Theological Review* 23 (1930): 251–74. Reprinted in *Essays on Religion and the Ancient World.*

———. "The Emperor's Divine *Comes*." *Journal of Roman Studies* 37 (1947): 102–16. Reprinted in *Essays on Religion and the Ancient World.*

———. *Essays on Religion and the Ancient World.* Edited by Zeph Stewart. 2 vols. Cambridge, MA: Harvard University Press, 1972.

Noethlichs, Karl Leo. "Zur Einflussnahme des Staates auf die Entwicklung eines christlichen Klerikerstandes." *Jahrbuch für Antike und Christentum* 15 (1972): 136–154.

Norton, Peter. *Episcopal Elections, 250–600: Hierarchy and Popular Will in Late Antiquity.* Oxford: Oxford University Press, 2007.

Nouhailhat, René. *Saints et patrons: Les premiers moines de Lérins.* Université de Besançon: Centre de Recherches d'Histoire Ancienne 84. Paris: Belles Lettres, 1988.

Nourrir la plèbe: Actes du colloque tenu à Genève les 28. et 29. IX. 1989 en hommage à Denis Van Berchem. Edited by Adalberto Giovannini. Schweizerische Beiträge zur Altertumswissenschaft 22. Basel: F. Reinhardt 1991.

O'Donnell, James J. *Augustine: A New Biography.* New York: Harper Collins, 2005.

———. *The Ruin of the Roman Empire: A New History.* New York: Harper Collins, 2008.

Omar, Irfan. "Khidr in the Islamic Traditions." *The Muslim World* 83 (1993): 279–94.

Oort, Johannes van. "The Young Augustine's Knowledge of Manichaeism: An Analysis of the *Confessiones* and Some Other Related Texts." *Vigiliae Christianae* 62 (2008): 441–66.

Orlandi, Silvia. *Epigrafia anfiteatrale dell'occidente romano.* Vol. 6, *Roma.* Vetera 15. Rome: Quasar, 2004.

Osborne, Robin. "Introduction: Roman Poverty in Context." In *Poverty in the Roman World,* 1–20. Edited by Margaret Atkins and Robin Osborne. Cambridge: Cambridge University Press, 2007.

O'Sullivan, Jeremiah F. *The Writings of Salvian, the Presbyter.* Fathers of the Church 3. New York: CIMA, 1947.

Otranto, Giorgio. "Paolino di Nola e il Cristianesimo dell'Italia Meridionale." In *Anchora vitae: Atti del II Convegno Paoliniano nel XVI Centenario del Ritiro di Paolino a Nola,* 35–58. Edited by Gennaro Luongo. Naples: Redenzione, 1998.

Padovese, Luigi. "Considerazioni sulla dottrina cristologica e soteriologica di Paolino di Nola." In *Anchora vitae: Atti del II Convegno Paoliniano nel XVI Centenario del*

Ritiro di Paolino a Nola, 209–24. Edited by Gennaro Luongo. Naples: Redenzione, 1998.

Paesaggi e insediamenti rurali in Italia meridionale fra tardoantico e altomedioevo. Edited by Guiliano Volpe and Maria Turchiano. Bari: Edipuglia, 2005.

Pagans and Christians in the Roman Empire (IVth–VIth Century A.D.): The Breaking of a Dialogue. Proceedings of the International Conference at the Monastery of Bosé, October 2008. Edited by Peter Brown and Rita Lizzi Testa. Münster: Lit, 2011.

Panciera, Silvio. "Ancora sulla famiglia senatoria 'africana' degli Aradii." *Africa Romana* 2 (1986): 547–72.

Parkin, Anneliese. "'You do him no service': An Exploration of Pagan Almsgiving." In *Poverty in the Roman World*, 60–82. Edited by Margaret Atkins and Robin Osborne. Cambridge: Cambridge University Press, 2007.

Parry, Jonathan. "*The Gift*, the Indian Gift and the 'Indian Gift.'" *Man*, n.s., 21 (1986): 453–73.

Patterson, Helen. "The Tiber Valley Project: Archaeology, Comparative Survey and History." In *General Issues in the Study of Medieval Logistics: Sources, Problems and Methodologies*, 93–117. Edited by John F. Haldon. Leiden: Brill, 2006.

Patzold, Steffen. "Zur Sozialstruktur des Episkopats und zur Ausbildung bischöflicher Herrschaft in Gallien zwischen Spätantike und Frühmittelalter." In *Völker, Reiche und Namen im frühen Mittelalter*, 121–40. Edited by Matthias Becher and Stefanie Dick. Munich: W. Fink, 2010.

Peacock, D.P.S., Féthi Bejaoui, and Nejib Ben Lazreg. "Roman Pottery Production in Central Tunisia." *Journal of Roman Archaeology* 3 (1990): 59–84.

Peña, J. Theodore. "The Mobilization of State Olive Oil in Roman Africa: The Evidence of the Late Fourth-Century *Ostraca* from Carthage." In *Carthage Papers*, 117–238. Edited by Peña et al. Journal of Roman Archaeology Supplement 28. Portsmouth, RI: Journal of Roman Archaeology, 1998.

Pensabene, Patrizio. "Marmi e reimpiego nel santuario di S. Felice a Cimitile." In *Cimitile e Paolino di Nola. La tomba di S. Felice e il centro di pellegrinaggio: Trent'anni di ricerche*, 129–207. Edited by Hugo Brandenburg and Letizia Ermini Pani. Città del Vaticano: Pontificio Istituto di Archeologia Cristiana, 2003.

Percival, John. "Desperately Seeking Sidonius: The Realities of Life in Fifth-Century Gaul." *Latomus* 56 (1997): 279–92.

Les Pères de l'Église et la voix des pauvres. Edited by Pascal-Grégoire Delage. La Rochelle: Histoire et Culture, 2006.

Pergola, Philippe. "*Mensores frumentarii Christiani* et annone à la fin de l'Antiquité (Relecture d'un cycle de peintures)." *Rivista di archeologia cristiana* 66 (1990): 167–84.

Perler, Othmar. *Les voyages de Saint Augustin.* Paris: Études Augustiniennes, 1969.

Perrin, Michel-Yves. "*Ad implendum caritatis officium*: La place des courriers dans la correspondance de Paulin de Nole." *Mélanges de l'École française de Rome: Antiquité* 104 (1992): 1025–68.

Persic, Alessio. "La Chiesa di Siria e i 'gradi' della vita Cristiana." In *Per foramen acus: Il cristianesimo antico di fronte alla pericope evangelica del "giovane ricco,"* 208–63. Milan: Vita e Pensiero, 1986.

Peyras, Jean. "Le fundus Aufidianus: Étude d'un grand domaine romain de la région de Mateur (Tunisie du Nord)." *Antiquités Africaines* 9 (1975): 181–222.

Picotti, G. B. "Sulle relazioni fra re Odoacre e il Senato e la chiesa di Roma." *Rivista Storica Italiana,* ser. 5, no. 4 (1939): 363–86.

Picturing the Bible: The Earliest Christian Art. Edited by Jeffery Spier. New Haven, CT: Yale University Press; in association with Forth Worth, TX: Kimbell Art Museum, 2007.

Pietri, Charles. "Chiesa e comunità locali nell'Occidente cristiano (IV–VI d.C.): L'esempio della Gallia." In *Società romana e impero tardoantico.* Vol. 3, *Le merci, gli insediamenti,* 761–97. Edited by Andrea Giardina. Bari: Laterza, 1986. Reprinted in vol. I of *Christiana respublica.*

———. *Christiana respublica: Éléments d'une enquête sur le christianisme antique.* 3 vols. Collection de l'École française de Rome 234. Rome: École française de Rome, 1997.

———. "Damase, évêque de Rome." In *Saecularia Damasiana,* 31–58. Studi di Antichità Cristiana 39. Vatican: Pontificio Istituto di Archeologia Cristiana, 1986. Reprinted in vol. 1 of *Christiana respublica.*

———. "Donateurs et pieux établissements d'après le légendier romain (Ve–VIIe s.)." In *Hagiographie, cultures et sociétés, IVe–XIIe siècles,* 434–53. Paris: Études Augustiniennes, 1981. Reprinted in vol. 1 of *Christiana respublica.*

———. "Évergétisme et richesses ecclésiastiques dans l'Italie du IVe à la fin du Ve siècle: L'exemple romain." *Ktèma* 3 (1978): 317–37. Reprinted in vol. 2 of *Christiana respublica.*

———. "Recherches sur les *domus ecclesiae.*" *Revue des études augustiniennes* 24 (1978): 3–21. Reprinted in vol. 1 of *Christiana respublica.*

———. *Roma Christiana: Recherches sur l'Église de Rome, son organisation, sa politique, son idéologie de Miltiade à Sixte III (311–440).* Bibliothèque des Écoles françaises d'Athènes et de Rome 224. Rome: Palais Farnèse, 1976.

———. "Le Sénat, le peuple chrétien et les partis du cirque sous le pape Symmaque." *Mélanges d'archéologie et d'histoire* 78 (1966): 123–39. Reprinted in vol. 2 of *Christiana respublica.*

———. "Le serment du soldat chrétien: Les épisodes de la *militia Christi* sur les sarcophages." *Mélanges d'Archéologie et d'Histoire* 74 (1962): 649–64. Reprinted in vol. 2 of *Christiana respublica.*

Pietri, Luce. "Évergétisme chrétien et fondations privées dans l'Italie de l'Antiquité tardive." In *Humana sapit: Études d'Antiquité Tardive offeres à Lellia Cracco Ruggini,* 253–63. Edited by Jean-Michel Carrié and Rita Lizzi Testa. Bibliothèque d'Antiquité Tardive 3. Turnhout: Brepols, 2002.

———. "Riches et pauvres dans l'*Ad Ecclesiam* de Salvien de Marseille." In *Les Pères de l'Église et la voix des pauvres,* 149–61. Edited by Pascal Grégoire Delage. La Rochelle: Histoire et Culture, 2006.

Piganiol, André. *L'empire chrétien (325–395)*. Histoire romaine 4:2. Paris: Presses Universitaires de France, 1947.

Plassmann, Otto. *Die Almosen bei Johannes Chrysostomus*. Münster: Aschendorff, 1961.

Plinval, Georges de. *Pélage: Ses écrits, sa vie et sa réforme: Étude d'histoire littéraire et religieuse*. Lausanne: Payot, 1943.

Plumer, Eric. *Augustine's Commentary on Galatians*. Oxford: Oxford University Press, 2003.

Poglio, Federico Alberto. *Gruppi di potere nella Roma tardoantica (350–395 d.C.)*. Turin: Celid, 2007.

Pohl, Walter. "Rome and the Barbarians in the Fifth Century." *Antiquité tardive* 16 (2008): 93–101.

Polci, Barbara. "Some Aspects of the Transformation of the Roman *Domus* between Late Antiquity and the Early Middle Ages." In *Theory and Practice in Late Antique Archaeology*, 79–109. Edited by Luke Lavan and William Bowden. Late Antique Archaeology 1. Leiden: Brill, 2003.

Porena, Pierfranceso. "Trasformazioni istituzionali e assetti sociali: I prefetti del Pretorio tra III e IV secolo." In *Le trasformazioni delle "élites" in età tardoantica*, 325–56. Edited by Rita Lizzi Testa. Rome: Bretschneider, 2006.

Potter, David S. *The Roman Empire at Bay, AD 180–395*. London: Routledge, 2004.

Pottier, Bruno. "Entre les villes et les campagnes: Le banditisme en Italie du IVe au VIe siècle." In *Les cités de l'Italie tardo-antique (IVe–VIe siècle): Institutions, économie, société, culture et religion*, 251–66. Edited by Massimiliano Ghilardi, Christophe J. Goddard, and Pierfrancesco Porena. Collection de l'École française de Rome 369. Rome: École française de Rome, 2006.

Poveri ammalati e ammalati poveri: Dinamiche socio-economiche, trasformazioni culturali e misure assistenziali nell'Occidente romano in età tardoantica. Edited by Rosalia Marino, Concetta Molè, and Antonino Pinzone, with the collaboration of Margherita Cassia. Catania: Edizioni del Prisma, 2006.

Poverty in the Roman World. Edited by Margaret Atkins and Robin Osborne. Cambridge: Cambridge University Press, 2007.

Pricoco, Salvatore. *L'isola dei santi: Il cenobio di Lerino e le origini del monachesimo gallico*. Rome: Edizioni dell'Ateneo e Bizzarri, 1978.

———. "Paolino di Nola e il monachesimo del suo tempo." In *Anchora vitae: Atti del II Convegno Paoliniano nel XVI Centenario del Ritiro di Paolino a Nola*, 59–92. Edited by Gennaro Luongo. Naples: Redenzione, 1998.

Prinz, Friedrich. *Frühes Mönchtum im Frankenreich: Kultur und Gesellschaft in Gallien, den Rheinlanden und Bayern am Beispiel der monastischen Entwicklung (4. bis 8. Jahrhundert)*. Vienna: Oldenbourg, 1965.

Le problème de la christianisation du monde antique. Edited by Hervé Inglebert, Sylvain Destephen, and Bruno Dumézil. Paris: Picard, 2010.

Property and Power in the Early Middle Ages. Edited by Wendy Davies and Paul Fouracre. Cambridge: Cambridge University Press, 1995.

Prosopographie chrétienne du Bas-Empire.
Vol. 1, *L'Afrique chrétienne (305–533).* Edited by André Mandouze. Paris: CNRS, 1982.
Vol. 2, *L'Italie chrétienne (313–604).* Edited by Charles Pietri and Luce Pietri. 2 vols. Paris: École française de Rome, 2000.
Vol. 3, *Diocèse d'Asie (325–641).* Edited by Sylvain Destephen. Paris: CNRS, 2008.
The Prosopography of the Later Roman Empire. Edited by A.H.M. Jones, John Robert Martindale, and John Morris. 3 vols. Cambridge: Cambridge University Press, 1971–92.
Purcell, Nicholas. "The Populace of Rome in Late Antiquity: Problems of Classification and Historical Description." In *The Transformations of Vrbs Roma in Late Antiquity,* 135–61. Edited by W. V. Harris. Journal of Roman Archaeology: Supplementary Series 33. Portsmouth, RI: Journal of Roman Archaeology, 1999.
———. "Tomb and Suburb." In *Römische Gräberstrasse: Selbstdarstellung, Status, Standard,* 25–41. Edited by Henner von Hesberg and Paul Zanker. Bayerische Akademie der Wissenschaften: Philologisch-historische Klasse/Abhandlungen, NF 96. Munich: Bayerische Akademie der Wissenschaften, 1987.
Raeck, Wulf. *Modernisierte Mythen: Zum Umgang der Spätantike mit klassischen Bildthemen.* Stuttgart: F. Steiner, 1992.
———. "*Publica non despiciens*: Ergänzungen zur Interpretation des Dominus-Julius-Mosaiks aus Karthago." *Mitteilungen des deutschen Archäologischen Instituts: Römische Abteilung* 94 (1987): 295–308.
Raimondi, Milena. "Elezione *iudicio Dei* e *turpe convicium*: Damaso e Ursino tra storia ecclesiastica e amministrazione romana." *Aevum* 83 (2009): 169–208.
Rajak, Tessa. "The Gifts of God at Sardis." In *Jews in a Graeco-Roman World,* 229–39. Edited by Martin Goodman. New York: Oxford University Press, 1998.
Rapp, Claudia. "Charity and Piety as Episcopal and Imperial Virtues in Late Antiquity." In *Charity and Giving in Monotheistic Religions,* 75–88. Edited by Miriam Frenkel and Yaacov Lev. Studien zur Geschichte und Kultur des islamischen Orients, n. F. 22. Berlin: de Gruyter, 2009.
———. *Holy Bishops in Late Antiquity: The Nature of Christian Leadership in an Age of Transition.* Berkeley: University of California Press, 2005.
Rebenich, Stefan. *Hieronymus und sein Kreis: Prosopographische und sozialgeschichtliche Untersuchungen.* Historia Einzelschriften 72. Stuttgart: F. Steiner, 1992.
Rebillard, Éric. "Augustin et le rituel épistolaire de l'élite sociale et culturelle de son temps: Éléments pour une analyse processuelle des relations de l'évêque et de la cité dans l'Antiquité tardive." In *L'évêque dans la cité du IVe au Ve siècle: Image et autorité,* 127–52. Edited by Éric Rebillard and Claire Sotinel. Collection de l'École française de Rome 248. Rome: École française de Rome, 1998.
———. *In hora mortis: Évolution de la pastorale chrétienne de la mort aux IVe et Ve siècles dans l'Occident latin.* Bibliothèque des Écoles françaises d'Athènes et de Rome 283. Rome: Palais Farnèse, 1994.
———. "*Quasi funambuli*: Cassien et la controverse pélagienne sur la perfection." *Revue des Études Augustiniennes* 40 (1994): 197–210.

———. *Religion et sépulture: L'Église, les vivants et les morts dans l'Antiquité tardive.* Paris: Éditions de l'École des Hautes Études en Sciences Sociales, 2003. Translated by Elizabeth Trapnell Rawlings and Jeanine Routier-Pucci, as *The Care of the Dead in Late Antiquity.* Ithaca, NY: Cornell University Press, 2009.

———. "Sociologie de la déviance et orthodoxie: Le cas de la controverse pélagienne sur la grace." In *Orthodoxie, christianisme, histoire,* 221–40. Edited by Susanna Elm, Éric Rebillard, and Antonella Romano. Collection de l'École française de Rome 270. Rome: École française de Rome, 2000.

Rebuffat, René. "Enceintes urbaines et insécurité en Maurétanie tingitaine." *Mélanges de l'École française de Rome: Antiquité* 86 (1974): 501–22.

Rees, B. R. *Pelagius: A Reluctant Heretic.* Woodbridge, UK: Boydell, 1998.

Reinert, François, ed. *Moselgold: Der römische Schatz von Machtum.* Luxembourg: Musée national d'histoire et d'art, 2008.

Religion, Dynasty and Patronage in Early Christian Rome, 300–900. Edited by Kate Cooper and Julia Hillner. Cambridge: Cambridge University Press, 2007.

Reutter, Ursula. *Damasus, Bischof von Rom (366–384).* Studien und Texte zu Antike und Christentum 55. Tübingen: Mohr Siebeck, 2009.

Reynolds, Paul. *Hispania and the Roman Mediterranean, A.D. 100–700: Ceramics and Trade.* London: Duckworth, 2010.

Rilinger, Rolf. *Humiliores-Honestiores: Zu einer sozialen Dichotomie im Strafrecht der römischen Kaiserzeit.* Munich: Oldbourg, 1988.

Rio, Alice. "High and Low: Ties of Dependence in the Frankish Kingdoms." *Transactions of the Royal Historical Society,* 6th ser., 12 (2008): 43–68.

Rivière, Yann. "'Une cruauté digne des féroces barbares?' À propos du *De emerdatione servorum* (C.Th.IX.12)." In *Le Code Théodosien: Diversité des approches et nouvelles perspectives,* 171–208. Edited by Sylvie Crogiel-Pétrequin and Pierre Jaillette. Collection de l'École française de Rome 412. Rome: École française de Rome, 2009.

Robert, Louis, and Jeanne Robert. "Bulletin épigraphique." *Revue des études grecques* 97 (1984): 419–522.

Roberts, Michael. "Barbarians in Gaul: The Response of the Poets." In *Fifth-Century Gaul: A Crisis of Identity?* 97–106. Edited by John Drinkwater and Hugh Elton. Cambridge: Cambridge University Press, 1992.

———. *The Humblest Sparrow: The Poetry of Venantius Fortunatus.* Ann Arbor: University of Michigan Press, 2009.

Robins, William. "Romance and Renunciation at the Turn of the Fifth Century." *Journal of Early Christian Studies* 8 (2000): 531–57.

Rodá, Isabel. "Iconografía y epigrafía en dos mosaicos hispanas: Las villas de Tossa y de Dueñas." In *VI Coloquio internacional sobre mosaico antiguo,* 35–42. Palencia/Mérida: Associación Español del Mosaico, 1994.

Roda, Sergio. "Fuga nel privato e nostalgia del potere nel IV secolo d.C.: Nuovi accenti di un'antica ideologia." In vol. 1 of *Le trasformazioni della cultura nella tarda antichità,* 95–108. Rome: Bretschneider, 1985.

Roda, Sergio. "Polifunzionalità della lettera commendaticia: Teoria e prassi nell'epistolario simmachiano." In *Colloque genèvois sur Symmaque*, 177–207. Edited by François Paschoud. Paris: Belles Lettres, 1986.

Rome and China: Comparative Perspectives on Ancient World Empires. Edited by Walter Scheidel. Oxford: Oxford University Press, 2009.

Rossiter, Jeremy J. "Domus and Villa: Late Antique Housing in Carthage and Its Territory." In *Housing in Late Antiquity: From Palaces to Shops*, 367–92. Edited by Luke Lavan, Lale Özgenel, and Alexander Sarantis. Late Antique Archaeology 3.2. Leiden: Brill, 2007.

Rostovtzeff, M. *The Social and Economic History of the Hellenistic World.* 3 vols. Oxford: Clarendon, 1941.

———. *The Social and Economic History of the Roman Empire.* Oxford: Clarendon, 1926.

Roueché, Charlotte. "Acclamations in the Late Roman Empire: New Evidence from Aphrodisias." *Journal of Roman Studies* 74 (1984): 181–99.

———. "The Image of Victory: New Evidence from Ephesus." *Travaux et mémoires* 14: *Mélanges Gilbert Dagron*, 527–46. Edited by V. Déroche. Paris: Boccard, 2002.

Rousseau, Philip. *Ascetics, Authority, and the Church in the Age of Jerome and Cassian.* Oxford: Oxford University Press, 1978.

———. "Cassian: Monastery and World." In *The Certainty of Doubt: Tributes to Peter Munz*, 68–89. Edited by Miles Fairburn and W. H. Oliver. Wellington, New Zealand: Victoria University Press, 1995.

———. "The Preacher's Audience: A More Optimistic View." In vol. 2 of *Ancient History in a Modern University*, 371–408. Edited by T. W. Hillard et al. Grand Rapids, MI: Eerdmans, 1998.

Rousselle, Aline. *Porneia: De la maîtrise du corps à la privation sensorielle, IIe–IVe siècles de l'ère chrétienne.* Paris: Presses Universitaires de France, 1983.

Rowland, Robert J. "The 'Very Poor' and the Grain Dole at Rome and Oxyrhynchus." *Zeitschrift für Papyrologie und Epigraphik* 21 (1976): 69–73.

Rubin, Miri. *Charity and Community in Medieval Cambridge.* Cambridge: Cambridge University Press, 1987.

Rummel, Philipp von. *Habitus barbarus: Kleidung und Repräsentation spätantiker Eliten im 4. und 5. Jahrhundert.* Reallexikon der germanischen Altertumskunde, Ergänzungsband 55. Berlin: de Gruyter, 2007.

———. "*Habitus Vandalorum?* Zur Frage nach einer gruppen-spezifischen Kleidung der Vandalen in Afrika." *Antiquité tardive* 10 (2002): 131–41.

Ruokanen, Mikka. *Theology of Social Life in Augustine's De civitate Dei.* Forschungen zur Kirchen-und Dogmengeschichte 53. Göttingen: Vandenhoeck and Ruprecht, 1993.

Rutgers, L. V., M. van Strydonck, M. Boudin, and C. van der Linde. "Stable Isotope Data from the Early Christian Catacombs of Ancient Rome: New Insights into the Dietary Habits of Rome's Early Christians." *Journal of Archaeological Science* 36 (2009): 1127–34.

Sabw Kanyang, Jean-Anatole. *Episcopus et plebs: L'évêque et la communauté ecclésiale dans les conciles africains (345–525).* European University Studies 701. Bern: Peter Lang, 2000.

Saecularia Damasiana. Studi di Antichità Cristiana 39. Vatican: Pontificio Istituto di Archeologia Cristiana, 1986.

Sage, Michael M. *Cyprian.* Patristic Monographs Series 1. Cambridge, MA: Philadelphia Patristic Foundation, 1975.

Saint Augustin, la Numidie et la société de son temps. Edited by Serge Lancel. Bordeaux: Ausonia; Paris: Boccard, 2005.

Salamito, Jean-Marie. "Aspects aristocratiques et aspects populaires de l'être chrétien aux IIIe et IVe siècles." *Antiquité tardive* 9 (2001): 165–78.

———. *Les virtuoses et la multitude: Aspects sociaux de la controverse entre Augustin et les pélagiens.* Grenoble: Éditions Jérôme Millon, 2005.

Salomonson, J. W. "Late Roman Earthenware with Relief Decoration Found in Northern-Africa and Egypt." *Oudheidkundige Mededelingen* 43 (1962): 53–95.

———. *La mosaïque aux chevaux dans l'antiquarium de Carthage.* The Hague: Imprimerie Nationale, 1965.

Salona: Recherches archéologiques franco-croates à Salone. Vol. 3, *Manastirine: Établissement préromain, nécropole et basilique paléochrétienne.* Edited by Noel Duval, Emilio Marin, and Catherine Metzger. Collection de l'École française de Rome 194:3. Rome: École française de Rome; Split: Musée archéologique de Split, 2000.

Salzman, Michele Renée. "*The Making of a Christian Aristocracy*: A Response to Ralph Mathisen's Review Article." *International Journal of the Classical Tradition* 12 (2005): 123–37.

———. *The Making of a Christian Aristocracy: Social and Religious Change in the Western Roman Empire.* Cambridge, MA: Harvard University Press, 2002.

———. *On Roman Time: The Codex-Calendar of 354 and the Rhythms of Urban Life in Late Antiquity.* Berkeley: University of California Press, 1990.

———. "Symmachus and the 'Barbarian' Generals." *Historia* 55 (2006): 352–67.

———. "Symmachus and His Father: Patriarchy and Patrimony in the Late Roman Senatorial Elite." In *Le trasformazioni dell' "élites" in età tardoantica,* 357–75. Edited by Rita Lizzi Testa. Rome: Bretschneider, 2006.

———. "Symmachus' Ideal of Secular Friendship." In *Les frontières du profane dans l'antiquité tardive,* 247–72. Edited by Éric Rebillard and Claire Sotinel. Collection de l'École française de Rome 428. Rome: École française de Rome, 2010.

———. "Travel and Communication in *The Letters of Symmachus.*" In *Travel, Communication and Geography in Late Antiquity: Sacred and Profane,* 81–94. Edited by Linda Ellis and Frank L. Kidner. Aldershot: Variorum, 2004.

Samson, R. "Slavery, the Roman Legacy." In *Fifth-Century Gaul: A Crisis of Identity?* 218–27. Edited by John Drinkwater and Hugh Elton. Cambridge: Cambridge University Press, 1992.

Sánchez León, Juan Carlos. *Les sources de l'histoire des Bagaudes.* Paris: Belles Lettres, 1996.

Sanchez Velasco, Jerónimo, Antonio Moreno Rosa, and Guadalupe Gómez Muñoz. "Aproximación al estudio de la ciudad de Cabra y su obispado al final de la Antigüedad." *Antiquitas* 21, 135–80. Priego de Corboba: Museo Histórico Municipal, 2009.

Santilli, Roberto, Jens Ormö, Angelo P. Rossi, and Goro Komatsu. "A Catastrophe Remembered: A Meteorite Impact of the Fifth Century AD in the Abruzzo, Central Italy." *Antiquity* 77 (2003): 313–20.

Sardella, Teresa. "Continenza e uxorato del clero nell'Africa di Agostino." In *L'adorabile vescovo d'Ippona*, 183–226. Edited by Franca Ela Consolino. Soveria Manelli: Rubettino, 2001.

———. *Società, chiesa e stato nell'età di Teodorico: Papa Simmaco e lo scismo laurenziano.* Soveria Manelli: Rubettino, 1996.

Sarris, Peter. *Economy and Society in the Age of Justinian.* Cambridge: Cambridge University Press, 2006.

Savino, Eliodoro. *Campania Tardoantica (284–604 d.C.).* Bari: Edipuglia, 2005.

Savon, Hervé. *Saint Ambroise devant l'exégèse de Philon le Juif.* 2 vols. Paris: Études Augustiniennes, 1977.

Scheidel, Walter C. "Finances, Figures and Fiction." *Classical Quarterly* 46 (1996): 222–238.

———. "Germs for Rome." In *Rome the Cosmopolis*, 159–76. Edited by Catharine Edwards and Greg Woolf. Cambridge: Cambridge University Press, 2003.

———. "Stratification, Deprivation and Quality of Life." In *Poverty in the Roman World*, 40–59. Edited by Margaret Atkins and Robin Osborne. Cambridge: Cambridge University Press, 2006.

Scheidel, Walter C., and Steven J. Friesen. "The Size of the Economy and the Distribution of Income in the Roman Empire." *Journal of Roman Studies* 99 (2009): 61–91.

Schmidt, Manfred. "Ambrosii carmen de obitu Probi: Ein Gedicht des Mailänder Bischofs in epigraphischer Überlieferung." *Hermes* 127 (1999): 99–116.

Schmidt-Hofner, Sebastian. *Reagieren und Gestalten: Die Regierungsstil des spätrömischen Kaisers am Beispiel der Gesetzgebung Valentinians I.* Vestigia 58. Munich: C. H. Beck, 2008.

Schneider, Lambert. *Die Domäne als Weltbild: Wirkungsstrukturen der spätantiken Bildersprache.* Wiesbaden: F. Steiner, 1983.

Schofield, Malcolm. "Cicero's Definition of *res publica*." In *Cicero the Philosopher*, 63–83. Edited by J.G.F. Powell. Oxford: Clarendon, 1995.

Schöllgen, Georg. *Ecclesia Sordida? Zur Frage der sozialen Schichtung frühchristlicher Gemeinden am Beispiel Karthagos zur Zeit Tertullians.* Jahrbuch für Antike und Christentum: Ergänzungsband 12. Münster: Aschendorff, 1984.

Schrüfer-Kolb, Irene. *Roman Iron Production in Britain: Technological and Socioeconomic Landscape Development along the Jurassic Ridge.* British Archaeological Reports 380. Oxford: Archaeopress, 2004.

Schrunk, Ivančica, and Vlasta Begović. "Roman Estates on the Island of Brioni, Istria." *Journal of Roman Archaeology* 13 (2000): 252–76.

Schwartz, Seth. *Imperialism and Jewish Society, 200 B.C.E. to 640 C.E.* Princeton: Princeton University Press, 2001.

———. *Were the Jews a Mediterranean Society? Reciprocity and Solidarity in Ancient Judaism.* Princeton: Princeton University Press, 2010.

Scogin, Hugh. "Poor Relief in Northern Sung China." *Oriens Extremus* 25 (1978): 30–45.

Scott, Sarah. *Art and Society in Fourth Century Britain: Villa Mosaics in Context.* Oxford School of Archaeology Monographs 53. Oxford: Oxbow, 2000.

Serfass, Adam. "Slavery and Pope Gregory the Great." *Journal of Early Christian Studies* 14 (2006): 77–103.

Settipani, Christian. "Ruricius Ier évêque de Limoges et ses relations familiales." Prosopographica X. *Francia* 18 (1991): 195–222.

Settis, Salvatore. "Per l'interpretazione di Piazza Armerina." *Mélanges de l'école française de Rome: Antiquité* 87 (1975): 873–994.

Shanzer, Danuta. "Arcanum Varronis iter: Licentius' Verse Epistle to Augustine." *Revue des études augustiniennes* 37 (1991): 110–43.

———. "*Avulsa a latere meo*: Augustine's Spare Rib—*Confessions* 6.15.25." *Journal of Roman Studies* 92 (2002): 157–76.

———. "Jerome, Tobit, Alms, and the Vita Aeterna." In *Jerome of Stridon: His Life, Writings and Legacy*, 87–103. Edited by Andrew Cain and Josef Lössl. Farnham, UK: Ashgate, 2009.

Shaw, Brent D. "African Christianity: Disputes, Definitions and 'Donatists.'" In *Orthodoxy and Heresy in Religious Movements: Discipline and Dissent*, 5–34. Edited by Malcolm R. Greenshields and Thomas Robinson. Lampeter: Edwin Mellen Press, 1992. Reprinted in *Rulers, Nomads and Christians.*

———. "After Rome: Transformations of the Early Mediterranean World." *New Left Review* 51 (2008): 89–114.

———. "Bad Boys: Circumcellions and Fictive Violence." In *Violence in Late Antiquity: Perceptions and Practices*, 179–96. Edited by H. A. Drake. Aldershot: Ashgate, 2006.

———. *Bringing in the Sheaves: Economy and Metaphor in the Roman World.* Toronto, forthcoming.

———. "The Family in Late Antiquity: The Experience of Augustine." *Past and Present* 115 (1987): 3–51.

———. *Rulers, Nomads and Christians in Roman North Africa.* Aldershot: Variorum, 1995.

———. "Rural Markets in North Africa and the Political Economy of the Roman Empire." *Antiquités africaines* 17 (1981): 37–83. Reprinted in *Rulers, Nomads and Christians.*

———. *Sacred Violence: African Christians and Sectarian Hatred in the Age of Augustine.* Cambridge: Cambridge University Press, 2011.

———. "War and Violence." In *Late Antiquity: A Guide to the Postclassical World*, 130–69. Edited by G. W. Bowersock, Peter Brown, and Oleg Grabar. Cambridge, MA: Harvard University Press, 1999.

Shaw, Brent D. "Who Were the Circumcellions?" In *Vandals, Romans and Berbers: New Perspectives on Late Antique North Africa*, 227–58. Edited by A. H. Merrills. Aldershot: Ashgate, 2004.

———. "'A Wolf by the Ears': M. I. Finley's *Ancient Slavery and Modern Ideology in Historical Context*." Introduction to Moses I. Finley, *Ancient Slavery and Modern Ideology*, 3–74. Princeton, NJ: M. Wiener, 1998.

Shaw, Brent, and Richard P. Saller. "Close-Kin Marriage in Roman Society?" *Man*, n.s., 19 (1984): 432–44.

Shaw, Teresa M. *The Burden of the Flesh: Fasting and Sexuality in Early Christianity*. Minneapolis: Fortress Press, 1998.

Shelton, Kathleen J. *The Esquiline Treasure*. London: British Museum, 1981.

Shtaerman, E. M., and M. K. Trofimova. *La schiavitú nell'Italia imperiale: I–III secolo*. Rome: Riuniti, 1975.

Sillières, Pierre. "Approche d'un espace rural antique: L'exemple de Vila de Frades en Lusitanie méridionale." In *Du latifundium au latifondo: Un héritage de Rome, une création médiévale ou moderne?* 21–29. Publications du Centre Pierre Paris 25. Paris: Boccard, 1995.

Simões, Margarida Barahona. *Prisciliano e as tensões religiosas do século IV*. Lisbon: Universidade Lusíada, 2002.

Simonnot, Philippe. *Les papes, l'église et l'argent: Histoire économique du christianisme des origines à nos jours*. Paris: Bayard, 2005.

Sivan, Hagith. *Ausonius of Bordeaux: Genesis of a Gallic Aristocracy*. London: Routledge, 1993.

———. "The Death of Paulinus' Brother." *Rheinisches Museum für Philologie* 139 (1996): 170–79.

———. "On Hymens and Holiness in Late Antiquity: Opposition to Aristocratic Female Asceticism in Rome." *Jahrbuch für Antike und Christentum* 36 (1993): 81–93.

———. "The Last Gallic Prose Panegyric: Paulinus of Nola on Theodosius I." In *Studies in Latin Literature and Roman History*, 577–94. Edited by Carl Deroux. Vol. 7. Collection Latomus 227. Brussels: Latomus, 1994.

VI Coloquio internacional sobre mosaico antiguo. Palencia/Mérida: Associación Español del Mosaico, 1994.

Skeb, Matthias. *Christo vivere: Studien zum literarischen Christusbild des Paulinus von Nola*. Hereditas 11. Bonn: Borengässer, 1997.

Slootjes, Daniëlle. *The Governor and His Subjects in the Later Roman Empire*. Mnemosyne Supplements 275. Leiden: Brill, 2006.

Smith, J. T. *Roman Villas: A Study in Social Structure*. London: Routledge, 1997.

Smith, Rowland B. E. "'Restored Utility, Eternal City': Patronal Imagery at Rome in the Fourth Century AD." In *"Bread and Circuses": Euergetism and Municipal Patronage in Roman Italy*, 142–66. Edited by Kathryn Lomas and Tim Cornell. London: Routledge, 2003.

Snyder, Christopher A. *An Age of Tyrants: Britain and the Britons, A.D. 400–600*. University Park: Pennsylvania State University Press, 1998.

Social and Political Life in Late Antiquity. Late Antique Archaeology 3:1. Edited by
Will Bowden, Adam Gutteridge, and Carlos Machado. Leiden: Brill, 2006.

Società romana e impero tardoantico. Edited by Andrea Giardina. 4 vols. Rome: Laterza,
1986.

Sogno, Cristiana. *Q. Aurelius Symmachus: A Political Biography.* Ann Arbor: University
of Michigan Press, 2006.

———. "Roman Matchmaking." In *From the Tetrarchs to the Theodosians: Later Roman
History and Culture, 284–450 CE. For John Matthews on the Occasion of His 70th
Birthday,* 51–71. Edited by Scott McGill, Cristiana Sogno, and Edward Watts.
Yale Classical Studies 34. Cambridge: Cambridge University Press, 2010.

Sotinel, Claire. "Les ambitions d'historien d'Ennode de Pavie: *La Vita Epiphanii.*" In
La narrativa cristiana antica: Codici narrative, strutture formali, schemi retorici,
585–605. Studia Ephemeridis Augustinianum 50. Rome: Istituto Patristicum
Augustinianum, 1995.

———. *Church and Society in Late Antique Italy and beyond.* Farnham, UK: Ashgate/
Variorum, 2010.

———. "Le don chrétien et ses retombées sur l'économie dans l'Antiquité tardive."
Antiquité tardive 14 (2006): 105–16. Translated by Sotinel as "The Christian Gift
and Its Economic Impact in Late Antiquity." In *Church and Society,* article IX.

———. "Les évêques italiens dans la société de l'Antiquité tardive: L'émergence d'une
nouvelle élite?" In *Le trasformazioni delle "élites" in età tardoantica,* 377–404.
Edited by Rita Lizzi Testa. Rome: Bretschneider, 2006. Translated by Sotinel as
"The Bishops of Italy in Late Antique Society: A New Elite?" In *Church and
Society,* article VIII.

———. *Identité civique et christianisme: Aquilée du IIIe au VIe siècle.* Bibliothèque des
Écoles françaises d'Athènes et de Rome 324. Rome: École française de Rome, 2006.

———. "Le personnel épiscopal: Enquête sur la puissance de l'évêque dans la cite." In
L'évêque dans la cité du IVe au Ve siècle: Image et autorité, 105–26. Edited by Éric
Rebillard and Claire Sotinel. Collection de l'École française de Rome 248. Rome:
École française de Rome, 1998. Translated by Sotinel as "The Bishop's Men:
Episcopal Power in the City." In *Church and Society,* VII.

———. "Le recrutement des évêques en Italie aux IVe et Ve siècles." In *Vescovi e pastori
in epoca Teodosiana,* 193–204. Studia Ephemeridis Augustinianum 58. Rome:
Institutum Pontificium Augustinianum, 1997. Reprinted in *Church and Society,* VI.

———. "La sphère profane dans l'espace urbain." In *Les frontières du profane dans
l'antiquité tardive,* 319–349. Edited by Éric Rebillard and Claire Sotinel. Collection de l'École française de Rome 428. Rome: École française de Rome, 2010.

Spera, Lucrezia. "Un cubicolo monumentale nella catacomba di Pretestato." *Rivista di
archeologia cristiana* 68 (1992): 279–307.

———. *Il paesaggio suburbano di Roma dall'antichità al medioevo: Il comprensorio tra le
vie Latina e Ardeatina dalle Mura Aureliane al III miglio.* Rome: Bretschneider,
1999.

Spier, Jeffery. "A Lost Consular Diptych of Anicius Auchenius Bassus (A.D. 408) in the
Mould for an ARS Plaque." *Journal of Roman Archaeology* 16 (2003): 251–254.

Squatriti, Paolo. "The Floods of 589 and Climate Change at the Beginning of the Middle Ages: An Italian Microhistory." *Speculum* 85 (2010): 799–826.

Die Stadt in der Spätantike—Niedergang oder Wandel? Edited by Jens-Uwe Krause and Christian Witschel. Historia Einzelschriften 190. Stuttgart: F. Steiner, 2006.

Stancliffe, Clare. *St. Martin and His Hagiographer: History and Miracle in Sulpicius Severus.* Oxford: Clarendon, 1983.

Stanley, David J. "Santa Costanza: History, Archaeology, Function, Patronage and Dating." *Arte medievale*, n.s., 3 (2004): 119–40.

Statuen in der Spätantike. Edited by Franz Alto Bauer and Christian Witschel. Wiesbaden: Reichert, 2007.

Sternberg, Thomas. *Orientalium more secutus: Räume und Institutionen der Caritas des 5. bis 7. Jahrhunderts in Gallien.* Jahrbuch für Antike und Christentum, Ergänzungsband 16. Münster in Wesfalen: Aschendorff, 1991.

Stewart, Columba. *Cassian the Monk.* Oxford: Oxford University Press, 1998.

Stickler, Timo. *Aëtius: Gestaltungsspielräume eines Heermeisters im ausgehenden Weströmischen Reich.* Vestigia 54. Munich: C. H. Beck, 2002.

Stirling, Lea M. *The Learned Collector: Mythological Statuettes and Classical Taste in Late Antique Gaul.* Ann Arbor: University of Michigan Press, 2005.

Strobel, Karl. *Das Imperium Romanum im "3. Jahrhundert": Modell einer historischen Krise? Zur Frage mentaler Strukturen breiterer Bevölkerungsschichten in der Zeit von Marc Aurel bis zum Ausgang des 3. Jh.n.Chr.* Historia Einzelschrift 75. Stuttgart: F. Steiner, 1993.

Stroheker, Karl. *Der senatorische Adel im spätantiken Gallien.* Tübingen: Alma Mater, 1948.

Strothmann, Jürgen. "Königsherrchaft oder nachantike Staatlichkeit? Merowingische Monetarmünzen als Quelle für die politische Ordnung des Frankenreichs." *Millennium* 5 (2008): 353–81.

Suburbium: Il suburbio di Roma dalla crisi del sistema delle ville a Gregorio Magno. Edited by Phillippe Pergola, Riccardo Santangeli Valenzani, and Rita Volpe. Collection de l'École française de Rome 311. Rome: École française de Rome, 2003.

Syme, Ronald. *Ammianus and the Historia Augusta.* Oxford: Clarendon, 1968.

———. *The Roman Revolution.* Oxford: Clarendon, 1939.

Tanguy, Bernard. "De l'origine des évêchés bretons." In *Les débuts de l'organisation religieuse en la Bretagne Armoricaine,* 6–33. Brittania Monastica 3. Landevennec: Brittania Monastica, 1994.

Tauer, Johann. "Neue Orientierungen zur Paulusexegese des Pelagius." *Augustinianum* 34 (1994): 313–58.

Tedeschi, Carlo. *Congeries lapidum: Iscrizioni Britanniche dei secoli V–VII.* 2 vols. Scuola Normale Superiore di Pisa: Centro di Cultura Medievale. Pisa: Scuola Normale Superiore, 2005.

Terry, Ann, and Henry Maguire. *Dynamic Splendor: The Wall Mosaics in the Cathedral of Eufrasius at Poreč.* University Park: Pennsylvania State University Press, 2007.

Testard, Maurice. *Saint Augustin et Cicéron*. 2 vols. Paris: Études Augustiniennes, 1958.

Thébert, Yvon. "L'évolution urbaine dans les provinces orientales de l'Afrique romaine tardive." *Opus* 2 (1982): 99–131.

———. "Private Life and Domestic Architecture in Roman Africa." In *A History of Private Life*. Edited by Philippe Ariès and Georges Duby. Vol. 1, *From Pagan Rome to Byzantium*, 313–409. Edited by Paul Veyne. Translated by Arthur Goldhammer. Cambridge, MA: Harvard University Press, 1987.

———. *Thermes romains d'Afrique du Nord et leur contexte méditerranéen: Études d'histoire et d'archéologie*. Bibliothèque de l'École française d'Athènes et de Rome 315. Rome: École française de Rome, 2003.

Theologisches Wörterbuch zum Alten Testament. Edited by G. Johannes Botterweck and Helmer Ringgren. Stuttgart: Kohlhammer, 1973. Translated by John T. Willis as Theological Dictionary of the Old Testament. Grand Rapids, MI: Eerdmans, 1974.

Thier, Sebastian. *Kirche bei Pelagius*. Patristische Texte und Studien 50. Berlin: de Gruyter, 1999.

Thomas, Yan. "La construction de l'unité civique: Choses publiques, choses communes et choses n'appartenant à personne et representation." *Mélanges de l'école française de Rome: Moyen Age* 114 (2002): 7–39.

Thompson, E. A. "Peasant Revolts in Late Roman Gaul and Spain." *Past and Present* 2 (1952): 11–23.

———. *The Visigoths in the Time of Ulfila*. Oxford: Clarendon, 1966.

Tiersch, Claudia. *Johannes Chrysostomus in Konstantinopel (398–404): Weltsicht und Wirken eines Bischofs in der Hauptstadt des Oströmischen Reiches*. Studien und Texte zu Antike und Christentum 6. Tübingen: Mohr Siebeck, 2000.

Tomlin, R.S.O. "The Curse Tablets." In *The Temple of Sulis Minerva at Bath*. Vol. 2, *The Finds from the Sacred Spring*, 323–24. Edited by Barry Cunliffe. Oxford: Oxford University Press, 1988.

Toneatto, Valentina. "I linguaggi della ricchezza nella testualità omiletica e monastica dal II al IV secolo." In *Economica monastica: Dalla disciplina del desiderio all'amministrazione razionale*, 1–88. Edited by Valentina Toneatto, Peter Černic, and Susi Paulitti. Spoleto: Centro di Studi sull'Alto Medioevo, 2004.

Topographie chrétienne des cités de la Gaule, des origines au milieu du VIIIe siècle. Edited by Nancy Gauthier and Jean-Charles Picard.

    Vol. 4, *Province ecclésiastique de Lyon (Lugdunensis Prima)*. Edited by Brigitte Beaujard. Paris: Boccard, 1989.

    Vol. 5, *Province ecclésiastique de Tours (Lugdunensis Tertia)*. Edited by Luce Pietri. Paris: Boccard, 1987.

    Vol. 6, *Province ecclésiastique de Bourges (Aquitania Prima)*. Edited by Françoise Prévot. Paris: Boccard, 1989.

    Vol. 7, *Province ecclésiastique de Narbonne (Narbonensis Prima)*. Edited by Paul-Albert Février. Paris: Boccard, 1989.

    Vol. 8, *Province ecclésiastique de Sens (Lugdunensis Senonia)*. Edited by Jean-Charles Picard. Paris: Boccard, 1992.

Topographie chrétienne des cités de la Gaule, des origines au milieu du VIIIe siècle.
    Vol. 10, *Province ecclésiastique de Bordeaux (Aquitania Secunda).* Edited by Louis
    Maurin. Paris: Boccard, 1998.

Toscano, Santo. *Tolle divitem: Etica, società e potere nel De divitiis.* Testi e Studi di Storia
    Antica 19. Catania: Edizioni del Prisma, 2006.

The Transformations of Vrbs Roma in Late Antiquity. Edited by W. V. Harris. Journal
    of Roman Archaeology: Supplementary Series 33. Portsmouth, RI: Journal of
    Roman Archaeology, 1999.

Le trasformazioni delle "élites" in età tardoantica. Edited by Rita Lizzi Testa. Rome:
    Bretschneider, 2006.

Trelenberg, Jörg. *Augustins Schrift de Ordine.* Beiträge zur historischen Theologie 144.
    Tübingen: Mohr Siebeck, 2009.

Troncarelli, Fabio. *Il ricordo della sofferenza: Le Confessioni di sant'Agostino e la
    psicoanalisi.* Naples: Edizioni scientifiche italiane, 1993.

Trout, Dennis E. "Augustine at Cassiciacum: *Otium Honestum* and the Social Dimen-
    sions of Conversion." *Vigiliae Christianae* 42 (1988): 132–46.

———. "Christianizing the Nolan Countryside: Animal Sacrifice at the Tomb of St.
    Felix." *Journal of Early Christian Studies* 3 (1995): 281–98.

———. "*Lex and iussio:* The *Feriale Campanum* and Christianity in the Theodosian
    Age." In *Law, Society, and Authority in Late Antiquity,* 162–78. Edited by
    Ralph W. Mathisen. Oxford: Oxford University Press, 2001.

———. *Paulinus of Nola: Life, Letters, and Poems.* Berkeley: University of California
    Press, 1999.

Ullmann, Walter. *Gelasius I (492–496): Das Papsttum an der Wende der Spätantike zum
    Mittelalter.* Päpste und Papsttum 18. Stuttgart: Hiersemann, 1981.

Van Dam, Raymond. "Bishops and Society." In *The Cambridge History of Christianity.*
    Vol. 2, *Constantine to c. 600,* 343–66. Edited by Augustine Casiday and Frederick W.
    Norris. Cambridge: Cambridge University Press, 2007.

———. *Kingdom of Snow: Roman Rule and Greek Culture in Cappadocia.* Philadelphia:
    University of Pennsylvania Press, 2002.

———. *Leadership and Community in Late Antique Gaul.* Berkeley: University of
    California Press, 1985.

———. *The Roman Revolution of Constantine.* New York: Cambridge University Press,
    2007.

———. *Saints and Their Miracles in Late Antique Gaul.* Princeton: Princeton Univer-
    sity Press, 1993.

———. "Self-Representation in the Will of Gregory Nazianzus." *Journal of Theological
    Studies* 46 (1995): 118–48.

Van Ossel, Paul. "Rural Impoverishment in Northern Gaul at the End of Antiquity:
    The Contribution of Archaeology." In *Social and Political Life in Late Antiquity,*
    533–65. Edited by Will Bowden, Adam Gutteridge, and Carlos Machado. Late
    Antique Archaeology 3:1. Leiden: Brill, 2006.

Vandals, Romans and Berbers: New Perspectives on Late Antique Africa. Edited by
    Andrew H. Merrills. Aldershot: Ashgate, 2004.

Vaquerizo Gil, Desiderio, and José Ramón Carillo Díaz-Pinés. "The Roman Villa of El Ruedo (Almedinilla, Córdoba)." *Journal of Roman Archaeology* 8 (1995): 121–54.

Vasey, Vincent R. *The Social Ideas in the Works of St. Ambrose: A Study on De Nabuthe.* Studia Ephemeridis Augustinianum 17. Rome: Institutum Patristicum Augustinianum, 1982.

Vera, Domenico. "L'altra faccia della luna: La società contadina nella Sicilia di Gregorio Magno." *Studi Storici* 47 (2006): 437–61.

———. *Commento storico alle "Relationes" di Quinto Aurelio Simmaco.* Pisa: Giardini, 1981.

———. "Enfiteusi, colonato e trasformazioni agrarie nell'Africa romana proconsulare del tardo impero." *Africa Romana* 4 (1987): 267–93.

———. "Forme e funzioni della rendita fondiaria nella tarda antichità." In *Società romana e impero tardoantico,* 367–447. Edited by Andrea Giardina. Vol. 1, *Istituzioni, ceti, economie.* Bari: Laterza, 1986.

———. "Giustiniano, Procopio e l'approvvigionamento di Costantantinopoli." In *Politica, retorica e simbolismo del primato: Roma e Costantinopoli (secoli IV–VII),* 9–44. Edited by Febronia Elia. Catania: Spazio Libri, 2004.

———. "Massa fundorum." *Mélanges de l'École française de Rome: Antiquité* 111 (1999): 991–1025.

———. "I paesaggi rurali del Meridione tardoantico: Bilancio consuntivo e preventivo." In *Paesaggi e insediamenti rurali in Italia meridionale fra tardoantico e altomedioevo,* 23–38. Edited by Guiliano Volpe and Maria Turchiano. Bari: Edipuglia, 2005.

———. "Presentazione." In *Eburnea Diptycha: I dittici d'avorio tra Antichità e Medioevo,* 7–9. Edited by Massimiliano David. Bari: Edipuglia, 2007.

———. "Simmaco e le sue proprietà: Struttura e funzionamento di un patrimonio aristocratico del IV secolo d.C." In *Colloque genèvois sur Symmaque,* 231–76. Edited by François Paschoud. Paris: Belles Lettres, 1986.

———. "Terra e lavoro nell'Africa romana." *Studi Storici* 4 (1988): 967–92.

Verheijen, Luc. *Nouvelle approche de la Règle de Saint Augustin.* Vol. 1. Vie Monastique 8. Bégrolle-en-Mauge: Abbaye de la Bellefontaine, 1980.

Vescovi e pastori in epoca Teodosiana. In occasione del XVI centenario della consacrazione episcopale di S. Agostino, 396–1996. XXV Incontro di studiosi dell'antichità cristiana, Roma, 8–11 maggio 1996. Studia Ephemeridis Augustinianum 58. Rome: Institutum Pontificium Augustinianum, 1997.

Vessey, Mark. "Peregrinus against the Heretics: Classicism, Provinciality and the Place of the Alien Writer in Late Roman Gaul." *Studia Ephemeridis Augustinianum* 46 (1994): 529–65. Reprinted in Vessey, *Latin Christian Writers in Late Antiquity and Their Texts.* Ashgate: Variorum, 2005.

Veyne, Paul. "Les cadeaux des colons à leur propriétaire: La neuvième *Bucolique* et le mausolée d'Igel." *Revue archéologique* (1981): 245–52.

———. *L'empire gréco-romain.* Paris: Seuil, 2005.

———. *Le pain et le cirque: Sociologie historique d'un pluralisme politique.* Paris: Le Seuil, 1976. Translated by Brian Pierce as *Bread and Circuses: Historical Sociology and*

Political Pluralism. With an introduction by Oswyn Murray. London: Allen Lane Penguin, 1990.

——. *Quand notre monde est devenu chrétien (312–394)*. Paris: Albin Michel, 2007. Translated by Janet Lloyd as *When Our World Became Christian, 312–394*. Cambridge: Polity Press, 2010.

Vieillard-Troïekouroff, May. *Les monuments religieux de la Gaule d'après les oeuvres de Grégoire de Tours*. Paris: Champion, 1976.

Vigil-Escalero Guirado, Alfonso. "Granjas y aldeas altomedievales al Norte de Toledo (450–800 D.C.)." *Archivo Español de Arqueología* 80 (2007): 239–84.

Les villas romaines de São Cucufate (Portugal). Edited by Jorge de Alarcão, Robert Étienne, and Françoise Mayet. Paris: Boccard, 1990.

Villas Tardoantiguas en el Mediterráneo Occidental. Edited by Alexandra Chavarría, Javier Arce, and Gian Pietro Brogiolo. Anejos de Archivo Español de Arqueología 39. Madrid: Consejo Superior de Investigaciones Científicas, 2006.

Virlouvet, Catherine. *La plèbe frumentaire dans les témoignages épigraphiques: Essai d'histoire sociale et administrative du peuple de Rome antique*. Collection de l'École française de Rome 414. Rome: École française de Rome, 2009.

——. *Tessera frumentaria: Les procédés de la distribution du blé public à Rome à la fin de la République et au début de l'Empire*. Bibliothèque des Écoles françaises d'Athènes et de Rome 296. Rome: Palais Farnèse, 1995.

Vogüé, Adalbert de. *Histoire littéraire du mouvement monastique dans l'antiquité*. 12 vols. Paris: Le Cerf, 1991–2008.

Volk, Katharina. "Heavenly Steps: Manilius 4.119–121 and Its Background." In *Heavenly Realms and Earthly Realities in Late Antique Religions*, 34–46. Edited by Ra'anan S. Boustan and Annette Yoshiko Reed. Cambridge: Cambridge University Press, 2004.

Völker, Reiche und Namen im frühen Mittelalter. Edited by Matthias Becher and Stefanie Dick. Munich: W. Fink 2010.

Volpe, Giuliano. "Architecture and Church Power in Late Antiquity: Canosa and San Giusto (*Apulia*)." In *Housing in Late Antiquity: From Palaces to Shops*, 131–68. Edited by Luke Lavan, Lale Özgenel, and Alexander Sarantis. Late Antique Archaeology 3.2. Leiden: Brill, 2007.

——. *Contadini, pastori e mercanti nell'Apulia tardoantica*. Bari: Edipuglia, 1996.

Volpe, Giuliano, Giuliano De Felice, and Maria Turchiano. "Faragola (Ascoli Satriano): Una residenza aristocratica tardoantica e un 'villaggio' altomedievale nella Valle del Carapelle: i primi dati." In *Paesaggi e insediamenti rurali in Italia meridionale fra tardoantico e altomedioevo*, 265–97. Edited by Guiliano Volpe and Maria Turchiano. Bari: Edipuglia, 2005.

——. "La villa tardoantica di Faragola (Ascoli Satriano) in Apulia." In *Villas Tardoantiguas en el Mediterráneo Occidental*, 221–51. Edited by Alexandra Chavarría, Javier Arce, and Gian Pietro Brogiolo. Anejos de Archivo Español de Arqueología 39. Madrid: Consejo Superior de Investigaciones Científicas, 2006.

Volpe, Giuliano, Pasquale Favia, Roberta Giuliani, and Donatella Nuzzi. "Il complesso sabiniano di San Pietro a Canosa." In vol. 2 of *La cristianizzazione in Italia tra Tardoantico e Altomedioevo*, 1113–65. Edited by Rosa Maria Bonacasa Carra and Emma Vitale. Palermo: Carlo Saladino, 2007.

Vuolanto, Ville. "Male and Female Euergetism in Late Antiquity: A Study on Italian and Adriatic Church Floor Mosaics." In *Women, Wealth and Power in the Roman Empire*, 245–302. Edited by Päivi Setälä et al. Acta Instituti Romani Finlandiae 25. Rome: Finnish Institute, 2002.

Wacher, John. *Roman Britain*. 2nd ed. Stroud, UK: Sutton, 1998.

Waddell, Helen. *The Wandering Scholars*. London: Constable, 1929.

Wallace-Hadrill, Andrew. *Rome's Cultural Revolution*. Cambridge: Cambridge University Press, 2008.

Wallraff, Martin, and Cristina Ricci. *Oratio funebris in laudem sancti Iohannis Chrysostomi: Epitaffio attribuito a Martirio di Antiochia 40*. Spoleto: Centro Italiano di Studi sull'Alto Medioevo, 2007.

Ward-Perkins, Bryan. "407 and All That: Retrospective." *Journal of Late Antiquity* 2 (2009): 75–78.

———. *The Fall of Rome and the End of Civilization*. Oxford: Oxford University Press, 2005.

———. *From Classical Antiquity to the Middle Ages: Urban Public Building in Northern and Central Italy, 300–850*. Oxford: Oxford University Press, 1984.

Weaver, Rebecca Harden. *Divine Grace and Human Agency: A Study of the Semi-Pelagian Controversy*. Patristic Monographs Series 15. Macon, GA: Mercer University Press, 1996.

Weidemann, Margarete. *Das Testament des Bischofs Bertram von Le Mans vom 27. März 616: Untersuchungen zu Besitz und Geschichte einer fränkischen Familie im 6. und 7. Jahrhundert*. Römisch-germanisches Zentralmuseum, Monographien 9. Mainz: R. Habelt, 1986.

Weinfeld, Moshe. *Social Justice in Ancient Israel and in the Ancient Near East*. Minneapolis: Fortress; Jerusalem: Magnes, 1995.

Weisweiler, John. *State Aristocracy: Resident Senators and Absent Emperors in Late Antique Rome, c. 320–400*. D. Phil. diss., University of Cambridge, 2011.

Wermelinger, Otto. *Rom und Pelagius: Die theologische Position der römischen Bischöfe im pelagianischen Streit in den Jahren 411–432*. Päpste und Papsttum 7. Stuttgart: A. Hiersemann, 1975.

Wessel, Susan. *Leo the Great and the Spiritual Rebuilding of a Universal Rome*. Supplements to Vigiliae Christianae 93. Leiden: Brill, 2008.

Whittaker, C. R. "Circe's Pigs: From Slavery to Serfdom in the Later Roman World." *Slavery and Abolition* 8 (1987): 88–122.

Wickham, Chris. *Early Medieval Italy: Central Power and Local Society, 400–1000*. London: MacMillan, 1981.

———. *Framing the Early Middle Ages: Europe and the Mediterranean, 400–800*. Oxford: Oxford University Press, 2005.

Wickham, Chris. *The Inheritance of Rome: A History of Europe from 400 to 1000.* London: Allen Lane, 2009.

———. "Marx, Sherlock Holmes and Late Roman Commerce." *Journal of Roman Studies* 78 (1988): 183–93.

Wiesen, David S. *St. Jerome as a Satirist: A Study in Christian Latin Thought and Letters.* Ithaca, NY: Cornell University Press, 1964.

Wightman, Edith Mary. *Roman Trier and the Treveri.* London: Hart-Davis, 1970.

Wilkinson, Kevin W. "Palladas and the Age of Constantine." *Journal of Roman Studies* 99 (2009): 36–60.

———. "Palladas and the Foundation of Constantinople." *Journal of Roman Studies* 100 (2010): 179–94.

Williams, Daniel H. *Ambrose of Milan and the End of the Arian-Nicene Conflicts.* Oxford: Oxford University Press, 1995.

Williams, Megan Hale. *The Monk and the Book: Jerome and the Making of Christian Scholarship.* Chicago: University of Chicago Press, 2006.

Wilson, Andrew. "Urban Production in the Roman World: The View from North Africa." *Papers of the British School at Rome* 70 (2002): 231–73.

Wipszycka, Ewa. "Les aspects économiques de la vie de la communauté des Kellia." In *Études sur le christianisme dans l'Égypte de l'antiquité tardive*, 337–62. Studia Ephemeridis Augustinianum 52. Rome: Institutum Patristicum Augustinianum, 1996.

———. "Les formes institutionnelles et les formes d'activité économique du monachisme égyptien." In *Foundations of Power and Conflicts of Authority in Late Antique Monasticism*, 109–54. Edited by A. Camplani and S. Filoramo. Orientalia Lovaniensia Analecta 157. Louvain: Peeters, 2007.

———. "Le monachisme égyptien et les villes." *Travaux et mémoires* 12 (1994): 1–44.

Witschel, Christian. *Krise-Rezession-Stagnation? Der Westen des römischen Reiches im 3. Jahrhundert n. Chr.* Frankfurt: M. Clauss, 1999.

———. "Re-Evaluating the Roman West in the 3rd Century A.D." *Journal of Roman Archaeology* 17 (2004): 251–81.

———. "Statuen auf spätantike Platzanlagen in Italien und Afrika." In *Statuen in der Spätantike*, 113–69. Edited by Franz Alto Bauer and Christian Witschel. Wiesbaden: Reichert, 2007.

Witschel, Christian, and Barbara Borg. "Veränderungen im Repräsentationsverhalten der römischen Eliten während des 3. Jhrdts n. Chr." In *Inschriftliche Denkmäler als Medien der Selbstdarstellung in der römischen Welt*, 47–120. Edited by Geza Alföldy and Silvio Panciera. Stuttgart: F. Steiner, 2001.

Wood, Ian N. "The Exchange of Gifts among the Late Antique Aristocracy." In *El disco de Teodosio*, 301–14. Edited by Martín Almagro-Gorbea. Estudios del Gabinete de Antigüedades 5. Madrid: Real Academia de la Historia, 2000.

———. "Review Article: Landscapes Compared." *Early Medieval Europe* 15 (2007): 223–37.

Wood, Susan. *The Proprietary Church in the Medieval West.* Oxford: Oxford University Press, 2006.

Woolf, Greg. "Food, Poverty and Patronage: The Significance of the Epigraphy of the Roman Alimentary Schemes in Early Imperial Italy." *Papers of the British School at Rome* 58 (1990): 197–228.

———. "Writing Poverty in Rome." In *Poverty in the Roman World*, 83–99. Edited by Margaret Atkins and Robin Osborne. Cambridge: Cambridge University Press, 2007.

Wrede, Hennig. *Senatorische Sarkophage Roms: Der Beitrag des Senatorenstandes zur römischen Kunst der höhen und späten Kaiserzeit.* Monumenta Artis Romanae 29. Mainz: P. Zabern, 2001.

———. *Die spätantike Hermengalerie von Welschbillig.* Römische-germanische Forschungen 32. Berlin: de Gruyter, 1972.

Yü, Ying-shih. *Trade and Expansion in Han China: A Study in the Structure of Sino-Barbarian Economic Relations.* Berkeley: University of California Press, 1967.

Zangara, Vincenza. "Una predicazione alla presenza dei principi: La chiesa di Ravenna nella prima metà del sec. V." *Antiquité tardive* 8 (2000): 265–304.

Zanker, Paul, and Björn Christian Ewald. *Mit Mythen leben: Die Bildwerk der römischen Sarkophage.* Munich: Hirmer, 2004.

Zettler, Alfons. *Offerenteninschriften auf den frühchristlichen Mosaikfußböden Venetiens und Istriens.* Berlin: de Gruyter, 2001.

Ziche, Hartmut G. "Administrer la propriété de l'église: L'évêque comme clerc et comme entrepreneur." *Antiquité tardive* 14 (2006): 69–78.

Zuiderhoek, Arjan. "The Icing on the Cake: Benefactors, Economics and Public Building in Roman Asia Minor." In *Patterns in the Economy of Roman Asia Minor*, 167–86. Edited by Stephen Mitchell and Constantina Kaksari. Swansea: Classical Press of Wales, 2005.

INDEX

Abba Moses, 418

abbots, 412, 416, 420, 421–22, 516–17

Abellinum, bishop of, 81

Abelonii, sect of, 342

Abraham, 313–14

acclamation, 171, 209; and Ambrose, 126; and Augustine, 171, 324, 341; and church offering ceremonies, 318; and euergetism, 76; and games, 354; and Jerome, 318; and Magerius, 67; for Pinianus, 324, 342, 347, 482; of poor people, 234–35; and Proconsuls of Africa, 344; by theater crowds, 66

Achaemenid empire, 83, 85, 86

Actium, 269

Adalgisel Grimo, 524

Adam, 178–79, 180, 181, 255, 368, 474

Adeodatus, 168–69

Adrianople, battle of, 128, 135

Aemilius, bishop of Beneventum, 374

Aetius, 394, 447, 454, 461

Africa, xix, 118; and Ambrose, 148; and *annona civica,* 73, 110, 471; and aristocratization of church, 494; and Augustine, 149, 167, 322–31; and barbarian invasions, 360; baths of, 200; bishops of, 330, 336–37, 344, 357, 366, 371, 382, 529; building in, 65; Byzacena, 400, 401, 484; Catholic Church in, 170; Catholics and Donatists in, 328–36, 348, 349, 364, 382, 483; celibacy of clergy in, 519; ceramics of, 28–29, 401; Christianity

in, 288, 320, 322, 329–30, 331, 334–38, 335; church councils of, 326; and churches and theology, 369; churches of, xx, 325, 334–36, 355–56, 361, 366; church government in, 333; church of, 380–81, 494; cities of, 6–7, 8, 151, 330, 337; civil religion of cities in, 330; clergy of, 301, 307, 381, 519; and Constans, 333; conversions in, 46; and country bishoprics of fourth century, 520; and court of Ravenna, 529; development of churches in, 334–36; ecclesiastical government in, 425; as economic center of gravity, 65; and economy, 23; and emperor, 366–67, 381; estates in, 366–67; euergetism in, 64, 65–66, 67–68; farmers of, 367; giving in, xx, 357, 363–65; and imperial court, 381; and imperial games at Carthage, 353; and imperial system, 368; landholdings of nobility of Rome in, 366–67; landowners of, 364; local courts in, 394; Manichaeism in, 158; *mediocritas* of churches in, 325; mosaics of, 206; paganism in, 329; and Pelagius, xx; poor people in, 342; Proconsularis, 400, 401; Proconsulship of, 95; Proconsuls of, 344; provincial society of, 366–67; refugees from Rome in, 288, 300–301, 323, 330, 359–60; regions of, 326–28; reputation for novelty in, 369; role of *populus* in, 357; and Rome, 288; rural settlements in, 10; and Septimius Severus, 95; and taxation, 344, 381, 382, 383; tenants in, 367; theology in, 369; town